MOON HANDBOOKS®
PANAMA

FIRST EDITION

WILLIAM FRIAR

AVALON TRAVEL

Puerto Limón

C a r i b b e a n   S e a

Uatsi

Sixaola

Changuinola

Bocas

**Parque Nacional
Bastimentos**

Almirante

**Parque
Internacional
La Amistad**

*Laguna de
Chiriquí*

Chiriquí Grande

*Golfo de los
Mosquitos*

Río Sereno

**Parque Nacional
Volcán Barú**

Boquete

*Bosque
Protector de
Palo Seco*

**Parque Nacional
Omar Torrijos H
(El Copé)**

Volcán

La Concepcion

Santa Fé

Penonomé

1

1

Antón

David

Las Lajas

Tolé

San Francisco

Aguadulce

Puerto
Armuelles

1

Divisa

**PN
Sariguá**

*Bahía d
Parita*

*Bahía de
Charco Azul*

**Parque Nacional
Golfo de Chiriquí**

Santiago

Ocú

Chitré

2

Golfo de Chiriquí

Las
Minas

Las Tablas

Isla de
Coiba

**Parque
Nacional
Coiba**

*Refugio de Vi
Silvestre Isla
Cañas*

Arenas

Tonosí

**Parque Nacional
Cerro Hoya**

C
O
S
T
A

R
I
C
A

PACIFIC   OCEAN

MoON

© AVALON TRAVEL PUBLISHING, INC.

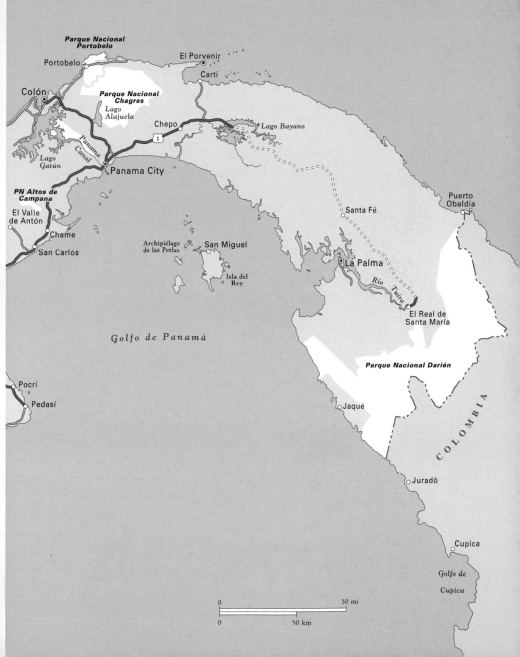

PANAMA

Parque Nacional Portobelo

Portobelo

El Porvenir

Cartí

Colón

Parque Nacional Chagres

Lago Alajuela

Chepo

Lago Bayano

1

Panama Canal

Lago Gatún

Panama City

PN Altos de Campana

El Valle de Antón

Chame

San Carlos

Santa Fé

Puerto Obaldía

La Palma

Archipiélago de las Perlas

San Miguel

Isla del Rey

Río Tuira

El Real de Santa María

Golfo de Panamá

Parque Nacional Darién

Pocrí

Pedasí

Jaqué

COLOMBIA

Juradó

Cupica

Golfo de Cupica

0   50 mi

0   50 km

CONTENTS

Discover Panama

Explore Panama

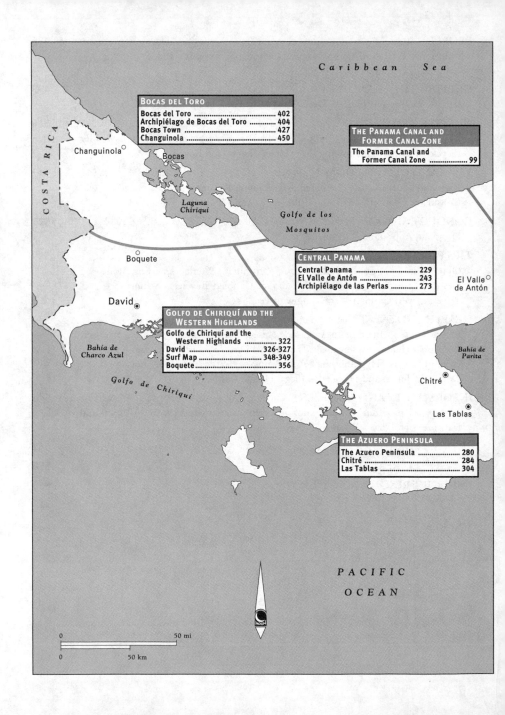

Caribbean Sea

COSTA RICA

Changuinola

Bocas

Laguna Chiriquí

Golfo de los Mosquitos

Boquete

El Valle de Antón

David

Bahía de Charco Azul

Bahía de Parita

Golfo de Chiriquí

Chitré

Las Tablas

PACIFIC

OCEAN

MOON

0   50 mi

0   50 km

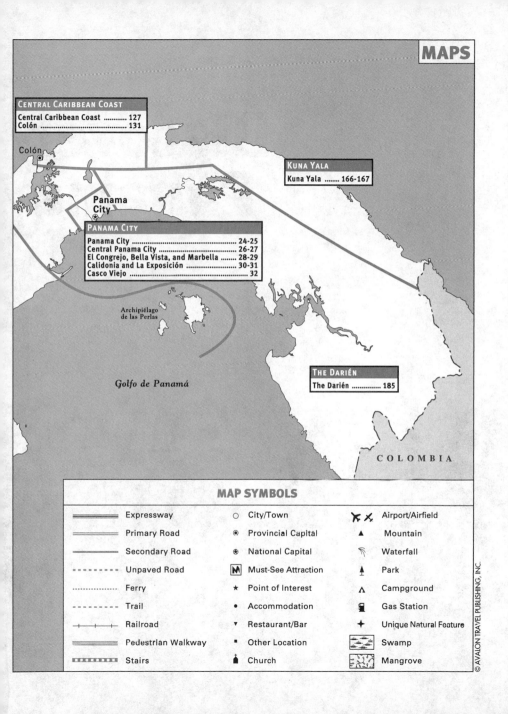

MAPS

Colón

Panama
City

Archipiélago
de las Perlas

Golfo de Panamá

C O L O M B I A

MAP SYMBOLS

═══	Expressway	○	City/Town	✈ ✈	Airport/Airfield
───	Primary Road	◉	Provincial Capital	▲	Mountain
───	Secondary Road	✪	National Capital	🕅	Waterfall
- - - -	Unpaved Road	Ⓜ	Must-See Attraction	♠	Park
·········	Ferry	★	Point of Interest	⋀	Campground
- - - -	Trail	●	Accommodation	⛽	Gas Station
┼─┼─┼	Railroad	▼	Restaurant/Bar	✦	Unique Natural Feature
▬▬▬	Pedestrian Walkway	▪	Other Location		Swamp
▪▪▪▪▪	Stairs	⛪	Church		Mangrove

© AVALON TRAVEL PUBLISHING, INC.

Discover Panama

The Republic of Panama lacks only one thing its overexposed neighbors have in abundance: hordes of tourists.

It's hard to think of a single country on the planet that has so much to offer visitors, yet so few actual visitors. Just for starters, it has incredible natural beauty, a modern infrastructure, good roads, clean water, year-round warm weather, a peaceful atmosphere, and a rich history.

Panama has long been known as "the crossroads of the world," which accounts for its international sophistication and ethnically mixed population. It also has eight indigenous peoples, some of whom still live as they did thousands of years ago. The Kunas of the San Blas Islands are widely recognized as having the most vibrant indigenous culture in the Americas.

An astonishing amount of history has played out on the narrow isthmus of Panama. Balboa discovered the Pacific here. Sir Francis Drake was buried at sea in a lead casket off the Caribbean coast. The '49ers risked malaria and yellow fever as they struggled across the isthmus on their way to the gold fields of California. Scandals that nearly destroyed France and Scotland began in Panama.

Reminders of that history pop up everywhere. The ruins of old Spanish forts still guard the coastlines of both oceans. The remains of ancient civilizations are being uncovered as you read this. Even in the heart of modern Panama City, the brick streets and colonial buildings of Casco Viejo transport visitors to a distant past.

But even though humans have passed back and forth across the isthmus for thousands of years, much of Panama remains untouched by development. A quarter of the country has been set aside as national parks and protected areas, from a rainforest just a half-hour drive from Panama City to the legendary Parque Nacional Darién, the last great wilderness in Central America, through which no road has ever crossed.

The natural riches of Panama are overwhelming. It has close to a thousand species of birds, more than in all of North America, and innumerable plant and animal species found nowhere else on earth. Its two oceans are so close together that one can swim in both in a single morning. Along the coast are 1,500 islands and some of the most intact coral reefs and mangrove forests in Central America. Panama has little-known but world-class diving, surfing, and white-water rafting, and more deep-sea fishing records have been set here than anyplace else on earth.

And then there's the Panama Canal, still one of the wonders of the modern world. A transit through the canal across the mountains and jungles of Panama is unforgettable.

Perhaps the best thing about Panama is that the world hasn't yet caught on to all it has to offer. It's easy to find a white sandy beach without another human being on it. Some spectacular sights are so little advertised that even Panamanians barely know of them.

Virgin turf comes at a price. Tourism is still so new to parts of Panama that visitors will face challenges they wouldn't find in more touristy parts of Latin America. At times visitors may feel like pioneers, with all the excitement and frustration that implies. But if the going gets rough, cosmopolitan Panama City is never more than a day's journey away.

Panama may be a small country, but it's an elongated one with rugged and varied terrain. Seeing all it has to offer can take far longer than one might expect. Fortunately, many of its top attractions are within an hour's drive of downtown Panama City. Its most spectacular natural attractions, however, are farther afield.

The quickest way to get around is by air. Panama City is the only true air hub, so getting from Point A to neighboring Point B often requires an intermediate stop in the capital. Since there are relatively few flights and most leave in the early morning, those who want to see a lot of the country will inevitably have layovers in Panama City. One way to work around this is to explore Panama City and its surrounding attractions in staggered intervals as one works one's way around the isthmus.

If possible, allow at least a week to see Panama City, the Panama Canal, and one or two nature destinations. Two weeks give visitors a chance to truly relax and appreciate Panama's great beauty and cultural complexity. A visitor with a month to spend can sample every region in the country.

Panama has good roads, cheap and frequent public transportation, clean water, and plenty of other evidence of a modern infrastructure one wouldn't expect of a developing country. But its tourist infrastructure is rudimentary. Good hotels and restaurants outside Panama City and a few other popular destinations are still limited. And while Panama is a great outdoor-recreation destination, it's not always easy to find an outfitter or qualified guide.

WHEN TO GO

Panama has two seasons, the rainy and the dry. The dry season lasts mid-December–mid-April and is Panama's "summer." Schools let out, families take vacations, and everyone's ready to party. This is also the high season for tourism. Hotels raise their prices, and occasionally they even fill up.

The weather is especially lovely at the beginning of the dry season. Flowering trees all over the country burst into bloom, and everything seems fresh and luminously green. January and February are among the best times to be in Panama. Later in the dry season the lowlands turn brown and slash-and-burn agriculture can fill the sky with smoke.

The rainy season lasts about mid-April–mid-December. Even during those months, though, the rains in most parts of Panama tend to come in the afternoon or early evening, so it's often possible to enjoy clear mornings. When the rains do arrive, they typically dump an unbelievable amount of water in an hour or even less and then move on. Storms tend to last longer, and come earlier, late in the rainy season.

Those who've never experienced a tropical downpour may want to visit

Panama in the rainy season; the storms can be stupendous and are often accompanied by earth-shattering thunderclaps. However, it's not a great time to go on long hikes or drive on rough roads, as the countryside turns to mud and rising rivers make some routes impassable.

The rain never stops completely in some parts of the country. Be prepared for some precipitation year-round along the Caribbean coast, in the western highlands, and on the islands of Bocas del Toro.

There are many different theories about the best time to dive and snorkel in Panama. Some argue the rainy season is ideal. In the dry season, strong winds stir up the ocean and bring sediment from the bottom, spoiling visibility. This is much less of a problem in the rainy season, and a light rain can actually help calm the waters. However, if you're diving in an area where many rivers empty into the sea, runoff following a rain can also wreck visibility. Late February–March is usually considered the best time to visit the islands of Kuna Yala. Bocas del Toro has its own odd microclimates: September–October and February–March are the driest times.

Temperatures in Panama don't change much during the year. In the lowlands, expect a high of about 32°C (90°F) in the day down to 21°C (70°F) in the evening. It never gets cold in the lowlands, and the dry-season breezes in the evening are pleasant. It gets considerably cooler in the highlands. Panama can be quite humid year-round, but especially so in the rainy season.

Panama's biggest holiday is Carnaval, held each year in the four days leading up to Ash Wednesday. The country comes to a complete halt during those days. This may appeal to those into massive parties, but hotels in the Carnaval hot spots book up months ahead of time, and plane reservations can be hard to come by. November is filled with *fiestas patrias* (national-independence holidays).

WHAT TO TAKE

Most parts of Panama are hot and humid year-round. Bring lots of thin cotton or breathable, moisture-wicking synthetic clothing. Be sure your travel wardrobe is not all shorts and skimpy tops, though; dress in Panama is conservative. Bring at least one semiformal outfit for restaurants, bars, or clubs in the cities.

Life is easier for those who travel light, especially if travel plans call for domestic flights, where there's a severe weight restriction on luggage. Launderettes aren't hard to come by once clean clothes are exhausted. But consider bringing a bunch of T-shirts, as many people on the move are more comfortable if they can change their sweaty tops two or even three times a day.

Those planning to do much hiking should bring along a waterproof anorak or rain poncho, preferably of breathable fabric. Bring lots of plastic bags for stashing gear to protect it from the elements. Consider taking along a small umbrella for use in town, or just do what the locals do—wait for the rain to stop.

Waterfalls near Los Pozos de Caldera are a good place to cool off after a dip in the hot springs.

It can cool off significantly in some regions of Panama, and air-conditioning can raise goose bumps in the lowland cities. Even parts of the Darién can get fairly chilly at night, and temperatures in the western highlands sometimes approach freezing. Bring some warm clothes. A light sweater or fleece along with a waterproof windbreaker or parka is a useful combination. If you think you'll spend much time island-hopping, consider bringing a life jacket. These are often not standard equipment.

Consider bringing along a bedroll or light sleeping bag even if you're not planning on doing serious camping. It can come in handy if you have to spend a night in a place without decent linens. And don't forget the binoculars.

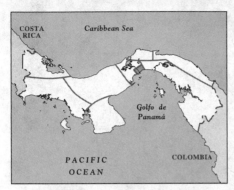

PANAMA CITY

The first European city on the Pacific coast of the Americas, 500-year-old Panama City is both rich in history and focused on the future. It is by far the most cosmopolitan city in Central America, a burgeoning metropolis of soaring skyscrapers, sophisticated restaurants, and international banks and businesses. At its heart is Casco Viejo, a charming and well-preserved old town that dates from the 16th century. It grew from the ashes of the original city, Panamá la Vieja, burned by pirate raids but whose ruins still stand facing the Pacific.

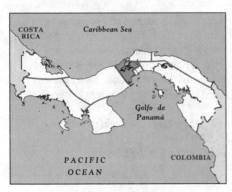

PANAMA CANAL AND FORMER CANAL ZONE

The building of the Panama Canal was the great engineering feat of its era, and the canal is still one of the wonders of the modern world. No one who comes to Panama should miss out on seeing and, if possible, transiting it. Miraflores Locks have the best visitor facilities and are a great introduction to how the canal was built and works. The builders literally moved mountains, and nowhere is this more vividly seen than at Gaillard Cut, a 14-kilometer-long manmade canyon through the Continental Divide. A ride on the Panama Railway is another unforgettable way to cross the isthmus from ocean to ocean. A walking tour of the old townsites of the former Canal Zone, particularly Balboa and Ancón, gives a glimpse of a unique, lost world of U.S. canal workers and their families. The Amador Causeway is a popular recreation and nightlife destination.

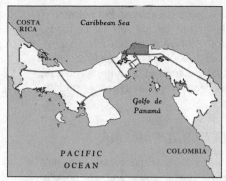

CENTRAL CARIBBEAN COAST

The ruins of Portobelo and Fuerte San Lorenzo, two of the most important forts in the Spanish empire, still stand along the coast near the Caribbean entrance to the Panama Canal. The conquistadors brought treasure from the looting of the Inca Empire here, only to have it looted from them by wave after wave of pirates and buccaneers. All that swashbuckling history competes for attention with some of the most impressive parts of the canal, including the mile-long Gatún Locks, the mouth of the mighty Río Chagres, and the massive, manmade Lago Gatún. Some of Panama's most accessible Caribbean dive spots and beaches are found here, notably around Portobelo and the popular Isla Grande.

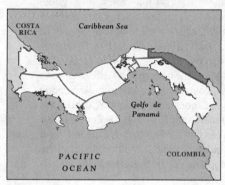

KUNA YALA

Only about 40 of the nearly 400 islands in the Kuna Yala, commonly known as the San Blas Archipelago, are inhabited. On these live the Kuna, arguably the most fascinating and intact indigenous culture in the Americas. Many of the deserted islands are palm-covered paradises of white sand and clear blue water that are straight out of *Robinson Crusoe*. The coral around the most remote islands, such as the Cayos Holandéses and Cayos Limónes, offers great snorkeling.

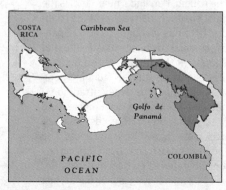

THE DARIÉN

The legendary Darién jungle has attracted adventurers from around the world in the half millennium since Balboa fought his way across it and became the first European to see the Pacific Ocean. Feared for its natural and human dangers, the Darién is also beloved for its natural and human riches. Parque Nacional Darién is one of the largest and most vital tropical forests in the Western Hemisphere. The wildlife at Cana and Pirre Station is spectacular and surprisingly accessible for a place that still has no roads. The forested coast, especially around Punta Patiño and the Bahia de Piñas, offers a completely different Darién experience, including astonishingly abundant sea life just offshore. The Darién is also crisscrossed by countless rivers, along which three nations of indigenous people cling to rugged ways of life they've sustained for centuries.

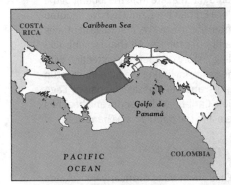

CENTRAL PANAMA

The central provinces contain Panama's most accessible highlands and popular beaches, some of which start within an hour's drive of Panama City. Coronado is especially popular, but the beaches become more gorgeous and less developed the farther west one goes, especially around Santa Clara and Farallón, which are just now beginning to take off as international beach destinations. From any of the beaches it's easy to head for the hills and escape the heat in the town of El Valle de Antón, nestled at the bottom of an extinct volcano and known for its waterfalls, square trees, golden frogs, and a popular Sunday crafts market. Those who want a more rugged mountain destination can hike and camp in the foggy forests of Parque Nacional Omar Torrijos H. (El Copé). Those who want a taste of lowland provincial life can find it in Penonomé, a modern town trying to hang on to traces of a quainter, quieter Panama. And the islands of the Archipiélago de las Perlas are just a short plane ride from Panama City.

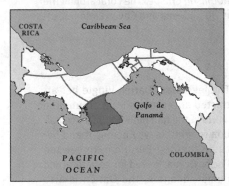

THE AZUERO PENINSULA

The Azuero, Panama's heartland, is the most culturally rich region of the country. Time has marched right by Spanish-colonial towns such as Parita and Pedasí. In the homes of the Azuero, master artisans still sew stunningly embroidered *polleras,* weave traditional hats, craft fearsome devil masks, and fire ceramic pottery whose designs date back more than a thousand years. The Azuero, known for its festivals, hosts the country's most important Carnaval celebration. The peninsula also has a ribbon of barely visited beaches that offer good surfing, snorkeling, and fishing. The 13-kilometer-long Isla de Cañas, just off the peninsula's southern tip, attracts more sea turtles than any other place along Panama's Pacific coast.

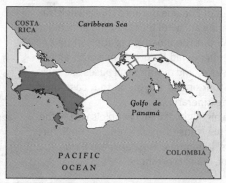

GOLFO DE CHIRIQUÍ AND THE WESTERN HIGHLANDS

Along Panama's western Pacific coast is a gulf so large and ecologically unique some consider it a small sea. Dominating the gulf is Parque Nacional Coiba, which conservationists have called the Galapagos of the 21st century. The jewel in the crown is gigantic Isla Coiba, the largest island in Panama and one as fabled for its Devil's Island–style penal colony as for the superabundant marine life that surrounds it. The region also includes Playa Santa Catalina, one of the best and largest surf breaks in all of Latin America, and the important provincial city of David.

The cool highlands of western Panama are home to the country's highest mountain, the 3,475-meter Volcán Barú. The dormant volcano's fertile volcanic soil produces gourmet coffee, gorgeous flowers, and delicious oranges and strawberries. But what really sets the region apart are its sprawling protected areas, most notably the gigantic Parque Internacional La Amistad. Five of Central America's six species of big cat are found here, as are 600 species of birds, including the resplendent quetzal, which ornithologists have called the most beautiful bird in the world. On the side of Barú is Boquete, one of Panama's most charming towns.

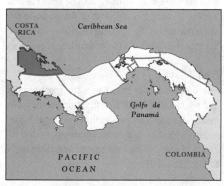

BOCAS DEL TORO

Panama's hottest tourist destination, the Bocas archipelago is a bohemian playground of white-sand beaches, big surf, frolicking dolphins, pristine coral reefs, and unusual creatures, including a bewildering array of tiny jewel-toned frogs. The humans are pretty fascinating, too, with new arrivals from North America and Europe adding to an already rich mix that includes indigenous and Afro-Caribbean inhabitants who've called Bocas home for hundreds of years. Every day seems to bring a new hotel or restaurant to Isla Colón, Carenero, and Bastimentos, but many of the beaches and forests of the archipelago are still undeveloped and barely visited.

21-Day Best of Panama

Those determined to touch on every part of Panama during a three-week trip can do it, but just barely. It means covering an awful lot of ground and, most likely, spending quite a bit of cash. All but the most energetic will be exhausted by the time they finish everything listed below. Those with ample time but limited money can take it more slowly and rely more on buses and their own planning and less on planes and tour operators, but in that case they should build about a week more into the itinerary.

A day transit of the Panama Canal is a highlight of many people's visit to the isthmus. The price is quite reasonable, but transits are offered only on Saturdays and can be hard to fit into travelers' itineraries. Most are partial transits, though even these take nearly a full day. Plan accordingly.

DAY 1

Arrive at Tocumen International Airport and transfer to a hotel in Panama City.

DAY 2

Visit the ruins of **Panamá la Vieja**, go for a walking tour of **Casco Viejo**, and have dinner in one of Panama City's elegant international restaurants.

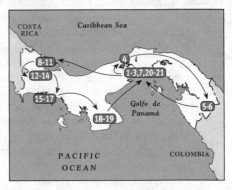

DAY 3

Begin a visit to the **Panama Canal** by exploring the former Canal Zone townsites of **Balboa** and **Ancón**. Tour **Miraflores Locks**, perhaps stopping for lunch on the balcony of the visitors center. Be sure to pass by the impressive **Gaillard Cut** and make at least a brief stop at **Gamboa** and **Parque Nacional Soberanía**, a true tropical rainforest just a short drive from downtown Panama City. End the day with a ramble along the **Amador Causeway**, a good place to stop for a drink or a meal as the lights of Panama City come on across the bay.

DAY 4

Take an early-morning ride across the isthmus on the **Panama Railway** and explore the Caribbean entrance to the canal. The Spanish ruins of **Portobelo** and **Fuerte San Lorenzo** transport visitors back to the days of pirates and conquistadors, and the mile-long **Gatún Locks** bring them back to the

high-tech present. If times allows, squeeze in a wildlife-viewing tour, by boat or kayak, down the lower reaches of the **Río Chagres**. Finish up in time to catch the train back to Panama City.

DAY 5

Board a charter flight to **Cana**, the most remote and spectacular wildlife destination in enormous **Parque Nacional Darién**. Follow species-rich jungle trails that pass by the overgrown, rusted remains of gold-mining equipment. Spend the night at the rustic lodge.

DAY 6

Hike up **Cerro Pirre** to Cana's cloud-forest camp, where temperatures cool off and the night is filled with sounds of forest animals.

DAY 7

Hike back down the mountain for the return flight to Panama City. Spend the day shopping for souvenirs and exploring the more cosmopolitan sides of the city.

DAYS 8–11

Reward yourself for all that exercise by flying off for a few days of Caribbean sun and sea. Choose between the booming bohemia of Bocas del Toro or the more rustic but culturally fascinating attractions of Kuna Yala; those with a few more days can visit both. The best way to see Kuna Yala is from the deck of a yacht sailing between the vibrant, crowded hubs of El Porvenir and Río Sidra. Stop along the way for snorkeling off remote cays, walks through traditional island villages, and forest hikes to powerful waterfalls and sacred cemeteries on the mainland. A visit to Panama's other great Caribbean archipelago, Bocas del Toro, can be split between funky Bocas town and the unspoiled beaches and coral reefs around Isla Bastimentos and its neighbors.

DAY 12

Head for the highlands of western Panama. Fly to David (those coming from Kuna Yala must go through Panama City) and take a bus or car to Boquete. Spend the afternoon exploring the town and its gardens and taking in the view of Volcán Barú.

DAYS 13–14

Those who need a break can opt for a gourmet-coffee tour or a stroll in the city's peculiar gardens. More active types can summit Volcán Barú in hopes of seeing both oceans at once, take a white-water rafting trip, search for quetzals on little-known forest trails, or hike through Parque Nacional Volcán Barú on the famous Sendero Los Quetzales.

DAYS 15–17

To see how the Pacific side of the isthmus

© WILLIAM FRIAR

Panama City's cathedral is in the heart of the Casco Viejo neighborhood.

© WILLIAM FRIAR

The Azuero Peninsula has more beaches than tourists.

compares with the Caribbean, head back down the mountain to the **Golfo de Chiriquí**. Those on a tight budget can find colorful backpackers' havens on **Isla Boca Chica**, the gateway to **Parque Nacional Marino Golfo de Chiriquí**, or popular **Playa Las Lajas**. For a splurge, book a scuba-diving or deep-sea fishing trip to magnificent **Parque Nacional Coiba** or the even more remote **Islas Secas**.

DAYS 18–19

Returning to the mainland at David, Santiago, or Panama City, you'll find it easy to arrange transfers to the **Azuero Peninsula**. Check into a hotel in Chitré and use it as a base to learn about Panama's crafts and folkloric traditions in nearby towns such as **La Arena, Parita, La Villa de Los Santos, Guararé,** and **Las Tablas.**

DAY 20

Head back to Panama City by land or air for last-minute shopping, sightseeing, and a farewell dinner.

DAY 21

Transfer to Tucumen International Airport for the flight home.

Panama is in many ways a kid-friendly country, and it's easy to find activities, accommodations, and restaurants that cater to families. The more rugged and remote parts of the country, however, are not always appropriate places for young children. This is especially true of most parts of the Darién.

DAY 1

Arrive at Tocumen International Airport and transfer to a hotel in Panama City or in the less-hectic former Canal Zone. The Gamboa Rainforest Resort is a particularly promising possibility for families.

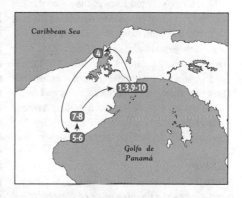

DAY 2

Spend the morning visiting Casco Viejo and the ruins of Panamá la Vieja. After lunch, head over to Amador Causeway and explore the aquariums at the Smithsonian's Centro de Exhibiciones

Small cruise ships offer a good way to see the islands of Kuna Yala.

Marinas. Have dinner in one of the causeway's open-air restaurants.

DAY 3

Take a tour of **Miraflores Locks** and then head to **Gamboa** for a ride up the Gamboa Rainforest Resort's **aerial tram**. Visit the flora and fauna exhibits, being sure not to miss the serpentarium and the butterfly pavilion. Another option is a boat trip on **Lago Gatún** to visit the islands of the **Primate Refuge and Sanctuary of Panama,** home to five species of monkeys. Have lunch at the resort's lakeside **Restaurante Los Lagartos,** where's there's a chance of spotting caimans and freshwater turtles. Stop by **Summit Botanical Gardens and Zoo** on the way back to Panama City. The highlight will probably be the harpy eagle exhibit.

DAY 4

Take the early-morning train across the isthmus and explore the Spanish ruins of **Portobelo** and **Fuerte San Lorenzo.** Stop by the mile-long **Gatún Locks** and, if possible, take a boat trip down the lower **Río Chagres,** which ends right below the fort at San Lorenzo. Take the train back to Panama City.

DAYS 5–6

Transfer to one of the resorts or smaller hotels at **Coronado, Farallón,** or **Santa Clara.** Spend a couple of days playing in the surf and splashing in the pool. It's generally easy to arrange other activities, from horseback rides on the beach to banana-boat rides in the ocean.

DAYS 7–8

Transfer to **El Valle de Antón** for cooler weather and a taste of the highland forests of Panama. For older kids, consider the **Canopy Adventure zipline tour.** Other possibilities include horseback riding, a visit to a small zoo with golden frogs and other exotic creatures, easy bike rides, walks to petroglyphs and waterfalls, and shopping at a bustling crafts market.

DAY 9

Return to Panama City for shopping and additional sightseeing.

DAY 10

Transfer to Tocumen International Airport for the trip home.

The ultimate Panama destination for the adrenaline set is the Darién. Attempting to hike through the Darién Gap these days is suicidal, but there are plenty of far safer but no less exciting ways to explore the forest. Ocean-to-ocean treks through the heart of the Darién are sometimes possible, but these are expensive, time-consuming, and logistically tricky.

However, there is a quicker and less complicated way to cross the isthmus on the west side of the Darién, and a possible way of tackling it is listed below. This is a short enough adventure to allow time to experience some of Panama's other well-known physical challenges.

For those who truly want to immerse themselves in the Darién, Ancon Expeditions offers an intense two-week trek that takes in the rivers, rainforests, and highlands of the region. Custom-designed trips are also possible.

Climbing to the top of Volcán Barú from the west side of the mountain is popular with outdoorsy types. Those who don't need to climb every mountain, however, may prefer to hike around Barú instead, on the prettier Sendero Los Quetzales. This can allow more time for other highland activities, such as white-water rafting.

The suggested itinerary below is meant only for the highly energetic and fit, and even then it should be attempted only with experienced naturalist guides.

© WILLIAM FRIAR

Most visitors to the Darién eventually end up on a river.

DAY 1

Arrive at Tocumen International Airport and transfer to a hotel in Panama City.

DAY 2

Transfer in the early morning to the **Bayano** area. If time allows, take a boat across **Lago Bayano** to explore the caves on the far side. This will probably only be possible if the tour includes transportation up to Burbayar. Otherwise begin hiking up to the **Continental Divide** from El Llano. Spend the night in Burbayar Lodge, about 15 kilometers north of the Interamerican Highway.

DAY 3

Explore the forest around Burbayar, then head over the Continental Divide through Kuna territory toward Cartí, on the Caribbean coast 22 kilometers from Burbayar. Camp in the forest.

DAY 4

Arrive in **Cartí** early in the morning and hire a boat to one of the islands around **El Porvenir**. Snorkel around **Achutupu** and spend the night in a Kuna hotel.

DAY 5

Fly back to Panama City. Spend the day sightseeing and resting.

DAY 6

Take an early-morning flight to David and transfer to **Cerro Punta**. Spend the afternoon exploring the area or hiking in **Parque Internacional La Amistad**.

DAY 7

Hike up **Volcán Barú** and set up camp in the afternoon. Pitch a tent close to the summit.

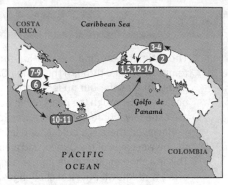

DAY 8

Arrive at the summit by dawn for the best chance of a clear view of both oceans. Head back down the mountain after breakfast.

DAY 9

Spend the afternoon relaxing around Cerro Punta. The truly energetic can hike in the forest in search of quetzals.

DAYS 10–11

Head back down to David and transfer, through a tour operator, to **Parque Nacional Coiba** for scubadiving. Spend two nights at the ranger station on Isla Coiba.

DAYS 12–13

Transfer to Panama City. Visit the **Panama Canal** and the remaining Panama City sights. This is also the time for souvenir shopping, a little pampering, and maybe a fancy meal or two after all that time in the boonies.

DAY 14

Transfer to Tocumen International Airport for the flight home.

Those on a tight schedule who want a broad introduction to Panama can see the capital, the canal, and the hottest highland and beach destinations in less than two weeks. This would be a jam-packed trip with little down time, but because these are popular destinations, there are good travel connections between them. Don't be surprised, however, if you wish you had more time in every place, particularly Boquete and Bocas.

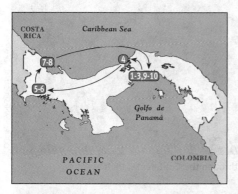

DAY 1
Arrive at Tocumen International Airport and transfer to a Panama City hotel.

DAY 2
Visit the Spanish ruins of Panamá la Vieja and take a walking tour of Casco Viejo. Splurge on dinner at one of Panama City's better restaurants.

DAY 3
Visit the Panama Canal, particularly Miraflores Locks, Gaillard Cut, and the Gamboa area. Stop by

Bocas del Toro

COURTESY PANAMA CANAL COMMISSION

The Panama Canal's Gaillard Cut was dug right through the Continental Divide.

the Amador Causeway in the morning or evening to admire the view and stretch the legs.

DAY 4

Take the early-morning train across the isthmus and explore the Spanish ruins of Portobelo and Fuerte San Lorenzo as well as Gatún Locks. Those who plan to be in Panama City on a Saturday can opt instead for a day-transit of the canal. Return to Panama City at the end of the day.

DAYS 5–6

Fly to David and transfer to a Boquete hotel. A quick visit might include either a hike in search of quetzals or a white-water rafting trip.

DAYS 7–8

Return to David early in the morning and fly to Bocas del Toro. Stay at a hotel in Bocas town, exploring the town the first evening and going for a boating and snorkeling trip to Cayo Crawl, Swan's Cay, and Boca del Drago the next morning.

DAY 9

Fly back to Panama City for last-minute shopping and sightseeing.

DAY 10

Transfer to Tucumen International Airport for the flight home.

Those fascinated by Panama's role as a crossroads of the world can cover 500 years of history in less than a week. This requires skipping most of the natural attractions of Panama and concentrating on the human efforts to conquer the isthmus by trail, railway, and canal. Most touring is within a narrow band no more than 100 kilometers or so from the capital, making this an especially economical and speedy introduction to the country.

DAY 1

Arrive at Tocumen International Airport and transfer to a hotel in Panama City.

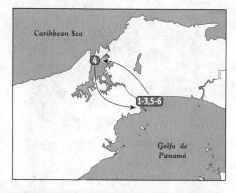

DAYS 2–3

Begin the first day with a morning visit to the ruins of **Panamá la Vieja**, and then spend the afternoon and next day exploring **Casco Viejo** and the greater **San Felipe area**. Those up for a long walk can begin at **El Museo Antropológico Reina Torres de Araúz**, and then walk up Avenida Central to Plaza Santa Ana, stopping for a snack and

Panamá la Vieja's cathedral tower is one of the country's most beloved icons.

view from the Panama Canal's Administration Building, July 4th, 1919, Balboa

a drink at Café Coca Cola. Continue into Casco Viejo and explore all the churches and little museums on the walking tour. The next day, after exploring the rest of central Casco Viejo, continue through the Terraplén, the public market, Salsipuedes, and the Barrio Chino. Be cautious, and, if possible, go with a guide who knows the area and its history well.

DAY 4

Take the Panama Railway across the isthmus and visit Portobelo, Fuerte San Lorenzo, and Gatún Locks. A boat trip down the Río Chagres is especially evocative for those who want a sense of what conquistadors, pirates, and '49ers faced when they first arrived on the isthmus. Take the train back to Panama City.

DAY 5

This day can be devoted to the history of the Panama Canal. Begin by exploring the old townsites of Ancón and Balboa, being sure to stop by the old high school, now the Centro de Capacitación Ascanio Arosemena, to see the many relics and mementos that date from the earliest canal-construction days. Have lunch at the Miraflores Locks visitors center, and then tour the locks and the center's exhibits. Continue to Pedro Miguel and Gaillard Cut, then head out to Madden Forest to see a bit of the fabled Camino de Cruces. Return to Panama City for dinner.

DAY 6

Transfer to Tucumen International Airport for the return flight home.

Explore
Panama

Panama City

Panama City surprises first-time visitors. When they cruise into Panama Bay or drive down Corredor Sur from the airport, they're stunned to see all the modern, closely packed towers rising out of the ocean. Panama City is far more cosmopolitan than many Latin American cities, certainly those in Central America.

But its vibrant modernity really shouldn't be surprising, given the capital's status as an international banking center and its location next to the Pacific entrance of the Panama Canal, the "crossroads of the world." Panama City has been important to world commerce since its founding nearly 500 years ago.

Because of all this, it's also in many ways an international city. The shops of Indian and Chinese merchants have been city institutions for generations. Any given day might find Colombian émigrés having a drink in a British pub, Japanese businessmen making a deal in a Brazilian steakhouse, and Canadian retirees looking for their place in the tropical sun.

The city's acceptance of its rich diversity can be seen in its houses of worship: Along with its

Must-Sees

Look for M to find the sights and activities you can't miss and M for the best dining and lodging.

M Panamá la Vieja: Founded nearly 500 years ago, this original Panama City was the first Spanish city on the Pacific coast of the Americas. Its stone ruins transport one back to the time of gold-hungry conquistadors and pillaging buccaneers (page 38).

M Casco Viejo: This charming colonial neighborhood is the cornerstone of modern Panama City. It was founded in 1673 after the sacking of Panamá la Vieja, and an ambitious renovation project has brought restaurants, theaters, and clubs to its historic buildings, sidewalk cafés to its quaint plazas, and new life to its crumbling churches. It's the most colorful part of Panama City (page 39).

© WILLIAM FRIAR

The streets of Casco Viejo lend themselves to fascinating walking tours.

M El Museo Antropológico Reina Torres de Araúz: The modest displays don't usually live up to the grand building, but the city's anthropology museum does have some fascinating pre-Colombian treasures. It's also a good place to start a walking tour from Plaza Cinco de Mayo down the pedestrian stretch of busy Avenida Central (page 44).

M Parque Natural Metropolitano: More than a city park, this 265-hectarce tropical forest within the city limits offers a glimpse of Panama's flora and fauna for those who can't make it to the country's enormous national parks (page 50).

M Calle Uruguay Area: Panama City's most dynamic nightlife destination lies along Calle Uruguay, where trendy new restaurants and clubs open and close constantly (page 53).

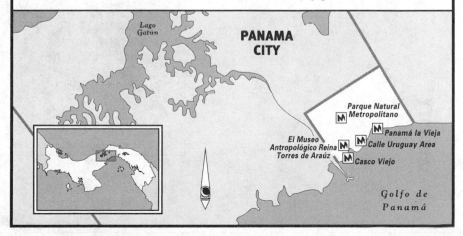

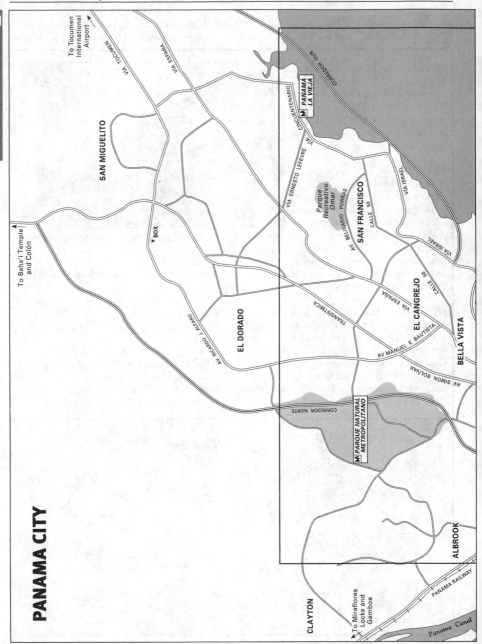

PANAMA CITY

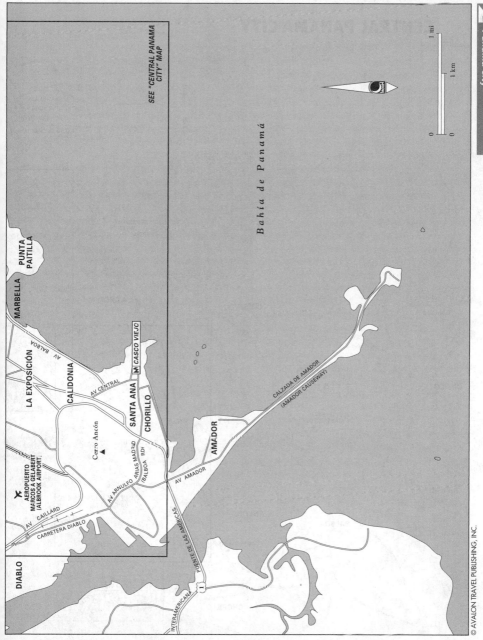

SEE "CENTRAL PANAMA CITY" MAP

Bahía de Panamá

DIABLO

PUNTA PAITILLA

MARBELLA

LA EXPOSICIÓN

CALIDONIA

AV BALBOA

CASCO VIEJO

SANTA ANA

AV CENTRAL

CHORILLO

Cerro Ancón

ARIAS MADRID
(BALBOA RD)

AEROPUERTO
MARCOS A GELABERT
(ALBROOK AIRPORT)

AV CAILLARD

CARRETERA DIABLO

AV ARNULFO

AV AMADOR

AMADOR

CALZADA DE AMADOR
(AMADOR CAUSEWAY)

PUENTE DE LAS AMÉRICAS

INTERAMERICANA

0   1 km
0   1 mi

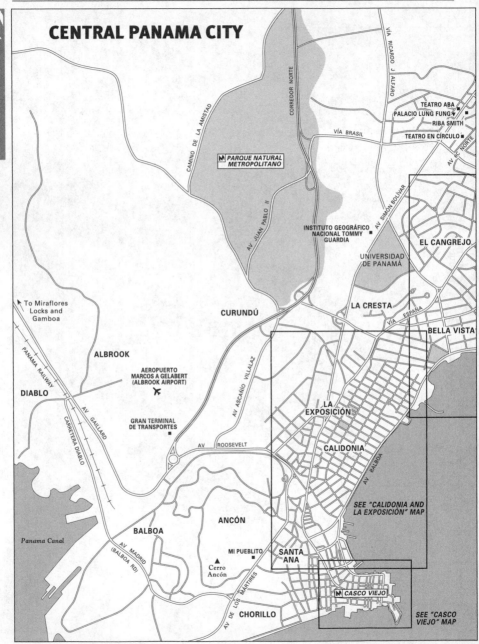

CENTRAL PANAMA CITY

Panama City

TEATRO ABA
PALACIO LUNG FUNG
RIBA SMITH
TEATRO EN CÍRCULO

VÍA RICARDO J ALFARO

CORREDOR NORTE

CAMINO DE LA AMISTAD

VÍA BRASIL

AV IC NORTE

PARQUE NATURAL METROPOLITANO

AV JUAN PABLO II

AV SIMÓN BOLÍVAR

INSTITUTO GEOGRÁFICO NACIONAL TOMMY GUARDIA

EL CANGREJO

UNIVERSIDAD DE PANAMÁ

To Miraflores Locks and Gamboa

CURUNDÚ

LA CRESTA

VÍA ESPAÑA

BELLA VISTA

PANAMA RAILWAY

ALBROOK

AEROPUERTO MARCOS A GELABERT (ALBROOK AIRPORT)

AV ASCANIO VILLALAZ

AV GAILLARD

DIABLO

GRAN TERMINAL DE TRANSPORTES

LA EXPOSICIÓN

CARRETERA DIABLO

AV ROOSEVELT

CALIDONIA

AV BALBOA

SEE "CALIDONIA AND LA EXPOSICIÓN" MAP

Panama Canal

BALBOA

ANCÓN

MI PUEBLITO

SANTA ANA

AV MADRID (BALBOA RD)

Cerro Ancón

AV DE LOS MÁRTIRES

CASCO VIEJO

CHORILLO

SEE "CASCO VIEJO" MAP

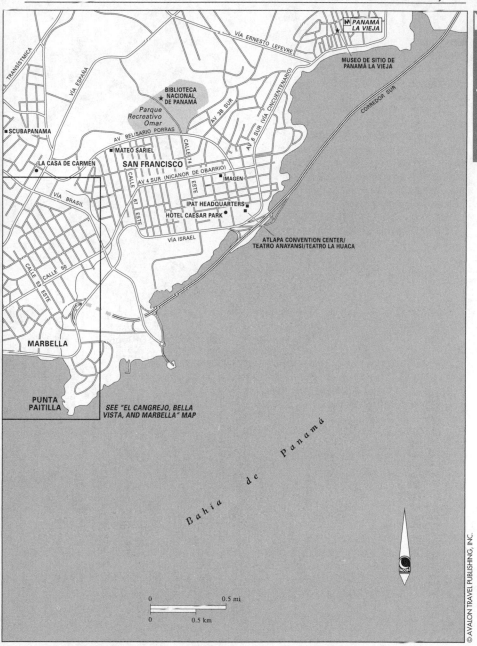

PANAMÁ LA VIEJA

MUSEO DE SITIO DE PANAMÁ LA VIEJA

CORREDOR SUR

VÍA ERNESTO LEFEVRE

BIBLIOTECA NACIONAL DE PANAMÁ

Parque Recreativo Omar

SCUBAPANAMA

AV BELISARIO PORRAS

MATEO SARIEL

LA CASA DE CARMEN

SAN FRANCISCO

AV 4 SUR (NICANOR DE OBARRIO)

IMAGEN

IPAT HEADQUARTERS

HOTEL CAESAR PARK

VÍA ISRAEL

ATLAPA CONVENTION CENTER/ TEATRO ANAYANSI/TEATRO LA HUACA

VÍA BRASIL

CALLE 50

CALLE 53 ESTE

MARBELLA

PUNTA PAITILLA

SEE "EL CANGREJO, BELLA VISTA, AND MARBELLA" MAP

TRANSISTMICA

VÍA ESPAÑA

AV 3B SUR

AV 6 SUR (VÍA CINCUENTENARIO)

CALLE 74

CALLE 67 ESTE

Bahia de Panamá

0   0.5 mi

0   0.5 km

© AVALON TRAVEL PUBLISHING, INC.

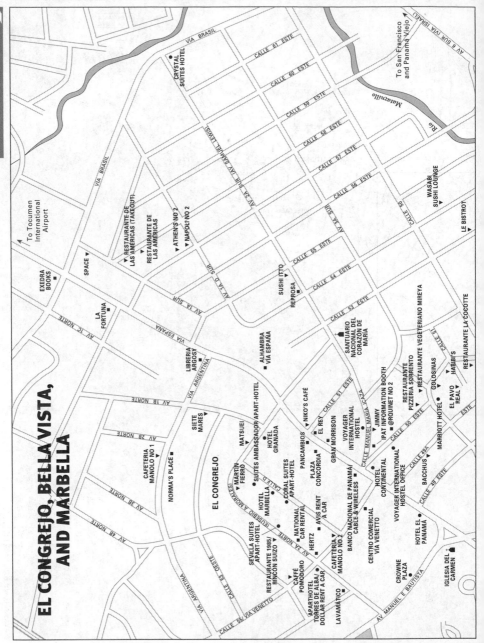

EL CONGREJO, BELLAVISTA, AND MARBELLA

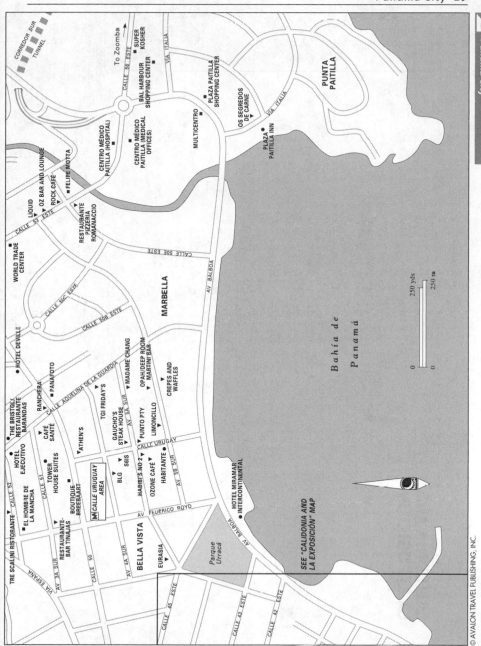

CORREDOR SUR TUNNEL

To Zoomba

SUPER KOSHER

CALLE 58 ESTE

BAL HARBOUR SHOPPING CENTER

VIA ITALIA

PLAZA PAITILLA SHOPPING CENTER

PUNTA PAITILLA

CENTRO MÉDICO PAITILLA (HOSPITAL)

CENTRO MÉDICO PAITILLA (MEDICAL OFFICES)

OS SEGREDOS DE CARNE

VIA ITALIA

MULTICENTRO

PLAZA PAITILLA INN

FELIPE MOTTA

OZ BAR AND LOUNGE

ROCK CAFÉ

LIQUID

CALLE 53 ESTE

RESTAURANTE PIZZERIA ROMANACCIO

CALLE 50E ESTE

WORLD TRADE CENTER

MARBELLA

AV. BALBOA

CALLE 50C ESTE

CALLE 50B ESTE

HOTEL DEVILLE

Bahía de Panamá

RANCHERA

PANAFOTO

CALLE AQUELINA DE LA GUARDIA

MADAME CHANG

OPAH/DEEP ROOM MARTINI BAR

THE BRISTOL

RESTAURANTE BARANDAS

CAFÉ SANTÉ

TGI FRIDAY'S

AV. 5A SUR

CREPES AND WAFFLES

HOTEL EJECUTIVO

ATHEN'S

GAUCHO'S STEAK HOUSE

PUNTO PTY

LIMONCILLO

CALLE 52

CALLE 51

TOWER HOUSE SUITES

BOUTIQUE BREEBAART

CALLE URUGUAY AREA

BLG

S6IS

CALLE URUGUAY

HABITANTE

HABIBI'S NO 2

OZONE CAFÉ

AV. 5B SUR

TRE SCALINI RISTORANTE

EL HOMBRE DE LA MANCHA

RESTAURANTE-BAR TINAJAS

AV. FEDERICO BOYD

HOTEL MIRAMAR INTERCONTINENTAL

VIA ESPAÑA

AV. 3A SUR

BELLA VISTA

CALLE 50

AV. 4A SUR

EURASIA

AV. BALBOA

Parque Urracá

SEE "CALIDONIA AND LA EXPOSICIÓN" MAP

CALLE 45 ESTE

CALLE 43 ESTE

CALLE 42 ESTE

0   250 yds
0   250 m

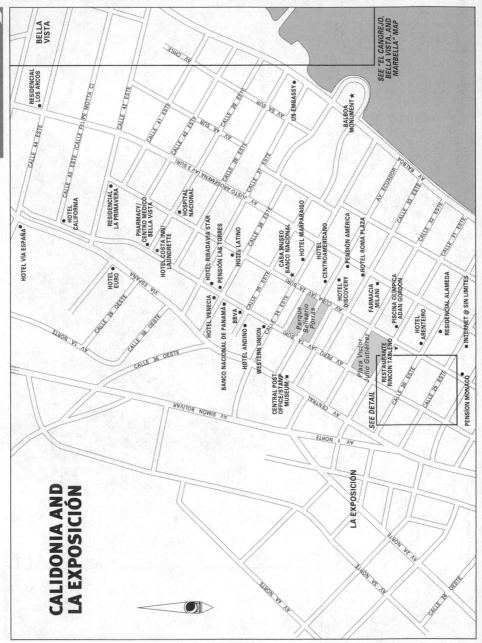

CALIDONIA AND
LA EXPOSICIÓN

LA EXPOSICIÓN

BELLA VISTA

SEE 'EL CANGREJO,
BELLA VISTA AND
MARBELLA' MAP

RESIDENCIAL
LOS ARCOS

AV CHILE

CALLE 42 ESTE

CALLE 43 ESTE (CALLE FELIPE MOTTA CI)

CALLE 44 ESTE

HOTEL
CALIFORNIA

RESIDENCIAL
LA PRIMAVERA

CALLE 41 ESTE

CALLE 40 ESTE

CALLE 39 ESTE

AV 4A SUR

AV 3A SUR

US EMBASSY

BALBOA
MONUMENT

AV BALBOA

AV ECUADOR

CALLE 33 ESTE

CALLE 32 ESTE

CALLE 31 ESTE

HOTEL VÍA ESPAÑA

HOTEL
EURO

VÍA ESPAÑA

PHARMACY/
CENTRO MÉDICO
BELLA VISTA

HOTEL COSTA INN/
LAUNDRETTE

HOSPITAL
NACIONAL

AV JUSTO AROSEMENA/AV 3 SUR

CALLE 38 ESTE

CALLE 37 ESTE

HOTEL MARPARAISO

HOTEL
CENTROAMERICANO

PENSIÓN AMÉRICA

HOTEL ROMA PLAZA

CALLE 38 OESTE

CALLE 37 OESTE

AV 1A NORTE

HOTEL VENECIA

HOTEL RIBADAVIA/ STAR

PENSIÓN LAS TORRES

HOTEL LATINO

CALLE 35 ESTE

CASA MUSEO
BANCO NACIONAL

AV CUBA/AV 2A SUR

HOTEL
DISCOVERY

FARMACIA
MILANI

PISCINA OLÍMPICA
ADAN GORDON

RESIDENCIAL ALAMEDA

INTERNET @ SIN LIMITES

BANCO NACIONAL DE PANAMA

BBVA

HOTEL ANDINO

WESTERN UNION

CALLE 34 ESTE

AV PERÚ/AV 1A SUR

Parque
Belisario
Porras

Plaza Víctor
Julio Gutiérrez

HOTEL
ARENTEIRO

CALLE 36 OESTE

CENTRAL POST
OFFICE/STAMP
MUSEUM

AV CENTRAL

RESTAURANTE
RINCÓN TABLEÑO

SEE DETAIL

CALLE 30 ESTE

CALLE 29 ESTE

PENSIÓN MÓNACO

AV SIMÓN BOLÍVAR

AV 1 NORTE

AV 2A NORTE

AV 3A NORTE

AV 4A NORTE

CALLE 38 OESTE

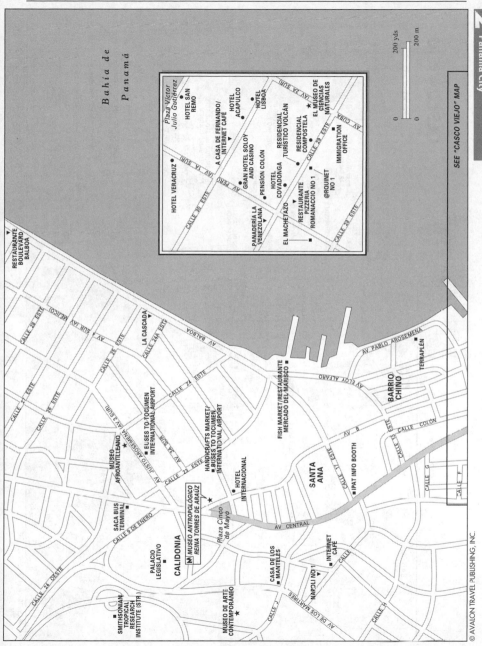

Panama City

*Bahia de
Panamá*

SEE "CASCO VIEJO" MAP

© AVALON TRAVEL PUBLISHING, INC.

CASCO VIEJO

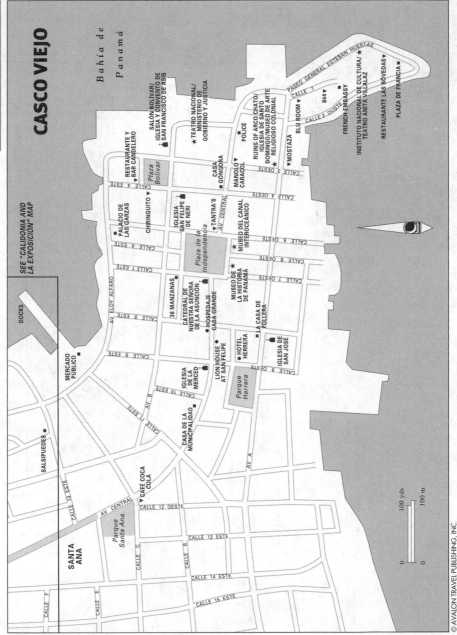

Bahía de
Panamá

SEE "CALIDONIA AND
LA EXPOSICIÓN" MAP

DOCKS

MERCADO
PÚBLICO

SALSIPUEDES

PASEO GENERAL ESTEBAN HUERTAS

SALÓN BOLÍVAR/
IGLESIA Y CONVENTO DE
SAN FRANCISCO DE ASÍS

RESTAURANTE Y
BAR CANDELERO

Plaza
Bolívar

PALACIO DE
LAS GARZAS

CHIRINGUITO

IGLESIA
SAN FELIPE
DE NERI

TANTRA'S

CASA
GÓNGORA

★ TEATRO NACIONAL/
MINISTERIO DE
GOBIERNO Y JUSTICIA

POLICE

MANOLO
CARACOL

RUINS OF ARCO CHATO
IGLESIA DE SANTO
DOMINGO/MUSEO DE ARTE
RELIGIOSO COLONIAL

MOSTAZA

BLU ROOM

CALLE 1

844

CALLE 2 OUISTE

FRENCH EMBASSY

INSTITUTO NACIONAL DE CULTURA/
TEATRO ANITA VILLALAZ

RESTAURANTE LAS BÓVEDAS

PLAZA DE FRANCIA

Plaza de la
Independencia

MUSEO DEL CANAL
INTEROCEÁNICO

CALLE 3 OESTE

CALLE 4 OESTE

CALLE 5 OESTE

AV. CENTRAL

CALLE 4 ESTE

CALLE 5 ESTE

CALLE 6 ESTE

CALLE 7 ESTE

AV. ELOY ALFARO

CALLE 8 ESTE

38 MANZANAS

CATEDRAL DE
NUESTRA SEÑORA
DE LA ASUNCIÓN

HOSPEDAJE
CASA GRANDE

MUSEO DE
LA HISTORIA
DE PANAMÁ

LA CASA DE
POLLERA

CALLE 6 OESTE

CALLE 7 OESTE

CALLE 9 ESTE

IGLESIA DE LA
MERCED

LION HOUSE
AT SAN FELIPE

HOTEL
HERRERA

IGLESIA DE
SAN JOSÉ

Parque
Herrera

CALLE 9 OESTE

CALLE 10 ESTE

AV. B

CASA DE LA
MUNICIPALIDAD

CALLE 11 ESTE

AV. A

CAFÉ COCA
COLA

SANTA
ANA

Parque
Santa Ana

AV. CENTRAL

CALLE 13 ESTE

CALLE C

CALLE B

CALLE 12 OESTE

CALLE 13 ESTE

CALLE 14 ESTE

CALLE 15 ESTE

CALLE F

CALLE E

100 yds

100 m

0

0

© AVALON TRAVEL PUBLISHING, INC.

Roman Catholic churches are synagogues, mosques, one of the world's seven Bahá'i houses of worship, the Greek Orthodox Metropolitanate of Central America, a prominent Hindu temple, and gathering houses for every conceivable Protestant congregation.

The one faith that draws all these people together is business. Deals are being made everywhere at all times, from the kids hawking cell-phone accessories at congested intersections, to the developers determined to build on every square centimeter of open space. Life is fast-paced compared with the rest of Panama, and the city's residents are comparatively assertive, street-savvy, and no-nonsense. Panama City is to, say, the Azuero peninsula as New York City is to rural Nebraska. Everyone on the road is in a great hurry, and skyscrapers pop up seemingly overnight.

Still, by the standards of many other countries' capitals, Panama City is a mellow, fun-loving place. Any excuse for a party will do, and big celebrations, especially Carnaval, can shut down the whole city.

Those who come to Panama solely for its natural treasures will be tempted to blast right through the capital on their way to the country's forests, mountains, islands, and beaches. But it'd be a shame not to spend at least a day or two in Panama City. Hundreds of years of history live on in its streets, and its more modern attractions and international restaurants are especially appealing after roughing it in the wilderness for a while. Besides, it has its very own tropical forest. Even city streets aren't far removed from nature; an entire book has been written on the birds of Panama City.

PLANNING YOUR TIME

Those in a big hurry can see Panama City's main tourist attractions, from Casco Viejo to Panamá la Vieja, in a single day. But anyone with a bit more time should plan on spending at least a couple of days in the capital. That's the only way to get a sense of its rhythms and to experience its less-showy charms: feeling a tropical evening breeze at a sidewalk café, splurging

on dinner at an elegant restaurant, bargaining for *molas* with a Kuna Indian, dancing at an all-night club, or just people-watching along its streets.

The ruins of **Panamá la Vieja** can be explored in about two hours, including a visit to the little museum and the handicraft kiosks on the site. Plan on a half day for a walking tour of the historic quarter of **Casco Viejo** that includes visits to its major museums and churches and lunch or a drink at one of its restaurants or cafés.

A second day in the city could include a walking tour of its major **shopping streets.** In rough ascending order of priciness, these include: Avenida Central, Vía España, Calle 53 in Marbella, and Avenida 2 Sur/Samuel Lewis in Obarrio. Trying to get to all these areas in a single day would make for a long, hot, tiring slog.

Avenida Central is crowded with discount stores that don't have much to offer foreign visitors, but it's a fun place to explore. The section that extends from **Plaza Cinco de Mayo** to **Parque Santa Ana** has been closed to most traffic and is now a walking street. One possible way to see it is to walk up one side of the street, stop for a drink at the venerable Café Coca Cola next to tiny Parque Santa Ana, then come back on the other side of the street. Allow time to visit the **handicrafts market** on Plaza Cinco de Mayo and the anthropology museum, **Museo Antropológico Reina Torres de Araúz,** next to it. Covering all this ground could take a couple of hours to half a day.

The more modern and somewhat more upscale **Vía España** also lends itself to wandering, though it's not exactly pedestrian-friendly and the street is congested with traffic. This is more an area to find trip supplies than to get interesting souvenirs, but again, the people-watching is fun. The posh shops on **Calle 53** and **Avenida 2 Sur/Samuel Lewis** are concentrated in a smaller area.

Those not planning to visit the Azuero peninsula or indigenous villages should consider spending an hour or two at **Mi Pueblito,** which contains idealized recreations of a late-Spanish-colonial rural town, housing for West Indian laborers on the Panama Canal, and the traditional dwellings of the Kuna, Emberá-Wounaan, and Ngöbe-Buglé. It's a tourist site, but it's reasonably well done and I've never seen it crowded.

If time and budget allow, plan on at least one evening out on the town. Good areas to combine dinner and clubbing include **Casco Viejo,** the **Calle Uruguay** area, **Calle 53 in Marbella,** and **El Cangrejo. Vía Argentina** also has a mix of good restaurants and late-night cafeterias. The tourist restaurant **Tinajas** is a traditional place to go for a taste of Panamanian food and folkloric dances (dancing on Tuesday, Thursday, Friday, and Saturday nights only).

Insatiable museum buffs who've seen the anthropology museum and exhausted those in Casco Viejo can add on a visit to **El Museo de Arte Contemporáneo** and **La Casa Museo Banco Nacional.** An hour at each should be plenty.

A morning or early evening stroll along **Avenida Balboa** near the statue of Balboa overlooking Panama Bay is pleasant and offers good photo possibilities. **Parque Natural Metropolitano** offers a chance for a true tropical-nature walk within the city limits. It's a short drive from downtown, and the longest trail takes two hours to walk.

Intrepid travelers who want to immerse themselves in a grittier but undeniably colorful part of Panama City could consider spending a few hours wandering around the public markets and ramshackle kiosks in the area around Casco Viejo, most of which is in the **Santa Ana** district. Highlights include a modest **Chinatown (Barrio Chino),** the crowded shopping street of **Salsipuedes,** the **fish market (Mercado de Mariscos),** the **meat and produce market (Mercado Público),** and the repair and bric-a-brac stalls of the **Terraplén.** Note: Parts of this area are fairly rough and definitely not for everyone. Dress down, don't wear jewelry, and try not to look touristy. Explore it only during the day.

Those compelled to see and do it all can cover everything listed above in about four full days, after which they'll definitely be ready for a rest. However, most will be content to hit the highlights over the course of two or three days.

Panama Canal Sights

Because downtown Panama City is so close to the Panama Canal, many visitors prefer to extend their stay in the city and make day trips to explore the canal area rather than shift their home base to lodging in the former Canal Zone. (Others prefer to do just the opposite: Make a canal-area hotel their base and explore Panama City from there.)

In that case, plan on an extra day or two to see **Miraflores Locks, Gaillard Cut,** the **Amador Causeway (Calzada de Amador),** and **Gamboa.** Those interested in visiting **Isla Taboga** should budget a full day for that alone. (See the *Panama Canal* chapter for details on all these.)

It's also possible to see the highlights of the Caribbean side of the canal during a day trip, though it can be a pretty long day given the distances involved—it's 80 kilometers each way just to cross the isthmus, most of it on slow roads in need of repair. Plan on getting an early start to visit **Gatún Locks, Gatún Lake,** the **Colón Free Zone,** and **Fuerte San Lorenzo.** Adding **Portobelo,** about 60 kilometers from Colón, mostly on a windy two-lane road, would make for a very crammed day trip. Consider spending one night on the Caribbean side of the isthmus to see everything. (See the *Central Caribbean* chapter for details.)

These time estimates assume travel in a taxi or rental car. Doing all this by bus and local taxi is logistically tricky and slower. However, consider going over or coming back by the **Panama Railway;** it's pricey and the times are inconvenient, but it's a memorable trip.

HISTORY

Panama City has had three distinct incarnations. The original city, the first European city on the Pacific Ocean, was founded on August 15, 1519, by Pedro Arias de Ávila, better known as Pedrarias. The Spanish governor of Castilla de Oro (the conquistadors' name for all their Central American possessions), Pedrarias was notoriously cruel and bloodthirsty, responsible for the slaughter of many of the isthmus's indigenous people as

"PANAMA": AN ABUNDANCE OF THEORIES

The country of Panama gets its name from the city of Panama, but what does "Panama" mean? No one knows for sure.

The Spanish first used the name in conjunction with a native fishing village they soon claimed as the cornerstone of their new capital. It's little wonder, then, that the most common explanation is that Panama (or, to be proper, *Panamá*), is a forgotten indigenous word for "abundance of fishes." Another theory is that the word means "abundance of butterflies." Yet another posits that the striking (and abundant) Panama tree lent its name to the city and then the republic. Some say the word just meant "abundance," hence the odd variety of plentiful things associated with it. A personal favorite is that it means "to rock in a hammock."

Take your pick: All definitions still fit.

well as the execution of his rival Balboa on a fabricated charge of treason.

Pedrarias moved the capital from the town of Santa María de Antigua in the Darién to the site of an Indian fishing village on the Pacific coast one of his lieutenants had discovered four years earlier. The Spaniards reported that the village was called Panamá, which according to one theory was the Cueva Indian word for "place where many fishes are caught."

The town quickly gained in importance as the Pacific port of the Camino Real and later the Camino de Cruces, trails across the isthmus over which treasure from the looting of the Inca Empire was brought from South America.

All that treasure attracted pirates, and in 1671 the Welsh buccaneer Henry Morgan, having taken the Caribbean-side Spanish fort of San Lorenzo, led his men on a brutal trek across the isthmus to sack Panama City. The city, built mainly of wood, burned to the ground during a vicious battle between the buccaneers and Spaniards on January 28, 1671. No one knows whether it was the buccaneers or the Spanish who started the fire. Morgan's own chronicler said the pirate did it but blamed it on the Spaniards. In another version, the Spaniards inadvertently destroyed the city while blowing up a munitions dump they didn't want the pirates to capture. In any event, much of its wealth and nearly all its buildings were destroyed.

The furious buccaneers, deprived of their expected riches, tortured city residents suspected of hiding treasure. They hardly left empty-handed:

A contemporary account claims they crossed back over the isthmus with 165 mules weighted down with silver plate and coins. Today all that remains of the original Panama City, now known as Panamá la Vieja or, as it's more commonly known, Panamá Viejo (Old Panama), are the ruins of a few stone buildings, including what's left of the cathedral's tower, which has become a national symbol.

One treasure survived, however: a church's golden altar that, according to isthmian lore, was painted black by a quick-thinking priest to fool the buccaneers into thinking it was made of base metal. The altar now sits in a church in Casco Viejo.

After Morgan's rampage, the Spaniards decided to rebuild the city in a more easily defensible site. The site chosen was a small peninsula near the base of a hill, Cerro Ancón, less than 10 kilometers to the west. Founded on January 21, 1673, the entire new city was ringed by a thick wall and other fortifications. Though some still argued the city's defenses were inadequate, Panama City was never sacked again.

Casco Viejo, the modern name for the second Panama City, is surprisingly well preserved, but time, neglect, and fires have done plenty of damage even without the help of pirates. The walls have mostly come down, though visitors can still walk along the intact and impressively massive seawall in the area now known as the Plaza de Francia. A major restoration is turning this area of narrow brick streets, quaint plazas, and flower-draped balconies into one of Panama City's prime tourist attractions.

Panama City declined along with the Spanish Empire during the 18th century. It became a sleepy provincial backwater, awakening from its tropical torpor just twice in the 19th century: during the California Gold Rush years, when Panama City became the Pacific terminus of the Panama Railroad, and during the failed canal-building effort of the French, who made their headquarters in Panama City (their administration building, now a museum, still stands in Casco Viejo).

But it wasn't until after Panama became an independent republic in 1903, with Panama City as its capital, that the modern city began to emerge. This had much to do with the arrival of the United States to build the Panama Canal. As one of its first acts, the United States had the city paved, fumigated, sanitized, and supplied with running water. This eventually led to the eradication of the most virulent diseases afflicting the city and country, especially yellow fever and malaria. The opening of the canal in 1914 ensured Panama City's reemergence as a center of world commerce, which it remains to this day.

Casco Viejo continued to be the heart of the city during the first decades of the 20th century. But the city's tremendous growth, particularly since the 1980s, has turned the San Felipe district, as it's also known, into a charming old neighborhood tucked away from the mainstream of a sprawling modern metropolis. Most of its massive walls have long since been knocked down as the city spilled out to the north and east.

In modern times, the biggest upheaval to face Panama City was the 1989 U.S. invasion, dubbed "Operation Just Cause," that removed the dictator General Manuel Noriega from power. The hardest-hit area of the city was El Chorrillo, an impoverished neighborhood of wooden tenements that lay right next to the Comandancia, Noriega's headquarters. The area was devastated by fire during the U.S. attack on the Comandancia. An estimated 2,000 homes were destroyed and an estimated 15,000 residents left homeless. No one knows for sure how many died here, or during the invasion as a whole. Estimates of total civilian deaths during the invasion range from about 200 to 4,000. Many of these occurred in El Chorrillo, which had been a center of anti-Noriega sentiment. There has been some rebuilding in El Chorrillo, but it remains a poor, neglected, and crime-ridden neighborhood.

Panama City has enjoyed considerable peace, prosperity, and political stability in the years since the invasion. A forest of tall office towers and condominiums has transformed the skyline in the last few years, and with the U.S. turnover of the Panama Canal on December 31, 1999, the city has spilled over its traditional limits and, for better and worse, is absorbing and transforming the former Canal Zone as well.

Sights

ORIENTATION

Panama City is a growing metropolis of 708,000 people, all of whom seem to be in cars 24 hours a day. Roads and public transportation have not kept pace with the city's growth, and the streets are choked during morning and evening rush hours. In recent years the city has grown east toward Tocumen International Airport, and with the city's absorption of the former U.S. Canal Zone, urban sprawl has been creeping north and west as well.

Note that Panamanians typically drop the "city" when referring to Panama City and call it simply Panama (in English) or Panamá (in Spanish—pah-nah-MA). Formally, it's la Ciudad de Panamá.

The city is bounded by the Bahía de Panamá (Bay of Panama) and the Pacific Ocean to the south and the Panama Canal to the west. The terrain is fairly flat—the United States dug the canal nearby because the Continental Divide is particularly low-lying here—though a few isolated hills, most notably Cerro Ancón, jut near the canal's Pacific entrance. The climate is hot and humid in the dry season (approximately mid-December to mid-April) and hot, very humid, and wet in the rainy season. But for most of the rainy season storms don't sweep in until midafternoon and generally come down in short, powerful bursts that race on as quickly as they arrive. Because of the high ratio of concrete to trees, midday can be wiltingly hot, especially at the height of the dry season. Early mornings and evenings, though, are often pleasant and relatively mild. And few things are as soothing as a dry-season breeze at night.

The section of the city of most interest to visitors runs along the coast from Casco Viejo, the cornerstone of modern Panama City, east to the ruins of Panamá la Vieja, eight kilometers away. The most cosmopolitan parts of the capital lie between these two boundaries.

Getting one's bearings can be tricky in Panama City, given its confusing mass of winding streets and its topsy-turvy geography (some never get used to seeing the Pacific Ocean lying to the south, for instance).

The city is organized into a series of loosely defined neighborhoods, and thinking in terms of these helps make sense of the place. The only ones most travelers will be concerned with are **Punta Paitilla, Marbella, Bella Vista, El Cangrejo, Calidonia/La Exposición,** and **San Felipe/Casco Viejo.** (Former Canal Zone townsites such as Balboa and Ancón, and former U.S. military bases such as Albrook and Amador—which are all now technically part of Panama City—are covered in the *Panama Canal* chapter.)

Vía España, a busy commercial street, has long been the heart of modern Panama City. In recent years, though, the action has spread just north to El Cangrejo and south to Bella Vista and Marbella. Most of Panama's upscale hotels, restaurants, and shops are in these areas.

An area of about three square blocks between Bella Vista and Marbella, centered on **Calle Uruguay** (also called Calle 48 Este), is a booming nightlife destination of restaurants and clubs, as is, to a lesser degree, the main strip through Marbella, **Calle 53.**

An older commercial center is found along **Avenida Central** in the Calidonia district, a neighborhood that contains most of the budget hotels. The west end of Avenida Central, from Plaza Cinco de Mayo to Parque Santa Ana, is now a walking street. Its shops deal mainly in electronics, jewelry, discount clothing, and the like, but it's worth a stroll for the people-watching even for those not in a shopping mood. On a typical day one can spot Kuna women going about their business in traditional clothing, juice vendors crushing sugarcane in old-fashioned presses, and hawkers trying to lure customers into stores. The area is well patrolled by police, but be alert for pickpockets anyway.

Below this area is the district of **San Felipe,** which contains the historic neighborhood of **Casco Viejo,** tucked away on a small peninsula. This once *was* Panama City, and it's still the capital's administrative and cultural hub. The walls that once protected it from pirates have mostly come down, but its brick streets and colonial buildings remain. A large-scale renovation is rescuing it from decades of neglect.

Avenida de los Mártires, formerly known as **Fourth of July Avenue,** used to mark the boundary between Panama City and the former Canal Zone. Most of the shops on the Panama City side closed with the departure of the Zonians who used to do business there. The area is now mainly notable for the proximity of the rather homely building, the **Palacio Legislativo,** which houses the Asamblea Legislativa (Panama's national legislature) on one side and the **Museo de Arte Contemporáneo** (museum of modern art) and headquarters of the **Smithsonian Tropical Research Institute** on the other.

A few other major arteries are worth mentioning. Broad **Avenida Balboa** borders Panama Bay from Casco Viejo to the posh condo towers of Punta Paitilla. The bustling commercial street of **Calle 50** runs between and parallel to Vía España and Avenida Balboa. North of all three of these is the **Transístmica (Avenida Simón Bolívar),** which cuts across the city and then heads north across the isthmus. However, those planning to head north toward the Caribbean are much better off taking the new toll road, **Corredor Norte,** which extends about a third of the way and supposedly will one day be completed clear across the isthmus to the city of Colón. Taking it saves a lot of time and hassle for $2.50. Another toll road, **Corredor Sur,** leads from Tocumen International Airport to Panama City, where it meets Avenida Balboa. Again, it's well worth the maximum toll of $2.40.

HISTORIC SITES

 Panamá la Vieja

These extensive ruins are all that's left of the original Panama City. The ruins are on the eastern outskirts of the modern-day city, an easy drive east along Vía Cincuentenario. The Corredor Sur arcs right by it, making for an especially impressive sight at night, when the ruins are illuminated. Note that the site is commonly

The ruins of Panamá la Vieja's cathedral tower, one of the few structures to survive Henry Morgan's sacking of the city in 1671, is one of the country's national symbols.

known as Panamá Viejo, though that's not its proper name.

The city was founded on August 15, 1519, by the notorious conquistador Pedro Arias de Ávila, better known as Pedrarias, and burned down during a battle with the equally notorious Welsh pirate Henry Morgan in 1671. After that disaster, the Spanish moved Panama City to a more defensible site a few kilometers southwest, in the area now known as Casco Viejo.

Since most of Panamá la Vieja was made of wood, only the partial remains of a relatively few stone buildings were left standing. Two of the best-preserved structures are near the main entrance. The first is the tower of the **cathedral,** which is largely intact. It's one of Panama's national symbols and was built between 1619 and 1626. The other, a bit farther in, is the Casa Alarcón, also known as the **Casa del Obispo** (bishop's house). Built in the 1640s, it was a three-story building with a wooden top floor. It's the largest and most intact house on the site, but it's still just fragments of walls. There are other ruins worth exploring, but try not to wander too far—the more distant ruins border a neighborhood plagued by crime and gangs.

The site is open 9 A.M.–5 P.M. daily. Admission is $2 for adults, $.50 for students. A booklet with a map and history of Panamá La Vieja is available at the museum entrance for $2.50.

A restoration project is buttressing the crumbling, rough-hewn stone walls with red bricks completely out of keeping with the original architecture. There are now signs in English and Spanish that explain the history of some of the ruins.

There are lots of souvenir kiosks in the buildings next to the ruins that sell devil masks, *molas,* Ngöbe-Buglé necklaces, and various other trinkets. There's a cafeteria inside as well. An IPAT information booth is on the premises, but you'll probably have a better chance turning up lost pieces of eight than finding anyone actually working there.

During the restoration archaeologists have found Spanish pots, plates, and utensils dating from the 16th and 17th centuries as well as a much older Indian cemetery with bones dating from 50 B.C. Examples of some of these are on display at the **Museo de Sitio de Panamá la Vieja** (tel. 226-9815 or 224-6031, www.panamaviejo.org, 9 A.M.–5 P.M. Tues.–Sun., closed Mon., $3 adults, $.50 students), which has been moved to a new, modern building about a kilometer before the main complex. (See *Museums* in this chapter for details.) Note that you have to pay only a single admission fee to get into both the ruins and the museum.

Casco Viejo

The "Old Part," also known as Casco Antiguo or the San Felipe district, is the most colorful part of Panama City. UNESCO declared it a World Heritage Site in 1997. It's a city within the city, and one from a different age. It's a great place for a walking tour. You can wander down narrow brick streets, sip an espresso at an outdoor café, visit old churches, and gaze up at wrought-iron balconies spilling over with bright tropical plants. It has an unusual blend of architectural styles, most notably ornate Spanish- and French-influenced buildings.

Casco Viejo has always had a romantic look, but for decades the romance has been of the tropical-decadence, paint-peeling-from-rotting-walls variety. Now, though, it's in the midst of a tasteful and large-scale restoration that's giving the old buildings new luster and has turned the area into one of the city's most fashionable destinations for a night out. Elegant bars, restaurants, and sidewalk cafés are opening. Amazingly, this is being done with careful attention to keeping the old charm of the place alive. In some places the district now resembles the French Quarter of New Orleans. It also looks very much like a smaller Cartagena. Unfortunately, the renovation is squeezing out the poorer residents who've lived here for ages.

Please note: Even with the makeover, Casco Viejo is not the safest part of Panama City. There's no reason to be overly concerned, but use common sense. I cringe when I see obvious tourists wandering around here. If you're pale and gringo, you're going to stand out, but try to look as though you're a resident foreigner. Don't wear shorts, fanny packs, Hawaiian shirts, or the like,

The colonial neighborhood of Casco Viejo is being spruced up after years of neglect.

and be discreet with the cameras and maps. Don't come dripping jewelry and dressed in expensive clothes. Don't wander around at night, and be cautious on deserted side streets or when venturing beyond the major activity hubs (Plaza Bolívar, Plaza de la Independencia, and Plaza de Francia). In particular, at night avoid the block of Calle 4 between Avenida Central and Avenida B, as well as the area around Parque Herrera. The decay and the renovation work present their own hazards: Watch out for foot-eating potholes, missing drain covers, and so on.

However, the neighborhood is well patrolled by the *policía de turismo* (tourism police), who cruise around on bicycles and are easy to spot in their short-pants uniforms. They've been trained specifically to serve tourists, and they're doing an impressive job. It's not unusual for them to greet foreign tourists with a handshake and a smile and offer them an insider's tour of the area or help with whatever they need. Visitors have reported many pleasant encounters with them. Don't hesitate to ask them for help or directions. Their office is next to Manolo Caracol and across the street from the Ministerio de Gobierno y Justicia (Avenida Central between Calle 2 Oeste and Calle 3 Este, tel. 211-2410 or 211-1929).

There's also a heavy police presence around the presidential palace, but those guys tend to be more stern and no-nonsense. Their main job is to protect the president, not help tourists.

A good way to explore the area is to come with a knowledgeable guide or taxi driver who can drop you in different areas to explore on foot. Safety aside, you'll probably save time this way, as the streets are confusing and it's easy to get lost. Do major exploring only during the daytime; those who come at night should taxi in and out to specific destinations. Restaurant and bar owners can call a cab for the trip back if visitors have trouble finding one.

Advice and guides are available at the new **Tourism and Internet Café** (Avenida Central between Calle 8 Este and Calle 9 Este, tel. 228-9903, tel./fax 228-7006, tourisminfo@cw-panama.net, 7 A.M.–10 P.M. Mon.–Sat., 6 A.M.–10 P.M. Sun.), on the ground floor of the Lion House hostel. The place is run by Rich Cahill, a

top Darién guide, and his wife, Gaby. They're friendly, helpful people. They can arrange for local guides to give a three-hour walking tour of the neighborhood ($5–10 per person, depending on group size). The guides have lived in Casco Viejo all their lives and really know the ins and outs of the place. A map painted on the wall highlights important sights in the district. There's also an Internet café ($.50 an hour), a place to make international calls ($.10 a minute to the United States, Canada, and the United Kingdom), fax and copying services, and a separate video-game center for kids. English and Spanish are spoken.

Below are the main points of interest in the neighborhood, organized as a walking tour that starts in the heart of the heart of the district and circles counterclockwise, finally ending up back at the starting point. This is not the only way to tour the area, of course, and not everyone will want to be this thorough. Highlights of the area include the Iglesia de San José (also called the Church of the Golden Altar), Plaza de la Independencia, Plaza de Francia, Plaza Bolívar, the area around the Palacio de las Garzas, and (if it's ever rebuilt) the Arco Chato, also known as the Flat Arch.

In some respects Sunday is a good day for a walking tour. For one thing, it's the likeliest time to find the churches open and in use. However, it's practically impossible to find a place to eat or drink on Sunday, or even visit many museums—just about everything is closed. Friday and Saturday nights are the best bet for dining and partying. Getting a look inside historic buildings and museums is easiest during the week, especially since some of these house government offices that are open only during normal business hours. Churches open and close rather erratically.

(A few places to eat and drink are mentioned below in passing, but see *Food* for details. For information on the area museums, see the *Museums* entry elsewhere in this chapter.)

In the center of Casco Viejo is the **Plaza de la Independencia,** where Panama declared its independence from Colombia in 1903. Construction began on the cathedral here, the

Catedral de Nuestra Señora de la Asunción, in 1688, but it took more than 100 years to complete. It has an attractive marble altar and a few well-crafted stained-glass windows, though otherwise the interior is rather plain. The towers are inlaid with mother of pearl from the Perlas Islands. The bones of a saint, Santo Aurelio, are contained in a reliquary hidden behind a painting of Jesus near the front of the church, on the left as one faces the altar. Visitors have been known to nudge the painting aside to take a peek when no one's looking.

The **Museo del Canal Interoceánico** (Avenida Central between Calle 5 and Calle 6, tel. 211-1995 or 211-1649, 9:30 A.M.–5:30 P.M. Tues.–Sun., closed Mon., $2 for adults, $.75 for students), is on the left as one faces the cathedral. Dedicated to the history of the Panama Canal, it's housed in what was once the headquarters of the French canal-building effort. The **Museo de la Historia de Panamá** (Avenida Central between Calle 7 and Calle 8, tel. 228-6231, 8 A.M.–4 P.M. Mon.–Fri.), in the building next door, is a small museum containing artifacts from Panama's history as a republic. It's in the Palacio Municipal, a neoclassical building from 1910 that is now home to government offices.

Head up Avenida Central past the museums and then past the cathedral to Calle 9. The church here, with the crumbling brown facade and white-washed sides, is **Iglesia de la Merced,** which was built in the 17th century from rubble salvaged from the ruins of Panamá la Vieja. The neoclassical building next to it, the **Casa de la Municipalidad,** is a former mansion now used by the city government.

Head west down Calle 9 past the little park, **Parque Herrera,** which was dedicated in 1976. The statue of the man on horseback is General Tomás Herrera, an early hero of Panama's complex independence movements.

Turn left onto Avenida A. On the left is the **Iglesia de San José** (Avenida A between Calle 8 and Calle 9, 7 A.M.–noon and 2–8 P.M. Mon.–Sat., 5 A.M.–noon and 5–8 P.M. Sun.). The church's massive **golden altar** *(altar de oro)* is a prime tourist attraction. Legend has it that the altar was saved from the rapacious Welsh pirate

Henry Morgan during the sacking of the original Panama City when a quick-thinking priest had it painted black, hiding its true value.

Across Avenida A from the church is **La Casa de la Pollera** (Avenue A and Calle 8, tel. 228-8671, home tel. 223-5375—ask for Evelina de Herran, 9:30 A.M.–5:30 P.M. Mon.–Sat.), which sells both machine-made and (very expensive) hand-embroidered *polleras,* Panama's stunning national dress. (For more details, see *Shopping.*)

Continue down Avenida A. On the left near the corner of Calle 3 are the ruins of the **Iglesia de Santo Domingo.** The original church was built in the 17th century, but it burned twice and was not rebuilt after the fire of 1756. But it remains famous for one thing that survived, seemingly miraculously: the nearly **flat arch (Arco Chato).** Since it was built without a keystone and had almost no curve to it, it should have been a very precarious structure, yet it remained intact even as everything around it fell into ruins. One of the reasons a transoceanic canal was built in Panama is that engineers concluded from the intact arch that Panama was not subject to the kinds of devastating earthquakes that afflict its Central American neighbors.

But on the evening of November 7, 2003, just four days after Panama celebrated its first centennial as a country, the arch finally collapsed into rubble. Predictably, attempts to find someone to blame for its neglect—it had been left exposed to the sun, rain, and rumbling traffic of Panama for ages—began almost before the dust settled. So did vows to restore it. It may possibly be rebuilt by the time you read this, though of course its main appeal, its gravity-defying properties through the centuries, can never be restored.

Next to these ruins is the **Museo de Arte Religioso Colonial** (Avenida A and Calle 3, tel. 228-2897, 8 A.M.–4 P.M. Tues.–Sat., closed Sun. and Mon., $.75 adults, $.25 students), a little museum with miscellaneous religious artifacts from the early Spanish era. It's worth a quick visit.

Continue two more blocks to Calle 1 and make a right. This strip of road has become a popular nighttime destination, with trendy restaurants, nightclubs, and bars including the Blue Room, 844, and Macarena. The road ends at the **Plaza de**

Francia (French Plaza), which has seen a great deal of history and was among the first parts of Casco Viejo to be renovated, back in 1982.

The obelisk and the marble plaques along the wall commemorate the failed French effort to build a sea-level canal in Panama. The area housed a fort until the beginning of the 20th century, and the *bóvedas* (vaults) in the seawall were used through the years as storehouses, barracks, offices, and jails. You'll still hear gruesome stories about dungeons in the seawall, where prisoners were left at low tide to drown when the tide rose. Whether this actually happened is still a subject of lively debate among amateur historians. True or not, what you will find there now is one of Panama's more colorful restaurants, Restaurante Las Bóvedas. Also in the plaza are the French Embassy, the headquarters of the **Instituto Nacional de Cultura** (INAC, the National Institute of Culture) in what had been Panama's supreme court building, and a small theater, **Teatro Anita Villalaz.** Visitors are not allowed into the grand old building that houses INAC, but it's worth peeking into from the top of the steps. Next to the restaurant there is now an **art gallery** (tel. 211-4034, 8 A.M.–5:30 P.M. Mon.–Fri., closed Sat. and Sun.) run by INAC that displays works by Panamanian and other Latin American artists.

Walk up the staircase that leads to the top of the vaults. This is part of the old seawall that protected the city from the Pacific Ocean's dramatic tides. There's a good view of the Panama City skyline, the Bridge of the Americas, and the Bay of Panama, and the breeze is great on a hot day. The walkway, **Paseo General Esteban Huertas,** is shaded in part by a bougainvillea-covered trellis and is a popular spot with smooching lovers. Continue to the end of the walkway and come down on Avenida Central. Turn right at the first corner and walk a block. Along the way notice the building on the waterfront to the right. By the time you visit, this may be the site of a large hotel being planned for the area. But it's on the site of what was once the officers' club of the Panamanian Defense Forces; it was largely destroyed during the 1989 U.S. invasion.

Turn left onto Avenida B. The building to the left, between Calle 3 and Calle 4, is the intimate **Teatro Nacional,** or national theater, where classical concerts and other posh events are held. It was built in 1908 on the site of an 18th-century monastery. It's housed in the same building as the **Ministerio de Gobierno y Justicia** (Ministry of Government and Justice), which has its entrance on Avenida Central, across the street from Manolo Caracol, a fun restaurant. Inaugurated on October 1, 1908, the neobaroque theater is worth a brief visit between concerts to get a glimpse of its Old World elegance. The first performance here was a production of the opera *Aida,* and for about 20 years the theater was a glamorous destination for the city's elite. But after that it gradually deteriorated, and at one point was rented out as a movie house. A 1974 restoration brought it back to life until the rainy season of 2000 wrought serious damage. The ceiling is covered with faded but still colorful frescos of cavorting naked ladies, painted by Roberto Lewis, a well-known Panamanian artist. Leaks in the roof destroyed about a quarter of these frescos, and the roof partially collapsed. It was finally reopened in mid-2004. (A bit of local color: Old-timers remember the days before air-conditioning was installed, when performances were sometimes drowned out by the sound of traffic noise and heavy rains that wafted through the doors, which were opened to provide some circulation. Occasionally a bat would zoom into the gallery, adding a bit of unplanned excitement.)

Turn right on Calle 3. The elegant square is **Plaza Bolívar.** It's been undergoing a charming restoration, and several cafés and restaurants have sprung up (and folded) here. It's especially pleasant to hang out on the plaza in the evening, when tables are set up under the stars. It's a good rest stop for a drink or a bite. The new Restaurante y Bar Candelero, on the north side of the plaza, was the best bet at the time of writing. (See *Food.*) Refresquería Chiringuito, on the west side, is a simple but clean hole-in-the-wall that offers daily lunch specials for less than $2. It's open 11 A.M.–6 P.M. Monday–Saturday, closed Sunday.

The plaza was named for Simón Bolívar, a legendary figure who is considered the father of

Latin America's independence from Spain. In 1826 Bolívar called a congress here to discuss forming a union of Latin American states. Bolívar himself did not attend and the congress didn't succeed, but the park and the statue of Bolívar commemorate the effort.

The congress itself was held in what is now a small museum called **Salón Bolívar** (Plaza Bolívar, tel. 228-9594, 9 A.M.–4 P.M. Tues.–Sat., 1–5 P.M. Sun., $1 adults, $.25 students), attached to the massive **Palacio Bolívar.** The latter was built on the site of a Franciscan monastery that dates from the 18th century, but the current structure was built in the 1920s and was a school for many years. Now it's home to the Ministerio de Relaciones Exteriores (foreign ministry). During regular business hours (about 8 A.M.–3 P.M. Mon.–Fri., 9 A.M.–1 P.M. Sat.) it's possible, and well worthwhile, to explore the huge inner courtyard, which has been outfitted with a clear roof that's out of keeping with the architecture but protects it from the elements. The courtyard is open to the surf in the back, where part of the original foundation can be seen. Be sure to notice the beautiful tilework, and the posh chandelier at the entrance.

Next door but still on the plaza is a church and former monastery, **Iglesia y Convento de San Francisco de Asís.** The church dates from the early days of Casco Viejo but was burned during two 18th-century fires, then restored in 1761 and again in 1998. Another church, **Iglesia San Felipe de Neri,** is a block away, on the corner of Avenida B and Calle 4. It dates from 1688 and, though it has been damaged by fires, it's one of the oldest standing structures from the Spanish colonial days. It was being renovated when I last visited. It looked as if it were going to be quite lovely when finished.

Head back past Plaza Bolívar on Calle 4. Make a left at the waterfront. The presidential palace, the **Palacio de las Garzas** (Palace of the Herons), is on the left at Calle 5, overlooking Panama Bay. It's an attractive place that houses the presidential office and residence. The president lives here, and visitors are not permitted. The place and the neighboring streets are surrounded by guards, who may ask for your passport but more likely will just wave you by. Be polite and deferential—they should let you walk by the palace. Walk slowly and take a quick peek inside at the courtyard, visible from the street, and try to spot the herons around the fountain.

Make a left at the next street, which is Calle 6 but goes by several other names just to make things confusing. Head straight for three blocks to Plaza de la Independencia, where this tour began.

Near Casco Viejo

The area that leads into Casco Viejo from the northeast, centered around the waterfront strip of Avenida Eloy Alfaro, is one of the most colorful, lively, squalid, and—especially at night—intimidating parts of Panama City. There are plans to clean up the area, but little had changed by the time this book went to press.

The municipal government is determined to clean up this bustling area of commerce—legal and otherwise—since it is the main entrance into the rapidly gentrifying Casco Viejo.

Small fishing boats have for ages pulled up to the deteriorating docks here, but now seafood is sold through the clean, modern fish market, the **Mercado de Mariscos,** nearby at the west end of Avenida Balboa. (See *Food.*) The other merchants and tiny repair kiosks in the waterfront area, known as the **Terraplén,** are being nudged out.

Meat and produce is sold at Panama City's **Mercado Público** (public market), at the intersection of Avenida Eloy Alfaro and Calle 13, which has been a national institution since it opened in 1914. Early Sunday morning has traditionally been the time to come here, but the bustling place opens daily at 2 A.M. However, the entire market is eventually supposed to be moved to nearby Avenida B, in what had been an old freight house built by the United States. It's being renovated and modernized. The new place will undoubtedly be less colorful, but let's hope it will also be more hygienic—the meat section on the ground floor of the old place was a dirty and nonrefrigerated place and one of the best arguments for vegetarianism.

In front of the old market, up Calle 13, is the crowded shopping area of **Salsipuedes** (a contraction of "get out if you can"). This is mostly of interest for those into people-watching. The area is crammed with little stalls selling clothes, lottery tickets, and bric-a-brac. To the right as one faces away from the public market is a small **Chinatown,** called Barrio Chino in Spanish (make a right at Calle Juan Mendoza), which frankly has little to interest tourists. Most of the Chinese character of the place has been lost through the years; the ornate Chinese archway over the street is one of the few remaining signs of a less-assimilated time.

MUSEUMS

You'd never get a sense of the rich history of Panama if all you had to go on were the museums of its capital city. They are all neglected and underfunded, and what few exhibits they contain are generally poorly presented and contain almost no explanation of their significance.

That said, Panama has paid more attention to its cultural treasures in recent years. The city's imposing anthropology museum, Museo Antropológico Reina Torres de Araúz, is slowly being reopened after a modest renovation. The modern art museum, Museo de Arte Contemporáneo, once an art gallery more than anything else, is emerging as a respectable repository of Panama's better-known and emerging contemporary artists. And everyone's excited by the ambitious new Museum of Biodiversity, designed by Frank O. Gehry, that was slated to open on the Calzada de Amador in 2007. It's the latest in Panama's endless bids to come up with something to truly put itself on the jet-setter map.

Most of the museums—Museo de Arte Religioso Colonial, Museo del Canal Interoceánico de Panamá, Salón Bolívar, Casa Góngora—are in Casco Viejo and can be visited as part of a walking tour of the area.

El Museo Antropológico Reina Torres de Araúz

Panama's anthropology museum (Plaza Cinco de Mayo, tel. 212-3079 or 212-3089, 9 A.M.–4 P.M. Mon.–Fri., closed Sat. and Sun., $2 adults, $.25 students), sometimes known as MARTA, is housed in a massive building that

was built in 1912 as the terminus of the Panama Railroad. It was reopened in 2000 after several years of renovation. Or rather, a couple of small halls were opened; most of the building remains bare. New halls are being opened at a glacial place, and others that have been recently renovated mysteriously close for re-renovation. It's a crap shoot which halls may be open during any particular visit.

As long as one's expectations are low, the place is worth a visit. It does have some unusual displays, and the guides, whose services are included with the entrance fee, are friendly and helpful though they speak little English. It's possible to see the whole place in less than an hour. The museum is right on Plaza Cinco de Mayo near the beginning of the pedestrian section of Avenida Central, so a visit can be combined with a shopping/walking tour.

The main exhibit, in the room next to the entrance, is dedicated to the Barriles culture, believed to be Panama's earliest major civilization. It grew up around Volcán Barú in western Panama before 700 B.C. and came to a sudden end with the eruption of Barú in A.D. 600. Little is known about this culture, though it's believed to have been both agrarian and dominated by warriors. The figures on display came from a ceremonial center that dates from around 60 B.C. The site is on a farm just west of the town of Volcán that's open to visitors but today contains little worth seeing.

The exhibit here consists of about a dozen and a half carved stone figures and fragments. Because these pieces were discovered in 1947–1948 through *huaquería* (grave robbing), nearly all their historic context has been lost.

The exhibit is modest and little is known about this culture, but the mystery surrounding the pieces adds something to their appeal. Especially memorable are the strange stone statues depicting a proud figure wearing a conical hat who is being carried on the shoulders of a stockier man. Not surprisingly, this has been taken as evidence of a stratified society, with chiefs figuratively or perhaps literally supported by their subjects. The other notable piece is an unusually large (2.3 meters long) ceremonial *metate,* a stone table used for grinding corn. Because of its similarities to *metates* throughout pre-Colombian Central America, and the grim carved human heads lining its edges, it's believed to have been used for sacrifices.

The gold room upstairs contains a small collection of gold figures of animals, gold-armor plates, ceramics, jewelry, breast plates, a crown, and other items made by ancient indigenous peoples and recovered from archaeological sites around the country.

Most of the items are *huacas*, ceremonial treasures buried with prominent indigenous people. The oldest item, a copper and gold nose ring found on Cerro Juan Díaz on the Azuero peninsula, dates from 180 B.C. It's displayed in a small window near the entrance to the main room. As part of Panama's centennial celebration in 2003, the Reprosa jewelry store, well-known for its replicas of *huacas,* made reproductions of some of the prized ones in this collection. One especially impressive item here is a large spider made of gold and copper. Also notice the especially fine work on the tiny *cascabels* (string of small bells). Several of the pieces in the displays are broken, which is believed to have been part of an ancient funeral rite to make sure no one in this world could use the objects again. There is also a display of human bones and *huacas* dating from A.D. 1500 that were dug up at Sitio Conte in Coclé.

Two new halls have recently been opened on the third floor. The first is the **Salón de las Huellas,** which attempts to depict the traditional dwellings, utensils, and clothing of some of Panama's peoples. The exhibit is somewhat amateurish and contains little written information, but it's worth a quick look.

The second hall is the **Salón de la Etnografía** (Ethnography Hall). The displays include pre-Colombian *metates* used in rituals and to grind corn; fishing gear; pre-Colombian ceramics, including a few impressive pieces; a century-old *pollera;* a variety of traditional hats; and so on.

El Museo de Arte Contemporáneo

Panama's contemporary-art museum (Avenida San Blas, tel. 262-3085, 262-3380, or 262-8012, info@macpanama.org, www.macpanama.org,

9 A.M.–5 P.M. Tues.–Sun., closed Mon., $1 adult, $.50 children) is one of Panama's best and best-maintained museums. Bear in mind, though, that it doesn't take much to reach that level in Panama. This one still more resembles an art gallery than a museum (many of the pieces are for sale). But it does present a reasonable cross-section of Panama's best-known and emerging modern artists as well as some work from other parts of Latin America. It sometimes presents film series. The museum is housed in a two-story building on the edge of the former Canal Zone in Ancón, next to the old Ancón Elementary School and not far from the headquarters of the Smithsonian Tropical Research Institute (Instituto Smithsonian de Investigaciones Tropicales).

El Museo de Arte Religioso Colonial

This tiny museum in Casco Viejo (Avenida A and Calle 3, tel. 228-2897, 8 A.M.–4 P.M. Tues.–Sat., closed Sun. and Mon., $.75 adults, $.25 students) contains religious relics dating from the earliest days of the Spanish-colonial era. While its offerings are sparse, it's improved in recent years and is worth a quick visit. Its centerpiece is a massive wooden altar from Sevilla, Spain, with a figure of the Virgin of Rosario at the top, covered in 23.5-karat gold, that dates from 1575. The gold leaf was added later—it was originally just painted red, blue, green, and black. It was salvaged from the ruins of Panamá la Vieja after Morgan sacked the city. The altar was moved to Casco Viejo in 1673. The museum has an enthusiastic and knowledgeable guide, but she speaks only Spanish.

El Museo del Canal Interoceánico

This museum dedicated to the history of the Panama Canal (Avenida Central between Calle 5 and Calle 6, tel. 211-1995 or 211-1649, 9:30 A.M.–5:30 P.M. Tues.–Sun., closed Mon., $2 for adults, $.75 for students) is a popular stop on sightseeing tours. It's on Plaza de la Independencia in Casco Viejo, housed in what was once the headquarters of the French canal-building effort. It's worth a visit, but be prepared for some frustration if you don't speak Spanish. Everything is in Spanish only, which is a problem for those who don't speak the language since the "exhibits" often consist more of text than anything else. However, an audio guide in English, Spanish, and French is available for $5. The displays tell the story of both the French and American efforts to build the canal, and throws in a little bit of pre-Colombian and Spanish colonial history at the beginning. There's some anti-American propaganda, and most of what's written about the canal from the 1960s on should be taken with a big chunk of salt. Sadly, history here gives way to polemics. There's a good coin collection upstairs, as well as a few Panamanian and Canal Zone stamps. There's also a copy of the 1977 Torrijos-Carter Treaties that turned the canal over to Panama. You can do the whole place in about an hour.

El Museo de la Historia de Panamá

This small museum about the history of Panama (Avenida Central between Calle 7 and Calle 8, tel. 228-6231, 8 A.M.–4 P.M. Mon.–Fri., $1 general admission, $.25 for kids), next to the Museo del Canal Interoceánico, is housed in the Palacio Municipal, a neoclassical building that dates from 1910. It contains mementos from various periods in Panama's history, from the colonial period to the modern era. It was being renovated when I last visited, so I can't say if it's worth a visit, but it can easily be combined with a visit to the canal museum.

Salón Bolívar

Attached to the Palacio Bolívar on Plaza Bolívar in Casco Viejo is a small, modern museum (Plaza Bolívar, tel. 228-9594, 9 A.M.–4 P.M. Tues.–Sat., 1–5 P.M. Sun., $1 adults, $.25 students) attached to the Palacio Bolívar that commemorates the 1826 congress Simón Bolívar called to try to create a union of Latin American republics. The congress took place from June 22 to July 15, and though Bolívar himself didn't attend and the talks ended in failure, the attempt is still considered an important moment in Latin American history. While the museum is attractively designed, there's little in it. The room upstairs contains the text of the protocols of different congresses called during the independence movement. There's also a replica of Bolívar's jewel-encrusted sword, a gift from Venezuela (the original is now back in Venezuela). The actual room where the congress took place is below this one, but it was being renovated during my last visit. There may be more to see once the renovation is complete.

Casa Góngora

Built in 1756, this stone house (Avenida Central and Calle 4, tel. 212-0338, 8 A.M.–4 P.M. Mon.–Fri., closed Sat. and Sun., free admission), is the oldest in Casco Viejo and one of the oldest in Panama. It was originally the home of a Spanish pearl merchant. It then became a church and has now been turned into a small, bare-bones museum. It's had a rough history—it has been through three fires, and the current wooden roof is new. A 20th-century restoration attempt was botched, causing more damage. There isn't much there, but the staff can give free tours (in Spanish) and there have been noises about making it more of a real museum in the future. There's an interesting, comprehensive book on the history of the house and neighborhood (again, in Spanish) that visitors are welcome to thumb through while visiting. It contains rare maps, photos, and illustrations. Ask for it at the office. The museum hosts jazz and folkloric concerts and other cultural events in the tiny main hall on some Friday and Saturday nights.

El Museo de Ciencias Naturales

Panama City's natural sciences museum (Avenida Cuba and Calle 29 Este, tel. 225-0645, 9 A.M.–3:30 P.M. Tues.–Sat., closed Sun. and Mon., $1 adults, $.25 students) is a modest place consisting of four rooms mainly containing some stuffed and mounted animals and geological specimens. It's worth a quick visit, at least if you're in the neighborhood, to get a close-up look at some of Panama's more interesting animals, including a jaguar, harpy eagle, howler and spider monkeys, and a huge iguana. It's also fun to get a close look at the amazing hanging nest of an oropendola (a common bird in Panama). But the most interesting display is probably a handful of fossilized bones of a 50,000-year-old sloth (*Eremotherium rusconi),* estimated to have been four meters long. The remains were found on the Azuero peninsula in 1991. Only the geology and paleontology room is air-conditioned, ensuring that the rocks stay nice and cool while the snake exhibit, for instance, rots away in the heat and humidity.

Museo Afroantilleano

The Afroantillean museum (Calle 24 Este off Avenida Justo Arosemena/Avenida 3 Sur, 8:30 A.M.–3:30 P.M. Tues.–Sat., closed Sun. and Mon., $1 adults, $.25 children) preserves the memory of the thousands of West Indian workers, mostly from Barbados, who supplied most of the labor for the building of the Panama Canal. These workers, who had the most dangerous and punishingly grueling jobs during canal construction, are often little more than a footnote in accounts of the building of the canal. Their descendants today make up a significant part of the population of the country. The museum is tiny, but it would be worth a quick visit if I didn't have concerns about its location: It's on one of the diciest streets in Panama City, not the sort of place a tourist should be wandering around. If you do come, take a taxi and have the driver wait outside the entrance for you; you can see everything the museum has to offer in about a half hour. It's installed in an old wooden house stocked with canal construction–era furnishings and photos meant to give a sense of what construction-era life might have been like for these workers, though it is certainly much more comfortable than the shacks many of the workers had to make do with in those days.

Casa Museo Banco Nacional

This elegant little house (Calle 34 Este and Avenida Cuba, tel. 225-0640, 8 A.M.–12:30 P.M. and 1:30–4:30 P.M. Mon.–Fri., free admission), the former residence of a doctor, dates from 1925 and is now owned by the Banco Nacional de Panamá. It has rotating exhibits of arts and crafts for sale, though those I've seen have been quite poor. It does have a tiny but interesting collection of Panamanian commemorative coins, including a silver 20 balboa piece about the size of a fist,

a small gold 100 balboa piece, and a tiny 2.5 centavo piece. Other coins date from 1904, some of the earliest days of the republic. It's worth visiting just to see how the well-heeled lived in early 20th-century Panama City. The house is lovely, with marble staircases, ornate wrought-iron fixtures, and several types of tile floors.

Museo de Sitio de Panamá la Vieja

Relics from the ruins of Panamá la Vieja have been moved to a new, modern building (tel. 226-9815 or 224-6031, www.panamaviejo.org, 9 A.M.–5 P.M. Tues.–Sun., closed Mon., $3 adults, $.50 students) about a kilometer before the ruins themselves. It's one of Panama's best museums, a modern, two-story place with attractively presented displays of items dug up around Panamá la Vieja. Start on the top floor and work your way down. Displays include indigenous artifacts from the hundreds of years before the Spanish conquest, when the site was a fishing village. One of the more haunting exhibits is that of the skeleton of a woman, believed to have died at around age 40 and apparently an important figure, whose grave also included the skulls of nine males. Other displays include items from the early Spanish colonial days, such as shards of cooking pots, coins, lead musket balls, trinkets, and so on. There's also a model of the city as it looked before Morgan's incendiary visit. The ground floor has details on the restoration of the site. There is limited information in English, and no English-speaking guides.

Mi Pueblito

This is a charming, if idealized, re-creation of a typical Panamanian town on the Azuero peninsula, Panama's heartland. The architecture is Spanish colonial, which is especially noticeable in the red-tile roofs and whitewashed walls, the mission-style church, and the central plaza and fountain. The builders have included lots of small, loving touches, from the lesson plan on the blackboard of the schoolhouse to the telegraph office that looks as though the operator has just left for a siesta. There's even a rustic outhouse behind the buildings.

Mi Pueblito (which translates to "my little

town," and which is also known as Los Pueblitos) includes a small *pollera* museum, where a *pollera*-wearing semibilingual docent is on hand to give you a detailed description of this lovely traditional dress and, if you're lucky, an utterly wacky theory of Christopher Columbus's ethnic background.

There is also a folkloric dance school where one can sometimes see small children learning the steps to traditional Panamanian dances. Performances by grown-ups are sometimes given. Call tel. 228-7154, 228-2361, or 228-7178 for information.

The Mi Pueblito complex has in recent years been expanded to recognize the traditional dwellings of some of the other peoples that make up modern Panama. These are directly across the street from the Spanish colonial village. The first site honors the West Indian immigrants who provided most of the labor force for the building of the Panama Canal. The brightly painted two-story wooden buildings are an extremely fanciful take on what the laborers' accommodations were really like. A walk through a little forest takes you to more accurate re-creations of the way three indigenous peoples—the Kuna, Emberá-Wounaan, and Ngöbe-Buglé—lived, and in many cases still do.

Souvenirs are on sale at shops throughout the complex. There are three simple open-air restaurants—in Mi Pueblito proper, the West Indian village, and the Kuna village—specializing in seafood and offering a few "native" dishes. Prices range from inexpensive to moderate. The complex also offers a good view of Panama Bay and the Pacific entrance to the Panama Canal, as well as an eavesdropper's peek into the ramshackle apartment buildings of El Chorrillo, a nearby barrio.

Mi Pueblito is near the base of Cerro Ancón (also known as Ancón Hill), just off the westbound side of Avenida de Los Mártires. It's a quick right turn off this busy road and easy to miss because there are no signs. Taxi drivers should know where it is. The complex is open 10 A.M.–10 P.M. Tuesday–Sunday. Admission is $.50. There's an out-of-date and minimally informative Spanish-only brochure. Most of the signs in the complex are in Spanish.

CHURCHES AND SHRINES

Panama City's cathedral and most of its historically significant Catholic churches are in Casco Viejo (see that section for details). A couple of other prominent churches are scattered around modern Panama City.

Santuario Nacional del Corazón de María

The Santuario Nacional del Corazón de María was dedicated on August 22, 1949. It's a relatively simple church with pretty stained-glass windows and a modern interior. Peacocks and a riot of other domesticated birds wander around a fountain near the crypts, which are a bit creepy but worth a peek; they're out the side entrance to the right as one faces the altar. The church's facade is attractive at night, when it's illuminated and provides a striking contrast to the glittery modern buildings that surround it. It's not worth making a special trip for, but given its central location it might be convenient to pop in briefly.

Iglesia del Carmen

The Iglesia del Carmen, at Vía España and Avenida Federico Boyd, across the street from the Hotel El Panamá, is the most conspicuous church in modern Panama City. A cream-colored, neo-Gothic confection with tall twin towers, it was built in 1947.

Baha'i Temple or House of Worship

Despite being an overwhelmingly Catholic country, Panama has a live-and-let-live attitude toward the many minority faiths brought by immigrants from around the world or still practiced by its indigenous peoples. Two non-Catholic places of worship are especially prominent and draw curious visitors.

Panama's Baha'i Temple or House of Worship (9 A.M.–6 P.M. daily, free admission), the only one in Latin America and one of only seven in the world, is an impressive structure that resembles an egg, with huge, open arched entrances that let the breezes blow through but keep the rain out. The temple interior is entirely unadorned. It has an

© WILLIAM FRIAR

Plaza de la Independencia and Panama City's cathedral, Nuestra Señora de la Asunción, are at the heart of Caso Viejo.

unusual panoramic view of the city, the Pacific Ocean, and the surrounding countryside.

The temple is northeast of Panama City, near Las Cumbres. To get there, head east and then north on the Transístmica (Vía Simón Bolívar) from downtown Panama City. After about 15 kilometers there's a big intersection with Tumba Muerto (Avenida Ricardo J. Alfaro). Continue north on Transístmica. About four kilometers past the intersection there should be a Bacardi rum factory on the left. Turn left here and head uphill for 1.5 kilometers to the temple.

Hindu Temple

The Hindu Temple (7:30 A.M.–noon and 4–8 P.M. daily, no admission fee) is less impressive but easier to get to. It's a rather modern, spartan place that looks more imposing from a distance than it does close up. The most interesting thing about it, at least when worshipers are around, is the sense it gives you of how extensive and well-established Panama's South Asian community is. The temple is off Tumba Muerto (Avenida Ri-

cardo J. Alfaro). Head east a couple of kilometers past Calle de la Amistad (Friendship Highway) and make a left turn. Visitors must sign in at the gate. The temple is a short drive uphill.

PARKS

Other than Parque Natural Metropolitano, Panama City isn't blessed with much in the way of impressive or well-tended open spaces. Even little plazas are hard to find outside of Casco Viejo and the walking section of Avenida Central—they're one bit of the city's Spanish heritage that, sadly, it's letting slip away.

Avenida Balboa

Panama City's grandest avenue also offers some of the most dramatic views. It sweeps along the edge of Panama Bay from Casco Viejo to ritzy Punta Paitilla, home to tony high-rise condominiums and a few noteworthy stores and restaurants. It offers good views of the modern skyline of Panama City, Panama Bay, and the old seawall, churches, and historic buildings of Casco Viejo. A well-maintained promenade along Avenida Balboa, with a little park that contains an enormous statue of Balboa "discovering" the Pacific midway, makes this a pleasant place for a morning or evening stroll. Try to time that stroll to coincide with high tide, when the view is nicer and the smell less potent. (Panama City dumps its untreated sewage into the bay. The government says it's planning to build an incredibly expensive sewage treatment system one day, but don't hold your breath—or rather, do.)

Parque Belisario Porras

Though not worth a special trip, those staying in Calidonia who need a little open space can visit Parque Belisario Porras, between Calle 33 Este and Calle 34 Este and Avenida Perú and Avenida Cuba. It's a rather austere, formal plaza with a monument to Porras, thrice president of Panama and one of its founding fathers, looking rather dapper and jaunty. The plaza is surrounded by attractive old buildings housing various government offices and the Spanish embassy. A series of kiosks serve greasy fast food to office workers on Avenida Perú near Calle 35, next to the Ministerio de Economía y Finanzas.

Parque Natural Metropolitano

Amazingly enough, you don't even have to leave the limits of Panama City to find a tropical forest. This 265-hectare park is just minutes from downtown, and it's a lovely little place with a surprising amount of wildlife given its location and size. Only brief day hikes are available here. Skip this park if time is short and you plan to venture out at least as far as Parque Nacional Soberanía, which is only about a half-hour drive away from the city. But if not, Parque Metropolitano gives a quick sample of what Panama's forests have to offer.

Most of the park is dry lowland Pacific forest, now rare in Central America because of deforestation, and it's home to about 45 species of mammals, 36 species of reptiles, and 14 species of amphibians. These include such colorful creatures as two- and three-toed sloths, *monos tití* (Geoffroy's tamarin), and boa constrictors. As usual, however, don't be surprised if you see only

birds during a hike. The park has recorded 227 bird species.

Having an urban center this close to a nature park has its drawbacks: A new highway, Corredor Norte, cuts right through the park's eastern edge, and other busy streets run by its borders. You're never far from the roar of the road. Sadly, there have also been reports of muggings. Don't wander on a trail alone.

There are about four kilometers of trails spread among three main loops. Not surprisingly, the most strenuous one, **La Cienaguita,** also offers the best chance of seeing animals. It takes about two hours to walk. It's an interpretive trail; the visitor's center sells an informative booklet about it for $2. The **Mono Tití Road** is, as the name suggests, a rocky road. Mountain biking is allowed on it, which would be great if there were a place to rent mountain bikes. It's named for the *monos tití* (Geoffroy's tamarin), a small primate that lucky visitors may see while hiking the trail. The easiest trail is **Los Momótides,** across an extremely busy road—be careful crossing the street. It's short and level, designed for people in a hurry or who have difficulty walking, and it is a nice little walk.

The entrance to the park is on Avenida Juan Pablo II in the Curundu district of Panama City. Trails are open 6 A.M.–6 P.M. every day. There is no fee, but donations are encouraged. The visitors center offers a free brochure, but ask for the glossy color trail guide ($.50), which has a much-needed map. The visitors center is open 8 A.M.–4 P.M. weekdays and 8 A.M.–1 P.M. Saturday. Guided tours in English and Spanish are available for $6, but you have to call at least a day or two in advance. Call tel. 232-5552 or 232-5516.

Cerro Azul/Cerro Jefe

This hilly area about an hour east of Panama City has long been popular with more affluent city dwellers looking to escape the hot lowlands—the elevation reaches 950 meters, high enough to cool things off significantly. Attempts have been made to attract tourists to the area, but only serious birders are likely to find it of great interest. They come for the foothill species, including some one normally has to venture into the Darién to find. There are some stretches of elfin forest, but getting to the less-developed areas requires a four-wheel drive with high clearance, and some places can only be approached on foot. Birders should go with a knowledgeable naturalist guide. Other than that, this is mostly an area of suburban homes and little else. There is one nice place to stay on Cerro Azul, the Hostal Casa de Campo Country Inn and Spa (see *Accommodations.*)

To get to Cerro Azul, take the Corredor Sur toll road toward the international airport. When the road ends at the Riande Aeropuerto Hotel and Resort, turn left onto the Interamerican Highway. Make another left at the Super Xtra supermarket and follow the Cerro Azul signs. Casa de Campo is about a 20-minute drive up the hill. Turn left at Urbanización Las Nubes and follow the signs. To get to Cerro Azul by public transportation, take any bus going to 24 de Deciembre. Get off at the Super Xtra supermarket and transfer to a Cerro Azul bus.

Entertainment

NIGHTLIFE

Panama City has experienced a nightlife boom in recent years, concentrated in four main areas around the city.

One popular area is a densely packed grid of restaurants, clubs, cafés, and bars bounded by the Bella Vista district to the west and Marbella to the east. The center of this area is **Calle Uruguay,** with businesses that seem to come and go overnight lined along the streets leading off of it for several blocks, up to Calle 50.

Calle 53 Este, the main street through the upscale business district of Marbella, draws young people on the prowl to its music clubs.

The renovation of **Casco Viejo** has turned it into a trendy place for clubs, sidewalk cafés, bars, and seafood restaurants. Most action at the time of writing was on Calle 1 leading into the Plaza de Francia/Las Bóvedas area, and around Plaza Bolívar.

The newest entertainment area in Panama City is not actually in the city proper but along the **Calzada de Amador** (Amador Causeway) in the old Canal Zone. (See the *Panama Canal* chapter for details.)

Clubs start late in Panama City. Very late. Most don't really get going until midnight and others don't reach their stride until 2 A.M. The partying often lasts all night. Music is generally played at ear-shattering volumes; bring earplugs.

Oddly, in a country where kids tend to learn to dance to salsa and merengue as soon as they can walk and where partying is virtually a civil right, it's not unusual to see little or no dancing at a Panama City club these days. Even if the place is packed and the music deafening, most people may just be talking, flirting, and drinking.

Note: Be careful not to ask a taxi driver to take you to a good "nightclub," unless what you're looking for is a strip club or brothel. What gringos call "nightclubs" or "clubs" are still mainly known as "discos" in Panama.

A popular place for salsa lessons is **Bohío Florencia** (Vía España near ULACIT and Hospital San Fernando, tel. 221-7582), but it's in a busy industrial area that's a bit of a haul from downtown. Lessons are given Thursdays 6 P.M.–10 P.M. and cost $3, but call ahead of time to make sure the schedule hasn't changed. The place can also sometimes arrange private lessons at a place of the students' choosing. The area can be intimidating at night, and you're likely to be the only foreign visitor. But it's certainly an off-the-beaten path option for those who want an urban adventure away from the touristy parts of Panama City. Be alert, dress neatly, and leave the bling-bling behind.

Punta Paitilla

Zoomba (Calle 56 Este, tel. 215-1581, 10 P.M.–late Wed.-Sat.) is a pleasant, upscale place that attracts the young and the pampered. It has sleek, modern decor—split-level, projection screens, whimsical lighting fixtures that might have been designed by Tim Burton, and so on.

STRIP CLUBS, BROTHELS, AND BATHHOUSES

Prostitution is legal and regulated by the Panamanian government. But prostitution in Panama is hardly free from exploitation, and AIDS and other sexually transmitted diseases are a major concern.

Those toying with the idea of partaking should bear the following in mind: Panama has an estimated 30,000 people living with HIV, which, given the country's small population, gives it the third-highest rate in Central America. HIV in Panama is more often transmitted through heterosexual than homosexual sex. And according to a United Nations agency in Panama, HIV rates have skyrocketed 500 percent in the last decade.

Panama has plenty of "gentlemen's clubs," often also referred to as "nightclubs," with strip shows and the like. These usually have fancy names with words such as "elite" or "palace" in them. Those interested will have no trouble finding advertisements in tourist-oriented publications.

At last count, there were two gay bathhouses in Panama City, one of which is quite upscale. Again, those who are determined will likely find them, most likely through contacts at gay bars or the Internet.

The area from Avenida de Los Mártires to the section of the San Felipe district around the old public market has lots of rough and seedy bars, including some gay bars and places that are more or less brothels. This area can be quite dangerous, though, and one of the toughest Panamanians I know thinks it's a dumb move for a gringo to bar-hop around here—there's an excellent chance of getting mugged on the way home. You've been warned.

Salsa and merengue are popular here, and there's live music on Friday and Saturday nights. It's near the end of Calle 56 Este in a modern shopping plaza with a big Super 99 supermarket. It's almost at the tip of a peninsula and isolated from other nightlife areas.

Bella Vista

Bacchus (Ave. 3A Sur and Calle Elvira Méndez, tel. 263-9005, 10 P.M.–late Mon., Tues., Thurs., Fri., and Sat.), pronounced BAH-koos, has been around forever. It was a popular club, though at a different location, when I was in high school, which makes it practically a historical landmark. It's showing its age but is still popular with a mixed-age crowd. It's a fairly spacious split-level place with an indoor terrace that's good for people-watching. There's also a smaller room in the front of the building. It sometimes offers live music, mostly Latin rock. It has a more mellow vibe than in the days when it was a hot disco for dancing fools.

Miyake 1777 (Calle Elvira Mendez, tel. 269-2054, 6 P.M.–1 A.M. Tues.–Sat.) is a DJ bar/sushi bar that opened right next door to Bacchus in

December 2002. It has a white, minimalist semi-Japanese modern interior and a hipster vibe (by Panama standards). Fridays after 11 P.M. are the best times to catch a DJ at work—the owner claims these sometimes include English imports. There's sometimes unplugged live music. Saturdays are usually given over to Latin rock.

El Pavo Real (Calle 52, tel. 269-0504, 4:30 P.M.–late Mon.–Sat., closed Mon.) was once a nice upscale restaurant but is now a grungy, if popular, pub that reeks of smoke and has a carpet that seems mainly there to absorb cigarette burns. The place offers fish 'n' chips for $6.50 and Guinness for $2.75. There are a dart board and pool table.

Marbella

All but one of the clubs listed below are on Calle 53 Este, the main drag in Marbella. Wasabi Sushi Lounge is one street over.

Rock Café (Calle 53 Este, tel. 264-5364, 9 P.M.–until nearly dawn Tues., Thurs., Fri., and Sat., $10 cover after 11 P.M.) is a staple of the party scene. It's a fairly large, cavernous place but it has little atmosphere—it's purely functional. DJs spin a motley mix of music, including rock, trance, and típico. Whatever's playing, you can be sure it'll be deafening. There's sometimes live music by local bands on Thursday and Friday. There's no cover before 11 P.M. except on Friday nights, when it's open-bar night: all you can drink for a $10 cover. Women are admitted free except on Friday.

Oz Bar and Lounge (Calle 53 Este, tel. 265-2805, 9 P.M.–late Tues.–Sat., generally $5 cover), next to Rock Café, is a sleek and more upscale place with attractive lounge decor and big-screen TVs. DJs spin house and lounge music some nights.

Liquid (Calle 53 Este, tel. 265-3210, Tues.–Sat., www.liquidpanama.com), across the street from the World Trade Center, is a dark, modern club done up in steel and blue neon light strips. It's spacious, low-key, and well air-conditioned. It's probably the best place in Panama City to hear decent (by Panamanian standards) rock bands, though often this place just features recorded music. The cover averages around $8–10.

Wasabi Sushi Lounge (Calle 54 near Calle 50, tel. 264-1863) is a new club that's aiming for a retrofuturistic 1960's look. It's not well marked—look for the green, stylized "W" above the entrance—and can look a bit intimidating from the street. It's mellow inside. It starts heating up after 10 P.M. Wednesday–Friday.

Casco Viejo

Historic Calle 1, which leads into the Plaza de Francia, packs several trendy bars, clubs, and restaurants onto a single narrow street, but other nightspots have begun to pop up elsewhere in Casco Viejo. Besides the places mentioned below, be sure to check out the bar at **Restaurante Las Bóvedas** (see the *Food* section) in Plaza de Francia itself, even if you don't plan to eat there. It's built into the old stone vaults of the seawall and is quite a cool, atmospheric place. There's live jazz Fridays and Saturdays after about 9:30 P.M.

844 (Calle 1 near Plaza Francia, tel. 211-1978, Wed.–Sat. until late) consists of four intimate rooms, two downstairs and two upstairs.

This used to be the house of the owner's grandmother, who would no doubt be scandalized by the goings-on here. The main room is dark and cavelike with low tables and sofas and a raised cushioned platform in one corner. For some reason, it also has plaster casts of people's butts on the wall. One of the room upstairs has zebra-print couches and chairs and is hung with translucent drapes that create a casbah/makeout-room effect. The second room downstairs has a big-screen TV and a sushi bar, operated by the owners of Sushi Itto restaurant, with food $4.50–10.50 or $42 for a platter. Sake is $6. The cover is usually $5. Friday and Saturday are the big nights, when festivities can last until dawn. Wednesday is an all-you-can-drink night for a $12 cover. Thursday is ladies' night.

Blu Room (Calle 1 near Plaza Francia, tel. 228-9059, Tues. Sat. until late) is a small, dark martini lounge with a chill-room vibe. It's lit by a subtle indigo glow. It offers 22 kinds of huge (10.5 ounces) martinis for $6–7. DJs tend to spin classic salsa on Tuesday, hiphop on Thursday, and house and trance on Friday and Saturday. On Wednesday there's a hard-core drink special: 10 drinks for $15, liver transplant not included.

Further east, **Tantra's** (Avenida Central and Calle 5 in Casco Viejo, tel. 262-8788, 9 P.M.–late Thurs., Fri., and Sat., $5 cover on Fri. and Sat.), is a cocktail lounge with a kind of Arabian Nights theme, including a canopied interior and cushions to sit on. DJs spin and there's sometimes live music. The cover charge includes bar food on Friday and Saturday.

Calle Uruguay Area

Popular clubs and bars in the Calle Uruguay area fold and new ones pop up at a rapid rate, so it's impossible to say what will be there when you visit. The best bet is just to stroll around late on a Thursday, Friday, and Saturday night and follow the crowds.

S6is (Calle Uruguay/Calle 48 Este between Avenida 4A and 5A, tel. 264-5237, Tues.–Sun. nights until late), pronounced "seis" (the number six), is a DJ bar/cocktail lounge/sushi bar near

Gaucho's Steak House. It's upstairs in what had been an old house and projects the air of a party in a pleasant, minimalist apartment. It attracts a midtwenty-something and older crowd. A happy hour starts at 5 P.M.

Punto PTY (Avenida 5A and Calle Uruguay/Calle 48 Este, tel. 265-1230, Wed.–Sun. until late) was until recently a small, minimalist club called Dot, but I haven't been back since it changed names. It's worth giving a shot late at night.

TGI Friday's (Avenida 4A Sur near Calle Aquilino de la Guardia/49 Este, tel. 269-4199), ghastly though it may be, is mentioned here just because it's a perennially popular destination for young singles on the prowl or just hanging with their friends. There's another one attached to the Country Inns and Suites on the Calzada de Amador (Amador Causeway).

Opah (Avenida 5B between Calle Uruguay/Calle 48 Este and Calle Aquilino de la Guardia/49 Este tel. 265-8041), formerly Café Dali, was a new hot spot on my last visit. The place features all aluminum, space-agey minimalist decor, exposed ventilation ducts, and hostesses wearing tight bustiers. There's a smaller room at the back of the club. The attached cocktail lounge, the **Deep Room Martini Bar,** has a more intimate vibe and revs into gear after 2 A.M.

Gay Bars and Clubs

Panama City is still a place where gay bars have to keep a low profile, but you don't hear horror stories of police raids, gay bashings outside of clubs, and so on—not, at least, among the relatively affluent. It's more a matter of people wanting to be cautious and discreet. Gay bars and clubs are either in remote locations or hidden in plain sight—it's possible to walk right past one and not know anything's there at all.

The three listed below are the most prominent and popular spots. They draw mostly a gay male clientele (the one lesbian bar closed years ago), but lesbians and straight singles or couples are welcome. Visitors will likely find the vibe at these places friendlier, more low-key, more inclusive, and less macho than that at many of the city's straight bars and clubs.

There are also so-called "camouflage" bars—ostensibly straight bars that draw closeted gays—and rough dives. Neither kind is included here, for reasons of privacy and safety.

Panama City's biggest gay club, **Box** (off Tumba Muerto, no telephone, 11 P.M.–late Wed., Fri., Sat., and Sun. 11 P.M.–6 A.M. Sat., 11 P.M.–4 A.M. Sun.), is well-hidden in a warehouse district quite a hike east of downtown Panama City. It's a converted warehouse with minimal atmosphere, deafening music, and a scene that frequently lasts until dawn. This is the only gay club in Panama City that, when everything clicks, can resemble a happening, high-energy night in New York or San Francisco. The cover charge ranges $6–10 on the weekends. Wednesday, Saturday, and Sunday tend to be "open bar" nights (all you can drink for the price of the cover charge). Saturday is the big night here. Sunday can also be surprisingly well-attended. Regulars caution that this place can get kind of wild and rough, and fights sometimes break out, which may explain the police presence during my one visit (they wandered in to monitor the scene but did not hassle anyone). That night, at least, the crowd was friendly and low-key.

To get to Box, head east on Tumba Muerto (Avenida Ricardo J. Alfaro) for four kilometers past the turnoff to Calle de la Amistad (also called Friendship Road); you should see that road to the left as you pass it. When you're near the turnoff to the club, look for the Universidad Santa María la Antigua (U.S.M.A.) to the left. If you come to a major cloverleaf intersection, you've gone too far; turn around and try again. It's a right turn into a deserted warehouse area. Look for a warehouse with corrugated aluminum siding near an ice plant (*hielera*).

Given the remoteness of the area and the difficulty in finding the place, I do not recommend that foreign visitors look for it solo. It's possible a cab driver would recognize the place with enough hints, but you may need to take a map and point it out.

BLG (Calle 49 and Calle Uruguay/Calle 48 Este, tel. 265-1624, 10 P.M.–late Wed.–Sun., $5 cover most nights) has two bars, ample room for dancing, and bad acoustics. It's a fairly simple place, but by virtue of its location in the heart of one of Panama City's more affluent nightlife areas it has the most upscale vibe of the gay bars in the city. It draws men, women, and some straight couples. The music is mostly electronica. It has drag shows *(transformistas)* and comedians some Wednesday, Thursday, and Sunday nights. There are sometimes special events on Friday and Saturday nights. It's easy to walk right by this place and not see it, as it's designed to fade into the background. The facade is painted blue. Look for a metal wedge that resembles the brow of a ship jutting out from a wall. There's a small neon *abierto* sign that's illuminated when the place is open. The bar has good security.

Space (Calle 70, tel. 265-7320, Tues.–Sat.) is a small, cozy bar in Obarrio near Magnum Pub and Bar. It has some aluminum tables, a little dance floor, a video screen, a pool table, and that's about it. It has a low-key and friendly vibe. There's a $3 cover on Friday and Saturday. Friday is the biggest night. The place is unmarked. The entrance is a metallic silver door.

CINEMAS

There are plenty of movie theaters in Panama City. Mostly these are multiplexes showing recent Hollywood spectacles and are generally in English with Spanish subtitles rather than dubbed. Ticket prices for adults are less than $4. Theaters generally charge half price on Tuesdays and/or Wednesdays.

The daily newspapers carry a list of current movies, locations, and showtimes. A good online list is at www.epasa.com/cartelera/cartelera.html.

Popular, centrally located multiplexes include **Alhambra Vía España** (Vía España, tel. 264-3217), **Extreme Planet** (Vía España, tel. 214-7022), **Kinomaxx** (next to Extreme Planet in the new Multicentro mall, tel. 236-9585), and **Cinemark 8 Los Pueblos Albrook** (Albrook Mall, next to the Gran Terminal de Transportes, tel. 314-6001).

THEATERS AND CONCERTS

Panama City has an active theater scene, with regular productions featuring plays by Panamanian playwrights as well as classic and contemporary plays from other countries. The easiest music performance to find on any given night is a *típico* combo, though salsa, Latin pop/rock, and other high-energy music forms are also popular. Most of these are local acts that perform in clubs, but with the opening of more modern, high-capacity venues such as the **Figali Convention Center** at the Panama Canal Village, the city is beginning to attract more big-name international pop acts. Classical music and dance groups come through less often. (See the *Panama Canal* chapter for information on the Panama Canal Village and other canal-area entertainment venues near downtown.)

Tickets for major concerts and other events are usually available through TicketCenter (tel. 279-1010, www.ticketccenterpa.com), which has outlets in CD Place and AudioFoto stores scattered around the city.

Panama's elegant old **Teatro Nacional,** or national theater (Avenida B between Calle 3 and Calle 4 in Casco Viejo, tel. 262-3525, 262-3582), hosts visiting classical music ensembles and other arts events.

Teatro en Círculo (Avenida 6C Norte near Vía Brasil, tel. 261-5375), near Scubapanama in a quiet residential area east of downtown, presents many of the city's highest-profile plays, from Spanish-language renditions of Shakespeare to well-received original productions by Panamanian playwrights. The small **Teatro Anita Villalaz** (tel. 211-4017 or 211-2040), in Plaza de Francia in Casco Viejo, is another prominent playhouse. Performance groups often rent out the **Teatro ABA** (Avenida Simon Bolívar/Transístmica near Avenida de los Periodistas, tel. 260-6316) for their productions. It's near the Chinese restaurant Palacio Lung Fung and not far from Teatro en Círculo.

The **Atlapa Convention Center,** next to the Hotel Caesar Park off Vía Israel, has two theaters, the 3,000-seat **Anayansi** and the 600-seat **La Huaca.**

Shopping

Panama certainly has no shortage of shopping malls and commercial centers—at last count there were about two dozen of various sizes. Many of these, however, look better stocked from the outside than they do on closer inspection, and the city is not the best place to look for the latest fashions (many better-off Panamanians fly up to Miami to do their shopping). However, those in the market for cosmetics and perfumes can find better deals than they would in the United States at the nicer department stores, such as the **Stevens, Figale, Collins, Felix B. Maduro,** and **Dante** chains. There are branches of these on Vía España, on Tumba Muerto (Avenida Ricardo J. Alfaro) in El Dorado, and in some of the malls.

The newest and glitziest of the malls is the youth-oriented **Multicentro,** on the west end of Avenida Balboa near Punta Paitilla. There's a gringo-style food court on the top floor that has a great view of the city and the bay. Another new and growing complex is the **Albrook Mall,** sometimes also called Los Pueblos II, next to the Gran Terminal de Transportes, the main bus terminal, which is near the domestic airport in Albrook, a former U.S. Air Force base.

Other upscale shopping destinations include the **Plaza Paitilla** and **Bal Harbour** minimalls in the Punta Paitilla area, the designer-name shops along **Calle 53 in Marbella** (especially in the **World Trade Center**), and the tony jewelry stores and galleries on **Avenida 2 Sur/Samuel Lewis** in Obarrio. More bargain-oriented stores tend to be along **Vía España** and the malls and strip malls of the **El Dorado** neighborhood, though both places have higher-end shops as well. **Punta Pacifica** is a new area of condominium towers, stores, and at least one hotel that's going up rapidly west of Punta Paitilla and should have some upscale shopping options when you visit.

Avenida Central is a busy shopping district with an extensive walking street that extends from **Plaza Cinco de Mayo** to **Parque Santa Ana.** Just about the only things for sale on Avenida Central are cheap clothes and jewelry, electronics, and photo-development services. Even those not interested in these things should consider a stroll, though, as the people-watching is fun and the area gives one a real sense of daily life in Panama City. For the full Central experience, try a glass of sugarcane juice from one of the vendors who crush the cane in a hand-cranked press while you watch. Visitors are often warned to beware of pickpockets around here, which is probably a good idea, but this place is well-patrolled by police and you're unlikely to have an unpleasant encounter, at least during the day. It has an IPAT information booth at the intersection of Avenida Central and Calle I that's unlikely to be staffed.

(For information on the Mercado Público and Salsipuedes, see the *Casco Viejo* section.)

Below are some individual stores that may be of interest.

DEPARTMENT STORES

The **Gran Morrison** department store chain is a bit like a Kmart in the United States. The Vía España branch (Vía España near Calle 51, tel. 269-2211, www.panamainfo.com/Artesania/, 9 A.M.–6:30 P.M. Mon.–Sat., closed Sun.) is close to many of the city's more popular hotels. In addition to a wide assortment of low-end household goods and such, the store has a music department with a decent selection of *típico, rock en español,* salsa, merengue, and some gringo music. It also carries some souvenirs, local books, and an extensive collection of magazines in English and Spanish.

There's a huge, five-story outlet of the **El Machetazo** discount department-store chain in the Calidonia area (Avenida Perú between Calle 28 Este and Calle 29 Este, tel. 227-3014, 8:30 A.M.–7:30 P.M. daily). There's a grocery store on the ground floor. Other departments include a pharmacy, cheap clothing, and lots of assorted junk.

THE REAL TAILOR OF PANAMA

La Fortuna (Vía España at Calle 55 Este near Vía Argentina, tel. 263-6434, 9 A.M.–6 P.M. Mon.–Sat., closed Sun.) is Panama's best-known destination for tailored men's suits. It's been around since 1925 and has dressed ambassadors and presidents. A custom-made suit or tuxedo made from high-quality imported fabric can be had for around $500; knock $100-200 off that estimate for less-expensive material. One of the nifty things about having a suit made here is that the tailors sew a panel inside the suit with the buyer's name and the statement that it was made *exclusivo* for him. Another cool thing is that if you don't care for any of their styles, you can bring in a photo of what you like and they'll create it for you. I've had jackets and suits made here based on ads from fashion magazines and photos downloaded from the Internet, and I've been pleased with the results. (And no, I didn't get a price break for writing that.) They carry a range of fabric from famous European and North American designers.

José Abadí, the "tailor of Panama" (at left) and his son

© BONNIE KAY SPINDLER

The late dictator Omar Torrijos reportedly once declared that the owner, José Abadí, was the only man who could make him drop his trousers. There are autographs on display from Geoffrey Rush, Jamie Lee Curtis, and Pierce Brosnan, who were in Panama to make the dreadful movie adaptation of John le Carré's "The Tailor of Panama"—inevitably, Brosnan's note dubbed Abadí the "real tailor of Panama." It's said he was in fact the inspiration for le Carré's book, about a tailor to powerful Panamanian politicians who is forced by a British agent to spy on his customers. Fittingly enough, the first time I was there the head of the Asamblea Legislativa (the national legislature) was in the store buying suits for his five bodyguards, and another member of the legislature was having a suit made for himself on a more recent visit. It's a nice coda for a family of Jewish immigrants that has gone through some rough times in Panama, including a bleak period during the 1940s when Jews and other minorities had their civil rights stripped away.

Visitors should place an order at the start of their travels, as the process requires two fittings, and the shop normally needs at least 10 days to make a suit, more during peak seasons, such as before the independence holidays in November, when they're busy making uniforms for bands and such. Those pressed for time can sometimes have a suit made in 24 hours, but don't expect a perfect fit. Try to give it at least a week.

PHOTO SUPPLIES

Panafoto (Calle 50 and Calle 49A Este, tel. 263-0102, 9 A.M.–7:30 P.M. Mon.–Sat., noon–6 P.M. Sun.) is a modern, glass-enclosed consumer electronics store and photo-development place. One-hour photo developing costs $8.50 for 24 exposures or $12.50 for 36 exposures.

You can have carnet photos—passport-sized shots—taken here for $3 for six. There's an espresso bar upstairs.

MUSIC STORES

Panama lacks good record stores. Outlets of the **CD Place** chain are dotted throughout the city, but they have meager offerings even of Panamanian music. I once asked a clerk at a record store why it's easier to find music by Colombian pop stars than Panamanian ones anywhere in Panama, and he explained that stores can buy Colombian CDs for considerably less than they can Panamanian ones. Go figure. CD prices are about the same as those in the United States, meaning that a single disc costs more than most Panamanians earn in a day. **El Puente del CD** (tel. 223-8455, Calle 50 between the Btesh clothing store and National Car Rental, 9 A.M.–6 P.M. Mon.–Sat., closed Sun.) has a modest collection of Panamanian music, plus music from other Latin American countries and a decent jazz selection. Gran Morrison outlets carry some music.

CRAFT SHOPS AND BOUTIQUES

The **Reprosa** (Avenida 2 Sur/Samuel Lewis and Calle 54 Este, 9 A.M.–6 P.M. Mon.–Sat., closed Sun.) jewelry store is a Panama institution. It's a great place to go for unique presents or souvenirs. There's a second Reprosa store in the Flamenco Shopping Plaza on the Amador Causeway (see the *Panama Canal* chapter).

Reprosa is most famous for its reproductions of *huacas,* figures recovered from pre-Colombian graves. The figures are created by using molds made through the so-called "lost wax" process, which creates exact replicas, including the imperfections in the original. This process is virtually the same as that used to produce the ancient original pieces. Prices are very reasonable—some start at less than $10, though the cost goes straight up from there depending on the purity of the gold. Pieces include replicas of some of the finest and oldest *huacas* in the collection of Panama's anthropology museum. The store carries other jewelry as well—including replicas of pieces of eight and the pearl-encrusted broaches known as *mosquetas,* the latter of which is traditionally worn with the *pollera*—and there are other jewelry shops on the same street.

Reprosa was planning to offer tours of its factory near Panamá la Vieja, and they should be under way by the time you read this. A visit to the factory is well worthwhile for anyone with the least interest

making replicas of pre-Colombian *huacas* at the Reprosa factory

© BONNIE KAY SPINDLER

in the blend of ancient and modern techniques that go into crafting this jewelry. From a catwalk above the factory floor, visitors will be able to watch technicians go through every step of the process, from creating the molds to polishing the final pieces. Tours will likely include a visit to the casting room and a chance to buy finished pieces. Reprosa planned to have its own guides to explain the process, but tours will be booked through the city's major tour operators. (See *Organized Tours* for a partial list of likely candidates.)

Casa de la Pollera (Avenue A and Calle 8, tel. 228-8671, home tel. 223-5375—ask for Evelina de Herran, 9:30 A.M.–5:30 P.M. Mon.–Sat., closed Sun.), across the street from the church of the golden altar, is the place to go in Panama City for Panama's beautiful national dress, the *pollera.* The shop sells mainly machine-made *polleras* ($125) on which the patterns are printed rather than embroidered on the cloth. However, the shop does take orders for custom, handmade *polleras.* These start at $2,000 and take months to make. The shop takes your measurements and mails the completed dress by DHL. The shop also sells traditional Panamanian men's shirts, including a *camisilla de lujo* with gold buttons for $70 and a hand-embroidered *montuna campesino* (or country shirt that's still worn in folkloric dances) and matching cutoff pants for $120. **Boutique Breebaart** (#36 Calle 50 near Calle Uruguay/Calle 48, tel. 264-5937, 9 A.M.–6 P.M. Mon.–Fri., 10 A.M.–5 P.M. Sat., closed Sun.), upstairs in a what was once a charming old house in Bella Vista, offers unusual skirts, dresses, bathing suits, pillows, place settings, napkins, and other items designed by a French artist, Helèné Breebaart, whose work is inspired by the colorful *molas* of the Kuna Indians, who actually stitch the clothing and other pieces. Some of the work, which generally features floral patterns that are appliqued onto the items, is quite lovely and elegant; some is rather kitschy. Each piece is custom-made, requires a week to 15 days to make, and can cost anywhere from $10 to $500. Bergdorf-Goodman and Saks Fifth Avenue in the United States have commissioned beautifully embroidered purses from the boutique. These are not for sale at the shop.

A few items are on display. If you visit, peek in the back to see the dozen Kuna women (and perhaps a gay Kuna man—gay men in Kuna society take on traditional women's roles) at work. Bit of trivia: Breebaart designed the cheerful nature flags in the lobby of the Gamboa Rainforest Resort.

Casa de los Manteles or Linen House (Avenida de los Mártires near Calle J, tel. 262-0822, 9 A.M.–6 P.M. Mon.–Sat., closed Sun.) is known for its lovely embroidered tablecloths, napkins, and other linens. It also carries good-quality guayaberas (the semiformal traditional Latin American shirt). This area is not the safest these days, though it should be fine in the daytime and the store has a parking lot behind the building.

There is a **handicrafts market** in Plaza Cinco de Mayo, behind the anthropology museum, that offers hats, *molas*, hammocks, sandals, and the like. Hats are especially well-represented. There's also a place here that takes passport photos for $1 the half-dozen. Most stalls open by 9 A.M. daily and stay open until sundown. If you have trouble finding this place, ask for the *artesanía* near Plaza Cinco de Mayo. Better handicraft markets are in Balboa, in the old Canal Zone. (See that chapter for information.)

ART GALLERIES

Panama's best art gallery is **Imagen** (Calle 50 and Calle 77, tel. 226-8989, 9 A.M.–1 P.M. and 2–6 P.M. Mon.–Sat., closed Sun.). It's in a lovely old building and the staff is gracious. It's small, but it's a good place to go just to get a sense of what's happening in the local art scene. **Habitante** (Calle Uruguay/Calle 48 Este, tel. 264-6470, 9 A.M.–6 P.M. Mon.–Sat.), in the Calle Uruguay nightlife area, is also small, but less interesting. **Mateo Sariel** (Vía Porras and Calle 66 Este, tel. 270-2404, 9 A.M.–6 P.M. Mon.–Fri., closed Sun.), though also well known, often feels more like a framing shop than an art gallery.

Sports and Recreation

Panama City is really not the best spot for either spectator or participant sports. Generally only the most expensive hotels have tennis courts, pools big enough to swim laps in, or decent gyms. Most sports clubs are upscale places open to members and their guests. The best options for those interested in golf are Summit Golf and Resort in the former Canal Zone or, for those going to the Pacific beaches, the course at the Coronado Hotel and Resort. They are well-maintained, championship courses with good facilities. Other courses are being built around the country.

Piscina Olímpica Adan Gordon

Piscina Olímpica Adan Gordon (between Calle 31 and Calle 32 and Avenida Cuba and Avenida Perú, 8:30–11:45 A.M. and 1–3:45 P.M. Tues.–Sat., 8:30–11:45 A.M. and 12:30–2:45 P.M. Sat. and Sun., closed Mon.) is a decent, Olympic-sized swimming pool across from the national lottery plaza in the heart of the budget hotel district. Tourists are welcome to go for a splash for $.50, but passports must be left with the attendant. Don't leave valuables unattended.

Panama City

THE LOTTERY

The Lotería Nacional de Beneficencia, or national lottery, is a tenacious carryover from a time when Panamanians had a lot fewer entertainment options. The first lottery on the isthmus was held in 1882, and the current system dates from 1919. It's still hugely popular.

Every Sunday and Wednesday at 1 P.M., a crowd gathers for the drawing, which is broadcast live throughout the country on TV and radio. Drawings are held in Plaza Víctor Julio Gutiérrez, which is covered by an open-sided shed that takes up an entire block between Avenida Perú and Avenida Cuba and Calle 31 and Calle 32. Anyone can drop by to watch the drawings, which are held on a stage at the back of the shed.

The ritual is as solemn and unwavering as a church service. First, the lottery balls are turned incessantly back and forth in a shiny steel cage by a designated official. This seems to last for hours. At last, the cage is stopped and a ball extracted by a child dressed in his or her very best for the honor. The ball is twisted apart to reveal a number printed inside, which is held up for all to see, read aloud by the emcee, and then carefully recorded on a board behind the stage. Three sets of four numbers are chosen, corresponding to the first, second, and third prize. A ticket holder must have all four numbers in the correct order to win a prize.

Often, the ball can't be easily unscrewed and must be loosened with a special contraption, heightening the suspense. (In 1991 lottery officials tried to update the system with a fancy new pneumatic machine, but a suspicious and tradition-minded public rebelled.) The lottery staff goes through the whole process twelve times, once for each number, which turns the drawing into an event long enough to allow for all kinds of side shows: beauty queens in *polleras,* folkloric dances, musical performances, visiting dignitaries, and so on.

All this for a first prize of . . . $2,000. That's still a lot of money for the average hard-working Panamanian, and there are special drawings that pay considerably more. Drawings called *Gordi-*

tos del Zodíaco (little fat ones of the Zodiac) are held on the last Friday of each month, unless the month ends mid-week, in which case the drawing is held on the first Friday of the following month.

Besides, the lottery is considering raising the first prize to a whopping $2,500. Second prize will remain $600 and third prize $300.

Four-number tickets cost $1. *Chances,* tickets with two numbers, go for $.25. These pay off if the numbers correspond to the last two numbers of any of the winning combinations. First prize is $14, second prize is $3, and third prize is $2.

Tickets are sold by freelance vendors around the country. Those interested in playing should have little trouble finding a vendor on any street with lots of foot traffic. A whole battalion has stalls set up on the Avenida Perú side of the plaza, between Calle 31 and Calle 32. There are nearly 10,000 vendors throughout the country.

© WILLIAM FRIAR

Lottery vendors sell tickets outside the Mercado Público near Casco Viejo.

Hipódromo Presidente Remón

Panama has a well-established horse-racing industry. The national racetrack, Hipódromo Presidente Remón (tel. 217-6060, www.hipodromo.com) is on the outskirts of the city. It's about eight kilometers east of Punta Paitilla in the Juan Díaz area, on the way to the international airport. It holds races Thursdays, Saturdays, Sundays, and holidays. The quickest way to get there is via the Corredor Sur. It's also accessible from Vía España, which becomes Vía José Agustín Arango east of the city. The racecourse is just past the national stadium, **Estadio Rommel Fernández.**

Scubapanama

Scubapanama (Avenida 6C Norte, tel. 261-3841 or 261-4064, fax 261-9586, www.scuba-panama.com, rene.gomez@wcom.com), Panama's largest dive operator, also rents and sells snorkeling and diving gear. Those who plan to do a fair amount of snorkeling should know that most of the equipment available on Panama's beaches and islands is mediocre at best. This is a decent place to buy some if you don't bring your own.

Casinos

Gambling is legal in Panama and casinos are scattered throughout the city, primarily in the better hotels. One of the nicest and newest is in the centrally located **Hotel El Panamá.** Another good possibility is the casino at the **Hotel Caesar Park,** though it's more out of the way for those not staying there. Both casinos offer a range of table games and slot machines and attract gamblers until the wee small hours.

Accommodations

Panama City offers plenty of good lodging options for almost any budget. A couple—or two friends who don't mind snug conditions—can find a decent if bare-bones room for as little as $10 a night. Those in the mood for a splurge can choose from several five-star options for what they'd most likely pay for a more modest hotel in a big city back home.

WHAT TO EXPECT

At the low end of the scale, every $5 extra can mean dramatically better digs. For $10 s/d a night, don't expect much more than a bare room with a cold-water bathroom and a fan, though occasionally even these places offer air-conditioning for a couple of bucks more. Air-conditioning is universally available once the price gets up to around $20 s/d per night; hot water kicks in at less than that. For about $25 s/d, it's possible to find some quite pleasant, clean hotels with modern furnishings, reliable air-conditioning, clean hot-water bathrooms, and sometimes cable TV.

By the $50 mark, you're getting into two-and-a-half and three-star hotel territory. At that price, it's possible to find lodgings with lots of character,

attractive rooms with good beds, and amenities such as cable TV, in-room telephones, a decent restaurant/bar, a small swimming pool (often on the rooftop), and so on. Some of these places are in high demand and should be booked several days or even weeks in advance if possible.

Many of the options between $50–100 a night are so-called "aparthotels," which offer furnished, usually large studio and one-bedroom apartments with a full kitchen and utensils, telephone, and washer and drier either in the apartment or in a laundry facility on the premises. These also sometimes have a business center and small pool. These can offer more for the money than more expensive traditional hotels, and they generally offer price breaks for long stays.

Four- and five-star hotels generally go for between $100–200 a night per couple. Prices vary wildly at this level, and deals are often available.

NEIGHBORHOODS

Most of the budget hotels are in and around the Calidonia/La Expoición district. This is a busy, older neighborhood near Panama Bay, with a high concentration of cheaper hotels, most of them concentrated in a 10-block area between Avenida Perú and Avenida Cuba. Note that Avenida 3 Sur is quieter than either of these two major avenues, something to consider when choosing a place to stay; it's just two blocks from the bay.

Though a poorer neighborhood compared with Bella Vista to the northeast, Calidonia is a bustling area and travelers generally feel safe enough here. Still, as always it pays to stay alert, especially at night, when it's probably a good idea to get around by taxi. The neighborhood deteriorates as the street numbers go down. I have found just a few places below Calle 28 Este I consider safe or decent enough to recommend. Adventurous types can try one of the rock-bottom pensions along the pedestrian section of Avenida Central, but these are known hangouts for prostitutes and their customers, drug addicts, and other sketchy characters. I don't recommend them. Central is also busy day and night, which can add a sense of safety but make for a noisy night's sleep. It's unquestionably a colorful place to stay, though. There are also three reasonably safe places in Casco Viejo.

Most of the midrange and high-end hotels are in or around El Cangrejo and Bella Vista/Marbella, in the center of Panama City. The streets immediately north and south of the heart of Vía España, the area near the Hotel El Panamá and Iglesia del Carmen, have an especially high concentration of these hotels. Many of the city's tourist services and better restaurants are in the area as well.

A FEW POINTERS

Hotels often charge the same for one or two guests, so those traveling solo can save money by buddying up with fellow travelers they meet along the way. A third or fourth guest often costs just a fraction more, so small groups can get deals even at the higher end of the scale.

The midrange and high-end hotels often offer "corporate rates" and promotional deals that can be significantly cheaper than their standard rates. It never hurts to ask for the discount, which one may get without having to produce so much as a business card.

The biggest problem with Panama City's cheaper hotels, as with those throughout the country, is management's belief that mattresses last forever. Given that they tend to be poor quality to begin with, it's not unusual to find thin, squishy, or plank-hard mattresses in otherwise decent-looking hotels. Try the beds in a few rooms before deciding to stay.

Prices quoted are generally for standard rooms. Luxury hotels all have more expensive options for those who can't burn through their money fast enough. As elsewhere in the book, all prices include Panama's 10-percent room tax.

UNDER $10

Hotel Herrera (Plaza Herrera in Casco Viejo, tel. 228-8994, $5.50 s, $7.70 d) is a 40-room pension on the edge of Casco Viejo, housed in a deteriorating landmark building that dates from the 1920s. The place is rather shabby, but it still has lots of attractive old features, including a beautiful wooden staircase, elaborate mouldings, vintage tiles, and a high-ceilinged common room that looks out on the plaza. Rooms have thin, sagging mattresses and are paneled with dark wood, making them rather gloomy. Some of the rooms have private bathrooms and all have fans. Because of the price and location, this place is popular and fills up. Warning: Be extremely careful around here at night, and do not venture into the plaza after dark. Youth gangs live in other rundown buildings in the neighborhood, including a notorious character who by age 14 had allegedly already killed three people. The police have so far been unable to pin anything on him. The entrance to the pension itself is gated.

Hospedaje Casa Grande (Avenida Central and Calle 8 Este in Casco Viejo, tel. 211-3316, $6 s/d, $7 s/d with balcony) has the feel of a squatters' hangout. The thin walls are made of plywood and reach only two-thirds of the way to the very high ceilings. Rooms have foam mattresses and fans and little else. Bathrooms are shared. Because of the price, this place is often full. It's on well-trafficked Avenida Central, which probably makes it a safer place to stay in Casco Viejo than Hotel Herrera. It has a gated entrance.

$10–25

Panama City's pioneering hostel is the **Voyager International Hostel** (Edificio Di-Lido, Apt. 8, Calle Manuel María Icaza, tel. 260-5913, tel./fax 223-3687, cell 636-3443, hostelpm@cableonda.net, www.geocities.com/voyagerih, starts at $9 per person with air-conditioning, $8 without; those without student IDs pay 10 percent more for the IPAT tax).

The hostel is actually divided between two buildings, both centrally located in the area just south of the busiest part of Vía España. The larger part of the hostel is on the top floor of the eight-story Di-Lido apartment/office building, down from the Hotel Continental on the same street as Restaurante Jimmy. It's a former apartment that's been turned into a stark hostel with 40 dorm beds, a spacious balcony, and communal bathrooms. It has a view of Vía España and the downtown cityscape. There's a TV room and communal kitchen. The elevator and intercom are poorly maintained, which can be quite a nuisance.

The other part of the hostel, which also contains the main office, is one street over, on Calle Ricardo Arias. It consists of 25 beds, some of them in private rooms, on the second floor of an old apartment building. This building is older, dirtier, has saggier mattresses, and is generally not as nice, but it does have a certain funky charm, a sitting room/library, and a balcony overlooking the busy street. The walls don't rise all the way to the ceiling in some of the dorm rooms. There are five private rooms for couples ($18 per couple with air-conditioning, $15 without), but these must be reserved ahead of time. There's a very small communal kitchen.

Voyager is not affiliated with any international hostel organization. The whole place is pretty disorganized and not terribly clean. But it has a friendly, hippiesh hostel vibe and it's easy to see why it's popular with young backpackers. You'll likely meet interesting people here, and some of the staff members speak English.

A continental breakfast is served 7–11 A.M. There's a laundry room in the high-rise: $1.50 to wash, $1.50 to dry. Internet access at both lo-

cations is free. There's a book swap at the Ricardo Arias location.

The whole show is run by Guadalupe Peralta, a warm and friendly woman with the air of a harried but caring mom. Note that the hostel has moved before, and Guadalupe was considering relocating at least the high-rise part of it yet again; call ahead before showing up.

This is also a good place to get hooked up with unusual opportunities. Those who stay a week can teach English to beginning tour guides in exchange for free tours. For those who want a free and unusual way to transit the canal, the hostel may be able to help make arrangements to be a line-handler on a transiting yacht. The staff can also sometimes arrange boat trips to Cartagena for $150, though be cautious in setting something like this up.

The new, 40-bed **Lion House at San Felipe** (Avenida Central between Calle 8 Este and Calle 9 Este, tel. 228-7257, lionhousepanama@hotmail.com, $10 per bed, including continental breakfast) is a three-story hostel in a wooden building that dates from 1860. The hostel was nearing completion during my last visit. All the rooms are different but average four bunk beds with new mattresses. Each has a table, chairs, and ceilings about four meters high. The rooms are spacious. There are a couple of private rooms for couples or those who just want less company. There's a common room with old-fashioned furnishings, shared cold-water bathrooms, laundry facilities, and a kitchen that guests are free to use. Note that the walls between the rooms don't go all the way to the ceiling, but this does improve ventilation. It looked like the choice rooms would probably be on the top floor, as they have balconies with a partial view of the cathedral and Cerro Ancón.

The Lion House (named in honor of its original owners, the León family) looks out on a building across the street with a beautiful wrought-iron balcony. Built in 1868, it was reportedly a hardware store used by the French during their attempt to build a canal. It's owned by the Lion House and may eventually house additional rooms.

Though I wasn't able to see it in actual operation, this place is likely to be a great option for those who want to stay in Casco Viejo and don't mind simple digs. Avenida Central is well lit at night, and there's a security gate at the hostel entrance. The **Tourism and Internet Café,** a good source of local information, is on the ground floor.

Pensión Las Torres (Calle 36 and Calle Perú, tel. 225-0172, starts at $10 s/d) is a very friendly place. It consists of 24 rooms in a converted house, built in 1931, that retains its original Spanish tile and other old touches that give the place character and an almost Moroccan air. A tiny room with shared bathroom goes for $10 s/d. Large rooms with air-conditioning, cable TV, and private hot-water bathroom are also available. Rooms are spartan but funky and the beds are decent. This is a good budget place—the one weird thing about it is that the rooms with private bath don't have bathroom doors, which can be awkward if you're sharing a room. Note that the entrance to the place is hidden behind bushes and a bit hard to find.

Residencial La Primavera (Calle 42 Este and Avenida Cuba, tel. 225-1195, $10 s/d) has 18 basic rooms barely big enough for their (mostly okay) beds. Rooms come equipped with fans and small windows, a combination that doesn't help much on a hot afternoon. But the place has been converted from an old house in a great location on a quiet residential street close to the action on Vía España. The rooms are passable, the place has a mellow vibe, and the price is right. This is one of the better cheapo options. Note: The street signs along the side of the house claim it's on Calle 43, but it's actually on Calle 42.

Pensión Colón (Avenida Perú between Calle 29 Este and Calle 30 Este, no phone, $10 s/d with fan, $12 s/d with air-conditioning) has 47 basic, moderately clean rooms with cold-water bathrooms and local TV. This is a decent budget option if you're not put off by being buzzed in through a metal gate or sleeping in a bed with graffiti carved into the headboard. The low-security-prison aspects of the place may actually keep you safer.

Residencial Turístico Volcán (Calle 29 Este between Avenida Perú and Avenida Cuba, tel. 225-5263, $12 s/d with fans, $14 with air-con-

ditioning) is another prisonlike place with 24 fairly clean rooms with cold-water bathrooms. The rooms with fans for $12 s/d are dreary cells; $2 more gets you a bigger, better room with air-conditioning. This place is basic but okay.

The nine-story **Pensión Monaco** (Avenida Cuba between Calle 28 Este and Calle 29 Este, tel. 225-2573, $15 s/d) is one of the best budget hotels in Panama City. Opened in late 2002, it offers large modern rooms with a breakfast table, spacious bathrooms, air-conditioning, and cable TV. Mattresses are thin but okay. Rooms are unadorned but feature attractive wooden furniture. It's an outstanding value at $15 s/d, but be prepared for prices to increase as people discover this place.

Pensión América (Avenida Ecuador and Avenida 3 Sur, tel. 225-1140, $15 s/d) has 56 minimal but cheerful rooms—the walls are covered with nearly psychedelic swirls of blue paint. Rooms are decently clean, with air-conditioning, cable TV, and cheap but okay mattresses. There's a protected parking garage. One annoyance here is the constant buzzing from the laundry room. This place is a good value, and neohippie types will probably dig it.

Hotel Discovery (Avenida Ecuador near Avenida 3 Sur, tel. 225-1140, $15 s/d) is right next door to Pensión América and has the same owner and phone number. Its 79 rooms are virtually the same as those at its sibling, except the swirly walls are pink instead of blue. But Pensión América is a better bet since its room doors are steel and have deadbolt locks, while these are flimsy and have cheap locks.

Residencial Compostela (Calle 29 Este near Avenida Cuba, tel. 267-6394, $18 s/d), between the Museo de Ciencias Naturales and immigration office, offers 44 small but clean and modern rooms, soft but okay mattresses, and surly service.

The only real problem with the **Hotel Arenteiro** (Calle 30 Este between Avenida Cuba and Avenida Perú, tel. 227-5883, $18 s/d) is that it's five stories high but has no elevator. If you have a lot of luggage, ask for a lower floor. It offers 58 small, modern, minimalist rooms with thin mattresses. It may remind you of a European pension. All rooms have air-conditioning, cable TV, and phones. There's a restaurant/bar and a protected parking lot. The hotel was built in 1998 and still looks new. It's a good deal.

Residencial Alameda (Calle 30 Este between Avenida Cuba and Avenida Perú, tel. 225-1758, $18.50 s/d) offers 60 small, generic rooms with microthin mattresses. The place is newish and okay but lacks any character. There's a parking lot, and guests can send and receive in-country faxes for free.

Hotel Latino (Avenida Cuba and Calle 36 Este, tel. 227-3395, $15/20 s/d) offers old but reasonably maintained and fairly clean rooms, if you ignore the smudges on the walls. There's a small outdoor pool on the fifth floor that doesn't have much of a view. The mattresses are thin but it's an okay place otherwise. There's a simple bar/restaurant on the premises.

Residencial Jamaica (Avenida Cuba and Calle 38 Este, tel. 225-9870, $20 s/d) is nothing fancy, but it's a quite decent, modern place offering 35 clean, cheerful rooms with soft but okay beds, air-conditioning, and cable TV. It's in a reasonably quiet neighborhood.

Hotel Venecia (Avenida Perú and Calle 36 Este, tel. 227-7881, 227-5252, or 227-7673, $20 s/d) has 71 modern rooms with air-conditioning, firm beds, and local TV. Some effort has gone into making the rooms pleasant, but the mattresses are on the thin side and the bathrooms could be cleaner—ask to see several rooms. This is a newish place but it's not being well-maintained and is aging fast. There's a bar/restaurant on the premises.

The six-story **Hotel San Remo** (Calle 31 Este near Avenida Perú, tel. 227-0958, 227-2840, fax 227-6398, sanremo@cwpanama.net, $20 s/d), across the street from Plaza Víctor Julio Gutiérrez (the national lottery plaza), opened in early 2003 and offers 60 simple but clean, modern rooms with air-conditioning and good beds. Some of the rooms are quite small and look out on brick walls. The hotel also has a restaurant/bar, secure parking, and laundry service. Internet and fax services will allegedly be ready by the time you visit. This place is a good value.

Hotel Covadonga (Calle 29 Este between Avenida Cuba and Avenida Perú, tel. 225-5275,

fax 225-4011, $22 s/d) is a seven-story hotel with 65 older rooms that are a bit worn and smell of mothballs. Rooms have air-conditioning, cable TV, and phones. There's a small rooftop pool without much of a view. There's a basic restaurant on the premises. Overall, the place is okay but has little charm unless one counts the bright pink floral wallpaper (I don't). The hotel offers pick-up and drop-off service to Tucumen International Airport for $20 for one or two people.

Hotel Centroamericano (Avenida Ecuador between Avenida Cuba and Avenida Perú, tel. 227-4555, $16.50 s/d) has 61 old but reasonably maintained, air-conditioned rooms. Some beds are better than others. Rooms are decent and pretty clean but spare. They're proud here, for some reason, of having ice machines on every floor. There's a restaurant/bar on the premises.

The three-story **Residencial Los Arcos** (Avenida 3 Sur and Calle 44 Este, tel. 225-0569, 225-0570, or 225-0571, $22 s/d) offers simple but immaculate and tasteful modern rooms with air-conditioning in a quiet neighborhood close to the action. Bigger rooms are $27.50. Rooms can also be rented by the hour, but the place does not have a tawdry atmosphere at all.

The **Hotel Acapulco** (Calle 30 Este between Avenida Cuba and Avenida Perú, tel. 225-3832, $19.80/22 s/d) is an older but very well-maintained six-story place with 55 clean, pleasant rooms tastefully decorated with wooden furniture, tile floors, and new wallpaper. The beds are on the soft side but okay. This place is efficiently run by a proud, friendly staff. All rooms have air-conditioning and cable TV, and some have little balconies. There's a 24-hour restaurant. This is a great option in its price range.

Hotel Marparaiso (Calle 34 Este between Avenida Cuba and Avenida Perú, tel. 227-6767, $22 s/d) is on a relatively quiet stretch of road. It has 72 aging rooms of varying quality and appearance. Some are large, with king-sized beds and attractive bathrooms. You definitely need to shop around here—some beds are quite old. There's a parking lot, and Internet access for $2 an hour.

Hotel Andino (Calle 35 Este between Avenida

Perú and Vía España, tel. 226-1162, $22 s/d) has 40 large, spartan air-conditioned rooms with beds that have seen better years. The word "functional" comes to mind at this worn but okay place. It's a decent value. Guests get a free half hour of Internet time. There's a bar/restaurant on the premises.

Hotel Lisboa (Avenida Cuba and Calle 30 Este, tel. 227-9916, $20/24.20 s/d) is another older place with 55 clean, salmon-colored, reasonably well-maintained rooms that show some wear. Some beds are in better shape than others—ask to see several rooms. All have air-conditioning and some have a partially blocked view of the Bay of Panama. The hotel connects with Restaurante Rincón Tableño #5.

Euro Hotel (Vía España next to Hotel Bella Vista, tel. 263-0802 or 263-0927, eurohotel@cw-panama.net, $20 s, $25 d), the successor to the old Hotel Europa, opened at the end of 2004. It has been spruced up by a renovation but is not terribly different-looking from its older self. It offers 103 rooms, a small pool, a bar, and a roomy cafeteria. Rooms are simple, plain, and dark but otherwise perfectly okay. The furnishings are older but in good shape, and the beds are firm. Don't waste money on the suites, which are just connecting rooms featuring bedrooms barely big enough to contain the bed.

$25–50

The **Hotel Internacional** (off Plaza Cinco de Mayo, tel. 262-9760, $27.50 s/d) is a six-story place with 80 moderately clean, bright and simple air-conditioned rooms with firm but thin mattresses. Some rooms smell of smoke. This is an older place, but it's being moderately well-maintained. Some rooms have a view of the Bay of Panama and the towers of Punta Paitilla. If you stay here, ask for a room on the top floor, which offers the best view. There's a rooftop terrace with a view of the bay, a casino, a parking lot, and a basic bar/restaurant. Its main appeal is that it's right on Plaza Cinco de Mayo and next to the pedestrian stretch of Avenida Central, for those interested in being in the thick of an older, bustling part of Panama City.

Hotel Veracruz (Avenida Perú between Calle 30 Este and Calle 31 Este, tel. 227-3022, $25/27.50) offers 64 older rooms with so-so mattresses and chipped, cream-colored wooden furnishings. If this is meant to be "shabby chic," the hotel has only gotten the first part of the equation right, but it's still an okay place. The restaurant here is one of the most attractive in the neighborhood.

La Casa de Carmen (#32 Calle Primera between Vía Porras and Vía Brasil, tel. 263-4366, serviturisa@cableonda.net, lacasadecarmen.com, $13.75 per person in a dorm, rooms start at $29.70, prices include continental breakfast) is one of those nifty "for those in the know" places. It's a bed-and-breakfast in a very cute house. It's one block off Vía España and close to downtown but far enough away, in the well-off El Carmen residential area, to offer some peace and quiet. It's a fantastic find. It has eight rooms plus a dorm room with three beds and a bathroom. All have air-conditioning and fans and all but two have private baths. Each room is decorated according to a different theme, some fancier than others; all are modern and cozy. The place is clean and well-maintained. There's a communal kitchen, or the place can make lunch for $3. Laundry service is also available: $.50 to wash, $.75 to dry. There's also a TV room, a small library, and free Internet access. Dining tables are set on a terrace in the backyard, which has a little garden and lawn chairs and hammocks to relax in. Rooms vary from tiny to huge. The atmosphere is friendly and welcoming. Since prices are per room and the larger rooms can sleep four or five for $44–55, small groups can actually get a private room for less than the dorm.

The 60-room, five-story **Hotel California** (Vía España and Calle 43, 263-7736, fax 264-6144, info@hotel-california.ws, www.hotel-california.ws, start at $25 s/d including a welcome cocktail, discount for longer stays) has long been popular as a place to get a decent room at a great price. Beds are somewhat hard but rooms are nicely maintained, clean and cheerful and have air-conditioning, hot-water bathrooms, and televisions. Some have a bay view partly obstructed by high-rises. Rooms are somewhat small and some smell of smoke. The hotel is on loud, crowded Vía España without being conveniently close to anything. (If you stay here, try to get a room at the back of the building.) Note: If you stay more than one night, the rate is $20. Rooms with two beds are $33. Internet access in the lobby is $2.50/hour. There's also laundry service and a bar/restaurant.

Hotel Vía España (Vía España at Avenida Martín Sossa /Calle 44, tel. 264-0800 or 264-2873, fax 264-8802, $25/30 s/d), opened in mid-2002, is on one of the busiest intersections in the city. Buses rocket by day and night, but the rooms are surprisingly quiet, especially with the air-conditioning on. Still, it'd be worth trying to get a room at the back of the building. This place is centrally located, clean, modern, and a good deal. Four of the rooms are "sweets" with an in-room whirlpool baths and are worth asking about since they were being promoted at the same price as regular doubles. At the time of writing, only the first two floors had been finished, with a total of 60 rooms. The hotel isn't in the nicest location by any means, but the security is pretty attentive—guests must be buzzed in, and there's a walled parking lot for those with cars. The hotel has a cafeteria. Internet access in the lobby is $2/hour.

Hotel Ribadavia Star (Avenida Perú between Calle 36 Este and Calle 37 Este, tel. 225-7422, fax 225-2520, www.ribadaviapanama.com/page10.html, hotel@ribadaviapanama.com, $27.50/33 s/d) is a glossy, modern place built in 2000 that offers 52 cheerful, clean rooms with firm beds, air-conditioning, and cable TV. It also has laundry service, a parking lot, and a pleasant bar/restaurant. This is quite a nice place and a good deal, though it's already showing a few early signs of wear.

Hotel Costa Inn (Avenida Perú and Calle 39 Este, tel. 227-1522, $24/49.50 s/d) is a seven-story hotel offering 87 air-conditioned rooms, a 24-hour bar/restaurant, a parking lot, room service, and a small rooftop pool with a good view of the city and the Bay of Panama. It was in the middle of a renovation on my last visit that should be finished by the time you visit. The remodeled rooms were cheerful, with new beds

and furnishings and cable TV. The old ones were worn and had saggy beds—don't get stuck with one of these. This place often has promotional deals. Internet computers are available for $3 an hour, three times the going rate. The hotel also has self-serve washers and dryers ($.75 per load for either).

Hotel Roma Plaza (Calle 33 Este and Avenida 3 Sur, tel. 227-3844, $49.50 s/d) would be considered a decent three-star hotel if Panama used such ratings. Its rooms are light and airy and have dressing tables, larger-than-normal TVs with cable, and phones. Some of the rooms smell of smoke. There's a pleasant 24-hour cafeteria, restaurant, bar, safe-deposit boxes, an attractive rooftop pool with a good view, a small gym, and free Internet access. This place fills up. The hotel offers airport pick-up and drop-off for $18/35 one-way/round-trip.

Tower House Suites (Calle 51 between Avenida Federico Boyd and Calle 39 Este, tel. 269-2244 or 214-3719, fax 269-2869, $45 s/d, $30 for stays of a month or more), near Restaurante-Bar Tinajas. It's a great find. Not only is it a good deal among the "apart-hotels," it's also more appealing than some conventional hotels that charge twice as much. Rooms are immaculate and tastefully decorated. Some have a view of Panama Bay. The standard accommodations are "junior suites" that include sitting areas and small fridges; suites with fully equipped kitchenettes are the same price. There are a pool, laundry room, parking garage, and attractive restaurant, Restaurante Barba Roja (I haven't yet tried it). Fax and Internet services are available.

Hotel Marbella (Calle D near Avenida Eusebio A. Morales, 507/223-2220, fax 507/263-3622, $35/$40 s/d), near the Hotel Granada, is generally considered one of the better economy hotels. It's a clean, modern, five-story place on a pleasant residential street but close to a lot of urban action. However, I find the rooms dark and austere, and most look out on blank walls. There's a restaurant.

The **Gran Hotel Soloy and Casino,** (Avenida Perú between Calle 29 Este and Calle 30 Este, tel. 301-1155 or 301-1133, fax 227-0884, soloyger@cableonda.net, 39 s, $42d) is not really all that

Panama City

gran, but it has a few things going for it. There's a rooftop disco, Bar Mai Tai, that may be appealing. Ditto for the small rooftop pool with its big view of Panama Bay and the city skyline. Rooms are clean and basic, with mattresses that have seen better days. There's a casino on the premises. Note that the Panaline bus from Costa Rica no longer stops here.

$50–100

Hotels in this price range and higher often offer "corporate" rates and other promotional deals that can be substantially lower than their standard rates. Be sure to ask.

M Las Huacas Hotel and Suites (Calle 49 a half block from the corner of Vía Venetto and Vía Argentina, tel. 213-2222 or 800/001-0109, www.bestwestern.com, starts at $70 s/d) is not as good a deal as it was before it was acquired by Best Western, but it's still a pleasant surprise tucked away near the Aparthotel Torres de Alba and not far from the Hotel Panama. It offers 33 cheerful rooms, most with a small balcony. It has a kind of safari theme, with lots of bamboo, leopard-print cloth upholstery, furniture made from driftwood, bathrooms tiled with rock, and so on. It's meant to be vaguely Panamanian but ends up more like a Disney-themed hotel, though it's done well enough that it comes across as cute rather than cheesy. The rooms vary in size but feature okay beds, a bar area, and a kitchenette with microwave, coffeemaker, a two-burner stove, and a sink. Rates include a room-service breakfast, Internet access in the business center, a welcome cocktail, and laundry service. A restaurant was in the works when I visited. Internet access in the room is $.25 a minute, which is absurd by Panama standards, so you're better off padding down to the business center and using the hotel's computer for free.

The 180-room **Hotel Granada** (Avenida Eusebio A. Morales, near Vía España, tel. 269-1068, 265-1962, or 265-1963, toll-free U.S. tel. 877-434-1212, fax 263-7197, www.hotelsreiande.com/hotelgranada.asp, $110 s, $120 d including an "American breakfast," corporate rates are $77 s, $88 d) is a long-established hotel that enjoys a solid reputation. It's part of the Riande chain, which also owns Hotel Continental and the Riande Aeropuerto Hotel and Resort near Tocumen International Airport. Rooms are pleasant, clean, and modern, though they're on the small side and showing some signs of wear. There are a swimming pool, casino, and cafeteria.

M Hotel Ejecutivo (Avenida Aquilino de la Guardia between Calle 51 and Calle 52, tel. 265-8011 or 264-3989, toll-free U.S./Canada tel. 866-876-0915, fax 269-1944, onlinereservations@executivehotel-panama.com, http://executivehotel-panama.com/, $100 s/d, $65 s/d corporate rate) has long been a favorite with Latin American businessmen, and it's easy to see why. The Ejecutivo (roughly eh-HEC-oo-tivo, known as the Executive in English) is a solid good value. Rooms are similar to what you'd expect at a Best Western–style hotel: clean, pleasant enough, but nothing fancy. All come equipped with refrigerator, TV, coffeepot, free Internet connection, telephone, desk, and balcony. The hotel is centrally located just down from Vía España and some rooms have terrific views of the lights of the city and Panama Bay. The 24-hour coffee shop offers big portions at low prices. It's a popular place for breakfast (which is served day or night); in the morning there's a breakfast buffet. There's also a free daily happy hour. Guests are allowed to use some of the business center's facilities for free. There are a tiny pool and fitness center. Special deals are often available; be sure to ask.

Aparthotel Torres de Alba (Avenida Eusebio A. Morales, tel. 269-5180 or 269-7770, fax 269-3924, reservaciones@torresdealba.com.pa, www.torresdealba.com, $95 s/d, $85 for stays of five nights or more) offers what are essentially small modern apartments, each of which has a bedroom, sitting room, fax machine, full kitchen, and washer and dryer. The place consists of twin 13-story towers and is mainly aimed at short-term residents. But even tourists who don't need all that stuff might consider the place, especially those staying five days or more; it's simple but quite nice. There's a small gym and a pool that's borderline big enough for lap swimmers. Corporate rates are $10 less. A third person is $5 per night.

Rooms at **Sevilla Suites Apart-Hotel** (Avenida Eusebio A. Morales, tel. 213-0016 or 213-1312, fax 223-6344, sevillasuites@sevillasuites.com, www.sevillasuites.com, $71 s/d), built in 2000, are smaller and darker than those at the Torres de Alba, but the furnishings are quite nice. Accommodations lie closer to the hotel end of the apartment-hotel spectrum, but all the suites have minikitchens and some have terraces. There's a small gym and pool. Two of Panama's best restaurants, Restaurante 1985 and Rincón Suiza, are right across the street.

The **Suites Ambassador Apart-Hotel** (Calle D, tel. 263-7274 or 263-6068, fax 264-7872, starts at $63 s/d, including continental breakfast) is right next door to Hotel Marbella and has some of the same pluses and minuses (on a pleasant and centrally located street, but in the shadow of neighboring buildings). The 31 suites and eight studios are well maintained and have kitchens, but the beds need replacing. The suites, which often cost just a few dollars more, are good-sized apartments with sitting room, bedroom, and kitchenette with fridge, oven, and microwave. There's a small rooftop pool without much of a view, coin-operated washers and dryers, and a cafeteria.

Coral Suites Apart-Hotel (Calle D, tel. 269-2727, fax 269-0083, coralsuites@coralsuites.net, www.coralsuites.net/default.html, $71.50 s/d including continental breakfast) is a modern, nicely maintained place built in 2001. It features 63 rooms with very firm beds, full kitchenette, 125-channel cable TV, in-room Internet access ($.10 a minute), in-room safe, ironing board, and a sitting area with table. There's no restaurant, but the place offers room service. Stays include an hour of free Internet use in the business center, after which it's $2 an hour. There's a decent-sized rooftop pool without much of a view and a small but reasonably equipped gym. Service is rather disorganized, but this is a good place at a good price.

Crystal Suites Hotel (Avenida 2 Sur/Samuel Lewis and Vía Brasil, tel. 263-2644 or 263-5111, fax 264-8125, $71.50 including breakfast) was built in 1999 and has been aging quickly ever since. It has 59 suites with kitchenettes equipped with small fridges and stovetop burners in lieu of ovens. The suites are spacious and have a dining area, firm but okay beds, in-room safe, cable TV, and Internet connections for $.10 a minute. It features a pleasant pool and pool deck. The "grand suites" sleep four and are a good value for a small group at $126.50. The hotel has parking and a pleasant, sunny dining room that's open to 10 P.M. Its main drawback is its location: It's on the eastern edge of Marbella a fair hike from downtown and with little around it but nondescript stores and apartment buildings. It's an easy taxi ride to more interesting places, traffic permitting, but you're likely to feel removed from the flow of city life here.

The all-inclusive **Avalon Grand Panama** (Vía Transístmica, Las Cumbres, tel. 268-4811 or 800/261-5014, www. avalonvacations.com, $58 per person Sun.–Thurs., $89 per person on the weekend, including all meals and activities) is actually outside of Panama City, in the suburban Las Cumbres area about 15 kilometers from downtown. Las Cumbres is on the road to Colón, near Las Lajas. It's really not that far away, but it feels like the boonies. This place is more a weekend getaway for Panamanian families that want to stay close to home than a place likely to appeal to most foreign visitors curious to explore Panama. For one thing, it's isolated, with virtually nothing around it, unless you count a Bacardi rum factory and Panama's landmark Baha'i Temple.

It has extensive grounds, though its claims to be a "majestic jungle resort" are extremely fanciful, to put it charitably. The 8.5 hectares of land look more like a big, shrubby garden gone to seed than a forest. Its main attraction is an extensive aquatic park with water slides, a climbing wall, tennis and volleyball courts, and so on. Day passes are available. There's a display of golden frogs and other amphibians in a glass display case in the lobby, plus aquariums filled with both Caribbean and Pacific fish species. A few small wild animals are kept in cages on the property.

The large yellow "villas" consist of 36 rather cluttered guest rooms of different sizes. Each features a small bedroom with very firm but okay beds, a nice bathroom, a breakfast table, a minifridge, and a balcony that looks out on trees but has no view. As an "all-inclusive," rates include three meals, snacks, access to the water park and other facilities, taxes and tips, and all the domestic liquor you can drink.

The Avalon is northeast of central Panama City, so those coming from Tocumen International Airport can head straight to the hotel without passing through downtown traffic. At the interchange between Tumba Muerto (Avenida Ricardo J. Alfaro) and the Transístmica (Vía Simón Bolívar), head north on the Transístmica, in the direction of Colón. The Avalon will be on the left 3.8 kilometers north of the Bacardi rum factory.

Out on Cerro Azul, **Hostal Casa de Campo Country Inn and Spa** (#39 Avenida Los Cumulos, tel. 270-0018 in Panama City, 297-0067 in Cerro Azul, inform@panamacasade campo.com, www.panamacasadecampo.com, starts at $72.50 s/d) is a large, upscale country home that's been turned into a pleasant, well-maintained inn with lots of character and extensive grounds. All rooms are different, and some are considerably nicer than others. There's a small swimming pool, a full-service spa, and good views of the surrounding forested hills and Lago Alajuela. The inn offers a variety of spa and outdoor-adventure packages, including bird-watching trips. Meals are available for an extra charge. Round-trip transportation from Panama City, about an hour away, can be arranged for $20. The staff speaks English, Spanish, and Italian here.

$100–150

Hotel Continental (Vía España and Calle Ricardo Arias, tel. 263-9999, toll-free tel. 877-434-1212, fax 263-5143, www.hotelsriande .com/HotelContinentalCasino.asp, $140 s, $150 d, corporate rates $85 s/d, including American breakfast) right on busy Vía España, is another old Panama City landmark, but it's benefited from a tasteful remodeling that has made it an upscale business hotel. It's part of the Riande chain, which also owns the Hotel Granada and the Riande Aeropuerto Hotel and Resort near the international airport. All the rooms are nice, but some are bigger and more elegantly appointed than others; ask to see several. The hotel has a restaurant, cafeteria, small pool, and casino. You can probably make a deal here.

The **Four Points Sheraton Panama** (Calle 53 and Avenida 5 B Sur, tel. 236-3636, fax 265-3550, www.starwood.com, starts at about $114 s/d, though deals are often available) has taken over from the Radisson, which seemed to fold almost as soon as it opened. The eight-story hotel is another in a seemingly endless parade of new hotels catering to the upscale business crowd. The rooms are, of course, attractive and comfortable, but the suites are a considerable step up in quality. There's a pool, gym, sauna, and lighted tennis court. It's a good location for businesspeople, but it's not the most scenic part of town. Le Bistrot, one of Panama's better restaurants, is right across the street.

Hotel DeVille (Calle Beatriz M. de Cabal near Calle 50, tel. 206-3100 or 263-0303, fax 206-3111, reservaciones@devillehotel.com.pa, www.devillehotel.com.pa, starts at $115.50/ $126.50 s/d for a junior suite with breakfast) is an elegant, rather formal boutique hotel with four types of rooms: junior suites, luxury suites, grand suites, and "grand suites luxury." The junior suite, as usual, is a spacious room rather than a true suite and has the simplest furnishings. It features a marble-tiled bathroom, high ceilings, an Internet connection, sitting area, and in-room safe. The luxury suite adds elegant dark woods, antique Vietnamese furniture inlaid with mother of pearl, a large bathroom with two sinks, a fax machine, and so on. The grand suite resembles the luxury suite but has an upper level with a bedroom and second bath. The "grand suite luxury," oddly, isn't quite as luxurious as the grand suite. Amusingly enough, given the (at best) ambivalent feelings about the man in Panama, one of the suites is named for Teddy Roosevelt. The business center offers free Internet access. In-room Internet connections cost $5 an hour. The junior suite actually compares well in price to much simpler hotels. The most expensive suite costs $258.50/$269.50 s/d. Given that extra people in the room cost just $11 more per person, even the fanciest suites can be a decent value if you can squeeze enough people in. Art from local galleries is displayed in the lobby. Restaurante La Cocotte shares the same building.

OVER $150

The **Marriott Hotel** (Calle 52 at Calle Ricardo Arias, tel. 210-9100, fax 210-9110, www.marriott.com, rack rate $160 s/d) is quite an elegant place with 296 rooms, a small pool, and a pleasant, upscale cafeteria but no formal restaurant. The breakfast buffet at the cafeteria ($12) is extensive but not memorable. There's also a deli with sandwiches and salads. Ask for a corner room; they're the largest of the standard rooms, which come with the usual business-hotel amenities. Corporate and other special rates are often available. This place has proved to be one of the most popular of the higher-end hotels. It's an attractive place in a central location, with lots of dining, shopping, and entertainment options an easy walk away. Be alert wandering near the hotel at night. (Note that the Caesar Park was once a Marriott in a former incarnation. At this point it's unlikely a taxi driver would confuse the two, but it wouldn't hurt to specify you want the Marriott "en Bella Vista.")

Panama's newest destination hotel is the ultramodern **M Radisson Decapolis** (behind the Multicentro mall on Avenida Balboa, tel. 215-5000, reservas@decapolishotel.com, www.decapolishotel.com, starts at $160, including breakfast buffet, $20 in drink credits per night, and $25 in gambling credits per stay for use in the casino). The hotel is "inspired by the avant-garde hip hotels" of Europe and North America, to quote the marketing materials. It's quite an impressive place that will appeal to those who like the sleek and streamlined over Old World elegance. Opened in mid-2004, it's a 29-story concoction of brushed stainless steel and glass, including a glass elevator that goes to the 14th floor and is worth the ride just for the view. Traditional Panamanian elements—*mola* patterns, devil masks, ships—inform the modern decor. The standard rooms are quite large, sleek, attractive, and minimalist, with photo blowups of Panama's indigenous peoples over the beds

and large windows looking out on the view. The view is spectacular on the ocean side (an extra $10 a night), particularly on the higher floors, offering a panorama that encompasses Panama Bay, the towers of Paitilla, and, in some rooms, Casco Viejo. Each room has a safe, ironing board, hairdryer, coffeemaker, Internet connection, cable TV, and so forth, and English- and Spanish-language newspapers are delivered daily. The junior suites ($215 s/d) have a living room, walk-in closet, 1.5 baths, and two television sets.

Other features include the equally striking Fusion restaurant, a martini/sushi lobby bar, a tiny pool on the fourth floor with a hot tub and bar, and several executive floors, including two exclusively for businesswomen. The hotel's spa, Aqua (6 A.M.–10 P.M. daily), has some exercise machines and offers a full range of spa services, including facials, sauna, steam baths, and so on. There's a free shuttle to the airport at 8:30 A.M. and 3:30 P.M. Otherwise airport transportation is $10 per person.

Rooms can reportedly be difficult to find here when the hotel fills up with groups splitting their stay between the Decapolis and the Decameron beach resort; make reservations as far ahead of time as possible. The hotel connects through a walkway with the new, glitzy Majestic Casino and the Multicentro mall.

Built in 1951, the **Hotel El Panamá** (Vía España next to Iglesia del Carmen, tel. 215-9000 or 215-9181, fax 223-6080, reservas@elpanama.com, www.elpanama.com, $154/170.50 s/d) was for many years Panama's premier hotel. It has 340 rooms, including some cabañas by the large, attractive pool. The hotel has changed hands and been renovated several times over the years, but no matter how many times it's made over one thing remains constant: The service is lousy. Because of its international name recognition it still draws a lot of guests, many of whom compete to see who can be louder and more obnoxious. On the weekends especially, the place is bedlam. For the money you can do far better elsewhere. However, frequent promotional offers can slash the rates, and it is centrally located. It also has a lovely pool. Its newish casino is large, modern, and worth a visit for those in a gambling mood.

The **Crowne Plaza** (between the Hotel El Panamá and Iglesia del Carmen on Avenida Manuel E. Bautista, tel. 206-5555 or 206-5556, fax 206-5557, holidayinn@holidayinnpanama .com, www.holidayinnpanama.com, starts at $110 s/d), formerly the Holiday Inn Hotel and Suites, is among the more upscale specimens of the chain: Standard rooms are spacious, well-appointed, and have minibars. It opened in early 2000. There are a small pool and gym, a computer room that offers Internet access, and a sports bar.

From the outside, the **Bristol** (Calle Aquilino de la Guardia between Calle 51 and Calle 52, just down from the Hotel Ejecutivo, tel. 265-7844, fax 265-7829, www.bristol.com, bristol@thebristol.com, start at $192.50 s/d) is a nondescript, salmon-colored building that's easy to overlook. But inside it's a lovely boutique hotel. It's quite a luxurious place, and it even offers limited butler service. Standard rooms are "deluxe," and they truly are. All the rooms are lovely and tastefully done. The furnishings are elegant, with local touches such as *mola* pillows and lamp bases made from Ngöbe-Buglé sandstone figurines. The attached Restaurante Barandas is attractive and one of Panama City's most ambitious. Note that this isn't a huge resort. If you want a pool and several restaurants to choose from, try the Caesar Park or Miramar Intercontinental; this place is more low-key. Service is so intensely attentive you may feel stalked, which is not to say you won't also find it inept at times.

Ⅶ Hotel Caesar Park (Vía Israel and Calle 77 across the street from the Atlapa Convention Center, tel. 270-0477, fax 226-2693, reservations@caesarpark.com, www.caesarpark.com,

$195 s/d, corporate rates are $150) has the most loyal clientele of Panama five-star hotels, and even with newer, flashier hotels to choose from it remains the most beloved. It's a huge complex with 353 rooms, eight suites, three restaurants, a deli/pastry shop, a shopping gallery, an appealing casino that has been expanded in recent years, an athletic club, a pool, a sauna, and so on. It's changed hands several times through the years; currently it's part of the Starwood chain. Note: Large tropical birds are kept on the premises, including a toucan in a painfully small cage. Standard rooms are arguably not quite as attractive as those at the Bristol and Miramar Intercontinental, but they're of course quite comfortable. Note that the hotel is on the outskirts of town, quite a hike from everything but the convention center, the ruins of Old Panama, and the international airport. The hotel provides an hourly shuttle service to the airport, a 15-minute drive away, 4 A.M.–noon for $10 per person.

The **Hotel Miramar InterContinental** (Avenida Balboa, tel. 214-1000, fax 223-4891, panama@interconti.com, www.interconti.com, $240 s/d, corporate rates are $185) dominates the middle of Avenida Balboa and has great views of the Pacific and the Panama City skyline. It's a 206-room luxury hotel that's part of the Inter-Continental chain and comes with the works: two restaurants, a largish pool, a health spa, tennis court, several bars, and so on. The standard rooms are quite nice, naturally, but not as fancy as one might expect given what this place charges. The best things about the hotel are its views and attractive pool. The place also gets good marks for service. Gossip item: Mick Jagger spent the night in a suite here in February 2000, which got Panama City residents quite excited.

Food

The restaurants are among the best things about Panama City. It's easy to find excellent food, gracious service, and pleasant surroundings, not to mention a surprisingly wide variety of cuisine. For the higher-end restaurants, expect to pay close to what you would for a similar place in the United States. It's also quite possible to stuff yourself on tasty, simple food for about $2 if ambience means nothing to you. Panamanian *comida corriente* (literally "current food," meaning typical dishes served cafeteria style) places are scattered around the city, as are all kinds of American fast-food franchises.

Many of the upscale restaurants are found in two general areas on either side of Vía España: El Cangrejo to the northeast of the Hotel Panamá, and the booming nightlife area around Calle Uruguay (also known as Calle 48 Este).

The Calidonia/La Exposición area, home to most of Panama City's budget hotels, is not overrun with good restaurants. Best bets in this area include the Calidonia branch of Romanaccio (a pizza place), A Casa de Fernando, the restaurant at Hotel Veracruz, and Rincón Tableño #5. A bonus for those staying in this area is that Romanaccio offers free room service to hotels.

Reservations are a good idea at the fancier places, if only to be sure the restaurant is actually open. However, even the best restaurants can be surprisingly empty, especially in the early evening. Things can be busier at lunchtime, when the upscale eateries draw a schmoozing business clientele. Many restaurants, including some of the fancier ones, are closed for lunch on Saturday and all day on Sunday.

Those planning to spend much time exploring Panama may want to pass on sampling traditional Panamanian fare in Panama City, since there'll be plenty of that in the hinterland. By the end of the trip, you'll likely have had your fill of *patacones* and *maduros* and such. Might as well take advantage of the international offerings in the big city. Those who don't have time to see much outside the city, however, can get a taste of old-fashioned Panamanian cooking at the tourist restaurant Tinajas, or try a *nouvelle cuisine* spin on it at the elegant Barandas. Those on a tight budget can sample heartland food at any number of basic places, including the Rincón Tableño and Niko's Café chains.

Below is just a sample of the city's culinary treats.

ASIAN

Chinese immigrants have been an important part of Panama since long before it was even a country, so it's not surprising that Chinese food is popular everywhere. Japanese food has gradually caught on—there are even outdoor sushi kiosks scattered around the city, about the scariest food concept I can imagine for a tropical country—and Thai food is finally making some inroads, though with more mixed results.

Madame Chang (Avenida 5A near Calle Uruguay/Calle 48 Este, tel. 269-1313, 269-9654, noon–3 P.M. and 6–11 P.M. daily), is Panama's most upscale Chinese restaurant. The seafood here is excellent. Try the clams in black bean sauce to start. The *guabina* (a kind of mild-flavored fish) steamed in soy sauce and Chinese vegetables is light and delicious. The atmosphere is pleasantly upscale, with tile floors and peach walls and tablecloths, but it's not particularly dressy. Main courses average about $12. The restaurant recently has taken a stab at Thai food, including salads, soups, and curries.

Palacio Lung Fung (Vía Simón Bolívar/Transístmica and Calle 62C Oeste, tel. 260-4011, 6:30 A.M.–11 P.M. daily) has been around a million years and is still one of Panama City's favorite places for Chinese food. The atmosphere is old school—ornate decor, heavy furniture. Dim sum (Chinese buffet-style breakfast, brought around on carts) is served 6:30 A.M.–noon daily. It's delicious, and you can fill up for around $5. Family-style dinners go for $14–18 for two people.

Panama City's most established Japanese restaurant is **Matsuei** (Avenida Eusebio A. Morales, tel. 264-9562 or 264-9547, 11 A.M.–11 P.M.

Mon.–Sat., 4:30–10:30 P.M. Sun.), a small, simple place with a sushi bar. It has an extensive menu of sushi and sashimi, as well as tempura and other cooked food, but far from budget prices. Two pieces of sushi cost $3.25–7.25, and platters start at $15. Expect to pay around $20 per person, not including drinks. Cooked options include corvina prepared "Japanese style," tempura, and so on. The sushi's okay, but nothing special. The *ebi* (shrimp) is tasty, but avoid the California rolls, which taste kind of funky. Unless you like your sushi with cream cheese, watch out for that on the menu, as the combo seems popular with Panamanians. Imported fish is more expensive. The ravenous can opt for an odd all-you-can-eat "open sushi" deal for $19.75 per person noon–8 P.M. Monday–Saturday. The catch is you have to pay extra for anything you leave on your plate, to discourage waste. Mother would approve.

Sushi Itto (Avenida 2 Sur/Samuel Lewis and Calle 55 Este, tel. 265-1222 or 265-1136, noon–10 P.M. Mon.–Thurs., noon–11 P.M. Fri. and Sat., 12:30–10:30 P.M. Sun.), right next to the Reprosa jewelry store, is a new, modern place with an extensive sushi menu as well as tempura, rice dishes, pastas, soups, and even a few Thai dishes. The sushi's okay.

Royal Thai (Avenida 4A Sur and Calle Uruguay/Calle 48 Este, tel. 263-2323 or tel. 263-2888, noon–3 P.M. and 6 P.M.–11 P.M. daily) replaced the venerable seafood restaurant La Toja in late 2002. Panama is still struggling to get a grip on the concept of Thai food, and many of the offerings here taste more like a Chinese cook's conception of Thai food than the real thing. If you can get beyond that, it's a pleasant place for a meal. Whatever its origin, the food is tasty, the veggies are fresh and cooked just right, and the atmosphere manages to be both formal and simple, with tablecloths, subdued lighting, and fast, polite service. The average entrée costs $12. The green curry *langostinos* are reasonably authentic and quite spicy by Panama standards. The satay, on the other hand, tastes like plain grilled meat and doesn't even come with peanut sauce. Save room for the fried bananas for dessert; they're deadly.

CAFÉS

Restaurante y Bar Candelero (Calle 4 Este at the north corner of Plaza Simón Bolívar in Casco Viejo, tel. 262-6598, 8 A.M.–midnight Mon.–Sat., closed Sun.) is a little café and bar on Plaza Simón Bolívar. Cafés have been coming and going rapidly on this picturesque plaza, and at the time of writing this was the best place there to sip a drink in the evening. It serves breakfast (a rarity in Casco Viejo), lunch, and dinner, with most main dishes less than $10. Patrons are encouraged to borrow a pen and scrawl graffiti and messages all over the walls.

The new **38 Manzanas** (Calle 7 Este at the side of Catedral de Nuestra Señora de la Asunción in Casco Viejo, tel. 263-3776, cafe38manzanas@yahoo.es, 7 A.M.–midnight Mon.–Sat., closed Sun.) is a bright, pleasant, white-walled café with tile floors and black-and-white photos by a locally famous photographer, Sandra Eleta, on the walls. The food is fair, but the more-than-fair prices are a major draw of the place. A full breakfast starts at $2.75. An executive lunch consisting of soup, main course, salad, juice, and a sweet is $4.50. It's popular at night, when tables are set outside and the café is transformed into a tapas bar, with most plates going for around $5.

Café Santé (Ave 3A Sur near Calle Aquilino de la Guardia/49 Este, tel. 264-6886, 11:30 A.M.–11 P.M. daily) is a small sidewalk café near the Ejecutivo and Bristol hotels. It doesn't have a whole lot of atmosphere, but it's a pleasant place to hang out in the evenings, when it's popular enough to make for fun people-watching. Offerings include pastas, salads, and various meats, some in unusual sauces (guava, anyone?) The *birra con pollo* ($3.75) is a chicken dish sautéed in a rich mushroom cream sauce laced with onion, garlic, and a little dark beer. It's quite good. Except for the seafood dishes, most items cost less than $5. There's live music every night 7 P.M.–11 P.M.—most likely a guitarist/singer. The café does takeout here. A new outlet recently opened up on the plaza at the front of the Multicentro mall.

Crepes and Waffles (Avenida 5B near Calle

Uruguay/Calle 48 Este, tel. 269-1574, noon–11 P.M. Mon.–Sat., 9 A.M.–11 P.M. Sun.) serves—guess what?—in a sunny, modern brick-and-glass building with an air-conditioned interior, outdoor terrace, and yuppie vibe. Only the '70s soft rock mars the pleasant atmosphere. Its large selection of savory and sweet crepes include some vegetarian options. Other offerings include lots of coffee drinks, a salad bar, pita sandwiches, and other café goodies. Most items are $4–6.

The menu at **Ozone Café** (Calle Uruguay/Calle 48 Este between Avenida 5A Sur and Avenida 5B Sur, tel. 214-9616, 11 A.M.–3 P.M. and 6–10 P.M. or so daily) is almost comically eclectic: Among other things it features Indian, Iraqi, Indonesian, German, Lebanese, Senegalese, Italian, Tunisian, and Alabaman(!) cuisine. Of these, the Middle Eastern fare is probably the safest bet, and you'd probably also do okay with the pastas, salads, and grilled meats. The food is tasty but the chef has a fondness for oil. This is a cozy, popular little place with a low slanting ceiling and little lamps that hang above the tables. Prices range $5–15. The service I've had here has been gracious and attentive.

CAFETERIAS AND DINERS

The small Vía España branch of the **Niko's Café** chain (Vía España to the side of the El Rey supermarket, tel. 223-0111), is centrally located and open 24 hours a day. These cafeterias have proven to be quite popular because of their wide selection of simple and tasty food, fast service, cleanliness, long hours, and cheap prices. A few dollars buy heaps of meat, starches, and some veggies from long rows of steam tables. Niko's also offers fresh sandwiches, soups, individual pizzas, and desserts. Most breakfast items are under $2.

There are three 24-hour cafeterias within a five-minute walk of the Hotel Continental. The best known of these is **Restaurante Jimmy** (Calle Manuel María Icaza, tel. 223-1523, open 24 hours), just down from the hotel. It's a neighborhood institution that moved to new digs across the street in 2003. It has a spartan but clean and modern diner atmosphere that's several

steps up from its old greasy-spoon ambience. It serves a wide range of items, including its own take on Greek food (pita, *tzatziki,* fried eggplant, *keftedakia,* and so on), which can be odd but rather tasty. Other possibilities include *sancocho,* pasta, sandwiches, seafood, pizza, various meats, and so on. Most things cost $3–6.

If you're just looking for a simple place for breakfast or a snack, try **Cafeteria Manolo** (Vía Argentina #12 at Avenida 2B Norte, tel. 264-3965, 7 A.M.–1 A.M. daily). There's a second Manolo's in El Cangrejo near the Hotel El Panamá (Calle 49B Oeste, tel. 269-4514, 6 A.M.–1 A.M. daily). But the one on Vía Argentina is the homey original. Though recently given a somewhat austere remodeling, it still has an unpretentious coffee-shop atmosphere that has been attracting both locals and resident foreigners for years. (It was one of my haunts in high school.) It's hard to explain our fondness for this place. The food quality goes up and down; the only things you can really count on are the *churros* (a sugary fried pastry shaped like a hotdog; served only at the Vía Argentina Manolo) and the decent cappuccinos, though the sandwiches are usually tasty. The yummiest churro is the *manjar blanco*—it looks disgusting, but it's toe-curlingly good. For a real sugar buzz, order the *churros* along with Spanish hot chocolate *(chocolate a la española),* which is thick and delicious. Mainly, though, Manolo's is just a relaxing place to hang out on one of few streets in the city that strike a nice balance between bustle and mellowness. A full breakfast costs around $4.50. Sandwiches ($2.50–4.50) are the best prospect at other mealtimes. Other offerings include pasta, meats, and seafood. The more ambitious dishes average $6.50–9.

The coffee shop of the **Hotel Ejecutivo** serves breakfast 24 hours a day in a cozy, friendly atmosphere. A full Panamanian-style breakfast including lots of fried things bad for your health costs $5.25. Most other breakfasts cost less than that. It also offers an all-you-can-eat breakfast buffet.

A Casa de Fernando (Calle 30 Este between Avenida Perú and Avenida Cuba, tel. 225-2378, 24 hours daily) is a pleasant tavern likely to be of interest to those staying in the Calidonia/La Exposición area, mainly because it's got a central location and is open 24 hours a day. It serves an absurdly ambitious variety of food, including salads, soups, sandwiches, and all the usual meats, seafood, and pasta. The average main dish goes for around $8, but options vary from simple bites for $1.75 up to fancy prawn dishes for $13.50. It's not air-conditioned, but there are ceiling fans. There's live music Thursday and Friday nights starting around 9 P.M. Genres vary but include salsa and merengue. This is a good find.

Restaurante Boulevard Balboa (Avenida Balboa and Calle 31, tel. 225-0914, 7 A.M.–1 A.M. Mon.–Sat., closed Sun.) is a Panama institution that's been around since 1959 and has waitresses who've worked there almost since the beginning. It attracts a mix of power-breakfasting politicians and regular josés. It's known for its grilled sandwiches, the most expensive of which is $4, and its *batidas* (milkshakes). If you have breakfast here and you're a meat-eater, you've really got to go for a breakfast steak just for the experience. The place doesn't have much atmosphere—it's a nondescript, smoky, air-conditioned diner—but it's good value for the money and a small slice of Panama City history. A disturbing chapter in that history was added in July of 2001, when a prominent lawyer, Roque Alberto Pérez Carrera, was assassinated here. He was shot twice in the face by a man who then escaped by taxi. To date, the killer has not been found.

Café Coca Cola (Calle C and Calle 12 Oeste, tel. 228-7687, 7:30 A.M.–11 P.M. daily), across the street from Parque Santa Ana, is a slightly grungy, air-conditioned diner and a Panama City institution. This place has been here forever—the building it's housed in was erected in 1907, just four years after Panama became a country—and is a good spot for people-watching and soaking up the atmosphere of a slower, quainter Panama City from an earlier era. Full hot lunches go for about $2.50. Other offerings include sandwiches, chop suey, and pasta. Nearly everything on the menu is less than $4. The espresso drinks are palatable.

INTERNATIONAL

⋈ Golosinas (Calle Ricardo Arias near Calle 50, tel. 269-6237, 269-2028, noon–3 P.M. and 5:30–11 P.M. Mon.–Sat., closed Sun.) has long been considered one of the finest restaurants in Panama City, and you'll get no argument here. The food is delicious and the service is excellent. The atmosphere is pleasant, too. It's a quiet oasis in the *area bancaria* (banking district) that attracts the local beautiful people. The decor tends toward the floral but is quite cozy and romantic, with candles everywhere. The inventive menu might be described as eclectic continental. Italian dishes, seafood, and assorted meats are particularly well represented. Main courses are $10–19. Try the *guabina* (a delicate-flavored local fish) in champagne sauce and capers. The crab cakes in cranberry chutney are a light and unusual appetizer. There's a patio dining area that's inviting on dry-season nights.

⋈ Manolo Caracol (Calle 3 and Avenida Central in Casco Viejo, tel. 228-4640 or 228-9479, manolocaracol@psi.net.pa, noon–3 P.M. and 7–10 P.M. Mon.–Fri., 7–10 P.M. Sat., closed Sun.) is the namesake restaurant of Manolo Maduño. Manolo promises *cocina con amor*—food made with love—and he delivers. There is one menu a night (seafood-oriented, though if you talk to Manolo ahead of time he'll try to accommodate vegetarians) and food starts arriving as soon as you sit down. The menu changes with the season, but a typical offering might include seafood salad, portabella mushrooms, grilled shrimp, mussels, marinated tomatoes, red snapper, tuna, and something exotic for dessert. Price for the whole thing? $16. The lunch menu is $8. You definitely have to be in a receptive mood for this kind of food bombardment, but if you're willing to surrender to the experience it offers ones of the more entertaining dining options in Panama City.

The open kitchen sits right in the dining room, under a copper smoke hood and behind mounds of fresh produce set on a counter. In front of this is a dugout canoe filled with bottles of Spanish wine (the only kind served). Modern art hangs on the walls. The only real problem with this place are the acoustics—the restaurant is a stone and concrete box, so when it's crowded, it's loud. Manolo himself, a Spaniard by way of Colombia, is a kinetic character likely to be one of the loudest people in the restaurant. He presides over everything unless he's away on a special assignment (last time I was there, he said he was preparing to jet off to cook for Mick Jagger, whose rumored purchase of land near Coiba has been a source of great gossip in Panama). He'll likely greet you as a long-lost friend with a crushing hug, and slip you a glass of wine on the house if he sees your cup is empty—just because you're such a terrific person.

As its name suggests, **Fusion** (Decapolis Hotel, tel. 215-500, 6:20 A.M.–11 P.M. daily), offers a fusion of different cuisine, especially Asian and Peruvian. The food isn't particularly memorable and the service can be inept, but this is easily the most striking-looking restaurant in Panama City. At least stop by for a drink. Be sure to sit inside the cone-shaped room, which shoots up for three floors and is dominated by a seven-meter bust that vaguely resembles an Easter Island statue and supposedly is meant to represent the fusion of the world's different races. The hotel's swimming pool is on the floor above it. The pool has a partial glass bottom, which allows light to stream through and gives the feel of dining in an underwater temple in Atlantis. Main dishes cost about $9–25. Avoid the house wine. The passion fruit dessert is delicious.

Restaurante Las Bóvedas (Plaza de Francia in Casco Viejo, tel. 228-8058 or 228-8068, 6 P.M.–late Mon.–Sat., closed Sun.) is worth visiting for the ambience at least as much as for the food. It's built right into the historic stone vaults *(bóvedas)* of the old city's seawall, so you're dining in what was once a dungeon. (See the *Casco Viejo* section for more information.) A redecoration a few years back made the place slightly less cozy but a little more elegant. French-inspired main dishes are $15–32. The second room in the place is a bar called Los Piratas. The house drink is the *caipirinha*, a potent Brazilian concoction. Friday and Saturday nights after about 9:30 P.M. there's live jazz in the bar. Owner Ricardo "Richie" Traad, a senior Panama Canal pilot and

now director of Panama's national maritime service, was a major mover behind the renovation of Casco Viejo—Las Bóvedas was one of the first places in Casco Viejo to get a makeover, helping spur the whole renaissance of the area. If he's around, try to chat with him, as he is a great resource for the history of the neighborhood.

Near Las Bóvedas is the new, Spanish-owned **Macarena** (Calle 1 near Plaza de Francia in Casco Viejo, tel. 228-0572, noon–midnight Mon.–Sat., closed Sun.), which specializes in—surprise!—Spanish food. The revolving menu includes tapas, *montaditos* (open-faced sandwiches), tortillas, *cazuelitas* (ministews), and so on. Bigger plates go for $7–12. I haven't yet had a chance to sample the food; the restaurant was having a grand-opening party when I last visited the area, and I wasn't able to fight the crowd to the goodies. It serves only Spanish wines here. The atmosphere is quite appealing. The decor is a blend of mementos of Pamplona and local touches: Many of the fixtures are made of *jira* palm; there's a canoe from the Darién, a *pilón* (large pestle) from Bayano, and so on. The bright tiles are vintage, imported from Colombia to fit into the historic neighborhood.

Le Bistrot, (Calle 53 Este, tel. 264-5587 or 269-4025, 11:30 A.M.–11:30 P.M. daily), tucked away in a nondescript office building across from the World Trade Center in Marbella, is a Panama institution that's been around for nearly 25 years. The chairs on rollers may remind you of Siete Mares, which makes sense since they're both owned by the same folks. It's a good place for a romantic dinner, as the banquettes and mood lighting offer lots of privacy. Food tends toward the usual array of seafood, fish, and meats, but it's quite well prepared. Main dishes range $10–23. The *calamari a la plancha* (grilled squid) is a bit oily but delicious. Also try the *langostinos a la thermidor* (prawns thermidor), or the very tender *filete a la pimienta* (pepper steak). And give in to the *flan de queso* (cheesecake flan).

Restaurante 1985 (Avenida Eusebio A. Morales near Vía Venetto, tel. 263-8541, 263-8571, www.1985.com, 11:30 A.M.–11:30 P.M. Mon.–Fri., 5–11:30 P.M. Sat.–Sun.) is one of Panama's best restaurants, and one of its most expensive. It's under the command of Chef Willy Diggelmann, who also oversees Rincón Suizo and Caffé Pomodoro. It specializes in French cuisine and seafood but also offers German, Swiss, Spanish, and gourmet vegetarian dishes (note to vegans: These tend to be loaded with cheese). The atmosphere is kind of floral country French, and not at all stuffy. Entrees average $18. Fixed-price menus range $49–57. Steak lovers should consider Les Trois Filets ($22), which consists of three slices of filet in a mushroom, green peppercorn, and cheesy white sauce. It's delicious. This is a good place for a splurge. If you're going by taxi, tell the driver you want to go to *restaurante mil noveciento ochenta y cinco*, or just point to this entry.

Rincón Suizo (Avenida Eusebio A. Morales near Vía Venetto, tel. 263-8310, www.1985.com, 11:30 A.M.–11:30 P.M. Mon.–Fri., 5–11:30 P.M. Sat.–Sun.) is upstairs from Restaurante 1985, in the same building, and serves good Swiss and German food in a darker, cozier atmosphere. Offerings include raclette, *berner rösti,* and cheese fondue. The food tends to be a bit cheaper here than at 1985.

Just what was missing from Panama City's restaurant scene wasn't obvious until **Limoncillo** (Calle 47 and Calle Uruguay/Calle 48 Este, tel. 263-5350 or 263-5334, www.limoncillo.com, noon–3 and 7–10:30 P.M. Mon.–Fri., 7–11 P.M. Sat., closed Sun.) appeared to close the gap. It has a sleek, modern bistro look that would fit in perfectly in New York, and owners who truly understand that mood, music, and lighting are nearly as important as food in creating a memorable dining experience. Limoncillo has 11 tables in a room done up in rich lavender, aquamarine, and red, with lovely orange-red wooden furnishings. The walls display a rotating collection of interesting and quite good art by local artists. The well-chosen music alone, a mixture of chill-room lounge and unexpected international sounds, makes this place a standout in Panama City.

The food tends toward "contemporary American," with lots of fresh local ingredients and organic fare when possible. The menu changes every few months, but popular offerings include portabella mushrooms stuffed with pesto, goat cheese, and potatoes; breaded coconut prawns; pan-roasted grouper with grilled asparagus and tamarind vinaigrette; and a filet mignon that some reckon surpasses that offered by the steak houses. Save room for the ginger crème brûlée if it's available; it's excellent. Main courses at dinner go for about $8–16; lunch prices are lower. This places gets packed on the weekends; make a reservation or come early.

In the kitchen is Clara Icaza, a Panamanian whose 15 years as a chef in New York included work at the acclaimed Aqua. A Colombian magazine named her one of the best chefs in Latin America a few years back. Working the room is her partner, Jennifer Spector, a New York transplant who's constantly attentive to the ambience and the restaurant's many regulars.

Clara is also a baker, and though the service isn't advertised, those starved for real bread in Panama can place an order for a loaf and pick it up at the restaurant the next day. A loaf goes for about $5 and can include foccacia, rustica ciabatta, cornbread, and whole-grain breads.

Eurasia (Calle 48 between Avenida Federico Boyd and Parque Urracá in Bella Vista, tel. 264-7859, noon–3 P.M. and 7–10:30 P.M. Mon.–Fri., 7–11 P.M. Sat., closed Sun.), opened in 2002, has quickly emerged as one of Panama City's better restaurants. It's an elegant place in a lovely house built in 1936, with wrought-iron grillwork, tile floors, high ceilings, and antique mirrors and chairs. It's worth visiting just for a glimpse of what posh Panama City houses used to look like.

The kitchen is under the direction of chef Fabien Migny, formerly of La Cocotte, and the food is a fusion of French and various Asian cuisines. There are about a dozen and a half first courses ($5.50–9.50). Try the lobster and seafood bisque with tamarind, lemongrass, and basil. The more than two dozen second courses ($9.50–27.50) include unusual combinations such as the Japanese glazed salmon with tender spinach and water-chestnut fricassee.

Those with a sweet tooth can really indulge here; $5.50 gives you access to an all-you-can-eat dessert buffet. It's a full table filled with all kinds of delicious cakes, flans, and tarts, from the traditional Panamanian *(tres leches)* to the exotic (passion-fruit cake).

Restaurante La Cocotte (Calle Beatriz M. de Cabal near Calle 50, in the Hotel DeVille, tel. 263-2050, 7 A.M.–10:30 P.M. daily), across from the Tower Bank building just off Calle 50, gets a lot of hype for its French cuisine. However, the food these days is just average and, in the case of its desserts, sometimes well below average. Its celebrity chef, Fabien Migny, left in 2001 to start up Restaurante Eurasia, which is a better place to go for a fancy meal. That said, La Cocotte is quite pleasant. The small, low-ceilinged dining room has a tasteful nautical theme and blond-wood floors, the food is prettily presented, the service is warm, and the bar in front is cozy. The only time you may want to come here, though, is the last Wednesday and Friday of the month, when the restaurant hosts classical music concerts and literary and cultural discussions. Tickets for these cost $25, including dinner, which is a good deal on the right night. Tickets must be bought in advance. For information on the performances, call tel. 269-9147. On other nights, main courses range $12–18. Be sure to avoid the crème brûlée and apple tart.

The upscale **Restaurante Barandas** in the Bristol hotel (Calle Aquilino de la Guardia between Calle 51 and Calle 52, tel. 265-7844, 6:30 A.M.–11 P.M. daily) is noted for its nouvelle Panamanian cuisine. Traditional Panamanian fixtures such as *carimañolas,* corvina, and yuca are given the fusion treatment, with unusual sauces and generally lighter, healthier recipes. The executive chef is Coquita Arias de Calvo, who has her own local cooking show, books, and magazine. She is sort of Panama's answer to Martha Stewart before the legal troubles. The dining room is quite pleasant, especially the large, glass-enclosed room, which resembles an elegant greenhouse. Food is not always consistent here, however, though it seems to be on an upswing recently.

Mostaza (Avenue A and Calle 3, tel. 228-3341 or 228-8775, noon–3 P.M. and 5 P.M.–midnight Mon.–Sat., closed Sun.) is a restaurant and bar in Casco Viejo across the street from the ruins of the Iglesia de Santo Domingo, which

contained the famous, ancient *arco chato* (flat arch), until it finally crumbled into rubble in late 2003. The food when I visited was okay but nothing special, though I've since heard good reports. In any case, this is a nice spot to stop for a drink or a snack. It's a charming, cozy little place decorated with orchids, green linen tablecloths, and other nice touches. The Spanish-era stone walls have been left exposed. It offers salads, grilled meats, seafood, and pasta for $6–14. Service is included.

ITALIAN

Tre Scalini Ristorante (Calle 52 in Bella Vista, tel. 269-9951, 269-9952, noon–3:30 P.M. and 6–11 P.M. daily) offers decent Italian food and friendly service in a cozy faux-Italian atmosphere near the old Hotel Costa del Sol. Most dishes are around $8. It's a favorite standby for many a Panama City dweller. There's a second Tre Scalini in the El Dorado district (Boulevard El Dorado and Calle Miguel Brostella, tel. 260-0052 or 236-5303), if you happen to find yourself out that way. Avoid the house wine at either place.

Caffé Pomodoro (corner of Vía Venetto and Avenida Eusebio A. Morales, tel. 269-5936, 7 A.M.–midnight or later daily) continues to be one of the hottest restaurants in Panama City for reasons that escape me. The pasta here is pretty good and the atmosphere is pleasant, but it sure inspires a lot of affection for an outdoor café with plastic chairs that's wedged in the shadow of several unattractive high-rises. Still, it's a good place to go if you want to get a glimpse of the local scene. It boasts that it prepares pasta 120 different ways (prices range $4–10). It also offers 20 types of cheese served with bread, plus a variety of pizzas. There's a takeout window with the same hours.

The fairly new, overpriced wine bar next door—called, creatively enough, **The Wine Bar** (tel. 265-4701)—has the same owner and has proved quite popular. The wine selection is similar to what you'd find at a run-of-the-mill supermarket in California. It also serves food.

Restaurante de Las Américas (Calle 58 and

Avenida 1 Sur, tel. 223-7734 or 223-4676, Tues.–Sun. 11 A.M.–10:30 P.M., closed Mon.) is a long-established, upscale Italian restaurant in the long-established, upscale Obarrio neighborhood. It features subdued lighting, tablecloths, elegant draperies, and a quiet, genteel atmosphere. Most dishes are $9–14. The food is adequate but not exceptional and the restaurant gets by to some extent on its name and pleasant atmosphere. Most main dishes are $9–14. The restaurant also has a takeout window around the block with similar food at lower prices.

MEDITERRANEAN

A second branch of the Lebanese café **Habibi's** (Calle Uruguay/Calle 48 Este and Avenida 5A, tel. 264-3647, 10 A.M.–12:30 A.M. daily) has taken over from the defunct Petit Café, housed in a lovely old home that's been redecorated in an attractive modern style. I haven't yet eaten there, but it looked to offer much the same menu as the original Habibi's (Calle Ricardo Arias near Golosinas and the Marriott Hotel, tel. 213-9919 or 672-0131), which offers tasty Middle Eastern food, complete with hot pita bread. Most dishes are less than $8. It also serves pizzas and sandwiches and such for less than $4. It has a more upscale atmosphere than the original Habibi's, plus a pleasant front courtyard for those who'd rather dine al fresco—a good option on dry-season evenings. It's kitty-corner to Guacho's, on a busy corner that makes for good people-watching on the weekends. This is also a good place for drinks and appetizers before a meal elsewhere.

Athen's (Calle 50 and Calle Uruguay/Calle 48 Este, tel. 265-4637, 11 A.M.–11:30 P.M. Thurs.–Tues., closed Wed.) is a popular place for pizzas ($2.75–3.50 for a nine-inch pie), Greek salads, gyros, souvlaki, and other Greek dishes for $2.50–5. It's a casual, fast-food kind of place with an air-conditioned interior and an outdoor terrace overlooking Calle 50 and Calle Uruguay. (And yes, sadly, it really is spelled "Athen's.") Each table has a phone customers can use to place an order, a gimmick undercut by the fact that the waitresses come around unprompted.

The pizzas are just so-so. The pita sandwiches are huge and drowned in yogurt sauce but otherwise tasty. There's a second Athen's in the Obarrio neighborhood (Calle 57, tel. 223-1464) that's open on Wednesday when this branch is closed; its night off is Tuesday.

NORTH AMERICAN/FAST FOOD

There are plenty of U.S. theme restaurants (TGI Friday's, Bennigan's, Hard Rock Café), fast-food joints (McDonald's, Burger King, KFC, etc.) and other prefab American eateries to choose from in Panama City, if that's your thing. The theme restaurants tend to be popular with Panamanians, so, ironically, they can be good places to meet locals and people-watch. The **TGI Friday's** at the corner of Calle 49 Este and Avenida 4A Sur is practically a singles bar. (See the *Nightlife* section for details.)

In the last couple of years, coinciding with the downturn in the world economy, a chain of fast-food trailers has popped up on the streets for those who find the fare at McDonald's and their ilk too expensive. Called **Rancheras,** they serve cheap American-style grub, the most popular of which is a hamburger and soda combo for a buck. A centrally located one is near the corner of Calle 49A Este and Calle 50. More recently a similar chain of *churros* trailers has popped up, selling an absurd number of the sugary pastries for $1.

La Cascada (Avenida Balboa and Calle 25, tel. 262-1297, 11 A.M.–11 P.M. daily) is worth visiting purely for its bizarre vibe, which you'll notice even before being handed the tome of a menu. (Fans of Dr. Bronner's soap will detect a kindred spirit in its text.) It's an outdoor place decorated with what looks like leftover Elk's Club furnishings and lawn ornaments circa 1958. To call a waitress, you flip on a light switch at the table that also lights up a console by the cashier. The food? Oh yeah, the food: Think Sizzler on an off night. But you can't beat the portion size; food here is measured by the pound. A typical "high-end" offering is a huge platter of fried steak, breaded shrimp, salad, rolls, and pretty tasty French fries for around $10.

Fast-food stands on Avenida Perú and Calle 35, near the Ministerio de Economía y Finanzas, cater to office workers who want cheap deep-fried goodies. They're convenient to those staying in Calidonia.

PANAMANIAN

Restaurante-Bar Tinajas (Calle 51 near Avenida Federico Boyd, tel. 263-7890 or 269-3840, www.panamainfo.com/tinajas, 11 A.M.–11 P.M. daily) is an unabashed tourist restaurant. It's worth checking out for its folkloric dance performances at 9 P.M. on Thursday, Friday, and Saturday. The cover for the show is $5 per person, and you must make reservations. The cuisine is Panamanian, with main dishes in the $8–14 range. The restaurant is decorated with touches meant to remind you of a traditional town on the Azuero peninsula.

Restaurante Rincón Tableño #5 (Avenida Cuba near Calle 31 Este, tel. 227-5649, 5:30 A.M.–4:30 P.M. Mon.–Sat., 5:30 A.M.–2:30 P.M. Sun.) is a basic *comida corriente* cafeteria except that the waitresses wear pretty *pollera*-style blouses. Full meals here go for $2.50, or half that for lunch specials. The menu changes daily.

PIZZERIAS

Restaurante Pizzeria Romanaccio is one of the best places for pizza in Panama City. It has two locations, one in bustling Calidonia and the other in the more upscale environs of Marbella. Both are pleasant places for a casual meal.

The pizza is thin, toasty, and quite tasty. Individual-size pies cost $4–6 and are actually big enough to feed two moderately hungry people. Family-size pizzas cost $8–11 and bite-size minis $3–4.25. They also serve two dozen kinds of pasta, plus meat, chicken, and fish dishes. The *pizza cuatro stazioni* has ham, olives, mushroom, and artichokes and is quite good ($5.75).

The Calidonia branch (Calle 29 Este between Avenida Perú and Avenida Cuba, tel. 227-8737 or 227-8738, 10:30 A.M.–10 P.M. daily) shares a building with Hotel Benidorm (which is a touch too shabby to recommend). It's an air-condi-

tioned place with bright, cheerful decor, tablecloths, and plate-glass windows overlooking the street scene one floor below. It offers free room service to hotels 10 A.M.–4 P.M. and 6–9 P.M. Monday–Saturday. The one in Marbella (Avenida 5B near Calle 53 Este, tel. 264-9482 Marbella, noon–3 P.M. and 5:30–11 P.M. Mon.–Sat., noon–11 P.M. Sun.) is similar, though slightly cozier and more upscale.

There are also two branches of the beloved **Napoli** pizzeria. Napoli is famous for its clam pizza, but I've always been partial to its wonderfully charred, greasy pepperoni pies. I consider it some of the best pizza in Panama, but it's impossible to be objective about it since I was practically raised on this stuff. There are plenty of pastas and such on the menu, but both are places for wood-oven–baked pizza.

The older and much plainer **Napoli,** (Calle Estudiante and Calle I, one block from Avenida de los Mártires, tel. 262-2446 or 262-2448, 11:30 A.M.–11:30 P.M. Wed.–Mon., closed Tues.) is a good place to grab lunch for those on a walking tour of Avenida Central. It's a short walk from the heart of Central, just before the street, Avenida de los Mártires, that was the informal boundary between Panama City and the old Canal Zone (specifically, the townsite of Ancón). This branch has been around since 1962 and is an institution. It has an air-conditioned interior and an outdoor seating area where you can look out on what's left of the street life in this once bustling, now declining area. It serves a variety of pizzas and pastas, with most items $2–5.

Napoli No. 2 (Calle 57 and Ave. 1 D Sur, tel. 263-8799 or 263-8800, noon–midnight Tues.–Sat., closed Mon.) is the somewhat more upscale younger sister in the quite a bit posher neighborhood of Obarrio. It's air-conditioned and pleasant. The service is lame—an army of waiters stands around ignoring customers—but the food comes fast once you finally talk someone into waiting on you. A 10-inch pizza ranges $3.50–8, 15-inchers $8–17. The "Super Napoli" comes with a whole lot of stuff, and the 10-inch version can feed two.

Restaurante Pizzeria Sorrento (Calle 50 Este, tel. 269-0055, 11 A.M.–11:30 P.M. daily) offers mediocre pizza and very little atmosphere, but it does have a central location near the Hotel Continental, Voyager International Hostel, Internet cafés, and several other tourist haunts. Individual-sized pizzas go for $3–5. It also serves pasta.

SEAFOOD

Most of Panama City's better restaurants do a good job with seafood, but there are a couple of notable ones that specialize in it. My favorite place for seafood is **Siete Mares** (Calle Guatemala near Vía Argentina, tel. 264-0144 or 264-32032, 11:30 A.M.–11:30 P.M. daily). One of the most consistent and consistently popular restaurants in the city, it's a cozy, tranquil place and the service is good. An unusual house specialty is fried ceviche, a light and tangy appetizer. Most main dishes are in the $10–14 range. The fish is so tasty you won't need to order anything fancier than *corvina a la plancha* (grilled corvina). The restaurant moved down the street from its original home a few years ago and now has a sleek, modern decor to match its delicious food. The centerpiece of the new digs is an artificial waterfall near the entrance. It does have one peculiar touch left over from its old home: chairs on rollers, like those you might find in a plush conference room. A pianist performs in the evening.

Restaurante Mercado del Marisco (Avenida Balboa, tel., 212-0071, 11 A.M.–about midnight daily) is just upstairs from the city fish market, which is at the west end of Avenida Balboa. It boasts that it has the "best and freshest fish and seafood in Panama," and one would hope so, given its downstairs neighbor. (The fish market is modern and clean, so you shouldn't have to worry too much about a fishy smell wafting upstairs.) It's certainly reasonably priced; most items run $5.50–7. Offerings include ceviche, seafood soup, corvina, jumbo shrimp, and octopus in garlic sauce. An all-day "executive menu" includes salad, fish, soup, rice, and plantains for $4.50. If you don't see anything on the menu you like you can buy your own fish downstairs and have it cooked for you here. The restaurant is a spartan place with little atmosphere, but there's a partial view of the bay and the Panama City skyline. The waitresses are friendly and speak a little English.

STEAK HOUSES

It's a mystery why Panama steak houses haven't discovered candles or anything else to soften their atmosphere. Maybe it has something to do with catering to the loud, cigar-chomping businessmen with whom these places are most popular. If you don't mind your meal in manly surroundings, try one of the places below. But if atmosphere is important to you, consider one of the city's elegant international restaurants, all of which tend to prepare beef well.

An old standby, **Gaucho's Steak House** (Calle Uruguay/Calle 48 Este and Avenida 5A, tel. 263-4469 or 263-1406, noon–3 P.M. and 6–10:30 P.M. daily) serves decent steaks for those who don't expect much more in a dining experience. Both the atmosphere (brightly lit, chain–steak house vibe) and the food (this is a place for *meat;* you won't find much green outside the potted plants) are unadorned. The service tends to be fast but perfunctory. Though ostensibly an Argentine steakhouse, Gaucho's imports its meat from the United States. Prices for beef dishes average about $13, though the protein-deprived can always pop for the "Gaucho's Special," which consists of 20 ounces of beef ribs or strip loin for $25. Chicken and seafood are also on the menu, but that's not why people come here.

For starters, try the *picado de chorizo* (a plate of sliced sausages, $4.50). It's delicious. The sangria ($2.50) is also good, and the house red wine ($2) is quite drinkable.

The atmosphere at **Martín Fierro** (Avenida Eusebio A. Morales, tel. 264-1927 or 223-1333, noon–3 P.M. and 6–11 P.M. Mon.-Sat., noon–3 P.M. and 6–9:30 P.M. Sun.) is a bit nicer than Gaucho's, but this is still a brightly lit place where decor runs a distant second to simply serving slabs of meat—grilled beef, chicken, and pork. Domestic meats go for $7.50–14 and imported for $14–25. The imported meats come from Omaha, Nebraska. The restaurant also serves pasta, seafood, and fish, but that's not why anyone comes here. Meals include access to a meager salad bar, but who's kidding whom? If you really feel like punishing your heart, try the tasty *mozzarella frita* (fried mozzarella—oh, go ahead, you're on vacation). Then try the quite good *tres leches*. Book your angioplasty ahead of time.

The most glittery of the steak houses is **Os Segredos de Carne** (Vía Itália, tel. 263-0666, noon–11:30 P.M. daily) in Punta Paitilla. It's a Brazilian-style *churrascaria*—a veritable showcase of grilled meats. The restaurant's name is Portuguese; in Spanish it's Los Secretos de la Carne, that is, "the secrets of meat."

You pay $20 for all-you-can eat meat, meat, and more meat, plus a crack at a very fancy international salad bar that also includes sushi, seafood . . . and even more meat. After the salad bar, waiters glide by with endless skewers and slabs of every kind of meat you can imagine, complemented by breaded potato balls, onion rings, and the like. Some of the cuts are tasty, others dry and tough. Hard-core carnivores will love this place, though the best food is at the salad bar. Note that service is included, though the bottles of water enticingly placed on the table, and the even more enticing dessert cart (avoid the cheesecake, which tastes like pure butter), are not.

VEGETARIAN

The basic **Restaurante Vegeteriano Mireya** (Calle Ricardo Arias and Avenida 3 Sur, tel. 269-1876, 7 A.M.–8 P.M. Mon.–Sat., closed Sun.) is a truly vegetarian restaurant, though the veggies consist mostly of tired steam-table offerings that may remind former college hippies of the stuff they used to cook up at their old co-op houses. Offerings include soy chops, dried-out eggplant, *guandu, platanos,* yuca torts, vegetable soup, and loaves of soy bread. Most items are $1.25. Come early in the day before everything gets too soggy.

SUPERMARKETS AND SPECIALTY FOODS

Supermarkets are everywhere in Panama City, and in recent years their selection has vastly improved. They now more closely resemble megamarkets in the United States, with an array of imported and local goods, including a better choice of fresh produce (difficult growing conditions can make much beyond tropical fruit hard to come by in the tropics).

Panama's biggest grocery-store chain is **El Rey.** At last count it had 16 stores, most of them in Panama City. The one on Vía España (tel. 223-7850) is centrally located, is open 24 hours a day, and has a pharmacy and many other services. The more upscale **Riba Smith** supermarket has two locations in Panama City: in Bella Vista (Calle 45, tel. 225-6247) and on the Transístmica (tel. 299-3999).

There's a kosher cafeteria/bakery, a kosher deli, and even a kosher supermarket clustered together in Punta Paitilla. All three have good, unusual (for Panama) offerings that may be of interest even to those who don't keep kosher. They are great options on Sunday, when many other places are closed, but expect crowds. **Pita-Pan Kosher** (Vía Italia, tel. 264-2786 or 265-1369, 7 A.M.–9 P.M. Mon.–Thurs., 7 A.M.–5 P.M. Fri., 9 A.M.–9 P.M. Sun., closed Sat.) is an air-conditioned kosher cafeteria in the upscale Bal Harbour shopping center just off Avenida Balboa. It serves fish, salads, pasta, sandwiches, pizza, quiche, hummus with falafel, and so on. It even has kosher sushi. Most items are $3.50–6. The food here is tasty. Another plus is that it serves pita and other fresh bread by the loaf. It's closed Friday evening–Sunday morning for the Sabbath. Right next door is **Deli Shalom Kosher** (tel. 263-2805, noon–3 P.M. and 6–10 P.M. Mon.–Thurs., noon–3 P.M. Fri., 7–10 P.M. Sat., and noon–10 P.M. Sun.). Until recently it was a tiny kosher deli but has recently expanded to become a fairly large and often packed place that serves Middle Eastern and Jewish comfort food, including kibbee, falafel, hummus, tabbouleh, *shwarma,* and pastrami sandwiches. Most items are $6–9. The baba ghanouj is delicious, as are the falafel sandwiches. The kebobs are just edible. Like its neighbor, it's closed Friday evening–Saturday evening for the Sabbath. **Super Kosher** (Calle 56 Este, tel. 263-5253, 8:30 A.M.–8:30 P.M. Sun.–Thurs.,

8:30 A.M.–4:30 P.M. Fri., closed Sat.) is an upscale kosher supermarket one street north of the Bal Harbour shopping center. Among other things, it offers good veggies and products from the United States. There's a cafeteria inside that serves breakfast items, sandwiches, and other goodies, all kosher. Panama City residents also like to come here for gringo and gourmet groceries that can be hard to find elsewhere.

Fruteria Bal Harbour in Punta Paitilla (Bal Harbour shopping center, 7:30 A.M.–8P.M. Mon.–Fri., 8 A.M.–7 P.M. Sat., 9 A.M.–8 P.M. Sun.) next door to Deli Shalom Kosher, has good veggies and fruit.

Some of Panama's best coffee is at **Café Ruiz,** (World Trade Center on Calle 53, tel. 265-0779, www.caferuiz.com, 7 A.M.–6 P.M. Mon.,

Tues., Wed. and Fri., 7 A.M.–5 P.M. Thurs., closed weekends). It's a café and shop that carries all kinds of roasts and flavors of coffee, both whole bean and ground. Attractive gift packages and mugs are available. Café Ruiz coffee is also available at some supermarkets—including Casa de la Carne, Riba Smith, El Rey, and Super 99—but the gourmet roast is available only at the Café Ruiz shops. There are two other shops in the town of Boquete, in the western highlands.

Felipe Motta in Marbella (Calle 53, tel. 269-6633, 9 A.M.–7 P.M. Mon.–Fri., 9 A.M.–6 P.M. Sat., closed Sun.) has a good selection of wines at prices comparable to what you'd find in the United States. It also has some gourmet foods and fresh bread and pastries.

Information

Panama's government tourism institute, Instituto Panameño de Turismo (IPAT), has its administrative headquarters at the Atlapa Convention Center next to the Hotel Caesar Park off Vía Israel, but it's not really set up to deal with actual visitors. If you're eternally optimistic, you can try calling the office at tel. 226-3544 or 226-7000.

There are several IPAT information booths set up around town, including ones at the ruins of Old Panama, on Vía España next to the Hotel Continental, and on the Avenida Central pedestrian strip near Calle I. However, I've never seen anyone actually working in them. There's also an information booth between Immigration and Customs at Tocumen International Airport that's sometimes staffed, though don't expect much more than a handful of hotel fliers. It's rare to encounter an IPAT attendant who has much useful information to offer, and most speak only Spanish.

Tour operators and guides are the best bet for information about Panama City. Most of Panama's tour operators have their headquarters in Panama City, and nearly all offer city tours of different kinds.

Taxi drivers often double as tour guides. Don't

expect a scholarly lecture on the sights, but it can be a reasonable way to cover a lot of ground. Agree on a price ahead of time. The going rate is about $6–7 an hour.

Focus Magazine, a free monthly published in English and Spanish, contains brief, enthusiastic articles on various attractions around the country, as well as maps, hotel and restaurant listings, and general tourist information. It's widely available at hotels and other locations that cater to travelers.

MAPS

Tourist maps of Panama City are still a halfhearted affair. They tend not to be widely available, user-friendly, or terribly accurate, and they often seem little more than a guide to advertisers who paid to be put on the map, literally. Other than the maps in this book, your best bet at the time of writing were the fold-out ones that come with the free *Focus* tourist magazine, copies of which are easy to find in hotels and tourist-oriented sights around the city. A variety of city maps are sometimes for sale at bookstores (try Libreria Argosy, El Hombre de la Mancha, or Exedra Books), pharmacies (try one of the ubiquitous Farmacias Arrocha), and department stores (such as Gran Morrison). The stores also may carry one of several pictorial maps of Casco Viejo that have popped up in the last few years; these can make navigating around its maze of streets a bit easier.

The Instituto Geográfico Nacional Tommy Guardia on the Transístmica near the Universidad de Panamá sells large maps that will be too detailed for most visitors. (See the *Know Panama* chapter for information.)

HOSPITALS, POLICE, EMERGENCIES

The emergency number for the police (*policía nacional*) is 104. The emergency number for the fire department (*bomberos*) is 103. Directory assistance (*asistencia al directorio*) is 102. The national operator can be reached at 101. To reach the international operator, dial 106.

The *bomberos* have a reputation for arriving on the scene of an emergency before the police. But there is no real "911"-type emergency response for medical emergencies. The two major private-ambulance services in Panama City are SEMM (tel. 264-4122 for emergencies) and Alerta (tel. 269-9778 or 800-0911 for emergencies).

Panama City has first-world medical facilities and excellent doctors, many of whom were trained in the United States and speak English. Even those without medical insurance can receive good care for far less than in the United States.

Centro Médico Paitilla (Calle 53 and Avenida Balboa, tel. 265-8800 or 269-0333) has long been considered Panama's best medical center. The Hospital Nacional (Avenida Cuba between Calle 38 and Calle 39, tel. 207-8100 or 207-8102, emergency room tel. 207-8110, ambulance tel. 207-8111, www.hospitalnacional.com) opened a modern facility in 1998 and has been positioning itself as catering to the expatriate and foreign tourist market.

The pharmacy at the centrally located El Rey supermarket on Vía España (tel. 223-1243) is open 24 hours a day. Farmacia Milani (Calle 33 and Avenida Justo Arosemena/Avenida 3 Sur, tel. 225-0065), across the street from Hotel Roma Plaza in Calidonia, is also open 24 hours a day. The pharmacy at Centro Medico Bella Vista

(Avenida Perú and Calle 39, tel. 227-4022, 7:30 A.M.–10 p.m. Mon.–Fri., 7:30 A.M.–8 P.M. Sat., 7:30 A.M.–4 P.M. Sun.) is across the street from the Hotel Costa Inn, in the Bella Vista/Calidonia area. Farmacia Arrocha is a large drugstore chain. Centrally located branches include one just off Vía España (Calle 49 Este, tel. 223-4505), about midway between the Hotel Ejecutivo and the Hotel El Panamá, and in the Albrook Mall attached to the main bus station (Gran Terminal de Transportes, tel. 315-1728).

BOOKS AND NEWSPAPERS

Panama City is not a great town for readers, but the bookstore offerings have gotten somewhat better in recent years. Don't expect any bargains, though—shipping heavy books to Panama is expensive, and that's reflected in the prices. Panama City has few bookstores. Both the Gran Morrison department store and the Farmacia Arrocha drugstore chains carry books and magazines. Offerings are hit-or-miss, though occasionally a rare find surfaces. The Gran Morrison on Vía España is particularly promising. The city's major bookstores are listed below.

Libreria Argosy (Vía Argentina near Vía España, tel. 223-5344, 10 A.M.–6 P.M. Mon.–Sat., closed Sun.), run by a friendly Greek émigré named Gerasimos (Gerry) Kanelopulos, has been a Panama City institution for more than three decades. It's a small, crowded place that sometimes feels as though it still has the first book it ever stocked. Be sure to dig below the piles—a lot of books are buried under each other. It carries a substantial collection of works about Panama or written by Panamanian authors. Be sure to note Gerry's extensive collection of autographed photos of actors, writers, and musicians. Pride of place belongs to Dame Margot Fonteyn, who spent her twilight years in Panama.

There are several outlets of **El Hombre de la Mancha,** a local bookstore chain. The one downtown, across from the old Hotel Costa del Sol near Vía España (Calle 52 E at Avenida Federico Boyd, tel. 263-6218, 263-2593, www.books hombredelamancha.com, 10 A.M.–7 P.M. Mon.–Sat., closed Sun.) has a small English-language book selection with a few bestsellers and a lot of bulk discount–type books. It also has a reasonable selection of Spanish-language books by Panamanian authors. There's a café upstairs and Internet access for $2 an hour. The branch near the Country Inns and Suites in El Dorado (Central Comercial Camino de Cruces, tel. 360-2063, 10 A.M.–10 P.M. Mon.–Sat., 11 A.M.–8 P.M. Sun.) has a better overall selection of books than the downtown branch, but its English section is even more limited. It carries lots of Panamanian authors and a decent selection of literary fiction from other Spanish-speaking countries, as well as some English-language books translated into Spanish. There's also a branch in the Hotel Caesar Park and the new Multicentro shopping mall.

Exedra Books (Vía España and Vía Brasil, tel. 264-4252, noon–7 P.M. Mon.–Sat., closed Sun.) is modeled after U.S. chains such as Borders, minus the books. For such a large, attractive store, most of its offerings are odd and very limited. The English-language books in particular seem to consist of by-the-pound leftovers. It does have a decent selection of Spanish-language fiction, though, and on my last visit it seemed to be making a genuine effort to become a real bookstore. It also carries some used books at better prices. Upstairs there's an Internet café that actually has a café. It's also a ticket outlet for local concerts and other events. Literary talks, in Spanish, are given on Monday nights at 7 P.M.

All of Panama's daily newspapers are published out of Panama City and are widely available at newsstands and in shops. Most are in Spanish (there are three long-established Chinese-language papers for the Chinese immigrant population). There are currently no English-language newspapers. (See the *Know Panama* chapter for information on the various papers.)

Panama's national library, the four-story **Biblioteca Nacional de Panamá** (Parque Omar off Vía Porras, tel. 224-9466 or 221-8360, 9 A.M.– 6 P.M. Mon.–Fri., 9 A.M.–5 P.M. Sat., closed Sun.) may be of interest to those who want in-depth information on Panama. It's off Vía Porras in the middle of Parque Recreativo Omar (4 A.M.–8 P.M. daily), a small but pleasant city park with unmemorable modern-art sculptures and some tall shady trees. The collections include books by Panamanian authors or about Panama, and newspaper morgues dating from the 19th century. A wall of filing cabinets contains biographical information on prominent Panamanians and expatriates. The library is open to the public, but the stacks can't be browsed: Visitors search the electronic catalog on the third floor and then request their selection from a librarian. All books must be perused on the premises; borrowing privileges have been "suspended" because too many people did not return books. There are several quiet, comfortable areas to read inside the library.

Local Histories

Spanish-speakers interested in learning more about Panama City's history will have their best chance of finding locally written books at one of the stores listed above. However, these generally are academic works produced on a minimal budget and containing far more minute detail than the average reader will have much use for. (For general-interest books in English, which are easier to find through the Internet or in North American bookstores than in Panama, see the *Know Panama* chapter.) A few titles that may be of interest include:

Leyendas e Historias de Panamá la Vieja, Ernesto J. Castillero Reyes (Producciones Erlizca, 2nd edition 1998). The history and legends of Old Panama from its founding to its sacking by Henry Morgan, with crude illustrations and a blurry map of the city during its heyday.

Génesis de la Ciudad Republicana, Damaris Díaz Szmirnov (Agenda del Centenario, 2001). A detailed account of the emergence of modern Panama City in the late 19th and early 20th centuries. Though likely to be of most interest to residents, it fills in many gaps in Panama's recent history, something that has not been well documented, especially from a Panamanian perspective. It contains some small but interesting historical photos.

Panamá: Resumen Histórico Illustrado del Istmo, 1501–1994, Ricardo de La Esprriella III (Antigua Films, 1994). A slender coffee-table book with historic photos and brief summaries of major events in Panama's history.

NAUTICAL CHARTS

Islamorada Internacional (Bldg. 808, Avenida Arnulfo Arias Madrid/Balboa Road, tel. 228-4348 or 228-6069, info@islamorada.com, www.islamorada.com, 8 A.M.–5 P.M. Mon.–Fri., 8 A.M.–1 P.M. Sat., closed Sun.) is the place to go in Panama for nautical charts, books, software, instruments, flags, and pendants. It's actually in Balboa, in the former Canal Zone, across the street from the huge fountain of Arnulfo Arias. It lays claim to being the largest nautical bookstore in Panama. It also has general guidebooks to the Caribbean and elsewhere. Yachties can reach it in Balboa harbor at VHF channels 12 and 16; in Cristóbal try VHF 65 and 85, "Radio Balboa." The staff speaks fluent English here.

Services

Any business that visitors need to transact, from visa extensions to flight changes, is best done in Panama City. It has far better facilities and options than are generally available in the hinterland.

You can find most things in Panama City you'd find in any other cosmopolitan city, from DJ bars to pizza delivery in your hotel room.

CHANGING, RECEIVING, AND SENDING MONEY

Strangely enough for an international banking capital, there are only two places in Panama City where visitors can exchange a range of currencies (the main Western Union office exchanges just Latin American currencies, and only a few of these). One is the Banco Nacional de Panamá branch in Tocumen International Airport, which is open 7 A.M.–11 P.M. daily. It exchanges most major currencies. The other is a small office in central Panama City, Pancambios (Vía España, tel. 223-1800, 8 A.M.–5 P.M. Mon.–Fri.), toward the back of the Plaza Regency next to Plaza Concordia. It exchanges Costa Rican colones, euros, British pounds, and Canadian dollars for U.S. dollars.

Banks with ATMs are all over Panama City. For those staying in the Calidonia area, branches of Banco Nacional de Panamá (8 A.M.–3 P.M. Mon.–Fri., closed Sat.) and BBVA (8 A.M.–3 P.M. Mon.–Fri., 9 A.M.–noon Sat.) are centrally located on busy streets near Hotel Venecia and Hotel Ribadavia Star. They both have 24-hour ATMs. The Banistmo at the Multicentro mall has unusually long hours during the week (10:30 A.M.–6 P.M. Mon.–Fri., 9 A.M.–3 P.M. Sat.).

For those who need to send or receive money, there are Western Union outlets all over Panama City. The main office is in the Plaza Concordia shopping complex (Vía España, tel. 800-2224, 8 A.M.–8 P.M. Mon.–Sat., 10 A.M.–5 P.M. Sun.). It's a nice modern place with facilities for making international calls, exchanging Latin American currencies, accessing the Internet, sending and receiving faxes ($1.85 per page to the United States), and making photocopies. Other centrally located offices include one in the Gran Terminal de Transportes in Albrook (tel. 314-6206, 9 A.M.–6 P.M. Mon.–Sat., closed Sun.), and an outlet in the Super Empeñas San Ramon store in Calidonia (Calle 34 near Avenida Perú, tel. 225-1952, 7 A.M.–5 P.M. Mon.–Sat., closed Sun.). For other locations, visit www.western union.com. MoneyGram has about three dozen outlets in Panama City. The one at the Plaza Concordia is in the Bambi Empeños stores (Vía España, tel. 263-4293, 8 A.M.–6 P.M. Mon.–Fri., 8 A.M.–3 P.M. Sat.).

POST OFFICE

Panama's main post office is in Calidonia (Avenida Central between Calle 33 and Avenida Perú), across from a church, Basílica Don Bosco. There's a kind of stamp museum in the complex, but it's in disarray and shows no signs of being open to the public any time soon. Other post-office branches include ones in the Plaza Concordia shopping center on Vía España and next to Restaurante Boulevard Balboa (Avenida Balboa near Calle 31).

All are open 7 A.M.–5:45 P.M. Mon.–Fri., 7 A.M.–5 P.M. Saturday.

COMMUNICATIONS

Internet cafés open and close frequently in Panama City. Most are just bare-bones air-conditioned rooms with terminals, but the rates are cheap—usually $1 an hour or less. Some offer international calling at good rates. A few also send and receive faxes; sending domestic faxes tends to be reasonable, but sending an international fax can cost $5 a page or more. Be sure to ask for rates before sending one. All the places below charge $1 an hour for Internet access unless otherwise indicated. It's often possible to pay for just a half hour or 15 minutes.

There are plenty of Internet cafés in the Calidonia area, where most of the budget hotels are. The one above A Casa de Fernando (Calle 29 Este between Avenida Cuba and Avenida Perú, tel. 225-3580, 9 A.M.–midnight Mon.–Sat., 1–10 P.M. Sun.) is a quiet, nicely air-conditioned place with new computers. It's a good place in a central location. @rquinet (Calle 29 Este between Avenida Perú and Avenida Cuba, no phone, 8 A.M.–midnight daily) is next to Restaurante Pizzeria Romanaccio in Calidonia. There's also a small Internet place at the back of Panadería La Venezolana (Avenida Perú between Calle 39 Este and Calle 30 Este, tel. 221-1335, 10 A.M.–8:30 P.M. Mon.–Sat., closed Sun.), between Gran Hotel Soloy and Pensión Colón. Internet @ Sin Limites (Calle 29 Este between Avenida Cuba and Avenida Justo Arosemena/Avenida 3 Sur, tel. 225-4936, 8 A.M.–10 P.M. daily) is a cordial, air-conditioned place that offers Internet access and has private booths for making international phone calls. Calls to the United States are $.20 a minute. It also sends in-country faxes and can receive faxes as well.

The Plaza Concordia shopping complex on Vía España has several places to access the Internet, the nicest of which are in the new Western Union office (tel. 800-2224, 8 A.M.–8 P.M.

Mon.–Sat., 10 A.M.–5 P.M. Sun.). There are also passport-photo shops in the same complex. There are plenty of other places in the heart of the Vía España area with Internet access. Four Internet cafés were in the shopping center to the side of the Hotel Panama on Vía Venetto, Centro Comercial Vía Venetto, when I last visited. It's hard to imagine they'll all be in business when you visit, but some should be. They tend to stay open quite late and charge $1 an hour for Internet access and $.20 a minute for phone calls to the United States. Other Internet cafés in the Vía España area include a couple on Calle Ricardo Arias off Vía España just south of the Hotel Continental, including a second @rquinet (tel. 265-7393, 8 A.M.–2 A.M. Mon.–Sat., 8 A.M. midnight Sun.) that charges $1 an hour for Internet access.

Norma's Place (Vía Argentina, no phone, 7 A.M.–midnight daily) is across the street from and just north of the Vía Argentina branch of Cafeteria Manolo. It charges $.75 an hour.

An unnamed Internet place (Calle I down from Avenida de los Mártires, tel. 212-4043, 8 A.M.–7 P.M. Mon.–Sat., 8 A.M.–late afternoon Sun.), across the street from the original Napoli pizzeria on Calle I and Calle Estudiante, offers Internet access for $.85 an hour, phone calls to the United States for $.20 a minute, and international faxes for $1.25 per page plus long-distance charges.

There's a Cable and Wireless office, with phone-card vending machines outside, next to the Banco Nacional de Panamá on Vía España (7:30 A.M.–5 P.M. Mon.–Fri., 7:30 A.M.–2:30 P.M. Sat.). "Telechip" phone cards are also sold at stores throughout the city. Panama is seeing an influx of phone providers, and there may well be more prepaid services when you visit.

Directory assistance (*asistencia al directorio*) is 102. The national operator can be reached at 101. To reach the international operator, dial 106.

IMMIGRATION OFFICE

Panama City's main Migración y Naturalización (immigration and naturalization) office is in Calidonia, close to most of the budget hotels (Avenida Cuba and Calle 29 Este, tel. 207-1800,

777-7777, or 227-1077, tel./fax 227-1227, 8 A.M.–3 P.M. Monday–Friday). Visitors who need to extend their tourist cards or visas should come here for the laborious process of getting a *prórroga de turista* (tourist extension). (See the *Know Panama* chapter for details, and for a list of embassies and consulates in Panama City.)

Tourists who extend their stay no longer have to go through the additional hassle of getting a *paz y salvo* (a document that certifies one doesn't owe Panama taxes) and *permiso de salida* (exit permit). That's a joy now reserved for some locals and resident expatriates.

LAUNDERETTES

Lavamáticos are not all that easy to find in central Panama City (as opposed to *lavanderías,* which are comparable to dry-cleaning places in the United States). Budget and business-oriented hotels often provide laundry service at quite reasonable rates; be sure to ask for prices ahead of time. Some hotels, especially aparthotels, have self-service washers and dryers. *Lavamáticos* generally charge around $2 total to wash and dry a load.

There's a nameless lavamático (Ave. 2 Norte/Eusebio A. Morales, tel. 633-2188, 7:30 A.M.–7 P.M. Mon.–Fri., 8 A.M.–7 P.M. Sat., closed Sun.) near the Aparthotel Torres de Alba and the Las Huacas Hotel and Suites in El Cangrejo. It charges $1 to wash, $1 to dry, and $.40 for detergent. It seems a bit odd, but the Hotel Costa Inn in Calidonia claims it allows nonguests to use its self-service laundry facilities ($.75 to wash, $.75 to dry). It probably depends on the whim of who's at the desk; look respectable.

Getting There and Away

Panama City is the main entry point for visitors to Panama. Most travelers come to and leave the country through Tocumen International Airport, 25 kilometers east of Panama City. The nearest cruise-ship port is at the end of the Calzada de Amador, which is near the Pacific entrance to the Panama Canal a few kilometers from downtown. The national bus terminal, for international and domestic long-distance buses, is the Gran Terminal de Transportes in Albrook. It's quite close to Panama City's domestic airport, Aeropuerto Marcos A. Gelabert, also in Albrook. (For detailed

© BONNIE KAY SPINDLER

Many visitors are surprised by the modern skyline of Panama City.

information on getting to Panama City by air, sea, and land, see the *Know Panama* chapter.)

Panama City, not surprisingly, is the country's transportation hub. It has its major international and domestic airports, its biggest bus terminal, its main ship ports, and plenty of rental car companies.

(For information on international travel, including buses to Costa Rica, see the *Know Panama* chapter. For information on the Panama Railway, which crosses the isthmus to the city of Colón, see the *Panama Canal* chapter.) Note that no roads or ferry service link Panama and Colombia; the only safe way to get there is by air.

DOMESTIC FLIGHTS

Panama City's small domestic airport, officially called Aeropuerto Marcos A. Gelabert, is near the Gran Terminal de Transportes in Albrook, a former U.S. Air Force base. It's just a couple of kilometers northwest of the heart of Panama City. Flights generally leave Panama City early in the morning, though some popular destinations have multiple daily departures scattered throughout the day. (See the *Know Panama* chapter for more information.)

Most taxi drivers won't know the airport by name: Ask to go to the *aeropuerto de Albrook*. Emphasize that you want to go to Albrook to avoid being taken to Tocumen, the international airport. The fare from most parts of Panama City should be only a few dollars.

Buses from downtown Panama City to Albrook leave from the SACA Bus Terminal in Calidonia every 10 minutes 4:30 A.M.–10:30 P.M. Monday–Saturday and every half hour during daylight hours on Sunday. The fare is $.15–.25. But it will generally make more sense, and even be more economical overall, to take a taxi directly to the airport than to fool with getting to the bus station for the short ride to Albrook.

Note: Some old maps still show the domestic airport in Paitilla, on the east side of Panama City, but it was moved to Albrook in 1999.

All three of Panama's domestic carriers fly out of the airport, the country's major domestic air hub. Good Boquete-grown coffee is available at Café Kotowa (5 A.M.–6 P.M. Mon.–Fri., 6 A.M.–6 P.M. Sat., 7 A.M.–6 P.M. Sun.). There's also a greasy-spoon cafeteria that opens before dawn. There are branches of the Thrifty, National, Avis, Budget, and Dollar rental-car companies at the airport, but whether they'll be staffed is a different question. There's an ATM near the airport entrance.

Aeroperlas (tel. 315-7500, fax 315-7580, info@aeroperlas.com, www.aeroperlas.com) is the dominant carrier, with the most routes and business.

Turismo Aéreo (tel. 315-0279 or 315-0300, fax 315-0300, www.turismoaereo.com) flies only to Contadora, Isla San José, the Darién, and Kuna Yala (the San Blas Islands).

Mapiex Aero (tel./fax 315-0888, reservaciones@aero.com.pa, www.aero.com.pa) flies only to David and to Changuinola and Bocas town in the province of Bocas del Toro.

Below is a sample of some of the flights offered by Aeroperlas to give a sense of what's available. The schedule is subject to change, especially the frequency of flights; call for updated itineraries. All the fares listed are one-way.

Achutupu: one daily, $39.90.

Bahía Piñas: one flight Tues., Thurs., and Sat., $50.40.

Bocas del Toro (Bocas town and Changuinola): two daily flights, $57.75.

Chitré: two flights Mon.–Sat., one on Sun., $36.75.

Colón: two flights Mon.–Thurs., one on Fri., $35.70.

Contadora: three flights Mon.–Fri.; four Saturday; five Sun. $29.40.

Corazón de Jesús: one daily flight, $33.60.

David: three flights Mon.–Sat., two on Sun., $58.80.

El Real: one flight Mon., Wed., Fri., $48.30.

La Palma: one flight Mon., Wed.., and Fri., $39.90.

Playon Chico: one daily flight, $37.80.

Porvenir: one daily flight, $31.50.

Río Sidra: one daily flight, $31.50.

REGIONAL BUSES

Most long-distance buses leave from the capital's impressive new terminal, the Gran Terminal de Transportes. It's pretty *gran*, all right—it's a more attractive and user-friendly space than the international airport.

The terminal is two stories high. All the ticket booths are on the ground floor. Destinations are posted on each booth, and a schedule of hours and intermediate destinations is often posted behind the ticket seller. Note there may be more than one bus headed to your destination at any given time. If a bus that has your destination as a final stop isn't convenient, look for one that has it as an interim stop. Those heading to Santiago, for instance, can buy a ticket at the Santiago booth or, say, the David booth (Santiago is on the way to David). There's a $.05 departure fee for long-distance bus service, payable at the turnstiles on the way to the buses; change machines are nearby. Using the bathrooms in the terminal costs $.25.

The terminal has shops, pharmacies, Internet cafés, banks and ATMS, a branch of the low-cost Niko's Café cafeteria, a U.S.-style food court, places to take passport-size photos, and other businesses likely to be of interest to travelers on the ground floor. It's also next to a shopping mall, Los Pueblos Albrook Mall, and a movie multiplex, Cinemark. A few notable services include:

Farmacia Albrook (10 A.M.–11 P.M. Mon.–Sat., 8 A.M.–10 P.M. Sun.), one of two pharmacies more-or-less next door to each other.

Banistmo bank (10:30 A.M.–5:30 P.M. Mon.–Fri., 9 A.M.–2 P.M. Saturday), which has a 24-hour ATM.

Telxpress (tel. 314-6406, 8 A.M.–10 P.M. Mon.–Sat., 10 A.M.–8 P.M. Sun.), which offers international phone-call service. But calls cost a pricey $.72 a minute to the United States; buying a phone card is a better deal. The place also has Internet computers.

A Western Union office (tel. 269-1055, 9 A.M.–6 P.M. Mon.–Sat., closed Sun.).

The bus terminal's information desk downstairs is useless, but those who need a complete schedule of departures can request one upstairs at the terminal's administration office.

Schedule

Below are some bus destinations likely to be of interest to visitors:

Almirante (port for Bocas del Toro archipelago) and Changuinola: One daily bus at 8 P.M. arriving about 6 the next morning at the Almirante crossroads ($23) and 7 A.M. at Changuinola ($24). Note: there's a two-suitcase maximum included in the fare.

Bayano: Every 45 minutes or so 5 A.M.–6 P.M. ($3, 2.5 hours).

Chitré: About once an hour 6 A.M.–11 P.M. ($6, 3.5 hours).

Colón: Every 20 minutes or less from 4:15 A.M.–10 P.M. for air-conditioned express ($2 for express, about 1.5 hours; regular bus is $1.50 but can be far slower). Note: Once in Colón the only convenient way to get around the area is by taxi. It can't be emphasized enough that Colón is a crime-ridden city and not safe for visitors. Be alert at the Colón bus terminal and do not explore the area on foot. Those who want to go to Portobelo or Isla Grande by public transportation should take a Colón-bound bus and transfer at Sabanitas, on the Boyd-Roosevelt Highway (Transístmica), well before reaching Colón.

Coronado: Every 15 minutes 6 A.M.–9 P.M. ($2, 1.5 hours).

Darién: 4:15, 5:15, 6:30, 8, 9:45, 11:45 A.M., 1:30 P.M., and 3:45 P.M. Because of road conditions, Meterí ($9, 6–7 hours) is usually the last stop. In dry season, early morning buses sometimes make it all the way to Yaviza ($14, about nine hours).

David: Three companies run large, long-haul, air-conditioned buses between Panama City and David. The normal fare is $10.60 one-way, or $15 for a one-way "express" bus, though the upstart Transporte Expreso Cinco Estrellas has been charging about $1.50 less to try to compete with the big boys. The round-trip fare for all three companies is double the one-way fare. The trip theoretically takes about 6.5 hours, but buses frequently run late; express buses can shave up to an hour off that time. Buses generally stop at provincial towns along the Interamerican Highway, most notably Aguadulce, Penonomé, and

Santiago. Other stops are made by request. In Santiago, buses usually take a half-hour break at the Hotel Pyramidal complex, where there is a cafeteria, restaurant, bathrooms, pharmacy, ATM, and other services. Seats are assigned, and passengers can request seat assignments. For safety's sake, avoid seats at the front of the bus. The bathroom is in the back, so avoid sitting near there as well. Note that the companies frequently tinker with their schedules, so don't rely too heavily on precise timing. However, buses leave virtually around the clock, and there is usually more than one option per hour during daylight hours. The largest of the companies, with the most frequent trips, is Terminales David-Panama (tel. 314-6228, tel. 314-6395 for cargo, terminal@cw-panama.net). Buses leave at 6:45 A.M., 7:30 A.M., 8:20 A.M., 9:10 A.M., 10 A.M., 11 A.M., noon, 1:15 P.M., 2:15 P.M., 3:45 P.M., 5 P.M., 6:30 P.M., and 8 P.M. Expresses are at 10:45 P.M., midnight, and 3 A.M. Padafront (tel. 314-6264) has departures to David at 6:30 A.M., 7:30 A.M., 9:30 A.M., 2:30 P.M., 4 P.M., 5:45 P.M., and 7:40 P.M., with expresses at 10:45 P.M., and midnight. Transporte Expreso Cinco Estrellas (tel. 314-6285) has departures at 10 A.M. and 7:30 P.M., with an express at 11:30 P.M.

El Copé: once an hour 6 A.M.–7 P.M. ($5, three hours)

El Valle: every 30 minutes 7 A.M.–7 P.M. ($3.50, 2.5 hours)

Farallón: every 20 minutes 5:30 A.M.–8 P.M. ($4, two hours)

Las Tablas: about once an hour 6 A.M.–7 P.M. ($6.50, four hours).

Paso Canoa (border crossing with Costa Rica): Two of the companies that make the Panama City-David run continue west to Paso Canoa, the main border crossing with Costa Rica. Padafront charges $12, or $17 for an express. Transporte Expreso Cinco Estrellas charges $11.50, or $15.50 for an express. The trip takes 8–9 hours, slightly faster for an express. Most travelers will be better off taking the international bus lines, Tica Bus or Panaline, which continue to Costa Rica and beyond (see the *Know Panama* chapter). But if someone just needs to make it to the border, these companies

make more frequent trips. Another possibility is to take any bus to David and switch to one of the small regional buses that run constantly between that city and the border.

Penonomé: every 20–30 minutes 4:45 A.M.–10:45 P.M. ($3.70, two hours).

Santiago: about once an hour around the clock ($6, about four hours). Note: Two companies, Expreso Veraguense and Sanpasa, work this route and compete aggressively with each other. Be prepared for *boleteros* (ticket touts) trying to get your business as you approach their counters.

Soná: 8:20 A.M., 10:20 A.M., 12:45 P.M., 2:20 P.M., 4:20 P.M., 5:45 P.M. ($6, about four hours).

CAR

New highways that crisscross Panama City are making it easier to bypass heavy traffic on the way out of town.

The Corredor Norte, a toll highway with several entrances on the north and west outskirts of the city, leads north one-third of the way across the isthmus toward Colón. Supposedly it will one day be completed all the way. For now, at Chilibre it meets the Transístmica (also known as the transisthmian highway, and as the Boyd-Roosevelt Highway, though no one calls it that), the old, slow, potholed road across the isthmus. Both roads border the east side of the Panama Canal, though neither actually has views of the canal.

The Corredor Sur, another toll highway that begins just east of Punta Paitilla, leads to Tocumen International Airport, where it links with the Interamerican Highway. There, at a clover-leaf intersection next to Hotel Riande Aeropuerto Hotel and Resort, the Interamerican "Highway" (really just a two-lane road) continues east toward Cerro Azul and the Darién. This road passes through the Darién and finally ends at Yaviza, the beginning of the Darién Gap, through which no road has ever been built.

To all points west of Panama City—the beaches, mountains, Azuero Peninsula, Bocas del Toro, Costa Rican border, and the rest—at the time of writing there was only one way to begin the journey by land: crossing the Bridge of the Americas near the Pacific entrance to the Panama Canal. This should change, however, when the Puente Centenario, a new bridge across the canal near Pedro Miguel, is finally opened. (The bridge was "inaugurated" but not actually opened in 2004—its access roads were still being built at the time of writing.)

West of the Bridge of the Americas, the road eventually connects with another toll road, the Autopista. This is now a divided highway for much of the way to the western frontier, though at the time of writing much of the stretch between Santiago and David was still a two-lane road with huge potholes. Nevertheless, this entire ribbon of road is officially part of the Interamerican Highway.

Most Pacific-side destinations in the former Canal Zone are accessible from Panama City by taking Gaillard Highway (now officially known as Avenida Omar Torrijos Herrera), which borders the east bank of the canal and runs past the domestic airport at Albrook, the Panama Railway terminal at Corozal, Clayton, Miraflores and Pedro Miguel Locks, and so on. The road forks outside Gamboa. Left leads to the attractions around Gamboa before Gaillard Highway dead-ends in Gamboa itself. Right leads through part of Parque Nacional Soberanía, including part of the historic Las Cruces Trail, before intersecting the Transístmica, the old road linking Panama City with Colón.

One canal-area attraction, the booming Calzada de Amador (Amador Causeway), is now easier to get to from Panama City thanks to highway ramps that lead onto and off Avenida de los Mártires near the foot of the Bridge of the Americas.

Getting Around

Traffic in Panama City is bad and getting worse all the time. If possible, avoid car trips during morning and evening rush hours, especially from about 8–9 A.M. and 4:30–6:30 P.M. A couple of new toll roads that cut through the city—Corredor Norte and Corredor Sur—are a quick escape from some of the congestion, since they're priced out of reach of the average Panama City driver. Unless you're on a severe budget (most tolls will run about $.35–$.75) you'll save a lot of time and aggravation by taking them.

Taxis are inexpensive and easy to find at all hours, making them the transportation of choice even for Panamanians of modest means. Buses are frequent and even cheaper, but they are a far slower and less convenient way to get around most parts of the city.

I don't recommend that those unfamiliar with Panama City, especially those unaccustomed to Latin American roads, attempt to drive in the city. It's a good way to spoil your day, if not your whole trip. Drivers are aggressive, streets are confusing and poorly marked, and there's a severe shortage of traffic signals, which most drivers treat merely as friendly suggestions in any case. Streets have been known to change from two-way to one-way literally overnight, without anyone's bothering to change the signs. It's no fun to turn a corner of what you thought was a two-way street and see a battalion of SUVs barreling down on you. Other nuisances include the occasional stolen manhole cover.

Traffic in the former Canal Zone remains more orderly, but it too is increasingly showing the effects of chaotic road expansion and urban sprawl. Taxis and in some cases buses are cheap and convenient options for trips into the canal area, particularly for Pacific-side destinations such as the Calzada de Amador (Amador Causeway), Albrook, Miraflores Locks, Balboa, and the ferry pier to Taboga.

Adding to the confusion of getting around is the fact that many streets have multiple names. The names used in this chapter are generally those most likely to be recognized by taxi drivers and other locals. Some destinations, especially in the former Canal Zone, are much more likely to be known by proximity to landmarks than by any street name.

TAXIS

Taxis offer by far the easiest way to get around the city. There are approximately two zillion of them in Panama City, all jockeying for your business. Most are small Japanese cars that will take you just about anywhere in town for $2 or less. Don't be put off by taxi drivers beeping their horns at you; it can be annoying, but it's just their way of finding out if you want a ride.

Taxis are not metered in Panama City or anywhere else in the country. In Panama City, taxis charge according to a government-mandated zone system. The city is carved up into six zones; fares are based on the number of zones crossed. Within the city limits, the maximum fare for one passenger is $2. Each additional passenger adds $.25 to the fare, regardless of the distance. There is also a $.15 surcharge for rides between 10 P.M. and 5 A.M. Most taxi drivers are honest, decent guys, but ask for the fare to your destination before getting in, just to be safe. Taxi drivers are required to present the zone chart on demand, but rather than hassle with a driver who seems unscrupulous, just refuse to give him your business and grab the next cab.

Don't be alarmed if your driver stops to pick up another fare heading the same way. It's a normal practice, but tell the driver not to do it if it makes you uncomfortable.

More alarming is the way many taxi drivers drive. Near misses are common. Fortunately, traffic congestion and moderate speeds mean most actual mishaps end up as fender benders.

Fares for rides outside the central city, for instance into the former Canal Zone, go up according to distance, but not as quickly as one might think. A taxi to the Calzada de Amador (Amador Causeway) or Miraflores Locks, for instance, should cost no more than about $4 from downtown Panama City. A ride as far as Gamboa, on the Panama Canal about halfway across the isthmus, should cost around $20. Taxis can also be hired for day tours, but bear in mind that few taxi drivers speak much English or are particularly knowledgeable tour guides, though all know the city well. The going rate is $6–7 an hour.

A few larger, air-conditioned cabs lurk around the more upscale hotels and charge several times what the smaller guys do. They are "tourist taxis," recognizable by the "SET" license plates. You can always just walk down the street to find a cheaper ride if you can do without air-conditioning and the sense of safety that comes from riding in a bigger hunk of metal.

Taxis are almost always easy to find, but "radio taxis" can be called as well. Hotels and restaurants will usually be happy to make the call for you.

RENTAL CARS

The major U.S. car rental agencies have outlets scattered around Panama City as well as at the international and domestic airports. Several outlets are within a few blocks of the Hotel Continental and Hotel El Panamá on or near Vía España.

Again, for most visitors, taking taxis will be a better option than driving around Panama City. But it's likely to be the best way of getting to the beaches within a couple hours of the city, and for exploring both the nearby canal area and distant locations it's a reasonable alternative to taxis, buses, and organized tours.

A few of the more centrally located offices are listed below. Most of these are within easy walking distance of each other near the Hotel El Panamá. (For some information on driving laws and rental car policies, and tips on driving in Panama, see the *Know Panama* chapter.)

Avis Rent A Car (Calle D, tel. 213-0556, 7 A.M.–9 P.M. daily) near the El Cangrejo branch of Cafeteria Manolo, not far from the Hotel El Panamá. At last count it had five other branches in the Panama City and Panama Canal areas. See www.avis.com.

Budget Rent A Car has two branches in the Vía España area. The larger one is on the western end of Vía España itself (tel. 263-9190, 7 A.M.–10 P.M. daily) just before Calle Gabrielle Mistral in Bella Vista. The other is at the entrance to the Hotel El Panamá (tel. 214-6806, 8 A.M.–5 P.M. daily). The central reservations number, for all locations in Panama City and nationwide, is tel. 263-8777, or try Reservaciones@budgetpanama.com, www.budget-panama.com.

Hertz (Vía Venetto and Avenida Eusebio A. Morales, tel. 264-1111, 8 A.M.–9 P.M. daily) has an office around the corner from Avis, next to the El Cangrejo branch of Cafeteria Manolo. There's another branch at the Marriott Hotel (tel. 210-9213, 8 A.M.–5 P.M. Mon.–Fri., 8 A.M.–4 P.M. Sat., closed Sun.). Including the international airport, Hertz at last count had five outlets in Panama City. For other locations, see www.hertz.com.

National Car Rental (Vía Venetto and Avenida Eusebio A. Morales, tel. 265-5092, 8 A.M.–5 P.M. Mon.–Sat.) is right across the street from the Hertz office in El Cangrejo, but the main office is some distance away on Calle 50 (tel. 265-3333, 7 A.M.–10 P.M. daily). For other locations, see www.nationalcar.com.

ORGANIZED TOURS

All of Panama's major tour operators have their headquarters in Panama City, and they all offer Panama City tours. They're more of an afterthought for the ecotourism outfits, though, so those looking for a group tour might consider going with a more traditional tour company that offers city tours as a more-or-less daily business. However, those planning an adventure outside Panama City with an ecotourism operator may want to add on a city tour with the same group for simplicity's sake.

Because Panama City is a relatively compact place, half-day and full-day tours typically give an overview of the entire city, including the ruins of Panamá la Vieja (Panamá Viejo), parts of the reviving colonial district of Casco Viejo, and at least a drive through the major sections of modern, central Panama City. The full-day tours in particular usually find time for a visit to the area of the Panama Canal close to the city. This part of the tour inevitably includes a visit to Miraflores Locks and sometimes throws in stops at the handicrafts market next to the YMCA in Balboa and the Administration Building of the Panama Canal Authority, a historic structure perched on a hill that has impressive murals depicting canal construction days in its rotunda and which offers dramatic views of the former Canal Zone. All

three canal stops are worthwhile, so look for tours that include more than just Miraflores Locks.

Pesantez Tours (tel. 263-8771 and 233-5374, fax 263-7860, pesantez@sinfo.net, www.pesantez-tours.com) is a long-established tour operator with a reputation for dependable service. Other possibilities include **Ecocircuitos** (tel./fax 314-1586, cell 617-6566, U.S. tel. 708/810-9350, annie@ecocircuitos.com, www.ecocircuitos.com), **Panama Travel Experts** (tel. 265-5323, fax 265-5324, toll-free U.S. tel. 877-836-5300, info@panamatravelexperts.com, www.panama-travelexperts.com), and **Gray Line Panama** (tel. 300-2333, fax 300-2340, tours@grayline-panama.com, www.grayline-panama.com).

Expect to pay around $40 per person for a half-day tour and $60–80 per person for a full-day tour that includes lunch.

Revelers may be interested in the *chiva parrandera*, a party bus that roams some of the city's scenic spots at night with a *murga*, a traditional Panamanian band that plays Panamanian folk music and salsa. The trip includes local booze and the bus is thoughtfully outfitted with cup holders so your drinks don't tip over even if you yourself do. *Parranda*, by the way, means both "strolling band of musicians" and "to go on a binge." Whether this all sounds like heaven or hell is obviously a matter of taste. Most tour operators who offer city tours can arrange for seats for about $25 per person. Bring earplugs and a spare liver.

BUSES

There are several bus hubs around Panama City, but the main three are in Albrook and Calidonia. Long-distance buses leave from the Gran Terminal de Transportes in Albrook (see *Getting Away* for details and schedules). Many city and regional buses also pass by the terminal, on the side opposite the long-distance buses. Plaza Cinco de Mayo in Calidonia, next to the walking section of Avenida Central, is the terminus for many routes within the city and greater metropolitan area. Most buses stop in front of the handicraft kiosks on the plaza. The SACA bus terminal, also near Plaza Cinco de Mayo, has buses to the former Canal Zone.

Taking buses within Panama City is an exercise in frustration, especially when travelers can zip around in a cab for very little. Buses make constant stops and are often crowded and hot. And they're not exactly safe. They're known by locals as *diablos rojos* (red devils) because of the way they so often barrel recklessly through traffic—whoever's biggest wins on the roads of Panama. (Few of them are red, incidentally. In fact, they're typically painted over with all kinds of bright-colored murals, especially at the rear of the bus, which makes for great photo possibilities.)

Buses are frequent and dirt cheap, however, so those with a lot more time than money might want to give them a try. Destinations are painted on the front windshield. The fare anywhere within the city limits is $.25. Passengers indicate their desired stop by shouting out *parada* (pah-RAH-tha; "stop"). For destinations outside the city center, look for buses that have "corredor" painted on the windshield or side. That means the bus uses the toll roads, which means fewer stops and much faster transportation. Note that two or three people traveling together will collectively pay the same for a bus as they would for a taxi to many destinations in the city.

Buses are a more reasonable option for destinations outside the central city, especially into the former Canal Zone. Buses to various points in the canal area leave from the SACA bus terminal (Calle 9 de Enero near Avenida Central, close to the Palacio Legislativo, tel. 212-3420). The orange *(naranja)* ones that resemble school buses (which is what they originally were) are not air-conditioned. Air-conditioned buses leave from the same terminal and run the same routes for $.05–$.15 more. Note that the schedules below are more ideal than exact. Popular routes include:

Albrook: every 10–30 minutes 5 A.M.–10 P.M. Monday–Friday, every 20–30 minutes 4:30 A.M.–7:30 P.M. Saturday, every 20–30 minutes 5 A.M.–5 P.M.; $.15 regular, $.25 air-conditioned. The bus stops at the domestic airport (Aeropuerto Marcos A. Gelabert, also called Aeropuerto de Albrook),the Gran Terminal de Transportes (main bus terminal), and Albrook Mall.

Amador: hourly 6 A.M.–6 P.M. Monday–Friday; every 15–45 minutes 4:30 A.M.–7:30 P.M. Saturday; every 15–30 minutes 7:30 A.M.–5:20 P.M. Sun., with final buses at 6:15 P.M. and 8 P.M.; $.40 regular, $.50 air-conditioned.

Gamboa: 5 A.M., 5:30 A.M., 6 A.M., 6:30 A.M., 7:30 A.M., 9 A.M., 10:30 A.M., noon, 1:15 P.M., 2:15 P.M., 3:15 P.M. 4:30 P.M., 6 P.M., 7:30 P.M., 9 P.M. and 11:15 P.M. Monday–Friday; 5:30 A.M., 6 A.M., 8 A.M., 10 A.M., noon, 2 P.M., 4:30 P.M., 6 P.M., 7:30 P.M., 9 P.M., and 11 P.M. Saturday, and 6 A.M., 8 A.M., 10 A.M., noon, 2 P.M., 4:30 P.M., 6:30 P.M., 9 A.M., and 10:30 P.M. Sun.; $.65 regular, $.80 air-conditioned. This bus can drop passengers off at Pedro Miguel Locks, Paraiso, Parque Nacional Soberanía, Summit Botanical Gardens, and other destinations en route to Gamboa.

Miraflores Locks (take the Paraiso, Gamboa, or Clayton bus): every 15 minutes or less 5 A.M.–8:15 P.M., plus final buses at 9:45 P.M. and 10:30 P.M. Monday–Friday; every 15–30 minutes 5:30 A.M.–midnight Saturday, every 15–30 minutes 5 A.M.–11 P.M. Sun.; $.35 regular, $.50 air-conditioned. Note: Only the 5:45 A.M., 6:10 A.M., and 2:30 P.M. Clayton-bound buses go all the way to the locks. All other buses stop along the main road, and passengers must walk about one kilometer to get to and from the locks.

The Panama Canal
and Former Canal Zone

The Panama Canal was being hailed as a wonder of the world even before it opened for business on August 15, 1914. It still stands as one of the most awe-inspiring of all human endeavors. If you come all the way to Panama without visiting the canal, you're cheating yourself—not to mention inviting puzzled looks from your friends and relatives when you return home.

Built across the isthmus of Panama at one of its narrowest and lowest points, the canal is 80 kilometers (50 miles) long, extending from the city of Colón on the Caribbean Sea to Panama City on the Pacific Ocean. To the bafflement of many a visitor, the Caribbean entrance is northwest of the Pacific entrance. What was once the Canal Zone ran the length of the canal, extending eight kilometers (five miles) on either side of it. The U.S. civilian townsites and military bases near the Pacific Ocean are now abandoned or being engulfed by Panama City, though some of the forested lands in the former Canal Zone have been set aside as protected

Must-Sees

Look for **M** to find the sights and activities you can't miss and **ΧΙ** for the best dining and lodging.

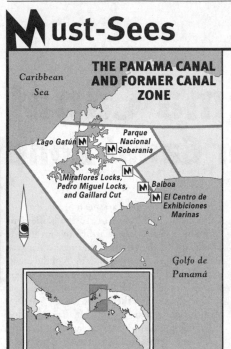

THE PANAMA CANAL AND FORMER CANAL ZONE

Caribbean Sea

Lago Gatún **M**

Parque Nacional Soberanía **M**

M

Miraflores Locks, Pedro Miguel Locks, and Gaillard Cut

Balboa

M El Centro de Exhibiciones Marinas

Golfo de Panamá

M El Centro de Exhibiciones Marinas: This little Smithsonian-run marine exhibit on the Amador Causeway is as notable for its views of the entrance to the Panama Canal as for its marine life (page 100).

M Balboa: A glimpse of what life in the former Canal Zone was like (page 106).

M Miraflores Locks, Pedro Miguel Locks, and Gaillard Cut: A close-up look at a one of the world's great engineering feats (page 107).

M Parque Nacional Soberanía: A species-rich tropical forest just a few minutes' drive from downtown Panama City (page 113).

M Lago Gatún: Once the world's largest man-made lake, Lago Gatún is the Panama Canal's major waterway, the home to important tropical-nature reserves, and a popular destination for water sports and recreation (page 115).

areas. (For a brief history of the building of the Panama Canal, see the *Know Panama* chapter.)

The canal itself is so impressive it's easy to overlook nature's equally astonishing handiwork on its banks and in its waters. Parque Nacional Soberanía is one of the most accessible tropical forests in the world. It has an astonishing amount of wildlife, especially considering that its trails start just a half-hour drive from Panama City. The park itself and surrounding forests have some of the best bird-watching in the country. There's also a surprisingly decent chance of coming across largish mammals, including three species of monkeys (white-faced capuchins, Geoffroy's tamarins, and howlers), sloths, kinkajous, coatimundis, and capybaras (the largest rodent in the world) in the extensive moist tropical forests still standing here. Even jaguars and harpy eagles are not unheard of, but the chances of spotting either are extremely slim. You may also see a green iguana or two.

All the attractions described here run along the east bank of the canal and are easily accessible from Panama City. (For information on Gatún Locks and other canal destinations near Colón, on the Caribbean side of the isthmus, see the *Central Caribbean* chapter.)

PLANNING YOUR TIME

It's possible to visit **Miraflores Locks, Pedro Miguel Locks, Gaillard Cut,** and the townsites of **Balboa** and **Ancón** in a single day. A good way to end that day is with an evening walk and a meal or a drink on the **Amador Causeway (Calzada de Amador).** A quick visit to **Gamboa** can be tacked on, but really exploring the area takes a second day. A **Panama Canal transit** is an all-day event; taking the **train** across the isthmus requires a half day to a full day, depending on the return trip. **Isla Taboga** is better for a day trip than an overnight visit, and those planning to visit other islands may want to skip it altogether.

The Panama Canal

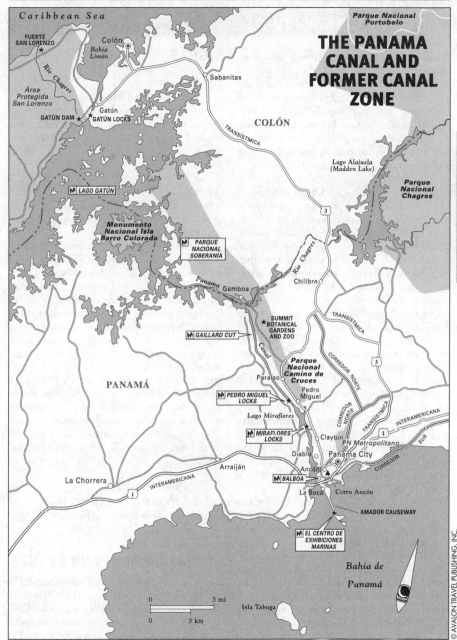

Caribbean Sea

FUERTE SAN LORENZO ★

Colón
Bahía Limón

Sabanitas

Área Protegida San Lorenzo

GATÚN DAM ★ Gatún
GATÚN LOCKS

COLÓN

Río Chagres

Parque Nacional Portobelo

THE PANAMA CANAL AND FORMER CANAL ZONE

Lago Alajuela (Madden Lake)

Parque Nacional Chagres

TRANSÍSTMICA

3

Ⓜ LAGO GATÚN

Monumento Nacional Isla Barro Colorado

Ⓜ PARQUE NACIONAL SOBERANÍA

Río Chagres

Panama Gamboa

Chilibre

Ⓜ GAILLARD CUT

SUMMIT BOTANICAL ★ GARDENS AND ZOO

TRANSÍSTMICA

3

PANAMÁ

Canal

Paraíso

Parque Nacional Camino de Cruces

CORREDOR NORTE

Ⓜ PEDRO MIGUEL LOCKS

Pedro Miguel

Lago Miraflores

CORREDOR NORTE

TRANSÍSTMICA

INTERAMERICANA

Ⓜ MIRAFLORES LOCKS

Clayton

PN Metropolitano

1

Diablo

Panama City ★

La Chorrera

Arraiján

INTERAMERICANA

1

Ancón

Ⓜ BALBOA

La Boca

Cerro Ancón

CORREDOR SUR

★ AMADOR CAUSEWAY

Ⓜ EL CENTRO DE EXHIBICIONES MARINAS

Bahía de Panamá

0   5 mi
0   5 km

Isla Taboga

moon

The Panama Canal

Amador Causeway

This beautiful breakwater extends more than three kilometers into the Pacific, calming the waters at the entrance of the Panama Canal and preventing that entrance from silting up. It was built from spoil dug from the canal and connects three islands: **Naos, Perico,** and **Flamenco.**

The causeway has gorgeous views. On one side the majestic Bridge of the Americas spans the Pacific entrance to the canal, so there's always a parade of ships gliding underneath it or waiting their turn in the anchorage. On the other side is the half moon of Panama Bay, ringed by the ever-growing Panama City skyline.

In the old Canal Zone days, the causeway was a major lover's lane and hang-out spot for high-school kids. It's seeing more action now than ever before: It's become a major nightlife destination for Panama City residents, and huge amounts of money are being poured into it in the hopes it will lure international visitors. In the last few years, restaurants, bars, and shopping centers have gone up, as have a hotel, cruise-ship terminal, marina, convention hall, and amphitheater. Most of these have been built on Isla Flamenco on one end of the causeway and in Amador proper, a former U.S. military base, on the other.

The causeway itself has gotten an understated and elegant makeover, with new street lights and a renovated walking path that left the palm trees along it intact but added benches for those who need a rest. Near the entrance to the causeway is a row of flags of many countries, though the U.S. one is conspicuously absent; flying the stars and stripes anywhere in Panama, especially a former gringo army base, would be loaded with controversial symbolism.

Much more is on the way, including a resort hotel, a casino, and the Museum of Biodiversity, designed by architect Frank O. Gehry, that was scheduled to open in 2007. Its boosters hope it will do for Panama what Gehry's Guggenheim did for Bilbao, Spain. Mockups make it look much gaudier than that museum, with ribbons of bold "tropical" colors.

SIGHTS

El Centro de Exhibiciones Marinas

There's a long-established little museum toward the end of the causeway, El Centro de Exhibiciones Marinas (Punta Culebra on Naos, tel. 212-8000, ext. 2366, $1 adults, $.50 children, 1–6 P.M. Tues.–Fri., 10 A.M.–6 P.M. Sat. and Sun., closed Tues.) that's well worth a visit. Try to call before going or arrive in the middle of the day, because opening and closing hours shift erratically. Expect longer hours in the dry season. It's always closed on Monday.

This nicely designed marine exhibition center is run by the Panama-based Smithsonian Tropical Research Institute. Exhibits set up along a beach-side path explain the extensive natural and human history of the area and touch on that of Panama in general. There's a small outdoor aquarium and an air-conditioned observation building. Free telescopes are set up along the path; check out the ships waiting to transit the canal. At the end of the path are a few hundred square meters of dry forest, once common all along the Pacific coast of Central America but now mostly wiped out since it's easy to burn. It's amazing what you may find in this little patch of forest. There are lots of iguanas, and the last time I was there I saw a shaggy three-toed sloth walking upside down along a branch just a few meters above my head.

The center is on Punta Culebra toward the end of the causeway. At the public beach on the first island, Naos, make a right when the road forks. There should be large signs.

ENTERTAINMENT AND EVENTS

The glitzy new **Panama Canal Village** (tel. 314-1414), on the Calzada de Amador (Amador Causeway) contains the Figali Convention Center, Panama's largest venue for extravaganzas. It hosts major international pop acts—ones that have gotten local fans revved up in the last couple of years include the Red Hot Chili Peppers, Shakira, and the Offspring—and other spectacles such as the 2003 Miss Universe beauty pageant. **Flamenco Shopping Plaza,** the shopping and dining center on Isla Flamenco, has several shoe-box-sized bars/nightclubs on the ground floor at the back of the complex. Each has a different theme—sports pub, Egyptian, "ciber"—but they're pretty interchangeable. Sometimes people dance a bit, but they're usually too crowded for that. These are mostly places to have a drink and hook up. The common denominator in all of them? Deafening music.

A larger and less claustrophobic place in the complex, also on the ground floor, is **Havana Rumba** (tel. 314-1197), which attracts pretty good Cuban and Panamanian musicians on Friday and Saturday nights and Sunday afternoons. This place attracts an older crowd that's passionate about Latin classics. This is not the place for those looking for a hot, hip scene. But it'll be fun for anyone curious to see Latin American musicians connecting with a knowledgeable audience.

Some of the restaurants on the second floor of Flamenco Plaza have live music combos on weekend nights and Sunday afternoons. Chances of hearing "Margaritaville" are good, though the combos I've heard haven't actually been that bad.

A **folkloric dance group** sometimes performs in the plaza when a ship is in port.

SHOPPING

Flamenco Shopping Plaza, a compact shopping mall at the end of the causeway on Isla Flamenco, might as well be in Miami, despite or because of which it has proven to be tremendously popular with locals and some foreign tourists, especially cruise passengers. It also contains about a dozen restaurants and bars. The shops are so well buried behind the restaurants that some visitors don't even know they're there. They stay open late on Saturday nights. The only notable shop is a branch of the famed **Reprosa** jewelry store (tel. 314-1034, 2–9:30 P.M. Tues.–Sat., 2–8 P.M. Sun., closed Mon.), which carries the *huaca* and Spanish coin replicas the store is known for, as well as a range of other attractive, reasonably priced jewelry. There's also a small cruise-ship terminal (passengers have to be taken by tender to and from ships) that has a few services.

The causeway can get packed with visitors on the weekends, particularly dry-season Sundays. The popularity of the bars and restaurants causes traffic jams on the two-lane road on weekend nights, as a result of which there's talk of widening the road.

SPORTS AND RECREATION

Walking, running, or biking the causeway are popular. It's especially pleasant to ramble about in the morning and early evening, when the weather is cool and the light is gorgeous. Bikes can be rented for $2 an hour from a kiosk next to Restaurante Pencas. It's open 8 A.M.–8 P.M. Monday–Friday, 7 A.M.–9 P.M. Saturday and Sunday. There can be long lines on the weekends. There's a little strip mall on Naos, next to Mi Ranchito, that has a couple of places to rent bikes, scooters, and roller blades, but this requires making one's way almost all the way to the end of the causeway.

You may see people splashing around in the little beaches along the causeway, but I don't advise you join them. Way back in high school I participated in a beach cleanup here that netted all kinds of disgusting stuff, including hospital waste, that had washed up from Panama City. No way would I ever set foot in the waters on the Panama Bay side. There's a little beach on the canal-facing side of the causeway we used to swim off of when I was a kid, but that's when there was a large shark net across the inlet to discourage hopeful scavengers from following ships toward the canal. The net rotted away years ago, after the demise of the Zone. The beach is being spruced up, but unless another net is erected I wouldn't recommend going for a splash.

The well-heeled, or large groups, can charter a 56-foot catamaran from the **Flamenco Yacht Club** (Isla Flamenco, tel. 314-0665, 225-3513, or 225-3514, fax 225-3515, marina@fuerteamador.com, www.fuerteamador.com). The yacht can hold up to 16 people. A day-cruise to Taboga costs $1,200–1,600. A night cruise around

© WILLIAM FRIAR

The Amador Causeway (Calzada de Amador) offers beautiful views of the Bridge of the Americas.

Panama Bay and the Bridge of the Americas is $800 including refreshments. Fishing trips and overnight charters to the Islas Perlas can also be arranged. Another outfit, Canal and Bay Tours, sometimes offers weekend night and Sunday afternoon bay cruises for $20 per person. Panama Marine Adventures charters the 119-foot *Pacific Queen* for large groups. (For information on either company, see *Panama Canal Transit* under *Pacific Side Locks and Townsites*.)

ACCOMMODATIONS

There is so far only one place to stay on the causeway, though that will likely have changed by the time you read this. That place is a **Country Inn and Suites** (tel. 211-4500, fax 211-4501, country.pma@unesa.com, www.panamacanal-country.com, starts at $98 s/d including breakfast), on the water near the entrance to Amador. It's a four-story, 98-unit hotel that resembles the other nondescript members of the chain. Standard rooms include cable TV, telephone, iron and ironing board, coffeemaker, and a balcony. It's worth paying an extra $10 to get the view of the Pacific entrance to the canal and the Bridge of the Americas, the proximity to which is the most

distinctive thing about the hotel. There's a TGI Fridays, an attractive swimming pool on the edge of the canal, a tennis court, a spa, and a business center. Tours of Panama City, the canal, and other attractions are easy to arrange.

FOOD

There are plenty of places to eat on and near the causeway, though I've yet to have a memorable meal at any of them. The restaurants below are listed in order, from Amador proper to the end of the causeway on Isla Flamenco. The TGI Friday's next to Country Inn and Suites is popular, though less of a singles scene than the one in downtown Panama City. It has the chain's usual mediocre food, but a great view.

Restaurante Pencas (tel. 211-2579, noon–11 P.M. Mon.–Thurs., 12:30 P.M.–12:30 A.M. Fri.–Sat., noon–10 P.M. Sun.) is just past the Panama Canal Village. It's a large open-air place with tables on a raised deck near the water, with a view of the ocean and Panama City skyline. The menu tends toward American comfort food and includes baby back ribs and other grilled meats, sandwiches, burgers, fajitas, pasta, and seafood. The *filete de canal frances* is a small but tender cut of beef.

Mi Ranchito (tel. 228-0116, 11 A.M.–11 P.M. daily) is a simple but clean open-air place under a thatched roof on Naos, just past the turnoff to the Centro de Exhibiciones Marinas. It has a view of the bay and is quite popular on the weekend. It serves mostly seafood and typical Panamanian fare. While many people have good experiences here, I've found the food to be just so-so—the corvina is not very flavorful and is drowned in sauce, and the soup is thin—but the prices are reasonable. A fixed-price lunch, including a drink, is $6. Most other main dishes are $6–9. The *patacones* are tasty.

Flamenco Plaza on Isla Flamenco has an impressive number of theme restaurants squeezed into a small space. Oddly, the complex has been designed so the parking lot is on the best real estate, with a view of Panama Bay and the Panama City skyline, while the restaurants are set so far back they really only have a view of the parking lot. Most are indoor/outdoor places on the second floor, and it's pleasant to sit outside in the evenings to enjoy the tropical breeze. Among the more notable eateries are:

Café Barko (tel. 314-0000, 11:30 A.M.–12:30 A.M. Mon. and Tues., 11:30 A.M.–1:30 A.M. Wed. and Thurs., 11:30 A.M.–2:30 A.M. Fri. and Sat., closed Mon.), which has a nautical theme and an outdoor seating area that's pleasant and breezy on a dry-season evening. It specializes in fish, with offerings including corvina, mahimahi, or snapper with a choice of 19 sauces. It also serves pastas and a variety of meats. The food is okay, but the chef is overly fond of salt. Most dishes range in price $12–18. The tables on the terrace have a partial view of Panama Bay.

Bucanero's Restaurante y Taberna (tel. 314-0880, noon–midnight Mon.–Thurs., noon–1 A.M. Fri.–Sat.) is kind of a corny, touristy place, with waiters dressed as pirates and glass-topped tables filled with sand and shells that are supposed to suggest the sea. It serves mostly fish, pasta, and grilled meat, with prices $5.75–16. The food is so-so. The corvina in dill sauce isn't bad, but it's quite rich. Consider asking for sauce on the side—the chef likes to drown his fish. The restaurant has a small air-conditioned room that's usually empty. There's

cheesy live music starting every night at 8 P.M., 1 P.M. on Sundays.

Crepes and Waffles (tel. 314-1108, noon–11 P.M. Mon.–Wed., noon–midnight Thurs.–Sat., closed Sun.) is a branch of the popular downtown café and offers the same menu of snacks and desserts. It's at the back of the complex, on the second floor.

M Alberto's Café (tel. 314-1132, noon–midnight Sun.–Thurs., noon–1 A.M. Fri.–Sat.) is an Italian place in the cruise-ship terminal on Isla Flamenco, so it's actually on the water and has a partial view of Panama Bay and the city skyline. It has an air-conditioned indoor dining room as well as sidewalk seating on the waterfront. It goes for a real Venice feel, complete with waiters dressed as gondoliers. It probably has probably the best food in the area. It's a good spot for a drink in the evening. Main courses are $5.50–14.

The internationally famous and much-beloved **Balboa Yacht Club,** a fancy name for a ramshackle little bar/restaurant, burned down a few years back, much to the horror of its devotees. So far all that's risen from its ashes is a little open-air bar and fast-food caravan near the pier. But it can still be a place to meet colorful people and perhaps wrangle a Panama Canal transit or a more distant trip on a passing yacht. It's across the street from Country Inn and Suites and TGI Friday's.

PRACTICALITIES
Information and Services

The cruise-ship terminal has a duty-free shop, but only cruise-ship passengers can buy from it. It also has a Western Union outlet and a small newsstand/gift shop. A minisupermarket and deli were in the works.

The Flamenco Yacht Club (Isla Flamenco, tel. 314-0665, 225-3513, or 225-3514, fax 225-3515, marina@fuerteamador.com, www.fuerteamador.com) is a well-equipped marina that offers moorings, repairs, maintenance, and supplies for everything from small pleasure boats to megayachts. Next to it is a marine-supply store, Nautipesca (tel. 314-0826, 9 A.M.–6 P.M. Mon.–Thurs., 9 A.M.–8 P.M. Fri. and Sat., closed Sun., www.nautipesca.net).

The Panama Canal

Getting There and Around

Amador, formerly the U.S. army base Fort Amador, begins near the east end of the Bridge of the Americas. The main road leads directly to the causeway. Taxis from downtown Panama City should cost around $3–4 one-way. Buses from downtown to the causeway leave the SACA Bus Terminal across from the Palacio Legislativo (national assembly building) in Panama City. (See the *Panama City* chapter for details.) Only those on a very tight budget will want to fool with the bus to go this short distance.

Drivers coming from downtown Panama City can reach Amador by two roads. The older route is to drive through Balboa on Avenida Arnulfo Arias Madrid (also called Balboa Road) and turn off it onto the road between the YMCA and the huge statue of Arnulfo Arias. This leads straight to Amador. A faster and more direct route is to take a new access road that links Avenida de los Mártires directly with Amador near the entrance to the Bridge of the Americas; follow the signs and stay alert—the intersections come up quickly and can be dangerous.

For those without cars, the main way to get around is on foot, though it can be a long walk in the sun from one end of the causeway to another. Fortunately, most of the attractions are clustered at the end of the causeway, on or near Isla Flamenco. Bikes can be rented at either end of the causeway (see *Sports and Recreation*.) It may also be possible to flag down a passing taxi or bus for a quick ride up or down the causeway.

Pacific Side Locks and Townsites

The Pacific side of the former Canal Zone comprises two of the Panama Canal's three sets of locks and the beginning of the approximately nine-mile (14-kilometer) **Gaillard Cut** through the Continental Divide, the toughest part of the canal to dig and the most dramatic to see. It also contains most of the former Zone "townsites," which were home to the civilian employees of the canal and their families. These include **Ancón, Balboa, La Boca,** and **Diablo.** It's home also to what were once its most important U.S. military bases, including Howard Air Force Base, Fort Clayton, Fort Amador, Quarry Heights, Albrook Air Force Base, and Rodman Naval Station.

Amador, as has been mentioned elsewhere, has become a major nightlife and tourism destination. Albrook has become a fairly upscale suburban residential area (and home to Panama City's domestic airport and bus terminal—see the *Panama City* chapter). Parts of Clayton have been converted into something called **La Ciudad del Saber** (the City of Knowledge), which aims to attract international academic and research institutions. But much of the rest of the former Zone has become a series of veritable ghost towns awaiting a development plan, or are being plowed under to make way for port facilities, highways, and other industrial developments.

SIGHTS

Cerro Ancón

This hill, which is just across what used to be the boundary between Panama City and the Canal Zone, has an impressive view from the top and a few interesting places to visit on its slopes.

The agency that runs the Panama Canal, now known as the Autoridad del Canal de Panamá (Panama Canal Authority), is headquartered in an imposing building perched on a small hill on the side of Cerro Ancón. Known simply as the **Administration Building (Edificio de Administración),** it's worth visiting for a couple of reasons.

First, there are dramatic murals inside the building's rotunda that depict the construction of the canal. These were painted by William B. Van Ingen, a New York artist who also created murals for the Library of Congress and the U.S. Mint in Philadelphia. They were installed in January 1915 and underwent a restoration in 1993. The four major panels of the mural show excavation at Gaillard Cut and the construction of Miraflores Locks, the Gatún Dam spillway, and a set

A FEW FACTS

The Panama Canal is a trivia buff's dream. The mind-boggling engineering details and the canal's colorful history make for an endless list of unusual factoids. Here are just a few:

• If all the rock and dirt dug from the canal were piled into boxcars, the resulting train would circle the earth four times at the equator.

• The toll record at the time of writing was set by the *Coral Princess* on Jan. 17, 2003. It pays $273,750 when it transits.

• The adventurer Richard Halliburton paid the lowest toll, $.36, to swim the canal in 1928. (No one else has ever been allowed to swim the entire canal; it's too dangerous.)

• The widest ships allowed to transit the canal are the USS *New Jersey* and her sister ships. They have a beam of 108 feet (32.9 meters). The lock chambers are 110 feet (33.5 meters) wide.

• The longest ship to transit was the *San Juan Prospector*, a bulk/oil carrier. It's 973 feet (297 meters) long. Each lock chamber is 1,000 feet (305 meters) long.

• The average transit takes 8–10 hours.

• The fastest transit time, 2 hours and 41 minutes, was set by the U.S. Navy hydrofoil *Pegasus*.

• Ninety-two percent of the world's ocean-going ships can still transit the canal.

• No pumps are used to raise and lower ships in the locks; it's all done by gravity.

• The United States is the major user of the canal.

• Containerized cargo is more commonly shipped through the canal than anything else. Grain comes in second place.

• The builders of the Panama Canal included 20,000 Barbadians and just 357 Panamanians.

• The record for the most transits on a single day, 65, was set on February 29, 1968.

• A ship traveling from New York to San Francisco saves 7,872 miles (12,674 kilometers) by using the canal instead of going around the tip of South America.

The Panama Canal

of lock gates. They give a sense of what a staggering task the building of the canal was.

Second, there's a sweeping view of part of the former Canal Zone, especially the townsite of Balboa, from the back of the building. Walk through the doors at the back of the rotunda, but note they may lock behind you; in that case just walk around the outside of the building to get back to the front entrance.

In the foreground is what was once Balboa Elementary School (on the left) and Balboa High School (on the right). The marble monolith between them is the Goethals Monument. The long, palm-lined promenade is the Prado. In the distance is the Bridge of the Americas and Cerro Sosa. Those feeling energetic can walk down the long flight of stairs and explore the townsite of Balboa.

Visitors are free to explore the rotunda any

time of the day or night, but they're prohibited from visiting other parts of the building without an appointment. Sign in with the guard at the door.

The **Administrator's House,** a wooden mansion set in a well-tended garden, is a short drive or an easy, pleasant walk farther up the road. When the road forks, head left. During construction days this was the home of the canal's chief engineer. It originally sat overlooking what is now Gaillard Cut, allowing the chief engineers (first John F. Stevens, then George W. Goethals) to keep an eye on the excavation even when they were home. In 1914 it was taken apart and moved by train to its present location. It has been the home of the canal's chief executive ever since. The large, nondescript house farther down the hill is the home of the canal's deputy administrator.

Double back on the same road. Stay straight

COURTESY PANAMA CANAL COMMISSION

The SS *Ancon* was the first vessel officially to transit the Panama Canal, on August 15, 1914.

and head into Quarry Heights, once the headquarters of the U.S. Southern Command. Go past the guard house (if there's actually a guard there he will probably just wave you in), then make a left past the headquarters of the environmental nonprofit ANCON. Access from this point on is by a one-way road. Guards at either end of the road tell you when it's safe to go, but honk the horn around curves anyway. The top of Cerro Ancón is two kilometers up from the Quarry Heights gate. It has a great view of Casco Viejo, Panama Bay, and the modern city skyline. Walk behind the communications tower to get a look at the entrance to the Panama Canal, the bridge of the Americas, Miraflores Locks, and the townsite of Balboa. It's also possible to walk up to the giant Panamanian flag, which was one of the first things to go up in the former Canal Zone after the ratification of the treaties that turned the canal over to Panama. This spot has the best view of the Panama City skyline. Historical footnote: The U.S. military dug a tunnel into the heart of the hill, the entrance to which still stands in Quarry Heights, as a secure command post for the Southern Command during times of crisis.

Balboa

Those who want a sense of what life was like in the former Canal Zone should consider spending an hour or two wandering around the townsite of Balboa. The unofficial "capital" of the Canal Zone, it was the most formally planned of the Zone communities. Today it's being squeezed between a container port and highway overpasses, and many of the old apartments are either unoccupied or have been converted into offices, but it retains much of its utilitarian elegance. (Make allowances for some personal bias here, since I spent most of my childhood in Balboa and Balboa Heights and am a graduate of both Balboa Elementary and Balboa High.)

Balboa extends from the base of the Administration Building to Cerro Sosa and makes for an easy walking tour. The marble monolith is the **Goethals Monument,** erected in honor of George W. Goethals, the chief engineer of the canal from 1907 to its completion in 1914. The three tiers of the fountain symbolize the three sets of locks. The monument was controversial when it was erected; some complained it didn't fit into the community's design.

Leading away from the monument is the palm-lined promenade of the **Prado.** Each of the two sections, if one includes the sidewalks, has the exact length and width of a lock chamber (1,000 by 110 feet). The whitewashed buildings with red-tile roofs along either side were built as multifamily apartments. In the foreground to the left is what was once **Balboa Elementary School.** On the right is what was once **Balboa High School.** Both are now offices used by the Panama Canal Authority.

Parts of the old high school, now known as the **Centro de Capacitación Ascanio Arosemena,** are open to visitors 7 A.M.–4:15 P.M. Monday–Friday. Outside is a breezeway dedicated to the Panamanians who died during the 1964 Flag Riots; their names are inscribed on the pillars. Just inside the building is a display about the riots, including some mementos from the old Canal Zone, that attempts to walk a delicate line between the still-polarized views on what exactly happened during the riots, the bloodiest and most controversial conflict between the United States and Panama until the 1989 U.S. invasion. Lining the halls on this floor and the one above is a wealth of rare artifacts from both the French and U.S. canal efforts, including railroad ties and pick-axes, clippings from 19th-century newspapers, bonds sold to finance the disastrous French effort, fascinating black-and-white prints dating from the 1880s, maps, Canal Zone stamps and seals, and historic china and silverware from the Canal Zone governor's house. On the second floor is the **Biblioteca Roberto F. Chiari** (open 10 A.M.–4 P.M. Mon.–Fri. for "investigators"). This is the library of the Autoridad del Canal de Panamá (Panama Canal Authority), housed in what was once the high-school library. It contains all kinds of technical and historical books and documents on the Panama Canal and Panama. It's not technically open to the general public, but those who fancy themselves "investigators" can certainly stop by and sign in.

Those who want a longer walking tour can continue down the Prado to **Stevens Circle,** a rather drab monument to John Stevens, the canal's chief engineer 1905–1907 and its master designer. On the left is the **Balboa post office.** Directly across the main road is what's left of a cafeteria that used to feed canal workers around the clock. Next to it is the **Teatro Balboa,** once a movie theater and now host to occasional concerts and other performances. Across the street from that is the former commissary for canal employees, now offices. Next to the old football stadium is Niko's Café, the best bet for a meal in the area.

As you head down Avenida Arnulfo Arias Madrid (also known as Balboa Road) in the direction of Amador and Panama City you'll head past the **Union Church,** an ecumenical church that is still in operation. Just past it is an enormous and rather weird **fountain** built in honor of Arnulfo Arias Madrid, who was elected (and overthrown) president of Panama four times. It was built by Mireya Moscoso, Arias's widow, after she became president in 1999 and depicts Arnulfo flashing a V for victory sign at figures representing the Panamanian people, who are struggling to their feet. Shortly after it was erected, some amateur art critics sawed off his index finger, changing the significance of the gesture considerably. The statue was quickly repaired. Across the street is the YMCA, next to which is a large **handicrafts market.** Farther up that same road is a Kuna-run *mola* **cooperative.**

Miraflores Locks, Pedro Miguel Locks, and Gaillard Cut

Miraflores Locks, completed in May of 1913, stand at the Pacific entrance to the Panama Canal. They link the Pacific Ocean with the manmade Miraflores Lake, raising and lowering ships 54 feet (16.5 meters) in two impressive steps. Of the canal's three sets of locks, these are the easiest to reach from Panama City and the best equipped to handle visitors.

The massive new **Centro de Visitantes de Miraflores** (Miraflores Visitors Center, tel. 276-8325, cvm@pancanal.com, www.pancanal.com, 9 A.M.–5 P.M. daily, $8 admission) is an out-of-place monolith from the outside, but inside it's rather impressive. It contains a four-story museum, an observation deck, a theater that shows

COURTESY PANAMA CANAL COMMISSION

The Panama Canal's locks are among the most massive structures ever built.

documentaries on the canal in English and Spanish, and a restaurant with good views of the locks. Hold onto your ticket to be admitted to the museum and theater. The first floor of the museum contains a history of the canal, starting with the failed French effort and continuing through completion by the United States. The second is an ecological exhibit that stresses the importance of the Panama Canal watershed and contains displays on the flora and fauna found within it. The third shows the operation of the canal and includes a full-scale pilot-training simulator and a topographical canal map. The fourth is the least interesting, with route maps that stress the importance of the canal to world commerce.

The restaurant has a terrace right on the edge of the locks, making it a great place to come for lunch or dinner. (See *Food*.) There's also an outdoor snack bar on the ground floor.

Admission to the entire complex is $8, $5 for kids ages 5–17, free for children younger than five. Admission just to the ground terrace and shops is $5, $3 for kids.

Pedro Miguel Locks, about a 10-minute drive farther down Gaillard Highway from Miraflores, raise and lower ships in one 31-foot (9.5-meter) step, linking Miraflores Lake and Gaillard Cut. These locks are not open to the public, but a little rest stop just beyond them gives a good view of the action. You can also see the beginning of Gaillard Cut (also called Culebra Cut), where the canal was dug right through the Continental Divide. It's a dramatic sight, though the widening of the cut has made it a bit less so by pushing back and lowering the rocky peaks through which the waterway runs. Construction also removed the viewing platform at the top of Gaillard Cut, so it's hard to get a good vantage point these days. The best way to see it is from the canal itself, during a transit. Farther up the road is the Puente Centenario, a dramatic new suspension bridge over the canal that was inaugurated in 2004, before any of the access roads to it were completed. Presumably the bridge will be in use when you visit (check out www.mop. gob.pa for current developments).

Panama Canal Transit

A transit of the Panama Canal is unforgettable, and fortunately you don't have to buy an entire cruise to have the experience. These days the most popular way to do it is with **Panama Marine Adventures** on the *Pacific Queen* (tel. 226-8917 or 270-4288, info@ptymarineadventures.com, www.ptymarineadventures.com). This is an air-conditioned 119-foot vessel equipped with a snack bar, souvenir shop, and television monitors on which cruisers can watch documentaries on the canal when they need a break from the action on deck. Transits are always on a Saturday. Usually this is a partial transit that starts in Gamboa, goes through Pedro Miguel and Miraflores Locks, and ends at Isla Flamenco on the Amador Causeway. The transit takes 4–5 hours and costs $99 for adults, $45 for children younger than 12. The price includes pickup at the Flamenco marina on the Causeway, lunch and soft drinks, and a bilingual guide. One Saturday a month the company offers a full transit. This starts at Flamenco and goes through the entire canal, ending at Colón after exiting Gatún Locks. The transit takes 8–9 hours and costs $149 for adults, $55 for children younger than 12. It includes all the above plus a continental breakfast and transportation back from Colón to Flamenco.

Another group that offers transits is **Canal and Bay Tours** (tel. 314-1349, 314-1350, or 314-1353, info@canalandbaytours.com, www.canalandbaytours.com), with a similar schedule and identical prices. It uses the 96-foot-long *Isla Morada* and 115-foot-long *Fantasia del Mar,* old ferry boats that made the run to Taboga for many years. The company has been sprucing them up.

Note: Transits generally start early in the morning, but it's impossible for either company to promise exact end times. Scheduling is entirely up to the Panama Canal Authority, and since these are smaller vessels they have to make way for larger traffic.

Panama Railway

A railway, the descendent of the famed Panama Railroad built for the '49ers during the California gold rush, ran constant daily trips back and forth across the isthmus during the Canal Zone days. It ran along and sometimes over stretches of the Panama Canal, was billed as the world's fastest and cheapest transcontinental journey, and was used as a commuter and cargo train. Panama's military government inherited the railroad and allowed it to fall apart during the 1980s. In 1998, though, the post-Noriega Panamanian government signed an agreement with two U.S. companies, including Kansas City Southern, a railroad holding company, to create the Panama Canal Railway Company and rebuild the rail link between the Atlantic and Pacific. The result is a 47.5-mile (76.5-kilometer) railway used primarily to move cargo across the isthmus.

However, the train does make one daily passenger trip, leaving the Pacific side of the isthmus at 7:30 A.M. and returning at 5:15 P.M. It's quite a step up from the utilitarian train of the old Canal Zone days: The cars in this one have dark wood paneling, leather banquettes set around tables, large observation windows, and waitresses in little conductors' outfits who serve coffee and muffins. Be sure to step onto the spacious platforms between cars, which offer great views and pleasant breezes. It's also quite a step up in price: The fare is $22 one-way, $38 round-trip, half price for those 12 and younger. The train serves mainly affluent business people and tourists. Seats are limited, so make reservations (tel. 317-6700, info@panarail.com, www.kcsi.com).

The train doesn't quite go from ocean to ocean. The new Pacific terminus is at the old Canal Zone townsite of Corozal, about a 15-minute drive away from downtown Panama City. The Caribbean terminus is at Colón. The train is an express and makes no stops en route. The trip takes about an hour. Those who take the train from Panama City to Colón can either hire a taxi and spend the day exploring Caribbean-side attractions such as the nearby Gatún Locks, Fuerte San Lorenzo, and the Colón Free Zone until it's time for the return train, or else catch a bus back to Panama City at the Terminal de Buses in Colón. (See the *Central Caribbean* chapter for details.) Do not try to walk between the train station and the bus terminal, or anywhere else in Colón. Muggings at knifepoint are a major problem in Colón, a city I strongly advise travelers to avoid except for a couple of relatively safe areas.

The Panama Canal

ENTERTAINMENT AND EVENTS

The **Theatre Guild of Ancon** (tel. 212-0060) is the only English-language playhouse that has survived the demise of the Canal Zone's once-thriving community-theater scene. The rickety old wooden playhouse was slated to be moved to Clayton, a former U.S. Army base, at the time of writing; call for location information. A bit of Hollywood gossip: Jennifer Aniston's dad, John Aniston, was an actor at the theater in the 1950's. **Balboa Theater** (tel. 228-0327), an aging former movie house off Stevens Circle in the heart of the former Canal Zone townsite of Balboa, hosts concerts and the occasional play and special event. In recent years, a **concert series** has been held near the steps of the Panama Canal Administration Building in Balboa on dry-season Tuesday and Thursday evenings.

SHOPPING

Balboa has a couple of good places to buy handicrafts. The first is the **Centro de Artesanías Internacional** (behind the YMCA on Avenida Arnulfo Arias Madrid/Balboa Road, 9 A.M.–6 P.M. Mon.–Sat., 10 A.M.–5 P.M. Sun.). It houses many stalls selling handicrafts from all over Panama—including *tagua* carvings, *molas, cocobolo* figurines, and Panama hats—as well as some from other parts of Latin America.

Those who won't feel satisfied with a visit to Panama unless they buy a "Panama hat" of the kind actually made in Ecuador will find some good-quality ones here. Ask for the stall of Segundo Reyes. His best ones sell for $100–200. He also has some coarser ones for $10. All come in attractive balsa-wood boxes and make good presents for the geographically challenged. They need blocking and there's a good place in Panama to do it, but it's in such a dangerous part of Panama City I'm not going to tell you where it is. Pay the extra money and have it done at home.

Note: An artesanía recently opened in the YMCA building itself, and those who work there aggressively lure in lost visitors who've heard there's a handicrafts hall near the YMCA but aren't sure where it is. By all means take a look, but don't be confused and miss out on the much bigger and better selection at the main artisans' center.

Farther up Avenida Arnulfo Arias Madrid/Balboa Road, on the right as one heads toward Avenida de los Mártires, is the **Centro Municipal de Artesanías Panameñas** (8 A.M.–6 P.M. daily). It's run by Kunas and has a wider and better selection of *molas* than the Centro de Artesanías. You can probably strike a better bargain here, since they see less business. The Kuna women sewing *molas* and wearing *mola* blouses aren't doing it for show. That's really how they dress and what they do.

SPORTS AND RECREATION

Summit Golf and Resort (tel. 232-4653, summit@summitgolfpanama.com, www.summitgolf-panama.com), 14 kilometers north of Balboa, is an upscale golf course that welcomes non-members. It's a 6,626-yard, par-72 course that was given a major makeover a few years back. It has a modern circular clubhouse with pretty views of rolling countryside, as well as a restaurant and bar. A hotel is in the planning stages. Greens fees are $50 for nine holes or $90 for 18 holes including cart 6:30 A.M.–2 P.M. Monday–Thursday. Rates are $10 more on weekend mornings, and significantly less any afternoon after 2 P.M. Club rental is $10–35, depending on quality of club and number of holes played. Summit is 7.5 kilometers north of Miraflores Locks. The turnoff is on the right 1.5 kilometers before the left turn toward Gamboa.

ACCOMMODATIONS

There are only a couple of hotels in the canal area so far. Most people will prefer to stay in downtown Panama City, which is quite close by, though the two places below offer quiet, out-of-the-way neighborhoods for those who find that appealing.

M La Estancia (tel. 314-1417, cell 651-6232, stay@bedandbreakfastpanama.com, www.bedandbreakfastpanama.com, starts at $45 s/d, including continental breakfast) is a new 10-room bed-and-breakfast in Quarry Heights, the former headquarters of the U.S. Southern Command, on the side of Cerro Ancón.

Rooms have air-conditioning, telephones, and private bathrooms. Two have their bathrooms down the hall rather than attached to the room but come with a balcony and hammock to make up for that slight inconvenience. Most rooms have a queen-sized bed. There's a common area for guests to relax in. The place is surrounded by trees, and there's a partial view of the Panama Canal and the Bridge of the Americas from some of the balconies. Two of the rooms are actually fair-sized apartments with sitting rooms, kitchenettes, and a small patio. These go for $75 a night or $395 a week, including breakfast.

The building was once used as apartments for military personnel and thus is a bit stark and utilitarian, but the bed-and-breakfast's owners have made attempts to soften the place and make it cheerful. To get to La Estancia, take the first left up the hill after passing the guardhouse at the entrance to Quarry Heights. The bed-and-breakfast is 400 meters past the guardhouse. It's house number 35, a peach-colored, three-story building on the right.

Albrook Inn (14 Calle Hazelhurst, tel. 315-1789, 315-1972, 315-1973, or 315-1974, fax 315-1975, gerencia@albrookinnpanama .com.pa, www.albrookinnpanama.com.pa, starts at $38/50 s, $44 d including continental breakfast) is a two-story, 30-unit hotel opened in early 2003 in a peaceful middle-class suburban neighborhood next to what had been the Albrook Officers' Club back when Albrook was a U.S. Air Force base. It has 27 rooms. Small, simple rooms with very firm beds, air-conditioning, and cable TV go for $44 s/d. Larger rooms with a sitting room and sink are $77 s/d. Some beds are hard as rock slabs. A restaurant is supposedly in the works, and spa treatments (including a "spiritual guide") are available by appointment.

FOOD

Since this area is still so much in flux, there are only a few places to eat. Fortunately, downtown Panama City and the Calzada de Amador are quite close if the restaurants below aren't appealing. There is also a range of places to eat at the Gran Terminal de Transportes/Albrook Mall in

Albrook. A new El Rey supermarket was going up at the entrance to Albrook during my last visit.

The best place for a meal in the canal area is the restaurant upstairs at the **N Centro de Visitantes de Miraflores** (Miraflores Locks Visitors Center, tel. 276-8325, 11 A.M.–11 P.M.). The food is decent—sandwiches, pastas, seafood, salads, and so on, ranging in price $6.50–20—but that's not the main attraction. Watching the ships go by from the terrace is. It's a unique experience day or night (high-mast lighting at the locks makes everything easy to see after dark). Come early or make a reservation to sit against the railing, where the view is best. Service charge is included.

Niko's Café (tel. 228-8888, 7 A.M.–11 P.M. daily) at the end of the Prado next to Stevens Circle in Balboa, is one of a small chain of successful cafeterias in Panama City that offer simple, tasty food at rock-bottom prices. This one is in the heart of the old Canal Zone, between what was once the high-school football stadium and the employees' commissary, built on the site of a bowling alley. Reflecting its location, the cafeteria has great panoramic black-and-white photos of the Canal Zone, U.S. military bases, and parts of Panama dating from the 1920s and 1930s. Much to the amazement of old Zonians, the seal of the Canal Zone is above the counter. Nothing on the menu is over $4, which will buy piles of local food. Most breakfast items are under $2. Ditto for sandwiches, soups, individual pizzas, and desserts.

Lum's Bar and Grill (tel. 317-6303, 11 A.M.–midnight daily), just off Gaillard Highway across the tracks from the railroad station in Corozal, is one of the last bastions of meat-and-potatoes Zonian spirit. Turn off the highway at the lovingly preserved Panama Railroad train cars. It's a converted warehouse that features a restaurant in the main room with pastas, salads, sandwiches and the like, most for $6 or less. Attached to it is a sports bar with pool tables, ESPN, and, on some nights, live local bands.

INFORMATION AND SERVICES

The Smithsonian Tropical Research Institute (tel. 212-8000) has its headquarters, the Earl S. Tupper Research and Conference Center, in Ancon.

The Panama Canal

It's a large building on Roosevelt Avenue across Avenida de las Mártires from the Palacio Legislativo. It has a small research library (9 A.M.–5 P.M. Mon., Wed., Thurs., and Fri.; 8 A.M.–5 P.M. Tues.; 9 A.M.–noon Sat., closed Sun.) that contains science periodicals and older research books and a bookstore (10 A.M.–4:30 P.M. weekdays) with some hard-to-find books on Panama's natural history. Both are worth a visit for those who want detailed information on Panama's flora and fauna. They are open to the public, but visitors must present an ID and sign in to get into the center. Visitors to Barro Colorado have to make arrangements through the center, but this can be done by phone or email. The center also has a cafeteria that serves lunch for less than $2.

GETTING THERE AND AROUND

Taxis are the most convenient way to get from downtown Panama City to most of the destinations described above, though they're easy to explore by rental car as well. Many tour operators offer day tours that include stops in Balboa, Miraflores Locks, and the handicrafts market next to the YMCA. A taxi tour can also be arranged for around $6 an hour.

Exploring by bus requires a lot of connections, but those who want to try it can start at the SACA bus terminal, near the Palacio Legislativo in Panama City. (See the *Panama City* chapter for information.)

The Administration Building is in Altos de Balboa (Balboa Heights), a short drive from downtown Panama City. It's hard to miss. A taxi ride from most parts of Panama City should cost about $2–3. Ask the driver to take you to *el edificio de administración en Balboa*. If that doesn't work, tell him it's *Cerro Ancón, cerca de McDonald's* (close to McDonald's, alas). It's easy to walk from the Administration Building to the Administrator's House, but walking to the top of Cerro Ancón is a serious hike. Those who want to take a taxi to the top will have to negotiate a tour.

Miraflores Locks are about a 20-minute drive from Panama City, just off Gaillard Highway. The road borders the canal for part of the way. The entrance to Miraflores Locks will be on the left less than 10 kilometers from Balboa. Pedro Miguel Locks are about five kilometers farther on. Just beyond Pedro Miguel is the beginning of Gaillard Cut, now sometimes referred to by its original name, Culebra Cut.

The road continues to Gamboa, so those heading that way should consider making a visit to the locks as a side trip. Taxis to Miraflores from Panama City cost about $4. Taxis sometimes hang out at the locks, but if you don't see any when you arrive, ask your driver to wait and take you back (agree on a price for this ahead of time, and don't pay him until the return trip). Those who want to continue by taxi to Pedro Miguel and Gaillard Cut will probably be better off negotiating for a half-day tour.

Gamboa and Surroundings

The townsite of Gamboa, on the banks of the Panama Canal about halfway across the isthmus, is surrounded by extraordinary natural beauty, especially given how close it is to Panama City. In it or nearby are world-famous birding trails, the tropical rainforest of Parque Nacional Soberanía, the powerful Río Chagres, botanical gardens and a zoo, and the huge, manmade Lago Gatún. That lake is at the heart of the canal and contains Barro Colorado Island, one of the world's foremost natural laboratories for the study of tropical nature.

Though Emberá Indians still live up the Río Chagres, Gamboa is the headquarters of the canal's engineering and dredging divisions and has a modern infrastructure. Two impressive eco-resorts are in the area, though today there is little else out there. There are few services, accommodations, or places to eat, but Panama City is less than a 45-minute drive away.

Note: Lago Alajuela (formerly Madden Lake) is a second artificial lake northeast of Gamboa that supplies water for the canal. Some people like to visit its impressive Madden Dam, but because

© WILLIAM FRIAR

The Gamboa Rainforest Resort's aerial tram provides great views of the canal area and a chance to spot wildlife.

The Panama Canal

of several instances of tourist muggings there I recommend avoiding it. Those who like dams should visit the even more impressive and easily accessible Gatún Dam, on the Caribbean side of the isthmus.

Also, on December 28, 2004, a large group taking a guided tour along the Camino de Cruces (Las Cruces Trail) was robbed by two masked men wielding machetes. Hopefully this will prove to be a freak occurrence, but as this book went to press the U.S. embassy in Panama was warning tourists to avoid the trail and exercise caution in the area.

SIGHTS
Summit Botanical Gardens and Zoo
These gardens (tel. 232-4854, 8 A.M.–4 P.M. daily, $1, children younger than 12 free) are worth a quick side trip on the way to or from the Canopy Tower or Gamboa Rainforest Resort. They were created by the Panama Canal Company in 1923 for the study of tropical plants and turned over to the Panama government in 1985. The place has deteriorated in recent years but some efforts are being made to fix it up. At last count there were 4,000 plants representing 366 species still growing in the gardens. Ask for a brochure/map at the gate. It's in Spanish and something resembling English.

There's also a small zoo that contains tapirs, caimans, jaguars, and other large animals. Their cages are small and antiquated, which will disturb many visitors.

The harpy eagle compound, Summit's showcase, is more encouraging. The harpy eagle is the world's most powerful bird of prey; it can grow up to a meter long from bill to tail. Sadly, it's also endangered. The bird is indigenous to Panama, and a major purpose of the compound is to try to get the birds to reproduce in captivity. The specimens here are magnificent, with thick plumage, fearsome hooked bills, and steely talons. They look like stoic high chiefs.

There's an audiovisual display at the compound that's supposed to be open 8:30 A.M.–12:15 P.M. and 1–3 P.M., but it was closed when I got there at 11 A.M. The best bet to find it open is to arrive on a weekend or holiday. Even if the display is closed, however, you can still see the eagles in their huge cage.

Parque Nacional Soberanía
This is a true tropical forest, and it's one of the most accessible in the world. Its 22,000 hectares extend along the east bank of the Panama Canal, ending at Lago Gatún near the town of Limón. The wildlife is amazing, especially considering how close the park is to population centers. Among its inhabitants are 525 species of birds, 105 species of mammals, 55 species of amphibians, and 79 species of reptiles.

All its well-maintained trails are a short drive from Panama City, making it quite feasible to go for a morning hike during which there's a chance of encountering such tourist-pleasing critters as sloths, coatimundis, toucans, and kinkajous, and then be back in the heart of the city in time for lunch in an air-conditioned restaurant. There are also two very different kinds of ecotourist resorts—the Canopy Tower and Gamboa Rainforest Resort—bordering the park, for those who'd like to stay overnight in comfortable surroundings.

A section of the famous **Camino de Cruces (Las Cruces Trail),** which has a history dating to the 16th century, runs through the park. To reach it by car, continue straight when the road forks just past the railroad overpass with "1929" carved in it. The road, Madden Road (don't expect a street sign), will pass through a forest which, sadly, is often strewn with litter. There's a parking area and picnic tables on the left after 6.3 kilometers. The trailhead is well marked. It's possible to hike this trail for about five or six hours to the Chagres and even camp along it. For just a glimpse of this storied trail, walk at least five minutes along it and you'll come to a section where the ancient paving stones that once lined the trail have been restored. In the dry season, you may have to brush aside dead leaves to find them. (Use your boot to do this, not your hand, as there are still some poisonous snakes in the forest.)

If you turn left toward Gamboa instead of continuing straight, the first major trail will be the wide, flat **Plantation Road.** It's a right turn off the highway; follow the Canopy Tower signs. The entrance to the trail is on the left at the base of the road leading to the Canopy Tower. (See *Accommodations and Food* for more information on the trail.)

Farther along the main road is **Sendero El Charco (Pond Trail),** also on the right. This is a very short (844 meters) trail that can easily be skipped. A little waterfall near the entrance sure looked a lot bigger and nicer when I was a kid. A barbecue area on the premises attracts hordes of families on the weekends.

The best trail for viewing bird life is the famous **Pipeline Road (Camino del Oleoducto).** To get there, cross over the one-lane bridge leading into Gamboa. Continue straight. After about three kilometers the road will fork; take the left fork onto the gravel road. The swampy area to the right, just before Pipeline Road, is worth checking out on the way back from an early-morning birding trip. At around 8–9 A.M., as the forest warms up, there's an excellent chance of spotting capybaras, the world's largest rodents, on the far side of the clearing. A couple of kilometers past this area there's a "Parque Nacional Sober-

anía" sign indicating you've reached Camino del Oleoducto. Make a right here and park. There's talk about eventually building a major interpretive center at the entrance to the road, but it hadn't happened the last time I visited the area.

For the first six kilometers or so the forest is mostly secondary growth. You'll see dozens of species of birds if you arrive early. There's a slight chance of finding anteaters, howler monkeys, white-faced capuchins, Geoffroy's tamarin, green iguanas, agoutis, coatimundis, or two- and three-toed sloths. Serious birders will want to continue past this area into old-growth forest, where there's a possibility of seeing such rare specimens as yellow-eared toucanets, crimson-bellied woodpeckers, sirystes, and other gorgeous birds that will impress even those who don't know a russet antshrike from a slaty-winged foliage-gleaner. The unbelievably lucky may see an endangered harpy eagle, but don't count on it. Pipeline Road continues for many kilometers, but the bridges over streams are not well-maintained these days. Bridge collapses can curtail a long hike. Note: Get here by dawn to see this famous birding road in all its feathered glory. It's worth the loss of sleep.

Hiking and camping permits are available at the ANAM office at the edge of the park, conveniently located before any of the trails. It's on Gaillard Highway at the fork just past the narrow overpass; you can't miss the huge Parque Nacional Soberanía sign. The office is officially open 8 A.M.–4 P.M. weekdays, but the staff live in the little house behind the office so there should always be someone there to take your money. Entrance fee is $3, which gives visitors access to all the trails for the day. The camping fee is another $5. Bear in mind there are no developed camping sites (though there are some facilities at Sendero El Charco) and this is a tropical forest. Those planning an early-morning hike can probably pay on the way back without a problem. But otherwise ask about the conditions of the trails, especially Pipeline Road, before venturing out. Note that the Camino de Cruces is quite a hike from the other trails; Gamboa-bound buses take passengers only as far as the fork to Gamboa, after which you'll have to hoof it for six kilometers unless you can flag down a ride. It's much more convenient to take a taxi from Panama City or go with a tour group to this trail.

Lago Gatún

Once the largest manmade lake in the world, at 422 square kilometers Lago Gatún is still a plenty impressive body of water. It was formed by damming the Río Chagres near its mouth, at Gatún, and is an integral part of the Panama Canal. Transiting ships still follow the submerged river bed of the Chagres, since it's the deepest part of the lake. It's long been a popular spot with boaters, water-skiers, fisherfolk, and even scuba divers. The diving here is unusual, to say the least. A Belgian locomotive and eight of its 40 train cars, abandoned during construction days, were recently salvaged from the bottom of the lake, and submerged trees and remnants of old towns are still there. Not surprisingly, however, the water is murky and in some places choked with vegetation. Divers often find the experience of poking around down there rather spooky.

These days, the only recreation I'd recommend on the lake is a boat ride or a fishing trip. Caimans have always shared the lake with people, but these days there are a lot more of the critters. An acquaintance whose idea of a fun family outing used to be playing catch-and-release with caimans—we're not talking a wimp here—told me she would not even go water-skiing in the lake today. "It's infested," she said. The lake now also has crocodiles. A friend of a friend who lives in Gamboa, a town right on the lake, took his dog for a walk a few years back and watched in horror as a crocodile lunged out of the water and ate it.

In other words, I advise you to stay in the boat. The fishing here is terrific—the peacock bass population, accidentally introduced decades ago, is so out of control fishermen are actually encouraged to catch them to restore some kind of ecological balance. It's not uncommon for an angler who knows the good spots to catch dozens of fish an hour.

A new highlight of a Lago Gatún boat trip is a visit to the **Primate Refuge and Sanctuary of Panama (PRSP),** a nonprofit monkey haven

scattered among about a dozen islands in the lake, known collectively as the Islas Tigre and Islas Las Brujas. Here visitors can spot tamarins, spider monkeys, white-faced capuchins, howlers, and night monkeys swinging or peering from trees just a few meters from the boat.

Only visit the sanctuary on a tour led by a responsible naturalist group such as Ancon Expeditions. Do not feed or have any physical contact with the monkeys. All but the night monkeys have been rescued from illegal captivity, and the project is trying to reintroduce them to the wild. The last thing they need is more human contact. Besides, some can be pretty aggressive, so don't get too close. For more information on the project, which attracts students and researchers, visit www.primatesofpanama.org. Some boat tours of the area include walks through small, forested islands, some of which have spooky ruins from the old Canal Zone days. Douse yourself with insect repellent before exploring them; the mosquitoes can be voracious.

a spider monkey at the Primate Refuge and Sanctuary of Panama, Lago Gatún

© WILLIAM FRIAR

BARRO COLORADO ISLAND

BCI, as it's commonly known, is one of the world's most famous biological reserves. Part of what makes it exceptional is that it's been left alone so long: It was declared a protected area in 1923, when such reserves in the neotropics were almost unheard of. Since then its flora and fauna have been more intensely studied than that of any other tropical area of comparable size. The island is administered by the Smithsonian Tropical Research Institute (STRI), which is based in Panama.

Barro Colorado Island was actually a hill until 1914, when the damming of the Chagres River to create Lago Gatún made that hill an island. The flooding of the lake left only 15 square kilometers of tropical forest on the island, but they contain 480 species of trees (more than in all of Europe), 70 species of bats, 384 species of birds, 30 species of frogs, 47 species of snakes, and on and on. Just accounting for the insects on the island is an overwhelming task. Take ants, for instance: More than 200 species have been identified so far.

Day visitors, as opposed to research scientists, can walk on only some trails, usually an interpretive loop that takes 2–3 hours to walk at an easy clip. It's fairly flat most of the way, but it does get muddy at times. There's a short side trail off the main loop that's well worth taking. It leads to the aptly named "Big Tree," a kapok (*Ceiba pentandra*) so huge other trees are growing on its branches.

Visitors are not allowed on the trails without a guide who knows the way. But consider buying *A Day on Barro Colorado Island* (Smithsonian), by Marina Wong and Jorge Ventocilla, anyway. It contains a trail guide and information on the island's flora and fauna that will help you get much more out of your visit. It's available for $7 at the little bookshop at STRI's main office in Panama City.

Note: BCI has the kind of wildlife many visitors come to the tropics to see, including tapirs, coatimundis, sloths, ocelots, anteaters, collared peccaries, and three species of monkeys. A jaguar made a brief appearance as recently as 1993. It swam over from the mainland, hung out for four months, and then vanished. But as STRI personnel will be the first to tell you, day visitors expecting a jungle crawling with creatures will likely be disappointed. One may see almost no animal life during a short visit to BCI. Chances will drop to near zero if you get stuck with a

© WILLIAM FRIAR

Barro Colorado Island, in the middle of the Panama Canal, is a world-famous tropical-biology reserve.

guide who insists on shouting nonstop, as a certain travel writer did. You have a better chance of seeing wildlife at the Canopy Tower, and day trips there are about the same price and much less hassle to arrange than visits to BCI.

The only mammals one is likely to encounter on a brief visit to BCI are agoutis and howler monkeys. It's actually hard not to stumble upon howlers. A 1977 census found 65 troops on the island, each with about 19 monkeys. Do the math. Their numbers haven't changed much since.

Access to the island is strictly controlled. Visitors must arrange a tour through STRI or an STRI-approved tour operator, and the few spaces available are often booked a year in advance. Cancellations are not uncommon, however, so even if you can't plan that far ahead it's worth checking with STRI to see if any last-minute spaces have opened up. Some tour operators offer trips to Barro Colorado Nature Monument, which includes the surrounding mainland as well as the island itself. Make sure the tour actually goes to the island if that's important to you.

The Smithsonian offers tours on Tuesday, Saturday, and Sunday. The cost is $70 per person ($40 for students) and includes a morning hike and lunch. This includes the launch from Gamboa to BCI, a 2–3-hour hike with a naturalist guide, a tour of the visitors center, and lunch at the field-research station (vegetarian food is available). It may be possible to chat up a research scientist over lunch. Reservations should be made as far ahead of time as possible. Credit cards and U.S. checks are accepted, but visitors can also pay in cash at the Earl S. Tupper Research and Conference Center, STRI's headquarters. (See the entry on STRI under *Information and Services* in the *Pacific Side Locks and Townsites* section for directions.) For reservations, contact tel. 212-8026, fax 212-8146, visitstri@tivoli.si.edu, www.stri.org. Ask for Patrizia Pinzón.

The launch to the island leaves from Gamboa, about a 45-minute drive from Panama City, at 7:15 A.M. on Tuesday and 8 A.M. on Saturday and Sunday. It's imperative that visitors arrive on time, as the launch to the island, about a 45-minute ride away, leaves on time. Visitors are responsible for their own transportation to Gamboa. (See the *Panama City* chapter for the schedule from the SACA bus terminal.) STRI can send would-be visitors an information sheet with directions and updated bus schedules.

RÍO CHAGRES

This powerful river supplies most of the water for the Panama Canal and much of the drinking water for Panama City. It once flowed unimpeded across the isthmus, emptying into the Caribbean below the ruins of Fuerte San Lorenzo near the city of Colón. The damming of the river near Gatún Locks created the massive Lago Gatún and today the river disappears into the lake at Gamboa and doesn't resurface until it approaches the Caribbean. But the upper reaches of the Chagres still wind their way through lovely rainforest. In the dry season, stretches of the river become little more than glorified puddles. In the rainy season, however, the Chagres can rise many meters in a single hour. Flash floods are not unknown.

Emberá Indians have been relocated from the Darién jungle in recent years to live in communities along the banks of the river surprisingly close to Panama City. The one most visited by tourists is Parara Puru. While these are true Emberá who cling to some of their traditional ways, visitors should note that the "village" is rather touristy and the elaborate traditional costumes they wear are put on for their benefit. Even the concept of a village is not a traditional part of Emberá culture; historically, families lived in relative isolation from each other. This community is reminiscent of La Chunga, in the Darién, in the way it caters to the tourist market.

Still, a trip up the river is beautiful and encounters with Emberá are always interesting. Visits to the community include dance demonstrations, a walk through a botanical garden, and a chance to buy *cocobolo* figurines, *tagua* nut carvings, woven baskets, and other handicrafts. Those inclined can have themselves painted with traditional *jagua* (a kind of vegetable dye) designs, but bear in mind the dye takes many days to fade and can't be washed off. Several tour operators offer trips up the Chagres to Parara Puru. **Aventuras Panama** (tel. 260-0044 or 236-5814,

The Panama Canal

fax 260-7535, info@aventuraspanama.com, www.aventuraspanama.com) offers an all-day excursion for $80 per person, three-person minimum. The trip includes lunch in the community. River rafting is also possible on the Chagres (see *Sports and Recreation*).

SPORTS AND RECREATION

Gamboa Rainforest Resort

The **aerial tram** is one of the star attractions of the resort. It's sort of like a ski lift that takes passengers up about 80 meters to a hill, passing through the canopy of a patch of secondary forest along the way. A bilingual naturalist guide travels along in each four- and five-person gondola to spot and describe flora and fauna. Passengers can get off at the top and climb a 30-meter observation tower that offers panoramic views of the canal, the Chagres, and the surrounding forest. The trip takes a little over an hour, not including the stop at the observation platform. Don't get your hopes up about seeing too much wildlife; these canopy trams are a comfortable way to experience tropical forest, but a quick zip through the trees is unlikely to net many encounters with animals. In two visits, my biggest scores have been a glimpse of the tail of a sleepy kinkajou in the crook of a tree, and a roadside encounter with a group of coatimundis on the ride back to the hotel. Unfortunately, the tram doesn't run in the early morning or evening, when chances of spotting wildlife would be best. The tram runs at 8:45A.M., 10:30 A.M., 1:30 P.M., and 3 P.M. Tuesday–Sunday, closed Monday. The ride costs $35 per person. Call tel. 314-9000 for reservations and information.

Before or after a tram ride it's worth wandering around the resort's **flora and fauna exhibits.** They're housed in a series of structures on the road leading up to the tram and include an orchid nursery, a serpentarium with impressive native and nonnative species, a butterfly house, and a small fresh-water aquarium that also contains crocodiles, caimans, and turtles. The "model Emberá village" nearby is rather hokey, but it's a chance to meet a few Emberá and buy their tightly woven baskets and other handicrafts.

You don't have to be a guest at the Gamboa Rainforest Resort (tel. 314-9000) to use its activities center or book its tours, which include bird-watching walks and night "safaris" on the lake. It rents kayaks ($10/hour), bicycles ($10/two hours), and other toys. The center is open every day 8 A.M.–6 P.M. You can also charter fishing boats here, but expect to pay a fortune. The cost is $125 for three hours or $175 for six hours for up to three people. This is several times what you'd pay to charter a more rustic boat and gear at the nearby public marina, even though these boats have access to the same fishing spots.

Fishing and Adventure Tours

That **marina** is just outside Gamboa, near the one-lane bridge across the Chagres River. Those wanting to fish should stop by at least a day ahead of time to work out a deal with one of the captains hanging around the dock. You need to be on the lake just before dawn; by midmorning the fish stop biting. A morning of fishing from about 5:30 A.M.–noon costs $40 for 2–3 people, $50 for four. Bait (about 100 minnows) is another $5. You can also just go for an exploratory cruise around Lago Gatún and/or the Chagres River. The price depends on how far you want to go.

Aventuras Panama (tel. 260-0044 or 236-5814, fax 260-7535, info@aventuraspanama .com, www.aventuraspanama.com) offers rafting trips on the Río Chagres. The rafting is usually quite gentle, with mostly Class II rapids and a few Class IIIs. It's not intended for those who need big white water. However, this is still a long, fairly rigorous trip and the Chagres, like any other powerful river, has seen its share of accidents and needs to be approached with respect. Clients are picked up from their hotel at 5 A.M. and driven into the highlands above Cerro Azul. From there, it's a 1.5-hour hike through the forest to the put-in spot. Rafters spend all day on the river, ending up in Lago Alajuela (also called Madden Lake) in the late afternoon. Clients are dropped back at their hotel around 7 P.M. The trip costs $125 per person, three-person minimum, and includes breakfast, lunch, and transfers. Clients must be between the ages of 12 and

70. The company offers many other tours, including rafting trips on the Mamoní and Río Grande and a boat ride up the Chagres to visit the Emberá community of Parara Puru.

ACCOMMODATIONS AND FOOD

To date there are only two hotels in the Gamboa area, but both are impressive, if expensive, places that are destinations in themselves. The only restaurants open to nonguests are at the Gamboa Rainforest Resort, though the Canopy Tower sometimes offers day passes that include a meal. It's also possible to camp in Parque Nacional Soberanía, but there are no facilities and this is a true tropical forest, with all the potential discomforts that implies.

Gamboa Rainforest Resort

The resort, (tel. 314-9000, U.S. toll-free tel. 877/800-1690, reservation@gamboaresort.com, www.gamboaresort.com, rates start at $132 s/d, including breakfast) is one of the boldest efforts to date to lure tourists to Panama. Spread over its 137 hectares are a slice of tropical forest with an aerial tram running through the canopy, a full-service spa, a 107-room hotel, an entire neighborhood of one- and two-bedroom "villas" converted from old Canal Zone housing, a huge swimming pool, tennis courts, three restaurants, traditionally dressed Emberá selling handicrafts at a pseudo-"model village," an orchid nursery, a snake house, an amphibian exhibit, several aquariums, a butterfly house, a marina, and on and on. Opened in 2000, it's a peculiar mixture of an ecotourism resort, luxury spa, and theme park.

The location couldn't be better: The resort was built right on the banks of the Chagres, one of Panama's most important rivers, and it is only a stroll away from Lago Gatún, where one can watch ships transiting the Panama Canal. It's bordered by Parque Nacional Soberanía, the major trails of which are just a few kilometers away, as is the Canopy Tower.

There are two basic kinds of accommodations. The first are in the main hotel overlooking the Río Chagres. There are four kinds of rooms

here, varying from a "garden view" room for $215 s/d to a "Tivoli master suite" for $440 s/d. All have balconies, air-conditioning, minibar, safe, cable TV, iron and ironing board, coffeemaker, and so on. Of these, the best cost-to-value ratio is achieved by the "deluxe river view" rooms, for $247 s/d. These are fairly spacious rooms with hammock-equipped balconies overlooking the Río Chagres and surrounding forest. Room quality is on a par with what one would find at a midlevel business hotel in the United States. All the rooms in the main hotel are pleasant and decorated in vaguely tropical style.

The price for the one-bedroom "villas" is a comparative bargain at $132 s/d. Whereas the rooms in the hotel are generic, these have character. They consist of renovated wooden buildings dating from the 1930s that actually housed Panama Canal employees and their families in the old Canal Zone days. The renovation was done in simple, cheerful good taste, from the rattan furniture to the historic canal clippings and sketches on the walls. All have sitting rooms and kitchenettes with microwaves, minifridges, and coffeemakers. They don't have a view of the river, but they're surrounded by trees. Why these are the "budget" accommodations is one of those mysteries of life in Panama. Two-bedroom villas run $187 s/d.

All kinds of multiday packages are available that combine stays with golfing, bird-watching, spa treatments, ecotours, and so on. The resort's activities center rents mountain bikes, kayaks, pedal boats, and other gear.

One bit of trivia worth mentioning: To the credit of the resort's builders, the plans for the main hotel were changed—apparently at considerable expense—to save an enormous tree growing on the site.

The food at the resort is hit or miss. Of the three restaurants, **Restaurante Los Lagartos** (tel. 276-6812) is the best option because of its terrific location. It's down the hill from the main hotel, built onto an attractive, open-walled wooden terrace that juts into the Río Chagres near where it empties into Lago Gatún. From their tables diners can sometimes see turtles, caimans, and the odd iguana sunbathing on the same log, peacock bass and tilapia nosing about in the shallows, and little blue herons and jacanas hunting for food among the floating vegetation. Though on my last visit the food seemed to have improved somewhat, this remains the only place in Panama I've ever had badly prepared corvina. Other offerings include attempts at variations on traditional Panamanian fare, such as a *sancocho* (a hearty stew) made with duck instead of chicken, but the simplest fare is probably the safest bet. Fixed-price menus that include an appetizer, main dish, dessert, and a drink cost $18. Sunday champagne brunch (11 A.M.–5 P.M.) is $25.

The **spa** at the Gamboa Rainforest Resort is also open to nonguests and offers a wide assortment of treatments and packages at U.S. prices, varying from manicures and massages to a full day of pampering.

Canopy Tower

The Canopy Tower (tel. 264-5720, 263-2784, or 214-9724 in Panama, U.S. fax 800/854-2597, birding@canopytower.com, www.canopytower .com, high-season canopy rooms cost $367.50 s/d including meals and guided walks; three-night minimum) is a special place. But prices in the high season (December–April) have skyrocketed as its fame has spread, and a stay now means a major splurge, especially during the high season.

The place is an old U.S. military radar tower that has been cleverly transformed into a 12-room hotel and wildlife observation platform high above the floor of a protected forest, Parque Nacional Soberanía. Visitors can look out the window of their room right into the forest or climb two more flights of stairs and actually look down on the canopy. In the middle distance one can see ships cruising through the Panama Canal and as far as Gaillard Cut. The Pacific Ocean and the high-rises of Panama City are in the far distance. The lights of the Puente Centenario, the new bridge over the canal near Pedro Miguel, make for an especially impressive sight at night. All this is just a half-hour drive from the city.

The five canopy rooms and the Blue Cotinga Suite are on the third floor. All are simple but cheerful and comfortable, with teak louvered doors and other touches that soften the utilitarian feel of the structure (the teak comes from a

commercial plantation belonging to the hotel's owner). Each room has two single beds with mosquito nets, ceiling fans, and a good hot-water bathroom. The Blue Cotinga Suite is a large room (34 square meters) that has a private balcony with a hammock swing. This is the fanciest place to stay at the tower. High-season rates are $420 s/d.

The tower is not air-conditioned so as not to scare away wildlife and separate guests from the sound of the forest. However, the elevation is high enough that, with the screened windows open and the ceiling fan on, it's quite comfortable. Those who like to sleep in late or are looking for a romantic getaway should note that the tower is made of metal and was not originally built as a lodge. Sound carries easily, and it's hard to sleep in with people clanking around above one's head. The walls and doors of the rooms are louvered to allow air to circulate, cutting down still more on privacy.

One flight up from the canopy rooms are the dining and living room, which offer a near 360-degree view. The living room has couches, ham-

The Canopy Tower is a unique eco-resort in the middle of a national park close to Panama City.

mocks, observation chairs, a telescope, and a small library. Guests can continue up to the roof, which is a great place to watch the sun rise and set over the forest, listen to the roar of howler monkeys, and watch for owls and other nocturnal creatures in the evening.

Another suite and five single rooms have recently been added on the level below the canopy rooms, about 5.5 meters above the hilltop. The Harpy Eagle Suite is a little smaller (27 square meters) and plainer than the Blue Cotinga Suite but goes for the same price: $420 s/d in the high season. The other five rooms were once used by guides. They are quite small (eight square meters, less than half the size of the canopy rooms), have a single bed, and share a bathroom. The high-season rate of $273 s/d is steep for such simple accommodations.

The rooms, however, are only a small part of a visit to the tower. Stays include all meals and two daily guided hikes into the national park on well-maintained trails. The food here is good, concentrating on simple but tasty local dishes. Tips for staff and birding guides are extra and encouraged.

Rates dip to $241.50/$304.50 s/d during the "migration season" (October–November) and to $183.75/$262.50 s/d in the "green season" (May–September). During these months, the minimum stay is two nights. There is no break for single occupancy during the high season. Special packages are sometimes available.

The chances of spotting birds and wildlife can plummet during or after a rain. But the "migration season," which occurs late in the rainy season, can actually be an exciting time to come. This is when raptors, including broad-winged hawks, Swainson's hawks, and turkey vultures, pass through Panama on their annual migration. Literally millions cross the isthmus in just a few weeks. On some days the sky is dotted with flocks so thick they look like black clouds. (See the *Know Panama* chapter for more information.)

The best way to get the most value for the money is to arrive at check-in time, 11 A.M., to settle in before lunch. Checkout is at 9 A.M., after breakfast.

The guided walks included with a stay are along Semaphore Hill Road and Plantation Road. The first is the 1.7-kilometer road leading down from the tower to the highway. The road can be deceptively slippery, so watch your step. Those not up to the walk down the hill and back, which some may find strenuous and steamy, can take the "rainfomobile" or "birdmobile" converted pickup-truck shuttles. The road meets up with the wide, flat Plantation Road, which leads back into Parque Nacional Soberanía. If it gets too hot, there's a lovely little waterfall 1.5 hours into the park where one can go for a splash. At sunrise the next morning guests can watch the forest action from the roof before a morning walk. The tower has a list compiled by the Smithsonian Tropical Research Institute that has identified 46 numbered tree species in the park.

Depending on how busy things are, the tower sometimes offers day tours for those who don't want to or can't afford to stay at the tower. Possibilities include a long breakfast (6:30–11 A.M.) or lunch (noon–5 P.M.) for $75 that includes a two-hour guided walk and a chance to view wildlife from the tower. An evening visit (5:30–9 P.M.), for $85, includes appetizers and dinner.

Guests are likely to see more wildlife while lounging in the tower than they would on many long hikes in remote areas. Within five minutes of my first visit I saw a tití monkey (Geoffroy's tamarin) and a host of other creatures. By the end of my second visit, I had seen a kinkajou, a dozen coatimundi moms and babies, a sloth, an unidentified snake, and innumerable birds (short-tailed hawk, three toucans in a single tree, dusky-capped flycatcher, white-whiskered puffbird, white-shouldered tanager, blue-crowned manakin, and on and on). At last count, bird-watchers had identified 283 species of birds just from the tower and Semaphore Hill Road.

The Canopy Tower is 25 kilometers from Panama City, about a half-hour drive. Those driving must take the left fork off Gaillard Highway after the railroad bridge and follow the road toward Gamboa. The well-marked turnoff to the Canopy Tower will be on the right 1.6 kilometers past Summit Botanical Gardens. There's a gate across the entrance to the tower road that you may have to open (and be sure to close). Go up the one-lane, well-maintained road 1.7 kilometers to the tower. Note: The tower is far from being wheelchair-accessible. Access to the top of the tower is by stairs—five dozen of them.

Call or email as far ahead as possible to make reservations, even for day trips, as the tower remains popular even as prices climb. Children 13 and younger are not allowed.

GETTING THERE AND AROUND

The end of the road in Gamboa is about a 45-minute drive from Panama City. Taxis charge around $20 one-way. Buses leave from the SACA Bus Terminal in Panama. (See the *Panama City* chapter for schedules.) Gamboa-bound buses take passengers within reasonable walking distance of every attraction in the area except for the Camino de Cruces. None of them is close to each other, though, so it's not feasible to walk from one attraction to the next. Buses to and from Gamboa stop at designated bus stops along Gaillard Highway about every half hour during daylight hours,

but this can be a time-consuming way to visit the various spots. Those who can afford it should consider hiring a taxi for a half-day or full-day tour.

Those driving from Panama City should head west on Gaillard Highway. Just past Pedro Miguel the road summits a small hill and then crosses under a narrow underpass, a railroad bridge with "1929" carved into it. The ANAM office that sells hiking and camping permits is at the fork. Straight leads into Madden Forest, a part of Parque Nacional Soberanía. Here's where you'll find the Camino de Cruces (Las Cruces Trail). A left turn at the fork keeps you on Gaillard Highway and leads to Summit Botanical Gardens, Plantation Road, the Canopy Tower, and Sendero El Charco, in that order. Just before the one-lane bridge over the Chagres River is the public marina, where boats and captains can be hired to explore the Chagres and Lago Gatún or do some fishing. Crossing over the bridge (caution: Be sure to stop if the red light is on) leads into the town of Gamboa, where the road ends. An immediate right turn leads up to the Gamboa Rainforest Resort. Staying straight leads to the launch to Barro Colorado Island and Pipeline Road.

Isla Taboga

Taboga is the most easily accessible island from Panama City. It's just 12 nautical miles away, a trip that takes about an hour by ferry. It's a pretty, quaint little island. If you squint, the look of the town—with its whitewashed walls, curving walkways and staircases, and flowering trees—may remind you of a Greek island.

Taboga is home to a full-time population and attracts many weekend visitors. It's an appealing place but inspires a nostalgic affection somewhat out of proportion to its modern-day charms, especially for those who like deserted, pristine shores. Beaches here are okay, if a bit rocky, but they can get relatively crowded on dry-season weekends, and some trash does wash up from Panama City.

Since you can explore Taboga's attractions in a day and there aren't many facilities on the is-

land, you may not want to bother spending the night. But it is a good place for a day trip, especially for those with limited time who need a quick island fix.

The ferry ride over is half the fun of a Taboga visit. It leads past the Pacific entrance to the Panama Canal, under the Bridge of the Americas, and along the Causeway. You can occasionally see dolphins on the way over, and if you're very, very lucky you may spot a Sei or humpback whale.

An awful lot of history has passed through Taboga since the Spaniards first came calling in the early 16th century. The current town was founded in 1524, and the simple white church on its high street claims to be the second oldest in the Western Hemisphere. Francisco de Pizarro is said to have stopped by Taboga on his way to destroy the Inca Empire. Besides the conquistadors, its visitors have numbered pirates, '49ers, and workers on both the French and American canals, including one by the name of Paul Gauguin. Canal workers recovered from their illnesses at a convalescent hospital that has long since disappeared.

A water festival in honor of the Virgen del Carmen is celebrated on Taboga every July 16.

SIGHTS

The main beaches are on either side of the floating pier, where the ferries arrive. The more attractive one, **Playa La Restinga,** is in front of the Hotel Taboga. A right turn as one leaves the pier leads along an ocean path shaded by tamarind trees. The path ends at the grounds to the hotel. Visitors can either pay $7 to use the facilities, or take a right turn down to the public entrance to the beach. Remember: All beaches in Panama are public. Avoid the stretch of beach on the far left side of the Hotel Taboga as you face the ocean; the smell of sewage will tell you why. At low tide it's possible to walk across a sandbar from Playa La Restinga to the neighboring islet of El Morro. Note that the sandbar disappears at high tide.

The town itself is quite attractive and worth exploring. There are two main roads, a high street and a low street, which are easy to walk on since there are few cars on the island. Both roads are to the left of the pier as one leaves the ferry. When the jasmine, oleander, bougainvillea, and hibiscus are in bloom, you'll understand why Taboga is called "the Island of Flowers." Houses tend to be well-maintained and quaint. When Paul Gauguin first left Europe for the tropics he was so taken with Taboga that he tried to buy land here. However, he was broke and ended up having to help dig the Panama Canal instead, a job that he detested. He never could afford Taboga's prices and soon sailed on. He eventually found Tahiti, and the rest is art history. There's a plaque commemorating his stay, from May to July 1887, on the high street one block uphill from the Hotel Chu. It's by some picturesque Spanish ruins that in turn are next to a lovely garden filled with a rainbow of flowering plants.

The quaint, white-washed **church** in the center of town was originally made out of wood, erected after the founding of Taboga in 1524. Taboga is a hilly island that lends itself to walks on which you're likely to come across old grave sites, abandoned U.S. military bunkers, and the overgrown remains of Spanish fortifications, in addition to a bit of wildlife. The cemetery, on the edge of the ocean toward the end of the road, makes for a picturesque amble.

It's possible to take a moderately strenuous walk to the top of **Cerro de la Cruz,** which, as the name implies, is topped by a cross. There's a good view of the ocean from here. The south side of the island, together with neighboring Isla Urabá, is part of a national wildlife refuge that protects the nesting area of an important brown pelican colony.

As with everywhere else in Panama, beaches are public and free. But many day-trippers opt to pay the $7 fee ($5 for kids) at the entrance to Hotel Taboga to use its beach-side facilities, which include access to shelters and hammocks, bathrooms, showers, and changing rooms. The fee also includes $3 in "Taboga dollar" vouchers to be used at the hotel, including the cafeteria. Use of the medium-sized pool is $2. Locker rental is $1. The hotel rents two-person sea kayaks for $7 an hour. There's a pleasant garden on the grounds, but macaws and toucans are kept in painfully small cages. The beach that faces the mainland is rocky and attracts some litter, not to mention an alarming smell of sewage at low tide. Those who want to go for a wade should do so on the side facing into the island.

ACCOMMODATIONS AND FOOD

Taboga has a dearth of decent places to stay and eat. Most people will be content with a day trip, and it's worth considering packing a lunch.

The main place to stay is **Hotel Taboga** (tel. 264-6096 Panama City reservations, or 250-2122 on Taboga, htaboga@sinfo.net, $50 s/d), down the path on the right as one leaves the ferry. It offers 54 basic and drab but otherwise passable rooms with air-conditioning. It's overpriced for what you get. There's a **cafeteria** offering greasy chow mein, fried food, and other basic items for about $4–9. It's open 7 A.M.–8:45 P.M. Sunday–Friday, 7 A.M.–9:45 P.M. Saturday and holidays. There are also several ultrabasic *fondas* at the entrance to the hotel.

The **Hotel Chu** (tel. 250-2035), about a 10-minute walk along the oceanfront road, is living a twilight existence, and it has been denounced in news reports the last couple of years as a place frequented by unsavory sorts. I can no longer recommend it as a place to stay. The terrace restaurant at the hotel also continues to deteriorate. If you eat there, don't peek in the kitchen. The **Bar El Galeon** is downstairs from the main hotel, with a back porch that overlooks the water. It draws a rough, hard-drinking crowd and is probably not the best place for a foreign visitor to hang out. The hotel is mentioned here simply because there are so few options for those who get stranded, though it's always possible the place will have been revamped by the time you arrive.

Donde Pope Si Hay (8 A.M.–9 P.M. Thurs.–Sun.) is easily the most pleasant place to eat on the island. Though that doesn't say much, the owner (nicknamed Pope) has created a cheerful, open-air café about 25 meters before the Hotel Chu. Food includes rice with *guandu* (a kind of bland pea), *patacones,* fried chicken, fried beef, pork chops, corvina, and so on. A full meal costs $3.25–5.

GETTING THERE AND AWAY

Ferries leave from Muelle 19 (Pier 19) in Balboa. A taxi from just about anywhere in Panama City should cost less than $4. There is parking near the pier for those who drive.

Ferry schedules are more theoretical than real; service is erratic. Make a reservation or show up early on dry-season weekends and holidays to be sure of getting a ticket—it's a popular day-trip destination for Panamanians. Also, since there's no assigned seating, be sure to board in time to claim a spot out of the sun—it's easy to get fried before you even hit the beach.

The *Calypso Queen* (tel. 232-5736 or 264-6096, fax 223-0116) goes to Taboga at 8:30 A.M. Tuesday–Friday, returning at 4:30 P.M. On Saturday, Sunday, and holidays it leaves at 7:45 A.M., 10:30 A.M., and 4:30 P.M., returning at 9 A.M., 3 P.M., and 5:45 P.M. It does not operate on Monday. The trip takes about an hour and the fare is $5/$10 one-way/round-trip.

The boat ride is part of the Taboga experience, but if you're in a hurry you can try a newer service, **Expreso del Pacifico** (tel. 261-0350 or 229-1742). For the same price charged by the slower ferries it offers a big speedboat and claims to make the trip in 20 minutes, but the first—and last—time I tried it the trip took 35 minutes. I can't recommend these guys because when the wind picks up just a little bit it's a wet, wild ride. Neither the captain nor crew inspired much confidence, and there was one life jacket for every dozen passengers. But those looking for an adrenaline rush can take their chances. It has departures to Taboga at 6 A.M., 8:30 A.M., 1:45 P.M. and 3 P.M. Monday–Friday. Return trips are at 9:45 A.M. and 3:45 P.M. Departures on Saturday and Sunday are at 8:30 A.M., 10:15 A.M., 3 P.M., and 5 P.M. The boat returns at 9:15 A.M., 2 P.M., 4 P.M., and 6 P.M.

Central Caribbean Coast

The strip of Caribbean coastline that stretches from the mouth of the Río Chagres east toward the border of the Comarca de Kuna Yala is rich in history and even richer in natural beauty. Evidence of the former include the well-preserved ruins of Spanish forts, built to protect looted Inca treasure, as well as some of the most awe-inspiring structures of the Panama Canal. The area's natural attractions can be found among the mangroves, coral reefs, beaches, and forests that still abound with wildlife. Scuba diving and snorkeling are popular and easily accessible in the warm Caribbean waters, home to brilliant tropical fish and ancient shipwrecks that are still being discovered. All this is within a two-hour drive from Panama City.

The Portobelo area in particular has long been a favorite place for Panamanian and American locals to enjoy water sports, especially scuba diving.

M ust-Sees

Look for **M** to find the sights and activities you can't miss and **N** for the best dining and lodging.

© WILLIAM FRIAR

The Real Aduana de Portobelo, Portobelo's custom house, held great treasure during the Spanish era.

M Gatún Locks: The largest (one mile long) and most impressive set of locks at the Panama Canal, raising and lowering ships 85 feet in three giant steps (page 138).

M Gatún Dam: Once the world's largest earthen dam, it's right next door to Gatún Locks and is an impressive sight when the spillway is open (page 140).

M Fuerte San Lorenzo and Área Protegida San Lorenzo: A surprisingly intact Spanish fort at the mouth of the Río Chagres and the end of the fabled

Camino de Cruces, in the heart of one of Panama's newest protected forests, Área Protegida San Lorenzo (page 140).

M Portobelo Ruins: The battered remains of one of the most important, pirate-pestered ports in the Spanish empire (page 143).

M Church and Museum of the Black Christ: Home to Panama's most revered Catholic icon, the Black Christ, and the epicenter of its most spectacular religious festival (page 145).

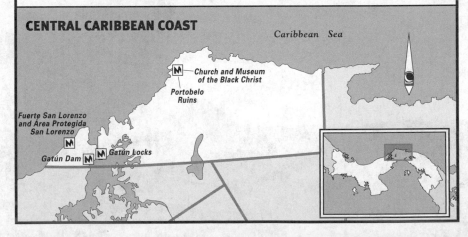

CENTRAL CARIBBEAN COAST

Caribbean Sea

Church and Museum of the Black Christ

Portobelo Ruins

Fuerte San Lorenzo and Área Protegida San Lorenzo

Gatún Dam Gatún Locks

CENTRAL CARIBBEAN COAST

Caribbean Sea

Isla Grande
La Guaira
Bahía San Cristóbal
Puerto Lindo
Nombre de Dios
Viento Frío
Palenque
Miramar
Cuango
Playa Chiquita
Santa Isabel
Palmira

Gulfo de San Blas
Cartí

COMARCA DE KUNA YALA

Río Cuango

PANAMÁ

INTERAMERICANA
El Llano
Chepo
1

Parque Nacional Chagres

To Panama City

Lago Alajuela (Madden Lake)

Parque Nacional Portobelo

Portobelo

⬛ CHURCH AND MUSEUM OF THE BLACK CHRIST

⬛ PORTOBELO RUINS

COLÓN

TRANS-ISTMICA

Sabanitas

3

Monumento Nacional Isla Barro Colorado

Colón
Bahía Limón

⬛ FUERTE SAN LORENZO

⬛ ÁREA PROTEGIDA SAN LORENZO

⬛ GATÚN LOCKS

Gatún

⬛ GATÚN DAM

Lago Gatún

10 mi

10 km

0

0

© AVALON TRAVEL PUBLISHING, INC.

While the diving and visibility is better elsewhere, it's quite convenient here. Other dive spots include the waters around Isla Grande, which also has one surf break.

This is prime bird-watching country. The Audubon Society once identified 350 species on a single day during its annual Christmas Bird Count. Other activities include organized walks through the forest and a short boat ride to the mouth of the historic Río Chagres.

PLANNING YOUR TIME

All the attractions described in this chapter are in Colón Province, which lies along the central Caribbean coast of Panama. Its capital is Colón, historically Panama's second-most important city. (Please note: Though this chapter includes information on Colón, it is a very dangerous city. Foreign visitors should avoid it.)

Though this area starts just 80 kilometers north of Panama City, it has long been neglected and has significantly fewer resources and facilities than the Pacific side of the isthmus. A few tour operators, especially dive operators, specialize in the area, but it is still relatively off the beaten track for most tourists. Consider renting a car to explore this area, as public transportation between different destinations can be a hassle.

The stretch of coast east of Colón is known as Costa Arriba, which includes Portobelo, Nombre de Dios and its neighboring villages, and La Guaira, the jumping-off point for Isla Grande. For most of the way this is a lovely drive: It's quite striking to zip along the lush, quiet coastline and suddenly come upon the ruins of ancient Spanish forts. A large swath of this area is part of Parque Nacional Portobelo, whose boundaries extend into the surrounding waters. The park is under a lot of pressure from the surrounding human populations.

Most visitors to the central Caribbean side of the isthmus come just for the day and return to Panama City at night. It's possible to take in **Portobelo**, the attractions near the Atlantic entrance to the Panama Canal (most notably **Gatún Locks** and **Gatún Dam**), and **Fuerte**

San Lorenzo in a single day. However, it would be a long day, with lots of driving, and it's probably too ambitious for those relying solely on public transportation. Consider striking either Portobelo or Fuerte San Lorenzo off the itinerary or plan to spend the night. One approach for a longer visit is to stay a night or two on Isla Grande, stopping at Portobelo on the way over and visiting San Lorenzo and the canal-area attractions on the way back to Panama City.

If at all possible, take the train across the isthmus at least one-way. It's by far the most scenic and pleasant way to make the trip. Since the **passenger train** is mainly for commuters, it's possible to take the train over in the early morning, hire a taxi to explore the area, and then take the train back in the late afternoon.

Those interested in adding outdoor activities such as scuba diving, birding, or boating to a visit should plan to spend at least one night in the area to have any time to see the sights.

Especially popular spots for birding include what is now the **Área Protegida San Lorenzo** and the **Achiote and Escobal Roads,** in Costa Abajo west of Colón. The roads to Achiote and Escobal start just past Gatún Dam, though they can be tough to drive, particularly in the rainy season. Bird-watchers should go with an experienced guide. Hard-core birders may be interested in spending the night in the area. There is now a rustic dormitory, supported by local residents, where birders can spend the night for a small fee. For details, contact the nonprofit CEASPA (Centra de Estudios y Acción Social Panameño) in Panama City at tel. 226-6602, ceaspa@cwpanama.net, or sherman@sanlorenzo.org.pa).

Rainfall is far more plentiful on the Caribbean side than the Pacific side of the isthmus. It averages 3.2 meters in Colón, nearly twice as much as in Panama City. For those not metrically inclined, that's more than 10 *feet* of rain a year. The dry season is also not as well-defined on the Caribbean as the Pacific side. In Portobelo, one of the wettest spots in Panama, it rains nearly year-round, as many a miserable Spanish soldier standing guard against pirates learned to his dismay in the days of the conquistadors.

HISTORY

In 1501, Rodrigo de Bastidas, the first European to stumble upon the isthmus of Panama, explored the coastline from the Darién at least as far west as what is now known as Nombre de Dios. One of the sailors on this two-ship voyage of exploration was Vasco Núñez de Balboa, who years later would lay eyes for the first time on the Pacific Ocean, changing this quiet stretch of coast, and the history of Panama, forever.

Christopher Columbus explored the rest of the Caribbean coastline during his fourth and final voyage to the New World, which left Spain on May 11, 1502. His most glorious days behind him, Columbus sailed with four dilapidated ships east down the Caribbean coast of the isthmus. He stopped first at Bocas del Toro, in western Panama near what is now the Costa Rican border, where he discovered indigenous people wearing gold jewelry. This fascinated his crew far more than his quest for a passage to Asia.

Columbus arrived at Portobelo on November 2, 1502, and traded with indigenous people until November 9, when he set out east again. But he was forced to halt his explorations at Nombre de Dios, where his ships sheltered from a terrible storm for 14 days. This essentially marked the end of Columbus's attempts to find a passage to the Indies.

Columbus sailed back west and anchored his remaining ships near the mouth of the Río Belén, on the border between the modern-day provinces of Colón and Veraguas, on Epiphany, January 6, 1503. He established the first European settlement on the isthmus, Santa María de Belén, and attempted to leave his brother Bartholomew in charge. Almost immediately, however, battles with the indigenous population, led by a chief known to history only as "the Quibián," brought this first Spanish foothold in Panama to a bloody end. Columbus

sailed back to Jamaica with two barely seaworthy ships, having been forced to abandon the *Gallega* at the mouth of the Belén and the *Vizcaina* somewhere near Portobelo, and died in Spain shortly thereafter, on May 20, 1506.

In 1998, an American yachtie who was lobster-diving with his son came across an ancient shipwreck off Playa Damas, near Nombre de Dios. The ship is believed to date from the early 16th century. Tests are still being conducted to determine if this is the wreck of the *Vizcaina*. These include such arcane methods as trying to trace the age and origin of the timbers and link them with the European forests Columbus's shipbuilders would have used. As a potentially priceless national and world treasure, the wreck is off-limits to divers. Even if it turns out not to be the *Vizcaina,* it's a historically important find.

During the Spanish-colonial era, this stretch of coast became one of the most strategically important areas in the entire Spanish Empire. It was here that most of the incredible treasure of the Incas was brought after being shipped up from South America. From there, Spanish ships transported them to Europe. The loot was carried across the isthmus by two different routes. The first was the **Camino Real,** a narrow, muddy trail to Nombre de Dios and, after that port was abandoned, to Portobelo. The second route was by land for about a third of the way across the isthmus and then down the Río Chagres to the coast. Parts of this second route, the **Camino de Cruces (Las Cruces Trail)** still exist and can be walked to this day.

All that wealth made the Caribbean coast a target of pirates and buccaneers for hundreds of years. The Spanish fortresses were constantly under siege and taken several times. The most famous adventurer of them all, Sir Francis Drake, died here in 1596. His leaded coffin, which has never been found, is said to be lying somewhere in the waters off Portobelo, the site of some of his most famous exploits.

Colón

Though the city of Colón (pop. 42,133, co-LONE in Spanish and kah-LAWN in English) has a long, colorful history, I strongly advise avoiding it. For one thing, it has little to offer tourists, and one can get to all the region's sights without ever stopping here. But more important, it's just too dangerous. Extreme unemployment and poverty give this crumbling city a terrible reputation as a place where it's a surprise if you *don't* get mugged at knifepoint. Colón loyalists argue these fears are exaggerated, but they tend to follow that up by saying visitors should have no problem—as long as they take taxis everywhere and never set foot on the streets.

Colón's dangers can be deceptive. On a sunny day, it looks like a colorful, mellow old place with wooden shanties, little different from any number of shabby Caribbean towns. During the week, one can see little schoolgirls in spotless uniforms traipsing to and from school alone. They're probably safe: You aren't. You're the one with money.

The mugging method of choice is to sneak up behind a victim and hold a knife to his or her throat. During a recent visit to Panama, I heard more of these violent stories than ever before. One happened to a friend of a friend, a former Colón resident who wanted to pay his beloved city a visit. He was robbed in the middle of the day while chatting with old friends on the sidewalk. I also heard a story, that I wasn't able to confirm, about some cruise passengers who were robbed inside a church while trying to do some sightseeing. Ships' crew members have been mugged walking to McDonald's. And on and on it goes.

Panama's 2000 census put unemployment in Colón at 18 percent, one of the highest rates in the country, though that still seems low compared with the evidence of one's eyes. And that was even before fallout from the recent downturn in the world economy. There's always talk about revitalizing Colón, but little ever seems to change for the better. The latest effort is a cruise-ship port at the heart of a controversial tourism project called **Colón 2000.** In its first few years of

The city of Colón has suffered from decades of neglect.

© WILLIAM FRIAR

COLÓN

Caribbean Sea

Bahía de Manzanillo

PASEO WASHINGTON

WASHINGTON HOTEL

CALLE 1
CALLE 2
CALLE 3
CALLE 4
CALLE 5
CALLE 6
CALLE 7
CALLE 8
CALLE 9
CALLE 10
CALLE 11
CALLE DE LESSEPS

MERYLAND HOTEL

PASEO GORGAS

COLÓN 2000 ★

AV ROOSEVELT

AV SANTA ISABEL

AV MELENDEZ

HOTEL CARLTON

PASEO DEL CENTENARIO

AV AMADOR GUERRERO

AV BOLIVAR

AV DEL FRENTE

CALLE 12
CALLE 13
CALLE 14
CALLE 15
CALLE 16
CALLE 17

ZONA LIBRE DE COLÓN

BUS TERMINAL

PANAMA CANAL YACHT CLUB

To Transístmica

Bahía Limón

0   400 yds
0   400 m

© AVALON TRAVEL PUBLISHING, INC.

Central Caribbean Coast

COLÓN'S NOTORIOUS, COLORFUL PAST

For most of its history, Colón has been known as a place to avoid. Even the intrepid Columbus decided to steer clear of the area when he and his crew became the first Europeans to see Isla Manzanillo. All they saw was a pestilential swamp filled with mosquitoes, snakes, caimans, and who knew what else.

Throughout the Spanish colonial era, the Colón area was largely ignored. The Spanish built their forts at San Lorenzo to the west and Portobelo and Nombre de Dios to the east.

It wasn't until an American company began work on the Panama Railroad in 1850 that people started living and working on the island and built the foundations of the city of Colón. The railroad had its Caribbean terminus nearby, and a settlement sprang up to house the employees and cater to the 49ers, who gladly paid the then-exorbitant sum of $25 to take the train to the Pacific side of the isthmus in their dash to the California gold fields.

A nameless boomtown sprang up on Isla Manzanillo, but it was a squalid place notorious as a sink of vice and filth. There was no sewage or drainage system. Everything, including dead animals, was just tossed onto the unpaved streets or into the sea. And during the French era, so much wine was consumed in Colón that an entire street, still known by some as Bottle Alley, was paved with inverted wine bottles.

"Searching for the specialty in which [the town] excelled," wrote a disgusted 19th-century historian, H.H. Bancroft, "we found it in her carrion birds, which cannot be surpassed in size or smell. Manzanillo Island may boast of the finest vultures on the planet . . . The very ground on which one trod was pregnant with disease, and death was distilled in every breath of air."

The town did not even merit a name until 1852, when it was dubbed Aspinwall in honor of one of the founders of the railroad. Panama was still a part of Colombia at the time, and officials in Bogotá rejected the name, insisting it be called Colón, the Spanish name for Colombus. A feud over the name erupted between the Panama Railroad Company and Bogotá, resulting in much confusion until 1890, when the Colombian government began rejecting any letters with "Aspinwall" on the envelope. The railroad company finally gave in.

Colón's fortunes declined following the gold rush, but they revived again in the 1880s when the French began their doomed attempt to build a sea-level canal. Colón residents would later reminisce about this as a time when champagne was in far greater supply than the suspect local water. Then Colón burned to the ground in 1885 during the so-called Prestán Uprising (see the *Know Panama* chapter) and was rebuilt, primarily by the Panama Railroad Company. It wasn't until the French effort collapsed and the U.S. effort began that Colón began to be cleaned up and transformed into a modern city. The gringos installed sewers and plumbing, paved the streets, drained the swamps, and sanitized the whole place.

For the first half of the 20th century, Colón became a rather picturesque little city of three-story wooden buildings with long verandahs, and white, neo-classical concrete buildings erected by the Isthmian Canal Commission. Front Street, which faced the railroad tracks and the port of Cristóbal, boasted elegant shops.

Since Colombus' full name in Spanish is Cristóbal Colón, the port town across the street from Colón in the Canal Zone was dubbed Cristóbal. During the French canal era Cristóbal was known as Cristophe-Colomb.

As Panama City and the Pacific side of the isthmus grew in importance, Colón again deteriorated. Toward the end of the 20th century, it became dangerous for visitors to wander past Front Street. Now, it's foolish even to venture that far. The fancy shops have long since disappeared.

operation, it hadn't seemed to have made a dent in Colón's poverty. The best bet for the foreseeable future, sadly, is to stay well away from the city.

For those who insist on visiting, perhaps because the near-certainty of a life-threatening attack sounds like fun, the hotels and restaurants below are the best bets. Shopping at the **Colón Free Zone** and **Colón 2000** is also reasonably safe.

At the very least, do not walk around Colón: Drive or take taxis everywhere.

Colón is technically built on a one-square-mile island, Isla Manzanillo, though it's separated from the mainland only by the overgrown Fork River. The city is essentially on a peninsula.

It's laid out on a grid, with streets running west-east and broad avenues running north-south. Avenida de Frente, or Front Street, delineates its western boundary, facing the old Canal Zone port town of Cristóbal. The venerable old Washington Hotel is to the north. The Colón Free Zone and the Colón 2000 cruise-ship port and shopping center are on its eastern edge.

ENTERTAINMENT AND EVENTS

One special day in Colón's history is November 5. On that day in 1903, separatists in Colón used a young woman, 18-year-old Aminta Melendez, to smuggle a message to conspirators in Panama City about a plot to disarm Colombian troops that had landed in Colón to put down Panama's incipient revolution. Melendez was the daughter of Porfirio Melendez, Colón's police chief and one of the separatists. The plot was never acted upon, but Aminta's bravery is still celebrated every November 5 as part of Colón's independence celebrations. Throughout her life, it was traditional for the president of Panama to visit her home to pay homage. Oddly, for a country that loves celebrations, this is not a national holiday, something that annoys beleaguered Colón boosters, who often lobby for the event's national recognition.

SHOPPING

There are only two places in Colón that are safe places for tourists to shop: the Zona Libre and Colón 2000.

Zona Libre de Colón

The Zona Libre de Colón is the world's second-largest free-trade zone, after Hong Kong. A free zone is an area where goods can be imported and exported free from customs duties. Each year about $10 billion worth of goods move through its 1,000 companies, which employ an estimated 15,000 permanent workers and thousands more temporary ones. It was opened in 1948.

This isn't just some sort of oversized shopping mall: It's a shopping city within a city, one far wealthier and better maintained than the real city that surrounds it. It's huge—400 hectares—and is one of the most important contributors to Panama's GNP. Goods come mainly from Hong Kong, Japan, and the United States and go mainly to Central and South America.

The downturn in the world economy, and the relaxing of tariffs throughout Latin America, has hit the Zona Libre hard. It's working quickly to find ways to remain competitive in the 21st century, partly by repositioning itself as a "global logistics center," taking advantage of its proximity to the canal and its expertise in handling merchandise to become a modern commercial distribution hub for the Americas.

The Zona Libre is primarily aimed at international wholesalers, not consumers. Individuals can shop at some stores there, but getting in and around the place, and getting purchases out, is a hassle. Think twice before going to the trouble: Many goods are just as cheap and far easier to get at airport duty-free stores or even at discount houses back home.

Cruise-ship passengers don't come here often, and stores aren't really set up to deal with them and deliver their purchases to ships. Passengers mostly go to the duty-free shops at Colón 2000, though the Zona Libre's prices are generally better.

Private cars and taxis are not allowed inside the free zone, which is just as well because the streets inside it are permanently gridlocked with commercial vehicles. There are parking lots just outside the zone. These are fairly safe, but be alert for muggers.

The main entrance to the Zona Libre is at the intersection of Avenida Roosevelt and Calle 13.

It's a maze inside, and streets are not well marked. Ask for directions to particular stores.

Visitors need a permit to enter the Zona Libre. The office is on the right as one faces the main gate. Have passports and return flight information handy. Be prepared for a long wait in line.

Good values inside the zone include 10-, 14-, and 18-karat gold, jewelry, cosmetics, liquor, high-end handbags, high-end scarves, watches, and stereo equipment. Digital cameras, at least so far, are not a great deal. Gold jewelry is sold by weight depending on the purity.

One store worth checking out is **Motta International** (tel. 433-6000, 433-2000, 441-5355, fax 441-4438, www.motta-int.com, info@motta-int.com), a major and long-established Free Zone player not far from the main entrance. Motta carries a little bit of a lot of things, including watches, perfume, liquor, electronics, clothing accessories, and crystal. Sample brand names: Cartier, Lalique, Mont Blanc, CK, Fendi, Limoges Castel, Baccarat, and Camusso. The atmosphere is pleasant and the service gracious. Several gold shops are nearby.

Once you've made a purchase, you can't just waltz outside the Zona Libre with it. Remember, this is a free-trade zone and purchases are meant for export only. For those flying out of the country, stores will deliver purchases to the airport for pick-up on the day of the flight. Stores tend to charge a minimum of $15 for delivery and need at least two days to deliver the goods.

Here's the drill: Give the store clerk the flight information after making a purchase. He or she produces a receipt. On the day of the flight, arrive at the airport early and take the receipt to the Equipaje Acompañado office, which is downstairs and to the right of the main terminal as one faces the airport. Present passports and tickets. The office is a sketchy-looking place and it'll feel like a minor miracle when someone actually produces the merchandise. There's a $3–5-a-day storage charge, so try not to buy things too far in advance of your departure. Allow plenty of time to transact all this business.

Some unwilling to jump through all these hoops smuggle goods out of the zone. After all, how can anyone tell when and where that gold necklace you're wearing was bought? But note that everyone leaving the zone is subject to search, and anyone caught with *contrabando* can be charged with a crime.

Restaurants are not allowed in the zone, but there's a falafel stand right outside a jewelry store called Super Gold and across the street from a large department store called Rosen. A falafel sandwich costs $3, which goes nicely with a $1 glass of fresh-squeezed orange juice.

Free Zone hours are generally 8 A.M.–5 P.M. Monday–Friday. Only a few shops are open on the weekend.

Colón 2000

The cruise port/shopping mall Colón 2000, opened in (surprise!) 2000, was supposed to attract fleets of cruise ships to Colón and breathe life into the local economy. So far it hasn't happened. Not many ships are stopping, and the complex itself ended up far more modest than glitzy artist renderings suggested. A planned Radisson hotel has so far failed to materialize.

Besides a handful of duty-free shops and some souvenir-trinket stores, the complex includes an enormous Super 99 grocery store, a Western Union branch, a Cable and Wireless office, and a couple of places to eat. (See *Accommodations and Food* and *Services* for information.)

During the main cruise season (approximately October–May), folkloric dancers perform for the tourists when a ship is in port. The place is pretty deserted when ships don't show up, and stores are having a rough time holding on.

ACCOMMODATIONS AND FOOD

There are several places to stay in Colón. The three listed below are the best and safest. Those staying in Colón should eat at their hotel. Otherwise, a reasonably safe dining option away from downtown Colón is **Café Iguana** (tel. 447-3570 and 447-3956, 10 A.M.–10 P.M. Mon.–Sat., closed Sun.), in the Colón 2000 cruise port/shopping center. It's upstairs and on the right as one faces the complex. It's a simple but pleasant place to eat if the air conditioner's working, with photos from the Panama Canal construction era on the wall and Middle Eastern music on the stereo. People come here for the Lebanese food, but other options include Mexican food, sandwiches, burgers, fish, meats, and pastas. Most dishes are $4–12. If nothing on the menu looks appealing, there's also a Subway sandwich shop in the Colón 2000 complex.

The nicest place to stay in Colón is the **☒ Meryland Hotel** (corner of Calle 7 and Santa Isabel next to Parque Sucre, tel. 441-7044, 441-5309, 441-7127, 441-7128, or 441-7149, fax 441-0705, $38.50 s/$44 d). The hotel was built in 2000 in a quiet, sparsely settled part of town. There's a long, narrow park outside and lots of schoolkids passing by on school days. It definitely feels like the safest place to stay in town. It's a modern, clean place with cheerful neo-Spanish colonial decor featuring lots of glossy tile and ornate iron fixtures. Amazingly, the paint in the rooms started peeling soon after the hotel opened. Mattresses are very firm. All rooms have air-conditioning, cable TV, and phones. There's room service from the restaurant on the premises, which is open until midnight. Internet access is $3 an hour. Some of the houses near the hotel used to be quarters for Panama Canal employees during the Canal Zone days.

The **Washington Hotel,** (2nd Street at the northwest end of Colón, tel. 441-7133, fax 441-7397, $38.50 s $44 d) is now officially known as the New Washington Hotel, but no one will ever call it that. Built by the United States in 1913 on the site of a Panama Railroad Company guesthouse erected in 1870, it was once one of Panama's grand hotels. It was built at the order of President William H. Taft, a frequent visitor to Panama during canal construction days, first as Secretary of War and then as president. The hotel has hosted two American presidents (Taft and Warren Harding), a British prime minister (David Lloyd George), Will Rogers, Bob Hope, Al Jolson, and others. But its decay has mirrored that of Colón itself. The Spanish-inspired colonial building and common areas are still lovely, if tattered, with brass railings, wrought ironwork,

chandeliers, painted wooden beams, and marble stairs. And the hotel is built right on the edge of the sea, with a view of ships at anchor waiting to transit the canal. But the "new" rooms are still drab and musty, with spongy beds. They're large, however, and come with a minifridge. There are a bar, casino, nightclub, and a large pool. It's definitely worth a quick visit for those in the neighborhood, but most would probably prefer staying in the less historic but more comfortable surroundings of the Meryland Hotel, which has comparable rates. Note that even though the hotel feels safely removed from downtown, there have been reports of muggings on its spacious grounds.

Those who really want to get a feel for Colón's sketchiness can try the **Hotel Carlton** (Calle 10 and Avenida Melendez, tel. 447-0459, 447-0111, 447-0349, 447-0446, or 447-0112, fax 447-0114, $35 s/$40 d), which is smack in the middle of a fairly rough neighborhood at the center of town. The guards at the door and the battery of video monitors at the reception desk may give a sense of security, but when I visited I saw a set of master keys left unattended on a maid's cart. The place is a drab, plain, low-ceilinged honeycomb of halls, and the service is sluggish. But it'll do in a pinch. Shop around here—the rooms vary dramatically. Some of them are quite small and feature mattresses that feel like stone slabs. But there are a couple of nicer, newly remodeled rooms with balconies overlooking the street. Hanging out on the balcony offers plenty of local color, plus it gives the local *maleantes* (bad boys) a chance to window-shop you. There are a restaurant and laundry nearby. The "suite," which is nothing fancy, comes with a kitchenette and runs $55.

SERVICES

Colón has banks and a post office and such, but again it's just too dangerous to transact business in this city. The possible exceptions are listed below.

The Colón 2000 cruise port/shopping center has a few facilities of interest to tourists. Internet access is available at $1/hour at Cable and

Central Caribbean Coast

BREAKING FOR BIRDS

Those who need a place to break their journey on the way to or from the sights on the central Caribbean coast should consider spending the night at **Sierra Llorona Panama Lodge** (tel. 638-9557, 442-8104, fax 441-5414, www.sierra llorona.com, info@sierrallorona.com).

Sierra Llorona means "crying mountain," an apt name for a place that sees rain 286 days a year. Even in the "dry" season expect predawn rains. The plus side of all that precipitation is evident in the lushness of the 200 hectares of private primary and secondary rainforest surrounding the lodge.

The owner of all this, Ida Herrera, is a dentist who has lived here more than 30 years and is determined to leave the forest as untouched as possible. She limits the number of visitors, which means you're likely to have the forest pretty much to yourself. There are four kilometers of well-maintained trails that start about a 10-minute walk from the lodge. Observation platforms and rustic shelters have recently been added along the way. There are two main trails, neither of which is very long. One, La Poza, leads down to a pretty little waterfall; you can go for a dip in the pool at its base.

Sierra Llorona and its forests are most popular with bird-watchers: More than 160 species of resident and migratory birds have been spotted in the forest surrounding the lodge. The lodge can supply a list. But also keep your eyes open for small mammals, butterflies, insects, and other critters. Scientists frequent the area to study its flora and fauna, some of which is not found elsewhere. A new species of frog, *Atelopus limosus*, was disovered here in 1995. This is its only known habitat. Go on walks with a local guide, which the lodge will arrange. The guide's services are included with a stay, but consider giving him a tip.

The lodge sits on a ridge 300 meters above sea level. Even this modest elevation is enough to give the place cool, pleasant breezes in the morning and evening as well as views of the Caribbean, Limón Bay, and, at night, the lights of Colón.

The "lodge" is really a sprawling house with an attractive indoor fish pond, a swimming pool and deck, and a separate building a short walk down the hill. The three rooms in the house each have twin beds. Only one of them has a private bathroom. The rooms are nothing fancy but they're clean and comfortable. The rooms near the pool have a view and are larger and nicer, with private baths and two double beds in each. None of the rooms has air-conditioning, TV, or telephones. There's also a deteriorating tennis court on the property.

One of the best things about this place is Ida and her extensive family. They couldn't be kinder and more welcoming. You'll immediately feel yourself at home, which is good because meals are

Wireless (tel. 882-4160 or 882-4347, 7:30 A.M.–5 P.M. Mon.–Fri., 9 A.M.–noon Sat., closed Sun.), which faces the water at the back of the complex. There are also telephone booths for making international telephone calls and banks of pay phones that accept prepaid phone cards sold here. If a ship is in port, prepare to wait in line with homesick crew members. There's a security guard outside.

The complex also has a Western Union office (tel. 445-2008, 9 A.M.–5:30 P.M. Mon.–Sat., closed Sun.), in the Treasure Island Souvenirs store. The Colombian consulate (tel. 441-8057, fax 441-00114) is in an upstairs office nearby.

Yachties can anchor their boats at the Panama Canal Yacht Club (tel. 441-5882, fax 441-7752, http://public.cwpanama.net/~yacht/bottom.htm, pcyachtclub@cwpanama.net). For landlubbers, the entrance is in Cristóbal off Front Street, near the docks just southwest of Colón. It's a pretty simple affair but a longtime favorite hangout and a good place to meet all kinds of seafaring characters. It has a bar, outdoor restaurant, Internet and fax services, and facilities for yacht owners. Again, it's probably safe inside, but wander outside the grounds and things quickly turn dicey.

GETTING THERE AND AROUND

In recent years a toll highway, the Corredor Norte, was completed across 25 kilometers of the isthmus, a little less than one-third of the way from served family style. Lunches and dinners consist of tasty local food, and plenty of it.

All-inclusive rates are $76 per person, two person minimum. This includes all meals, use of the pool and tennis court, and a guided hike. There's also a weekend rate (4 P.M. Fri. through 3 P.M. Sun.) of $180 for two people for two nights. An extra person on this package is $25, $12.50 for children 12 and younger. For those who just want a room, the rate is $49.50 s/d.

Day visits are possible. A guided hike, lunch, and use of all facilities is $22 per person for one or two people, $18 per person for three or more.

Sierra Llorona also offers tours to nearby destinations. Rates are per person, with a two-person minimum unless otherwise specified. These include bird-watching on Achiote Road ($95, four-person minimum), Fuerte San Lorenzo ($70), Portobelo ($70), Gatún Locks ($35, four-person minimum), Lago Gatún boat trip ($65, four-person minimum), and Colón and the Colón Free Zone ($35). All these include lunch and drinks. Tours of a couple of Pacific side destinations, including Summit Gardens ($60) and Pipeline Road ($105), are also available.

Sierra Llorona will arrange transportation between Tocumen International Airport and the lodge for $15 per person, four-person minimum. Pick-ups from other parts of the country are also possible. With advance warning, they can easily pick up those who travel by bus to Sabanitas; get off at the El Rey supermarket and call the lodge upon arrival. Add 3 percent to these prices if paying with Visa or Mastercard.

The lodge is located near the small community of Santa Rita Arriba (not to be confused with nearby Santa Rita). If you're coming from Panama City, it's reached by a right turn off the Transístmica a couple of kilometers before Sabanitas. The turnoff isn't marked and is easy to miss. Turn when you see a sign that says Ciudadela de Jesús y María. If you end up in Sabanitas, turn around and head back up the hill. This time you'll see a Santa Rita Arriba sign on your right; make a left turn there.

After the turn, head uphill about 2.5 kilometers, then make a left turn onto a rutted dirt road. The lodge will be on the left after another 1.5 kilometers or so. It's next to several radio antennas.

Visitors need a four-wheel-drive to get up this rough road in the rainy season. Call the lodge for current conditions. If you arrive in the nearby town of Sabanitas and for some reason the lodge can't pick you up, you can hire a pickup-truck taxi in front of the El Rey supermarket for $6-8. If they don't recognize the name of the lodge, ask them to take you to Santa Rita Arriba near the radio antenna towers (*cerca de las torres*).

ocean to ocean. Even that little bit of good road makes the drive from Panama City much quicker, easier, and scenic than it's ever been. The toll from Panama City to the end of the line is no more than $2.40. The toll road ends at Chilibre. Turn right at the end of the exit ramp, then left onto the old Boyd-Roosevelt Highway (commonly known as the Transístmica). If the toll road is ever extended all the way to the Caribbean, the drive will be a snap. Note that at the time of writing there was a lot of construction going on along the Transístmica outside of Colón.

The Terminal de Buses de Colón is on Avenida Bolívar, Colón's major shopping drag, and Calle 13. The bus terminal is a busy place and should be relatively safe, at least during the day, but be alert for pickpockets and backpack thieves. Routes include:

La Guaira: 9:30 A.M., 11:30 A.M., 12:30 P.M., 1:30 P.M., 3:30, P.M., and 5:30 P.M. The fare is $2.25. Return buses leave La Guaira every hour or two 5:30 A.M.–1 P.M. The schedule is much more restricted on Sunday, with buses running only at 7 A.M., 10 A.M., 1 P.M., and 4 P.M.

Panama City: 4:30 A.M.–10 P.M. Buses leave every 20 minutes or so. The fare is $1.50, or $2 for the express bus. Try to get the express, which takes about 1.5 hours. The slower buses can take up to twice as long to cover the same ground when traffic is bad.

Nombre de Dios: 6 A.M., 9 A.M., 10 A.M., 11 A.M., noon, 1 P.M., 3 P.M., 4 P.M., and 5:45 P.M.

Mon.–Sat., 9 A.M., 11 A.M., 1 P.M., 3 P.M., and 5:45 P.M. Sunday. The fare is $2.75. Return buses run once an hour 4 A.M.–3 P.M.

Portobelo: 16 buses daily 6:15 A.M.–9 P.M. The fare is $1.30. Return buses run about every half hour 4:30 A.M.–6 P.M.

It's also possible to fly from Panama City to Colón, but this is usually at least as time-consuming as traveling by land. **Aeroperlas** (tel. 315-7500, fax 315-7580 in Panama City, tel. 430-1038 in Colón, info@aeroperlas.com, www.aeroperlas .com) flies to Colón at 8:45 A.M. and 5:10 P.M.

Monday–Thursday and 5:10 P.M. Friday. The return flights are at 9:10 A.M. and 5:35 Monday–Thursday and 5:35 P.M. Friday. This is a commuter flight, and there is no weekend service. Time in the air is about 15 minutes. The fare is $35.70/$71.40 one-way/round-trip.

A taxi anywhere within Colón should cost less than $1. Take taxis everywhere. A tourist walking in Colón is begging for trouble. To visit area tourist attractions, consider hiring a taxi by the hour; it should cost no more than $5 an hour.

Panama Canal Area: Caribbean Side

Few visitors to Panama who aren't transacting business at the Zona Libre or arriving by cruise ship see the Caribbean side of the Panama Canal. But it has its charms, including the canal's most impressive set of locks, the well-preserved ruins of a Spanish fort, and lush tropical forest surrounding the mouth of the storied Río Chagres.

The area is worth adding as a side trip on the way to or from, say, Portobelo or Isla Grande, or for those taking the Panama Railway across the isthmus. As a destination in itself, it's likely of most interest to those with an especially keen interest in the Panama Canal or Panama's piratical past.

The area's few main sights—Gatún Locks, Gatún Dam, and Fuerte San Lorenzo—are all clustered close together in a relatively small area southwest of Colón. So are its natural attractions, the mouth of the Río Chagres and the bird-watching spots around Achiote and Escobal.

It's possible to cover most or all of these in a long day trip from Panama City. But there are a couple of lodging options for those who choose to spend the night.

Gatún Locks are at the end of a road that begins at the Cuatro Altos intersection off the transisthmian highway, outside of Colón. All the other attractions described below are on the west side of the canal, across a swing bridge at Gatún Locks that is the only land link between western and eastern Panama on the Caribbean side of the isthmus.

SIGHTS

The sights below are close together. To get to them, first head west at Cuatro Altos (you may see a sign that says "4 Altos"), a four-way intersection on the Transístmica, or transisthmian highway, just outside of Colón. A highway overpass was recently completed at this intersection, making Cuatro Altos ("four stops") a misnomer.

The road forks a little less than a kilometer past Cuatro Altos. Take the left fork. Stay straight on this road, which will snake around a bit and pass the old townsite of Margarita. After a few kilometers, the road will fork again. Take the right fork to Gatún Locks. The visitors center is well marked.

There is a swing bridge at the north end of the locks. Nearly everything else of interest to visitors is on the west side of the canal, across the bridge. That includes all the other sights listed below. The wait can be up to half an hour if a ship is transiting, but the bridge provides a fascinating fish's-eye view of the locks since one actually drives through a lock chamber.

Ⓜ Gatún Locks

On the Pacific side of the Panama Canal it takes two sets of locks, Miraflores and Pedro Miguel, to raise or lower ships 85 feet (26 meters). Gatún Locks, on the Caribbean side, do the job by themselves. Each lock chamber is the same size as those on the Pacific—1,000 by 110 feet (almost 305 by 34 meters)—but there are three pairs of them on this side, versus two (at Miraflores) and one (Pedro Miguel) on the Pacific. That makes Gatún Locks absolutely massive, a little less than a mile (more than 1.5 kilometers) from end to end. All this is by way of saying that the Gatún Locks are an especially impressive sight. An observation platform up a long flight of stairs gives an excellent view of the locks, the Caribbean entrance to the canal, and Lago Gatún.

There's another observation spot downstairs, next to a building on the edge of the locks. It has a small scale model of the entire canal. Bathrooms for tourists are in the building behind the model.

The locks are open to visitors 9 A.M.–4 P.M. seven days a week. The number of tourists visiting the locks was increasing at the time of writing, but the free bilingual talks on the canal offered regularly by the Panama Canal Authority at Mi-

raflores were still sporadic here. Best bets are Thursday, the occasional Friday, and whenever a cruise ship disgorges its passengers for a tour of the locks. Contact the Panama Canal Authority Guide Service at Miraflores (tel. 276-8325 or 276-3187, cwm@pancanal.com, www.pancanal.com) for information on the current guide schedule at Gatún Locks. Call at least a week ahead of time to arrange a tour.

If time and transportation allow, take a quick spin through the townsite of Gatún, next to the locks. The area is still under control of the Panama Canal Authority, and during my last visit it was still being well maintained—the grass was neatly cut, and the old houses and employee facilities were still in pretty good shape. A visit will give a taste of what life in the old Canal Zone looked like.

THE "OTHER SIDE"

In the old Canal Zone days, those on the Pacific side of the canal thought and spoke of the area around the Caribbean entrance to the canal as "the Other Side." (Naturally, those "other siders" in turn tended to apply that term to those on the Pacific side.) Though the farthest Pacific townsite was less than 80 kilometers away, the Atlantic side felt like another world. Its isolation was underscored because there were just two ways to get there by land: by the railroad or by a usually pothole-riddled "highway," known as the Transístmica, through the Panamanian countryside. As kids, many Pacific siders, including this one, rarely made what seemed like an epic journey to the Caribbean side: swim meets and the annual football jamboree against our arch rival, Cristóbal High School, were about the extent of it for me.

Actually, in those days we all thought in terms of the Atlantic rather than the Caribbean side, though the latter is more accurate. When Panama started trying to lure tourists, people began to be more careful about using the word "Caribbean," since it summons up balmier images than does "Atlantic."

Even in a tiny world, the Caribbean side was miniscule. It also tended to get less attention than the Pacific side. The canal organization had its headquarters on the Pacific coast, close to Panama City, and that's where most of the action was. Colón never had the advantages of Panama City, and the townsites had even fewer resources than those on the Pacific side. As a result, the Caribbean communities tended to be tight and socially active. With few diversions, Atlantic siders had to find ways to entertain themselves.

Residents lived in townsites with names such as Cristóbal, Gatún, Coco Solo, Margarita, and Rainbow City, dotted among which were U.S. military bases, such as Fort Sherman, Fort Gulick, and Fort Davis. Cristóbal was literally across the street from Colón, and partly for that reason the boundaries between the Canal Zone and Panama were especially fluid on this side.

When the gringos left, much of the Canal Zone became a virtual ghost town, and this is especially true of the Caribbean side. Whole townsites have grown silent, and in some places the tropical forest is taking over again, at least for now.

Central Caribbean Coast

Gatún Dam

This huge (nearly 2.5 kilometers long) earthen dam was built to create Lago Gatún (Gatún Lake), a vital part of the Panama Canal. It was the largest such structure in the world when the canal opened in 1914. The dam controls the flow of the mighty Río Chagres, a major obstacle to canal builders, and supplies electricity used at the locks and the surrounding communities. It's an impressive sight when the spillway is opened and the water comes roaring out. A small bridge runs right by the spillway, behind which there's a good view of the canal. To get to the dam, cross over the swing bridge that spans Gatún Locks. Take the first left after the bridge and head up the road for about two kilometers.

Fuerte San Lorenzo and Área Protegida San Lorenzo

This is one of Panama's newest protected areas. Its 12,000 hectares include a former U.S. military base (Fort Sherman), the impressive ruins of the Spanish fort of San Lorenzo, and four types of forest, including mangroves and freshwater wet-lands. The United States left most of this forest standing, and with the departure of the military all kinds of wildlife have returned even to formerly populated areas. The big question is what happens next.

Conflicting demands are being made on the area. On the one side are those who want to preserve this vital ecosystem, restricting its use as much as possible to ecotourism and scientific research. This area is a crucial link in the biological corridor that runs the length of Panama, especially since so much of the land to the east and west of it has already been deforested. That also makes it a linchpin in the even more important Mesoamerican Biological Corridor, which runs the entire length of Central America. On the other side are those who see this entire region as prime real estate. Also, slash-and-burn farmers, hunters, and loggers began to invade the area after the departure of the U.S. military.

Still, it seems likely that those pushing for conservation will be at least partly successful. In the short term, only organized groups are being allowed into most of the protected area. That's

Fuerte San Lorenzo, near the mouth of the Río Chagres, was sacked by Henry Morgan in 1671.

Central Caribbean Coast

probably just as well for now, because visitors really wouldn't want to wander around here by themselves. Besides the usual hazards found in a tropical forest, there is unexploded ordnance in the area. The U.S. military conducted jungle-warfare training and had a firing range here. For more information on the protected area, visit www.sanlorenzo.org.pa.

The ruins of Fuerte San Lorenzo (official name: Castillo de San Lorenzo el Real de Chagres) are impressive and surprisingly intact. They sit on the edge of a cliff with a commanding view of the Caribbean coast and the mouth of the Río Chagres, which the Spaniards built the fort to protect. The Welsh buccaneer Henry Morgan won a bloody battle here in 1671, destroying the then-wooden fort before crossing the isthmus to sack Panama City. San Lorenzo was rebuilt as a strong stone fort in 1680, but the British admiral Edward Vernon still managed to destroy it in 1740. It was rebuilt yet again in 1768, with more fortifications added in 1779. These are the ruins visible today. The ruins, along with those at Portobelo, were declared a UNESCO World Heritage Site in 1980. Note: Be careful wandering around the fort. There are few guard rails and it'd be easy to walk right off a roof or a cliff. Supposedly at least one tourist has.

The entrance to the area is 12 kilometers past Gatún Locks in the former U.S. military base of Fort Sherman; stay straight after crossing over the swing bridge at the locks. Fuerte San Lorenzo is another 11 kilometers up a rough but passable road. It's a left turn past the entrance to Fort Sherman. On the way to Fort Sherman, look for a water-filled channel near the road. This is the French Cut, a remnant of the doomed French effort to build a sea-level canal.

At the guardhouse at Fort Sherman, just tell the guard you're going to San Lorenzo and you'll be let in. Be prepared to show ID.

Once-popular Shimmy Beach, to the right, is covered in trash washed up from Colón— probably not the best spot for a swim. The turnoff to San Lorenzo is on the left. It's a 20-minute drive on a sometimes rough road from here. Those without a four-wheel drive can ask about road conditions at the gate. The guard might possibly know.

From this point on the road is surrounded by beautiful rainforest. It's easy to feel transported back in time and imagine conquistadors and pirates hacking their way through this jungle in their relentless pursuit of treasure. Follow the signs to the fort, which is where the road ends. Road conditions get fairly rough toward the end.

ACCOMMODATIONS AND FOOD

The two hotels in the area are close to each other, on two former U.S. military bases near Gatún Locks. To get to them from Panama City, turn left at the Cuatro Altos intersection outside Colón (see introduction to *Sights*). Stay straight on this road, which snakes to the right, then back left, for about 1.5 kilometers. To get to the Hotel Sol Meliá, take the second left onto Avenida de Las Naciones Unidas. Look for the Sol Meliá sign. To get to Davis Suites, instead of turning onto Avenida de Las Naciones Unidas, stay straight for about another four kilometers. The hotel will be on the left less than a kilometer after the entrance to Fort Davis.

Davis Suites Panama Canal (tel. 473-0639, cell 628-6454, davissuites@yahoo.com, www .davis.suites.iwarp.com or www.panama.does.it, $50 s/d), is a former U.S. military building that has been converted into a six-room guesthouse. It's a rather utilitarian place in the middle of the former Fort Davis, an abandoned U.S. military base near Colón that Panama has done little with. This may have changed by the time you visit, but if not you'll find yourself in a ghost town. The main reason to stay here is to avoid having to stay in Colón proper. The suites are spacious and offer a sitting room, a kitchenette with a hot plate, and cable TV. Rooms are plain but okay, though the beds are rock hard. The place was remodeled since my last visit and may be fancier now. Tours of the surrounding areas are available. There are no restaurants nearby, but the hotel can arrange for room service that consists of food cooked and delivered by a local woman for a few dollars.

The **Hotel Meliá Panama Canal** (tel. 470-1100, fax 470-1200, www.solmelia.com, $82.50 s/d), a Spanish-owned 310-room resort, is a prime example of Panama's undying faith that if you build it they will come. So far, they haven't. The hotel has a striking location on the forested banks of Lago Gatún near the Área Protegida San Lorenzo in Espinar (formerly Fort Gulick), close to Colón and Gatún Locks. But it's not an area that attracts many tourists.

The hotel was built from the remains of the U.S. military's notorious School of the Americas, which had a reputation for training Latin American dictators and torturers. Its parentage notwithstanding, it's quite an attractive hotel, with bright and cheerful Spanish-Mediterranean decor that tosses in a splash of Italian rococo. Rooms are large, with Spanish tile floors, cable TV, tasteful decoration, lots of dark wood, a minibar—and incredibly hard beds. There have also been complaints of wafer-thin walls. Amenities include an impressive swimming pool, pleasant restaurant, piano bar, casino, business center, and so on.

The restaurant at the hotel once offered good food in a pleasant atmosphere. During my most recent visit, however, the air-conditioning was broken and the sealed windows couldn't be opened, the breakfast buffet consisted of food that looked as if it'd been left to wilt for hours, the service was unfriendly and slow, and the whole place was not particularly clean. Let's hope things will be on the upswing when you visit.

The hotel also offers tours to Gatún Locks, motorboat and kayak rentals on Lago Gatún, fishing trips, and other activities. Note that special package deals, especially on the weekend and during the rainy season, are often available and can be a good deal.

A new restaurant called **Flieger's** was opening next to the Meliá during my last visit, but I have little information on it so far. It billed itself as a "grill, tavern, and breakfast" place and may be a better bet for a meal.

The area surrounding the hotel is rather ominous looking, since the former U.S. military base has been allowed to decay—there are lots of crumbling buildings, a swimming pool filled with stagnant water, and so on, though new apartment buildings are also going up.

M Spillway's Bar and Restaurant, formerly the Tarpon Club, which is how most still know it (tel. 443-5206, 3:30–11 P.M. Tues.–Sat., 11 A.M.–8 P.M. Sun.), is right next to Gatún Dam and two kilometers from the west side of Gatún Locks (i.e., across the swing bridge). This used to be a good place to stop for lunch while visiting the area's attractions, but now Sunday is the only day it's open for lunch. It's an old standby known for its seafood. It was renovated in 2000 and now offers a fancier menu and spruced-up atmosphere. Most dishes are under $10. The plate-glass windows look out on a great view of the dam and the fast-flowing waters it spills into the Río Chagres. When the spillway is open the view is particularly impressive. You'll probably also get a glimpse of some of the spectacular bird life for which the area is famous. Oddly enough, there's also a disco attached to the restaurant, with occasional live performances. It's open starting at 9 P.M. on Friday and Saturday.

The Colón 2000 complex and the Panama Canal Yacht Club are so close by they're also worth considering for a meal (see the *Colón* entry).

GETTING THERE AND AROUND

There's no direct public transportation from Panama City to the Área Protegida San Lorenzo and the other sights west of Colón. It's probably best to go with a guide or rent a car. It takes about 1.5 hours to get to this area from Panama City.

To get to the area from Panama City, take the Corredor Norte toll highway to the end of the line. That's now at Chilibre, a little under one-third of the way across the isthmus. The toll from Panama City to the end of the line is $2.40. Turn right at the end of the exit ramp, then left onto the old Transístmica, or transisthmian highway. (Officially it's the Boyd-Roosevelt Highway, but no one calls it that.)

As described in earlier sections, all these sights are to the west of the Cuatro Altos ("four stops") intersection. Roads aren't well marked, and highway construction, especially the new overpass at Cuatro Altos, has jumbled things up considerably.

If you miss the turn and end up in Colón, do not stop to ask for directions; it's just not safe. Turn around and head back out of the city; ask for help once well away from downtown Colón.

Nattur Panama (tel. 442-1340, fax 442-8485, panabird@cwpanama.net, www.natturpanama .com) offers a popular tour, the Conquerors' Path, that includes a boat trip down the lower Río Chagres to Fuerte San Lorenzo, a tour of the fort, and a trip to Gatún Locks. The cost is $75 per person, minimum of four people.

Portobelo

Though the Spanish ruins scattered all over this seaside town hint at its long history, it still may be hard to believe that Portobelo (pop. 3,867) was once one of the most important ports in the Spanish empire. Today it's sleepy and impoverished, the decaying houses of its current residents built near or in some cases into the crumbling stone ruins. It truly comes alive only on October 21, for the celebration of the Festival del Negro Cristo (see sidebar, *The Black Christ Festival*).

The town's poverty can be a bit intimidating, but visitors shouldn't have any problems if they come here during the day and stay alert. Note that Portobelo is one of the wettest spots on the isthmus.

Inca treasure brought from South America was carried across the isthmus and stored here, drawing European merchants to renowned trade fairs for nearly 150 years. Columbus discovered Portobelo Bay in 1502, naming it *puerto bello* (beautiful port) himself. The city, originally called San Felipe de Portobelo, was founded in 1597 after the Spanish abandoned Nombre de Dios farther east. Portobelo endured constant assault from those seeking its riches. It was first attacked, five years after its founding, by the English pirate William Parker. Sir Henry Morgan, for years the scourge of the isthmus, sacked the city in 1668. The assaults continued into the 18th century. Sir Francis Drake, the most famous thorn in Spain's side, was supposedly buried at sea in Portobelo Bay, though modern-day searches have failed to discover his leaded casket. Given the attacks, it's a wonder so much survives. But large sections of the forts still stand.

SIGHTS
M Portobelo Ruins
The first Spanish structure as one enters Portobelo from the west is **Castillo Santiago de la Gloria,** on the left side of the road. It's the last incarnation of a fort that was built, destroyed, rebuilt, and tinkered with for more than 150 years and never ended up defending the town particularly well. These ruins date from 1753.

In the town itself is **Castillo San Gerónimo,** which dates from the same period. The nearby Customs House, the **Real Aduana de Portobelo,**

The cannons are now silent, but the ruins of Portobelo still stand guard over the Caribbean.

© CLEA EFTHIMIADAS

THE BLACK CHRIST FESTIVAL

Every October 21 Portobelo comes back to life at the Festival del Cristo Negro, or Festival of the Black Christ. It's quite a spectacle. Thousands throng the Church of San Felipe, home to the life-sized wooden effigy of the Nazarene of Portobelo, otherwise known as the Black Christ. Some come by foot from distant parts of Panama. Others come crawling on their hands and knees, their friends sweeping the ground in front of them free of debris or rocking a small shrine before their faces to keep the pilgrims' eyes on the prize. Still others let their companions pour candle wax on them as they crawl, as a further act of penance.

What's this all about? There are several legends of the origin of the statue and its festival. One has it that the statue arrived in Portobelo on a ship bound for Cartagena, Colombia. A storm arose each time the ship tried to continue on, and the crew members decided the effigy wanted to stay in Portobelo. Variations on the story have the ship either sinking in the storm and the statue washing up on shore or the crew members throwing the statue overboard in fright. Then, the story goes, on October 21, 1821, Portobelo residents prayed to the Black Christ to be spared from a cholera epidemic sweeping the isthmus; they were.

Each October 21 since, people from all over Panama who have prayed to the Black Christ for help with an illness or other problem give thanks by making a pilgrimage to Portobelo, often performing some act of devotion or penance along the way. Most find just walking here from Sabanitas in the heat and humidity to be sacrifice enough. That's a walk of nearly 40 kilometers; health stations are set up along the way for those who need help, and the entire route is littered with water cups dropped by pilgrims. There are no portable toilets anywhere, so you can imagine what Portobelo is like by the end of the night.

Devotees often wear purple robes in emulation of the Christ statue. Those who have asked for a major favor make the pilgrimage for several years. Each year they cut a bit of cloth off the hem of their robes. Some of the robes end up awfully short, presenting the interesting paradox that the most pious also have the most scandalous attire.

The festival is a blend of the sacred and profane in other ways as well. For many, it's an excuse to get very drunk and dance all night. It's not unusual to see a pilgrim in resplendent purple robes making his way to town carrying a beer. Most who arrive on their hands and knees start crawling just at the outskirts of town, and some of these seem to be at least as interested in the attention they get as in the sacrifice. The whole vibe is sort of spring-break-with-self-flagellation.

Once in Portobelo, pilgrims crowd into the church to worship before the Black Christ. Many offer necklaces, which are draped around the effigy. Mass is held, and devotees burn hundreds of votive candles and sing songs about the festival and the effigy. Late at night the statue is carried out of the church and paraded through the streets on a litter. The procession takes a long time, as the statue is carried with a peculiar rocking, back-and-forth gait: three steps forward, two steps back.

Those in Panama on October 21 should make an effort to attend the festival. It's a fascinating spectacle. But be forewarned it's also a major mob scene. Be prepared for epic traffic jams and stay alert for pickpockets. Traffic is generally stopped several kilometers outside of Portobelo, forcing even non-pilgrims to walk in. It's best to drive or come with a tour operator. Trying to get a return bus is a nightmare; many pilgrims go back home right after they arrive, so the line for the bus is hours long even in the morning. One strategy is to hire a boat near Portobelo and motor into town, skirting the traffic. Suggest this to your tour guide ahead of time, or call a hotel, restaurant, or dive operator to arrange it. The Coco Plum Eco-Lodge is a good bet.

was restored in February 1998 by the Spanish government. If you hadn't seen its state before the restoration, you might have a hard time figuring out what was done to it. Still, the place has been through a lot: Originally built in or around 1630, it was seriously damaged in a 1744 attack, then rebuilt, then damaged again in an 1882 earthquake. Just a couple of walls were left standing before the restoration.

The one-room museum inside the building is nothing special. There's a bit of the original foundation in the middle of the floor, but "exhibits" consist mainly of cheap reproductions of period pistols (on sale) and some old tools, cannonballs, and mortars. There are also replicas of pre-Colombian Indian tools and weapons mixed in with a few pieces of real pottery shards. There's a small model of Portobelo's fortifications just outside the entrance.

For all the incredible treasure that came through this building—and which is still being found in the jungle—the museum has seen fit instead to display a collection of common, modern-day coins that tourists have tossed into the foundation pit. It's one of those goofy touches one often finds in Panama museums, as is the 1920s typewriter from a *colección privada* (private collection).

Upstairs from the museum is a large hall with a narrative display containing information on Portobelo, the Camino Real, the Black Christ Festival, and Panamanian folkloric dances. The display is fairly interesting if one speaks Spanish; there is no English translation.

If exploring these ruins and buildings doesn't satisfy your historical urges, hire a water taxi near **Castillo Santiago de la Gloria** for $2 per person to take you across the bay to visit what's left of **Castillo San Fernando,** which was designed in the 1750s to replace Castillo San Felipe, demolished in 1739 by Edward Vernon, a British admiral. Unfortunately, American builders used rock from the fort in the construction of the canal, further damaging what little that time, war, and pirates had spared. (See *Getting Around.*) Also, a short, steep hike above town leads to some fortifications with a good view of the bay; if you're heading east, it'll be on to the hill to the right just before town. Drivers can park by the side of the road.

 Church and Museum of the Black Christ

The large white church nearby is the **Iglesia de San Felipe,** which is still in use. It dates from 1814, but its tower wasn't completed until 1945. It's famous as the home of the life-sized effigy of the Nazarene of Portobelo, better known as the **Black Christ.** The effigy, depicting Christ carrying the cross, normally resides on a podium to the left of the altar, but it is brought out to the center of the church for the Black Christ Festival, by far Portobelo's biggest event. The handsome altar of the church is adorned with gold images depicting various emblems of the crucifixion, including nails, instruments of torture, and the dice the Roman soldiers cast for Christ's robe. Small wooden carvings ringing the walls depict the stages of the cross.

Behind this church is the recently renovated **Iglesia de San Juan de Dios,** home to the new

Pilgrims at Portobelo's Black Christ Festival often wear purple robes.

© BONNIE KAY SPINDLER

Central Caribbean Coast

Museo del Cristo Negro de Portobelo, which now displays 63 of the robes donated by Panamanians for the festival, some of which are more than 100 years old. Among the more famous is the one donated by the champion boxer Roberto "Manos de Piedra" (hands of stone) Duran.

The Black Christ figurine's robes are changed twice a year, and each is used just once. The statue is adorned with a red wine–colored robe for the Black Christ Festival held each October 21. This is changed to a purple one for Holy Week. Many of the robes are donated anonymously. Some are simple and others are quite ornate, done up in gold trim and the like. The priciest one on display here cost the donor an estimated $1,700 for the raw materials alone.

Admission to the entire complex is $1 for adults, $.25 for children. The price includes a guided tour of the displays, though the guides speak only Spanish. Hours are 8 A.M.–4 P.M. Mon.–Fri., 8:30 A.M.–3 P.M. Sat.–Sun.

SPORTS AND RECREATION

Portobelo has long been a popular spot for scuba divers and yachties. It's also possible to hike in the forests of Parque Nacional Portobelo, but this should be attempted only with an experienced guide. In 1996, John Collins, the creator of the original Ironman triathlon in Hawaii, visited the Portobelo area on a yacht and decided it would be a perfect place for a triathlon. The first Portobelo Triathlon was held in 1997, and it has become an annual event. It is held the second Sunday of March and increasingly attracts world-class athletes. The event includes an 1,800-meter swim from La Guaira to Isla Grande and back, a 35-kilometer bike ride to Portobelo, and a 10-kilometer off-road run in the Portobelo area. For details, visit www.triathlon.org.pa or contact Allan Baitel at tel. 612-2063 or ptyab@c-com.net.pa.

Diving and Snorkeling

There are 16 dive spots around the Portobelo area, with attractions that vary from coral reefs and 40-meter-deep walls to a small airplane and a cargo ship. The best diving in the area is off the rocky Farallones islands a fair boat ride away.

There's a chance of seeing nurse sharks, spotted eagle rays, and schools of barracudas there. But any honest dive operator will be the first to admit the diving around Portobelo is for the most part just average: Expect no more than 10 meters of visibility on a typical day. And visibility is quite volatile: up to 30 meters on a great day, and down to three when it rains (several rivers empty into the ocean here; the diving is better in the dry season). Portobelo does, however, have two major things going for it: The diving is inexpensive and it is easily accessible.

The Portobelo dive operations are within quick driving distance from each other about seven kilometers before (i.e., west of) Portobelo. The closing of the American bases at the end of 1999 hit them hard, as military personnel and their families constituted much of their business. There are only two full-fledged operations left. As always when you dive, bring evidence of certification and ask to see the dive master's credentials.

The operation that inspires the most confidence is the **Twin Oceans Dive Center** (tel. 448-2067, info@twinoceans.com, www.twin oceans.com), on the grounds of the Coco Plum Eco-Lodge and Restaurante Las Anclas, between the Los Cañones and La Torre restaurants.

This is a PADI dive center with two instructors and a PADI dive master. It offers all the PADI courses. There are five partners in the business, four Brits and one American. They really seem to know their stuff, and they enjoy a good reputation. They have new, good-quality equipment and put a premium on safety.

Trips are made in a 28-foot boat with twin 115-horsepower motors. A one-tank dive including all equipment is $60. A two-tank dive is $80. Prices are $30 cheaper for those with their own gear. They sell new equipment here, too. Twin Oceans also sometimes offers trips to Isla Coiba on the Pacific side of the isthmus.

Scubaportobelo, (tel. 448-2147 in Portobelo or 261-4064 and 261-3841 at the main office in Panama City), is five kilometers west of Portobelo. The spot is pleasant, with a wooden mirador built on rocks over the ocean. This is the Portobelo division of Scubapanama, Panama's largest dive operation.

Divers pay for everything separately here. Complete equipment rental is $25. Filling the first tank costs $6, $4 for each additional tank. Boat transport is about $4–20, depending on where you want to go.

There's a restaurant on the grounds that offers simple food for around $4–5.50. Six basic cabins are also available. (See *Accommodations*.)

The **Portobelo Bay Resort** (tel. 448-2248, 448-2040, 673-6601) is a fancy name for a minimal operation. As you head towards Portobelo from the west, make a left at the police station just past Restaurante La Torre. The operation is near the dock. Most recently this was the home of Diver's Haven, which has since moved to the Nombre de Dios area.

The place is leading a twilight existence these days. Mainly it's a place for certified divers with their own equipment to get transportation to dive spots, though the owner can arrange for instructors with some notice. Boat transportation costs $7–25, for a trip to the Farallones. They'll fill tanks here for $3.

Even nondivers may want to stop by this area briefly to check out pieces of cannon and bottles from an early Spanish-era shipwreck being desalinated by the Instituto Nacional de Cultura (INAC). Some believe this is the wreck of the *Vizcaína*, one of four ships used by Columbus on his last voyage. The relics, which are sitting in outdoor tanks, aren't much to look at, but it's kind of cool to be that close to history.

Other Activities

Selvaventuras (tel. 448-2143, www.geocities .com/selvaventuras, 9 A.M.–5 P.M. daily) is to the right of the CEFATI building at the entrance to Portobelo. It's a bootstrap operation started in 2001 by four eager guys from Colón. Excursions include jungle hikes to waterfalls, overnight camping in the forest, horseback riding, fishing trips, and boat transport to nearby beaches. Prices vary depending on the destination and length of trip. For instance, a tour of the closest forts (which you can really do yourself) costs $2 per person; a half-day hike is $18 per person. The guides speak a little English. There's a modest café on the premises.

ACCOMMODATIONS

The dive operations offer rooms, none of which come terribly cheap. There are no hotels in Portobelo proper. Those on a budget can save a few bucks by opting for a room without air-conditioning, but bear in mind this is a humid area and some of the nonair-conditioned rooms are sweat boxes. Also, be sure to stay only in a room with intact screens. Mosquitoes and *chitras* can be fierce, and Portobelo sometimes reports cases of mosquito-borne illnesses such as malaria and dengue fever.

The cabins at **Scubaportobelo** (tel. 448-2147, $30 during the week, $50 on the weekend, for up to five people) are meant primarily for divers, but during the frequent slow periods landlubbers can get a room here too. The rooms are basic, small, low-ceilinged, and crammed with beds. But they have air-conditioning. Up to five people can be squeezed into each room, but you'd better really like each other.

Rooms at the **Portobelo Bay Resort** (tel. 448-2248, 448-2040, 673-6601, $15 s, $35–45 d for air-conditioned rooms) are also meant for divers, but anyone can stay there. The place offers squishy beds in basic rooms with bathrooms. Rooms with fans but no air-conditioning are $3 cheaper per person.

The best accommodations around Portobelo are at **Coco Plum Eco-Lodge** (tel. 264-1338, 264-1975, or 269-7970, fax 223-9444 and 269-7971 for Panama City reservations; tel. 448-2102 or 448-2309, fax 448-2325 at the hotel; $33 s, $44 d). It's just before Restaurante La Torre on the way to Portobelo and shares the same complex with the Twin Oceans Dive Center. It's a cheerful place, with conch shells ringing the door frames of the rooms and murals of fish painted on the walls inside. Rooms are clean and pleasant though a bit dark. There are a dozen rooms, most with air-conditioning.

FOOD

Restaurante Los Cañones, (about six kilometers before Portobelo, tel. 448-2980, 11 A.M.–10 P.M. Mon.–Fri., 8 A.M.–10 P.M. Sat.–Sun.) is a charming little open-air place on a small bay.

Central Caribbean Coast

Looking out at the Caribbean, it's easy to imagine Sir Francis Drake's ships gliding past on the way to a sneak attack. Seafood is the specialty at this popular place, with most entrees going for $6–8. The food is good. Try the *pulpo en leche de coco* (octopus in coconut milk, $6).

A little farther down the road is **Restaurante Las Anclas** (tel. 448-2012, 10 A.M.–8 P.M. daily), at the Coco Plum Eco-Lodge. It's a cute place entirely decorated with detritus recovered from the sea, including sewing machines, the wheel of a boat, wheelbarrow parts, gas containers, and so on. Seafood is again the specialty here, with most dishes averaging $6.50. The chef is Colombian, so be sure to order the enormous, Colombian-style *patacones*. A "menu turístico" includes either corvina or *pargo* (red snapper) for $6.99.

Restaurante La Torre (tel. 448-2039, 10 A.M.–7 P.M. Mon.–Fri., 7:30 A.M.–7 P.M. Sat. and Sun.) is a cute little open-air restaurant just beyond Restaurante Las Anclas. It's easy to spot because of the stone tower that gives the place its name. Again, seafood is its main thing, though I've had better luck with Los Cañones and Las Anclas. Most dishes are around $6. The service is friendly and courteous. There's an illustrated capsule history of Portobelo, in Spanish and English, along one of the wooden walls.

INFORMATION AND SERVICES

Just as you enter Portobelo there's a large, unmarked wooden building, one of the biggest structures in town, at a fork in the road. This is yet another monstrous CEFATI (tel. 448-2200, 8:30 A.M.–4:30 P.M. Mon.–Fri.) building, a tourist center erected by IPAT, Panama's government tourism institute. It reportedly cost a quarter of a million dollars to build. When I last visited I found a barren place staffed by a friendly employee who speaks only Spanish and doesn't know a thing about the area's attractions. Paintings by local artists are sometimes displayed.

A better bet is the Selvaventuras tour office (tel. 448-2143), to the right of the CEFATI as one faces the building. The folks here are interested in selling guided tours, but they can give

some basic information for free. (See *Sports and Recreation* for details.)

There's a small *artesanía* (artisans' shop) to the left of the CEFATI. It may be worth a quick visit if you arrive when it happens to be open.

Note that the last gas station on this entire stretch of road is at María Chiquita, roughly halfway between Sabanitas and Portobelo.

GETTING THERE

Portobelo is about 100 kilometers from Panama City. Those coming by Colón-bound bus from Panama City will have to change buses in Sabanitas. Do not go all the way to Colón, and make sure ahead of time that the bus stops in Sabanitas, which is on the *transístmica* 60 kilometers from Panama City. Passengers are let off near the El Rey supermarket. Buses between Sabanitas and Portobelo run only during daylight hours. The fare is $1.25.

The main bus stop in Portobelo is next to the Iglesia de San Felipe. Colón-bound buses leave Portobelo every half hour 4:30 A.M.–6 P.M. To get from Portobelo to Panama City, take a bus to Sabanitas (Colón-bound buses stop there). Get off at Sabanitas, cross the highway, and take any of the frequent long-distances buses running from Colón back to Panama City.

For those with a car, the drive from Panama City is fairly straightforward. At the time of writing, the Corredor Norte toll road came to an end near Chilibre. Head right at the highway exit toward Chilbre, then make a left turn onto the *transístmica* (also known as the Boyd-Roosevelt Highway or transisthmian highway), and head north 40 kilometers to Sabanitas. The turnoff to Portobelo from Sabanitas is on the right side of the highway just past the El Rey supermarket as you head north, in the direction of Colón. Stay on this road to Portobelo, about 35 kilometers away.

GETTING AROUND

Portobelo is a small town and easily walkable, though be alert and try not to wander around alone, as with any impoverished town.

A water taxi (tel. 448-2266; ask for Carlos) is

on the edge of the bay next to Castillo Santiago de la Gloria, the first fort as one enters Portobelo from the west. It's next to the Restaurante Santiago de la Gloria. A trip across the bay to the ruins of Castillo San Fernando is $2 per person. Prices to area beaches range from $10 per couple to nearby Playa Huerta up to $25 per couple for a trip to Playa Blanca. Prices are likely negotiable if business is slow.

NEAR PORTOBELO

Playa Blanca is a pretty little beach, by far the nicest in the area, situated on a remote cove at the tip of a forested peninsula 20 minutes by boat from Portobelo. There are no roads leading to it and it is accessible only by sea, which gives it the feel of an island. Day trippers can hire a water taxi to the beach from the ruins of Castillo Santiago de la Gloria in Portobelo for $25 per couple.

Those who want to stay longer can get a room right on the beach at **M Tesoro del Caribe** (tel. 613-1558, radio phone 613-5749, tel. 232-4985 for messages, www.tesorodelcaribe.com, book@ tesororodelcaribe.com, rates start at $75 per person). This lodge is just about the only thing at Playa Blanca. Note: Don't confuse this area with the Playa Blanca beach community on the Pacific side of the isthmus.

The lodge is just a few feet away from blue-green ocean and a rocky beach; a sandier swimming beach is just behind it. There are coral gardens literally a one-minute swim away that are alive with colorful small- and medium-sized fish and the occasional bigger guy (I came across a rather large and curious barracuda when I visited).

Snorkeling equipment, beverages (including bottled water, wine, beer, soda, and juice), snorkeling equipment, Sunfish sailboats, canoes, and boat transportation from a dock near Portobelo are included with stays. Deep-sea fishing, horseback riding, and scuba diving (including a dive master and gear) can be arranged for an extra charge with enough notice. A trail through the forest leads to José del Mar (also called José Pobre; see *Near Isla Grande*), about an hour away, where there's a little restaurant. The Portobelo ruins are close by and easy to visit during a stay.

The place is owned by four North Americans who take pains to get everything right. It's simple but comfortable. Little lights and bedside fans run on 12 volts of electricity, mostly supplied by solar panels. The bathrooms have solar-heated warm water.

The main lodge is an attractive, open-sided wooden building with a corrugated roof. It's sunny and airy, but don't expect much privacy. (For one thing, the walls don't reach all the way to the ceiling.) There are four rooms and three bathrooms in the lodge; the room upstairs is a bit like a tree house. There's also a full kitchen.

The best rooms are in a separate building on a nearby point. Two spacious upstairs rooms with balconies are upstairs. The view is absolutely beautiful. There's a kitchen and third room downstairs.

All the (quite comfortable) beds have mosquito nets, which you need here. As with many beach areas the *chitras* can be a nuisance.

Tesoro del Caribe's boat takes passengers to Playa Blanca from a dock just before Portobelo. Make a left turn at the police station immediately past Restaurante La Torre as you head toward Portobelo. Park at the side of the road. Cars should be safe here, but don't leave any valuables behind.

The basic rate includes kitchen privileges, but guests must arrange for their own food. Another option is to pay $125 per person, which includes a room and four (count 'em!) meals a day, plus snacks. Both rates include all the extras mentioned above as well as boat transport to and from the dock. The prices are the same for the borderline rustic rooms in the main lodge and the significantly nicer ones in the new building.

Isla Grande

This is the most accessible of the Caribbean islands from Panama City. Those planning to go to Bocas del Toro or the San Blas Islands can easily give Isla Grande a miss; these archipelagos have much more to offer. If not, though, this is a good place to get a quick dose of natural Caribbean beauty and tranquility. It's quite a humid place; be prepared for some serious afternoon napping.

Isla Grande is not really all that grand—it's about five kilometers long and 1.5 kilometers wide and has around 1,000 inhabitants, most of whom live in the small town that runs along a single waterfront path facing the mainland. It consists mainly of a handful of simple hotels, some run-down houses, and a few tiny stores and open-air restaurants. The island is only a few hundred meters from the mainland.

© WILLIAM FRIAR

The often-calm waters of Panama's Caribbean coast are markedly different from the pounding surf found on the Pacific.

Though Isla Grande has a couple of beaches, a decent one in front of Hotel Isla Grande and a narrow strip at Bananas Village Resort, this is not the place for vast expanses of sand. What the island mostly offers is the chance to laze about and enjoy some beautiful views of the forested mainland, clear blue ocean, and palm-covered nearby islands.

The beauty of this place has in the past been marred by the trash inhabitants and visitors thought nothing of tossing into the crystal waters. Little wonder the coral nearby is in sad shape. Recently, however, clean-up campaigns have greatly improved the look of the area. Less-disturbed spots are a short boat ride away.

Isla Grande tends to be dead during the week, especially in the rainy season. At these times, there are few dining options, and some of the hotels may be closed. Those who visit during a dry-season weekend, however, will likely find plenty of people having a rowdy good time and blasting music late into the night. Bear that in mind when considering a hotel in town.

SIGHTS

The best, and most popular, stretch of beach on the island is in front of the Hotel Isla Grande. The hotel has fenced off most of it and now charges $3 for those not staying in the hotel in an attempt to limit the day-trippers who show up with their boomboxes and coolers. There's a little point on the left side of the beach as one faces the mainland that one can use for free, but it requires a little scrambling over rocks to get there.

A better and less crowded beach is on Isla Mamey, a tiny, uninhabited private island with relatively calm, shallow waters. It's possible to snorkel or scuba dive here. This is a popular destination for boat tours. These tours usually include a trip near the mainland through a channel lined with beautiful mangroves. This channel has come to be known locally as the "Tunnel of Love."

On the boat ride over from the mainland to Isla Grande there's a developed island that's largely deforested except for palm trees. This is **Isla Cabra,** a private island owned by a Spaniard who owns a great deal of property in the area. It is not open to visitors, but those with binoculars should keep their eyes open for macaw nests.

West of Isla Cabra is **Bahia Linton,** one of the safest anchorages between Colón and Cartagena, Colombia. At the entrance to this harbor is **Isla Linton,** another private island one should not set foot on. However, boat tours of the waters near Isla Linton are popular because of the monkeys that have been introduced here, which boatmen summon by clapping. Be careful: Tourists often feed the monkeys (something you should NOT do), which has made them bold around people. A monkey bit a woman in late 2002.

The owners of Isla Linton, Allan and Rosalind Baitel, are conservationists working in conjunction with Florida State University to create a research facility on the island.

The Baitels also run an animal rescue and rehabilitation program behind their home on the mainland (again, this is not open to the public). Here they try to heal animals wounded by hunters or otherwise injured or interfered with, after which they return them to the forest. In some cases, all they can do is give animals a safe home, as is the case with a couple of jaguars that some thoughtless people kept as "pets" before the couple rescued them. These jaguars would no longer be able to survive in the wild. Unfortunately, Panama has no program for breeding jaguars in captivity, so the Baitels have been trying to find a way to export the jaguars to a country that does have such a program. Ironically, the international CITES treaty, created to protect endangered species, prohibits the export of animals that were not actually bred in captivity, which has proved to be a major obstacle.

ENTERTAINMENT AND EVENTS

There is not much to do on Isla Grande at night other than booze it up, and there aren't even many places to do that. The best bet is probably **Punta Proa,** a festive, Rasta-themed bar along the town waterfront. It's a veritable shrine to Bob Marley. The bar is known for cocktails made

with fresh fruit. A friend who ordered a Bloody Mary here watched in amazement as the bartender squeezed fresh tomatoes for the drink. Another concoction is something called "the Paralyzer." Good luck.

Patron saint festivals are held on June 24 and July 16 and involve celebrations on both land and sea.

SPORTS AND RECREATION

Centro de Buceo Isla Grande (cell 656-6095 or 501-4374, buceoenpanama@tutopia.com, www .buceoenpanama.com) is in a small concrete building near Cabañas Super Jackson. The place is run by Andres Hernandez, an enthusiastic Chilean-Colombian who has lived in the region since the late 1980s and knows all the good spots. He's a very nice guy, and he has his own certified compressor. Andres doesn't speak much English, but he's made himself understood to legions of American military guys through the years. He's the only dive operator on the island. His operation is geared more toward trips to Coiba and the San Blas (diving outside the *comarca,* snorkeling inside), but he does still offer diving trips and courses around Isla Grande. Bananas Village Resort contracts its diving trips out to him. Snorkelers who need to rent equipment should be sure to visit him; he usually offers the best deal on the island.

There's a decent surf break along the rocky shore just down from Sister Moon (see *Accommodations*), but surfers have to bring their own boards.

There are also a few short, hilly forest hikes on the island. (See the Bananas Village Resort entry for details.)

Hotel Isla Grande offers a variety of boat tours around the island. A trip that includes Isla Mamey and the "Tunnel of Love" mangroves is $35. A circuit of the island is $20. Fishing trips are $20 an hour. All of these trips are for up to six or seven people.

Snorkeling, sea kayaking, and daily boat trips are included with stays at Bananas Village Resort. The hotel can also arrange scuba-diving trips. Other activities include deep-sea

© WILLIAM FRIAR

There is one surf break on Isla Grande.

fishing ($200, four hours), a boat tour of Portobelo ($200, four hours), and a private boat tour of several nearby islands and villages ($100, two hours). Prices for these trips are good for up to six people.

ACCOMMODATIONS

For such a small place, there's quite a range of places to stay on Isla Grande, though no great bargains. Only the lucky or the easy-to-please will think they're getting their money's worth, at any budget. It's easy to spend upward of $40 for a double room one could get for half the price in Panama City. In the hoteliers' defense, it's not cheap to offer big-city amenities in such a remote area. And the cheaper places tend to cater not to foreign couples on a budget but rather to Panamanian weekend partiers who shoehorn as many people as possible into a room.

Most of the hotels are clustered close together, especially the motelish cabañas at the lower end of the price spectrum.

Hotel Isla Grande is on the side closest to the mainland. Cabañas Super Jackson, Candy Rose, La Cholita, and Villa Ensueño are lined up one after another along the main strip overlooking the

water. Of these, La Cholita and Villa Ensueño are the farthest from "downtown," right next to each other. Sister Moon is farther along still, on an isolated bluff accessible by a rocky path. Bananas Village Resort is clear on the other side of the island, secluded from everything.

In addition to the hotels on the islands, as this book went to press a new motel was being built at Puerto Lindo, next to La Guaira on the way to Isla Grande. It was being built on the grounds of the old Panama Canal Yacht Club annex, and from early descriptions it appeared likely to be pleasant and comfortable. But contact information and even the final name of the hotel were unavailable at the time of writing.

$10–25

Cabañas Super Jackson (tel. 448-2311, $20 s/d without air conditioning, $35–55 with air-conditioning) offers four cramped, rustic rooms of varying quality. The place has little atmosphere and the matresses are saggy, but it's clean and will do in a pinch. The better rooms have air-conditioning. There's a restaurant and a small general store on the premises. Boat trips are offered here, starting at $15–20 for a circuit of the island.

$25–50

Cabañas La Cholita (tel. 448-2962, tel. 232-4561 in Panama City, no local phone, $38.50 s/d), offers 12 rustic rooms in a cheerful garden setting. There's no hot water, but there is air-conditioning. Again, this place is often packed on the weekend. You can rent kayaks here.

Right next door to Cabañas La Cholita is **Villa Ensueño** (cell 448-2964, $44.50 s/d), which offers 16 simple, spacious rooms ringing a garden. This place isn't fancy, but it's comfortable and it has some charm. Brightly painted, shell-encrusted picnic tables and little *ranchos* are set around the grounds. All the rooms have air-conditioning. There's a restaurant, and a little store that sells snacks and such. This is a very popular place with the party crowd on the weekend, so bear that in mind if you're looking for a quiet spot. Campers can pitch a tent in the garden for $10 for up to three people, which includes use of a bathroom and shower. This is the most colorful of the town's little hotels. Snorkeling equipment can be rented for $2.50 per hour.

Cabañas Candy Rose (tel. 656-6917, 448-2947, $25 s/d with fan, $45 s/d with air-conditioning), next to Cabañas Super Jackson, was closed when I last visited, though friends have rec-ommended it as the best place to stay and eat in its price category.

Hotel Isla Grande (tel. 225-6722, fax 225-6721 in Panama City, no local phone, $40–60 for up to four people) is the biggest hotel on the island, with 50 rooms. It also has the largest and best beach on the island, which curves in a half-circle in front of the hotel. The place is popular with Panamanians, and the hotel and beach can get quite busy on dry-season weekends. It's traditionally been a dreary place with torpid service. However, when I last visited, the five cabins set right on the beach had been given fresh coats of vivid paint and generally spruced up. Even the service seemed friendlier. Each cabin has four beds, separated into two semiprivate rooms. They're still basic but they're okay and clean. These go for $60 for up to four people. Avoid the rooms in the motel-style buildings set back from the beach. These feature two saggy double beds and exposed ducts in the ceiling. They run $40 for up to four people.

$50–100

Hotel Sister Moon, (tel. 226-9861, cell 687-9861 or 688-5320, www.hotelsistermoon.com, rates start at $68 s/d including breakast), also known as Moon Cabins, sits by itself on the hills

Central Caribbean Coast

© WILLIAM FRIAR

Hotel Sister Moon sits on a hillside with a lovely view of the sea around Isla Grande.

of a palm-covered point overlooking a picture-postcard bay, rolling surf, and the emerald green mainland. The main accommodations consist of a series of thatched-roof cabins on stilts dotted along the hillside. Each has a double bed. The cabins are simple but extremely pleasant and tastefully designed. It's like staying in a fancy tree house, and the breeze here is a welcome respite from the island's humidity. There are also eight cabins with bunk beds for backpacker-types. A small, rocky beach with a good surf break is close by. A sun deck juts out right over the surf break, and next to it is a little restaurant and a pub with a billiard table and dartboard. There's also a small, murky swimming pool that's more scenic than inviting. Packages that include meals are available. The one odd thing about this place is that it seems to live a perpetual twilight existence. In my many trips to Isla Grande, I've never been there when the place was in full swing. That can be great for those seeking seclusion, but those who make reservations far in advance should confirm before arrival to make sure everything's up and running.

$100–150

Bananas Village Resort, (tel. 263-9510, 263-9766, fax 264-7556 Panama City for reservations, tel. 448-2252 or 448-2959 at the resort, info@bananasresort.com, www.bananasresort.com, rates start at $64.30 s, $98.60 d), is the fanciest place on Isla Grande. It's on the north side of the island, tucked away in a lovely, isolated spot facing the ocean. It's accessible only by boat or forest trails. Rates are higher on the weekends and lower in the rainy season. There are sometimes promotional discounts, and packages that include some meals are available.

The place, which opened in 1998, is nicely designed, cheerful, and small. The rooms are in eight A-frame cottages on stilts. Each cottage has three units: two large rooms below and one very large room above. They're the same price, but the upstairs ones are nicer. All have balconies, hammocks, and air-conditioners, and all look out on the ocean (but palm trees block the view in some cases—shop around). There's a swimming pool, and guests have free access to sea kayaks, snorkeling equipment, beach chairs, and so on. Boat excursions to the surrounding area are included. Afro-Caribbean dancers sometimes entertain guests on Saturday nights with the "Congo" dances for which the region is famous.

For those in a group who want something even more exclusive, Bananas has a private villa on a secluded, rocky cove nearby. It has four bedrooms, a private pool, and a kitchen, and it includes access to all the facilities of the hotel. Rates are $50 per person, six-person minimum. There is a two-night minimum stay on the weekends, and discounted rates starting with the third night.

Note: Though the resort is attractive, every time I've visited the service has been poor and slow, and no one seems to be in charge. Also, it is not being well-maintained, and things started falling apart soon after it opened. Guests can't even count on hot water. Service may be better on the weekend, when the place is more likely to be fully staffed but also more crowded. Macaws, parrots, and other beautiful tropical birds are kept in cages on the grounds, which will be a turnoff to some.

For $15–25 each way, the hotel shuttles guests between Panama City or Tocumen International Airport and the dock at La Guaira. For $5 more each way, they'll pick guests up at their Panama City hotel.

There are two ways to get to or from Bananas and the rest of the island by land. The easier way is to climb the concrete steps that start to the right of the cabañas as you face the complex. Be prepared for a steep and muggy walk over the top of a hill. If you take the right fork at the summit, the trail dead-ends at a spot with a picturesque view of the ocean and islands. Double back to the left fork to head down into town, which comes out near a little town park a short walk from Candy Rose and Cabañas Super Jackson.

The other way is more of an obstacle course. Head past the dock to the left of the cabañas as you face the complex. The trail starts on the beach and continues over rocky terrain up into muddy and slippery vegetation. The trail is hard to follow: Follow the sound of the rooster uphill. When the trail splits, either head up to the island's lighthouse or head down into town.

FOOD

Food on the Caribbean side of the isthmus contains ingredients rarely found elsewhere in Panama. Finding a restaurant on Isla Grande that's both open and serves these dishes can be a challenge, though. Be on the lookout for seafood in coconut sauce and moderately hot red-pepper "congo" sauce.

At meal times, count yourself lucky just to find a place that's open, especially during a rainy-season weekday.

The hotels are the best bet for food. Several of the ones along the main drag have simple, open-air restaurants right on the water's edge. What they may lack in quality they somewhat make up for in rustic island ambience.

(Bad news for those who may have heard of Club Turqueza, a hotel that had the best—if priciest—restaurant on the island; it had been closed down for quite some time and looked unlikely to reopen any time soon, if ever.)

I haven't had a chance to eat at **Villa Ensueño** (tel. 448-2964), but friends who are Isla Grande regulars, and whose taste can be trusted, recommended the food as simple but good. It's not rock-bottom cheap, but most dishes are reasonable: Breakfast tops out at $4, and most seafood dishes hover around $7.50. **Cabañas Candy Rose** is similar.

Bananas Village Resort (tel. 448-2252, 448-2959) has a very limited menu. Entrées include the usual Panama trinity of meat, chicken, and fish ($7.50 to $15). The food is reasonably tasty but the chef has a fondness for fried stuff and strong sauces. The grilled shrimp ($12) is pretty good. The setting is nice. You can sit on a veranda near the ocean or dine upstairs in a circular open-air building with pleasant sea breezes. The staff sometimes blares dance music at high volume here, more interested in entertaining themselves than you. A full breakfast, including coffee and juice and a choice of omelette, pancakes, french toast, or steak costs around $6.25. (For information on getting there by land, see the Bananas listing under *Accommodations*.)

The restaurant at **Hotel Isla Grande** (no local phone) is large and drab. It serves all the usual Panamanian specialties, especially the fried ones. A burger with coconut rice and fried plantains goes for $3. Breakfasts run about $2.75. Lunch and dinner entrées average $7. There's a full bar.

PRACTICALITIES

There is no tourist office on the island. The island also lacks banks, ATMs, or much in the way of services at all. Bring cash.

Getting There and Around

Access to Isla Grande is from the down-at-the-heels village of La Guaira, 120 kilometers from Panama City. (Those planning to drive should see *Getting There* in the *Portobelo* section for directions.) La Guaira is 20 kilometers from Portobelo; just drive through town and continue along the same road. The trip from Panama City takes about two hours.

The road has some rough spots, especially just outside of the village. It's doable in a regular car, but drive slowly and watch for potholes. At the entrace to La Guaira look for a sign that reads Isla Grande. Take the left turn indicated. Park by the dock for free, or in the partially fenced-in area on the left, behind Doña Eme's kiosk, for $2 a day. The fee probably buys nothing but a specious sense of security, but I always go for it anyway. Obviously, don't leave anything valuable in the car. When you come back, one or more teenagers lounging about may hit you up for change for "watching" the car. It's up to you whether to give one of them anything, but they can be unpleasant if you don't.

Note that the last gas station between Sabanitas and the end of the road is at María Chiquita, about 40 kilometers from La Guaira.

Those coming by bus from Panama City should take a Colón-bound bus (less than $2) and make sure it stops in Sabanitas. Get off at the El Rey supermarket in Sabanitas, which is right on the highway, and switch to a bus bound for La Guaira ($2.25).

Any of the boatmen hanging around the dock at La Guaira will take you to the island (don't expect life jackets). The ride takes about five minutes. The fee is $1 per person to be dropped off in what passes for downtown, $1.50 to go to Sister Moon. Transportation is sometimes free for those staying at Bananas; check with the hotel for details. Expect to pay double if you come at night, which you should try to avoid since few boats in these waters have lights. Boatmen may try to charge more if they think you're a clueless gringo. Name the hotel near which you want to be dropped, settle on a price ahead of time, and clarify whether it's per person or per group.

Nearly every place on Isla Grande is easily accessible by foot. Those who want to visit Sister Moon or Bananas and don't feel like hoofing it can hire a boatman down by the town waterfront for a couple of dollars. Your hotel can probably arrange for a boat back to the mainland at the end of your trip, but if not it should be easy to find one along the waterfront.

a "pet" ocelot cub

NEAR ISLA GRANDE

If none of the places in this chapter sounds quite remote enough, there's always **José del Mar**, better known as José Pobre. Talk about the middle of nowhere.

This is an anchorage in a cove next to the isolated village of Cacique, between Portobelo and Isla Grande. It's mainly a hangout for yachties, who leave their boats here for months at a time under the care of the owners of a simple restaurant and a couple of rooms here. (For those in the market, the rates are $60 a month.)

As one might expect in a place like this, the owners—a foreign couple (he's from Switzerland; she's from Grenada) and their Panamanian partner—are rather colorful. The couple arrived by sailboat in the early 1990s and decided to stay. The Grenadian woman, Valerie Gloude, is an animated character who provides plenty of excitement in this quiet spot, as did the sight of a "pet" ocelot cub being carried by one of their children when I last visited the area. It was almost as big as him. One hopes for everyone's sake that they've found a more appropriate home for this wild, endangered creature by the time you visit.

The rustic restaurant, known simply as José del Mar, is perched over the water with a view of the sea and the boats. Seafood and meats run

about $4.50–6. It's essentially open 24 hours a day—whenever a boat arrives, it's ready to serve.

There are also two nonair-conditioned cabins for rent, each with electricity, shower and toilet, screens, and soft mattresses. Rates are $20 per cabin, $15 after the first night.

There's no phone, but those wanting more information can send email to the owners at konrad_markus2000@yahoo.de.

The view of the sea and the cozy cove is lovely, and it's a very tranquil spot. But there are few facilities, no appealing beach nearby, and lots of *chitras*. While it's a great stopover for yachties, it's hard to see why landlubbers would make the difficult trip way out here. The owners will, however, take certified divers out on their boat for around $50 a day. Divers must bring all their own equipment.

The turnoff to José del Mar is 14 kilometers east of Portobelo on the way to La Guaira. Turn left at the stop sign at Kiosco Joel. Head up to the village of Cacique. At the cross in Cacique, make a left onto a supremely rough road. Only a four-wheel drive with high clearance will make it from this point on, at least in the rainy season. The road ends about 2.5 kilometers on. Park here and look for the cove and restaurant to the left. It's a short walk away, over a couple of bridges.

Nombre de Dios and Vicinity

Eight tiny towns—villages really—run along the coast east of Isla Grande. Five of these are linked by a road in remarkably good condition. All look pretty dismal and deserted, especially during the day, when their inhabitants are out working in the fields or fishing in the ocean.

The first five—**Nombre de Dios, Viento Frío, Palenque, Miramar,** and **Cuango**—are lined up one after another on a lonesome, 30-kilometer stretch of road that runs along the edge of the sea. The last three—**Playa Chiquita, Palmira,** and **Santa Isabel**—are even more isolated, separated from the others by the Río Cuango. This river is known for gold, and it still attracts wishful-thinking prospectors today. The road ends at the river, and those final three towns are accessible only by boat. Santa Isabel is the last town before the Comarca de Kuna Yala (the San Blas Islands). All these towns are so sleepy they're practically comatose. However, they do wake up for parties. (See *Entertainment and Events.*)

Frankly, there isn't much reason for tourists to come to this part of Panama, at least these days. Though some entrepreneurs are making noises about opening up Costa Arriba to tourism, not much is happening so far and there doesn't seem to be a whole lot of potential for anything to happen. The beaches aren't that great, the area is in the middle of the boonies, and the lovely tropical forest covering its rolling hills is being hacked and burned as quickly as possible to make way for cattle farms.

Historically, this is the home of so-called *Afro-Colonials,* the descendents of escaped African slaves from the Spanish era, called *cimarrones,* who slipped away and established hidden towns called *palenques.* They emerged from the forest from time to time to raid Spanish mule trains along the Camino Real, more to harass their former captors than for treasure that was pretty much useless to them. It's fun to think that the fisherman chatting about the tides may very well be descended from *cimarrones* who helped Drake in one of his famous exploits. In modern times, Costa Arriba has attracted settlers from Los Santos province. They are famous or notorious, depending on your perspective, for their prowess at cutting down trees. Having mostly deforested their own province, they're diligently working on doing the same to this area, which borders a vitally important national park.

Even though the attractions of this area are meager, there is some scuba diving in the waters off the coast. Wrecks of Spanish ships are still being found out here, including a 500-year-old one discovered in 1998 just off Nombre de Dios that some believe is the *Vizcaína,* one of the four ships used by Columbus on his fourth and final voyage to the Americas. It's well documented the *Vizcaína* was in fact abandoned in these waters. However, shipwrecks off the Panamanian coast are off-limits to divers and scavenger-hunting around them is a serious crime. Some also use this area as a jumping-off spot for trips to the San Blas Islands. (See *Sports and Recreation* for information on hiring a boatman to make this trip.)

SIGHTS

The first, largest, and most famous of the little towns is **Nombre de Dios** (pop. 1,053), about 25 kilometers east of Portobelo. It was the original Caribbean terminus for the Camino Real, the overland route used by the conquistadors to transport plunder from the destruction of the Inca Empire. The first European to lay eyes on the area was Rodrigo de Bastidas, during his voyage of discovery of the isthmus of Panama in 1501. Columbus rode out a terrible storm here in 1502. Legend has it that Nombre de Dios ("name of God") got its name when the unlucky Spanish explorer Diego de Nicuesa ordered his beleaguered and starving crew to take refuge in the harbor, shouting, "Let us stop here, in the name of God!"

Nombre de Dios was a poor, shallow harbor and proved nearly impossible for the Spanish to defend. Sir Francis Drake attacked it in 1572, though a wound forced him to retreat. He returned in 1595 and sacked it. The Spanish abandoned Nombre de Dios and moved the

Caribbean end of the Camino Real to the far better and more defensible harbor of Portobelo in 1597. Nombre de Dios quickly faded away.

Today it is a poor, out-of-the-way, ocean-side settlement of squat cinderblock buildings connected by dirt roads, as are the other towns along this road. There's nothing left in town that recalls its rich past except a modern-era sign at the crossroads as you enter town that reminds you this humble place is one of the oldest surviving towns in the Americas. The left fork leads to the old part of town, inhabited mainly by fishermen. The right fork leads to the "new" side, which is where most of the settlers from Los Santos province live. There's a manmade water channel that runs right through the middle of town; the builders of the Panama Canal scooped up sand from Nombre de Dios to build Gatún Locks after the Kunas turned them away from beaches in the San Blas Islands.

Viento Frío (pop. 427) is even sadder looking. There's a noni plantation just beyond it; noni, for those who've missed out on the craze, is a fruit that looks like a potato, tastes and smells awful, and is believed to have all kinds of miraculous curative powers. The main importance of the next town, **Palenque** (pop. 400), is as the administrative headquarters of the district—the mayor of all eight towns lives here—and as the location of the best lodging option in this whole region. There's little memorable about **Miramar** (pop. 180) except for a simple restaurant, the new gas station that should be completed by the time you read this, and another place to stay. The road ends at **Cuango** (pop. 331).

ENTERTAINMENT AND EVENTS

These sleepy towns live for festivals, especially Carnaval and their *fiestas patronales,* the saint's day corresponding to the anniversary of the town's founding. These dates are the best bet to catch the colorful, African-derived dances known as Congos. Some *fiestas patronales* and other local celebrations in the region include April 27 (Nombre de Dios), June 8 (Santa Isabel), June 19 (Playa Chiquita), June 24 (Palmira), July 31 (Viento Frío), September 8 (Palenque), and September 24 (Río Indio). It's not worth making a trip all the way out here just for one of the celebrations, but those who plan to visit anyway should bear those dates in mind.

During my last visit to this area, residents told me that on October 12 Viento Frío celebrates a big "Día de la Raza" festival, the Latin American version of Columbus Day. In recent years, of course, people's attitude toward that day have become ambivalent throughout the Americas, with some seeing it as a more appropriate time for mourning than celebration. The festivities that the residents described to me—an elaborate mock battle between the races—suggest that ambivalence exists even way out here. I haven't attended the celebration and have had trouble getting reliable information on it, but it could be fascinating to attend such an unusual Columbus Day commemoration in an area Columbus actually visited.

SPORTS AND RECREATION

Watersports are the main attractions. If you go for a swim, beware of the undertow and rip currents. The only organized recreational services in this area are provided by **Diver's Haven** (tel. 505/891-9003 in Nicaragua, through which calls are routed, no local phone, G8919003@ alianza.com.ni), which moved here in 2000 from its old home in Portobelo. The place is run by a character named James Norris, an Alabama native who has been diving these waters for several years. He says the visibility is consistently far better out here than around Portobelo.

The turnoff is about four kilometers east of Nombre de Dios, before Viento Frío. The road is rough and steep, but it's doable in a non-four-wheel-drive vehicle. Make a left onto the gravel road, which heads through swampy terrain and ends at a T-intersection. Turn right here. The road ends at Diver's Haven.

Facilities include a large house built at the edge of an attractive stretch of beach. Norris rents out a rustic ground-floor room with six bunk beds and ceiling fans. There are no screens on the window, which is a shame because the *chitras* here are voracious. There's a toilet and hot-water shower at the back of the building. The bunks are meant for divers and are included in the price of the dives.

BOATS TO KUNA YALA

It's possible to hire local boatmen in these towns for trips to Kuna Yala (also known as the San Blas Islands). However, be advised that the trip takes a minimum of one hour in small, open boats on a sea that can quickly turn very rough. I've made longer trips out here on foolishly small craft—not the smartest thing I've ever done—but I've always felt pretty confident about the skill and good sense of my captains, if not the sturdiness and maintenance of their boats or the adequacy of their safety precautions.

All the above are in short supply in this area, and it may very well be risky to try to make the trip. At the very least, go with a captain who has life jackets, or bring your own. Also note that just because a boatman fishes for a living doesn't make him a good seaman; some around here are notoriously accident prone.

I've never traveled with the folks listed below. They're listed here because something about them, or at least about the quality of their gear, inspired a bit of confidence. But remember that some of the greatest navigators in history, from Columbus on down, have had harrowing experiences and lost ships and crew in these seas.

You can hire a boat and captain for a San Blas trip at Diver's Haven; see *Sports and Recreation.*

In Viento Frío ask for a boatman named Miguelón (no phone). He owns a tiny general store in town. Miguelón transports goods to and from Kuna Yala often and has a reputation as a capable captain. He does seem to know his stuff. He has access to three open boats, including a 25-footer, and uses a 55-horsepower motor. Sample rates are $180 to Porvenir, $250 to Río Sidra, and $300 to Corazón de Jesús for up to three people. The trip takes him an hour to Porvenir, another 75 minutes to go as far as Corazón de Jesús.

Niano Cuadro, the crusty owner of Isla Bella Vista near Miramar (tel. 651-7341) goes to the San Blas Islands for $25 per person, eight-person minimum—i.e, $200 per trip. Expect to pay more for trips far beyond the Porvenir area. He has a 23-foot boat that takes a little over an hour to get to the beginning of the archipelago. If he buys the more powerful motor he had his eye on, however, the trip would be significantly faster.

If you want to snorkel in the San Blas, bring your own equipment. The Kunas don't allow scuba diving in their waters.

Meals are served in the large *rancho* next door. The most expensive breakfast costs $3.25. Lunch and dinner runs to seafood, which costs around $6–7.50 for items other than lobster, which is $12.

Divers can splash around the reef right off the beach for $5. Most dive sights, however, are 10 kilometers out. Dives requiring boat transportation start at $15 and go up to $85 per person for a three-tank dive along a barrier reef at the border of Kuna Yala (the San Blas Islands). Norris also offers trips to Kuna Yala, but not to dive. The Kunas do not allow scuba diving in their own waters. The trip can take up to 1.5 hours each way and includes a sack lunch. He charges $6 to fill a tank.

Diver's Haven brings in instructors to teach courses. A Discover Scuba course costs $60, which can be used toward other full courses if the student gets hooked and wants to learn more. These cost $150.

For those into less rigorous fun, the place offers banana boat rides ($3) and sea-kayak rentals ($5 an hour for single kayaks, $10 an hour for doubles). It also can arrange half-day and full-day guided horseback-riding and hiking tours of the surrounding forest. A full-day horse tour, including lunch, costs $40.

ACCOMMODATIONS AND FOOD

There are a few basic places to stay in this area, and as usual camping on the beach is free. This area doesn't get many foreigners, though, so people may wonder what you're up to. It's probably a good idea to let the police and townspeople know you come in peace.

As always, camp only in a tent. *Chitras* are likely to be the least of your troubles. This is cattle country, which means vampire bats, and it's poor, which means a small but distinct possibility of disease-carrying mosquitoes.

Places to stay are listed by town, from west to east.

Diver's Haven, between Nombre de Dios and Viento Frío, provides food and lodging to divers. (See *Sports and Recreation.*)

Posada Palenque (tel. 448-2188, public pay phone—let it ring for a long time and ask for Sr. Ñolo, $8 s/d with shared bathroom, $20 s/d with air-conditioning and private bath), in the middle of Palenque, is a surprisingly decent place with eight rooms and a bit of charm. The owner has made an effort to prettify the place, including surrounding it with flowering plants. The rooms are dark and some have sagging mattresses. He can also arrange food.

Behind the gas station just east of Miramar, on a microscopic island about 50 meters from shore, is **Isla Bella Vista** (tel. 651-7341, $35 s/d). This consists of three utterly basic cinderblock cabins without screens or glass windows—which is not a good thing since the place is right next to *chitra*-infested mangroves, not to mention vampire bat–friendly cattle country. The rooms are essentially cells, and the bare-bones kitchen facilities include a gas hook-up but no gas (bring your own if you want to cook). There are an open-air shower and outhouses. Remarkably, there is electricity. There's nothing else on the island except plenty of time to wonder what the hell you're doing way out here.

This place is run by a former Panama Defense Forces sergeant named Niano Cuadro, a gruff character with a crushing handshake and a mouth full of gold teeth. He'll paddle you out to the island in a dugout canoe. Rates are an exorbitant $35 per couple per room, or $75 for a whole cabin, which allegedly can sleep a very crowded six people. This is incredibly high for what you get.

He also owns a small, open-air seaside restaurant in town that offers heaps of fried seafood and other simple fare for a couple of dollars.

PRACTICALITIES

There are few services of any kind in this remote, neglected part of the country. There's a pay telephone in each town, but that's about it. There are no banks or ATM machines. The best bet for official help if one encounters trouble is in Palenque, the administrative headquarters of the district.

Getting There

To get to this area by car, first drive through Portobelo. Continue east through Portobelo, i.e., in the direction of La Guaira and Isla Grande, for about eight kilometers. You'll come to a crossroads known, logically enough, as El Cruce. Turn right here. (Heading straight leads to La Guaira/Isla Grande).

After about 13 kilometers there's a rickety-looking suspension bridge. Grit your teeth and drive over it. The first sizable settlement is Nombre de Dios (15 kilometers from El Cruce, about 25 minutes). The paved road ends a little past Nombre de Dios, turning into a rocky dirt road that's passable in a regular car most of the way. The road continues through Viento Frío (8 kilometers past Nombre Dios), and then through nearby Palenque, Miramar, and Cuango, which are bunched together within a few kilometers of each other toward the end of the road. The road gets rough beyond Miramar, requiring a four-wheel drive in the rainy season, before coming to a sudden end at the especially rundown Cuango, on the edge of the wide mouth of the Río Cuango.

A small gas station just east of Miramar should be open by the time you read this. It is the only gas station in the entire region east of María Chiquita. Since María Chiquita is quite a ways away, about 20 kilometers west of Portobelo, those driving should be sure to start their exploring with a full tank.

Getting to these remote areas by bus can be a hassle, as service is neither frequent nor speedy. Those coming from Panama City can take a Colón-bound bus to Sabanitas and get off at the El Rey supermarket. Look for buses with "Costa Arriba" or the name of the particular destination painted on the windshield. Buses also run between Costa Arriba and the Colón bus terminal (see the *Colón* section for details). It's also possible to hire a taxi in Sabanitas or Colón, but the fare will probably be rather steep, depending on the destination.

Kuna Yala

Welcome to paradise. Cartoonists who love to picture tropical islands as dots of soft sand with a few coconut palms could have gotten the idea from Kuna Yala, otherwise known as the San Blas Islands. That image fits countless idyllic spots in this archipelago of nearly 400 islands off the eastern Caribbean coast of Panama. When the sun hits the sea here you'll think of emeralds and sapphires.

The islands are part of the Comarca de Kuna Yala, a semiautonomous homeland of the Kuna people. Kuna territory also encompasses a mountainous strip of mostly virgin forest on the mainland, along the Caribbean slope of the Darién. It runs the length of the archipelago, ending at the Colombian border.

Most visitors prefer to hang out on the islands. Nearly all the estimated 40,000 Kuna who live in the *comarca* (district) inhabit just 40 of the islands, none of which is very large. As one might imagine, things get pretty crowded: On many islands, the thatch roofs of the Kunas' cane huts almost touch, making walking around a bit of a challenge. Visitors generally spend as much time as possible on the uninhabited islands, but be sure to visit a village. The chance to meet the Kuna, who have one of the most vibrant

Must-Sees

Look for **M** to find the sights and activities you can't miss and **N** for the best dining and lodging.

M Achutupu: You'll find easy and accessible snorkeling in crystalline waters on this island (page 169).

M Cartí: Though one of the most touristed areas in Kuna Yala, this cluster of islands near El Porvenir has an interesting blend of traditional and modern Kuna life, as well as a museum that offers insight into that life (page 170).

M Isla Maquina: One of the most traditional, charming, and attractive inhabited islands in the archipelago, where the vibrant Kuna culture is going strong (page 174).

M The Uninhabited Cays: The Cayos Holandéses, Cayos Limónes, and Cayos Coco Bandero are among the archipelago's remote and stunning string of sparsely inhabited islands, with clear water and spectacular coral (page 181).

© WILLIAM FRIAR

Cartí Suitupu's small Kuna museum gives a glimpse of the mythology, history, rituals, and daily life of the Kuna.

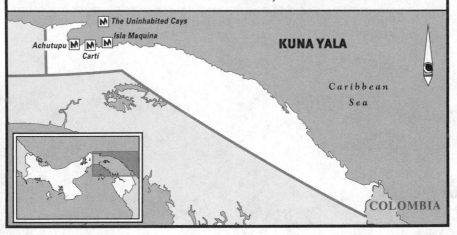

Kuna Yala

indigenous cultures in Latin America, is reason enough to visit the San Blas Islands.

A word of warning: If you're looking for Club Med, Kuna Yala is not for you. Even the most "exclusive" accommodations are quite simple, and there's little to do on the islands except swim, snorkel, laze in hammocks, and visit villages. The food is generally bland and basic.

More disturbing, any lingering romantic notions one has about indigenous people's harmonious relationship with nature gets a jolt upon realizing how severely the Kuna are overfishing their waters, or seeing the garbage and sewage they routinely dump into pristine blue waters.

On the other hand, there are still plenty of

lovely, uninhabited islands in the archipelago, more than anyone could possibly see during a visit. A big part of the charm of these islands is their very simplicity: no timeshare condos or tacky T-shirt shops here. Nodding off in a hammock slung between coconut palms, watching a Kuna woman sewing a *mola*, and showering by the light of a kerosene lantern can soon seem like a pretty good way to spend the day.

PLANNING YOUR TIME

The Comarca de Kuna Yala consists of a strip of mountainous coast and a nearby archipelago that stretch 226 kilometers down the eastern Caribbean side of the isthmus to the Colombian border. Nearly all the islands are within five kilometers of the mainland. Only a handful of the inhabited ones have much in the way of visitor facilities. Few tourists visit the coast, which is home primarily to Kuna farms and dense tropical forest.

After a general description of what to expect in the archipelago, the islands most popular with and accessible to visitors are listed below, organized in five clusters, starting with the westernmost islands and heading southeast down the archipelago. These also have the best facilities for visitors. This is followed by a description of the most popular of the lovely, remote, and sparsely inhabited outer cays. Farther down the archipelago, east of Corazón de Jesús, the reef ends and the islands are subject to higher seas. This area sees few tourists.

It's possible to visit more than one of these island clusters during a visit. However, distances are too great and the sea sometimes too rough to make a day trip from one cluster to another practical by the chief means of transportation for tourists: small wooden boats powered by outboard motors. Unless you have access to a large power boat or yacht, choose just one area to explore. If your schedule allows, you can also fly to a second area and spend one or more nights there, but that will increase your logistical hassles significantly; interisland flights are tricky to arrange.

Visitors will get the most out of their visit if they take time both to explore Kuna villages and escape to one of uninhabited islands for snorkeling or sunbathing. Most island groups offer an attractive combination of both. Those who stay around the busy hubs of **El Porvenir** and **Cartí,** for instance, have easy access to the uninhabited island of **Achutupu** and other pristine spots. Those who stay on the tranquil hotel islands around **Río Sidra,** on the other hand, can take a day trip to explore the nearby village islands, including traditional and picturesque **Isla Maquina.**

Try to stay a minimum of two nights on the islands. That allows enough time to explore a Kuna village, do some snorkeling, shop for *molas,* and lounge in a hammock. Three nights are better to get a taste of the rhythms and beauty of life on the islands. Time will go much faster than you expect.

Later in the dry season, from late February to March, is generally reckoned to be the best time to visit the islands. The winds are calmer then, improving snorkeling visibility. This calmer weather can last until mid-April. There are strong trade winds from December to February, which creates lots of chop in the sea. It also tends to be cloudy then, which drops snorkeling visibility even more.

There's less wind in the rainy season, which begins around mid-April and lasts until the end of the year. This calms the water, but underwater visibility near land can be poor because of runoff from the rivers. The lack of wind can also make it quite hot and humid. On the other hand, the seas are calm enough that it's possible to take a boat outside the reef that protects the western half of the archipelago from the open ocean. The fishing is also better then, and there are fewer tourists. December to March is the high season for tourists. According to experienced sailors, if there are hurricanes out in the Caribbean (Panama is beyond the hurricane belt) the weather in the San Blas tends to be good.

Holidays in Kuna Yala include the anniversary of the Revolución Tule (the Kuna war against Panama in 1925) on February 21, which is celebrated throughout the archipelago, and a celebration in honor of Charles Robinson, an important figure in the revolution, which is celebrated just on his native island of Narganá.

Kuna Yala

The Comarca

SPORTS AND RECREATION

Snorkeling, swimming, and visiting Kuna villages are just about the only things to do on the islands. Depending on where one stays, the hotel may be able to arrange a tour of the rainforest near the coast for an extra fee. Transportation within the *comarca* is mainly by small motorized boat. Don't expect to see a life jacket. The seas can get choppy, especially in the dry season. Those planning to travel significant distances by boat should bring a life jacket.

Underwater visibility in these crystalline waters can be better than 30 meters on a good day. The best snorkeling is found among the sparsely inhabited outer cays at the western end of the archipelago, where the coral is extensive and indescribably beautiful. The most popular of these are the Cayos Holandéses.

Unfortunately, the Kunas have banned scuba diving in the *comarca*. The hotels typically have snorkeling equipment to rent or borrow, but it's usually not in good shape. Bring your own if possible.

Don't swim around inhabited islands, as human and animal waste is allowed to flow out to sea; try even to avoid sea-spray during boat rides near them.

Hikes through the forest, usually to a waterfall or Kuna cemetery, have been added to many hotels' tour repertoires in recent years. Remember that these can be hikes through the true wilderness of the Darién. Be prepared, and do not attempt to explore the forests without a Kuna guide.

PRACTICALITIES

Note that island names can be confusing. Some are known alternately by Spanish and Kuna names, and there is rarely widespread agreement on how to spell the latter. There are even different islands with the same name. The most common names and their alternates are listed here.

It's tempting to take photos of the Kuna,

© WILLIAM FRIAR

Daily boat trips are part of the standard package at most hotels in the archipelago.

particularly the colorfully dressed women. But always ask first, and expect to pay $1 for the privilege. If the Kuna are going to be treated as curiosities, they figure the least tourists can do is compensate them for it. Be sure to bring lots of small bills, particularly $1 and $5 bills, to buy souvenirs; change can be hard to make on the islands. You may feel more comfortable taking a photo of a Kuna woman you've just bought something from, and she may not even charge you in that case. You won't be charged for photos of village scenes that don't focus on an individual. Even with the hassle, the San Blas Islands are so photogenic you'll probably burn through a lot of film. Take more than you expect to use.

Accommodations

Most of the phone numbers listed for lodgings are in Panama City, where nearly all the hotels have offices. When you make a reservation, the staff will also arrange for a boat to pick you up from the nearest airstrip. Just about all the hotels offer packages that include room, meals, pickup and drop-off at the airstrip, and a daily boat tour to snorkel or visit a Kuna village. Some will also make plane reservations for you.

Some hotels allow guests to opt out of the full package and fend for themselves for meals and transport. However, unless you have your own boat you'll probably find it cheaper, and certainly simpler, to go with a package deal. Remember that accommodations on the islands vary from fairly rustic to very rustic.

The life span of hotels is particularly unpredictable in Kuna Yala. It sometimes seems the more successful the hotel, the better its chances of being shut down. It's one of those things that makes Kuna society such a mystery to outsiders. Make sure your hotel of choice still exists before making too many plans.

Camping on the islands is not generally a good idea unless you're with an organized group. There are no developed campgrounds, so the only real option is pitching a tent or slinging a hammock on a deserted island. That may sound appealing, but smugglers, including drug traffickers, have been known to run these waters. You really wouldn't want them accidentally to stumble upon you in the middle of the night. There has also been some concern in recent years of Colombian guerrilla and paramilitary activity spilling into the *comarca*. Just to be on the safe side, it's probably a good idea to be under a Kuna roof close to a population center during your visit if you're traveling alone or in a small group.

Food

Don't expect any real restaurants in Kuna Yala. Those staying on the islands will probably eat all meals in the hotel's simple dining area. As mentioned above, often the food is not very good. Consider bringing snacks to tide you over. Beer is widely available on the islands, but wine and spirits are not.

Once you've had your third straight meal of tasteless fried fish and rice, you may be tempted to accept your hotel's offer of lobster. Bear in mind that lobster, once a subsistence food for the Kuna, has been so commercially overexploited it's in danger of extinction in these waters. At the very least, do not eat lobster during the mating season, which runs from March to July. Also, even if you have a package deal you'll probably pay extra for lobster, something you may not realize until you're presented the bill.

It's probably also a good idea to avoid squid. Kuna fishermen typically chase squid out of aquatic caves by dumping bleach into them. Bad for the environment and bad for you.

Information and Services

There are few modern services of any kind on the islands. Bring just about anything you'll need during your stay, as only the most basic supplies are sold anywhere in the *comarca*.

Bring enough cash to cover any expenses you expect to incur on the islands. There's a branch of the Banco Nacional de Panamá on Nargana. It's open 8 A.M.–2 P.M. weekdays, 9 A.M.–noon on Saturday. There's no ATM, but it's the only place in the archipelago that cashes travelers checks.

Telephone booths that accept Cable and Wireless calling cards are popping up on the inhabited islands. But expect to be more or less cut off from the rest of the world during your stay.

Kuna Yala

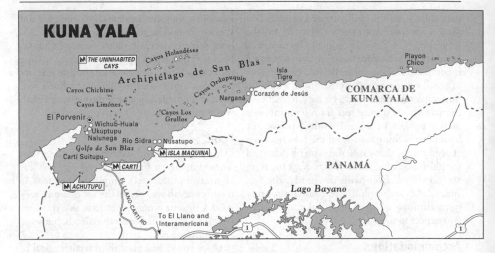

GETTING THERE AND AROUND

Unless you're a glutton for punishment and have access to a great four-wheel-drive vehicle with a winch, or you are up for a major hike, you can't get to the San Blas Islands by land. A road of sorts leads from El Llano, on the Interamerican Highway, over the mountains to the west end of the *comarca*. But for most of the way it's little more than a brutally rugged trail, though there's talk of one day improving it. It's sometimes impassable with any vehicle. (See *To the Darién by Road* in the *Darién* chapter for details.)

By Sea

The best way to explore the islands is by yacht. I have found **San Blas Sailing** (tel. 232-7598, cell 674-8860, info@sanblassailing.com, www.sanblassailing.com) to be an excellent way to go for those who can afford it. It charters a range of yachts with competent, experienced captains. Trips are custom-designed depending on the interests and time of the passengers, but typically in Kuna Yala they're made on comfortable 34- to 42-foot catamarans and include all meals, wine, visits to villages, and use of snorkeling gear. Most yachts have a two-person kayak, and all have a dinghy with outboard motor. Rates run about $85–100 per person per night for 4–8 people in a boat in the low season up to about $225 per person per night for two people who want a boat to themselves in the high season. There's also a $20 per person charge (per trip, not per night) to cover all local taxes and fees. The company can do quick trips, but it recommends at least a four-day cruise, which in my opinion is the minimum to truly unwind and enjoy all the islands have to offer when visited by boat. You'd be amazed how quickly a week slips by out there.

The catamarans have a very shallow draft, allowing them to explore a wide variety of remote and beautiful spots. If they want, clients can explore Kuna villages by day and then come back to the yacht at night, which generally anchors well away from population centers. Weeklong cruises include a forest hike. Airfare from Panama City to the islands is not included, but it can be arranged by the company, as can hotel stays and a day tour in Panama City.

The second best way to explore the islands is by small, adventure-type cruise ship. Outfits that often include Kuna Yala as part of their itineraries include Tauck World Discovery, Cruise West, and American Canadian Caribbean Line (see sidebar, *Expedition and Adventure Cruises,* in the *Know Panama* chapter for details). Several of the huge cruise ships that transit the Panama Canal also stop in the islands. Tourists can outnumber Kunas during these brief visits, which are hardly the ideal way to experience the islands or Kuna culture.

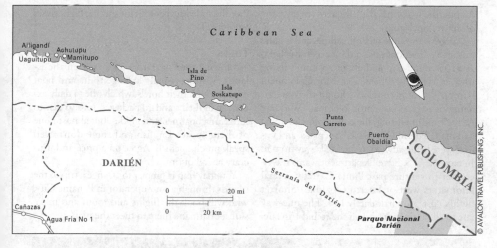

Centro de Buceos Isla Grande (tel. 501-4374, cell 656-6095, buceoenpanama@tutopia.com, www.buceoenpanama.com) offers a three-day snorkeling and diving trip that includes two dives near Isla Grande and snorkeling in Kuna Yala (again, the Kuna have banned scuba tanks from their waters). The cost is $460 per person ($40 less if just snorkeling), including one night in a Panama City hotel, all transportation including flights between Panama City and the islands, meals, equipment, and a night's stay at Hotel San Blas.

Note: Some tourists are under the misimpression that it's easy to buy passage on a boat from El Porvenir to Colombia. This is not the case. Though I don't recommend hitching a ride in these waters, which are known drug-trafficking routes, it's far easier to do so from Colón or Isla Grande. Tourists have been known to get stranded on Porvenir for days waiting for a ride, if they get one at all. It may be possible to buy passage down the archipelago, or trade a ride for work, on a private yacht, a Colombian trader, or a 75-foot-long Kuna supply boat. The latter two options are quite rustic, slow, and most likely unsafe. It's also possible to arrange boat transportation from the area around Nombre de Dios, but this is generally on small motorized fishing boats and is a quite risky way to get to the islands. There is no commercial boat transport to and from the islands.

By Air

Most visitors who want to stay on the islands come by small plane from Panama City. Flying on these tiny, sometimes aged-looking contraptions can be an adventure in itself, especially while crossing the coastal range. But on a clear day the views are breathtaking, and the flights are mercifully short—usually less than an hour.

Two airlines fly from Panama City to islands and coastal airstrips in the *comarca*. Each generally offers one daily, early-morning flight to and from the major island groups. The planes make several stops, so be careful to get off at the right place—on my last visit, a couple got off at the wrong place and spoiled their entire yacht trip. For those staying at one of the island hotels, transportation by small boat between the closest airstrip and the hotel is included with a stay. There are no true airline offices in the archipelago, but hotels can sometimes make or change reservations for guests. However, it's best to come to the islands with a round-trip ticket and stick to the itinerary.

Aeroperlas (tel. 315-7500, fax 315-7580, info@aeroperlas.com, www.aeroperlas.com) has daily flights to the main islands in the chain. Don't be concerned if you're booked on Aero Taxi or ANSA—these are Aeroperlas subsidiaries.

The new **Turismo Aéreo** (tel. 315-0279 or 315-0300, fax 315-0300, www.turismoaereo.com) is providing increased competition for

Kuna Yala

Aeroperlas. It also has daily flights to many parts of the archipelago.

Airfare is the same on both airlines and is quite reasonable. The longest and most expensive flight, at $105 round-trip and about an hour's flying time, is to Puerto Obaldía, near the Colombian border. The only travelers who go there are attempting to cross over into Colombia. (Warning: At the time of writing, the conflict in Colombia had made Puerto Obaldía a dicey place, and visitors were being advised to stay well away from it. In fact, the U.S. State Department warns travelers not to venture past Punta Carreto, several kilometers west of Puerto Obaldía.) Shorter flights cost proportionately less. The one-way fare to all destinations is half the round-trip fare.

(See the individual entries for specific flight times and fares.)

Tours

No formal tour operators are based on the islands. Visitors usually arrange tours and boat trips through their hotels, which offer a daily excursion in their standard packages. It's also easy to hire Kuna boatmen and guides, but almost none of them speaks English and some don't even speak much Spanish. Agree on a price and itinerary ahead of time.

You may find it simpler to arrange a trip to the islands through a tour operator in Panama City, who will book the flights and room and make sure a boatman's there to meet the plane.

El Porvenir and Surroundings

The small island of El Porvenir is the western point of entry for the archipelago. It has a landing strip, a couple of government offices, and a basic hotel. There's also an **artisans' cooperative** that sells *molas* and other arts and crafts. The **Museo de la Nación Kuna** (Museum of the Kuna Nation) was nearing completion on the far side of the island during my last visit. Housed in a two-story yellow building, it was going to have displays on Kuna art, history, and culture. There's little else on the island. But because it's isolated from the densely populated islands nearby, its

Kuna villages often have houses of worship in a variety of non-indigenous faiths.

PARADISE UNDER PRESSURE

The spectacularly clear water around the islands makes the *comarca*'s underwater flora and fauna the big draw for most visitors. For starters, consider the coral reefs that can make navigating these waters so treacherous: According to the Smithsonian Tropical Research Institution, which until recently had a research facility on the islands, Kuna Yala has more coral species than just about anywhere else in the Caribbean. It's easy to spot colorful staghorn, brain, fan, and leaf coral, among many others. Nearly 60 species of marine sponges grow on the western side of the *comarca*.

Sadly, however, over-fishing and reef destruction have decimated marine life. Five types of lobster are found here, but they are in danger of local extinction because Kuna divers catch them to sell to outside commercial interests. The same thing is happening with other marine creatures, including sea turtles and, beginning in the early 1990s, even small tropical fish, which are ending up in household aquariums in the United States. Marine life in the region, while still impressive, is not what it was even a decade ago.

The Kuna also lost nearly 80 percent of their remaining coral in the last three decades of the 20th century, according to a study conducted in 2003, due mainly to "coral mining" to build seawalls and landfill to expand islands, as well as some natural causes.

About 90 percent of the *comarca*'s territory on the mainland is still covered with forest. Though these forests are under pressure, animals found in them include the collared and white-lipped peccary, Baird's tapir, red brocket (a kind of deer), and iguana.

little beach is clean and pleasant. For most people, though, this island is just a transit point.

NEARBY ISLANDS

Clustered just to the south of El Porvenir are Wichub-Huala, Ukuptupu, and Nalunega. Wichub-Huala and Nalunega both have villages. All these islands usually have generator-powered electricity 6 P.M.–midnight, and it's much easier to find English speakers here than elsewhere in the archipelago. All three islands are just a couple of minutes from each other by motorized boat.

Ukuptupu is entirely covered with a sprawling wooden complex connected by boardwalks that was the home of a Smithsonian research facility for 21 years. The Kuna, ever suspicious of foreigners in their *comarca*, finally kicked the Smithsonian out of Kuna Yala in 1998. The research facility is now a rustic hotel. **Nalunega** is most popular with visitors because it's home to the Hotel San Blas, the oldest hotel in the archipelago. The villages here and on Wichub-Huala make the islands worth a visit, but the surrounding water is too polluted to swim in.

Wichub-Huala has the attractive Hotel Kuna Niscua, a health center, and a small community.

Popular day trips from the hotel islands include snorkeling around the uninhabited island of Achutupu or exploring the densely inhabited islands of Cartí, especially the large community of Cartí Suitupu.

◪ ACHUTUPU

The idyllic uninhabited and semi-inhabited islands around the El Porvenir area are all east or northeast of this busy hub. The most popular with visitors is Achutupu, also known as Isla de Los Perros (Dog Island). It's a private island with just one small family living on it. (Note: Don't confuse this Achutupu with the large, crowded island of the same name much farther east.) Everything about this pristine speck of sand and palm trees is straight out of a postcard. The water is calm and crystalline, with great snorkeling visibility. And the snorkeling here is fun: There's an old shipwreck in shallow water just off the south side of the island. It's overgrown with brilliant coral and has become a playground for a variety of small and medium-sized tropical fish.

Kuna Yala

© WILLIAM FRIAR

Achutupu is the most popular boat trip from the El Porvenir area, offering a deserted beach and snorkeling in crystal clear water.

Achutupu is surrounded by other lovely islands, with rustic Kuna sailboats and the occasional sleek foreign yacht gliding around them. If Achutupu isn't perfect enough, ask the boatman to do some more exploring. Resist the urge to use up your entire stock of film in this area.

CARTÍ

South of the Porvenir area, about a 40-minute motorized boat ride away, is a cluster of islands and a bit of coast known collectively as Cartí (Gardi). There's a large, vibrant village on Cartí Suitupu (Gardi Sugdup), which makes it a popular cruise-ship destination. This place sees more foreigners than any other part of the archipelago, so it's perhaps not surprising it has an estimated two dozen bars/soda stands. There is generator-powered electricity 6 P.M.–midnight.

Especially noteworthy is a small **Kuna museum** (tel. 299-9002 or 299-9074, 8 A.M.–4 P.M. daily, $2) housed in a thatch-roofed hut. It has its own dock, so small boats can go there directly. The displays are modest but include an interesting mix of traditional implements, exhibits on the Kuna puberty ritual (only girls go through

this, and it's a huge, drunken party for the whole village), vintage *molas,* and so on. It gives a glimpse into the mythology, history, rituals, and daily life of the Kuna. A Kuna man named José Davis, who established the museum along with his father, gives guided tours of the exhibits in English and Spanish, with lots of intricate and sometimes hard-to-follow explanations of Kuna history and religion. One of the more interesting tidbits is a description of Kuna burials. (The cemeteries are on the mainland, where the Kunas dig underground rooms and string them with hammocks into which the deceased are placed.)

Visitors are welcome to stop by the other islands in the group as well, which are not quite as modernized or heavily touristed as Cartí Suitupu.

PRACTICALITIES
Accommodations and Food

Nearly all visitors fly into El Porvenir and stay at one of the basic hotels on the surrounding islands. Hotel stays generally include all meals, transfers to and from the airstrip on El Porvenir, and daily boat trips. These trips are generally to Achutupu or Cartí, but jungle hikes on the mainland or boat rides to the remote Cayos Holandéses are sometimes possible for an extra fee. Expect to pay at least $50 per boat for a trip to the Holandéses. The Hotel San Blas offers a three-hour hike through mainland forests that leads to a village and a waterfall for $60 per person.

The 🎝 **Hotel San Blas** (tel. 257-3311, cell 582-1221, hotelsanblas@hotmail.com or hotelsanblas@nativeweb.com, $35 per person including all meals and two daily boat trips with an English-speaking guide), on Nalunega, is the old stalwart among the archipelago's hotels. It consists of a couple of dozen rooms on the southern side of Nalunega. There are three kinds of accommodations here. The huts right on the beach have sand floors and offer slightly more privacy, as they are a few centimeters away from their neighbors. If a breeze is more important than privacy, for the same price one can get a room in the large building behind the huts, which has eight rooms upstairs and six downstairs. The nicer, breezier ones are upstairs. Be warned, though, that this is essentially a dormitory with cane dividers that don't reach all the way to the very tall thatch roof. If anyone up there snores, you'll soon find out about it. Also, there's not much of a view from the rooms even though the building is only a few steps from the beach. There's also a concrete building with three rooms and a private bath on the second floor, plus a private dining area, but this is meant for families or large groups.

The hotel is owned by Luis Burgos, a laid-back Kuna who speaks English and Spanish, but it's more likely your host will be Juan Amado, who is fully bilingual and used to work for a travel agency. Meals are served in a large common dining area downstairs or on a more open and breezy terrace upstairs that has a view of the sea. Seafood is the staple diet, but basic vegetarian meals can be arranged. One thing that sets the hotel apart is that it offers two daily boat trips rather than just one.

The rest of the island is taken up by a village of about 450 inhabitants. One of the charms of this place is staying in such close proximity to the Kuna. Guests are free to wander around the village, but there's enough of an invisible divide between the hotel and the rest of the island to ensure both the Kuna and guests a certain degree of privacy from each other. There's a general store with basic supplies and several kiosks that sell sodas, cookies, beer, and such. As with other Kuna villages, this one is none too clean, but the hotel staff rakes the sand around the hotel every day, ensuring its little patch is tidy. Still, the outhouses over the water on either side of the hotel's small beach should be a tip-off that this isn't a good place to go for a swim (the hotel's own bathrooms are shared, rustic, and not terribly clean, but they do have plumbing).

The hotel rents snorkeling equipment (mask, snorkel, and fins) for $6. But you may find yourself drawn to the hotel's most popular activity: snoozing in shaded hammocks right at the edge of the lapping sea. This is a very relaxing place. You should know, however, that rats are a fact of life on the islands, and they tend to make an appearance here more often than at some other Kuna hotels. I've never heard of anyone's being bitten, but the rustling critters have been known to upset a good night's sleep.

Hotel Kuna Niscua (tel. 259-3471 or cell 681-3167, $35 per person including all meals and a daily boat tour), on Wichub-Huala, is the most attractive hotel in the region. It's still quite simple, but it's a tidy, well-cared-for place. The main building is concrete, but softened by intricately woven cane walls. There are a half-dozen rooms with shared bath, plus a common area and a balcony strung with hammocks. The rooms in the second building (also with shared bath) are darker and offer less privacy. Most have just a single window, so try to get the corner room overlooking the water; it has more windows.

There's little else on the island except for village houses, a health center, and a school. A kiosk near the pier sells beer, water, soda, and other basic goods.

Cabañas Ukuptupu (tel. 293-8709 or 299-9011, ukuptupu@hotmail.com, $35 per person including all meals and a daily boat trip) is the only thing on the rocky island of Ukuptupu, nestled between Wichub-Huala and Nalunega. The hotel, which until 1998 was a Smithsonian research facility, consists of 15

Kuna Yala

THE KUNA PEOPLE

Some still refer to the Kuna as the San Blas Indians, because of the Spanish name for the archipelago where most Kuna live. But Kuna is the preferred term, and the archipelago is increasingly known by its official name, Kuna Yala (land of the Kuna). To confuse matters, the Kuna call themselves the Tule, though they refer to themselves as Kuna when dealing with *uagas* (outsiders).

No one knows for sure where the Kuna originally came from, but surprisingly enough they have only been on the islands a few hundred years. Before that they lived in the Darién forest, but wars with the Spanish, the Emberá-Wounaan, and descendants of escaped African slaves gradually pushed them toward the Caribbean coast and islands. Some Darién rivers that are now part of Emberá and Wounaan territory still bear Kuna names.

Some Kuna remain in the mainland forests, mostly in two other *comarcas,* Madungandí and Wargandí. The mainland Kuna were historically known as the *Kuna Bravo* (fierce Kuna, for their warriorlike ways). The most remote of these see few visitors, cling especially tightly to their

traditional ways, and tend to exclude outsiders, whom they view with considerable suspicion. A distinction is still made between the more open and adaptable "island Kuna" and the traditional "mainland Kuna."

Most of the inhabitants of the Comarca de Kuna Yala are island Kuna, but even they travel by *cayuco* to the mainland to farm, hunt, and bury their dead. About 40,000 of the estimated 61,700 Kuna live on the islands. The rest live in the mainland forests, in Panama City, and scattered around the country.

The Kuna have done a remarkable job over the centuries of keeping invaders out and holding onto their rich culture. They even fought and won a re-

Toucans and macaws are popular pets on the islands.

basic but spacious cane-and-wood rooms over shallow water, connected to each other by boardwalks. Because it's very easy to walk off the boardwalks into the ocean, this is not a place to bring small children. The hotel completely covers the tiny island, so it's more private and isolated than the other hotels in this region, without the pros and cons of sharing an island with a Kuna village. Beds consist of foam mattresses in a wooden frame. Bathrooms are shared but have flush toilets. Guests take bucket baths from barrels filled with rainwater. There's an open-air bar with a pool table,

and a little library with battered books. The hotel has good views of the ocean and the surrounding inhabited islands. Hammocks are strung up around the place, which tends to get a nice breeze. An underwater rock corral houses the lobsters, crab, and other sea creatures guests may be offered for dinner. The owner, a sexagenarian named Juan García, worked in a U.S. military mess hall for five years and speaks fluent English.

volt against the Republic of Panama in 1925, which eventually earned them their semiautonomous status. Today, no foreigner is allowed to own land in Kuna territory.

Kunas have gained a greater voice in Panamanian government in recent years. In 1999 a Kuna, Enrique Garrido, became the head of Panama's general assembly.

Visitors are inevitably struck by the beautiful traditional dress of the Kuna women, which is not worn to impress tourists. The Kuna themselves cite the preservation of women's traditional clothing and ornamentation as vital to maintaining their culture.

The most famous part of this dress are the panels of intricately worked cloth that decorate the front and back of the woman's blouse. Known as *molas* (*mola* is Kuna for blouse), these panels are prized by collectors around the world. (See the *Art of the Mola* sidebar.) Older women in particular also wear gold rings through the bottom of their nose and tight strings of beads around their forearms and lower legs.

The Kuna are physically striking in other ways. For one thing, by European standards they are short, growing to about 150 centimeters (five feet), but have what to outsiders seem to be disproportionately large heads and limbs. In spite of their short stature, basketball is the most popular sport on the islands. Kunas also have the highest rate of albinism in the world for reasons that are still not well understood. Known as "moon children," albinos are treated as special people but, sadly, have a shortened life expectancy because of their susceptibility to skin cancer. Why a people so close to the equator should have such a high rate of albinism has fascinated scientists for years.

The Kuna have always been wary of outsiders, and that's a major reason they still exist. One can have a relatively inexpensive stay in the San Blas Islands, but nothing is free; even taking a photo of a Kuna usually costs a dollar. The Kunas' reticence, and a belief that visitors should pay for the privilege of visiting their homeland, can be off-putting to those who come with stereotyped notions of fun-loving, generous Indians. It's not hard to see the Kunas' point of view, though. Outsiders have been trying to take their home away from them for centuries, and even visitors with more benign intentions often treat them as colorful parts of the scenery. One Kuna official I chatted with a few years back angrily recounted instances in which he felt Kunas were treated, at best, as so much travel-brochure fodder, concluding: *No somos animales* ("We are not animals").

Try to bear that in mind during your stay. At the very least, never take a photo of a Kuna without asking permission first. You'll probably find that if you're willing to accept the Kuna on their own terms, you'll get a glimpse of a fascinating world.

If all the above are full, the 13-room **Hotel El Porvenir** (tel. 221-1397 or 221-1392, cell 697-2008 or 698-4471, U.S. tel. 954/486-1776, hotelelporvenir@hotmail.com, vivi_archibold@hotmail.com, $30 per person, including all meals and a daily boat tour) may have to do. Rooms here are drab, dark, and run-down, and they have worn mattresses and zero charm. The staff is friendly, though, and there are toilets and showers in the rooms, though they're not especially clean. There's a gazebo area strung with hammocks for guests to use. As the name suggests, the hotel is on the island of El Porvenir, which is also home to the area's airstrip and some small government offices. There's nothing else on the island, which means you'll have plenty of peace and quiet—at least until an airplane lands, since the hotel is almost on the airstrip. The little beach here is pleasant, and the water seems much cleaner than that surrounding the crowded islands nearby. But you'll likely feel quite isolated.

Getting There

Nearly all visitors fly into El Porvenir and transfer to the surrounding islands. Flights from Panama City to El Porvenir cost $31.50/$63 one-way/round-trip. Both Turismo Aeréo and Aeroperlas have a daily flight that leaves at around 6 A.M., arriving in Porvenir about 25 minutes later. The return flights leave at about 6:35 A.M.

Kuna Yala

Río Sidra and Surroundings

Río Sidra is a densely packed island of about 2,000 inhabitants that has seen more and more visitors in recent years thanks to a growing range of accommodations in the area.

Río Sidra actually comprises two communities, Mamartupo and Urgandí, that have distinctive identities. The school is the unofficial dividing line between the two. Mamartupo faces the sea; Urgandí faces the land. It's quite crowded, with huts packed tightly together over the entire surface of the island. Some of the inhabitants sport modern clothing; it's jarring to see a teenage Kuna kid in gangsta-inspired street wear.

NEARBY ISLANDS
⋈ Isla Maquina
One island well worth a visit is Isla Maquina (Mormarketupo in Kuna), about a 10-minute boat ride from Río Sidra. It's the quietest and most purely traditional of the islands in the region and one of the most traditional in the archipel-

hanging on the dock at Mamartupo

ago. It's known for its *mola* makers. Huts aren't as squashed together, and it's quite tidy and significantly cleaner than other islands. There are a school and water supplied by an aqueduct, but very little else in the way of facilities—no hotel, no health center. It's pleasant to wander around the narrow paths lined with cane fences that border homes. There are a few places to buy sodas and snacks.

Kuanidup
Kuanidup is a gorgeous island a half hour away by motorized boat from Río Sidra. Actually, there are two Kuanidups. The first is Kuanidup Grande, which is home just to Cabañas Kuanidup, a sandy beach, a sand volleyball court, and hammocks strung between coconut palms. About the same size as tiny Isla Robinson, it's "grande" only in comparison to its little sister, Kuanidup Chico. There's nothing but a single hut, sand, and palm trees on Kuanidup Chico, which is an easy swim away (maybe 300 meters) for a moderately fit swimmer. The hotel staff on Kuanidup Grande can also ferry guests over.

There's pretty good snorkeling around the islands. It's fun to circumnavigate Kuanidup Chico and explore the coral shelf that rings the island; it has surprisingly diverse coral species. Take it slow and really check things out: There are lots of small, hidden natural treasures. Watch out for sea urchins, fire coral, and sudden shallows. Visibility plummets after a rain because of the proximity to mainland rivers.

Other islands in the area include **Nusatupo (Isla Ratón),** a populated island next to Río Sidra, and the small, private **Isla Robinson,** between Río Sidra and Kuanidup.

ACCOMMODATIONS AND FOOD
As usual, hotel stays generally include all meals and daily boat tours, though room-only options are available. Typical tours go to Achutupo (the uninhabited one with the shipwreck, not the

THE ART OF THE MOLA

Molas are made from several layers of brightly colored cotton cloth. Kuna women create these works of art using a technique of cutting and sewing sometimes referred to as reverse appliqué. The way the cloth is cut reveals the layers beneath, which all go into creating the overall design. Designs can be abstract or representational. The best are such works of art that *mola*-making has been described as being like painting with a needle.

What should you look for in a *mola*? Anthropologist Mari Lyn Salvador conducted a study in which she asked Kuna women themselves that question. A few of her findings:

1. The design should be balanced and all the spaces filled.
2. The lines should be thin and evenly spaced, with smooth edges.
3. Stitches should be small, even, and nearly invisible.
4. The design should stand out and be easy to see, which is largely a matter of the proper use of contrast and color.

For more information on Kuna arts and culture, see *The Art of Being Kuna: Layers of Meaning Among the Kuna of Panama* (UCLA Fowler Museum of Cultural History), edited by Mari Lyn Salvador.

one farther down the archipelago) or Río Sidra. With at least one day's notice and permission from local authorities, it's possible to visit a mainland cemetery. This requires a guide, which will probably be an extra fee. Visitors are not allowed to take photos at the cemetery.

$25–50
Cabañas Isla Robinson (tel. 299-9058 public phone on Río Sidra, $17.50 per person) is a private island between Río Sidra and Kuanidup that's about half the size of a football field. It's about 15 minutes by boat from Río Sidra. There is nothing on it but palm trees, seven cane-walled huts, a ramshackle outhouse over the water, an outdoor shower, and a plastic common table with some chairs. The huts are sand-floored and equipped only with hammocks. It's a place for those who don't need much more than a rustic shelter from the elements. It's popular with backpackers because it offers the cheapest appealing accommodations on the islands, but once one starts adding in the extras the savings quickly become marginal. Meals are $3 each and transfers from the landing strip on the mainland are $10 each way. Do some calculating before deciding to stay here, as the relatively more upscale Kuanidup may be a better deal, particularly if one wants boat tours. To make a reservation, call the public

phone on Río Sidra (tel. 299-9058) and ask for Sr. Robinson. Be prepared for a long wait while someone looks for him, or else say you'll call back in 5–10 minutes. This place fills up, so try to book a hut at least several days in advance, and confirm before arriving.

Refresquería Petita (tel. 299-9058 public phone, $25 per person, including all meals and a boat tour, or $15–20 just for the room), in the Mamartupo community on Río Sidra, is right next to the main pier and may appeal to those who want to get a taste of Kuna community life. It offers three small, wood-paneled upstairs rooms, one with bunk beds and two with balconies, with foam beds and shared flush toilet and shower. There are no fans and the rooms are pretty airless. But they look down on the neighboring houses, which lets one snoop on the daily life of the neighbors. It's owned by Humberto Ayarza, a friendly man who worked for the U.S. military in Albrook for 45 years and speaks English and Spanish. To make a reservation, call the public phone (tel. 299-9058) and ask for him. The *refresquería* itself sells homemade cakes and muffins as well as other snacks.

$50–100
Two minutes by boat from Río Sidra is Nusatupo (Isla Ratón), most notable for the recently

Kuna Yala

expanded **Hotel Kuna Yala** (tel. 315-7520, 315-0570, or 315-0279 in Panama City, $40 per person, including all meals and a boat tour), a three-story concrete building on the water's edge that offers 11 rooms with foam mattresses. The place was in the middle of a major overhaul on my last visit and it was hard to tell exactly what the end product would be like, but it appeared it would be an okay place if not for the long line of outhouses on the water right next door. The hotel has a view right down into them, and when the breeze blows the wrong way there's a strong sewage stench. The hotel itself was having flush toilets installed. The owner, Manuel Alfaro, works with Turismo Aéreo, and the place is managed by his daughter, Inilda, and her partner Rogelio López. Visitors are asked to make a "voluntary contribution" to visit the island—$1 per couple should do it.

The best place to stay in the region, **Cabañas Kuanidup** (tel. 227-7661, fax 227-1396, $75 per person, including all meals and a daily boat tour; kids ages 5–10 are $45) is a good bet for those who want the beauty of a remote island without spending a fortune for the privilege of living simply. The location is gorgeous. Because the nearest sizable settlement is a half-hour boat ride away, the sea here is clean and the beaches free of trash. There are 10 cabañas with foam mattresses, sand floors, and the usual thatched roofs and cane walls. They are spaced a few feet away from each other to offer a bit of privacy. Accommodations vary from a small cabaña with a double bed to a couple of large ones with four single beds. The cabañas are rustic but comfortable. There are shared toilets and showers with very weak water pressure in a separate hut and a small open-sided dining room on the opposite end of the island. Guests can buy beer, wine, water, and *seco* at a little bar area. Lights in the dining room are powered by solar panels, but the cabañas are lit only by kerosene lanterns. Try to make reservations well ahead of time in the dry season, and confirm before arriving. The standard package includes daily boat trips to tour Río Sidra or snorkel and laze around Achutupu. The only other entertainment will be looking at the blue ocean, the occasional small fishing boat, and the islands off in the distance. You have to be truly in the mood to get away from everything to come here.

GETTING THERE

Río Sidra is about an hour from the Porvenir area by motorized boat, but few people go all that way just for a day trip. Most travelers arrive by air. Río Sidra's airstrip is actually on the mainland coast rather than the island itself. Airfare is $31.50/$63 one-way/round-trip. Both Turismo Aéreo and Aeroperlas have a daily flight that leaves Panama City at around 6 A.M. The flight takes about 45 minutes. The return flights leave around 6:55 A.M. An office near the bright red Centro Deportivo Mamartupo on Río Sidra sells Turismo Aéreo tickets (6 A.M.–5 P.M. daily), though it's a better idea to book the entire trip in Panama City before leaving.

Corazón de Jesús and Narganá

Another hub of island life lies about 40 kilometers east of El Porvenir, centered around the inhabited islands of Corazón de Jesús and Narganá (pop. 12,685), which are linked by a footbridge. These are the least traditional islands in the archipelago. There are more concrete buildings than thatch-roofed huts, and most younger women do not wear traditional clothing. There's electricity around the clock, and at night residents gather in the homes and stores of those with TVs to watch shows, with great enthusiasm.

These islands are unlikely to interest most travelers. Since the closing a few years back of the Kwadule Eco-Lodge, once the archipelago's most upscale hotel, there is no appealing place to stay here. Only those who've spent a great deal of time on the more traditional islands are likely to find these more modern and less colorful ones of great interest, and only then for the contrast they provide.

The more southerly island, Narganá, has the archipelago's one true bank, a small branch of the Banco Nacional de Panamá. The central square has a statue of Charles Robinson, a pivotal figure in Kuna Yala's 1925 war against Panama. Public phones are at the side of the square, and there's a hospital, school, church, and police station nearby. It also has the best place to eat and the only hotel. With quite a bit of humor, residents have named the "barrios" of this small island after those in Panama City—the vicinity of the lone bank thus becomes the *area bancaria* (banking area), the posher homes are in "Paitilla," the poorer ones are in "Chorrillo," the main walkway is "Avenida Central," and so on.

THE SPIRIT OF THE *UAGA*

All things come from Mother Earth. Nothing exists that is more necessary than she is. Without her, life is not possible. Our ancestors fought for her because they recognized her value. "I am nothing without the earth. I would be poor without her," so they said . . .

We always left medicinal plants in the fields when we cleared and cut trees. The elders give us advice about how to take care of useful plants. Therefore, in Kuna Yala we still have forests. The foreigners don't do this. They thoughtlessly destroy nature for their livestock.

The jungle and the forests provide us with meat, as well as wines, poles, and medicinal plants. In them lie our history and our culture. We know that Europeans don't have the same resources because their scientists come to the Comarca to see what is in our forests. I want it to stay this way, but I'm afraid that one of them will arrive with a chainsaw.

The lobster traders are responsible for the deterioration of our main resources—only for the money. Even if we want to control the fishing of lobsters, we won't succeed, because the young people who are involved in this activity are making their living from it.

Our tradition of working together no longer exists. Once, when a decision was made to address a problem, everyone complied unanimously. Now they follow money. We are acquiring the spirit of the *uaga* (foreigner, outsider).

Once everything is evaluated in terms of money, it changes one's way of being, it makes one selfish. So said our forefathers. Thus we are beginning to deceive our forefathers. That's what I think.

From "The Spirit of the *Uaga*" by Cacique General Carlos López, recorded by Valerio Núñez from *Plants and Animals in the Life of the Kuna* by Jorge Ventocilla, Heraclio Herrera, Valerio Núñez, edited by Hans Roeder, translated by Elisabeth King, © 1995. Courtesy of the University of Texas Press.

Kuna Yala

Corazón de Jesús is across a short footbridge (watch for loose planks) on the seaward-facing side of the island. It has the airstrip, a simple restaurant, a pool hall, and little else.

Isla Tigre, also called Río Tigre, is a few kilometers east. A visit to the traditional Kuna community here is the most common day trip for visitors.

PRACTICALITIES

The only hotel on either island is **Hotel Noris** (tel. 299-9009 or 299-9090 public phones, $10 s or $15 d with fan, $15 s or $20 d with air-conditioning), a pink, two-story concrete building facing the mainland that has seven spartan but okay rooms. Some have air-conditioning and private toilets and showers; the rest are more basic, with fans and shared baths. Room number one is the nicest. The location isn't very nice, however—it's right on a somewhat swampy shore that smells of sewage. Boat rides to a nearby beach are $5 per person; trips to Isla Tigre are $15. Meals can also be arranged. Laundry is $3 a load. Call one of the public phones and ask for Paco, the half-Kuna, half-Spanish owner of the place.

Restaurante Nali's Café (6:30 A.M.–10:30 P.M. daily) is the nicest place to eat on either island. A full seafood meal costs no more than $4, and the food is both good and nicely presented. More basic din-ners cost $2.50. Breakfast offerings include eggs, ham, and sausage. Diners, if they want, can rent a film at the café and watch it on the TV inside. But most will probably prefer to sit in the open-air area, which is right on the beach overlooking the channel between Narganá and Corazón de Jesús.

Minisuper Lelia, one of a couple of tiny stores near the café, sells cheese, butter, chicken, fruit, basic supplies, and so on. **Tienda Eidi,** a kiosk near the volleyball court, sells fresh produce and chocolate as well as other more commonly found goods.

Over on Corazón de Jesús is **Fonda Delicias de Mi Pueblo** (6:30 A.M.–10 P.M.), a basic but pleasant open-air restaurant next to the pool hall, **Billar Akuanusa,** which can look intimidating from the outside but is actually a friendly place to have a beer and knock balls around.

Narganá has a small branch of the Banco Nacional de Panamá (8 A.M.–2 P.M. Mon.–Fri., 9 A.M.–noon Sat.). It has no ATM.

It takes about 2.5 hours by motorized *cayuco* to reach these islands from El Porvenir. Except for those on a yacht, it's much more practical to come here by plane. The airstrip is on Corazón de Jesús. Aeroperlas and Turismo Aéreo have daily flights that leave Panama City at 6 A.M. The return flight leaves around 6:40 A.M. Airfare is $33.60 one-way, $67.20 round-trip on either airline. The flight takes about half an hour.

Playon Chico and Surroundings

Playon Chico (Ukupseni in Kuna) is a fairly large, somewhat bedraggled village island of about 3,000 inhabitants. It's a relatively modern community with a two-story health center, the churches of a half-dozen religions, some houses made of concrete, and even a group of allegedly drug-dealing teens who hang out in a graffiti-covered "youth hall." But there are still lots of traditional huts and traditional ways. Though none too tidy, Playon Chico is full of life, and it's fascinating to walk down the main drag and watch kids romping, a father playing a flute for his children, local dancers practicing for a festival, women sewing *molas,* and old men playing dominoes. A concrete footbridge connects the island with an airstrip on the mainland.

There are two hotel islands, **Sapibenega** and **Yandup,** a few minutes' boat ride away from Playon Chico.

Isla Iguana (Arridup) is a private island 20 minutes by boat from Sapibenega. It's cared for by the hotel, whose staff rakes the sand and clears debris and trash to make it appealing for guests. It's a nice place to hang out on the beach by a coconut palm and look at the sea or the forest-covered mountains, but the snorkeling isn't very good. The coral has been decimated, the water is

The Kuna have their own trading vessels to bring supplies from the mainland.

often turbulent and cloudy, especially after a rain, and the fish are scarce.

There are other islands nearby, both uninhabited and with traditional villages, that can be visited with guides from the hotels. Trips to the nearby cemetery on the mainland can also be arranged, as can more ambitious forest hikes.

PRACTICALITIES

There are few facilities, no hotels, and no appealing places to eat on Playon Chico. Visitors generally stay on one of the two hotel islands.

Accommodations and Food

Yandup (tel. 261-7229, 261-6347, or 220-0467, cell 606-6917, yandup@cableonda.net, www.yandup.tripod.com, $60 per person, including meals and daily tour; discount for kids), a small island about five minutes by boat from Playon Chico, offers four bungalows with wooden floors, bamboo walls, decent mattresses, and front porches overlooking the sea. There's an open-air dining room, and shared toilets and showers outside. It's quite a simple place with few extras, which will suit some people just fine. The main

problem is it's near a mangrove forest, and the *chitras* can be a serious nuisance.

Sapibenega: The Kuna Lodge (tel. 226-8824, cell 676-5548, fax 226-9283, thekunalodge@sapibenega.com, www.sapibenega.com, $90 s, $180 d, $240 t, plus a one-time charge of $20, including all meals and daily boat tour; there are discounts for children), just a few minutes by boat from Playon Chico, has the best accommodations and service in the archipelago. Formerly known as Iskardup, it's a small island with seven bungalows, each with two units. Most have double beds, but one larger bungalow can accommodate three or four people in each unit. The bungalows are spacious, with wooden floors, cane walls, comfortable beds, flush toilets, and tiled showers with good water pressure. All look out on the sea, and hammocks are strung up just outside the back doors, on the edge of the water. Like everyplace else in Kuna Yala, though, accommodations are still rustic and close to nature. Don't be surprised to find small crabs in the shower or geckos hiding in the soap dish.

Sapibenega has a large, attentive staff eager to make sure guests are entirely comfortable. There is an attractive dining room, a bar, and a lounge area

Kuna Yala

with rough-hewn furniture inside a large thatched-roof building with high ceilings and open sides. Another bar is in a little *rancho* set on pilings above the water, connected by a walkway with the island. There is electricity 24 hours a day, supplied by solar cells and a generator. Food here is very good, and tiki torches are set up on the grounds at night so guests can dine under the stars. The island is within hailing distance of the shore, but far enough away from everything to feel remote and tranquil.

Getting There and Away

Playon Chico is far down the archipelago, and most people arrive and leave by airplane. The airstrip is on the mainland, connected by a footbridge with Playon Chico. Aeréo Turismo and Aeroperlas have daily flights that leave Panama City at 6 A.M. They return from Playon Chico around 6:50 A.M. The fare is $37.80/$75.60 one-way/round-trip on either airline. The flight takes about 45 minutes.

Achutupu and Surroundings

Don't confuse this Achutupu with the little private island described elsewhere. This is a densely populated island quite a bit farther east and south down the archipelago, less than 100 kilometers from the Colombian border. It's an interesting place to visit, although as usual be considerate about where you poke your nose and always ask permission before snapping a photo. In the middle of the island is a huge gathering house. These long thatch-roofed buildings are the center of community life in Kuna villages. If you're lucky,

a puberty ceremony or community meeting will be taking place on the island during your stay. If you're very lucky, you'll be allowed to observe some of it.

Immediately to the east of Achutupu, about a minute away by boat, is **Uaguitupu,** also known as Dolphin Island. About half the island is taken up by Kuna huts, while the other half is home to Dolphin Island Lodge. This part of the island is pretty and offers tranquil views. However, it doesn't offer much in the way of a beach. This is

Guests at Dolphin Island Lodge can get a close-up look at Kuna life.

primarily a place to collapse in a hammock for hours on end, and for that it's just about perfect.

About 20 minutes north of these islands are a series of coral heads. If the sea is calm and the visibility good, the snorkeling here is okay. Sadly, though, intensive fishing in the area makes it unlikely you'll see much besides tiny fish.

Those who stay at the Dolphin Island Lodge—and there's probably nowhere else here they'd want to stay—will probably be offered a trip to the peculiarly named **Islandia.** (That's right: Iceland. Go figure.) This is a microscopic uninhabited island with a thin strip of beach. One would have more of a sense of getting away from it all if beer cans, plastic bags, and other garbage from the inhabited islands didn't wash up on the shore. Still, it's worth a visit if only for the scenic boat ride, which gives good views of the islands, both uninhabited and packed with huts. There's a good chance of passing a Kuna sailboat gliding by, with the deep forests of the coastal mountain range as backdrop. The major inhabited island of **Ailigandí** is a short distance west of Islandia, closer to the mainland. The curious can ask the boatman to stop there. Other possibilities include forest hikes and a tour of a Kuna cemetery.

Potential visitors should note that it's harder in this part of the archipelago to get completely away from the inevitable garbage and sewage that plague the islands.

PRACTICALITIES
Accommodations
Ⓜ **Dolphin Island Lodge,** also called Cabañas Uaguitupu (tel. 225-8435 or 263-7780, fax 225-2521, info@uaguinega.com, www.dolphin-lodge.com, $110 s, $190 d, including all meals and a daily boat trip; rates are $15 per person cheaper after the first night), is in some ways a good blend of the other accommodations in the archipelago. It offers seclusion and comfortable surroundings, yet there's an interesting Kuna village just minutes away on Achutupu. The only thing on the island is the lodge, which consists of nine bungalows and a dining area. The bungalows are large, attractive, and comfortable. They have concrete floors instead of the more typical

sand ones, plus cold-water showers, sinks, and toilets. Most have a back porch right on the water, where one can lie in a hammock or write postcards at a little table.

The open-air dining room is on the northern edge of the island, looking out on open sea. The site is pleasant enough to take your mind off the food, which when I visited was bland and uninspiring. The dining room and grounds have electricity, but the rooms themselves don't. You're brought a lantern at night, which adds to the romantic charm of the place.

The lodge is owned and run by a Kuna family, the de la Ossas, and service here is personal and friendly. The patriarch is Jerónimo, but you're likely to have more contact with his sons and daughters. One of the sons, Horacio, learned English during a three-month visit to the hippie enclave of Bolinas in Northern California, which he found a fascinating anthropological experience. (He thought it was *muy interesante* that there are 60-year-old North American women who smoke marijuana.)

While the cabañas are all thatch-roofed, management decided a few years back to convert their walls from cane to longer-lasting wood, which is a shame because it's delightful to look through the cane slats in the morning and see the sun sparkling on the blue water. Avoid the new cabañas with two units; they offer very little privacy.

Getting There and Away
This section of the archipelago is quite a hike from the more touristed areas, and distances are much too great to take a small boat from any of them. As usual, Turismo Aeréo and Aeroperlas have one daily flight to Achutupu. They leave Panama City at around 6 A.M. and return about 7:05 A.M. The flight takes about an hour. Airfare is $39.90/$79.80 one-way/round-trip. Note that Turismo Aeréo usually refers to this as the Mamitupo/Ailigandí flight, but request a flight to Achutupu and make sure you get off at the right place.

Ⓜ THE UNINHABITED CAYS
The loveliest and most unspoiled islands in the archipelago are fairly remote, and they can

be difficult to visit unless one has access to a yacht. There are no accommodations on these remote cays.

The **Cayos Holandéses** are the best-known of the many gorgeous uninhabited and lightly populated islands toward the western end of the archipelago. They are 15 kilometers north of the mainland, farther offshore than any others in the archipelago. Yachts like to hang out here, as do snorkelers. The coral in some areas is beautiful, though even out here the waters have been overfished and the coral damaged.

To the west of the Holandéses, and closer to the Porvenir area, are the also lovely **Cayos Chichime,** the **Cayos Limónes,** and, farther south, the **Cayos Los Grullos.**

About 40 minutes east of the Holandéses by large motorboat (the smallest thing one should be in this far out) are the **Cayos Coco Bandero** (Ordupuquip in Kuna). It's a pristine group of more than a half dozen islets that's rarely visited by anyone other than yachties. It's stunningly beautiful out here. A Spanish galleon supposedly sank around this area, but neither the ship nor the gold have ever been found. There's also a modern-day wreck, a cargo ship, that's lodged upright on the nearby reef. It makes for quite a haunting sight. The waters are calm, protected by the same reef that snagged the ship, making it an appealing spot for snorkelers.

The Cayos Holandéses are accessible by boat from the Porvenir, Río Sidra, and the Corazón de Jesús/Narganá areas, but it's quite a haul on open sea that can turn rough. Coco Bandero is much closer to Narganá/Corazón de Jesús. None of the hotels offers a visit to the more distant of these island groups as part of their standard packages, but they may be able to arrange a trip for an extra free. Do not attempt the trip without a life jacket. Most visitors will be content with exploring islands closer to where you're staying.

The cost of a boat trip, and the time it takes, obviously depend on where you're coming from and how many islands you want to explore. From Kuanidup, for instance, the trip to the Cayos Holandéses takes at least two hours each way and will cost $60 just for gas, plus a bit more for the boatman's time. From the Porvenir area it's about $50 per boatload. For those who can afford it, a far better way to explore this area is by private yacht.

The Darién

The Darién: It's a name filled with magic.

In many people's minds the magic is of a dark and sinister kind. The Darién has historically been seen as a foreboding, dangerous place, a Conradian wilderness into which explorers venture, never to return. But the Darién is magical in many more positive ways as well. It is one of planet earth's last great bastions of pristine tropical nature. Its biodiversity is so incredible it's been named both a World Biosphere Reserve and a Natural World Heritage Site by UNESCO.

The province of Darién is, at 16,671 square kilometers, by far the largest in Panama. It's extremely sparsely inhabited; only 40,000 people live in the entire province. Parque Nacional Darién alone is enormous, covering 579,000 hectares of wilderness that sprawl across the isthmus near the Colombian border. It contains the most extensive lowland tropical forest left along Central America's Pacific coast. Balboa stepped out of this forest in 1513 and became the first European to set eyes on the "South Sea."

The great attraction of the Darién is its magnificent forests and the incredible biodiversity they contain. Hiking, trekking, and bird-watching are what draw most nature tourists. But there are a couple of places along the coast of the Darién with accessible beaches and coral reefs. And,

© WILLIAM FRIAR

Must-Sees

Look for ▶ to find the sights and activities you can't miss and ◀ for the best dining and lodging.

▶ **Santa Cruz de Cana:** The most remote part of Panama and one of the most beautiful, with extensive trails through pristine foothills up to a cool cloud forest, and around the jungle-choked remains of an old mining camp. One of the world's top birding destinations (page 207).

▶ **Pirre Station:** The entrance to the famous Parque Nacional Darién, Central America's grandest tropical forest (page 209).

▶ **Punta Patiño Nature Reserve:** The largest private nature reserve in the country, and the most comfortable place from which to visit the coast and rivers bordering the Golfo de San Miguel (page 212).

▶ **Mogue:** The best bet for those who'd like to spend the night in an Emberá village (page 217).

© WILLIAM FRIAR

Coastal Darién, particularly around the Bahia de Piñas, suprises visitors who expect nothing but humid jungle.

▶ **Bahia de Piñas:** Considered by many the best deep-sea fishing destination on the planet, it also has stunning forests, colorful villages, and the only luxury hotel in the Darién (page 221).

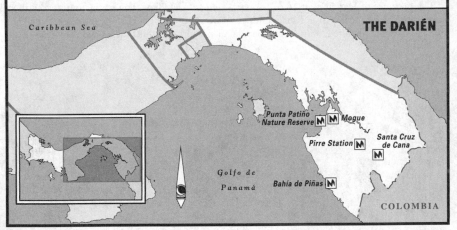

THE DARIÉN

Caribbean Sea

Punta Patiño Nature Reserve ▶ ▶ Mogue
Pirre Station ▶   Santa Cruz de Cana ▶
Golfo de Panamá   Bahía de Piñas ▶
COLOMBIA

for those into such things, the waters off Piñas Bay offer world-class deep-sea fishing.

What's commonly thought of as "the Darién" extends beyond Darién province itself. It encompasses all of eastern Panama except the islands of Kuna Yala. Traditionally, the Darién starts at the town of Chepo, just 50 kilómeters east of Panama City, though the city has expanded so much it's hard to believe this area was pure wilder-

ness less than three decades ago. It's possible to drive into the Darién as far as the town of Yaviza, but there's little reason to do so other than to say you've done it. Though the road has recently been much improved, the drive still takes a solid day, and all one encounters along the way are vast expanses of deforested land.

The part of the Darién of most interest to visitors lies toward the southeast section of the

COLOMBIA

Parque Nacional Darién

Caribbean Sea

COMARCA DE KUNA YALA

Área Silvestre de Nargandí

Archipiélago de San Blas

Puerto Obaldía

Río Chico

Boca de Cupe
Unión Chocó
Vista Alegre
Pinogana
El Real de Santa María
Pijí Basal
Yaviza

Río Tuira
Cerro Setetule

SANTA CRUZ DE CANA
Cerro Pirre

PIRRE STATION

Río Balsas
Río Jaqué
Ensenada El Guayabo
Puerto Piñas
Playa Blanca
Biroquera
Jaqué
BAHÍA DE PIÑAS

DARIÉN

Río Chucunaque
Río Tuira
Río Sabanas
Río Sambú
Río Sambú

Puerto Quimba
Metetí
INTERAMERICANA
Agua Fría No 1
Agua Fría No 2
Santa Fé
Cañazas
Torti
Ipetí

La Palma
MOGUE
Punta Alegre
PUNTA PATIÑO NATURE RESERVE
La Chunga
Golfo de San Miguel
Punta Patiño
Ensenada de Garachiné
Punta Garachiné

El Llano
Cañita
Chepo
To Panamá City
Lago Bayano
BAYANO CAVES

PANAMÁ

Golfo de Panamá

Archipiélago de las Perlas

Isla del Rey
Bahía del Rey
San Miguel
Isla Saboga
Isla Pedro González
Isla San José
Isla Chepillo

Icantí
Cañita
El Porvenir
Cartí

15 mi
15 km
0

THE DARIÉN

N

The Darién

© AVALON TRAVEL PUBLISHING, INC.

province, where there are no roads. The only way to get around here is by plane, boat, and foot. This contains the most accessible entry points into Parque Nacional Darién.

Two of the best spots in the park are Cana, on the east side of 1,615-meter-high Cerro Pirre, and Pirre Station, on its west side. These are right in the middle of barely inhabited tropical forest. Cana, the most remote point in Panama, is especially impressive.

The most popular coastal areas are Punta Patiño, on the Golfo de San Miguel, and the Bahía de Piñas, farther down the coast near the Colombian border. Those looking for a trip up a Darién river usually find themselves on the Sambú, Mogue, Balsas, Pirre, or Tuira, though innumerable others crisscross this part of the Darién.

There seems to be a saying about the Darién for every tree in the forest, some of which contain useful insights. My favorite, and one likely to resonate for any visitor, is this: Though many have come before you, it always feels as though you're the first to enter the Darién.

Flora and Fauna

From rainforests to sandy beaches to cloud forests to mangroves, the Darién has a greater variety of ecosystems than any other place in tropical America. Lush doesn't even begin to cover it. Flying over the Darién opens up an endless expanse of forest broken only by an occasional snaking river or a lone flowering tree trying to add a splash of bright red, orange, or yellow to the sea of green.

The wildlife is spectacular. Mammals alone include jaguars, ocelots, pumas, margays, jaguarundi, giant anteaters, capybaras, white-lipped and collared peccaries, howler monkeys, white-faced capuchins, spider monkeys, Geoffroy's tamarins, two- and three-toed sloths, and Baird's tapirs. And unlike so many other parts places in the neotropics, there's a fair chance of spotting at least a couple of these.

However, don't get your hopes up too much. Most creatures in a tropical forest have evolved to stay hidden. A hiker could be standing right next to a jaguar and never know it's there.

On the other hand, the Darién is one of the

GOD'S HAND

"Cuando entres al Darién, encomiéndate a María. En tu mano está la entrada; en la de Dios la salida."

—An anonymous bit of verse, said to have been carved into the walls of a Spanish fort at the edge of the Darién. It reads: "When you enter the Darién, commend your soul to the Virgin Mary. In your hand lies the way in; in God's the way out."

best places in the world to spot birds. More than 400 species have been identified, including plenty to impress those who don't give a hoot about birds. In some places it's actually hard not to see flocks of flamboyant blue-and-yellow, red-and-green, great green, and chestnut-fronted macaws. The rare harpy eagle, the world's most powerful bird of prey, lives here, as does the lovely golden-headed quetzal.

Reptiles and amphibians abound as well, including caimans, crocodiles, and jewel-like poison-arrow frogs. Then there are the creatures that make some people nervous when they think of visiting the "jungle": snakes. Yes, there are lots of them, including some very venomous ones. The wisdom is it's rare to spot them, and those who do should count themselves lucky. My personal experience is that if you do any amount of serious hiking in the tropics, you will eventually come across at least one, probably several. Most are not aggressive, and if you leave them alone they won't bother you.

The most common venomous snake in the Darién is also one of the most lethal: the fer-de-lance, a tan pit viper with a diamond pattern on its skin. They are everywhere in the Darién, though again you probably won't see one. If you do, don't play with it.

PLANNING YOUR TIME

Where one goes and how long one chooses to stay in the Darién depends on how deeply one wants to enter into this formidable world. It may help to think of there being three Dariéns: the coast, the rivers, and the foothills and highlands of Parque Nacional Darién. Ecosystems, accommodations, and the overall experience are quite different in each of these.

Those with the time and ability to do some serious trekking should consider an organized trip that touches on all three Dariéns. This requires at least a week and perhaps two and involves all-day hikes in rugged, hot, and humid conditions. These trips are really miniexpeditions and do not come cheap. The best way to arrange one is through a good tour operator that can provide qualified guides, keep trekkers safe, and handle the considerable logistics.

Visiting just one part of the Darién can be done in as little as two or three days, particularly if one flies. Given the time and expense involved in getting around this part of the country, visitors will not get much out of the experience if they attempt a stay shorter than that. Visitors to Tropic Star Lodge, the only true resort in the entire Darién, generally stay for a week, though half-week packages are sometimes available.

The only parts of the Darién one can consider visiting without a guide are the towns along the Interamerican Highway or those that can be reached by air, which also happen to be among the least appealing and attractive places in the Darién. No one should set foot in the forest or venture far on a river without experienced guides.

The coast tends to be the most accessible part of the Darién, and the least rugged. The most comfortable accommodations are found here as well. This area includes the **Bahia de Piñas, Jaqué,** and **Punta Patiño,** as well as the town of **La Palma,** the provincial capital of the Darién. Most people fly in or come by ocean-going vessel.

The rivers are the main means of transportation in the interior of the Darién, and most visitors will spend at least a little time on them. It can be a pleasant way to get around, and it's certainly scenic, but boat travel can also be hot, humid, and wet. Most transport is by long, dugout canoes called *piraguas,* which can get a bit uncomfortable after an hour or two. It can take a long time to get anywhere by boat, depending on conditions: The crew may need to clear tree falls or drag the *piragua* through shallow stretches of some rivers.

Possibilities include the **Río Sambú, Río Balsas, Río Mogue,** and **Río Marea,** all of which

© WILLIAM FRIAR

Tropic Star Lodge is by far the most luxurious place to stay in the entire Darién.

The Darién

SOME WORDS OF WARNING AND ADVICE

Unlike other chapters, this one is written with the idea you will travel to the Darién only with experienced, respected nature guides. I strongly urge you to do so (unless you're going to the Tropic Star Lodge, which offers modern accommodations and lots of pampering).

Those who don't speak Spanish and know the area will find it hard to get logistics set up for a Darién trek. A naturalist guide can spot and describe animals and plants the uninitiated will miss. Most importantly, those who venture off by themselves have a great chance of getting lost and dying. Seriously. The Darién is a fantastic place and definitely worth visiting. But it must be treated with respect.

There are human hazards as well. Colombia's civil war has spilled over the border into the Darién, and there are guerrillas and paramilitaries working in some areas. Drug traffickers and bandits also hide out in the forest. All these baddies have done unwitting good for conservation: Even hunters with guns are afraid to enter some areas.

Knowing which regions are unsafe is tricky. Again, experienced guides can be helpful, since it's in their interest to know the dangerous spots. Border police and park rangers are also sources of information. Be sure to check the U.S. State Department's travel warnings and Consular Information Sheet at tel. 202/647-4000 or www.travel.state.gov/travel/warnings.html.

These advisories are not always accurate or up to date. However, they include a useful rule of thumb that should still be accurate when you read this. Look at a map of the Darién and picture an imaginary line drawn from Punta Carreto (west of Puerto Obaldía in the Comara de Kuna Yala, on the Caribbean coast) through the town of Yaviza in the heart of the Darién, down to Punta Piñas on the Pacific coast. The State Department considers travel east of this imaginary line to be dangerous.

This was roughly accurate at the time of writing, with some caveats. El Real and the area around Pirre Station and Cana in Parque Nacional Darién were not considered high-risk spots. Neither was the Tropic Star Lodge fishing resort on Piñas Bay, nor nearby Jaqué, which now has a significant police presence.

Travel up the Río Tuira as far as Boca de Cupe was also relatively okay given the strong police presence in the area, though going past this point was dangerous. Ditto for travel up the Río Jaqué past the village of Biroquera, which is off-limits to foreigners. Travel to Puerto Obaldía was considered unsafe. The situation in the Darién is fluid, and a quiet spot today can be an area of concern tomorrow, and vice versa.

Those who know the Darién well feel the risk of coming across warring Colombian factions is exaggerated. They point out that combatants use the forests on the Panamanian side of the border as a place to hide out and rest. The last thing they want is to draw attention to themselves by provoking conflict.

Yet even Darién experts say it is crazy to hike through the Darién Gap into Colombia. Despite or perhaps because of all the warnings, some still insist on trying it. It's an extraordinarily dangerous thing to do.

An English orchid-hunter, Tom Hart Dyke, and his friend, Paul Winder, were captured by Colombian guerrillas while trying to cross the Gap in March of 2000. They were held for nine months. Anyone who thinks trying this is an exciting lark should read their account of their horrific ordeal, "The Cloud Garden."

In January 2003 Robert Young Pelton, an adventure-travel writer, and two 22-year-old American backpackers were kidnapped by a right-wing paramilitary group near the Kuna village of Paya, close to the Colombian border. They were held for nearly a week before being released unharmed. Less fortunate were four Kuna village leaders in Paya and Púcuru, who were tortured and murdered during this attack. A fifth Kuna was reported missing, and hundreds of refugees from the villages poured into the police-patrolled village of Boca de Cupe. Panama and Colombia pledged to beef up security around the border in the wake of these tragedies.

After his release, Pelton, the author of "The World's Most Dangerous Places" and "Come Back Alive," called the Darién Gap "probably the most dangerous place in the Western hemisphere."

Other Tips
Those going on a multi-day trek in the Darién, versus staying in a lodge with screens, should start taking anti-malaria medication in advance of the trip.

There are three hospitals in the Darién, in Yaviza, La Palma, and El Real. There are also six *centros de salud* (health centers), in Boca de Cupe, Metetí, Santa Fé, Garachiné, Jaqué, and Sambú, plus a subcenter on the Río Balsas. Both should have antivenin for venomous snakes. The El Real hospital sees 12–15 snake bites a year, mostly fer-de-lance. The hospitals are reasonably well stocked, but serious cases are stabilized and flown to Panama City.

Be careful in the forest during and after a rain. Tropical trees have shallow roots and fall all the time. You can hear them crashing all around you.

Keep your passport with you at all times. There are police checkpoints throughout the Darién and you'll be asked repeatedly to present your papers. As always in Panama, be polite and respectful toward the police. To keep the passport dry, double-bag it in ziplock plastic bags.

The Darién is one of the few places in Panama where water can be unsafe. Bring a good water purifier or water purification tablets. (See the *Know Panama* chapter for a list of suggested expedition gear and clothing.)

Campers should always sleep in tents. Always. Among the dangers of sleeping in the open are malaria, which is endemic to the Darién, and rabies from vampire bat bites. There is no cure for rabies, and only one person in history has survived it (though taking a series of vaccinations after exposure can usually prevent infection). On one trek, an experienced Darién guide got so hot he ignored his own advice and unzipped his tent a speck. He woke up the next morning with congealed blood in his hair and little bite marks on his scalp—a vampire bat had feasted on him. Back in Panama City a doctor gave him his shots and told him to wait. For what? To see whether he died or not. He didn't, but he'll never leave his tent open again.

Flight times in the Darién are rough approximations at best. Be ready to leave an hour early but prepared to wait as long as it takes, which can be hours.

Some cell phone networks reach only as far as Chepo. Others carry as far as Punta Patiño. None penetrates deep into the forest. But even some remote villages have a pay phone. Buy a prepaid local phone card in Panama City, as these phones get choked with change.

With few exceptions, transactions are cash only, and there are no ATMs anywhere east of Metetí. Those traveling independently should calculate a rough budget ahead of time and bring a stash of cash with them, including lots of small bills.

CHOOSING A GUIDE

The most prominent guide outfit for the Darién is **Ancon Expeditions** (tel. 269-9415, fax 264-3713, info@anconexpeditions.com, www.anconexpeditions.com). The company also runs the ANCON lodges at Cana and Punta Patiño.

They are known to have some of the best Darién guides in the country. At the top of the heap is Hernan Araúz, a third-generation Darién explorer with a passion for this place. His credits include many trans-Darién expeditions, and he's considered one of the premier birding guides in the entire country. Rich Cahill is another experienced Ancon guide who also has multiple trans-Darién expeditions under his gear belt. They speak both English and Spanish fluently.

I've traveled extensively with both Hernan and Rich in the Darién and found them both to be conscientious, knowledgeable, safe, and friendly guides with an infectious love of the forest. They're also just highly entertaining characters. I've literally put my life in their hands, and I feel confident recommending them, and Ancon Expeditions generally, to those who want to have an adventure, learn a lot about the Darién, and get home safely.

Ancon Expeditions offers a number of packages in the Darién in addition to those described elsewhere in this chapter. Among these are major expeditions, including a 14-day Darién Explorer Trek. This trek takes clients by foot and dug-out canoe to the best-known nature hot spots in the Darién. It costs $2,400 per person, with a minimum of four people.

When conditions permit, Ancon Expeditions occasionally offers a Trans-Darién Trek. This involves traveling by foot and dug-out canoe from the Caribbean to the Pacific, following a route similar to that taken by Balboa when he discovered the "South Sea." It costs $2,495 per person, with a minimum of four people.

These major treks are true adventures, but you'll be traveling in a certain amount of style. Porters carry all your gear (it's for your safety, as you wouldn't want to trip and break a leg in the middle of the Darién—it has happened), and the guides bring along a paramedic and satellite phone. Still, trekkers must be in good shape and willing to rough it a bit.

Guerrilla and paramilitary activity along the Colombian border can affect these treks, particularly the Trans-Darién one. Contact Ancon Expeditions for current conditions and schedules.

Though I have yet to travel with him, Michel Peuch and his company, **Exotics Adventures** (tel. 223-9283, cell 673-5381, www.panamaexoticsadventures.com), come strongly recommended by a number of people whose opinions I trust. He specializes in coast-to-coast treks in western Darién that follow the El Llano-Cartí Road for part of the way. He offers other trips of varying degrees of difficulty.

Another top Darién guide, and one of the finest birding guides in Panama, is Willie Martinez. His company is **Nattur Panama** (tel. 442-1340, fax 442-8485, panabird@cwpanama.net, www.natturpanama.com). These days he focuses on trips elsewhere in Panama, but the company may be able to arrange Darién trips by request.

Travelers arranging their own expeditions should try to buy basic provisions in the larger towns at the start of a trip rather than just bringing everything in from Panama City. This supports the depressed local economy and lightens the load in getting this far, which is especially important if one is flying in: Airline passengers are restricted to a total of 25 pounds (a little over 11 kilos) of checked and carry-on luggage. Those who avoid insulating themselves completely from the local communities earn good will for themselves and future visitors. While anything having to do with modern technology, including batteries, can be hard to come by in the Darién, food and basic trekking supplies are easily found.

As has been mentioned elsewhere, **Narciso "Chicho" Bristán** in El Real (tel. 299-6566) has a well-deserved reputation as the most able boatman in the Darién. Those who want to cobble together their own expedition would do well to contact him.

Those who need a driver with a good four-wheel drive for trips to the Darién via the Interamerican Highway should consider **Benigno Calderón** (cell 643-7819). He's a safe, responsible driver who knows the road well. He charges $175 from Panama City all the way to the end of the road at Yaviza.

have Emberá-Wounaan villages along their banks. The Río Pirre is far less densely settled and quite beautiful. The **Río Tuira** is wide and lightly populated between La Palma and El Real, then narrows and is lined by villages as it flows farther east. For their own safety, visitors are not allowed to travel up the Tuira past the village of **Boca de Cupe.** The same goes for the **Río Jaque** (near the Bahía de Piñas) past the village of **Biroquera.** Those who want to spend a night on the river will probably camp in a village with few facilities. Only **Mogue** and **La Chunga** have true visitors' accommodations; staying in any other village requires negotiating for a spot in someone's hut or a place to pitch one's tent. The town of **El Real,** on the Río Tuira near the Río Pirre, also has guest accommodations and a couple of basic places to eat and drink.

The foothills and highlands of Parque Nacional Darién are among the wildest and most beautiful parts of the country. Most visitors go to the area around **Cerro Pirre,** usually making their base at **Rancho Frío,** in the lowlands just northwest of the mountain, or **Cana,** on its eastern slope. Hikers can stay at **Pirre Station** (the ranger station at Rancho Frío) or the rustic lodge at Cana. This area is particularly treasured by bird-watchers, but the magnificent primary and secondary forests will impress anyone.

Cana has more trails and facilities, it's more comfortable, and it has a nifty cloud-forest camp. Conditions at Pirre Station are more rustic, but a trip there can be arranged far more cheaply. Those on a moderate budget will find Pirre Station the most accessible part of the national park. (Pirre Station and Cana are only about 20 kilometers apart, but no trails connect them.)

The average temperature in the Darién is 26°C, but as usual in the tropics that average sounds milder than it feels. The Darién lowlands are hot and humid year-round. Be prepared to feel wet and sticky even in the dry season, and don't expect ever to get completely dry in the rainy season. The Pacific and central parts of the Darién can see as much as 2.5 meters of rain a year. The Caribbean side gets up to 3.5 meters a year. Trekkers on long expeditions often take just two sets of clothing, which after the first day can be categorized as "wet" and "wetter." Sleep in the former; hike in the latter.

The highlands, however, can get surprisingly cool at night. You'll probably need a light jacket or windbreaker, for instance, at Cana's cloud-forest camp.

To the Darién by Road

TRAVELING THE INTERAMERICAN HIGHWAY

The Interamerican Highway extends east from Panama City to Yaviza, about 270 kilometers away. Here the "highway"—really a two-lane road nearly all the way from Panama City—comes to an abrupt end about 50 kilometers from the Colombian border, and the famous Darién Gap begins.

There are only two things likely to compel visitors to enter the Darién by land: 1) an unreasoning need to drive to the end of all roads, and 2) a severely limited budget.

Going into the Darién by four-wheel drive or bus is not convenient, to say the least. By the time you read this, the final stretch of road leading into Yaviza may finally be paved, turning what had been an all-day, vehicle-punishing journey into a somewhat shorter and smoother ride. But it will still be a long, tiring trip through unlovely countryside. Anywhere the road has been extended deforestation has followed, and the view out the windows is of sad little towns, villages, farms, and cattle pasture, not the majestic rainforest most come to the Darién to see. It takes about eight hours by four-wheel drive, including stops for breakfast and lunch, to cover the approximately 270 kilometers from Panama City to Yaviza in the dry season, which gives some sense of the road conditions.

But traveling by bus is the cheapest way to get into the Darién. There are frequent daily buses from Panama City that go at least as far

The Darién

as Metetí and make interim stops at all the towns and villages along the highway.

Budget travelers can take a bus from Panama City to Metetí, switch buses to the nearby river port of Puerto Quimba, and then cross the wide mouth of the Río Tuira to La Palma, the capital of Darién province. From there it's possible to arrange expeditions to explore the Emberá-Wounaan and Afro-Colonial villages and the coasts and lowland forests of southwestern Darién province. It's also possible to hire a boat to go far up the Río Tuira toward Parque Nacional Darién.

Alternatively, when road conditions allow, those on a budget can continue all the way to Yaviza, take a motorized *piragua* to the nearby town of El Real, and from there plan trips to visit villages up the Río Tuira or to Pirre Station, the most accessible part of Parque Nacional Darién.

Once one gets off the bus, however, expenses mount quickly. Expect to pay up to $200 round-trip per small group for transportation any significant distance upriver to forest destinations. That doesn't include the cost of food, guides, park fees, and so on. And a competent, knowledgeable guide is pretty much a must even for the most independent-minded traveler.

For most travelers, flying into the Darién is the only reasonable option. Except to places served only by charter planes, such as Cana, it's not expensive and is a much faster and less exhausting way to get to the most interesting parts of the Darién.

The entries below contain information on towns and villages offering food, lodging, and services road-trippers may need on the way to the frontier. With the exception of the Llano-Cartí Road and the area around Lago Bayano, however, the places mentioned are unlikely to

THE END OF THE ROAD

No road has ever penetrated all the way through the Darién, and many hope none ever will. The Interamerican Highway comes to a complete stop in Yaviza, and from there the road doesn't pick up again for another 100 kilometers, well inside Colombia. The Darién Gap is the only missing piece in a system of roads that links North and South America from Alaska to Patagonia.

The completion of the highway was long stalled by fears that hoof-and-mouth disease would spread from South America to Central and North America. Those fears have abated, but environmental ones have grown.

Wherever there is a road, massive deforestation has followed. Logging, ranching, farming, and hunting have decimated enormous tracts of the Darién. If the Interamerican Highway is completed, it is all but certain the days of the Darién as a magical place will be numbered.

So far, building those last 100 kilometers of road continues to be put on hold, due to conservation concerns, the war in Colombia, and worries about giving drug traffickers yet another route to the north.

But even without the road, the Darién is under enormous pressure. How well protected the Darién, and particularly Parque Nacional Darién, is depends on the whim of the particular government in power. The consensus among environmentalists is that in the first few years of the 21st century, the Darién has been sadly neglected at best.

Even in better times, Parque Nacional Darién never had more than about a dozen rangers to protect an area the size of some countries. Now there are only two ranger stations being staffed in the entire park, Pirre Station and Balsas Station. The Cruce de Mono Station (a.k.a. Cruzamono Station) has been abandoned and poachers have moved in. There have been reports of hunters almost all the way to Cana, which is among the most remote and pristine areas in the entire country. Wild peccary meat is being sold everywhere, illegally.

For now, however, it remains a fantastic nature destination. Try to get there if you possibly can.

interest many travelers. Most people will not choose to spend the night in any of the towns along the highway unless they're stranded on the way to somewhere else.

Those who choose to drive should attempt it only in a four-wheel drive with high clearance, a couple of spare tires, a winch, and plenty of fuel. The road has in the past been tough or impossible to navigate the whole length in the rainy season, but the entire road may be paved by the time you visit and this may no longer be a major issue. Still, there are tire-repair stands at regular intervals along the road, which may very well come in handy. Note also that, while there are police checkpoints all along the highway, these are at widely spaced intervals. Those who get stranded or have an accident may be in for a long, long wait before help arrives. There is exactly one transit police station along the entire 200 kilometers between Chepo and Yaviza, and it doesn't even have a phone. It's in the tiny town of Zapallal, just east of Santa Fé, about 80 kilometers from the end of the road.

From Panama City, take the Corredor Sur toward Tocumen until it peters out, then follow the signs east to Chepo and the Darién. If you forget something, stop at the town of 24 de Deciembre, at the turnoff to Cerro Azul. There's a mall here with a supermarket, gas station, and the last McDonald's until Colombia (talk about entering the wilderness . . .).

CHEPO TO LAGO BAYANO

Chepo

Though actually in eastern Panama province, Chepo (pop. 12,734) has traditionally been thought of as the starting point for the Darién. This view persists today, despite the fact that Panama City has grown so far east and this area has been so heavily settled Chepo now seems more like a suburb of the city. It's a big, sprawling town with a hospital, filling station, ATM machine, and stores where travelers can stock up on provisions.

The first police checkpoint on the road is just before the turnoff to town. Chepo itself is five kilometers south of the Interamericana. It's not a scenic place, however, and because it's just 50 kilometers from Panama City, there's little reason to stop here on the way to or from the Darién. It's locally popular during Carnaval, though.

The **Río Mamoní** crosses the Interamericana just east of Chepo. At the beginning of the 1970s, it marked the beginning of the Darién Gap. There was solid rainforest from this point east, pure wilderness. It's sobering how quickly and completely all that has vanished.

Along the El Llano–Cartí Road

Shortly before Lago Bayano is a road that heads north over the Continental Divide and down into the Comarca de Kuna Yala, otherwise known as the San Blas Islands. It is the only land access to the islands, but calling this a "road" is extremely generous. Though the islands start less than 30 kilometers due north of the Interamerican Highway, the serpentine, unpaved road is in many places little more than a trail. It starts off brutal on the Pacific side of the hills and quickly turns all but impassable the closer one gets to the Caribbean. Even in the dry season, a four-wheel drive with a winch can have a tough time making it even halfway in.

From time to time there is talk of paving the road, but the Kuna and environmentalists fear that it could prove disastrous, greatly accelerating deforestation in the area and even threatening the autonomy of the island Kuna, which is preserved in part by their isolation.

Even the existing road, rough as it is, encourages squatters, cattle ranchers, and poachers to invade Kuna land. To try to stop this encroachment, the Kuna established a nearly 100,000-hectare forest reserve in this area called the **Área Silvestre de Narganá.** With funding from international organizations, they built a rustic lodge along the Continental Divide in an area called Nusagandí, hoping to attract ecotourism. The Kuna ecotourist project never quite got off the ground and the lodge was pretty much abandoned at the time of writing.

However, there is another ecolodge along the road that attracts birders and other nature lovers. **Burbayar Lodge** (tel. 264-1679, 654-0952, or 674-2964, burbayar@cwpanama.net, www.burbayar.com, $115 per person for the first night, including all meals, transportation, and guides; $85 per person for subsequent nights) lies along the San Blas mountain range 14.5 kilometers north of the Interamericana and 22 kilometers south of the Caribbean coast. I have not yet been able to visit the lodge—the road was impassable when I tried—but an experienced naturalist guide whose opinion I trust calls it his favorite rustic nature lodge in the country. It's at 375 meters above sea level, high enough for cooler temperatures, pleasant breezes, and, apparently, no mosquitoes. There are electricity and running water, and the accommodations appear simple but comfortable. The lodge can accommodate just 14 people at a time, in shared rooms. Meals are served family-style on a terrace in the main lodge. The lodge appears to be making a genuine effort to be as ecofriendly as possible.

The lodge borders the Narganá forest reserve and offers six forest trails of varying degrees of difficulty. The lodge also offers tour packages. These include visits to Lago Bayano and the Bayano caves as well as a tough all-day hike all the way to Cartí, in Kuna Yala. There hikers can spend the night in a Kuna hotel on one of the islands. Tour packages generally include transportation to and from Panama City, boat transportation, a local guide, and meals. Helicopter transportation between the lodge and Panama City is also available for a hefty extra fee.

This area has the finest birding in eastern Panama after Cana and Pirre Station. This is the best place in Panama, for instance, to see the speckled antshrike, black-headed antthrush, and black-crowned antpitta. An estimated 400 bird species pass through the area, of which birders at Burbayar have so far counted about 300. The dry season is the best time for birding.

Those who choose not to stay at the lodge can also do some exploring along the road on a day trip. The view from even a few kilometers above the Interamericana is sweeping and lovely, though the sight of hill after deforested hill now covered with teak plantations on the Pacific side is a clue to just what the Kuna are so worried about.

It's also possible to trek from the highway all the way to Cartí, but this means two long days of hiking. Hikers can arrange to spend the night either at Burbayar or strike a deal with local Kuna to crash at what's left of the Nusagandí lodge. Plan to arrive at Cartí, on the Caribbean shore, early in the morning; after the morning planes come and go, there probably won't be anyone around to take hikers to the islands until the next day. It's possible to do this hike without a guide, but it's not a good idea. In any case, the usual mantra applies: Do not hike alone. Exotics Adventures offers a three-day ocean-to-ocean hike and kayak trip that begins in Cartí, crosses the Continental Divide down to El Llano, and continues all the way to the Pacific. Only truly fit people should attempt this one.

The unmarked turnoff to the El Llano–Cartí road is about 15 kilometers east of Chepo, just before the flyspeck town of El Llano (pop. 2,839). There's a rice field on the right. Turn left onto the unpaved road. It's possible to pick up some provisions in El Llano, but Cañita, eight kilometers farther east, is better stocked.

Cañita

Cañita (pop. 2,140), a little over 20 kilometers east of the Chepo turnoff, is a good place to stop for a break. It has a few basic restaurants and stores.

If you get stranded there are a couple of places to stay.

Pension Villareal (no phone, $5/8 s/d for fan-cooled rooms, $7/10 for a double bed instead of two singles, $12 s/d for one of the two air-conditioned rooms), at the Y intersection toward the end of town, offers basic, not terribly clean rooms with cold-water bathrooms and showers down the hall.

Hospedaje Santa Cecilia (tel. 298-9067, $6/8 s/d with fan, $10/12 s/d with air-conditioning) is also basic, but the owners have made a modest effort at decoration. This includes the bizzaro irony of sticking a save-the-environment poster next to an ocelot pelt. Two of the rooms have private toilets and showers for the same price as those with shared bath. Those on an extremely tight budget can get a microscopic cell here for $3. The *hospedaje* is hidden in a residential area near the Pension Villareal; ask someone to point it out.

El Descanso, a pleasant open-air restaurant on the north side of the road, is a popular place to eat. It's owned by immigrants from Los Santos province and is known for its soups, such as *sancocho* and *sopa de carne* (beef soup). A breakfast of steak, tortilla, juice, and coffee costs less than $2. The old ocelot, jaguar, and peccary pelts hanging from the rafters is a disturbing reminder of the toll humans have taken on nature in this area, and the endangered turtle eggs that may be for sale is an equally disturbing reminder that the trend continues. Please don't buy them; for one thing, it's against the law. In fact, if they're being sold you can always boycott the place and tell the management why you're doing so. If you do stop for a bite, be careful the house sparrows don't poop in your food.

LAGO BAYANO

Even those who'll pass on a drive all the way into the Darién might be interested in going at least as far as the Bayano Dam area, where there are a couple of places to check out. It's about 90 kilometers east of Panama City. Note that there's an active police checkpoint at Bayano, and your papers will definitely be scrutinized here.

Lago Bayano is an artificial lake, created when the Río Bayano was dammed in 1976. It flooded 350 square kilometers of tropical forest and displaced thousands of Kuna and Emberá. It is the second-largest source of power in the country, after the Fortuna Dam in western Panamá.

Those coming on their own can drive or take any Darién-bound bus to Lago Bayano, getting off at the checkpoint just before the bridge, Puente Bayano. Buses from Panama City that go only as far as Lago Bayano leave from the Gran Terminal in Albrook daily every 40–50 minutes between 4 A.M. and 4:45 P.M. The fare is $3 and the trip takes about 2.5 hours. Bayano, by the way, was the name of a famous leader of the *cimarrones,* rebel African slaves, who held the conquistadors at bay for two years before he was finally captured.

Icantí

The 10 Kuna communities in this area banded together and in 1996 gained *comarca* (semiau-

Exploring the caves of Lago Bayano makes for an exciting day trip.

tonomous reservation) status. Called the **Comarca Kuna de Madungandí,** its government office is right at the checkpoint, along with a little stand selling (rather poorly made) *molas.* Sometimes the name is spelled Madugandí.

The *comarca* is trying to get some ecotourist projects off the ground, though when I last visited plans were in the early stages and everything was pretty casual. Those interested in visiting a Kuna village on their own should contact ORKUM, Organización Kuna de Madungandí (tel./fax 298-9319; ask for Manuel Martínez). This may be of interest to those who don't have time to go to the San Blas archipelago, or who just want to see how the mainland Kuna compare with their island cousins.

If you show up without an appointment, ask around for ORKUM (or-KOOM) at the checkpoint. Day trips to the village of Icantí, near the mouth of the Río Icantí on the north side of the lake, cost around $50 for two people, which includes the boat ride and entrance to the reserve. Note that both the river and the village are sometimes known as Aguas Claras. The boat trip takes half an hour each way.

Bayano Caves

There are also some caves on the south side of the lake that make for a pretty cool day trip for the adventurous. These are best explored with a good guide, but it's possible to arrange a trip on your own.

There's a boat-launching ramp to the right of the Bayano bridge and usually a few boatmen hanging around. Ask near the checkpoint for Mateo Cortéz, who probably knows the caves as well as anyone. The trip across the lake takes about half an hour in his 30-foot boat and costs $40 for a single person or small group. If Mateo isn't around, ask around for someone willing to go to *la cueva*.

There are actually three caves, though nearly everyone just explores the first one. The second one requires crawling through narrow passages on hands and knees—pretty intense. Even Mateo hadn't yet explored the third. He's been trying to find someone crazy enough to go with him.

The first has a river flowing through it, the Río Seco, which is fed by creeks and underground springs. At the height of the rainy season, it's possible to steer the boat a fair distance inside the cave. At other times visitors have to get out of the boat and wade in through chest-high water—make sure valuables are sealed in plastic bags and be prepared to carry them over your head, or else leave them behind. Carrying a camera is a pain, and it's hard to get good photos in there; it's dark, and the humidity fogs up the lenses.

This trip requires lots of scrambling over slippery rocks, and it's remarkably easy to break an ankle or crack your head. Scuba or surfing booties work well here. Second-best are sneakers with good traction. There are some aggressive fish with sharp, pointy teeth swimming around in the dark; I saw one actually capture and eat a large frog. It's probably best not to wear open-toed shoes.

Wear a bandanna or T-shirt over your nose and mouth. There are lots of bats in this cave, and there's always a chance of contracting something unpleasant from the droppings, such as histo-

plasmosis, a potentially serious or even fatal infection. Chances of this are minimized by the fast-flowing river that washes out the cave.

Flashlights are a must; it's utterly dark in some sections. After a couple of minutes you'll hear a roar of water and the squeaking of thousands of wings. Shine the flashlight straight ahead and you'll likely see a solid wall of agitated bats. This is what a guide friend of mine likes to call "a high-adrenaline moment." Some may have second thoughts at this point, and probably with reason. Those who continue shouldn't be bothered by the bats—they'll flit right by—and will be rewarded by a large open area, with shafts of light streaming down from high above. Impossibly long tree roots hang through the cracks overhead and otherwordly mounds formed by calcium deposits cling to the walls. It's all very Indiana Jones.

The cave is about two kilometers long, though the water is usually too deep to go the whole way except at the height of the dry season.

It's a spooky but beautiful place. No wonder the locals have stories about troll-like creatures that live in the cave, and a human skeleton somewhere in the forest above it. Real, live creatures may be enough to keep the cautious (sane?) out, though: After coming back out of the cave, my little group spotted the head of either an unusually large caiman or a rather small crocodile lurking about the entrance. It could easily have come inside to swim with us.

LAGO BAYANO TO YAVIZA
Ipetí to Santa Fé

The small Kuna village of **Ipetí** is right on the road 45 kilometers east of the Bayano bridge. It's possible to buy fruit and *molas* here. A turnoff to the south leads to its Emberá sister village about 15 minutes away, but those planning to visit the heart of the Darién, where the villages are more traditional, can easily skip it.

Tortí (pop. 8,030), 13 kilometers farther east on the Río Tortí, is a sizable town with two gas stations, a few stores, a couple of restaurants, and an okay place to stay.

A leather shop, **Tablateria Echao Palante,** is

on the north side of the road. It's interesting to poke around here for a few minutes and check out the saddles, sandals, and sheaths for machetes and knives. A beautifully ornate saddle costs $110. Sandals go for $7 and knife sheaths and belts for $3. Those planning to eat at the restaurant next door might consider ordering a pair of *cutarras,* traditional sandals from Los Santos. They're very simple, but they can custommake them on the spot for $2. There's another leather shop across the street.

Those in need of a bed can try **Hospedaje Tortí** (no phone, $5/6 s/d with fan, $10/12 s/d for air-conditioning). It offers 35 cell-like but clean rooms that lock on the outside with flimsy padlocks. Toilets and showers are down the hall.

Next door to Tableteria Echao Palante is **Parrillada Ñata,** a basic but okay place to eat that resembles Descanso back in Cañita.

Cañazas, 16 kilometers farther east, is really just a roadside rest stop with a police and immigration checkpoint, a restaurant, and a minisupermarket.

Another 11 kilometers east brings us to **Agua Fría No. 1** and the start of Darién province. The only thing here are a couple of houses, an agriculture checkpoint, some transit police, and an ANAM office. Still, that's more than you'll find three kilometers farther on in the rather unimaginatively named **Agua Fría No. 2.**

Four more kilometers east is **El Tirao,** most notable for its pay telephones and minisuper, followed 13 kilometers east by **Arimae,** formerly known as Los Monos, an Emberá-Wounaan village with a population of about 400. Note the Pepsi sign on the side of one of the thatch-roofed huts.

All buses going at least as far as Metetí pass by these towns, though few travelers will be inclined to stop unless stranded for some reason.

Santa Fé

Santa Fé (pop. 5,764), about 200 kilometers east of Panama City, is a surprisingly large and lively town, though not a scenic one. There's little trace of it today, but the town has a long history thanks to its accessibility: It's possible to navigate from the Pacific all the way to Santa Fé by river.

Though the place can draw an interesting mix of people from neighboring areas during a festival, there isn't much to reason to visit it. It does, however, have a hospital and other services one would expect to find in a remote provincial town. All buses going at least as far as Metetí pass by it.

There are a few options for those in need of a bed.

Hospedaje Las Guacamayas (tel. 299-6727, $10 s/d/t) is a 14-room guesthouse above a store, which may be the best dining option. All the rooms have fans and their own bathrooms. Rooms are dark and have the charm of prison cells, but they're otherwise perfectly fine. There's a launderette next door.

Further into town is **Hospedaje Casa La Esperanza** (tel. 299-6529, $6 s, $10 d), which offers six rooms with fans, spongy mattresses, local TV, and shared bath. Visitors can rent Playstations and computers downstairs in the same building, but there's no Internet access so far. **Cabañas Evelyn,** (tel. 299-6529, $20 s/d) are next door but have the same owner. They consist of airconditioned cabins with private bath and small TVs with cable reception. The AC is a big plus, but you'll feel every single spring in the beds.

To get to Santa Fé from the Interamericana, take the right fork near the gas station as you head towards Yaviza. The town is two kilometers away.

Metetí

The last real town before Yaviza is Metetí (pop. 6,244). Most residents are colonists from the province of Chiriquí, of all places—it's clear on the other side of Panama, on the Costa Rican border.

Metetí is mainly of interest to travelers as the crossroads for travel to Puerto Quimba on the Río Tuira. From there it's possible to take a water taxi to La Palma or, with more difficulty, arrange boat trips to El Real and Yaviza. Along with other services, there are several hole-in-the-wall restaurants and places to stay.

Hotel Felicidad, the most substantial hotel in the region, was closed for repairs after a fire but may be reopened by the time you visit. It's on the Interamericana just before the crossroads.

Hotel Hermanos Ortíz (tel. 299-6534, $8/10 s/d for nonair-conditioned rooms with shared bath), near the crossroads, offers 16 dark, dingy, none-too-clean rooms with spongy mattresses. Three of the rooms have air-conditioning and private bath for $15 s/d. Take $2 off that rate if you don't use the air conditioner. But you will. A rustic restaurant and general store are attached to the hotel.

Hospedaje Las Nashiras (tel. 299-6393, $11 s/d with fan, $16 s/d for air-conditioned rooms upstairs), on the left side of the road leading toward Puerto Quimba, has 10 rooms varying in quality from very basic and dreary to somewhat more spruced-up rooms. The fan-cooled rooms are grimmer than the ones with air-conditioning. The place isn't terribly clean, but it'll do in a pinch. Note that the "reception" telephone is actually a pay phone just outside the *hospedaje;* let it ring a long time, as the ringer is quiet but the stereo the staff likes to play isn't.

There's a branch of Banco Nacionál de Panamá (tel. 299-6052 or 299-6054, 8 A.M.–3 P.M. Mon.–Fri., Sat. 9 A.M.–noon) at the Metetí crossroads. It has an ATM and can supposedly cash American Express travelers checks. There's also a large police post and checkpoint, filling station, and pay phones. There's an ANAM station a right turn off the road before the crossroads as one heads toward Yaviza. You'll likely find the staff absolutely useless.

Buses to Metetí leave from the Gran Terminal de Transportes, the Panama City bus terminal in Albrook, every day at 4:15 A.M., 5:15 A.M., 6:30 A.M., 8 A.M., 9:45 A.M., 11:45 A.M., 1:30 P.M., and 3:45 P.M. The trip costs $9 and takes 6-7 hours. Return buses leave Metetí at 5 A.M., 7 A.M., 8:15 A.M., 9:30 A.M., 11 A.M., 12:30 P.M., 2 P.M., and 4 P.M.

Most services are at the crossroads outside Metetí rather than in the town itself. To get to the town, turn south off the Interamericana. The road continues to Puerto Quimba.

Puerto Quimba (KEEM-buh) is Metetí's "port." Some people know it as Kimball. Pickup "buses" link Puerto Quimba and Metetí

A water taxi runs from Puerto Quimba to La Palma from 7:30 A.M. to 6:30 P.M. and from La Palma to Puerto Quimba from 5:30 A.M. to 5 P.M. The water taxi to La Palma theoretically runs every hour to hour and a quarter, but in re-

ality only the first one of the day is reliable. After that, the boat leaves when it gets a full load. The trip costs $2.50 one-way and takes about 30 to 45 minutes.

Those who need a boat up the Río Tuira to El Real, Yaviza, or Parque Nacional Darién may find someone willing to make the trip at Puerto Quimba, but the chances are better in La Palma. How much this will cost depends on the number of passengers and whether the boat was already going that way. It may be possible to hitch a ride for about $5 per person, but hiring one's own boat can cost around $40–100 per small group.

YAVIZA

Welcome to the end of the road. And not just any road: Yaviza (pop. 3,177) marks the abrupt end of the Interamerican Highway, which those in a less environmentally aware time once dreamed would link North and South America. Fortunately, sanity has so far prevailed and the road has been indefinitely halted, which is at least delaying the ecological destruction that would inevitably follow. The famous Darién Gap begins here. Depending on how one measures it, the gap consists of about 100 kilometers of unbroken wilderness near the borders of Panama and Colombia, through which no road has ever been built.

Just paving the existing stretch of road between the Lago Bayano area and Yaviza, which may be completed by the time you read this, will likely bring dramatic change to this backwater, which until recently was tough to get to even in the dry season.

Only a true optimist would be confident those changes will be for the better. On the other hand, it's hard to imagine Yaviza getting much sketchier. It's got the vaguely menacing, unpredictable vibe one expects from a frontier town in the middle of nowhere. It's also hot and humid, the very essence of jungle rot.

When the first vehicles ever to make it to Yaviza emerged from the jungle in 1960, on a brutal expedition to study the feasibility of a road through the Darién Gap, some townspeople were so frightened by the sound and sight of these mechanical beasts that they jumped into the

Workers in Yaviza load yams brought downriver in piraguas. Each basket holds 60–90 kilos.

river. Not a whole lot has changed since then. Yaviza still looks like a backwater Panamanian town from 100 years ago.

Yaviza is certainly colorful, and it's an interesting place to spend an hour or so on the way to somewhere better. That's all the time needed to get the flavor of this tiny town. Those who need to spend the night in the area are better off in the nearby (and much friendlier) town of El Real, or in Metetí, back west along the Interamericana. That said, if you get stuck here there is one semi-okay place to stay.

Yaviza has a long history. A Spanish fort, **Fuerte San Jerónimo de Yaviza,** was built by the Spanish in the 18th century to prevent pirates from raiding the gold mines of Cana by river. What's left of the fort's crumbling walls can still be seen perched on the edge of the Río Chucunaque. Erosion is wearing away the riverbanks, and this haunting bit of history is slowly tumbling into the murky waters, with no attempt to preserve it. It's the only real sight in town and is worth a quick visit. It's a short walk towards the water from the Hotel Trés Americas. It's easy to find, but if you have trouble ask anyone where the *fuerte* is.

The Chucunaque snakes around the edge of Yaviza, making for a natural boundary. There's a **boat landing** on the right as you enter town where 45-foot-long *piraguas* loaded with *platanos* (plantains) and *ñames* (yams) from riverside plantations unload their cargo onto trucks, which carry them to Panama City. These same boats are the main source of transportation for those venturing deeper into the Darién.

Watching the *piraguas* in "port" makes for just about the only other entertainment in town. The wiry stevedores who do the unloading are impressive guys. They carry huge, handwoven baskets on their backs up a slippery incline to the trucks. There the baskets are weighed on a mechanical scale, and the weight is shouted to a supervisor sitting comfortably in the shade, who makes a note in his ledger. Each basketful weighs 60–90 kilos. It hurts just watching them.

Party days in Yaviza include the Festival de San Francisco Javier, the town's patron saint, on March 12 and the Festival de la Virgen del Carmen, celebrated throughout the province and the country on July 16, though sometimes it comes earlier here.

TRAVELING BY RIVER

Because there are (thankfully) still few roads in the Darién, most travel is done the old-fashioned way: on the river. Spend much time in the Darién and you'll become intimately familiar with *piraguas*, 30- to 45-foot-long dugout canoes that are still the best way to get around on the rivers. Their shallow drafts and tough bottoms allow them to skim over water that's just a few centimeters deep or be dragged across rocky bottoms without springing a leak. The only concession to modernity are the outboard motors that make upriver trips much easier. Making a *piragua* is a long, labor-intensive job, which is why they can sell for as much as $1,500.

The indigenous people also use *cayucos*— small, paddled dugout canoes for shorter trips— and rafts made from lightweight balsa wood. The rafts are one-way, makeshift affairs used to travel downriver with the current, after which they're abandoned.

Travel by *piragua* is nothing fancy. One sits on a wooden plank along the bottom, often in a puddle of water. They're completely exposed to the elements, which means it can be broiling hot and humid in the sun and startlingly chilly in the rain. Some sort of cushion to sit on and, in the rainy season, a poncho with hood will make long *piragua* trips more comfortable. Consider bringing a life jacket; flashfloods are possible on some rivers. Don't forget to wear sunscreen on the open river. And stay alert: Tree falls and other obstacles can suddenly appear on a fast-flowing river, requiring a quick limbo to avoid getting knocked out of the boat.

It's possible to arrange a river trip on one's own, but it will entail a great deal of planning and hassle, particularly for those who don't speak decent Spanish. Life will be a lot easier and safer if you go with a qualified guide who knows the good boatmen and can make all the arrangements.

If you do decide to go it alone, the main points of entry for the rivers discussed here are El Real, La Palma, Punta Patiño, and the area around Sambú. See those entries for more information, and for advice on contacts to help arrange river trips.

How much a river trip costs depends primarily on how far you want to go, as the main expense is fuel. Expect to pay up to $100 one-way per group for a solid couple of hours of motoring, which will actually take you pretty far, probably as far as you'd like to go in a day. Note that this just covers the cost of the boat, fuel, and crew. The crew will consist of at least a captain and a poleman. The latter stands up front with a long pole, on the lookout for snags and shallows. Food, supplies, guides, porters, and tips are all extra, as is lodging for those who plan to spend the night.

The best "cultural" rivers, which give a taste of Emberá-Wounaan village life, are the Río Sambú and the Río Balsas. The farther upriver, the more traditional the villages. Other possibilities are the Río Mogue and Río Marea. The sparsely inhabited Río Pirre is a good bet for sheer natural beauty; those venturing up to Pirre Station in Parque Nacional Darién can take the river most of the way to the station in the rainy season.

At the time of writing, rivers to avoid because of Colombian guerrilla and paramilitary activity included the upper reaches of the Río Jaqué and the stretch of the Río Tuira upriver from Boca de Cupe. As with all travel in the Darién, the closer one gets to the Colombian border, the greater the risk of coming across a dangerous situation.

Because the Río Balsas starts so far from any population center—it's between La Palma and El Real—a trip up the Balsas is considerably more

© WILLIAM FRIAR

Traveling by river is often the easiest way to get around in the Darién.

The Tuira is the longest river in Panama (with the possible exception, depending whom one asks, of the unbelievably tortuous Chucunaque), and carries the greatest volume of water. It's easy to imagine you're on the Amazon on this stretch of the river. The water is brown with sediment and the river too wide to see much wildlife, though the one time I took this trip we spotted a four-meter-long American crocodile sunning itself on a sandbar.

That may suggest this is not a place to go for a swim (few rivers in the Darién are in any case, especially those near human settlements, because of the risk of disease). Because the wide mouth of the Tuira opens into the Golfo de San Miguel, saltwater animals including hammerhead sharks also venture pretty far up the river. Tides affect the river as far east as El Real.

Note: Be sure any boat you take on the Tuira between El Real and La Palma has an extra outboard motor. There is virtually nothing and no one on this part of the river, so it's not a great place to get stranded.

expensive than many of the other rivers. Normally, visitors fly into La Palma and then travel by boat up the Río Balsas to the Balsas ranger station, about 4–5 hours upriver.

Those traveling between La Palma and El Real might consider a trip along the Río Tuira as an alternative to flying, though a longer and more expensive one. It takes about two hours and can cost up to $200 per group to hire a boat, though it may be possible to hitch a ride for considerably less. It's a different kind of river experience, as the Tuira is quite wide for most of the way, especially the closer one gets to La Palma. Being out on open water near the ocean is incredibly refreshing after the heat and humidity of the forests and towns.

Spending the Night in a Village

It's generally possible to spend the night in an Emberá-Wounaan village, though I don't recommend it. Malaria is endemic and you'll probably be sleeping in an open-sided hut without screens. If you do stay in a village, sleep in a tent, no matter how hot it gets, stay indoors in the evenings (or as close to indoors as feasible), and douse yourself with insect repellent. Also, plan to start taking anti-malaria medicine well before a visit; it takes several weeks to kick in. You must ask permission to stay in a village, and you'll probably have to pay. Ask to speak to the *dirigente* (leader, pronounced dir-ee-HEN-te); $10 per night for a couple should do it.

The Darién

Practicalities

The town consists mainly of dilapidated two-story wooden buildings, incongruously well-paved streets, and a large, fenced-in police station. Ask for the *cuartel*. Travelers should register their passport information and intended destination at the station as soon as they arrive. It's the law, and it's probably an excellent idea in any case. Those who go missing out here—and, sadly, it does happen—have a better chance of being found if there's a record of where they were last spotted. Travelers will need to register at every town, village, or checkpoint they pass through from this point on. Drivers can park their vehicles at the police station, where it should be safe.

Hotel Trés Americas (no phone) is the only real option for those who get stuck in Yaviza, and it's not a great one. It's by the basketball courts in the plaza at the center of town and offers rooms with fan for $8/11 s/d. A couple of the rooms are okay; the others aren't. The shared bathroom is icky. Air-conditioned rooms are in a separate building behind the main hotel. These are actually grimmer and literally stink. They smell like someone just died in there, and in this town you just never know. They cost $20 s/d. The hotel also has a basic bar and restaurant.

Those who forgot something in Panama City can find all kinds of basic provisions at hole-in-the-wall stores in Yaviza: food, equipment, machetes, rope, ammo—everything one needs for a Darién expedition. Yaviza also has a small hospital.

Getting There and Away

Buses to Yaviza leave Panama City from the Gran Terminal de Transportes (the bus terminal in Albrook) daily at 4:15 A.M., 5:15 A.M., 6:30 A.M., 8 A.M., 9:45 A.M., 11:45 A.M., 1:30 P.M., and 3:45 P.M. In the dry season, only the first two buses in the morning are guaranteed to run all the way to Yaviza. In the rainy season, none of them goes that far, though that may change when the road is finally paved all the way. The fare to Yaviza is $14 and the trip takes about nine hours.

Normally Metetí is the end of the road, and getting to Yaviza from there often means traveling up the Río Tuira. (See *Metetí* under *To the Darién by Road* for details.) Even in the dry season, plan on taking a return bus to Panama City from Metetí, not Yaviza. Road conditions make the chances of actually getting a bus from Yaviza too unreliable.

It takes about eight hours by four-wheel drive, including stops for breakfast and lunch, to cover the approximately 270 kilometers from Panama City to Yaviza in the dry season, which gives some sense of the state of the road.

It may be possible to hire a driver with a four-wheel drive in Panama City to make the trip to Yaviza. I've found Benigno Calderón (tel. 643-7819) to be a safe, reliable, and friendly driver who knows the area well. He charges $175 one-way from Panama City.

As has been mentioned elsewhere, the eventual paving of the road all the way to Yaviza should make the trip to Yaziva faster and easier to make year-round, and it may mean faster and more frequent bus service by the time you read this. Check at the Panama City bus terminal.

There are only two ways to venture farther into the Darién from Yaviza: by foot or by river. Continuing east towards the Colombian border is highly dangerous. Those foolish enough to try run a real risk of meeting Colombian guerrillas, paramilitaries, or plain old bandits. The far better option is to head southwest by boat, first on the Chucunaque and then onto the mighty Río Tuira, to El Real. It's a good base for reaching the national park and other parts of the Darién. The closest airport in this whole region is in El Real.

Cargo-carrying *piraguas* charge $5 a head to El Real, a trip that takes less than an hour with a 30-horsepower motor. Those attempting this trip on their own should note that *piraguas* aren't always available, and even when they are it can take hours to unload the thousands of kilos of produce before the boatmen are ready to head back out.

Into the Darién

EL REAL DE SANTA MARÍA

Known by everyone simply as El Real, this sleepy town (pop. 1,185) sits on the edge of the Río Tuira and is mainly of interest to travelers as the staging ground for trips into Parque Nacional Darién or up and down the enormous Río Tuira. The town is friendlier and more laid-back than nearby Yaviza. Still, few visitors use El Real as anything other than a stepping-stone to someplace else.

The Spanish founded El Real in the early 17th century. Today it boasts little more than an airstrip, a small hospital, a couple of places to stay, three utterly basic restaurants, a few bars, and one billion roosters, all of which are eager to rouse exhausted travelers insanely early.

A big party day around here is August 15, the festival of La Virgen Santa Maria la Antigua. It's a good excuse for cockfighting and drinking.

Practicalities

El Real's ramshackle houses are connected by a short network of streets and footpaths. It takes maybe 10 minutes to see the whole place. All the places listed below are within shouting distance of each other. If any are closed when you arrive, ask around: The owner is probably nearby and would be happy to open up for a potential customer.

Cana Blana (no phone) is the most attractive and interesting of the town's bars. It's a 60-year-old cantina with a thatched roof and cane walls, a local institution that's a popular place to begin or end an expedition.

Hotel El Nazareno, (tel. 299-6567 or 299-6548, $5 s, $7 d), is an old wooden tinderbox of a place on what passes for the main street on what passes for downtown. If you stay here, don't light a match, and pray no one else does, either. It's rustic and the plumbing doesn't work well—one flushes the toilets by dumping a bucket of water down them. Rooms are equipped with fans, and some have private baths. The best rooms are on the balcony facing the street. Reception is at the small general store next door.

A better though not more attractive lodging option are the very basic rooms rented out by Narciso "Chicho" Bristán (tel. 299-6566, $8 per person). However, these are generally only available to those using Chicho's expert boatman services (see *Getting There and Around*). Rooms have foam mattresses, plywood walls that don't extend all the way to the ceiling, fans, and that's about it. Showers and toilets are down the hall. This is basically a rustic barracks, but they're about as good as it gets in this part of the Darién.

The most appealing of the three hole-in-the-wall eateries in town, **Fonda Maná** (no phone) consists of a few tables in what is essentially someone's living room. The food is pretty good, considering, and as in all *fondas* consists of whatever's on hand that day. Nothing costs more than a buck or two.

The general store next to Hotel El Nazareno and a similar one just up the street carry the bare necessities for a Darién adventure, from machetes to dry noodles.

Those heading into the national park, including Pirre Station, must pay the park entrance fee at the ANAM office in town (tel. 299-6965, 8 A.M.–4 P.M. Mon.–Fri.). The entrance fee is $3 per person. A bed in the dormitory at Pirre Station costs $10 per person per night. Make that $5 if you just want to pitch a tent on the grounds.

There's an office of the Servicio Nacional para la Eradicación de Malaria (SNEM) in town (tel. 299-6299; ask for Glovis Garrido, the friendly woman who heads the office). It can supply antimalaria pills for free if you're running low.

Getting There and Around

Most tourists travel to and from El Real by small plane. **Aeroperlas** (tel. 315-7500, fax 315-7580 in Panama City, no local phone, info@aeroperlas.com, www.aeroperlas.com) flies between El Real and Panama City on Monday, Wednesday, and Friday. There's just one flight each way on those days, allegedly leaving Panama City at 9:30 A.M. It leaves El Real for the return trip to Panama City at about 10:55 A.M. There's often

A VERY BRIEF HISTORY
OF THE PEOPLES OF THE DARIÉN

The earliest known inhabitants of the Darién were the Cuevas, who were wiped out by the conquistadors. The Kunas moved in to fill the void and managed to resist the Spanish, in part by helping English and French pirates in their constant raids against the Spanish forts, towns, and gold mines. Many of the rivers in the Darién still bear Kuna names.

In the 18th century, a new group of indigenous peoples, traditional enemies of the Kuna, moved into the region. Once known collectively as the Chocó, because they came from the Chocó region of Colombia, they were actually two linguistically distinct though culturally similar peoples, the Emberá and the Wounaan. They spoke the same language an estimated 3,000 years ago and a third of their vocabulary still overlaps, but their languages have grown so far apart that today the Emberá and Wounaan tend to speak Spanish when they want to communicate with each other.

Centuries of conflict with the Spanish, Emberá-Wounaan, and so-called "Afro-Colonials" resulted in the Kuna being pushed north toward the Caribbean coasts and islands, which is where most Kuna live today. Some traditional-minded Kuna still live in the Darién. Historically they were the most formidable warriors, known by their enemies as the *Kunas Bravos* (fierce Kunas). Some attribute the Emberá-Wounaan success in their wars against them to superior war technology: They, unlike the Kuna, knew how to use blowgun darts tipped with the toxin from the tiny golden poison frog, *Phyllobates terribilis*. It's the most lethal poison of any known land animal; the toxin on the skin of a single frog is said to be powerful enough to kill 100 adult humans.

There are an estimated 22,000 Emberá and 7,000 Wounaan in Panama, though some place their numbers at just half that. Most still live in the Darién, generally along rivers that flow into the Golfo de San Miguel. Other villages are inhabited by Afro-Colonials, the descendants of African slaves who escaped from the Spanish. They are also known as *darienitas* or *costeños*. The Emberá-Wounaan have integrated into some of these villages.

an intermediate stop at La Palma. The trip length depends on the itinerary, which can change with no notice, but count on about an hour or so each way. The fare is $48.30/$96.60 one-way/round-trip.

Passengers who plan to return to Panama City by plane should reconfirm reservations as soon as they arrive in El Real. Plan to be at the airstrip at least an hour before flight time. If a plane happens to arrive early, it will also leave early. But chances are it'll leave late, so get comfortable. Those needing help carrying luggage between the airstrip and town, which is just a few minutes' walk away, can hire unofficial porters for about $1 a bag.

El Real is the closest transportation hub to Pirre Station, an ANAM ranger station in the most accessible part of Parque Nacional Darién. There are two ways to get to Pirre Station from El Real: by boat up the Río Pirre and on foot along

a forest trail. (See *Pirre Station* under *Parque Nacional Darién* for details.)

Most transportation around here is by river. It shouldn't be tough to hitch a ride on a *piragua* to Yaziva, the closest point for picking up the Interamerican Highway back to Panama City. The fare is $5 a head.

Longer river trips require more planning and considerable expense. Fuel costs a lot in the Darién, shallow waters take a toll on motors, and the rivers are often blocked by logjams that have to be cut through with chainsaws.

Narciso "Chicho" Bristán (tel. 299-6566) has a well-deserved reputation as the most able boatman in the Darién. He's a sharp, serious guy who shows up on time and hires a top crew. He lives in El Real; everyone knows him. Chicho charges $75 each way for a trip up the Río Pirre to Piji Basal, the closest village to Pirre Station. A day

The Emberá-Wounaan still tend to live in thatched-roof, open-sided huts on stilts. The stairway leading up to the living quarters is a log with steps chopped into the side. If the log is inverted, with the notched steps pointing down, it's a sign the family wants privacy. The log is pulled up at night to keep out unwelcome visitors, both two-legged and four-legged. As befits the climate, they traditionally wear very few clothes, but the influx of "civilization" has eroded this practice.

Village life is a relatively new thing for the Emberá and Wounaan. Traditionally, families set up house in relative isolation from others along a river. The patriarch of a clan would live upriver, with his children in homes some distance away downriver. They lived a semi-nomadic existence, settling into an area and practicing slash-and-burn agriculture and hunting, then moving away to fresh territory, allowing the depleted area to recover. This worked as long as the human pressures on the land were small. This mobile way of life changed in the 20th century, when the Panamanian government pressured the Emberá-Wounaan to form villages.

The Emberá-Wounaan continue to have land conflicts with loggers, cattle ranchers, poachers, and small farmers from outside the Darién who followed the building of the Interamericana and devastated the rainforest in western Darién from Chepo to Yaviza. The subsistence ranchers and farmers are known as *colonos*, many of whom moved to the Darién from heavily deforested Los Santos province.

The Panamanian government has established about 25 percent of the Darién as Emberá-Wounaan *comarcas*, semiautonomous reservations, giving them much greater control over their land and lives. The issues of land stewardship are complex. Parts of the *comarcas* as well as other areas the Emberá-Wounaan have traditionally seen as theirs overlap with the boundaries of the Parque Nacional Darién, where they are no longer legally allowed to hunt, farm, or extract timber. Poor Emberá-Wounaan increasingly log their own land and sell the timber, helping them survive in the short run but endangering their future.

trip up the Río Tuira to visit the villages along the river costs $160 round-trip to go as far as Unión Chocó. A voyage down the Tuira to La Palma, the provincial capital of Darién province, costs $200 one-way (expensive because he has to go back to El Real at the end of the trip). All prices are for up to five people and do not include tips (a good guide will advise whom to tip, and how much; at the very least, tip the hard-working poleman).

Caution: The steps leading down to El Real's "port" are incredibly slippery.

UP THE RÍO TUIRA TOWARD BOCA DE CUPE

Those with a morning to kill and an interest in the flavor of village life in the Darién should consider a trip up the Río Tuira from El Real. The riverbanks are dotted with small communities of Emberá and Wounaan Indians and *darienitas* (descendants of African slaves).

These villages have far too much contact with the modern world to be particularly "traditional." Their narrow streets tend to be paved, for instance, and the Emberá and Wounaan do not traditionally live in villages, period. Those who want to immerse themselves in an older era of indigenous life should consider an expedition far up the Río Sambú or Río Balsas.

This stretch of river is certainly colorful and interesting, but it's too densely populated to be particularly pretty. The river is brown with silt, which is probably a good thing since everything gets dumped in the river. It's not clogged with trash, but it's disheartening to see bottles and foam cups floating by in what used to be Eden. I once even saw a cooler bobbing along. Villagers bathe in the river, which is not something you'll want to try.

Still, green forest lines the banks, unbroken except for the occasional little rice and plantain field. Towering *cuipos* and bizarre-looking kapoks, which can have a crown broader than the tree is tall, jut up from time to time, and majestic neotropical cormorants and other water birds fish along the banks.

Boats are welcome to put in at any community. Villages here tend to be laid-back to the point of torpor, and visitors will likely be looked upon with mild curiosity but little enthusiasm. As always, be respectful and courteous. Do not, for instance, take a photo of anyone without asking permission.

Travelers must register at every police outpost along the river. This means regularly scrambling up muddy banks to present passports and answer a few questions. This is not meant as harassment but rather as a way to tightly monitor all movement in the area. Any boatman with any sense will automatically pull in at every post. Trying to slip by without stopping would be a very, very bad idea.

Officially these guys are police, but a stranger might be forgiven for thinking they were soldiers in a combat zone. They're big dudes with black T-shirts, khaki fatigues, and aging AK-47s, and they spend their days fighting boredom inside semicamouflaged compounds lined with sandbags.

Heading up the Tuira means getting closer and closer to the frontier with Colombia and thus to areas frequented by guerrillas, paramilitary troops, and other characters you won't want to meet. At the time of writing, traveling east past **Boca de Cupe,** about four hours upriver from El Real, was dangerous. Boca de Cupe, sometimes known as Boca de Cupé, has the last police post on the river, and thus the last semblance of law and order. The village itself (pop. 902) saw some serious ugliness on November 15, 1997, when a group of unidentified gunmen—some say Colombian guerrillas, others say bandits masquerading as guerrillas, no one knows for sure—attacked the police post and killed one of three officers manning it.

The main reason visitors come here is to hike into or out of Cana, a two-day trek southwest. Boca de Cupe was once the supply town for the gold-mining camp in Cana and, though it's hard to believe today, a railroad once linked the two areas.

At the height of the dry season, the river level can drop so low that boat transportation all the way to Boca de Cupe is impossible. Most day-trippers will probably be satisfied in any case with touring the river and the villages closer to El Real.

It's easy to distinguish Emberá and Wounaan villages from Afro-Colonial ones. The houses of the former, made either of planks or (more traditionally) of cane, are built on stilts. The latter are built right on the ground. There are representative examples of each well before Boca de Cupe.

Pinogana, an Afro-Colonial village about a half hour upriver from El Real by motorized *piragua,* is the first village upriver. Though it has a population of only about 350, that's apparently big enough to support three cockfighting rings, which is pretty much the only entertainment option in town unless you arrive on a festival day. The Fiesta de la Virgen de la Candelaria, held around the end of January and beginning of February, is a big one. There's a tiny place to eat and no official place to sleep. It's kind of a sad little town. There's a police checkpoint here.

Vista Alegre, about an hour farther upriver, is a Wounaan village that has another police checkpoint. This is a good place to buy one of the Wounaan's world-famous hand-woven baskets, since every girl in the village age 12 and older makes them. Expect to pay $60–70 for one the size of a bowling ball. Before haggling too much, look around at how poor this place is and bear in mind it takes two months to weave a basket that size. That's about all the place has to offer.

Union Chocó, less than half an hour farther up, is most notable for the sizable police station in the heart of the village.

All these villages have pay telephones. Remember to bring calling cards in case of an emergency; phones tend to fill up with coins.

The trip back downriver is much faster, thanks to the current. A *piragua* with a 30-horsepower motor can cut trip time in half on the way back down.

Parque Nacional Darién

⩕ SANTA CRUZ DE CANA

Those who can possibly spare the time and money should make a trip to Santa Cruz de Cana, in the heart of Parque Nacional Darién. More commonly known simply as Cana, it's the most remote spot in all of Panama: The nearest human settlement, Boca de Cupe, is two to three days away by foot, and there are no roads. Cana is a truly amazing place that offers genuine wilderness amid relative comfort, a rare combination. It's my favorite spot in the Darién.

Cana sits in a forested valley up against the eastern slope of the 1,615-meter-high Cerro Pirre. Given its extremely isolated location in the middle of dense, uninhabited forest, it's hard to believe Cana has been a major player in the history of the isthmus for at least 500 years. Even more astonishing is that at various times in that period it has hosted large, important settlements. During the Spanish colonial era it grew to be a town of 20,000. Later, it became the first place in all of Panama to have electricity, not to mention an ice plant.

The reason for all this attention was gold. The early conquistadors founded a settlement here and named it Santa Cruz de Cana, but it wasn't until 1665 that they discovered the area's fabulous gold deposits. "The richest gold mines ever yet found in America," the buccaneer historian William Dampier called them in 1684. You can almost hear him drooling.

The Spaniards forced slaves to work the mines, which came to be known as Las Minas del Espíritu Santo de Cana. At their height, they produced 100,000 troy ounces of gold a year. But repeated attacks by English pirates, Indian rebellions, and disease forced the Spanish to abandon the mines in 1727.

They were lost to the jungle for many years before they were reopened in the 19th century. Their most productive period was from 1887 to 1912, when they were run by an Anglo-French outfit called the Darien Gold Mining Company. During this era there was a railroad linking Cana with Boca de Cupe, and from there to the outside world.

The mines were abandoned once again, and once again the jungle swallowed up most traces of human habitation. But in 1962 the last survivor of the Anglo-French operation, a hearty 73-year-old named Medardo Murillo, guided an expedition to the mines. He had started working as a mule driver in 1904, when he was 15, and he still remembered the way. The whole place was overgrown, naturally, but they did find one house still completely intact and still stocked with viable dynamite.

Though mining was revived once again for a spell starting in the 1960s, today Cana is treasured for different kinds of natural riches: amazingly diverse and abundant flora and fauna. Two of Murillo's grandsons now work at an ecological field station at Cana, which, except for a tiny border-police post, is the only inhabited facility of any kind in the entire region. Though in the middle of Parque Nacional Darién, Cana is operated by ANCON, a nonprofit environmental organization, and the tourist concession is operated by Ancon Expeditions, its for-profit tour-operator sister. Other tour operators can use the facilities, but arrangements have to be made through Ancon Expeditions. The imposing abandoned mines (do not try to explore them; for one thing, it's the perfect lair for jaguars and other beasties) and rusted mining equipment overwhelmed by vegetation give the place a slightly spooky *Heart of Darkness* feel. But for the most part it's an open, airy, and inviting spot that doesn't square with stereotypes the uninitiated may harbor about the forbidding jungle.

Flora and Fauna

The wildlife here is breathtaking. As usual in the forest, those who come expecting a Discovery Channel cavalcade of big critters will likely be disappointed. The only thing you're guaranteed to see are some of the most gorgeous birds in the world. But there's a better chance of coming across tropical mammals and other impressive

⩕ The Darién

animals here than in most parts of Panama. There's an especially good chance of finding troops of Central American spider monkeys, and it's a near certainty you'll be surrounded by the uncanny bark of howler monkeys. It's not uncommon to come across fresh jaguar prints. Jaguars have been known to take a leisurely stroll down Cana's landing strip, but you'd be extremely lucky to spot one during a brief visit.

Herds of literally hundreds of white-lipped peccaries sometimes descend on the station and tear up the turf, rooting for food. When this happens, the staff and visitors have to lock themselves in the lodge. Peccaries, the only creature I've seen Darién guides get nervous about, can be aggressive, and they run faster than you do. Don't make the mistake of thinking they're just cute little pigs.

The very lucky few might also come across a Baird's tapir, the largest land mammal in Central America. At the cloud-forest camp above Cana, a tapir once sat on a guide's tent while the guide was sleeping in it. Both recovered from the surprise.

Cana has been called one of the 10 greatest bird-watching spots on the planet. Even those with only the slightest interest in feathered creatures will likely be bowled over by what they encounter here. Blue-and-yellow, red-and-green, great green, and chestnut-fronted macaws streak across the valley all day long. Keel-billed toucans, looking as if they just flew off a Froot Loops box, peer down at visitors from the trees.

From the porch of the lodge it's possible to spot an incredible array of stunning birds, many of them rare elsewhere, searching for food on the ground a few meters away.

The lodge is a barely converted mining camp building that dates from the 1960s. It's a rustic wooden structure containing six basic rooms with little in them besides a bed and a few shelves. Fresh linens are supplied and there are screens on the windows. There are shared bathrooms and showers with running water. A generator provides electricity 7 P.M.–9 P.M., after which everyone switches to candles and flashlights. A plan to upgrade the facilities has been put on indefinite hold because there are not yet enough visitors to justify the cost.

Trails

Since Cana's elevation is nearly 500 meters, the forest here is premontane, and it's neither as hot nor as buggy as one might expect. The valley offers beautiful views of the surrounding hills, which are covered with lush virgin forest. There's also a cloud-forest camp on the mountain itself, at 1,280 meters, where it can get cool in the evenings.

Five main trails originate from Cana, not counting a short trail near the station that follows railroad tracks to an abandoned locomotive. The **Boca de Cupe Trail** is the longest. It continues for a solid two days, all the way to the village of Boca de Cupe. Hiking in for at least a few kilometers is well worthwhile. It's a mostly flat trail offering spectacular birding and the chance of seeing larger wildlife. The **Machinery Garden Trail** is a lovely and exotic two-kilometer loop that features both nature and the rusting remains of the 19th-century mining operation. The **Seteganti Trail** leads down to the Río Seteganti. Vis-

The trails around Cerro Pirre offer some of the best bird-watching in the world.

itors can easily explore all these trails during a brief visit.

The Pirre Mountain Trail is a somewhat strenuous nine-kilometer hike that leads three-quarters of the way up Cerro Pirre to a cloud-forest camp. The hike takes four to five hours at a reasonable clip. The hike down takes about three hours and can actually be a bit more painful, as the trail is often fairly steep and hard on the legs.

But it's absolutely worth the effort. The trail itself leads through beautiful primary forest alive with animals. On a single trip I encountered large groups of spider monkeys crashing through the trees 40 meters overhead, crossed paths with a fer-de-lance snake (we both minded our own business), and, of course, saw dozens upon dozens of flamboyant birds.

The cloud-forest camp itself is a pretty impressive operation. A full field kitchen is set up in one large thatch-roofed hut, and tents with pads are set up in another. The camp can accommodate about two dozen guests. It's relatively cushy for its location. Generally all you have to take is a day pack; the cook and staff bring the food and water and set up the tents. (Tips are much appreciated; the guides can suggest amounts.) The view of nearby Cerro Setetule and the forested valley is breathtaking, and the nights are a riot of forest sounds. Big animals have been known to wander through camp at night.

The truly dedicated can continue a bit farther up the mountain on the **Cloudforest Trail,** but the summit can't be reached from this side of the mountain. There's a slim chance of spotting the rare golden-headed quetzal on this trail.

Guides lead all these hikes. Do not attempt to venture out anywhere alone. The trails are well marked so you probably wouldn't get lost, but there are small but real dangers to avoid in the forest. Travelers have a much better chance of staying out of trouble if they go with a good guide.

Plenty of venomous snakes are in the area. On a single trip, a guide recently spotted a coral snake, fer-de-lance, and bushmaster. But such sightings are unusual, and none of the snakes bothered the group. They're highly unlikely to bother you, either.

It's hard to exaggerate just how special Cana and its surroundings are. It's an enormous expanse of nearly pristine tropical forest, an overwhelming oasis of biodiversity. It's not cheap to get there and the trip is a bit of adventure, but nature lovers will likely find it the highlight of their trip to Panama.

Getting There

The easiest, though by far the most expensive, way to visit Cana is by airplane, since only small chartered planes make the trip. Visits are generally arranged through tour operators, who offer package deals that include everything from airfare to guides and food. The trip over takes about an hour and a quarter. The view is incredible. Planes land on a grass landing strip that ends in the mountain, which makes takeoffs and landings adventures in themselves.

Ancon Expeditions offers a five-day all-inclusive package to Cana for $1,327 per person for two people, $961 per person for four people, $993 per person for six people, or $999 per person for eight or more people. Prices do not include sales tax, currently 5 percent. Eight-day trips are also available, and a visit to Cana is sometimes included as part of other packages.

A far cheaper though far more strenuous way to visit is on foot. It's a two- to three-day trek from Boca de Cupe, following the route of the old railroad. Most get to Boca de Cupe by river from El Real or Yaziva. This is a popular leg of many multiday Darién treks and definitely something that should be tried only with well-equipped, knowledgeable guides.

◤ PIRRE STATION

The area around Pirre Station, an ANAM ranger station in Parque Nacional Darién, offers an experience of the Darién similar to that found at Cana. While Pirre is in the lowlands and Cana is in the foothills, they are on opposite sides of Cerro Pirre and share many of the same birds and other wildlife. Both have good trails, including ones that lead up onto Cerro Pirre.

Pirre Station is just within the boundaries of Parque Nacional Darién, in an area known as **Rancho Frío.** The forest here is lush and primeval;

The Darién

© WILLIAM FRIAR

Pirre Station (Rancho Frío) in Parque Nacional Darién

it has never been cut. The birding is excellent. Specialties include such beauties as lemon-spectacled and scarlet-browed tanagers, white-fronted nunbirds, and crimson-bellied woodpeckers. Those who wouldn't know a white-fronted nunbird from a nun should keep their eyes and ears open for flocks of macaws, an impressive sight by anyone's standards. Mammals include sloths, spider and howler monkeys, white-faced capuchins, and Geoffroy's tamarins. A 150-kilogram jaguar has been seen in the area, but as usual the chances of spotting it are extremely slim.

The station is surrounded by primary forest and little else. Facilities are minimal, consisting of a dormitory, an outhouse with flush toilets and showers, a field kitchen, and a couple of picnic tables. The dormitory is basic, to say the least. It consists of two bedrooms and a bare common area with concrete floors. Visitors sleep on bunk beds that are nothing more than foam mattresses on wooden frames. The rangers sleep in the second bedroom. There is no electricity at the station.

The site itself, however, is beautiful. The crystal waters of the Río Peresenico run by the camp, which sits in a clearing ringed by verdant forest.

Trails

Two main trails originate from the station. One is an easy two-kilometer **loop trail** that leads to a series of waterfalls just 15 minutes away from the station. It's a real *Blue Lagoon* scene. The first waterfall is about five-meters tall and pours into a deep pool filled with cold, clear water and surrounded by deep green vegetation.

Those feeling adventurous or foolish or both can climb the sheer, slippery face of the first waterfall and follow the river to two more falls. Be aware that there are several ways to get seriously hurt doing this, and it's a long, long way to a hospital from here.

Hernan Araúz, probably the top Darién guide in the country, nearly bit it not once but twice here. The first time he scrambled to the top of the waterfall only to come face to face with an annoyed fer-de-lance snake. He had to dive back down the waterfall and was lucky not to break his neck. The second time he slid down the face of the waterfall in a more measured way, only to get pushed underwater by the fast-flowing current; his companion had to dive in and pull him out.

So don't attempt to clamber around without a good, strong guide to help you. Throw rocks into the brush at the side of the falls to scare away venomous snakes. Watch your step at the higher falls; it's easy to step out into space and fall into a chasm. Be prepared to swim hard when you slide back down the first waterfall, especially if wearing lots of jungle gear. And make sure someone's always nearby in case of an emergency.

A fork in the middle of the loop trail leads up to a clearing that has a communications tower, but it's a tough, two-hour climb up a 45-degree incline, and clouds usually obscure the view.

The **Cerro Pirre trail** leads up the mountain, starting in the forest and coming out onto an exposed ridge that skirts the mountain rather than climbing to its summit. It's a fairly steep hike, very steep at times, with lots of ups and downs. Expect the trail to be muddy and slippery. It's a moderately strenuous trail and only reasonably fit hikers should attempt it.

It takes about two hours at a rapid clip to get to **Rancho Plástico,** which, despite its name, is only a reference point and has no facilities. There's a view of the valley of the Río Balsas from here. Theoretically one could continue along the ridge for two days before turning back. Note that this trail does not link up with the Cana Cloudforest Trail on the other side of the mountain.

It's possible to camp along the ridge, but hikers have to bring everything they need with them.

It's especially important to have a guide on this hike. The trail is not well-defined and is not being maintained. It's easy to get lost, and tree falls sometimes completely block the way. If you're alone and get lost or hurt, you have a real chance of not making it back out.

In 1996 a lawyer from San Francisco hiked the trail on his own. He not only got lost but also ended up separated from his tent and had to spend the night in the forest without any protection. One can only imagine what that was like. When he finally found his tent the next day, it had been devoured by army ants.

Note: The environmental nonprofit ANCON owns 300 hectares of land between the village of Piji Basal and Pirre Station and keeps it undeveloped as a buffer zone between Parque Nacional Darién and El Real. Ancon Expeditions, its sister tour-guide outfit, has bought 50 hectares of land close to Piji Basal from ANCON and has plans to build a small eco-retreat, which if completed could make for a much more comfortable, albeit more expensive, alternative to staying at Pirre Station. Contact Ancon Expeditions to check on the status of the project.

Practicalities

Pirre Station is too far from El Real, or anywhere else you'd want to spend the night, for a day trip. Plan to spend at least one night here, two if possible.

Visitors have to bring their own towels and will probably want to bring their own sheets, though the latter can be rented at the station for $3. Because there is no electricity, or even kerosene lanterns, bringing lots of extra flashlight batteries is a good idea. Bring a good water purifier or purification tablets unless you don't mind toting all the water you'll need for your stay all the way from El Real.

The rangers keep the grounds of the station well groomed and clear of debris. But within about 100 meters of the station the forest is literally crawling with venomous fer-de-lance snakes. You're unlikely to come upon one, but never wear sandals and shorts outside the immediate station area. In the Darién I generally wear boots and long pants even in camp, especially at night.

Visitors should pay the national park fees ahead of time at the ANAM office in El Real (tel. 299-6965, 8 A.M.–4 P.M. Mon.–Fri.). The park entrance fee is $3 per person. A dormitory bed costs $10 per person per night. Those with tents can camp on the station grounds for $5.

Travelers must bring in all their own food, usually from El Real. The rangers will cook and wash dishes for a small tip. Around $5 a day for a small group is about right. It'd be a nice gesture to bring enough food for the rangers, too. Remember that these are forest guards, not hotel staff. They're your hosts during your stay, and you'll have a more enjoyable time if you've won their good will. If you've come without a guide, you may be able to hire a ranger to take you on the trails, though their wilderness skills and

The Darién

knowledge of the area vary. Again, do not venture far on a trail without a competent guide.

Getting There

Unlike many places in the Darién, it's possible to visit Pirre Station on one's own without tremendous hassle or expense. However, I recommend going with a good tour operator, as you're likely to have a safer, more enlightening trip and won't have to deal with making all the considerable arrangements.

Getting to Pirre Station can be an adventure. The usual point of entry is El Real (see *Into the Darién* in this chapter). It's possible to reach El Real by boat, but most visitors coming from Panama City fly in.

There are two ways to get to Pirre Station from El Real: by boat up the Río Pirre and on foot along a forest trail.

The trail leads directly to Pirre Station. Do not hike it without a knowledgeable guide. Hiking in takes about 2.5 hours in the dry season, when it is generally the only option because the Río Pirre drops to an unnavigable trickle. In the rainy season, though, the trail to Pirre Station turns into a boot-sucking ribbon of mud and the hike becomes a miserable four-hour slog. There was talk at the time of writing of improving the road between El Real and Piji Basal to allow four-wheel drives to make the trip, but concerns about the deforestation that would likely follow if this isn't done carefully may delay the plan indefinitely.

When it's runnable, the river is definitely the way to go for those who can afford it. Chicho Bristán in El Real is an excellent boatman and the obvious first choice. The trip costs $75 for up to five people each way and takes travelers up the Río Pirre to the poor little Emberá village of Piji Basal. This leg of the journey can take up to three hours if the river is choked with fallen trees, which it frequently is. Watching a boatman chainsawing a massive trunk in the middle of a fast-flowing river suddenly makes the fare seem quite reasonable.

It takes about an hour and a half to hike the trail from Piji Basal to Pirre Station, a little less if one takes an overgrown shortcut for the first part of it. Again, go with a knowledgeable guide. It's good politics (and karma) to hire a porter in Piji Basal. It'll cost about $5 up to Pirre. Don't count on the porter's knowing the way, oddly enough.

The trip back down the Río Pirre is much faster. Stay alert throughout the lovely ride. It's remarkably easy to get your face raked by treefalls or even have your head taken off if you're dozing. An experienced poleman on one trip I took was nearly brained by his own pole and knocked out of the boat this way.

Coastal and Upriver Darién

⬛ PUNTA PATIÑO NATURE RESERVE

Punta Patiño is, at 30,000 hectares, the largest private reserve in the country. It's owned by ANCON, a Panamanian environmental nonprofit, and operated by its for-profit sister organization, Ancon Expeditions. It's a great place to come to get a taste of "coastal Darién," which has a much different feel from the interior. Punta Patiño offers quite a range of vegetation and wildlife, and it's the most comfortable place to stay in the Darién outside of the Tropic Star Lodge fishing resort. It's on the Golfo de San Miguel, a little under an hour by boat from La Palma.

Large swaths of Patiño, about a third of the reserve, were used for a cattle, coconut, and lumber operation before it became a protected area. The coconut plantation is still standing but nothing is being done with it. Nature is making a surprisingly strong recovery in the disturbed areas. A large reforestation project is under way, and ANCON is also working to preserve red and black mangrove here.

"Punta Patiño" translates to "Point Patiño." The point itself is off to the left as you face the beach, where the lighthouse is. The closest settlements from here are the small Afro-Colonial town of Punta Alegre, between Punta Patiño and La Palma, and an Emberá village up the Río Mogue.

Flora and Fauna

The forest around the lodge is secondary growth, but it's possible to hike into primary forest from there. Notable trees include the massive *cuipo,* whose blossoms burst into bright red or orange at the end of the dry season, and the spiny cedar, which has sharp spikes covering its trunk.

Unlike most parts of the Darién, there's a decent chance of seeing at least one kind of exotic critter that doesn't have wings. You're almost guaranteed to see capybara, the world's largest rodent (picture a giant guinea pig), and gray foxes at night toward the end of the rainy season (late December through January). Sightings drop off thereafter. Other largish mammals include *tayras* (a lanky weasel with a long, bushy tail), Geoffroy's tamarins, night monkeys, and collared peccaries. Caimans lurk in the swampier areas, and there are also lots of iguanas. Pilot and humpback whales and bottlenosed dolphins can sometimes be spotted in the Golfo de San Miguel. Bird specialties at Patiño include black-tailed trogons, boat-billed herons, and night herons. A jaguar has been known to hunt capybara in the area, but don't expect to see it.

Sports and Recreation

There are several well-developed trails—in some cases they lead to old roads—leading into a variety of ecosystems.

The **Sendero Piedra de Candela (Flintstone Trail),** is named for the reddish quartzes along this stretch; striking them with a machete sets off sparks. It's a loop trail that takes about an hour to walk. It goes through secondary-growth coastal forest where birders can hunt for mannakins, common black hawks, woodpeckers, and tanagers. It's also a good place to spot Geoffroy's tamarin and, at night, red-eyed tree frogs. It's a flat, easy trail. After 2.5 kilometers it meets a coastal road that eventually leads to the Afro-Colonial town of Punta Alegre in one direction and back to the lodge in the other.

A trail that starts behind Cabin 10 merges with a road leading to the back part of the reserve, which consists of primary lowland forest. There's also a road/trail that leads through the coconut plantation into some wetlands, and another short one leading onto the airstrip.

While walking the trails is the main activity

PANAMA'S MAGNIFICENT NATIONAL BIRD: THE HARPY EAGLE

The Darién is one of the last Panamanian homes of the harpy eagle (*Harpia harpyja*), the world's most powerful bird of prey. It is Panama's national bird. Deforestation has endangered this magnificent creature, which inhabits lowland tropical forests from southeastern Mexico to parts of Argentina and Brazil. So has hunting, especially since harpy eagles don't generally fear humans. It doesn't help that they produce at most one chick for every nesting attempt, and that they nest only once every three years. This is the longest known breeding period for any raptor.

Conservation programs are underway in Panama, including a breeding program to reintroduce harpy eagles into wilderness areas where they've disappeared. The first harpy eagle bred in captivity in Panama, or anywhere else in Central America, was born in January 2002 at the Peregrine Fund's Neotropical Raptor Center near Panama City.

The eagle can grow to over a meter long from fierce hooked bill to tail, more than half the height of a tall man. Its wingspan can reach 2.1 meters, as wide as a basketball player is tall. Its talons are the size of a grizzly bear's claws. Adults have a distinctive two-pronged crest, making them easy to distinguish from other eagles.

You'd be extremely lucky to spot a harpy eagle even in the Darién, as they rarely soar above the treetops. They hunt within the canopy with remarkable agility given their great size. They favor monkeys, sloths, and other hefty mammals, which they scoop up in their powerful talons at speeds up to 80 kilometers per hour.

The Darién

here, don't forget the beach just down the hill from the lodge. It's black sand but pleasant, and you'll have it all to yourself. There's a second beach a 10-minute boat ride away.

Accommodations

Guests stay in ANCON's lodge, high on a hill behind a long, deserted beach. It's a steep walk, but the reserve has a "tractor taxi," a tractor with a wagon hitched to it, to transport guests and luggage. The lodge has a dining hall with a wraparound balcony fitted with strategically placed hammocks. There's a mirador upstairs. Both have gorgeous views of the Golfo de San Miguel and the point where Balboa is believed to have stepped out of the forest to become the first European to see the Pacific. On the left there's a sweeping view of the old coconut plantation. Sunsets can be spectacular here, especially during the dry season. The lodge is high enough up that mangrove black-hawks sail by at eye level. It's an incredibly tranquil spot, especially when it's breezy.

The 10 simple but pleasant cabins are behind the lodge. They're surrounded by flowering trees, and all have a view out over the coconut plantation from their balconies. Six of the cabins have air-conditioning. Each has two beds, high ceilings, and a private cold-water shower and toilet. Towels and soap are provided. A generator supplies electricity in the lodge and cabins 6 P.M.–6 A.M.

The place is well managed and guest-oriented. Thoughtful touches include being greeted with a *pipa* (fresh coconut), finding fresh-cut flowers in the cabin, and discovering that a staff member has fired up the air conditioner in the cabin (if you're lucky enough to get an air-conditioned one) before you turn in for the night. Lime trees are everywhere, so there's always plenty of fresh limeade ready to cool you off.

However, because Patiño is surrounded by mangroves, it's much buggier than places such as Pirre Station and especially Cana. The mosquitoes are intense in the late rainy reason, and insect repellent just seems to make them thirstier. As annoying as this is, Patiño has so many charms it's worth a little crazed scratching and a welt or two.

This place is a good compromise for those who'd like a taste of the Darién but don't want to rough it too much.

Getting There and Around

There is a private airstrip at Punta Patiño, but only chartered aircraft land there. The nearest commercial airstrip is in La Palma. From La Palma it's about an hour down to Patiño by boat, which will be arranged for those who go with a tour operator. Ancon Expeditions offers a three-day, two-night package to Patiño for $595 per person for two people, $495 per person for four people, $450 per person for six people, and $425 per person for eight or more people. The price includes lodging, airfare, guided hikes in the forest, tours of the Emberá village on the Río Mogue, a visit to Punta Alegre, and meals. It's $100 per person for an additional night, spent in Mogue, regardless of group size. Sales tax is extra. The company also includes Punta Patiño as part of some of its treks and other trips.

LA PALMA

La Palma (pop. 3,884) is the provincial capital of the Darién, with the accent squarely on "provincial." Branches of the major government offices are here, including ANAM (the environmental regulatory agency), a police headquarters, a grim jail, even an outpost of the national lottery.

La Palma's location is striking. It's at the wide mouth of the Río Tuira, just where it races into the Golfo de San Miguel. Balboa became the first European to discover the Pacific near here. The ruins of Spanish fortifications are on craggy islets topped with emerald vegetation a few minutes' boat ride away.

Look away from the water, though, and the view becomes less appealing. La Palma is a hot, humid town where garbage piles up on the side of the road or is just chucked into the fast-flowing river. It consists of a strip of road wedged between an unbroken chain of hole-in-the-wall restaurants, bars, stores, and hotels perched above the river mouth on one side and a steep hill crowded with shanties on the other side. A remarkable number of minibuses ply this single road, which leads to the village of Setegantí, about 20 kilometers south of the airstrip. Walking the length of "downtown," from the airstrip at one end to the Cable and Wireless office at the other, takes about 10 minutes at a slow pace. The town doesn't have a friendly vibe. Be prepared for lots of poker-faced stares.

As with Yaviza and El Real, most visitors use La Palma as a way station and provisioning post on the way to somewhere else. Still, town life in La Palma can be fascinating for an hour or two: a drunk staggering around at 10 in the morning, a surly Colombian shop owner grumbling about being ostracized by the locals, a tailor working his foot-pedaled Singer on the street, kids setting off to school in neat blue-and-white uniforms, the local hottie strutting her stuff in painfully tight clothes, dreaming of the big city.

An important festival day here is the Fiesta de San José, held on March 19.

Sights

Other than the town itself, the only thing in the area that constitutes a sight are the ruins of the **Fuerte de San Carlos de Boca Chica,** five minutes by motorboat from La Palma on the island of Boca Chica. It shouldn't be too difficult to find a boatman willing to make the trip. Wander down by the boat ramps and ask around. La Palma isn't exactly a hot tourist destination, so it may be a challenge to explain what you want, especially if your Spanish is limited. Ask about *el fuerte de Boca Chica*. Once that's established, the boatman may have a hard time figuring what to charge. About $5–10 for a small group should do it, especially if you explain you want to be over there only for a half hour (*media hora*) or so. That's all the time you'll need.

Note there's a small battery on a neighboring islet, but the main fortifications are on Boca Chica. The Spanish built El Fuerte de San Carlos de Boca Chica in the mid-18th century as part of their network of defenses for the Espíritu Santo gold mines in Cana. It's not a big fort and the jungle has devoured much of it—a strangler fig has practically melded with what's left. But it's an impressive, photogenic sight, and it brings history vividly to life. It doesn't take much imagination to

picture a poor, homesick Spanish soldier on lookout here, sweating in the jungle and keeping an eye out for pirates. The fort is a couple of minutes uphill from shore and so shrouded by forest it's no longer easy to see from the water.

There are two Afro-Colonial towns a few minutes by boat from La Palma, Punta Alegre on the Golfo de San Miguel to the southwest and Chepiagana near the mouth of the Río Tuira to the southeast, though they're little more than collections of zinc-roofed shanties on the water's edge.

Accommodations and Food

M Hotel Biaquirú Bagará (tel. 299-6224, $10/$15 s/d for a room with fan and shared bath, $20/25 s/d with air-conditioning and private bath), near the end of town heading away from the airstrip, is by far the best place to stay in La Palma. The place is a local institution and has been the home base of many expeditions. It offers 13 tidy little rooms, some of which are surprisingly cheerful. A few have balconies. The two best rooms have air-conditioning and private bathrooms. There are satellite TV, a pay phone, and free drinking water. It's by no means a fancy place, but if one comes here after spending time in the jungle, it'll feel like the Ritz. There's a lovely view of the river from the balcony, though management was building new rooms that promised to block most of the view except for those who happen to have one of the new rooms. This place has quite a bit of character. The name of the place, by the way, means "beautiful macaw" in Emberá.

Meals can be arranged at the hotel with notice. The price depends on what you want. The place is run by Prof. Lesbia Alarcón, who can also arrange river trips to other parts of the Darién. (See *Getting There and Around*.)

Pension Takela, (tel. 299-6490, $8/16 s/d with shared bath or $10/20 s/d with private bath; ask for Ignacio Turner, the owner), the closest lodging to the airport, offers 10 windowless cells, each with fans and two single beds with thin mattresses. The balcony has a view of the river. Three of the rooms have private bathrooms. This is a very basic place.

M The Darién

Pension Tuira (tel. 299-6316, $10 s, $15 d, ask for Sra. Petra Rodriguez), near the middle of town, offers 11 dark and windowless rooms with fans and private bathrooms. They'll do in a pinch.

All the "restaurants" in La Palma are **fondas,** little holes-in-the-wall that serve whatever they happen to have on hand that day for a buck or two. Sometimes this includes peccary (usually called *puerco de monte,* mountain pig). Hunting and eating peccaries and other wild animals is illegal and punishable by jail time. Do not order it.

Locals reckon the best of the bunch is **Restaurante y Refresqueria Genesis,** across the street from Pensión Tuira, a hole-in-the-wall that actually has air-conditioning. Whether someone will turn it on is another matter.

Another possibility is **Restaurante El Regocijo,** a very basic place near Pension Tuira that serves heaps of food for less than $2. Its best feature is the huge plate-glass window overlooking the street, which makes for great people-watching while dining. A cantina with a large deck overlooking the river is attached.

Services

All the services in town are squeezed together one after another on La Palma's main road. The exception is the hospital. Though the old hospital building is on the main street, the hospital itself is now in a new structure on the hill at the far side of the town's airstrip, outside of town. The airstrip doubles as a road when planes aren't landing or taking off. Every bus running between La Palma and Setegantí drives near the place.

La Palma carries just about anything you'd need for a Darién expedition. It's also one of the few places in the Darién with fresh produce. Stock up at vegetable stalls set up on the main street.

The general store attached to the Hotel Biaquirú Bagará is the most complete in town. Las Paisas, next door to the hotel, is a small Colombian-owned general store that also offers a range of provisions, from machetes to sodas.

Banco Nacionál de Panamá (8 A.M.–3 P.M. Mon.–Fri., 9 A.M.–noon Sat.), near the airstrip, cashes American Express travelers checks.

The Cable and Wireless office (8:30 A.M.– 4:30 P.M. Mon.–Fri.), at the far end of town from the airstrip, sells "Telechip" phone cards.

Getting There and Around

The crumbling "airport" at the edge of town doesn't inspire much confidence, but most visitors come and leave by air.

Aeroperlas (tel. 299-6651 in La Palma, 315-7500, fax 315-7580 in Panama City, info@aeroperlas.com, www.aeroperlas.com) flies between La Palma and Panama City on Monday, Wednesday, and Friday. There's just one flight each way on those days, which is supposed to leave Panama City at 9:30 A.M. The return flight leaves around 10:30 A.M. Sometimes there's an intermediate stop in El Real, usually on the way back to Panama City even though El Real is in the opposite direction. The trip length depends on intermediate stops, which can change with no notice, but count on a little over an hour if the flight's nonstop and about an hour and a half if there's an intermediate stop.

Turismo Aéreo (tel. 315-0279 or 315-0300, fax 315-0278 in Panama City, no local phone) flies to La Palma from Panama City at 9 A.M. Tuesday, Thursday, and Saturday. The return flight leaves around 9:55 A.M. The fare is $39.90/$79.80 one-way/round-trip on either airline.

These times are approximate at best. Arrive at least an hour early in case by some miracle the plane shows up early. Once it's loaded it'll probably just take off again, with or without you. Most likely, though, the plane will be late, perhaps very late. On one trip to La Palma, the Aeroperlas flight to Panama City was so late I calculated I could have gotten back faster by boat and bus.

Which brings us to the other commercial link between La Palma and Panama City. A water taxi shuttles back and forth between La Palma and Puerto Quimba, the port for Metetí, on the Interamerican Highway. Some people know it as Kimball. A shuttle bus links Puerto Quimba and Metetí, which is the last stop for most buses that run between Panama City and the Darién. (See *Metetí* under *To the Darién by Road* for details on the water taxi and buses.) This route is the cheapest way to reach the Darién from Panama City.

To avoid getting stuck overnight in Metetí on the way to La Palma, leave Panama City early. Factor in time to make the connection to Puerto Quimba and the water taxi to La Palma. The 8 A.M. bus should be safe, but the 9:45 A.M. one is cutting it too close for the Darién, where little happens on time. As noted earlier, the paving of the road all the way out here will probably mean faster and more frequent service by the time you read this.

La Palma's location at the mouth of the Río Tuira and the edge of the Golfo de San Miguel makes it a natural launching point for trips by water into the heart of the Darién. As always, the best way to do this is with a knowledgeable guide who'll make all the arrangements. Otherwise, contact Prof. Lesbia Alarcón at Hotel Biaquirú Bagará, who is nice, prompt, experienced, and may be able to set up a river trip to places varying from the nearby Emberá village of Mogue on the Río Mogue; much farther east to the Emberá village of La Marea; or even all the way to El Real, which can be used as a base for further exploration.

⚅ MOGUE

The Emberá village of Mogue (MOE-gay), up the river that gives it its name, welcomes visitors and in fact has become a tourist destination for the area. It's about midway between Punta Patiño and La Palma.

It takes about a half hour by boat from either Patiño or La Palma to get to the mouth of Río Mogue. It's a potentially bumpy boat ride on the ocean. The Mogue is a beautiful river, in a slightly spooky, Conradian sense. It's swampy, still, and serpentine, with towering black mangroves on either side.

Boats have to take it slow up this murky river to avoid damaging the engine. It's about a 25-minute cruise from the mouth of the river to Mogue village. On the river and the trails around the village birders might spot white ibises, willets, whimbrels, mangrove black-hawks, roseate spoonbills, red-throated caracaras, laughing falcons, black oropendolas, orange-crowned orioles, and other gorgeous birds.

CAREFUL WITH THAT *JAGUA*

Emberá-Wounaan men, women, and children sometimes decorate themselves with a black dye drawn from the *jagua* fruit (*Genipa americana*), creating a kind of temporary tattoo. The fruit is pulped, and the liquid from the pulp is painted onto the face and body. The liquid appears clear at first, but as it dries it gradually turns black and the pattern emerges. Traditionally this consists of a geometric pattern across the body up to the lower jaw.

These days Emberá-Wounaan typically only go in for *jagua* decoration at festivals or special occasions. But they've discovered that offering to paint tourists is a good way to entertain them when they visit.

One little catch, though: The dye doesn't wash off. It wears off gradually, usually in a week to 10 days. Sheepish-looking tourists heading home with their faces tattooed-up like Maori warriors can be an amusing sight at the airport. One wonders what the immigration officials make of them back home.

Maybe the Emberá-Wounaan actually came up with a way to entertain *themselves,* not the tourists.

If you decide to get painted, think about where you have to go and what you have to do in the next two weeks. At the very least, you might want to skip the face.

The village is near when the mangroves give way to plantain fields. It's a 15-minute walk from where the boat puts in to **Paraíso Mogue** (Mogue Paradise), as a welcome sign in the village puts it.

The Emberá established Mogue in the late 1960s. It's a relatively pretty little village reminiscent of La Chunga in that it caters to tourists, putting on traditional dances and opening handicraft stalls when tour groups arrive. But it feels relatively more "traditional," at least given that the Emberá do not traditionally live in villages at all.

It's possible to spend the night in Mogue in relative comfort. There's a huge version of a traditional Emberá open-sided thatched-roof hut raised on stilts about 15 feet off the ground, where visitors can pitch tents and relax in hammocks. It's breezy up there and has an eavesdropper's view of the surrounding village, as well as a vista of the forest-covered hills in the distance. If you stay here, drown yourself in insect repellent and be prepared to be awakened early by roosters and crying babies.

Primary forest starts 15 minutes from the village. An hour hike from here leads to a harpy eagle nest. An hour hike in the opposite direction leads to the nest of a crested eagle. You'll need a guide to show the way in either case.

A big festival in these parts is held on November 14, the anniversary of the building of the local school.

Practicalities

Because of Mogue's proximity to Punta Patiño, most visitors come here with Ancon Expeditions as part of a stay at Patiño. Ancon Expeditions brings in food, which the villagers cook. Depending on the itinerary, visitors either spend the night or just pay a short day visit.

But it also may be possible to come here on your own from La Palma. Contact Prof. Lesbia Alarcón in La Palma (see *Getting There and Around*) for help in arranging this.

Mogue has showers for tourists that may actually work, and a rather scary-looking latrine.

THE RÍO SAMBÚ AND LA CHUNGA

The Río Sambú makes for a memorable boat ride. Its wide, muddy mouth opens into the Ensenada de Garachiné, a cove that in turn opens into the Pacific Ocean. The mouth is about midway between Punta Garachiné to the south and Punta Patiño to the north. The river is bordered by an intricate tangle of mangroves, behind which rise lush green towering trees. It's a beautiful sight. Even though there are settlements along the banks and many small fishing boats plying the waters, there's no doubt you're in Mother Nature's living room here.

It's easy to spot birds sailing overhead or hanging by the water as you motor upriver, particularly such water-loving fowl as herons, egrets, frigate birds, pelicans, and cormorants. You'll probably see at least a couple of hawks perched high atop the tallest trees. Toucans and parrots are a bit

setting up for tourists at La Chunga

© WILLIAM FRIAR

EMBERÁ-WOUNAAN ART

The Emberá-Wounaan are famous for their artistic abilities. This is especially true of the Wounaan, who are generally thought to produce the finest works. Three items are especially popular with travelers, and are a major source of income for the Emberá-Wounaan:

1. **Decorative baskets** made from the fine leaf fibers of the *chunga,* or black palm. They are made using a coil technique, the basket spiraling out from around a base made from *nahuala* (*Carludovica palmata*), the so-called Panama hat palm. They are made by women, and it's a long, painstaking process. The finest are so tightly woven it's been said they can hold water. This is probably apocryphal, though, since there's no indication the baskets were ever actually used for that purpose. You won't want to spoil yours by testing the theory.

Traditional baskets are plain or contain black-and-white geometrical patterns. But brightly colored ones depicting detailed scenes of butterflies, macaws, and forest animals have become popular, and the artisans are always experimenting with new ideas. The most sought-after baskets use natural dyes for the vivid colors. The one problem with these baskets is the destructive way in which they're made. The chunga tree is covered with long, sharp spines, making it extremely tricky to get to the top of the tree to harvest the leaves needed for the fibers. As a result, the Emberá-Wounaan chop down the trees to get at the leaves. Three trees can go into making a single basket. However, realizing the toll this is taking on their environment, the Emberá-Wounaan are working on practical ways to harvest the leaves while leaving the trees standing.

The Emberá-Wounaan make other items using the same technique and materials, including platters and decorative masks. Using a weaving method and different natural fibers, they also make a variety of baskets for everyday use, such as carrying produce or trapping fish.

2. **Carved tagua nuts.** Tagua nut, also known as "ivory nut" or "vegetable ivory," is the seed of a variety of palm tree that grows throughout the tropics. These were once a major export crop for parts of Central and South America, since the developed world used them to make a variety of goods such as dice, dominoes, and, especially, buttons. The nut is about the size of a chicken egg. In the 1920's, a fifth of all buttons produced in the United States were made from tagua. Then plastics came along, and now tagua is used only for the occasional piece of high-fashion clothing. The Emberá-Wounaan have learned how to carve beautiful and delicate miniature sculptures of forest animals out of the nut, depicting everything from ants to jaguars. These can be remarkably detailed and lifelike. They are made by the men, who primarily use the particularly hard nut of *Phytelephas seemannii,* often leaving the bottom half of the nut intact as a base. Because a good crop of tagua nuts requires healthy tagua trees, this is a particularly sustainable, environmentally friendly source of income for the Emberá-Wounaan.

3. **Cocobolo statues.** Cocobolo (*Dalbergia retusa*) is a kind of rosewood. It's remarkably hard, heavy, and dense. It doesn't float in water, and it takes years to rot in the rainforest. Emberá-Wounaan men carve blocks of cocobolo into sculpture—usually, as with the tagua nuts, these depict forest animals (the same sculptors often work with both cocobolo and tagua). When polished, the wood is a deep, lustrous red.

Perhaps the most amazing thing about all three of these, given the high level of artistry, is what a short time the Emberá-Wounaan have been making them. Basket-making has been a part of Emberá-Wounaan culture since their earliest days, but it wasn't until the 1990s that the tourist trade sparked the ornate, elaborate baskets one sees today. As late as the mid-1980s, the only cocobolo statues I remember seeing were rather crude and simple, nothing like the works of art made now. And the Emberá-Wounaan didn't even begin carving tagua nuts until the 1980s.

The Darién

harder to spot, but they're around. And the occasional splash and burble in the river will set your mind wondering exactly what is lurking in there.

The heavily touristed Emberá village of La Chunga (la CHOON-guh) is about an hour upriver. It's along the banks of the Río Chunga, a sluggish but no less scenic little river that empties into the Sambú. (A *chunga* is a kind of black palm with sharp spines, used by the Emberá-Wounaan to make decorative baskets. Ask a villager to point one out.) The village is about a 20-minute walk down a wide, flat path from where the boat lands.

You may have mixed feelings about visiting La Chunga. The village, which has a population of about 300 people, has obviously been shaped with tourists in mind. Most of the tourists come from small cruise ships that offer a taste of the Darién as part of a transcanal itinerary. Those who slip into the village ahead of a tour group may see women taking off their blouses and bras and men kicking off their jeans to look appropriately Indian for their visitors. Decked out in little more than short skirts or loin coverings, they dance around as tourists snap photos. The whole thing looks as uncomfortable for the villagers as it will probably feel to you.

When a tour group is expected, Emberá and Wounaan come from nearby settlements to join the villagers in selling handicrafts at tables set up around the village. Those in the market for a souvenir can find some well-made items at good prices, and the money is going right to the needy source. Popular items include *cocobolo* (rosewood) figurines, tightly woven baskets and bowls, and *tagua* nuts (also known as ivory nuts) carved in the shape of forest animals.

Sports and Recreation

Your host is Ricardo Cabrera, *cacique* (chief) of La Chunga and 11 other villages. Ricardo is a friendly guy who speaks great English. (He's the only one in the village who speaks more than a word or two.) It's startling to hear American slang from him until you learn he spent six months in Southern California helping a missionary document the Emberá language. He can arrange guided hikes on which you might see all kinds of critters, including crocodiles in a nearby lake, golden-headed quetzals, peccaries, and, of course, snakes.

A group of up to five people can hire a fishing boat for about $200 and pursue corvina, a delicious saltwater fish that's a Panama staple. Those caught here can weigh in at a little over two kilos. If you do decide to fish, one hopes you'll avoid the practice that at least one villager told me was great sport: hooking a manta ray and watching its frantic efforts to escape.

Practicalities

The residents of La Chunga have managed to turn their village into one of the more comfortable places to stay in the Darién. "Comfort" is a relative term where the Darién is concerned, but amazingly enough this place has real flush toilets and running water. Four solid thatch-roofed, bamboo-sided cabins on stilts are rented out to visitors. The rooms, officially known as the **Hotel Emberá**, are a short walk from the village proper, set in a little clearing where medicinal plants are being grown for the edification of visitors. The cabins have two rooms, each equipped just with two wooden beds topped by a foam mattress and mosquito nets. One of the cabins has double beds; the rest are singles. Showers are in a neighboring hut and consist of a cold-water spigot. Rates are $150 for one person, $60 for each additional person. This includes lodging, meals, and tours, but not airfare to Sambú.

With the exception of those who come by boat from Punta Patiño or elsewhere, most visitors fly to Sambú. From there they can hire a boat to La Chunga if they haven't arranged for someone to meet them. **Aeroperlas** (tel. 315-7500, fax 315-7580 in Panama City, no local phone, info@aeroperlas.com, www.aeroperlas.com) makes the trip on Tuesday, Thursday, and Sunday.

Turismo Aéreo (tel. 315-0279 or 315-0300, fax 315-0278 in Panama City, no local phone) flies over at 9 A.M. on Monday, Wednesday, Friday, and Saturday. The return flight is around 10:10 A.M. The price is $42 one-way, $84 round-trip, for either airline. The flight takes about 45 minutes.

It's probably best to book a trip to La Chunga through a tour operator, who will arrange flights, rooms, food, tours, and boat transportation. But independent travelers can also try booking their stay directly through Ricardo Cabrera, the *cacique.* The price is the same, minus the airfare. Ricardo can be reached through the one telephone in the village. The number is 299-6083. However, be advised that the phone is often out of order. If so, try calling tel. 649-6686 or 659-3905 and asking for Cabrera. Those are cell phones and will only be answered if Cabrera is in Panama City. Otherwise send a telegram from a post office to: Ricardo Cabrera, La Chunga, Darién, Zona 4. List your date of arrival, number in the party, and how long you want to stay. If Ricardo knows you're coming, he'll arrange for a boat to pick you up and take you to La Chunga, but don't be surprised if you have to wait around for a while.

BAHIA DE PIÑAS

The Bahia de Piñas (Piñas Bay) is far down the Pacific coast of Panama, southeast of the Golfo de San Miguel and just 56 kilometers from the Colombian border. It is world-famous for deep-sea fishing, but the area is so extraordinarily beautiful that even those who don't want to be anywhere near a fish will likely enjoy a visit. It's also a culturally interesting area.

Approximately 200 deep-sea fishing world records have been set in this area, more than anywhere else on the planet. More than 40 records were still held at the time of writing, mostly for black, blue, or striped marlin and Pacific sailfish.

The best fishing is about 20–25 kilometers offshore. During the 2003–2004 season, guests at the Tropic Star Lodge, the bay's legendary fishing lodging, caught and released 479 marlin. In June 2002, a group staying at the lodge caught an astounding 1,257 sailfish in just six days. (Billfish, the generic term for all these magnificent creatures, are caught and released.)

What accounts for this? It has a lot to do with **Zane Grey Reef,** a dramatic seamount (underwater mountain) that rises from the 100-meter-deep sea bottom in three peaks, two of which top out within 45 meters of the surface. The current sweeps plankton around the reef, which

feeds huge amounts of baitfish, which in turn attract large predators. The area is a giant natural aquarium filled with, among other things, sharks, rays, jacks, snappers, dorado, tuna, and, of course, billfish. The reef is particularly renowned among fisher folk for black marlin. The area is carefully protected: Panama enforces a 32-kilometer exclusion zone around the bay, into which commercial fishing vessels with their huge nets are not allowed. Panama's marine authority keeps a small ship stationed in the area that investigates any suspected infractions; violators are fined and can lose their fishing licenses.

The Bahia de Piñas itself is a small, narrow bay formed by two fingers of land that jut to sea. Between are the landscaped grounds of Tropic Star Lodge. Close to 6,000 hectares of the surrounding land is owned by Tropic Star, and nearly all of this has been left undeveloped and pristine. It is heart-stopping gorgeous: Emerald forests filled with massive trees spill down the hilly countryside to the very edge of the coast, which ends in sheer, rocky cliffs broken by the occasional waterfall. Dolphins like to romp around inside the bay, and humpback whales are sometimes spotted outside it. Indigenous people still pan for, and sometimes find, gold nuggets on the Río Piñas. **Playa Blanca,** a small but gorgeous white-sand beach just north of the bay, offers clear blue water and snorkeling near a coral reef just offshore. It's on property owned by Tropic Star Lodge, but as with all beaches in Panama it's open to the public. However, only guests of the lodge may hike into the forest.

Nearby are two small coastal towns, **Puerto Piñas** and **Jaqué,** which have a mixed population of Afro-Colonial and Emberá inhabitants. Several indigenous villages are up the Río Jaqué, one of which, the Wounaan village of **Biroquera,** is open to day visitors.

Puerto Piñas

To the southeast of the lodge, about 10 minutes by boat, is the small fishing village of Puerto Piñas (pop. 819). It's a dilapidated place, but the people are friendly and laid-back and it's right on a gray sandy beach. A little more than half

© WILLIAM FRIAR

basket-weaving in Puerto Piñas

its residents are estimated to be Emberá and the rest Afro-Colonial. Dwellings consist of modest cinderblock houses next to traditional cane or plank thatch-roofed huts. There is also a good airstrip, a police bunker, an ultrabasic place to stay, a couple of equally basic places to eat and drink, an Aeroperlas "office," a primary school, a tiny general store, several churches, a volleyball court, a sand soccer field, and not a whole lot else. An odd little factoid: The town and its environs have a dog population of about 400, one for every two residents. A census was taken in 2004 in advance of a visit by a team of veterinarians to try to rein in the prolific pooches, many of which are in sorry shape.

Electricity around the clock is coming to the village but hasn't quite made it yet. A concrete path links everything. Past the soccer field, on the far end of the village, is an enormous open-sided thatched-roof hut used for village meetings and Emberá dances presented to tourists. About half of the adult residents of the village

work at Tropic Star during the fishing season. Otherwise, they sustain themselves through fishing and subsistence agriculture, especially bananas, plantains, and rice. One encouraging development is the establishment of a Centro de Educación y Capacitación Amibental (center for environmental education and training), supported by Tropic Star, to teach villagers about their fragile ecosystem.

The area surrounding Puerto Piñas has been turned into farmland. It and the neighboring village of Jaqué are both at the edge of swampy plains backed by hills; the flatlands have largely been deforested, but the hills are mostly intact. Reaching primary forest requires a moderate hike back from the coast. I've been told by several people there is a large, beautiful waterfall a two- to three-hour hike into the forest (and a much easier boat ride back), but I have not yet had time to check it out. It goes without saying that this should not be attempted without a good guide.

Jaqué

The area around the town of Jaqué (pop. 2,244) is even more deforested. They actually graze cattle here—thankfully the only place along this stretch of coast that does. They mainly fish and grow crops that include rice, plantains, yuca, and yams. It's considerably larger and relatively more affluent-looking than Puerto Piñas, with some fairly substantial houses, but it's still a place where people live pretty close to the bone. There's an airstrip, a hospital, two *hospedajes,* a soccer field, and a handful of basic places to get a bite or a drink. A police bunker is at the edge of town near the mouth of the Río Jaqué, and there's a camouflage netting–covered main *cuartel* (police station) in the center of town. In 2000, the Colombian civil war pushed hundreds of refugees from the Colombian town of Juradó over the border into Jaqué and its surroundings. Stories appeared in the Panamanian press at that time saying that some of these refugees had been placed on Colombian death lists, and there was concern the war might spill over the border into this area. This didn't happen, and a beefed-up police presence in town and up the Río Jaqué has apparently kept things peaceful in the years since. The town is mellow and the people non-intrusively friendly to strangers.

Those who come to Jaqué by boat must get from open sea to the mouth of the Río Jaqué, and doing so often means riding waves that can be three meters high or even bigger. Managing this requires an experienced captain with a feel for surfing, and no one should attempt it without life jackets. This wave actually can be surfed, though few have made it all the way down here with their boards.

Near Jaqué

There are four indigenous villages on the Río Jaqué within about 20 kilometers of the town of Jaqué: Biroquera, Lucas, El Coco, and El Mamey. There are police posts in each village, but the upper reaches of the Río Jaqué beyond El Mamey are not patrolled and are supposedly used as a rest spot by combatants in the Colombian civil war. All the villages are Emberá except the first one, Biroquera, which is Wounaan. It's about 15 minutes by fast boat from Jaqué and at the time of writing was the only village Panamanian authorities allowed foreign travelers to visit. For your own safety, do not attempt to travel farther upriver. Note also that getting to the Río Jaqué by sea can be rough.

Biroquera is a fairly tidy and spacious village built right on the edge of the river. It's worth a quick visit. Houses are a mixture of traditional white cane–walled huts on stilts and more "modern" huts with walls made of wooden planks. A concrete path winds through the village, which is lit for a couple of hours in the evening by a small generator. The Wounaan are renowned for their crafts, particularly woven baskets, carved *tagua* nuts and *cocobolo* figurines, and it should be possible to buy directly from their makers. However, all the artists were in a meeting when I visited so I couldn't check out the quality of the local wares. It should be possible to hire a boat from Jaqué to Biroquera for about $20 for a small group.

About 20 kilometers southeast of Jaqué there's a small bay, **Ensenada El Guayabo,** that I have not yet visited but which I've been told has a white sand beach even prettier than Playa Blanca. All that's there are a handful of indigenous huts.

It makes for an easy day trip from Jaqué or Piñas. Visitors can trade fishing hooks and sodas with the residents for fresh coconut milk. It's probably not a good idea to head much farther down toward the Colombian border.

Tropic Star Lodge

Most foreign visitors to this area stay at the Tropic Star Lodge (U.S. tel. 800/682-3424, other countries tel. 407/423-9931, fax 407/839-3637, bonnie@tropicstar.com, www.tropicstar.com), a four-decades-old institution that looms large over the area and has made the Bahía de Piñas world-famous in fishing circles.

An exclusive fishing resort that can accommodate no more than 36 guests at a time, the lodge is set on lovely, landscaped land right above the bay. There's a small beach in front, flowering trees all around, a swimming pool with a bar, and a river that cuts across the grounds.

It's the kind of place pop stars, screen idols, and famous athletes frequent—notable guests have included John Wayne, Walter Peyton, and, more recently, George Strait. Ask about the time Lee Marvin was kicked out for throwing a chair through the restaurant window. It's entertaining to thumb through the old guest books looking for familiar names.

This was originally the vacation home of a Texas oil millionaire named Ray Smith, who turned it into a fishing lodge in 1965. It has been owned by the Kittredge family since 1976. The current owners are Terri Kittredge Andrews and her husband, Mike Andrews.

Accommodations are, as one might expect, quite comfortable, though this is definitely a fishing lodge and not an ultraposh hotel. Given the lodge's remote location, however, it is remarkably well-maintained and filled with creature comforts. It's easy to forget the nearest road is more than 100 kilometers away.

Most rooms are in two-unit cabins with wrap-around wooden porches or in a single long building near the beach. The rooms are spacious, with air-conditioning, twin beds, and large private bathrooms/dressing rooms. All have a view of the bay. Up the hill is El Palacio, a three-bedroom house with a sunken living room that was

The Darién

the original owner's home. It can accommodate up to six guests. It's reachable by climbing 122 stairs or taking the more popular cable car.

The food is delicious, with multicourse candlelit dinners served at night in the circular, air-conditioned restaurant/bar or out on the veranda. There are no telephones, fax machines, or televisions at the lodge so guests can have a true sense of getting away from it all. Expect pampering: A staff of 80 serves the 36 guests.

The lodge still has a '60s vibe about it, though a 2004 updating of the facilities has meant some welcome changes—such as replacing wall-to-wall carpet in the cabins with tile—while retaining the vintage feel of the place.

Daily fishing trips are made on 31-foot Bertrams, of which the lodge owns 14. The prime black-marlin season runs from mid-December through April. Pacific sailfish are caught year-round, with April through July especially good months. The recent building of the new airstrip in Piñas has allowed Tropic Star Lodge to extend its season from December 1 to September. Guests have free use of kayaks to explore the bay or travel up the Río Piñas.

There are also several kilometers of trails through primary and secondary forest. These are well worth walking, especially in the early morning when there's the best chance of spotting wildlife. I came across a group of curious coatimundis during a hike shortly after dawn. Don't expect to see that many animals, as hunters from surrounding villages have taken their toll through the years. But a puma hung out for a while just behind the lodge in July 2004, three-toed sloths live in the trees just behind El Palacio, foxes sometimes nose around, and the staff has found jaguar prints on the beach.

A wide ridge trail leads to a point at the end of the peninsula overlooking the bay. Hikers need to be in reasonable shape to walk the trail any distance, as there are lots of ups and downs, some of which are steep. It's also terribly slippery—I wiped out repeatedly when I walked it, so be careful. But it's wide and is being maintained again after being allowed to grow back for some time. I hiked it for more than an hour at a fast pace, but I had to turn back before reaching the end of the trail. There's apparently a good view of the ocean and bay at the end, which is on the tip of the point. Those who are feeling less ambitious can just hike up to a communications tower about 15 minutes or so from the lodge. It, like the few other lookout points along the way, offers only partial views through the canopy.

Another trail has been cut through the forest down to Playa Blanca, a lovely white-sand beach about a half-hour walk away, on the far side of the peninsula. This also has steep, slippery sections. Most guests prefer to take a 20-minute boat ride to the beach instead. There's snorkeling around the reef near the shore.

The staff can also arrange a trip up the Río Jaqué to visit the Wounaan village of Biroquera.

None of this comes cheap, of course. The basic fishing package includes seven nights of lodging, six days of fishing, and three meals a day, including wine with dinner. The rate depends on the number of people in the boat. During the highest season, January through March, the weekly per-person rates range from $3,395 for four people in a boat to $7,995 if a single person wants a boat all to him- or herself. Those who prefer not to fish pay $1,650 per person, double occupancy, during those months. The lodge is small and popular, with lots of repeat business. Reservations must often be made a year or two in advance.

The fishing package includes boat, crew, and fishing tackle but not tips for the crew ($300 per boat per week is recommended). It also doesn't include land transfers and flights from Panama City to Piñas. This is an extra $450 per person when arranged through Tropic Star Lodge, which provides VIP transfers and charter flights. There are commercial flights between Panama City and Piñas for considerably less, but these often run late and could interfere with your plans. The rates also do not include hotel stays in Panama City, which will probably be necessary at the start and end of the trip. Guests typically fly to Panama City Friday night, fly to Piñas on Saturday morning, and stay through the following Saturday morning.

Rates are considerably cheaper April–September and in December. Expect frequent rain during these months, though the fishing can still be exceptional. Half-week trips are also available then, which drops the rate even more. The cheapest basic fishing package is $1,695 per person, for three days' fishing and four nights' lodging in the lower season. The cheapest nonfishing rates are $1,000 per person double occupancy, for four nights' lodging. Again, transfers and Panama City lodging are not included in those rates.

Practicalities

Visitors can enjoy many of the natural attractions of this area for a tiny fraction of the cost of staying at Tropic Star Lodge, as long as they are willing to take a giant leap down in quality. However, the lodge's extensive primary forests and trails are on private property and are available only to guests. Only Playa Blanca, a public beach, is accessible to the general public. Relatively untouched forest that's not on private land begins a considerable distance inland and should be hiked only with a knowledgeable guide.

There are two basic *hospedajes* in Jaqué and an ultrabasic one in Puerto Piñas. The owners should be able to help guests find a boat and captain for trips up and down the coast. If none of these appeals, enterprising souls can probably strike a bargain to rent a room in someone's house upon arrival. The only places to eat are rustic to say the least; this is a good place to come with one's own food supply.

Hospedaje Kenia (tel. 267-4911 or cell 628-8734 in Panama City, tel. 333-0506 public phone in Puerto Piñas, $5 s, $7 d) is a rockbottom place to stay in Puerto Piñas that offers four rooms upstairs with plywood walls, unfinished plank floors, and a shared bathroom that consists of a toilet and spigot for bucket baths. The place was remarkably dirty when I visited, but the mattresses were in okay shape and this is the only hotel in town. Bring your own bedding and cleaning supplies. An Aeroperlas office is in the same building, and a meager general store is on the ground floor. Food and drink are available just across the path at a simple *fonda* and at Cantina Kenia, which belongs to the owner of the *hospedaje.* The police bunker is around the corner and the beach is a coconut's toss away.

There are two places to stay in Jaqué. **Aventuras**

Anamar (tel. 233-7623, 221-7423, cell 698-5413 in Panama City; ask for Sr. Herman Torres or Sra. Praxedes Torres, $10 s/d) offers the best rooms in either town. The *hospedaje* is a two-story building on a rather attractive stretch of beach past the east edge of town. It's completely basic but surprisingly okay, with three rooms that look out on a porch facing the ocean and four darker ones behind them. Room 1 is the nicest. It's a corner room with lots of glass windows and a partial view of the ocean. Bathrooms are shared. Management here is friendly and animated.

Hospedaje Chavela (cell 694-4095, tel. 259-7370 in Panama City, $5 a bed), in the middle of town close to the airstrip, offers six basic rooms with fans and foam-mattress beds. The shared toilet and spigot-shower is downstairs. The owners have made some effort at decoration, but accommodations are still threadbare. The better rooms face the front and share a balcony. To reserve a room, call the Panama City number and ask for the owner's daughter, Jasmina González. Otherwise call the public phones in Jaqué (tel. 333-0508 or 333-0503) and ask for Sr. González with the *hospedaje* (os-peh-DA-hay). **Cinema Chavela,** on the ground floor, is a claustrophobic room with wooden risers and a big-screen TV that shows Hollywood videos at deafening volume for $.25.

Food and booze are available at a handful of nondescript kiosks, *fondas,* and cantinas in Jaqué. Near the river is **Hermanas Hurtado,** a tiny general store with an airless little bar next door.

Getting There and Away

Commercial flights from Panama City stop at both Jaqué and Puerto Piñas, though the order of arrival varies. The two airstrips are about two minutes' flight time away. Turismo Aéreo may make an intermediate stop at Isla San José as well.

Aeroperlas (tel. 315-7500, fax 315-7580 in Panama City, no local phone, info@aeroperlas .com, www.aeroperlas.com), makes the trip on Tuesday, Thursday, and Saturday at 9:30 A.M. The return flight leaves around 11:10 A.M. on Tuesday and Thursday and 10:45 A.M. on Saturday.

Turismo Aéreo (tel. 315-0279 or 315-0300, fax 315-0278 in Panama City, no local phone)

© WILLIAM FRIAR

boatman's son, Río Jacqué

flies over at 9 A.M. Monday and Friday. The return flight leaves around 10:15 A.M.

The flights take about an hour. Make sure to get off at the right airstrip. All these departure times are optimistic estimates—flight times to the Darién are notoriously erratic. The fare is $50.40/$108.80 one-way/round-trip on either airline to Piñas; it's about $2 cheaper each way to Jaqué.

The new concrete airstrip at Piñas is in great shape. The Jaqué airstrip is not, and it gets quite muddy in the rainy season—an acquaintance compared landing here by small plane to taking an off-road spin in a four-wheel drive.

Guests at Tropic Star Lodge generally arrive at Piñas by charter flight. Staff members then transport them and their luggage in a tractor-pulled trailer with sheltered benches a short distance up the coast. They then transfer to a boat at the mouth of the Río Piñas or, if the tide is low, at the shore.

A little-known transportation option, by far the cheapest and longest way to get to this area, is to book passage on *The Ventura,* Tropic Star Lodge's 80-foot supply boat. It leaves Panama City Friday night and arrives at Piñas midday Saturday. It returns to Panama City the following Monday or Tuesday. The vessel sleeps 14 and the fare is $15 each way. For more information and to make a reservation, contact Tropic Star's office in Panama City (tel. 232-8375 or 232-8379).

Central Panama

The section of Panama that stretches roughly from Altos de Campana in the east to the Fortuna Road in the west contains Panama's most popular beaches, its most accessible highlands, and some of its most important and historic provincial towns.

The Cordillera Central, Panama's central mountain range, forms the backbone of most of this long stretch of land. Its steep, saw-toothed peaks form a fortresslike wall between the Pacific and Caribbean slopes, making it especially easy to discern the Continental Divide here.

The Pacific side contains some of the longest-settled parts of Panama. Significant population centers include the quaint provincial town of Penonomé, the industrial outpost of Aguadulce, and the major transportation hub of Santiago. These and most of the other sizable towns are in the lowlands right on the Interamerican Highway—also known as the Pan-American Highway or, in Spanish, the Interamericana—and most of the beaches are just a couple of kilometers south of it. Lovely beaches are also found on the Archipiélago de las Perlas, an archipelago of more than 90 Pacific islands that begins just a 15-minute plane ride from Panama City.

The highlands are all north of the highway, though many of them are easy to get to on good roads (the sections that aren't easy to reach make up for the rough trip in their untrammeled

Must-Sees

Look for **M** to find the sights and activities you can't miss and **M** for the best dining and lodging.

M Santa Clara: White sand beaches not yet overrun with tourists and weekenders (page 238).

M Farallón: Panama's fastest-growing Pacific beach destination (page 240).

M Sunday Market: El Valle's market is a popular weekend destination for Panama City residents in search of crafts and plants, and an excuse to enjoy the cool weather and natural attractions of El Valle (page 246).

M Parque Nacional Omar Torrijos H.: Known as El Copé, this eastern outpost of Panama's rugged western highlands has good facilities for campers (page 259).

M Basílica Menor Santiago Apostól de Natá: A modest church with a history that stretches back five centuries, the basilica is the oldest church along the Pacific coast of the Americas (page 263).

© WILLIAM FRIAR

The remote Parque Nacional Omar Torrijos H. (El Copé) has the best visitors facilities of any of Panama's national parks.

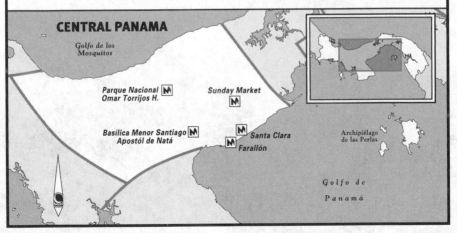

CENTRAL PANAMA

Golfo de los Mosquitos

Parque Nacional **M** Omar Torrijos H.

Sunday Market **M**

Basílica Menor Santiago **M** Apostól de Natá

M Santa Clara **M** Farallón

Archipiélago de las Perlas

Golfo de Panamá

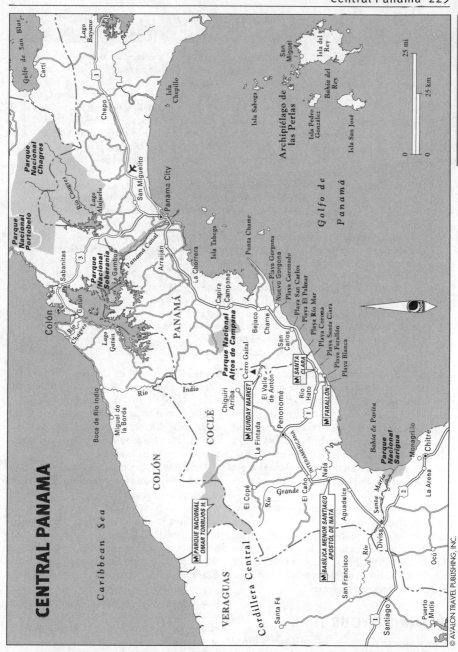

CENTRAL PANAMA

TRAVEL TIPS

Drivers should take it easy on the windy, hilly stretch of the Interamericana that heads west past Altos de Campana. The curves are deceptively sharp and many cars lose control. Take the speed signs seriously—they're really not being conservative.

All the mainland areas mentioned in this chapter are well served by buses from Panama City. Try to travel in the morning, when service is more frequent and it's easier to find one's way around. It's much tougher to get transportation to more remote areas after dark. For beach and lowland areas, it's not necessary to take a bus that has your destination on the windshield; any bus plying the Interamericana that goes at least as far as your stop will drop you off. Buses to highland destinations are generally less frequent, though it's easy to get a bus to El Valle.

Renting a car is also a reasonable option, especially to get to the beaches. The road from Panama City is good the whole way, if more than a bit dangerous. Speeding is a problem on the Interamericana, so drive defensively. It's possible to get to El Valle, La Pintada, Santa Fé, and San Francisco in a regular car; just about every other highland spot described here requires a powerful, high-clearance four-wheel-drive vehicle.

It's not a good idea to drive through the countryside at night, when visibility is poor and help harder to come by if you get into trouble. Note that there's a toll booth about 30 kilometers from Panama City ($.50), at the start of the *autopista*.

There are still (thankfully) few places along the coast to rent boats, ATVs, Jet Skis, and other recreational toys. Those who want a little boat ride can always hire a fisherman and putter around. And *campesinos* (country folk) all along the beaches rent horses, especially on the weekends. If you have trouble finding a likely candidate, ask for help at your hotel. Except at resorts, it shouldn't cost more than a few dollars an hour. Please be considerate about where you ride; horses can muck up the beach for sunbathers.

beauty). Attractive and accessible highland spots with lush forests and cool waterfalls are within a couple hours' drive of Panama City. The most popular of these spots is El Valle de Antón. More isolated spots are not much farther away, and their beauty makes it worth the trouble to get there. All are dotted along the Cordillera Central, which means visitors at the higher elevations get to experience both Pacific and Caribbean flora and fauna.

Once one reaches the Continental Divide, most roads end and the only way forward is on foot through dense tropical forest. Much of the Caribbean slope is less well known and more lightly settled than some remote parts of the Darién. Exploring it requires a serious organized trek through rugged wilderness.

PLANNING YOUR TIME

The destinations in this chapter cover a broad swath of central Panama, and only those with

boundless time will be able to cover them all. Which to choose will depend on your taste and where else in Panama you're planning to go.

Those who want a little beach time within easy driving distance of Panama City have lots of options. Plan to spend at least a couple of nights to have time to truly relax.

For big full-service resorts with lots of facilities, go for **Coronado** or **Farallón.** The resorts at more distant Farallón are newer and, though a construction explosion is rapidly transforming it, the area is still not as densely developed as long-established Coronado. The white-sand beaches there are also among the prettiest on the coast, though the surf can be rough. **Santa Clara** has smaller but still comfortable lodgings on an equally gorgeous beach. The other beach spots generally offer cheaper but less attractive places to stay, on beaches that have calmer surf but aren't going to grace a postcard anytime soon.

It's easy to add a day or overnight trip to **El**

Valle de Antón from any of these beach spots; Santa Clara and Farallón are especially close to it. If at all possible, plan to visit El Valle on a Sunday, when its famous little market is bustling.

El Valle has the largest selection of lodgings, restaurants, and activities in the central highlands, and it's the easiest to get to of the mountain spots discussed in this chapter. **Parque Nacional Omar Torrijos H. (El Copé)**, by contrast, is the most remote and wild of these spots, but it has better visitor facilities than any other national park in the country. It's a good place to spend the night and enjoy some evening and morning hiking and bird-watching. It can get surprisingly chilly in the highlands—take a windbreaker and rain gear at any time of year. As attractive as the central highlands are, those short on time who are planning to head to the wilder and even more beautiful western highlands won't miss too much by skipping them.

The **Archpiélago de las Perlas** is the closest major island group to Panama City. It offers beautiful beaches and lots of aquatic activities. However, it tends to get overshadowed these days by the tourists hotspots of Bocas del Toro and the culturally rich Kuna Yala, and only those with a need to experience both Pacific and Caribbean island life will opt to visit all three.

Parque Nacional Altos de Campana

Established in 1966, Altos de Campana is Panama's oldest national park. Its 4,817 acres are spread over hillsides that range from 400 meters above sea level to the 850-meter-high Cerro Campana. Birders come up here for a chance to see the gorgeous orange-bellied trogon and other striking species. But the countryside is heavily settled, with just fragments of intact tropical and premontane forest left. There's a mirador just up from the park's ranger station, on the left, though the view is plenty dramatic just from the road. That view is the main reason to come up here; this place will appeal to most people more as a highway vista point than as a park to hike and camp in. It offers a breathtaking panorama of the Pacific Ocean, Punta Chame, craggy hills, an estuary that snakes up through the green countryside, and, on a clear day, Isla Taboga in the far distance.

PRACTICALITIES

The **ANAM ranger station** is four kilometers uphill from the turn off the Interamericana, on the left. Pay the $3 entrance fee here, plus $5 more to camp. For the same $5, you may be able to rent a bunk in a cabin on a ridge behind the station. It's meant for ANAM staff, but if there's room you're welcome to stay. The cabin has two basic rooms, each with four bunk beds, a common room, and a shared cold-water bathroom. Bring bedding. It's nothing special, but the price is right and you can't beat the location: perched right above a steep, craggy valley, with sweeping views all the way down the hills and out to sea.

The ranger at the station can answer basic questions (in Spanish only) about the area and the single developed trail, **Sendero La Cruz.** Five kilometers up from the ANAM station, or nine kilometers from the turnoff, you'll see a *senderos* sign on the right. Turn there onto a brutal road that requires a four-wheel drive with high clearance and a good warranty. Head up toward the

A ROADSIDE ATTRACTION

Restaurante D'Liza's Café (tel. 244-6082, 7 A.M.–10 P.M. Mon.–Sat., closed Sun.) in greater Chorrera is a good place to stop for a cheap meal between Panama City and the beaches. It's a particularly convenient spot for breakfast when you need to leave Panama City early to beat the traffic. It's clean, air-conditioned, and pleasant, and the cafeteria food is decent and plentiful. A full meal and drink costs around $2. It's in the Plaza Nuevo Milenio shopping plaza, on the north side of the road next to the Texaco station. It's near kilometer marker 40, before the road west starts climbing uphill.

towers as far as possible, then park. The trail leads through mostly secondary forest to a cross 700 meters away and 800 meters above sea level. The hike up and back takes about two hours.

Back on the main road, another kilometer uphill (6 kilometers from the ANAM station, 10 kilometers from the turnoff) is **Richard's Place** (tel. 601-2882, $3 per person to camp, $10/$20 s/d), a hostel-like guesthouse on a ridge at 762 meters. It contains five basic but spacious rooms that can house couples or friendly groups. Every room is different, but they all have hot-water bathrooms. The common area and dining room are simple but pleasant, and there's a breezy deck out back that overlooks the valley and has a barbecue grill.

The whole place is stocked with vintage gizmos—a collection of electric meters that date back to 1927, a 50-year-old emergency-response tape recorder—that hints at the owner's life as a radio and TV repairman before he went on to run three power plants for the old Panama Canal Company. That owner, Richard William Froehle (FRAY-lee) is in his late 70s and manages to be simultaneously funny, mellow, friendly, and profane. He's quite a character, the epitome of an eccentric type the Canal Zone used to attract. He's owned the place for 30 years.

Those who camp on the grounds get access to hot showers and all the other facilities. Richard has six old tents that campers are welcome to use. Richard's Place will cook meals here for a couple of dollars, or guests can bring their own food and use the kitchen to prepare it.

GETTING THERE

The turnoff to Altos de Campana is less than an hour west of Panama City. The right turn up

---

ANOTHER ROADSIDE ATTRACTION

Artesanias Tipicas Panameñas (8 A.M.– 6 P.M. daily, tel. 248-5313) on the westbound side of the Interamericana, east of Capira near kilometer marker 50, has long been a convenient place to stretch one's legs and do a little shopping on the way to and from the beach. It's a large, open building with a moderate selection of fancy hammocks (the most elegant of which are the white ones from Nicaragua, which sell here for about $130), tooled-leather chairs, traditional Azuero ceramics and devil masks, and other souvenir possibilities. With enough warning, they can make hand-painted ceramic signs with house numbers, family name, or personalized messages. Those with their own transportation can place an order when heading west and pick up the completed sign on the way back east.

---

from the westbound side of the Interamericana, about six kilometers west of Capira, comes up fast, and the road turns bad instantly. Be careful, and approach the turn very slowly. The drive starts steep, on a rough dirt and rock road and requires a four-wheel drive.

To get to the park from Panama City by public transportation, take a bus that goes at least as far as Capira, which is where you'll switch buses. Buses make the trip from Capira up to Altos de Campana every day about 8 A.M.–6:30 P.M. Look for "Capira-Chicá" on the windshield—Altos de Campana is an intermediate stop. Buses make the run every hour or two; service is erratic. Buses head back down to Capira 5 A.M.–4 P.M. The fare is $1. Taxi fare from Capira is $18.

Beach Towns and Resorts

Wide, sandy, and accessible beaches start a little under an hour's drive from Panama City and stretch west for 50 kilometers. This strip of coast is where most people who live in and around Panama City, at least those who can afford it, go for a weekend at the beach. These beaches are great for swimming, body surfing, and lazing about. Some offer decent surfing. Those interested in diving and snorkeling need to head farther west or to the Caribbean side of the isthmus. One spot, Punta Chame, is known for windsurfing and kitesurfing.

The area has undergone major development in the last couple of decades, however, and now the most popular beaches have a few condo towers looming over them. One sometimes has to contend with weekend personal watercraft riders, all-terrain-vehicle riders, and boom-box blarers, though some effort has been made to control these nuisances. But it's still quite possible to find clean, secluded spots without another soul on the beach for as far as you can see, especially if you come during the week.

Note: If only pure white sand makes you happy, these beaches may be disappointing. The sand mostly comes in shades of brown, gray, and even black. But those who can get beyond their postcard preconceptions of a tropical beach will find these quite inviting. They're wide, long, and sandy, and the water is warm.

Many of the places to stay along the beach have restaurants attached. There are lots of other simple places to eat along the side of the road on the way to or from the beaches. But those with their own cars should consider doing what local weekenders do: Pack a cooler. Some of the places listed below have kitchen facilities. The most popular beach areas have small grocery stores with basic supplies. Playa Corondo has a large 24-hour supermarket.

The Pacific coast of Panama is completely different from the Caribbean coast. For one thing, where the Caribbean tides average 30 centimeters, the Pacific's massive tides range about 3.5–5.5 meters. Some of the beaches have strong rip cur-

rents and pounding surf, so watch out. The beaches below are listed in order of their distance from Panama City, with the closest described first.

PUNTA CHAME

Punta Chame (Poon-tah CHA-meh) is at the end of a dry and rather barren peninsula that curves up toward the mainland to the east, forming Bahía de Chame, a long, narrow bay that from shore looks like a quiet strait. The turnoff to Punta Chame is about 70 kilometers west of Panama City, a drive that takes a little under an hour. From there it's another 25 kilometers to the beach on a potholed road that's unpaved in sections. This is a popular windsurfing spot, though unfortunately there is no longer a place to rent sailboards and kitesurfing gear.

In the middle of the bay between the tip of Punta Chame and the mainland is Isla Taborcillo, which was once owned by John Wayne. An ambitious project to build vacation cottages for Europeans on the island—with a peculiar Wild West theme in honor of its former owner—appears to have faded.

Punta Chame is likely to appeal only to avid sailboarders, who have to bring their own gear. The beaches aren't that nice (the best ones are

A NOTE TO BEACH CAMPERS

Campers considering sleeping on the beach along this strip of coast should be careful. As usual, sleep in a tent as a precaution against the small but real chance of being bitten by vampire bats, which carry rabies. Locals also warn about *maleantes* (thugs). Given that there are several guarded, inexpensive places with good facilities on or near the beach, you're better off pitching your tent there than on a secluded stretch of beach. The best camping facilities are at Santa Clara.

on the side facing the ocean, not the bay), the limited facilities are unappealing, and the village is depressed and nondescript. But the area does offer solitude and lovely views of the sea, islands, and hilly mainland. If you do go, notice the signs around Motel Chame warning not to swim at low tide. They're supposedly there because of the danger of stepping on a stingray.

Practicalities

Motel Punta Chame (tel. 223-1447 Panama City reservations, tel. 240-5498 at the motel, rooms start at $44 s/d) near the tip of Punta Chame, is a shabby, gloomy place that suggests what a trailer park might look like if it went on a beach vacation. It's far too expensive for its meager offerings. But for windsurfers who need a roof over their heads, this place is pretty much the only option. (Those with tents can find a secluded stretch of beach away from the motel and camp for free.)

There are seven quite different rooms, all with air-conditioning. These include four rooms in a trailer with fake wood paneling ($44 s/d). The best bet is probably one of the two rooms in a stand-alone building on the motel grounds. They're basic and cold-water only, but the beds are passable. They have a good view of the ocean, islands, and mainland and a sitting room ($55 s/d). The motel has a little restaurant/bar that serves food 7 A.M.–9 P.M. in the dry season, until 8 P.M. in the rainy season. It has a large, pleasant *rancho* that overlooks the beach. Most items are $4–8.

There are few services in Punta Chame itself. The town of Chame, near the Interamericana, has a branch of the Banco Nacional de Panamá and a little store with basic supplies next to a soccer field. Bejuco has a pharmacy and launderette.

Getting There

The turnoff to Punta Chame is about 70 kilometers west of Panama City. The drive takes a little under an hour. Don't confuse the turnoff to Punta Chame with the town of Chame, which is a few kilometers farther west along the Interamericana. If you see a sign for Chame, you've gone too far. From the Punta Chame turnoff it's

another 25 kilometers down to the beach on a potholed road that's unpaved in sections.

To get to Punta Chame from Panama City by public transportation, take a bus that goes at least as far as Bejuco (beh-HOO-coh), about a kilometer past the Punta Chame turnoff. The fare is $2.15. Get off at Bejuco, which is little more than a way station on the Interamericana, and take either a "bus" (really a pickup truck, $1) or a taxi (asking $15, but try bargaining) to Punta Chame. The pickup-buses are by the Texaco station; the taxis are a little farther west, near an underpass. The bus service runs 6 A.M.–about 7:30 P.M.

PLAYA GORGONA

The next beach area along the coast is Playa Gorgona, about seven kilometers past the Punta Chame turnoff. Gorgona has the feel of a modest weekend beach destination that's past its prime and hovering on the brink of abandonment—which is exactly what it is. There are better hotels and nicer beaches farther west.

The place will mainly be of interest to surfers. **Playa Malibu,** right next to Gorgona, has a reputation for offering the best and most reliable ride along this whole stretch of coast. To get there, take the Gorgona turnoff from the Interamericana and head straight down to the beach. The break is to the left, near the mouth of a river. Those traveling by car should take a four-wheel drive and park it on the beach near the break. Otherwise, there's a good chance someone may break into the car while you're surfing.

Accommodations and Food

There are several basic places to stay in and near Gorgona. The ones listed below are the best of the bunch, which isn't saying much. All are overpriced.

Cabañas Playa Gorgona (tel. 233-2469 Panama City reservations, tel. 240-6160 at the cabins, $44 s/d) consists of rows of low concrete buildings that house 43 dreary and bare-bones rooms. It's straight down the road that leads from the Interamericana to the beach, three kilometers south. The rooms have kitchenettes with stoves, air-conditioning, and cold-water bathrooms. They're pretty grim, aimed at Panamanian groups on a budget who stuff as many people as they can into each room. This is not an attractive place.

The Canadian (tel. 240-6066, $40 per bungalow weekdays, $50 on weekends) consists of eight cinderblock bungalows with zinc roofs, each with a kitchen, in a compound surrounded by a six-foot-high wall. To get there, take the road from the Interamericana toward Cabañas Playa Gorgona, then make a left when the road forks and follow the signs. The place is right next to the beach. The bungalows are all different and sleep 3–6 people. All are air-conditioned and have a sitting area, but they're old, rustic, and have squishy beds. They're passable, in a ramshackle country cabin kind of way, but not very nice. It's a poor deal for a couple but a decent one for a group that needs fortresslike security. The small, basic restaurant is open on the weekends. The bar is always open.

Cabañas Villanita (tel. 240-5314 or 228-0138, $45 for up to three people), a two-minute walk from the beach, consists of three multiroom cabañas in a beachy suburban setting. The cabañas are made of cinderblocks and the place is surrounded by a barbed-wire fence. It seemed to be the most pleasant place to stay in the area, but it was locked up when I visited. This is a quieter and more isolated stretch of beach. To get there, head down from the Interamericana toward Cabañas Playa Gorgona. When the road forks, go left about two kilometers. Go past the turnoff to The Canadian. Cabañas Villanita are on the right, near the beach.

My last time through I had the bad luck to catch **Rincón Catracho** (tel. 240-5807, 9 A.M.–8 P.M. Mon.–Thurs., 7:30 A.M.–9:30 P.M. Fri.–Sun.) between meal hours, but it comes recommended and it'd be a big surprise if it's not the best place to eat in town. It's run by—and out of the house of—a Honduran woman and her German husband and their kids, who have created a friendly sidewalk café ambience in the middle of this down-at-the-heels village. The menu includes chili, pastas, seafood, chicken tacos, and various meats, with dishes ranging $5–10.50. It's a little tricky to find. It's behind a little beer garden called Jardín Nacira on the west side of the soccer field in the village.

Club de Playa Gorgona Resort (tel. 695-9763, 9 A.M.–5 P.M. Mon.–Fri., 7 A.M.–10 P.M. Sat., 7 A.M.–7 P.M. Sun.) is a fancy name for a basic place to eat. It's an open-air restaurant that serves questionable-looking meals, mainly seafood, for $5–15. It's just west of Cabaña Playa Gorgona and can be reached by walking along the beach.

Getting There

The turnoff to Playa Gorgona is on the Interamericana about seven kilometers west of the turnoff to Punta Chame and four kilometers east of the Coronado turnoff.

Any bus from Panama City that goes at least this far can drop passengers off by the turnoff. From there it's three kilometers down to the beach and Cabañas Playa Gorgona. The Canadian and Cabañas Villanita are a couple of kilometers down a left fork off this road, a short distance before the beach. Rincón Catracho is in "downtown" Gorgona, which is a right turn before the beach as one heads toward Cabaña Playa Gorgona. Those without their own wheels will probably have to hoof it from the Interamericana to any of these places. Alternatively, in the likely event there are no taxis around, visitors can get off the bus at the Coronado turnoff and get a taxi back to Gorgona from there. During the weekend this should be no trouble; during the week, it's more of a gamble. There are also taxis near the underpass back in Bejuco.

PLAYA CORONADO

Playa Coronado, about 10 kilometers past the Punta Chame turnoff, is the most (over)developed beach in Panama. Because the beach is a long sweep of pure sand, this has long been a favorite place for those living in Panama City to build a weekend beach house. Growth here has exploded in the last couple of decades. It has condo towers, mansions, housing developments, several simple restaurants, and a major resort hotel. Every centimeter of beachfront property has been built on. However, even here there's a good chance of not having to deal with crowds. Note that the sand is blackish.

The turnoff to Coronado is well marked; look for the El Rey supermarket sign, which is just about the tallest thing for kilometers around. There's a guardhouse at the entrance to the area, and on the weekends access is controlled. Gringos, fairly or not, should have little trouble getting past the guard at the gate—if stopped, just say you're going to the Coronado Hotel and Resort or Club Gaviota; you don't have to produce evidence of a reservation. It's a nuisance, especially since all beaches in Panama are open to the public, but it does keep the crowds down.

Accommodations and Food

A moderate deal in pricey Coronado is the recently expanded **Club Gaviota** (tel. 224-9053 or 224-9056 Panama City reservations, 240-4526 in Coronado, $50/$65 s/d). It's to the right of the white condo towers toward the end of Paseo George Smith (also called Paseo Lajas). It offers eight rooms, most of which are in a motel-style building set back from the beach with no view. The ones in this building are fairly new, simple, and pleasant. Each has air-conditioning, two good double beds, and attractive cold-water bathrooms. Avoid rooms 1 and 2, which are old and small, set in a separate building. Main dishes in the simple restaurant range in price $7–15. The restaurant is allegedly open 8 A.M.–5 P.M. daily, but that's likely only the case on dry-season weekends. The place has two swimming pools set in a well-tended, flower-filled garden on a rise overlooking the ocean. There are a bar on the premises and a large new open-air dining room. Warning: Daytrippers from Panama City are shipped in by the busload on dry-season weekends.

The small, upscale **Corowalk Inn** (tel. 240-1516 or 240-1517, $66 s/d), in the shopping complex on the Interamericana, is a 14-room hotel built in 2002. It offers 14 modern, attractive rooms with good beds and air-conditioning. The rooms are small and simple but pleasant. Some rooms have no windows, and others are on a terrace overlooking the El Rey parking lot. The staff is refreshingly friendly. The only real problem with this place is that it's on the highway, not the beach. **La Dolce Vita Spa** (tel. 240-1480,

9 A.M.–6 P.M. Mon.–Sat., 1–5 P.M. Sun.) is right next door.

Coronado Hotel and Resort (Avenida Punta Prieta, tel. 264-3164 or 264-2724 Panama City reservations, 240-4444 at Coronado, fax 223-8513, corogolf@sinfo.net, www.coronadoresort.com, rates start at $181.50/192.50 s/d) a short drive past the Coronado guard house, is one of the biggest resort hotels outside of Panama City. It has a health spa, 18-hole golf course, four tennis courts, three bars, three restaurants, a large swimming pool, and so on. Its latest addition is a huge equestrian club on a separate property, with its own steak house, **Restaurante Estribos de Plata.** Its 76 rooms (they're all suites) are modern and cheerful, ranging in size from large to gigantic. The least expensive are the "standard suites," which have a king-sized bed, a sitting room with two sofa beds, minibar, telephone, hot-water bathroom, and TV. These go for $181.50 for one person or $192.50 for two, but they can sleep up to four people for $16.50 more per person. Children 12 and younger are no extra charge. Package deals are sometimes available.

One drawback about this place is it's not actually on the beach. A frequent shuttle bus runs between the hotel and its private "beach club" on the water two kilometers away. A nice place to grab a simple lunch is **La Terraza,** a casual open-air place near the pool. The food is nothing special, but the atmosphere is pleasant. It offers sandwiches, pasta, steaks, seafood, a few veggie dishes, and so on. Most items cost around $5–10. The most formal place to eat at the resort is **Le Club,** an air-conditioned restaurant upstairs with tablecloths and such and a small but fancy menu. I confess I haven't eaten there in a while so can't comment on the food these days. Main dishes are $11–25. Theoretically, only guests are supposed to eat at the restaurant, but nonguests have been known to eat there anyway.

Guests can rent bicycles, golf carts, ATVs, horses, and more. All kinds of tours are available.

Restaurante Malibu (no phone, 8 A.M.–10 P.M. daily) is a large, basic outdoor place just behind the shopping complex on the road into Coronado. It serves middling but edible food for a rather pricey $6–12. In case you're curious what *pollo Americano* (American chicken) might be, apparently we gringos like our chicken drowning in barbecue sauce. The fried yuca is good.

El Rincón del Chef (no phone, 7 A.M.–3:30 P.M. Tues., 8 A.M.–8 P.M. Wed. and Thurs., 7 A.M.–10 P.M. Sat. and Sun., closed Mon.) is a cute open-air place offering dishes varying from corvina to *pulpo a curry* (curried octopus). The average entrée goes for about $6. It's on the right as one heads toward the gatehouse.

Resaurante Los Che's, on the north side of the Interamericana near the Coronado entrance, has long been a popular pit-stop with local residents and weekenders from Panama City, but there have been complaints about the quality of the food recently.

Services

There's a modern shopping complex at the turnoff to Coronodo that has a huge 24-hour El Rey supermarket whose sign on a tall pole is visible for kilometers. There's a pharmacy inside the supermarket.

The complex also includes the Corowalk Inn, a gas station, a Global Bank (8:30 A.M.–3 P.M. Mon.–Fri., 9 A.M.–2:30 P.M. Sat.), and other stores.

A Western Union outlet (tel. 240-4691, 8 A.M.–5 P.M. Mon.–Sat., 8 A.M.–4 P.M. Sun.) is in the *ferretería* (hardware store) across the street from the complex on the road leading into Coronado.

Getting There and Around

Buses run constantly between Coronado and Panama City, about 80 kilometers east ($2.30). From the turnoff you can take a taxi or minibus to the beach or your hotel for a few dollars.

A taxi from the shopping complex on the Interamericana to the beach, three kilometers away, costs $3. Minibuses make the same run from in front of the hardware store on the road leading into Coronado, across from the shopping complex, for $.50.

BETWEEN PLAYA CORONADO AND PLAYA CORONA

The 15 kilometers of beach between Coronado and Corona are relatively undeveloped and have few facilities. The area is most popular with surfers. All are a left turn off the Interamericana, then a couple of kilometers drive or hike to the beach.

The best known spots are **Playa Teta,** about three kilometers west of the Coronado turnoff onto an unmarked dirt road; **Playa El Palmar,** just after the town of San Carlos; and **Playa Río Mar,** two kilometers past San Carlos onto a well-marked road. The sea bottom tends to be rocky in this area, so booties are a must. (Nonsurfers will not find most stretches of these beaches very attractive.) There are 2–3 breaks at each spot. Teta and Río Mar are the most popular.

San Carlos, 11 kilometers west of the Coronado turnoff, is the only sizable town along the Interamericana between Coronado and Corona. It's about at the midpoint of the surfing beaches along this part of the coast. There's little of interest in town. It has its own beach, about a kilometer south of town, but it's rocky, attracts a lot of trash, and is mainly used by fishermen to launch their boats. The main significance of San Carlos for tourists is that buses run frequently between it and the highland town of El Valle de Antón. However, these buses pick up and drop off passengers right on the Interamericana, not in the town itself.

Skip the last beach, **Playa Corona.** The beach is rocky with black sand, and the one hotel and camping spot, Hotel Playa Corona, is run-down.

Practicalities

Surfers are probably best off camping on the beach in tents. However, keep an eye on valuables around here. At the time of writing, the only place to stay worth considering on this whole stretch of coastline was **Hotel Playa Río Mar,** (tel. 223-0192 or 264-2272 Panama City reservations, or tel. 240-8027 at the hotel, $42.90 s/d). Set on a ridge overlooking the ocean near the end of the road leading to the beach, the hotel offers rather rustic and shabby rooms that are overpriced for what you get. Try haggling. The grounds are pretty, though—there's a small, attractive pool surrounded by flowering bushes next to the open-air restaurant. There are 20 rooms, some in cottages with a sea view. The rooms are rundown and have air-conditioning, cold-water bathrooms, and local TV. Some of the beds are squishy, others are passable. It's a pleasant spot to stop for a drink. The food varies from fish to fried rice. Main dishes are pricey, at $7–16. To get there, take the Río Mar turnoff two kilometers west of San Carlos on the Interamericana. The hotel is about a kilometer down the road.

Getting There

Surfers without their own transportation will probably have to hoof it with their boards at least a kilometer or two from the bus stop on the Interamericana to any of these beaches. Bus fare from Panama City to any of these turnoffs is no more than $3.

Buses between San Carlos and El Valle run constantly during daylight hours. The fare is $1. The last bus down from El Valle leaves at 8 P.M. Bus fare between San Carlos and Panama City is $2.70.

ℕ SANTA CLARA

Santa Clara has it all: pleasant places to stay, a few decent places to eat, a beautiful white-sand beach, and not too many people. During the week, the only signs of life you may see are a few fishing boats motoring by in the distance. The short road from the highway to the beach has lots of potholes but is drivable in a regular car if you're careful.

Accommodations and Food

There are three pleasant places to stay in Santa Clara, two of them on the beach. None of them is a bargain, however. This is also the best area on this part of the coast for camping. There are several places where backpackers can pitch a tent in secure surroundings with good facilities for a few dollars. As usual, you can also just claim any open stretch of beach for free, but keep an eye on your gear.

ℕ Cabañas Las Sirenas (tel. 223-5374, 263-7577, 263-8494, or 263-9478 through Pesantez Tours in Panama City, tel. 993-3235 in Santa Clara, traducsa@cwp.net.pa, www.panamainfo.com/lassirenas, $88 for one-bedroom cottage)

is my favorite place to stay on my favorite Pacific coast beach. It offers the quietest, coziest, and most secluded lodging around. To get there, head down the paved main road from the Santa Clara turnoff and follow the "Las Sirenas" signs, which will lead you onto a dirt road. Both roads are potholed but drivable. Las Sirenas is just beginning to get a slightly weathered look, but it's still well-functioning and tastefully designed. It's not luxurious but it offers quite comfortable and large beach cottages. The cabañas above the beach all have sitting rooms, well-equipped kitchens, barbecue areas, patios with hammocks, TV/VCRs, and a view of the ocean. The cottages on the beach are similarly equipped. I prefer these because they're more private and the porch looks out on the beach a few steps away. Only the bedrooms are air-conditioned. The grounds are home to peacocks as well as bougainvillea and other beautiful flowering bushes. The one thing this place lacks is a restaurant. One-bedroom cottages are $88 and can sleep five. Two-bedroom cottages go for $110 and can sleep eight.

Restaurante y Cabañas Las Veraneras (tel. 993-3313 or fax 993-2528 in Santa Clara, tel. 317-6594 in Panama City, reserva@lasveraneras.com, www.lasvereneras.com, rates start at $55 per cabin), is a newer place that continues to grow. It's just to the right of Las Sirenas as one faces the beach; the road is well marked. It offers a range of accommodations, some quite pleasant though plain. My favorites are the three quaint split-level cabins with thatch roofs on a bluff overlooking the ocean. They're a bit rustic and don't have air-conditioning or hot water, but they do have private bathrooms and hammock-equipped balconies that look out on the surf. Each goes for $55 and can sleep five. (Management now calls these Modelo Las Trillizas, though the name keeps changing.) Some of the other cabins on the property have air-conditioning and hot water, but none of them have the rustic charm of these and some are set far back from the beach and have no view. These latter go for $55 (five-person cabin with kitchen but no air-conditioning), $65 (five-person cabin with air-conditioning and hot water), and $110 (10-person house with air-conditioning and a kitchen).

© WILLIAM FRIAR

The split-level cabins of Restaurante y Cabañas Las Veraneras have a great view of the ocean.

A warren of very rustic cabins with a tree-house feel has recently been built on stilts right above the outdoor restaurant on the beach; expect plenty of noise on dry-season weekends if you stay in one of these ($40/$45 s/d).

Campers can pitch a tent for $10 per person, which includes use of all facilities. The site is not as nice as that at Balneario Santa Clara, though, and it's next to the mouth of a slow-moving river that looks like a great mosquito breeding ground.

A pool was being built the last time I visited. The large open-air restaurant, right on the beach, is open for breakfast, lunch, and dinner. It serves seafood, meats, and chicken, with most things going for $4–6.

For those not spending the night, $1 buys you entrance, a *rancho,* and use of the bathroom, changing room, and outdoor shower for the day. **Restaurante y Balneario Santa Clara,** (tel. 993-2123, 11 A.M.–6:30 P.M. Mon.–Fri., 9 A.M.–7 P.M. Sat. and Sun. in the dry season) is a restaurant, bar, and campsite that gets packed on dry-season weekends. During the week, you're likely to have it all to yourself. The restaurant is little more than a large thatch-hut on the beach. The food isn't memorable, but it'll do in a pinch and the lo-

cation is cool. The place is on the beach right between Cabañas Las Sirenas and Cabañas Las Veraneras. The restaurant specializes in seafood and pizzas. *Pulpo a ajillo* (octopus in garlic sauce), $7.50, is chewy but tasty. Everything but lobster is $7.50 or less. You'd better be in the mood to eat early, as the last order has to be in by 6 P.M. You'd be wise to come by ahead of time to make sure the cook's around and has what you want. Place your order for a specific time and then go for a swim.

Campers can stay here for a very reasonable $2 per person. The rate includes use of a *rancho*—a little open-air thatched-roof hut—right on the beach and clean bathrooms and outdoor showers. There's a guard on duty at night.

The place can get you a horse for $3 an hour on the weekends. You can also rent a boat any day of the week for $30. Trips last "until the gas runs out."

XS Memories (tel. 993-3096, fax 993-3069 xs-memories@hotmail.com, www.xsmemories.com, $60.50 s/d) is a secure and comfortable place to pitch a tent, park the RV, or rent a room. It's run by a friendly couple from Las Vegas who have built a tidy walled compound with a pool set on well-tended grounds.

The cost to camp is $2 per person or $4 per tent. Campers should note, however, that the site is a couple of kilometers from the ocean, on the other side of the Interamericana from the Santa Clara turnoff. Motor homes can hook up here for $6–10 a day, a price that includes water, electricity, septic service, and access to a small shop for repairs. Campers and RVers are also welcome to use the pool, shower, and all other facilities.

This place is popular with the RV crowd that drives the Interamerican Highway down from North America until it comes to a dead end in eastern Panama. The place gets 100 RVs a year, including some that come down in caravans.

XS Memories also offers three wheelchair-accessible cabins, each with air-conditioning and hot water. One of the cabins has a kitchenette. Rooms are simple but clean, though the mattresses are thin. There's a restaurant and sports bar with a big-screen TV. The restaurant concentrates on simple, hearty American fare and bar food, such as hamburgers, chips with guacamole, and a variety of chicken, beef, and pork dishes. The price range is $2.25–9.50. The restaurant is open 8 A.M.–8 P.M. Mon.–Thurs., 8 A.M.–10 P.M. Friday–Sunday. There's a tiny zoo on the premises. Bikes can be rented for $6 a day. XS Memories is on the north side of the Interamericana opposite the turnoff to Santa Clara. The turn is well marked.

Getting There and Around

The poorly marked turnoff to Playa Santa Clara is 13 kilometers past Corona. It's about a 1.5-hour drive from Panama City, 108 kilometers east. Buses from Panama City make the trip every 20 minutes or so from early morning until mid-evening, though it's best to go during daylight hours. The fare is $3 and the trip takes around two hours. Any west-bound bus heading to Río Hato, Antón, Penonomé, or points farther west can let passengers off here. Buses will often drop passengers off at the beach for an extra $1; be sure to ask the driver ahead of time. Otherwise passengers will have to walk a couple of kilometers from the highway to the beach unless a taxi happens to be hanging around.

The Santa Clara turnoff is about seven kilo-meters east of the depressed town of Río Hato. Next to that town is a huge old airstrip built by the United States military and the growing beach resort of Farallón. The closest large town is Penonomé, 36 kilometers west.

Those who want to do a bit of exploring under their own steam can rent bikes at XS Memories.

FARALLÓN

The Farallón (far-ah-YONE) area, which starts about three kilometers west of the Santa Clara turnoff, didn't get much attention until the Colombian-owned Decameron hotel chain built a mammoth resort there in late 2000.

Before then, Farallón was just a quiet fishing village with a pretty beach that attracted some weekenders. Next door is a large airstrip built years ago by the U.S. military, since this is one of the driest places in Panama. In the 1980s it was the site of a Panamanian military base that housed some of Noriega's elite troops. U.S. forces wiped out the base during the 1989 "Just Cause" invasion.

Now, suddenly, it's the hot beach destination. The Decameron refers to this area as Playa Blanca, the name of one stretch of beach here, but most everyone in Panama still thinks of the area simply as Farallón. The Spanish Barceló chain opened its own resort down the beach in 2003, and new condominium buildings are sprouting up as far as the eye can see. The days of Farallón and the other sleepy beach villages around here seem numbered.

As with its neighbor, Santa Clara, the beach is lovely and it's a wonder it was neglected so long. There are a few other simpler and cheaper places to stay and eat in the village of Farallón and around the town of Río Hato, back on the Interamericana, a few kilometers farther west. Río Hato is the nearest semiurban center, but it's down at the heels and has little to offer other than a few services. The presence of the new resorts hasn't helped it much, a fact the townspeople still grumble about.

Accommodations and Food

The **Royal Decameron Beach Resort and Casino** (tel. 214-3535 Panama City reservations, tel. 993-2255 at the resort, reservas.pa@decam eron.com, www.dccameron.com, all-inclusive packages for $119/$198 s/d, half off for kids 11 and younger in double rooms) is by far the biggest beach resort in Panama. Its name keeps mutating, but most know it simply as "the Decameron." It's enormous—600 rooms set in three-story units above a large, gorgeous stretch of beach. All rooms have the same layout and feature either two full beds or a king-sized bed. The rooms are medium-sized, cheerful, and modern, if fairly nondescript, and the beds are comfortable. The resort features eight restaurants and cafes, eight bars, nine pools, a duty-free shop, and so on.

The Decameron is an all-inclusive place that features "unlimited consumption" of food and booze, including taxes and tips. Also included are daily activities, performances, and use of non-motorized water-sports equipment such as ocean kayaks and snorkeling gear. Other goodies include a free scuba-diving minicourse and aerobics and dance classes. Tours, fishing trips, and other activities are available for an extra charge. One unusual tour takes visitors to one of Manuel Noriega's old beach houses, right next door.

Transportation to and from Panama City is sometimes included in package deals arranged through travel agents. The resort caters mainly to large Canadian, European, and South American groups that are shipped over on charter flights, get a sunburn, and are shipped out a few days later. The resort sometimes offers special packages aimed at the local market, and rates can be lower during the week and off-season. Call the hotel or check for ads in Panama City newspapers.

The Decameron got some competition with the opening in October 2003 of the **Barceló Playa Blanca** (tel. 264-6444, fax 264-3972 Panama City reservations, tel. 993-2910 or 993-2911 at the hotel, reservaciones@playablancaresort.com, www.barceloplayablanca.com, $120/$160 s/d), two kilometers farther west down the beach. This all-inclusive features 219 rooms in seven three- and four-story buildings set around an attractive swimming pool.

The decor is kind of faux-Mediterranean, with the buildings done up in white with blue trim. Facilities include two main restaurants (one

seafood, one buffet) plus a sailboat-shaped outdoor restaurant on the beach that's open on the weekends, a spa/beauty parlor, an Internet café, a small open-air theater, gift shops, a nine-hole putting course for golfers, a late-night disco, and so on. There's an activities center that offers personal watercraft, ATV vehicles, kayaks, mountain bikes, sailboarding gear, surfing lessons, fishing trips, sailboats, and tours of El Valle, Panama City, and other sights.

Rates include all meals, domestic liquor, use of nonmotorized aquatic gear (kayaks, pedal boats), and daily activities. The simple but pleasant rooms have one queen-sized or two double beds, safes, cable TV, and balconies. Try to get a room in buildings 600 or 700, which are right on the edge of the beach; the others are set around the swimming pools. Day passes, weekday discounts, and other special offers are sometimes available. Service so far is cordial and friendly. The turnoff to the hotel is just before the town of Río Hato. The hotel is three kilometers from the highway, surrounded by new condo developments.

Club Casa Blanca, between Hospedaje Farallón and the Decameron, is a walled-in compound that's a combination restaurant, disco, and sports bars. It's a rowdy locals hangout that features ear-melting music and a lot of macho attitude. Just down from it is **Sapo Rojo Club,** a more mellow open-air bar with a great view of the ocean and island.

A little closer to the Decameron is **Restaurante La Fogata** (no phone, noon–10 P.M. Thurs.–Tues., closed Wed.), a simple but cute place with a thatched roof and bright and cheerful decor. It serves meat and seafood dishes for a top price of $4.50.

Restaurante Bar Rancho Río (tel. 932-2740, 9 A.M.–10 P.M. daily) is a large, thatched-roof *rancho* set back from the beach. To get there, make a right 0.5 kilometer past the Decameron. It's the "fanciest" of the eateries around the beach, but it's still pretty simple. Dishes are $5–10 and consist mainly of seafood.

My favorite place to hang out in this area is **Pipa's Beach Bar** (no phone) two kilometers past the Decameron. It's a relaxed, friendly place that's open from about 11:30 A.M. daily until the last person passes out. Pipa's serves seafood ($5–20). There's also a volleyball net on the beach. To get there, turn right at the Decameron and stay straight. After two kilometers the road turns to sand. Keep going. The bar will be up ahead on the left, right on the beach. Party down.

If staying on the beach isn't important to you but saving money is, consider **Hospedaje Las Delicias** (tel. 993-3718, starting at $12 s/d with fan, $20 s/d with air-conditioning) just off the north side of the Interamericana on the eastern outskirts of Río Hato. It's set in a yard with flowering trees and has a bright and cheerful facade. Rooms are simple but okay with firm beds. Seven rooms have air-conditioning; five have fans. Note that this place is about 7–8 kilometers from the beach at Farallón.

Information and Services

There's an IPAT office (tel. 993-3241, fax 993-3200, 8:30 A.M.–4:30 P.M. Mon.–Fri.) on the road that runs past the west side of the airstrip leading from the Interamericana to the Decameron.

Just about anything guests at the Decameron or Barceló could want is provided at the resorts. A couple of the services at the Decameron are also available to nonguests. These include CB Tours (tel. 993-2255, ext. 3067, or tel. 688-8445, 8 A.M.–6 P.M. daily), in the parking lot of the Decameron. It rents mountain bikes with helmets for $5 for 1.5 hours or $20 for a two-hour bike tour. Visitors can also rent ATVs for $25 for a half hour, $35 for an hour, $50 for

two hours, and $70 for three hours. Guided tours by ATV are also available. Near the entrance to the Decameron parking lot is a Banco Nacional de Panamá ATM.

There are also a few services in the town of Río Hato, which is divided by the Interamericana four kilometers west of the Decameron turnoff. Plaza Río Hato, in the center of town on the south side of the Interamericana, is a minimall with a grocery store, bakery, and Río Cyber Café (10 A.M.–9 P.M. daily), an Internet café with (at the time of writing) very slow computers. It charges $1.25 an hour for Internet access. This is a real Internet café, if you count burgers, hotdogs, and other cheap fast food as café fare. There are a couple of other grim-looking places to eat in town.

Getting There and Around

To get to this area from the direction of Panama City, continue west past the Santa Clara turnoff for three kilometers. On the far (west) side of the airstrip, turn left. The road runs past an IPAT office, then to the Decameron resort on the beach two kilometers from the highway. A right turn at the resort leads to the fishing village of Farallón.

Buses to Farallón from Panama City, about 110 kilometers to the east, cost $4 and leave every 20 minutes or so 5:30 A.M.–8 P.M. The trip takes around two hours. Buses should drop passengers off at the Decameron or Barceló by request.

A National Car Rental (tel. 265-2222, 8 A.M.–1 P.M. and 2–5 P.M. Mon.–Sat., 8 A.M.–4 P.M. Sun.) is in the parking lot of the Decameron.

El Valle de Antón

When the steamy heat of Panama City is too much even for locals, they head to the hills of El Valle de Antón, which everyone simply calls El Valle. It's a pleasant little town nestled in the valley of a huge extinct volcano. The valley floor is about 600 meters above sea level, high enough to make this area significantly cooler and fresher than the lowlands. This is one of the few places in Panama where you'll find houses with fireplaces.

El Valle proper lies along the wide, flat valley floor, and most of the sights are within town or

on gentle slopes not far away. That makes it easy to get almost anywhere on foot or by bicycle, a pleasant way to get around given the mild climate and the flower-lined streets. Watch out for monster potholes.

The first thing one sees upon entering El Valle is a *supermercado* (supermarket) with a gas station, to the right. This and the **public market** in the center of town are common landmarks, and most of the directions in this section will use them as starting points. A single main road, sometimes

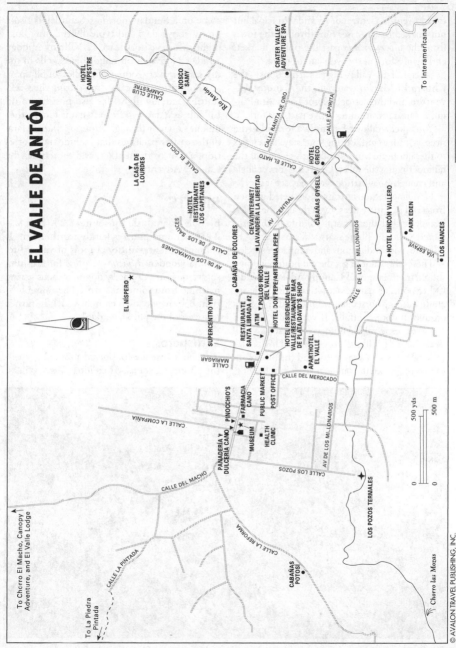

EL VALLE DE ANTÓN

HOTEL CAMPESTRE

KIOSCO SAMY

CALLE CLUB CAMPESTRE

Río Antón

CRATER VALLEY ADVENTURE SPA

CALLE RANITA DE ORO

CALLE CAPIRITA

To Interamericana

LA CASA DE LOURDES

CALLE EL CICLO

HOTEL Y RESTAURANTE LOS CAPITANES

CALLE EL HATO

HOTEL GRECO

CIEVA/INTERNET/ LAVANDERÍA LA LIBERTAD

CABAÑAS GYSELL

AV. CENTRAL

CALLE DE LOS SAUCES

AV. DE LOS GUAYACANES

CABAÑAS DE COLORES

CALLE DE LOS MILLONARIOS

HOTEL RINCÓN VALLERO

PARK EDEN

VÍA ESPAYÉ

LOS NANCES

EL NÍSPERO

POLLOS RICOS DEL VALLE

HOTEL DON PEPE/ARTESANÍA PEPE

SUPERCENTRO YIN

RESTAURANTE SANTA LIBRADA #2

ATM

HOTEL RESIDENCIAL EL VALLE/RESTAURANTE MAR DE PLATA/DAVID'S SHOP

CALLE MARIAGAR

APARTHOTEL EL VALLE

CALLE DEL MERCDADO

PUBLIC MARKET

POST OFFICE

FARMACIA CANO

PINOCCHIO'S

CALLE LA COMPAÑÍA

CALLE DEL MACHO

PANADERÍA Y DULCERÍA CANO

MUSEUM

HEALTH CLINIC

CALLE LOS POZOS

AV. DE LOS MILLONARIOS

LOS POZOS TERMALES

To Chorro El Macho, Canopy Adventure, and El Valle Lodge

To La Piedra Pintada

CALLE LA PINTADA

CALLE LA REFORMA

CABAÑAS POTOSÍ

Chorro las Mozas

500 yds
500 m
0
0

© AVALON TRAVEL PUBLISHING, INC.

called **Avenida Central** or Avenida Principal but not marked in any case, runs through the town from the *supermercado* past the public market, ending in a fork at the west end of town.

Several of El Valle's biggest attractions—the **Chorro El Macho** waterfall, the **Canopy Adventure,** and the petroglyphs of **La Piedra Pintada**—are a few minutes' drive past this fork.

You'll hear talk of **La India Dormida** (the sleeping Indian girl) during your stay. This refers to the silhouette some see along a section of the hilltops ringing the valley. Given the correct angle and enough imagination, you may see it too.

El Valle is famous for its endangered **golden frogs** and its square trees. Even though the area is heavily settled there is still wildlife in the protected forests. There's also a small zoo, **El Níspero,** with indigenous and nonnative species.

Those who want to get the old heart pounding should try the unusual **Canopy Adventure** ride. Other popular nature activities in El Valle include hiking, horseback riding, and splashing around under waterfalls. If you come early in the week, especially Monday or Tuesday, you'll likely have El Valle all to yourself. This is nice in some ways, but some may find the place a bit too sleepy. To see the public market in full swing,

come on a Sunday morning. Saturday is also a pretty active day, and typically the only busy night. Most visitors leave El Valle by midday Sunday. Note that on holiday weekends in the dry season, every room in El Valle can fill up.

Room prices typically drop during the week, starting Sunday night. It's also possible to do El Valle as a day trip from Panama City, either on one's own or through a tour operator. Many of these offer packages that include transportation, a visit to the market, and sometimes the Canopy Adventure.

SIGHTS

El Valle's bare little **museum** ($.25, 10 A.M.– 2 P.M. Sat. and Sun.) is hardly worth a visit. It contains a few traditional tools of valley life, from a wooden *trapiche*—a press for crushing sugarcane—to a decidedly nonindigenous sewing machine from someone's attic. The museum is right behind the town church, which in turn is just west of the public market.

El Níspero

Though it's usually considered a zoo, El Níspero (no phone, $2 adults, $1 children, 7 A.M.–5 P.M.

© WILLIAM FRIAR

The Canopy Adventure is a quick, high-adrenaline ride across an El Valle waterfall.

El Valle's little zoo, El Níspero, has some striking native species.

daily) is really more of a plant nursery with caged creatures. Even if you have qualms about animals confined in small places—and some of the cages here are painfully small—consider visiting this one. For one thing, it's a good place to see Panama's endangered **golden frogs** *(Atelopus zeteki)*. There are dozens of the little guys here. It's hard to believe something this color can exist in nature.

Other indigenous creatures here include the capybara, the world's largest rodent—it can grow up to a meter long and weigh up to 45 kilograms; several species of primates, including Geoffroy's tamarin and the white-faced capuchin; sleepy-looking sloths; a tapir; and two species of felines, the margay and ocelot. Among the decidedly nonindigenous critters here are some emus, of all things.

The zoo also has a greenhouse stuffed with orchids, extensive gardens, and a fish-filled wishing well.

Heading into El Valle, continue west along Avenida Central 1.4 kilometers past the *supermercado* at the entrance to town. Take a right turn at the sign that says El Níspero. Follow the winding road 1.1 kilometers. The road is rough

but doesn't require a four-wheel drive. El Níspero is on the left.

There's no guide, but Wednesday through Sunday you can try imposing on one of the caretakers. A small tip would probably be appreciated but is not necessary. The caretakers speak only Spanish.

La Piedra Pintada

El Valle has an impressively large boulder covered with hieroglyphics that is locally known as La Piedra Pintada ("the painted rock"). No one is sure what all the squiggly designs carved (not painted) into the face of this boulder mean, or even who made them, though everyone has a theory. Maybe it's just the doodling of the gods. The boulder is easy to get to and thus worth a visit. It's just a five-minute walk up a trail that follows a pretty little stream.

Drive west on the main road, Avenida Central, past the public market and out of town. Take a left after the bridge. Make the first real right, then follow the road until it ends at a cul-de-sac at a small church. (The whole way is well marked.) Small boys will mysteriously appear, eager to show you the rock—for a fee, of course. Being surrounded by a swarm of tykes can be intimidating, but you shouldn't have a problem. As soon as you choose one the others will back off. He'll probably be pleased with a quarter. By the way, they're not leading you astray if they steer you left rather than straight up, as the misleading sign would have you go.

Golden Frogs and Square Trees

The **Hotel Campestre** has a path with a golden-frog enclosure at the beginning and a few square trees at the end. Facing the hotel in the middle of its spacious grounds, you'll see a large glass display case to the right. There are golden frogs in there, but they're so tiny and the case is so huge they're hard to spot. Look carefully. A "trail" has been built behind it that leads to the square trees, but the first part of it is really just a path through scrub. Instead of fooling with this, just walk toward the hotel and head over to the right, by the pool. The real trail, which is often muddy, starts on the right side of the white cinderblock building behind the pool. This runs by a brook and a bit of secondary-growth forest. The trail isn't well marked and has forks, but if you follow your intuition about the "main" trail, you should be okay. After 5–10 minutes, you should see a collapsing bamboo fence on the right. Walk over it into the little clearing. The most convincing specimens are more trapezoidal than square, but at least you can say you've seen El Valle's famous square trees.

Hotel y Restaurante Los Capitanes now has what I've been told is the best display of golden frogs in the area, but I haven't been back to the hotel since the terrarium was built. The hotel is more centrally located than either the Campestre or the Níspero, so golden-frog hunters should begin their quest here.

SHOPPING

 Sunday Market

Some visitors come to El Valle just for the public market. Here you'll find crafts from many parts of Panama, in addition to fresh fruit, vegetables, and plants. While the kind and quality of crafts vary week to week, this is usually a good place to buy Panama hats. Note that these are not the el-

El Valle's public market is popular on Sundays.

© WILLIAM FRIAR

egant, tightly woven hats that most people think of—those "Panama hats" are actually Ecuadorian, as has been mentioned elsewhere. The ones here aren't usually even the more finely woven ones made in some parts of the Azuero Peninsula. These are more coarsely woven, usually of white and black fibers, and are the most common kind worn in Panama. Prices range $8–25. You should expect to pay about $20 for a decent one. Other items to consider include carved soapstone figures, which range in price $2–15. The limiting factor isn't the price but the weight you have to lug around. Note that the market is quaint and lively but is not big. While a popular weekend destination for lots of Panama City residents and the old Canal Zone crowd, and much-trumpeted by tour outfits, it's unlikely to blow your socks off.

The public market is 1.7 kilometers down the main road as you enter El Valle. You can't miss it—it's smack in the center of town. The market operates on a limited scale during the week, but it's in full swing on Saturdays and especially Sundays. There are also a few souvenir kiosks directly across the street. If you're not in town on Sunday, there are some newer souvenir shops to the east of the market.

Other Craft Shops

David's Shop (tel. 983-6536, 7 A.M.–7 P.M. Sun.–Thurs., 7 A.M.–10 P.M. Fri. and Sat.) has a better selection of crafts than the market itself. There's a little workshop at the back where you can peek in at artisans at work. The shop can also dispense tourist information, arrange horse rentals and trips to the Canopy Adventure, and rent bikes ($2 an hour or $10 for the day). It's affiliated with Hotel Residencial El Valle upstairs.

Artesanias Pepe (tel. 983-6425, 7 A.M.–7 P.M. daily) next door, below Hotel Don Pepe, is a similar place, though the quality and selection is better at David's Shop.

SPORTS AND RECREATION

El Valle is popular with middle-class and wealthy Panamanians as a weekend getaway. As such, most entertainment takes place inside people's weekend homes. There is almost nothing in the way of nightlife in El Valle. Hiking, horseback riding, and bird-watching are the main things to do around here. It's possible to take hikes and horseback trips up into the mountain, but these tend to be on old forest paths used for years as commute routes rather than on developed trails and shouldn't be attempted without a knowledgeable guide. Be sure to bring rain gear, warm clothing, and long-sleeved shirts (to avoid getting cut up by the brush).

Canopy Adventure

The outdoor activity that's gotten the most attention in recent years is the Canopy Adventure (tel. 983-6547 in El Valle, tel. 264-5720, 612-9176, or 264-8951 in Panama City, tel./fax 263-2784, stay@canopytower.com, www.canopytower.com/adventure, open approximately 6 A.M.–5 P.M. daily). It's a lot of fun, as long as you're not too uncomfortable with heights.

The Canopy Adventure is sort of a cross between a nature hike and a zip-line thrill ride. The hike part comes at the beginning, when you head uphill through steamy forest on a trail that's steep and slick at times. The hike takes about an hour. You're hiking through protected private land that borders a private forest reserve, so there's a good chance of seeing some wildlife.

Now for the really fun part, the zip-line ride. Up ahead you'll see a steel cable attached to a series of enormous trees in the middle of the forest. It's attached toward the top of the trees, to be specific. You, in turn, will be attached to the cable by harness and pulley. The cable is strung at a gentle downward angle, so you go flying back down to the trailhead in five stages. Even better, you cross over the lovely Chorro El Macho waterfall on the way down. You're about 30 meters above the base of the falls at the beginning of the ride.

Riders zip through the trees under their own power. Brake by grabbing firmly—but not too firmly—to the cable (the guides give you a heavy-duty glove for the purpose). The first run is the most dramatic, when you're also the most nervous about slamming into a tree.

The ride on all five platforms costs $40. Those who don't care for heights can opt instead for a three-hour guided walked ($15), a swim in the pool below the waterfall ($2), or just walk the little trail along the base of the waterfall ($2). For $95 the Canopy Adventure provides transportation to and from Panama City, lunch, and a tour of El Valle in addition to the ride. Part of the proceeds go to maintaining the nature preserve. You will get muddy, but wear long pants to protect your legs. Also, wear sturdy, closed shoes with decent traction. The guides offer water and insect repellent during the hike. Sunday is the busiest day, so show up before 10 A.M. to avoid long lines. Allow two hours for the whole thing.

The Canopy Adventure is three kilometers past the public market (heading west) on the main road. Follow the blue signs reading "El Macho." At the west end of town, the road forks after a bridge. Take the right fork, which is Calle El Macho. The ride's office, a thatched-roof hut, will be on the left.

Other Recreation

El Valle's other main waterfall, **Chorro Las Mozas,** is mainly a place for locals to wash their clothes and splash around a bit. It attracts trash and there's a strong smell of horse manure at the main waterhole. If you follow the river to the right, the view gets prettier and you'll come to a couple of waterfalls. However, the water looks none too clean. Note also there have been reports of robberies around here. If you're still tempted, it's one kilometer past Cabañas Potosí, the last third of which is down a deeply rutted road that requires a high-clearance four-wheel drive.

You can rent horses at **Kiosco Samy** (tel. 983-6628 or 646-5813, 8 A.M.–6 P.M. daily) at the fork in the road one kilometer up Calle El Hato, the road leading to Hotel Campestre. It's hard to miss—there's a colorful mural of a horse on the side of the kiosk and a big sign that says "Horseback Riding." The price is $3.50 an hour, which includes a Spanish-speaking guide. You can request a destination or just take the staff's advice; many trails lead up through the wooded hills.

A group of supposed thermal pools, **Los Pozos Termales** (8 A.M.–noon and 1–5 P.M. daily, $.50 for adults, $.25 for kids) is really not worth a visit. We're talking three small pools with cloudy, greenish water. The temperature is supposedly 36°C (97°F), which you'll note is below body temperature. There's an unappealing picnic site on the grounds. It's for the thermal pool–obsessed only. From the public market, head west on the main road for .6 kilometer. Take a left and head straight down for another kilometer. The only pool you might dare stick your feet in costs another $1 for adults, $.50 for children.

Adventure Tours

Nature tours can often be arranged through your hotel. **Hotel y Restaurante Los Capitanes,** (tel. 983-6080 or 687-8819, fax 983-6505, www.los-capitanes.com), for instance, offers a variety of hikes guided by local school kids for $2-3, including a two-hour hike to the top of La India Dormida, stopping at three waterfalls along the way.

The **Panama Explorer Club (PEX)** (tel. 983-6939, fax 983-6243 in El Valle, tel. 215-2330, fax 215-2331 in Panama City, info@pexclub.com, www.pexclub.com) offers a range of tours of El Valle and the surrounding area. These include hikes, rock climbing and rappelling, and mountain biking. Except for mountain biking ($10), all these tours cost $20 per person, or $45 if you need transportation to and from Panama City. It also offers rafting and river kayaking trips to more distant spots.

The **Centro de Investigación Ecológicas de El Valle de Antón (CIEVA)** is a loose-knit tour guide outfit (tel. 629-3722, 8 A.M.–5 P.M. daily) that started up just two weeks before my last visit. At that time, it drew upon a couple dozen local residents, about half of whom spoke some English and three of whom had biology training, to lead tours of the area. Among their more ambitious tours are a 4.5-hour moderate hike up Cerro Gaital and a 3.5-hour hike up La India Dormida. They also offer tamer tours of the surrounding attractions. Tours cost $5 an hour for up to five people. The place is on the north side of Avenida Central, one block past Calle El Ciclo, the street that leads up to Hotel Los Capitanes.

ACCOMMODATIONS

Hotel options used to be quite limited in El Valle, as much of the potential clientele own vacation homes here. But now, in addition to the old stalwarts, visitors can choose among simple but pleasant budget accommodations, a quaint bed-and-breakfast, a couple of relatively upscale hotels, and even a resort spa. Rates at some places go down after the high season, which runs approximately from November to March.

In addition to the places described below, the owner of the Canopy Adventure was planning to open a 10-room ecolodge modeled after his highly regarded Canopy Tower in Gamboa. **El Valle Lodge** will be in the middle of the private forest reserve that's home to the Canopy Adventure. It's being built 300 meters below Chorro El Macho and should be open by the time you read this and will likely be one of the best lodging options in the area, as well as one of the priciest. Contact the Canopy Tower for information. Another new addition, scheduled to open sometime in 2005, is the **Lion House at El Valle,** a sister to the Lion House hostel in Panama City. It will be on Calle de los Millonarios.

$10–25

The centrally located **Hotel Residencial El Valle** (Avenida Central, tel. 983-6536, residencialelvalle@hotmail.com, www.hotelresidencialelvalle.com, rooms start at $20 s/d) is above David's Shop, a souvenir store near the market that's affiliated with the hotel. It offers 17 simple but fine rooms with new beds, hardwood floors, local TV, and hot-water bathroom. The rooms have fans and are cheerful, clean, and quite nice. The friendly general manager, Luis Enrique Tiban, worked on the U.S. military bases for 10 years and speaks some English. He can help arrange guides and has a map for guests. (See *Shopping* for more information.) His talented family constructed the building, the beds, even the room mirrors with butterflies and birds painted around their borders. The place has a spacious terrace with a view of the mountains, including Cerro Gaital and Cerro Cara Iguana and a good profile of La India Dormida. Laundry service here is $1 to wash and $1 to dry. Small rooms are $20 s/d. Larger ones are $45 s/d on the weekend, $35 s/d during the week. Use of the kitchen is included with your stay. This place is a good value.

Hotel Don Pepe (Avenida Central, tel. 983-6425, tel./fax 983-6835, hoteldonpepe@hotmail.com, www.pmaol.com/hotelpep.thm, $15/25 s/d) offers 11 clean rooms with local TV, fans, hot-water bathrooms, and new beds. There's a terrace with a good view of the mountains. If all this sounds a bit like Hotel Residencial El Valle, right next door, the similarities don't end there—both are also above a handicrafts shop and a simple restaurant that serves Panamanian and Peruvian food. This one is run by Pepe Galarza, who gives the impression of being a bit of a wheeler-dealer and may be flexible on prices. The Hotel Residencial El Valle has a warmer and more laid-back atmosphere, but it may be worth shuttling between the two places to see which has more appealing rooms and prices available. Internet access is available for $1.50 an hour, bike rentals for $2 an hour, and laundry service for $1.50 to wash and $1.50 to dry.

$25–50

Cabañas Gysell (Calle El Hato near Avenida Central, tel. 983-6507, $20–25 s, $30–35 d) is a cute little place run by friendly folks who've decorated it with lots of love—something that's always a treat to find in Panama, where so many budget accommodations are functional at best. Rooms are painted blue and white and are decorated with nice touches, such as hand-painted murals on the walls. Its eight rooms are set in a garden with an outdoor kitchen, hammocks, and rocks scattered about with words of wisdom inscribed on them. The rooms are simple but clean and perfectly okay, with good beds and hot-water bathrooms. Some rooms are more attractive than others, so ask to see a few. For couples who don't mind quirky accommodations, there's also an old camper sans wheels on the property that goes for $20 a night.

Cabañas Potosí (Calle La Reforma, tel. 983-6181 in El Valle, tel. 226-3914 in Panama City, $40 s/d) is run by a friendly *doña* named Patria Greco. The place offers four cabañas and one room in the family house, all set on two well-tended hectares just west of town. The rooms, all of which have a double and a single bed, are plain and very simple, but they have high ceilings and porches with a good view of the hills. Try the mattresses before agreeing on a room. Be warned you'll be sharing the grounds with some roosters. It's about one kilometer west of town on the main road. At the end of town, take the first two lefts you come to. The cabañas will be on your right. Doña Greco can arrange meals for an extra charge. (Camping is also possible; see *Camping* in this section.)

Cabañas de Colores (Avenida de los Guayacanes, tel. 983-6613, $40 s/d) consists of three cabins set in the front yard of a private home, which can itself be rented by the night. It's north of but not far from the market. The whole place is decorated in a sort of unintentionally kitschy bucolic style, as though everything was ordered from a country-cottage collection in a '70s Sears catalog. The cabins have hot water. Some beds are passable, but others are beyond saggy. The house has a kitchen.

Ⓜ Hotel y Restaurante Los Capitanes (Calle El Ciclo, tel. 983-6080 or 687-8819, fax 983-6505, capitanes@cwp.net.pa, www.loscapitanes.com, www.panamainfo.com/loscapitanes.com, rooms start at $27.50 s, $44 d including continental breakfast) is an inviting place set on lovingly tended grounds in the heart of the valley. There's not much else around it, so you get sweeping views of the mountains ringing the valley. It's a spotless, peaceful place that gives you room to breathe. It's run by a retired German sea captain (hence the name of the place) named Manfred Koch. Be sure to chat with him—he has lots of interesting tales. The cheapest rooms are in a long, one-story building next to the main hotel. They're pretty simple and a bit dark, but they're wheelchair-accessible, which is almost unheard of anywhere in Panama. Larger rooms with queen-sized beds go for $55–71.50. The best rooms are the family suites upstairs in the tower ($93.50 for up to four adults). They have lofts and balconies and are a good deal for what you get. All rooms have TVs, fridges, and hot water. There's a common lounge area equipped with cable TV.

Note: If you're in Panama around Oktoberfest, check to see if there's a big celebration here; there has been in the past, and it's been the place to be. To get to Los Capitanes, head down the main road into town .8 kilometer past the *supermercado*. Turn right at the big anchor. (There should also be a sign.) You'll soon see the hotel on your left. The hotel can arrange pick-up and drop-off in Panama City. Prices can go down significantly during the week.

If you're looking for an unusual bed-and-breakfast experience, try **Los Nances** (Vía Espavé, tel. 983-6126, rates start at $50 s/d including breakfast). The place is owned by an older couple, the Nances, who offer 4–6 rooms (depends on demand) in their house in the hills above town. The husband is retired from the U.S. Air Force; the wife came to Panama in 1930 (she calls herself "an old Vallero"—valley resident). Each of the four rooms normally rented out has a kitchenette with a refrigerator, stove, and TV. All have a soul-soothing view of the valley. The best room in the house is large, with a queen-sized sofa bed and a stunning view. Ask for "the room with a view." A couple of the rooms are on the dank side. As this is a residence, you have to call for directions. It's not far from the Rincón Vallero, on a rough

road that's just barely navigable without a four-wheel drive.

The grand old lady of El Valle is **Hotel Campestre** (end of Calle El Hato, tel. 983-6146, fax 983-6460, $27.50 s, $55 d), and like most such places in Panama she's not aging gracefully. I don't recommend staying here, but since many tour operators still do you should know what awaits you. The hotel, which has 40 rooms, looks rather grand from a distance, like a wooden hunting lodge with extensive grounds. It's on a hill at the end of Calle El Hato, a right turn off the main road shortly after you enter town. The best thing about it is an enormous fireplace in the lobby.

Close up, however, it's dingy and tired. The rooms are drab, overpriced, and in desperate need of new mattresses. A recent "renovation" consisted of some cosmetic changes that left the rooms bare and the mattresses as worn out as ever. The swimming pool is fed by a stream and artificial waterfall that gushes forth water so opaque you'll enter at your own risk. For many years the place was well-known for its golden-frog pond, but in recent years it has had trouble keeping them alive. They are now (cross your fingers) in a large glass enclosure on the grounds, to the right as one faces the hotel. (See *Sports and Recreation* for information on the golden frogs, square trees, and a short trail on the grounds.)

The **Hotel Rincón Vallero,** (off Calle Los Millonarios, tel. 983-6175, fax 983-6968 in El Valle or tel. 264-9119, fax 269-0944 in Panama City, rooms start at $82.50 s/d including continental breakfast) is a hotel of fairly recent vintage surrounded by flowering trees. A human-made waterfall and fish-filled stream runs through an enclosed patio, which contains the dining room and lobby. All rooms have color TVs, air-conditioning, and hot water. Most of the rooms are in cabins set around a garden with an artificial duck and fish pond. There are 14 rooms. The standard rooms ($82.50) are on the small side and rather dark. For another $22 or so you can get a "junior suite," which is really just a largish room. Full suites are $137.50. All these prices are for double occupancy. A third person in any of the rooms costs $11 more. The hotel is too close to the hills to offer a view. Directions to the hotel are well-marked. As you enter El Valle, make a left turn off the main road 0.2 kilometer past the *supermercado*. Follow the road 0.6 kilometer, then make a left. Follow that road another 0.2 kilometer. The hotel is on the left.

$100–150

Crater Valley Adventure Spa (Calle Capirita at the corner of Calle Ranita de Oro, tel. 215-2328, fax 215-2329 in Panama City, info@crater-valley.com, www.crater-valley.com, rates start at $103 per person, including continental breakfast) is a new spa resort built into an elegant old Spanish-style villa that belonged to a grandmother of one of the current owners. To get there, upon entering El Valle make the first right past the *supermercado* and follow the signs. Pass the two asphalt roads on the right. The spa will be on the left.

Amenities include an attractive swimming pool with tanning deck, a sauna, a large and amazingly turbulent hot tub, spa services, yoga classes, small library, and a souvenir shop. Its large, attractive grounds have a view of Cerro Gaital and are filled with trees, flowering plants, and three fish ponds. A continental breakfast is included, and lunch ($6.50) and dinner ($7.50) are available for guests. There's also a bar.

The spa has eight modern rooms with good beds, hot-water bathrooms, and cable TV. Each of the rooms is completely different. Some are surprisingly plain though still fine, and others are large and tastefully appointed. Prices range $103–130 on weekends and holidays. Rates drop an average of $10 Monday–Thursday. My main complaint about this place is that, oddly for a health spa, just about every room I checked out smelled of cigarette smoke.

Crater Valley is affiliated with the Panama Explorer Club (PEX), which explains the climbing wall, campsite, and adventure tours offered. (See *Sports and Recreation* for information on these, and *Information and Services* for the spa services.)

M Park Eden (Vía Espavé, tel. 983-6167 in El Valle, cell 680-9400, tel./fax 226-8858 in Panama City, parkeden@cwpanama.net, www.parkeden.com, rooms range in price from $66 for a small room to $214.50 for an entire house, including breakfast and afternoon tea) is a charming bed-and-breakfast in a lovely garden setting. For 18 years it was the country home of Lionel Alemán Toledano and his wife Mónica, who turned it into a bed-and-breakfast in 2000. Both speak fluent English and Spanish. Staying with them is like visiting your favorite country aunt and uncle: They couldn't be more friendly and attentive.

There are six places to stay, all quite different. Breakfast and afternoon tea are served in a cozy glassed-in porch in the main house, where the couple lives. It has a view of the garden. La Vie en Rose ($93.50) is in the front of the main house and has a private terrace and a full and twin bed. As befits its name, it's rose-colored and frilly. La Casita ($104.50) is the designated honeymooner's room. The Linda Vista ($214.50) is a two-story house with two bedrooms upstairs and a downstairs living room and sunny kitchen. It features big windows that let in a lot of light, a sofa bed, outdoor fountain, and a large terrace with a barbecue grill. Guests usually book the entire house, but the individual bedrooms are also available by themselves. The first is the Nicole Room ($132), which has a vaulted ceiling, four-poster bed, and balcony. It connects with the Tiffany Room ($104.50), which has two twin beds and a balcony. They share a full bathroom with a skylight. There are lovely views of the garden and Cerro Gaital and other mountains from the upstairs rooms. Los Limoneros ($104.50) has a queen bed, sleeper couch, and small private terrace. Mi Cuartito is a room behind the house and has two bunk beds. It's quite small but has its own bathroom.

Most rooms have some combination of TV/VCR, coffeemaker, small fridge, microwave, etc. All are decorated with quaint and sometimes quirky knickknacks and homey touches.

Camping

A few of the hotels sometimes offer casual camping options. Campers can pitch a tent next to a river on land belonging to the owners of **Cabañas Potosí** (tel. 983-6181 in El Valle, tel. 226-3914 in Panama City). The site, which is undeveloped, is across the street from the cabañas. Theoretically this will cost a whopping $20, but if owner Patria Greco likes your looks you can probably haggle her down. Manfred Koch, the owner of **Hotel y Restaurante Los Capitanes,** (tel. 983-6080, capitanes@cwp.net.pa), had plans when I last visited to run camping trips up to a thatched-roof hut up in the hills. These would be by horseback, and Koch would provide the hammocks and barbecue. Contact him ahead of time to see if this is really happening. **Crater Valley Adventure Spa** (tel. 215-2328, fax 215-2329 in Panama City) has a basic area on its property that's generally used by Panama Explorer Club trips, but it doesn't hurt to ask if it can make room for you.

FOOD

El Valle still doesn't have many food options, but the choices are far better than they were just a few years ago. There's a decent option in just about every price range. There's now even a genuinely gourmet restaurant.

Restaurante Santa Librada #2 (Avenida Central, tel. 983-6376 or 645-5310, 7 A.M.–9 P.M. daily) is a favorite place for simple Panamanian fare at good prices. It's a popular locals hangout (Santa Librada #1, by the way, no longer exists). The decor is nothing fancy, but it's a pleasant open-air place. A full breakfast costs less than $3. Seafood and grilled meats top out at less than $8. The big bowl of *sancocho de gallina* (chicken stew, $2) has a nice flavor but is a little light on the chicken and veggies. The papaya *batido* (shake), however, is killer. The restaurant is on the right as you head into town, down Avenida Central about 1.5 kilometers from the first *supermercado.* The restaurant also rents out a few basic rooms.

Restaurante Mar de Plata (Avenida Central, tel. 641-9472, res_mardeplata@hotmail.com, 7 A.M.–7 P.M. Mon.–Thurs., 7 A.M.–late on Fri. and Sat.), beneath the Hotel Residencial El Valle and next to David's Shop, is a simple eatery that offers some Peruvian food, *comida criolla* (national dishes), seafood, and fruit juices and shakes. I haven't eaten there yet, but the chef told me she once worked in the Hotel El Panamá in Panama City. Most dishes are $3–7. There's a very similar

place with a similar menu next door, below Hotel Don Pepe. It's open 7 A.M.–10 P.M. daily.

Pinocchio's (Avenida Central, tel. 983-6975, noon–9 P.M. Mon.–Sat., noon–8 P.M. Sun.) serves quite tasty if somewhat greasy thin-crust pizzas. Individual pizzas cost $5–5.50 and are actually big enough to feed two reasonably hungry people. The English-speaking owner is friendly and takes a justifiable pride in his cooking. Other items on the menu include chicken, pork chops, burgers, tacos, shakes, and fruit juices.

Pollos Ricos del Valle (Avenida Central, no phone, 10 A.M.–7:30 P.M. daily) is a warehouse of a place that sells entire rotisserie chickens for $5, as well as burgers, hot dogs, and such. It's just east of the Melo store on Avenida Central.

Hotel y Restaurante Los Capitanes (Calle El Ciclo, tel. 983-6080) is a small, pleasant open-air octagonal restaurant separate from the hotel. The menu is limited and the fare hit or miss, but you'll find German cuisine here along with more typical Panamanian fare. The German owner prepares homemade sauerkraut. ("Even the Germans like it, and that is something.") It costs $10. Dishes range about $7–13.50. A full American breakfast costs $5. There's also a bar.

Stop by **Rincón Vallero** (off Calle Los Millonarios, tel. 983-6175, 7 A.M.–9 P.M. Mon.–Thurs., 7 A.M.–11 P.M. Fri.–Sun.) for a meal even if you're not staying there. It's very pleasant to eat on its enclosed patio, which has an artificial waterfall and a fish stream running through it. It's a cute place, and the decor is attractive. Fortunately, the food is good, too. You can make a meal just on the appetizers. Try the *plato típico,* which consists of favorite Panamanian finger food: *patacones, carimañolas, chorizos,* and *bollas*—all basically fried death, but tasty and worth experiencing at least once if you haven't been served the stuff a zillion times already. Also go for the fried ceviche, which is a rarity in Panama and quite delicious. Main dishes run the range of meat, chicken, fish, and seafood, for $7–12.50.

M La Casa de Lourdes (off Calle El Ciclo, tel. 983-6450 or cell 612-2028 in El Valle, tel. 269-6237 in Panama City, golosinas@cable onda.net, 6 or 7 P.M.–midnight Fri., noon–

midnight Sat., noon–4 P.M. Sun., some holiday hours) gives El Valle its first gourmet restaurant. It's the latest project of Lourdes Fábrega de Ward, the owner-chef of one of Panama City's favorite upscale restaurants, Golosinas. It literally is her "casa"—the upstairs is her weekend retreat, which is why it's open only on the weekends and some holidays.

Sadly, I've yet to eat there, since I last visited El Valle during the week. But I've eaten at Golosinas, which has delicious food, a pleasant atmosphere, and good service, and friends who are regulars at both places tell me that, if anything, La Casa de Lourdes now surpasses Golosinas, which would make it one of the finest restaurants in Panama. It's certainly elegant—it somewhat resembles a salmon-colored Italian villa, with a colonnade that leads to a terrace with a lovely pool. For those in the mood for a splurge, this is the place. La Casa de Lourdes sits by itself in a relatively undeveloped area north of the town center. Head north on Calle El Ciclo, pass Hotel y Restaurante Los Capitanes, and make a left at the next major intersection. Make another left and wind your way down to the restaurant. Note that last few hundred yards are on a gravel and dirt road that should be navigable in a regular car.

Panadería y Dulcería Cano (Avenida Central, no phone, 7:30 A.M.–8 P.M. daily, more or less) is a bakery and pastry shop across the street from the church.

INFORMATION AND SERVICES

There's an IPAT kiosk at the west end of the public market, though it quite likely won't be staffed. If it is, don't expect the staff to speak any English or have much information.

The tour-guide outfit Centro de Investigación Ecológicas de El Valle de Antón (tel. 629-3722, 8 A.M.–5 P.M. daily) offers free tourist information even for those who don't take its tours. It is on the north side of Avenida Central, one block past Calle El Ciclo, the street that leads up to Hotel y Resaurante Los Capitanes.

Farmacia Cano (tel. 983-6940) next to the museum has no fixed hours. If you need some-

thing and it's closed, just call the number. Someone should come by to open up and serve you.

There are no banks in El Valle, but there is now a Banco Nacional de Panamá ATM next to the Melo store on Avenida Central, kitty-corner from Hotel Don Pepe.

The post office (7 A.M.–5 P.M. Mon.–Fri., 8 A.M.–noon Sat.) is behind the public market, off Calle del Mercado.

Internet access (tel. 983-6688, 8 A.M.–noon and 1–5:30 P.M. Mon.–Sat., 9 A.M.–noon Sun.) is available in the same building as Centro de Investigación Ecológicas for $1.50 an hour. You can send overseas faxes here ($3.50 per page to the United States).

Also in the building is Lavanderia La Libertad (8 A.M.–4 P.M. daily) which charges $.50 to wash a load of laundry in cold water, $.80 to wash in hot water, and $.75 to dry.

Supercentro Yin (7 A.M.–7 P.M. daily) is a basic grocery store across the street from Hotel Residencial El Valle.

The **Crater Valley Adventure Spa** (see *Accommodations*) services include massages, facials, manicures/pedicures, shampoo treatments, and so on. The most expensive of these is a 55-minute massage for $50, given in pleasant surroundings: a thatched-roofed bamboo hut next to a fish pond. Yoga, meditation, and aerobics classes cost $5 or less. Use of the pool, hot tub, and a dressing room is about $6. A private sauna is $5 but requires an appointment. The spa is associated with the Panama Explorer Club (PEX).

GETTING THERE AND AROUND

El Valle is 120 kilometers from Panama City, a drive that takes a little under two hours. If you're driving, head west on the Interamerican Highway for 95 kilometers, which takes about an hour and a quarter. The turnoff to El Valle will be on the right. It's better marked than it used to be, but keep an eye open. If you're coming from Panama City and you see a sign for Gaucho's Steakhouse, you've just missed the turn. If you get to Playa Corona, you've gone even farther astray. Double back at the first turnoff.

Turn off the Interamericana and head north up

the winding two-lane road over the hills and into the valley. The road leads straight into El Valle, about 25 kilometers from the highway. It's a lovely drive, with a craggy ring of lush, forested hills before you and a good view of the Pacific behind. This road used to have more craters than the moon but is now in great shape, though it floods in heavy rains. Watch out for tire-eating roads in the town itself.

Buses to El Valle from Panama City leave every 35 minutes 7 A.M.–6:30 P.M. every day except Sunday, when they run 6:45 A.M.–9 P.M. The fare is $3.50.

Taxis are near the public market, or you can ask your hotel to track one down; $1–1.50 should get you just about anywhere in town, though you'll usually find it just as easy to walk around the central part of the town. A taxi tour of the area, including El Níspero, the Piedra Pintada, and the waterfalls should cost no more than $10 per person. Taxis charge $25 from downtown back to the Interamericana, which is an awful lot considering a bus ride costs $1.

Those leaving El Valle to go somewhere other than Panama City can just take a bus toward San Carlos, get off on the Interamericana, and catch a bus from there to most destinations that are near the Interamericana. Buses between San Carlos and El Valle run constantly during daylight hours. The fare is $1. The last bus down from El Valle leaves at 8 P.M.

Penonomé

There isn't actually that much to see in Penonomé (pop. 15,840), the capital of the province of Coclé, but it is one of Panama's quaintest towns. It has made way for modern industrial bustle without entirely giving up its quiet Spanish colonial charm, at least in the heart of town.

Penonomé is in the middle of wide expanses of flat, humid lowland, with the Interamericana curving north to meet it before dropping back down south on its way west. Visible off to the distant north are the tantalizingly lush highlands. Trinidad Spa and Lodge is in the highlands northeast of Penonomé. Access to Parque Nacional Omar Torrijos H. is farther west along the highway, as are the cultural sights of the central provinces. One interesting note about Penonomé is its longstanding appeal among immigrant merchants—including Turks, Chinese, and Arabs—who are so woven into the life of the town you probably won't even notice them.

Mercado de Artesanias Coclé (Interamericana, 9 A.M.–4 P.M. Mon.–Fri., closed Sat. and Sun.) is about a half kilometer east of the Hotel Dos Continentes. It's hard to miss since the building is in the shape of a Panama hat. It has a decent though hardly exceptional selection of Ngöbe-Buglé bags, assorted ceramics, and small souvenirs.

SIGHTS

In the evenings it's pleasant to wander around the town plaza, which sometimes attracts a surprisingly cool breeze and, more often, the neighborhood skater kids. The plaza has a gazebo and (miraculously) a few shade trees. It faces the **Catedral de Penonomé,** whose most distinctive features are its small, modern stained-glass windows, which look pretty when the sun is right. To the side is the **Casa de Gobierno,** the municipal government offices, which has some fine wrought-iron grillwork on the outside. This is all ringed by a few old, sloping red tile–roofed buildings, some of which feature bright green doors that somehow fit into the scene. There is also a small museum, **El Museo de Penonomé** (Calle San Antonio near Parque Ruben Dario Carles, tel. 997-8490, 9 A.M.–4 P.M. Mon.–Sat., 9 A.M.–noon Sun., $1, $.25 for kids) several blocks from the plaza in the direction of the Interamericana. It seems always to be closed when I visit.

That's about it for the historic charms of Penonomé, though, which can be exhausted in about an hour. Other than that, there are two main commercial drags: Avenida Juan Demóstenes Arosemena, which leads up to the Interamericana a kilometer or so away, and about three kilometers of the Interamericana itself that skirts the edge of town. The first is mainly a busy shopping street for cheap goods. The latter strip has the better hotels and restaurants, plus street vendors selling Panama hats. Those in the market should find a good selection outside the Restaurante Universal, which is near Hotel and Suites Guacamaya.

ACCOMMODATIONS

Pension Estrella Roja (Calle Damian Carles, no phone, $8/$10 s/d) offers ultrabasic rooms, some with fans, and shared bathrooms.

Residencial La Paisa (Avenida Juan Demóstenes Arosemena, tel. 997-9242, $7.70/$15.40 s/d) has seven rooms, each with two beds. The rooms are basic and small, the beds are spongy, and the bathrooms are cold water only. However, the place is centrally situated near the town plaza. It's set back from the street and a bit hard to spot.

Hotel Dos Continentes (Interamericana, tel. 997-9325, $22 s/d) right next to the Guacamaya, has been around 30 years and looks it. It offers 61 old, worn rooms with hard beds, air-conditioning, and cable TV. A few rooms have balconies overlooking the highway. It has a cafeteria.

Hotel y Suites Guacamaya (tel. 991-0117, fax 991-1010, $18.70/$22 s/d) on the Interamericana just east of the entrance to town, is a modern 40-room hotel built in 2001. Rooms are simple but pleasant and have air-conditioning and cable TV. It'd be a great deal if it weren't for the cheap beds, which sag so badly in the middle it's like sleeping in a soft ditch.

On the western outskirts of town is the modern **Hotel La Pradera** (Interamericana, tel. 991-0106, $26.40 s/d). Built in 2001, it has 30 clean rooms with air-conditioning, hot water, cable TV, and good beds. Half the rooms have one double bed, and the other half have two double beds. There's a restaurant and bar and a small pool set in a back yard. It's the best hotel in Penonomé.

FOOD

The restaurant at **Hotel y Suites Gucamaya** (Interamericana, tel. 991-0117, 6:30 A.M.–10 P.M.

daily) serves mainly Chinese food. Most items are in the $4–8 price range.

Panadería y Refresquería Romellini (Avenida Juan Demóstenes Arosemena, 7 A.M.–10 P.M. daily), just down from Hotel Dos Continentes on the way toward downtown Penonomé, offers sandwiches for $1.50 and delicious smells for free.

Parrillada El Gigante, (Interamericana, tel. 997-1864, 10 A.M.–9 P.M. daily), on the north side of the Interamericana just west of Hotel Dos Continentes, offers grilled meats, seafood, Middle Eastern food, pizzas, and sandwiches in a friendly atmosphere. Most of the grilled goodies are $6–8. This is what passes for an upscale restaurant in these parts, but the food isn't great. The signature dish, the Parrillada El Gigante, is a heap of five kinds of meat that could easily feed two ravenous carnivores, but the meat's tough and not that tasty. Judging by the falafel, the Middle Eastern food is also marginal.

There arc five outlets of the local **Gallo Pinto** chain (6 A.M.–9 P.M. Mon.–Sat., 6 A.M.–2 P.M. Sun.) in the area. Each serves basic *comida corriente* (fast food) in an equally basic atmosphere. Everything on the menu costs $2.25 or less. The ones likely to be most convenient are Gallo Pinto #1, on Calle Nicanor Rosas near the center of town, and Gallo Pinto #2, on Avenida Juan Demóstenes Arosemena near its intersection with the Interamericana.

Restaurante Las Tinajas (Interamericana, tel. 997-9606, 7 A.M.–10 P.M. daily) is a cafeteria with a quaint thatch-roofed dining area with traditional Panamanian designs on the walls. Most dishes are less than $2.

There's a **public market** between Calle Damian Carles and Avenida Juan Demóstenes Arosemena near the town plaza.

SERVICES

Super Farmacia Coclé (Avenida Juan Demóstenes Arosemena near its intersection with the Interamericana, tel. 997-9849, 8:30 A.M.–7:30 P.M. Mon.–Sat., 8:30 A.M.–12:30 P.M. Sun.) is a pharmacy just down from the Hotel Dos Continentes. There's a supermarket, Supercentro Coclé, next door.

A branch of the Banistmo bank (Avenida Juan Demóstenes Arosemena, 8 A.M.–3:30 P.M. Mon.–Fri., 9 A.M.–noon Sat.) is just a bit farther down on the way into town. Banco Nacional de Panamá (Avenida Juan Demóstenes Arosemena, 8 A.M.—3:30 P.M. Mon.–Fri., 9 A.M.–noon Sat.) is about halfway down the same road, where it forks near the Delta gas station. There's a Western Union outlet in a store called Casa Peter (Avenida Juan Demóstenes Arosemena, tel. 997-7117, 9 A.M.–5 P.M. Mon.–Sat., closed Sun.).

The post office (Calle Damian Carles, 7 A.M.–5:45 P.M. Mon.–Fri., 7 A.M.–4:45 P.M. Sat.) is about a block south of the town plaza.

The Hobby Chat Internet K'fe (tel. 9961-0637, 9 A.M.–10 P.M. daily) is an Internet place upstairs from the Delta gas station.

GETTING THERE AND AROUND

Penonomé is 143 kilometers west of Panama City, a drive that takes about two hours. Buses to Penonomé leave from Panama City every 20 minutes 4:55 A.M.–9:15 P.M. The one-way fare is $3.70.

Buses to other parts of Panama leave from different places in Penonomé depending on the destination.

Buses to Panama City leave from the large building with the "Terminal Deutrapep, S.A." sign emblazoned on the front. It's across the Interamericana from the Hotel Dos Continentes. They depart every 20 minutes 4 A.M.–7 P.M. Fare is $3.70.

Regional buses (e.g., to Santiago, Chitré, Las Tablas) stop at the Restaurante Universal, near Hotel y Suites Guacamaya on the Interamericana. Buses to David have to be flagged down at bus stops on the Interamericana.

Most of the more-or-less local area buses leave from a loosely defined terminal area near the public market between Calle Damian Carles and Avenida Juan Demóstenes Arosemena just south of the public market. Below are some of the routes most likely to be of interest:

Aguadulce: every 10 minutes, 6 A.M.–7 P.M., $2. The trip takes about 45 minutes.

El Copé: every 25 minutes, 4:45 A.M.–6 P.M., $1.50. The trip takes about an hour.

La Pintada: every 20 minutes, 6:20 A.M.–8 P.M., $.70. The trip takes 15 minutes.

Chiguirí Arriba: every 15 minutes, 6 A.M.–6:30 P.M., $1.50. The trip takes about an hour. Note that the last bus down on the return trip leaves at 1 P.M.

Around Penonomé

There are a couple of places worth noting around Penonomé. The little town of La Pintada, in the nearby foothills, has natural beauty and interesting human artifacts both ancient and modern. Trinidad Spa and Lodge is a comfortable mountain spa that's a good base for exploring the surrounding highlands, though it can be a bit tough to get to.

LA PINTADA

Because it's so close to Penonomé, those in the area should consider a half-day trip to La Pintada (pop. 3,700), in the foothills northwest of town. It's a pleasant, mellow town ringed by hills, including some big ones by Panamanian standards. The most storied of these is Cerro Orarí, a low,

jagged-toothed peak that has inspired Panamanian poets and musicians but would go unnoticed by those from a truly mountainous country.

It's a pleasant, quiet town with some nearby petroglyphs, a pretty little river, a cigar factory, and even a fledgling guide service. The hat makers in this district are famous for a variety of Panama hat called a *sombrero pintado* (painted hat), named for the rings of black fibers woven into it.

Popular festivities in La Pintada include the district's famous El Topón procession, a Christmas-day parade featuring effigies of Mary and the baby Jesus; Carnavalito, a mini-Carnaval celebration held the month before the actual Carnaval; and October 19, the anniversary of the town's founding.

Sights

The best way to see the sights is through the auspices of the **Asociación de Guías de Turismo La Pintada** (no phone, 8 A.M.–noon daily), which consists of about a half dozen young local guys who seem more interested in helping out their community than getting any kind of profitable business going. Tour possibilities include the petroglyphs, the cigar factory, and the hat-making communities around La Pintada. At the time of writing the group was still so new there were no set prices. Assuming this is still the case when you visit, $5 for a brief tour should do it. If this cooperative doesn't last, it should still be possible to hire someone in town to show you around for the same price or less.

To find them, look for the *información turistica, servicios de guía* sign on a house near the church, on the left side of the road as you enter town. If no one's there, head up to the little market in the center of town and ask the staff member there. It's in a house about halfway down and on the left side of the soccer field as one enters town.

That **artisans' market** (9 A.M.–4 P.M. Tues.–Sat., closed Mon.) has a decent selection of hats of different weaves made in the surrounding area. The best ones cost $90 and up. A pretty decent one can be had for around $25. A few pieces of pottery and some bric-a-brac are also on sale. There's a small **restaurant** attached that serves nothing that costs more than $1.75. It serves local food including *gallo pinto,* a kind of stew with rice, beans, and meat.

Even if you prefer to explore the area on your own, you'll need a guide at least to get to the **petroglyphs.** For one thing, they are on private property, the small cattle pasture of the Tuñon family, and you shouldn't just wander around without permission (the local guides have that permission). For another, it would be a friendly gesture to support this area's fledgling attempts to support itself through celebrating its attractions. Third, asking for the *piedras pintadas* may get you nowhere—many locals don't know where they are, even though they're less than three kilometers from the center of town.

Getting to the petroglyphs involves a short walk and a little scrambling over rocks. The closest petroglyphs are across a *quebrada* (brook) that only has water in the rainy season. They consist of a few dim figures of some kind of animals, though they're too abstract to identify. The second set are farther upstream. These are clearer, seemingly depicting two reptiles. The third set, a little farther up, are just a bunch of squiggles. The one next to it has a couple of figures. The most interesting thing about all of these is trying to guess what they might have once signified to the pre-Colombian indigenous people who carved them. Are they maps? Messages? Simple artistic expression? No one knows.

The **Río Coclé del Sur** is a pretty little river that runs by the edge of town. Locals claim it's clean, but bear in mind this is cattle country. It's hard to believe questionable things don't get washed into this river upstream. To get there, make a right turn past the church as you head into town and look for the *balneario* sign. The river will be on the right about 100 meters down. You can hire a little painted boat and captain to paddle you around for $.50 at Balneario J. Los Algarrobos, the river's popular little waterhole.

Those interested in seeing how Panamanian cigars get made can visit **Cigarros Joyas de Panamá** (tel. 692-2582, 634-4437), a small factory right before town on the way up from Penonomé. To get there, look for a sign on the outskirts of town. Make a hard left turn, which will double back onto a side road in the direction from which you just came. The cigar factory is a couple hundred meters down on the right.

Getting There

To get to La Pintada by car, take the road leading west from the plaza in downtown Penonomé and stay straight for 13 kilometers. The road ends at La Pintada. The road to the petroglyphs is two kilometers before town, on the left. But again, to find them you're best going with a guide.

Buses from Penonomé to La Pintada leave from near the town market every 20 minutes 6:20 A.M.–8 P.M. The fare is $.70, and the trip takes 15 minutes.

TRINIDAD SPA AND LODGE

Formerly known as La Posada del Cerro la Vieja (tel. 264-5379 in Panama City, tel. 983-8900 at the lodge, contacto@posadaecologica.com, www.posadaecologica.com, $40/$50 s/d), this place is a pleasant surprise. It's a combination mountain inn and off-the-beaten-path spa resort in a spot one wouldn't expect to find either. Those with limited time who are heading up to the western highlands can give it a miss, but it has several things to recommend it.

For one thing, it's perched atop a 470-meter ridge with a terrific view of a huge forested valley and the green peak of the 520-meter-high Cerro La Vieja ("old lady mountain"), which looks close enough to touch. The breezes here blow strong and cool, but when they stop it can be as hot and humid as the lowlands. The surrounding land is heavily settled by farmers—the drive up will give a real flavor of Panamanian country life—but the lodge is attempting to bring back native vegetation on its 250 hectares.

The lodge's owner, Alfonso Jaén C., also owns the tourist restaurant Las Tinajas in Panama City.

He takes understandable pride in this place. Spa services are available in a new building constructed in 2003. Rates are quite reasonable: A 50-minute massage is $20, and the most expensive service, something called a *limpieza termal* (thermal cleansing), tops out at $45.

There are 23 rooms, all with hot water, and some are definitely nicer than others. The best are in the new pair of modern two-story cabañas perched right on the edge of the ridge. The day after my first visit to the area, one of these was scheduled to host the president of Panama. Ask for Chihibalí or El Turega; the rooms on the top floor are best of all, but all have balconies and hammocks. Package deals that include meals are also available.

The lodge offers many different excursions for its guests. It can arrange hiking or mule-riding trips to, among other places, Cascada El Tavidá, a 30-meter waterfall, and nearby petroglyphs; to the top of Cerro Congal, a peak from which one can see both oceans on a clear day; and to Vaquilla, where there's a campsite by a river. The latter hike supposedly takes about 1.5 hours (I didn't have time to check it out myself), and I was

© WILLIAM FRIAR

Trinadad Spa and Lodge is a combination mountain inn and off-the-beaten-path spa resort in a spot one wouldn't expect to find either.

told the campsite consists of a riverside wooden hut that can hold up to 28 people. There are a kitchen and running water but no electricity.

For those who feel ambitious, the lodge sometimes offers a five-day, four-night trek to the Caribbean. Guests spend the first night at the lodge, then head north by mule and riverboat, camping out in hammocks at night. Total one-way cost (you can get a bus back from the coast) including mules, guides, all meals, and the boat is around $500 per person. This is a demanding trip. Far less grueling is a day hike or mule ride to El Valle, where the lodge can arrange for guests to spend the night at a hotel.

The food at the lodge is simple but tasty. A full lunch or dinner should cost no more than $10. The restaurant has a spectacular view of the valley and Cerro La Vieja.

The lodge is 28 kilometers northeast of Penonomé on the Chiguirí Arriba road. Those driving from Panama City should turn right off the Interamericana at the Hotel Dos Continentes. Look for a sign reading "Churuquita, Toabre, y Caimito" and turn right. Continue straight up into the hills. The paved road ends at the town of Caimito. Continue straight on the dirt road to the lodge. At the time I visited, the upper stretch was impassable except by four-wheel-drive vehicle, though it's supposedly in better shape these days. The drive takes about 45 minutes. Buses leave from the public market in Penonomé during daylight hours ($1.50). Look for the "Chiguirí Arriba" bus. You can also come by taxi from Penonomé, which will cost you $20–30 depending on the condition of the road and the driver's mood.

Ⓜ PARQUE NACIONAL OMAR TORRIJOS H.

This somewhat hard-to-reach park consists of more than 25,000 hectares of forested highlands stretching down the Pacific and Caribbean sides of the Continental Divide. Its full name is Parque Nacional General de División Omar Torrijos Herrera, but most people know it simply as **El Copé,** and that's how it'll be referred to here.

The park was created to honor the late military dictator Omar Torrijos, who died in a mysterious plane crash in these mountains on July 31, 1981. Supposedly some charred remains of the plane are still intact on Cerro Marta, a peak you'll see to the right as you enter the park, but you'd have to be a major bushwhacking mountain-climber to prove it.

Because this park is hard to get to, it's filled with thousands of acres of primary forest you're likely to have to yourself. It's a beautiful place with sweeping vistas, as long as it's not too foggy. Even when it is, the morning mist rising off the mountains is quite dramatic.

El Copé is about as far east as the bird life of the western highlands venture, so if you're a bird nut and you're not heading west this is a place for you. If you're not an experienced bird-watcher or guided by one, however, you may not spot many species. El Copé is well known as a place to see hummingbirds, especially the snowcap and green thorntail. The rare bare-necked umbrellabird—which looks as though it's wearing a thatch roof—has been spotted here in the last few years. Its call sounds like the roar of a bull.

All the feline species of Panama are still found in the park, but chances are slim you'll bump into any. Ditto for Baird's tapirs, white-lipped peccaries, and collared peccaries.

Yes, there are venomous snakes here, but as is true throughout the tropics you're unlikely to see one and extremely unlikely to be bothered by one. That said, in the interest of full disclosure you should know that the day before my first visit, a U.S. Peace Corps volunteer nearly stepped on a deadly bushmaster while cutting a trail. The volunteer also once found an eyelash palm pit viper coiled in the cyclone-fence wall of the shelter that served then as visitor quarters. These are cute little devils, but also venomous. And during one hike, a group of experienced hikers ahead of me thought they came across a coral snake. In other words, watch where you step and sleep. And let someone else go first.

Note: This area gets rain and fog year-round and is quite a bit cooler than the lowlands, so bring warm, waterproof clothes. You'd be surprised how easy it is to get hypothermia even in this relatively mild climate.

Trails

There are several good, wide trails that start from the entrance to the park. Facing into the park, with the visitor shelter and park sign to your right, you'll see two trails. The one to the left heads straight up to the top of a mountain with views of both oceans (about a half-hour's walk). The one to the right heads down toward the Caribbean slope (endless). The latter trail is rocky and rutted, and you'll have to cross several streams. Be prepared for ankle-deep mud. An hour into it there's a far more rugged, strenuous trail that leads you back to the shelter. The umbrellabird has been spotted here (as have venomous snakes). Do not take this trail without a guide: You will get lost. It takes about an hour to get back to the shelter. There is also a half-kilometer interpretive trail that starts behind the shelter. There's a rudimentary trail map posted on a signboard. The ranger may be available to guide you; as always, a small tip is always appreciated.

Practicalities

You'll see the ranger station on the left just as you come to the official entrance to the park at the crest of the hill. The park entrance fee is $3, another $5 to camp. There's also an ANAM administrative station in the small town of El Copé, below the park, that's theoretically open 8 A.M.–3 P.M. Monday–Friday.

In 2002 the glorified tool shed that served as a visitors shelter was replaced with what may be the nicest cabin in the entire Panama national parks system. It's simple but modern and pleasant and has a bathroom with running water.

Just 128 paces behind the shelter is an attractive visitors center that's allegedly open 8 A.M.–5 P.M. daily. It's on a ridge with an awe-inspiring view of mountains, the valley, and the Caribbean.

Getting There

The turnoff to El Copé is 20 kilometers west of Penonomé. The turnoff may not be marked when you visit, as it wasn't the last time I did. If you're coming from the direction of Penonomé, turn right when you see the Accel gas station and a building marked "Casa Río Grande." They're before the pedestrian bridge that spans the Interamericana. From here it's a 33-kilometer drive into the mountains, a trip that takes over an hour. The last seven kilometers are on a dirt road that used to be horrendous. It's now much improved, but it's still a rough, bumpy drive that requires a four-wheel drive. The trip can take more than an hour from Penonomé even with a powerful vehicle, depending on road conditions.

Direct buses from Panama City to El Copé run once an hour 6 A.M.–6 P.M. The trip takes about 3.5 hours and costs $5. If you're coming from Penonomé, you can take an El Copé bus ($1.50) from there as well. In either case, switch at the little town of El Copé to the Barrigón bus ($.40). The destinations will be painted on the windshield. From Barrigón you can hike uphill into the park, a rocky four kilometers that takes about an hour.

Santos Navas and his daughter, Nuris, may also be able to give you a lift in their pickup the last few brutal kilometers from the tiny settlement of Barrigón to the park entrance. Call tel. 983-9130, or look for the house with the sign that says Albergue Navas in Barrigón. It'll be on the right as you face uphill. It'll cost you $10 one-way; you can arrange a time for them to pick you up. Be sure to ask them about progress at La Rica, far into the park. They own 100 hectares of primary forest there, and have been trying to get an ecotourist lodge off the ground.

Aguadulce

The industrial town of Aguadulce (pop. 7,700), 53 kilometers east of Santiago in Coclé Province, lies on a vast, dusty, sun-blasted plain that may remind Californians of the wasteland around Bakersfield. It has just about as much charm and can easily be skipped. None of the few sights, restaurants, or hotels here are anything special. The area is known for producing salt, shrimp, and sugar, and there's a big dairy on the edge of town. At the time of writing, the divided highway shrank to the old two-lane road just west of Aguadulce, though construction on the highway extension was well under way and will likely be finished by the time you read this.

SIGHTS

Museo de la Sal y el Azúcar (Avenida Sebastián Sucre, tel. 997-4280, 8:30 A.M.–noon and 1–4 P.M. Tues.–Fri., 8:30 A.M.–12:30 P.M. Sat., closed Sun., $1 for adults, $.25 for kids) is a tiny museum housed in a turn-of-the-20th-century building that was once the town post office. It's on the plaza, facing the cathedral. An earnest, Spanish-speaking guide will explain the simple displays and tell you more than you're likely to want to know about how salt and sugar are produced in the area. One interesting note is that salt has been harvested in the province since pre-Colombian times using much the same method: Sea water is diverted into manmade channels near the shore and allowed to evaporate. The current elaborate, mazelike channel system has been used for more than 100 years. The best thing about this museum is how hard the staff tries to make do with such very limited resources.

Las Piscinas is one of those surreal, only-in-Panama projects. Because the "beach" around here is really gooey mudflats, the community has seen fit to build four tile swimming pools, the largest of which is about 15 meters long, smack in the middle of a rocky part of those flats. At low tide the pools drain out. At high tide during the dry season, local folks splash around in them. Others come here to check out the plentiful shorebirds.

To get to the pools, take the unmarked road to the left of the church in Aguadulce. You should see an old building on the left inscribed "El Capitolio Entre Dos Pueblos Hermanos." Las Piscinas are down this road. The road runs past some shrimp farms. Park two kilometers later at Kiosco Piscinas del Mar. Mangroves will be on the left. Walk about 200 meters until the path turns rocky. The pools are up ahead on the right. A taxi here costs $4 each way.

ACCOMMODATIONS AND FOOD

The **Hotel Interamericano** (Interamericana, tel. 997-4148, $16.50 s/d) is on the south side of the Interamericana near the entrance to Aguadulce. It offers 25 old and drab rooms with firm beds, balconies, air-conditioning, and cable TV. The place is far from spotless—the walls in particular need a good scrubbing—but it's okay. Its restaurant (7 A.M.–11 P.M. daily) serves Chinese food plus basic Panamanian fare in an almost air-conditioned room that's on the dreary side and not particularly clean. The shrimp chow mein isn't bad, and there's plenty of it. Most dishes cost less than $5.

The **Hotel Plaza Aguadulce** (Interamericana, tel. 986-0728, $16.50/$18.70 s/d), right next door to the Interamericano, is a better deal. Its 39 smallish rooms aren't winning any cleanliness awards either, but they're significantly nicer and newer, with air-conditioning, cable TV, a coffeemaker, and good beds. The cafeteria attached to it serves steam-table fast food and short-order items for $1.50–5. Offerings include Chinese food and the usuals. It's open for lunch and dinner only.

As you head into town, the **Carisabel Hotel** (Calle Eduardo Pedreshi, tel. 997-3800, $23.10/$26.40 s/d) is a 21-room motel with air-conditioning, TV, and a bathtub-sized swimming pool. It's a modern but spartan place and the walls are a bit smudged. Some of the beds are good, some aren't—shop around. The restaurant right next door looked promising but was closed when I visited.

Restaurante La Tablita, next to the Texaco station and across the street from the two hotels on the Interamericana, serves cheapo food in a large thatch-roofed building 24 hours a day. The steam-table offerings are rather ominous looking, but diners can order decent grilled sandwiches and French fries for a couple of bucks.

INFORMATION AND SERVICES

There are no tourist offices in Aguadulce. The best bet for general information is to ask a staffer at the Museo de la Sal y el Azúcar.

Aguadulce has three banks with ATMS, all on Avenida Rodolfo Chiari, the main road that leads to the cathedral. The closest to the church is Banistmo. The other two, Banco Nacional de Panamá and Global Bank, are next to each other a couple of blocks up toward the highway.

A Moneygram outlet (Calle San Juan Bautista, tel. 997-6772, 8 A.M.–noon and 1–6 P.M. Mon.–Fri., 8 A.M.–noon Sat., closed Sun.) is near Lavamático Fajardo. The local Western Union outlet (corner of Avenida Alejandro T. Escobar and Avenida Rodolfo Chiari, tel. 997-4979, 8 A.M.–5 P.M. Mon.–Fri., 9 A.M.–5 P.M. Sat., closed Sun.) is in a small shopping complex on the right as one turns down Avenida Rodolfo Chiari toward the center of town. Next to it is a pharmacy, Farmacia Megacentro (tel. 997-4880, 8 A.M.–8 P.M. Mon.–Sat., 8 A.M.–noon Sat., 8 A.M.–noon and 7–8 P.M. Sun.).

The shoebox-sized post office (7 A.M.–6 P.M. Mon.–Fri., 7 A.M.–5 P.M. Sun.) is around the corner from the museum, in the same building.

Lavamático Fajardo (Avenida Alejandro T. Escobar, 8 A.M.–7 P.M. Mon.–Sat., 8 A.M.–noon Sun.) charges $.50 to wash and $.75 to dry a load of laundry. There's another launderette (7:30 A.M.–9 P.M. Mon.–Sat., 8 A.M.–8 P.M. Sun.) in the Plaza Aguadulce, around the corner from the Hotel Plaza Aguadulce and Hotel Interamericano. This one's self-serve and charges $.50 to wash ($.75 for hot water), and $.60 to dry. There's also a supermarket, Supercentro Hawaii, in the same complex.

Cine Más is a small multiplex across the street from Hotel Carisabel and Restaurante Caribe.

GETTING THERE AND AWAY

It's a couple of kilometers from the Interamericana to the center of town, an awfully long walk in the hot sun. If you get dropped off by the highway, consider a cab into town. It costs $.65.

Regional buses leave from the town plaza. Buses to Panama City, David, and other distant spots don't come into the city; go to the Interamericana to catch one of these.

Buses to El Copé leave from the side of the museum every 45 minutes 6 A.M.–6 P.M. The fare is $1.50.

Minibuses to Santiago leave every 15 minutes 5:45 A.M.–7 P.M. from the town plaza. $2. Large, David-bound buses stop at Santiago, but these must be caught on the Interamericana.

A taxi back to the Interamericana to catch a long-distance bus is $.65. The fare to Natá is $3. A trip all the way to Penonomé is $20. If you have trouble flagging a cab in town, there's a taxi cooperative, Radio Taxi Cooperativa de Transporte El Sol (tel. 997-4519), a few streets behind the museum. Another taxi stand is next to Restaurante La Tablita on the Interamericana.

Around Aguadulce

There are two sites of some historical interest near Aguadulce: Natá, which has one of the oldest churches in the Americas, and El Caño, which has an archaeological dig nearby. Natá is nine kilometers east (actually, given the bend in the road, it's really more north) of Aguadulce; El Caño is another nine kilometers past that. They're both just off the Interamericana on the way to Penonomé and can be visited as a side trip from either of those large towns in a couple of hours. Rather than fool with buses, those without their own transportation should consider hiring a cab in Aguadulce (or Penonomé, as the case may be—it's just 21 kilometers east of Natá). Any bus running between Aguadulce and Natá can drop visitors off along the Interamericana at the edge of these towns. In that case, it's worth going to Natá first; it's a short walk to the church, and it'll probably be easier there to get a taxi to pop over to El Caño than vice versa. It's unlikely visitors will find enough in either town to compel them to spend the night; better to head on at least as far as Penonomé or Aguadulce.

NATÁ DE LOS CABALLEROS

The Spanish founded Natá on May 20, 1522, which makes it the oldest surviving town in Panama and one of the oldest in the Americas. Its origins are older than that, however—it was the center of an important indigenous chiefdom. Its last leader was named Natá; the Spanish took his name for their new town, then used the town as a base from which to conquer the native peoples of western Panama. Legend has it that it got its full name, Natá de los Caballeros, when the king of Spain sent 100 *caballeros* (knights) to help in these wars. The town remained an important regional center of Spanish power throughout the colonial period.

Basilica Menor Santiago Apostól de Natá

Natá's past is far more impressive and interesting than its present, however. Today it's a sleepy village of onion and tomato farmers. Pretty much the only attraction left is its famous, ancient

© WILLIAM FRIAR

Natá's church lays claim to being the oldest along the entire Pacific coast of the Americas.

church, the Basilica Menor Santiago Apostól de Natá. Though built over several decades after the founding of the town, it lays claim to being the oldest church along the entire Pacific littoral of the Americas. While of interest to historians, it's actually a rather simple if attractive stucco church with a plain wooden ceiling and red-tile roof. Its most notable features are its elaborate carved wooden altars. It was renovated in 1998. Every July 25, a statue of Santiago Apostól, the patron saint of Natá, is paraded through the streets of the town for the faithful. The nearby chapel, Capilla de San Juan de Dios, is supposed to be renovated eventually.

If the church is closed during the week, ask for help at the *alcaldía* (mayor's office), on the right side of the plaza as you face the church. The church isn't really all that impressive or worth making a special trip for, but the Interamericana is less than a kilometer away from the church and village center, making it an easy place to swing by for those with their own transportation. Visitors can easily walk to the church from the highway if need be. There are a few facilities for tourists in Natá, but there are better options in Aguadulce or Penonomé.

EL CAÑO

This little town nine kilometers northeast of Natá has an important archaeological dig that's open to visitors, but there isn't much to see today. Its centerpiece was a ring of carved stone columns, about six meters high, in the shape of human and animal figures. In the 1920s a North American adventurer, A. Hyatt Verrill, removed nearly all of them, 150 in total, and shipped them to museums in the United States along with gold and ceramics found at the site. Only the stone pedestals from which the figure were cut remain in the field today. Nearby is an excavated cemetery where five exposed skeletons can still be seen at the bottom of a four-meter-deep pit. The site dates from about A.D. 800–A.D. 1100.

There's a small museum on the site in the quaint house with the red-tile roof. It's worth a quick visit. While most of the few pieces that were not taken out of the country aren't displayed here, for security reasons, there are a few small stone statues and ceramics. There are some photos of statues that were removed, a crude model of the site, and some pieces that date from the Spanish era.

The complex is open 9 A.M.–noon and 12:30–4 P.M. Tues.–Sat., 9 A.M.–1 P.M. Sun., closed Monday. Entrance is $1 for adults, $.25 for kids. The site is three kilometers from the Interamericana and is accessible by a dirt road that runs by the left side of El Caño's church, Iglesia San Lorenzo, as one faces it. Keep left at the fork. The site is kind of isolated. Those without their own transport are probably best off hiring a taxi in Natá.

Note that in the rainy season the entire site is a virtual swamp swarming with ferocious mosquitoes. If possible, wear rubber boots and douse yourself with gallons of insect repellent.

Santiago

Though it's one of Panama's main cities and the provincial capital of Veraguas, most people treat Santiago (pop. 32,480) as a place to break their journey to somewhere else. Usually that somewhere else is either David or Panama City, since Santiago falls just about midway between the two. It's about a 3.5–4 hour drive to either city from here.

Santiago is a homely commercial and transportation hub on the Interamerican Highway with little to offer tourists. But it does have the facilities and bus connections one would expect of a growing Panamanian town with such a strategic location. And it has a real town life, some decent places to stay and eat, and even some entertainment possibilities. It's a good place to stop for the night on cross-country trips.

The Interamericana forks at the eastern outskirts of town. Taking the left fork off the Interamericana leads into town via Avenida Central, also known as Avenida Hector A. Santacoloma, though few call it that. The road leads through a busy commercial stretch before splintering by the town church, the Catedral Santiago Apóstol. Left turns at the church lead down to the surfing beaches of Playa Santa Catalina and to Puerto Mutis, a launching point for trips to Parque Nacional Coiba.

Most of the hotels, restaurants, shops, and services of interest to visitors are not in Santiago proper but rather on the Interamericana. Instead of turning in to Santiago at the fork, stay right; facilities are on either side of the Interamericana.

A little farther west the Interamericana is intersected by Calle 10A Norte, also called Calle Polidoro Pinzón. This cuts southwest into Santiago (a left turn, if coming from the direction of Panama City) and is where the main bus terminal and a few other facilities for visitors can be found.

Celebrations in Santiago include the religious festivals of Jesús de la Misericordia on April 8 and the Virgen del Carmen on July 16, the Patronales de Santiago Apóstol (patron saint's day) on July 25, and the Grito de Separacíon de Panamá de Colombia (the town's call for independence from Colombia) on November 9.

SIGHTS

Santiago's few sights can be taken in on a self-guided walking tour that shouldn't last longer than a couple of hours, including people-watching.

The **Museo Regional de Veraguas,** on the north side of the plaza next to the cathedral, was closed for renovation during my last visit, and there was no telling when it would reopen or whether it'd be worth a visit.

The **Catedral Santiago Apóstol,** on the west end of Avenida Central, contains the remains of General José de Fábrega, a key figure in Panama's decision to declare independence from Spain and become a part of Gran Colombia in 1821. As always, it's interesting to see how lively churches in Panama can get on a given day, but it's unadorned by Catholic standards and isn't worth a special trip.

La **Escuela Normal Superior Juan Demóstenes Arosemena** (Avenida 5A Norte between Calle 6B Norte, also called Calle Domingo García, and Calle 8A Norte, also

© WILLIAM FRIAR

Santiago's teachers college, La Escuela Normal Superior Juan Demóstenes Arosemena, is noted for its ornate architecture and murals painted by Roberto Lewis.

called Calle Eduardo Santo) is an imposing teachers college and pretty much the proud symbol of Santiago. It's worth a quick look if you're in the neighborhood, which is several blocks northeast of the cathedral. It's a bulky structure with a red-tile roof, but what will grab your attention is the flamboyantly ornate entrance, which features nudes frolicking up the columns and across the arch. Visitors are welcome to peek inside, where there are more ornate columns and, across the hall, a theater with murals painted by Roberto Lewis, the famous Panamanian artist who also painted the ceiling of the Teatro Nacional in Panama City. They're not in great condition and, frankly, aren't terribly impressive in any case, but you've got to admire the ambition: The murals depict key moments from pretty much the whole span of human history, from the discovery of

ANOTHER ROADSIDE ATTRACTION

Eight kilometers west of Santiago, on the south side of the crossroads near the town of La Peña, are two small souvenir shops that may be of interest. The **Mercado Artesenal de Veraguas** (7:30 A.M.–noon and 12:30–4 P.M. Mon.–Fri., 7 A.M.–noon Sat., closed Sun.). has some nice traditional ceramics and a few Panama hats, some Ngöbe-Buglé bags, and a few other, less interesting knickknacks. **Cerámica La Peña,** right next door, sells some traditional ceramics, though a more limited selection than you'd find on the Azuero Peninsula.

fire to the Code of Hammurabi to Copernicus to the crucifixion of Christ. He tossed in the Spanish enslavement of Native American peoples for good measure.

SPORTS AND RECREATION

Santiago's de facto port, **Puerto Mutis** is the jumping-off point for boats to Coiba (see the *Golfo de Chiriquí and the Western Highlands* chapter) and other fishing and diving spots. It's 24 kilometers southwest of Santiago on a good road and is easily accessible from Santiago by bus or taxi. The "town" is just a few houses, hole-in-the-wall restaurants, gas stations, and shops lining the road, which ends at a pier on an estuary.

Right at the end of the road is **Montijo's Bay Restaurante, Bar, y Gasolinera** (tel. 999-8174), where you can dine right across from a huge gasoline tank. It's a surprisingly pleasant, modern, open-air place on stilts that looks out on a pretty view of the estuary.

Coiba Adventure Sportfishing (Panama tel. 998-8108 or 628-0810, U.S. toll-free tel. 800/800-0907, info@coibadventure.com, www.coibadventure.com) is based in Rincón Largo, three kilometers up the road from Puerto Mutis. This is the home of Tom Yust and Tyra Ford, the friendly U.S. couple that owns the business. I haven't traveled with them yet, but they come highly recommended by people I trust.

They run trips on a 31-foot Bertram and a

21-foot Mako. They also have a 14-foot inflatable and two sit-on-top sea kayaks. The outfit offers 3–6-day package deals, but it's also possible to do day trips. These cost around $800 on the Mako and $1,200 on the Bertram. Prices include use of fishing tackle and snorkeling gear.

As has been mentioned elsewhere, it's also possible to work out cheap trips to Coiba with local fisherman, but it's a risky proposition and I do not recommend it. These are small, open boats on seas that can quickly turn rough. The boats are unlikely to have a backup motor, life jackets, or a radio, let alone sportfishing gear. One of these boats goes adrift at sea every other month. Even if you make it, you won't be able to do much more than snorkel (with your own gear) from these boats.

The road to Puerto Mutis is not well marked. To get there by car, follow Avenida Central (Avenida Hector A. Santacoloma) toward the cathedral and take the left fork once you reach it. Turn left behind the church onto Calle 2 Norte. The Hotel Santiago will be on the left. Take the second right (it's Avenida 5B Sur, but it's not marked) and then stay straight all the way to Puerto Mutis. (For information on buses and taxis from Santiago, see *Getting There and Around.*)

ACCOMMODATIONS

$10–25

Motel Residencial Camino del Sol (Calle 10A Norte, also called Calle Polidoro Pinzón, across the street from the bus terminal, tel. 998-2114, $11 s/d with fan, $16.50 s/d with air-conditioning) offers the best cheap rooms in town. It's a newish place with good beds in spartan but clean and modern rooms. The air-conditioned rooms are good value. The rooms with fan are an even better deal, but be warned—the fans are small, desk-style affairs that are mounted to the ceiling, and don't push a lot of air. You may be reluctant to open the windows given that they don't have screens and the hotel is on a bustling street. If you can spare the cash, go for the air-conditioning.

Hotel Santiago (Calle 2 and Avenida 1, tel. 998-4824, starts at $11 s/d), one block south of the cathedral, is a 30-room hotel in an 80-something-year-old building. As one might expect, the place is tattered, but it does have a touch of character. The rooms are basic and worn and the beds are spongy, but it's an okay place for the price. Rates are $11 s/d for a room without air-conditioning or fan, things you are likely to want. A room with a battered air conditioner is $13.20. This is a sister hotel to Motel Residencial Camino del Sol, which is a far better place for about the same price.

Hotel Hong Kong (Interamericana, tel. 998-0671, $13 s/d with fan, $16.60 s/d with air-conditioning), across the street from the Hotel Gran David, has 39 dark, utterly plain rooms that smell of disinfectant. But the beds are firm and the place is clean.

Hotel Pyramidal (tel. 998-3213, 998-3124, $21 s/d) is on the north side of the Interamericana as the roads forks at the entrance to town. It's a 62-room maze of corridors in the Centro Pyramidal. Rooms are worn and a little dreary and the beds are hard, but the place is clean and the location couldn't be more convenient for cross-country bus travelers. It's part of the Centro Pyramidal complex, which also includes the stop for cross-country buses, an air-conditioned restaurant, outdoor cafeteria, ATM, gas station, pharmacy, and gas station. All the rooms have air-conditioning and cable TV. There's a sizable pool in the courtyard. It's a reasonable value.

$25–50

Hotel Gran David (Interamericana, tel. 998-4510, 998-2622, or 998-2622, tel./fax 998-1866, $18.70/$26.50 s/d), easily confused with the nearby Hotel Plaza Gran David, is on the north side of the Interamericana just past the turnoff to Santiago as one heads toward David. It offers simple but pleasant rooms with firm beds set in a maze of hallways. The rooms are a little older and more worn those at the Hotel Galeria, but they're fine and, amazingly, are designed to let light in rather than keep it out. All the rooms have air-conditioning and TV. There's a small pool on the premises. This is a popular place and often fills up; reservations are a good idea.

Hotel Galeria (Interamericana, tel. 998-7950, 958-7951, or 998-7953, tel./fax 998-7954,

$38.50 s/d), formerly known as Hotel Camino Real, is on the north side of the Interamericana just east of the Hotel Gran David. It's next to a small mall and offers 40 rooms, a bar, and a restaurant. It's not a fancy place, but it's long been popular with business travelers and tourists who can afford it because it offers clean and modern rooms with comfortable beds, hot showers, air-conditioning, and cable TV. There's even a weight room. The restaurant is open for breakfast, lunch, and dinner.

The new **M Hotel La Hacienda** (Interamericana, tel. 958-8580 or 958-5477, fax 958-8579, $38.50 s/d) is the best hotel in the whole region. On the Interamericana less than three kilometers west of town, it offers 42 bright and cheerful rooms carefully decorated with furnishings that seem imported directly from Pueblo, Mexico. There's a small gym, a small but attractive swimming pool, laundry facilities, a restaurant and bar, and an Internet café. Rooms come with double, queen, or king beds, and suites are moderately priced. All rooms have air-conditioning and cable TV. There's (awful) live music in the bar on Tuesday nights. Day passes and special deals are often available.

FOOD

The restaurant at the **Hotel Gran David** (Interamericana, tel. 998-4510, tel. 998-2622) is simple and a bit dingy, and the waiters are harried and overworked, but it's a good place to go with a big appetite and small budget. There's no menu, but lunch and dinner offerings tend to include a variety of beef, pork, spaghetti, and chicken dishes with a salad and *patacones* or potatoes on the side for $3–4.50. This place is best for breakfast. A plate of delicious, nongreasy tortillas and white cheese with a cup of coffee costs a couple of bucks. It's open for breakfast, lunch, and dinner.

Restaurante Tropicalismo (Avenida Hector A. Santacoloma and Avenida 14A Sur near the IPAT office, tel. 998-3661, 9 A.M.–11 P.M. daily) is a simple but clean indoor/outdoor place that's a decent option for a budget meal. It specializes in Cuban food and also offers an assortment of pastas, sandwiches, seafood, meats, fresh juices, and so on. Breakfast is $2 or less, and there's a daily lunch special of meat, chicken, or fish with side dishes for $1.75. The Cuban sandwich ($3) tastes like the real thing.

The restaurant at **Hotel Galeria** (Interamericana, tel. 998-7950 or 958-7951) has an ambitious menu of meats, seafood, and pasta, but this is a place to keep things simple. The average main dish costs around $7–8. The food is okay but nothing special by any means. It's open for breakfast, lunch, and dinner.

The best place to eat in Santiago is **Ⓜ Restaurante Delicias del Mar** (across the Interamericana from the Centro Pyramidal, tel. 998-6455, noon–3 P.M. and 6–11 P.M. Mon.–Sat., 1–9 P.M. Sun.). It has upscale aspirations and does a surprisingly good job of meeting them. It specializes in Peruvian seafood, of all things, and offers a range of other ambitious fish and meat dishes. The *langostinos* here are excellent. The ceviche is prepared Peruvian style, with red onions and a yam on the side to cool things off. It's also good. Most dishes are $9–14. The atmosphere is austere but semiformal, and you're served by a polite waiter sporting a bow tie.

Restaurante Los Tucanes (Interamericana, tel. 998-6490, 11:30 A.M.–10:30 P.M. daily), is in a gas-station plaza on the Interamericana just west of the Hotel Gran David. It's a quiet, pleasant air-conditioned place with tablecloths that takes a stab both at international cuisine and local food. Offerings include meat, pasta, chow mein, conch, and rice every which way. Just about everything on the menu is $7 or less. The *filete a la plancha en salsa chimi-churry* is a chewy but tasty piece of grilled steak in a brown sauce, served with *petit pois*. The service is gracious.

The food at the new **Hotel La Hacienda** (Interamericana, tel. 958-8580, 6 A.M.–10 P.M. daily) is passable but disappointing. It features Mexican and Peruvian dishes as well as the usual meat and seafood offerings. Most main dishes average $6. The guacamole is bland, though the chips are homemade. The burritolike tacos are okay. Don't order anything too ambitious here. The restaurant itself is attractive.

INFORMATION AND SERVICES

The IPAT office (Avenida Central, also called Hector A. Santacoloma, tel. 998-3929, fax 998-0929, 8:30 A.M.–4:30 P.M. Mon.–Fri.) is in Plaza Palermo, a small strip mall across and down the street from Restaurante Tropicalismo. The staff here is friendly, understands a couple of words of English, and may have a little more marginally useful printed material than usual.

Farmacia Veraguas, in the Centro Pyramidal bus stop on the Interamericana, is a 24-hour pharmacy.

A few banks with ATMs are clustered along Avenida Central in the blocks leading up to the cathedral, starting with Global Bank (Calle Rogelio Girón R., 8 A.M.–3 P.M. Mon.–Fri., 9 A.M.–noon Sat.).

Right next to the IPAT office is R&R Solutions (8 A.M.–10 P.M. Mon.–Sat., closed Sun.), which has a few computers with Internet access for $.75/hour. Hal's Internet Café (Calle 10A Norte, also called Calle Polidoro Pinzón, near the corner of Avenida Central, tel. 998-0996, fax 998-2663, 8:30 A.M.–11 P.M. Mon.–Sat.) is often crowded. Internet access is $1/hour. Sending or receiving faxes here costs $1/page within the country or a whopping $10/page internationally.

There are several launderettes near the cathedral. Lavamático El Sol (8 A.M.–10 P.M. daily), a short walk behind the cathedral on Avenida Central, is a self-service place that charges $.50 to wash ($.75 for hot water) and $.75 to dry a load. The little store next door sells detergent.

The Galeria on the Interamericana resembles any small strip mall in the United States, complete with American fast food and American blockbusters playing at the little muliplex, Cines Moderno.

GETTING THERE AND AROUND

Because Santiago is about midway between Panama City and David, it's an important transportation hub with excellent, frequent connections to many destinations. It takes about 3.5 hours to drive the 250 kilometers between Panama City and Santiago at a safe clip, and, depending on road conditions, about three to four hours to drive to David on a far worse stretch of road. Those heading west should note there are few gas stations beyond Santiago. The first one at the time of writing was about 90 kilometers west of Santiago, and they're far scarcer after that. Fill up in Santiago.

Buses

Santiago has two bus depots: the main terminal, in Santiago itself, and the Centro Pyramidal on the Interamericana near the east entrance to town.

The latter is the place to go for large buses to Panama City and all buses to David or the Costa Rican border. It's a common rest and food stop for long-haul buses running between Panama City and David or Costa Rica. Terminales David-Panama (tel. 998-4006, 8:30 A.M.–5 P.M. daily), the main long-haul carrier between David and Panama City, has an office on the west end of the complex. You can buy tickets or get information there.

Buses to David leave every hour to 1.5 hours 9:30 A.M.–11 P.M. There are also two express buses at 1:30 A.M. and 2:45 A.M. Fare is $6.

Buses to Panama City leave approximately every hour on the half hour 9:30 A.M.–10:30 P.M. There are also two express buses at 1:15 A.M. and 2 A.M. Minibuses to Panama City leave more frequently from the main bus terminal in Santiago, but they are smaller and less comfortable than these, and there's less metal between you and the dangers of the road.

The Pyramidal also has a hotel, air-conditioned restaurant, outdoor cafeteria, ATM, gas station, pharmacy, and gas station.

The main bus terminal, the Terminal de Transporte de Santiago, is on Calle 10A Norte, also called Calle Polidoro Pinzón. It has a small bakery and pharmacy. There's a little 24-hour grocery store across the street.

Those heading to Playa Santa Catalina should note that there are no direct buses from Santiago. Take the bus to Soná and transfer to a Santa Catalina bus there. Note that there are only three daily buses from Soná to Santa Catalina, at 5 A.M., noon, and 6 P.M.

Below are some of the more popular routes:

Chitré: Every half hour 5:30 A.M.–8 P.M.; $2. The trip takes about an hour and a half.

Ocú: Every 20 minutes during daylight hours; $1.50. The trip takes a little less than an hour.

Panama City (by minibus): Every half hour 24 hours a day; $6. The trip takes 3.5 hours. (The large, long-distance buses don't run from here; go to the Centro Pyramidal on the Interamericana).

Puerto Mutis: Every 15–20 minutes 6 A.M.–9 P.M. Monday–Friday. On the weekends they depart every 20–25 minutes 6 A.M.–8 P.M. on Saturday and until 6:45 P.M. on Sunday; $1. The trip takes a little less than an hour.

Santa Fe: Every half hour 5 A.M.–6:40 P.M., returning 4:40 A.M.–6 P.M.; $2. The trip takes about an hour. The bus stops by San Francisco on the way up and back.

Soná: Every 20 minutes 6 A.M.–9:40 P.M., 6 A.M.–8 P.M. Saturday–Sunday; $1.50. The trip takes a little less than an hour.

Taxis and Rental Cars

Those who want to take a taxi to Playa Santa Catalina should be prepared to pay $50, but this may be negotiable—this isn't a common trip, and taxi drivers don't have a fixed idea of the price. Taxis to Puerto Mutis are $12 each way. Taxis within town should cost less than $1 for most destinations.

There's an office of Budget Rent a Car (tel. 998-1731, tel./fax 998-1746) on the Interamericana just west of the Hotel Galeria. It's the only rental car place in the whole region.

SAN FRANCISCO AND SANTA FÉ

There are two highland towns north of Santiago that may be of interest to some visitors. The first is San Francisco, less than 20 kilometers above Santiago. The second is Santa Fé, a little under 40 kilometers farther north on the same road.

San Francisco

San Francisco is a small (pop. 2,220) and not very scenic town except for its unusual church and its local water hole. The church, **Iglesia San**

© WILLIAM FRIAR

San Francisco's church, which dates from 1727, is noted for its unusual fusion of European and indigenous images and traditions.

Francisco de la Montaña, dates from 1727, more than 100 years after the town was founded. It's one of the most charming churches in Panama. It's noted mainly for its nine baroque cedar altars, painted in rich reds and golds, which in their carvings depict unusual syncretisms, fusing European and indigenous images and traditions. The outside is brick at the bottom, with a more modern whitewashed tower planted incongruously on top. Part of a very slow renovation of the church was supposed to restore the whole outside to a semblance of its former appearance. With luck, it'll finally be done when you visit. To get to the church, make a right turn off the main road to Santa Fé at the police station. Make another right upon entering town. The church will be straight ahead.

For those who need to cool off, there's a water hole near the church, **El Salto de San Francisco,** that's fed by a couple of small waterfalls. Note that this is a popular place and thus far from pristine—expect to encounter trash on the banks. There's a simple place overlooking the water to get a drink or a bite. To get there, take the road on the right as you face the front of the church. At the T-intersection, turn right. The road ends at the water hole, which is less than one kilometer from the church.

Santa Fé

The highland town of Santa Fé (pop. 2,800) is 54 kilometers north of Santiago, or 37 kilometers past the turnoff to San Francisco. Founded around 1557, it and the surrounding hills were the scene of fierce battles between the Spanish and indigenous peoples under the command of Urracá, an especially skilled warrior who managed to beat back the conquistadors for a time and today is commemorated on Panama's one *centavo* coin.

Santa Fé is 470 meters above sea level, which is high enough to get some cooling breezes and fog. Those who plan to go to the Western Highlands or El Valle can easily skip it. It scores low on the quaintness scale: It's really a sprawl of nondescript houses and little else. It doesn't have much character, and deforestation has degraded its natural attractions. This is a well-settled area, and one has to head pretty far up into the hills to get away from the cattle pastures and into the forest.

That said, the area does have its charms and at tracts some birders. The countryside is pretty, the denuded hills notwithstanding. The rolling pastureland is ringed by a sparsely forested, scrubby mountain range that becomes green with dense forest as it heads up toward the Caribbean side, which is still lightly settled and in some places less well known than it was hundreds of years ago.

The main road up from the south forks just as it enters town. Staying straight leads into the heart of town, where there are a couple of markets, the town church and plaza, a couple of places to eat, and not much else. The left (west) fork leads to a simple place to stay and the trail head to Alto de Piedra.

There are few roads and trails up here, and it's really not a place to explore without a guide. One possible exception is a hike around Alto de Piedra. The turnoff is marked; heading north into town, take the left (west) fork and follow the signs. Turn left at the Cable and Wireless communications tower. This is a densely settled area, but some forest begins two kilometers west of town and gets denser farther up. Access is by a road that's slippery mud even in the dry season. Driving it can be challenging even for a four-wheel drive. This is a good place to use a horse.

Accommodations and Food

All the facilities for visitors listed here are in Santa Fé; there isn't much of anything in San Francisco. Even in Santa Fé there are few services of any kind. There also aren't many food options besides the simple restaurants at the two hotels in the area, and don't expect a memorable meal no matter where you eat. There are a couple of markets that sell fresh produce.

There are two places to stay in Santa Fé.

Jardín Santafereño (tel. 954-0866, $11 s/d) offers four cold-water cinderblock cabins set on a pleasant, forested ridge with a view of the mountains. The rooms are utterly bare and have spongy beds, but they're clean. There's a basic restaurant/beer garden on the premises. To get there, follow the sign to Alto De Piedra on the west side of town. Turn right at the Cable and Wireless communications tower. Go straight. A short,

steep dirt road on the left leads to the cabins. It's a bit of a walk from the center of town.

The **Hotel Santa Fé** (tel. 954-0941, starting at $13 s/d), a 20-room motel a few hundred meters south of the town entrance, is a far more pleasant place to stay. It's right off the main road, but it's a little tough to spot. Clean, cold-water rooms are set in a breezy yard with a lovely view of the surrounding hills. Tiny spartan rooms without TV, air-conditioning, or fans are $13 s/d. Larger rooms with air-conditioning and cable TV are $25 s/d. Note that you may not need air-conditioning or fans here. The beds are soft and the rooms are simple, but this place is quite okay. There's a restaurant on the premises.

Restaurante El Condor (north end of town, no phone, 6 A.M.–9 P.M. daily) is a basic open-air place offering the usual assortment of fried heart-stoppers, plus sandwiches and pizza. You can fill up here for a couple of bucks.

Mercado Agricola y Artesanal Santa Fé (in the center of town, on the east side near the church, no phone, 7:30 A.M.–6:30 P.M. daily) is an open-air market with some fruits and vegetables for sale, as well as a very few handicrafts, mostly Ngöbe-Buglé. There's also a rough map of the area and bit of tourist information posted on one wall.

The **Centro de Mercadeo de Productos Agropecuario, Orgánico, y Artesenal** (no phone, 8 A.M.–5 P.M. daily, closed during lunchtime) has a name bigger than the enterprise. It's a cooperative that sells a few veggies and beans, straw hats, Ngöbe-Buglé handicrafts, and the local coffee. To get there, keep right at the fork as the road leads into town. Continue up to the northern edge of town, then turn right onto the dirt road. The cooperative is on the right. The restaurant (no phone, 5:30 A.M.–9 P.M. daily) below it is pleasant and breezy, and the food is basic and cheap. A substantial lunch here costs less than $1.25. It's a marginally nicer place than El Condor.

Information

One thing Santa Fé is known for is orchids, and the person most responsible for that is **Berta de Castrellón** (tel. 954-0910), an orchid grower who lives in town. She's the head of the Asociación de Orquideología de Veraguas, which every August puts on a three-day orchid festival in town. She's also the closest thing the town has to a tour guide and information service. Those who come here on their own would be well advised to get in touch with her. She often lets visitors tour the huge collection of orchids at her house.

It's a little tricky to spot the house. As you come into town, stay right at the fork and continue to the north side of town. Take the right turn down the road toward Río Mulabá. Her house is on the right a couple hundred meters down. It's set back from the road and her orchid sign is tough to see. Ask anyone you see for *la casa de Berta*. Everyone knows her.

Getting There

The road is good all the way from Santiago to Santa Fé. Buses from Santiago make the 54-kilometer run every half hour 5 A.M.– 6:40 P.M., returning 4:40 A.M.–6 P.M. The fare is $2. The same bus passes by San Francisco and can drop passengers off; just tell the driver ahead of time. After visiting the church, catch another bus the rest of the way to Santa Fé or back down to Santiago.

For those driving themselves, the turn off the Interamericana toward San Francisco and Santa Fé is at the crossroads just west of Santiago. Turn north and head up into the hills for 17 kilometers and turn right at the police station to get to San Francisco. Stay straight on the main road for another 37 kilometers to get to Santa Fé.

Those who prefer just to take a quick tour of Santa Fé as a side trip from Santiago can hire a cab for $20. Make sure to specify it's a round-trip ride (*ida y vuelta*).

Archipiélago de las Perlas

Ninety named islands and more than 130 unnamed islets make up this archipelago, which begins just 15 minutes by plane or a couple of hours by fast boat from Panama City. "Perlas" is Spanish for pearls, and pearls are what first brought these beautiful islands international fame. When Vasco Nuñez de Balboa crossed the Darién looking for the "South Sea," one of his motives was to find and conquer the islands he had heard were overflowing with the precious little oyster byproducts. The conquistadors eventually brought back a treasure that presumably made the king of Spain quite happy. In the process they wiped out the islands' indigenous population.

The archipelago has a way of periodically achieving brief international notoriety. In 1983, the island of Contadora was the site of the first meeting of the Contadora Group, formed by the leaders of several Latin American countries to try to promote democracy in Central America and influence U.S. foreign policy in El Salvador, Nicaragua, and Guatemala, which were being torn apart by bloody military conflicts. In 1979, the same island briefly played host to the exiled shah of Iran. Most recently, the archipelago was the location for the 2003 season of the U.S. reality-TV series *Survivor* as well as a *Survivor All-Stars* bout.

There are lush forests on the islands, lovely sandy beaches on their shores, and healthy coral reefs a short swim away. The latter attract a wealth of brilliant small fish and impressive larger creatures, including sea turtles, manta rays, white-tipped reef sharks, and moray eels. The Perlas are considered one of the better spots in the country for divers in search of big fish.

CONTADORA

By far the most developed and visited of the islands is Contadora, named for its role as the counting-house island for the Spanish pearl trade. Wealthy Panamanians have beach homes here, and it has nearly all the accommodations, places to eat, and tour operations in the archipelago. It's a small island—just 1.2 square kilometers. It's easy to explore just about all of it on foot in a couple of hours. It has several nice beaches, including one, **Playa de las Suecas** (Swedish Women's Beach), where one can sunbathe nude.

My favorite, **Playa Cacique,** is a pretty, secluded beach behind Villa Romántica and away from the crowds. Contadora's largest and busiest beach, the aptly named **Playa Larga,** is somewhat rocky at low tide. Snorkeling is possible just off Playa de las Suecas, **Playa Galeón, Playa Ejecutiva,** and Playa Larga. There's very little else to do on the island, though Hotel Contadora has a nine-hole golf course and tennis courts for those so inclined.

Entertainment and Events

There's little to do at night except drink. **Julius** (tel. 250-4134, noon–3 P.M. and 8 P.M.–late daily) is a rather cozy, nautical-themed disco/bar on a little hill overlooking the sea and operated by Hotel Punta Galeón. There's a pool table inside. It's mainly a place to have a drink, especially on its breezy balcony, but food is also served. Behind Super Mercado Contadora is **Billar El Marguito,** a little cinderblock pool hall where locals drink and dance. **Mi Kiosquito,** a little kiosk near the airstrip. is primarily a place to get a cup of coffee or an elaborate alcoholic potion.

Sports and Recreation

Boat tours of Contadora and the surrounding islands are a popular activity. There's usually a four-person minimum for these, which might possibly be hard to come by during quiet times on the island, such as a rainy-season work day. Scuba diving, snorkeling, and fishing trips are easy to arrange. Dive operators can take guests to nearly two dozen scuba-diving spots within a 45-minute boat ride from Contadora. Most are only 10 minutes away. The diving in the Perlas can be impressive, especially for those fond of big fish: There's a quite good chance of spotting white-tipped reef sharks, manta rays, and moray eels. Among the many other critters

you may come across are angelfish, parrotfish, grunts, snappers, amberjack, sergeant majors, and triggerfish. Personal-watercraft rental is also available for those who feel the need to shatter the peace of the fish and fellow visitors.

Las Perlas Sailing (tel. 250-4214 or 250-4186) on the road leading into Hotel Contadora, offers four-hour boat tours for $35 per person, including soft drinks. The tour can include snorkeling stops, with gear supplied, for those interested. A one-hour tour that just circumnavigates Contadora is $12 per person. The operation also rents two-person personal watercraft for 15-, 30-, and 60-minute increments for $1 a minute. The one-person personal watercraft are the same price, for 30 or 60 minutes. Deep-sea fishing is $150/$300 half day/full day

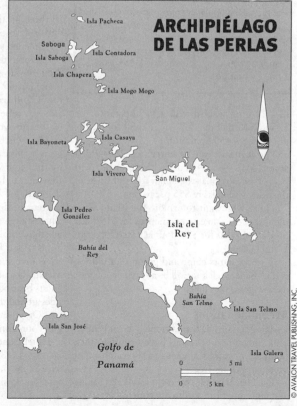

ARCHIPIÉLAGO DE LAS PERLAS

Isla Pacheca

Saboga
Isla Saboga
Isla Contadora

Isla Chapera

Isla Mogo Mogo

Isla Bayoneta
Isla Casaya

Isla Vivero
San Miguel

Isla Pedro González

Isla del Rey

Bahía del Rey

Bahía San Telmo
Isla San Telmo

Isla San José

Golfo de Panamá

Isla Galera

0   5 mi

0   5 km

AND ANOTHER ROADSIDE ATTRACTION

Restaurante Los Camisones (tel. 993-3622, daily 11 A.M.–"until the last client leaves"), also known as El Rincón de los Camisones, is a pleasant and popular open-air place that gets absolutely packed on a dry-season Sunday. It's located near kilometer marker 104, which is about 7 kilometers west of the turnoff to El Valle and about 10 kilometers east of Santa Clara. The place isn't visible from the road, but the turnoff is marked. As you head west, it's a steep right (north) turn up a narrow road—slow down as you approach the turn, and watch out for cars coming down from the restaurant. It's set back from the road and has no view, but it catches a welcome breeze. It serves a range of typical Panamanian dishes. The food's not bad, but the restaurant's popularity stems more from being part of many families' weekend-getaway ritual than for the quality of its fare. The average dish goes for about $6. The brave—at least those carrying pepper spray—can try the *creeps de la casa* for dessert.

4214 or 250-4186, $30 s/d, $15 for a third person, including continental breakfast) with hot water, cheap beds, local TV, minifridge, and gas stove. Guests have free use of bikes, snorkeling equipment, and a computer with Internet access. The units are small and stark, but they're fairly new (opened in 2000) and in decent shape. Note they're not on the beach; they're on a rise above the airstrip, but they do not have a view of the ocean.

Villa Romántica (tel. 250-4067, contadora@villa-romantica.com, www.contadora-villa-romantica.com, rooms start at $77 s/d in the main house, $66 s/d in the old annex), formerly Casa Charlito, is a quirky place that has to be approached with the right attitude to be enjoyed. It's on the south side of the island right above beautiful Playa Cacique and offers eight rooms in two houses. Two of the modern, rather glitzy rooms in the main house have waterbeds, and all three on the ground floor have tile floors, mirrored closets, and air-conditioning. Discounts are sometimes available for those traveling alone.

Rooms in the main house are far nicer than the three run-down and dreary rooms in a second house farther inland that has a kitchen, dining room, and bar. However, on my last visit this annex was being expanded and may be better by the time you read this.

The owner seems to be going for a romantic getaway vibe. That atmosphere is helped a lot by the large veranda and open-air restaurant, Restaurante Romántico, that look right out on the secluded beach. But it's diminished by the clutter and air of cheerful chaos about the place. There's a spa in the middle of the dining room, which is emblematic of the odd aura of '70s hedonism that lingers about the place. The Austrian owner is an enthusiastic, effusive, and friendly character named Charley, who offers his guests boat rides for $5 per person per hour and rides around the island on a "train" for $3 per person. On my last visit, he was building a miniature golf course on the property.

Hotel Contadora (tel. 214-3710 or 214-3720, fax 264-1178 in Panama City for reservations, tel. 250-4033, fax 250-4038 on Contadora, reservas@hotelcontadora.com, www.hotelcontadora.com, $110/$160 s/d including all meals, use of

in a 22-foot Seabird with a 115 hp motor or $250/$500 half day/full day in a 30-foot Uniflight with a 450 hp motor.

The **Aquatic Sport Center** (tel. 250-4033) at the Hotel Contadora offers boat tours for $30 per person. Personal-watercraft tours of three of the nearby islands are $55 per person.

Those who want to explore the island with minimum exertion can rent mopeds for $15/hour or four-wheelers for $20/hour at a stand next to Hotel Galeón.

Dive operators come and go on Contadora, and it's hard to tell if there'll be any when you visit or how good they'll be.

Accommodations

Lodging options have traditionally been limited on Contadora, but things have begun to pick up in recent years. Campers can also pitch a tent on any beach for free.

The French couple that owns Las Perlas Sailing also rents four plain **studio apartments** (tel. 250-

sports equipment, and local liquor) is a worn behemoth of a place on Playa Larga that's not much loved by discriminating locals. It was already feeling its age when I first stayed there in the mid-1980s, and these days most of its clientele consists of large tour groups flown in from overseas. The 354 rooms are scattered among two-story motel-like buildings out of keeping with the tropical ambience. The rooms are aging and some smell of mildew and have worn-out beds; try several. The single rooms are quite small. The place has been notorious for years for such unpleasant surprises as running out of water. On my last visit, dead, fumigated roaches were lying about the grounds.

The hotel offers only all-inclusive packages, which means guests are stuck eating its substandard food. There's a nine-hole golf course, a swimming pool, and tennis and volleyball courts. Special deals are often available.

N Hotel Punta Galeón (tel. 214-3710 or 214-3720, fax 214-3721 Panama City reservations, tel. 250-4134, fax 250-4135 on Contadora, reservas@puntagaleon.com, www.punta galeon.com, $114/$166 s/d, including breakfast) is the best place to stay on the island. It has a lovely location on a low rocky bluff above Playa Galeón, next to a pretty but overbuilt beach. Rooms are in a series of white-washed one-story buildings topped with thatch (purely for aesthetics—they're not real thatch roofs) and perched on the edge of the point. Rooms are simple but cheerful, modern, and attractive. All are air-conditioned and have small TVs and minibars. The whole place is ringed by an elaborate boardwalk that offers lovely views of the deep-blue ocean and nearby islands. Stairs lead to the rocky surf, but it's too rough for safe swimming here. Walk to the beach next to the point instead. There's an attractive swimming pool surrounded by a patio on the premises.

Food

Contadora is not known for good restaurants. What's worse, diners have to pay quite a bit even for mediocre food, since everything has to be brought over from the mainland. All the places to eat on the island at the time of writing are listed below, roughly in order of their distance from

the airstrip, with the closest first. Gerald's and Restaurante Romántico are the best bets for getting a decent meal. There are also two grocery stores near the airstrip. This is a good place to arrive with lots of snacks stashed in the luggage.

Fonda Sagitario (6:30 A.M.–8:30 P.M. daily), near the police station, is a basic but clean locals' hangout that serves simple food at cheap prices. A plus for those into fishing is the place will cook your catch for $5–6.

The food at the restaurant attached to **Punta Galeón** (tel. 250-4134) is mediocre and generates lots of complaints. Prices are in the $6.50–14.50 range. It's open for breakfast, lunch, and dinner.

N Restaurante-Bar Gerald's (cell 654-1804, noon–3 P.M. and 6–11 P.M. or so daily), in a large, attractive *rancho* on a hill just above the Hotel Contadora, mainly offers seafood and the occasional German dish, such as bratwurst with real German mustard. Prices range $8–22. The food's pretty good, though the chef is too fond of salt.

The poor quality of the food at the **Hotel Contadora** (tel. 250-4033, 7–9:30 A.M. breakfast, 12:30–2:30 P.M. lunch, 7–9:30 P.M. dinner) has long been a source of grumbling. There's an open-air dining area next to the main dining room that at least has a breeze and a view of the nearby surf. Meals are included with a hotel stay. Though it's unclear why they'd want to, nonguests can eat from the buffet for $8 for breakfast and $15 for lunch or dinner.

N Restaurante Romántico, (tel. 250-4067, 8–10 A.M. breakfast, 11 A.M.–2 P.M. lunch, 6–10 P.M. dinner daily) the restaurant attached to Villa Romántica, offers expensive food in a good location: It's an open-air place right above a pretty beach that's likely to be deserted when you visit. It's known for its "hot rock" shtick, in which you're given a piece of meat and a hot plate to grill it on. This is allegedly romantic, which may be why you're expected to pay $19–22 for a meal you cook yourself. Other offerings include prawns, shrimp, and various meat and fish dishes. The seafood is good, but fare here tends to be a little heavy and rich. The kitchen is run by a German-trained cook who used to work at Rincón Suizo, one of Panama

City's better restaurants. This place is a bit of a hike from the main hotels.

Services

There are few services of any kind on Contadora. Hotel Punta Galeón has a minimall with a series of small shops carrying souvenirs, liquor, and necessities. It's open 9 A.M.–1 P.M. daily. Next to it is a playground with a nifty tree house in a huge old tree.

Getting There and Away

Aeroperlas (tel. 315-7500, fax 315-7580, in Panama City, 250-4026 on Contadora, info@aeroperlas.com, www.aeroperlas.com) flies between Panama City and Contadora at 8:45 A.M. and 5 P.M. Monday–Friday, at 8:50 A.M., 9:45 A.M., and 5 P.M. on Saturday, and 8:50 A.M., 3:30 P.M., 4:40 P.M., and 5:30 P.M. on Sunday.

Return flights are at 9:10 A.M. and 4:25 P.M. Monday–Friday, 9:15 A.M. and 4:25 P.M. Saturday, and 9:15 A.M., 4:15 P.M., 5:50 P.M., and 6:10 P.M. on Sunday. That's the theory, anyway. Aeroperlas flights are never that exact, however, so double-check flight times and arrive early.

Turismo Aéreo (tel. 315-0279 or 315-0300, fax 315-0278 in Panama City) flies to Contadora at 9 A.M. Monday–Saturday and 4:30 P.M. Friday and Sunday. Return flights are a half hour later.

The fare is $29.40/$58.80 one-way/round-trip on either airline. The flight takes 15-20 minutes.

Commercial boat service to Contadora is occasionally offered, especially during the dry season, but don't count on it. New services pop up and disappear overnight. Those who'd rather not fool with the flight can contact Expreso del Pacifico (tel. 261-0350 or 229-1742) to see if it's restarted its Contadora service. However, after taking one wild ride with this outfit over to Isla Taboga, on a boat sorely lacking in life jackets, I would be reluctant to make the much longer trip over to Contadora this way. It's your call whether you think a small plane is safer.

ISLA SAN JOSÉ

This remote, 44-square-kilometer private island, the second-largest in the archipelago, saw few visitors before the opening of the 14-cabaña **Hacienda del Mar** (tel. 269-6634 or 269-6613, fax 264-1787 in Panama, U.S. tel. 866/433-5627, U.S. fax 305/233-9933, info@haciendadelmar.net, www.haciendadelmar.net, $363 for up to four people, including breakfast) a few years back. It's easily the most exclusive place to stay in the archipelago.

The cabañas look rather rustic from the outside, with their cane walls and red zinc roofs. But inside they're quite modern and feature air-conditioning, hot-water bathrooms, ceiling fans, and balconies. The resort's "clubhouse" has a sports bar with satellite TV, pool table, sauna, and so on. It leads out to an attractive swimming pool. All this is on the southeast side of the island, perched above a sandy beach.

Possible activities at Hacienda del Mar include hikes or ATV tours through the island's forests, snorkeling and scuba diving, mountain biking, water-skiing, banana boat rides, and airplane tours of the islands. All of these activities are extra, ranging from $10 per person for a banana boat ride to $180 per person for a half-day scuba-diving tour including equipment for certified divers (dive master is an extra charge). Boats can be chartered for inshore and deep-sea fishing trips for $320 for a half day and up to six people. There's an extensive trail system through the island's forests, which are home to white brocket deer, peccaries, iguanas, anteaters, and other wildlife.

Most guests arrive by plane from Panama City, 90 kilometers away. A boat ride over from Panama City would take about two hours, but there's no commercial service to the island.

Turismo Aéreo (tel. 315-0279 or 315-0300, fax 315-0278 in Panama City) flies to Isla San José at 9 A.M. on Tuesday, Thursday, and Saturday and 4:50 P.M. on Friday and Sunday. The flight takes 20–30 minutes. Return flights leave as soon as the plane is ready on the same days. Note there's sometimes an intermediate stop. The resort can handle the plane reservations. The fare is $30/$60 one-way/round-trip.

Beautiful as Isla San José is, it has a less than peaceful history. During and immediately after World War II, the United States, with support from Canada and Great Britain, dropped or detonated thousands of chemical weapons on the island to test their use in tropical warfare, according to a 2002 article in *Bulletin of the Atomic Scientists.* A 2001 inspection team found several unexploded chemical bombs on the island. The Panamanian government temporarily placed the island in quarantine, but a more thorough inspection to search for other weapons has not taken place. A conflict between the United States and Panama over who should pay for the inspection and possible clean up had not been resolved as this book went to press.

Resort management says all these weapons tests took place many kilometers from Hacienda del Mar. I have heard no reports of guests being harmed in any way.

OTHER ISLANDS

The islands listed below are just a sampling of what else the archipelago has to offer. However, most of the islands are not easily accessible. There's no commercial air or ferry service among the islands. Most visitors use Contadora or San José as a base to explore the nearest islands on a boat tour.

Pacheca, immediately north of Contadora, is also known as Isla de Los Pájaros (Bird Island) because it's a sanctuary for magnificent frigate birds, brown pelicans, and cormorants, among other seabirds. **Mogo Mogo,** less than five kilometers south of Contadora, is a picturesque island with nice beaches. The one time I snorkeled here there wasn't much to see, but supposedly there are extensive coral fields off a part of the island I didn't visit. **Casaya,** about three kilometers farther south, still has a small village of pearl divers. One can shop for pearls here, but don't expect any great treasures; those days are long over. **Isla del Rey** is, at nearly 240 square kilometers, the giant of the islands. To its south is **San Telmo,** a private nature reserve owned by the nonprofit environmental group ANCON. It's home to a large brown pelican colony as well as to boobies, cormorants, magnificent frigate birds, and endangered moist premontane forest. A Japanese submarine, abandoned during World War II, still lies grounded on one of its beaches. As this was written, plans to open up San Telmo to ecotourism were on hold. If you're interested in visiting, contact ANCON or Ancon Expeditions to find out if that's changed.

The Azuero Peninsula

The Azuero Peninsula is a paradoxical place. It's a heavily settled, terribly deforested land where wilderness has largely been supplanted by farms. In some places erosion has transformed forest into wasteland. Yet it still feels isolated from modern Panama, frozen in an idyllic past, and there's lots of charm and natural beauty left. It's a land both much beloved and much abused.

The Azuero is inevitably called Panama's "heartland," a designation that tends to exclude the country's widely scattered indigenous populations, not to mention, for instance, those of African descent. If asked, many of these peoples would say their hearts belong to other parts of Panama.

Still, the peninsula occupies an important, almost mythological, place in the Panamanian psyche. It is the wellspring of Panama's favorite folkloric traditions, many of which originated in Spain but have taken on a uniquely Panamanian form—often thanks, ironically enough, to borrowings from the above-mentioned indigenous and African peoples.

Beautiful traditional clothing, such as the stun-

Must-Sees

M La Catedral de San Juan Bautista: Chitré's cathedral, at the heart of this cozy provincial town, has an understated elegance that's rare in Panama (page 285).

M Museo de Herrera: Housed in a quaint Spanish-colonial building in Chitré, this little museum attempts to document the history of the central provinces from 2400 B.C. to the present (page 285).

M La Arena: An entire town devoted to making ceramics with pre-Colombian designs that are eternally popular around the country (page 286).

M Parita: Visiting this immaculately preserved Spanish-colonial town is like stepping through a time portal to the Azuero of a hundred years ago (page 287).

Parita is a Spanish-colonial town that time forgot.

M Iglesia de San Atanasio: Notable for its ornate, 18th-century interior, this church is the best-preserved bit of the historically important town of La Villa de Los Santos (page 296).

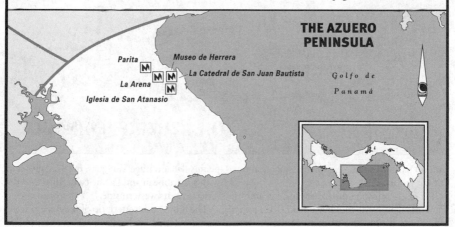

THE AZUERO PENINSULA

Parita
Museo de Herrera
La Catedral de San Juan Bautista
La Arena
Iglesia de San Atanasio
Golfo de Panamá

ning *pollera,* and handicrafts, such as ceramics based on pre-Colombian designs, originated and are still made on the Azuero. The same is true of some important musical and literary traditions. Even Panama's national drink, the sugarcane liquor known as *seco,* is made here. Traces of Spanish-colonial Panama—rows of houses with red-tile roofs and ornate ironwork, centuries-old churches overlooking quiet plazas—are easy to

find, especially in well-preserved little towns such as Parita and Pedasí.

Most of all, the Azuero is known for its festivals. It has the biggest and best in the country, from all-night bacchanals to sober religious rituals. At the top of the heap is Carnaval, held during the four days leading up to Ash Wednesday. No Latin American country outside of Brazil is more passionate about Carnaval than Panama,

THE AZUERO PENINSULA

and no part of Panama is more passionate about it than the Azuero.

For all the affection the Azuero inspires among Panamanians, most who live outside the peninsula know it only as a place to come for festivals. It usually flies below the radar of foreign visitors altogether. But those who want a taste of an older, more stately Panama should consider a visit. In some places, it's as though the 20th century never happened.

The Azuero is large enough to be shared by three provinces. The nearly landlocked Herrera province, Panama's smallest, is to the north; Los Santos to the southeast has an extensive coastline ringing the eastern and southern sides of the

peninsula; and huge Veraguas, the only province with a Caribbean and Pacific coast, dips into the Azuero on its western side.

The hilly southwestern tip of the Azuero is the least developed, with a few patches of unspoiled wilderness left. These are extremely hard to get to, which is why they're still lovely. The accessible lowland areas are now mostly farm country.

Slash-and-burn agriculture and logging have been more extensive in the Azuero than in any other part of Panama, and the inevitable result has been both dramatic and sad. Deforestation has turned some parts of this region into barren desert.

The east coast of the Azuero, as well as a strip of coast in Coclé province to the north, is known as the *arco seco* (dry arc), because of its lack of rainfall. While good news for sunbathers, that scarcity is bad news for the environment, showing the effects of creeping desertification.

The east-coast beaches resemble those within a couple of hours of Panama City, minus 30 years of development. They're easy to get to—in some cases, visitors can drive on good roads right up to the beach—yet for dozens of kilometers at a stretch there's little sign of human habitation. No condo towers here. At least, not yet.

As with the beaches closer to Panama City, don't expect pure white sand. In fact, the beaches here tend to be even darker. But those who don't mind brown, gray, and in some cases black sand will have no trouble finding a deserted seaside paradise. The beaches are wide and long, often backed by rugged cliffs and facing rolling surf. Their waters are filled with big fish and, in some places, extensive coral. Isla Cañas, off the south coast of the Azuero, is the most important nesting spot for sea turtles on Panama's Pacific coast: Tens of thousands lay their eggs there each year.

The interior of the peninsula is taken up mostly by farmland, cattle pasture, and towns. There are few facilities for visitors, but visiting this heart of the "heartland" is like stepping back in time.

PLANNING YOUR TIME

It's possible to explore the biggest towns of the Azuero—**Chitré** and **Las Tablas**—and their surrounding attractions in a couple of days. It's a straight shot, for instance, to pull off the road for a quick look at **Parita,** shop for pottery in **La Arena,** visit **La Catedral de San Juan Bautista** and **El Museo de Herrera** in Chitré, then pop by La Villa de Los Santos before ending up in Las Tablas for the night. All that can be done in a day for those with their own transportation. Those relying on buses and taxis, however, should plan on spending at least two days in the area, probably making Chitré home base for excursions to the surrounding area. And those who arrive during festival times should probably plan to stay longer than that, as many of the festivals are several days long. The biggest

Carnaval celebration is in Las Tablas; Chitré runs a close second. Try to allow time before or after any festival to shop or visit museums, as just about everything shuts down during big celebrations. Add at least one more day to visit more remote destinations, especially along the coast, where you'll want time to enjoy the beach. Be sure to make time for a quick visit to the historic town of **Parita.**

Nearly the entire Azuero is well served by buses. Bus service between the peninsula and other parts of Panama is also good. Buses run constantly, for instance, to and from Panama City and Chitré and Las Tablas.

Las Tablas and Chitré are the major transportation hubs on the Azuero. They can be used as bases for exploring the east coast of the peninsula, but those looking for good beaches should head all the way down to **Pedasí,** near the southeast tip of the Azuero. It's a quiet, peaceful, and colorful little town that makes a great springboard for exploring a number of nearby bathing and surfing beaches, and a major sea-turtle nesting spot.

To drive to the Azuero Peninsula from Panama City, head west on the Interamerican Highway until Divisa, which is little more than a crossroads. Divisa is about 215 kilometers from Panama City, a drive that takes around three hours. Make a left at the fork, which heads down to the peninsula (straight leads to the city of Santiago and from there to western Panama).

Most of the notable towns in the Azuero are on a single main road, an ambitiously named *carretera nacional* (national highway) that runs down the east coast of the peninsula. The stretch of road from Divisa all the way to Pedasí is about 100 kilometers long and takes a little under two hours to drive.

The interior of the peninsula has a confusing network of roads of various quality. But a closer look reveals reasonably well-maintained loops that link up the towns of most interest to travelers. These are also served by buses. The largest of the loops connects Chitré, Las Tablas, Pedasí, Tonosí, and Macaracas before linking back up with Chitré. This route and others are detailed elsewhere in the chapter.

HISTORY

The Azuero Peninsula has an incredibly ancient history. Evidence of an 11,000-year-old fishing settlement, the earliest sign of human habitation in all of Panama, has been found in what is now Parque Nacional Sarigua. Ceramics found around Monagrillo date to at least 2800 B.C., possibly much earlier. It's the oldest known pottery in all of Latin America.

Excavations taking place right now at Cerro Juan Díaz, near La Villa de Los Santos, indicate the site was used as a burial and ceremonial ground off and on for 1,800 years, from 200 B.C. until the arrival of the Spanish brought a bloody end to the indigenous civilizations.

THE PEOPLE AND CUSTOMS OF THE AZUERO

The people of the Azuero are among the friendliest in Panama, and the percentage of smiles per capita seems to go up the farther south you head. People seem not just content but genuinely happy. It'll probably rub off on you.

This is a region of farmers, cattle ranchers, and, on the coast, fishermen. It's hard to picture the wilderness that once existed in this now nearly tamed pastoral land. Residents of Los Santos province are especially well-known for their tree-chopping prowess. Having cut down most of the trees in their own province, *santeño* farmers and cattle ranchers have spread out to deforest other parts of the country, including, most sadly of all, the forests of the Darién.

No part of Panama is as devoted to big, spectacular events as the Azuero. It's rare for a single week to go by without some festival, fair, holy day, or other excuse for a major party somewhere on the peninsula.

Carnaval is celebrated throughout the country, but those who can get away try to come to the Azuero during those four days of partying. The Carnaval celebration held in the town of Las Tablas, in the southeastern Azuero, is the most famous in the country. For those who don't mind a madhouse, this is the place to be. Smaller but no less enthusiastic Carnaval celebrations are held in other towns and villages throughout the peninsula.

Another big event is the Festival de Corpus Christi, which takes over the tiny town of La Villa de Los Santos for two weeks between May and July every year. Ostensibly an allegory about the triumph of Christ over evil, it's most notable for its myriad dances, especially those featuring revelers in fiendishly elaborate devil costumes. Then there's the Festival Nacional de la Mejorana, Panama's largest folkloric festival, which takes over the sleepy town of Guararé each September. It draws performers and spectators from around the country.

That's just for starters. Los Santos alone has more religious festivals than any other province in the country.

Dates for some of these festivals change yearly. IPAT, Panama's government tourism institute, publishes updated lists of festival dates and details each year. Check with IPAT in Panama City or any of the several government tourist offices scattered throughout the Azuero. This is one part of the country IPAT does a decent job of covering, especially when it comes to the parties.

It sometimes feels as though the entire peninsula is dedicated to preserving the past, at least symbolically. This includes maintaining the charming but definitely antiquated custom of the *junta de embarre* (rough translation: "the mudding meeting"), in which neighbors gather to build a rustic mud home for newlyweds. Miniature versions of these are sometimes made during folkloric events. Some tradition-minded music festivals go so far as to ban, by town decree, the use of newfangled instruments—such as the six-string classical guitar.

As is so often the case in Panama, it's easy to drive right by a quaint town that time forgot without noticing it. That's because the part of the town abutting the main road is often quite ugly and industrial. It's worth pulling off the highway from time to time to explore the older part of the towns, which are set back from the road. The best bet for finding a slice of colonial quaintness is to head for the town church and check out the buildings set around its plaza.

Just how complete that victory was can be seen in the modern-day residents of the Azuero. They are by and large the most Spanish-looking people in Panama, with lighter skin and eyes than residents of most other parts of the country.

The Azuero has continued to play an important role in the history of the country in the modern era. On November 10, 1821, for instance, residents of the little town of La Villa de Los Santos wrote a letter to Simón Bolívar asking to join in his revolution against the Spanish. This *primer grito de la independencia* (first cry for independence) is still commemorated today. It was the first step in Panama's independence from Spain and union with Colombia.

Chitré

The provincial capital of Herrera province, Chitré (pop. 7,756 in town, 42,467 in district; pronounced sort of like chee-TRAY) is one of the largest towns on the peninsula. The other is Las Tablas, which usually gets more attention but can't compete with Chitré in charm. By Panamanian scale, both qualify as "cities."

This is a mellow place that's clinging to its Spanish-colonial past. The high-curbed streets are still lined with row houses that have red-tile roofs and ornate iron window screens. Each house is tiny and melds seamlessly with its neighbors. Life is lived and observed in the front rooms and porches of these modest homes, which overlook the streets.

Many men wear traditional straw hats, without affectation, as they go about their daily business. On dry-season evenings, people still gather in the town plazas to sit and enjoy the breeze.

The town was founded October 19, 1848, though according to some historians it was first settled by the conquistadors in 1558, which would make it one of the oldest surviving towns on the isthmus.

There isn't much to see in Chitré beyond its attractive cathedral and small museum. But it's a pleasant place to do some people-watching and get a sense of life on the Azuero. It's also a good base for exploring the surrounding area, including the well-preserved Spanish-colonial town of Parita, the pottery shops of neighboring La Arena, and three unusual natural attractions. Villa de Los Santos is just four kilometers south, which makes this a convenient place to stay during that town's Festival de Corpus Christi and other big events.

For those coming from the north, the main road into Chitré starts at the little town of La Arena, about two kilometers west of Chitré. The road forks here.

To get to downtown Chitré, keep going straight. The road will lead through La Arena into Chitré, where it becomes Paseo Enrique Geenzier, the main west-east promenade, before morphing into Calle Manuel María Correa near the cathedral downtown.

The right fork circumvents downtown and heads toward Los Santos province. This is the more direct route to Chitré's IPAT information center, Hotel Barceló Guayacanes, the bus terminal, and Restaurante DKDA's. They are all on Calle 19 de Octubre (also called Avenida Roberto Ramírez de Diego) before the road links up again with the main road leading south toward Villa de Los Santos and Las Tablas.

The cathedral is at the heart of downtown Chitré, and most of the town's hotels, restaurants, and services are within a few blocks of it.

Avenida Herrera cuts across town from north to south. It starts near the ocean, at Playa El Agallito, then runs down past the airport and the east side of Chitré's cathedral. Several of the cheaper places to stay are on this avenue, near the cathedral.

SIGHTS

Sightseers can take in Chitré's few landmarks in a couple of hours. The best way to do this is on foot, if the heat's bearable. Soaking up the street life on the way is at least as interesting as seeing the landmarks.

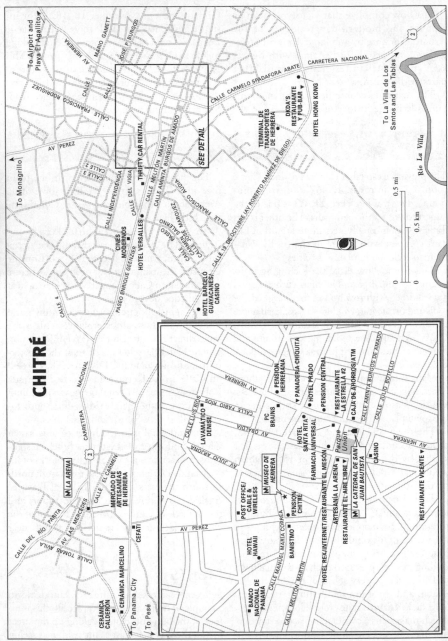

CHITRÉ

© BONNIE KAY SPINDLER

The Azuero Peninsula

Panama hats for sale on the streets of Chitré

To get a quick overview of Chitré, start at the cathedral, then head west past Parque Union (the church plaza) on Calle Melitón Martín. Turn right on Avenida Julio Arjona and walk north one block, to the Museo de Herrera. After visiting the museum, head east down Calle Manuel María Correa, a busy shopping street. Finish the tour by wandering up and down Avenida Herrera, another shopping street. There may be a vendor or two selling Panama hats here. The tour ends back at the cathedral. That's pretty much downtown Chitré.

The ceramic shops of La Arena, the historic towns of Monagrillo and Parita, and the natural attractions of Playa El Agallito, Parque Nacional Sarigua, and the Refugio de Vida Silvestre Cenegón del Mangle are all outside of Chitré. They're accessible by car or bus.

La Catedral de San Juan Bautista

Chitré's cathedral was built between 1896 and 1910 on the site of an earlier church. With its tall twin towers, it's an easily spotted landmark. Inside, it's most notable for what it lacks: overwrought decorations. Instead, it makes tasteful, restrained use of dark woods, gold trim, attractive frescos, and stained glass. An arched ceiling made from thick beams, some of them hand-hewn, gives the cathedral a cozy feel.

Museo de Herrera

Chitré's museum is housed in a lovingly preserved Spanish colonial building (Calle Manuel María Correa and Avenida Julio Arjona, tel. 996-0077, 8 A.M.–noon and 1–4 P.M. Tues.–Sat., 8–11 A.M. Sun., closed Mon., $1 adults, $.25 children). The collection downstairs is devoted to archaeological finds from all around the central provinces, including stone tools from Monagrillo dating 2400–1000 B.C. Be sure to check out the collection of ancient ceramics. Local artisans are still inspired by the same designs the indigenous peoples used more than 1,500 years ago. In the middle of the ground floor is a recreation of the burial site of an Indian *cacique* (chief) found by the Spanish in 1517, including exact replicas of beautifully wrought gold jewelry, made by the Reprosa jewelry company in Panama City. The displays upstairs are devoted to the history of Herrera Province, from Spanish times to the modern era, represented by a signed baseball and Chicago White Sox cap donated by major-leaguer

Chitré's little Museo de Herrera is one of the better museums in the country.

water. These are used as decorative items all over Panama. One of the country's most famous painters, Sheila Lichacz, has made a career out of her pastel images of and montages using these *tinajas,* which fascinate her. She was born in nearby Monagrillo. When she was a child she'd swim in the river on her family's ranch and accidentally kick up shards from broken pots that dated back 500 years or more.

The oldest designs made in La Arena are based on pre-Colombian patterns, mostly abstract, painted in earth tones on the reddish-brown piece. More modern designs start with these patterns but incorporate bright colors, glazes, and representational images, and these have become popular in recent years. It can now be difficult to find more traditional pieces. The factories are constantly trying new designs. After a little comparison shopping it's easy to spot the distinctive style of each *taller* (workshop/factory).

La Arena is also known for its bread, though remember what's called good bread in Panama is usually what other countries call "hotdog buns." Stop by one of the bakeries if you're peckish, but don't get hopes up too high.

© BONNIE KAY SPINDLER

Olmedo Sáenz, who is from Chitré. Other exhibits include devil masks, *polleras,* and traditional musical instruments from the area. There's a diorama outside depicting a traditional local kitchen garden and sugarcane press. As small and simple as this museum is, it's one of the better ones in the country.

La Arena

This town two kilometers west of Chitré could be renamed Ceramics City. All along the main street that passes through the little town (pop. 6,429), which is practically a suburb of Chitré, are small shops selling the pottery this area is famous for throughout Panama. These include pots, mugs, ashtrays, plates, vases, pitchers, and so on. Entire tableware sets are sometimes available (see *Shopping.*)

The pottery is based on designs created by the indigenous residents of this area thousands of years ago. The most traditional piece is the *tinaja,* or pot, that was once used to store household

Monagrillo

One of the most ancient known inhabited spots on the isthmus can be reached from Chitré by heading north on Avenida Pérez two kilometers from where it intersects Paseo Enrique Geenzier. Avenida Pérez runs past the Cable and Wireless office; look for the tall communications towers. Ceramics found in this area date from at least 2500 B.C., the oldest found in Central America and among the oldest anywhere in the Americas. There are no archaeological displays or other traces of that ancient history, but those with spare time who just like the idea of being near that much history should consider a quick drive-through. The town (pop. 9,549) does have a quaint little church with some well-preserved old homes with red-tile roofs. It's similar to Parita, though not quite as scenic. The taxi ride from Chitré will cost at most $1. Buses also make the run between Monagrillo and Chitré, and if it's not too hot you can even walk it.

Parita

This amazingly well-preserved Spanish colonial town is 10 kilometers northwest of Chitré. As you drive up from Chitré, the turnoff is on the left at a gas station.

There's nothing much to do here but walk around and take photos, but Parita hints at what towns in the Azuero must have been like in olden days. It's also home to a nationally famous devil-mask maker (see *Shopping.*)

Parita was founded in 1556 as Santa Elena and was later renamed. The town church, **Iglesia Santo Domingo de Guzmán,** was built a century later. It's a simple but attractive church filled with ornately carved woodwork. It's worth a quick visit. A little museum in the back that houses silver ceremonial pieces and other artifacts from the Spanish era was closed during a lengthy renovation of the church, but the town was trying to get it reopened during my last visit.

The townspeople live adjacent to each other in narrow, block-long buildings with red-tile roofs set around the plaza and church. The pride residents take in the place is evident in the spotless streets and the riot of flowering plants that cover the whole front of some buildings. It's a supremely mellow place, and so removed from the flow of modern life that many Panamanians don't even know it exists.

Parque Nacional Sarigua

An 8,000-hectare national park (tel. 996-7679 in Chitré, no local phone, open 8 A.M.–4 P.M. daily, entrance fee $3) established in 1985, Sarigua stretches east toward the coast and out to sea. It's 10 kilometers northwest of Chitré, near Parita.

Sarigua was the site of a fishing settlement an astonishing 11,000 years ago. That's the oldest trace of human habitation on the entire isthmus. It was also home to the country's oldest known farming community, which tilled the land here up until about 1,500 years ago.

That long history makes one all the sadder to realize what modern humans have done to this area in just a few decades in the 20th century. Sometimes tourist officials try to bill this place as a desert. That misses the point entirely. It's not a desert: It's a wasteland. It's a vivid, horrifying example of just what deforestation in the tropics can look like. This area used to be covered by species-rich mangroves and dry coastal forest. They were chopped and burned away. Strong winds blow

© WILLIAM FRIAR

Parita's church, Iglesia Santo Domingo de Guzmán, dates from the 17th century.

The Azuero Peninsula

© BONNIE KAY SPINDLER

campesino and dog near Parita

here in the dry season; without the buffer of the mangroves, the wind blew sand inland, hastening the deforestation.

The average temperature now is around 36°C, far above the norm for the surrounding areas that still have vegetation, and it can get even hotter. The area gets less than a meter of rain yearly, a fraction of the precipitation in other parts of the Pacific coast. Note the garbage sticking out of the mounds around the ranger station; Parita used the area as a dump before 1980.

There's a mirador near the station visitors can climb to get a good view of the sweeping nothingness. The ranger will probably come up and give a little lecture; he may speak a little English.

It's possible to drive around here even when the ranger station is closed, but it's not a good idea to come by in the late afternoon in any case. It's too hot. Visitors can drive only about two kilometers into the park. After that there's a private shrimp farm that's not open to the public.

To get to the park from Chitré, head northwest on the main road toward Parita for about 10 kilometers. Turn right before Parita at the large park sign. After about three kilometers, turn left onto the dirt road and follow some more signs into the park.

Refugio de Vida Silvestre Cenegón del Mangle

Cenegón del Mangle is a 776-hectare wildlife refuge that's worth a quick visit on the way to or from Chitré or Las Tablas. There's no admission fee or set opening hours. It's best to go in a four-wheel-drive vehicle.

The part that's accessible to visitors consists of a half-kilometer-long boardwalk that loops through tall black mangroves near the shore. It makes for a short, scenic walk that's halfway between spooky and pretty, since it's easy to imagine all kinds of creatures in the mangroves and the murky marsh below one's feet.

This is a major heron hangout. In fact, some of the herons that grace the fountain in the Palacio de las Garzas ("palace of the herons"), the presidential palace in Panama City, are captured here. The area attracts what birders call "mixed colonies" of herons, including the great egret, tricolored heron, and cattle egret.

It's also easy to spot caimans here, especially when some of herons nest, from June to September. The toothy critters wait patiently under the nests, like dogs by the dinner table, in hopes the odd egg will fall from a nest and into the marsh. Yum. Also be on the lookout for iguanas and the occasional crocodile. Herons can be spotted here year-round.

Access to the refuge is from the village of París, the turnoff to which is at a gas station seven kilometers north of Parita. If you're heading up from Chitré, which is 17 kilometers southeast of París, the turnoff is to the right. There's no sign marking the turn from this direction. París is one kilometer down this road.

Once in París, which won't remind you of the one in France, take the right fork when the road splits at the church. Then make a right turn 0.3 kilometer past this fork onto a road that quickly turns to dirt. Go six kilometers, until the road forks at the none-too-scenic garbage dump.

The left fork leads to the mangroves. Park just past the dump. There'll be a dirt trail on the left. Follow this to the boardwalk, about a five-minute walk away. This area is parched in the dry season, but even then there are plenty of marshy areas as one gets closer to the shore.

If you have trouble finding all this, ask around back in París. A local kid will probably hop in your car and show the way for a quarter or two.

The right fork back at the dump, by the way, leads to some so-called thermal pools said to have medicinal properties. These consist of shallow, foot-wide puddles with nasty-looking stagnant water. They look like boils on the face of a sunbaked patch of earth. To say this is easily skipped is a wild understatement.

It takes about 45 minutes to drive to the refuge from Chitré.

Playa El Agallito

This is not a bathing beach, though the municipality has made a halfhearted attempt to dress it up as one, with a crumbling archway at its entrance and a modest recreational area near the water. Rather, it consists of mudflats that lead into mangroves. This becomes obvious at low tide, when the muck stretches nearly two kilometers out into the distance. The mudflats are so extensive and the tide so great (six meters), one can literally see the tide coming in and out. When it's in, there's no beach at all—the water comes right up to the road.

The beach, such as it is, is artificial. It dates from 1967, when the residents of Chitré

Darío López is nationally famous for his fearsome *diablicos* (devil masks).

BIG CHALLENGES FOR A LITTLE BIRD

I n 1980, biologist Francisco Delgado, a Chitré native who studied in Leningrad, in the former Soviet Union, began coming out to the beach at low tide to band the legs of western sandpipers (*Calidris mauri*), a palm-sized, rather nondescript gray shorebird with long legs and beak.
He and his assistants band 30 birds a day; early risers can often spot the researchers wading out
in the shallow waters. Next to the beach is the ecological station he runs, Estación Ecologica Alejandro von Humboldt, housed in a modest cinderblock building. Driving towards Playa El Agallito, it's on the left as the road ends.

The western sandpiper's home turf and breeding ground is western Alaska and northeastern
Siberia. There are an estimated 3.6 million western sandpipers, which makes them the most populous shorebird along the Pacific coast of North America.

In the fall, they begin their southern migration. It's an amazing journey. The little birds can
fly 20 days without a stopover of more than a few hours in a few key spots, including British Co-
lumbia and the San Francisco Bay. And they travel enormous distances: These Arctic dwellers
have been found as far south as Chile.

An unbelievable number make their way to Panama's Pacific coast, where they spend the winter or just stop briefly on their way to South America: Bird-watchers have been stunned to
watch throngs of literally hundreds of thousands of them at a time, especially around eastern
Panama Bay.

Many of them, not surprisingly, like to spend the winter in Panama. What's more surprising
is something else researchers are finding out about their migrations. To say they're creatures of
habit is putting it mildly: Year after year, the birds come back to the same spot.

This is true on the larger scale—western sandpipers that winter in Panama, for instance, always go to Panama; those that winter in Peru always go to Peru. But Delgado has found that the
same holds true on a very much smaller scale. The same birds don't just come back to Playa El
Agallito each year; they come back to the same part of the beach. If they're chased away by a
predator such as a falcon, they'll return in a few minutes. Delgado has tracked two birds that have
come back to the exact same spot for 10 years.

One theory of why the birds are so wedded to such a seemingly rigid migration pattern is that,

---

decided they wanted a town beach and cut down mangroves to create one. The main reason to come out here is to watch the impressive bird life. Playa El Agallito attracts 35 species of shorebirds, including sandpipers, black-bellied plovers, willets, whimbrels, American oystercatchers, yellowlegs, ospreys, and warblers. Most of all, it attracts western sandpipers. (See the sidebar, *Big Challenges for a Little Bird.*) The sight of large flocks of these little birds swooping low over the water is impressive even to those not normally taken with our feathered friends.

To get to Playa El Agallito from downtown Chitré, head north on Avenida Herrera for six kilometers past the cathedral, until it ends at the beach.

ENTERTAINMENT AND EVENTS

The **Carnaval** celebration in Chitré is the biggest in the Azuero after Las Tablas. As usual, it takes place in the four days leading up to Ash Wednesday. (To get a sense of what's in store for would-be Carnavalites, see the *Las Tablas* entry.)

The town celebrates two events tied to its origins. The first is **October 19,** the day on which the district of Chitré was founded in 1848. This is cause for a big parade and festivities. The other commemorates the town's patron saint, **San Juan Bautista** (John the Baptist), on June 24. This latter celebration also dates from the 19th century, when an image of St. John was brought to town.

Nightlife when no festival takes over the town is normally very limited, consisting mainly of because their grueling transcontinental trip requires enormous stores of energy, once they touch down they need to replenish themselves urgently. Those that survive a migration have learned where food is plentiful and safe and stick with the same location year after year. If their normal stopover points and wintering grounds are damaged or destroyed, the loss could be fatal for whole populations of the little birds.

There is considerable evidence this is happening. The global population of western sandpipers dropped dramatically in the 1990s. A good part of this is likely attributable to the El Niño phenomenon. But pollution and habitat destruction is believed to play a significant role as well.

Delgado estimates that 10,000 western sandpipers come to Playa El Agallito each year, in flocks that average 300. They start showing up in late October and leave in early March. Delgado worries what will happen to them if their habitat is destroyed.

This has already happened to some extent. While the area still has mangrove forests, large tracts have been hacked away. Recently, for instance, environmentalists lost a battle with commercial interests that went on to destroy mangroves and flood shallow salt ponds to create a 600-hectacre shrimp farm. The ponds are now too deep for the sandpipers to roost or hunt for food, and the population that wintered there, who knows for how many years, has been scattered. As usual when it's sandpipers against humans, the sandpipers didn't stand a chance.

"Money is money," Delgado says.

Money is not something Delgado and his team have much of. He doesn't even have enough to patch the tattered net he uses to trap birds for banding.

Still, he has high hopes. He has mapped out plans for a **Centro de Interpretaciones de Recursos Marinos y Costeros,** an interpretive center at Playa El Agallito he hopes will attract the public and teach it more about the natural beauty around them and the need to preserve it. Among other things, he'd like it to have a seawater aquarium with a coral reef and many displays for children. He also has one particularly spooky display in mind: the skull of a huge crocodile that killed a friend of his. He's in the process of trying to get government approval and funding for the center. Those interested in finding more about Delgado's work can email him at delgadofrancisco2410@yahoo.com or call him in Chitré at tel. 996-1725.

---

some grimy bars. There's a large **casino** at the Hotel Barceló Guayacanes and another one, ironically enough, two blocks south of the cathedral.

The **Cines Modernos** is a gringo-style multiplex complete with Hollywood blockbusters and the mall rats they attract. It's west of and across the street from Hotel Versalles on Paseo Enrique Geenzier.

The **Festival de Corpus Christi** is held in neighboring La Villa de Los Santos sometime between May and July. The dates change yearly.

SHOPPING

The best place in La Arena to get a sampling of the range of available items is at the **Mercado de Atesanías de Herrera** (8:30 A.M.–4:30 P.M.

daily), the white two-story building at the fork in the middle of town. It sells pieces from a variety of *talleres.* The prices are highly reasonable; a small pot costs less than $2.

It's also possible to stop by the workshops themselves during work hours, and this is where you can find the best pieces. The most garish pieces are often displayed outside. Don't be dissuaded by this; go in and poke around. Visitors are welcome to step back into the workshop to see the wood-burning ovens, the drying rooms, the painting workshops, and so on. **Cerámica Marcelino** (tel. 974-4801, 7:30 A.M.–6 P.M. daily) is at the west end of La Arena, where the road from Chitré meets the road from Los Santos. I especially like the work at **Cerámica Calderón** (tel. 974-4946 or 974-4157, cell 695-4195, early morning to late evening daily), a few houses closer to Chitré on the main road. Pieces here are well made, with clean designs and striking patterns. Those with the time can design their own pieces and have them made here. Proprietor and lead designer Angel Calderón and his son, also called Angel, will pull out books of photos and sketches of actual pre-Colombian ceramics, some of them museum pieces, and let you pick and choose the designs you like. It's possible to order a full, custom-made 12-piece dinner set for around $250. They deliver to Panama City, but you may have to make your own arrangements to ship the pieces out of the country. Making a set takes several weeks.

In Chitré, **Artesanía La Arena** (Calle Melitón Martín, 996-0090, 8 A.M.–6 P.M. Mon.–Sat., closed Sun.) is a little storefront a block and a half west of the cathedral that carries a fair selection of the ceramics for which the area is famous.

While in Parita, consider paying a visit to the home workshop of **Darío López** (tel. 974-2015, 7 A.M.–5 P.M. daily). He's nationally famous for his fearsome *diablicos* (devil masks), which are worn by dancers during the Corpus Christi Festival in nearby Villa de Los Santos. He's been making them for nearly 40 years, helped out in recent years by his nine children.

The large masks cost $25 and take two days to make. Don't expect to find them in stock close to Corpus Christi or other festivals, when they're much in demand, but smaller models—including ones barely big enough to mask a finger—are usually on sale for significantly less.

López's house, which is also his workshop, is back on the highway, across the street from and north of the Shell station, near Calle José Angel Bosquez B. His home is next to Kiosco Chely. Look for devil masks hanging on the front of the house.

ACCOMMODATIONS

Chitré has the biggest array of accommodations on the Azuero. These include a number of budget hotels and *hospedajes* as well as a few relatively upscale choices. Those planning to visit during Carnaval, the Corpus Christi festival, or

other big events should book several months in advance. At other times, there should be plenty of options to choose from.

$10–25

Pension Chitré (Paseo Enrique Geenzier and Avenida Perez, next to the Museo de Herrera, tel. 996-1856, $8 s, $12 d) is a basic six-room place with cold-water bathrooms. Prices during Carnaval jump up to $20 s/d. Book at least a month in advance for festivals.

Hotel Hawaii (Calle del Vigia, just off Paseo Enrique Geenzier, tel. 996-3524, $16.40 s, $23 d) is a pleasant, modernish hotel in the commercial district that offers 33 rooms with cable TV, air-conditioning, and telephones. It's clean enough. Guests can send and receive faxes for $.50 (send) and $.25 (receive) per page, plus tolls. Carnaval packages are available.

Hotel Prado (Avenida Herrera, tel. 996-6859 or 996-4620, $10/$16.80 s/d with fan, $16.80/ $22 s/d with air-conditioning) is a very simple 27-room hotel saved by a generally pleasant and friendly atmosphere. Some rooms are dark and have old, thin mattresses, while others are much cheerier and more comfortable; shop around. The place is moderately clean and has a spacious open-air lobby/restaurant/sitting area overlooking a busy street. The restaurant serves breakfast, lunch, and dinner.

The 18-room **Hotel Santa Rita** (Calle Manuel Correa near Avenida Herrera, tel. 996-4610, fax 996-2404, $11/$15.40 s/d with fan, $15.40/ $19.80 with air-conditioning) is a clean, neat, old-fashioned place with character. Rooms are dark and offer thin mattresses, tiny TVs, and cold-water bathrooms that must be shared with the room next door. That aside, the rooms are pleasant enough. Some have balconies overlooking the loud, busy commercial street below. Rates during festivals are $23.10 s/d with fan and $30.80 s/d with air-conditioning.

The centrally located **M Hotel Rex** (just north of the cathedral on Calle Melitón Martín, tel. 996-4310, 996-2408, fax 996-2391, $16.50 s, $24.20 d) has 37 bright, simple rooms with hot-water bathrooms, cable TV, and air-conditioning. The rooms on the top floor are the cheeriest.

A pleasant terrace upstairs overlooks the cathedral plaza. There's a restaurant and Internet café on the premises. The hotel offers five-day Carnaval packages; reservations must be made a month ahead of time. Though the Rex is not as fancy (or expensive) as the Barceló Guayacanes or Hotel Versalles, its location right in the heart of Chitré will appeal to those who want to soak up the local atmosphere. This is the best of the budget hotels.

$25–50

Hotel Karla (Calle Carmelo Spadafora A., tel. 996-9972 or 996-7149, $16.50 s, $27.50 d) also known as Hotel Carla, is a dark, concrete structure offering 32 plain rooms with firm mattresses, air-conditioning, and cable TV. Some are windowless. It's a clean, okay place, but for the price Hotel Rex is a better value. Attached is a rather ornate Chinese restaurant I haven't yet tried (most items $3–8), which also has an outdoors dining area with simpler and cheaper offerings.

Hotel Hong Kong (Calle Carmelo Spadafora A., tel. 996-4483 or 996-9180, $22 s, $33 d), on the southern outskirts of town, offered two kinds of rooms on my last visit: old and older. Since my last visit, however, the place has undergone a renovation and friends tell me the rooms are much improved. Even before the most recent sprucing up the place was clean and perfectly okay. There are 28 rooms in all, all with air-conditioning, cable TV, and telephones. The decor is vaguely Chinese. The hotel has a mini aquatic park—a water slide and three small pools—that's extremely popular with kids. Nonguests can use the pool area for $3 for children and $5 for adults. Rates at Carnaval and other festivals leap to $45 s/d. Those interested in staying here during that time should book by the first of January.

M Hotel Versalles (Paseo Enrique Geenzier, tel. 996-4422, 996-3133, 996-4563, or 996-8958, fax 996-2090, info@hotelversalles.com, www.hotelversalles.com, $23 s, $34 d) is a solid three-star hotel, a modern, clean, and fairly cheerful place with 60 rooms featuring good mattresses, cable TV, and air-conditioning. There's a small pool and an attractive lobby, bar, and restaurant (open 6:30 A.M.–10 P.M. daily, though it may close earlier on Sun.). Reservations for Car-

naval should be made by December or January. Its one real drawback is its isolated location on the west end of Paseo Enrique Geenzier, the main avenue that heads east into town.

At the time of writing, **Hotel Barceló Guayacanes** (Calle 19 de Octubre, tel. 996-9758, $38.50 s, $49.50 d, including welcome cocktail and full breakfast) was the fanciest place to stay in the entire Azuero Peninsula. It's a member of the Spanish Barceló chain, which is increasingly well-represented in Panama. Built in 2001, it's kind of an odd place. Rooms are in several two-story buildings set around an artificial duck pond with an artificial waterfall. The hotel has a pool that's popular with day groups, plus a restaurant, bar, large casino, and little garden in back. It started having problems, such as perpetual shortages of hot water, within its first year of opening. During my last visit, the duck pond was turning into a swamp, the infrastructure already appeared to be crumbling, and the room I stayed in was invaded by tiny ants. In spite of all that, it was still an okay place to stay. The hotel is in a sparsely populated area a short drive from downtown Chitré. It's quite insulated from its surroundings, which may not appeal to those who come to the Azuero to mix with the locals.

FOOD

The restaurant in the Hotel Barceló Guayacanes, **Restaurante Las Brisas** (tel. 996-9758), has an outdoor dining room covered by a large wooden roof held up by massive wooden pillars. There's also a fancier, air-conditioned dining room, but no one ever seems to use it. During my last visit, a souvenir shop had been built along one side of the outdoor area, blocking what had been the restaurant's best feature: a strong, pleasant breeze that gave the restaurant its name. The menu is limited—pastas in addition to the usual assortment of meats—and the dishes are hit or miss. The spaghetti marinara and spaghetti bolognese, for instance, are fairly good, while the *hongos al ajillo* (garlic mushrooms) are vulcanized rubber.

The restaurant at the **Hotel Hong Kong** (tel. 996-4483 or 996-9180) is decorated in pink and white, making it resemble a young girl's birthday cake. It theoretically offers Chinese food, though it's really just bland Panamanian food gussied up with a few semi-Chinese touches. The fried wontons are tasty, though.

Restaurante Vicente (two blocks south of the cathedral on Avenida Herrera, tel. 996-8106, 9 A.M.–11 P.M. daily), serves mediocre Chinese food in a pleasantly modern atmosphere. There's an outdoor eating area and an allegedly air-conditioned indoor dining room, though the air conditioner wasn't working when I visited. Most dishes are $3.50–7. Avoid anything with sweet and sour sauce, as it tastes as if it came straight out of a can. Meat lovers should note that the restaurant fires up the grill here 5–11 P.M. Friday–Sunday.

Panadería Chiquita (two blocks north of the cathedral on Avenida Herrera, tel. 996-2411, 5 A.M.–10 P.M. daily) serves pastries, coffee, and juices as well as fast-food options that include sandwiches, chicken, burgers, and pizza. The most expensive thing on the menu is $5.

Restaurante La Estrella #2 (no phone, 6 A.M.–10 P.M. daily) is housed in an attractive older building with wrought-iron window fittings on the corner of Avenida Herrera and Calle Melitón Martín. It offers a large array of sometimes scary-looking cafeteria items, plus pizzas and sandwiches. Most full lunches are $1.75 or less. Breakfasts cost $1.25 or less. It's open for breakfast, lunch, and dinner. Come early before the food becomes too decrepit.

Restaurante El Aire Libre (no phone, 6:30 A.M.–10 P.M.) is a simple, open-air place near the corner of Calle Melitón Martín and Avenida Obaldia, to the west of and overlooking the cathedral and plaza. It offers meats, seafood, and Chinese dishes. The food is basic but okay. The most expensive item is $3.75. It's open for breakfast, lunch, and dinner.

DKDA's Restaurante y Pub-Bar (Calle 19 de Octubre, tel. 996-3339, 9 A.M.–11 P.M. Mon.–Thurs., noon–midnight Fri. and Sat., noon–11 P.M. Sun.), pronounced deh-ca-DAHS, is a pleasant enough outdoor place despite the mounted TVs playing shows at full volume. It serves all the usuals—meat, fish, seafood, and poultry—at prices that hover around $5–7. The *filete mignon* ($6) is big and edible. Avoid the wine.

M Restaurante El Mesón (tel. 996-4310, 7 A.M.–11 P.M. daily), on the ground floor of the Hotel Rex, has an extensive menu that varies from burritos and tacos to lasagna and pastas to seafood, meats, and salads. It also offers two dozen sandwiches for $1–3.50. Patrons can sit outside on a front deck overlooking the church or in the nicely air-conditioned dining room. The food's pretty good here, definitely one of the better and relatively fancy dining options in town. It's not expensive, though. Most dishes are in the $4–7 range, and an ample "executive lunch" is available during the week for $2.50. The tacos here actually look and taste like tacos. Try the *tacos de carne ropa vieja*. They're not spicy, but they're pretty yummy.

INFORMATION

IPAT's attractive new CEFATI tourist information center (Calle 19 de Octubre, tel. 974-4532, 8:30 A.M.–4:30 P.M. daily, including holidays) actually has some tourist information. The staff is friendly and eager to help—or at least it was when I visited, shortly after the grand opening.

Displays in the building give some information on the history and culture of the Azuero in Spanish and something that bears a faint resemblance to English. Sample: "The rival 'tunes' are very meticulous in that their Queen and the cars leaves in everyone an unforgettable experience." No doubt.

The CEFATI is one kilometer east of the Los Santos/Chitré fork at La Arena. Take the right fork toward Los Santos. The CEFATI is off the road to the right. It's a two-story building with a red-tile roof.

Farmacia Universal (Calle Melitón Martín and Avenida Herrera, tel. 996-4608, 8 A.M.–8 P.M. Mon.–Sat., 8 A.M.–noon Sun.) is a drugstore across the street from the north end of the cathedral.

SERVICES

Banistmo (Paseo Enrique Geenzier, 8 A.M.–3:30 P.M. Mon.–Fri., 9 A.M.–noon Sat.) is across the street from Pension Chitré, near the museum.

The Caja de Ahorros, just east of the cathedral across Avenida Herrera, has a 24-hour ATM.

Banco Nacional de Panamá (8 A.M.–3 P.M. Mon.–Fri., Sat. 9 A.M.–noon) is on the west end of Calle Manuel María Correa, just as it enters downtown. There are several other banks with ATMs nearby.

The post office (Avenida Perez, 7 A.M.–6 P.M. Mon.–Fri., 7 A.M.–5 P.M. Sat.) is a long block north of the museum. It's around the corner from, but in the same building as, the main Cable and Wireless office.

The business center at the Hotel Rex. (tel. 996-4310, 7 A.M.–11 P.M. daily) offers air-conditioned Internet access for $1.50 an hour. Sending and receiving faxes within the country costs $.50 a page.

PC Brains (Avenida Herrera, tel. 996-5438 or 996-7510, pcbrains@hotmail.com, 8 A.M.–11 P.M. daily) offers Internet access for $1.50 an hour. It's two blocks north of the cathedral, across the street from Panadería Chiquita.

Lavamático Denise (Calle Fabio Ríos, no phone, 5 A.M.–8:30 P.M. daily) charges $.50 to wash and $1 to dry a 10-pound load. It's a fair hike from downtown on a hot day, though it's convenient to those staying at the cheapo places on Avenida Herrera. The easiest way to get there on foot is to walk north on Avenida Herrera and turn left on the fourth street past the cathedral. It's a block and a half down.

GETTING THERE AND AROUND

Bus Terminal

The Terminal de Transportes de Herrera is a large regional bus terminal two kilometers south of downtown on Calle 19 de Octubre (also called Avenida Roberto Ramírez de Diego), the street that runs past Hotel Barceló Guayacanes. It has a 24-hour greasy spoon and a few little shops selling snacks, pharmaceuticals, and knickknacks.

Below is information on some of the more common destinations.

Las Tablas: Every 10 minutes, 6 A.M.–9 P.M. Monday–Friday, until 8 P.M. on the weekends. The trip takes about 45 minutes and costs $1. The bus also stops in **Guararé** ($.80). Those

heading to **Pedasí** have to take a bus to Las Tablas and catch a Pedasí-bound bus there.

Pesé: Every 15 minutes, 6:40 A.M.–6:45 P.M. The trip takes half an hour and costs $.75.

Los Pozos: Every 25 minutes, 6 A.M.–7:25 P.M. Monday–Friday and 6:40 A.M.–7:25 P.M. Saturday and Sunday. The trip takes 45 minutes and costs $1.50.

Las Minas: Every half hour, 6 A.M.–6:15 P.M. The trip takes an hour and costs $2.

Ocú: Every half hour, 6:30 A.M.–7 P.M. The trip takes an hour and costs $2.

Tonosí: Every 1.5 hours, 6 A.M.–7 P.M. The trip takes two hours and costs $4.

Santiago: Every half hour, 5 A.M.–6:30 P.M. The trip takes about 75 minutes and costs $2. Those going to David can change buses in Santiago; they leave constantly. The alternative is to take a bus to Divisa. It lets passengers out near the Interamericana, where it's easy to catch a westbound bus to Santiago or David.

Panama City: The Tuasa bus company (tel. 996-8652) has a departure every 45 minutes in the morning and every hour in the afternoon from 1:30 A.M. to 6 P.M. The trip takes 3.5 hours and costs $6. Look for the ticket booth with the *boletería* sign.

Airport

The airport is three kilometers north of downtown on Avenida Herrera, the avenue running by the east side of the church. **Aeroperlas** (tel. 996-4021 Chitré; tel. 315-7500, fax 315-7580 in Panama City, info@aeroperlas.com, www.aeroperla.com) flies from Panama City to Chitré at 7:40 A.M. and 3:30 P.M. Monday–Saturday and 3:30 P.M. Sunday. The return flight to Panama City is at 8:25 A.M. and 4:15 P.M. Monday–Saturday and 4:15 P.M. Sunday. The trip takes about 35 minutes and costs $36.75/$73.50 one-way/round-trip.

Getting Around

A Thrifty Car Rental office (Paseo Enrique Geenzier, tel. 996-9565, 996-5093, 8 A.M.–noon and 1–5 P.M. Mon.–Sat., closed Sun.) is just east of and across the street from Hotel Versalles. It may be able to arrange pickup and drop-off at the airport or bus station, though taxi fare is so cheap it's probably easier just to grab a cab than fool with this.

A taxi ride anywhere in town costs less than $1. The fare between town and the bus terminal is $1. Other destinations include the airport ($1.50), Villa de Los Santos ($1), Parque Nacional Sarigua ($6), Playa Monagre ($5), and Las Tablas ($10).

Buses between Chitré and Villa de Los Santos, four kilometers away, run constantly. The fare is $.25.

La Villa de Los Santos

Four kilometers south of Chitré lies La Villa de Los Santos, which, as the name suggests, is in Los Santo province. Río La Villa, which the road crosses just northwest of town, marks the border between Los Santo and Herrera provinces.

La Villa de Los Santos is commonly known simply as La Villa. It's also sometimes called Los Santos, which makes it easy to confuse with the whole province.

This tiny town has played a big role in Panama's history through the years. Founded by the conquistadors, its moment of glory came on November 10, 1821. On that date a group of La Villa residents wrote a letter to Simón Bolívar, who had recently defeated the Spanish and won independence for Gran Colombia. In it, they complained of exploitation by the Spanish governor and voiced their wish to sign onto Bolívar's revolution.

This Primer Grito de la Independencia (first cry for independence) was followed just 18 days later by Panama's actual declaration of independence from Spain and union with Gran Colombia, decided at a meeting in Panama City.

The house in which this letter was signed is now a museum, where each year La Villa commemorates the Primer Grito, also known as La Grita de La Villa (the cry of La Villa) with a solemn ceremony attended by dignitaries, often including the president of Panama.

The area's history goes much deeper than that, though. Indigenous peoples used nearby Cerro Juan Díaz, a hill at the edge of the Río La Villa, both as a village and as a burial and ceremonial ground off and on for 1,800 years, from 200 B.C. until the arrival of the Spanish. There's an archaeological dig at the site, but it's not set up for tourists. Ornaments made from gold, shells, pearls, and the like have been excavated, along with a more grisly find: human jawbones from which the teeth have been pried (postmortem, thankfully). Because teeth with holes drilled in them have been found at other sites, it's believed the missing teeth were used to make grim necklaces.

The main town of La Villa de Los Santos consists of just a few blocks of homes and businesses, some quite old and well-preserved, on the northeast side of the Chitré-Las Tablas road. Places to stay and eat are in the newer suburban area directly across from town, on the southeast side of the road.

SIGHTS

Most of La Villa's few sights surround Parque Simón Bolívar, the town plaza. Unless a festival has taken over the town, which happens pretty frequently, visitors can see La Villa's attractions in about an hour.

Iglesia de San Atanasio

La Villa's church, sometimes spelled Iglesia de San Atanacio, was declared a national monument in 1938, though what's inside is more impressive than the building itself. It has a huge main altar, an ornate wooden affair in gold and blue, that was erected in 1733. That makes it older than the current church, whose beginnings date from 1773. The altar and other fixtures were undergoing a major restoration when I last visited, and from the looks of things work may well be continuing when you visit. Even if the church hasn't officially reopened, though, it may be possible to slip inside and watch the restorers at work, which is interesting in itself. Among

the church's other features is a tall, fantastically ornate archway, also erected in 1733, that is covered
with gold arabesques and splashes of reds and
blues. It looks almost Chinese. The church is in
the center of town, next to the plaza.

El Museo de la Nacionalidad

This little museum (tel. 966-8192, 8:30 A.M.–
4 P.M. Tues.–Sat., 9 A.M.–noon Sat., closed Mon.)
is next to the IPAT office on the northwest side
of the church plaza. As is so often the case with
Panama's museums, its name (translation: "the
museum of nationality") is far grander than its
offerings. Ostensibly tracing the history of the
area from its earliest days to its role as the first
town in Panama to call for independence from
Spain, in reality it makes the most it can with a
few scraps of history and little explanation of
their significance.

The museum is installed in the house where
the town leaders signed their famous letter to
Bolívar, declaring they wanted in on his revolutionary movement. The centerpiece of the
museum is a display commemorating La Grita
de La Villa. It attempts to replicate the room
where the letter was signed, using furniture
from the period. Other than that, the displays
consist mainly of a few pieces of pre-
Columbian pottery, some random 18th-cen-
tury religious objects, rusty conquistador
swords, and the like.

Centro de Estudios Superiores de Folklore Dora Pérez de Zárate

This school for students of folklore is run by
the Instituto Nacional de Cultura (INAC).
While not set up to receive tourists, it's housed
in a pretty old blue and white building that's
worth a quick peek. Lucky visitors might hear,
through the upstairs balcony doors, the strains
of students practicing traditional music. It's a
couple of blocks southwest of the plaza, toward
the highway.

Beaches

There are a couple of beaches within easy driving
distance of La Villa de Los Santos, neither of
which is particularly nice. The sand's not very

pretty, and they attract a town crowd and the
trash they leave behind.

The turnoff to **Playa El Rompío** and **Playa
Monagre** is six kilometers southeast of La Villa de
los Santos, in the direction of Las Tablas. As you
drive south from Chitré, it'll be a left-hand turn.
After another 8.5 kilometers the road forks. The left
fork heads to Monagre, a gray-sand beach covered
in litter, with several open-air bars and restaurants.

Playa El Rompío, at the end of the right fork,
is a bit more low-key and clean. The road ends at
a small residential community and fishing village with a few simple places to eat and a stretch
of gray beach just beyond.

All in all, those who need beach time should
head farther south, at least as far as Pedasí.

ENTERTAINMENT AND EVENTS

La Villa lives for its festivals. At other times, there's
little in the way of entertainment in this sleepy little town. The main party is the Festival de Corpus
Christi. La Grita de La Villa, the town's other nationally known event, is a more serious affair.

Festival de Corpus Christi

This is the biggest celebration in La Villa, drawing revelers from all over Panama. Though celebrated elsewhere, no place can compete with La
Villa. The festival lasts nearly two weeks and is
quite a production.

Pope Urban IV sanctioned the Corpus Christi
("body of Christ") festival in A.D. 1264, though
its origins go back even further. It is still celebrated throughout the Catholic world, with lots
of local variation.

The festival officially commemorates the Eucharist, but in La Villa it is far more elaborate
and far-reaching than that. By incorporating
"pagan" dances into the celebration, Spanish colonial priests in Panama used the celebration both as
a colorful way to attract converts and as a graphic
lesson in the Church's views on good vs. evil.

These dances are at the heart of the festival
and have evolved through the years. Keeping
them alive is practically the main industry of La
Villa. The dances include **el Gran Diablo, el
Torito, los Diablícos Sucios, la Montezuma**

Española, la Montezuma Cabezona, el Zacarundé, and several others.

Many of these seemingly have little or nothing to do with the Eucharist, the sacrament in which Catholics consume the body and blood of Christ. El Zacarundé, for instance, remembers the African slaves who escaped from the Spanish in the Darién. La Montezuma Española is about the conquest of Mexico. El Torito involves a predawn search for a bull effigy whose significance I, for one, have never quite gotten a handle on.

The main story line that holds the two-week celebration together is the battle between the forces of evil, led by the Gran Diablo, against the forces of good, led by the Archangel Michael. The diabolical side of the struggle tends to get most attention and energy. Artisans compete to outdo each other in making the most frightening and horrendous devil masks for the dancers.

The two-week celebration always kicks off at noon on the first day with huge explosions and music and the appearance of a band of devils. They have a plot to terrorize the world and carve up the cosmos into four pieces they will then divvy up among themselves. Eventually, of course, the forces of good prevail.

The whole thing involves more than 100 dancers, actors, and musicians. The festivities take place up and down the streets of La Villa, in people's homes, and inside the town church. At one point, the devils ask and receive permission from the Archangel Michael to enter the church, something that fascinates scholars.

By tradition, only men are allowed to perform, though, in a mild concession to the excluded, there's a *día de la mujer* (woman's day) tacked on to the end of the celebration during which women are allowed to dance. In recent years a *día del turismo* (tourism day) has also been added to the end of the festivities. It compresses the highlights into a single day for those unable to get away for two weeks of partying.

The dates of the celebration vary considerably from year to year, since they're based on several Catholic holy days. Generally it's held sometime between late May and early July. Check with IPAT for dates.

La Grita de La Villa

Every November 10 local and national dignitaries, often including the president of Panama, gather to reenact La Grita de La Villa, the town's call for independence from Spain on November 10, 1821. This date is a national holiday. The ceremony starts in the morning at El Museo de La Nacionalidad, the house in La Villa where the historic letter was signed. It's a pretty solemn occasion, but a parade and music performances have been added to the event through the years. Santeños love to party.

ACCOMMODATIONS AND FOOD

La Villa is so close to Chitré that visitors can easily stay in either town. In fact, those who like to party but want to get away from the action when it's time to sleep should consider staying in Chitré for the big La Villa events, such as the Corpus Christi festival, and staying in La Villa for the big Chitré festivals, such as Carnaval. On festival days, of course, visitors may feel lucky to get a room anywhere.

Hotel La Villa (tel. 966-8201 or 966-9321, $16.50 s, $20 d and up) has 38 rooms with air-conditioning and cable TV in a quite pleasant garden setting. There's also an attractive restaurant attached that serves breakfast, lunch, and dinner daily.

The place is clean, the beds are firm, and this is generally one of the better lodging options in the whole area. The place is decorated with love. The owner is high on folkloric art, particularly *tinajas* (the earthenware pots this part of the Azuero is famous for). They're everywhere: in the lobby, hanging from the rafters, used as planters, on the tables, and so on. It's no surprise to see a poster in the lobby signed by Sheila Lichacz, the local artist internationally famous for her depictions of *tinajas*.

Price start at $16.50 (single) and $20 (double) for the most basic rooms and can be twice that for the nicer ones. Add a few dollars for weekend visits and take off a few for longer stays. You can probably haggle here. The newer rooms are significantly more pleasant than older ones, which have tired furniture and dreary fake-wood paneling.

The hotel is at the end of a quiet cul-de-sac 700 meters southwest of the main road. To get there from Chitré, look for the signs as you enter La Villa; it's a right turn off the road.

Toward the weekend, a rustic but fun place to eat in this area is **Ⓜ Kiosco El Ciruelo** (no phone, 6 A.M.–10 P.M. Fri.–Sun. only). It's 4.5 kilometers southeast of La Villa on the road to Las Tablas; look to the left for a large, open-air shed with a corrugated zinc roof. Food is cooked in an old-fashioned wood oven fueled by a mountain of wood stacked at the back of the place. Disappointingly bland *sancocho* is, at $2, the most expensive thing on the menu. The delicious tamales, for $.40 each, are the reason to come here. Bet you can't eat just one.

The place has a lot of character. Chickens wander through the "restaurant" among the diners, waiting for their turn to end up in the pot. It's easy to imagine food being prepared the same way at the same spot a hundred years ago.

INFORMATION AND SERVICES

Because of its long history, tiny La Villa merits its own IPAT office (tel. 966-8013, fax 966-8040, 8:30 A.M.–4:30 P.M. Mon.–Fri.) that may offer Spanish speakers a modicum of information, especially about the festivals. The town's police station is on the town plaza, near the museum. The Banco Nacional de Panamá (8 A.M.–3 P.M. Mon.–Fri., 9 A.M.–noon Sat.) is about a half block southwest of the plaza. It has a 24-hour ATM. Farmacia Hermanos Moreno (tel. 966-8249) is on the plaza, just south of the church. Buses to Chitré ($.25) stop near the IPAT office.

Loop Road: Pesé to Ocú

Those who want to truly immerse themselves in the culture and rhythms of the Azuero peninsula should consider exploring the loop road that circles through the heart of the peninsula. Even though the wilderness long ago surrendered to cattle pasture, farms, and teak plantations, the drive is still scenic and the rolling countryside quite pretty. The road is in good shape most of the way, and new stretches of it should be paved by the time you visit.

One festival or another always seems to be happening in one of these towns. A few are mentioned below, but, since many of them change yearly, check with IPAT (the main office is near the start of the road, on the outskirts of Chitré) for a current calendar of the major events. Without some sort of festival taking place, the towns themselves don't hold much interest.

The loop starts at **Pesé,** about 25 kilometers southwest of Chitré. To get to Pesé, turn west off the main road just north of La Arena (north of where the main road forks at Cerámica Marcelino). The turn is marked.

From Pesé traveling clockwise, the road leads through the towns of **Los Pozos, Las Minas,** and **Ocú.** Note that these are also names of districts, of which the towns are the *cabecera,* sort of the Panama equivalent of a county seat. The loop can also be driven counterclockwise. Those without wheels can explore this area by bus. They run frequently between each of the towns and Chitré.

The clock itself seems to turn back with every kilometer along the road. Towns here—really rural villages—probably don't look much different than they did 100 years ago. This is the real heartland of the heartland. Be prepared for curious stares. Not many foreigners make it this far into the interior.

Distances below assume driving the loop counterclockwise. Even though the distances aren't great, allow a half day just to drive the loop, or a full day to stop and explore what the towns have to offer. Each has some claim to fame.

PESÉ

The cutest of the towns is Pesé (pop. 2,547), 19 kilometers from the turnoff. It has a quaint little church surrounded by red-roofed buildings half-hidden behind flowering trees. Horse carts are still used to haul goods around here.

In the odd juxtaposition one sometimes sees in small Panamanian towns, across the street from the church is a Seco Herrerano factory. *Seco* is sugarcane liquor, and Panama's national drink. There are no official tours of the factory, but curious visitors who show up on a normal work day, which also includes Saturday before noon, can probably convince someone to let them poke around.

Given this cozy combination of the sacred and profane, it's only fitting that Pesé is noted for a live reenactment of the suffering and final days of Jesus Christ during Semana Santa (Holy Week), the week leading up to Easter. This may sound pretty somber, but in recent years the Catholic Church has chided the town for, essentially, having too much fun during what is supposed to a religious observance.

LOS POZOS AND LAS MINAS

There's really not much to see in Los Pozos (pop. 2,268), the next significant town. It's 19 kilometers south of Pesé. Las Minas (pop. 2,209), 13 kilometers west of Los Pozos or 51 kilometers from the start of the loop, is kind of cute, though not as cute as Pesé. At this point, the road has turned hillier and the surrounding countryside greener and more lush. The big party in Las Minas is on December 4, in honor of the village's patron saint, Santa Barbara.

OCÚ

Ocú, 21 kilometers farther north on a potholed road, is not quaint. The houses and church are made from cinderblocks, for instance. But the town, which has a population of 8,150, works hard to preserve the old ways, and it's often considered the folkloric center of Herrera province.

The town and its namesake district are known for producing lovely *polleras* that are quite unlike those made in Los Santos province. The area is also known for producing distinctive white hats with a black band that more closely resemble the famous "Panamas" made in Ecuador than do other traditional Panamanian hats. A national folkloric festival, the **Festival del Manito,** is held here annually on the second weekend in August. A highlight of the festival is the chance to see a traditional country wedding, with the bride on horseback in a beautiful white *pollera*, her proud groom mounted behind her, protecting her from the sun with an umbrella. The town's other big multiday celebration is **la Feria de San Sebastián,** a country fair that overlaps with the town's patron saint day, January 20.

BACK TO CHITRÉ

The fastest way back to Chitré is to finish the loop to Pesé, 30 kilometers away. From there it's a 19-kilometer drive to the main road leading into Chitré. Getting back to Pesé from Ocú can be a bit tricky. Don't be shy about asking for directions if you get lost; the people are friendly, and they know roads get confusing out here.

The road to Pesé starts past a supermarket to the east of downtown. The road was being paved the last time I was in the area and should be in good shape by the time you visit. After 13 kilometers, make a right. This will lead south into Pesé. From there just continue east to Chitré.

Note this also means that those wanting to go straight from Chitré to Ocú can take this more direct route rather than drive the whole loop described above. Those not already on the Azuero peninsula can also drive directly to Ocú from the Interamerican Highway. The turnoff is west of Divisa.

Guararé

This small (pop. 3,883), not particularly scenic town is famous throughout Panama for the **Festival Nacional de la Mejorana,** a huge folkloric festival held annually in September. There's little reason to visit the town between festivals.

Guararé is right on the main highway linking Chitré, 25 kilometers to the north, and Las Tablas, five kilometers to the south. The main town is just east of the highway. It boasts a tiny **folkloric museum,** a couple of **fireworks factories** that are probably worth staying well clear of on a hot day, and an elaborate open-air stage on the church plaza that was built for the Mejorana.

A quite decent hotel is on the west side of the highway and a quite basic *hospedaje* is on the east side. The hotel is the best bet for food, though there are some other basic eateries in town.

La Enea (pop. 1,128), sometimes called La Enea de Guararé, is an even tinier town tucked away just north of Guararé, toward the coast. It's sort of a suburb of Guararé and is famous for producing beautiful *polleras.* Beyond it are a couple of mediocre beaches, **Playa Bella Vista** and **Playa El Puerto,** that aren't worth a special trip. That's just about it.

SIGHTS

This backwater town holds a few surprises even when no festival has invaded the place. While there's not enough to justify an overnight stay between festivals, those with a spare hour or two should consider exploring the town's modest attractions. At the top of the list is the chance to see a master *pollera* maker at work.

Casa-Museo Manuel F. Zárate

Two blocks past the church as you head into Guararé from the highway, a small folkloric museum (tel. 994-5644, 8 A.M.–4 P.M. Mon.–Sat., 8 A.M.–noon Sun., $.75 adults, $.25 children) has been installed in the home of the late Manuel F. Zárate. He was a chemistry professor who, along with his wife, Dora Pérez de Zárate, and a few colleagues founded the Mejorana festival in 1949. He is nationally known for his work to revive and preserve Panama's folkloric traditions.

The museum's offerings are, as usual, meager. Displays consist mainly of folkloric costumes, including some old but not especially fine *polleras,* as well as photos of traditional homes, a few impressive devil masks, and so on. It's worth a very quick visit.

Cohetería La Negra Vieja

This fireworks factory (tel. 994-5424) makes fireworks used at major celebrations throughout the country. It's not set up for tourists, and it's not probably not smart to smoke within a kilometer of the place, but it's mentioned here just in case you're curious to know what that building near the church is.

Polleras

One of Panama's most famous *pollera* makers, **Ildaura S. de Espino** (tel. 994-5527), lives in La Enea, the teeny town between Guararé and the beaches. It takes her six months to make a *pollera,* Panama's heavily embroidered national dress, and each sells for $1,500–$2,000. She takes orders, but be prepared for a long wait. Those just curious to see an artist at work are welcome to stop by for a visit.

La Enea is about two kilometers past Guararé on the way to Playa El Puerto. Look for the church steeple in the distance on the right. That's where the town square is.

Once in La Enea, look for the house with a green-tile front right on the town square, near the statue of the Virgin Mary. Don't be shy about asking for directions—everyone knows Ildaura and will probably point her out without prompting; she's the main reason out-of-towners stop by. She's gracious and happy to show visitors her work. She's now in a wheelchair and looking a bit frail, but she still spends her days diligently making beautiful costumes.

ENTERTAINMENT AND EVENTS

Guararé is synonymous with the Mejorana Festival, which is just about the only reason visitors come to this remote town. There's little in the way of entertainment at nonfestival times.

Every September, Guararé hosts **La Festival Nacional de la Mejorana,** Panama's biggest and most important folkloric festival. The weeklong Mejorana festival was started in 1949 by a small group of local folklore preservationists, and through the years it has ballooned into one major party. It overlaps with the festival of La Virgen de las Mercedes, Guararé's patron saint.

The festival is named in honor of a Panamanian song form called the *mejorana,* which is played on a small, five-string guitar called a *mejoranera.* Just to make things confusing, the instrument itself is sometimes called a *mejorana,* as is a traditional dance that it accompanies.

The festival's celebrants are so determined to preserve tradition that the town has banned by law all modern or foreign music and dance during the festival. Even playing a six-string guitar is forbidden.

However, the festival does attract hundreds of folkloric dancers and musicians whose styles diverge from the *mejorana* tradition. They come from far beyond the Azuero heartland, varying from performers from Bocas del Toro in western Panama to the African-inspired Congo dancers of Colón in eastern Panama.

Competitions are held for the best performer in all kinds of categories, including competitions for both the best spoken-word and song-form *décima,* a traditional Spanish poem consisting of 10 eight-syllable lines, and a *saloma* competition for the best Panamanian-style yodeler.

A queen is chosen each year. She wears a pointed crown and presides over the festivities from her throne when not dancing with different groups in her gorgeous *pollera.*

Other attractions include bullfights, a parade of super-elaborate floats pulled by oxcarts, fireworks, strolling musicians, and handicraft booths. Each day an *abandadero,* a standard-bearer, is chosen to lead that day's events.

Probably the wackiest part of the festival is **La Atolladera,** which very loosely translates to "Day of the Mud Fight." It's a day to sling mud at your friends. The queen and her court show up in pure white outfits just so winging mud balls at them is all the more satisfying. Good times.

The festival is a big deal and attracts Panamanian tourists from all over the country. Give up all hope of finding lodging in Guararé without a reservation made months in advance. Las Tablas is the nearest town, but it may be necessary to look for a place in Chitré, 25 kilometers away, or maybe even farther afield.

The Mejorana Festival is always held in September, though the dates and length of the festival vary yearly. It's always pegged to the town's commemoration of its patron saint, La Virgen de las Mercedes, which lasts for nine days, climaxing on September 23–24. The Mejorana generally dovetails with the end of that religious observance and lasts about a week. Check with IPAT for exact dates and a schedule of events.

ACCOMMODATIONS AND FOOD

The red tile–roofed **Hotel La Mejorana** (tel. 994-5794, fax 994-5796, $12.10/$14.30 s/d for small rooms, $22 s/d for larger rooms) is lovingly decorated with Guararé's role as a folkloric center in mind. The walls of the common areas are adorned with devil masks, sketches of women in *polleras,* paintings of sugarcane presses—all the traditional touchstones. Its 22 rooms are much simpler and dark, with tiny windows, but they're clean and pleasant enough, with pretty good beds, hot-water bathrooms, air-conditioning, local TV, and telephones. Reserve 2–3 months in advance for all festivals.

The cheerful open-air restaurant at the hotel serves most of the usuals, but it also offers a surprisingly extensive seafood selection, including calamari, octopus, lobster, clams, and prawns. Don't expect gourmet preparation, however. Most entrees are $4–9.50. The combination chow mein (chicken, pork, clams, and shrimp) is edible.

A half order is plenty for a normal appetite and costs a couple of bucks.

Hospedaje Eida (tel. 994-5411, $8.80 s/d with fan, $14.30 s/d with air-conditioning) is a huge leap down in quality. It's a rock-bottom place right on the highway meant for those who don't expect more from lodging than a space to get horizontal. Some of the rooms have shared bathrooms.

Las Tablas

Las Tablas (pop. 7,980 in town, 24,298 in the district) has more sprawl and less charm than Chitré, its sister town 30 kilometers north in Herrera Province. It feels more like a city in miniature, sacrificing coziness for a somewhat more urban feel and advantages, such as better dining options than Chitré can muster. However, the *tableños* are just as mellow and easygoing as the people you'd find in smaller towns.

Most visitors come here for exactly one reason: Carnaval. Las Tablas hosts Panama's biggest, wildest celebration, which is saying a lot for a country known for the fervor of its Carnaval spirit.

Las Tablas is built up around an "L" formed by two roads. The first is the stretch of highway that runs north to south from Chitré to Las Tablas. It intersects in downtown Las Tablas with Avenida Belisario Porras, which runs east through town and turns back into highway outside the town limits.

Most of the restaurants, hotels, and services are along these two streets or within a block or two of them. At the base of the "L" is the town church, plaza, and a museum dedicated to favorite son Belisario Porras, a three-time president of Panama. A stroll from the plaza east down Avenida Belisario Porras is a good way to get a sense of town life.

As is true of every town in Panama, most streets have multiple names, none of which may appear on a road sign or be known even by those who live on the street. The only street that people may know by name is Avenida Belisario Porras, which is basically the town's main drag.

SIGHTS

Though Las Tablas is an important provincial "city," it has very little in the way of sights. After taking in the museum and church around Parque Porras in downtown Las Tablas, there's little left to do but wander around and people-watch. A good place to start is along Avenida Belisario Porras, which begins at Parque Porras and heads east.

Museo Belisario Porras

The town museum (Avenida Belisario Porras and Calle 8 de Noviembre, tel. 994-6326, 8:30 A.M.–5 P.M. Monday–Friday, 9:30 A.M.–5 P.M. Saturday and Sunday, $.50 adults, $.25 children), on the south side of the church plaza, contains personal effects, important documents, and memorabilia from the life of Porras, a national hero who is considered one of Panama's founding fathers and was its president three times. He was born in Las Tablas in 1856 and died in 1942. The displays have been damaged in recent years, according to preservationists, through neglect and smoke from Carnaval fireworks.

Parque Porras and Iglesia Santa Librada

The name of the town plaza is Parque Porras, though it contains more *cemento* than *parque*. It's at the heart of Las Tablas, where the north-south highway into town intersects Avenida Belisario Porras, which runs west-east. This is ground zero during Carnaval.

The town church, Iglesia Santa Librada, on the west side of the plaza, is more notable for the constant devotion of the worshipers inside than for the building itself. The centerpiece is a large altar covered with gold leaf.

Playa El Uverito

When the heat impels visitors to find a beach, the nearest one is Playa El Uverito. As usual with this stretch of coast, its proximity is the most attractive thing about it. It's a huge, gray-sand

The Azuero Peninsula

LAS TABLAS

© AVALON TRAVEL PUBLISHING, INC.

beach with a couple of basic places to eat. It's not much to look at.

The road to Playa El Uverito starts at the bus terminal. Take Avenida Emilio Castro, the street that runs past the south side of the bus terminal, east for 12 kilometers, until the road forks. Take the left fork.

ENTERTAINMENT AND EVENTS

To say that the **Carnaval** celebration in Las Tablas is its biggest annual party is putting it far too mildly. It's one of the biggest parties in the entire country. Other major Carnaval locations on the Azuero include Chitré, Parita, Ocú, and

Villa de Los Santos, but none can compete with Las Tablas.

Carnaval officially lasts from the Saturday before Ash Wednesday until what we gringos call Fat Tuesday, the last hurrah before the forty abstemious days of Lent.

In Las Tablas, though, things get started on Friday, with the coronation of the town's two Carnaval queens. Las Tablas's first Carnaval queen was crowned in 1937, but since 1950 the town has had two rival queens and their attendant courts, or *tunas:* that of Calle Arriba (high street) and Calle Abajo (low street).

Throughout Carnaval, the two retinues try to outdo each other in the beauty, opulence, splen-

© WILLIAM FRIAR

a Christmas parade in Las Tablas, famous for its festivals

dor, and ingenuity of their costumes and floats *(carros alegóricos)*. It's easy to imagine more resources go into creating these than the entire town produces in a year. They also compose songs, called *tonadas*, that, among other things, praise the beauty and grace of their chosen queen and mock the supposed ugliness and witchiness of the rival one. These *puyas*, or taunts, are part of the fun and usually taken in stride, but the *tonadas* are approved ahead of time by a censorship board to make sure they don't get too nasty and personal.

Both *tunas* take to the streets every day for a huge parade, with different jaw-dropping floats and costumes each day. These are usually incredibly flamboyant and elaborate, reminiscent of those found at Rio's Carnaval.

Neither costumes nor behavior tend to get as risqué as that at Rio's Carnaval or even New Orleans's Mardi Gras. Carnaval everywhere in Panama, while it certainly has a lot of booze and steaminess, is still considered a family affair. In fact, when some revelers acted lewd and showed too much skin during the Carnaval celebration in neighboring Chitré in 2002, their "immoral" and "pornographic" behavior caused a public outcry and lots of official tsk-tsking.

Still, this is a decidedly secular celebration with deep pagan roots. The reigning deity is Momo, also known as Momus, the Greek god of laughter and mockery. This is a huge party, the goal of which seems to be to make sure everyone has something to atone for come Lent.

Though masks were featured in Panama's early Carnaval celebrations, which were officially recognized nationwide in 1910, they quickly faded out and are rarely seen during Panama's Carnaval today. One Panamanian addition is for the queens to include stunning *polleras*—Panama's flowing, embroidered national dress—among their many costumes.

Another important part of the Carnaval celebration, in Las Tablas and throughout the country, is the *culecos*. Each morning of Carnaval, to the cry of *¡agua, agua!*, large water trucks with hoses spray revelers with thousands of gallons of water, cooling them off as they dance in the heat. Some participants also flirtatiously squirt each other with water guns. The tradition is somewhere between a mild version of a wet T-shirt contest and the ritual opening of fire hydrants during a summer heat wave in a U.S. city

The *culecos* are such a beloved part of the

STAYING SAFE AND HEALTHY DURING CARNAVAL

The Carnaval celebrations in and around Las Tablas were canceled in 2000 because of an outbreak of hantavirus, which is spread by rodents. This was taken very seriously by the Panamanian government, which launched an aggressive campaign to control the disease.

Between the outbreak of the virus in early 2000 and mid-2003, a total of 31 cases had been reported, 7 of which were fatal. This is a much lower mortality rate than found, for instance, in the strains of the disease endemic to the United States. Most cases were diagnosed in the first year, and the infection rate has been slashed drastically since then.

Because of the economic importance of Carnaval, and the huge influx of people from around the country who come to Las Tablas for it, Panama's public health officials now conduct extensive house-to-house inspections of the area before signing off on the area's Carnaval celebrations.

The government has not had to cancel Carnaval since 2000. But those considering a trip to the area around Las Tablas and Guararé may want to check for updated information with the U.S. Centers for Disease Control, tel. 877/FYI-TRIP

(394-8747), www.cdc.gov/travel, or the U.S. State Department, tel. 888/407-4747 or 317/472-2328, www.travel.state.gov/panama.html. The most up-to-date information, though, will probably be in the Panama press. Those who speak a little Spanish can also try searching for "hantavirus" in the archives of *La Prensa* (www.prensa.com) or other Panamanian newspapers. Only registered users can search *La Prensa's* archives, but registration is free.

The entire country stops working and starts playing hard during Carnaval. Naturally, this involves the consumption of vast quantities of booze. Try to avoid the roads as much as possible during those four days. And foreign visitors inclined to join in should remember that alcohol plus unfamiliar heat and humidity can easily add up to dehydration. Drink lots of water and don't go nuts. Also be on the lookout for amateur fireworks displays set off at random in crowded areas.

Those planning to visit Panama during Carnaval should also note that international and domestic flights get booked solid far in advance, as do hotels, which jack up their prices for the festivities. Plan accordingly.

celebration they're officially sanctioned even during water shortages, though officials urge residents to conserve water in the days leading up to the celebration.

Music played at maximum volume is an important part of the proceedings, as it is at every Panamanian festivity. Temporary discos sprout up, and *murgas* (strolling musicians) march in the processions. At night, fireworks light the skies—and maybe houses and partiers, too, given the drunken knuckleheads that sometimes fire off rockets in the middle of downtown.

The celebration climaxes on Tuesday night. Or rather, it climaxes at dawn on Ash Wednesday, since the final party goes all night long.

There's a saying in Panama, kept alive by its own citizens, that the only thing Panamanians take seriously is Carnaval. In that sense *tableños* are the most serious people in the country.

No sooner is Carnaval over than plans begin to

select the following year's queens. These are introduced on **New Year's Eve,** another huge party that resembles the last night of Carnaval. The two new queens are greeted and the two retiring queens seen off with fireworks and a parade.

ACCOMMODATIONS

For a place that attracts what seems like the entire country for Carnaval, Las Tablas doesn't have many hotel rooms. Most visiting Carnavalites stay with friends or family, or else rent houses during the nearly weeklong celebration. At that time, residents looking to make some quick bucks rent out even the most modest homes to eager revelers.

There are other official hotels and *hospedajes* than those listed below, but these are the best—and least sketchy—of the limited bunch.

The centrally located **Hospedaje Zafiro**

(Avenida Belisario Porras and Calle 8 de Noviembre, tel. 994-8200, $14.30 s, $18.70 d) offers nine worn, cold-water rooms with old mattresses, air conditioning, and local TV. All the rooms are upstairs, and the best feature of the place is a common area with a little balcony overlooking the action on the town plaza. The *hospedaje* is dreary but okay, though those willing to part with just a few dollars more can do much better elsewhere.

Hotel Las Tablas (Avenida Carlos L. Lopez and Calle Ramón Mora, tel. 994-7422, $19.80 s, $27.50 d) is so well-hidden it's almost as though it doesn't want the business. It's above Supermercado Las Tablas, across the street from the bus terminal on the main road that leads south into downtown Las Tablas. Prospective guests must ask one of the supermarket's cashiers for help. There's no sign and no visible management. The 14 rooms are dark and have cold-water bathrooms, squishy mattresses, and local TV. They're clean enough but seem unused. Given the hotel's proximity to the bus terminal and distance from downtown, this place is best for people arriving late or leaving early by bus.

Just south of the town center is **Hotel Sol del Pacifico** (Calle Agustin Cano Castillero, tel. 994-1280, cell 675-7318, $22 s/d and up); it has 13 rooms and three apartments, with 18 more rooms on the way. Rooms are spartan but okay, with air-conditioning, local TV, and private baths. The hotel is on Calle Agustin Cano Castillero, which runs west-east at the southern end of downtown Las Tablas. It's two blocks south of Belisario Porras and about two blocks southeast of the town plaza.

Formerly known as Hotel Piamonte, **Ⅿ Hotel y Restaurante Manolo** (Avenida Belisario Porras, tel. 994-6372, cell 640-4648, $17 s, $20 d) is a better value than Hotel Sol del Pacifico if the prices stay the same. Its nine cold-water rooms are quite clean and simple, though so stark white they're almost sterile. There are a bar, restaurant, and Internet access for $1/hour. The friendly and attentive owner speaks fluent English; he lived in the United States for years. The hotel has a central location a block and a half east of the town plaza.

FOOD

Dining options are severely limited in Las Tablas. The restaurants listed below are the best bets.

Ⅿ Restaurante y Bar Jorón Moravel (Avenida Rogelio Gáez, tel. 994-7250, 7 A.M.–11 P.M. daily), two blocks southwest of the bus terminal, is a cute little place that, with its thatched roof, resembles a giant *rancho*. Lunch offerings include lasagna, chicken, spaghetti, and *sancocho*. The lasagna is pretty good. It also does seafood, meat, Chinese fried rice, pizza, and sandwiches. Prices range about $2–8. Breakfast costs $2 or less. The place does a thriving takeout business. While there are several things to recommend this place, be warned that serving food hot isn't a priority here.

The food is okay at **Hotel y Restaurante Manolo** (Avenida Belisario Porras, tel. 994-6372, cell 640-4648, 7 A.M.–11 P.M. daily). It offers the usual suspects, plus 10 kinds of sandwiches ($1–2.75) and, allegedly, beef and chicken tacos. Don't start jonesing too hard for the latter, though. The *si hay tacos* sign posted on the wall doesn't necessarily mean a thing. Best bet to find them is probably in the evening. Most things on the menu are $5 or less.

Housed in an old home in the center of town, **Restaurante Los Portales** (Avenida Belisario Porras, 6 A.M.–10 P.M. Mon.-Sat., 6 A.M.–3 P.M. Sun.) has a certain rustic charm. It features high ceilings, arched doorways, sloping red-tile roof, and tables set around a porch right on Avenida Belisario Porras, kitty-corner to Hotel y Restaurante Manolo. It's a basic place but offers a wide range of food, including prawns, calamari, octopus, corvina, spaghetti, and various meats. Most items are $2–8. The *bistec picado* ($3) comes in a kind of sweet-and-sour sauce and is surprisingly tasty.

Restaurante El Caserón (Avenida Moises Espino, tel. 994-6066, 7 A.M.–11 P.M. daily) is a pleasant-enough open-air place known for its heaps of meat. The *parrillada mixta* (grilled meat) costs $5.75 and offers a pile of chicken, pork, beef, and local sausage. It's reasonably tasty, especially the sausage, though it's a good way to use up a whole year's quota of grease and cholesterol. The restaurant also serves pizza, seafood,

Ⅿ The Azuero Peninsula

chow mein, pasta, and more meat. Prices range from $2 for a small pizza up to $10 for fancier offerings. The restaurant is on Avenida Moises Espino, which is parallel to and one block north of Avenida Belisario Porras. It's about two blocks northeast of Hotel y Restaurante Manolo.

SERVICES

Farmacia Novedades (Calle 8 de Deciembre, tel. 994-6300, 7 A.M.–10 P.M. Mon.–Sat., 7 A.M.–1 P.M. and 5–10 P.M. Sun.) is half a block south of Avenida Belisario Porras, near the town plaza and Museo Belisario Porras.

Most banks are set around or close to the town plaza. Other services are spread out around the downtown area.

A branch of Banco Nacional de Panamá (Avenida Carlos L. Lopez, 8 A.M.–3 P.M. Mon.–Fri., 9 A.M.–noon Sat.) is next to the bus terminal on the main street running south into downtown. Banistmo (Avenida Belisario Porras and Calle 8 de Noviembre, 8 A.M.–3:30 P.M. Mon.–Fri., 9 A.M.–noon Sat.) is at the intersection of Las Tablas's two main streets. It didn't have an ATM at the time of writing. BBVA Banco (Avenida Belisario Porras, 8 A.M.–3 P.M. Mon.–Fri., closed Sat.), across the street from Banistmo, does have an ATM.

The main post office (Calle Ramón Mora, 7 A.M.–6 P.M. Mon.–Fri., 7 A.M.–5 P.M. Sat.) is a block and a half west of the bus terminal.

Interchat (9 A.M.–10 P.M. Mon.–Fri., 9 A.M.–9 P.M. Sat., closed Sun., $.75/hour) is an air-conditioned Internet café that sells some snacks. It's on an unmarked street a half block east of the north end of the town plaza.

There's a self-service launderette (Calle 3 de Noviembre, 8 A.M.–noon and 1–6 P.M. Mon.–Sat., 8 A.M.–1 P.M. Sun., $.75 to wash, at least $1 to dry) a block north and east of Hotel Sol de Pacifico.

GETTING THERE AND AWAY

Taxis are easy to find in Las Tablas, and there are taxi stands all over. The taxi stand (tel. 994-8532 or 994-8533) near the launderette on Calle 3 de Noviembre is open 24 hours a day. Sample fares include Guararé ($2), Playa El Uverito ($5), and Pedasí ($15). For those who can't afford the cab fare, buses to Guararé leave from downtown every 10 minutes ($.30) from early morning to evening. They can be flagged down on Avenida Carlos L. Lopez, the main road heading north out of Las Tablas.

Buses to more distant locations leave from the town bus terminal at the north end of town, shortly after the national highway morphs into Avenida Carlos L. Lopez. The cross street is Avenida Emilio Castro. There's a taxi stand at the bus terminal. Though it's just a half kilometer to the center of town, it can feel like a major hike in the heat when you're toting luggage. Avoid the misery and cough up the $.75 cab fare.

A few of the most important routes:

Pedasí: Buses run every 45 minutes 6 A.M.–7 P.M. The trip takes 45 minutes and costs $2.

Tonosí: The first buses to Tonosí leave Las Tablas at 8 A.M., 10 A.M., and 11 A.M. Monday–Saturday and 8:30 A.M. and 10 A.M. on Sunday. They then run about every hour 12:30–5:30 P.M. The trip takes about an hour and 20 minutes and costs $3. Note that this is an inland route and does not lead down the coast near Pedasí, Playa Venao, or Isla Cañas.

Panama City: The first bus leaves at 6 A.M. every day. After that, buses leave every hour on the half hour 7:30–11:30 A.M. and every hour and a quarter 12:15–4:30 P.M. There are two additional early departures at 2 A.M. and 4 A.M. Monday–Friday. On Friday and Sunday there's a final departure at 5:30 P.M. Got all that? Never mind—all times are more theoretical than real in any case. The fare is $6.50 and the trip takes 4.5 hours.

Pedasí

Like Parita, Pedasí (pop. 1, 830) is a Spanish-colonial town that time forgot, with the same kind of architecture and the same civic pride in keeping the place clean and quaint. There's little shaking in this friendly town 43 kilometers south of Las Tablas, and that's part of its appeal: It's a haven of tranquillity surrounded by natural beauty. I can't think of a more pleasant place to discover heartland Panama.

That kind of peace comes at a price. Pedasí offers only basic rooms, though ones with character. The few restaurants are el cheapo places whose backbone clientele are the local laborers. But now may be the time to visit it, while there's still little traffic on its narrow, tree-lined streets. A tourism push keeps threatening to come to Pedasí, helped along by a new airstrip, a French condo development under construction nearby, and the fact that this is the hometown of Mireya Moscoso, Panama's president 1999–2004.

A cynic might believe Pedasí has benefited in the last few years from the presidential connection. A large, modern branch of Banco Nacional de Panamá now gleams at the north entrance to town. It looks bigger than the town itself. There's also an attractive new government tourist information center, or CEFATI, with an Internet café attached. Not bad for what's essentially a fishing village.

How much the town has actually benefited, however, is debatable. The tourists have been slow to arrive, and in 2003 the town council announced it was near bankruptcy.

Developers and entrepreneurs also make the occasional noise about building hotels out here, though so far little has happened.

Most of Pedasí is on either side of a one-kilometer stretch of quiet two-lane road that runs north-south through the town. The ocean is just a couple of kilometers to the east. The town church and plaza are on the southeast side of town.

Visitors can take in the town itself in less than an hour. The main attractions are its nearby **beaches,** a couple of unusual islands, **Isla Iguana** and **Isla de Cañas** (see *Islands Near Pedasí*), that

There are still lots of Spanish-colonial touches in Azuero towns.

LABORATORIO ACHOTINES

About 30 kilometers south of Pedasí on the way to Playa Venao, a gated entrance on the left side of the road bears the sign "Laboratorio Achotines." This is a tuna-research facility, which is only fitting given that this area is sometimes known as "the tuna coast."

The laboratory is affiliated with the Inter-American Tropical Tuna Commission, a group that's more impressive and powerful than its humdrum name might suggest. Supported by a dozen member countries, ranging from the U.S. and Japan to Peru and Vanuatu, the commission regulates tuna fishing in the entire eastern Pacific Ocean, usually through setting quotas. In 2002, the commission closed the entire eastern Pacific to tuna fishing for a month, and sent out observers to enforce the ban. Tuna fishing is a multi-billion-dollar industry.

Since its establishment in 1985, the Achotines Laboratory has become an important research facility. It raises and studies yellowfin tuna, snapper, corvina, and other fish in a half dozen giant tanks at the laboratory. Yellowfin tuna are huge; they can easily top 100 pounds, and have been known to reach four times that weight. Other buildings have facilities for incubating eggs or growing algae and rotifer to feed the fish.

One purpose of the Achotines Laboratory is to study the spawning of yellowfin tuna in captivity to get a better understanding of their lifecycle in the ocean, and thus learn how to protect them from over-fishing. One experiment involves implanting radio-transmitting computers in yellowfin specimens and releasing them back into the ocean.

The Achotines Laboratory (tel. 995-8166, fax 995-8282, achotine@cwp.net.pa, www.iattc.org) offers tours of its facilities by appointment. It's closed weekends and holidays.

November 25 is the celebration of Pedasí's patron saint, Santa Catalina. The town also has its own elaborate Carnaval celebration.

SPORTS AND RECREATION

Pedasí is a beach town that sometimes seems to have more beaches than tourists, which is one of its charms. It's also a good base for planning trips to nearby diving, snorkeling, and surfing spots.

Nearby Beaches

Pedasí is only a couple of kilometers from the ocean, and it offers a choice of good, easily accessible beaches. The ones listed below are a sampling of the better options.

Playa Arenal is three kilometers east of town on a good road. To get there, follow the road behind the gas station that leads past the CEFATI. Arenal is absolutely massive. You have to take a short hike across the sand just to get to the water, and it stretches along the coast farther than the eye can see. Fishermen anchor their boats here, but there's more than enough beach and surf to go around.

Getting into and out of boats through the pounding surf at Playa Arenal can be a bit of an adventure. The Japanese government is building a boat ramp in quieter waters near the mouth of the Río Pedasí, though exactly why it has donated it is a subject of much gossipy speculation. To get to the ramp, head down the road to Playa Arenal and make a left just before the beach. It's one kilometer down that road.

Playa El Toro is another big beach, 2.7 kilometers southeast of town on a well-marked dirt road. When the road forks, head left; the right fork leads to **Playa La Garita,** which is okay but too rocky to recommend. El Toro is also a bit rocky, and there are huge boulders just offshore. But it gets nicer the farther north you walk. The sand here is brown. Warning: El Toro is the most popular beach with townsfolk, which means it's the most crowded on dry-season weekends.

My favorite beach in the area is **Playa Los Destiladeros,** 10 kilometers south of town. Head south down the main road through town until you get to Limón, three kilometers away. The turn will be on the left.

aren't too hard to get to, and a surfing spot, **Playa El Venao,** about 30 kilometers south of town that's great for beginners. The waters off Pedasí offer good diving and fishing, and Pedasí now has an outfitter to take advantage of that fact. Humpback whales can be spotted offshore from around August to October.

© WILLIAM FRIAR

The Azuero Peninsula

The Azuero Peninsula has kilometers of beaches with no one on them.

When that road forks, take the right fork. The road dead-ends at Los Destiladeros, seven kilometers away. It's a wide brown beach with a great view. Locals don't tend to come here since there are no facilities or shade, so you'll likely have it to yourself. However, a French company is building a large, gated residential community less than a kilometer from the beach, so it may be a more popular spot by the time you visit. It's a Southwestern-themed condo development with extensive landscaped grounds, but the fortresslike walls around it aren't too inviting.

Sadly, in 2003 Panama's government environmental agency was forced to investigate the illegal extraction of truckloads of sand from this pretty beach. This is a problem all along the east coast of the Azuero, and environmental and tourist groups complain that little is done to stop it. Let's hope there'll still be a beach at the beach when you visit.

The left fork back near Limón leads to **Punta Mala,** an exposed point at the southeast tip of the Azuero that's *mala* because of the rough seas as one rounds the point. Former Panamanian president Mireya Moscoso, a Pedasí native, took over an abandoned U.S. military building here after taking office in 1999 and set about turning it

into Panama's answer to the U.S. presidential retreat at Camp David. It became her weekend getaway. The whole project was quite mysterious and sparked a lot of controversy. The president was close-mouthed about the source of the funds used to renovate the place, for instance.

Though the compound is off-limits, there's public beach access next to it. Head down the road for 5.7 kilometers past the fork. A fairly wide stretch of the Río Caldera (note: This is not the same Río Caldera that bisects Boquete, in the Chiriquí highlands) runs right across the road at kilometer 4. Presidential clout was driving the construction of a bridge across the river, which should be completed by the time you read this.

If not, be careful about timing the crossing. At low tide, the stream is fordable in a four-wheel drive, but at high tide it's impassable except by boat. It's easy to get stranded for hours on the beach side of the stream, so those without a four-wheel drive or a tide table should park on the inland side and wade or swim across, then walk the last 1.5 kilometers or so.

The road ends at the presidential compound. There's a parking area. The beach starts down a short path to the left, though to get there may require another swim across the Caldera, since its wide mouth empties into the sea here. The beach is pretty, a half-moon arc of sand partly protected by a rocky point.

Playas El Toro and La Garita are a fairly easy hike from town, or a $3 taxi ride. A trip to Los Destiladeros or Punta Mala should run $5. If no taxis are around, call for one at 995-2275.

Day visitors can also use the secluded cove at La Playita Resort, about 30 kilometers south of Pedasí on the way to Playa Venao, for a small fee. The resort rents snorkeling gear, rowboats, and kayaks, and it can arrange fishing and boating trips to nearby areas. (See *Accommodations* for details.)

Diving and Sportfishing

The main dive destinations are the waters around **Isla Iguana** and the **Islas Frailes.**

Isla Iguana has extensive coral fields, though human pressures and El Niños have damaged them. The Islas Frailes, considerably farther out, off the southeast tip of the Azuero, are a pair of rock outcroppings that offer good open-water diving. There is no beach on either of the Frailes; all diving is from the boat. There are also two wrecks south of Punta Mala, in 20-meter-deep waters: a U.S. Navy ammunition ship that dates from before World War II and a shrimper.

Diving is best during the rainy season, from around April to December. From December to mid-March, dry-season winds stir up the sea and limit visibility. Wetsuits are necessary in January as protection from the cold waters of the Humboldt Current. They also fend off the stings of tiny jellyfish.

Buzos de Azuero (tel. 995-2405, fax 995-2412, bdazuero@hotmail.com, www.divenfish-panama.com, 8 A.M.–5 P.M. Mon.–Fri., 7 A.M.–7 P.M. Sat. and Sun.) is a reasonably well-equipped diving and deep-sea fishing outfit. It's situated between the Accel gas station and the CEFATI building at the north end of town.

It's owned by Jeffrey Hopkins, a friendly and laid-back gringo from Southern California, and his wife, Cristina Sosa de Hopkins, a Nicaraguan general-practice physician. Jeffrey has been diving since 1970 and became a diving instructor in 1977. Cristina divides her time between her practice in Costa Rica and her husband in Pedasí. Though at the time of writing she wasn't licensed to practice in Panama, it's worth keeping her in mind in a medical emergency.

Buzos de Azuero rents a dive equipment package, which includes one tank, weights, regulator, BCD, and wetsuit, for $30. A second tank is another $5. The shop has its own compressor. Snorkelers can rent a mask, snorkel, and fins for $10 a day.

Boat transportation is the same for divers/snorkelers and those who just want a boat ride. The trip to Isla Iguana costs $40. To the Islas Frailes it's $50. Trips are made on a 23-foot fiberglass boat with outboard motor. Your captain will be a local fisherman. Add $25 to the above prices for a diving guide.

There's more demand for sportfishing than diving around here. This area has been nicknamed the "tuna coast," and there's even a major international tuna research facility, **Laboratorio Achotines,** on the coast 30 kilometers south of Pedasí. Other big fish found in these waters include sailfish, wahoo, and black, blue, and striped marlin.

Buzos de Azuero charges $50 for a fishing trip around Isla Iguana. To Islas Frailes it's $70. The shop rents trawling rods for $20. Other equipment, such as lures and ice chests, can also be rented.

Jeffrey contracts out boat transportation for the above trips through local fishermen. For any trip, consider making arrangements through him rather than dealing directly with a fisherman. The price will probably be the same, and Jeffrey knows better than a first-time visitor which captains are reliable and likely to be sober at 8:00 in the morning (not all of them are).

One fisherman Jeffrey often works with is **Negro Garia,** who lives next to the Texaco station. He's much in demand for fishing and diving tours—when there is a demand.

Buzos de Azuero also has its own 33-foot boat that it uses for fishing and diving trips in the rainy season, from April to December. A trip to Isla Iguana in this boat costs $120 for up to 12 sunbathers or six divers. To Islas Frailes it's $185 for up to six divers. These prices don't include diving or snorkeling equipment. A half-day fishing trip to Islas Frailes in the boat costs $200 without fishing equipment or $350 with equipment. For a full day it's $275 without equipment or $425 with equipment.

The shop rents out life jackets for $1 a day, which is definitely a good investment. It also sells sunblock, film, insect repellent, and ice. The shop takes cash or travelers checks.

Buzos de Azuero also offers diving courses, including NAUI certification courses.

Surfing

Playa Venao (also called Venado), 34 kilometers southwest of town on the main road, is a popular surfing beach, and it's easy to see why. The beach describes a huge, easy arc, and the surf offers an exceptionally long and gentle ride that breaks left and right. It's a good place for beginners. The beach itself is not exceptionally pretty, so only surfers will likely find going all this way worthwhile.

The turnoff is poorly marked, so be careful not to overshoot it. Heading south, it's a left turn 1.4 kilometers south of the La Playita Resort turnoff. The road is good and it's possible to drive right up to the beach. There's a simple, open-air place that serves food and drinks. A taxi here costs about $12–15 one-way from Pedasí. Serious surfers, at least those with their own transportation, may want to check out two other popular spots farther west, along the bottom of the peninsula near the town of Tonosí. These are **Playa Guánico** (about 75 kilometers from Pedasí, 1.5 hours by car) and **Playa Cambutal** (a little under 100 kilometers, two hours by car). (See the *Tonosí* entry for details.)

ACCOMMODATIONS

Try to call ahead for hotel reservations. The risk is not so much that places will fill up as that business may be so slow the manager may not even be around to check guests in.

$10–25

Residencial Moscoso, (tel. 995-2203, start at $14 s, $16.50 d), on the main road toward the south end of town, is a simple but pleasant pension run by friendly folks. Both the people and the place possess lots of old Azuero character. Just to remind you how small Panamanian society really is, the place is owned by an uncle of Mireya Moscoso, the president of Panama 1999–2004. Rooms vary a lot. Some are quite dark and small. Some have air-conditioning. None has hot water. There is no restaurant on the premises, but there are places to eat nearby.

Hotel Residencial Pedasí (tel. 995-2322, $16.50 s, $22 d), on the main road at the north end of town, offers 16 clean, spartan rooms. The beds are a bit saggy and the rooms tend to be somewhat dark. But the spot is nice and quiet. There's an open-air dining hall on the premises, but it's not in use these days.

The nicest place to stay in town is **M Dim's Hostel** (tel. 995-2303, mirely@iname.com, $16.50 s, $24.20 d, including breakfast). It's on the west side of the main road about midway through town. Accommodations consist of five air-conditioned rooms with private bath in the aging home of the owner, Mirna Batista. Rooms are pretty basic, but they have character and were recently renovated. None of the rooms has hot water. Guests are served full breakfasts out on an attractive, if odd, thatch-roofed patio area with a massive mango tree as the centerpiece. Guests can bring their own food for lunch and dinner and use the house kitchen to prepare it. Mirna is an energetic, attentive, and helpful host who speaks pretty good English (though she's shy about using it) and is eager to see more tourists come to Pedasí. She's very friendly and will cheerfully take guests under her wing if they want her to. For a while, she tried to get a tour guide service going, but that faded away from lack of tourists. But she's still the go-to person for help setting up a trip to Isla de Cañas and other area attractions. This place is popular, so make reservations as far in advance as possible, especially during the dry season and holidays.

There are four very rustic cabins on the beach at **Playa Venao** that have showers and electricity. They go for $14 a night, which is high for what they offer, especially when campers can just pitch a tent on the beach for free. Those who must have a roof over their heads should ask for the proprietor at the basic restaurant/bar next door. The phone number (it's a pay phone) is tel. 995-8107.

$25–50

La Playita Resort (tel. 996-5491 in Chitré; there's no local land line, though you can also try calling cell 639-2968; $45 s, $50 d, $55 t but may go up when the place is finished) is 30 kilometers south of Pedasí, halfway between the Achotines Laboratory and Playa Venao. It has by far the most attractive accommodations in the entire area.

The "resort" is a small, well-appointed *finca* owned by Lester Knight, a horse-racing jockey with a Panamanian mother and an American father. His land is secluded and the *finca* is built right above a lovely beach that, given its location, is essentially a private cove. A couple of islets offshore form a natural breakwater, so the surf is calm here. A short marble staircase leads down to the sand. The whole complex features lots of whimsical tilework.

The *finca* offers two large "cabañas" and five other rooms in a new building that should be ready by the time you read this. The finished rooms were quite nice, done up in Spanish style with teak furniture. They're cold-water only.

A huge *rancho* with kitchen and bar was being built during my last visit. The staff cooks simple meals for the guests that range from about $2.50 for breakfast to $4 for dinner. Guests can also bring their own food and use the kitchen. This is a quite casual place.

Knight is a bit of a character, which shows in the way he's designed his sanctuary. He always wanted a zoo when he was a kid, and now he's got one. He lets all kinds of exotic creatures roam free on his land, including emus, turkeys, a Geoffroy's tamarin (a small primate), and seven macaws, including a rare scarlet macaw. There's also a large cage filled with all kinds of other birds. Mornings around here are pure cacophony.

Most incongruous of all are two enormous ostriches, which wander wherever they please and pack a hell of a kick for those who'd dare bother them; stay well away from them. Their numbers may have dropped to one by now. During my last visit, one of them snatched up and ate a plastic T-connector pipe before workers could stop it. It was painful to watch the large piece of plumbing make its way slowly down the poor animal's long throat.

All the creatures wandering around make this a less tranquil, if more colorful, place than it was a couple of years ago. So does management's encouragement of day trippers. This little place averages 200 day visitors during dry-season weekends and can sometimes draw 500 or more partiers. Those looking for a secluded spot should try to come during the week and should definitely avoid the place during holidays.

Day use of the beach for nonguests, including access to the quite nice public bathrooms, is $3 for adults, $1 for kids.

The *finca* rents snorkeling gear ($6/day), rowboats ($5/hour), and kayaks ($1/hour). It's also possible to hire a boat and captain for trips varying from a jaunt to Playa Venao ($5 per person) to a fishing trip ($30/hour). Guests can borrow fishing rods and buy lures from the *finca*.

The turn off the main road toward La Playita Resort leads onto a dirt country road that's okay in the dry season but requires a four-wheel drive in the rainy season. Taxis from Pedasí make the trip for about $12 one-way. If the driver doesn't recognize the name of the resort, ask for "la casa de Lester." Bus service from Pedasí, which was always very limited, has become even more so with the dropping of service all the way to Tonosí. At the time of writing there was just one morning bus, at 8 A.M., and one afternoon bus, at 4 P.M. The fare is $1.75. This is the bus to Cañas, which will stop at the resort by request (again, ask for "casa de Lester" if the driver's puzzled). If the driver's in a good mood, he may take visitors all the way to the *finca*. Otherwise it's a short hike in.

Camping

There are a few informal options for campers. As has been mentioned elsewhere, it's not a good idea to camp outside a tent because of the slight risk of being bitten by a rabies-carrying vampire bat. The area around Pedasí is very mellow, so campers probably don't have to be as worried about being molested by bad guys as they would closer to urban areas. Still, solo campers may want to think twice about pitching a tent in a very remote area, just as they would in their home country.

Camping on any beach is free and legal. Playa Venao is an easily accessible spot that's popular with surfers.

It's also possible to camp overnight on Isla Iguana, but make sure the fisherman who takes you over is reliable and will show up for the return trip to shore. Except on dry-season weekends, the island doesn't get a lot of traffic and it's possible to get stranded there for days. The usual fee to camp on protected land is $5, but again it will probably not be easy to find someone to pay the fee to.

If business is slow, campers may also be able to work out a deal to pitch a tent on the lovely beach at La Playita Resort. The fee had been $10 a night, which includes access to bathroom facilities, but policy on this may change once the resort is fully functioning.

FOOD

Pedasí is not the place for fine dining. In fact, sometimes it's not the place for any kind of dining. Despite their alleged opening hours, it's quite possible to find every eatery in town closed at meal times. This is a good place to bring a well-stocked cooler.

The restaurants are all essentially *fondas*, holes-in-the-wall that cater to workers who get an early start and are willing to eat whatever's on hand, served at rock-bottom prices. The best bet for breakfast is to show up no later than 8 A.M. The restaurants start shutting down shortly after nightfall.

Restaurante Brisas de Pedasí serves breakfast, lunch, and dinner and makes a modest stab at an atmosphere. It actually has tablecloths, for instance. Offerings can include *bistec picado* (chopped steak), spaghetti, rice and lentils, grilled chicken, and so on. A filling meal of beef, rice, lentils, and a couple of beers comes to $3.50.

Restaurante Angela, (tel. 995-2275), right next to Dim's Hostel, is a bare bones place that serves hearty local food. Nothing on the menu is

more than $2. It opens at dawn and closes at sunset; if Angela knows you're coming she may stay open a little later.

Restaurante Marisco del Faro (tel. 995-2317) by the Texaco station at the end of town, is an ultrabasic place where you can get a more-or-less edible breakfast for next to nothing.

The peach-colored place 100 meters south of Residencial Moscoso is officially called **Las Delicias,** though there's no sign. It's another basic *fonda* that's open for breakfast, lunch, and dinner.

Panadería y Refresquería Betel (6 A.M.–2 P.M. and 4–10 P.M. Mon.–Sat., 6–10 A.M. and 4–10 P.M. Sun.), on the town plaza, offers bread, sweets, and ice cream.

Refresquería y Dulcería Yely (9 A.M.–8 P.M. daily, and maybe open until 9 P.M. on Sat.), across the street from and south of Residencial Moscoso, is a clean sweets shop locally famous for its cakes. Slices are just $.25. The *nueces* (nut) cake is good; the rum one is just so-so. It also offers *flan, tres leches,* and other temptations.

There's a minimally stocked supermercado on the town plaza next to Restaurante Brisas de Pedasí. The minisuper near the Texaco station is the only store open late at night. There's also a little *rancho* two kilometers south of town that serves seafood, but I've yet to have the pleasure.

INFORMATION AND SERVICES

The CEFATI tourist information center (tel. 995-2339, 8:30 A.M.–4:30 P.M. daily; the building is sometimes left open until 10 P.M.) is at the north end of town. To get there as you drive south into town, go past the Hotel Residencial Pedasí and the sad little park and make a left at the gas station. Whether there'll actually be someone in this attractive tourist information office who has tourist information to share is, as usual, dubious. Chances of that person's speaking English are even less. Those who strike out here will have a much better chance of getting solid information, in English and Spanish, at Buzos de Azuero, the dive shop next door, and from Mirna Batista, the owner of Dim's Hostel, in the middle of town.

The mammoth Banco Nacional de Panamá

(8 A.M.–3 P.M. Mon.–Fri., 9 A.M.–noon Sat.) is hard to miss at the north end of town.

The post office (7 A.M.–6 P.M. Mon.–Fri., 7 A.M.–5 P.M. Sat.) is behind the ambitiously named Palacio Municipal, across the street from Restaurante Angela.

Infoplaza, the Internet café attached to the CEFATI, has erratic hours. It will probably be open during daylight hours Monday–Wednesday, Friday, and Saturday, starting sometime between 8:30 and 10 A.M. It will probably be closed Thursdays. It will definitely be closed Sundays. Rates are $1/hour. Save files often and keep emails short; the computers crash regularly. There's a public bathroom in the building.

Buzos de Azuero rents out life jackets for $1 a day, which is definitely a good investment. It also sells sunblock, film, insect repellent, and ice.

GETTING THERE AND AWAY

Buses to Las Tablas leave from the main street every 45 minutes 6 A.M.–5 P.M. The fare is $2. There is no longer bus service between Pedasí and Tonosí, though a bus goes as far as Cañas, the jumping-off point for Isla de Cañas, at 8 A.M. and 4 P.M. The fare is $2.25.

The town is easily walkable; the main street is just a kilometer long. There's a taxi stand (tel. 995-2275) on that street just north of Residencial Moscoso for longer trips. One-way fares include Playa Arenal for $2.50, Playa Garita or Playa El Toro for $3, Playa Destiladeros or Punta Mala for $5, Playa Venao for $15, and Tonosí for $25. Those on a tight budget can also hike to Arenal, Toro, or Garita without much trouble. They're about three kilometers from the center of town.

Islands Near Pedasí

REFUGIO DE VIDA SILVESTRE ISLA IGUANA

Isla Iguana is a small, narrow island that, along with its surrounding waters, was declared a wildlife sanctuary in 1981. It's accessible by boat from Playa El Arenal in Pedasí. The island is a popular spot for snorkeling since it has the biggest (15 hectares) and oldest (500 years) coral reef in the Gulf of Panama, and it's the only one that's nominally protected. It contains more than a dozen species of coral and attracts about 200 species of reef fish.

Among the dozens of bird species drawn to the island, the most important is a colony of 5,000 magnificent frigatebirds, the largest colony in the eastern Azuero.

Sadly, the island and its waters are far from pristine. The current brings garbage from as far away as Panama City, as do some thoughtless visitors who junk up the beach, drop anchors on the coral, and take back souvenirs.

Also, the U.S. military used this island for target practice during World War II, as evidenced by the craters in the middle of the island. More than half a dozen bombs have been found and deto-

nated on the island since then; there may be more that haven't been discovered, so don't wander off the trail.

Still, there's lots of natural beauty left that humans and coral-damaging El Niños haven't yet destroyed.

Snorkeling is best off the west side of the island, where the longest beach is. Known as **Playa El Cirial** or simply La Playa, it's a pretty, long, light-sand beach as long as you ignore the motor-oil bottles, tires, plastic buckets, and so on that can wash up and spoil the scene. Swimmers should not venture out past the reef, as the water quickly turns rough.

A 200-meter trail leads to a tiny beach on the east side of the island that seems to attract less trash. There's a small lighthouse in the middle of the trail. It has a rusty ladder that those who don't suffer from vertigo or a fear of a broken leg this far from civilization can climb to check out the view and a few bomb craters.

Divers may be able to find moray eels off the north end of the island, octopus and large jewfish around the rocky outcroppings on the southern end, and big schools of fish among the mushroom coral fields off the southeast side.

Note that the waters around the island can get quite turbulent.

The boat ride takes about 20 minutes from Playa El Arenal, 30 minutes if the water is choppy. Be prepared for one hell of a bouncy adventure on a windy dry-season morning; it feels more like a watery roller-coaster ride than a boat trip. On those days, the return trip can be much faster, as the wind and waves practically blast the boat back to shore.

Since Isla Iguana is a government wildlife refuge, there's allegedly a $3 charge to visit, though as usual with remote parks, finding someone to pay it to can be difficult.

Fishermen charge $40 round-trip for the boat ride to Isla Iguana from Arenal. (See *Diving and Sportfishing* for recommendations.) **Iguana Tours** in Panama City (226-8738 or 226-4516, fax 226-4736, iguana@sinfo.net, www.nvmundo .com/iguanatours/index.htm), specializes in trips to the island from Panama City and may be able to tell you about current reef conditions.

REFUGIO DE VIDA SILVESTRE ISLA DE CAÑAS

Isla de Cañas is the most important nesting site for sea turtles on Panama's Pacific coast. Five species come here. By far the most numerous is the olive ridley *(Lepidochelys olivacea)*, the smallest of the turtles that come to Panama, weighing in at about 35–45 kilograms and with a shell about 70 centimeters long. The second-most frequent visitor is the Pacific green *(Chelonia mydas)*, followed, in very limited numbers, by the loggerhead *(Caretta caretta)*, leatherback *(Dermochelys coriacea)*, and hawksbill *(Eretmochelys imbricata)*.

To make things confusing, the green turtle is known colloquially in Panama as the *tortuga negra* (black turtle) and the olive ridley as the *tortuga mulata* (mulatto turtle).

Every year between 20,000 and 30,000 turtles show up to lay their eggs in successive waves, which makes for a spectacular sight if one times a visit right. That's not necessarily an easy thing to do, since no one seems to agree on the best time to come. Visitors should be able to see the best ac-

tion between September and November, though nesting season can begin as early as April or May, and islanders say that massive inundations of turtles have occurred as late as the end of December. Very few turtles nest during the dry-season months of January through March.

Getting to the island is kind of complicated, but the trip is fun. From Pedasí, head south on the main road to the town of Cañas, about 40 kilometers away, or 11 kilometers south of Playa Venao. The turnoff is on the left, and it's easy to miss because the sign faces the northbound traffic. Head down the rocky but okay road until it dead-ends at the shore 2.5 kilometers away. Isla de Cañas is a long, narrow barrier island parallel to and quite close to shore. It's an unusual island: Its ocean-facing beach is 13 kilometers long, but the island is just 175 meters wide at its narrowest point.

From the landing it's a five-minute boat ride through mangroves to the island ($.50 per person each way). Go at high tide if you don't want to slop around in muck. If there's no boat waiting, call the island's one phone; it's a pay phone and the number is tel. 995-8002. Ask for Neyla or for a *lancha* or *bote.* The closest pay phone to make the call is back in Cañas.

The biggest pain in all this is getting to the flyspeck village of Cañas, on the mainland. The area is not well served by buses, especially since a route running between Pedasí and Tonosí was dropped in recent years. Only two buses make the trip from Pedasí, at 8 A.M. and 4 P.M. The fare is $2.25. Taxis from Pedasí are about $20 each way; make sure to arrange a pickup time, try not to pay until the return trip, and hope for the best.

Given the logistical hassles involved in getting here, many will find it worthwhile to arrange a guided trip. Most of these will have to be arranged with a tour operator back in Panama City, but those near Pedasí should contact Mirna Batista at Dim's Hostel, who if she has time may be able to arrange a trip for a quite reasonable fee, probably no more than the cost of a taxi. She knows the area well.

The island is a colorful place with a population of about 900, most of whom live in cane houses. The community has been here since the

sugar-cane farmers and a sugar-cane press on Isla de Cañas

1920s, drawn from mainland towns and the surrounding countryside. They protect the turtles and their eggs, in exchange for which they're legally allowed to harvest some eggs (but not the turtles).

There are a few ultrabasic, no-name huts for rent near the beach for $10–15 per night, but those who want to hang out here are better off pitching a tent on the beach for free. A local sugarcane farmer, Señor Fernando, will take visitors for a ride on his cane cart for $8 per group, but the beach where the turtles do their thing is just a five-minute walk across the island.

Sea turtles lay their eggs only late at night, but trying to get to the island alone after dark can be tricky, not to mention spooky. Camping on the beach is probably the best bet for those not traveling with a guide. Do not use flashlights or wear light-colored clothing at night; the turtles are easily disoriented and scared off by anything brighter than moonlight.

Those visiting the island without a guide should still hire a villager to guide them to the turtles. It likely will cost less than $10 per group (arrange the price ahead of time) and the tourism dollars help ensure the turtles are left in peace to procreate rather than end up on someone's dinner plate.

Tonosí

Really little more than a glorified crossroads, Tonosí (pop. 2,272) will be of interest mainly to surfers going to or coming from nearby Playa Guánico and Playa Cambutal. It's not a pretty town, though it does have some facilities, including one surprisingly decent place to stay, as well as a couple of more basic but cheaper options. There are also a post office and a few gas stations and pharmacies.

Most everything in town is built around a Y-shaped intersection. The northeast road forks six kilometers east of town. Its right fork heads north to Isla de Cañas, Playa Venao, and Pedasí,

and continues from there to Las Tablas. The left fork is a more direct route to Las Tablas that cuts out the intermediate stops.

The south road leads to Playa Guánico and Playa Cambutal, on the southern coast of the Azuero. It also heads toward Parque Nacional Cerro Hoya, but the park is virtually inaccessible, especially by land. There are no facilities of any kind.

Only one thing passes for a sight in Tonosí. One kilometer south of town on the road to the beaches, make a quick stop at the overpass over the Río Tonosí. Look left down at the pond: It's absolutely crawling with caimans. Locals some times feed them bread as though they were ducks. Those who have trouble spotting the pond should ask in town where to find the *lagartos*.

BEACHES

Playa Guánico and **Playa Cambutal** are known for good surf. Cambutal is the more attractive of the two, but it's also much harder to get to. Only serious surfers should bother coming all the way down to this remote part of the Azuero. Those just looking for a little beach time would do better to visit the beaches around Pedasí or even Playa Venao.

To get to either beach, head south from Tonosí (the bottom of the Y intersection). After about 15 kilometers there'll be a marked left turn into the town of Guánico. There's a green iguana-breeding project in town, but there's no real facility to visit. Those with sharp eyes may see one of the big guys up in a tree. Head straight through town to find the beach, which is eight kilometers away down a dirt road. There's a little open-air restaurant. The beach has black sand.

Back on the main road, take the left fork that appears five kilometers past the Guánico turnoff. (The right fork leads to the nearly inaccessible Parque Nacional Cerro Hoya.) The town of Cambutal is 10 kilometers past the turnoff. The paved road quickly turns into a very rough dirt one that follows the beach. It's impassable by regular car in the rainy season, but may just be manageable in the dry season. Be prepared, however, to ford two streams. This beach is more picturesque than Guánico, and it's certainly isolated. There are no facilities.

PRACTICALITIES

Residencial Mar y Selva (tel. 995-8003, $16 s/d), between two gas stations on the north end of town, has 10 small, barely passable rooms with air-conditioning, hot water, and telephones.

They're not terribly clean, but they're okay. There's an open-air restaurant downstairs.

Pensión Boamy (tel. 995-8142, $18.70 s/d and up), a pleasant surprise on the road to Playa Cambutal, has 11 rooms with air-conditioning, TVs, and hot-water bathrooms. It's a clean, perfectly fine place by a church on the edge of town. It also has a cheerful little restaurant. It's the best place in town.

Camping on the beaches, as usual in Panama, is free. Only do so in a tent, however, and it's not a good idea to camp alone in such isolated spots.

Banco Nacional de Panamá (8 A.M.–3 P.M. Mon.–Fri., 9 A.M.–noon Sat.), near the center of town, lacked an ATM at the time of writing.

GETTING THERE AND AWAY

Buses to Las Tablas leave from the center of town every hour and a half or so 6 A.M.–4 P.M. Monday–Saturday and 7:30 A.M.–4:30 P.M. on Sunday. The trip costs $3 and takes an hour and 20 minutes. Buses no longer run between Tonosí and Pedasí, oddly enough.

The northwest road out of Tonosí winds through the still relatively unspoiled southwest tip of the Azuero. It starts out hilly, with sweeping views of deforested but still scenic hills, passes through the town of Macaracas, and ends up in the flatlands as it gets close to Chitré, about 100 kilometers away. Those who drive this way should watch out for tire-eating potholes and one-way bridges.

MACARACAS

One note on Macaracas: For nearly two hundred years the town has celebrated Epiphany (January 6) through a staged reenactment of the gift of the Magis to the baby Jesus, starring the townspeople themselves. The **Fiesta de los Reyes Magos,** as it's called, is pegged to January 6 but lasts for several days. Dates vary each year; check with IPAT.

Golfo de Chiriquí and the Western Highlands

Western Panama offers some of Panama's most spectacular, and diverse, attractions.

On the one hand, there are the verdant highlands, home to the country's tallest mountain and the picturesque town of Boquete, which now rivals Bocas del Toro as Panama's hottest destination for foreign tourists and retirees. On the other, there are the remote Pacific islands and beaches of the Golfo de Chiriquí, which is so large and species-rich some consider it a small sea.

The Golfo de Chiriquí extends from Punta Burica at the western edge of Panama toward the Azuero Peninsula to the east, encompassing the entire coast of Chiriquí province and much of the Pacific coast of Veraguas. It's a region of superlatives. It contains the richest mangrove forests in Central America, the largest island in Panama, and one of the largest coral reefs in the Pacific. It offers truly world-class diving, surfing, and sportfishing.

Conservation organizations have targeted this area as one of the most ecologically important in Central America. It has so far seen relatively little

Must-Sees

M Parque Nacional Marino Golfo de Chiriquí: A remote and still little-known tropical paradise lightly peppered with deserted islands, bohemian hangouts, and an exclusive resort (page 338).

M Parque Nacional Coiba: Panama's answer to the Galapagos, Coiba is the crown jewel of the country's islands, with virgin forest covering it, rich sealife surrounding it, and a Devil's Island mystique about it (page 342).

M Playa Santa Catalina: Panama's top spot for surfers, remote Catalina has one of the most consistently awesome breaks in all of Latin America (page 347).

M Finca Lérida: It's pricey to visit and not easy to get to, but this highland coffee farm is one of the best places anywhere to see the resplendent quetzal (page 359).

M Parque Nacional Volcán Barú: Panama's tallest mountain is visible from everywhere in the western highlands, and on a clear day adventurous hikers can see both oceans from its summit. Don't miss Sendero Los Quetzales—the most popular hike in the highlands—while you're here (page 366).

© WILLIAM FRIAR

Parque Internacional La Amistad is a gigantic park with trails that lead to magnificent waterfalls.

M Parque Internacional La Amistad: A gigantic national park, with some of the most diverse flora and fauna in Panama (page 379).

M Cañon Macho de Monte: An impressive and accessible canyon that appeals both to bird watchers and inner-tube rafters (page 389).

Golfo de Chiriquí

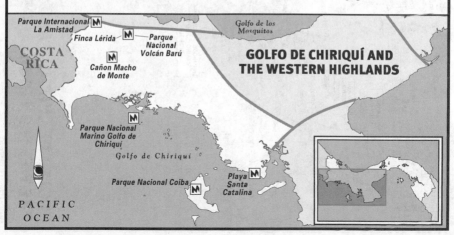

Parque Internacional La Amistad

Finca Lérida

Parque Nacional Volcán Barú

COSTA RICA

Cañon Macho de Monte

Golfo de los Mosquitos

GOLFO DE CHIRIQUÍ AND THE WESTERN HIGHLANDS

Parque Nacional Marino Golfo de Chiriquí

Golfo de Chiriquí

Parque Nacional Coiba

Playa Santa Catalina

PACIFIC OCEAN

El Copé

COCLÉ

Divisá

San Francisco

Santiago

La Peña

Puerto Mutis

La Mesa

HERRERA

Las Minas

Ocú

Auzero Peninsula

Arenas

Cerro Hoya

Parque Nacional Cerro Hoya

VERAGUAS

Santa Fé

Cordillera Central

Cañazas

La Mesa

Soná

Golfo de Montijo

Isla Cébaco

Santa Catalina

Hicaco

M PLAYA SANTA CATALINA

20 mi

20 km

BOCAS DEL TORO

Golfo de los Mosquitos

Río Caña

Río Cricamola

INTERAMERICANA

Tolé

El Cruce

Las Lajas

Isla Silva de Afuera

Isla Silva de Adentro

Morro Negrito

PENAL COLONY

M PARQUE NACIONAL COIBA

Isla de Coiba

Isla Jicarón

Islas Contreras

Chiriquí Grande

Bosque Protector de Palo Seco

CHIRIQUÍ

Soloy

Horconcitos

Islas Secas

Isla Las Ladrones

Golfo de Chiriquí

Isla Montuosa

FORTUNA RD

To Almirante

Boquete

Gualaca

Caldera

Río Caldera

Chiriquí

Boca Chica

Isla Boca Brava

M PARQUE NACIONAL MARINO GOLFO DE CHIRIQUÍ

Cordillera de Talamanca

Alto Quiel

M FINCA LÉRIDA

Río Caldera

David

Dolega

Chiriquí

Isla Parida

Islas Las Ladrones

M PARQUE NACIONAL VOLCÁN BARÚ

Guadalupe

Cerro Punta

Nueva Suiza

Bambito

Volcán

Santa Cruz

Río Chiriquí

★ **M** CAÑÓN MACHO DE MONTE

La Concepción

Pedregal

Playa Barqueta

Dolega

Río Sereno

M PARQUE INTERNACIONAL LA AMISTAD

COSTA RICA

Paso Canoa

Progreso

Puerto Armuelles

Viejo

Bahía de Charco Azul

Limones

Bella Vista

Punta Burica

PACIFIC OCEAN

GOLFO DE CHIRIQUÍ AND THE WESTERN HIGHLANDS

development, but human pressures are mounting. Panama has reacted by establishing protected areas, most notably two huge marine parks: Parque Nacional Marino Golfo de Chiriquí and the newly created Parque Nacional Coiba.

Because the Golfo de Chiriquí is still so remote and untouched, facilities for visitors in the most scenic areas are limited and getting around can be laborious. But the region also includes Panama's second-largest city, David, near the coast not far from the Costa Rican border.

Most visitors simply pass through David on the way to somewhere else, usually the highlands, but it has all the services one would expect of a busy, modern provincial capital. There are a few large beaches within a couple hours' drive of David, the most popular of which are Playa Barqueta and Playa Las Lajas. Farther east, remote Playa Santa Catalina is internationally famous as one of the best surfing spots in Latin America.

Those who visit the western highlands after a trip to the beaches and islands feel they have entered a different world, a world filled with powerful rivers, gigantic waterfalls, imposing mountains, secluded hot springs, and green forests bursting with life. The highlands are also home to Volcán Barú, a dormant volcano that, at 3,475 meters, is Panama's biggest and most dramatic mountain.

There's plenty to keep outdoorsy types busy, including hiking, horseback riding, biking, the country's best white-water rafting, kayaking, even rock climbing and rappelling. The western highlands are popular with bird-watchers, since the forests attract hundreds of species, including many spectacular ones.

Most of the highland sights are clustered on the west and east sides of Volcán Barú. While the west side of Barú is a bit cooler and more dramatic looking, the east side has both great beauty and something its western neighbor lacks: a charming little town called Boquete.

Boquete is booming. As a result, there are more options for lodging, food, outfitters, and guided tours on this side of the mountain. The west side of Barú is quieter, less densely populated, and more rugged. It also has easily accessible trails through the enormous Parque Internacional la Amistad.

PLANNING YOUR TIME

Most visitors to western Panama choose to spend their time in the highlands, either on the west side or the east side of **Volcán Barú**. To truly do justice to both sides of the mountain would require up to a week. The eastern side, centered around **Boquete,** is more popular. Allow at least three days to explore the town, go for a hike, and do at least one of the activities the area is known for, such as a coffee tour, white-water rafting trip, or search for quetzals. The highlights of the western side, including a long hike, can be covered in two days. Physically fit visitors who want to see both sides of the mountain should consider hiking the **Sendero Los Quetzales** from one side to another when they're ready to relocate; allow a full day for this.

It's fun to combine a trip to the highlands with a visit to the beaches and islands of the Golfo de Chiriquí. It's quite a contrast. Those who just want a little beach time can spend a night or two at the mainland beaches of **Barqueta** or **Las Lajas,** or make day trips there from **David.** David itself can be explored in half a day, and most people give it even less time than that. Getting just about anywhere else in the Golfo de Chiriquí takes time and planning, especially for those of us who don't own private yachts.

Parque Nacional Coiba is about two hours by boat from the nearest mainland ports; only private planes can fly there, and only then with special permission. Reaching **Playa Santa Catalina** or **Parque Marino Golfo de Chiriquí** by land means driving considerable distances on brutally bad roads. Most guests arrive at the **Islas Secas Resort** by private plane arranged by the resort.

Few will have the time or inclination to visit both marine parks. Coiba and its surrounding waters and islands are stunning, at the top of most visitors' wish lists. **Parque Nacional Golfo de Chiriqúi** is not as uniquely impressive as Coiba, but it has plenty of small, deserted islands to explore, and it's easier and cheaper to get to.

Most people get to the islands of the gulf through a tour, dive, surf, or fishing operator, though some areas close to shore can be reached by taking a taxi, bus, or private vehicle to the coast, where fishing boats can generally be hired. Even Coiba can be reached this way, though it's not the safest and certainly not the fastest way to go. Plan to spend at least two nights on the islands to enjoy the surroundings and recover from the hassle of getting there.

Exploring the **Fortuna Road area** makes most sense for travelers who are driving or taking a bus to or from Bocas del Toro. Otherwise, combining it with a visit to the Volcán Barú or Golfo de Chiriquí areas would mean more traveling than most are likely to want.

David

Depending on where one draws the boundaries, David (dah-VEED), the provincial capital of Chiriquí province, is the second- or third-largest city in Panama (pop. 77,734 in the central city, 124,280 in the entire district). It's the lowland hub for visits to the highlands and other parts of western Panama and has the largest concentration of visitor services in the region.

David is a busy, congested commerce and transportation center for Chiriquí province, which has the most productive farmland in the country. Every year the city hosts the Feria Internacional de David, an enormous agriculture and livestock fair that draws participants from around Latin America, Europe, and even Asia.

Few foreign visitors who aren't into farming or business spend much time in the city, however. Though David was settled by the Spanish in 1602 and has a history of indigenous inhabitation far older than that, few traces of all that rich history remain and most of the contemporary buildings and byways are utilitarian at best. Its lowland location close to, but not close enough to, the coast can also make it wiltingly hot and humid.

Those who spend much time on this side of the country, though, will likely have to spend at least one night here. Fortunately it has decent places to stay and eat, and even a few city-style diversions. It can offer a good change of pace after time spent in the boonies.

Although there has been local concern in the last couple of years about a rise in youth gangs, David is a pretty safe and mellow town. I've walked all over the place at all hours of the day and night and never felt threatened. *Davideños* are generally easygoing and cordial, and there just isn't enough tourism here for scams and rip-offs to be a serious concern. But David is a growing

city, and visitors should keep their city smarts about them, particularly women traveling alone. Also, streets beyond the center of town are poorly lit and deserted at night.

SIGHTS

David is not a particularly scenic town, and it has little that qualifies as a true sight. The best way to get a feel for the place and its people is to wander around, especially near **Parque Cervantes,** the plaza at the center of town. The church on the northwest side of the plaza, **Iglesia de la Sagrada Familia,** is said to date from 1810, but the current interior is newish and generic and has all the ambience of an income-tax office.

There are some colonial-era buildings on the southeast side of town in an area of a few square blocks known as **Barrio Bolívar.** This area is also sometimes known as **El Peligro** (the danger). There are different theories about how it got that name. My favorite is that the barrio is in the vicinity of a church, a cemetery, a funeral home, and a jail. Don't let the name put you off: It's worth roaming around a bit here.

Most notable of these buildings is the **Museo de Historia y de Arte José de Obaldía** (Avenida 8 Este between Calle Central and Calle A Norte, tel. 775-7839, 8 A.M.–4 P.M. Mon.–Sat., closed Sun., $1 adults, $.25 children), a small museum housed in the 150-year-old wooden, red tile–roofed home of José de Obaldía (1806-1889). An important figure in 19th century Panamanian history, he was instrumental in the founding of Chiriquí province in 1849. Among his other notable accomplishments was a stint as acting president of New Granada, which encompassed Panama and Colombia, 1854–1855.

This "history and art" museum is an extremely modest place, though not especially so by Panamanian museum standards. The displays, which have virtually no descriptions, include a *metate* (a flat stone used for grinding corn) and a broken statue from the ancient Barriles culture, whose roots in Chiriquí date to 734 B.C. There are also some Spanish colonial swords and wooden church figures. Some mementos from the War of a Thousand Days are upstairs. Several items in the museum's collection have been stolen over the years. The attendant can give a little information about the place to those who speak Spanish.

A couple of blocks farther down, near Avenida 10 Este and Calle A Norte, is the crumbling **tower of the Catedral San José de David,** which dates from 1891. Its bell hasn't rung since Panama's centennial celebration, but the local padre says that has nothing to do with fear the tower might collapse. There are rumblings about restoring the tower some day.

ENTERTAINMENT AND EVENTS

Discoteca La Boom (on Avenida Obaldía near the intersection of Calle E Norte and Avenida 9 de Enero/1 Este, tel. 777-3520) is a popular disco near the bus terminal that tends to close during the dry season, preferring not to compete with the many festivals, parties, and Carnaval celebrations during that time. Wednesday is ladies' night and Friday is all-you-can-drink night for a cover charge of $8 (men) and $5 (women).

Pool players can knock balls around at **Billar Top Place** (Calle Miguel A. Brenes/F Sur and Avenida 5 Oeste), next to Restaurante Jenny #19, for $1.50 an hour.

Super Strike David (Avenida 5 Oeste between Calle B and Calle C, tel. 775-7172 or 775-7142) is a bowling alley one block behind the Purple House Hostel. It charges $1.75 a game, $.50 for shoes.

There's a casino in the Gran Hotel Nacional. A new 24-hour casino recently opened in the same building that houses Restaurante Jenny #19.

The best bets for movies are the **Gran Hotel Nacional** and the new **Chiriquí Mall,** both of which have six-screen multiplexes. Movies cost $2.50, or $1.80 for matinees.

The **Feria Internacional de San José de David,** usually shortened to the Feria Internacional de David or simply the Feria de David, is a huge trade fair that draws thousands of attendees from all over the country and abroad for 10 days in mid-March. It's essentially a giant agriculture, livestock, and commerce convention, though it does make room for folkloric crafts and dances. The fairgrounds take up 12 hectares on the western outskirts of town near Avenida 9 de Enero /1 Este, the road that leads to Playa Barqueta. In recent years it's drawn 500 exhibitors from around Panama, Latin America, and beyond, including some from Europe and Asia, as well as 600 prize livestock specimens. It's said to draw a staggering 300,000 attendees a year, though that's hard to believe. One suspects a few of these get counted more than once over the 10 days.

David's Barrio Bolívar celebrates the **Festival del Tambor** at the end of November, around the time of Panama's celebration of its independence from Spain on November 28. This is a traditional festival that features *tambores* (drums), *tunas* (marching bands), folkloric dances in colorful local costumes, and traditional *chiricano* food.

David and its surrounding communities celebrate **Carnaval** along with the rest of the country. A particularly popular place to go for the celebration is Dolega, a small town about midway between David and Boquete. It's less than 20 kilometers up the David-Boquete road. It's a more mellow affair than Carnaval in Las Tablas and Panama City.

March 19 is the *fiesta patronal de San José,* David's patron saint's day.

SHOPPING

Vendors near the Migracíon y Naturalización office sell Ngobe-Buglé dresses and other items varying from fresh produce to hammocks. **Avenida 3 de Noviembre** (Avenida 4 Este), which runs past Parque Cervantes northeast towards Avenida Obaldía, is a busy commercial street with many shops hawking inexpensive clothes and household goods and such. The big new **Chiriquí Mall,** a few kilometers west of David on the Interamercana, opened in May of 2003 with a multiplex, a branch of El Hombre de la Mancha bookstore (tel. 774-1174, 11 A.M.– 8 P.M. daily), fast-food stalls, clothing stores, and so on. **CD Place** (Avenida Obaldía near the intersection of Avenida 9 de Enero/1 Este and Calle F Norte, tel. 777-0729, 10:30 A.M.–8 P.M. Mon.–Sat., closed Sun.) has a decent but expensive collection of Panamanian *típico,* rock (including some *rock en español*), and salsa. It's near the bus terminal.

Those who'd like to take back some good-quality Chiriquí highland coffee without going to the Chiriquí highlands can buy gourmet-roast Café Ruiz coffee, one of the finest in Panama, at the **Super Barú** supermarket. It's the only store in Panama, except for the Café Ruiz shops in Boquete and Panama City, that carries the gourmet roast. Other kinds of Café Ruiz are more widely available.

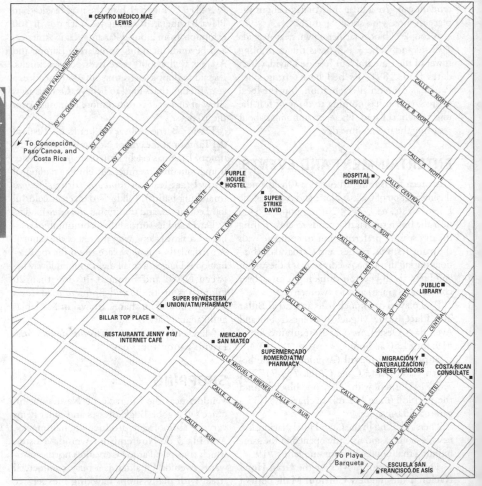

SPORTS AND RECREATION

The **swimming pool** at the Gran Hotel Nacional (tel. 775-2221 or 775-2222) is usually reserved for guests but they sometimes make an exception. Look respectable, ask at the pool rather than at the reception, and expect to pay a couple of dollars. The pool's nothing fancy, but it's fairly large. There are changing rooms nearby.

The most popular beach within easy driving distance of David is **Playa Barqueta,** a wide,

black-sand beach with pounding surf that's usually far too rough for swimming. Think seriously before going into these waters above your calves. I grew up body surfing in fairly big surf on Panama's Pacific beaches, and I wouldn't dare go for a splash in what I've seen at Barqueta.

A wildlife refuge, **Refugio de Vida Silvestre La Barqueta** (8 A.M.–4 P.M. daily, $3) stretches for 10 kilometers down the beach and includes two estuaries and a .75-kilometer boardwalk. The area attracts shorebirds and sea turtles that lay their

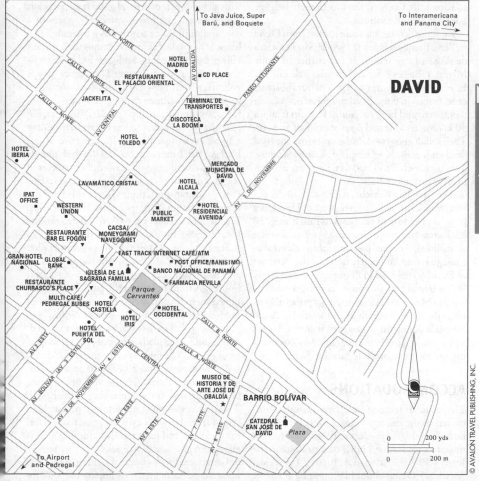

eggs from around June to November. Visitors with high-clearance four-wheel-drive vehicles can drive onto the refuge, but be prepared for lots of slippery sand and paint-scratching brush. The refuge has a rather shaky existence; at the time of writing, there was concern that lots were being carved right out of the refuge and being sold for development.

To get to Playa Barqueta by bus, take the Guarumal bus from the David bus terminal at 8 A.M., 11:20 P.M., and 3:30 P.M. For this service, ask for Tita (tel. 775-9943 or 630-6123) at Kiosco de Colores, next to the left-luggage booth at the bus terminal.

For those driving, the main turnoff from David to Playa Barqueta is at the Escuela San Francisco de Asís, a large school at the corner of Calle Miguel A. Brenes/F Sur and Avenida 9 de Enero/1 Este. There's no name on it, so look for the statue of St. Francis in front. Head southwest on Avenida 9 de Enero and keep on going. The trip is about 30 kilometers long and takes about half an hour. The asphalt ends two kilometers before the road dead-ends at the hotel here (see *Accommodations*). This last stretch is rock and dirt, navigable in a regular car driven carefully.

The wide **Río Gariche,** which runs under the Interamericana 40 kilometers west of David, is a popular place to cool off. Buses to Paso Canoa, 10 kilometers farther west, can drop you off if you're so inclined. Another popular spot is **Balneario Majagua,** four kilometers north of the outskirts of David on the road to Boquete. There's a pretty little waterfall here that pours into the slow-moving Río Majagua. Unfortunately, its popularity attracts the inevitable trash in and around it. Avoid this place during the weekend or holidays. There's a pleasant-looking bar/restaurant. Any bus heading to Dolega or Boquete can stop here.

ACCOMMODATIONS

The range of lodging in David has much improved in the last few years, with good options both for budget travelers and those with a bit more to spend. A new hotel next to Restaurante Jenny #19 (Calle Miguel A. Brenes/ F Sur near Avenida 5 Oeste) should be open by the time you read this. It seemed as if it would be one of the more upscale options.

$10–25

Opened in February 2002, the **Purple House Hostel** (Calle C Sur and Avenida 6 Oeste, 774-4059, purplehousehostel@yahoo.com, www.purplehousehostel.com, rates start at $6.60 per person) is a true hostel in a—you guessed it—purple house. Though it's in a residential area 10 hot blocks from the heart of the city, it's within easy walking distance of a commercial district with all kinds of services and good transportation connections. The hostel offers 19 spaces in a configuration that's constantly changing. The house is simple but clean and comfortable and totally geared toward the budget traveler. Its owners, Andrea Aster, a former U.S. Peace Corps volunteer from New York, and José Alexander Zapata, a Panamanian citizen, are sources of useful area information and travelers' tips. Staying here gives guests access to lots of extras, including a book exchange, storage lockers, use of the kitchen, free Internet access, all the fresh orange juice you can squeeze (in season), free coffee and tea, and discounts on some area services, restaurants, and transportation. Guests also have the option of stashing luggage here during side trips. English and Spanish are spoken. There's no curfew, but quiet time starts around 11:30 P.M.

Rates are $6.60 per person in a fan-cooled dorm room, $17 s/d in a private room with fan, and $21 s/d in a private room with air-conditioning. A third person in the largish air-conditioned room is another $6. Try to call in advance to reserve, especially for the private rooms.

Laundry service here costs $3 for a washed, dried, and folded load. A special plus for longer-term guests: The owners can arrange for dance (salsa, merengue, and *típico*) and Spanish language lessons. Purple House also offers a free bed in exchange for volunteering at the hostel. Those interested must speak some Spanish, have stayed at the hostel as a paying guest to get a feel for the place, and have traveled around Panama enough to give advice to guests.

Guests heading to Bocas should note that one bus a day to Almirante, the jumping-off point for

Bocas, stops by the Purple House Hostel between 9 and 10 A.M. Besides sparing you the trip all the way to the bus terminal, the fare is $1 cheaper. Ask at the Purple House for details. They are also working on arranging shuttle service to Boca Brava.

Hotel Residencial Avenida (Avenida 3 Este/Bolivar between Calle D Norte and Avenida Obaldía, tel. 774-0451 or 774-4720, fax 775-7279, $9/$10 s/d with ceiling fan, $12.50/$15 with air-conditioning) is the older sister to Hotel Alcalá across the street. It's a much simpler place that offers basic but large and okay rooms. The beds are actually better here than at the more upscale Alcalá. All the rooms have cable TV and phones.

Hotel Toledo (Avenida 9 de Enero/1 Este between Calle D Norte and Calle E Norte, tel. 774-6732, 774-6733, 775-0694, 775-2446, rooms start at $18 s/d) has 39 old but well-maintained rooms, some with good beds. Try the mattresses in several rooms. The rooms offered at $18 s/d are small; about $7 more gets you a substantially larger one. All rooms have air-conditioning, a phone, and cable TV. There's a restaurant/bar attached.

Hotel Occidental (Avenida 3 de Noviembre/4 Este between Calle A Norte and Calle B Norte, tel. 775-4068, 775-4695, 775-8340, fax 775-7424, $17/21 s/d), on the southeast side of Parque Cervantes, seems older than its 20 years but offers 61 well-maintained and clean rooms with air-conditioning, phones, and some character. The service is friendlier and the rooms are more pleasant than at the similarly priced Hotel Iris. One nice feature is the spacious balcony that overlooks the plaza.

Hotel Alcalá (Avenida 3 Este/Bolivar between Avenida Obaldía and Calle D Norte, tel. 774-9018, 774-9019, 774-9020, fax 774-9021, hotel alcala@cwpanama.net, $19.80/$22 s/d) is a newish, modern hotel that offers 55 pleasant rooms with air-conditioning, cable TV, and phones. Surprisingly, the mattresses aren't very comfortable. The hotel is close to the public market and has a restaurant that's open until around 10:30 P.M. daily.

Hotel Iberia (Calle B Norte and Avenida 1 Oeste, tel. 777-2002 or 775-7395, fax 774-1950,

hoteliberia@hotmail.com, $25 s/d) opened in 2002 with 34 spare but modern, comfortable, and clean rooms with air-conditioning, cable TV, and telephones. The hotel has a computer with free Internet access and a bar and restaurant. This place is a good value.

$25–50

Hotel Puerta del Sol (Calle Central and Avenida 3 Este/Bolivar, tel. 774-8422, fax 775-1662, puertadelsol@cwpanama.net, $26.40/$29.70 s/d) is a glossy hotel built in 2001. It has 86 modern, pleasant rooms with good beds. This place is kind of dark and rooms are small, though—the "junior suite" would be an average-sized room in other hotels—but it's otherwise quite nice. It has a nondescript restaurant, a smoky bar, guarded parking, and safety deposit boxes.

Though not the bargain for two it used to be, **M Hotel Castilla** (Calle A Norte between Avenida 2 Este and Avenida 3 Este/Bolivar, tel. 774-5236, 774-5260, 774-5261, 774-5262, fax 774-5262, inmisa@cwp.net.pa, $27.50/$38.50 s/d) remains popular with business travelers and is a good option for those who want a quiet, comfortable place in the heart of town (it's across the street from Parque Cervantes). The Castilla offers 78 pleasant, clean rooms with air-conditioning, phones, and cable TV. It has an underground, gated car park, which is a plus for those driving these busy streets. The restaurant here is decent though windowless. Internet access is $2 an hour.

The **Gran Hotel Nacional** (Calle Central between Avenida Central and Avenida 9 de Enero/1 Este, tel. 775-2221 or 775-2222, fax 775-7729, hotnacional@cwp.net.pa, $48/$57.20 s/d) remains the fanciest place in town, with a swimming pool, a full casino, a cafeteria, a pizzeria, and a six-screen theater that shows first-run movies. The place is designed to vaguely resemble a Spanish-colonial hacienda, with red-tile roofs, white-washed walls, and breezy corridors. It has 75 modern, rather glitzy rooms. The no-nonsense Castilla is a better deal (and the simple rooms are more tastefully appointed), but the Nacional will appeal to those in the mood for a little provincial flash. Laundry service is available.

$100–150

There's an all-inclusive 48-room hotel at Playa Barqueta, **Las Olas Beach Resort** (U.S. toll-free tel. 800/346-1329, tel. 772-3000 at the hotel, fax 772-3619, lasolas@cwpanama.net, www.lasolasresort.com, $130 s, $160 d). A wildlife refuge is right next door.

The hotel, which is far away from anything, feels more lonely than cozily secluded, and, though the beach is certainly huge and uncrowded, those who expect powdery white sand and gentle emerald waves lapping at their toes will not find them here. The rooms are rather small and have firm beds, cable TV, air-conditioning, and small refrigerators. The rooms aren't luxurious, but the yellow décor is tasteful enough. All rooms have a sea view and terrace. The hotel has a sauna, a tiny gym, a restaurant, an outdoor grill, bars, and karaoke at night. There's also a small pool that was none too clean when I visited. Use of these facilities, and food and drink, is included in the price.

Sit-on-top kayaks are free for the brave. Spa services are extra, as are horseback riding tours, tours of the wildlife refuge, and sports fishing. More ambitious tours include day trips to Volcán, Fortuna, and Caldera.

Rates vary wildly, sometimes week to week. They drop considerably in the rainy season and shoot up around Christmas, when special packages are offered. The place generally offers day or night passes ($25 adults, $15 kids), which includes everything but the room.

FOOD

Restaurants and Café

Ⓜ Restaurante El Palacio Oriental (Calle E Norte and Avenida Central, tel. 777-2410, 10 A.M.–11 P.M. daily) serves the best Chinese food in town in a bustling atmosphere. Most dishes are $2.50–6.

Restaurante Jenny #19 (Calle Miguel A. Brenes/ F Sur near Avenida 5 Oeste, tel. 774-8826, 11 A.M.–11 P.M. daily) gets lots of gringos from the Purple House Hostel. It serves mediocre but cheap and plentiful Chinese food. Most dishes go for $3–5. A half order of chow mein

costs $2 and should stuff even the most ravenous backpacker. There's an Internet café next door. Several other Chinese restaurants, plus a couple of fried chicken places, are nearby if nothing looks appealing.

The no-frills **Restaurante Churrasco's Place** (Avenida 2 Este between Calle Central and Calle A Norte, tel. 774-0412, open 24 hours daily) is around the corner from the Hotel Castilla. It's popular for its cheap, simple meals. You can stuff yourself silly with tasty but greasy food for around $2. Prices top out around $6, and Monday through Saturday Chuarrasco's offers a full *comida corriente* meal for $1.75. This is a good place to have *arroz con pollo* if the mood hits. The restaurant downstairs is open-air and sweltering. A fancier dining room upstairs is air-conditioned, but you're likely to be the only one up there. This is a good place to mingle with the locals, though you'll have to put up with desultory service.

The cafeteria at the **Gran Hotel Nacional** (tel. 775-2221 or 775-2222, 6:30 A.M.–10:30 P.M. daily) offers pizza, pasta, and fancier meats and fishes than usual for $3.25–8. Monday through Saturday from around noon to 2 P.M., the cafeteria offers a great deal: an all-you-can-eat buffet of pretty good food and a glass of wine for $4.50. The buffet includes several salads, a variety of meat and fishes dishes, some veggies, and several desserts. From around noon to 2:30 P.M. on Sunday there's a popular brunch buffet with a glass of champagne for $8.50. The hotel's pizzeria, across the street, offers an *almuerzo del dia* (lunch of the day) from around noon to 2 P.M. Monday–Saturday for $3.25 with soup or $2.75 without, including dessert. From 11 A.M. to 4 P.M. during the week, there's a two-for-one pizza deal.

Restaurante Bar El Fogón (Avenida 9 de Enero/1 Este between Calle A Norte and Calle B Norte, tel. 775-7091, noon–1 A.M. Mon.–Sat., 4 P.M.–midnight Sun.) is a popular open-air place with a beer-garden atmosphere. It offers meats and lots of seafood dishes, plus pasta, soups, and sandwiches. Main dishes are $3–7. The food is farily good, and it's a pleasant place to enjoy a welcome evening breeze over a beer. Huge mugs *(jarras)* of beer on tap cost $1.75. For an unusual appetizer, try the *patacones rellenos* (stuffed fried plantains).

The restaurant at the **Hotel Castilla** (tel. 774-5236 or 774-5260, 7 A.M.–3 P.M. and 4–11 P.M. Mon.–Sat., 7 A.M.–3 P.M. Sun.) is pleasant though windowless, and the food is decent. It's worth eating here just for the fascinating "English" translations of the dishes. For $4–8.50 you can feast on such mysterious delicacies as "beef steak in the horse," "rice with sailor," or "filet of fish in the white lady." Yum. Breakfasts are big and plentiful, but the coffee is awful.

Ŋ Jackelita (Calle E Norte between Avenida 1 Oeste and Avenida Central, tel. 774-6574, 7:30 A.M.–11 P.M. Mon.–Fri., 4–10 P.M. Sat., 8 A.M.–11 P.M. Sun.) is a simple open-air place near Restaurante El Palacio Oriental that's locally famous for its homemade ice cream, yogurt, and juices. They're all made with fresh fruit, including *zarzamora* (blackberry), *guanabana* (usually called "soursop" in English, if that helps), *piña* (pineapple), mango, *fresa* (strawberry), and both *pipa* and *coco* (fresh and dry coconut). The yogurt isn't on the menu, oddly enough, but the place has got tons of it. This is a great place on a hot day (i.e., every day). Try the *yogurt de fresa*—it's delicious. It also carries *duros,* a kind of fruit popsicle in a cup I have fond memories of from my childhood in Panama. Jackelita also makes cheap breakfasts and fast food, including burgers and chicken. Nearly everything on the menu is $1 or less. There are other outlets near the bus terminal, Supermercado Romero, and the Chiriquí Mall.

Markets and Supermarkets

The **Mercado Municipal de David** (Avenida Obaldía between Calle E Norte and Avenida 3 de Noviembre/ 4 Este, open daily during daylight hours) sells fruit, vegetables, meats, and dried goods. There's another **public market** (near Calle D Norte and Avenida 2 Este, 6 A.M.–8 P.M. daily) that sells just fruit.

Mercado San Mateo (Calle Miguel A. Brenes/ Calle F Sur between Avenida 3 Oeste and Avenida 4 Oeste), 5 A.M.–9 P.M. daily) is a fresh fruit and vegetable market within walking distance of the Purple House Hostel. At night ven-dors set up huge vats of oil and cook fried-death snacks until 5 the next morning.

Super Barú (Interamericana and Avenida Obaldía, 8 A.M.–10 P.M. Mon.–Sat., 8 A.M.–1 P.M. and 4 P.M.–9 P.M. Sun.) is a large grocery store with a bakery, gringo-oriented packaged foods, and good veggies. It also has a bank with an ATM, a pharmacy, and a real Internet café with actual pastries and espresso drinks. The computers are upstairs, but you pay downstairs at the bakery ($1/hour). The hours are the same as the store's.

Super 99 (Calle Miguel A. Brenes/F Sur near Avenida 5 Oeste, 24 hours daily) is a large grocery store with a pharmacy, ATM, and one-hour photo developing. It also has a Western Union outlet (tel. 774-7405, 9 A.M.–6 P.M. Mon.–Sat., 9 A.M.–3 P.M. Sun.).

Supermercado Romero (a half-block northeast of Calle Miguel A. Brenes/F Sur between Avenida 2 Oeste and Avenida 3 Oeste) is a 24-hour grocery and dry goods store behind the McDonald's on Calle Miguel A. Brenes. It has a bakery, pharmacy, and ATM. It cashes travelers checks.

INFORMATION AND SERVICES

The local IPAT office (Avenida Central between Calle A Norte and Calle B Norte, tel. 775-4120, 8:30 A.M.–4:30 P.M. Mon.–Fri.) has little to offer other than hotel brochures. There's also an IPAT booth at the airport. The Purple House Hostel has far more free information and advice to offer, and its owners are enthusiastic David boosters.

The regional office for ANAM, (tel. 775-2055 or 775-3163, 8 A.M.–4 P.M. Mon.–Fri.) is on the road to the airport. Heading into town from the airport it'll be on the right. Hikers can get permits to visit Parque Internacional la Amistad and Parque Nacional Volcán Barú here ($3 to enter, $5 to camp), but it usually makes more sense to get them at the ranger stations in the highlands.

Farmacia Revilla (Calle B Norte between Avenida 3 Este/Bolívar and Avenida 3 de Noviembre/4 Este, tel. 775-3711, 7 A.M.–11 P.M. Mon.–Sat., 8 A.M.–10 P.M. Sun.) is a large pharmacy on the northeast side of Parque Cervantes that sells lots of general goods as well.

Hospital Chiriquí (Calle Central and Avenida 3 Oeste, tel. 774-0128, 775-8999, fax 774-0144, hchiriqui@pananet.com) is a modern hospital with a 24-hour pharmacy. A comparable option is Centro Médico Mae Lewis (Interamericana near Calle B Sur, tel. 775-4616).

Receiving and Sending Money

A branch of Banistmo (8 A.M.–3:30 P.M. Mon.–Fri., 9 A.M.–noon Sat.) is across the street from the post office. It has an ATM.

A Banco Nacional de Panamá (Calle B Norte between Avenida 3 Este/Bolívar and Avenida 3 de Noviembre/4 Este, 8 A.M.–3 P.M. Mon.–Fri., 9 A.M.–noon Sat.) with an ATM is at the northeast side of Parque Cervantes.

Global Bank (Calle A Norte between Avenida 9 de Enero/1 Este and Avenida 2 Este, 9 A.M.–3 P.M. Mon.–Fri., 9 A.M.–noon Sat.) is near the Hotel Castilla. Its ATM booth is open 10 A.M.–5 P.M. Monday–Friday, 9 A.M.–2 P.M. Saturday, closed Sunday.

The CACSA office (Avenida 2 Este between Calle A Norte and Calle B Norte) has a 24-hour ATM. There's also a Moneygram outlet here (8:30 A.M.–5:30 P.M. Mon.–Fri., 8 A.M.–noon Sat.).

There's a Western Union downtown (Calle B Norte between Avenida Central and Avenida 9 de Enero/1 Este, tel. 774-9910, 9 A.M.–6:30 P.M. Mon.–Sat., closed Sun.).

Post Office

The post office (Avenida 3 de Noviembre/4 Este and Calle C Norte, 7 A.M.–5:30 P.M. Mon.–Fri., 7 A.M.–4:30 P.M. Sat.) is one block northeast of the plaza.

Internet Services

Internet places open and close all the time in David. Most charge $.50–1 an hour. The following may well be closed by the time you visit, but others should be easy to find. Naveg@net (Avenida 2 Este between Calle A Norte and Calle B Norte, 8 A.M.–midnight Mon.–Sat., 8 A.M.–10 P.M. Sun.) charges $.75 a minute for Internet access. Fast Track (8 A.M.–1 P.M. daily), right across the street, charges $1 for two hours of Internet time. Pars Computer Technology

(Calle Miguel A. Brenes/F Sur near Avenida 5 Oeste, 8:30 A.M.–12:30 a.m. Mon.–Sat., 10:30 A.M.–12:30 A.M. Sun.) next to Restaurante Jenny #19 charges $.75 an hour for Internet access.

Immigration Office and Consulate

Those who need their tourist card or visa extended can apply for a *prórroga de turista* (tourist extension) at the Migracíon y Naturalización office (Calle C Sur and Avenida Central, tel. 775-4515 or 794-1332, fax 775-6823, 8 A.M.–3 P.M. Mon.–Fri., closed weekends). It's in a residential area southwest of downtown. (See the *Know Panama* chapter for details on the procedure.) It's worth calling or visiting the office to get the latest requirements before starting on the laborious process since the particulars seem to change depending on the government in power, the immigration office, and the mood of the official dealing with you.

The Costa Rican consulate (**Consulado de Costa Rica**) is in a house two blocks down from the immigration office (Calle C Sur and Avenida 2 Este, tel. 774-1923, 9 A.M.–noon, 1 P.M.–5 P.M. Mon., Fri., closed weekends).

Launderette

Lavamático Cristal (Calle D Norte and Avenida 9 de Enero/1 Este, tel. 775-9339, 7 A.M.–7 P.M. Mon.–Sat., 8:30 A.M.–1:30 P.M. Sun.) washes clothes for $.75 a load, including soap, and dries them for another $.75.

GETTING THERE AND AWAY

David is the transportation hub for all of western Panama, with good connections to the highlands around Volcán Barú, Bocas del Toro, the Costa Rican border, and Panama City. It has a large bus terminal, a domestic airport, and several rental car agencies.

By Air

David's airport, Aeropuerto Enrique Malek, is less than five kilometers south of downtown off Avenida 3 de Noviembre (Avenida 4 Este) on the way to Pedregal. Two of Panama's three airlines fly out of here, though the destinations are limited. Most traffic is to and from Panama City.

Aeroperlas (tel. 721-1195, info@aeroperlas.com, www.aeroperlas.com) flies from David to Panama City and to Bocas del Toro province (Isla Colón and Changuinola).

Mapiex Aero (tel. 721-0841 or 721-0842, fax 721-0843, reservaciones@aero.com.pa, www.aero.com.pa) is a newer airline that offers flights for the same price as Aeroperlas. Its only direct flights from David are to Panama City. To get to Bocas or Changuinola from David, you'd have to fly clear across the country to Panama City first, which wouldn't make any sense even if the connections synced up well, which they don't.

Note: The airline sometimes goes by the name Aero, and it recently formed a "strategic alliance" with a third airline, **Turismo Aéreo** (tel. 315-0279 or 315-0300, fax 315-0300), through which its flights can also be booked.

Several rental car companies—National, Budget, Thrifty, and Hilary—have desks at the airport. Café Kotowa, a gourmet coffee producer based in the Chiriquí highlands, has a coffee bar at the airport with Starbucks-style drinks and prices. There is also an ATM.

By Bus

David's busy Terminal de Transportes is east of downtown on Avenida Estudiante, which begins near the corner of Avenida 2 Este and Avenida Obaldía. Buses for destinations throughout Chiriquí province and the rest of the country leave from here.

There's a left-luggage facility (6 A.M.–8 P.M. daily) near the Almirante bus stall. Look for the sign that says *Custodia de Maletas, Servicio de Enconmiendas, Chiriquí-Bocas*. Travelers can leave bags here for $.40–.50 a day, depending on size, and bicycles for $1 a day.

There's a stark Internet café (7 A.M.–10:30 P.M. daily) in the bus terminal that offers Internet access for $1 an hour. Those in need of visa-sized photos can have them taken here for $1 for a half-dozen prints.

Below are some of the more popular routes.

Almirante (Bocas del Toro): Almirante is a port town, the jumping-off point for water taxis

to the archipelago of Bocas del Toro. Buses run every half hour 4 A.M.–7 P.M., but to catch the last water taxi to Bocas (they run only during daylight hours) take the 2 P.M. bus at the very latest. Even that is cutting it close; to be safe, take an earlier bus. Those who miss the last water taxi will have to spend the night in Almirante, which has severely limited accommodations and appeal. The trip takes about four hours and costs $7. Note that the bus stops at the crossroads outside of Almirante, and it's a long walk to the water-taxi pier. A taxi from the crossroads costs $.50 per person and is well worth it.

Boquete: Buses run every 20–25 minutes 5:45 A.M.–9:45 P.M., though slightly less frequently in the evenings. The trip takes 45 minutes and costs $1.20.

Changuinola: Those crossing into Costa Rica at the Guabito-Sixaola crossing must first get to Changuinola. Buses run every half hour 4 A.M.–7 P.M. The trip takes about 4.5 hours and costs $8. (Same schedule on the way back.)

Las Lajas (town): Buses leave at 11:45 A.M. and 12:45 P.M. and return at 2 P.M. and 3 P.M. The trip takes 1.5 hours and costs $2. Then it's a $4 taxi ride to Las Lajas beach. The timing doesn't work well for beachgoers, especially those who don't plan to spend the night. A better option is to take a San Felix or Tolé bus, which run about every 20 minutes, to the crossroads leading into Las Lajas and then catch a taxi from there. (See the *Playa Las Lajas* entry for more logistics information.)

Panama City: Three companies run large air-conditioned buses between David and Panama City. The normal fare is $10.60 one-way, or $15 for an express bus, but Transporte Expreso Cinco Estrellas has been charging about $1.50 less to try to compete with its more established rivals.

The trip is supposed to take about 6.5 hours, but buses often run late. The bus makes stops at provincial towns along the Interamerican Highway, most notably Aguadulce, Penonomé, and Santiago. Other stops are made by request. In Santiago, buses generally take a half-hour break at the Hotel Pyramidal complex, where there is a cafeteria, restaurant, bathrooms, pharmacy, ATM, and other services.

Especially on the expresses, those heading somewhere short of Panama City should ask the ticket

Golfo de Chiriquí

seller—and double-check with the driver—that the bus will, in fact, stop at that destination.

Note that these companies frequently shift their schedules, so call ahead if you want to make sure of getting the bus you need. However, there's almost always a bus to Panama City within the hour, especially during the day.

Terminales David-Panama (tel. 775-7074 or 775-2974, tel. 775-2923 for cargo, terminal@cw-panama.net) is a large bus company and the main way those without their own wheels travel between David and Panama City. It has its own air-conditioned waiting room at the bus terminal. It has depatures at 6:45 A.M., 8 A.M., 9 A.M., 10 A.M., 11 A.M., noon, 1:15 P.M., 2:15 P.M., 3:45 P.M., 5 P.M., 6:30 P.M., and 8 P.M., with expresses at 10:45 P.M., and midnight.

Padafront (tel. 774-9205) has departures at 7:15 A.M., 8:30 A.M., 9:30 A.M., 11:30 A.M., 12:45 P.M., 3:15 P.M., 5:15 P.M., and 7:30 P.M., with expresses at 11 P.M., and midnight.

Transporte Expreso Cinco Estrellas (tel. 774-8017) has three daily departures to Panama City, at 10 A.M., 10:45 A.M., and 4 P.M..

Paso Canoa: This is the border crossing with Costa Rica, and buses have *frontera* written on the front. They run continuously 6 A.M.–8 or 9 P.M. daily. The trip takes about 75 minutes and costs $1.50. The Padafront and Transporte Expreso Cinco Estrellas buses from Panama City also continue from David to the border.

Puerto Armuelles: Those heading to Punta Burica must first get to this port town. Buses run every 15 minutes 4 A.M.–10 P.M. The trip takes about 2.5 hours and costs $2.65.

Playa Barqueta: Take a Guarumal bus at 8 A.M., 11:20 A.M., and 3:30 P.M.. For more information, ask for Tita (tel. 775-9943 or 630-6123) at Kiosco de Colores, next to the left-luggage booth.

Río Sereno: This little-used border crossing with Costa Rica is in the Chiriquí highlands. Take this bus to get to Finca Hartmann (about 2.5 hours into the trip, $3.65). The trip all the way to Río Sereno takes a little under three hours and costs $4.

San José, Costa Rica: Agencia Tracopa (tel. 775-7269 or 775-0585 in David, tel. 727-6581 in Paso Canoa, tel. 506/222-2666 San Jose, Costa Rica) has one bus departure to San José daily, at 8:30 A.M. The trip takes about eight hours and costs $12.50. The bus lets passengers off at the Coca-Cola bus terminal in San José. Be careful on arrival in San José, as the area around the terminal has a reputation as a haven for thieves and other sketchy characters. Also note that Costa Rican time is always one hour behind Panama time. Tracopa's office at the David bus terminal is open 7:30 A.M.–noon and 1 P.M.–4 P.M. Monday–Friday, 7:30 A.M.–2 P.M. Saturday, and 7:30 A.M.–noon Sunday.

Volcán, Bambito, Cerro Punta, and Guadalupe: Look for the minibuses with "Cerro Punta" on the windshield. These make all the highland stops on the west side of Volcán Barú. Buses generally continue past Cerro Punta all the way up to Guadalupe, but ask to be sure. Fares are $2.30 to Volcán, $2.50 to Bambito, and $2.65 to Cerro Punta/Guadalupe. The trip all the way up takes about two hours. Buses run every 15 minutes 5 A.M.–8 P.M. daily.

By Car

David is just south of the Interamerican Highway. Depending on road conditions, it takes about 7–8 hours to drive the nearly 450 kilometers between it and Panama City at a reasonable clip with few stops. It takes a little over an hour to drive between David and the Costa Rican border crossing at Paso Canoa.

The road is a mostly well-maintained divided highway from Panama City to Aguadulce. From Aguadulce to David, however, it's mostly two-lane road with huge, axle-eating potholes that suddenly emerge right in front of the car. The highway is gradually being widened, but on my most recent trip it was worse than ever, with lots of poorly marked washouts and detours, shoulderless stretches, and blind corners. It's almost as though the building of new lanes is being used as an excuse to let the existing road fall apart. Perhaps this will all be smoothed over, literally, by the time you take to the wheel. If not, beware not only of road obstacles but also of oncoming traffic swerving into your lane.

A NOTE ON THE ROADS

Many of the highland roads are newly resurfaced and in great shape. Ironically, that can make them even more dangerous than usual. New roads are oily, and the lack of potholes encourages drivers to see how fast they can take those hairpin turns. If you drive, be extremely careful. Honk the horn at blind curves. Drive with low beams and hazard lights even in the daytime. (Don't forget to turn them off when you park.) If you're visiting in the rainy season, try to drive in the morning, when you're less likely to be hit by torrential rains. If at all possible, stay off the roads at night or when it's foggy.

If you take a taxi, don't be shy about asking your driver to slow the heck down. Remember, you're paying. A firm *Despacio, por favor* (des-PAW-see-o, por-fah-VOR) should get results. If you take a bus, just shut your eyes and hope for the best.

Gringo paranoia? Nope. One road in the highlands - fortunately, not one you're likely to take - is nicknamed La Carretera de la Muerte (Death Highway). Another one has a sign tallying the dozens of annual fatalities along a single stretch of road. I learned to drive on Panamanian roads and have the local survival skills, yet on a trip to Cerro Punta a few years back my car was totaled by a speeding, hydroplaning truck coming down the mountain. The 3.5-hour wait for the cops on a dark, rainy night gave ample time to wonder what would have happened if someone had been hurt, which luckily no one was.

The one consolation for all this is the scenery. The drive between David and Santiago is through lovely countryside, with little but farmland, blue sky, and, close to David, rolling hills that lead to fog-shrouded mountain ranges in the distance. Passengers should keep their eyes open for the occasional mammoth waterfall pouring down from those mountains. Drivers should keep their eyes on the road.

There are two good places to stop for a break within a couple of hours' drive of David: the Ngöbe-Buglé artisan stands set up along the Interamericana near the the town to Tolé, and the Casa Artesenal Ngöbe-Buglé, a cooperative that offers many of the same kinds of crafts, near El Cruce. (See the *Las Lajas* entry for details.)

There are few gas stations between Santiago and David; fill up before driving anywhere in western Panama.

Rental Cars: It's easy to rent a car in David. Those wanting a four-wheel drive should book a reservation as far ahead of time as possible, as these are popular and can be in limited supply. Rental cars cannot be taken across the Costa Rican border. The companies listed below have outlets both in town and at the airport.

- Avis: tel. 774-7075 or 774-7076, 771-0844 at the airport, fax 774-7250.
- Budget Rent A Car: tel. 775-5597 or 775-1667, 721-0845 at the airport, fax 775-1667.
- Hilary Rent A Car: tel. 775-5459.
- National Car Rental: tel. 721-0974.
- Thrifty Car Rental: tel. 721-2477, 721-2478 at the airport.

GETTING AROUND

Downtown David is concentrated in a small, congested area, so walking is the most practical way to get around. The rest of the town is sprawling, however, and those who walk for any distance in the daytime can get broiled quickly. The best way to get around is by taxis, which are everywhere. A ride anywhere in town should cost no more than $1. The fare from the town center to the airport is $2. A trip to Pedregal, David's entryway to the Pacific Ocean, is $2.

The only area bus one may want to fool with goes to the riverside port of Pedregal. Buses leave outside the Multi Café near the town center, at Calle A Norte and Avenida 2 Este. They run constantly 6 A.M.–11 P.M. The fare is $.25.

BANANAS AND OIL

The economy of the Puerto Armuelles area has always been dominated by the banana industry, in the shape of the Puerto Armuelles Fruit Company (PAFCO), a subsidiary of Chiquita Brands International. In 2002, the company moved 6.6 million 40-pound boxes through the port, accounting for 6 percent of the huge multinational corporation's banana supply in Latin America.

Still, after complaining of steady losses—$90 million over six years—that led to layoffs and strikes, Chiquita decided in 2002 to pull out of the area. This was potentially devastating to the region, as PAFCO employed 3,500 people working 3,000 hectares of land.

In June of 2003, however, Chiquita concluded a deal to sell all its assets, including the land, to a local banana workers' cooperative for $19.8 million. The workers got help from the Panamanian government and a loan from Chiquita itself. As part of the deal, the cooperative agreed to sell bananas to Chiquita at market prices for 10 years.

It'll be interesting to see how this latest chapter in the long history of Chiquita (formerly the United Fruit Company, which has played a powerful and controversial role in Latin America for more than a century) in Panama unfolds. Chiquita still owns a huge division in Bocas del Toro.

Puerto Armuelles' other claim to commercial fame is its proximity to the Pacific terminus of an oil pipeline at Charco Azul operated by Petroterminal de Panamá, a "cooperative alliance" between Northville Industries, a petroleum storage company based in Long Island, New York, and the Panamanian government. The pipeline cuts northwest across the isthmus, crossing over the Continental Divide and ending on the Caribbean coast at Chiriquí Grande, in Bocas del Toro province.

The 131-kilometer pipeline was built, at a cost of $150 million, to transport Alaskan crude oil to the Gulf Coast of the United States. It operated from 1982 to 1996, when the oil dried up. An unbelievable 2.7 billion barrels of oil were transported during those years. During its peak, 900,000 barrels a day moved through the pipeline.

The pipeline reopened on November 13, 2003, this time to transport Ecuadorian crude—a reported 100,000 barrels a day. Ecuador, which lacks an Atlantic coast, has long depended on the Panama Canal to transport its goods from ocean to ocean.

WEST OF DAVID

There are a few notable places between David and the Costa Rican border, though they are not high on most people's list of tourist attractions. The industrial port of Puerto Armuelles is important in the shipment of bananas and oil, Paso Canoa is the major border crossing with Costa Rica, and Punta Burica is an extraordinarily remote spot for surfers who truly want to get away from absolutely everything.

Paso Canoa

This grim little frontier outpost has nothing to interest visitors, no places to stay, and sketchy-looking greasy spoons that will appeal only to the brave or starving. But many tourists are forced to visit it every day, as it is the main border crossing with Costa Rica. They spend as little time there as possible. (See the *Know Panama* chapter for information on border formalities.)

As with the two other border crossings in western Panama, it's hard to tell where Costa Rica ends and Panama begins. A barren stretch of road is the only thing separating the two.

Immigration, customs, an IPAT government tourism office, a post office, and a branch of Banco Nacional de Panamá are all crowded next to each other at the border. There were plans to build a new border complex to spruce up what some Panamanians consider a national embarrassment, but it's unclear when this might be completed.

The attendant at the IPAT office (tel. 727-6524, 6 A.M.–11 P.M. daily) will likely say new brochures are due from the printer any day now. It's kind of a mantra at IPAT offices. The main function of this tiny place is to sell tourist cards. As usual, it doesn't have much tourist information to offer. At least the person running the place the last time I passed through was nicer than the surly grandpa who used to work there and was more interested in watching TV than helping visitors.

The small Banco Nacional de Panamá branch (8 A.M.–3 P.M. weekdays, 9 A.M.–noon Sat.) is behind the immigration/customs office. There's an ATM. The post office (8–11 A.M. and 2–5 P.M. Mon.–Fri., 8 A.M.–noon Sat.) is next to immigration.

There's a bus and taxi stand about 50 meters east of the immigration/customs building, with a small grocery store and hole-in-the-wall restaurant nearby.

A taxi between Paso Canoa and David costs about $20, but if business is slow haggling may be possible. However, bus service to downtown David is frequent and fairly quick. Buses run continuously 6 A.M.–8 or 9 P.M. The trip takes about 75 minutes and costs $1.50.

Padafront (tel. 727-7230 in Paso Canoa, tel. 774-9205 in David) has multiple buses to Panama City, with intermediate stops along the Interamerican Highway. The trip takes about 8–9 hours, somewhat less for an express. The fare is $12, or $17 for an express. Alternately, travelers can take any bus to David and board a bus to Panama City there.

Those with their own transportation can just head straight on the Interamerican Highway to get to David and points east.

Note: Panamanian police routinely set up roadblocks on the highway between David and Panama to check for smugglers and illegal immigrants. This is normal and no cause for alarm. Just make sure your papers are in order.

Punta Burica and Puerto Armuelles

The Burica Peninsula is a finger of land that separates Panama's Pacific coast from Costa Rica's. Most of the peninsula falls on the Panamanian side. At its very tip is Punta Burica, which consists of a stretch of sandy beach broken by occasional wide slabs of striated rock that reach out to sea. The shoreline is fringed by palm trees and the occasional fisherman's house. That's about it.

The beach itself isn't all that great. The only draw for visitors—other than the area's extreme isolation and the adventure of getting there—is

the surf. This is still a spot little known to all but a few pioneering surf dudes and dudettes. Long, tubing waves break left along the tip of the point; those who've ridden it say Burica is better than Pavones in Costa Rica. I've been told there's usually something to ride, but the one time I visited the tip the sea was like glass. Have some kind of backup entertainment planned (picnic, games, cooler of liquid refreshment) in case the surf's not happening, as there is absolutely nothing else out there but sand and sea.

Access to Punta Burica is through Puerto Armuelles, a surprisingly tidy little town considering the especially rough times this sleepy little place has been through in recent years. It holds little of interest for visitors, but even those just passing through may be curious to know a bit more about the place, which has been the center of quite a bit of international economic activity. (See sidebar, *Bananas and Oil.*)

Note: This area is near the border, so be sure all your papers are in order, as there are frequent checkpoints along the Interamerican Highway to search for illegal aliens and smugglers.

Buses to Puerto Armuelles leave from the David bus terminal every 15 minutes 4 A.M.–10 P.M. ($2.65, 2.5 hours). Buses makes the return trip to David 4 A.M.–9:30 P.M. Those driving should head west toward the border. At Paso Canoa, about 50 kilometers from David, make a left. Puerto Armuelles is another 40 kilometers south.

From Puerto Armuelles there are two ways to get to Punta Burica: by boat and by car. At the waterfront in Puerto Armuelles, it should be possible to hire a fisherman and his boat to go down to Punta Burica. Expect to pay $30 each way, plus gas, just to get to the point. The trip takes about 1.5 hours.

It's also possible to get to Punta Burica by land, but this is even more of an adventure than a boat trip. A road is being extended toward Punta Burica, but chances are good at least part of the trip will still involve driving on the beach itself. There's a big old Ford pickup "bus" that makes the trip between Puerto Armuelles and Punta Burica at low tide. In central Puerto Armuelles, ask around for *el carro de la costa*. The fare is $1.50.

Driving to Punta Burica: It's also possible to drive oneself, but until and unless the road is completed the whole way, this requires some tricky off-road maneuvering. Only attempt it in a high-clearance four-wheel drive with a powerful engine. Don't go alone. For one thing, you'll need a second person to scout out the route at some points.

In Puerto Armuelles, you may have to ask for directions toward Punta Burica—the town's a bit of a maze. The first stretch of the drive leads to a guardhouse at the oil pipeline. It's 7.6 kilometers from Puerto Armuelles, the last four kilometers of which is on a dirt road. Sign in at the guardhouse. Then drive to the second guardhouse, at the other end of the complex.

The road ends at the beach. At the time of writing, this was about 16 kilometers from Puerto Armuelles, but the road was being extended and may be much closer to Punta Burica by the time you visit. If not, you'll have to drive the last 16 kilometers on the beach itself. It's essential to time the trip there and back with the low tides. Drive on the damp sand, which is more solid and holds traction better. To make the trip the whole way, the tide has to be quite far out. Otherwise, you'll round a bend and find your way blocked by the sea. If so, get comfortable and wait for the tide to go out some more.

This is a hairy drive at times. There are some wide stretches of slippery, jagged, stratified rock that have to be navigated. Here's where the scout comes in; have him or her hop out and plot a course.

Some of the worst bits toward the end can be avoided by taking a detour up a dirt loop road between the microscopic villages of Limones and Puerto Balsa. Ask anyone you see to point out the road, which can be hard to spot from the beach. The road is rough and steep, leading through some desolate fields, but it's better than the rock obstacle course.

Punta Burica itself is the tip of the peninsula. Costa Rica begins on the western side of the tip. This is a rather pretty spot, and it's certainly away from it all, but there's just about nothing here except a palm-lined beach and the sea. It may be possible to hire a fisherman at Puerto Balsa to run you out to Isla Burica for another $30 plus gas, if you're so inclined.

Note: Be sure to park well above the high-tide line. It'd be a serious bummer to go play in the water only to return to find your car washed out to sea or sunk up to the axles in wet sand. Also be sure to bring all the food, water, and supplies for your stay; there are no stores or restaurants of any kind in the area. Those camping should bring a tent.

In the Golfo de Chiriquí

PARQUE NACIONAL MARINO GOLFO DE CHIRIQUÍ

Parque Nacional Marino Golfo de Chiriquí is a 14,740-hectare marine park that encompasses two dozen islands and their surrounding waters. The park is a refuge for all kinds of wildlife, including howler monkeys, leatherback and hawksbill turtles, and tiger-herons.

It's a bit of an adventure to get to the islands that start just off the coast east of David; that's half the fun of visiting this area. You get the sense of being in the middle of nowhere without actually being that far from civilization or having to spend a lot of money to get there. The easiest access to the islands is through the little town of Horconcitos, the turnoff to which is 40 kilome-

ters east of David. From there it's a nearly one-hour drive on a rough road to the fishing village of Boca Chica, then a short ride by fishing boat to Isla Boca Brava, the jumping-off point to the other islands. There are two quite unusual places to stay on Boca Brava, catering to clients traveling on budgets ranging from starvation to luxury.

If all this sounds more like fun than hassle, you have the right attitude to visit this place. The islands and ocean here are beautiful, and you can enjoy them with a certain degree of comfort while being quite intimate with nature. But be prepared for some rusticity.

Another plus about this whole region: Dry season tends to start earlier than in other parts of Panama, around November, and ends at about the same time, in April.

Isla Boca Brava

Isla Boca Brava is the first island you'll come to, and it's most likely where you'll be staying. The island is 14 kilometers long, six kilometers wide, and overflowing with wildlife. It's right on the edge of the park.

From Boca Brava you can explore an endless maze of mangroves in the estuaries of several rivers that empty into the sea here. Or you can snorkel and swim in the clearer waters of the surrounding islands, including idyllic uninhabited ones. The closest are **Linarte, Saino,** and **Las Ventanas** (*ventana* means window; the name refers to the caverns that run straight through their rocky sides).

The best islands are farther out. The snorkeling is decent around **Isla San José,** a short boat trip away, but it's definitely worthwhile to head out even farther. **Isla Bolaños** is 13 kilometers from Boca Brava, about 45 minutes by small boat equipped with a decent outboard motor. This is a lovely little deserted island with a couple of sandy beaches, lots of coconut palms, and snorkeling when the tide's low. It's easy to arrange a camping trip here. Twenty minutes from Bolaños is **Isla Gámez** (sometimes spelled "Gámes"), also lovely and even smaller. This one, however, tends to attract yachts and the weekend personal watercraft crowd, while Bolaños is rarely visited. (Sadly, though, even Bolaños has its share of trash.) Both these islands are tended by the nonprofit environmental group ANCON.

Other Islands

The biggest island here is **Isla Parida,** just across from Gámez. It's an inhabited island with lots of trash and can easily be skipped. There's an ANAM station on Parida next to a bunch of ramshackle huts and a dirty beach. You can spend the night at the station, but it's hard to see why you'd want to.

The scuba diving is said to be terrific around **Islas Las Ladrones** and **Islas Secas,** where the water is clearest and the sea life the richest. The diving visibility is supposedly up to 30 meters at Las Ladrones. The islands are very far away: Las Ladrones are 40 kilometers southwest and the Islas

Secas 30 kilometers southeast of Boca Brava. Do not attempt to go this far on the open sea without something more substantial than the little *pangas* common around here. If you do find a way to get there, the snorkeling's supposed to be good, too. A high-end resort on the Islas Secas was recently completed out here, which, though expensive, is by far the easiest way to visit the islands.

Sports and Recreation

How to get to all this stuff? This area is not exactly crawling with tour operators. Best bet for an economical tour is **Restaurante y Cabañas Boca Brava** (tel. 676-3244), which offers a wide variety of boat tours to all the attractions in the area. A half-day snorkeling and hiking trip to Isla San José, for instance, costs $25. A night tour through the mangroves to search for caimans is $30. A grand day-tour of all the major islands, including Bolaños and Gámez, costs $85. An expedition all the way to Islas Secas costs $110. Prices are for up to four people; there's a slight additional charge for an extra person. Snorkels and masks can be rented for $1.50 and bodysurfing boards for $2. There is also a $3 per person fee to enter the national park. The folks at the restaurant should also be able to fix up those who'd like to camp on an uninhabited island. They can supply tents and food and boat transportation to and from Bolaños. (Keep the food away from the island's voracious crabs.) Price varies depending on the number of people and provisions required.

Pricey deep-sea fishing packages and other trips are offered by the Panama Big Game Fishing Club (see *Accommodations*) and by the Boquete-based **Exploration Panama** (tel. 720-2470, info@explorationpanama.net, www.exploration panama.com) which offers boat trips around the Golfo de Chiriquí on a converted 50-foot U.S. Coast Guard search and rescue vessel. Possibilities include sightseeing, kayaking, scuba-diving, and deep-sea fishing charters. (See *Sports and Recreation* in the *Cerro Punta and Surroundings* section for details.)

Accommodations and Food

There are now two places to stay on Boca Brava: the funky Restaurante y Cabañas Boca Brava and its new, dramatically more upscale neighbor, the Panama Big Game Fishing Club. There's also an ANAM ranger station on Isla Parida that can provide lodging for a small fee, but the island is inhabited and quite junked up. There's no reason to stay here when one can sleep in a hammock at Cabañas Boca Brava for next to nothing, or camp on a deserted island with a little planning. The two lodgings are the only options for food.

Restaurante y Cabañas Boca Brava (tel. 676-3244, $3.30–19.80 s, $6.60–33 d) is one of my favorite places to stay in Panama, but it's definitely not for everyone. It's certainly not for those skittish about creepy-crawlies. I hadn't been there an hour on my first visit when a snake dropped from the rafters of the hotel's open-air bar. The owner instantly started slashing at it with a machete; fortunately or not, it got away. An armadillo on the island has been known to race across the dance floor in the evenings.

The cabins and restaurant are on a cliff 20 meters and a long flight of stairs above the ocean on the eastern edge of the island, giving it striking views of the Pacific and the surrounding islands. The place has a wild and woolly vibe, but it's a good deal and surprisingly comfortable given its remote location, as long as you don't mind some rusticity and living close to nature. It's owned by a German character named Frank Köhler and his Panamanian wife, Yadira Pinzon de Köhler. Frank is an architect who built the place himself, as well as, more recently, the Panama Big Game Fishing Club. (He was also a snow-ski instructor for 10 years; it's hard to imagine a more radical change than coming to this place).

The couple owns 48 hectares of Boca Brava, and through their land they've built more than 10 kilometers of trails that lead into the forest and down to the island's beaches. He also offers tours to all the surrounding islands and other natural attractions. The forests on the island are home to monkeys, anteaters, coatimundis, all kinds of birds, and a wealth of trees and plants. Frank proudly maintains that the island has "no poisonous spiders, but every kind of poisonous snake." He says they're mellow, but don't go for a forest hike without good boots. And watch your step. The place has five cabañas ($17.50–28.50 s,

$19.80–33 d), all with private baths, electricity, and fans. They're very simple—mattresses lie on raised platforms on the floor—and far from immaculate but perfectly fine, especially considering this remote location. The newest room, cabaña 1, is the nicest and most expensive.

A step down in quality and prices are the two thatched-roof *ranchos* ($8.80–11 s, $12.10–14.30 d), which put guests a bit closer to nature and rusticity. The bathroom and showers are shared. Those on a tight budget can also rent a hammock in an open-sided hut for $3.30. The price includes access to the showers and bathroom. Only same-day reservations are accepted for any accommodations. This place has become well known on the backpackers' circuit and sometimes gets more business than the couple wants.

The restaurant and bar is an open-air affair on the edge of the cliff, and the panoramic view is terrific. The food isn't fancy, but it's fine. *Cambute,* a kind of conch, is the house specialty. (If you're into that kind of thing, you can row out with Frank to the underwater net where the live critters are kept and help him extract them from their shells—definitely not for the squeamish.) The most expensive thing on the menu is lobster, for $6.50. Most other dishes are $3–5.50. Vegetarian meals can be arranged with notice. The piña coladas here are amazing, and the homemade papaya liquor ($2) is refreshingly sweet but deadly.

The place takes travelers checks but charges a 2.5 percent fee for the service. The Köhlers can also arrange bus pickup from David.

The **Panama Big Game Fishing Club** (tel. 683-0359, U.S. toll-free tel./fax 866/281-1225, biggame@panafishing.com, www.panamabig gamefishingclub.com) shares the same general idea as its neighbor—cabins and a restaurant/bar perched high up on the edge of Isla Boca Chica—but the result couldn't be more different. The Big Game Fishing Club is an upscale (impressively so, given its remote location) sportfishing lodge intended for fishing-package clients who'll spend more for a night here than the backpackers at Frank's and Yadira's place probably spend on their whole overseas adventure, airfare included. Frank actually built the place,

The high-end Panama Big Game Fishing Club offers panoramic views from its roof.

on a budget far bigger than he could afford for his own little hotel.

It's owned by two retired charter-boat captains from Miami who seem to be living out many a skipper's dream. The place was just getting off the ground when I last visited the area, making it impossible to comment on service and such, but the place sure looked nice. The four modern, cheerful cottages are similar except for the bright, hand-painted murals. Each is 600 square feet, big enough for two queen-sized beds in different wings of the cottage. The beds are separated from each other by a partial partition (but not doors). The cottages are air-conditioned, and hot water runs in their huge, glass block–walled showers. Each cottage can sleep up to six people.

Up the hill from the cottage is an attractive, semicircular bar and restaurant with plate-glass windows overlooking the sea, nearby islands, and the forested mainland. It looked like a pleasant place to sip a cocktail in air-conditioned comfort. There is also a TV with satellite reception. Above the restaurant, a ladder leads to an observation tower with an even more sweeping view. The club is reached by a steep flight of stairs

that's a pretty good workout on a hot, humid day. Fortunately for more sedentary fishing folks, the club was installing a funicular system to glide up and down the hill that should be running when you visit.

The club offers packages that vary from a busy weekend to a leisurely week. Per-person rates for weekend packages that include two days of fishing are $2,000 (two anglers), $1,700 (three anglers), and $1,500 (four anglers). Per-person rates for a week package, which includes five or six days of fishing, are $4,500 (two anglers), $3,200 (three anglers), and $2,700 (four anglers).

All packages include domestic air transportation to David, a one-hour boat ride from David to Boca Brava, all ground transportation, meals, lodging, beverages, crew, tackle, and fishing on a twin-diesel Sportsfisherman. No boat has more than two anglers, unless you want one or two more buddies in the boat. The week package includes a night in a five-star Panama City hotel on arrival.

Getting There

Those who've arranged a package at Panama Big Game Fishing Club will have transportation taken care of. Everyone else is in for an adventure.

Golfo de Chiriquí

The turnoff to Horconcitos is about 40 kilometers east of David on the Interamerican Highway. The turnoff is poorly marked; if you're coming from David it'll be on the right, not far from a rustic restaurant on a little hill. Horconcitos is five kilometers from the Interamerican Highway on a good road. Then it's a 16-kilometer drive south on a formerly horrendous, now merely brutal, rock and dirt road to the fishing village of Boca Chica. Do not attempt this drive even in the dry season without a four-wheel drive. This short drive still takes about 50 minutes and gets especially steep and rutted toward the end. About 10 kilometers from Horconcitos, the road forks. The left fork leads to a beach, Playa Hermosa. Straight continues to Boca Chica. Once in Boca Chica, ask around for a fisherman to take you in his boat ($1 per person) to Isla Boca Brava, which is just offshore. This will probably be your base during your stay. There's a pay phone at the pier in case you get stranded and need to call for assistance.

A bus driver in David regularly shuttles visitors between David and Boca Chica in his air-conditioned minibus. His name is Victor Rivera (tel. 603-7511) and he charges a very reasonable $7 per person, two-person minimum, each way. Ask for him at the David bus terminal around the Horconcitos stall. His cell phone number changes often, so those planning to stay at funky Restaurante y Cabañas Boca Brava who have trouble finding him can ask Frank or Yadira to make the arrangements (the owners of the Purple House Hostel in David also work with him). Failing that, a taxi is probably the best bet. Expect to pay at least $30, probably quite a bit more if the Horconcitos-Boca Chica road is in rough shape. It's hard on cars.

Buses from David to Horconcitos are easy to come by, but there is no longer any reliable transportation between Horconcitos and Boca Chica, so just showing up there without arranging a ride the last 16 kilometers is probably not a good idea.

Any bus plying the Interamerican Highway, including the long-distance ones that run between David and Panama City, can drop passengers off at the Horconcitos turnoff as long as the bus runs past that point. From David, these include a few buses with Horconcitos as the final destination, as well as the Tolé, San Felix, and Remedios buses. The fare from David is $1.25. Note, though, that the turnoff is five kilometers from Horconcitos itself. Most buses don't go into the town.

Also, plan ahead of time how to get back to civilization from Boca Chica. Victor should be able to pick you up. Frank at Restaurante y Cabañas Boca Brava sometimes gives his guests lifts in his pickup truck when he's got business on the mainland, but be prepared for Mr. Toad's Wild Ride.

⚓ PARQUE NACIONAL COIBA

Everything about Parque Nacional Coiba is big. It's one of the largest marine parks in the world. The island at the center of the park, **Coiba,** is Panama's largest—a massive 493 square kilometers. It has the second-largest coral reef in the eastern Pacific Ocean. And the waters are filled with big fish—very big fish, as in orcas, dolphins, humpback whales, whale sharks, manta rays, barracudas, amberjack, big snappers, three kinds of marlin, moray eels, and white-tip, hammerhead, and tiger sharks. Sharks and mantas are especially common, and there's a decent chance of coming face to face with a sea turtle. Visibility can be unpredictable, but even on "bad" days one is likely to see some impressive creatures. The diving here has been described as a cross between that off the Galapagos Islands in Equador and Cocos Island in Costa Rica.

The park became even larger in 2004 when Panama enacted a law that raised its status and nearly doubled its area, to 430,821 hectares. Besides Coiba, the park includes the comparatively tiny (242-hectare) island of **Coibita** just off its northeast tip, the 20-square-kilometer island of **Jicarón,** the **Islas Contreras,** and many other smaller islands and their surrounding waters, mangroves, and coral reefs.

Coiba itself is still mainly covered in virgin forest—it's reportedly 85percent intact—though there has been some deforestation and forest disruption. As with most islands, there isn't a huge diversity of animal species on Coiba itself, but there are least 36 species of mammals, including howler monkeys, and dozens of amphibians and reptiles, including the deadly fer-de-lance snake. You're much more likely to come across beautiful birds, however, of which there are about 150 known species. Coiba is just about the last stand in Panama of the gorgeous scarlet macaw, which are concentrated in an area called **Barco Quebrado.** Other impressive birds common on Coiba include the bicolored hawk and the enormous king vulture. Coiba also has several endemic species, including the Coiba spinetail (a bird—*Cranioleuca dissita*), Coiba agouti *(Dasyprocta coibensi),* and a local variety of howler monkey *(Alouatta palliata coibensis).*

Coiba attracts visitors largely on the strength of its world-class diving and deep-sea fishing. But the impact of human pressures, including the appearance of commercial fishing vessels that trawl these waters illegally, is beginning to mount.

Two things have so far kept nature more or less intact on and around Coiba: It's quite remote and hard to get to, and it's the home of a Devil's Island–style penal colony with convicted murderers, rapists, and other serious criminals. Prisoners are confined to a series of colonies around the massive island, but they're not locked in. Instead, guards lock themselves in with their guns at night. The island jungle and shark-filled ocean keeps prisoners from straying too far.

Naturally, a place such as this inspires endless stories, some of which may even be true. There's a legend, for instance, about the "mud man," a runaway prisoner who roams the island, covered in mud. He's said to steal up on other prisoners and strangle them to death, a "mercy killing" accompanied by whispered apologies.

The Panamanian government has been making noises for years about moving the colony and developing the island for tourism, but for better or worse, definite plans have been slow to materialize. That may at last be changing, however. The prison camp, along with its legacy of horror and misery, is slowly being phased out—there were reportedly just 60 prisoners left at last count—and the future of Coiba is being passionately debated.

Conservationists were fearful in 2003 that the new law extending the park's boundaries was just a smokescreen to allow the commercial exploitation of the island. A lobbying campaign by environmentalists and subsistence fishermen on the mainland appeared at the time of writing to have halted this scheme.

The passage of the new law was met with guarded optimism, and everyone was waiting to see what the new government that came to power in the second half of 2004 would eventually do with the park. There was lots of talk, as there has been for years, of building "low-impact" tourist developments on the island. Whether these will be built, and how truly low-impact they might be, is unknown. And there is still concern that commercial tuna boats have been using massive nets to fish the waters in and around the park limits, damaging fragile ecosystems. It was unclear what, if anything, was going to be done about this. One hopes that common sense and long-term self-interest will prevail. Losing this Garden of Eden would be a tragedy not only for Panama but also for the world.

The island is still relatively little known even by scientists. It's hilly in the center and crisscrossed by many rivers, including the 20-kilometer Río Negro. But because of the penal colony, access to the island itself is tightly controlled. Visitors are restricted to the area around an ANAM field station on the northeast tip of the island. It's well away from the prison camps, though one model prisoner works as a cook there. The guest cabins are decent and air-conditioned, and the station is on a sandy cove.

There is a landing strip on Coiba, but at the time of writing only charter flights made the trip. Otherwise, access to the island is a long haul by land and sea. The logistical hassles in getting to Coiba almost force travelers to go with some kind of tour operator. This can get quite expensive, but you'll see a lot more and have a far more comfortable—and safe—trip than if you tried to get there on your own.

Sports and Recreation

Dry season is the best time to see monkeys and other animals on shore. Diving can be good year-round, though visibility can vary dramatically

© WILLIAM FRIAR

The waters around Parque Nacional Coiba are famous for spectacular fishing and diving.

day to day. Access to most of the island is restricted for visitors' own safety.

The waters off **Bahía Damas,** a bay on the east side of the island, has the largest coral reef in Central America (135 hectares) and the second-largest in the eastern Pacific. That and the density and diversity of large sea creatures have made the park famous among scuba divers. The sealife in some spots is what a nature guide friend calls "aggressive—everyone in town comes by," including turtles, orcas, and sharks that zip right past divers. Because of the fragility of the environment here, and the necessity of knowing these waters well, diving trips should be arranged through reputable professionals. As my friend put it, anyone found tossing an anchor onto the reef will likely get an anchor tossed at his head.

A good and accessible spot for snorkeling is **Granito de Oro,** a lovely islet a short boat ride from the ANAM field station. There are coral fields, including brain and fan coral, and schools of pretty little tropical fish just off the islet's sandy beach. The current becomes very strong just beyond the rocky cove—even strong swimmers should be careful not to swim out too far.

There are two trails—short walks, really—around the ANAM ranger station. The **Sendero del Observatorio** (Observatory Trail) is a 15-minute walk at a very slow pace that leads to an elevated bird-watching station. It's not a particularly good place to watch birds, but the view is nice. The trail starts behind cabin 6. Note the sign that says the trail is "approximately" 527.81 meters long. Another brief walk behind the kitchen leads up to a second lookout point on a small hill. It has a lovely view of the sea and Isla Coibita.

The **Sendero de Los Monos** (Monkey Trail) is not accessible from the ranger station. It requires a boat ride to the area near the Granito de Oro islet. It takes about an hour to walk and curves inland from one beach to another. There are howlers and white-faced capuchins along the trail, but you'd be lucky to spot them; best bet is in the dry season. Other flora and fauna found along the trail include fiddler and hermit crabs, coconut trees, the guinea-piglike *ñeque de Coiba (Dasyprocta coibae),* boa constrictors, and fer-de-lance snakes.

There is a trail on the southeast side of the island that leads to some thermal pools, but a trip there requires special permission from both ANAM and the police. Those interested can try to make arrangements through ANAM.

Hannibal Bank, between Isla de Coiba and Isla Montuosa, is especially famous among deep-sea fishing folk.

Adventure Tours

Travelers planning to visit Playa Santa Catalina may be able to arrange day or overnight trips to Coiba through **Casa Blanca Surf Resort.** However, its biggest boat is a 24-foot *panga* with a 75 hp and 15 hp motor and is most suitable for snorkelers, casual fishermen, and day-trippers. Note also that this is a very roundabout way to get to Coiba if your travels aren't already taking you to Santa Catalina.

Twin Oceans Dive Center (tel. 448-2067, info@twinoceans.com, www.twinoceans.com), though based far away in Portobelo, on the Caribbean side of the isthmus, sometimes offers Coiba scuba-diving trips and has a reputation as a safe, professional operation. However, it was probably going to suspend trips in 2005 because of a staff shortage; contact it to see if trips have started back up. Possiblities include a three- or four-day package including transportation from Puerto Mutis to Coiba, three nights' lodging and food at the ANAM station, and eight dives, including weights and tanks. Longer trips are sometimes available. Fishing, kayaking, hiking, and snorkeling are also possible during these trips.

Another dive operator that offers trips to Coiba is **Centro de Buceo Isla Grande** (cell 656-6095, tel. 501-4374, buceoenpanama@tutopia.com, www.buceoenpanama.com). It's based in Panama City and the Caribbean island of Isla Grande, but it offers Coiba as a specialty. A five-day package that includes two nights in Panama City (usually at the Costa Inn), food and lodging at the ANAM station, and all transportation goes for $1,000 per person. Snorkelers pay $760. Those who don't need the Panama City hotel pay less. Shorter or longer trips are offered on request.

Several operators offer multiday deep-sea fishing trips to the waters around Coiba. It's worth doing some research before settling on a package, as they tend to be quite expensive and some of the operations are not well run and either use dilapidated boats or go out of business overnight. Operations tend to be run out of either Puerto Mutis, a port 24 kilometers southwest of Santiago, or Pedregal, David's port. (See the *Puerto Mutis* and *Pedregal* entries.)

A fishing group that enjoys a good reputation is **Coiba Adventure Sportfishing** (Panama tel. 998-8108 or 628-0810, U.S. toll-free tel. 800/800-0907, info@coibadventure.com, www.coibadventure.com). The operation is run by Tom Yust and Tyra Ford, a fun and friendly gringo couple. Tom has been running fishing trips to Coiba since 1991 and was the skipper on the original *Coiba Explorer* mothership. Their current operation doesn't use a mothership but rather a 31-foot Bertram and a 21-foot Mako. They also have a 14-foot inflatable and two sit-on-top sea kayaks.

The outfit offers two- to six-day fishing trips. A two-day fishing package costs $2,300 (two anglers) or $1,700 (three anglers) on the Bertram or $2,000 (two anglers) or $1,360 (three anglers) on the Mako. Rates include a round-trip charter flight between Panama City and Coiba, all meals, and a room at the ANAM lodge or a berth on the Bertram (depending on the package). Subtract $800 from the rates to go by land from Panama City to Puerto Mutis and then by boat from Puerto Mutis to Coiba. Day trips are also sometimes possible. These cost around $800 on the Mako and $1,200 on the Bertram.

The **Panama Big Game Fishing Club** (Panama tel. 683-0359, toll-free U.S. tel./fax 866/281-1225, panamabiggame@aol.com, www.panama biggamefishingclub.com) offers several fishing packages. Their boats run out of Pedregal, and guests stay at their new, high-end cabins on Isla Boca Brava. (See *Accommodations* under *Parque Nacional Marino Golfo de Chiriquí* for details.)

Another group to consider is **Pesca Panama** (U.S. toll-free tel. 800/946-3474, fax 623/362-2732, anglerfishing@aol.com, www.pescapanama.com). This fishing operation is run out of Pedregal and uses a 70-foot-long "floating lodge" that sleeps up to 12 in three air-conditioned guest cabins. Fishing is from 27-foot Ocean Masters. The standard package consists of six days of fishing. The package includes a five-star hotel room in Panama City on the first and last nights and food and accommodation during the five nights on the floating lodge. The outfit will make flight reservations from Panama City to David, but the fare is not included in the package rate. Food and transportation in Panama City are not included. Per-person rates are $2,295 (four anglers per boat and four people in a cabin), $2,795 (three anglers, triple), and $3,295 (two anglers, double). It also offers snorkel gear and scuba tanks and a compressor. Scuba divers must be certified.

Practicalities

Because of the penal colony, only the northeast tip of the island is usually open to the public. It's separated from the colony by many, many kilometers of forest filled with fer-de-lance snakes and other nasty critters, a barrier generally reckoned to be far more formidable than any walls. Rumors persist that escaped prisoners still hide out in the forest, but officials deny this.

The publicly accessible part of the island has an ANAM field station on a pretty, sandy cove backed by hills. Even day visitors must register here and pay a $10-per-person national park entrance fee. The complex includes a boat anchorage, guest cabins, a kitchen and dining area, and a small museum. The museum contains the skeleton of a humpback whale and specimens of other critters recovered from the park, including pickled fer-de-lance and coral snakes.

Each of the six cabins for guests has two rooms with separate entrances. The cabins are quite basic and bare-bones, but they're perfectly fine, especially given the extreme isolation of this place. They're even air-conditioned. Rates are $10 per person, plus the one-time $10 per-person park entrance fee.

The station will supply diesel for electricity 6 P.M.–midnight. Those who want air-conditioning through the night have to bring their own diesel supply. About 15 gallons of diesel per cabin should last through two nights.

Independent travelers should also note the need to bring not only food but also the gas to prepare it (stoves are provided). It's possible to hire the cook, the only model prisoner working at the ANAM station, to prepare the food. Meals are eaten in an open-air *rancho.* Be prepared for mosquitoes and *chitras,* which are fierce around here. There's nothing to do in the evenings but enjoy the tranquility. A few little souvenirs made by prisoners with what few materials they have to work with—a shell, a couple of small feathers, a bit of pipe cleaner—are generally sold at the station for a few dollars. Since this is a national park, taking shells from the beach is illegal, though it's hard to begrudge their attempts to make a couple of bucks.

Anchorage cost depends on the size of the boat. Those up to 17 feet pay $5 per day. Boats 18–24 feet pay $10.

It will be much less hassle to arrange a visit through a tour operator that frequents the island. To set up a visit on your own, contact ANAM in Santiago (tel. 998-4271; try asking for Soriya Herrera). You can also try calling the field station on the island (tel. 999-8103; ask for "Willy").

Though this place is paradise, it's easy to see that living here could get a bit tedious. No wonder the ANAM rangers have befriended some of the local wildlife. The most impressive is Tito, a three-meter crocodile *(Crocodylus acutus)* that emerges from the water when called to dinner. Another is Pancho, a Geoffroy's tamarin. Sara is a fat and lazy deer—not surprising, since her diet now includes junk food.

Warning: Boaters should be extremely careful in these waters. I've heard many tales, some of them from reliable sources, of prisoners swimming out to boats or posing as shipwreck victims and luring good Samaritans in toward shore. The horrors that followed are straight out of a bad thriller. If you see someone bobbing in the water and calling for help, throw out a life ring and radio for official assistance. Do not let him in the boat.

Getting There

Most visitors to Coiba come by boat from Puerto Mutis. The trip takes two to three hours, depending on the power of the boat. Other trips originate from Pedregal or Playa Santa Catalina. There's a landing strip on Coiba, but at the time of writing only charter flights made the trip.

Those whose goal is just to get to Coiba can work out cheap trips from Puerto Mutis with a local fisherman, but I don't advise it. You will be on open ocean that can quickly turn rough, riding in a small boat that probably won't have a backup motor, life jackets, or a radio. One of these boats goes adrift at sea every other month. Even if you make it, you won't be able to do much more than snorkel (with your own gear) from these boats.

ℕ PLAYA SANTA CATALINA

Santa Catalina is the best surfing spot in Panama, with one of the most consistent breaks in Central or South America. There's something to ride here every month of the year.

While Santa Catalina is of great interest only to serious surfers, it's a pretty place even for those who just want to watch the rollers from a distance. However, much of the beach is strewn with rocks and boulders, and it's a remote and isolated spot west of the Azuero Peninsula at the tip of sparsely settled farmland. It's a long, rough road away from anything approaching civilization. It's definitely a get-away-from-it-all kind of place. Lodging and dining options are basic. Those who just want some beach time have many better, more accessible options elsewhere.

The best time for really big waves is February to August, when wave faces get as high as 6–9 meters. At other times the average is 2–3 meters. There are several other breaks, some within walking distance, some requiring a boat ride to reach, that have breaks that can get even bigger.

The nearest sizable settlement on the drive down to the beach is Soná, an unattractive crossroads town with nothing to offer travelers. You can get some provisions here, but you're better off stocking up back in Santiago, on the Interamerican Highway a two-hour drive from the beach.

Surfing

The internationally famous surf break at Santa Catalina has been described as a "perfect" point break with long, powerful hollow waves that break left and right. The sea bottom is volcanic rock, so bring booties. This place is strictly for experienced surfers; it's all too easy to bust a board or a head on those rocks. There's also a **sand beach**

break next to town with hollow lefts and rights that are somewhat smaller than waves at the point.

There are several other breaks in the area that are less well known. **Punta Brava,** about a half-hour walk southeast of Santa Catalina point, is a hollow left-hand, rock-bottom break I've been told can get twice as big as those at Santa Catalina. **Punta Roca,** about a half-hour walk northeast of Catalina, is another left-hand point break, about the same size as Catalina. **Isla Cebaco,** which is accessible only by boat, is an island with a beach break and point break, with left- and right-breaking waves that tend to be somewhat bigger than Catalina point.

Except for the Santa Catalina point break, which can be surfed at medium or high tide, experienced surfers say these other waves can be ridden only at medium to low tide.

Surfers should bring their own boards. However, Rolo at Cabañas Rolo rents boards for $5 a day, though you're responsible for any damage to them. Ricardo Icaza, the owner of Casa Blanca Surf Resort, will sometimes let guests rent his boards if he's convinced they're experienced enough not to break them on the rocks.

Adventure Tours

Punta Brava Lodge (tel. 614-3868) charters a boat and captain to explore the immediate area starting at $10 plus gas and tip. Kayaks and mountain bikes are also available there for $10 a day. These services are intended for guests, but it never hurts to ask even if you're not staying there.

Casa Blanca Surf Resort (Panama City tel./fax 226-3786 or 226-3787, no local phone) offers trips to surrounding islands for fishing, snorkeling, and diving. Again, bring your own gear. It has some snorkeling equipment, but not much.

The more ambitious trips are made on a 24-foot *panga* with six seats and a 75 hp and 15 hp motor. Maximum capacity for fishing and surfing trips is three people. There's also a 20-foot *panga* with a 45 hp engine that's usually used for fishing trips.

Prices are per group and include the services of the captain, deck help for fishing trips, and gas. Tips are not included. There are a few life preservers, but to be safe bring your own. It's foolish to take to these seas—which can quickly turn

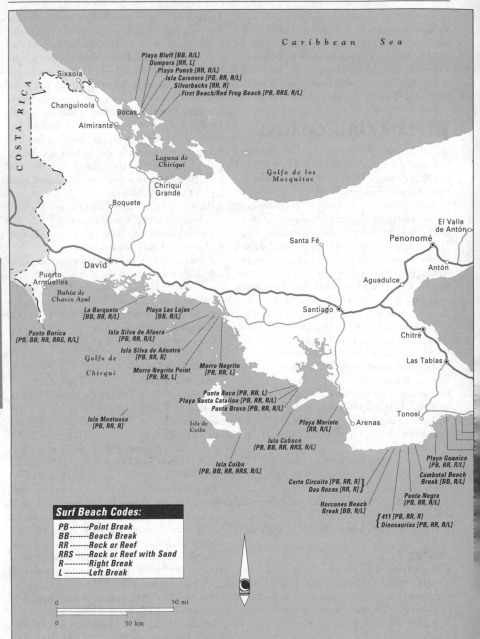

Golfo de Chiriquí

Caribbean Sea

Sixaola

COSTA RICA

Changuinola

Bocas

Almirante

Laguna de
Chiriquí

Golfo de los
Mosquitos

Chiriquí
Grande

Boquete

El Valle
de Antón

Santa Fé

Penonomé

Antón

David

Aguadulce

Puerto
Armuelles

Bahía de
Charco Azul

Santiago

Chitré

La Barqueta
[BB, RR, R/L]

Playa Las Lajas
[BB, R/L]

Punta Burica
[PB, BB, RR, RRS, R/L]

Isla Silva de Afuera
[PB, RR, R/L]

Las Tablas

Isla Silva de Adentro
[PB, RR, R]

Golfo de

Chiriquí

Morro Negrito Point
[PB, RR, L]

Morro Negrito
[PB, RR, L]

Isla Montuosa
[PB, RR, R]

Punta Roca [PB, RR, L]
Playa Santa Catalina [PB, RR, R/L]
Punta Brava [PB, RR, R/L]

Isla de
Coiba

Playa Mariato
[RR, R/L]

Arenas

Tonosí

Isla Cebaco
[PB, BB, RR, RRS, R/L]

Isla Coiba
[PB, BB, RR, RRS, R/L]

Playa Guanico
[PB, RR, R/L]

Cambutal Beach
Break [BB, R/L]

Corto Circuito [PB, RR, R]
Dos Rocas [RR, R]

Punta Negra
[PB, RR, R/L]

Horcones Beach
Break [BB, R/L]

411 [PB, RR, R]
Dinosaurios [PB, RR, R/L]

Playa Bluff [BB, R/L]
Dumpers [RR, L]
Playa Punch [RR, R/L]
Isla Carenero [PB, RR, R/L]
Silverbacks [RR, R]
First Beach/Red Frog Beach [PB, RRS, R/L]

Surf Beach Codes:

PB -------- Point Break
BB -------- Beach Break
RR -------- Rock or Reef
RRS ----- Rock or Reef with Sand
R --------- Right Break
L --------- Left Break

0   50 mi

0   50 km

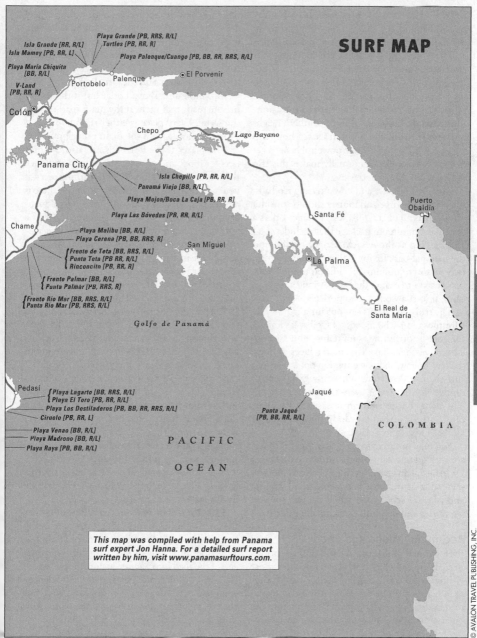

SURF MAP

Playa Grande [PB, RRS, R/L]
Turtles [PB, RR, R]
Isla Grande [RR, R/L]
Isla Mamey [PB, RR, L]
Playa Palenque/Cuango [PB, BB, RR, RRS, R/L]
Playa María Chiquita [BB, R/L]
Palenque
El Porvenir
V-Land [PB, RR, R]
Portobelo
Colón
Chepo
Lago Bayano
Panama City
Isla Chepillo [PB, RR, R/L]
Panamá Viejo [BB, R/L]
Playa Mojon/Boca La Caja [PB, RR, R]
Puerto Obaldía
Playa Las Bóvedas [PB, RR, R/L]
Santa Fé
Chame
Playa Malibu [BB, R/L]
Playa Cerena [PB, BB, RRS, R]
San Miguel
Frente de Teta [BB, RRS, R/L]
Punta Teta [PB RR, R/L]
Rinconcito [PB, RR, R]
La Palma
Frente Palmar [BB, R/L]
Punta Palmar [PB, RRS, R]
Frente Rio Mar [BB, RRS, R/L]
Punta Rio Mar [PB, RRS, R/L]
El Real de Santa María
Golfo de Panamá
Pedasí
Playa Lagarto [BB, RRS, R/L]
Playa El Toro [PB, RR, R/L]
Jaqué
Playa Los Destiladeros [PB, BB, RR, RRS, R/L]
Ciruelo [PB, RR, L]
Punta Jaqué [PB, BB, RR, R/L]
Playa Venao [BB, R/L]
COLOMBIA
Playa Madrono [BB, R/L]
Playa Raya [PB, BB, R/L]
PACIFIC
OCEAN

This map was compiled with help from Panama surf expert Jon Hanna. For a detailed surf report written by him, visit www.panamasurftours.com.

Golfo de Chiriquí

rough—without a life preserver. It's a bumpy ride year-round, but look out for strong storms in the rainy season, usually in the midafternoons.

The closest trip is to **Isla Cebaco,** known for clear waters and good coral. The trip costs $180. (Kenny's Surf Camp offers surfing trips to Cebaco on a less-powerful boat for $15 per person). Sport-fishing and snorkeling trips to the astonishing **Isla de Coiba** and its little southern neighbor, **Isla Jicarón,** cost $330. It's a 1.5-hour trip over open ocean in the more powerful boat to get to Coiba. Casa Blanca normally makes this trip between November and May.

Given the distance and how amazing Coiba is, those with the time and money should consider staying overnight at Coiba. Casa Blanca offers a two-night-minimum package that includes food and lodging at the ANAM ranger station and the national-park fee for $40 per person per day, two-person minimum, in addition to the $330-per-day cost to charter the boat. Arrangements require at least a week or two notice.

The truly ambitious can opt for a trip to **Isla Montuosa,** three hours west of Coiba. It's known for good sportfishing, snorkeling, and surfing. The waves here have five-meter faces and are shallow, hollow, and powerful. Do not attempt to surf them unless you really know what you're doing. This is far, far away from any hospital. The boat charter to Montuosa is $400 a day, plus $40 for one night's lodging and food at Coiba. This is a two-day trip.

You may not have to go nearly that far to encounter spectacular sealife. During my last visit, I watched as an enormous humpback whale submerged near my boat between Santa Catalina and Isla Cebaco. Closer to Coiba, we spotted sea turtles and dolphins cruising alongside us.

Accommodations and Food

Even the best of the lodging and dining options here are nothing fancy, which is fine with most visitors, who come here to surf or fish. Other than Cabañas Rolo, which is at the end of the road leading into Santa Catalina, just up from the open-air bar overlooking the beach, the accommodations listed below are all outside the village. They're accessible by a single road, most of

which is best attempted only in a four-wheel drive. As you drive into town, it'll be the steep, rocky road to the left. It quickly levels off, but beware of car-eating mudholes—it's not unusual to get stuck up there. The first place you'll come to is Casa Blanca Surf Resort. It, Kenny's Surf Camp, and Punta Brava Lodge are at the end of private roads that veer off the main road toward the water. Every place is either right above or a short walk away from the main point break.

The places that offer beds are also the best bets for food, and you may be able to convince them to serve you, with enough warning, even if you're not staying at the place. However, there is a pizzeria in the area that somehow, sadly, I managed to miss on my last visit. Anyone should be able to tell you how to get there. The pizza's alleged to be great—an Italian acquaintance called it the best in Panama. Supposedly the pizzeria is open only in the afternoons. Please have a slice for me. Still, overall, Santa Catalina is a good place to come with a well-stocked cooler.

Rike Waldschmidt, the former owner of Mondo Taitú, a surfers' hostel in Bocas del Toro, was planning to relocate to Playa Santa Catalina when I last visited. Her plans were uncertain but could include a (desperately needed) breakfast café, a surfers' camp, or even a place similar to Mondo Taitú. Given that she's a fount of local surfing knowledge, impressively resourceful, and ran a great, cheap place in Bocas, surfers may want to contact her to see what she may be cooking by the time they visit. She can be reached through the pay phone in Santa Catalina (tel. 998-8600, ask for Rike—REE-kah or REE-kay—or Paco). Her email, which she checks only once a month, is rikepaco@yahoo.de.

$10–25: Cabañas Rolo (tel. 998-8600—it's the town's public phone, so let it ring a reeeeally long time and ask whoever answers for "Rolo,"—$7 per person). This surfers' hangout is near the end of the road into Santa Catalina proper, where the bus stops near the beach. Rolo is a friendly young guy and his place is simple and basic but cheerful and clean. It consists of five rooms, with three more on the way. All have shared bathroom. The basic **Restaurante Vielka** on the property serves breakfast for $2 and lunch and dinner for $3. This place is ideal for surfers. Rolo also rents surfboards for $5 (or a lot more if you damage one on the rocks).

Kenny's Surf Camp (tel. 672-0089, info@ panamasurftours.com, www.panamasurftours .com, starts at $8/$16 s/d) is a little house that's been turned into a surfers' crash pad. Like its neighbors, it's in a primo spot above the surf, on a bluff overlooking a rocky beach. Main accommodations are dorm-style, consisting of five cramped beds in one upstairs room, separated by a thin wall from a room with another six beds. The rooms have fans. Beds here cost $8–10 per person. Making up somewhat for the cramped conditions is a nice big deck just outside. There's also a room downstairs with air-conditioning for $22/$25 s/d. This room can sleep up to five. There's no meal service, but a kitchen is available to guests. The place is affiliated with Panama Surf Tours, which offers surf packages that include transportation to and from Tocumen International Airport and lodging but no food. These start at $315 per person (four-person minimum) to $400 (single person) for four nights in the dorm rooms. Longer stays are possible.

$25–50: Punta Brava Lodge (tel. 614-3868, fax 229-7755, info@puntabrava.com, www.punta brava.com, starts at $25 d) consists of two buildings on a point overlooking the surf and a rocky beach. The main lodge is a modern, two-story building with three bedrooms and a bar/dining area with cable TV in the common area. It also has a satellite phone and Internet connection. The second building is a single-story, motel-type affair with five dark rooms, each with bunk beds, private bathrooms, and air-conditioning. The rooms are simple but the common area is cheerful and has a view of the ocean. Walk-up rates start at $25 for two people, $35 for three people, and $45 for four people, with a maximum of 4–6 people per room. Meals are available at $2.50 for breakfast and $4 for lunch or dinner. Package surf tours start at $399 per person including transportation from Tocumen International Airport in Panama City, three meals daily, boat rides to surf spots, and seven nights' lodging. Renting a boat and captain to explore the area starts at

$10 plus gas and tip. Kakyaks and mountain bikes are available for $10 a day.

At the end of the road is **Oasis Surf Camp** (no phone, surfoasis@hotmail.com, $15/$30 s/d), on Playa El Estero, a beach at the estuary of a small river. The camp, which opened in 2002, is right on a wide, black-sand beach. It's not the prettiest spot, but it's certainly away from it all and it's one of the few beaches in the immediate vicinity that's covered in sand rather than rocks. It offers eight pleasant rooms in four cabañas facing the beach, with hammocks in front. Each has three beds, a bathroom, fan, and electricity. Sheets and towels are included. The owner, Victor Bortoletti, is a retired Rome policeman who has the air of someone you wouldn't want to mess with. He doesn't allow tents on his property, as he's had bad experiences with campers. He's looking for calm, well-behaved guests. He's a bit gruff at first, but he warms up with time. Meals are available for $3. I haven't eaten there, but when I visited a delicious-smelling marinara was simmering. Victor takes his cooking quite seriously (*Soy Italiano!*—"I am Italian!"—he says, and what more explanation is needed?). There's a barbecue on the property. Subtract $5 per person from the rates in the rainy season.

Ⓜ Casa Blanca Surf Resort (Panama City tel./fax 226-3786 or 226-3787, no local phone, $20–60 d), is tucked away on an isolated bluff; take the first right above the village of Santa Catalina. It's a surprisingly pleasant and comfortable place to stay, given its location. Though not truly a "resort," Casa Blanca offers a rather random assortment of 16 rooms that vary in quality from basic but okay to simple but decent. Rooms are spread among several cabins on a spacious (six-hectare) property with a spectacular view of the ocean. The property is big enough that one small part of it has a soccer field on which the owner lets the local girls' team practice. The view of the surf is impressive, but the beach at the base of the bluff is choked with rocks—those wanting to sunbathe or go for a swim have to hike farther along the coast.

Rates run $10 per person for a quite basic room with a fan and shared bathroom up to $25 per person in a "colonial cabin type 'A,'" which is a large, simple room with air-conditioning, single beds, private bath, and a porch. There is a two-person minimum in every kind of room; single clients pay double the per-person rate. There is also a "colonial house" for rent that has two bedrooms, air-conditioning, and private bath for $30 per person, three-person minimum. Not all the windows have screens and none of the rooms is fancy.

But the rooms don't matter nearly as much as the lovely surroundings. There's an open-air restaurant on the premises where you can get all your meals and watch satellite TV. Food is good here, and two meal plans that include breakfast, lunch, and dinner are offered. The first is a basic plan that costs $10 and includes rice and beans, pasta, fish, chicken, and so on. The other costs $30 and steps things up to include offerings such as shrimp, lobster, steak, fresh fruit, desserts, and so on

The owner, Ricardo "Ponky" Icaza, is a surfer who's been riding waves in Panama for three decades. He's an easygoing, dependable guy who speaks fluent English thanks to his 12 years in California where, funnily enough, he learned to surf. He offers fishing and surfing boat trips to various locations in the region.

Camping is best done in the dry season, as it can get awfully wet and mucky around here in the rainy season. Campers can pitch a tent for free on the beach, but I'd suggest working out a deal at one of the surfing camps or with a farmer to camp on his land. (You won't be the first. During surf competitions—big international ones are sometimes held here—there's a real run on places to sleep). Maybe it's just me, but it doesn't feel safe to camp on this beach, at least near the village itself. Some of the characters who hang out around there give off bad vibes. Part of it is just the usual surf territorialism, but there's also a hint of a real *maleante* (rough translation: hooligan) air about some of them.

Getting There

By Bus: There are no direct bus connections to Playa Santa Catalina from major towns or cities. Travelers must first get to Soná, then take a bus or taxi from there to Santa Catalina, about 50 kilometers away.

Buses from Panama City to Soná ($6, about 4.5 hours) leave at 8:20 A.M., 10:20 A.M., 12:45 A.M., 2:20 P.M., 4:20 P.M., and 5:45 P.M. from the Gran Terminal Nacional de Transportes. Buses from Soná to Santa Catalina ($3) leave at 5 A.M., noon, and 6 P.M., returning at 7 A.M. and 8 A.M. A taxi from Soná to Santa Catalina should cost $25–30.

There are many more connections for those who go first from Panama City to Santiago, then from Santiago to Soná. Santiago-bound buses leave the Gran Terminal in Panama City round the clock, usually every half hour to an hour ($6, around 4 hours). Buses from Santiago to Soná leave from the Terminal de Transportes every 20 minutes 6 A.M.–9:40 P.M. Monday–Friday, 6 A.M.–8 P.M. Saturday–Sunday ($1.50, a little under an hour).

Those coming from David will probably have to take a bus to Santiago ($6) and then switch to a Soná-bound bus. Any bus going at least as far as Santiago will drop passengers at the Santiago bus terminal. Best bet are the long-haul buses to Panama City. (See the *David* entry for information.)

By Taxi: Travelers who decide to take a taxi from Santiago to Santa Catalina should expect to pay up to $50, but the price may be negotiable—this is not a common trip, so there aren't really established prices.

Driving to Santa Catalina: Those coming by car must pass through Santiago, the provincial capital of Veraguas. It's on the Interamerican Highway between Panama City (250 kilometers, about 3.5 hours) and David (190 kilometers, about four hours). As you drive west, the highway forks just before Santiago. Take the left fork and drive into Santiago, making a left turn toward the town of Soná at the church. The streets here are confusing, and you may need to ask for directions. Soná is 50 kilometers southwest of Santiago on a mostly excellent road. Beware, however, of the one-way bridges. Watch out for oncoming traffic, and keep your fingers crossed on some of the rustier ones. One bridge that was being replaced when I last visited looked ready to go. Let's hope the new one's finished before it does.

The road is in great shape and very scenic. It gets prettier the farther you go, winding past glimmering rivers, rice paddies, grazing cattle and horses, and coffee plantations. It's especially lovely in the rainy season, when everything is verdant. Though little pristine nature is left, emerald-green forested hills still ring the lowlands.

To continue to Santa Catalina, make a left at the gas station just before Soná; the turn is marked. Make a note of the mileage here. Make a left turn onto a rough road after 48 kilometers, at which point you make another left turn onto a rough road. Note: This turnoff is not marked. You'll have to rely on mileage, though there may be a sign for "Kenny's Surf Camp," which is in Santa Catalina. If you get lost, you should eventually find someone to ask directions.

After another nine kilometers you'll come to the village of Hicaco. Make a right at the Hicaco police station onto a rough, potholed dirt road that's been improved in recent years. It was navigable by regular car even in the rainy season when I last visited, but it's still not a great idea to come here in anything but a four-wheel drive or a bus. The road ends at Playa Santa Catalina, eight kilometers away. Driving straight through, the entire trip from Panama City takes about 5.5 hours.

The road ends right at the beach, where there are a couple of bars, a few simple homes, and little else. This is part fishing village, part surfers' hangout. A left turn up a steep, bad road leads to most of the area's accommodations. That's about all there is to Santa Catalina other than the amazing surf.

ISLAS SECAS

The M **Islas Secas Resort** (U.S. tel. 805/729-2737, info@islassecas.com, www.islassecas.com) consists of 16 small private islands far away from just about everything. The resort itself is on Isla Cavada, where there are six *casitas* (little houses) for guests, a dining/lounging area, and a spa. There are generally no more than 12 guests at a time. The *casitas* are on a cove facing the ocean and are circular, yurt-style buildings that provide a panoramic view of the surroundings. Each has a queen-sized bed, minibar, and bathroom. The largest, the Casa Grande, has a full kitchen.

While it's possible to do nothing but relax on a deserted beach, the resort's location is spectacular and lends itself to lots of nature activities. Possibilities include scuba diving or snorkeling, surfing near Morro Negrito, ocean kayaking, deep-sea and inshore fishing, and hiking on the islands. Diving and fishing in this region are outstanding. Rates are $299 per person, double occupancy, four-night minimum. This includes room, all meals, and excursions. Surfing, fishing, and scuba-diving trips, as well as massages at the spa, are extra and average about $100 per person per hour.

There is an airstrip on Isla Cavada. While boat transportation from David (about 1.5 hours) is sometimes available, nearly all guests arrive by private plane from Panama City (1 hour, $400 per person round-trip). The plane can also pick up and drop off guests at David (10 minutes, $200 each way). Pickup and drop-off from San José, Costa Rica, is also possible, for about $500–600 round-trip.

A unique tour offered by the resort is a private flight to hard-to-reach Isla Coiba, only 10 minutes by air away. Pricing was still in flux at the time of writing but a flight was likely to cost about $200 round-trip.

LAS LAJAS

The most popular mainland beach in the region is at Las Lajas, the turnoff to which is about 75 kilometers east of David (or 35 kilometers east of Horconcitos) on the Interamerican Highway. It's a long, wide, gray-sand beach with few facilities. It's not all that pretty or otherwise special, but it's the most accessible large expanse of sand around and it's big enough to offer seclusion even on busy dry-season weekends.

The crossroads of the Interamericana and the road leading down to Las Lajas is known, logically enough, as **El Cruce.** This is a common pit stop for buses and private cars making the long haul across the country. Here you'll find a gas station. Skip the hole-in-the-wall greasy spoon and hotel, and don't take your eyes off your stuff for a second.

It's a 13-kilometer drive south down a paved but pitted road from El Cruce to the beach, a drive that leads through the town of Las Lajas itself. Curve right when the road forks at a small yellow building; if the road turns to dirt, you've missed the turn. From this point on the drive is through cattle pasture lined with living fences that have become tall trees arching over the road. The road ends at the beach.

Shopping

Those looking for souvenirs can stop at the **Casa Artesenal Ngöbe-Buglé** (tel. 727-0783 or 727-0929, artesaniagnobe@hotmail.com, 8 A.M.–5 P.M. daily), an artisans' cooperative 300 meters west of El Cruce, the crossroads on the Interamerican Highway where the Las Lajas turnoff is. There's a small sign on the road. The shop is south of the highway, across a rickety suspension bridge. It has a small collection of Ngöbe-Buglé (Guaymi Indian) crafts, including their popular handwoven bags *(chácaras)*, pottery, clay pipes, traditional dresses at good prices, and *chaquiras,* necklaces made from bright beads, which make for dramatic jewelry or that can be framed and displayed. Note that 25 kilometers east of here, just east of the little town of Tolé, Ngöbe-Buglé vendors set up **roadside stands** that sell many of the same kinds of items.

Accommodations and Food

There are a few basic little open-air restaurants here (bring a cooler if possible), but only two places to stay. One is **Cabañas de Playa Las Lajas** (tel. 720-2430, cell 618-7723, starting at $5/$10 s/d), 1.4 kilometers down a dirt road to the right as one faces the beach. It's a fenced-off property with nine cabins—bamboo huts, really—right along the beach. Each has foam mattresses, concrete floors, and a loft for sleeping bags. They're rustic but adequate for a no-frills stay. They don't have bathrooms; a separate building houses basic shared toilets and showers. There are six more modern rooms in a building set back from the beach. These do have bathrooms but zero charm: they're basically four concrete walls and a floor. A restaurant and bar on the premises prepares meals in the dry season. At other times of the year, dinner is whatever you bring in a cooler. Rates are $5 per person in the cabins and $8 in the rooms back from the beach.

That buys a 24-hour stay. Camping on the property is $3 a day. Those who want to park a car for day use of the beach must pay $5; the fee is waived for overnight guests.

Interestingly, the rates are for foreigners. Reversing what one normally sees in national parks, museums, and the like, rates for Panamanians are higher—$10 per person in the cabins and a whopping $30 in the rooms. The signs at the entrance to the facility warning against loud music and all-terrain vehicles on the property suggest the motivation for this unusual policy. Apparently, the owner has dealt with one rowdy local bunch too many.

Las 3 Palmeras (tel. 727-0010, cell 690-7275, contact@las3palmeras.com, www.las3palmeras.com, $10 s, $15 d for beach houses) is rapidly staking its claim to be a bohemian destination to rival Restaurante y Cabañas Boca Brava. Officially opened in 2005, it's on the beach about 2.5 kilometers west of Cabañas de Playa Las Lajas. It was still being finished when I last visited, but when fully completed it should have a restaurant, bar, and 10 cabins. An unusual feature of the place are the parachute roofs over the bar and some of the cabins. Camping is possible, and two- and four-person tents with mattresses, pillows, and sheets are supplied. Rates are $10 s and $15 d for beach houses, $5 s and $9 for tent camping, and $3.50 for a hammock strung under a *rancho*. This place prides itself on its New Year's Eve parties, which feature all-night dancing to imported DJs. It's a bit of a hike from the T-intersection, but the owner shuttles visitors back and forth on the beach via dune buggy. Contact Las 3 Palmeras for details.

Getting There and Around

Buses to the town of Las Lajas leave the David bus terminal at 11:45 A.M. and 12:45 P.M. and return at 2 P.M. and 3 P.M. The trip takes 1.5 hours and costs $2. From the town, sun worshippers then have to take a taxi (about $4) to the beach. Any bus running along the Interamericana at least as far as El Cruce, the Las Lajas crossroads, can drop passengers off there, but then it's a taxi ride to the beach 13 kilometers away, which shouldn't cost much more and should be easier to find than a taxi from Las Lajas town. This will likely be a better option than the awkward timing of the bus to Las Lajas proper. Good bets include the San Felix and Tolé buses, which run about every 20 minutes.

MORRO NEGRITO SURF CAMP

Started in June 1998, Morro Negrito Surf Camp (U.S. tel. 760/632-8014, fax 760/632-8416, panasurfing@getresponse.com, www.surferparadise.com) is a place for adventurous surfers. It's on two islands in the Gulf of Chiriquí, due north of Isla de Coiba. It's just off the opposite (northwest) side of the same little peninsula where you'll find Playa Santa Catalina, and it's even more remote. The actual surf camp, Morro Negrito, is on an island that the locals call **Ensenada.** The camp has rustic cabañas, running water, and a dining area. Electricity is generated in the evenings. The waves here are smaller than

on the second island, with faces that range 1.5–2.5 meters on average. The other island is **Isla Silva de Afuera,** a half hour away by boat. This is the main surfing island, with wave faces that average 3.5–5.5 meters. There are both left and right breaks on both islands. Ten breaks have been discovered so far. The best time to find big waves is from April to October. For nonsurfers there's a long beach, ocean kayaking, horseback riding, snorkeling, and fishing (bring your own gear for the last two). It's also possible to hike to a 15-meter waterfall.

Only weeklong package deals are offered, and the place can accommodate a maximum of 20 people at a time. Packages cost $500 per person and include airport pickup and drop-off, a night in a Panama City hotel, transportation to the camp (a five-hour drive from the city), all food, and daily boat trips to surf spots. The package runs from Saturday to Saturday.

Boquete

The main attraction on the east side of Volcán Barú is Boquete (pop. 3,833 in central Boquete, 16,943 in the district), a pretty little town that faintly resembles a village in the Alps. At a little over a kilometer above sea level, it doesn't get quite as chilly here as it does in the higher mountain towns on the west side of Barú, but it's still pleasantly cool compared to most of Panama, and it can sometimes get surprisingly cold. Expect the foggy drizzle known as *bajareque* year-round. Again, bring warm, waterproof clothes. Though it's growing and becoming busier, the town is still tiny and laid-back, a relaxing place to hang out and plan day trips to the many attractions nearby.

Boquete has long been famous in Panama for its coffee and oranges, and for a flower festival that each year draws visitors from around the country. An influx of foreigners in recent years has given the area's fledging outdoor-adventure outfits a boost. The most popular activities are whitewater rafting, hiking the **Sendero Los Quetzales,** and climbing **Volcán Barú.**

What most people think of as Boquete is officially **Bajo Boquete** (Lower Boquete), so called

because it's in the middle of a picturesque valley surrounded by mountains. On a clear day, the Barú volcano dominates the landscape to the northwest. The town is bordered on the east by the churning waters of the Río Caldera.

Boquete's main drag is **Avenida Central,** which descends from Alto Boquete (Upper Boquete), runs north through town, and continues past a small church to the hills beyond. The plaza midway through town, on the east side of Avenida Central, is the town hub. Just east of it is a little square, **Parque de Las Madres,** with a statue depicting a mother with two small children who appear to be squirming in agony. Just south of it is another square with a cute fountain and a railroad car from the old train that used to run to the highlands.

Areas near Boquete of possible interest to visitors include **Bajo Mono,** northwest of Bajo Boquete, which has a lovely loop road and the trailhead for Sendero Los Quetzales; **Caldera,** which is southeast of Boquete and has good hot springs, some petroglyphs, and a bunch of little waterfalls; and the road to **Volcancito,** which

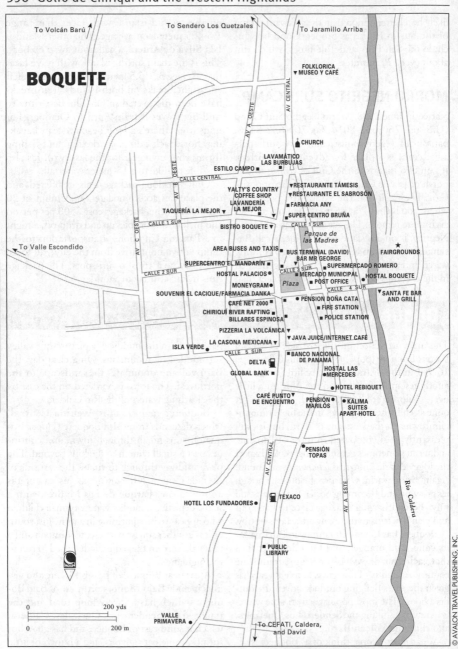

BOQUETE

To Volcán Barú

To Sendero Los Quetzales

To Jaramillo Arriba

FOLKLORICA
MUSEO Y CAFÉ

CHURCH

LAVAMÁTICO
LAS BURBUJAS

ESTILO CAMPO

AV A OESTE

AV CENTRAL

CALLE CENTRAL

AV B OESTE

YALTY'S COUNTRY
COFFEE SHOP

RESTAURANTE TÁMESIS
RESTAURANTE EL SABROSÓN
FARMACIA ANY

LAVANDERÍA
LA MEJOR

TAQUERÍA LA MEJOR

SUPER CENTRO BRUÑA

AV C OESTE

CALLE 1 SUR

BISTRO BOQUETE

CALLE 1 SUR

Parque de
las Madres

To Valle Escondido

AREA BUSES AND TAXIS

BUS TERMINAL (DAVID)
BAR MR GEORGE

FAIRGROUNDS

SUPERCENTRO EL MANDARÍN

CALLE 3 SUR

SUPERMERCADO ROMERO

CALLE 2 SUR

HOSTAL PALACIOS

MERCADO MUNICIPAL

HOSTAL BOQUETE

MONEYGRAM

Plaza

POST OFFICE

CALLE 4 SUR

SOUVENIR EL CACIQUE/FARMACIA DANKA

SANTA FE BAR
AND GRILL

PENSIÓN DOÑA CATA

CAFÉ NET 2000

CHIRIQUÍ RIVER RAFTING

FIRE STATION

BILLARES ESPINOSA

POLICE STATION

PIZZERIA LA VOLCÁNICA

LA CASONA MEXICANA

JAVA JUICE/INTERNET CAFÉ

ISLA VERDE

CALLE 5 SUR

BANCO NACIONAL
DE PANAMA

DELTA

HOSTAL LAS
MERCEDES

GLOBAL BANK

HOTEL REBIQUET

CAFÉ PUNTO
DE ENCUENTRO

PENSIÓN
MARILÓS

KALIMA
SUITES
APART-HOTEL

PENSIÓN
TOPAS

AV CENTRAL

AV A ESTE

Río Caldera

HOTEL LOS FUNDADORES

TEXACO

PUBLIC
LIBRARY

0   200 yds

0   200 m

VALLE
PRIMAVERA

To CEFATI, Caldera,
and David

Golfo de Chiriquí

© AVALON TRAVEL PUBLISHING, INC.

THE NATURAL TREASURES
OF THE WESTERN HIGHLANDS

The western highlands of Panama start at the Costa Rican border and head east for hundreds of kilometers along the Cordillera de Talamanca and the Cordillera Central. Much of Parque Internacional La Amistad and all of Parque Nacional Volcán Barú are in the highlands.

This chapter deals mainly with the Pacific slopes of the Continental Divide, since the parks and other sights are more accessible from that side. But the highlands extend north into Bocas del Toro Province, where they descend toward the Caribbean.

The western highlands harbor more virgin forest than any other region of Panama. The area's huge national parks are home to a bewildering array of plant and animal life, much of it endemic and some of it endangered. The mountain forests are threatened by encroaching farmland, which in turn is threatened by erosion. But there's a growing sense among highland dwellers that they're surrounded by something special that needs to be carefully preserved.

Spend any time up here and you'll soon know how cloud forests got their name. At the highest elevations you are literally in the clouds, and it's quite a dramatic sight to see puffy white billows blowing through the moss-draped trees in the afternoons.

Some parts of the woods may remind you of a temperate forest, but don't be fooled; you are still in the tropics. The forest has many of the same dangers and attractions as the lowland jungles, including venomous snakes.

This is one of the best places in the Americas to see the resplendent quetzal, an absolutely stunning bird. In the dry season, visitors often see several on a single outing. You're likely to see several species of jewel-toned hummingbirds among the hundreds of other bird species that make their home here.

Though you'd be very lucky to spot one, the forests are home to all five species of endangered felines found in Panama, including the jaguar. They are also home to one of the last stands of the endangered Baird's tapir, the largest land mammal in Central America.

Boquete is famous for its coffee and oranges, and the streams on the west side of Barú are filled with human-introduced trout. Flowers, strawberries, race horses, and dairy cows are also raised in the highlands.

It's refreshingly cool in the highlands, with temperatures that dip down to 7°C and sometimes lower. And it's wet: rainfall can exceed five meters. Even in the dry season, the mountains and valleys are often shrouded in what's affectionately known as *bajareque,* a foggy drizzle that can create photogenic rainbows. No matter when you come, bring rain gear.

Golfo de Chiriquí

starts near the CEFATI building in Alto Boquete and has some lodging and eating options.

A coffee tour, a stroll through Boquete's surreal gardens, a hike along a mountain trail, and a quest for quetzals are all worthwhile ways to spend time in this area. Try to find time to do them all. After that, a dip in Caldera's hot springs is a great way to soothe chilled, aching muscles.

SIGHTS

The best chance of seeing Panama's highest mountain in all its glory is at dawn. Shortly thereafter, its upper reaches and sometimes nearly the whole thing is usually obscured by clouds. Those wanting to see the mountain up close can hike to the top. (See *Sports and Recreation* in this section and the entry on the park under *Volcán and Surroundings.)*

El Explorador

This peculiar private garden (tel. 720-1989 in Boquete or 775-2643 in David, 9 A.M.–6 P.M. Fri.–Sun., $1 admission) in the hills above town is worth a visit if approached with a sense of humor. A winding path leads through two

El Explorador is one of two quirky gardens open to Boquete visitors.

hectares of terraced land with orange and lemon trees, a rose garden, stands of papyrus, a bonsai nursery, and much more. But what's most striking about this place are the human touches. All kinds of junk—shoes, bottles, shopping carts, TVs—have been turned into planters. Cartoon eyes peer out from trees and topiary shrubs. Classical music is pumped throughout the place. And dotted around the garden are wise sayings and encouraging words in Spanish. One tells you, "If before you die you plant a tree, you haven't lived in vain." Another sign leads the way to the "greatest miracle in the world." When you get there, you find—what else?—a mirror. What starts off seeming kitschy ends up making you feel rather, well, loved. This is a good place to recharge your batteries. If you see a gardener, thank him: They take great pride in the place. There's a great view of the valley from the rose garden.

El Explorador is about three kilometers northeast of town, near La Montaña y el Valle: the Coffee Estate Inn. Head north through Boquete on Avenida Central, pass the church, and then take the right fork toward the Panamonte Inn and Spa. Look for the signs. The road gets rocky toward the end but a four-wheel drive isn't nec-

essary if you're careful. It's also possible to walk from town, but it's uphill most of the way, steep at times. On days when the garden is officially closed, it may be possible to get in by appointment. There's a small food stand on the premises.

Mi Jardín Es Su Jardín

There must be something about the Boquete air that makes folks' dream gardens come out a little wacky. Mi Jardín es Su Jardín ("my garden is your garden") is a formal garden as it might have been conceived by the designer of a miniature golf course. We're talking a topiary dinosaur, brightly painted cow statues, a toy windmill, and so on, set on a sloping lawn crisscrossed by fountains and artificial streams. There's an impressive view of the valley and surrounding mountains from the observation tower. It's a toss-up whether this garden or El Explorador is quirkier. The garden is on private land, but it's open to the public and entrance is free, no reservations necessary. From the plaza, head north on Avenida Central past the church, keeping left at the fork. You'll soon see the entrance on the right. It's open daily 9 A.M.–6 P.M. Drivers must park outside.

Finca Lérida

This is the most famous birding spot on the whole east side of Barú. Though a working coffee plantation that produces some of the finest coffee in Panama, the *finca* contains primary and secondary forest that is home to hundreds of species of birds, as well as howler monkeys, peccaries, deer, and other mammals. There's a good chance of seeing resplendent quetzals here between January and August. The *finca* is up in the hills of Alto Quiel northwest of town, in a setting so picturesquely alpine you may find yourself humming the theme from *The Sound of Music*. That's part of the secret of the coffee's success: It's grown at elevations up to 1,600 meters, on the highest plantations in Panama.

Birding tours lead to a part of Lérida above the main estate, along a brutal road that leads through coffee and vegetable plantations that give way to dense, beautiful secondary cloud forest. The road ends at an even more gorgeous grove of primary forest, where you're likely to encounter quetzals, howler monkeys, and nasty mosquitoes.

Because Finca Lérida is private property and you must go with an authorized guide, this entry does not contain directions on how to get to the *finca*. These are usually arranged through tour guides. Visitors can also book a quite pricey tour directly through the Finca (tel./fax 720-2285, leridaestate@hotmail.com) that includes birdwatching, a nature walk, tour of the coffee facilities and lunch. Rates are $290 for one person, $310 for two people, $330 for three people, and so on. Groups of six or more are $65 each. Visitors can also hike a five-kilometer trail system on the finca for $10 per person, including trail map. The chances of spotting quetzals without a good guide, however, are not great.

Coffee Tours

A tour of one of Boquete's many coffee operations is a pleasant way to spend a few hours, and it'll deepen your appreciation of the area and its people, not to mention the incredible amount of work that goes into that morning caffeine buzz. It's not necessary to be a coffee addict to enjoy one of these tours, but it does help.

The tour of **Café Ruiz** (tel. 720-1392, Panama toll-free tel. 800-CAFE—800-2233, info@cafe ruiz.com, www.caferuiz.com) is best for those

A tour of Café Ruiz takes visitors through the whole process of growing and preparing coffee. The best coffee is sun dried, a process that takes 8–12 days.

Golfo de Chiriquí

MADE IN THE SHADE

Boquete is coffee country, but as you look around you may wonder where they're hiding the farms. Scanning the hillsides, all you see are shady trees, particularly orange trees. Look closer: If it's a coffee farm, you'll see tall shrubs below the trees. In the picking season, these will have ripe, cherry-red berries. The seeds are coffee beans.

Most of the coffee here is shade-grown, a traditional method in which coffee bushes grow in the shade of a forest or among trees planted by farmers. Farther west, especially around Río Sereno near the Costa Rican border, coffee is grown in open fields. This method produces a greater yield, but conservationists say it's a poor trade-off.

They argue that trees protect the crop from pests, produce natural mulch, preserve the chemical balance of the soil, and prevent erosion. Shade-grown coffee therefore requires less pesticide and fertilizer and is less disruptive to the environment. The money saved on fertilizer helps offset the lower productivity of shade-grown coffee. Also, the trees provide a habitat for mammals and hundreds of bird species, particularly migratory birds. This habitat becomes ever more important as forests are cleared in coffee-producing countries.

In Boquete, orange trees are commonly planted along with coffee and provide an extra source of income for the farmers. You can almost always find good oranges in Boquete. Navel oranges grow eight-ninth months out of the year. Valencias take over from February to March. This also helps make up for the lower productivity of the shade-grown method.

It's a pretty efficient system. The pulp of the berry that surrounds the bean is even used as compost, and the dried husk encasing the bean is used as fuel.

But even eco-friendly coffee processing has its limitations. Processing uses a great deal of water, which is then flushed into the rivers. The runoff is filled with pulp and sugar compounds that upset the biological balance of the rivers and streams. You won't find any trout splashing around in these rivers. Some of the more forward-thinking companies have begun purifying their runoff before dumping it; by law the entire industry will have to follow suit by 2006.

It's also hard to grow coffee completely organically. Few farms in Boquete use herbicides, but the orange trees attract Mediterranean fruit flies, which farmers do fight with pesticides. Still, the main enemy in the highlands is fungal disease, not insects. Because it's so wet up here, farmers plant coffee so that air flows through the rows of bushes, keeping everything a bit drier.

Bitter Times for Coffee Growers

A large workforce of migrant Ngöbe-Buglé farm workers is critical to the coffee industry in Panama. Harvesting is all done by hand. Workers search for fully formed red beans - the green ones are immature - and they have to twist the beans off carefully to keep the living stems intact. Try it if you get a chance - it's not easy. And it's tedious work.

Due to overproduction of coffee around the world, the market has become saturated in recent years. Prices have become so depressed it sometimes costs farmers more to pick the crop than they can hope to make from selling it. The Panamanian government has stepped in to tide farmers over with loans.

Hardest hit, naturally, are the coffee pickers. They're paid by the *lata*, a measure that has been used throughout Latin American for a hundred years. It's based on the size of a traditional cooking-oil can that holds around 20 liters, or 5 gallons. In better economic times, a worker could make as much as $1.85 per lata. In 2003, that amount was slashed to $.85. The market has recovered somewhat, and at the time of writing workers were making about $1.15-1.25. Still, a Ngöbe-Buglé worker can pick an average of six to seven *latas* of beans a day. Do the math. Even in Panama that's hard to live on.

It's All in the Timing

Coffee in Boquete is normally harvested from October to February. The beans of the best coffee are sun dried, a process that takes eight to twelve days. The beans are then stored for at least three months to cure them. The whole process is delicate; any misstep from bush to roaster can degrade the quality of the coffee.

Coffee is ready to sell in late March or early April. That's when the buyers come and the "cupping," the coffee equivalent of wine tasting, begins. The different farms compete to see who will have the highest-rated crop that year.

April to June is the best time to come to Boquete if you want to taste ultra-fresh coffee. Even then, you should aim for coffee that's been roasted within the last two weeks, if possible. If you grind the beans, you've got two days to taste it at its best.

Higher is Better

The two most widely produced types of coffee in the world are robusta and arabica. Robusta is a lowland coffee with twice as much caffeine and a more bitter taste than arabica, which is a highland coffee. Robusta has its defenders, and it's often mixed with arabica to create espresso blends. But good-quality arabica beans are generally considered to produce a better cup of coffee than good-quality robusta beans. All the coffee in Boquete is arabica.

Coffee grown at higher elevations, such as arabica, matures more slowly because of the lower temperatures. This makes for a more complex, less bitter brew. Generally, the higher the elevation, the better the coffee. Boquete coffee is grown at 1,000–1,600 meters, which is quite high.

Experts consider Boquete coffee among the best in the world, though its lower profile means it's often undervalued and less expensive compared with more famous rivals such as Jamaica Blue Mountain and Kona.

Don't Burn the Beans

Like many a would-be coffee snob, I'd always preferred hearty dark-roast coffee over the bitter stuff Americans traditionally consumed or the scorched water they now drink at Starbucks. As true coffee connoisseurs in Boquete will point out, though, dark roasts are often used to mask bad coffee. Gourmet coffees tend to get a lighter roast, allowing you, in the catch phrase of one Boquete grower, to "taste the coffee, not the roast." If you like your coffee strong, just brew more beans per cup. Those with sensitive stomachs should also note that dark roasts are more acidic. Another tip: coffee made from somewhat coarse grounds often tastes better than finely ground stuff.

who want a real nuts-and-bolts look at the whole coffee-production process. Ruiz produces 22 million pounds of coffee each year, a drop in the coffee cup compared with Panama's two biggest coffee companies, Duran and Sitton, who produce most of the coffee sold throughout the country, but enough to make Ruiz Panama's largest producer of gourmet coffee.

The full tour takes visitors to one of Ruiz's coffee farms; through its impressive mill in Palmira, near Alto Boquete; and ends up at its roasting facility, where one can taste two of its coffees and see how the coffee is roasted, ground, and packaged.

A three-hour tour costs $14 per person and is offered at 9 A.M. Monday–Saturday or by special arrangement. Sign up on the list posted at the door of the main café in Bajo Boquete (see *Food* for directions). A 30-minute tour just of the roasting facility is $4 and hours are flexible; call tel. 720-1392 or just show up during business hours.

The tour of **Café Kotowa** (tel. 720-1430, kotowa@myroaster.com, www.myroaster.com) is less dramatic but more charming and scenic. Its small mill is up in Palo Alto, a few kilometers north of Boquete, behind which its coffee farms run far up the steep slopes of emerald hills until they're lost in the clouds. The mill faces a breathtaking view of Barú across rolling pasture. This is cloud-forest country, and it gets quite wet up here.

Kotowa is the Ngöbe word for "mountain," and the company is named in recognition of the indigenous people who work the farms. The operation is owned by Ricardo MacIntyre, the grandson of a Scot who moved here from Canada after reading a newspaper article about Boquete in 1918. The original wooden coffee mill, powered by water and brought all the way over from Scotland, has been lovingly preserved and is part of the tour, as is the modern-day mill.

Coffee is roasted in small batches at the back of the tiny family chapel—talk about a religious devotion to coffee. It's done by hand, in a roaster not much bigger than a toaster oven.

The tour concludes at an espresso bar at the back of the wooden mill, where Ricardo MacIn-

tyre and his wife, Benita, are sometimes on hand to serve visitors a free cup.

Coffee Adventures (tel. 720-3852, cell 634-4698, habbusdekwie@cwpanama.net), a local guide service, gives excellent tours of Café Kotowa. Tours last three hours and cost $17.50 per person, two-person minimum, and includes transportation from hotels. Children younger than 10 are not allowed for safety reasons. To make a reservation, contact Coffee Adventures. Visitors can also visit Café Kotowa on their own, but only with warning.

Finca Lérida also offers tours of its coffee facilities, which consist of several quaint wooden buildings that house both the coffee mill and the family, set in pretty countryside. It's a highly photogenic place. These are usually included as part of a pricey bird-watching package, but it may be possible to tour the mill by itself. (See the *Finca Lérida* entry above for information).

Los Pozos de Caldera

These hot springs are a fair haul southeast of Boquete near the town of Caldera, famous in Panama as a home of cowboys and witches. Those who love hot springs will enjoy the Pozos de Caldera. Those who can take them or leave them will find the trip here a bit of a hassle for the payoff. That said, the springs are attractive, situated in a secluded stretch of forest near the bank of the roaring Río Chiriquí.

Unlike hot springs that belch forth a sulfurous stench, these barely smell at all. There are four pools. The first one is the warmest, supposedly 42°C. There's one closer to the river that's hard to spot but quite nice. It's not as warm as the first one, but it's surrounded by trees and is less developed (the others are lined with large, flat rocks).

Not far from the springs is a tributary to the Río Chiriquí which, if you don't mind quite a bit of scrambling over slippery rocks and muddy banks, you can follow upriver to five waterfalls, each more picturesque than the one before. This hike is best done with a guide. At the very least, as with any other forest hike in Panama, don't go alone. A dip in the hot springs is especially pleasant after splashing about in these brisk waters.

© WILLIAM FRIAR

The Piedra Pintada, a boulder covered with mysterious petroglyphs, is worth a quick visit on the way to Los Pozos de Caldera.

Golfo de Chiriquí

To get to the *pozos* from Boquete, head south out of town on Avenida Central. After about 12 kilometers look for a blue sign that says Caldera. Turn left here and continue past the town of Caldera. Another blue sign indicates a right onto a gravel road. Those with a four-wheel drive can follow this road to within a 15-minute walk of the springs. Otherwise, park and hike the rest of the way, about a 40-minute walk. Do not leave anything of value in the car; cars get broken into around here. After crossing the cable-and-plank bridge, make a left turn uphill (there should be a sign). Make the first left at the barbed-wire gate, which is easy to miss because there's no sign. From here the springs are about 15 minutes straight down the trail. Admission is $1, which goes to keeping the area clean.

On the way to the hot springs, it's worth stopping to check out the **Piedra Pintada.** This is yet another huge, riverside boulder etched with mysterious squiggles by a pre-Colombian people about which little is known. Just before "downtown" Caldera, look for a "Piedra Pintada" sign on the right side of the road. Pull over and park. Duck under the barbed wire and bamboo fence

behind the Jardín La Fortuna beer garden and walk across a pasture toward the water. Head in the direction of a metal post with the number 80 painted on it. On the left as you face the river is a three-meter-high boulder just above the river that is covered with crude faces and figures (and some modern-day idiots' graffiti).

Buses and taxis between Boquete and Caldera cost $3 per person each way.

Museum

The *museo* part of the **Folklorica Museo y Café** (11 A.M.–7 P.M. Sun.–Thurs., noon–8 P.M. Fri.–Sat., closed Tues.) contains a small collection of vintage postcards from around the country, as well as some old *molas* and a few other items. It's worth a quick stop, especially given the price of admission: free. The shop in the front of the museum offers an odd assortment of knickknacks.

ENTERTAINMENT AND EVENTS

Boquete is hurtin' for real nightlife. The nicest watering hole in town is the bar at the **Panamonte Inn and Spa,** which thanks to a recent renovation has made it both cozy and sleek, a very pleasant place to sit with a drink at either of its two stone fireplaces (one indoors, one out). Be sure to check out all the antiques. The only unwelcome addition is a big-screen TV. Another possibility is the spacious bar at **Santa Fe Bar and Grill,** which has a pool table. It's next to the fairgrounds. **Bar Mr. George,** next to the bus-station office on the north side of the plaza, is a blue-collar dive with zero atmosphere but a friendly, drunken vibe. A pool hall, **Billares Espinosa** (3 P.M.–midnight Mon.–Fri., 10 A.M.–midnight Sat.–Sun.) is on Avenida Central just south of the plaza. If you're feeling optimistic and it's a weekend, you can stop by the subterranean bar/disco at **Hotel Los Fundadores.** It's a cramped dungeon of a place, but it's got a dance floor and pretty lights. Good luck.

Valle Escondido

This gated community (tel. 720-2824, 720-1450, info@valleescondido.biz, www.valleescondido.biz) in a valley close to central Boquete is attracting expatriate retirees from North America eager for insulated first-world living at prices made possible by a third-world setting. The development plan calls for 150 homes, a small nine-hole golf course, tennis courts, a country club, a 600-person amphitheater, a clinic, and 24-hour security.

Some of the facilities are open to visitors, though the place was still being completed and it was unclear at the time of writing exactly what will be available for nonresidents when everything is finally done. On my last visit, day guests could pay $2 ($1 for kids) at the gate for admission to a small shopping complex and some of the grounds from 8:30 A.M. to 7 P.M. daily, which included a voucher that could be used to buy a soda or water. Most of the shops were not yet occupied, but those that were included a pro shop, a couple of artisan shops with modest offerings, and a coffee shop. There's also a **Cantina** (2–9 P.M. Mon.–Fri., noon–9 P.M. Sat. and Sun.), but revelers must be sure to make it through the front gate before 7 P.M.

The community is a short drive west of Boquete. Heading north on Avenida Central, turn left on Calle 5a Sur, just before downtown, to-

ward Isla Verde. Continue past the cabañas and follow the signs to the security checkpoint.

Fairs

The **Feria de las Flores y El Café** is Boquete's showplace event. The Fair of Flowers and Coffee draws an estimated 90,000 people from all over Panama to view the stunning flowers that carpet Boquete's fairgrounds on the east side of the Río Caldera. The fair has its roots in a celebration first held in 1950. Though gardens all over Boquete are spruced up for the event, the fairgrounds are the epicenter, transformed each year into a floral playground with fanciful landscaping. The festival also includes concerts, folkloric dancers, handicraft exhibits, and a chance to sip gourmet coffee and chug vast amounts of other liquids. It's held for 10 days in the middle of January. Check with IPAT for exact dates, which change annually.

After the Feria de las Flores y El Café in January, the fairgrounds remain open until April, when a smaller festival, the **Feria de las Orquídeas** (Orchid Festival) closes out the season with a four-day celebration. Again, check with IPAT for exact dates. The entire country celebrates Panama's independence from Spain on November 28, but Boquete's celebration is the biggest, presided over by the president of Panama and drawing people from far beyond the highlands for a huge party. No one's yet explained to me why Boquete's **Día de la Independencia** celebration is so grand. My favorite theory came from a tour guide who explained that was the date Boquete got its very own team of firefighters; he neglected to mention Spain at all.

SHOPPING

The small **Valle Escondido shopping plaza** should be well-established by the time you read this.

Packages of good coffee are easy to come by in Boquete, as you might imagine, in an overwhelming variety of roasts, qualities, and flavors. You can choose either whole bean or ground coffee, though whole beans preserve the coffee's flavor longer. Attractive souvenir packs are often available, which make for nice gifts. Finca Lérida, Café Ruiz, and Café Kotowa all offer excellent coffee.

The most widely available boutique coffee is Café Ruiz, which you can buy at either of the company's shops in Boquete. (See *Food* for directions.) The best-quality Ruiz is the gourmet, which is a lighter roast and is sold in gold bags. Ruiz coffee is increasingly easy to come by throughout Panama, but its gourmet coffee is sold only at its two Boquete shops, its shop in Panama City, and the Super Barú supermarket in David. La Berlina Estate is arguably the best of the gourmet varieties.

Some companies will ship coffee overseas. You can also order Café Kotowa coffee through its website (www.myroaster.com), and Café Ruiz may finally be following suit by the time you visit (www.caferuiz.com). Shipping costs for either of these options can exceed the cost of the coffee itself.

Estilo Campo (tel. 630-5404, 9 A.M.–noon, 2–6 P.M. Tues.–Fri., 10:30 A.M.–6 P.M. Sat. and Sun.) is a little shop at the north end of town, around the corner from Lavamática Las Burbujas, where you can buy simple but cute hand-painted birdhouses and wall ornaments.

Souvenir El Cacique (tel. 720-2217, 10 A.M.–1 P.M. and 2–9 P.M. Fri.–Wed., 1–9 P.M. Thurs.) is a new place that sells Ngöbe-Buglé necklaces, *molas*, *cocobolo* statues and other crafts from Panama, as well as a few things from Guatemala and Peru. The staff speaks English here.

The Bookmark (tel. 776-1688, 9 A.M.–5 P.M. Tues.–Sun., closed Mon.) is in Dolega, a small town about midway between David and Boquete. As you head up toward Boquete, look for it on the left 17 kilometers after the turnoff from the Interamericana. This tiny place is one of Panama's few used bookstores, and it has a little bit of everything—bestsellers, true crime, science fiction, nonfiction, romance, and so on. There are some used first editions from the old Canal Zone library, and a small Spanish-language section. This is a good place to sell or swap that tattered beach book. It's worth stopping by even if the place seems closed. It's run by an American who lives in the back of the house and he might be around when you stop by.

SPORTS AND RECREATION

There are plenty of options for outdoor activities around Boquete. The most popular and impressive of these are white-water rafting, hiking the Sendero Los Quetzales, and climbing Volcán Barú.

During my last visit, Café Kotowa was nearing completion of its **Boquete Tree Trek** (tel. 720-1635, cell 615-3300, info@aventurist.com, aventurist.com), a zip-line ride through the forest similar to the Canopy Adventure in El Valle. This one will have 12 stages spread over three kilometers and will pass by two waterfalls. It starts up the hill from the Café Kotowa mill in Palo Alto, but guests can be picked up from an office on Avenida Central in downtown Boquete. Rides were going to be offered at 8 A.M., 11 A.M., and 2 P.M. and cost $60 per person. The whole thing, including transportation from downtown, will last about three hours.

White-Water Rafting

Western Panama has fantastic whitewater, some of it truly world class. The main commercially run rivers are the powerful Río Chiriquí (east of Boquete) and Río Chiriquí Viejo (west of Boquete, near the Costa Rican border). Even experienced rafters will likely find the runs here pretty darn thrilling. They feature very long wave trains, relentless runs, hair-raising moments, and lots of variety. There are much more peaceful sections of the river where timid beginners can get their feet wet.

One of the great things about rafting on these rivers is the sense of solitude. Yours may be the only raft on the river, and you may not see a soul along the banks. Other than the occasional cow, all rafters are likely to encounter are forest, gorges, tributaries, and huge, beautiful birds. And, of course, big water.

Chiriquí River Rafting (tel./fax 720-1505 or 720-1506, cell 618-0846, rafting@panama-rafting.com, www.panama-rafting.com), enjoys a great reputation as a highly professional operation and the best white-water outfit in Panama. It is still the only white-water operation I can recommend as reliable and safety-conscious.

The company is run by Hector Sanchez, who

was for years in charge of recreational services for the U.S. military bases in the old Canal Zone. He's fully bilingual, as are some of his staff members. The rest speak enough basic English to get you through the rapids.

The company offers four different day trips on these two rivers, with rapids varying from Class IIs and IIIs to solid Class IVs. The most hard-core of these is the Palon section of the Chiriquí Viejo, a 4.5-hour blast through deep canyons. It costs $100 per person. The gentlest is the Avila section of the Chiriquí, a three-hour ride through Class II rapids suitable for families with young children. The price is $75 per person.

The Chiriquí Viejo can be run only from December to April, the same months that the Chiriquí is usually too dry to run.

For those who like gentle water, the company also offers 2.5-hour trips on the nearby Río Majagua ($55/person), which has Class II rapids.

From May to November, another gentle option is the Río Grande ($75/person) near El Caño, between Aguadulce and Penonomé in central Panama, though this requires a road trip of at least two hours. These are appropriate for families with small children.

The company also rents white-water kayaks for $30 a day, including all equipment.

All trips include a picnic lunch by the river. Trips to other rivers and sea-kayak expeditions are sometimes possible through special arrangement.

Note: Contact the company as far ahead of time as possible. Trips require a minimum of three people, so advance warning helps the company coordinate groups of sufficient size.

Every fall and winter a group of top-notch kayakers from North Carolina's highly regarded **Nantahala Outdoor Center (NOC)** comes to the western highlands for a "residency" with Chiriquí River Rafting. These guys are still making first descents throughout western Panama, including some scary world-class ones.

From October to November they offer advanced white-water kayak clinics in conjunction with Sanchez's group. For more information, contact NOC's Adventure Travel Office (U.S. tel. 800/232-7238, ext. 333, adtrav@noc.com, www.noc.com).

 Parque Nacional Volcán Barú

There are plenty of hiking trails in the area, the most popular of which is the gorgeous **Sendero Los Quetzales,** which skirts the north side of Barú and links Boquete with Cerro Punta.

Note that Cerro Punta is nearly a kilometer higher in elevation than Boquete, so you'll be walking uphill most of the way. Because of that, most people choose to hike in the other direction. (See the main *Sendero Los Quetzales* entry in *Cerro Punta and Surroundings* for more details on hiking in that direction.)

However, some reckon the uphill hike, though strenuous, is actually easier than hiking downhill since the steep descent is rough on the knees and can set you up for a case of the "wobbles," which is no fun when you still have hours of downhill hiking ahead of you. And some of those who regularly hike the trail claim there's a better

The western highlands of Panama offer world-class river rafting.

© WILLIAM FRIAR

Volcán Barú, Panama's tallest mountain, towers over Boquete Valley on a clear day.

chance of outrunning the rain hiking uphill, since it often rains in the morning on the Cerro Punta side and in the afternoon on the Boquete side. Besides not getting wet, you'll have a much better chance of seeing birds.

It's best to go with a guide when hiking the trail up to Cerro Punta, as there are a couple of places where it's easy to miss a turn. Get an early start.

Hiking uphill also takes longer than hiking downhill. Allow six hours just to hike between the two ANAM ranger stations—Alto Chiquero (Boquete side) and El Respingo (Cerro Punta side). And bear in mind the stations are a long way from any town. It's also possible to camp here or stay in a dorm room. (See *Accommodations* in the *Cerro Punta and Surroundings* section.)

Access to the Boquete entrance is from the scenic Bajo Mono loop road; the turnoff onto the road leading to the trailhead is marked. Note that from this turnoff it's a three-kilometer uphill walk to the ranger station, a walk that will add at least 1.5 hours to the hike. The trail officially starts past this station. Some guides drive all the way to the ranger station; be sure to ask where the tour begins and ends. The road has been recently

paved and is in excellent shape. Those with their own vehicles can park at the station. Don't leave any valuables in the car.

Hike down the dirt road for about 45 minutes. The Los Quetzales trailhead is on the left. There was a sign marking it the last time I was there, but you can't count on that; keep your eyes open, as it's possible to miss the turnoff and walk too far on the dirt road. The trail gets far steeper about 2.5 hours into the hike. After another hour, there's a campsite with vista points but few facilities. This is a good place to take a break and eat lunch.

Once at El Respingo, it's another 1.5-hour hike downhill to the road linking Cerro Punta and Guadalupe. From here you may be able to flag down a bus or taxi. If this doesn't sound like a fun way to end a hike, consider arranging for a taxi to meet you at El Respingo station. The fare to Cerro Punta should be about $10.

Those who choose to hike from the Bajo Mono turnoff all the way to the Cerro Punta-Guadalupe road should plan on a nine-hour hike.

Arrange transportation back to Boquete ahead of time or plan to spend the night in the Cerro Punta area. The trip by bus takes at least three hours, not including waiting time in David, where travelers must change buses. One-way trippers: Consider shipping luggage ahead to meet you. You can hire a taxi to do so, or make arrangements through your hotel or guide. Those who choose one of the latter options should find out exactly how the luggage will be sent and when it will arrive. There have been cases of tourists getting stuck waiting for bags that had been sent by courier services that make the trip only once a day. No fun.

Climbing to the Summit: The summit of the dormant volcano that gives the park its name is, at 3,475 meters, the highest point in Panama. Those wanting to climb to the top of Barú will find the Boquete summit trail easier to manage than the one on the west side of Barú. When the road is in slightly less horrendous shape than normal, which means the dry season, it may even be possible to drive to the summit from this side. Even then, however, this requires a good four-wheel drive with a winch. The "road" more closely resembles a steep river bed. It's an absolutely brutal drive.

If you hike instead, allow at least 4-5 hours up and 3-4 hours back down. The hike is strenuous but not technically difficult. Remember, there's a risk of hypothermia, especially for those who get stranded on the mountain, so be sure to bring warm, waterproof clothing. (See *Sports and Recreation* in the *Volcán and Surroundings* section for hiking and camping tips and more information on Barú.)

Unless you're looking for a marathon hike, drive or hire a taxi ($4) to the ranger station at the trailhead. A four-wheel drive is needed even to get this far. From Boquete, head north through town and take the second left past the church (look for the blue "Volcán Barú" sign). Continue straight past the first intersection then take the right fork uphill. There's a fork after 6.7 kilometers. Take the right fork. The road forks again in about 800 meters. Take the left fork. After another 600 meters, take the right fork up the very steep gravel road.

Entrance is $3, payable at the little ranger station at the entrance to the park, which is in an area called Camiseta. There's an outhouse at the station. It's another $5 to camp in the park, but there are no facilities. From the station (elevation 1,840 meters) it's another 13.5 kilometers to the top. The trail is fairly steep and very rocky. Those determined to start their trek in downtown Boquete should add another nine kilometers. (For more information on the park, see the entry under *Volcán and Surroundings*.)

More Hiking

A less-ambitious hike is along a stretch of the **Bajo Mono loop,** a scenic, 20-kilometer paved road. It features lush forest, dramatic volcanic cliffs, and a valley with a pretty river flowing through it. A plus is it's easy to flag down a bus if you get tired of hiking. Be careful—many of the truckers plying these roads seem to have a death wish. The Bajo Mono Loop starts north of Boquete. Follow Avenida Central and keep left at the fork past the church. The loop is well marked. Its also possible to bike or drive the road.

Nature Tours

A guide is a good idea for more ambitious hikes, such as summiting Volcán Barú or hiking the Sendero Los Quetzales. A knowledgeable birding guide also greatly increases the chance of spotting quetzals. Many guides have access to four-wheel-drive vehicles, a plus for those without their own transportation. Several of the hotels, especially the more upscale ones, can arrange tours for their guests. The Panamonte Inn and Spa offers tours to nonguests as well.

Please note: Though most of the guides in Boquete are good, safe, and reliable people, there have been some complaints about dangerous practices as well as inappropriate behavior toward women. This is likely a function of the relatively thriving tourism business in Boquete versus other parts of the country—there are just more people trying to break into the business, not all of them competent or professional.

To cite one example, though this area is a natural for horse riding, I have been unable to find a riding guide I feel comfortable recommending. If you do go for a ride, play it safe and go only in groups.

Some also let the desire for business overcome common sense. No matter what a tour guide might tell you, for example, a hike to the top of Volcán Barú or the length of Sendero Los Quetzales is too much for young children or adults who aren't in reasonably good shape. All the guides below have good reputations.

Coffee Adventures (tel. 720-3852, cell 634-4698, habbusdekwie@cwpanama.net), is a guide outfit that consists of Terry van Niekerk and Hans van der Vooren, the warm and eminently dependable Dutch couple who own Tinamou Cottage. They offer an excellent, well-organized guided hike along Sendero Los Quetzales. The usual drill is for Hans to drive you and Terry to the Alto Chiquero ranger station (Boquete side) early in the morning, then pick you up at El Respingo ranger station (Cerro Punta side) in the afternoon. This ensures that you hike only the trail, not the kilometers of road leading to and from the trail that can turn this into a marathon hike. The tour includes breakfast at the start of the day and a picnic lunch about two-thirds of the way through the hike. Terry is an accomplished bird-watcher who speaks English, Dutch, and Spanish. The cost is $95 for two people; discounts are available for groups of three or more.

They also offer less strenuous hiking trips for $22/person, minimum three people. These last about three hours and include refreshments.

Terry and Hans take a first-aid kit and cell phone along on all their hikes. As the name Coffee Adventures suggests, they also offer excellent tours of coffee facilities. (See *Coffee Tours.*) Other trips include half-day hiking and bird-watching tours ($32.50 per person) and a scenic drive from Boquete to Almirante in Bocas del Toro ($99 per person, two-person minimum), which, for those who can afford it and don't want to fly, is a quicker and much more enjoyable way to get to the islands than taking buses.

Santiago "Chago" Caballero (tel. 720-1075, fax 720-1075) has been guiding people in the highlands for 18 years and is often employed by top guide outfits. He is generally acknowledged as the best quetzal spotter around; if your main aim is to see a quetzal, he's your guy. He's a kind, gentle man and can be depended on to show up on time. He's got his own four-wheel drive and is a careful driver. His bird-watching tours cost $120 for 1–2 people, $40/person for 3–5 people.

Chago also offers tours to the summit of Volcán Barú ($150 for 1–2 people, $50/person 3–5 people) and Sendero Los Quetzales ($170 for 1–2 people, $60/person 3–5 people). Other offerings include tours of the Cerro Punta side of the mountain, including either Parque Internacional La Amistad or Cañon Macho de Monte and the Lagunas de Volcán (both $140 1–2 people, $50 per person for 3–5 people). All tours include a box lunch and transportation. Chago also offers transfers to David ($20), Cerro Punta ($70), and Almirante ($180), which is the jumping-off point for Bocas del Toro.

Michael Cooling, an easygoing gringo who speaks English and Spanish, has been hiking around here since 2000 and has discovered several little-known hikes. However, he works only with guests of La Montaña y El Valle: The Coffee Estate Inn; tours must be booked through the inn. He charges $50 for two people, $10 more for each additional person, and $15 more if he uses his own four-wheel drive.

ACCOMMODATIONS

Lodging below is in or near downtown Boquete unless otherwise specified. There are some good options in the outlying area, but those without their own transportation may find getting around inconvenient.

Though it was not slated to open until 2007, the planners behind the **Cielo Paraiso** (tel. 720-2431, www.cieloparaiso.com) development near Boquete are building Boquete's first true resort hotel. It's set to go up in La Estrella, a short drive southeast of downtown Boquete, on four former cattle farms that are being converted into a 180-lot housing development, 18-hole golf course, and 72-room hotel spread out among a main lodge and 18 two-story villas.

Under $10

Pensión Marilós (tel. 720-1380, $6.60/9.90 s/d with shared bath, $9.90/$15.40 s/d for one with a private bath) remains one of the best deals in all of Panama. It offers seven simple but clean and

© BONNIE KAY SPINDLER

Panamonte Inn and Spa

tidy rooms at bargain prices. It's two blocks south of the plaza, on Avenida E Este, which is parallel to and two blocks east of Avenida Central. Guests can use the kitchen and dining room.

$10–25

El Bajareque Lodge (tel./fax 720-1505 or 720-1506, cell 618-0846, rafting@panama-rafting.com, www.panama-rafting.com, $10 per person) is tucked away among the coffee plantations in Palmira, a short drive from Alto Boquete. It's run by the Sanchez family, the folks who run Chiriquí River Rafting, and is in fact on their farm, right next to their quite attractive, modern home. The hostel-style rooms are simple but comfortable, with bunk beds, plenty of blankets and private, hot-water bathrooms. The place caters mainly to kayakers, who can stash their kayaks in a secure shed on the property, but rooms are available to anyone. Guests can use the kitchen for free or arrange meals. All-you-can-eat breakfasts are $5, dinners are $7.50, and you're on your own for lunch. The turnoff to the lodge is near the Café Ruiz *beneficio* (processing mill); call for directions. The last stretch of road is rough and requires a four-wheel drive.

Taxis from Boquete cost about $2; ask the driver to take you to *Hector Sánchez en Palmira*.

Pension Doña Cata (tel. 720-1260, reservaciones@pensiondonacata.com, www.pensiondonacata.com, starts at $6/$12 s/d) is a new place in an old building—a two-story wooden building that dates from the 1950s and has tons of charm. This place used to be the Pension Virginia. It's right on the south side of the town plaza. There are 13 rooms in all. The cheapest room is quite small with a shared bathroom and an okay mattress for $6/12 s/d. Another room with shared bath upstairs goes for $10/$20 s/d and may be worth it for all the windows and a view of the plaza. A room with bath for $25 s/d is not much of a step up except for the private toilet and shower.

Hostal Las Mercedes (tel. 660-3138, rdarios44@hotmail.com, $10 s/d to $15 s/d, depending on size of the room) is a bare-bones but friendly six-room hostel. It's a short walk from the center of town, just south of the police and fire stations near the corner of Avenida A Este and Calle 5a Sur. The smallest room is barely big enough for its bed. Guests can use the kitchen and laundry room and the TV in the common room. Management can arrange tours of nearby attractions.

The German-run **Pensión Topas** (tel./fax 720-1005, schoeb@chiriqui.com, starts at $8.80/11 s/d) is three blocks south of the plaza on Avenida Belisario Porras, which is parallel to and one block east of Avenida Central. This is a cheerful place with eight rooms set in a garden filled with flowering trees. A full breakfast (8–11 A.M.) on the terrace is $3.90. The owner, Axel Shöb, speaks English and is helpful on advice about where to go and what to see. There's a volleyball net and small swimming pool on the premises. Very simple and small rooms with shared bath cost $8.80/11 s/d. Rooms with private bath start at $15.40/19.80 s/d, about $6 more for larger rooms. Allow 10 days for an answer to email; Axel hates computers.

Hostal Boquete (tel. 720-2573, 226-6042, starts at $15/20 s/d), on Calle 4a Sur near the west bank of the Río Caldera and just north of the bridge spanning it, offers seven rooms, most with a double and single bed and a tiny TV tuned to local stations. The rooms are dark and the beds are hard, but this place has two things to recommend it. One is its picturesque location on the banks of the Río Caldera, with a view of the fairgrounds on the east bank. The property slopes to the river, and guests can sit back here if they like. The other is Otilde de Aguilar, an absolutely delightful and ebullient person and one half of the friendly couple that owns the place. If she can't make you smile, you're a lost cause. She speaks English. Note that even if you could get a room here during a festival, you probably wouldn't want to—the music blasting across the river from the fairgrounds would render you deaf in seconds. The best rooms are numbers 6 and 7, romantic "crow's nest" rooms with balconies up a steep staircase. Rates are $15/20 s/d, $5 for each additional person. Rates for rooms 6 and 7 are $25 s/d.

Mozart Petit Hotel (tel. 720-3764, 646-1577, coyaldps@chiriqui.com, starts at $20 s/d) is on the winding road to Volcancito. This road intersects the main road from David to Boquete at the CEFATI building in Alto Boquete. As you approach Boquete from David, you'll see the CEFATI on the right. Make a left turn toward

Volcancito. The little hotel is two kilometers down, on the right. This is a bright and cheerful place with pleasant rooms. Camping is also possible here. The hotel offers tours and hiking trips to the surrounding areas. The owner speaks English, German, and Spanish.

$25–50

The 40-room **Hotel Los Fundadores** (tel. 720-1298, starts at $24 s/d) is another Boquete stalwart. It's on the left side of Avenida Central just before you come into town; its faux Arthurian-castle facade is hard to miss. Rooms here are small, drab, and well past their prime, but a babbling creek runs right through the middle of the place, which makes up for a lot. Rates are $24 s/d, $33 s/d for a queen-sized bed.

Just up the street from Pensión Marilós is **Hotel Rebiquet** (tel. 720-1365, $33 s/d), a modern place with nine large, pleasant rooms set around an interior courtyard. All have small TVs and refrigerators.

Kalima Suites Apart-Hotel (tel. 720-2884, 623-4530, $35/45 s/d) is a new, modern place across the street from Pension Marilós and Hotel Rebiquet. It consists of six spare apartments with a bedroom, sitting room with TV, and a kitchenette. The apartments could use more windows and furnishings, but everything was brand new as of 2003 and the young Colombian owners are friendly. A third person in the room is $5.50.

Valle Primavera (tel. 720-2881, cell 675-5761, valleprimavera@boquetehotels.com, www.pargorojo.net/valleprimavera, $16.50 s/d with shared bath, $38.50 with private bath) is a little place in a residential neighborhood just south of downtown. It's run by the Bruña twins, two friendly and perpetually laughing young women from Boquete. There are four rooms at the *hospedaje*. Two are in a little house with a faux Mexican adobe-style exterior. The rooms are cute, with high ceilings, tile floors, and private bath. The mattresses are quite firm but okay. There are two less expensive rooms with shared baths in the family's home. Breakfast is served out on the house's car park for about $2.50. To get there, turn west off the main road at Pizzeria Salvatore. It's one block down.

Golfo de Chiriquí

Isla Verde (tel. 720-2533, cell 677-4009, islaverde@cwpanama.net, http://islaverde.escapetoboquete.com, starts at $55 s/d), two blocks west of Avenida Central on the south end of town, is an unusual place. Its most notable feature is its six hexagonal cabañas set in a garden and connected by paths. Each cabin has a comfortable bed downstairs, another one up in a loft in the center of the cabin, and a kitchenette. Three of the cabañas sleep a maximum of four people; the other three sleep six, have a more extensive kitchen area, and are wheelchair-accessible. The decor in all is bright and cheerful. Two new suites, in a rectangular two-story building, have kitchenettes and balconies. Rates are $55 s/d in the smaller cabañas and lower suite and $15 more s/d in the larger ones and upper suite. Additional people are $10 each. A continental breakfast ($5) is served in an open-sided geodesic dome in the middle of the "village." The owners speak English, Spanish, and German. If you're heading into Boquete from the south, Isla Verde is a left turn off Avenida Central onto Calle 5a Sur just as you enter downtown. You'll see it on the right after two blocks.

$50–100

La Via Lactea (tel. 720-2376, info@lavialactea.biz, www.lavialactea.biz, $55 s/d), which opened in 2003, consists of 10 units in five peach-colored, two-story hexagonal cabañas in a pleasant garden setting along the Rio Palo Alto. There's a gazebo right by the river. Rooms are simple but pleasant, with good mattresses, kitchenettes, dining tables, ample bathrooms, and the sound of the rushing river. The place is run by a friendly Spanish-Italian couple. A third person in each unit is $11 more. Larger rooms are an additional $10. Children of guests must be at least 10 years old. The owners speak English, Spanish, and Italian. La Via Lactea is northwest of downtown. Cross over the bridge near the Panamonte Inn and Spa and make a left. It's about 1.5 kilometers north on this road, past the Restaurante Palo Alto.

Villa Marita's Lodge (tel. 720-2165, www.panamainfo.com/marita, villamarita@cwpanama.net, $55 s/d) is about four kilometers northeast of downtown Boquete in an area called El Santuario. It offers seven attractive, hardwood-paneled cottages set on a 1,200-meter-high plateau with a panoramic view of Barú and the surrounding hills and valleys. The cottages have sitting rooms and firm beds, and two of them have fireplaces. There's a dining room in the main building ($3 for breakfast, $6–8 lunch or dinner) and a common area that's open 24 hours a day. Internet access is free to guests. Each additional person in a room is $11. Cottages sleep a maximum of four. To get to Villa Marita, head north up Avenida Central past the church, bearing left when the road forks. The road will fork again two kilometers past the church, and you'll see a sign pointing left to Los Naranjos and right to Arco Iris. Take the right fork. Cross the bridge and head up the hill. After one kilometer you'll see a sign pointing right off the main road toward Villa Marita. Take that right and follow the signs. The lodge is less than a kilometer uphill.

Tinamou Cottage, (tel. 720-3852, cell 634-4698, habbusdekwie@cwpanama.net, $55 s/d) is a one-room place on a coffee farm, **Finca Habbus de Kwie.** It's southeast of Boquete in Jaramillo Abajo, a little more than five minutes by car or a hefty hike from downtown. It belongs to Hans van der Vooren and Terry van Niekerk, a charming and friendly Dutch couple who also are among the best tour guides in Boquete (see *Nature Tours*). The cottage is simple but pleasant, offering two comfy single beds that can be pushed together and a kitchenette with fridge, oven, and sink. The owners' home is just next door, as are their three good-natured dogs.

Of the 8.5 hectares on the *finca,* a little under half of it still grows coffee. The rest has been allowed to revert to nature, and the couple has built 1.5–2 hours of trails through the secondary growth, through which run several creeks and little waterfalls. There's some good birding here.

Breakfast is available for $5 per person. Hans and Terry will pick up and drop off guests in downtown Boquete for free. If guests prefer, they can call for directions on how to hike to the farm. It takes about half an hour from downtown. They'll also transport guests between David and the farm for $30. They can arrange hikes of any of the area's attractions, some of which they lead themselves. They speak Dutch, English, Spanish, and some German.

M Panamonte Inn and Spa (tel. 720-1327 or 720-1324, fax 720-2055, www.hotelpanamonte .com, panamont@cwpanama.net, starts at $64.90 s/d) is a Boquete institution—it dates from the early 20th century and has been owned by the Collins family since 1946—that has lots of Old World charm and has benefited from a recent renovation. Famous guests have included Charles Lindbergh and Admiral Richard Byrd, who wrote an article about his Arctic exploits for *National Geographic* while relaxing here.

The hotel's 19 rooms are quaint and clean. The least expensive ones are on the small side, but there are also four spacious garden cabañas ($132, sleeps four), and an especially appealing three-bedroom house, El Fresal, with a wraparound porch across the street from the main hotel ($198, sleeps six).

The hotel's charming, semiformal restaurant makes it worth a visit even if you don't stay here. The hotel can arrange tours, but these can be pricey. The Panamonte Inn and Spa is about .7 kilometer north of the town center. Follow Avenida Central past the church and head right when you come to a fork. It's the blue wooden building on the left. Rooms are $64.90 s/d to $77 s/d, depending on the size of the room.

If you do a lot of traveling, you soon meet innkeepers who have hospitality wired into their genetic code. Meet Jane Walker and Barry Robbins, Canadian expatriates who have turned their 2.5 hectares of forested land above Boquete valley into the most comfortable place to stay on this side of the mountain, if not the highlands, period. They call it **M La Montaña y El Valle: The Coffee Estate Inn** (tel./fax 720-2211, information@coffeestateinn.com, www.coffeestateinn .com, $99 s/d). You get a sense of the couple's obsessive attention to detail as soon as you make a reservation. They immediately send out a fat information package filled with solid advice on what to do and how to get around in Boquete and other parts of Panama.

The inn consists of three large, modern, immaculate bungalows set on a hillside just north-

east of Boquete. They're essentially small apartments, and they're tastefully decorated. Each has a balcony, sitting room, full kitchen, DirecTV, safe, and, on a clear day, a terrific view of Barú and the valley. (The estate is at 1,300 meters.)

Guests can dine in their cottage by candlelight on fancy meals you wouldn't expect to find outside Panama City (moussaka, homemade cannelloni stuffed with veal and spinach, Indonesian chicken, and so on). Main dishes cost around $11–14.

The property is a working coffee farm that produces more than 2,000 kilos of coffee a year. The coffee grows in the shade of a pretty, well-tended little forest that attracts more than 100 species of birds and lots of other highland critters. More than 50 indigenous trees have been identified so far. As usual, though, orange trees are especially well-represented. They produce 45,000 oranges a year, so help yourself to as many as you like.

Stays includes a free, optional tour of the owners' coffee operation from soil to cup. The (free) coffee you drink here has never been out of the roaster more than two days. You can buy souvenir packs to take home.

Barry and Jane are a great source of information on the area's attractions. Guests are invited to walk the kilometer of trails on the property and use the library in the house. The house also has free Internet access.

Note to those who like things funky: Barry and Jane run a tight, gleaming ship. The inn has more in common with a modern first-world country getaway than some bohemian third-world tree house. But this is a great place to pamper yourself, which can be especially fun if you've been roughing it for a while. Stay here a couple of days and you may find yourself thinking of Jane and Barry as Mom and Dad. Still, if you want to be left completely alone, they'll respect your privacy. This is a popular place with Panamanian honeymooners.

To get there, take Avenida Central north past the church and follow the signs. The entrance gate is near El Explorador. The last stretch of road is rough and rocky but doesn't require a four-wheel drive if driven carefully. A third person in the room is another $27.50. Children must be nine or older.

$100–150

Hotel Los Establos (tel. 720-2685, losestablos@comtetoboquete.com, www.valleescondido.biz/losestablos, $121 s/d, including breakfast and use of all facilities) is a golf-oriented bed-and-breakfast owned by the developer of the Valle Escondido gated community, and continues its Spanish mission theme. It's .7 km farther up the hill from La Montaña y El Valle: The Coffee Estate Inn at an elevation of 1,200 meters. It started life as horse stables, and its pastoral setting is stunning: It has a panoramic view of Volcán Barú and the surrounding countryside. Set on its four hectares are a glass-enclosed hot tub, a bar area with pool table, a lighted putting green and driving range, and a "clubhouse" with a barbecue pit. An elevated walkway leads from the latter to a large tree towering over some coffee bushes, where one can listen to the sound of a stream that flows into the Caldera.

There are just four rooms downstairs and two suites upstairs. The suites are more spacious: They consist of a small bedroom attached to a small sitting room, though the latter is glass-enclosed and gets a lot of light.

Each of the downstairs room has a tiny terrace, but, oddly enough, only one of them looks out on the volcano. All the rooms have cable TV and a DVD player, but guests need to bring their own DVDs (they can be rented in downtown Boquete). Guests also have free access to a computer with Internet access in the common areas. The hotel can pick up or drop off guests in David for $20 per group. Note: Children 14 and younger are not allowed in the hotel.

Camping

Though it's not as cold around Boquete as it is in the higher elevations on the west side of Barú, it can still get plenty chilly. As always in the highlands, campers should bring plenty of warm, waterproof clothing and a waterproof tent if planning to camp. Expect drizzle even in the dry season.

Camping is possible in **Parque Nacional Volcán Barú,** but those who pitch their tents high up should be prepared for weather that can approach freezing. Also, the elevation is high enough that altitude sickness is a possibility. If you feel nauseated or get a bad headache, head down the mountain immediately. It will only get worse. Be sure also to bring plenty of water; there are no facilities in the park itself. Campers can get a camping permit from the ranger station at the start of the Volcán Barú summit trail. Camping permits are $5, plus the $3 park entrance fee. (See the *Volcán Barú* entry under *Sports and Recreation.*) It's also possible to camp at the **ANAM ranger station** at Alto Chiquero, the Boquete-side end of the Sendero Los Quetzales. The station has two dorm rooms upstairs, each of which has four bunk beds and lockers for storing gear. There's also a kitchenette. The cost is $5 per bed. Parking is $1.

Mozart Petit Hotel (tel. 720-3764, 646-1577, coyaldps@chiriqui.com), on the road to Volcancito, offers camping on its grounds for $5, $2 more if you need to borrow a tent. Note that it's drier in these parts than down in Boquete.

FOOD

Restaurants come and go quickly in Boquete. A half dozen places I liked disappeared between my last two visits, and it's likely some of the ones listed below will be gone by the time you visit.

Restaurants

The restaurant at the ⚅ **Panamonte Inn and Spa** (tel. 720-1327 or 720-1324, 6–10 A.M., noon–3 P.M., and 6–9 P.M. Mon.–Fri., 7:30–11 A.M., noon–3 P.M., and 6–9 P.M. Sat. and Sun.) is the fanciest in town, with tablecloths, fresh flowers, candles, fine china, and lots of fascinating antiques. It's got an almost dollhouse charm, and the waitresses serve guests in frilly old-country uniforms. When everything comes together, this is the best restaurant in Boquete. In the past it's suffered from the usual Boquete problem of consistency, but in the last couple of years it's been going strong. Entrees are $8–12 and the food tends toward continental cuisine. There are also vegetarian options and a budget menu of burgers and sandwiches. The soups can be delicious—

try the spicy pumpkin soup if it's available—and if you want to sample the highland trout this is a great place to do it. Save room for dessert, as they tend to be done well. The rum cake is excellent, as is the "chocolate decadence," and I've heard good things about the key lime and apple pies.

Bistro Boquete (tel. 720-1017, 11 A.M.–11 P.M. daily) at the corner of Avenida Central and Calle 1a Sur, had a rather chaotic opening in late 2002 but has settled down into one of Boquete's better dining options. It's an airy, high-ceilinged place with large windows open right onto Avenida Central. The atmosphere is relatively upscale by Boquete standards. It offers a wide selection of bar-food items such as chicken wings, quesadillas, and burgers as well as a few fancier dishes. The curry chicken salad is tasty. Prices range from about $3 for burgers up to $10 for filet mignon. Avoid the house wine.

La Casona Mexicana (cell 685-4120), on the left side of Avenida Central as you enter town, is a funky little Mexican restaurant with so-so food. It consists of a honeycomb of brightly painted rooms in a slightly ramshackle wooden building. Everything on the menu is $7 or less. As with every place in Boquete, the food is inconsistent. The last time I had the mixed fajitas ($6.50) they were rubbery, and the margaritas were essentially snow cones. Still, it's a fun little place if you're not too picky.

Palo Alto Restaurante (tel. 720-1076, noon–9:30 P.M. Sun.–Thurs., noon–10:30 P.M. Fri. and Sat.) is housed in a large, glass-enclosed building that resembles a greenhouse. It has a view of the pretty Río Palo Alto that runs right by it, the view of which makes lunch the best time to come. There are some tables outside right by the river. The food is inconsistent here, but the location makes it worth a try. Offerings include steaks, chops, barbecued ribs, kebobs, and fish. Avoid the Thai spring rolls, which taste like Chicken McNuggets. Main dishes are $5.50–14. A small hotel by the same owners was going up next to the restaurant and may be completed by the time you visit.

Taquería La Mejor (cell 659-1063, noon–10 P.M. Tues.–Sun.) serves surprisingly good Mexican fast food in unadorned surroundings. Most dishes are $3. It's one block west of Avenida Central at the corner of Calle 1 Sur and Avenida B Oeste.

If you have an irresistible craving for pizza, **Pizzeria La Volcánica** serves the best in town, which isn't saying much. (Avoid Ristorante Salvatore, on the outskirts of town; both the pizza and service are bad.) Fairly tasty but greasy pizzas with thin cracker crusts range in size from *chica* to *gigante*. A *chica* will feed two moderately hungry adults; the most expensive is $3.50. You can also get sandwiches, or a whole roast chicken for $6. It's one block before the park on the main road.

The restaurant at the **Hotel Los Fundadores** (tel. 720-1298) has a good reputation for its way with the usual assortment of meats and seafood, priced from about $6–9. And again, it's got that cool creek running right through it.

Restaurante El Sabrosón (tel. 720-2147, 6:30 A.M.–10 P.M. Mon.–Fri., 6:20 A.M.–midnight Sat. and Sun.) is a popular place with low-budget diners. It's on the east side of Avenida Central at the north end of town, just down from where the road forks at the church. Nothing on the menu costs more than $3.50. Its steam-table offerings include the usual, plus some Chinese dishes. It's best known for its fresh trout ($3.50), which the cook will prepare however you like. It's good.

Restaurante Támesis, just up from Restaurante El Sabrosón, serves basic Panamanian food at rock-bottom prices: You'd have to be awfully hungry to spend more than $2 here, but the food is better at El Sabrosón.

Cafés

The gourmet coffee company **Café Ruiz** has two coffee shops in Boquete. The main one (tel. 720-1392, 7 A.M.–6 P.M. Mon.–Sat., 10 A.M.–6 P.M. Sun.) is at its roasting and packaging plant just north of town on Avenida Central. Keep left at the fork past the church. It's the white complex on the right, near Mi Jardín es Su Jardín. It offers cappuccinos, lattes, mochas, and so on. The espresso is among the best I've ever tasted—strong but not bitter. You can also buy a wide range of packaged coffees fresh from the plant.

Golfo de Chiriquí

They come whole bean (*grano*) or ground (*molido*), sealed in plain packaging or a variety of gift packs. You can book tours of the entire Ruiz operation here. (See *Coffee Tours.*) The other shop is in the CEFATI building in Alto Boquete. **Yalty's Country Coffee Shop** (tel. 720-2470, 8 A.M.–4 P.M. Mon.–Sat., 8 A.M.–1 P.M. Sun.) has minimal atmosphere but is popular for its waffles with fresh strawberries and cream as well as its soups. Other offerings include salads, sandwiches, juices, and shakes. Most items are around $3. It's on the west side of Avenida Central near Calle 1 Sur.

Café Punto de Encuentro, one block west of Pension Marilós, is a cute little outdoor breakfast café attached to a home. Pancakes, French toast with or without fruit, well-stuffed omelets, and other offerings cost $1.50–3.25. It's a simple, friendly place. It's open 7 A.M.–noon daily, though the owner was making noises about opening in the afternoon. There's a book swapping corner here where you can trade in your beat-up bestseller for another one.

Anyone can come for a full breakfast on the terrace at **Pension Topas** (tel./fax 720-1005, 8-11 A.M. daily), which costs about $4, but guests staying at the pension get priority. The pension does not serve other meals.

Folklorica Museo y Café (11 A.M.–7 P.M. Sun.–Thurs., noon–8 P.M. Sat., closed Tues.), on Avenida Central at the north end of town, serves pastas, sandwiches, desserts, and "New York bagels" no New Yorker would ever recognize. Prices are $3.50–5.50.

Java Juice (tel. 720-2502, 10 A.M.–10 P.M. daily), across the street from La Casona Mexicana on the south end of town, offers burgers, shakes, salads, juice, and blaring music. Everything on the menu is less than $3. There's an Internet café here.

Ⓜ Pasteleria Alemana Marianne's Café (11 A.M.–8 P.M. Thurs.–Mon., closed Tues. and Wed.), a little German pastry shop on the main road through Alto Boquete, is a popular place to stop for a sugar fix on the way to or from downtown Boquete. Its pies, cakes, and other sweets are delicious, and the prices are great— about $.25 for a slice, or less than $5 for an entire

pie. Try the lemon meringue pie, the choco-vanilla cake, or the chocolate chip cookies. It's about a kilometer south of the CEFATI building. The café is closed in June.

Ⓜ Fresas Mary (tel. 720-3394, 9 A.M.–7 P.M. daily) is an attractive snack kiosk built into the front of a house just a half kilometer down the Volcancito road from the turnoff at the CEFATI building. It'll be on the left as you head toward Volcancito. The strawberry shakes here are so good and fresh they'll make your knees buckle. The other nine flavors of homemade ice cream here include papaya, banana, *zarzamora* (blackberry), and *guanábana* (a tropical fruit sometimes known in English as soursop). You can also get hamburgers and other hot bites, coffee, and sweets. There's a comfortable indoor sitting area if it's raining.

Markets

If you're in the market (so to speak) for fresh vegetables, fruit, or meat, the **Mercado Municipal** (also known as the Mercado Público), is on the northeast corner of the plaza. Note that there are two entrances, one on the south side and one on the east side of the building. It's worth exploring the whole complex to see who's got the best stuff that day. It's open 6:30 A.M.–6 P.M. daily.

There are several supermarkets within a couple of blocks of the plaza. Besides groceries, **Supercentro El Mandarín,** on Avenida Central at the Calle 2a Sur, carries a range of toiletries, hardware, and other dry goods. **Supermercado Romero,** behind the post office, has a bakery and pharmacy.

INFORMATION AND SERVICES

IPAT's Centro de Facilidades Turisticas e Interpretación Volcán Barú-Boquete (CEFATI, tel. 720-4060) is in Alto Boquete on the main road just before it heads downhill into the town of Boquete. The place, almost as imposing as its name, was a costly undertaking for a glorified information booth, especially since the information it has to offer is quite thin. Three good things about it: It has bathrooms, there's a great view of the Boquete valley and Río Caldera behind the building, and there's a Café Ruiz shop next door.

Boquete maps come and go. A fairly current and useful one was available in some shops during my last visit. Try the Café Ruiz coffee stores.

Boquete's tiny public library (no phone, 8 A.M.–6 P.M. Mon.–Fri., 9 A.M.–noon Sat., closed Sun.) is on the right as you head north into town, about a half block before Hotel Los Fundadores. The limited offerings are all in Spanish. If you do speak Spanish, and are curious about the minutiae of Boquete's history, you can buy a copy of the 400-page *Boquete: Rasgos De Su Historia,* by Milagros Sánchez Pinzón, 2001, Colección Culturama, for $12.50.

Farmacia Danka (tel. 775-1788, 8 A.M.–8:30 P.M. Mon.–Sat., 8:30 A.M.–6:30 P.M. Sun.) is a pharmacy on Calle 3 Sur next to Pension Doña Cata. Farmacia Any (tel. 720-1296, 8 A.M.–9 P.M. daily) is just north of Super Centro Bruña on the east side of Avenida Central.

The post office (7 A.M.–5:45 P.M. Mon.–Fri., 7 A.M.–4:45 P.M. Sat., closed Sun.) is on the east side of the plaza.

Banco Nacional de Panamá and Global Bank are across the street from each other as you come into town on Avenida Central. They're open 8 A.M.–3 P.M. weekdays, 9 A.M.–noon Saturday. A Moneygram office (tel. 720-1398, 9 A.M.–4:30 P.M., 8 A.M.–12:30 P.M. Sat., 9 A.M.–1:30 P.M. Sun.) is in the CACSA building on the southwest corner of the plaza.

Lavamático Las Burbujas (no phone, 8 A.M.–5:30 P.M. Mon.–Sat., 8 A.M.–4 P.M. Sun.), on the west side of Avenida Central across the street from the church at the north end of town, charges $1.30 including soap to wash and $1.25–2.50 to dry. Lavandería La Mejor (tel. 720-1280, 8 A.M.–5 P.M. daily) charges $3 to wash and dry. It's a half block west of Avenida Central on Calle 1 Sur.

Java Juice has Internet computers that can be rented for $.50 an hour. Nearby is Cafe Net 2000, on the west side of Avenida Central at the entrance to Boquete. It's on the second floor, next to Chiriquí River Rafting.

Those who would like some pampering have a couple of options. The Panamonte Inn and Spa has an airy **day spa** (tel. 720-1327 or 720-1324, 8 A.M.–7 P.M. daily) where one can relax to the tune of the Río Caldera rushing by. It offers a variety of massages (average price $30 for 50 minutes), as well as facials, mud therapy, and the like. Room/spa packages are also available. Though I've yet to get a spa treatment from her, I've heard excellent reports about **Mariellen Serracín** (tel. 720-1239), who has worked at spas in Florida and Hawaii and offers a range of massages and facials. She charges $30 per hour or $45 for 90 minutes. Male clients are by referral only.

GETTING THERE AND AWAY

The city of David, in the lowlands, is less than 40 kilometers from Boquete and is the transportation hub for buses and planes to and from other parts of the country, most notably Bocas del Toro and Panama City. (See the *David* section for transportation information.) Some hotels and guides offer transportation to David, the west side of Barú, the Costa Rican border and Almirante, the port of entry for the archipelago of Bocas del Toro.

Boquete is 45 minutes by car from David, seven hours from Panama City. Those driving west from Panama City should turn right at the first major intersection upon entering David. The turn is not well marked, but it's at the first major crossroads for many kilometers. Follow the road all the way into Boquete, which is less than 40 kilometers north of David.

Boquete-bound buses leave the David bus terminal about every 25 minutes 5:45–9 P.M., with a final bus at 9:45 P.M. David-bound buses leave Boquete approximately every 20 minutes (slightly less often in the late afternoon) 4:50 A.M.–7 P.M. Catch the bus to David in front of the Hostal Palacio on the northwest side of the plaza. The trip costs $1.20 each way and takes about 45 minutes. The Oficina de Transporte Boquete-David, a fancy name for a tiny office on the north side of the plaza, has a bus schedule and may even have a staff member who speaks English.

Taxis between Boquete and David cost about $12 (downtown or bus station) and $15 (airport), $3 more for night trips. Expect to pay

Golfo de Chiriquí

around $40 for trips to Cerro Punta or the Costa Rican border, though I've heard quotes as high as $70 and as low as $30; shop around.

GETTING AROUND

You probably won't need transportation in town since it's easy to walk from one end of Boquete to another in just a few minutes. Buses and taxis to surrounding areas are plentiful and cheap. Drivers should be careful at night. The streets outside of town are dark and have no sidewalks. People often walk down the streets at night, and some are very drunk.

Urbana minibuses that roam around the nearby hills leave from Avenida Central just north of the plaza, but taxis here are generally so cheap you should try them first. Sample fares include $1 to Bajo Mono, where the Los Quetzales trail starts, and $3 to Los Pozos de Caldera. Note that *El Bajo* written on the windows of minibuses refers to Bajo Boquete.

It's easy to catch a taxi along Avenida Central. Taxis within town shouldn't cost more than $.50. Taxis to places just outside of Boquete, such as El Explorador and Mi Jardín es Su Jardín, shouldn't cost more than a buck or two. The drive to the ranger station *caseta* for the climb up Volcán Barú is $4 and should be made in a pickup taxi.

Daniel Higgins, tel. 617-0570 (cell), is a fully bilingual Panamanian taxi driver with a good reputation for reliability. He'll drive you around in his new 4Runner for $10/hour, which includes a commentary on the history of the area. Longer trips include Cerro Punta ($50) and Almirante ($100), the jumping-off point for the islands of Bocas del Toro.

I've also heard good things about **Juan Carlos Contreras,** tel. 633-0358 (cell), 720-1140 (dispatcher; ask for Juan Carlos), who doesn't speak English but understands a fair amount. He charges $10/hour.

Both Higgins and Contreras also offer regular taxi service to the surrounding areas for the going rates.

Cerro Punta and Surroundings

A phrase that sums up the west side of Volcán Barú is "pastoral paradise." As the road winds its way up the foggy mountains, it passes one tranquil dairy farm after another. Soon there are neat quilts of green-and-brown farmland clinging at impossible angles to mountain slopes. Down in the valleys, race horses romp in vast pastures. It's all so picturesque you have to remind yourself that the developed land borders two of Panama's most spectacular parks, and in some cases encroaches on them. The hikes through these parks are among the great attractions of the area. Cerro Punta has the most accessible entry into Parque Internacional la Amistad, a park so important UNESCO declared it a World Heritage Site in 1990.

All the towns and tourist sights on the west side of Barú are linked by a single road that starts in the lowland town of Concepción and ends at Guadalupe, elevation 2,130 meters. The first town is Volcán, officially known as Hato de Volcán, which has most of the visitor services but little else.

The road forks here. Straight leads to a Costa Rican border crossing at Río Sereno. A right turn leads farther up the mountain toward Bambito, Cerro Punta, and Guadalupe. Bambito has hotels and a few places to eat, but the "town" itself is really just a few roadside stands. The vistas open up at little Cerro Punta and tiny Guadalupe just beyond it. You're up in the clouds here, and you may feel you've found Shangri-la.

The town of Cerro Punta consists of little more than a small commercial strip in the middle of a heavily developed agricultural area. There are gas stations, a couple of dreary bars and pool halls, a few greasy-spoon restaurants, a grocery store, and a launderette.

SIGHTS

Natural beauty is the major draw of this area, particularly hikes in the mammoth Parque Internacional la Amistad or along the popular

THE RESPLENDENT QUETZAL

The resplendent quetzal has been called the most beautiful bird in the world, and it's easy to see why. The male in particular is just incredible. It's luminous green above and scarlet and white below, with tail feathers that can grow almost a meter long, twice the size of its body.

The resplendent quetzal's range extends from southern Mexico to the highlands of western Panama, where it's easier to spot than just about anywhere else. During the nesting season, which runs from February to May, you may see more than one during a hike. A popular saying among birders in Panama is that while 20 people might see one quetzal in Costa Rica and Guatemala, which are famous as quetzal habitats, in Panama one person might see 20 quetzals. That doesn't mean they're always easy to find, though. They can spend

a long time sitting quietly and inconspicuously. Quetzals often hang out at the edge of forests and in trees near clearings. Look for trees with holes in the side; they like to make their nests there.

Sadly, deforestation has forced quetzals higher and higher up into the mountains, and their numbers are dwindling. Conservation efforts and ecotourism dollars may help them survive.

Quetzals are spottable year-round, but the easiest time to see one is between December and April. The quetzal's tail is in full feather between December and August (in other words, it's a somewhat less dramatic sight between August and November). They're easier to spot on the Boquete side of the mountain, especially in Parque Nacional Volcán Barú and Finca Lérida. Sendero Los Quetzales, ironically enough, is not the best place to see them.

Sendero Los Quetzales. Visitors will get more out of the hikes with the help of a naturalist guide; it also greatly improves the chances of spotting quetzals. Those with extra time should consider a visit to the impressive Finca Dracula orchid farm. The strawberry and flower farms are also worth a quick visit.

M Parque Internacional La Amistad

The enormous and magnificent Parque Internacional la Amistad (PILA), which lies along the Talamanca mountain range, was established in September 1988 and declared a UNESCO World Heritage Site in 1990. It's "international" in that a little less than half of it is in Costa Rica. That leaves 207,000 hectares on the Panama side. Nearly all of this land is in the province of Bocas del Toro, but the 3 percent of it that pokes into Chiriquí province is far more accessible.

The park's plant and animal life are among the most diverse in Panama. The forests vary from lowland tropical to subalpine, and much of the vegetation is virgin. Five of the six species of Central American felines—the jaguar, puma, ocelot, jaguarundi, and margay—are still hanging on here, as is the also-endangered Baird's tapir. Among the nearly 600 types of birds identified in

the area are such spectacular species as the resplendent quetzal, the three-wattled bellbird, and the rarely seen bare-necked umbrellabird.

All that said, you may not see much wildlife other than birds on a day hike near Cerro Punta. But the park is well worth a visit even if you're not a birding fanatic. The forests are dense and varied and there are several kilometers of well-maintained trails near town.

The main entrance to the park is at Las Nubes, about seven kilometers west of Cerro Punta. There's an ANAM ranger station on the right at the end of the road, where the trails start. Pay the entrance fee here ($3) and get trail maps from the friendly staff. There's also a small display on the park and a few of its denizens.

The Las Nubes entrance to PILA is about a 10-minute drive from Cerro Punta. If you're heading up to Cerro Punta from the south, look for the sign indicating a left turn off the main road just before one enters "downtown." Make another left at the Las Nubes sign. The road gets a bit rough, but a four-wheel drive is not essential to get to the first gate. The short uphill drive past the gate to the ANAM ranger station and trailheads does require a four-wheel drive. Round-trip taxi fare from Cerro Punta is $5–7. The station is open from about 8 or 8:30 A.M.–4 P.M. every day. Entrance is $3. For information, call the ANAM regional office in David, tel. 775-3163 or 775-2055 (there's a radio but no phone at the station itself).

Finca Dracula

Don't worry, you don't need to bring garlic. It's named for the 30 varieties of the *Telipogon vampirus* that are among the more than 2,000 species of orchids found in this famous botanical garden. It has one of the most important collections in Latin America—it claims to be one of the 10 largest in the world—and is known for its experiments in propagating endangered species. The lovely landscaped grounds, which are crisscrossed with streams and ponds, make for a pleasant walk.

The *finca's* collections are contained in three areas, separated according to climate, from those that thrive at the local temperature of 14–20°C up to those that need a temperature of 25°C or higher.

Even if you're not a flower freak, you're likely to find this collection worth a visit. Specimens include carnivorous orchids, orchids the size of a nail head, orchids that disguise themselves as bees, orchids with a delicious fragrance, and orchids that bloom for only one day.

Finca Dracula is in Guadalupe, about a 20-minute walk or very short car ride past Hotel y Cabañas Los Quetzales. When the road splits past the hotel, take the right fork and then turn left onto the gravel road. You'll need a four-wheel drive if you're driving. You'll see a sign across the *finca's* gate on the left, at the turnoff to the entrance to the dirt road that leads to the Los Quetzales cabañas. Call tel. 771-2070 or send an email to fdracula@chiriqui.com to arrange a tour, or just drop by. Guides speak little English. Minimum tour length is half an hour, but can go quite a bit longer depending on the level of detail you're interested in. Tours are available 8 A.M.–5:30 P.M. daily. The cost is $7 per person.

Farms

Those who want to get a closer look at some of the crops the rich volcanic soil and mild weather of this region produce may be interested in paying a quick visit to Panaflores, which cultivates a variety of beautiful flowers, and Finca Fresas Manolo, which grows strawberries (*fresas* in Spanish) and some vegetables. Both are a few minutes from each other in the Entre Ríos area a short drive west of Cerro Punta.

Panaflores (tel. 771-2080 or 771-2015) is the first place you'll come to. It consists of a large field sheltered from the elements by a huge plastic-tarp roof. The rows of flowers look like an enormous yellow, white, red, and pink carpet. Quite photogenic.

Those coming from the south should make a left off the main road just before Cerro Punta, at the sign for Parque Internacional La Amistad. Go past the Las Nubes turnoff, then turn left at the sign for Entre Ríos. Look for the large enclosed field.

Three kilometers farther up the road, which quickly turns steep and rugged and requires a four-wheel drive, is **Finca Fresas Manolo** (cell 671-4871). The strawberries are also under plastic tarps, arranged in rows on the sharply sloping

© WILLIAM FRIAR

Finca Dracula has one of the largest orchid collections in the world.

hillside. Try to come during the week, when you're likely to encounter workers tending the field with great care.

There's no need to make an appointment at either place. Just stop by during regular business hours and tell them you want to poke around. They might think you're a little strange, but they'll probably let you.

Finca Fernández, on the road to Sendero Los Quetzales, has long been famous as a prime place to see quetzals. Sadly, there have been so many reports of thefts from tourists' cars here I can no longer recommend the *finca* as a safe place to visit. There are plenty of other places to see quetzals and plenty of other guides to find them for you.

SPORTS AND RECREATION

Hiking and looking for quetzals in the national parks are the big activities here, but there are a few other outdoor possibilities. White-water companies are headquartered in Boquete, on the other side of Barú, but they can usually pick clients up here for trips on either side of the mountain. (See *Sports and Recreation* in the *Boquete* section for details and recommendations.) Cerro Punta produces the finest horses in the country. Visitors can arrange rides on much more modest steeds for around $5–6 an hour. Hotel y Cabañas Los Quetzales charges $8/hour. The hotel also rents mountain bikes for $4/hour.

Genover "Negro" Santamaria is a friendly, reliable local guide who works with Hotel y Cabañas Los Quetzales. He specializes in long hikes, including ones to the summit of Volcán Barú ($80 for two people) and Sendero Los Quetzales to Boquete ($40 for two people). He's also available for multiday treks. Ask for him at the hotel. (See *Nature Tours* under *Volcán and Surroundings* for other guide suggestions.)

A good guide is essential on wilderness trails, particularly up Volcán Barú. But for nearby, less rugged destinations, it's simpler to make arrangements on your own than go through a guide. This is especially true of visits to Finca Dracula, which supplies its own tour guides for a fraction of what third-party outfits charge.

Hiking in Parque Internacional La Amistad

Three main trails start from the ANAM ranger station at Parque Internacional La Amistad (see *Sights* for general information on the park). **Sendero La Cascada** is a 3.4-kilometer, two-hour round-trip hike that leads to a picture-perfect 55-meter waterfall. The trail is wide and well-maintained. It's a 1.7-kilometer uphill hike to the falls, with the elevation climbing from 2,180 to about 2,500 meters. There are three miradors (observation platforms) along the trail with sweeping views of the mountains and valleys. However, if it's a foggy day you won't see a thing from them.

The first mirador is unmarked, but it will be on the right as the trail levels off and comes out of the woods. Mirador La Nevera is on the left a little farther on. The trail forks at Mirador El Barranco. To get to the falls, head down the steep wooden staircase to the right. (Note: Some of the stairs are loose and slippery. Watch your step.) Those in the mood for more exercise can take the left fork. If it's a clear day, a two-hour hike from here offers a view of the Caribbean.

Sendero El Retoño, a two-kilometer loop trail, is much less strenuous but even more beautiful. The trail is mostly level and remarkably varied. It leads through lush green forest, over bridges spanning rushing streams, and into a tunnel formed from leaning stands of bamboo. The hike takes about an hour at a very leisurely pace.

There are a few forks along the trail: to stay on the main trail, just take every left fork. For a longer hike, there's a loop within the loop that starts halfway down the trail at a marked fork to the right. It ends near the exit to the main trail.

A newer trail, **Vereda La Montaña,** leads up the side of Cerro Picacho. I have not yet hiked this rustic trail (*vereda* is Spanish for footpath), but it's allegedly four kilometers long and a quite strenuous uphill trek, though the rangers told me there's a wooden cabin with a kitchen and bathroom at the top. Ask them about it before attempting this hike. Allow six hours for the trip up and back.

Golfo de Chiriquí

For those who just want to take a little stroll, **Sendero Panamá Verde** is a 400-meter walk near the ranger station that takes about 15 minutes to walk.

Do not attempt any of the longer hikes without a good guide. The forest here is rugged wilderness, and it's very easy to get lost. Those who speak Spanish can ask the forest ranger at Las Nubes for guidance. It's possible to camp in the park or stay in a dormitory at the ANAM station. (See *Camping.*)

Serious trekkers may be interested to know there's an eight-hour hike through the forest to some hot springs. That's one-way; you'd have to camp out by the springs. For the truly hard-core, there's also the possibility of multiple-day treks over the cordillera toward the Caribbean coast. Hotel y Cabañas Los Quetzales may be able to help arrange an eight-day trek for those feeling brave. Be warned this is an extremely hard-core trip through mountainous wilderness and deep mud. You'll spend the last two days traveling in *cayucos* (dugout canoes) through Naso (also called Teribe) Indian territory. For food and shelter you'll mostly rely on lonely, friendly folk living in huts in the woods. Trekkers must have their own tents, sleeping bags, and all other equipment. Los Quetzales has booked this trip only once. Even the Naso who live in this forest will probably think you're nuts.

Sendero Los Quetzales

This popular trail through Parque Nacional Volcán Barú curves around the north side of Barú, linking Cerro Punta with Boquete to the east. Hiking it in either direction is far less challenging than a climb to the top of Barú, but it's still a serious hike. It is also described in the Boquete section, but more information is included here since most people hike it in this direction, and the logistics are a bit different.

It's not essential to have a guide, at least in this direction, but do not attempt it alone. Bring a first-aid kit. Do not hike the trail in shorts; it's cool in the forest, and if it rains it gets downright cold. A walking stick can come in handy.

The trail gives a taste of real wilderness but is well-defined enough it's not technically diffi-

cult to walk. And, because of the rapid change in elevation, it offers a vivid lesson in life zones, starting with mossy cloud forest dotted with towering oaks and picture-postcard streams that quickly give way to palms, bamboo, and serpentine lianas and vines. You'll encounter some forest giants, but most of the forest is secondary growth. Despite its name, this trail is not the best place to see quetzals.

It's a developed trail, with bridges and steps and the like, but it's not being well maintained so watch your step. There are lots of signs along the trail, though whoever put them up has a fanciful sense of distance; don't pay much attention to them.

About a third of the way down, there's a designated campsite with few facilities other than an open-sided wooden shelter and some rotting benches. The ground slopes at a pretty steep angle; campers who want to pitch a tent here are best off doing it in the relatively level shelter. A short walk behind this campsite are a couple of miradors, the second of which has a beautiful, expansive view down toward Boquete. The red-roofed building off in the distance is the little ranger station at the Boquete entrance to the trail.

It's less grueling to hike the trail from Cerro Punta to Boquete than vice versa since it's downhill most of the way, descending nearly a kilometer in altitude (though there is an uphill stretch at the end, just when you think you're literally out of the woods). The uphill route does have its supporters (see *Sports and Recreation* in the *Boquete* section).

The hike requires some planning since you end up far away from Cerro Punta, on the other side of the mountain. The bus ride back takes at least three hours, not including waiting time in David, where you have to switch buses. The best strategy is to leave early in the morning and either have someone meet you with a car at the end of the trail or plan to spend the night in Boquete. Some who choose the latter option arrange to have their luggage shipped ahead to Boquete, usually through their hotel or guide, but, as has been pointed out elsewhere, be sure to nail down exactly when the luggage will arrive. Some tourists have had their luggage sent by couriers who only make the trip once a day, leaving them stranded without their belongings, waiting for their luggage to catch up with them.

So how long will the hike down take? This question trips up a lot of hikers, who end up with a much longer outing than they bargained for. It takes an average of five hours to get from El Respingo ranger station (near Cerro Punta) to the Alto Chiquero ranger station (near Boquete, sometimes known as La Roca), but that doesn't take into account getting to and from the ranger stations.

El Respingo station is at the end of 5.5 kilometers of uphill road that branches off the main road that links Cerro Punta and Guadalupe. The turnoff is halfway between Cerro Punta and Guadalupe, or about 1.5 kilometers past the Hotel Cerro Punta. As you head toward Guadalupe, there's a huge trail sign on the right just after a little bridge. Turn here and follow the road toward the Bajo Grande area. This road was in sad shape the last time I took it, but I've since heard it's been paved within one kilometer of the ranger station.

If you want to walk to the station from the turnoff, add about two hours to the hiking estimate. You may want to opt instead for a taxi, which will cost about $10 from Cerro Punta to the station. Guests at Hotel y Cabañas Los Quetzales can get a ride to the El Respingo station for free.

Those who drive will need a four-wheel drive with high clearance. Park near the station. Don't leave anything of value in the car.

Park entrance is $3, $1 to park, and $5 more either to camp or to use a bunk in the quite nice ranger station. (See *Accommodations* for more information.)

From the Alto Chiquero ranger station at the Boquete end it's another 1.5-hour hike to get to the Bajo Mono loop road. From there you can catch one of the frequent buses to downtown Boquete for $1.

Boat Tours

For those who want a break from the highlands, **Exploration Panama** (at Yalty's Country Coffee Shop, tel. 720-24/0, info@explorationpanama.net, www.explorationpanama.com, 8 A.M.–4 P.M.

Mon.–Sat., 8 A.M.–1 P.M. Sun.) offers boat trips around the Golfo de Chiriquí, just off the Pacific coast. Trips are made on the M/V *Little Ship,* a converted 50-foot U.S. Coast Guard search and rescue vessel that has a sleeping cabin with bunk beds, a galley, and a main "salon." It's air-conditioned and has three heads (toilets) with showers. Every Saturday morning the company offers an all-day cruise through Parque Nacional Marino Golfo de Chiriquí that includes a beach picnic on Isla Gámez. The price is $119 per person, 10-person minimum. The company also offers all-day and multiday kayaking, scuba-diving, and deep-sea fishing charters. Dive and fishing trips start at $225 per person, four-person minimum for a two-tank dive around the Islas Ladrones or fishing close to shore (big-game fishing requires more time and greater distances). A two-day, one-night kayaking trip is $3,600 per trip, maximum six clients, and includes guides from Chiriquí River Rafting. The group is operated by Ron Mager, a U.S. Army Special Forces veteran who has been married since 1969 to Yalty Mager, the owner of Yalty's Country Coffee Shop.

ACCOMMODATIONS

There are only a few, widely scattered places to stay around Cerro Punta. Fortunately, these include a couple of appealing possibilities.

$25–50

Hotel Cerro Punta (tel. 771-2020, $22.$27.50 s/d) is on the left just as one approaches downtown Cerro Punta. It offers 10 decent rooms with okay beds. Six of the rooms are in an annex facing a gorgeous view of the mountains. Perversely, the windows are in the back, looking out on nothing. The rooms in the main building are nicer, and two have a good view for no extra charge. The service here is friendly.

$50–100

Easily the best-run place to stay on the entire west side of the mountain is **N Hostal Cielito Sur Bed and Breakfast** (tel./fax 771-2038, cell 642-5038, info@cielitosur.com, www.cielitosur.com, starts at $66 s/d). Along with Hotel y

Cabañas Los Quetzales, it is also the coziest and most pleasant. Actually four kilometers south of Cerro Punta and 10 kilometers north of Volcán in a postage stamp–sized "community" called Nueva Suiza, Cielito Sur sits by itself on 2.5 hectares of land just off the main road but within easy driving distance of most of the area's attractions. It consists of four modern, spacious rooms, each with decor inspired by one of Panama's indigenous peoples—the Kuna and Teribe rooms, and the larger Ngöbe-Buglé and Wounaan-Emberá rooms, which also have a minifridge and microwave. Even if you don't stay in the Wounaan-Emberá room, you should ask to check out the especially beautiful examples of Wounaan baskets mounted on the wall.

Everything here is done just right. The back patio of the bed-and-breakfast overlooks a spring-fed stream that runs through a carefully tended garden that attracts 10 species of hummingbirds. A stay includes an enormous breakfast in a sunny dining room and use of a private, enclosed hot tub. There's a common lounge with a fireplace, CD player and CDs, library, and Internet computer ($2/hour).

Your hosts are Janet and Glenn Lee, a Panamanian-American couple who speak fluent English and Spanish and are a good source of information on just about anything you'd like to know about the whole area.

Rates are $66 s/d in the smaller rooms and $77 s/d in the larger rooms. A third person in the larger rooms is $16.50. The bed-and-breakfast is closed in October.

The Lees can arrange transfers to or from David for $30 each way. They can also arrange ground transportation to or from just about anywhere else in western Panama, including Bocas and the Costa Rican border, as well as make domestic plane reservations and ground-transfer arrangements to or from Panama City. Rates depend on the destination.

Hotel y Cabañas Los Quetzales (tel. 771-2182 or 771-2291, cell 671-2182, fax 771-2226, stay@losquetzales.com, www.losquetzales.com, starts at $55 s/d) is the place to stay for nature lovers, so much so it's really a destination in itself. Mostly this is because the cabañas are in a 350-

© WILLIAM FRIAR

The cabañas at Hotel y Cabañas Los Quetzales are popular with nature lovers. They're inside one of Panama's most important protected areas.

acre private cloud-forest reserve that's inside both a national park (Parque Nacional Volcán Barú) and an international one (Parque International la Amistad). The owners bought land here in 1968, before the parks were founded.

As the name suggests, there are actually two Los Quetzales. The hotel is in the little town of Guadalupe, three kilometers past Cerro Punta. It's an attractive place with lots of handsome woodwork, on the edge of a fast-flowing river. It features 10 rooms, five large suites, a duplex, and dorm rooms. It resembles a comfy ski lodge. The smells wafting up from the bakery/pizzeria on the first floor of the main building add to the cozy feel. The paintings you'll see everywhere, some of them rather spooky, are by Brooke "Cookie" Alfaro, your host's brother and one of Panama's most famous artists.

Rates start at $55 s/d, including continental

breakfast, for small rooms with one queen and one single bed and a shower. Larger, nicer rooms are $65 s/d/t. Suites go for $80–90 and sleep up to four people. These are quite large and have fireplaces and balconies.

There are also three dorm rooms crowded with bunk beds but otherwise pleasant, featuring the same warm wood as the private rooms. Each has a shared toilet and shower. The smallest dorm room has lockers. Dorm beds are $12, including a continental breakfast.

There's a health spa right next to the river where you can recover from a grueling hike with a massage, sauna, or dip in an outdoor hot tub. An hour-long massage and sauna is $30, not including tip. Use of the hot tub (when it's working) is $20. A sauna by itself is $5.

The four cabañas in the park are slightly rustic in the mountain-cabin sense, but three of them are very comfortable and nicely designed. None has electricity, but all have wood-burning stoves or fireplaces, hot water, and a kitchen. Ten kinds of colorful hummingbirds are among the more than 100 species of birds identified near here. You'll see them buzzing around like mosquitoes.

Cabañas 2 and 3 are large, wooden, two-story structures built at more than 2,020 meters above sea level, right in the middle of a stunning cloud forest. The Chiriquí Viejo River runs through the property. Cabaña 2 can accommodate six people. It's slightly smaller than Cabaña 3, which sleeps up to eight.

Cabaña 4 is a short walk farther up into the park. It's huge and a bit fancier than the other wooden cabañas, with three bedrooms, two fireplaces, and a modern living room. The drawback here is you're actually above most of the surrounding forest, so you're not in the thick of the bird action as you are at Los Quetzales.

You can probably pass on Cabaña 1. It's a much more basic two-story concrete structure just as you enter the property, shrouded by trees and therefore dark and rather gloomy. It's close enough to town it's better to stay at the hotel and hike or drive to the trails in the park. Each floor has a separate entrance and can sleep two groups of five.

Prices for the other cabins are the same re-

gardless of group size, so larger groups can get a great deal. Rates are $125 in Cabaña 2 (sleeps five), $135 for Cabaña 3 (sleeps 6–7), and $150 in Cabaña 4 (sleeps eight). Cabaña 1 costs $90 per floor (sleeps five). All cabañas offer enough privacy that friendly acquaintances who meet on the road can share them to save money. Daily guided hikes and meals are included.

There is also a transparent geodesic dome tent on a raised platform that has two queen beds and an outside toilet ($45, sleeps four).

Because you're a hike from the hotel, there are four eating options at the cabañas: Have the hotel deliver food you cook yourself, have the restaurant deliver hot meals, get chauffeured back and forth to the restaurant, or hire a cook to prepare meals. The last option costs $15 per meal, not including the cost of the food.

Eight trails originate from the area around the cabañas. Foggy mountains, trees draped in moss, waterfalls, orchids, the lovely songs of countless birds—it's like a fairy kingdom up there. Two tours a day, led by Ngöbe-Buglé guides who speak only Spanish, are free to cabaña guests. Los Quetzales can supply boots, rain jackets, and horses. There's a very good chance of seeing quetzals here between January and May.

The cabañas are only 2.5 kilometers from the main hotel in Guadalupe, but the road is so ferociously bad it takes about 25 minutes to get there by four-wheel-drive vehicle. (Transportation is included with cabin rental.) Among other things, vehicles must ford a shallow river. That's something to bear in mind if you decide to hike in. Even if you go by four-wheel drive, it's a short but steep walk up to Cabañas 2 and 3. You may have to carry your own bags. One strategy for staying at Los Quetzales is to spend a night or two at the hotel, seeing the nearby sights, then head up to the cabañas. The hotel can arrange taxi pickup in David for $30.

A couple of caveats about Los Quetzales: It's a comfortable place, but attention tends to be focused on constantly innovating and expanding rather than perfecting the potentially delightful things it already offers. For instance, the shattered glass enclosing an attractive wood-burning stove has gone unrepaired for several years and has since been joined by other damaged stoves, including those in the suites. Food is hit-or-miss.

While the hotel had made an effort to become more efficient during my last visit, guests still complain about disorganized service. On the other hand, the staff means well. When an acquaintance had her laundry done here, not only did the laundress refuse to charge her for a full load, she also returned $60 she found in a pair of jeans. And the owner, Carlos Alfaro, is a gentleman in both senses of the word.

In short, if you come expecting a resort, you'll likely be disappointed. But if you come expecting a rustic mountain hideaway, you'll be pleasantly surprised by all the extras and creature comforts of this mostly magical place.

Camping

It's possible to camp in **Parque Internacional la Amistad** for $5, but as usual with Panamanian parks don't expect developed campsites. There's also a surprisingly pleasant dormitory at the **ANAM station** at the main entrance to the park for the same price. It offers bunk beds in shared rooms, a large fireplace, and a kitchen. Bring your own bedding. For more information, ask at the station, or call the ANAM regional office in David, tel. 775-3163 or 775-2055 (there's a radio but no phone at the station itself). This place is a great deal.

There's a similar setup at **El Respingo ranger station** at the trailhead for Sendero Los Quetzales. It'll cost $5 either to camp or to use a bunk in the quite decent ranger station, which is on a hill surrounded by nicely landscaped grounds. The view from here is stunning, and it's a great place to pitch a tent. The bunks are in a small, dark wooden room that's quite okay and has lockers.

FOOD

There are few dining options this far up the mountain. More possibilities are farther down, around Bambito and Volcán. Many small kiosks also offer fruit shakes and burgers and the like along the road from Volcán all the way to Guadalupe.

The quality of the fare at **Hotel y Cabañas**

Los Quetzales (tel. 771-2182 or 771-2291, 7:30 A.M.–8 P.M. daily) is variable but can be decent. The hotel features trout from its own pond, produce from its own garden, and tasty pizza from its own pizzeria. Other dishes include pasta and the usual array of meats. Because of the owner's concern over the forest devastation wreaked by cattle farming, the restaurant does not serve red meat. Entrée prices are in the $4–8 range.

The decor is plain in the dining room of the **Hotel Cerro Punta** (tel. 771-2020), but the food is surprisingly tasty and the service is refreshingly warm and friendly. The veggie rice dish *(arroz jardinero)* will be a godsend for those tired of meat and deep-fried starches. There's also the usual assortment of meats and fish, with most dishes going for $5–9. On my last visit the fresh-fruit shakes *(batidos)* weren't as amazing as I remembered, but they're still pretty good.

GETTING THERE

The lowland city of David is the bus and airline hub for the western highlands. It takes 6–7 hours by car to get from Panama City to David. From there it's about a two-hour drive to Cerro Punta. If you're driving from David, take the Interamerican Highway west to Concepción, 26 kilometers away. Turn right and head uphill. After another 34 kilometers you'll come to Volcán. Turn right at the fork to get to Bambito, Cerro Punta, and Guadalupe. There may be no sign at the intersection except one pointing toward Hotel Bambito. Follow it. Cerro Punta is about 74 kilometers from David, a distance that takes a little over two hours to cover by bus and a bit less by car. The village of Guadalupe is three kilometers farther uphill.

Bus fare from David is $2.65 to Cerro Punta and Guadalupe. Look for the bus with "Cerro Punta" painted on the windshield; it stops at all the towns along the way. The Cerro Punta bus goes all the way to Guadalupe, but ask to make sure. If not, taxi fare from Cerro Punta to Guadalupe is $1. Buses bound for Cerro Punta leave David 5 A.M.–8 P.M. David-bound buses leave Cerro Punta 4:45 A.M.–6:45 P.M. Buses run every 15 minutes. Those coming from Costa

Rica can also catch the Cerro Punta bus at Concepción rather than go all the way to the David bus terminal. Taxis between David and Cerro Punta charge around $30 one-way.

GETTING AROUND

This is a pleasant place to go for a walk, though attractions, hotels, and restaurants tend to be rather spread out. You can flag down any long-distance minibus running along the main road, since they all make stops between Cerro Punta/Guadalupe and Volcán on their way to or from David. For destinations off the main road, taxis are the best way to go. Sample fares include $1 between Cerro Punta and Guadalupe, around $5 between Cerro Punta and the Las Nubes entrance to PILA, and $10 from Cerro Punta up the brutal road to El Respingo, the trailhead for Sendero Los Quetzales.

Volcán and Surroundings

Volcán is what passes for an urban center on the west side of Barú. It's really little more than a homely crossroads, but there are several sights and an entrance to Parque Nacional Volcán Barú nearby. It also has the only banks, Internet cafés, launderette, and other services for many kilometers, as well as most of the dining options.

There are a couple of decent places to stay between Volcán and Bambito, but for the most part the choice is between lousy "budget" hotels that charge too much and overpriced "luxury" hotels that aren't that luxurious. Unless you plan to explore the area extensively, you may want to head up toward Cerro Punta, 14 kilometers up the mountain, where the lodging and scenery are more attractive.

SIGHTS

Parque Nacional Volcán Barú

Though only a fraction of the size of its imposing neighbor, La Amistad, this park is still plenty impressive. Its centerpiece is the dormant volcano that gives the park its name and whose summit, at 3,475 meters, is the highest point in Panama. The park was founded in 1976.

This is a good place for long hikes, camping, and bird-watching. Because of the change in elevation, the park has quite a range of life zones for its size (14,000 hectares). You'll pass through several different kinds of forests before reaching its barren and rocky summit. In the bushes near the top you can spot the rather plain-looking volcano junco. This is its only Panamanian habitat. Other birds you might encounter at the higher elevations before the forest ends include the timberline wren, black-and-yellow silky-flycatcher, and large-footed finch. (For more information, see *Hiking* in this section and *Sports and Recreation* entry in the *Boquete* section.)

Lagunas de Volcán

These picturesque lakes are part of a protected area comprising Panama's highest wetlands (the elevation is 1,200 meters). They're famous for good bird-watching. On the lakes there's a chance of seeing masked ducks and northern jacanas. Look for pale-billed woodpeckers, flycatchers, antbirds, and the rare rose-throated becard in the woods.

To get to the *lagunas*, turn left off the main road toward Río Sereno at the sign for the Oasis Place Hotel. Pass the hotel and go straight for .9 kilometer. Turn right at Casa Elsa and continue straight for 1.7 kilometers on the severely potholed road until you get to the old airstrip. Here you have two choices. You can cross the airstrip and continue straight, but the road is awful. You'll need a powerful four-wheel drive with high clearance. A better option is to head over to La Torcaza Estate and ask to use the shortcut on a better road that runs behind the facility. Ask nicely, because someone has got to unlock a gate for you. It might help your cause if you buy some coffee and take the coffee tour. (See the entry for directions.)

The *lagunas* are a 15-minute drive from "downtown" Volcán, more if the road's in bad shape (which it usually is), and you need a four-wheel drive in the rainy season. Note: Vehicles have been broken into here. If you drive, keep an eye on the car. Admission is free and there are no facilities.

La Torcaza Estate

This mill and farm (tel./fax 771-4306, janson-coffees@earthlink.cnet, www.estatecoffee.com/family), near Volcán's decaying and more-or-less abandoned airstrip, offers free tours of its facilities, in English or Spanish, 8:30 A.M.–noon, 1–5:30 P.M. Monday–Saturday, closed Sunday except by arrangement. It's run by the Janson family and is still known to some as Janson Family Coffee. There's also an espresso bar/shop on the premises where one can sip a cup and watch the beans being roasted. You can buy souvenir packages of coffee here or, if you want to avoid schlepping kilos of coffee around the country, you can wait until you get home and buy it (for a heftier price) through the Internet. To get to the mill, turn left off the main road toward Río Sereno at the sign for the Oasis Place hotel. Pass the hotel and go straight for .9 kilometer. Turn right at Casa Elsa and continue straight for 1.7 kilometers on the torn-up road until you get to the old airstrip. Turn right onto the airstrip and look for the large building on the right with "Café Volcán Barú" painted on its roof. That's your destination. A taxi from central Volcán costs about $2.50 each way.

Sitio Barriles

This field, on Finca Landau near central Volcán, is one of Panama's most important archaeological sites, but as usual the site itself has little to offer visitors but a view of some holes in the ground. Most of the items recovered here are now in Panama City's anthropology museum, which makes for a better visit. Still, those with an archaeological bent may want to take a quick look to help them connect the pieces with their place of origin.

The Barriles culture is intriguing, mostly because so little is known about it. It's believed to have been an agrarian, warrior-dominated society with roots extending back to 734 B.C.

It consisted of about four dozen human set-tlements that extended from this area to the north and east as far as Cerro Punta. The highland settlements are the most ancient. The relatively lowland Barriles site is much more recent, dating from around 60 B.C. It was the ceremonial center of the Barriles society.

The pieces found here are mysterious. The most numerous are odd stone statues depicting a proud figure wearing a conical hat who is being carried on the shoulders of a stockier man. Because these pieces were discovered in 1947–1948 through *huaquería* (grave-robbing) rather than professional excavation, nearly all their historic context has been lost. But later research has helped to date the site and its treasures. An authorized archaeology dig in 2001 uncovered more pieces.

Barú's last major eruption, in A.D. 600, scattered the Barriles culture, though the Barriles site itself was far enough away from the volcano that it may have remained populated until A.D. 800. There's some evidence it was recolonized in A.D. 1200.

Just about the only thing left here of all that history are some petroglyphs near the home of the Landau family, which owns the *finca* the site is on. They're trying to make it a tourist attraction—including neatly embedding some pottery into the walls of a hole in an attempt to simulate what a dig might look like. If you're pressed for time, and even if you're not, you can easily skip the place. They do have some tasty homemade cheese and jams to sell, though. The site is open 7 A.M.–6:30 P.M. daily. Call cell 633-2911 or 640-4388. There's no charge to visit, at least so far.

To get to the site from Volcán, head toward Río Sereno for one kilometer past the crossroads. (If you get to Hotel Don Tavo, you've gone too far.) You should see a sign on the left; make a left turn onto that road. The site is just down the road; look for the sign. A taxi from "downtown" Volcán costs $3.

Los Pozos Termales de Tisingal

These undeveloped hot springs are set among countryside within easy driving distance of Volcán. The road is in surprisingly good shape the whole way, though there are mud traps and steep sections that require a four-wheel drive. A creek runs right across the road near the hot springs, and in the rainy season it can rise high enough to be impassable. If the creek's not too high, you can park on the near side and wade across, hiking the rest of the way. The one time I visited the area it was too high and I was unable to reach the springs themselves.

The turnoff to the hot springs is 10 kilometers from the Volcán crossroads on the road to Río Sereno. You'll see a sign on the right as you crest a hill. Turn right and follow the winding road until you come to the springs.

Cañon Macho de Monte

This dramatic canyon, which features sheer faces, waterfalls, and the boulder-choked Río Macho de Monte at the bottom, is a prime bird-watching area. You have a decent chance of spotting orange-collared manakins, riverside wrens, fiery-billed aracaris, and orange-bellied trogons. Those into higher adrenaline outings might be interested in the inner-tube rafting or rappelling trips offered by High Lands Adventures. It's also just a great place for photos. The turnoff to Macho de Monte is about 12 kilometers south of Volcán at the tiny community of Cuesta del Piedra. If you're heading downhill, the unmarked turn will be on the left. Look for Restaurante El Porvenir and Mini Super Meinor; the road to the canyon is between them. Head down this road for less than three kilometers, past the guardhouse for the hydroelectric plant. You'll cross two bridges. Park by the tin-roofed *rancho* on the right. For a spectacular vista, walk down the slippery path, climb over the barbed wire fence, and scramble over a few boulders until you come to a vertiginous drop-off. Needless to say, watch your step. There's also a path near the guardhouse that leads down to the river. Ask the guard to point it out.

Truchas de Bambito

If shooting fish in a barrel sounds too challenging, Truchas de Bambito is for you. This is the Hotel Bambito's trout farm (*trucha* is Spanish for trout). Tons of the big guys swim about in a series of concrete tanks, and you're welcome to fish one out or ask the workers to catch one for you. Note: Catch and release is not allowed.

The trout farm is on the left .4 kilometer past Hotel Bambito as you head uphill. Rent a fishing

© WILLIAM FRIAR

Cañon Macho de Monte is a prime spot for bird-watching, inner-tube rafting, and rappelling.

pole for $5 an hour, or use your own for $2.50 an hour. Then you have to pay for what you catch, at $2.60 a pound. The place is open 7 A.M.–4 P.M. daily.

SHOPPING

Wild Adventures of Panama (tel. 771-5501, 8 A.M.–4:30 P.M. Wed.–Mon., 9 A.M.–1 P.M. Sun., closed Tues.), on the right just as you enter Volcán from the lowlands, is a camping supply store, amazingly enough. It's possible to rent or buy a decent array of camping stuff here. Sleeping bags rent for $2.50/day, but note that they weigh three pounds and have a comfort rating of just 45°F/7.2°C, well above how cold it can get in the highlands. It also rents bulky two- or three-person tents for $4/day and four- or five-person tents for $7/day. Propane lanterns go for $2/day and propane stoves for $3/day. Reserve gear as far in advance as possible; it doesn't have many items in stock. Other supplies include waterproof matches, light sticks, knives, insect repellent, and some cold-weather clothing.

SPORTS AND RECREATION

Summiting Volcán Barú is the big physical challenge around here, but there are plenty of other high-adrenaline possibilities, as well as gentler options. Hotel Bambito rents mountain bikes for $5 an hour and horses for $8 an hour. El Manantial Spa and Resort rents mountain bikes and fishing equipment for $5 an hour and horses for $10 an hour. It'll also rent you a bow and arrow for target practice on its land for $5 an hour. The resort, as its name suggests, offers massages and other spa services, but I haven't visited the place since these were added.

Hiking

There are three major trails in **Parque Nacional Volcán Barú.** One of these is Sendero Los Quetzales, which is described elsewhere. The other two lead to the summit of Barú from either side of the mountain. On a clear day (hah!) you can see both oceans from the summit.

From either of these last two trails reaching

the summit takes about five or six hours up and four or five hours down. It's a strenuous climb but not technically difficult. (See *Sports and Recreation* in the *Boquete* section for information on the very rough road that serves as a trail on the east side of the mountain. Neither trail is suitable for children.)

Do not attempt the summit trail on this side of the mountain without a safety-conscious and knowledgeable guide. There are lots of forks and it's easy to get lost, especially when the fog rolls in. It's also essential that you plan well. The average temperature at the higher elevations is 7.2°C and it can get down to freezing; hypothermia is a real possibility. And, like every place else in the highlands, it's often incredibly wet. Plan either to start very early or else camp out on the mountain. As an incentive, the best chance of a clear view is to be at the top close to dawn.

Dress warmly in waterproof clothes, and if you plan to camp bring a good tent and a second set of clothes. Bring plenty of water, as there are no facilities anywhere near the summit. Also, bear in mind that the elevation is high enough for altitude sickness to be a possibility. If you feel nauseated or get a bad headache, head down the mountain immediately.

One bummer about this hike is that many thoughtless people have scrawled graffiti all over the rocks near the summit. Try to ignore it; concentrate on the view and your sense of smugness for having made it to the top.

If you have a cell phone that works in this part of Panama, bring it. There's a communication tower at the summit, so it might be possible to make a call if you get into trouble.

For the hike to the summit of Barú you should drive to the trailhead, unless you're up for a marathon trek. The trailhead is at the end of 7.4 kilometers of dirt and gravel road, half of it horrible, that heads east across the plains from the main road between Volcán and Bambito. The road is not marked but your guide will know the way.

Admission to the park is theoretically $3, $5 more to camp, but there are usually no rangers around to collect it. This is yet another reason to exercise caution in climbing the mountain; don't expect the Mounties to come to the rescue if you get in trouble. Make sure there's someone back in town who knows where you are and is prepared to call for some sort of help if you don't return at a specified time. Again, a summit climb is absolutely not appropriate for young children.

Other Activities

A number of hotels and guides offer **white-water rafting trips.** You should note that all of them contract out to rafting companies in Boquete, on the east side of Barú, so find out if the tour planner is charging you a premium just to book the trip for you. You might do better to contact the company directly. The companies can usually pick rafters up and take them to rivers on either side of the mountain. (See *Sports and Recreation* in the *Boquete* section for details and recommendations.)

A couple of places offer **inner-tube rafting** along relatively gentle stretches of the roaring Chiriquí Viejo. El Manantial Spa and Resort rents tubes for $10 for use in the stretch in front of the hotel. High Lands Adventures (see *Guides*) charges $30/person, two-person minimum, for a higher-adrenaline trip in Cañon Macho de Monte.

Climbing sports are attempting to get a foothold (sorry) in this area. High Lands Adventures (see *Nature Tours*) offers rappelling off the vertiginous cliffs of Cañon Macho de Monte and rock climbing up the 42-meter face of a huge boulder near Bambito. Personally, I wouldn't go rock climbing or rappelling around here even if my guide showed me home movies of his one-handed ascent of El Capitan, but you may be more adventurous.

Nature Tours

High Lands Adventures (tel. 771-4413, cell 685-1682, jcaceres@chiriqui.com) is the most established and organized guide and outdoor-adventure outfit on the west side of Barú. The operation is run by brothers Nariño and Gonzálo Aizpurúa, who are trying to learn a bit of English and German. Their foreign-language skills are still basic, but they try to bring along an English or German translator if guests don't speak Spanish. Their prices average around $40 per person, going up to $70 per person for a hike to the top of Barú. They offer the usual hikes and tours,

plus rappelling and inner-tubing down the Río Chiriquí Viejo. There's a two-person minimum on all excursions.

Their office is in Volcán, next to the Shell station at the fork in the road. Look for the building with *turismo ecológico* and *EcoTour* painted on the front. If they're not guiding you should be able to find them in the office between 7 A.M. and 5 P.M. daily. Otherwise call their cell phone, which is always on. They also work with some of the area hotels. I still haven't gone adventuring with them, but they've always struck me as good guys who know what they're doing.

Abdiel Baules (cell 649-6223, abaules@hotmail.com) is a friendly, reliable, and professional birding guide (note that he does not lead other kinds of tours). An electrician by trade, he's also a biologist with a particular interest in the birds of western Panama. His tour destinations include Macho de Monte, Finca Hartmann, the forest around Cabañas Los Quetzales, Sendero Los Quetzales, the Fortuna area, and Bocas del Toro including the Río Teribe. He leads tours to other destinations by request. He generally charges $90 a day, with a maximum group size of 10 people. He's well-respected as a birder, and I've enjoyed traveling with him.

Several of the hotels in the area can arrange nature tours and outdoor adventures whether or not you're staying with them. At the time of writing these included El Manantial Spa and Resort and Hotel Bambito. Often, they subcontract out to the guides listed above.

(See the *Cerro Punta and Surroundings* section for more guide possibilities.)

ACCOMMODATIONS

Lodging around Volcán is generally unsatisfying. Consider heading farther up the mountain to the area around Cerro Punta. There are a couple of places worth checking out, however. And budget travelers may want to contact El Manantial Spa and Resort to see about getting a bunk bed in its "Las Barrackas" dorms. These are intended for large student groups, but if no one else is using them it may be possible to get a bed for about $10.

Golfo de Chiriquí

$25–50

Hotel y Restaurante Don Tavo (tel./fax 771-5144, Volcán @chiriqui.com, www.chiriqui.com/hotel/dontavo, $27.50/36.30 s/d) is on the right just past downtown. It's set around a pretty courtyard and offers 16 simple but clean rooms with TV. It's by far the best moderately priced place to stay in the area, and the best value overall.

$50–100

Hotel Barceló Dos Ríos (tel. 771-5555, hdosrios@chiriqui.com, $58.30 s/d including a minimal continental breakfast), on the outskirts of the Volcán area 2.7 kilometers from the crossroads on the road to Río Sereno, is the fanciest, and priciest, place to stay in Volcán. Recently renovated by the Spanish Barceló chain, it's an attractive place consisting of 14 rooms, two suites, and two slightly cheaper *casitas* (here meaning tiny bungalows with bunk beds, $52.50 s/d/t) set in a garden with a creek flowing by. Rooms are dark but have cheerful touches, especially the painted vines and startled-looking toucans that adorn the walls. Windows can't be opened so forget about ventilation, and the rooms are already showing signs of wear thanks to a casual attitude toward maintenance and cleaning. Rooms have TVs that get fuzzy local channels. All the polished wood everywhere is a mixed blessing. It

looks nice, but it makes the place resonate like the soundbox of a guitar, ensuring that anyone who walks by sounds like an army of storm troopers. Try to get a room on the second floor.

Hotel Bambito(tel. 771-4251, 771-4373, or 771-4374, fax 771-4207, bambito@chiriqui .com, starts at $82.50/96 s/d) is an aging luxury hotel that's pretty imposing but which you may find out of keeping with the natural beauty of the surroundings. It was built in 1981 and almost nothing about it has been changed since then, including the Last Days of Disco decor. It offers surprisingly plain standard rooms and several varieties of large suites. The place has seen better days. There are tennis courts, an indoor/outdoor swimming pool, sauna, hot tub, and a few pieces of gym equipment. Rates start at $82.50/96 s/d for a standard room during the week, $20/25 s/d extra during the weekend. Add another $5/7 s/d if you want breakfast included. Standard rates are excessive, but discount packages are often available.

You can choose from 19 quaint cottages at **Cabañas Kucikas** (tel./fax 771-4245 in Bambito or 269-0623 in Panama City, starts at $60 per group), .7 kilometer up from Hotel Bambito, just past the trout farm. It's on the left, but there's no sign so it's easy to miss the turn. The cottages are on forested grounds snug up against the mountains. It's a pleasant, if aging, place. All the cottages are

Cabañas Kucikas are among the more unusual lodging possibilities on the west side of Volcán Barú.

© WILLIAM FRIAR

different, with some more cheerful and well appointed than others. There's no restaurant on the premises, but all the cottages have full kitchens. This place is a good deal for larger groups. Rates run $60–150 for cottages that hold 2–10 people. There's a fancy "honeymoon" cottage for $60.

$100–150

El Manantial Spa and Resort (tel. 771-5126, fax 771-5127 at the resort, info@manantialspa.com, www.manantialspa.com, suites start at $110 s/d), formerly known as the Bambito Forest Resort or Bambito Camping Resort, is a place for wealthy Panamanian families to get close to the woods without giving up any comfort. The location is pretty, with the Río Chiriquí Viejo racing by the front of the hotel. It's about nine kilometers past the Hotel Bambito; look for the large sign by the side of the road. Turn left and continue along the one-lane dirt road for .6 kilometer. You don't need a four-wheel drive.

Most of the rooms here are elegantly wood-paneled, high-ceilinged suites, ranging in size from big to gigantic. They have all the amenities you'd expect in an upscale hotel. So in a place this fancy you wouldn't find thin walls, hard beds, toilets that don't flush right, five minutes' worth of hot water, and light switches that electrocute you, right? Wrong. If you stay here, inspect the room carefully.

A major step down in quality are the basic and musty rooms in the resort's Explorador cabins. You can do much better for less money elsewhere.

This place also offers nature tours and other outdoor activities and has a cushy campsite nearby. (By the way, the "canopy adventure" the resort brags about is much tamer than it sounds. It's basically a glorified playground ride. You can easily skip it, especially if you're planning to do the real thing in Boquete or El Valle.)

Rooms in the Explorador cabins are $44 s/d. Suites start at $110 s/d. Rates are sometimes even higher.

Camping

Be sure to bring plenty of warm clothing and a good tent if you camp out. It can get quite cold and drizzly even in the dry season.

As mentioned earlier, it's possible to camp in **Parque Nacional Volcán Barú,** which you may want to do if you hike to the summit. The fee is $5, but good luck finding someone to pay it to. If you want to do things by the book you can buy a permit ahead of time at the ANAM office in David or Panama City.

If you want to camp in cushier surroundings, you can pitch a tent on the 170-hectare grounds of **El Manantial Spa and Resort.** The resort also has a developed campsite a few minutes farther up the mountain by four-wheel drive. It offers hot-water showers and a bathroom. For $30 (two-person tent) or $50 (four-person tent) the resort will supply a tent, sleeping bags, pads, lanterns, transportation to and from the site, and a meager continental breakfast back at the hotel. If you have your own gear, you can camp at the site for $10, but you have to hike in and you're on your own for breakfast.

FOOD

Café Cerro Brujo (cell 629-5604, noon–"late" Mon.–Sat., closed Sun.) is on the left side of the road 300 meters from the crossroads as one heads toward Río Sereno. It's a cute little café with a boho vibe that's surprising for this area. It has a limited menu that makes a stab at relatively haute cuisine and changes daily. Main dishes come with delicious soups and salads. Offerings tend to include steak, pastas, *langostinos,* and *pulpo* (octopus, which is a popular dish here). Most dishes are $8–9.

Café Acropolis (tel. 771-4162), next to Super Centro La Fuente, serves a variety of Greek food, though don't be surprised if not everything on the menu is available when you visit. The *tzatziki* yogurt dip and the hummus, both served with fresh, hot pita bread, make good appetizers. The moussaka is tasty if oily. The café also serves the usual meats, plus pastas, burgers, and fresh shakes and juices. Most dishes are $2.50–7.50.

Cafeteria El Sombrero, three kilometers south of Cerro Punta or one kilometer up from the Cielito Sur bed-and-breakfast, is a cute little rustic roadside café that sells delicious fresh fruit shakes, as well as burgers, sandwiches, marmalades, and such. You'll see it on the left as you head uphill. There are some vegetable stands nearby if you feel like stocking up on produce.

Restaurante Lorena, (tel. 771-5086, 6 A.M.–9 P.M. daily), two kilometers from the crossroads on the road toward Río Sereno, is a plain place that offers a choice of beef, pork, or chicken with soup, a couple of plantains, beans, and rice for under $3. It's a good choice when you need something quick, plentiful, and cheap. The most colorful part of the establishment is Lorena herself, who serves patrons day or night in an evening gown, high heels, and lots of makeup.

The restaurant at **Hotel Barceló Dos Ríos** (tel. 771-5555) is the fanciest in town, which isn't saying a whole lot. It's pleasant to sit out on the patio, but the food is so-so at best. My dinner there was memorable for overcooked and chewy beef complemented by undercooked rice. Options include steaks, pasta, and pizzas, with most main dishes going for $5.50–11.50. The brave can opt for *la sorpresa de la casa* (house surprise). Yikes.

Restaurante Las Truchas, in the Hotel Bambito (tel. 771-4265) farther up the mountain, features plate-glass windows that look out on the artificial terraced pond in front of the hotel and the side of a mountain right across the street. The house specialty, as the name of the restaurant implies, is trout from its own trout farm up the street, prepared any way you can think of for $11. Pasta here is around $6, and most other dishes are $10–12. If you're feeling terribly hungry, tuck into the ample Sunday brunch for $14 a head.

The fare at the **El Manantial Spa and Resort** (tel. 771-5126) includes most of the usual suspects (beef, pork, chicken, and so on). Most dishes are $8–9. The trout is fine as long as you don't mind staring a big ol' fish in the face. The restaurant is housed in an attractive building that also has a fireplace, bar, and small lounge. If nothing else, this is a good place to stop for a drink.

Super Centro La Fuente is a big two-story supermarket at the crossroads. It has dry goods upstairs and an attached bakery.

INFORMATION AND SERVICES

The High Lands Adventure office in Volcán can give information on sights and nature activities in the area. (See *Sports and Recreation*.) It also sells a detailed area map with sights and points of interest marked on it for $2.50. You can get information about Parque International la Amistad at the ANAM ranger station at the Las Nubes entrance to the park.

Farmacia Don Bosco (tel. 771-4317, 8 A.M.–8 P.M. daily) is near Banistmo. Farmacia Volcán (tel. 771-4651, 7:30 A.M.–10 P.M. Sun.–Thurs., 7:30 A.M.–6 P.M. Fri., 6–10 P.M. Saturday) is on the left one kilometer from the crossroads on the way to Río Sereno.

The only banks on the west side of Barú are in the town of Volcán. As you head up from the lowlands, Banistmo (8 A.M.–3:30 P.M. Mon.–Fri., 9 A.M.–noon Sat.) is on the right shortly before the road forks. There's no ATM, but it cashes travelers checks. A branch of the Banco Nacional de Panamá (8 A.M.–3 P.M. Mon.–Fri., 9 A.M.–noon Sat.) is on the left straight past the fork, on the road to Río Sereno. It has an ATM, and you can cash travelers checks. The local Western Union outlet (tel. 771-4258, 8 A.M.–9 P.M. daily) is next to Hotel y Restaurante Don Tavo. The door is always locked; ask at the restaurant for service.

CyberCafé (tel. 771-4461 or 771-4055, 8 A.M.–11 P.M. daily), is attached to the Hotel y Restaurante Don Tavo. It offers fast Internet access for $.75/hour. Volc@net (tel. 771-5482, 8 A.M.–10 P.M. daily) on the right less than one kilometer from the crossroads on the road to Río Sereno, offers Internet access for $.80/hour. You can also send faxes here. A fax to the United States costs $5/page plus long-distance charges.

Lavandería Mollek (no phone, 9 A.M.–6 P.M. Mon.–Sat., closed Sun.), across the street from the Church of Jesus Christ of Latter-Day Saints four hundred meters from the crossroads on the way to Río Sereno, washes clothes for $1.25 and dries them for $1.

GETTING THERE

The city of David, in the lowlands, is the bus and airline hub for the entire western highlands.

It takes 6–7 hours to drive from Panama City to David. From there it's about a 1.5-hour drive to Volcán. If you're driving from David, take the

Interamerican Highway west to Concepción, 26 kilometers away. Turn right and head uphill. After another 34 kilometers you'll come to Volcán.

Buses between Cerro Punta and David all stop in Volcán ($2.30) and Bambito ($2.50). Look for the bus with "Cerro Punta" painted on the windshield. David-bound buses leave Cerro Punta 4:45 A.M.–6:45 P.M. Buses run every 15 minutes. Those coming from Costa Rica can catch the Cerro Punta bus at Concepción rather than going all the way to the David bus terminal.

Buses run between Volcán and Río Sereno about once an hour 5 A.M.–5 P.M. daily. The fare is $2.65. The bus stops at Finca Hartmann by request.

Taxi fare from David to Volcán is $20, a bit more to go farther up the mountain. Some of the highland hotels will arrange pickup at the airport or bus terminal, for a fee. Check with your hotel. Taxi fare from Volcán to Finca Hartmann is $15, $20 to Río Sereno.

GETTING AROUND

It's easy to walk around central Volcán, but those staying at a hotel on the road to Río Sereno without their own transportation will probably have to rely on taxis. There's a taxi stand at the crossroads, next to Super Centro La Fuente. Taxis anywhere within the vicinity of Volcán are $.75. Between Volcán and Cerro Punta the fare is $5, $3 more to get to Las Nubes entrance to PILA. Other fares include Sitio Barriles ($4), Lagunas de Volcán ($5), and Los Pozos Termales de Tisingal ($15). Catch the Cerro Punta-David bus if you want to take a bus between Volcán and the Bambito area.

WEST OF VOLCÁN

If you stay straight on the road through Volcán rather than turning right toward Cerro Punta, you'll head west and eventually end up in Río Sereno, a tiny town (population 3,289) with nothing to offer visitors but a little-used border crossing with Costa Rica that is not always open to foreign travelers. The main reason to come this way is to visit Finca Hartmann, a combina-

tion gourmet coffee farm and private forest reserve with a couple of cabins for birders and other nature lovers. It's 27 kilometers west of Volcán, 15 kilometers east of Río Sereno.

The road to Río Sereno is one of the prettiest in Panama. Bright, tiny flowers dot the shoulders. The road crosses over rivers and winds past splashing waterfalls, forested hills, coffee plantations, tall stands of evergreens, and plump cows grazing in fields.

But the road also features blind curves and trucks that barrel down the hills without a thought for what might lie around the bend. Count on landslides and washouts in the rainy season, though the road was repaved recently and should be in good shape when you visit. Be careful.

Though the countryside is attractive, Río Sereno itself isn't. It consists of a couple of basic stores (the best bet for food), a central plaza, a bank, the border crossing, and little else. There's an open-air market by the plaza with modest offerings, catering to Costa Rican day-trippers. Given the limited services here, and the fact that even the immigration officials don't quite know what to make of tourists, visitors should enter or exit Panama through the far less attractive but much more convenient crossing at Paso Canoa. (See the *Know Panama* chapter for detailed information on all Costa Rican border crossings.)

Finca Hartmann

This family-owned coffee farm (tel./fax 771-5144, fincahartmann@hotmail.com, www.angelfire .com/pa2/hartmann) is a great favorite with birders—more than 280 species have been identified—but even if that's not your thing you may want to consider visiting for its away-from-it-all natural beauty, for a tour of its coffee operation, or just for a cup of coffee with some friendly folks. The Hartmanns have two remote cabins, one of them surprisingly comfortable, for guests who want to stay overnight. The *finca* is in the community of Santa Clara, 27 kilometers from Volcán on the road to Río Sereno.

The Hartmanns offer tours of their small coffee mill. The coffee here, not surprisingly, is excellent, and there's a small coffee shop with an attractive wooden *rancho* where you can buy a cup or pick up some souvenir packs to take home. A tour of the coffee operation and/or access to the grounds for birding or hiking is $7.50 per person.

The patriarch of the clan is the friendly and gregarious Ratibor "Chicho" Hartmann, now in his 80s but in fantastic shape. He's an entomology enthusiast who worked for years in the Canal Zone at Gorgas Hospital, an important center for tropical medicine. Ask him about it; he's got interesting stories. Research scientists have been studying the farm's rich flora and fauna for years. Their gratitude has included naming two new beetles species and a new species of cloud-forest bee after Hartmann.

Reflecting his hobby, he has built a tiny museum in the compound that contains an impressive insect collection from the area and around the world. There's an incredible array of bizarre specimens. There's also a small collection of pre-Columbian pottery and stone figures, mostly from Chiriquí.

The real treasure of the place is the fragmented primary cloud forest 3.7 kilometers up from the main *finca* on a brutal road that requires a four-wheel drive with high clearance. It's called **Ojo de Agua** (eye of water) for the spring that runs between the two cabins in a clearing at the end of the road. Besides the incredible array of birds, the lucky might encounter a few of the 62 species of mammals that have so far been identified on the *finca,* including red brocket (a kind of deer), peccaries, armadillos, porcupines, opossums, and close to 20 species of mice, as well as white-faced capuchin, red spider, and howler monkeys.

Ojo de Agua borders Parque Internacional La Amistad (PILA). To the west one can see clear to Costa Rica. Five trails start from near the cabin: a one-kilometer uphill one that connects with the road, a three-kilometer trail that leads up a hill and that skirts PILA, another three-kilometer one that leads to a small river, a 350-meter walk to a 50-meter waterfall, and a 500-meter trail that leads to an enormous ficus tree.

The two cabins are quite different. The larger one is a two-story building that's been used as a research station, so creature comforts have not been a main concern. It's a basic place with a concrete floor, kitchen with gas stove, dining/sitting area, fireplace, and five bedrooms. There's no electricity, just kerosene lamps, but it does have hot-water showers. The smaller cabin is quite a bit nicer. It's still rustic, but it features finished wood, a snug bedroom, a kitchenette, and hot-water bathroom. Electricity is on the way; expect prices to go up when it arrives.

Rates run from $10 for a bunk bed to $30 for a cabaña for two. Optional food service is $20 a day. If you need transportation from the *finca* to the cabins, the Hartmanns will take you there for $10 round-trip.

Río Sereno Practicalities

The **Posada Los Andes** (no phone) is the only option for those stranded in Río Sereno on the way to someplace more interesting. It's in the building that looks like a factory looming over the plaza; rooms are upstairs from the shops. It offers rooms with shared bath for $8 per person or rooms with bath for $12 s/d. Don't expect the Ritz. Finca Hartmann is a better but more remote alternative.

A branch of Banco Nacional de Panamá (8 A.M.–3 P.M. Mon.–Fri., 9 A.M.–noon Sat.) is next to the plaza in the center of Río Sereno.

Getting There and Around

To drive to Finca Hartmann from Volcán, continue straight at the crossroads rather than turning right toward Cerro Punta. The drive takes about a half hour. You'll see a sign on the left side of the road; make a quick right onto the gravel road. The 42 kilometers from Volcán all the way to Río Sereno takes about 45 minutes by car. Just stay straight on the main road.

Buses run between Volcán and Río Sereno about once an hour 5 A.M.–5 P.M. daily. The fare is $2.65. The bus will stop at Finca Hartmann if requested. Taxi fare from Volcán is $15–20 to either place.

Buses between David and Río Sereno run every 45 minutes 5 A.M.–5 P.M. The trip takes nearly three hours and costs $4. Tell the driver if you want to get off at Finca Hartmann (about 2.5 hours, $3.65).

Río Sereno is tiny. You can walk from one end

of "downtown" to the other in five minutes. You can also wander right over to Costa Rica for a minute, if you want that weird little thrill of crossing a border. The crossing is wide open and not even marked; you'll only know which country you're in from the flags flying at the tiny *migración* offices.

ALONG THE FORTUNA ROAD

The area around the Fortuna reservoir, farther east along the cordillera, is known for its sweeping vistas and great bird-watching, but so far it doesn't see many visitors or even have that many residents.

Because the Fortuna Dam generates more than 30 percent of Panama's electricity, there's an economic incentive to keep its watershed well protected. That's good news for nature lovers, as the forests here are overflowing with life. It can get cool at the higher elevations, down to about 14°C (57°F), but it's significantly warmer than the area around Volcán Barú.

The reservoir, just south of the Continental Divide, is surrounded by the Reserva Forestal Fortuna (Fortuna Forest Reserve, 19,500 hectares), which in turn is bordered by the enormous Bosque Protector de Palo Seco (Palo Seco Buffer Forest, 244,000 hectares) to the northwest. The Continental Divide marks the border between the provinces of Chiriquí and Bocas del Toro.

A good, though dangerous, road—often referred to as the Fortuna Road—cuts north across the mountains from the town of Chiriquí on the Interamerican Highway to the oil port of Chiriquí Grande on the Caribbean coast, less than 100 kilometers away. A new road links Chiriquí Grande with Almirante, the jumping-off point for water taxis and ferries to the archipelago of Bocas del Toro. Along the way there are rugged access roads into the forest, making it relatively easy to explore the area.

More than 1,000 plant species have been identified just in the Fortuna Forest Reserve, which is also home to 40 mammal and 70 amphibian and reptile species. Endangered mammals here include the white-lipped peccary and Baird's tapir. The area has some of the best bird-watching in

Panama. Besides the ever-popular resplendent quetzal, there's a chance of seeing such spectacular specimens as the bare-necked umbrellabird, azure-hooded jay, black-bellied hummingbird, lattice-tailed trogon, and yellow-eared toucanet, to name just a few. Some of these are rare and nearly impossible to spot, so you'll get a lot more out of a hike if you go with a good guide. Fortunately, one of the best bird guides in Panama owns a campsite in this area. (For details, see *Accommodations.*)

Sights

Finca La Suiza is on the right about 40 kilometers up the Fortuna Road from Chiriquí. Those with time to kill should consider taking a hike in the *finca's* private reserve; the trails are good and well marked. The **Continental Divide** is at kilometer marker 60; flora and fauna quickly change as one heads down the Caribbean slope. The road also leads over the impressive **Represa Fortuna** (Fortuna Dam), whose hydroelectric plant supplies more than 30 percent of Panama's power. The road goes across the top and offers lovely views of the reservoir and the hills that ring it.

For a break, pull off the road at the bridge near kilometer marker 67. On the west side just past the bridge is a gorge. Walk down the little trail by the side of the road; it's not marked, but it's near a sign that says "Celestine." Do not open this gate and go up the steps; that's private property. The trail is to the left of it, starting at the guard rail. The trail leads down to a little *quebrada* (brook) with a **swimming hole and waterfall,** El Suspiro, in a narrow box canyon. The waterfall is at least 30 meters high and is absolutely stunning and pristine. Those so inclined can slip behind the waterfall. Even though this is all close to the road, as usual travelers shouldn't wander around solo. Even at low water you'll get wet; wear swim trunks and reef sandals, and bring plastic bags for the cameras. There's not a scrap of trash anywhere; please keep it that way. This is probably not the safest place to be during a heavy rainstorm.

Sports and Recreation

You do not have to stay there to hike the **Finca La Suiza trail.** It's one of my favorites in all of

Panama, both because of its beauty and because it's so well marked and maintained. For much of the trail you're in the thick of the forest, then suddenly you come upon spectacular waterfalls or sweeping valley views. The forest is alive with sights and sounds. On my first visit I had hiked in only a few hundred meters when a group of white-nosed coatis scampered through the trees right above my head. There are big cats in the forests here, but it's very unlikely you'll have the good fortune to see them. However, a puma attacked a neighbor's cattle in 1997.

Be advised that this is a somewhat strenuous hike that goes from an elevation of 1,150 to 1,700 meters. It's relentlessly uphill for the first half, and the trail "down" has lots of uphill parts. It crosses several streams, which can be tricky in the rainy season when the water is high and the trail is slippery. As with any forest trail in Panama, do not hike alone. If you get lost, the rescue fee is $100. Officially it takes 5.5 hours to hike the trail, but that's being very conservative. Going at a reasonable clip shaves at least an hour off that estimate. By the way, don't eat the things that look like blueberries growing along the side of the trail. They're poisonous.

The trail fee is $10. Finca guests pay only once no matter how many times they hike. If you're just planning to hike the trail, pay the fee to one of the Ngöbe-Buglé women in the house just up the hill and get a map of the trail from her. You must start the trail between 7 and 10 A.M. This is for your own protection, as you don't want to be stuck out there at night. The trailhead is a steep, seven-minute walk up the dirt road. The trailhead is to the left.

There's a newer trail at the *finca* that starts from an area called **Alta Vista** and heads up through a cloud forest, past a huge waterfall to the top of **Cerro Hornito.** I have not hiked it, but I'm told it is extremely tough, and it would be hard to retrieve a hiker if there's an accident. Unlike the rest of the trails, the Cerro Hornito is true wilderness. If you get lost, you're finished. This can only be hiked with a guide from the *finca;* you will get lost on your own. The fee for this is $72 for 1–4 people, $18 for each additional person. It takes about six hours to get to the

top. The elevation changes from about 1700 meters at Alta Vista to 2100 at Cerro Hornito (the lodge is at 1,220 meters).

Accommodations

Two appealing places to stay are aimed at ecotourists and are essentially nature sights in themselves. They are also good bases for exploring the area.

Sort of a cross between a mountain bed-and-breakfast and a nature reserve, **Finca La Suiza,** (tel. 615-3774, fincalasuiza@hotmail.com, $30.80/$39.60 s/d) is well worth a visit. It consists of 205 hectares of mountainous primary and secondary forest through part of which the friendly Swiss owners have built a terrific trail. Those owners, Herbert Brullmann and Monika Kohler, rent out three large and cheerful bedrooms with private bath in their small house, which is set on a ridge 1,220 meters above sea level. The views are spectacular. On a clear day, one can see lovely valleys, Pacific islands, Volcán Barú, and even a slice of Costa Rica.

The food here is gourmet and includes such unexpected treats as pesto, gnocchi, watercress and endive salad, and blackberry parfait. The produce is from the *finca's* garden. The full four-course dinner, which I recommend, is $10. A big breakfast featuring homemade jams is around $4. You're on your own for lunch. It's bring-your-own-bottle if you'd like wine with dinner.

Maximum capacity of each room is four people; the third and fourth person pay an additional $8.80 each. Rooms are not rented out in June, September, and October, during which time the trail is closed. Email is checked only once a week. Please confirm email reservations by phone upon arrival in Panama. The best time to phone is between 7 and 9 P.M.

Finca La Suiza is 55 kilometers from David on the road to Chiriquí Grande, just past Los Planes and the one gas station on the right. A sign for the *finca* is on the right. The lodge is not visible from the gate. Try not to arrive after sundown. The gate is always closed at 6:30.

Only those with a four-wheel drive that has high clearance can drive up to the lodge. Otherwise park just inside the fence, watching out for muddy stretches, and walk up the steep dirt road. You'll pass the trailhead on the left. *Finca* guests can continue straight to get to the house. If you don't have a four-wheel drive, leave the luggage in the car or at the house up the hill. The owners will help you retrieve it. Do not venture onto the property without permission; large dogs patrol the premises when the owners are out.

Owned by Wilberto (Willie) Martínez, one of the top birders in Panama, **Rancho Ecológico Willie Mazu** (tel. 225-7325, tel./fax 225-7314, panabird@cwpanama.net, www.nattur.com, packages start at $42 per person) is a unique camping retreat. This lovely campground is 31 kilometers north of Finca La Suiza, just on the other side of the Continental Divide, and borders protected forest. There are two main trails into the surrounding forest that originate from the campground. One leads to a 90-meter waterfall an hour's hike away. The second leads to a cloud forest about 1.5 hours away.

The main campsite is a *rancho* (open-air thatched hut) with a number of large and small tents. It's set in a garden next to a river and has electricity and a hot-water bathroom. There's a kitchen and dining area, and food service is included. Reservations are required.

Martínez is also building a botanical garden to protect indigenous local plants, some of which are endangered. He's gathered more than 250 species of orchids and is adding bromeliads, heliconias, ferns, and other plants. It's also a sanctuary for the poison-dart frog, with 13 varieties of the species identified on the property.

The most basic package is $42 per person per day, including three meals but no guide or transportation. A three-day stay including meals, transportation to and from Panama City, and guided tours is $290, two-person minimum. Martínez's tour company, Nattur Panama, offers other tours that include stays at the *rancho*.

The campground is 86 kilometers from David, or 29 kilometers south of Chiriquí Grande. It's not easy to see from the road, but it's on a river just before the road makes a steep, sweeping turn. If you're heading north, you'll see an orchid booth on the right side of the road a few dozen meters before the campground. The booth is run by the Martínez family (no relation to Willie), which also acts as caretaker for Rancho Ecológico. The camp will not be able to accommodate you if you show up without a reservation. Willie Mazu is near kilometer marker 69.

Information and Services

This is a remote area with few services of any kind and certainly no tourist information booths. The best bet for information and guides are Finca La Suiza and Rancho Ecológico Willie Mazu. Don't attempt a hike into the forest without a guide.

Getting There

The Fortuna Road begins at the town of Chiriquí, 15 kilometers east of David on the Interamericana. Turn north off the highway at Chiriquí and head straight past town. Keep left when you come to the fork at Gualaca. The two-lane route, unofficially known as the Fortuna Road, soon starts winding through the highlands and the views become spectacular. Beware of landslides and washouts. Returning to the Interamericana on the way back down can be a bit confusing. At Gualaca, be sure to turn left at the crossroads, following the signs that say "CPA" (apparently for Carretera Pan-Americana, i.e. the Interamericana).

Any bus running between David and Chiriquí Grande or Almirante uses this road and can drop off and pick up passengers anywhere along it. The trip from David to Finca la Suiza takes about an hour and costs $2.50. To return to David or Almirante you'll have to flag down a bus by the side of the road.

Note to those driving to or from Boquete: A road links Caldera and the Fortuna Road that can potentially shorten the trip considerably since it spares you from having to drive all the way down to the Interamerican Highway. It has recently been paved most of the way and should be in good shape when you visit. However, it's prone to landslides and washouts, so ask locals about conditions before attempting. The road is about 38 kilometers long. It's a pretty drive.

Golfo de Chiriquí

Bocas del Toro

It's hard to leave Bocas del Toro. It's a terribly relaxing place, and at the same time it exudes a funky, romantic charm that has something untamed about it. The place is filled with colorful characters nursing drinks in dilapidated wooden bars or running rustic hotels on remote beaches. It's the kind of Caribbean hideaway one expects to find only in old Bogart films.

And it's just gorgeous. It has an abundance of emerald islands, pristine beaches, turquoise waters, dense forests, barely explored mountains and rivers, extensive coral gardens, spooky mangrove channels, and exotic wildlife. Four species of endangered sea turtles still visit the waters of Bocas. They come ashore by the hundreds during nesting season to lay their eggs on the north side of the islands and some stretches of the mainland coast. Little Swan's Cay, really just a rock in the ocean, is the only Panamanian nesting site of the beautiful red-billed tropicbird. It's just one of the more than 350 species of birds attracted to the region. Sloths, caimans, dolphins, neon-colored frogs, and, of course, lots of small tropical fish are easy to spot in the archipelago. No wonder a dozen countries have shot their versions of the *Survivor* TV series here.

The people help make Bocas special. More ethnicities and nationalities are represented on the

ust-Sees

M Swan's Cay: A picture-postcard islet, and one of the last stands of the red-billed tropicbird (page 410).

M Laguna Bocatorito: Experience close encounters with bottle-nosed dolphins in this lagoon (page 410).

M Cayo Crawl: The quintessential Bocas scene: rustic restaurants floating just above the surface of a glassy sea, tropical fish swimming just below (page 437).

M North Shore Beaches: Isla Bastimento's north shore beaches offer pristine sand, monster waves, and brilliant red frogs (page 437).

M Parque Nacional Marino Isla Bastimentos: The highlight of this marine park are the Cayos Zapatillas, which offer cave diving and a pair of undeveloped islands (page 440).

Little Swan's Cay is a popular destination for boat tours.

M Proyecto ODESEN (Wekso Ecolodge and Center): Formerly a military jungle-survival school, now a base to discover the forest world of the Naso, an indigenous people fighting for their own survival (page 454).

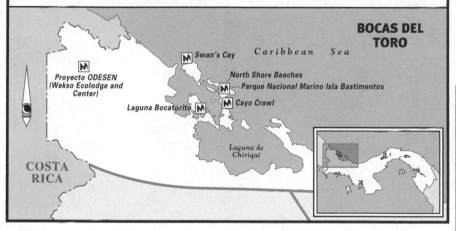

islands than anywhere in the country outside of Panama City. And one is more likely to hear English spoken here than anywhere in the country, period. The islands have long been home to the Ngöbe-Buglé, as well as the descendents of Afro-Caribbean immigrants from the English-speaking islands of Jamaica, San Andrés, and Providencia, many of whom came down to work on the region's enormous banana plantations.

Most of the hotels and restaurants on the islands are owned by Europeans and North Americans. And the mostly young and boho tourists Bocas attracts are coming from all over the world.

For most visitors, Bocas del Toro means the archipelago that stretches about 100 kilometers from Boca del Drago in the west to Isla Escudo de Veraguas in the east. For them the mainland is just a place to fly over or drive through on the

BOCAS DEL TORO

Caribbean Sea

Golfo de los Mosquitos

Isla Escudo de Veraguas

Boca de Río Caña

Río Caña

Río Cricamola

BOCAS DEL TORO

Guariviara

Río

Peninsula Valiente

Laguna de Chiriquí

Cayo de Agua

Chiriquí Grande

Quebrada de Sal

Isla Bastimentos

Isla Popa

PARQUE NACIONAL MARINO ISLA BASTIMENTOS

NORTH SHORE BEACHES

Old Bank

Isla Colón

Bocas

Isla Cristóbal

Punto Róbalo

FORTUNA RD

To David

Bosque Protector de Palo Seco

RD

Río Róbalo

SWAN'S CAY

Almirante

CHIRIQUÍ GRANDE – ALMIRANTE

Humedales de San San Pondsack

ALMIRANTE – GUABITO RD

Río Changuinola

Boquete

Alto Quiel

Cerro Punta

Parque Nacional Volcán Barú

Manzanillo

Sixaola

Guabito

Changuinola

El Silencio

Sieykin

Guadalupe

Bambito

Volcán

Río Sereno

Puerto Viejo

Bribri

PROYECTO ODESEN (WEKSO ECOLODGE AND CENTER)

Cahuita

Parque Internacional La Amistad

Cordillera de Talamanca

Río Teribe

COSTA RICA

CHIRIQUÍ

© AVALON TRAVEL PUBLISHING, INC.

10 mi

10 km

0

way to the islands. But the rest of the province of Bocas del Toro has plenty of spectacular natural beauty, such as the Caribbean side of the enormous Parque Internacional la Amistad and the wetlands of San San Pondsack. Lucky hikers, at least those who venture far up into the mainland forests, may encounter endangered mammals such as Baird's tapir. All five species of cats found on the isthmus, including jaguars, are hanging on in the most remote reaches of the forest, but the chance of coming across one is slim. The forests are also still home to indigenous peoples trying to hold onto their culture and ancestral lands. This includes the little-known Naso, who welcome visitors to a unique ecotourist project on the edge of their communities up the Río Teribe.

More than just about anyplace else in Panama, the Bocas archipelago is taking off as a tourist destination. Backpackers are spilling over from Costa Rica, and more affluent expatriates from the United States and Canada are buying up beachfront property and building their fantasy tropical getaways. Everyone is in the real-estate business these days. There are even luxurious planned communities in the works. But the funk factor is still strong and the islands are hardly a tourist trap. Long-term expats are already grumbling that Bocas isn't what it used to be, but so far the new arrivals have mainly just brought more international flavor and a broader range of lodging, dining, entertainment, and activity possibilities. For now, backpackers and surfers can still find a bed for five bucks and a meal for $1.50, but those with more money to spend can stay in relatively luxurious surroundings and dine on surprisingly good Thai, Indian, Mexican, Italian, and other international cuisine.

Bocas's biggest shortcoming is the rain. Bocas is one of the wettest regions in Panama. The rain never completely stops, though the best chance of a dry visit are in the minidry seasons of September/October and February/March. Happily, that's during Bocas's low season, when prices are cheaper and everything less crowded. But as with the rest of Panama, even in the rainy season storms usually blow through quickly. Rainfall tends to be heaviest in December and July.

The islands are evolving rapidly from a great backpackers' secret into a more upscale destination. Two bits of advice for those contemplating a visit: 1) Hurry and visit while they still have that quirky, rustic Bocas charm and beauty, and 2) do your part to make sure they always do.

PLANNING YOUR TIME

Given both the area's remoteness and its many attractions, getting anything out of Bocas requires a bare-minimum stay of two nights. Three or four is better. There is enough to keep visitors happy for a full week, especially since the Caribbean heat and pace of life has a tendency to slow even hyperactive types down and make significant hammock time seem pretty appealing.

The **Archipiélago de Bocas del Toro** is only part of the province of Bocas del Toro, but it's the part that the great majority of visitors come to explore. The islands have far better accommodations, food, and attractions and a more pleasant climate than any of the mainland towns.

Most visitors stay in **Bocas town** on **Isla Colón.** Everyone has to at least pass through Bocas town, since it has the only airport in the archipelago, and water taxis from the mainland come only here. (It's easy to make day trips from the islands to mainland destinations, though visitors to Wekso Ecolodge and Center should consider spending one night at the lodge.)

Note: Here's where the names start getting confusing. The town, the archipelago, and the province share the same name, often shortened simply to "Bocas." And just to really mess you up, the whole of Isla Colón is sometimes referred to as "Isla Bocas."

The other commonly visited islands in the archipelago are east of Isla Colón, which is the point of departure to all of them. The services diminish the father east one goes. **Isla Carenero** is the second-most developed island, and it's just a few minutes by boat from Isla Colón. The western tip of **Isla Bastimentos** has the second-biggest town in the archipelago, **Old Bank.** Most of the rest of the island, the largest in the archipelago, is sparsely populated, but its natural attractions draw many visitors. **Isla Solarte,** though

ARCHIPIÉLAGO DE BOCAS DEL TORO

Caribbean Sea

NORTH SHORE BEACHES

PARQUE NACIONAL MARINO ISLA BASTIMENTOS

Playa Segunda
Playa Larga
Red Frog Beach
Playa Primera

Punta Vieja

Cayos Zapatillas

Cayo de Agua

Quebrada de Sai

CAYO CRAWL

Isla Bastimentos

Isla Popa

Punta Laurel

Old Bank

Isla Solarte

Cerro Brujo

Laguna de Chiriquí

SWAN'S CAY

Isla Colón

LA GRUTA

DUMPS
PAUNCH
Isla Carenero
Bocas

LAGUNA BOCATORITO

Isla Cristóbal

Playa Bluff

Boca del Drago

Bahía de Almirante

Darkland Peninsula

CHIRIQUÍ GRANDE – ALMIRANTE RD

To Chiriquí Grande and David

Humedales de San San Pondsack

Canal de Soropta

Almirante

Río Changuinola

To Changuinola and El Silencio

Bosque Protector de Palo Seco

Río Changuinola

5 mi

5 km

0
0

© AVALON TRAVEL PUBLISHING, INC.

WATER QUALITY

Bocas del Toro is one of the few places in Panama that can't depend on safe drinking water coming out of the tap. It's been a source of contention, with *bocatoreños* citing it as an example of how the central government neglects this remote province, which despite the tourism boom remains one of the poorest in Panama. Protests, including violent confrontations in 2000 and 2004, have flared up in the province for more than a decade over the need for new waterworks as well as improved schools, roads, bridges, hospitals and schools. It doesn't help that the aging infrastructure is occasionally damaged by earthquakes in this seismically active area, and pretty much annually by floods during the rainy season.

Even on the islands, with their developing tourist infrastructure, water remains iffy. Modernization efforts began in 1999, and the water is now allegedly safe, but it still tastes bad. In late 2003, a water outage left Isla Colón and Isla Carenero dry. When the water started flowing again, it was murky. As for mainland Bocas, residents were promised in 2000 that a new water system was on the way. They're still waiting for it.

Some establishments on the island still filter their water. Consider erring on the side of caution and bring a water purifier, use purification tablets, or buy bottled water. Local shops sell water for about $1 a liter. Avoid the temptation to rely on beer as a thirst quencher, as that's a great way to get dehydrated in this hot, sweaty climate.

---

it starts just 10 minutes by boat from Isla Colón, still mainly draws visitors just to Hospital Point, a snorkeling/diving spot at its western tip. The other islands are more remote and still largely undeveloped. So far only Isla Colón has cars, and even it has very few.

Those who want to cover a lot of ground or have any kind of nightlife should probably stay in Bocas town or Isla Carenero. Most of the tour operators and inter-island water taxis are based in Bocas town, which also has the only water-taxi services to the mainland, not to mention the archipelago's only airport. Carenero is so close to Bocas town it's actually easier and quicker to get to and from town from there than it is from other parts of Isla Colón.

Getting back and forth to Bocas town from other parts of Isla Colón and the other islands can easily become time-consuming and expensive, though some hotel packages in the more remote areas include daily trips. Those staying in the remote parts of Bastimentos should plan on spending most of their time in that general area, as Bocas town is a long boat ride away. One strategy would be to stay in Bocas town for part of the time and include a night or two in a more distant spot before or afterward.

The first two days could include boat tours to the islands' most popular destinations: **Swan's Cay, Boca del Drago, Hospital Point, Crawl Cay, Cayos Zapatillas, Red Frog Beach,** and **Laguna Bocatorito.** These trips generally include snorkeling and lunch stops. Afternoons and evenings are the best time to explore Bocas town, which is generally dead during the day; many restaurants are even closed for lunch. The restaurants and few nightspots start to wake up as the sun goes down. It's also easy to arrange a night turtle-watching trip to **Playa Bluff** during nesting season.

A third day could be used to explore the islands more thoroughly. This could be a good time to move bases to someplace out of Bocas town. Things to do on Isla Colón include a forest hike, a trip to the eastern beaches, or a trip across the island with a stop at **La Gruta.** One could easily spend a full day or two exploring Bastimentos, including Old Bank, the northern beaches, **Quebrada de Sal,** and the interior forest, caves, and lake. **Playa Larga** is the place to watch sea turtles at night during nesting season.

The above time estimates don't factor in time for surfing or scuba diving, so surfers and divers should plan extra time for that or cut out some of the excursions. Throughout the archipelago, the great beaches and pounding surf tend to be on the north side of the islands, where there's nothing but ocean until Jamaica. Generally the sea is too rough for safe swimming. The water tends to be glassy on the southern side of the islands and in sheltered bays on the eastern sides. Here's where the good snorkeling is.

That covers the top draws of the islands. A fourth day could be a time to explore the mainland's attractions, including **Wekso Ecolodge and Center (Proyecto ODESEN), San San Pondsack,** and the **Canal de Soropta.** Wekso requires a full day and preferably an overnight stay. This can be combined with a visit to San San Pondsack and a trip down the canal on the way back.

Those with plenty of time to spend could consider branching out still farther. Possibilities include an all-day boat trip out to **Isla Escudo de Veraguas** (between August and October, the only time when the seas are calm enough), a hike on the **Darkland Peninsula (Tierra Oscura),** or **Peninsula Valiente.** These trips generally require planning and skilled guides.

High season on the islands is December–April. Prices are higher then and everything is more crowded; some places get booked up. But weather in Bocas is best during the minidry seasons of September–October and February–March. Turtles nest on the beaches from about March to October. In other words, if all the planets align correctly, those who visit between September and October may find lower prices, fewer people, dry weather, and some busy turtles.

Don't forget to factor in the time needed to get to and from Bocas, which is still quite isolated from the rest of Panama. The quickest way is to fly from Panama City to Isla Colón or, for the few who are more interested in exploring the mainland than the islands, to Changuinola. The flight takes less than an hour.

Getting to Bocas by land is a much longer affair, though there are now good roads and frequent bus service. A road leads east from the Sixaola-Guabito border crossing with Costa Rica to Changuinola and Almirante, the jumping-off points to the archipelago.

A new road links Almirante with Chiriquí Grande and from there to the rest of Panama. The building of this road has greatly diminished the importance of Chiriquí Grande; there is no longer any water-taxi service from there to the islands, and no reason for travelers to visit it. Outside of Chiriquí Grande, the Fortuna Road heads south over the Continental Divide and to the Interamericana (Interamerican Highway). This is the road link between Bocas and the rest of Panama.

HISTORY

When Christopher Columbus sailed into what is now Bahía Almirante in 1502, on his fourth and final voyage, he likely would have found a land long settled by several indigenous peoples. Columbus barely mentions the area, however, and he soon pushed on east with his worm-eaten ships and exhausted, demoralized crew. One of the few things that seems to have interested him here were natives wearing large gold discs around their necks, who told him there were rich gold fields on the mainland. Today's indigenous peoples still talk of lost gold mines in the remote highlands.

It's often said that Columbus gave the Bocas islands and other geographical features their names, but there is no evidence of this. It appears they were later named in his honor, such as Isla Colón (i.e., "Columbus Island"), Isla Cristóbal ("Christopher Island") and Bahía Almirante ("Admiral's Bay"). Columbus does refer to a place called Bastimentos, but this is believed to be the name he gave to Nombre de Dios in eastern Panama.

The earliest evidence of habitation on the coast and along the river valleys dates from 600 B.C. For years the best-known archaeological site was Cerro Brujo on Peninsula Aguacate, an oddly shaped peninsula that juts out between Isla Cristóbal and Isla Popa. It appears to have been a small village whose inhabitants subsisted on farming and fishing, including the hunting of manatees. But in 2002 archaeologists discovered evidence of what appears to have been a large and culturally sophisticated settlement at Boca del Drago on Isla Colón. They believe it was occupied A.D. 900–1150. Excavation is ongoing and the significance of the site is still being determined.

During the days of Spanish exploration and conquest, the Naso people, also known as the Térraba or Teribe, appear to have been the dominant group, living by the rivers of the mainland, along the coast of Bahía Almirante, and even as far north as Isla Colón. Today they are barely hanging on, with a population of just 3,800 in Panama and a few hundred over the border in Costa Rica. They are now vastly outnumbered by the Ngöbe-Buglé, the largest indigenous group not just in Bocas but in all of Panama. Tiny populations of Bri Bri and Bokota also remain.

Pressure from the Spanish, tribal warfare, and the introduction of European diseases decimated the indigenous populations. Some, including the Dorasque, were wiped out altogether.

But unlike in other parts of Panama, the Spanish never consolidated their hold on Bocas del Toro. That allowed the incursion of enterprising pirates and traders from England and other countries, the beginning of the international mix the region retains to this day. Early traders dealt in such items as the shell of the hawksbill turtle and coconut, but bananas eventually became the region's most important commodity.

The descendants of English-speaking Afro-Caribbean immigrants are among the longest-established residents of the islands. The earliest of these were brought over as slaves by English traders, but later arrivals came to work for the banana companies. Most trace their ancestry to Jamaica and the Colombian-owned Caribbean islands of San Andrés and Providencia. They are still a dominant cultural force in both Bocas town and, especially, Old Bank on Isla Bastimentos, where Guari-Guari, a Bocas-specific variety of so-called Panamanian Creole English, is still widely spoken.

The banana business began to take off in Bocas toward the end of the 19th century, attracting American and German planters. In 1899 the giant United Fruit Company (now known as Chiquita Brands International; the local division is called the Bocas Fruit Company) took over the whole show. It established its headquarters in Bocas town, which was founded in 1826 but until that point

was a sleepy village. The company built a hospital on the tip of Isla Solarte, an isolated area now known as Hospital Point, to quarantine patients with infectious diseases such as yellow fever and malaria. The hospital is long gone, but a headquarters building the company constructed in 1905 became Hotel Bahía, which was recently renovated but retains a few reminders of its history, such as the huge safe in its office.

The early 20th century was a boom time for Bocas del Toro. Bocas town became a hub for international commerce and one of the most important "cities" in Panama. It was prosperous enough to attract foreign consulates and support three (by some counts five) newspapers.

The islands' prosperity didn't last long, however. A fungus wilt that came to be known as Panama disease decimated the banana plantations on the islands and coastline. The company was forced to shift its operations to the mainland, to the area between the Changuinola and Sixaola Rivers, and over the border into Costa Rica. By 1920 the importance of the islands had declined dramatically. Even the hospital was shut down, as it was too far a trek for company employees on the mainland. The mainland banana plantations continue to thrive, however, and are still owned by Chiquita.

The province saw a few other notable events in the 20th century, including some grim ones. In 1902 it was a scene of a battle in the Thousand Days War, a Colombian civil war fought mostly in Panama (at that time still part of Colombia). And in 1921, Costa Rica occupied Guabito and Almirante as part of a border dispute with Panama. The United States put an end to both these conflicts.

In 1904 a fire in Bocas town, then as now built mostly of wood, destroyed an estimated 160 buildings. Three other major fires followed in the next 25 years.

The province is one of the most seismically active parts of Panama. On April 22, 1991, the border area between Costa Rica and Panama was struck by an earthquake measuring 7.5 on the Richter scale that was felt as far away as El Salvador. Costa Rica was hardest hit, but Bocas del Toro suffered greatly. The earthquake killed two dozen people in the province, injured hundreds more, and left thousands homeless. Changuinola and Almirante, on the mainland, sustained most of the damage.

For most of the 20th century, though, Bocas remained a rather placid place. It has long been seen in Panama as a backwater province, and it still feels culturally and geographically quite separate from the rest of the country. It is now experiencing its second major boom, though this time the lucrative crops are tourists and retirees rather than bananas.

Isla Colón

By far the most developed island in the archipelago is Isla Colón, and by far the most developed part of Isla Colón is the town of Bocas del Toro, at the southeast tip of this large (61 square kilometers) island. Bocas town is nearly an island in its own right; it's connected to the rest of Isla Colón by a causeway.

Almost all the archipelago's hotels, restaurants, tour outfits, and visitor services are in Bocas town. Most of the action is on either side of Calle 3, the broad main street that runs along the water's edge on the east side of town. The busiest section extends from the town plaza, Parque Bolívar, down to the ferry pier. The area west of Calle 3 is mainly residential, as is the section on the northwest waterfront, which is known locally as "Saigon."

Bocas town is laid out in a grid pattern, with numbered streets running more-or-less north to south and lettered avenues running more-or-less west to east. But the streets aren't well marked and there isn't even universal agreement on which road is which: the avenues above Avenida D are called different things on different maps. Fortunately, the town is small enough it's hard to get lost.

A road leads north out of town, past the fairgrounds, where the annual Feria Internacional del Mar is held, and over a causeway. The road forks north of town. The east fork heads up the east coast of the main island, becoming increasingly rough but leading to the island's best beaches. The west fork leads to a road that cuts diagonally across the island. About halfway along the road is La Gruta, a cave popular with those into bats. The road dead-ends at Boca del Drago, a little beach area on the northwest side of the island about 14 kilometers from Bocas town.

Several of the sights on and around Isla Colón are most easily—or only—accessible by boat. A typical boat tour includes Swan's Cay and Boca del Drago. For an extra fee it's often easy to add a quick cruise up the Canal de Soropta, which is close to Boca del Drago. Trips to Laguna Bocatorito (Dolphin Bay) are generally arranged as a separate tour.

Except for those who bring a car over by ferry, which is not worth it for most people, getting around on land requires hiring a taxi, renting a bike, or hoofing it. The east coast beaches are easily accessible by bike, depending on road conditions. Crossing the island to La Gruta or Boca del Drago by bike is more of a workout.

Isla Colón has forests and other caves to explore, but don't attempt this without a knowledgeable guide. Night trips to turtle-nesting spots are popular during nesting season, from about March to September. Just wandering around little Bocas town night or day can be a colorful experience in multicultural people-watching. Be sure to venture beyond Calle 3 to get a feel for the nontouristy parts of town.

Attractions on or around other islands, such as Cayo Crawl and Cayos Zapatillas, are discussed elsewhere in the chapter, though trips to most of these are generally easily arranged in Bocas town.

SIGHTS
Isla Colón Beaches

There are no real beaches in Bocas town, and the waterfront is too busy to make wading in the water here much fun. True beaches start north of the causeway, on the main part of Isla Colón. The best beaches start about a 15-minute drive from town up the east coast. The surf is too rough to land boats anywhere along this part of the island. You can bike to them, but the rocky dirt road gets a bit rough in places. The land along the coast has been gobbled up in the last few years, mostly by gringos building dream homes, so you may also have to contend with construction equipment along the road. A taxi may be the best bet. Expect to pay about $10 round-trip to get to the best beaches, near the end of the road. Arrange for a time to be picked up and don't pay until the driver returns. Taxis don't cruise this strip looking for passengers, so without previous arrangements, walking or hitching would be the only way back.

The nicest beach is **Playa Bluff,** about a 25-minute drive from town. It's absolutely gorgeous and often deserted during the week. This is also an important nesting site for endangered sea turtles. The surf can get rough here and is usually too dangerous for swimming, though it's a good spot for surfers. At the time of writing, the road ended at a stream just past Playa Bluff, after which the only way farther up the coast was by foot. About an hour hike away is **La Piscina** (the swimming

pool), a protected lagoon on the north side of the island. If you go without a guide, ask for directions at Rancho Paraíso, on Playa Bluff.

La Gruta

Halfway across the island on the road to Boca del Drago is La Gruta ("the cavern"), home to zillions of bats. It's at the little settlement of Colonia Santeña, near the Coca-Cola sign. There's a little store there that sells drinks. If your idea of fun is to wade through guano in a claustrophobic cave and inhale disease-carrying particulates, then by all means walk through the thing. The rest of us will be happy with a snapshot of the highly photogenic entrance to the cave, a green grotto with a little statue of the Virgin standing guard. Round-trip taxi fare from Bocas town should be about $10.

Boca del Drago

This is another popular beach area, mainly because it's easily accessible by boat. It lies on the

A FEW WORDS OF ADVICE

The archipelago is a friendly, mellow place, and reports of violent crime are rare. But the increase in tourism has brought an increase in petty theft. Don't leave valuables unattended on beaches, particularly near the surf spots on the north side of Bastimentos.

I've also heard a report of at least one robbery at the ATMs in Bocas town. Use caution when withdrawing money at night. Though I haven't been able to verify it, several people have told me about a machete killing outside El Encanto, a fairly rough bar in Bocas town. This was allegedly the result of a feud among residents, but treat dive bars in the archipelago with as much caution as you would those back home. Be respectful, and certainly don't look for a fight.

Land scams have been a problem in Bocas. Be skeptical of great deals on beachfront property or get-rich-quick teak- and noni-plantation schemes. Establishing land ownership is tricky in Bocas, Panamanian land-use laws are complicated, and successful tropical forestry requires a great deal more knowledge and hard work than many think. Do plenty of research and get legal and technical

advice from trustworthy sources before buying. As always, if it seems too good to be true, it is. Locals like to share stories about the unfortunates who "bought" a chunk of paradise that turned out to be in a cemetery. Just how extreme and unscrupulous real-estate fever can get became clear on my last visit, when a sketchy-looking guy sidled up to me and muttered, "Property. I've got property, grass." A true Bocas original: a combination drug dealer and real-estate agent.

The water tends to be so placid in Bocas it's easy to get casual about boat safety. But the sea can get rough, especially on the north side of the islands, and the distances between the islands can be deceptively great. Never go on a boat trip of any length without a life jacket. Be especially cautious at night, since few boats have lights. Some places on the islands let visitors tool around in *cayucos* (traditional dugout canoes). This is fun, but they're surprisingly easy to flip so watch out.

All these warnings aside, the only dangers most visitors will have to worry about are a bit too much sun and an impulse to stay in Bocas forever.

northwest side of the island. Boca del Drago is also the name of the canal separating this part of Isla Colón from the mainland. The water is tranquil, so landing a boat is not a problem; many of the island tours include a stop here. It's also possible to take a scenic drive across the island from Bocas town.

This beach isn't as nice as Bluff, but it's much better for swimming and splashing about. There are coral gardens close by that extend all along the west side of the island. The snorkeling can be decent, but the coral is not in great shape and the visibility isn't always the best.

There's now a biological field station and some cabins for rent, so Boca del Drago is not as isolated as it used to be, but it's still a mellow place.

There's a little thatch-roofed, sand-floored seafood restaurant on the beach called **Restaurante Yarisnori** (tel. 615-5580, 8 A.M.–6:30 P.M. Wed.–Mon., closed Tues.). The mixed ceviche is pretty good. Other items include red snapper, shrimp, octopus, lobster, and prawns. Most dishes cost around $9. Through the restaurant you can rent a small boat for $5, a pedal boat for $3.50, or snorkel gear for $6 all day.

Access to Boca del Drago is by boat or car. There's one road that extends across the island from Bocas town to Boca del Drago, about 14 kilometers away. A round-trip taxi ride costs around $25, including a stop at La Gruta for those interested. Water taxis from Bocas Marine and Tours now stop at Boca del Drago several times a day on the way to and from Changuinola. Those who time it right can get a ride to or from Bocas town, or both.

© WILLIAM FRIAR

A skilled boatman can slip through a narrow passage on Swan's Cay—if he times it right.

Swan's Cay

A standard boat tour around Isla Colón includes a stop at lovely Swan's Cay, a craggy rock that juts out of the ocean north of the island, about a half hour by motorboat from Bocas. It's so impossibly picturesque that when an acquaintance saw it he said it looked like it was designed by Disney. Swan's Cay is also called **Isla de los Pájaros** (Bird Island) for reasons that become obvious when you visit it. Most notably, it's the only known nesting grounds in Panama for the red-billed trop-

icbird, an elegant white bird with tail feathers about a meter long. Do not disturb the birds by walking on the island; you can, however, snorkel around it. The current isn't too strong, but the water can get pretty churned up at times, creating a washing-machine effect that drastically reduces visibility.

The boatman may ask if you'd like him to motor through the narrow cleft in the western crag. It may not look it, but it's possible if the boatman times the waves right. It's a fun thing to do—you can see crabs scuttling along the rocky walls centimeters from the boat. Go for it if you trust his boating skills.

Laguna Bocatorito

Otherwise know as **Dolphin Bay,** this lagoon, formed by the east side of Isla Cristóbal and an odd-shaped peninsular blob that juts from the mainland, starts about 10 kilometers south of Isla Colón. A labyrinth of shallow channels

SEA TURTLES

Four species of endangered sea turtles find Bocas as attractive as the tourists do: the hawksbill (*Eretmochelys imbricata*), leatherback (*Dermochelys coriacea*), green (*Chelonia mydas*), and loggerhead (*Caretta caretta*). Most lay their eggs on the beaches between March and October.

Night trips to the beach are popular during nesting season. The most accessible site is Playa Bluff on the east side of Isla Colón. Other good places are Playa Larga on Isla Bastimentos and the Cayos Zapatillas. An important spot on the mainland is the strip of coast between the mouth of the Río Changuinola and Peninsula Soropta, just across from Boca del Drago. Sometimes called Playa Changuinola, it's part of the protected wetlands of San San Pondsack.

Female turtles lay eggs several times in a season. The incubation period lasts about 60 days. Only one in 1,000 to 10,000 baby turtles survives to adulthood.

Only the leatherbacks and hawksbill are easy to find. Few greens nest in Bocas; those that do come from about June to August, their numbers peaking in July. Loggerheads rarely nest anywhere in the tropics. When they're spotted, it's usually as they're swimming by.

Bocas was once the most important nesting ground in the Caribbean for the relatively small hawksbill (about a meter long, up to 80 kilograms), especially on the remote Playa Chiriquí, a vast beach on the mainland east of Peninsula Valiente. They nest from June to October, peaking in August and September. Hawksbills (*carey* in Spanish) are what first drew traders to Bocas. Because they're prized for their meat and shell, their populations are critically endangered worldwide. Most that come to the islands nest on the Cayos Zapatillas.

The enormous leatherbacks, known locally as the *baula* or *canal,* are the largest of all sea turtles (up to 2.5 meters and 900 kilograms). They nest from March to June, peaking in April and May. Though most numerous on Playa Chiriquí, believed to be the most important leatherback rookery in Central America, they nest on beaches throughout the archipelago and coast.

Turtles are legally protected, but enforcement is lax and they're still poached for their meat, eggs, and shells. Even the leatherback, which lacks a valuable hard shell and palatable meat, is hunted for its eggs. Monitoring teams from the Institute for Tropical Ecology and Conservation, which has a field station in Boca del Drago, have investigated the annual slaughter of 30–40 leatherbacks on the mainland beach near the mouth of the Río Changuinola. Poachers slit off the flippers of the female turtles to make it easier to turn them over, gut them to remove their eggs, and leave them to die slowly on the beach, which is part of a nominally protected area.

Eating turtle eggs and meat is illegal, as is possessing anything made of tortoiseshell. But there are more subtle ways to harm the turtles.

Pollution is a threat to turtles. Even a floating plastic bag can choke to death a giant leatherback, which can't distinguish between it and jellyfish, its sole source of food.

Do not use flashlights, take flash photos, or even wear light-colored clothing near nesting spots. This can scare away nesting females or disorient baby turtles trying to make it to the sea.

Stay out of sight while the turtles lay their eggs. Never touch them, which disturbs them and can be dangerous—some have strong jaws and a nasty bite.

Don't handle eggs or disturb the nests. This can introduce bacteria or damage the eggs.

To ensure a responsible visit and support conservation efforts, go with qualified local guides.

formed by mangroves screens its northern entrance, helping to make it a kind of giant natural aquarium, six kilometers across at its widest. Day trips to Laguna Bocatorito are popular because of the possibility of spotting bottle-nosed dolphins close up. The best chance of seeing them is from June to July, when rough seas drive them into the calm waters of the bay. They tend to hang around an unusually long time, which isn't surprising when one considers what a smorgasbord the bay offers them: The mangroves act like a kind of net, drawing fish into the bay. There's a small town, also called Bocatorito, on the east side of Isla Cristóbal, but there's not much there.

An unusual place to stop for a bite or a drink near Laguna Bocatorito is **Restaurante El Morro,** a simple restaurant built around a rock right in the middle of the channel between the east side of Isla Popa and Isla Cayo de Agua. It was being renovated when I last visited. The little rock in the center is covered with philodendrons and can be climbed—there's a little *rancho* perched on top. Other, thatched-covered dining *ranchos* are built at the end of walkways leading off from the rock, like spokes jutting from a wheel. This area has some of the better snorkeling around. The visibility isn't great, but the coral fields are pretty. They get healthier and more abundant the farther out you go into the channel (watch out for boats). The best ones are too far away to swim from the restaurant—have your boatman explore a bit.

Canal de Soropta

If you're looking for a break from the beaches and snorkeling, a boat trip up the Canal de Soropta, on the mainland east of the town of Changuinola, is an interesting off-the-beaten-track jaunt. The 12-kilometer canal was built in 1903 by Michael T. Snyder, a pioneering plantation owner, to shelter his banana barges from the open sea on their way between the mainland and the islands. Sometimes referred to as the Changuinola Canal, it parallels the coastline from the mouth of the Río Changuinola to Almirante Bay.

When the canal was bordered by forest on either side it was a prime birding spot. Unfortunately, slash-and-burn farmers and cattle ranchers have cut away much of the forest in recent years. But it still attracts quite an array of birds. Manatees are occasionally spotted here as well. It makes for a tranquil jungle cruise, though the boats motoring up and down the canal probably don't make the local fauna very happy; at least ask the boatman to take it slow.

It takes about a half hour by boat to reach the entrance to the canal from Bocas town. Heading all the way up to the Río Changuinola takes about 45 minutes at a leisurely pace, but you don't have to go that far to get a good look at the wildlife that's left; there are tons of birds at the very entrance of the canal. Early morning or late afternoon is the best time to go. You may want to include this as part of an Isla Colón tour, since the entrance to the canal is just opposite Boca del Drago. Expect to pay an extra charge, but agree on a price ahead of time.

The Canal de Soropta, dug in 1903 for banana barges, makes for a scenic day tour.

ENTERTAINMENT AND EVENTS

Part of the charm of Bocas del Toro is that there's so little to do besides splash around in the water or laze in a hammock. In the daytime, Bocas town is more or less deserted, since most visitors are out snorkeling, boating, surfing, and so on. Things liven up a bit in the evening, though the action is more or less confined to the restaurants and bars.

The epicenter of Bocas nightlife, at least for visitors, is **El Barco Hundido** (Calle 1 between Avenida E and F, near Cable and Wireless), a fun and funky bar whose name, Spanish for "shipwreck," comes from the sunken boat just offshore. Some people call it the Wreck Deck. The bar is an open-sided wooden patio with a view of the *barco hundido,* which is illuminated at night. Semicompetent DJs spin on busy nights, and there's actually dancing. The bar doesn't serve food, but entrepreneurs set up stands outside the place and grill burgers and meat on a stick on big nights.

A centerpiece of the place is a floating deck moored to the bar. It's perched precariously on top of canoes— a *piragua* and two *cayucos*—that serve as pontoons. When the owner is in the mood, he sometimes takes this unwieldy party craft for a cruise; it's perfectly possible to be hanging out and drinking some night and suddenly find yourself motoring away from the bar. I've heard tales that this thing has been taken insanely long distances, including as far as Costa Rica and Isla Escudo de Veraguas, with the party in full swing. It's an absolutely nutty thing to do—not to mention dangerous—but quite believable given the character that runs this place.

The **Buena Vista Bar and Grill** (Calle 1 between Avenida C and Avenida D, tel. 757-9035, 10 A.M.–9:30 P.M. Wed.–Sun., closed Mon. and Tues.) remains a popular hangout, especially for gringos. Older visitors would tend to feel most comfortable here.

El Encanto (Calle 3 between Avenida A and Avenida B) is a rougher and basic locals bar and can be rather intimidating. It's definitely a place to get up close and personal with residents, but use the same caution you would at any tough

dive back home. And bring earplugs, because the music is played at ear-bleeding volume.

The place to be on Monday nights is Cantina La Feria, in Old Bank on Isla Bastimentos, for its **Blue Monday** party. (See *Entertainment and Events* under *Isla Bastimentos* for information.)

The biggest annual party in Bocas is the **Feria Internacional del Mar** (international festival of the sea), held for about four days in the second half of September (dates vary). It can feature such activities as a beauty contest, boat races, fireworks, volleyball and other games, various cultural events and displays, and, of course, lots of drinking and dancing.

For the last few years, Al Natural Resort on Isla Bastimentos has thrown an all-night **New Year's Eve beach party** in which, for a quite reasonable price, the staff provides boat transportation, refreshments, and DJs who are flown down from overseas for the occasion. Everyone eventually crashes wherever he or she likes. Those planning to be in Bocas on the New Year's holiday should contact Al Natural for details and reservations.

Other celebrations include:

May 1—**Palo de Mayo.** Maypole dance in Bocas town and Isla Bastimentos.

July 16—**Dia de la Virgen del Carmen.** Parade in honor of the patron saint of Isla Colón. **La Peregrinación a la Gruta,** a pilgrimage to the virgin's shrine at La Gruta, halfway across the island, takes place on the following Sunday.

October 12—**Columbus Day.** Though the date commemorates Columbus's discovery of America in 1492, Bocas has borrowed it to remember his visit to the archipelago in 1502.

November 16—**Founding Day** of the province of Bocas del Toro.

SHOPPING

A **souvenir stand** at the north end of Calle 3 has some cheap jewelry and *molas.* Oddly, it doesn't sell any Ngöbe-Buglé crafts. There are other souvenir stands around the town park.

Panchama (in the same building as Starfish Coffee on Calle 3, open during the day except 12:30–3 P.M. Tues.–Sat., closed Sun. and Mon.) sells some unusual crafts. Organic chocolate bars

Bocas del Toro

TREAD LIGHTLY

Bocas del Toro is one of the loveliest parts of Panama, and it's still relatively unspoiled. The protected areas of the mainland include a large chunk of the enormous Parque Internacional La Amistad and the buffer forest that surrounds it, as well as the wetlands of San San Pondsack. The islands are home to an important national park, Parque Nacional Marino Isla Bastimentos. Bocas is a crucial link in the Mesoamerican Biological Corridor that extends from southern Mexico to eastern Panama.

Even the unprotected parts of the province are still largely undeveloped. Most of the land remains covered with forest, including primary evergreen forests with century-old trees that soar above 30 meters. The hundreds of animal and thousands of plant and insect species here include many that are endangered and some that are found nowhere else on earth.

But Bocas del Toro is under increasing human pressure.

For decades the main disrupters of the environment were vast banana plantations. These were created by clearing forests and wetlands and kept alive through the unregulated use of pesticides, fungicides, and fertilizers to which workers were exposed and which ran off into the rivers and sea.

Now other troubling developments are coming to Bocas, and coming fast. New roads are allowing the incursion of subsistence farmers and cattle ranchers to formerly inaccessible areas. A vivid example of the rapid deforestation that follows can be seen along the new Chiriquí Grande-Almirante highway, where lush evergreen forests are already disappearing. The waters are also being over-fished, with lobster in particular locally threatened. The national mania for teak farming has spread to Bocas; there have been reports of acres of diverse, species-rich native trees being illegally cut down to plant this non-native tree, which local wildlife has little use for as a habitat. And there is a strong push to dam the powerful mainland rivers, which have the highest hydroelectric potential in the country but which run through land that is home both to indigenous peoples and important ecosystems.

But on the islands at least, the greatest human impact is caused by tourists and resident expatriates. Seeing tourism come to an area as relatively untouched as Bocas del Toro always provokes mixed feelings. It's so easy to destroy what attracts people to a place like this in the first place. But ecologically sensitive tourism might, with luck, help preserve its natural beauty and maybe even help its people.

made by the local **Caribbean Chocolate Company** are also sold in the store and a few other spots around town. A 100-gram bar sells for $2. It's crumbly, intense, and delicious.

Artesanias Bri-Bri Emanuel (Calle 3 between Avenida B and Avenida C, tel. 757-9652, 10 A.M.–8 P.M. Mon.–Sat., closed Sun.), right across the street from Bocas Marine and Tours, carries Ngöbe-Buglé crafts such as traditional dresses and handbags, as well as a variety of trinkets and figurines.

SPORTS AND RECREATION

Few leave the archipelago without taking at least one boat tour, which is by far the most popular outdoor activity. These tours usually include snorkeling, but those not interested in that can just splash around in the water or sun themselves on the boat or the beach during snorkeling stops. Scuba diving and surfing are also popular, and as tourism takes off in Bocas more and more outfitters with more and more toys are showing up. Though of interest to just a minority of visitors, forest hikes and camping are also possible.

Nearly all the guides and outfitters in the archipelago are in Bocas town, and most of these are found along Calle 3.

Diving and Snorkeling

Diving and snorkeling in Bocas can be good, but those with a lot of experience in the Caribbean may not find it as spectacular as other parts of the Caribbean. Several rivers empty into the sea here, so visibility tends to be 15 meters on a good day, 22 meters on an excellent day, and less than three meters when I visit. It's a good place for beginning divers and snorkelers because

A few suggestions:

1. Do not touch coral. Coral is alive and can take years to recover from even minimal contact.

2. Hire local boatmen and guides. This offers them an alternative to fishing and hunting and gives the local community a stake in preserving their surroundings.

3. Stay at small, low-impact places such as the environmentally friendly Al Natural.

4. Team up with others for boat tours. It saves money and lessens the disturbance caused by boats that motor through the same popular spots day after day.

5. Do not take "souvenirs" of any kind from the beaches or forests.

6. Stick to established trails.

7. Do not eat sea turtle meat or eggs, or any other endangered species. For one thing, it's illegal. But avoid lobster as well, which is over-fished and endangered. There are more decent vegetarian alternatives on the islands than in most parts of Panama.

8. Buy indigenous handicrafts, if possible directly from the makers.

9. Visit community-development projects such as Proyecto ODESEN (the Wekso Ecolodge and Center).

10. Consider a donation to legitimate projects. U.S. residents can make a tax-deductible contribution to the non-profit Nature Conservancy, which works with Wekso and several other projects in Panama: The Nature Conservancy, Attn: Treasury, 4245 N. Fairfax Drive, Suite100, Arlington, VA 22203, tel. 800/628-6860, comment@tnc.org. http://nature.org.

11. Report poaching or signs of environmental destruction to ANAM (tel. 757-9244 in Bocas town, tel. 758-6603 in Changuinola). If enough visitors complain it may have an impact. The non-profit ANCON runs a hotline, *La Linea Verde,* for reporting endangered animals in need of rescue. The number in Panama City is tel. 314-0060.

12. Not littering should go without saying. But consider picking up and packing out trash left by others.

---

there's so much calm, accessible water and lots to explore at shallow depths.

Bocas has extensive coral and sponge gardens that are easy for even novice snorkelers to explore. There is also more challenging cave, wall, and wreck diving for experienced scuba divers. Popular spots include **Hospital Point,** the **Cayos Zapatillas, Cayo Crawl,** and **Cristóbal Light** (a reef marked by a navigation light on the north side of Isla Cristóbal). A **ferry boat wreck** is off the tip of Bocas town, and nurse sharks can sometimes be spotted there. More ambitious spots include **Cayos Tigre (Tiger Rock),** off the north tip of Peninsula Valiente more than 40 kilometers southeast of Bocas town, and **Isla Escudo de Veraguas,** which is more than twice that far away. Dive operators sometimes offer trips to Cayos Tigre, but a trip to Escudo de Veraguas is a major undertaking and the sea is too rough to attempt

it much of the year. For other spots, see the dive-site maps on the website of Bocas Water Sports (www.bocaswatersports.com).

The best snorkeling tends to be in the placid, protected waters on the south side of the islands. The north sides are open to the sea and pounding surf. Because of this, the most satisfying spots for snorkelers tend to be Hospital Point and the area near Cayo Crawl, which are quite calm and have lots to see near the surface. There's also some snorkeling between **Boca del Drago** and **Big Bight** on the west side of Isla Colón, but the coral isn't that healthy and the visibility can be poor.

Two well-established groups offered scuba-diving trips and courses at the time of writing.

Bocas Water Sports (Calle 3 and Avenida A, near the ferry dock, tel./fax 757-9541, bws@bocaswatersports.com, www.bocaswatersports.com)

offers two-tank, two-site dives for $50 per person, including everything but lunch. The trip lasts all day and includes a stop at one of the Crawl Cay restaurants. Snorkelers can come on the same trip for $15, including equipment.

The company also offers PADI scuba classes ranging from a half-day Discover Scuba course ($65) to multiday, advanced certification courses. Instruction is in English or Spanish. It can arrange package deals with local hotels.

Starfleet Eco Adventures (Calle 1 next to the Buena Vista Bar and Grill, tel./fax 757-9630, scubastar@hotmail.com, www.explorepanama .com/starfleet.htm), under new management as of late 2004, offers two-tank, two-site dives for $50 per person. It's $10 more if a lunch stop and a dolphin-spotting visit to Laguna Boca-torito are thrown in. Snorkelers pay $20 per person, including equipment. PADI classes range from a half-day Discover Scuba course ($65) to advanced certification courses. The company can also help arrange accommodations.

Surfing

Bocas del Toro has good surfing, some of the best in the country. Waves are best from about December to March and least consistent from around August to October. There are three well-known breaks on Isla Colón, as well as some little-known, unnamed ones that local surfers still keep more or less to themselves. The three main spots, all of which are along the east coast, are listed below, in order of their distance from town. (See the *Isla Bastimentos* section and *Isla Carenero* in the *Beyond Colón and Bastimentos* section for information on other good breaks.)

Paunch (PUNCH) breaks left and right. It has long, "rippable" waves that are appropriate for all levels and attract beginners. It's a reef break, so wear booties.

Dumps (also known as Dumpers) is a reef-bottom left break with big tubes and short but dramatic rides. This is a dangerous break that should be attempted only by advanced surfers. Waves can get up to 3 meters. The reef is sharp, so wear booties. There's also an inner break known, logically enough, as **Inner Dumps.** It's another left-breaking, reef-bottom wave. It's faster and longer than the outside wave, but not as big.

Playa Bluff is, as has been mentioned elsewhere in the chapter, a gorgeous, several-kilometer-long beach at the end of the road, where the Rancho Paraíso surf resort is. It's a powerful beach break known for destroying surfboards. It features fast-breaking waves and long tubes. Kristian, the surfer who runs Rancho Paraíso, says the waves are best when they're no more than about 1–2 meters high. Even when the swell isn't big, the waves are too powerful for beginning surfers and swimmers.

Renting boards is an iffy proposition in Bocas, as they're not always available or in good shape. **Taller Joan Paul** (near the north end of Calle 5, 8 A.M.–6 P.M. daily), next to Casa Amarilla, rents them for $10 a day. **Tropix Surf** (Calle 3 between Avenida D and Avenida E, near the southwest end of the park, tel. 757-9727, 9 A.M.–noon and 3–7 P.M. daily) sells Tropix-brand surfboards made in Panama for $350–500. It also may rent boards eventually. The **bike/scooter rental stand** next to Douglas' Golden Grill on Calle 3 near Avenida E sometimes rents banged-up surfboards for $8 a day.

Mondo Taitú (north end of Calle 5, tel. 757-9425), because it's run by and offers accommodations for surfers, sometimes offers surfboard repair and dispenses surfing tips. The **Rancho Paraíso** (tel./fax 757-9415, info@ranchoparaiso.biz, www.ranchoparaiso.biz) surf resort on Playa Bluff rents surfboards and offers surf lessons.

Other Water Sports

Bocas Water Sports rents single kayaks for $3 an hour or $10 for a half day and double kayaks for $4 an hour or $12 for a half day. It also offers water-skiing for $25 for a half hour or $40 an hour (see *Diving and Snorkeling*). Hotel El Limbo on the Sea also rents sea kayaks.

Hiking

There are undeveloped forest trails on Isla Colón and other islands in the archipelago, but as usual only hike in the forest with a knowledgeable guide. Certainly don't hike alone. Be especially careful on any hike to Isla Popa, which is locally notorious for being infested with fer-de-lance snakes and other poisonous creatures. (Isla Bastimentos enjoys the best reputation among the snake-phobic; a species of nonaggressive coral snake with a mouth too small to be much threat to humans is the only known venomous snake on the island.)

A local forest guide who enjoys a strong reputation is **Oscar Gaslin.** He has been exploring the forests of Bocas since he was seven and has led jungle tours for more than a dozen years. He speaks English and Spanish and has worked with the cast and crew of several countries' *Survivor* TV series that have been shot on the islands. I haven't yet traveled with him, but a naturalist friend who knows the area well told me Oscar has an uncanny ability to find wildlife, especially snakes. He doesn't have a phone. Ask for him at Hospedaje Heike (tel. 757-9708) or ask around on Calle 9 for his house.

A typical half-day tour of Isla Colón takes people to two different primary forests to look for sloths and monkeys and includes a walk through La Gruta. His full-day tour typically takes guests to the northern tip of Isla Colón through primary forest and includes an exploration of three caves, including one that Indians supposedly called home 1,500 years ago. Neither tour is strenuous. The cost is $15 per person for a half-day tour, $40 minimum, or $20 per person for a full-day tour, $60 minimum. He also leads birding tours of the Darkland Peninsula (Tierra Oscura), which is south of Isla Cristóbal on the mainland, for $25 per person.

When I last visited Bocas, Oscar was thinking about offering five-day trips far up the Río Teribe to Palenque, the ancestral, long-abandoned homeland of the Naso. This would be a serious and very strenuous trek that even the Naso rarely attempt.

Tom and Ina Reichelt, the laid-back German couple who own Pension Tío Tom, offer nature tours of Isla Bastimentos, with a focus on hunting for frogs and exploring caves. (See the *Isla Bastimentos* section for information.)

Boat Tours

There is no shortage of boatmen offering tours of the islands and snorkeling spots. Usually these are organized as day trips with fairly standardized itineraries. A popular tour takes you around Isla Colón to Swan's Cay for bird-watching and snorkeling, stops for lunch at Boca del Drago, then

© WILLIAM FRIAR

Gallardo Livingston has offered boat tours to visitors for years.

Bocas del Toro

lets you snorkel some more down the west side of Isla Colón. Other trips go to the popular snorkeling spots of Cayo Crawl, Hospital Point, and/or Cayos Zapatillas; to the Bastimentos beaches; up the Changuinola Canal; and so on. A few also offer a tour around the waters of Laguna Bocatorito (Dolphin Bay) off Isla Cristóbal, where's there a chance of seeing bottle-nosed dolphins. Expect to pay about $15–20 per person. There's generally a minimum fee, so couples and singles often link up with others or let the tour operator organize groups.

Those planning to snorkel who don't have their own gear should make sure decent masks, snorkels, and fins are included. (A few places in town also rent snorkeling gear, including **Taller Joan Paul,** for $5 a day.)

Also, take a look at the boat before you seal the deal. Does it have life jackets, appear to be in good condition, and have a decent motor? (Some guidelines on horsepower: 75 hp will move you as fast as you're likely to want to go in these little boats, while 15 hp will give you a slow-motion leisure cruise. Time estimates in this chapter are based on a boat equipped with a 75-hp motor unless otherwise stated.)

Transparente Tours (Calle 3 near Avenida C, tel. 757-9915, transparentetours@hotmail.com, www.bocas.com) has offered snorkeling and sightseeing boat tours for several years. (It has joined forces with the competing J&J Tours, and it's sometimes listed as J&J Transparente.) Tours include Laguna Bocatorito (Dolphin Bay), Cayo Crawl, Hospital Point, and Red Frog Beach for $15 per person; Cayo Crawl, Punta Vieja, and the Zapatillas for $20 per person plus $10 per person marine-park admission; Boca del Drago and Swan's Cay or Canal de Soropta for $15; and Red Frog Beach, Hospital Point, and Old Bank for $7 per person. There's a six-person minimum on all these trips, but that doesn't mean you have to round up the full group yourself; as long as six total sign up, the trip will run. Tours start at 9:30 A.M. and return around 4:30–5:30 P.M. They include snorkeling equipment and an ice chest for any drinks/snacks guests bring.

Transparente also offers sport-fishing for $125 (half day) and $200 (full day), including fishing equipment and ice chest.

Bocas Water Sports and **Starfleet Eco Adventures,** though primarily scuba outfits, offer snorkeling trips for $15, including gear (see *Diving and Snorkeling*).

Those traveling alone or in a small group, or who just want to custom-design their own tour, may be better off with one of the many freelance boatmen in the area.

Boteros Bocatoreños, also called Boatmen United (tel. 757-9760, boterosbocas@yahoo.com, www.bocas.com) is a group composed of boatmen who have organized to stay afloat amid growing competition from tour operators. They offer the usual assortment of tours, most for $10–15 including snorkel gear.

One popular boatman is **Gallardo Livingston** (tel. 757-9388), a big guy with a booming voice who goes by Cabrioli or just plain Livingston. He's easygoing and professional, knows the islands well, and swears very colorfully in three languages. I've traveled with him several times and found him reliable, safe, and pleasant to deal with.

Livingston goes to all the usual destinations for about $15–20 per person, depending on distance. It's also possible to customize tours with him, including fishing trips for those with their own equipment, but he doesn't do forest treks ("I don't fool with the jungle"). One ambitious trip is to Escudo de Veraguas. The trip takes several hours each way and is possible only from August to October; waves and wind are too much for small boats at other times. He charges $350 for 1–2 people or $500 for 3–4 people, including sandwiches and drinks. He makes the trip in a sizable boat with a 75-horsepower motor and a 15-horsepower backup, but this would still be a serious, adventurous trip. If you can't reach Livingston by phone, try tracking him down through Boteros Bocatoreños, the Bocas Inn, Cocomo-on-the-Sea, or other hotels. Everyone knows him. His brother also does tours.

Bola Smith (tel. 757-9680) is another popular, well-regarded boatman. His specialty is a boating/walking tour of Isla Bastimentos that begins in the early morning, during which there's a good chance of spotting sloths, monkeys, and other wildlife. He charges $20 per person, $50 minimum. Bola can be contacted through Boteros Bocatoreños as well.

BOCAS TOWN ACCOMMODATIONS

Most of the hotels in the archipelago are in Bocas town, and most of these are built right on the water. But there are more and more options around Isla Colón and on the other major islands of the archipelago. There's quite a variety of accommodations, ranging from simple but clean hostels to modern midrange hotels and bed-and-breakfasts to rather upscale and exotic bungalows. All have hot water unless otherwise indicated. Rates are climbing faster in Bocas than in other parts of the country and the rates quoted below may well have changed significantly by the time you visit. However, low-season breaks and other deals are often available. There will likely be several more options by the time you read this. (See the *Isla Bastimentos, Isla Carenero,* and *Isla Solarte* sections for accommodations on those islands.) Many of the hotels have websites that are accessible through www.bocas.com.

$10–25

◪ Mondo Taitú (north end of Calle 5, tel. 757-9425, beds start at $5 per person), at the northern outskirts of town, is a great place for surfers and backpackers. There are two dorm rooms, each with four beds, for $5 per person. The dorms are "absolutely basic," as the former owner once described them, but they're clean and perfectly fine. Rooms with two single beds or a double bed go for $6 per person. These can be shared with another traveler or turned into a private single or double for $12. All rooms have a shared bathroom. There's a communal kitchen downstairs, and a morning juice bar was in the works on my last visit. Cross your fingers the tradition of daily fresh German bread didn't leave with the original German owner. This is also a place to get surfing information or surfboard repairs.

Hospedaje Heike (Calle 3 just west of the park, tel. 757-9708, suanagg1@yahoo.co.uk, www.bocas.com, $7 s, $12 d) is no longer actually owned by Heike, but everyone still knows it by that name—look for the place with the "hostel with kitchen" sign. Rooms are basic but cheerful—they're brightly painted, designed to let light in, and feature lots of pretty wood. The seven rooms all have fans and shared bathrooms. They can get hot during the day. Guests are welcome to use the kitchen.

Hospedaje Maritza (Calle 1 east of the post office, no phone, $10/12 s/d) offers basic and dark but clean rooms with fans and cold-water bathrooms. It's directly across from the Barco Hundido. It's not on the water and has no view.

Hospedaje Koral E.Y.L. (Calle 3 between Avenida A and Avenida B, tel. 757-9206, $12 d) is a surprisingly cheerful place with five basic rooms, all with fans, firm mattresses, and private bathrooms. Rooms are in the tiny home of a warm family (the "E.Y.L." stands for "Emiliano y Ligia," the couple who own the place), and guests are welcome to use the kitchen. Single travelers can sometimes get a price break.

Hotel Hipocampo (Calle 1 between Avenida A and Avenida B, tel. 757-9073, hotelhipocampo@yahoo.com, wwwbocas.com, start at $15 s, $20 d), across the street from Starfleet Eco Adventures, offers spare but clean rooms with air-conditioning, squishy mattresses, and cold-water bathrooms. Nicer rooms with cable TV cost $20/25 s/d. The management is friendly.

Hotel Dos Palmas (Avenida Sur west of Calle 5, tel. 757-9906, $22 s/d with fan, $27.50 s/d with air-conditioning), at the south end of town, offers nine rooms, all with hot-water bathrooms and thin mattresses. Seven have air-conditioning. It's a clean but basic wooden place run by proudly "100 percent bocatoreños." The furnishings are old-fashioned and the place is overpriced for what it offers. The main reason someone would stay here is to live close to the townspeople. It's something of a hangout for those who live in the neighborhood, as this place is slightly removed from the touristy part of Bocas town. To get there, walk all the way south on Calle 3, then turn right at the ferry dock and head up Avenida Sur, a waterfront road, for a couple of blocks.

Casa Max (Avenida H near the north end of

Calle 4, about a block west of the Bocas Inn, tel. 757-9120, casamax1@hotmail.com, $20 s, $25 d) is a bright and cheerful Dutch-owned place in a wooden building with 11 simple but clean rooms with private bath, fans, hot water, and firm beds. A bigger room with a view of the water is $5 more. Coffee and fresh fruit is served in the morning. The place has a colorful facade that's hard to miss, even at night, when it's lit up prettily.

$25–50

Next door to the Bocas Inn is **Hotel Las Brisas** (Avenida I/Avenida Norte near the north end of Calle 3, tel. 757-9248, $15.40-$38.50 s/d), a Bocas institution that is feeling the weight of its years. It offers 29 rooms of wildly different quality scattered among three buildings. However, the hotel seems to be in a slow, perpetual upgrade and rooms may be nicer (and pricier) when you visit. The main building has a certain weathered charm, but it's a bit gloomy and most of the 12 rooms have definitely seen better days—they tend to be old, musty, and have thin mattresses. Most of these have fans and all have hot-water bathrooms. There are some better rooms in the main building, with cable TV, air-conditioning, and minifridges. A recently renovated room with a skylight was the nicest. The seaside veranda is pleasant, with hammocks, wooden rocking chairs, and a breeze that lives up to the hotel's name. There's a second building set back from the water that has the seven cheapest rooms in the hotel. In these two buildings, expect to pay about $15.40 s/d for a room with a fan, $20 s/d with air-conditioning, and $28.50 for a room with cable TV, air-conditioning, sea view, fridge, and telephone.

A modern two-story annex down the street has 10 motel-style rooms with shared terraces and better mattresses for $38.50. Only the ones upstairs have a view, and it's partly obscured by houses.

Hotel del Parque (Calle 2, on the southeast side of the park, tel. 757-9008, $27.50 s, $33 d) offers eight rooms—four doubles and four triples—in an attractive wooden house right on the park and surrounded by flowering trees. Rooms are simple but pleasant with okay mattresses, cable TV, air-conditioning, and private hot-water bathrooms. There's a view of the park from the veranda and a nice little garden on the property. Guests are welcome to use the kitchen. This is a friendly place.

Along with Las Brisas, **Hotel Bahía** (south end of Calle 3, across from the ferry landing, tel. 757-9626, info@hotelbahia.biz, www.hotelbahia.biz, $44 s, $49.50 d) is one of the grand old ladies of Bocas. Built in 1905, it was once the headquarters building for the United Fruit Company. It had declined over the years into a rather dreary old hotel, but a recent renovation has preserved the building's historical character (the fruit company's massive old safe still sits in the office, for instance) while cheering up the place considerably. The 16 rooms are simple but pleasant and have air-conditioning, hot-water bathrooms, cable TV, and lots of attractive wood. Though the hotel is only one block from the water, not a single room has an ocean view. There's a restaurant downstairs and a terrace upstairs where guests can watch the scene on the street. Be warned that a rowdy bar across the street, El Encanto, often blasts music until late at night. A funny story about that safe: It's said that when the last guy who knew the combination died, workers had to drill into the safe to get at its contents. When they cracked it open, they found a piece of paper that had (wait for it . . .) the safe combination.

La Veranda (Calle H near the corner of Calle 7, tel./fax 757-9211, info@laverandahotel.com, www.laverandahotel.com, $28.50–49.50 s/d) is a Caribbean-style wooden house with a wrap-around veranda that gives the place its name. It's at the north edge of town about a block southwest of Cocomo-on-the-Sea. It offers seven pleasant rooms of various quality. The cheapest have shared bathrooms, no air-conditioning, and somewhat thin mattresses. The nicest are cheerful and large, with private bathrooms and air-conditioning available for an extra $5 a night. Air-conditioning may not be necessary since this place often gets a nice breeze, though sometimes the neighbors insist on blasting their music. All the rooms have mosquito nets. Guests are welcome to use the kitchen. Note to those who have stayed here before: The place changed hands in

November 2003 and no longer has the spa or the chocolate shop/café.

The appropriately named **Casa Amarilla** (Calle 5, tel. 757-9938, $45 s/d) is a bright yellow house just west of Mondo Taitú on the north end of town that offers four rooms with air-conditioning, private baths, fridges, and safes. Low-season rates can be significantly cheaper. The parrots in the private quarters upstairs can scream their heads off, but fortunately the guest rooms are downstairs. Coffee and fruit are served in the morning. One plus of staying here is the chance to rent bikes, snorkeling gear, and surfboards for half the normal rates.

Lula's Bed and Breakfast (Avenida I/Avenida Norte and Calle 6, tel. 757-9057, lulabocas@msn.com, www.lulabb.com, $46.20 s/d including breakfast) is a pleasant, clean bed-and-breakfast that features lots of handsome wood and rooms with attractive bathrooms, air-conditioning, and somewhat soft mattresses. The place has two doubles and four triples (the triples cost about $5 more). The nicest rooms are the two triples overlooking the balcony. It's run by Jean Barnett, who grew up in Bocas and whose American parents worked for the United Fruit Company.

Hotel Angela (Avenida I/Avenida Norte and Calle 6, tel. 757-9813, claudio@hotelangela.com, www.hotelangela.com, starts at $38.50 s/d including breakfast), once a backpackers' haven, was renovated and reopened in November 2002 as a considerably more upscale place. It contains 12 pleasant, modern rooms, all different and all with air-conditioning and private hot-water bathrooms. Meals are served in an attractive open-air wooden dining room built into a pier behind the hotel. There's also an open aquarium with lobster, shellfish, and turtles (the last were rescued from hunters, according to the owner).

$50–100

Posada Los Delfines (Calle 5 and Avenida H, tel. 757-9963, posadalosdelfines@posadalosdelfines.com, www.posadalosdelfines.com, start at $49.50 s/d), on the northern outskirts of town, is a clean and newish place (built circa 2001) that has 11 pleasant rooms with colorful Peruvian bedspreads, air-conditioning, hot water, cable TV, and squishy beds. Some of the rooms are quite dark. The nicer rooms cost $5–10 more. Price breaks are possible for those who opt for a fan instead of air-conditioning.

Cocomo-on-the-Sea (Avenida I/Avenida Norte between Calle 6 and Calle 7, tel./fax 757-9259, cocomoonsea@cwpanama.net, www.panamainfo.com/cocomo, $65.50–71.50 s/d including continental breakfast) has changed hands a couple of times in the last few years, but it remains a cozy place to stay. The current owners are from Cincinnati, Ohio. It's right on the water about a five-minute walk northwest of the town center. It offers four large, cheerful rooms in a wooden building designed with simple comfort in mind. The two rooms in front, Calypso and La Palma, have an ocean view, but all four rooms have access to a comfortable veranda, strung with hammocks, that juts into the water.

Hotel Laguna (Calle 3 about a block south of the park, tel. 757-9091, fax 757-9092, hotellaguna@hotellaguna.net, www.hotellaguna.net, $58 s/d) offers 16 modern, clean, and air-conditioned rooms in the center of "downtown." There's also a small bistro/café. Rooms are dark but cheerful with wood paneling and colorful bedspreads. All have hot water, cable TV, firm beds, and telephones. The nice "suite" ($100 s/d) and "junior suite" ($80 s/d) are really just larger rooms with balconies.

The **Bocas Inn** (north end of Calle 3, Bocas tel./fax 757-9600, Panana City tel. 269-9415 and fax 264-3713, info@anconexpeditions.com, www.anconexpeditions.com, rooms start at $66 s/d including breakfast) is an attractive, two-story wooden lodge owned by Ancon Expeditions, which has its field office in the building. The place is meant primarily for visitors who've arranged package tours with Ancon Expeditions, but it's also available for those who just want a room. The nicest rooms face the ocean and go for $77 s/d. These open out on a terrace with hammocks (the terrace can be used by all guests). All the rooms are attractive and have air-conditioning and hot-water bathrooms.

On the ground floor is a breezy veranda/pier that has a dining room and bar right on the water and quiet jazz and modern lounge music playing on the stereo. It's a good place to stop for a drink even for those not staying at the inn.

Guests generally book tours and lodging through Ancon Expeditions' main office in Panama City, though it's also possible to book a room directly through the lodge.

Suite Hotel Costes (Calle 3 next to Don Chicho, tel. 757-9848, cell 659-9851, fax 757-9864, info@suitehotelcostes.com, www.suitehotelcostes.com, $66 s/d), which opened in 2004, is a vibrantly painted Caribbean-style building that offers six rooms with good beds, a fridge, TV, air-conditioning, and private baths. The rooms are simple but pleasant. One wall in each is painted to match the rooms' bright bedspreads, all of which are different. This used to be a basic hostel called La Concha, but the renovation has made it quite a nice place. It's owned by an Italian man and his *bocatoreño* wife.

Hotel El Limbo on the Sea (Calle 1 next to Hotel Bocas del Toro, tel. 757-9062, ellimbo@hotmail.com, www.ellimbo.com, starts at $66 s/d) has 17 clean, modern rooms with air-conditioning, minibar fridge, cable TV, and telephone. Larger rooms go for $88 s/d and those with a sea view are $104.50 s/d. None of the rooms is very big. The hotel rents sea kayaks and snorkeling gear. Guests can also stay at El Limbo's rustic sister hotel, El Limbo on the Beach, on Bastimentos.

The newish **Hotel Bocas del Toro** (Calle 1 next to the Buena Vista Bar and Grill, tel. 757-9018, h_bocasdeltoro@hotmail.com, www.bocas.com, $71 s/d including breakfast) resembles its neighbor, El Limbo on the Sea: Both are Caribbean-style wooden buildings built right on the water. This one has 11 clean, modern rooms, all with air-conditioning, TVs, telephones, and in-room safes. Some have balconies that look out on the water. The hotel has already been given an upgrade thanks to new management that took over in mid-2004. It's an attractive place, featuring nine kinds of dark, polished wood. The restaurant on the premises serves mainly pasta and seafood for $5–15. The hotel has kayaks, and it should have sailboarding and other equipment by the time you visit.

The **Hotel Swan's Cay** (Calle 3 just north of Parque Bolívar, tel. 757-9316, 757-9090, tel./fax 757-9027, swanscayisla@cwp.net.pa, www.swanscayhotel.com, rooms start at $72/$85.25 in the main building) was the first fancy hotel in Bocas. The whole place is thoroughly air-conditioned and features such city-style touches as a carpeted lobby with wood-paneled walls. Rooms are comfortable and modern, with TV, telephones, and Italian furniture, but the smaller ones are a bit cramped and the whole place is dark. Somewhat cheaper rooms ($55 s/$66 d) are available in the hotel's annex. There's also a rather uninviting aboveground pool a few minutes' walk from the main hotel. Some find the hotel staid and out of sync with the bohemian ambience of the rest of Bocas. The hotel offers area tours. Its formal, air-conditioned restaurant is usually empty.

ACCOMMODATIONS AROUND ISLA COLÓN

There are also places to stay just north of Bocas town in "Saigon," on the eastern beaches, among the mangroves on the south side of the island, and in Boca del Drago.

$25–50

Cabañas Estefani (tel. 626-7243 or 624-3155, starting at $18 s, $25 d), at Boca del Drago, consist of nine rooms of varying quality spread among two-story cabins. Some of the rooms are rustic but pleasant; some are just rustic. All have fans. The setting is nice—the cabins are set among shade trees right next to the ocean. The cabins are used by students enrolled in field courses offered at the biological station next door, run by the Institute for Tropical Ecology and Conservation, so rooms may be hard to come by during winter and summer sessions. The nicest cabins, with an inside bath, can sleep up to six people for $55. Basic ones with an outside bath can accommodate up to five people for $25.

Those staying in Boca del Drago can arrange tours through Cabañas Estefani. Boat tours range from $5 per person for a visit to Swan's Cay to $20 per person to Bastimentos, Cayo Crawl, and Cayos Zapatillas. Overnight trips to Wekso on the Río Teribe are $70 per person, five-person minimum. Guests can also hire a horse for $30 per day.

© WILLIAM FRIAR

Punta Caracol Aqua Lodge, built over the water off the south tip of Isla Colón, is one of the most exclusive hotels in the archipelago.

$50–100

Bahía del Sol (west end of Avenida H, tel. 757-9060, cell 646-9772, info@bocasbahiadelsol.com, www.bocasbahiadelsol.com, start at $50 s/d including breakfast) offers five rooms in a private house in the "Saigon" section of Isla Colón. The house is modern and attractive—it's an open, polished-wood affair that gives the feel of being in the belly of a huge sailboat. All the rooms are cheerful and have private bathrooms and fans. Two have balconies. The best room has a large balcony with a whirlpool tub and goes for $100. Guests are welcome to use the kitchen and living area, which has a large TV with cable. This is a good option for those who want to stay away from the touristy areas and in a local neighborhood, but note that the neighborhood is a bit squalid and dirty—the house itself is nice, but some of the neighboring ones aren't and the shoreline is littered with garbage; you wouldn't go swimming around here. The place was for sale when I last visited Bocas and offerings may well have changed by the time you do. It's also about a 15-minute walk to downtown, though a quick, $.50 cab ride. To get there from town, head up Calle 3, which

curves left at the north end of town and becomes Avenida H. When that road forks, stay straight and head to the end of the dirt road (the right fork leads to the fairgrounds and the rest of Isla Colón). Bahía del Sol is down the concrete path on the right, overlooking the bay.

About five minutes by boat from Bocas town, around the southern tip of the island, is **Punta Manglar** (tel. 757-9541, cell 595-2665, reservas@puntamanglar.com, www.puntamanglar.com, $35–60 s/d, including continental breakfast). Formerly known as the Mangrove Inn, it consists of a series of very basic wooden cabins built on stilts over the water and connected by boardwalks to an open-sided bar/restaurant, also on stilts. Because there are no guardrails, this is not a place for young children. The cabins can accommodate 3–6 people, have cold-water bathrooms, and feature balconies that look out on the ocean. The view is lovely: The water is like clear glass, and the place is next to a series of coral reefs. But the place, as its name suggests, is right next to the mangroves, and the *chitras* have been ferocious when I've visited. This place is really geared for scuba divers who are more interested in being close to the water

Bocas del Toro

than in having fancy accommodations. Dive packages are available through Bocas Water Sports, which now operates the lodge.

$100–150

Tropical Suites (Calle 1 near Avenida D, tel. 757-9081 or 757-9880, cell 689-9451, bocaslasolas@cwpanama.net, www.tropical-suites.com, starts at $100 per apartment) is a three-story apartment building near the CEFATI office that offers 16 modern, somewhat stark studio apartments that can be rented by the day, week, or month. Those looking for the funky, Caribbean side of Bocas won't find it here, but it will probably appeal to those who want something more than a hotel room, particularly those who need a long-term place to stay while building their dream home. Each apartment has a balcony, air-conditioning, fully equipped kitchen, cable TV, bathrooms with his-and-her sinks and whirlpool bath, wireless Internet connection, and so on. Utilities and daily maid service are included. There are a coin laundry, security cameras, a marina, and a tiny restaurant nook that's open for breakfast, lunch, and dinner and provides room service. Rates are $100 (daily), $600 (weekly), and $40 per night (monthly) for apartments that look out on the street, and $125 (daily), $750 (weekly) and $55 a day (monthly) for ones with a sea view. Tropical Suites also has the distinction of being the first place in the archipelago with an elevator.

Rancho Paraíso (tel./fax 757-9415, info@ranchoparaiso.biz, www.ranchoparaiso.biz, $120 s, $150 d, $195 t including all meals and transport to and from airport, surf spots, and attractions) is an upscale surf lodge on Playa Bluff, the prettiest beach on the island. The main building is a huge, well-crafted, two-story octagonal structure with cane walls and thatched roof. It's based on a Panama-style *rancho,* but it's much larger and cushier. It has three bedrooms upstairs and two shared bathrooms (hot-water showers are outside). Downstairs there's a deck with hammocks and a dining area. On my visit I was devoured by *chitras* in the evening, so be prepared. The place isn't just for surfers. Playa Bluff has powerful waves and is too dangerous for swimming, but there's a calmer beach a 10-minute walk away.

There are also forest trails nearby, and horses can be rented for $7/hour. The lodge also has a front-row seat for turtle-nesting season on Playa Bluff. The place was built and is run by Kristian Salkovich, who was born in Croatia, grew up in Canada, and moved to Bocas in the late 1990s. An avid surfer, he's a calm, friendly guy and is fluent in English and Spanish.

Over $150

Punta Caracol Aqua Lodge (tel. 612-1088 or 676-7186, puntacaracol@puntacaracol.com, www.puntacaracol.com, starts at $240 s/, $265 d) is a quite lovely and unusual spot. It consists of six bungalows built off the west side of Isla Colón, right on the calm waters of Almirante Bay. Boardwalks link the bungalows to each other and to an attractive open-air restaurant where at night guests dine by the light of kerosene lanterns. That's all that's out there: The little resort feels as though it's floating off by itself in the shallow sea.

Opened in 2001, it's a Spanish-owned place run by a family from Barcelona. Cabins are cheerful, spacious, two-story wooden bungalows with thatched roofs. Upstairs is a large master bedroom with mosquito nets over a king-sized bed. A window is cut into the thatch to give a view of the water. Downstairs is a sitting room with a couch that converts into a bed. This leads onto a back porch with a landing from which guests can go snorkeling or swimming right from their rooms. The clear, shallow sea is your backyard, and it's great to sit out there and watch fish jumping or flocks of birds winging by. There's nothing between you and the low forested mountains on the mainland in the far distance. It'd be an ideal writer's retreat—there are even little desks upstairs—if a writer could afford it. The place is run on solar power, and there's a septic system (toilet paper must be disposed of in a trash can, not the toilet).

Five of the bungalows are identical and can sleep up to four people; the sixth is a suite that's twice as big and can accommodate up to six people ($310 s, $390 d). There are price breaks for small groups, and rates are lower from mid-May to mid-December. The resort does not recommend bringing children younger than 14.

Rates include breakfast, dinner, transfers to and from the airport, a welcome cocktail, snorkeling gear, and use of dugout *cayucos*. Food is delicious here, and a huge breakfast is served in the morning. Drinks are expensive by Bocas standards ($5 for cocktails, $3 for sodas).

As striking and special as this place is, there are a few things that may bother some guests, especially given the amount they're paying. The staff is casual, sometimes to the point of near rudeness. The dining-room staff likes to play the radio for its own entertainment, not that of the guests, and the sound can carry into the bungalows. It's not too annoying but it can mar the tranquility of the place. There's a whiff of mangrove stench when the wind blows from shore. Despite the proximity of the mangroves, though, the *chitras* aren't too bad. If you stay here, you really have to be in the mood for isolation without too much entertainment. It's a long boat trip back to town, and the resort charges $15 per person round-trip to ferry you. It's $5 more at night, $10 more after midnight.

Tours of the surrounding area range $70–160. A tour to Swan's Cay and Boca del Drago, for instance, is $100. A full-day tour to the Cayos Zapatillas, is $160. The tours are pricey, but they're conducted in a speedy fiberglass boat.

Camping

It's possible to camp in **Parque Nacional Marino Isla Bastimentos** for $5 per tent in addition to the $10-per-person park entrance fee. Entrance fees for both can be paid at the ANAM office in Bocas town. This entitles you to pitch a tent anywhere in the park. That includes the forest on Bastimentos itself, but as always it's not a great idea to camp in a tropical forest without a qualified guide. Most campers prefer to stay on one of the **Cayos Zapatillas,** which is part of the park, for a romantic, deserted-island experience. It's theoretically possible to buy permits directly from the ranger stationed on the Zapatillas. However, check at the ANAM office about current camping conditions and restrictions before venturing out that far. You'll also need to hire a boatman you can trust to pick you up when you're ready to return.

FOOD

Bocas town offers a fair range of cuisine, considering its size and location. Some places serve surprisingly good international fare. Pizza is particularly easy to come by, and some of it's quite tasty. A number of fast-food stalls are set around the perimeter of the park. Note that many restaurants are closed for lunch, when the tourists are usually out snorkeling and sunbathing.

Please boycott any restaurant that serves sea turtle meat or eggs or any other endangered species protected by law. It does still happen—one place in Bocas town has turtle on the menu.

Restaurants and Cafés

Restaurante El Pecado (Calle 3 across from the south end of the park, tel. 757-9088 or 597-0296, 5–10 P.M. Tues.–Sat.) is a bohemian dining dream—it has just the right combination of class and funkiness. It occupies the upstairs of an old wooden two-story building and has a wraparound porch where diners can survey the scene on Calle 3 as they eat. The food is good and includes Thai, Mexican, Lebanese, and Panamanian dishes. The Thai soups ($6–9) are to die for, as is the fried camembert. The menu of the day consists of an appetizer, main plate, dessert, and drink for $11.95. The "Drink El Pecado" is concocted from rum aged for weeks with whatever tropical fruit happened to be lying around; it's a little sweet but delicious (it used to be called "the Killer," but it didn't sell too well). The sangria is also good. The only things I've been disappointed with here are the desserts. The French-Canadian owner, Stefan, is quite a character and a lot of fun. One evening I spent here ended very late with Stefan spraying the restaurant with champagne before he led the whole group to even later debauches at the Barco Hundido.

On the north side of the park right next to Hotel Swan's Cay is **La Ballena** (Calle 3, tel. 757-9089), a pleasant street-side restaurant that serves pretty good pasta but whose prices are steep for such a simple place. Fish and pasta dishes go for $10–17.50. However, the restaurant also offers a "menu turístico" with simpler fare for $5–7. Sandwiches are $5.

The dining room at Swan's Cay is called **Restaurante Alexander,** where one can dine in air-conditioned comfort. The place is rather formal, with white tablecloths and so on, which doesn't fit too well with the bohemian vibe of the islands. I've never seen more than a couple of customers in the restaurant. The cuisine here is Italian, with prices hovering around $10.

Alberto's Pizzeria (Calle 5 between Avenida F and Avenida G, tel. 756-9066, 11 A.M.–3 P.M. and 5–11 P.M. Mon.–Sat., closed Sun.) has the best pizza on the island. Ingredients are fresh and the pizzas are made with love by its dedicated Italian owner. How dedicated? The last time I was there, Alberto had to tell a client he was out of pepperoni. But a few minutes later, he heard a plane coming in for a landing; realizing his pepperoni was on the plane, he grabbed his bike and pedaled to the airport to pick it up rather than disappoint a customer. As you might imagine, he's a bit of a character. Pizzas cost $4.75–7.50 and pasta $4.25–6.25. A pizza feeds two moderately hungry people. The only drawback of this place at lunchtime is that, even though the dining area is open-sided, it doesn't have fans and can't catch a breeze, so it can be blazingly hot. Fortunately, it offers fresh lemonade and orange juice. There's also a full bar.

M Om Café (Avenida H near Calle 4, near the Bocas Inn at the north end of town) serves authentic Indian food—basically unheard of anywhere else in Panama—in a cozy, funky bohemian atmosphere with world beat and electronic music for the soundtrack. The café is shoehorned onto the open-air porch of a tiny, ramshackle house. It's pretty at night, when it's candlelit. The food tastes like Indian home cooking, which is kind of what it is—the owner is a woman from Chandigarh who was raised in Canada. The portions aren't large, but that leaves room for dessert: The *gulab jamuns* are good. Vegetarian dishes are $3–3.50 and meat dishes are $5.50–6.50. Breakfast options include homemade yogurts. The café also offers lots of fresh juices and unusual kinds of *lassis* (India's answer to milkshakes), including banana, *maracuya,* papaya, and coconut.

The **Buena Vista Bar and Grill** (Calle 1 between Avenida C and Avenida D, tel. 757-9035) is *the* gringo hangout in Bocas town. It serves basic American comfort food, from burgers and hotdogs to brownies and cheesecake. Other offerings include nachos, taco salads, cheeseburgers, enchiladas, filet mignon, chicken, tuna steak, pork, sandwiches (the Jamaican jerked chicken is good), dinner salads and—wonder of wonders—veggie food. Meals are reasonably priced, ranging $4.25–12, for lobster. Margaritas are a house specialty, but the one I tried wasn't very good. The staff will pack a lunch in a cooler for you to take on boat excursions. Please order it the night before you need it. Be warned: The satellite TV is always tuned to a game and, since the couple who runs the place is from San Francisco, emotions run high when the 49ers are playing.

Pizzeria y Spaghetteria da Claudio (Calle 3 and Avenida D, tel. 757-9091, 7:30 A.M.–10 P.M. daily), in the same building as Hotel Laguna, offers nearly two dozen plate-sized pizzas, many of which are available in larger sizes, as well. It also serves more than two dozen pasta dishes, as well as fish, chicken, meats, and even goulash. Individual pizzas are $4–8. Other items are $4–12. The *pizza de la casa* has tomato, onions, olives, mushrooms, garlic, pepperoni, and ham. It's pretty good. It also boasts 20 kinds of beer, including Dutch, German, and Mexican ones. It also has a bakery.

M Cocina del Mar (Calle 1 between Avenida C and Avenida D, tel. 757-9156, 4:30–9:30 P.M. Mon.–Sat., closed Sun.), upstairs from Starfleet Eco Adventures and next to the Buena Vista, opened in late 2004 and immediately became one of the best restaurants in town. It's an open-air place on the second floor of a wooden building, which gives it a nice view of the water and Isla Solarte. The atmosphere is pleasant, with teak floors, candles on the tables, and fiesta-colored chairs. Offerings include shrimp, pasta, chicken, lobster, and shish kebobs. Most dishes are $9–12.50. Tuna sushi is sometimes available, and it's delicious. So are the brownies. There's a daily happy hour 4:30–6 P.M. and half-priced drinks for women on Thursday. There's sometimes live music.

The indoor/outdoor restaurant at the **Hotel**

BOCAS TOWN

Bahía Sand Fly

Caribbean Sea

AV NORTE/AV I

To Cemetery, Playa Bluff, and Boca del Drago

LA VERANDA

COCOMO-ON-THE-SEA

HOTEL ANGELA

LULA'S B&B

TALLER JOAN PAUL

SUPER EL EPICENTRO DEL AHORRO

MONDO TAITÚ

LAVAMÁTICO

OM CAFÉ

BOCAS INN

HOSPEDAJE EMANUEL

AV H

CASA AMARILLA

POSADA LOS DELFINES

CASA MAX

HOTEL LAS BRISAS

CALLE 7

AV G

SOUVENIR STAND

CALLE 3

CALLE 2

CALLE 1

SUPER GOURMET

ALBERTO'S PIZZERIA

AIRPORT

LA BALLENA

BANCO NACIONAL DE PANAMÁ

AV F

CALLE 5

DON CHICHO/INTERNET CAFÉ

HOTEL SWAN'S CAY/ RESTAURANTE ALEXANDER

ANAM OFFICE

SUITE HOTEL COSTES

HOSPEDAJE HEIKE

PALACIO MUNICIPAL

HOSPEDAJE MARITZA

EL BARCO HUNDIDO

CALLE 6

MCDOUGLAS' GOLDEN GRILL

Parque Bolívar

CABLE AND WIRELESS

SPA FLORA BELLA

BUBBLES COIN LAUNDRY

BIKE/SCOOTER RENTAL

HOTEL DEL PARQUE

EXPRESSO TAXI 25/ATM

POLICE STATION/JAIL

AV E

TROPIX SURF

RESTAURANTE EL PECADO

CEFATI/ INTERNET CAFÉ

HOTEL LAGUNA/PIZZERIA Y SPAGHETTERIA DA CLAUDIO/BAKERY

ESTRELLA DE BOCAS

TROPICAL SUITES

AV D

SUPERMERCADO ISLA COLÓN

STARFLEET ECO ADVENTURES

HOTEL HIPOCAMPO

BUENA VISTA BAR AND GRILL

HOTEL BOCAS DEL TORO

HOTEL EL LIMBO ON THE SEA

CALLE 4

RESTAURANTE Y BAR KUN-JA

LA PIRATE

AV C

PRODUCE STAND

J&J/TRANSPARENTE TOURS

BRAVO CENTER

AMERICAN AND CARIBBEAN FOOD TO GO

BOCAS MARINE AND TOURS

ARTESANIAS BRI-BRI EMANUEL

FARMACIA ROSA BLANCA

HOTEL BOCAS CARIBE/MONEYGRAM

AV B

STARFISH COFFEE/ PANCHAMA/CARIBBEAN CHOCOLATE COMPANY

HOSPEDAJE KORAL EYL

CALLE 3

BAR EL ENCANTO

FARMACIA CHEN

BOCAS WATER SPORTS

AV A

BOTEROS BOCATOREÑOS

Bahía de Almirante

HOTEL DOS PALMAS

SPANISH BY THE SEA

HOTEL BAHÍA

REEF RESTAURANT AND BAR

AV SUR

FERRY PIER

SCALE NOT AVAILABLE

© AVALON TRAVEL PUBLISHING, INC.

Bocas del Toro

Bahía (Calle 3 and Avenida A, tel. 757-9626, 7:30–9:30 A.M., 11:30 A.M.–2:30 P.M., and 5:30–10 P.M. daily) has a blinking neon sign that will quickly drive you insane if you sit in the front garden at night. Pizza starts at $4 for a medium pie and $6 for a large. Fish and meat dishes go for $6.50–14. The food is okay. It's among the few nicer places open for lunch.

The **Reef Restaurant and Bar** (Calle 3, no phone, 7 A.M.–midnight daily), at the south end of Calle 3 next to the ferry dock, is essentially a large pier with a restaurant. It's pleasant to sit outside on the water and watch the boats pass by. The food is okay, but the kitchen tends to overdo the sauces here. Offerings include pastas, seafood, steak, chicken, and a few veggie dishes. Entrées average about $6.

Restaurante y Bar Kun-Ja (Calle 1 next to Buena Vista Bar and Grill, tel. 757-9362, noon–11 P.M. Wed.–Mon., closed Tues.) is a Chinese place that offers lots of noodle and rice dishes. The food is somewhat greasy but tasty and the portions are big. Veggie combos cost around $3, but seafood dishes can range $14–20.

Le Pirate (Calle 3 near Avenida C, no phone), a bar/restaurant on the water next to the downtown water-taxi piers, has enjoyed a good reputation, but I find its offerings so-so. It's in a colorful location, though, and it offers a good-value "executive lunch" 11 A.M.–4 P.M. that consists of fish, chicken, or beef with coconut rice, salad, and *patacones* or boiled potatoes for $3.50. Most dinner items are $8.

McDouglas' Golden Grill (corner of Calle 3 and Avenida E, no phone, 7:30 A.M.–11 P.M. daily) is a basic but clean open-air place that offers cheap gringo food such as burgers, hotdogs, and individual-sized pizzas. A fried chicken, fries, and soda combo is $3. It also has ice cream.

The **Coffee Bar** (Calle 1, tel. 757-9062) at Hotel El Limbo on the Sea serves breakfast for $3 or less. Eggs are cooked well here—a rarity anywhere in Panama. Fresh-squeezed juices are available. Other offerings include sandwiches, burgers, chicken, and hotdogs for $2–4.

Starfish Coffee, on Calle 3 near El Encanto, sells frozen coffee drinks and other caffeine fixes.

El Pargo Rojo and **Sunset Grill** on Isla Caren-ero are such a quick boat ride from Isla Colón that they're a good dining option for those staying in Bocas town, even at night.

Markets

In addition to its restaurants and cafés, Bocas town also has several stores that sell food. **Super Gourmet** (Avenida F and Calle 2), while not really offering much in the way of gourmet food, has been a godsend for expatriates hungering for something beyond the usual local fare and may appeal to those staying in a place with kitchen facilities. Supplies include Old El Paso salsa, chili spices, ramen noodles, olive oil, Vienna sausages, instant grits, good coffee from Boquete, paté, hummus, and a modest selection of wine. **Supermercado Isla Colón** (Calle 3 at the east corner of Avenida D, 7:30 A.M.–11 P.M. Mon.–Sat., 8 A.M.–10 P.M. Sun.) is a grocery store in the center of town. A second one, **Super El Epicentro del Ahorro** (Calle 6 and Avenida H, 8 A.M.–9 P.M. daily), is farther away. **American and Caribbean Food to Go** (Calle 3, tel. 757-9964, 6 A.M.–7 P.M. daily), the place next to the Bravo Center with the "world's best turkey sandwiches" sign, packs sandwiches to go for around $4–5, convenient for those heading out on tours. There are a few small **fresh-produce stands** in town, including one next to J&J/Transparente Tours.

INFORMATION

The Panama government's huge CEFATI tourist information center (Calle 1 near Avenida D, tel. 757-9642, 9 A.M.–5 P.M. Mon.–Fri., closed Sat. and Sun.) is, as usual, heavy on the "center" and light on the "tourist information." The huge, two-story, Caribbean-style complex—situated, oddly enough, next to the town jail—is one of the biggest buildings in the archipelago. The staff member I dealt with on my last visit was unfriendly, had no useful information to offer even in Spanish (the only language he spoke), and only grudgingly gave up what printed material the place had, which consisted of little more than a blurry photocopy of an out-of-date map. However, there's a somewhat informative display detailing the human and natural history of Bocas in

Spanish and English upstairs. The center also has public bathrooms and an Internet café.

The tiny ANAM office (Calle 1, on the water northeast of the park, tel. 757-9244, 8 A.M.–noon and 1–4 P.M. Mon.–Fri.) issues park permits and sometimes has marginally useful maps and brochures of Parque Nacional Marino Isla Bastimentos. Entrance to the marine park is $10 per person. The fee to camp is another $5 per tent. The fees can also be paid to the ranger on the Cayos Zapatillas, but those planning to camp there should check in with ANAM in any case to check on current conditions and rules. The office sometimes has information on other natural attractions of the area, including San San Pondsack. It's one block east of Parque Bolívar.

There is increasingly useful information about Bocas on the Internet. A good starting place is www.bocas.com, which contains links to many of the archipelago's hotels, restaurants, and services as well as dates of special events and holidays, interactive maps, and practical information on visiting the islands. The website for the Bocas Marine and Tours (www.bocasmarinetours.com) water-taxi service contains a nifty, detailed interactive map of Bocas town that's kept up to date. A printable version is available at the site, which also contains useful travel tips and detailed information on getting around. The company's office, on the pier near Le Pirate, is a good place to go for transportation information, especially to Costa Rica, during regular weekly business hours.

If no one seems to be working at Farmacia Rosa Blanca (Calle 3 next to Bocas Marine and Tours, tel. 757-9560, 9 A.M.–12:30 P.M., 3–6:30 P.M., and 8–9:30 P.M. Mon.–Sat., 9 A.M.–noon Sun.) ask at the store next door for help. Another possibility is Farmacia Chen (Calle 3 and Avenida A, tel. 757-9280).

SERVICES

Nearly all the services in the archipelago are in Bocas town.

Banks

There are exactly two places to withdraw cash in the entire archipelago, and both are in Bocas town. A branch of Banco Nacional de Panamá (Avenida F between Calle 1 and Calle 2, 8 A.M.–2 P.M. Mon.–Fri.), northeast of Parque Bolívar, has a 24-hour ATM and cashes travelers checks. There's another 24-hour ATM in the same building that houses Expreso Taxi 25, the water-taxi service near the jail.

While credit cards are becoming more widely accepted in Bocas, most transactions are still cash only. Even hotels and restaurants that claim to accept credit cards sometimes don't when it comes time to pay, or charge an extra fee for their trouble (be sure to ask ahead of time). If the two ATMs go on the blink simultaneously, which occasionally happens, visitors can be caught short. This is a good place to come well stocked with travelers checks and/or dollars.

There's a Moneygram office (tel. 757-9154, 8 A.M.–6 P.M. Mon.–Sat., closed Sun.) in the dry goods store on the ground floor of Hotel Bocas Caribe.

Post Office

The post office (8 A.M.–noon and 2–5 P.M. Mon.–Fri., 7 A.M.–noon Sat.) is in the Palacio Municipal.

Internet and International Telephone Services

Bravo Center (Calle 3 near Avenida C, tel. 757-9229, cell 648-9237, fax 757-9204, bravocenter@bocasmail.com, 8 A.M.–7 P.M. Mon.–Sat., closed Sun.) offers Internet access for $2 an hour, as well as international calls and faxes, Fed Ex shipping, phone cards, video rentals, used books, and so on. Calls to the United States are $.25 per minute, plus a $1 connect charge.

Internet Don Chicho (Calle 3 and Avenida F, tel. 757-9829, 8 A.M.–9 P.M. Mon.–Fri., 9 A.M.–8 P.M. Sat., closed Sun.) is attached to the Don Chicho cafeteria. It charges $2 an hour for Internet access.

Bocas Internet Café (Calle 3 near Avenida D, tel. 757-9390, 8 A.M.–10 P.M. daily) offers Internet access for $2 an hour, chocolate and other snacks, and service with a frown.

The Cable and Wireless office (Calle 1 due east of the park, tel. 882-7817, 8 A.M.–noon,

1–4:30 P.M. Mon.–Fri.) sends and receives faxes. The cost is $.50 per page (domestic) and $1 per page (international) plus long-distance charges and a $1 surcharge to send faxes. The cost of receiving a short fax is $1. The office also has pay phones and sells telephone cards. A phone card vending machine is outside the building and available 24 hours a day.

Immigration Office

There is a Migración y Naturalización (immigration and naturalization) office (tel./fax 757-9263, 8 A.M.–4 P.M. Mon.–Fri.) in the Palacio Municipal at the north end of the park for those who need to extend their tourist card or visa or have some other immigration concern. Note: The fax machine picks up if no one's around to answer the phone. If so, try again later. In any case, it will likely be less hassle to try to handle this at the main office in Changuinola, or in Panama City.

Launderettes

Bubbles Coin Laundry (Avenida E between Calle 3 and Calle 4, 8 A.M.–8 P.M. Mon.–Sat., 8 A.M.–5 P.M. Sun.), near Spa Flora Bella, offers self-service washing and drying for $3.25 a load, or full service, plus folding, for $4.25. There's another *lavamático* on Avenida I/Avenida Norte between Casa Max and Om Café.

Marinas

The archipelago, long a haven for yachties, now supports two marinas. Bocas Yacht Club and Marina (tel. 757-9800, fax 757-9801, www.bocasmarina.com, bocasyachtclub@yahoo.com, 8:30 A.M.–noon and 1:30–5 P.M. Mon.–Fri., 8:30 A.M.–1 P.M. Sat., closed Sun.) is just southwest of Bocas town, across a small bay. It has floating docks that accommodate boats up to 100 feet long. Docking fees are $7–9/foot from May to December, $1 less from December to April. Year-round daily rates are $.50–.60/foot. Electricity is charged at $.20/kwh; water is free. The marina also offers some boat maintenance, laundry, charter, and brokerage services. A restaurant and pool are in the works.

Marina Carenero (tel./fax 757-9242, mar-car@swp.net.pa, www.careeningcay.com), on the west side of Isla Carenero close to Bocas town, can accommodate boats up to 60 feet long. Laundry, boat maintenance, and Internet services are also available. The marina is part of the Careening Cay Resort, which also has cabins and a restaurant, the Sunset Grill.

Spa

Those in the mood for pampering after their exertions can visit **Spa Flora Bella** (Avenida E between Calle 3 and Calle 4, tel. 757-9086, spaflorabella@yahoo.com, www.spaflorabella.com, 10 A.M.–6 P.M. Mon.–Sat., closed Sun.). It offers a full array of luxury spa services, including massages, facials, body scrubs, manicures, pedicures, and so on, in pleasant surroundings. Many of the treatments have a tropical flavor to them, including facials that use avocado, papaya, coconut, and even chocolate or beer (that last one for men, of course) and "after sun soothers" for those who spent a little too much time snoozing on the beach. Massages cost $30 for 45 minutes or $40 for 75 minutes. For an experience of sheer decadence, splurge on the four-hand massage ($50). It's best to make an appointment, but walk-ins are possible 2–6 P.M.

Courses

Spanish by the Sea (Calle 4 and Avenida A, tel. 757-9518, info@spanishbythesea.com, www.spanishbythesea.com) is a flexible Spanish-language program run by a friendly staff that operates out of a home in the heart of Bocas town. Prices depend on course length, size of group, and hours per day of instruction. Longer courses cost less per week. A five-day group course, with two hours a day of instruction, is $70 per person. A four-week, six-hour-a-day private course would cost $896. Minicourses are also available, including a six-hour "Travelers' Survival Spanish" course for $40, held over two or three days.

Several other things make the school appealing. Students can spend part of their course at the school's sister facility, Spanish by the River, in Turrialba, Costa Rica. It also offers reasonably priced activities and overnight excursions. The school can organize volunteer work, including help with a sea-turtle conservation project from March to September, for those who want to practice their Spanish in meaningful situations or just help out.

Students can stay at the school in very basic rooms with fans and shared bathrooms for $7.50 for a shared room or $12 for a private room. Laundry service is available ($2.50 a load), and guests can use the kitchen. The school can also arrange home stays with a family in Bocas town for $12 per person for a private room, including breakfast and laundry at the school.

A Florida-based nonprofit called the **Institute for Tropical Ecology and Conservation (ITEC)** has a biological field station in Boca del Drago. It's a private outfit unaffiliated with any university, but it draws its faculty from various U.S. and Latin American universities. It offers three-week winter and four-week summer courses in tropical biology and anthropology. Tuition is $1,400 and $1,700 respectively. The fee includes room and board—students are housed in Cabañas Estefani and fed at Restaurante Yarisnori. There is also a two-week "travel session" that takes students around Panama ($900). Contact the group's headquarters for information: ITEC, 1023 S.W. 2nd Ave., Gainesville, FL, 32601, U.S.A., tel. 352/367-9128, itec@itec-edu.org, www.itec-edu.org.

GETTING THERE AND AWAY BY AIR

There are several daily flights between Panama City and the archipelago ($57.75 each way, about an hour). There is also one flight to and from David during the week ($31.50 each way, about 50 minutes). The only airport in the archipelago is on Isla Colón, on the edge of Bocas town. The little airport is on the west side of town, along Avenida F. Those without too much luggage will probably find it easy to walk to most of the town's hotels, but a taxi or *transporte cooperativa* van to the airport costs $.50 per person. There's a little snack bar in the airport. Transportation to the other islands is by boat only.

Note that flights sometimes make an intermediate stop at Changuinola; be sure to get off

at the right place. These flight schedules are subject to change, so check with the airlines well ahead of time.

Aeroperlas (tel. 315-7500 and fax 315-7580 in Panama City, tel. 721-1195 in David, 757-9341 in Bocas town, info@aeroperlas.com, www.aeroperlas.com) has two daily flights to Bocas from the Albrook airport in Panama City. They leave Panama City at 8:30 A.M. and 1 P.M. Monday–Friday, 7 A.M. and 3 P.M. Sat., and 8 A.M. and 3 P.M. Sunday. Its two daily flights to Panama City from Bocas leave at 9 A.M. and 2:30 P.M. Monday–Friday, 8:40 A.M. and 5 P.M. Saturday, and 9:25 A.M. and 5 P.M. Sunday. Flights from David to Bocas leave at 8 A.M. Monday–Friday. Flights from Bocas to David leave at 9:40 A.M. Monday–Friday.

Mapiex Aero (tel./fax 315-0888 in Panama City, tel. 757-9841 and fax 757-9842 in Bocas town, reservaciones@aero.com.pa, www.aero.com.pa) has two daily flights between Panama City Monday through Saturday and one on Sunday. Flights leave from the Albrook airport at 6:45 A.M. and 2 P.M. Monday–Friday, 6:30 A.M. and 1 P.M. Saturday and 1 P.M. Sunday. Flights leave Bocas for Panama City at 8:15 A.M. and 3:30 P.M. Monday–Friday, 8 A.M. and 2:30 P.M. Saturday and 5 P.M. Sunday.

GETTING THERE AND AWAY BY LAND/WATER TAXI

The logistics of getting to the islands from the mainland aren't that complicated, but to those unfamiliar with the area they can be confusing. It may be helpful to refer to a map when making plans. (See the *Guabito, Almirante,* and *Changuinola* entries in the *Mainland Bocas* sections for more information.)

Getting to the Bocas del Toro archipelago by the land/sea route increasingly involves dealing with taxi drivers and *boleteros* (ticket touts) who work for commissions from specific hotels and water-taxi operations. This can be a nuisance and sometimes a rip-off, if you end up being overcharged or taken to a place you really don't want to go.

There have been reports of touts claiming one

of the water-taxi services (the one not paying him a commission) is shut down or temporarily closed. Taxi drivers sometimes try to overcharge passengers, for instance by charging as much per person as locals would pay per carload—be sure to clarify the deal before getting in the cab.

Some enterprising characters have set up a kind of tourist shuttle business at the Costa Rican border in which they meet travelers—sometimes before they even cross over to Panama—and offer to usher them all the way to the islands by taxi and water taxi.

The going rate for this when I last checked was $10 per person, four-person minimum, including the water taxi ride. This is significantly more than four people would pay on their own, but those who don't want to fool with the logistics may be tempted. Be aware, though, that the friendly guide works on commission: He'll try to steer you to places that suit him, not you. Be prepared to stand your ground if you don't like the hotel he takes you to.

Almirante Vs. Changuinola

The most common way to get to the archipelago is by water taxi from Almirante to Bocas town, on Isla Colón. The trip takes about 25 minutes. A much slower, less-frequent ferry also makes the trip. (Note: There is no longer any transportation service between Chiriquí Grande and the islands.)

One of the water-taxi outfits, Bocas Marine and Tours, now also runs water taxis from Changuinola to Isla Colón. This means that those coming from the Costa Rican border no longer have to travel all the way to Almirante if they don't want to. This shortens the overland trip from the border by about 25 winding kilometers, though the boat ride from Changuinola is about half an hour longer than from Almirante.

Those on a tight budget will still find it marginally cheaper to go all the way to Almirante from the border if they stick to buses the whole way, since the water-taxi ride from Changuinola costs $2 more than from Almirante, and the longer bus ride to Almirante costs them just $.60 extra.

However, those traveling by taxi from the border can save some money by going through Changuinola, depending on the size and nego-tiating skills of the group: Expect to pay about $3 per person from Guabito to the water-taxi pier in Changuinola or $10–12 per carload (*not* per person) to Almirante. Those with their own transportation should definitely go all the way to Almirante, where the vehicle can be left in a guarded parking lot for a daily fee. Another advantage of going through Almirante is the competition: You can choose to go with whichever water taxi is ready to leave or looks better to you.

Warning: The last water taxis of the day leave Changuinola at 5:30 P.M. and Almirante at 6:30 P.M. After that, travelers will have to spend the night in Changuinola or Almirante, both of which have a certain backwater-town funkiness but neither of which has much in the way of charm or things to do, especially compared with the islands. Changuinola has the broader range of accommodations and services, but it's not the safest place at night. (Neither is Almirante, for that matter.)

Almirante Water Taxis

Those arriving by bus from Changuinola will be dropped off at the Almirante bus terminal. The water-taxi services aren't visible from the terminal but are within easy walking distance. Look for the train tracks. Cross over them and head left along the waterfront. Bocas Marine and Tours is the first place you'll come to. Expreso Taxi 25 is farther down. The fare is the same at either place.

In Almirante you'll be approached by *boleteros* (ticket touts) who will offer to carry your luggage and lead you to the water taxis. They work on commission from one of the companies and will insist on taking you to that one. They can be hard to shake off and it may be easier just to let one haul your bags and show the way for a tip of about $.25. It's up to you to decide whether you're encouraging the entrepreneurial spirit of folks without many other job options or contributing to a tourism nuisance. Once at the pier, you can always choose to take your business and luggage to the competition if the wait's too long or you don't like the look of the place.

The fare is $3/5 one-way/round-trip at either place. Only those on a really tight budget should fool with saving a buck by buying the round-trip ticket. It's just one more thing to keep track of, and it forces you to stick with that company even if the other company's boat is leaving sooner. **Bocas Marine and Tours** (tel. 758-4085 in Almirante, 758-9033 in Changuinola, tel./fax 757-9033 in Bocas town) has departures for Isla Colón approximately every hour from 6 A.M. to 6:30 P.M. The schedule is the same on the return.

Expreso Taxi 25 (also called Marino Taxi 25, tel. 758-3498 Almirante, 757-9028 in Bocas town) has departures at approximately 6 A.M., 6:30 A.M., 7:30 A.M., and 8:30 A.M. After that, boats leave approximately every hour, depending on demand, usually at around 45 minutes after the hour. The last boat leaves at 6:30 P.M. The schedule is the same on the return.

Almirante Ferry

Few will want to fool with the painfully slow ferry (tel. 615-6674, 261-0350, and 229-1742 in Bocas town, tel. 229-1639 in Almirante) that runs between Almirante and Bocas town. It doesn't run often in any case. Only those who insist on bringing a vehicle to Bocas town—something there is very little reason to do—should bother. The ferry runs Tuesday–Sunday. It leaves Almirante at 8 A.M. and returns from Isla Colón at 4 P.M. except on Wednesday, when it returns at 5 P.M. The trip takes 1.5 hours. The fare is $1.50 for foot passengers, $2 for a bike, $10 for a motorcycle, $15 for a car, and $45 for a four-wheel drive. The ferry pier in Almirante is past the turnoff to the water taxis; look for the Texaco sign. The Bocas town ferry dock is at the southern end of Calle 3, across the street from the Hotel Bahía.

Changuinola Water Taxis

The **Bocas Marine and Tours** (tel. 758-4085 in Almirante, 758-9033 in Changuinola, tel./fax 757-9033 in Bocas town) water-taxi pier is at Finca 60, a banana plantation near the mouth of the Río Changuinola. The trip to Bocas town takes about an hour and is quite a scenic ride, leading through part of the Río Changuinola and Canal de Soropta, so taking this route can be a way to combine getting to the islands with a quick boat tour.

About half of the departures to and from Bocas town include a 10-minute stop at Boca del Drago, and passengers can get off here if they prefer. The fare from Changuinola is $5 to either place.

Getting from the Sixaola-Guabito Border Crossing to Finca 60/Changuinoala

After clearing customs and immigration in Guabito, walk down from the railroad tracks to get a bus or taxi.

Buses from Guabito to Changuinola run about every 20 minutes from 5:30 A.M.–7:30 P.M. The trip takes a half hour and costs $.70. From the Changuinola bus terminal take a *colectiva* bus to Finca 60 ($.40 per person).

Taxis can take travelers straight from Guabito to the water-taxi pier at Finca 60, saving time and the hassle of moving luggage. Taxis from Guabito charge $3 per person to Finca 60, $5 per ride (*not* per person) to the Changuinola bus terminal.

Getting from the Sixaola-Guabito Border Crossing to Almirante

There are no direct buses from Guabito to Almirante. To get there, take a bus to the Changuinola bus terminal and switch to an Almirante-bound bus, which drops passengers off at the Almirante bus terminal. They leave about every 25 minutes from 6 A.M. to 10 P.M. The trip takes a half hour and costs $1. Taxi fare from Guabito to Almirante is $10–12 per ride (not per person). Those who time it right can also take the slow, rickety banana train from Changuinola to Almirante. (See *Changuinola* in the *Mainland Bocas* section.)

Getting from Elsewhere in Panama to Almirante

Direct buses from Panama City to Almirante leave from the Gran Terminal de Transportes in Albrook just once a day, at 8 P.M. The bus arrives at 5:45 A.M. the next morning. The fare is $23. Those who don't relish a red-eye should consider taking a bus from Panama City to David

Bocas del Toro

and switch to an Almirante-bound bus there. However, this means a longer trip and tight connections. Plan to get a very early start or spend the night in David. Passengers are allowed a maximum of two suitcases without an extra charge. Plan to arrive before the last water taxi of the day, which leaves Almirante at 6:30 P.M. Remember that buses often run late.

Buses from David to Almirante run every half hour from 4 A.M. to 7 P.M. The fare is $7 and the trip takes about 4 hours. The 2 P.M. bus is the latest possible one to take, if it's running on time, and still have a chance of catching the last water taxi. To be safe, take an earlier bus.

If they have room, buses heading to Almirante can be flagged down along the Interamerican Highway or the Fortuna Road. But in most cases it will probably be quicker and more reliable to take a bus to David and catch an Almirante-bound bus from there.

Note: Long-haul buses from David, Panama City, and other parts of Panama still do not go into Almirante itself. They drop passengers at the crossroads outside of town and head on to Changuinola. It's a long walk, especially with luggage, from the crossroads to the water-taxi piers. It's worth the $.50 per person to take a taxi to the pier area.

Driving to Almirante

Those with their own transportation will need 9–10 hours from Panama City or 3.5 hours from David to drive straight through to Almirante. Those coming from Panama City should consider breaking the trip somewhere along the way and spending the night. Finca la Suiza is a good option for those who can afford it. Another possibility is Santiago, the provincial capital of Veraguas, on the Interamericana a little under four hours from Panama. It has a range of services and places to stay but is not exactly a scenic or exciting town.

There is only one road that links the province of Bocas del Toro archipelago with the rest of Panama. This is the Fortuna Road. It connects Chiriquí, a small Pacific-side town on the Interamerican Highway about 15 kilometers east of David, with Chiriquí Grande, about 100 kilometers away on the Caribbean coast. The route takes travelers over the Continental Divide and the huge Fortuna dam and hydroelectric plant. It's a scenic drive on a good road, but be careful as it averages more than one auto accident a week, which is a lot given how little traffic it sees. Driving the length of the Fortuna Road takes a little under two hours at a reasonable speed.

The road descends the Caribbean slope quickly and soon reaches the hot and humid flatlands near the coast. Pass the village of Punta Peña. There'll be a crossroads ahead, with a 24-hour gas station and restaurant. Straight leads to the oil-port town of Chiriquí Grande, which has little to offer travelers now that water-taxi service to the islands ended with the opening of the road to Almirante.

Turn left at the gas station onto the new road to Almirante. This is a lovely, 70-kilometer drive that takes about an hour. But slash-and-burn farmers and subsistence ranchers have followed the road, and the lush tropical evergreen forest along this entire strip of coast is disappearing fast. Entire hillsides are sliding down into the road, so be careful. It's a disturbing example of how quickly nature can be devastated in the tropics; at this rate, the land here will be of little value to anyone in a few years.

There's a bridge between kilometer markers 8 and 9. For another worthwhile stop, pull over on the right just after the bridge, or turn left and park near the bank of the little river. About five minutes upriver is a huge boulder in the middle of the stream with petroglyphs near the top. There are trails on both sides of the river; the petroglyphs are easiest to see from the east side. When the trail gets very rocky, head uphill, which allows one to look down on the boulder. If you can't find it, and an Indian is hanging around, ask him or her to show the way. A tip of $.25–.50 for this would be appreciated. The trail on the west side of the river leads into some lovely forest and, I've been told, a waterfall about a half hour away that I haven't visited yet.

Back on the road, the turnoff to Almirante, the jumping-off point to the islands, is about 60 kilometers farther west. The turn to Almirante is on the right and comes up quickly. The main road continues to Changuinola and the Costa Rican border. After the turn, the road will fork. Be sure to take the gravel road to the right. Stay straight, with the train tracks on the right, and turn right just before the bus terminal—it should be the first right after the old Bocas Fruit Company sign. The water-taxi piers are up this road.

You'll probably encounter a *boletero* eager to show you the way and take you to the water-taxi service he works for. Park in the fenced-in lot for $3 a day. It should be possible to pay when you leave, though you may be asked to pay in advance. I've parked here without problems, as have many other travelers.

Getting Away

Those heading to Costa Rica can take a water taxi from Bocas town either to Changuinola or Almirante. Changuinola is closer to the border. At the time of writing, only Bocas Marine and Tours offered water-taxi service to Changuinola. Those traveling to nearly all destinations in Panama should take a water taxi to Almirante instead.

There is one direct bus a day from Changuinola to San José, Costa Rica. It leaves at 10 A.M. and arrives around 4 P.M. No direct buses to Costa Rica leave from Almirante. It's also possible to get a bus to San José from the Sixaola-Guabito border crossing; they leave Sixaola at 7 A.M., 9:30 A.M., and 2:30 P.M. Another option is to take a bus from Sixaola to Puerto Limón and transfer to a San José bus from there. Confirm these connections before making plans, as routes are subject to change; Bocas Marine and Tours can provide current information on bus transportation.

The pier for **Expreso Taxi 25** (tel./fax 757-9033) is near the town jail and the CEFATI tourist information office. Boats leave at 6 A.M., 6:30 A.M., 7:30 A.M., and 8:30 A.M. After that, boats leave approximately every hour, depending on demand, usually at around 45 minutes after the hour. The last boat leaves at 6:30 P.M.

The pier for **Bocas Marine and Tours** (tel./fax 757-9033) is midway down Calle 3, near Transparente Tours and Restaurante Le Pirate. Boats to Almirante leave approximately every hour from

6 A.M. to 6:30 P.M. The fare is $3. Boats to Changuinola leave at approximately 7 A.M., 8 A.M., 9:30 A.M., 11 A.M., 12:30 P.M., 2 P.M., 3:30 P.M., and 5:30 P.M. The boats at 9:30 A.M., 11 A.M., 12:30 P.M., 3:30 P.M., and 5:30 P.M. make a 10-minute stop at Boca del Drago. The fare is $5.

Getting from Finca 60 in Changuinola to the Costa Rica Border: On arrival at the Finca 60 pier, take a *colectiva* bus ($.40) to the Changuinola bus terminal and catch a bus to Guabito ($.70) from there, or else take a taxi straight to the border crossing in Guabito ($3 per person).

Getting from Almirante to Elsewhere in Panama: Buses from Almirante to David and Panama City leave from the crossroads at the edge of town. Take a taxi ($.50 per person) to get there. There is now only one direct daily bus to Panama City. It leaves Almirante at 8 A.M., arriving about 5:30 P.M. The fare is $23. Passengers are limited to two bags each. David-bound buses leave every hour or so from 5 A.M. to 7 P.M. The fare is $8 and the trip takes about four hours. Buses from Almirante to Changuinola leave from the Almirante bus terminal every 25 minutes from 6 A.M. until late in the evening. The trip takes a half hour and costs $1. It makes more sense, however, to take a water taxi directly from the islands to Changuinola.

GETTING AROUND
By Land

There are only two major roads beyond Bocas town: one that extends up the east coast of Isla Colón, dead-ending at Playa Bluff, and a second that cuts diagonally across the island to Boca del Drago. There's no need to ferry a car over, as it's easy to get around the island by taxi or rented bike or motorcycle. Bocas town is pedestrian friendly—there's so little traffic one can usually walk down the middle of Calle 3—and small and flat enough it's easy to walk everywhere in town.

Taxis troll Calle 3 looking for customers. The fare to the airport and anywhere in town, including all the way to the northern waterfront at Saigon, is $.50 per person. Round-trip fare to Playa Bluff is $10 per group (to be sure the taxi will return, don't pay until the return trip). A round-trip ride to Boca del Drago is $25 per group. *Transporte colectiva* vans, the closest thing Bocas town has to buses, operate in town and to the airport, also for $.50 per person. Flag them down just as you would a taxi, and pay when you board.

A bike/scooter rental stand next to Douglas' Golden Grill on Calle 3 near Avenida E rents bikes for $1 an hour or $5 a day and motorscooters for $8 an hour. Taller Joan Paul (near the north end of Calle 5, 8 A.M.–6 P.M. daily), next to Casa Amarilla, rents bikes for $1.50 an hour or $8 a day.

By Water

Many places on Isla Colón are more cheaply and easily reached by boat, which is the only way to get to the other islands in the archipelago.

Freelance boatmen operate a casual water-taxi service between the islands. These boats stop constantly throughout the day at the town piers. Boats operate less frequently at night, and the lack of proper lighting on most boats can make it a more risky prospect; try to travel in daylight. Boats leave when they fill up. The per-person fare is $.50 to Isla Carenero and $2 to Old Bank in Isla Bastimentos. Carenero is less than five minutes away; it takes about 10 minutes to get to Solarte or Old Bank. Negotiate with boatmen for other destinations. Less-common destinations may require hiring the whole boat; it may be more economical and efficient to visit these as part of a full-fledged boat tour.

Isla Bastimentos

This big, beautiful island (52 square kilometers) has a lot to offer nature lovers. The north shore has pounding surf and miles of gorgeous sandy beaches, some of which attract sea turtles in nesting season. The protected waters on the southeast side of the island, between Cayo Crawl and Punta Vieja, are shallow and glassy, making it easy to explore a large underwater playground of coral and sponges. To the southwest are mangrove islands. And the island itself is home to forest that harbors many exotic and endangered species, including the famous red poison-dart frog *(Dendrobates pumilio)* that many come to the island to see. The midsection of the island and some of its surrounding waters are part of a national marine park, Parque Nacional Marino Isla Bastimentos.

Though about 1,350 people live on the island, most are concentrated in the largely Afro-Caribbean town of Old Bank on its western tip, sometimes called simply Bastimentos, and in the Ngöbe village of Quebrada de Sal (Salt Creek in English). They're rather ragged places and there isn't much to see, but they're both culturally interesting and worth a visit. The name Bastimentos, by the way, comes from the Spanish word for "supplies" or "provisioning."

Bastimentos is a large, oddly shaped island, and its attractions are spread widely apart. The town of Old Bank, just 10 minutes by boat from Bocas town, is the closest to Isla Colón. Cayo Crawl is at the southern tip, separated by a shallow channel from Isla Popa. The southeast side is sheltered, with glassy water, coral gardens, the Ngöbe village of Quebrada de Sal, and access to the Cayos Zapatillas. Lovely beaches with pounding surf, the famous red frogs, and turtle-nesting spots are on the northern side. Exploring the forested interior, part of which belongs to the marine park, requires a guide to reach caves and a fresh-water lake.

SIGHTS

Old Bank

The town of Old Bank, known to some simply as "Bastimentos," is on the west tip of the island, not far from Isla Carenero and Bocas town. Most of its residents live crowded close to each other in modest, zinc-roofed homes perched on the waterfront or on the hillside behind it. Its residents are mostly descendents of West Indian immigrants, and the place has a mellow, strongly Caribbean vibe. There's always loud music playing—sometimes live, if you're lucky.

The town is poor and has little to see, but it still has lots of local color, and it's the best place in the islands to hear Guari-Guari, a Bocas-specific variety of so-called Panamanian Creole English. It's fascinating to listen to and nearly impossible for the uninitiated to make much sense of, even though it derives primarily from English. Residents are used to and tend to pay little attention to tourists, but a little friendliness can be warmly reciprocated. Roots Bar and Restaurant is a good place to meet local folks.

Two parallel concrete paths extend the length of town. It's not the most attractive place; there's trash strewn along the shore and a fair amount of squalor. There are several places to stay, the best of which are described below. There are also a couple of restaurants and bars. A trail to the north-side beaches starts at the east end of town.

⚑ Cayo Crawl

Boats from Isla Colón that approach Bastimentos from the south pass a series of idyllic mangrove islands, protected as part of the marine park, before coming to Cayo Crawl, a shallow channel between Isla Bastimentos and Isla Popa. In keeping with the Bocas name game, Cayo Crawl is sometimes called Cayo Coral, and in English it's called Crawl Cay or Coral Cay. Got that? It's about a half hour by boat from Bocas town.

The water here is a luminous light green, smooth as glass, and in some places only a meter deep before hitting sandy bottom. The area attracts lots of tropical fish. It's an easy, relaxing place to snorkel or splash around.

Note: Some tour operators, wanting to save on gas, take snorkelers only as far as Cayo Crawl and call it a day. Given that coral gardens don't start until one rounds the point and heads up the southeast coast of Bastimentos—at which point there are kilometers of them—don't agree to this. Find out ahead of time exactly where the boat is heading.

The channel harbors three rustic thatched hut restaurants, built on stilts over the water, that are tourist destinations in their own right. Tours to Cayos Zapatillas and around Bastimentos usually include a stop at one of these photogenic spots. These places are bare-bones

establishments, but at least you know the seafood is fresh.

The three restaurants—**Restaurante Adonis, Restaurante Alfonso,** and **Restaurante Cayo Crawl**—offer similar experiences and fare. They specialize in seafood, naturally, with prices ranging from about $6 for fried fish to $15–20 for lobster. Other offerings may include octopus and shrimp in coconut milk. Restaurante Alfonso is the newest, built in June 2004. Both it and Restaurante Cayo Crawl, which is arguably the most attractive, have some tables set off by themselves on their own little hut "islands." The last restaurant also now has cabañas for those who want to spend the night.

The water is so shallow and clear that diners can watch slender needlefish and brilliant parrotfish, angelfish, snapper, and other aquatic life cavort just off the boardwalk. The fish in the area are so spoiled by free feedings that the Restaurante Cayo Crawl once boasted a "tame" barracuda.

A good strategy for those who want to eat at any of these places, since service tends to proceed at a languorous Caribbean pace, is to place orders an hour ahead of time and then go snorkeling.

Cayo Crawl to Punta Vieja

The sheltered waters from Cayo Crawl to Punta Vieja, a point about eight kilometers up the southeast coast of Bastimentos, offer some colorful snorkeling. The sea here is so shallow and calm it's like swimming in a tropical aquarium. There's a variety of coral and sponges and lots of small but dazzling fish. However, as elsewhere in the archipelago, the visibility can be disappointing. A few small hotels have been built along the coast, but this is still a remarkably isolated and tranquil spot. Waves are so gentle here that fish swim right up to the narrow strips of sandy beach.

⚑ North Shore Beaches

The beaches along the north side of Bastimentos are generally much too rough to do more than get one's feet wet. But there are several spectacularly beautiful beaches here. The one most popular with sea turtles is **Playa Larga.** (See *Parque Na-*

The north shore beaches of Isla Bastimentos are among the loveliest in Panama.

cional Marino Isla Bastimentos and sidebar, *Sea Turtles,* in this chapter.) Warning: There have been reports of thefts from these beaches, particularly Playa Primera (First Beach). Do not leave valuables unattended.

The sea is often too choppy to land boats on the beaches. An exception is **Playa Polo,** which is partly protected because waves break on rocks about 100 meters offshore. This means it's easier to go for a swim here, but it also means it's more likely to have visitors than some of the other beaches, and it's far too small to accommodate many people comfortably. There's a little house that sells cold beer, but there are nicer beaches farther west.

If the sea is rough, the best way to get to these beaches is to walk across the western neck of the island from Old Bank.

The trail to the beach starts toward the eastern edge of town, just past the soccer field and trash pile. You'll have to walk through townspeople's yards to get to the trail. There are now signs pointing to the start of the trail, but ask for directions to the beach or *playa* (PLY-yah) if you can't find the way. It's a very pretty walk over a hill to the beach, with panoramic views

from the summit. The walk takes less than half an hour at a moderate pace. Part of the trail leads through private property, and if the owner is around pay him a $1 toll to pass through it. The trail can get muddy and slippery near the beach.

The first beach you'll come to is called, logically enough, **Playa Primera (First Beach),** also known as Playa Wizard. It's a wide, stunning stretch of sand and big rollers and, if you're lucky, very few people. Again, beware of the strong surf here. Walk east to get to **Playa Segunda (Second Beach)** and **Red Frog Beach.**

Silverbacks, the biggest surf break in Bocas, is off this stretch of coast and is accessible by boat. It's a huge, barreling reef-bottom right break that is often compared to big Hawaiian waves such as Backdoor. Wave faces can exceed seven meters. It's strictly for expert surfers. There are also beach breaks off First Beach and Red Frog Beach that are appropriate for intermediate surfers.

Red Frog Beach's namesake is a tiny creature also called the strawberry poison-dart frog *(Dendrobates pumilio)* that's easier to spot here than anywhere else in Panama. The toxins in its skin are only a danger to animals who try to eat it. In

DON'T EAT THE STRAWBERRY FROGS

What is locally called the red frog is more widely referred to as the strawberry poison-dart frog. But neither name does justice to a species that comes in a jewel box of colors. Though in its best-known form it's red with blue legs, the tiny frog can be green, yellow, purple, orange, black, white, or a combination of these and other colors, with or without spots.

A safer bet is to call it by its scientific name, *Dendrobates pumilio*. It lives along the Caribbean coast from Nicaragua to Panama. Though common throughout Bocas del Toro, Bastimentos is famous for containing a remarkable number of forms, or morphs, on a single island.

The frogs can be hard to spot because of their small size: just 18–25 millimeters, or less than half as big as a man's thumb. They live in the forests of the islands and mainland but don't mind disturbed areas and are easiest to spot in dry leaf litter or near the forest edge. The males have a surprisingly loud call.

There are many other Dendrobates species, some still being found: *Dendrobates claudiae* was discovered on Bastimentos as recently as 2000.

Though its skin produces toxins for defense, *Dendrobates pumilio* doesn't pose a threat to humans, particularly those who don't eat one. It's nowhere near as potent as the golden poison-dart frog of Colombia, the aptly named *Phyllobates terribilis*. The skin of a single specimen of these is said to have enough toxin to kill 20,000 mice or a gruesome number of humans. Indigenous hunters of the Colombian rainforest traditionally tipped their blowgun darts with the deadly stuff.

Compared to these formidable creatures, *Dendrobates pumilio* is positively cuddly. But their own poison, or pumiliotoxin, is still potent. A group of visiting researchers discovered in 2004 where they get it: from munching a type of small ant.

reality the frog comes in a variety of vibrant colors besides red.

This beach can be approached by sea only when the water is dead calm. Otherwise, boatmen drop passengers off at one of the beaches to the west and tell them to walk over, or drop them at a trail east of Old Bank that leads over a narrow isthmus to Red Frog Beach. The last is the best option, as the trail is good and it's an easy 10-minute walk to the beach. There are lots of other frogs in the forest here. The noise they make is amazing; it's like a huge frog convention. Pay $1 a head at the end of the trail to get to the beach, as the access is across private land.

It can be hard to spot red frogs at first, though once you see one they suddenly seem to be everywhere. Look among the fallen leaves at the end of the trail near the beach. If a resident is around, ask him or her for help in finding the *rana roja* (RAH-na ROH-ha).

Note: A condominium resort and marina, with a road linking it to the south side of the island, was being planned for Red Frog Beach.

Construction was slated to start by the end of 2005. This place may look quite different in a couple of years.

Quebrada de Sal

This village of 450 people is not terribly scenic—it's a bit too simultaneously poor and modernized for that—but it's worth a visit, at least for those already on Bastimentos. It's approached by water on the southeast side of the island, between Cayo Crawl and Punta Vieja. The approach can be one of the best parts of the trip, as the boat has to pass through dense mangrove channels where there's a chance of spotting sloths. The boat docks next to a concrete path that peters out at the edge of the village. Visitors must pay $1 a head to enter, and sign a registry. There's a meager souvenir shop that has crude, painted wooden figures of animals, some *chácaras* (traditional woven Ngöbe-Buglé handbags) and a few other things, but nothing too memorable.

The center of the community is a spacious

field with a cinderblock school house, a dining hall, and a dance hall. A lot of the traditional Ngöbe culture has disappeared from the village. Women don't wear traditional dresses, for instance, though there are still some thatched-roof houses on stilts and residents who still adhere to their traditional religion. The villagers are courteous if a bit reserved, but those who speak some Spanish should have little trouble finding someone to chat with.

There isn't much else in the village, but there's a nice forest hike from here that leads to Playa Larga. The trail starts at the far side of the village. It's a good idea to hire a villager for a few dollars to lead the way and point out the flora and fauna. It's also possible to do this hike without a guide, but as always don't head off into the forest alone or in flip-flops. The walk takes about an hour each way and there's a chance of spotting armadillos, *conejos pintado,* and other small creatures.

ENTERTAINMENT AND EVENTS

Entertainment is mostly confined to the bars and restaurants along the waterfront in Old Bank. **Roots Bar and Restaurant** is a friendly place to hang out. **Bar El Gaviero** is a new, smaller place near Hotel Caribbean View. **Cantina La Feria** draws partiers, both local and visiting, from all over Bocas for its "Blue Monday" dance parties. This place has all the rough Caribbean character one could want. It's a basic cantina over the water that serves *seco* and beer at locals-friendly prices. The scene can be kind of intimidating at first, especially when the cops come around checking IDs and busting locals for mysterious reasons, but the vibe is generally low-key. Use common sense, go with a group, and be respectful, just as you would at any hard-drinking place back home. And bring earplugs.

Notable annual events, and excuses for a party, in Old Bank include **Palo de Mayo,** a Maypole dance on May 1 that's also held in Bocas town, and **Founding Day** on November 23. The place to be on **New Year's Eve** is the Al Natural Resort.

SPORTS AND RECREATION

Bar y Pizzeria Pelicano (tel. 757-9830), at the far end of Old Bank, rents kayaks for $2.50 an hour or $12 for the day, and dugout canoes for $1.50 an hour, $5 for a half day or $10 for a whole day.

Parque Nacional Marino Isla Bastimentos

This 13,226-hectare park is shaped like a bridge and, as its name suggests, most of it is underwater. It starts among the mangrove islands on the southwest side of Bastimentos, arcs across its midsection, and curves down to two lovely little islands.

These islands, the **Cayos Zapatillas,** are the most visited parts of the park thanks to the good snorkeling and diving among the nearby coral gardens and underwater caves, which start about 12 meters down. It's quite dramatic even to snorkel around here; the shallow waters suddenly give way to deep canyons. The coral heads inside the reef are in good shape, and there is a large variety and abundance of fish. Nurse sharks live in this area, as well as two different species of lobsters. Note that it's turbulent around here, which can make visibility cloudy. It's not a good place for snorkelers who aren't fairly strong swimmers. There's an attractive beach on the western island for those who would prefer to lounge, but the *chitras* can get nippy. The Zapatillas are about an hour by fast boat from Isla Colón.

There is an interpretive trail called **El Bosque Detrás del Arrecife** ("the forest behind the reef") on the more easterly of the Zapatillas (farther away from Bastimentos). It starts behind the ranger station. ANAM has put out a glossy booklet, in Spanish only, that describes the trail. The ranger at Zapatillas may have copies, but don't count on it. Before you leave Bocas town ask for the booklet at the ANAM office or CEFATI. Camping on either island is possible for $5 more per tent.

Most visitors to Isla Bastimentos come only for the beach, but the **inland forest** is a natural treasure trove, which is why a big swath of it is included in the marine park. For one thing, it is home to 28 species of reptiles and amphibians, more than half of which are threatened or endangered. There's a good chance of spotting sloths, monkeys, and many species of birds in a trip through the forest, especially in the early morning. The **Laguna de Bastimentos,** near the north coast midway across the island, is home to freshwater turtles, caimans, and crocodiles. Do not attempt a hike through the forest without a guide; you will get lost.

Playa Larga, which is part of the park, is an important sea-turtle nesting area, attracting four species of endangered turtles from about April or May through September.

Admission to the park is a whopping $10 per person. Even those just snorkeling or diving in the waters around the Cayos Zapatillas must pay this fee. Ask the tour operator if the fee is included in the price of the tour.

Nature Tours

Those staying in Old Bank should consider contacting Pension Tío Tom for tours of the island and the surrounding area. **Tom Reichelt,** half of the laid-back couple that owns the pension, is a landscape gardener and tree expert who is quietly passionate about this beautiful place. He leads tours of the interior of the island and has a special fondness for ones that involve searching for frogs (the pension has a cool frog terrarium) or exploring caves that he says are the largest in Panama—there's one on Bastimentos that is 1,475 meters long. Other tours include a trip to Swan's Cay, hikes through the island to a freshwater lake, hikes to the beaches, and *cayuco* trips through the mangroves. He charges $6 an hour for guide services. Trips that require use of the pension's motorboat are an extra $5/$10 half day/full day, plus fuel. Tom speaks English, German, and some Spanish, and he really knows his stuff.

Gallardo Livingston (tel. 757-9388) lives in Old Bank, making it easy to get in touch with him for boat tours. **Bola Smith** (tel. 757-9680) lives in Bocas town but specializes in boat/walking nature tours of Bastimentos. (See the *Isla Colón* section for information on both boatmen.)

ACCOMMODATIONS AND FOOD

Most places to stay and eat are in Old Bank, and most of these are budget options. Residents often rent out rooms in their houses to travelers for a few dollars. This is definitely a way to become immersed in the local culture, but these rooms are generally super basic and the surroundings noisy. Residents willing to rent rooms post signs on their houses, making it easy to wander around until something looks appealing. Be somewhat cautious in selecting lodging: When I last visited I got some seriously weird, unfriendly druggie vibes from one of the cheaper but not unattractive places, which for obvious reasons is not recommended here. Try to get a feel for the atmosphere before handing over money.

Cayo Crawl has a couple of restaurants that serve mainly those on boat tours (see *Sights* for descriptions), and there's now one place to stay there, too. The most upscale accommodations are quite a ways away, between Cayo Crawl and Punta Vieja on the southeast side of the island. Distances between these three areas are great enough that guests will usually end up eating at or near their lodgings.

Old Bank

All the places to stay and eat in Old Bank (Bastimentos town) are either right along the waterfront or along a concrete path on the hillside above it. The ones below are listed from right to left as one faces the water. The place is experiencing a building boom and there will likely be several more options when you visit.

A new place, **Casa del Sol,** was being built when I last visited. It looked as if it were going to consist of a two-story building with balconies, plus two more rooms set right on the rocky shore (there's no beach). These were being carefully built from wood and bamboo. The place looked like it was going to be relatively upscale. It should be open by the time you visit. The spot is very pretty, with a view of Isla Carenero. It's around the edge of the point and isolated from most of the surrounding houses, though a beer garden that attracts loud parties is nearby.

⋈ Pension Tío Tom (tel. 757-9831, tomina@cwp.net.pa, rooms start at $12 s/d) is a fun place to stay for anyone with a bohemian bent. Accommodations are basic and aimed at the backpacking set, but the place oozes rustic, piratical charm. The pension has three double rooms with shared bath (s/d $12) and a large room, the nicest, with a private bath ($20, or $7 per person for four people). It has a simple restaurant attached that can prepare vegetarian food. Breakfast costs $2.50–5; lunch and dinner go for about $5–6. The pension is built over the water, on a pier that attracts 38 species of colorful fish. Shortly before my first visit, a couple of guests tied fishing lines to their toes at night, tossed the hooks out their window, and fished while they slept. Fortunately for them, they didn't snag a barracuda. Though Pension Tío Tom has a secluded feel, bear in mind it's in the middle of the town's rather crowded waterfront, and trash along the shore and loud music played by neighbors are part of the local color. The pension is the home of the friendly, easygoing German owners, Tom and Ina Reichelt, and their teenage daughter, who speaks Guari-Guari. They've lived on Bastimentos for a decade and know the area well. They offer nature tours of Bastimentos and the surrounding islands. They speak English, German, and some Spanish.

Hospedaje Aislenis (tel. 757-9410 or 757-9383, $6 s, $12 d) is an utterly bare-bones place over the water. It's basically a large shed divided into rooms built from rough planks. Rooms have a fan and private bathroom and not much more. Rooms with shared bath are $2 cheaper. Other than price, the main thing this place has going for it is friendly management. The *hospedaje* offers boat tours of surrounding attractions for $7–15 per person.

Roots Bar and Restaurant is a pleasant thatched-roof place over the water with a friendly Caribbean vibe. This is a good place to try traditional Caribbean food with coconut sauce (ask for the "secret" Roots sauce). Dishes run toward seafood, including lobster and octopus.

The owner of the old Hospedaje Silvia now has a new hotel, **Hotel Caribbean View** (tel. 757-9442, $44 s/d), which was easily the most upscale lodging in Old Bank at the time of writing. It's a two-story, Caribbean-style building, white with gold trim, that's right on the water and has 11 rooms with modern bathrooms, TVs, and telephones. All the rooms have fans and six have air-conditioning.

Bar El Gaviero (tel. 516-9726, 4–11 P.M.), opened at the end of 2004, is a cute little thatched-roof place near the Hotel Caribbean View that's run by an Italian-Spanish couple. The husband is a DJ, so the music here is eclectic and fun. I haven't yet tried the food, but the

Pension Tío Tom in Old Bank is popular with backpackers.

menu runs toward Mediterranean and Caribbean dishes starting at $3.

There are five rooms at **Bar y Pizzeria Pelicano** (tel. 757-9830, $10s, $16 d), at the far end of town. Two of them are in the restaurant itself, which is on piles above the water, and three more are on the shore. The rooms are rustic and this isn't a very attractive spot; for one thing, the shoreline isn't too clean. A third person in a room is another $5. Pizzas are the specialty at the restaurant: They start at $3.50 for a medium pie, $5.50 for a big one.

Cayo Crawl

Cabañas Coral Cay (tel. 626-1919, 626-3269, caycoral@hotmail.com, www.bocas.com, $82.50 s/$165 d, including two meals, snorkeling gear, and *cayuco*) has recently been added onto Restaurante Cayo Crawl's boardwalk. It consists of a handful of rustic but charming little wood cabins with patchwork quilt covers and curtains made of shells and shards of coral. However, the *chitras* are ferocious—the place is right next to mangroves—and there are no screens on the windows. Each cabin has two units and the walls don't go all the way to the roof, so don't expect much privacy. The rustic bathrooms are shared. Stays here include breakfast, dinner, transfers to and from Isla Colón, and use of snorkeling equipment and a *cayuco* (dugout canoe). These extras do not make up for the exorbitant price of these rustic accommodations. However, prices and amenities seem to be fluctuating wildly as this place finds it niche, so be sure to check for current offerings. Tours are not included but can be arranged. Guests are isolated out here; there's nothing else around, and Bocas town is a half-hour boat ride away. The place has a tiny store with a few supplies.

Between Cayo Crawl and Punta Vieja

There are three appealing places to stay on the nearly 10 kilometers of beautiful curving coastline between Cayo Crawl and Punta Vieja. Each is quite secluded, both from each other and from everything else. Depending on boat speed, it can take up to an hour to reach them from Isla Colón.

Tranquilo Bay (renee@tranquilobay.com, www.tranquilobay.com, tel. 620-4179, tel. 713/589-6952 in the U.S., one-week all-inclusive stays start at $1,200 per person double occupancy) is a new all-inclusive place perched on a hill just around the point from Cayo Crawl. It consists of six air-conditioned, concrete-walled cabañas with zinc roofs, set in a clearing at the top of the breezy hill. Most have ocean views. There's also a two-story main lodge with a dining room and bar. A helicopter pad for emergencies and a swimming pool were in the works. The resort is situated on 50 acres of land that was a banana plantation for 100 years; the owners are building on six acres of land and letting the rest revert to forest. Note that the resort isn't on a beach. The hill is set above mangroves, but attractive beaches are a short boat ride away.

The project is the creation of two enthusiastic and friendly Texan couples who are clearly building their dream retreat. The basic weeklong package, for $1,200 per person, includes all transfers between airports, a Saturday-night stay at a Panama City hotel, round-trip airfare between Panama City and Bocas, transfers between Isla Colón and Tranquilo Bay, lodging in a cabaña from Sunday through the following Saturday, all meals and drinks, and water and land activities around the resort. These last include kayaking, snorkeling, swimming, hikes, and access to Tranquilo Bay's library and video library. Packages that include daily guided tours cost about $300–600 more per person, depending on time and distance. These can include snorkeling, diving, surfing, water-skiing, fishing, forest hikes, and so on.

Hotel El Limbo on the Beach (no phone on Bastimentos, tel. 757-9062 in Bocas town, www.el-limbo.com, ellimbo@hotmail.com, $65 per person, including breakfast, dinner, and kayak use) is the more rustic sister of Hotel El Limbo on the Sea in Bocas town. It lies about midway between Cayo Crawl and Punta Vieja. If the Swiss Family Robinson had built a hotel, it would have looked like this. It consists of a picturesque wooden building with four basic but comfortable rooms, two with stunning ocean views. This is a real get-away-from-it-all place; it's been all but deserted the times I've visited it. It's a colorful place, but bear in mind

Bocas del Toro

it's quite simple for the price and tours to surrounding attractions aren't included.

N Al Natural Resort (tel./fax 757-9004, cell 623-2217 or 640-6935, alnaturalbocas@cw-panama.net, www.bocas.com/alnatura.htm, rates start at $150 s, $200 d, including all meals, transportation, and use of recreation equipment) is a remarkable place. It consists of just a handful of bungalows (the warm and friendly Belgian owners never plan to build more than nine) on a secluded, pristine beach just below Punta Vieja on the southeast side of Isla Bastimentos. The bungalows are based on the traditional Ngöbe-Buglé house design: they're round, thatched-roofed wooden structures on stilts perched on the edge of the clear blue water. Inside, they're remarkably comfortable and well-appointed for such a remote spot. They have private, hot-water showers (a modern flush toilet is in a clean, well-maintained stall just outside each bungalow), good queen- or king-sized beds with mosquito netting fine enough to keep out *chitras,* and an electrical system powered by solar panels. Rain is collected and purified for drinking water.

One of the most attractive features of the bungalows is the way they're designed to put guests as close to the lovely natural surroundings as possible. The entire front of the bungalow is an open deck with gorgeous views of the sea, the Cayos Zapatillas, and the distant mainland. The back of the bungalows are partly open to the tropical forest behind the resort. But the area is so isolated, and the bungalows so well designed, that each has a great deal of privacy. They also tend to be surprisingly free of creepy-crawlies. I've never been any place where the margin between comfortable indoors and beautiful outdoors was so thin without ever making guests feel they're camping.

The bungalows are set on nine hectares of land, a former coconut plantation that is being allowed to revert to forest. Three species of primates, armadillos, boas, opossums, raccoons, and caiman have been spotted back here. A short, wide trail leads through this patch of secondary-growth forest to a north-shore beach. Guests have free use of sea kayaks, snorkeling gear, and fishing tackle in the calm, protected waters in front of the resort.

A recent addition is a large, three-story building—also wooden and thatch-roofed. The bottom

It's fun to take note of the little touches at the carefully designed Al Natural Resort.

floor is the dining/bar area. The second floor houses an open-air games area. There's an observation deck with expansive views on the top floor, 49 steps up from the dining room. It's a cool addition to the place. Meals are served family-style; the food is simple, but good wine is included with dinners. Some of the food—including bananas, pineapples, and ducks—is grown or raised at the resort. Occasionally a guest chef cooks; when he does, the quality of the food soars.

This is a great option for couples looking for a romantic spot, for adventurous families, or even for students of ingenious and environmentally appropriate architecture. The first few bungalows were designed and built over five years to make sure everything was done right. It's fun to note all the little touches. The showers are lined with pebbles laid out to form traditional Ngöbe-Buglé designs. The bungalows use a great deal of driftwood, with shapes carefully selected to fit into the overall design instead of being cut to fit. The bungalows are angled so that most storms blow in from behind; tarplike drapes can be clipped into place across the open front of the bungalows on those rare occasions when rain moves in from the sea. Pools of water around the bungalows' pilings keep termites out; seawater is used for this to keep from breeding mosquitoes.

There are three kinds of accommodations. The Natural House has a queen-sized bed and 12-volt electrical system. The Natural House Deluxe is larger, with a king-sized bed and 110-volt electrical system, sufficient to run a ceiling fan. There is also a two-story Natural House. It's well worth spending the extra money for a Natural House Deluxe, which are significantly nicer than the more basic Natural Houses.

Given how remote this spot is, it's not surprising maintenance can sometimes be a concern. On my most recent visit, there were glitches with the hot water and one of the boats. These problems were quickly resolved, but anyone who stays here should not expect everything to run like clockwork; it's still a bohemian Caribbean place, even given the exclusive prices.

Prices do get steep here by Bocas standards in the high season, but the experience is special enough to justify a splurge for those who can afford it. High-season rates start at $150/$200 s/d for the first night in a Natural House. After that, the rate drops about $25 per person. This includes transportation to and from Isla Colón in a fast boat, three meals a day including wine with dinner, and free use of snorkeling gear, kayaks, and fishing tackle.

Add about $20 per person for the two-story Natural House and about $25 per person for the Natural House Deluxe. "All-inclusive" packages that add daily half-day tours and all drinks are also available; there's a two-night minimum for these. Rates are about $5–10 cheaper per night during low season, from May through November. For extended stays, the seventh night is free. Children ages two and younger can stay for free; children ages 3–12 are half price.

The two-story Natural House and the Natural House Deluxe can sleep up to four people; rates are calculated per person, not per room, but the per-person rate is lower with three or four people, so families or friendly couples can get a price break by getting cozy.

PRACTICALITIES

Tranquilo Bay, El Limbo on the Beach, and Al Natural generally arrange all food, transportation, and activities for their guests. Make sure to clarify exactly what is being provided ahead of time, especially if you're staying at El Limbo, because there are no stores, water taxis, or services of any kind on this side of the island. Even Old Bank is a long boat ride away. In Old Bank there is a minisuper near Roots Bar and Restaurant and a police post above Pension Tío Tom. There is Internet access at Tío Tom; Hotel Caribbean View should eventually have it also.

Isla Colón is a 10-minute water-taxi ride from Old Bank; flag down passing boats. The fare is $2 per person.

Beyond Isla Colón and Isla Bastimentos

ISLA CARENERO

This little island is just a banana's throw across the water from Bocas town. Because it's so close to the busy waterfront and is pretty built up itself, it's not a popular tourist destination. It's more like a suburb of Bocas town. But it's home to several appealing places to stay and eat, and the **Galería Las Palmas** (tel./fax 757-9253), near El Pargo Rojo, is a small artisans' shop with a variety of crafts for sale.

The side of the island facing Isla Colón is rather densely populated, with lots of basic houses squeezed next to each other on the waterfront. The side that faces Bastimentos is more deserted; there's little there except for a couple of small hotels and a bit of beach. The north side of the island has pounding surf but the coastline is rather rugged and more mud and farmland than beach. Actually, the whole island is ringed by just a narrow band of sandy beach. Visitors have to travel to one of the other islands for big, spectacular beaches. The island seems especially popular with voracious *chitras*.

Residents will tell you it's possible to walk around the entire perimeter of the island. You can, but be prepared for a bit of an adventure rather than a leisurely walk. It can take up to two hours to walk the whole way around, and there are sections that require scrambling up muddy hills, dropping several feet, slipping through barbed-wire fences, avoiding pounding surf, and negotiating slippery, jagged rocks. It's no big deal, but it's not an easy stroll and it's not always obvious how to avoid obstacles. Consider hiring a local kid to lead the way for a quarter or two, and wear shoes with good traction.

Carenero is popular with surfers for a long, barreling reef break off the north side of the island that's considered one of the best waves in Bocas. Called simply Carenero, it's just a five-minute boat ride from Bocas town and thus can get crowded. The reef is shallow; wear booties.

That's about all there is in the way of activities on the island other than splashing and paddling around.

Accommodations and Food

Places to stay on Carenero vary from basic bungalows to fairly upscale miniresorts. Most have a restaurant attached. A walking path along the water links all of them. Places below are listed in counterclockwise order, starting from the west side of the island.

The family-run **Careening Cay Resort** (tel./fax 757-9242, $49.50 s/d) is on well-landscaped grounds on the water overlooking Isla Colón. It comprises four wooden cabins, Carenero's marina, and an open-air restaurant. The cabins are new and immaculate. One cabin has a king-sized bed. The other three have a master bedroom and a separate room that contains four bunk beds. The larger cabins can sleep up to six, $16.50 each after the first two people. Laundry service is available for $6 a load.

The restaurant attached to the resort is the **Sunset Grill** (tel./fax 757-9242, 8–9:30 A.M., 11 A.M.–2 P.M., 5–9 P.M. Mon.–Sat., 8–9:30 A.M. Sun.), which serves gringo-style food in a large, pleasant *rancho*. Offerings include burgers, grilled sandwiches, fish prepared a dozen ways, pork chops, surf and turf, and so on. It also boasts eight kinds of daiquiris. There are a Texas barbecue on Tuesday, Mexican food on Wednesday, and Asian food on Thursday.

Careening Cay can arrange boat transportation to and from Isla Colón for hotel and dining guests.

Restaurante Las Tortugas (tel. 757-9360, 9 A.M.–midnight daily), directly across the channel from Bocas town, serves mostly seafood at low prices. It'll send a boat to pick up diners from Isla Colón for $1.

M El Pargo Rojo (tel. 757-9649 or cell 685-2948, reservations@pargorojo.net, www.pargorojo.net), next to Restaurante Las Tortugas, has some of the best food in the islands and a few rustic but cheerful cabins. Even those staying on Isla Colón should consider making the short boat trip over; call ahead of time and a boat will pick you up ($.50 per person during the day, $1 at night). The owner, Bernard, is also the cook, and he's a good one. Possible offerings include hummus, chicken à la king, sushi, kebabs, Greek salad, and tandoori chicken. Most dishes are $6.75–12 (for lobster). Bernard is an Iranian who moved to Maryland after the revolution. The bandanna he wears gives him the air of a pirate, as do the tales of his many exploits. The restaurant is quite simple, built on a pier right over the water, as are the five cabins. These are Ngöble-Buglé style, with plank floors and walls and thatched roofs. The sea is visible through the floorboards. Cabins are basic but have hot-water private bathrooms, and the walls are decorated with hand-painted toucans, flowering vines, and such. Rates are $25 for up to three people, $30 for four, and $50 for five. An eight-person dorm is available for $40, which is a good deal for a large group. Free use of *cayucos* is included. Rates can double when there's high demand. This place has a lot of rustic charm. Note: Rumor at the time of writing had it that Bernard was planning to open a restaurant in Boquete; what this meant for the future of El Pargo Rojo was unclear.

Casa Acuario (tel. 757-9565, joberg1301@ cwp.net.pa, $82.50 s/d including breakfast) is a bed-and-breakfast built right over the water that offers four cute, spacious, and sunny wood-paneled rooms with modern bathrooms, air-conditioning, and cable TV. It has its own small stretch of beach. There's a balcony upstairs with a view of the ocean, Isla Colón, and the mountains on the distant shore. Guests are welcome to use the kitchen. A third and fourth person in the room are another $11 each. The place has a family vibe and not a whole lot of privacy, so pray that your neighbors are *simpático*.

Hotel Tierra Verde (tel. 757-9903, info@ hoteltierraverde.com, www.hoteltierraverde.com, $40–45 s, $50d including continental breakfast) is a somewhat incongruous place in these surroundings. It's a three-story modern hotel set well back from the beach that feels quite insulated from its surroundings. Built in January 2001, it has seven rooms, all with air-conditioning and hot-water bathrooms. The larger, nicer rooms are upstairs. There's a bar, and guests are welcome to use the kitchen. Guests can also use the

Internet computer in the lobby. The hotel can arrange boat tours.

The Panamanian-run **Doña Mara** (tel. 757-9551, donamara10@hotmail.com, www.bocas .com, $55 s/d), on the east side of the island, facing Bastimentos, is a cinderblock building with six simple but pleasant and brightly painted rooms, all with air-conditioning, cable TV, older furnishings, and tile floors. The place is well-maintained, but rates are excessive for such a simple place. It's on a small beach and has a bar and restaurant, with dishes going for $7.75–14.50.

The **Buccaneer Resort** (tel./fax 757-9042, tiothom@cwp.net.pa, www.buccaneer-resort .com, $71.60 s/d or $93.50 s/d for a bedroom suite, including breakfast), the last place to stay on this side of the island, is one of the archipelago's more upscale hotels. It consists of 12 units spread among four elevated cabañas and a pair of two-story buildings set on 10 acres of land. The two-story buildings have two large rooms downstairs and two upstairs (the resort calls these "bedroom suites." The downstairs rooms have screened-in porches. The upstairs rooms feature lovely wraparound verandas and wet bars, refrigerators, toasters, and coffeepots. The cabañas are standalone suites with one double and one single bed. All the rooms are air-conditioned with modern furnishings and bathrooms. There's a tiny beach in front of the resort and a little slice of forest behind it. An attractive restaurant and bar that serves seafood, meats, and pasta for about $6.50–15 is attached. Lunch is cheaper. The restaurant was closed but slated to reopen during my last visit, so check ahead of time. Note that a 15 percent service charge is added to the food bill. The place is run by an extremely colorful gringo named Thomas Williams, known locally as "Captain Tom."

Practicalities

There are few services of any kind on Carenero, but it's less than five minutes by boat from Bocas town. Water taxis run frequently between Carenero and the two town piers. The fare is $.50. To get to Bastimentos from Carenero, it's easier to take a boat back to Bocas town and get a Bastimentos-bound boat ($2) from there.

ISLA SOLARTE

Also known as **Nancy's Cay,** Solarte is a seven-kilometer-long island situated two kilometers east of Isla Colón. Its western tip, Hospital Point, is one of the most popular diving and snorkeling spots in the archipelago. There are coral reefs just a few meters from the surface, but there's also a wall that drops about 13 meters.

The point is named for the hospital the United Fruit Company built here in 1900 for its labor force, which was being decimated by malaria, yellow fever, and other tropical diseases. The hospital closed in 1920 after a fungus known as Panama disease wiped out the banana plantations on the islands and surrounding shore, forcing the company to move its operations farther west.

The house on the point is the home of Clyde Stephens, who for 32 years was a banana researcher for United Fruit. He gives lectures on the history of the banana industry, and his books include a history of Hospital Point, which he bought in 1970. His books are available in Bocas town. Try the Bravo Center or Buena Vista Bar and Grill.

Practicalities

There is almost nothing on Solarte at the moment, but plans are in the works for a major retirement development on the island. So far the only thing that has been built is the one place to stay on the island, **Solarte del Caribe Inn** (tel. 757-9032, fax 757-9043, steve@solarteinn.com, www.solarteinn.com, starts at $71.50 s/d, including breakfast and daily transport to and from Bocas town). It's a pleasant new bed-and-breakfast on a breezy hillside with a view of the ocean from the patio/dining area, which is done up in attractive woods. There are seven modern rooms with private hot-water baths. Staying here feels a bit like visiting an acquaintance's mountain home. Dinners, for $7–15, are possible with notice, and picnic lunches can be arranged for $5. The food is good. Boat tours of the islands can be arranged if the boat is available. Internet and fax services are available. Laundry is $3 a load. There's a rec room downstairs that has a television with DirecTV.

Isla Solarte is about 10 minutes by boat from Bocas town. A diving or snorkeling trip to Hospital Point is usually included as part of a tour of the islands.

ELSEWHERE IN THE ARCHIPELAGO

The islands and littoral in the rest of the archipelago are still sparsely populated and have no facilities for visitors, though this may well have changed by the time you visit. Each year more places are opened to tourism.

The **Laguna de Chiriquí** is huge and placid and a lovely place to boat around. The Talamanca mountain range and stacks of billowing clouds in the distance make for lovely vistas. On **Isla Cristóbal** two Ngöbe communities, **San Cristóbal** and **Valle Escondido,** are beginning to attract some visitors. **Isla Popa** is crawling with fer-de-lance and other poisonous snakes. It should be visited only with a good forest guide. The **Darkland Peninsula (Tierra Oscura)** is popular with birders. **Isla Cayo de Agua** is a distant but promising spot for scuba divers. The waters around **Isla Escudo de Veraguas** are supposed to be exceptionally clear and the coral reef healthy (I've yet to visit it). It's a serious all-day trip, however, and requires a good boat and experienced captain. It can be visited only between August and October. At other times, the wind and waves are too rough for boats. Getting there takes about two hours in a boat equipped with a 125-horsepower motor.

Mainland Bocas

Most visitors spend as little time as possible on the mainland of the province. The towns are generally poor and neglected and have just about nothing that qualifies as a "tourist attraction," but those who haven't experienced the Caribbean boonies may enjoy at least passing through. They have a bit of a rough, frontier feel and should be approached with some caution, at least at night, but one can also meet some kind people. For most travelers, however, Guabito is just a border crossing, Changuinola and Almirante just transportation hubs on the way to somewhere else, and Chiriquí Grande a name on a map.

Mainland Bocas outside the towns holds more appeal, thanks mainly to the gigantic Parque Internacional La Amistad and, increasingly, the Wekso Ecolodge and Center. Powerful rivers and magnificent evergreen forests lead down from the highlands, where indigenous peoples work to survive culturally and physically. Important wetlands line the coast, including the at least nominally protected San San Pondsack.

ALMIRANTE

You'd have to be bananas (ouch!) to choose to stay in the small, ramshackle port town of Almirante (pop. 12,430) rather than on the islands, but those who miss the last water taxi from town may end up stranded here for the night. (For transportation information, see the *Isla Colón* section.)

The main street into Almirante leads from the highway and parallels the railroad tracks as it reaches town. The water-taxi piers are to the right, across the train tracks and not visible from the road. There's a hotel, Hotel San Francisco, and a general store on the left side of the road and a bus terminal on the right. A second road crosses the main street just past the bus terminal. Most of the town's services are on or near this road.

Practicialities

The best bet for a night's stay is **Hotel San Francisco** (tel. 778-3779, fax 778-3761, start at $11 s, $15.40 d for older rooms with fans). It's close to the railroad tracks, near the bus terminal and water taxi piers. The hotel has 14 rooms, all with TVs and droopy beds. Room quality varies wildly. The cheapest rooms are basic and gloomy, with filthy shared baths. These cost $11/$15.40 s/d with fans or $15.40/$19.20 s/d with air-conditioning.

The most expensive ones are perfectly fine, at least for those without bad backs, and have air-conditioning and private hot-water bathrooms. They go for $27.50 s and $38 d/t. These rooms have been recently renovated, and the others may have been similarly spruced up and more expensive by the time you visit. Room prices may be subject to bargaining depending on demand. The hotel is above a general store that also serves as the hotel reception.

Restaurante Delimar (11 A.M.–midnight Mon.–Sat., 4–10 P.M. Sun.) looked like a pleasant enough place to eat, but it was closed when I last visited. It's just a few minutes' walk from the bus terminal and Hotel San Francisco. To get there, turn right off the main road at the intersection behind the bus terminal and look for a big store called Novedades La Flora de Almirante. The restaurant is just past that, on the left side of the street.

Around the corner from that big store is a Western Union outlet in Almacen Casa Rosada (tel. 758-3551, 8 A.M.–7 P.M. Mon.–Sat., closed Sun.) and a Banco Nacional de Panamá (no ATM). There's a Cable and Wireless office near the bus terminal. Turn left at the intersection behind the terminal.

CHANGUINOLA

This congested, unlovely provincial town (pop. 39,896) is not exactly what you'd call a tourist destination. It's little more than a single strip of road—Avenida 17 de Abril, commonly known as Calle Central—that's lined with shops offering cheap goods and basic services, plus a few hotels and restaurants. It's not even particularly colorful—it's a hot, humid, nondescript little town surrounded by banana plantations. But it is a commerce and transportation hub.

Those who haven't experienced this part of Panama may be curious to pass by for a quick visit. Primarily, though, it's a crossroads for those traveling between Costa Rica and the islands or heading up into Naso country (the Wekso/ODE-SEN project) and the Bocas entrance to Parque Internacional La Amistad. Only those who end up stranded on the way to or from those places will likely want to spend the night.

Central Changuinola is about a kilometer long from north to south, and nearly everything of interest is on or within a block of Avenida 17 de Abril, which runs parallel to the train tracks. Because of that, the town is easily walkable. But Changuinola isn't particularly safe after dark; take taxis instead of walking ($.50 or less). Unless otherwise noted, all the places listed below are on Avenida 17 de Abril.

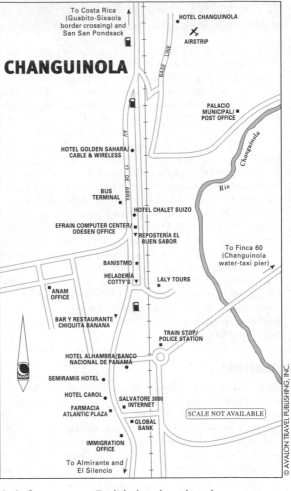

Accommodations

$10–25: Hotel Carol (tel. 758-8731, $11–18 s/d), near the south end of Avenida 17 de Abril, offers 37 air-conditioned rooms, some with hot water. The rooms are dark, basic, but okay, but they have smudged walls and concrete floors. The more expensive rooms are nicer, with cable TV, hot water, and tile floors, though they're still not the cleanest. A bar and restaurant were in the works. This is the best bet among the cheaper hotels.

Hotel Changuinola (Base Line, tel. 758-8678 or 758-8681, $13.50 s/d), at the north end of town near the airport, is a dark place with 30 hot-water rooms featuring old, spongy beds. Twenty of the rooms have air-conditioning, the rest have fans—the price is the same for either. There's a bar and restaurant on the premises. The management here is friendly and speaks some English, but the only real reason to stay here is to be next to the airport.

Golden Sahara (tel. 758-7478, 758-7908, or 758-7910, hotelgoldensahara@yahoo.com, $24 s/d), toward the north end of town, has 28 modern rooms with hot water, air-conditioning, and cable TV. Rooms are clean if a bit sterile. The rooms vary quite a bit—some are dark, and others are quite a bit cheerier; try to get one with a window. The hotel is well-run, and the staff members are attentive. They're happy to recommend places to eat and give other tips. Note that the hotel is right next to the train tracks, which could be a nuisance early in the morning, though it's on the edge of town and thus generally quieter. This place is a good deal.

$25–50: Semiramis Hotel (tel. 758-6006, 758-6009, 758-6013, $30/35 s/d), near the heart of town across the street from the Banco Nacional de Panamá, has fairly nice, clean rooms with air-conditioning, cable TV, and attractive bathrooms. It has a bar and restaurant that's open 7 A.M.–11 P.M. daily.

Food

Decent food is not easy to come by in Changuinola. The two places listed below are the best bets. Some of the hotels have restaurants, and a couple of Internet cafés serve ice cream and snacks.

Bar y Restaurante Chiquita Banana (tel. 758-8215, 7 A.M.–11 P.M. daily) is the best place to eat in town, which isn't saying a whole lot. It serves an extensive menu of Chinese and *criollo* food. Most items are $4 or less. There's a daily special—be sure to ask about it, since it's not written down anywhere. Most people eat on the enclosed front patio, which looks out on the busy street, but there's a fancier air-conditioned dining room inside, with a somewhat more upscale menu.

Repostería El Buen Sabor (tel. 758-8422), right next to the Efrain Computer Center, is a bakery and pastry shop that offers local specialties such as the *bon de Bastimentos*, which tastes like dry gingerbread, as well as fruit drinks, ice cream, and other goodies.

Information

The local ANAM office (tel. 758-6603, 8 A.M.–4 P.M. Mon.–Fri.) may have information on San San Pondsack and Parque Internacional La Amistad, but it's not really set up for travelers so don't get your hopes up. It's in a residential neighborhood a couple of blocks west of the center of town. Head west on the road that runs past the Hotel El Gran Hong Kong (which is grim and unfriendly and thus not listed). Turn left after two blocks. The office is a block down this road.

The police station is on an unmarked road east of the railroad tracks. It's parallel to and one block east of Avenida 17 de Abril. It's around the corner from the Hotel Alhambra and the Banco Nacional de Panamá. Farmacia Atlantic Plaza (tel. 758-7777, 24 hours daily), is a pleasant little pharmacy and ice-cream shop with an Internet café on the way.

Services

Global Bank (8 A.M.–3 P.M. Mon.–Fri., 9 A.M.–noon Sat.), about a block north of and across the street from the immigration office on the south side of town, has an ATM. The Banco Nacional de Panamá (8 A.M.–3 P.M. Mon.–Fri., 9 A.M.–noon Sat.) doesn't have an ATM, but the bank guard can point out a couple of standalone ATMs nearby if you can't spot them. One's across the street. Banistmo (8 A.M.–3:30 P.M. Mon.–Fri., 9 A.M.–noon Sat.), a couple of blocks south of the bus terminal on the east side of the street, has no ATM.

The post office is in the Palacio Municipal de Changuinola, on an unmarked road east of the airstrip on the north side of town.

Salvatore 3000 Internet, across the street from Farmacia Atlantic Plaza, charges $1 an hour. Heladería Cotty's (8:30 A.M.–11 P.M. daily), across the train tracks from Laly Tours, is another Internet café and ice-cream parlor. Efrain Computer Center next to Hotel Chalet Suizo (Avenida 17 de Abril, tel. 758-9137, 9 A.M.–10 P.M. Mon.–Sat. 11 A.M.–9 P.M. Sun. and holidays) charges $1 an hour. It also houses the headquarters of ODESEN, the Naso group that runs the Wekso Ecolodge and Center.

The local Cable and Wireless office (8 A.M.–noon and 1–5 P.M. Mon.–Fri., 8 A.M.–noon Sat.) is next to the Golden Sahara. It sells telephone cards.

An immigration office (tel. 775-4515, 8 A.M.–noon and 1–3 P.M. Mon.–Fri.) is at the south end of town, near Atlantic Plaza.

Laly Tours (tel. 758-5037), just east of Avenida 17 de Abril on the same street that runs past Heladería Cotty's, is a tiny local travel agency that sells tours to Bocas, Wekso, and San San Pondsack.

There are three gas stations on Avenida 17 de Abril.

Getting There and Away

Changuinola is a regional transit hub, with a busy bus terminal and a small airstrip. There's even a short train line, though it's not really set up for regular passenger service. Those traveling between the Costa Rican border and the islands must pass through this town.

By Air: There are several daily flights between Panama City and Changuinola ($58.80 each way, about 80 minutes). There is also one flight to and from David during the week ($31.50 each way, about 30 minutes). The airstrip is on the north end of town, just east of Avenida 17 de Abril. Taxi fare to and from town is $.50.

Note that flights usually make an intermediate stop in Bocas town on Isla Colón both on the way over and on the way back; be sure to get off at the right place.

Aeroperlas (tel. 315-7500 and fax 315-7580 in Panama City, tel. 758-7521 in Changuinola, info@aeroperlas.com, www.aeroperlas.com) has two daily flights to Changuinola from the Albrook airport in Panama City. They leave Panama City at 8:30 A.M. and 1 P.M. Monday–Friday, 7 A.M. and 3 P.M. Saturday, and 8 A.M. and 3 P.M. Sunday. Return flights from Changuinola to Panama City leave at 8:50 A.M. and 2:30 P.M. Monday–Friday, 8:45 A.M. and 4:40 P.M. Saturday, and 9:25 A.M. and 4:45 P.M. Sunday.

Flights from David to Changuinola leave at 8 A.M. Monday–Friday. Return flights from Changuinola to David leave at 10:10 A.M. Monday–Friday.

Mapiex Aero (tel./fax 315-0888 in Panama City, tel. 757-9841 and fax 757-9842 in Bocas town, reservaciones@aero.com.pa, www.aero.com.pa) has two daily flights between Panama City and Changuinola Monday through Saturday and one on Sunday. Flights leave from the Albrook airport at 6:45 A.M. and 2 P.M. Monday–Friday, 6:30 A.M. and 1 P.M. Saturday, and 1 P.M. Sunday. Return flights to Panama City leave at 8:15 A.M. and 3:30 P.M. Monday–Friday, 8 A.M. and 2:30 P.M. Saturday, and 5 P.M. Sunday.

Some of the above flights are scheduled to leave at exactly the same time from both Changuinola and the intermediate stop in Bocas town. Now that's some fast flying! As always,

confirm the flight time, be at the airport early, and hope for the best.

By Bus: There is one direct daily bus between Panama City and Changuinola. It leaves Panama City's Gran Terminal de Transportes at 8 P.M., arriving in Changuinola around 7 A.M. The return bus leaves Changuinola at 7 A.M., arriving in Panama City around 5:30 P.M. The fare is $24. Two pieces of luggage are allowed; additional luggage is an extra charge. Note this is the same bus that passes by the crossroads at Almirante.

Buses from David to Changuinola leave every half hour from 4 A.M.–7 P.M. The trip takes about 4.5 hours and costs $8.

Changuinola's bus terminal is near the north end of town across the street from Hotel Chalet Suizo. Other destinations include:

Almirante: every 25 minutes, 6 A.M.–10 P.M. The trip takes a half hour and costs $1.

Finca 60 water-taxi pier: every half hour or so. The pier is just outside of town and the trip costs $.40. The last water taxi leaves at 5:30 P.M.

Guabito/Costa Rican border crossing at Sixaola: every 20 minutes, 5:30 A.M.–7:30 P.M. The trip takes a half hour and costs $.70. There's also a *colectivo* taxi that works like a bus and runs between Changuinola and Guabito for $1 per person.

El Silencio: every 20 minutes, 5:30 A.M.–9 P.M. The trip takes 20 minutes and costs $.50.

By Taxi/Car: It shouldn't be hard to find a taxi on Avenida 17 de Abril. Expect to pay $.50 to the airport, $5 to El Silencio, $5 to Guabito, and $12 to Almirante.

To reach Changuinola by car from eastern Panama, stay left on the main road when it forks at Almirante. Changuinola is 21 kilometers farther west, on a scenic and curvy road. Watch out for speeding traffic and be careful crossing the bridges, which are really meant for the train and are falling apart.

By Train: A train still plies the ramshackle tracks between Changuinola and Almirante at a pace a turtle would find leisurely. It's meant for banana workers, but train nuts who happen to be at the train stop at the right time should be able to hop a ride. There are two trains on work days, leaving at 6–6:30 A.M. and 12:30–1 P.M. and returning around 11 A.M. and 3 P.M. The fare is $1. The train picks up passengers in an unmarked spot right across from the Changuinola police station. The 21-kilometer trip takes an hour. Cross your fingers when crossing the rusty bridge over the Río Changuinola.

HUMEDALES DE SAN SAN PONDSACK

These wetlands, established as a wildlife refuge in 1994, encompass a strip of coast that extends east and south from the Río Sixaola to the Caribbean. It comprises 16,125 hectares, but only a small part of it is easily accessible. The completely decrepit boardwalk that passes through its heart was being rebuilt when I last visited; if it's actually back in service, it will give visitors a close-up look at this otherworldly place. Animals found in the wetlands include an important population of manatees and leatherback and hawksbill sea turtles, but the manatees are shy and the turtles seasonal, so as usual don't get your hopes up. Birders come here for the 67 known avian species it attracts. The only things visitors are guaranteed to see, however, are mangroves, palms, and eerie, brackish water.

The wetlands can be visited either as part of a boat tour from the islands or by taxi from Changuinola. Arrange for the taxi either to wait or pick you up for the return trip. To be sure the taxi will show up at the appointed time, don't pay until the return to Changuinola.

(Note: There is not yet a consensus on how to spell the wetlands' funky name. You may see it as San San Pondsock, San San Pond Soc, San-San Pond Sak, and so on. It's all the same place, but don't confuse it—easier said than done—with Punta Pondsack, also known as Punta Pond Soc, east of Almirante.)

GUABITO

Even by the modest standards of mainland Bocas del Toro, the down-at-the-heels border town of Guabito (pop. 14,360) has little to offer visitors. It's simply a place to pass through on to the way to or from Costa Rica. There are no hotels and no appealing places to eat. The nearest place with significant services is Changuinola, about a 20-minute drive away.

The border crossing is on an elevated railway trestle on the edge of the Río Sixaola. The combination immigration, customs, and IPAT office is right on the train tracks next to the bridge

Bocas del Toro

© WILLIAM FRIAR

The Costa Rican border crossing at Guabito doesn't offer visitors the best first impression of Panama.

that crosses the river. (See the *Know Panama* chapter for entry requirements and detailed information on this border crossing.)

The border runs right down the middle of the Río Sixaola. Travelers must cross the railroad bridge on foot or in a vehicle. The bridge was built in 1908 and has been deteriorating ever since. It's a real embarrassment to Panama that the half of the bridge under Costa Rican control is freshly painted, at least superficially well-maintained, and has a protected walkway for pedestrians, while the Panamanian half is rusted, dilapidated, and forces pedestrians to walk right on the tracks. It's not the most inviting way to enter a country, but it makes for a comical photo. The border crossing is quite casual and anyone who wants to can wander out on the bridge to take a look.

Buses and taxis are available downstairs from customs and immigration.

Access to the Bocas del Toro archipelago is by water taxi from Changuinola or Almirante. (See the *Isla Colón* section for the pros and cons of both options and information on getting there.)

Buses to Changuinola run about every 20 minutes from 5:30 A.M.–7:30 P.M. The trip takes a half hour and costs $.70. There are no direct buses from Guabito to Almirante, Panama City, David, or anywhere else you're likely to want to go. Take a bus to the Changuinola bus terminal and change there.

Taxis should charge around $5 to Changuinola and $12 to Almirante. This is per ride, *not* per person. Taxi drivers and "tour guides" sometimes try to take advantage of clueless new arrivals at the border, so be polite but firm and don't get ripped off.

Buses from Sixaola, on the Costa Rican side, leave for San José, Costa Rica, at 5:30 A.M., 7:30 A.M., 9:30 A.M., and 2:30 P.M. The trip takes about 5.5 hours.

ⓜ PROYECTO ODESEN (WEKSO ECOLODGE AND CENTER)

A visit to Wekso is one of the most memorable experiences Bocas del Toro has to offer, and it makes for a nice change of scene for those getting island fever in the archipelago. It's a reasonable and accessible trip for those with the slightest sense of adventure, an interest in indigenous cultures, and a desire to explore a bit of tropical forest in rustic but relatively comfortable conditions. The climate is quite different from that on the islands and doesn't fit preconceived notions of a tropical rainforest. It can be rather mild and pleasantly breezy upriver.

Wekso is up the Río Teribe about an hour by land and water from Changuinola. It has a grim history as the former site of Pana-Jungla, a jungle-warfare/survival school that put elite Panamanian and foreign troops through legendarily difficult training. It was founded in 1977 and closed in 1990 following the U.S. invasion that ousted Manuel Noriega and disbanded the Panamanian military. Spooky remnants of the camp remain, including a cage that once housed a black panther, the ruins of barracks and officers' quarters, and a serpentarium that once held Panama's deadliest snakes for training purposes it's best not to speculate about.

Now, however, the site has a much more peaceful and cheerful purpose. It's the center of an ecotourism project run by the Naso, an indigenous people working hard to cling to their traditions and land.

The Naso are better known in Panama as the Teribe or Naso-Teribe. Some Naso say that "Teribe" is a mispronunciation of *tjer di,* which means "river of the Grandmother," the ancestral guiding spirit of the people. They are also sometimes known as the Térraba. At the beginning of the 17th century, Spanish missionaries moved most of the Naso to what is now Costa Rica, supposedly for their own protection. But only a few hundred remain in Costa Rica today, and the number who still speak their native language can be counted on one hand. There are about 3,800 Naso left in Panama. As one Naso man said to me with a sad smile, *Estamos en peligro de extinción* ("We are in danger of extinction").

There are 11 main Naso communities along the Río Teribe, all of which pay allegiance to a king who lives in **Sieyik,** a community about two hours up the Teribe. The royal palace today is an austere cinderblock house, but the Naso

NASO TALES

The Naso I've met have been gracious, open, and eager to share their culture with outsiders. They have great folktales, which are especially fun to listen to by candlelight at Wekso. ODESEN members don't speak English, but their Spanish tends to be remarkably clear. Visitors who speak a bit of Spanish will probably find it easier to communicate here than they do in, say, Panama City.

Some of the most evocative stories involve the *indios conejos* (rabbit Indians). They were nocturnal, had stripes down their backs, could see well in the dark, and could run superhumanly fast. Sometimes they ran through the forest at night bearing torches. They were also fierce and wild warriors who favored bows and arrows. The Naso say they waged wars with them near Palenque in the time of their grandparents. The only way they could get the upper hand with them was to attack at daybreak, while they slept.

What makes these tales especially intriguing is that the other indigenous peoples of western Panama have similar stories of going to war with *indios conejos*. Some versions are even more fanciful, describing them as white and just a meter tall, like mutant rabbits. One theory is that these stories are based on real battles with Miskito Indians. Some Naso don't believe the stories, but others are convinced the *indios conejos* did and still do exist, though today they're hidden away in the Chiriquí highlands.

Other tales are of lost cities and gold mines far up the Teribe beyond Palenque. Again, other indigenous people have similar stories. These may be purely fanciful, of course, but there is evidence the ancient inhabitants of this area had plenty of gold. Columbus was fascinated by the indigenous people he encountered during his brief visit to Bocas del Toro who wore little but mirror-like discs of gold around their necks. And some believe there was once a quite developed civilization in the highlands. A Panamanian guide told me that a park ranger, looking for survivors of a plane crash, once stumbled upon stone houses 40 kilometers upriver from Palenque.

Tales of evil spirits and sinister encounters are also popular with the Naso. One involves *Dö* (pronounced "doo"), a spirit that takes the shape of a monkey but has a scorpion's tale. It's said he abducts people, keeps them in his cave for eight days, and then drowns them in the river. Ask your hosts about this; on the way back down the river, they can point out the mouth of the cave where the spirit lives. The cave is supposedly hugely long, leading between the Sixaola and Changuinola rivers. The tales gets even better: they say an American found treasure in the cave 50 years ago. He took it, which would have been okay if he'd left something else behind in exchange. He didn't, and he didn't meet a happy end.

Then there's *Älu*, the spirit of the bongo tree, which takes the form of a monkey without a head. Its eyes are in its armpits, so in order to see it must raise its arms into the air. When *Älu* appears, blood gushes from around the bongo tree.

Wekso, by the by, is a Naso word that means "the place of bongo trees."

are proud that they are the last people in Latin America still led by a king.

History

Spanish records suggest that in the 16th century the Naso were already well-established in the region, including Almirante Bay as far north as Isla Colón, and may in fact have been the dominant power of the time. The Naso were gradually squeezed out of the area and by the latter half of the 19th century had retreated far up the Río Teribe in the highlands near the Costa Rican border, to communities that came to be known as *palenques* (Spanish for "palisade" or "stockade," the name given by the Spaniards to hidden villages). These villages have long been abandoned and are considered a kind of interim ancestral homeland, a connection with the Naso's ancient past.

By their own account, the Naso have fought just about all the former and present indigenous people in the region at one time or another. By the 17th century their numbers had declined drastically and have fluctuated ever since. A tuberculosis epidemic in the early 20th century killed many, including the king.

Today the Naso are among the most endangered of Panamá's eight surviving indigenous peoples. The cultural identity of the few Naso who remain is being eroded on all sides: by the dominant Latin culture, by missionaries, by intermarriage with other indigenous peoples, and so on.

The men tend to wear modern, nondescript shirts and slacks, but many women still wear distinctive dresses. These are cotton-print outfits in a single bright, bold color such as blue or yellow. They have puffy blouses and a tiny floral pattern that from a distance can look like polka dots.

The Naso still do not have *comarca* (reservation) status for their land. This is in stark contrast to their far more populous neighbors, the Ngöbe-Buglé, who now have a *comarca* that covers a huge chunk of western Panama. The Naso continue to tangle with them and others over land ownership, and they are also threatened by proposals to dam the Teribe and a tributary river for a hydroelectric project. A bill to create a 130,000-hectare *comarca* for the Naso has been moving through the Panamanian national assembly at a glacial pace.

Meanwhile, as with Panamá's other indigenous people, the Naso struggle with widespread poverty, though the Naso I've spoken with say that access to health care and education through the sixth grade have improved their lot somewhat.

Río Teribe and the Ecolodge

The ecotourism project is run by a Naso nonprofit called ODESEN, a Spanish acronym that translates to "organization for Naso sustainable ecotourism development." Assisted by Conservation International, the group uses proceeds from tourist visits to help the community. It has an office in Changuinola.

ODESEN members take visitors up the river to Wekso, where there's a large thatched-roof bungalow for guests, an outhouse with flush toilets, and a dining area. Two trails lead from the camp into the forest. Some guests also continue farther up the river to visit some of the communities, especially Sieyik, where there's a chance of meeting the king.

Just getting up to Wekso is a fun little adventure. In the days of the jungle-warfare school there was a forest road to the camp, but it has disappeared back into the forest and the ever-shifting river. Today visitors come by boat.

The departure point is El Silencio, a tiny community about 10 kilometers from Changuinola, where the Teribe meets the Río Changuinola. Transport is in a *piragua* powered by a 25-horsepower motor up the Teribe. The river flows so fast it can sometimes fight an outboard motor to a near standstill.

It's a beautiful trip. Small rapids ripple the river, and the air feels incredibly fresh and clean after the humidity of the towns and coast. Farm country at the beginning gives way to lush countryside and a view of the Talamanca mountains in the distance. Egrets, cormorants, and iguanas can be easy to spot. When the river is low, the boatmen sometimes have to get out and drag the *piragua* over rocks.

Only the odd hut is visible from the river, as the communities are set back into the forest; there's little sign of human habitation. It takes about 40 minutes to an hour to reach Wekso. The trip back down is twice as fast.

The Wekso camp is on a small hill overlooking the river. The dining area is on the edge of the hillside and has a great view of the river below and the forest beyond.

There is no electricity at the camp; candles and flashlights provide the only illumination at night. Meals are basic but okay and can include such traditional dishes as *palmito* and *plosón* salad. *Palmito* is heart of palm. *Plosón* is a fern that contains a tiny amount of cyanide—it's quite tasty.

The camp is frog heaven in the evening, when it's especially easy to spot incredibly cute red-eyed tree frogs. The guest bungalow, which resembles an oversized version of a traditional Naso thatched-roof house, is at the back of camp. It's rustic but perfectly acceptable and tidy, with foam-rubber mattresses, mosquito nets over the beds, and inviting hammocks on the front porch. Snakes are not unheard of around the camp; watch your step.

Just below the camp is a ranger station for

Parque Internacional La Amistad. This area is not technically in the park but rather in the buffer forest around it. But guests must pay the $3 park entrance fee anyway.

There is a good chance of spotting a variety of colorful birds in this area, including the white-fronted nunbird, blue-headed parrot, king vultures, long-tailed tyrants, Amazon kingfishers, snowy cotingas, and snowcap and green thorntail hummingbirds. As always, mammals in tropical forests are hard to find, but possibilities include water opossum, white-lipped peccaries, and neotropical river otters. Frogs are generally easy to spot, including red-eyed tree frogs (*Agalychnis callidryas*) and poison-dart frogs (such as *Dendrobates pumilio* and *Dendrobates auratus*).

Trails

A loop trail that starts at the camp takes about two hours to walk at a slow pace. A second trail forks off it about 40 minutes in. It cuts across the loop and provides a shortcut back to camp for those who want it. It's possible to walk either of these trails without a guide, but your visit will probably include a walk led by a Naso guide who can identify common flora and fauna and share a bit of Naso lore about them. As always, don't walk forest trails alone. The trail is pretty, leading at first along a ridge overlooking the river and then down toward a somewhat swampy and very muddy area criss-crossed with streams and four bridges. The forest alternates between primary and secondary growth. The patches of primary forest contain some huge, impressive trees, including bongo, almond, and ceiba. The trail can be good for birding, including crowd pleasers such as toucans, and there's a chance of spotting sloths. This area is too close to well-settled areas to draw much wildlife, however, and when I walked it even the birds had better places to be that morning. However, we did see peccary tracks, so there are still some big critters lurking around.

The Naso also have a system of narrow forest "commuter" trails that link the communities. Don't attempt to explore these without a Naso guide.

Farther Up the Teribe

About an hour upriver from Wekso is Sieyik, the Naso "capital." It's a village of about 500 people who live in houses scattered around a lovely hillside overlooking the river.

The center of the village is a clearing that contains the royal residence, a school, and the health post, all of which are made from cinderblocks. The royal symbol of power, a group of three arrows, is painted on the front wall of the residence. The king is assisted by a *consejo* (board of advisers) drawn from the communities. The Naso reserve the right to switch kings if they become unhappy with him. They can vote him out, but the replacement has to come from the royal family. The current king is Tito Santana; if he's around, there's a slight chance you might be granted an audience, but don't count on it. The graves of his grandfather and great-grandfather are in front of his residence.

A visit to Sieyik will likely include a walk around the village and a visit to a traditional home, which may include lunch. Traditional Naso homes are built on stilts of one kind of palm *(jira)* and the roofs are thatched with another kind *(palenquilla)*. Residents sleep on the soft bark of a rubber tree. Newer homes use wooden planks for walls and floor, and sometimes have corrugated zinc roofs.

Visits also include a display of and possibly a chance to buy handicrafts, including objects carved from cedar, which are interesting but rarely achieve the level of artistry one sees with Emberá-Wounaan and Kuna works.

The Naso now also offer the chance to visit the neighboring community of Sieykin, but I haven't yet had a chance to explore it and so can't say how it compares.

Much of the surrounding land is cultivated. Orange trees are everywhere; other crops include beans, rice, corn, and yuca. The Naso also hunt. One traditional method is to use spears, with different kinds of tips for fish, birds, and land animals.

Parque Internacional La Amistad

The Río Teribe is the Caribbean gateway of Parque Internacional La Amistad (PILA) and the

Palo Seco Buffer Forest that borders it. Far up in the headlands of the Teribe there are still jaguars, harpy eagles, tapirs, and macaws. That's because it's brutally hard to get to this area. The Caribbean side of PILA is far less accessible than the Pacific side, which lies in Chiriquí Province and has some developed trails close to population centers. Anyone who wants to enter the park from the Caribbean slope is in for a serious trek and needs a skilled guide and boatmen and considerable supplies. The terrain is steep, there are no trails, and the boat has to fight an increasingly fast and powerful river. Even for the Naso, the upper reaches of the Teribe are becoming a distant memory. Getting to the Naso homeland of Palenque, a long-abandoned village, requires a full day on the river. At the time of writing, Oscar Gaslin, a local guide based on the Bocas islands, was considering offering treks up to Palenque. (See the *Isla Colón* section for information.)

Practicalities

Visits can be arranged directly through ODESEN or through tour operators. The ODESEN office in Changuinola (Avenida 17 de Abril, tel. 758-9137, cell 658-5042 or 620-0192, eliseovargasgarcia@yahoo.com or turismonaso_odesen@hotmail.com, www.bocas.com, 9 A.M.–10 P.M. Mon.–Sat. 11 A.M.–9 P.M. Sun. and holidays) is in the Efrain Computer Center next to Hotel Chalet Suizo. The Naso staff speaks Spanish but no English. However, Eladio Beitia, the friendly director of the computer center, works with the group and speaks decent English. At the time of writing ODESEN's promoter, and probably the member you'll have most contact with, was Eliseo Vargas (eliseovargasgarcia@yahoo.com), a warm and earnest guy clearly dedicated to helping his people but with no illusions about the challenges that entails. It may also be possible to book a tour through a Bocas islands–based group called Bocas Aventuras (tel. 757-9367, boacasaventuras.com, www.bocas.com).

Visitors who book through ODESEN are charged cafeteria-style according to the services they need. Transportation between Changuinola

and El Silencio is $8 each way, and the boat trip between El Silencio and Wekso is $15 each way. Each meal is $2.50–4. Entrance to Parque Internacional La Amistad, which is payable to the ANAM park ranger, is $3. Overnight lodging is $12. A guided hike through the Wekso trails is $4. The above rates are per person for groups of 2–4 people; larger groups get a discount.

Tours from the camp to the surrounding area are charged per group. A full-day tour to Sieyik is $40, including boat and guide. A "traditional dance exhibition" is another $25. A full-day tour to Sieykin is $47. Visits to the nearby "botanical garden" is another $20.

In other words, a couple should count on paying about $150 total for transportation between Changuinola and Wekso, three meals, lodging, guides, and a hike. No one should come all this way without visiting at least one of the upriver communities, though, so add at least $40 on top of that total.

Visitors can lower the total by traveling with a small group. Going through a tour operator may be the simplest way to do this and will probably be logistically simpler as well. At least consider arranging your own transportation for the 10-kilometer drive between Changuinola and El Silencio; this is the one part of the ODESEN plan that is excessive, especially when buses make the trip for $.50 and taxis for $5.

A single night is sufficient to see and do all the above. It'd be tough to squeeze it all into a single day, but a day trip just to Wekso is quite doable.

Access to El Silencio from the islands is by water taxi to Changuinola (the better way) or Almirante. From either town, take a taxi and/or bus to El Silencio unless ODESEN or the tour operator has made other arrangements.

It rains year-round up the Río Teribe, but less so in January–March and August–October. March is the driest month. Bring rain gear and a light jacket regardless of when you come. It can get cooler and breezy during the "summer" (January–March). It's also a good idea to bring bottled water or water-purification tablets or filters.

Know
Panama

The Land

The Republic of Panama covers 75,517 square kilometers, which makes it slightly bigger than Ireland and slightly smaller than South Carolina. Panama is young in geological terms. It emerged from the sea just 2.5 million years ago, dividing the Atlantic from the Pacific and forming a natural bridge that connects the North and South American continents. The bridge has allowed North and South American species to intermingle. Known as the Great American Interchange, this mingling had a profound effect on the ecology of South America.

Panama's peculiar shape—like the letter "S" turned on its side—causes confusion for many visitors. It takes a while to get used to the notion that the Caribbean Sea is to the north and the Pacific Ocean to the south. Many also find it strange to be able to watch the sun rising over the Pacific and setting in the Caribbean, or to realize that when a ship transits the Panama Canal from the Pacific to the Caribbean it actually ends up slightly west of where it started.

Panama is at the eastern end of Central America, bordered to the west by Costa Rica and to the east by Colombia. It's far longer than it is wide. The oceans are just 80 kilometers apart at the Panama Canal, near the middle of the country, and that isn't even the narrowest spot on the isthmus. But the country stretches surprisingly far to the east and west; Panama has nearly 3,000 kilometers of coastline along its Caribbean and Pacific flanks.

People often wonder which body of water is the "higher" of the two. The reality is there's no difference in elevation—sea level is sea level. A locks canal was necessary in Panama not to keep the oceans from spilling into each other but to carry ships over the landmass of the isthmus. But there is a dramatic difference between the tides on each side. The Caribbean tide averages less than half a meter; Pacific tides can be more than 5 meters high.

Many visitors are surprised to discover how mountainous Panama is. The most impressive mountain range is the Cordillera Central, which bisects the western half of the country, extending from the Costa Rican border east toward the canal. It contains Panama's highest mountain, Volcán Barú, a dormant volcano that is 3,475 meters high. Another impressive range runs along Panama's eastern Caribbean coast, starting at the Comarca de Kuna Yala and ending at the Colombian border. It officially comprises the Serranía de San Blas to the west and the Serranía del Darién to the east, where it enters Darién Province.

Most parts of Panama experience few significant earthquakes, which is one of the reasons it was chosen as the site of an interoceanic canal. However, western Panama, particularly Bocas del Toro and Chiriquí, is far more seismically active. In 1991, an earthquake measuring 7.5 on the Richter scale struck along the Costa Rican-Panamanian border, leaving two dozen people dead in Bocas del Toro and thousands homeless.

Besides the humid tropical forests that people expect to find, which compose a third of Panama's remaining forests, Panama has a great variety of other ecosystems, ranging from cloud forests to a manmade "desert." Extensive mangroves, coral reefs, and hundreds of islands can be found on both the Pacific and Caribbean sides of the isthmus. Panama also has at least 500 rivers.

CLIMATE

Panama lies between 7 and 10 degrees north of the equator. The climate is mainly tropical, and days and nights are almost equally long throughout the year. Sunrise and sunset vary by only about half an hour during the year: the sun rises at about 6:00-6:30 A.M. and sets at about 6:00-6:30 P.M.

Temperatures in Panama are fairly constant year-round. In the lowlands, these range from about 32°C (90°F) in the day down to 21°C (70°F) in the evening. It never gets cold in the lowlands, and dry-season breezes are very pleasant there in the evenings. It gets considerably cooler in the highlands. At the top of Volcán Barú, temperatures can dip below freezing. Humidity tends to be quite high year-round, but especially so in the rainy season, when it approaches 100 percent.

Panama has two seasons, the rainy and the dry. The dry season, also known as summer (*verano*), lasts from about mid-December to mid-April. Rain stops completely in many parts then, especially on the Pacific side. Flowering trees burst into bloom around the country at the start of this season. Towards the end, vegetation turns brown or dies, and smoke from slash-and-burn agriculture and the burning of sugarcane fields can make the skies hazy.

The rainy season, also known as winter (*invierno*), generally lasts from about mid-April to mid-December. The rains tend to be heaviest and longest at the end of the season, as though the heavens were wringing out every last drop of moisture. October, November, and the beginning of December are especially heavy. Thunderstorms are a near daily occurrence during the rainy season.

Yearly rainfall averages around 3 meters. It's far wetter on the Caribbean side than the Pacific side. The rains in most parts of Panama tend to come in powerful bursts in the afternoon or early evening. Mornings are usually dry on the Pacific side.

Dirt roads and trails can become impassable in the interior during the rainy season, and paved roads and bridges are often washed out by mudslides and rising rivers. Flooding is a serious problem in parts of the interior, such as Bocas del Toro and Chiriquí.

The rain never stops completely along the Caribbean coast, in the western highlands, and on the islands of Bocas del Toro. Rainfall patterns in Bocas are quite different from other parts of Panama. It has no true dry season, but generally little rain falls during September–October and February–March.

Panama is south of the hurricane zone, so it's spared those terrible storms.

Flora and Fauna

Panama's shape and location—at the southernmost range of many North American species and the northernmost range of many South American species—makes it home to a particularly rich variety of plant and animal life. Sadly, the future of this abundant life is by no means secure: the World Conservation Monitoring Centre's Red List of threatened animals includes 112 species found in Panama.

Approximately 950 species of birds have been identified so far, more than are found in the United States and Canada combined. The country is also home to well over 200 mammal and 200 reptile species, close to 200 amphibian species, and more than 10,000 species of plants. Some of these are found nowhere else on earth.

TREES AND PLANTS

Panama's plant life is among the most diverse in the world. The country contains 12 of the planet's 30 Holdridge life zones. By far the most common is humid tropical forest, which accounts for about a third of Panama's remaining forest cover. All of these zones but one, humid premontane forest, are represented in a system of protected areas. Of Panama's estimated 10,000 species of plants, about 1,500 of them are found nowhere else on the planet. Panama also has extensive wetlands, mangroves, and coral reefs.

Panamanian environmentalists like to point out that, per square kilometer, Panama has 21 times the plant diversity of Brazil. Trying to

© WILLIAM FRIAR

mangroves near Isla Grande

identify the plants even in a small patch of rainforest is daunting. There are 480 species of trees just on the 15-square kilometers of Isla Barro Colorado, more than are found in all of Europe.

The Panama tree (*Sterculia apetala*) is widely thought of as the national tree, and some maintain it gave the country its name. It has a straight trunk that can grow up to 35 meters tall, with vertical buttresses around its base.

The *ceiba* or kapok *(Ceiba pentandra)* can reach 60 meters and often juts above other trees in the forest. One kapok specimen on Isla Barro Colorado is so huge other trees grow on its branches.

The *espavé* or wild cashew (*Anacardium excelsum*) has a trunk so straight and tall that indigenous peoples use it to make dugout canoes. One explanation of its name is that *espavé* is a contraction of *es para ver* ("it's for seeing"), meaning it's a good tree to climb to see what's off in the distance.

The *mata palo* or strangler fig (*Ficus obtusifolia*) starts as a seedling on a host tree that it eventually surrounds and engulfs. The mature strangler fig can be hollow inside, its original host completely decomposed. It's easy to spot because of its enor-

mously thick strangler roots, which can also engulf boulders and the ruins of buildings.

The massively thick trunk of the abundant *cuipo (Cavanillesia platanifolia)* also makes it easy to identify in the forest.

In the dry season, flowering trees burst into bloom around the isthmus, dotting the green canopy with brilliant colors.

Panama has more than 1,000 species of orchids, many of them endemic. The delicate white *espíritu santo* (holy ghost) orchid, also known as the dove orchid, is considered Panama's national flower.

BIRDS

Panama is especially well known for its incredible array of bird species. Besides its vast local populations, more than 120 species are migrants that regularly cross the isthmus on the way to and from their winter homes.

The famous (among birders) "raptor migration" of broad-winged hawks, Swainson's hawks, and turkey vultures is absolutely spectacular. During the fall and spring, particularly in Octo-

© CLEA EFTHIMIADAS

pet macaws in the former Canal Zone

ber to mid-November and March to early April, they pass overhead in flocks that can number in the many thousands. It's an unbelievable sight. The first comprehensive study of the migration was conducted in fall 2004, when researchers tallied more than 2.7 million raptors. One researcher counted 92,000 in a single day. They are easiest to spot around the former Canal Zone. Good places to see them include Cerro Ancón,the Canopy Tower, and the top of the aerial tram at the Gamboa Rainforest Resort.

Other species likely to impress non-birders include five species of macaws (blue-and-yellow, chestnut-fronted, great green, red-and-green, and the rare scarlet); several species of toucans and toucanets; the harpy eagle, the world's most powerful bird of prey; and the resplendent quetzal, which has been called the most beautiful bird on the planet.

LAND MAMMALS

The country's national parks are filled with animals that thrill foreign visitors, though many are hard to spot. There are five species of big cats on the isthmus: jaguars, jaguarundis, pumas, margays, and ocelots, but finding one in the wild is ex-

ceedingly hard. The forests harbor every species of non-human primate found in Central America: western night monkeys, mantled howler monkeys, white-faced capuchins, several types of spider monkeys, and Geoffroy's tamarins. Howlers are generally the easiest to spot (or at least hear) in the wild, but the Primate Refuge and Sanctuary of Panama (PRSP) has introduced four species of primates to islands in Lago Gatún, where the night monkey still occurs naturally. It's easy to spot several species during a boat tour of the lake.

Many visitors find white-nosed coatis (a.k.a. coatimundis) and kinkajous, with their long tails and furry bodies, terribly cute. They're reasonably easy to find, especially around Gamboa.

Capybaras are the world's largest rodents, but they're shy and more closely resemble giant guinea pigs than rats. They can grow to be a meter long and weigh up to 45 kilograms. They're easiest to spot in Gamboa and Punta Patiño.

Far smaller but equally cute are Central American agoutis, known locally as *ñeques*. They're generally less than half a meter long and weigh just 3–4 kilograms. They're covered in fur and have a rather large rump. They're among the easiest mammals to spot in Panama; they're diurnal and found just about anywhere there's forest. *Agoutis* are sometimes confused with pacas because of the latter's scientific name, *Agouti paca*. But pacas are quite a bit larger, and their brown fur is marked with rows of white spots, giving rise to their local name, *conejo pintado* (painted rabbit).

Small red brocket and white-tailed deer are common. Isla San José is the only place in Central America where gray brocket are found. Other notable land mammals include giant anteaters, white-lipped and collared peccaries, two- and three-toed sloths, and Baird's tapirs, the largest land mammal in Central America. The last can weigh up to 300 kilograms and are rather odd-looking creatures with a trunklike nose.

SEA LIFE

Five species of sea turtles can be found in Panama's waters, and four of them lay their eggs on its islands and coasts. They are the hawksbill, leatherback, loggerhead, olive ridley, and green.

Sea turtles are easiest to find in mating season on the islands and coasts of Bocas del Toro in the Caribbean (roughly March to October, with most activity in the later months), and Isla Cañas in the Pacific (most numerous between September and November). Nesting season varies by species, location, and the mood of the turtles, but dry season is generally the worst time to see them.

The hawksbill and leatherback are the most abundant in Bocas. All five species make their way to Isla Cañas, but by far the most numerous are the olive ridley. Many thousands make their way to the long island every year, making for a dramatic spectacle at night. The loggerhead rarely, if ever, lays eggs in Panama. (It's a subject of some debate).

The West Indian manatee can be found in the Panama Canal, most easily seen around the Gatún Yacht Club, and, to a lesser extent, the rivers and channels of Bocas del Toro.

The seas are filled with brilliant tropical fish as well as impressive large specimens, including orcas, several species of dolphins, humpback whales, marlins, manta rays, jewfish, moray eels, barracudas, big snappers, and white-tip, hammerhead, tiger, and whale sharks. The biggest creatures are found in the Pacific, especially around the Islas Perlas, the Golfo de Chiriquí, and the Bahía de Piñas, where dozens of deep-sea fishing records have been set. Small, radiant tropical fish are easiest to find among the coral gardens in the clear waters off the Caribbean islands.

AMPHIBIANS

Of the nearly 200 species of amphibians in Panama, the best loved and studied are the frogs and toads. Bocas del Toro is especially well-known for its many different morphs, or forms, of strawberry poison-dart frogs (*Dendrobates pumilio*). In addition to the distinctive red morphs that give the species its common name, these tiny frogs come in green, yellow, purple, orange, black, white, and multicolor forms, sometimes within a surprisingly small area. Panama is also known

for its endangered golden frogs (*Atelopus zeteki*), which are easiest to find in El Valle.

REPTILES

The country's many reptile species contain several that make visitors most nervous about the tropics: venomous snakes. It's unlikely you'll encounter any snakes at all during a hike, and highly unlikely any will bother you if you don't bother them.

That said, one of the country's most venomous snakes is also one of its most prolific: the fer-de-lance *(Bothrops asper)*, a pitviper known colloquially in Panama as *equis* for the diamond or X-pattern on its brown skin. A full-grown adult can be more than 2 meters long. The females give birth to up to 50 young at a time, which are born venomous and can actually be more deadly than an adult because they have not learned to regulate their venom. Fer-de-lance can be aggressive, especially during mating season.

Another forbidding creature is the bushmaster *(Lachesis muta)*, the world's largest pitviper. It can grow to be about 3 meters long but is much more rarely encountered. Other venomous snakes include the eyelash palm-pitviper (*Bothriechis schlegelli*), which comes in an assortment of brilliant colors, and a number of coral snakes. Assume any coral snake you encounter is dangerous—the rhymes used to distinguish venomous from non-venomous corals in the United States do not work in Panama.

Non-venomous but potentially dangerous snakes include the boa constrictor, which averages a little under 2 meters long and can bite if provoked. There are also plenty of harmless snakes, including a variety of vine snakes.

Caimans (*Caiman crocodilus*) are, despite their scientific name, a kind of alligator found in great abundance in some of Panama's rivers. They're easy to spot in Gamboa. They are generally small and rather placid, though some can grow to be about 2.5 meters long. There have been reports of the far larger American crocodile (*Crocodylus acutus*) in the waters of the Panama Canal, espe-

© WILLIAM FRIAR

Iguanas are officially protected in Panama.

cially around Gamboa, though this endangered species can be hard to find. It spends most of its time in estuaries on the Pacific side of the isthmus. On a recent trip to the Darién, I encountered an enormous one on a sandbank on the Río Tuira.

Green iguanas are a protected species in Panama but they are sometimes still hunted as food. Efforts are being made to reintroduce iguanas in various parts of the country.

INSECTS, ARACHNIDS, AND OTHER SMALL CREATURES

Visitors will most certainly have some encounters with insects, but many parts of Panama are not nearly as buggy as one might think. The mos-

quito population, for instance, is kept strictly controlled because of the risk of disease.

But the variety of insects found on the isthmus is staggering. It's estimated there are at least 10,000 species of beetles alone.

Most visitors would just as soon not encounter some of these insects, such as chiggers, bullet and army ants, giant cockroaches, Africanized bees, and stinging centipedes, not to mention the vast array of impressive arachnids, which include such creepy-crawlies as scorpions, tarantulas, and the stunning golden orb spider. But Panama is home to plenty of less-intimidating little creatures, such as 16,000 species of butterflies. One of the most spectacular of these is the huge and luminous blue morpho, which can often be seen floating slowly through the forest canopy.

Environmental Issues

Environmental destruction in the tropics is a terrible, disheartening thing to witness—and there's plenty of it going on in Panama. But anyone who's had a long association with Panama can't help but feel some optimism these days. While it's still a far-too-common sight to see citizens trashing their own country, there are also people out there cleaning up the mess—or at least refusing to add to it. Environmental protection laws and organizations are being created, and new protected areas are being set aside. It's true that resources and the political will to back up the good intentions are often lacking. It's also true that greed and the march of "progress" often undo the modest achievements that are made. But there is a genuine environmental movement in Panama now, a claim that would have been hard to make 20 years ago.

DEFORESTATION

About 40 percent of the Republic of Panama was still covered by forest at the beginning of the 21st century. That's the good news.

The bad news is that 50 years ago, the figure was 70 percent. In other words, in the last half of the 20th century Panama lost nearly half its remaining forests—about 2.2 million hectares (5.4 million acres) of wild, species-rich nature wiped out.

Even more disturbing, the trend continues in an era of increased environmental awareness. Though estimates vary, deforestation is believed to claim up to 50,000 hectares (123,500 acres) of forest a year.

These forests have mostly been converted into farms and cattle ranches, or paved over to make way for cities and towns. There is intense pressure on the remaining forests from subsistence farmers, ranchers, and large commercial interests. They have almost completely deforested the heartland provinces of Los Santos and Herrera on the Azuero Peninsula as well as the Pacific slopes of western and central Panama. Eventually this land becomes useless and barren—there is even a manmade "desert" on the Azuero Peninsula. This has driven people north to the Caribbean slopes and east and west to forests that were once nearly inaccessible.

burning mangroves along Panama's Caribbean coast

© WILLIAM FRIAR

Whenever a road enters a forest, the forest begins to disappear. So-called *colonos* (colonists)—slash-and-burn farmers in need of new land—follow the road. So do timber interests in search of magnificent old-growth giants. Once the forest cover is gone, the soil erodes easily under Panama's incredible downpours. This is worsened by the fact that nearly 78 percent of Panama's land is mountainous, with a high potential for erosion. The soil is generally of poor quality in any case—nearly all the nutrients in a tropical forest are contained in the trees themselves, not the soil—and is quickly overexploited, leading to the need for more land and thus more deforestation. Within just a few years the soil is exhausted and ranchers bring in cattle to graze on what is now sparse pastureland. The farmers, loggers, and ranchers move further into the forest, and the cycle continues.

Deforestation is proceeding at a particularly alarming rate in the Darién, Bocas del Toro, Colón province, and the new Ngöbe-Buglé *comarca*, all of which are rich in biodiversity and primary forests. Even the Kuna, who traditionally have been successful in keeping invaders off their land, have in recent years protested the incursion of *colonos* onto their mainland reservations in the Darién.

While much of the deforestation is driven by the needs of impoverished subsistence farmers, Panamanian and multinational commercial interests have also done substantial damage to the environment. Banana, coffee, and sugarcane plantations, for instance, have wiped out forests and contaminated rivers with pesticides and other kinds of chemical runoff. The government continues to grant gold and copper-mining concessions to corporations in the heart of important ecosystems. And large hydroelectric dams that flood forests, disrupt rivers, and displace indigenous people have been built, with more on the way.

Some efforts have been made in the last two decades to reforest parts of Panama where the soil has not become too degraded. Tax incentives have helped turn tree planting into a popular get-rich-quick scheme throughout the country.

Critics, including Panama's own environmental protection agency, point out that the policy has several flaws. The one most frequently cited is that about two-thirds of the trees planted so far have been teak, a non-native species that Panama's birds, animals, and other flora and fauna seem to have little use for. Teak is most often grown in plantations instead of being planted alongside native species, creating monocultures that do little for the local environment and, according to some, actually degrade it further. There have even been reports of species-rich native forest being illegally cleared to make way for teak plantations.

At the beginning of the 21st century, a total of 46,000 hectares (114,000 acres) of land had been reforested, less than is lost every year through deforestation.

The difference between the still intact Caribbean and heavily deforested Pacific slopes is startling, especially when seen from the air. But deforestation is creeping towards the Caribbean as well. The loss or fragmentation of these last forests, which some see as all but inevitable unless immediate steps are taken, would have profound, far-reaching effects. Panama is a vital part of the Mesoamerican Biological Corridor that links the ecosystems of North and South America. Consider birds alone: 122 migratory bird species regularly pass through Panama. What happens to them if the biological corridor disappears?

WATER RESOURCES

Water pollution and the shrinking of Panama's watersheds are also serious problems. Raw sewage and industrial waste are dumped directly into the Bahía de Panamá (Panama Bay), for instance, turning parts of what was once a tremendously vital body of water into toxic zones. It wasn't all that many years ago that kids swam in Panama Bay right across the street from bustling Panama City. Now doing so is a serious health risk. Fishing in the bay has long been banned. At low tide, the smell wafting off the bay can be overpowering.

The most remote, untouched islands and beaches of Panama sometimes have a ring of trash on the shores, carried there by currents that pass near cities and towns where garbage is dumped indiscriminately. Pollution and deliberate destruction is also decimating coral reefs, and over-fishing is doing even more damage to the biodiversity of the seas.

Mangroves are a vital and fragile component of marine ecosystems, and they help prevent coastal erosion. But in the last 30 years, Panama has lost 6,000 hectares of mangroves, cut down to make way for construction projects, resorts, cattle ranches, shrimp farms, and the like. Mangroves have also been lost through pollution and direct exploitation.

The Panama Canal watershed is the most important in Panama. It supplies the water needed to run the Panama Canal, and provides drinking water to the greater metropolitan areas of Panama City and Colón, where most of the country's population live. Slash-and-burn agriculture, urbanization, and pollution have done considerable damage to the watershed, diminishing the quantity and quality of its fresh water.

The purity of Panama's drinking water, a legacy of the Panama Canal Company's strict hygiene standards, has long been a source of pride. One can turn on a tap almost anywhere in the country and be sure the water is safe to drink. However, recent studies have concluded that if immediate steps aren't taken to curtail pollution, city dwellers may soon find themselves forced to drink bottled water.

AIR QUALITY

Those who've traveled extensively in the developing world will not be overwhelmed by air pollution even in Panama's most congested urban areas. But this problem is growing, particularly as more and more cars clog Panama's roads. Parts of Panama City register well above acceptable limits for airborne toxins. In the past, strong winds kept Panama City's air relatively fresh. In recent years, however, a brown haze hangs over the city more and more often.

PARKS AND PROTECTED AREAS

Panama has set aside nearly four dozen protected areas covering nearly two million hectares (close to five million acres) of land, or about 25 percent of Panama's total area, and a substantial portion of its territorial waters. Most of these protected areas are part of an extensive system of 13 national parks and marine parks and one international park, the giant Parque Internacional la Amistad (PILA), that extends over the border into Costa Rica. There are numerous wildlife refuges, buffer forests, protected wetlands, and so on. There are also laws on the books to protect endangered or threatened animals.

The protected areas are a relatively new phenomenon. The first national park, Parque Nacional Altos de Campana, was set aside in 1966, and all the others have been created just in the last 25 years. The parks and other protected areas are managed by the Autoridad Nacional del Ambiente (ANAM), which stands for "national environmental authority," which in 1998 replaced the even more imposingly named Instituto Nacional de Recursos Naturales Renovables (INRENARE).

As anyone who travels extensively in Panama's national parks will soon discover, just being named a protected area does not confer much protection. Illegal hunting, fishing, logging, and even farming continue in many of the protected areas.

All the parks have at least rudimentary ranger stations, but few have much in the way of visitors' facilities or developed trails. Large sections of some parks, notably the Caribbean slope of PILA and almost all of Parque Nacional Cerro Hoya, are almost inaccessible, which is the main reason they're still intact.

ANAM has only a couple hundred workers spread throughout the entire system of protected areas; there's an average of about one employee for every 7,000 hectares. Sometimes they're spread far more thinly than that: there are only a handful of rangers at two rustic ranger stations to guard the entire 579,000 hectares of Parque Nacional Darién. A third of the protected areas do not have a single ranger assigned to them.

CONSERVATION GROUPS

Panama's largest conservation group is the non-profit Asociación Nacional para la Conservación de la Naturaleza ("national association for the conservation of nature"), or ANCON. Since its founding in 1985 it has played an important role in Panama's attempts to protect its environment by taking on such basic but critical projects as demarcating park boundaries and training park rangers. ANCON does have its critics, who sometimes accuse it of giving a seal of approval to big development projects that are destructive to the environment.

ANCON owns the country's largest private nature reserve, the 65,000-hectare Punta Patiño Reserve on the Darién coast. Its other holdings include Isla San Telmo, in the Archipiélago de las Perlas, which protects endangered moist premontane forest and is a sanctuary for brown pelicans and other animals. It also owns several nature lodges around the country that are managed by Ancon Expeditions, a private for-profit organization that has been spun off as a separate entity.

ANCON welcomes foreign volunteers who'd like to work on its projects. Wild animals that are being abused, injured, or held in captivity illegally can be reported to ANCON by calling its *linea verde* (green line): tel. 314-0060, fax 314-0061.

ANCON, ANAM, and other Panamanian environmental organizations work with the U.S.-based Nature Conservancy on some projects in Panama. For more information contact the Nature Conservancy at 4245 N. Fairfax Dr., Arlington, VA 22203-1606, tel. 800/628-6860.

The prestigious Smithsonian Tropical Research Institute (STRI) is based in Panama. STRI is one of the leading centers for the study of tropical animals, plants, marine life, evolution, conservation, and much more. It's world famous for its research into lowland moist tropical forests on Isla Barro Colorado, which is in the middle of the canal. Access to the island is strictly controlled, but STRI does offer tours.

The Sociedad Audubon de Panamá (Panama Audubon Society) hosts regular bird-watching tours, and nonmembers are invited to join them. The society is also a good source of information on nature hikes and backcountry places to stay, and some of its members are freelance guides. For information write to Sociedad Audubon de Panamá, Apartado 2026, Balboa-Panamá, República de Panamá; or email info@panamaaudubon.org. The society's phone number is tel./fax 224-4740; its website is www.panamaaudubon.org.

History

It has been said of Panama there are few other places in the world where so much has happened yet left so little trace behind. The jungle has swallowed up whole civilizations, and graverobbers have made away with much of the remaining traces.

But some of the earliest evidence of human habitation in the Americas has been found in Panama. Remarkably advanced cultures flourished millennia after that. And since Spanish explorers discovered the isthmus, it has played an important role in determining the shape of the modern world. Over the last 500 years, Panama has helped establish Spain and the United States as great world powers, nearly bankrupted France, and forced Scotland to give up its sovereignty and become part of the United Kingdom.

ANCIENT HISTORY

Archaeologists estimate that humans have lived on the isthmus of Panama for 12,000 years, possibly longer. No massive structures, such as the pyramids found elsewhere in the Americas, have been discovered, and knowledge of the ancient inhabitants of Panama is sketchy. Many of the archaeological sites that have been uncovered have been damaged by the elements,

Know Panama

looters, and amateur excavations. But the surviving indigenous peoples of western Panama still tell intriguing if fanciful tales of lost cities in little-known and nearly inaccessible mountain forests—so who knows what may turn up one day? Archaeology in Panama is still in many ways in its infancy.

The earliest evidence of human habitation found to date is Clovis-type arrowheads found near what is now Lago Alajuela (Madden Lake) in the Panama Canal. Archaeologists have dated them to about 9,000 B.C. Agriculture appears on the Pacific coast of central Panama at around 5,000 B.C. Ceramics appear around 3,000 B.C. A particularly rich site was Monagrillo, on the Azuero Peninsula, where archaeologists have uncovered large numbers of decorated ceramics dating from at least 2,500 B.C., the oldest in Central America and among the oldest known in the Americas.

Most of the archaeological treasures dug up in Panama are far more recent. The roots of the Barriles culture of western Panama are believed to go back to at least 700 B.C., but the culture reached its zenith between about A.D. 400 and A.D. 600, when the eruption of Volcán Barú dispersed it. Intriguing, mysterious stone sculptures have been dug up that depict what appear to be chiefs or priests being carried piggyback by other men, as well as an elaborate and oversized *metate* (stone used to grind corn) that may have been used for sacrifices. Some of these are on display at Panama City's Anthropology museum, Museo Antropológico Reina Torres de Araúz.

But the bulk of the evidence of advanced civilizations, at least so far, is found in Central Panama. One of the most famous pre-Colombian archaeological sites in the Americas, Sitio Conte, was found between the Río Grande and Río Coclé near the town of Penonomé.

The site was a cemetery used for hundreds of years, from about A.D. 750-950. It was discovered when the Río Grande changed its course in the early 20th century and washed gold ornaments and pottery from the riverbanks. Excavated by scientists from Harvard in the 1930s, most of its treasures are scattered among museums in the United States and Europe. It's considered the

richest pre-Colombian site ever discovered in Central America. About 60 graves, more than 1,000 gold ornaments, and literally tons of pottery and carved stone were dug up there. One tomb, apparently that of a great leader buried around A.D. 750, contained about half the gold found at the site, as well as the remains of 22 followers. Nothing remains at the site today, which is on a private farm and cattle ranch and is not open to the public.

Another important archaeological site that raises more questions than it answers is Parque Arqueológico del Caño, on the outskirts of the town of Natá not far from Sitio Conte. It contained a cemetery and a large circular field marked off by carved stone columns in the shape of animal and human figures. Some of these statues are 6 meters high, and they may have been used to demarcate a ceremonial ground or playing field. Unfortunately, nearly all these figures were removed in the 1920s by an American adventurer and taken to museums in the United States. Only their pedestals remain. The site dates from about A.D. 800 to A.D. 1100.

Mysterious petroglyphs carved into boulders have been found near streams and rivers at dozens of sites around the country, including remote forests and islands. They consist mainly of abstract designs, especially spirals and squiggles, as well as crude animal and human figures. No one knows their purpose or when they were carved, but archaeologists have speculated they could be anything from ceremonial or sacrificial sites to "no trespassing" warnings. Wishful thinkers speculate they're maps to buried treasure awaiting someone clever enough to crack the code.

THE SPANISH CONQUEST

The arrival of the Spanish in 1501 spelled the end of the indigenous peoples' dominion over the isthmus and the beginning of the European conquest. The first arrival was an explorer named Rodrigo de Bastidas, who sailed along the Caribbean coast from the Darién at least as far west as Nombre de Dios. His crew included a seaman by the name of Vasco Núñez de Balboa;

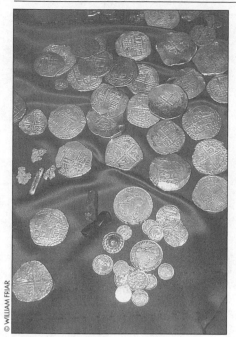

© WILLIAM FRIAR

Spanish coins, beads, gold nuggets, and pre-Colombian figurines found along old Spanish trails

12 years later Balboa would become the first European to hack his way through the Darién and lay eyes on the "Southern Sea," the Pacific Ocean.

In 1502 Christopher Columbus also explored the isthmus, on his fourth and final voyage to find a westward passage to the Indies. Columbus explored the part of the Caribbean coast that Bastidas had not seen, from Bocas del Toro in the far west of the isthmus to Nombre de Dios in the east. He attempted to establish a colony, Santa María de Belén, along the Caribbean coast near the mouth of the Río Belén, but it quickly failed. So did the next few Spanish attempts to gain a foothold on the isthmus.

Balboa and the Discovery of the Pacific

Balboa's career as a great explorer began inauspiciously. Though he was among the first Europeans to explore Panama, when he was a crewmember on Bastidas' voyage of discovery in 1501, he spent the next eight years in Hispaniola (modern-day Haiti and the Dominican Republic) getting into financial trouble. Determined to change his fortunes, he stowed away on a ship bound for the isthmus, slipping past his creditors by hiding in a cask that was loaded onto the ship. When he was discovered, the angry captain almost left him marooned on a desert island, but he soon made himself indispensable because of his knowledge of the isthmus.

When the early settlements began to fall apart, Balboa suggested a new colony be founded at a place in the Darién he remembered from his early days with Bastidas. This became Santa María de la Antigua del Darién, or Antigua, the first lasting European settlement. It was established in 1510 and eventually became the first capital of Castilla del Oro.

Balboa proved to be popular with the men and quickly moved into a position of power. He became the administrative head of Antigua and acting governor of Castilla del Oro, subjugating any indigenous peoples who opposed him. Though his methods were vicious, Balboa became known for his strategy of making peace with Indians who submitted to him. By the standards of his day, he was considered fair and merciful, particularly compared to his murderous contemporaries and successors.

Told by native allies of a sea to the south along whose coast were cities of gold, Balboa set out from Antigua on Sept. 1, 1513 with 190 of his men, an estimated (and probably exaggerated) 1,000 Indians, and a pack of dogs. Among his men was Francisco Pizarro. Along the way they had to fight both the hardships of the jungle and Indians on whose land they were trespassing. At 10 A.M. on Sept. 25, Balboa told the 67 of his men who had survived the brutal trek to wait while he climbed one last hill and became the first European to lay eyes on the "South Sea"— the Pacific Ocean. When he finally made it down to the shore four days later, he found himself on the edge of a large gulf off the Pacific coast of the Darién that he named the Golfo de San

Miguel. He waded out into the water in full armor and promptly claimed the entire sea and all the lands touching it for the Spanish crown, no doubt the biggest land grab in history.

The Founding of Panama City

Meanwhile, King Ferdinand of Spain had appointed a new governor of the isthmus, Pedro Arias de Ávila, better known as Pedrárias. On the isthmus, he had an even more fitting designation: *Furor Domini* (the wrath of God). He saw the popular and resourceful Balboa as a rival and had him beheaded for treason in January 1519 at Acla, a settlement on the Caribbean coast of the Darién.

Pedrárias decided to move the capital from Antigua to the site of a fishing village called Panama, on the central Pacific coast of the isthmus. He founded Panama City, the first European settlement on the Pacific coast of the Americas, on August 15, 1519. He also proceeded to slaughter the indigenous inhabitants of the isthmus.

His men met fierce resistance and sometimes suffered losses at the hands of warriors led by rulers impressive enough to have made it into Spanish records, such as París and Urracá. It was, of course, just a matter of time before the Spanish prevailed. París, for instance, died of natural causes, but he was hounded even in death: the Spaniards looted his grave of its gold. Urracá made peace with the Spaniards, but his people have long since vanished and his only lasting legacy is his profile on Panama's one *centavo* coin.

Panama was home to large, diverse populations of indigenous peoples when the Spanish arrived at the turn of the 16th century. Some put the population of the isthmus at that time at 2 million or even higher, two-thirds the modern-day population. The Spanish decimated these original inhabitants through war and disease. Today only eight groups of indigenous peoples remain, and three of these are barely hanging on.

COLONIAL ERA

During the colonial period, Panama's great importance to Spain was as a transshipment point

for the silver, gold, pearls, and other treasures plundered from South America once the conquest spread to include the Inca Empire. These riches were taken to Panama City, and then had to be carried over to the Caribbean coast, where Spanish ships transported them to Europe. They were carried across the isthmus by two main routes, both of which had their Pacific terminus at Panama City and were established by the Spanish in the early 16th century.

The Camino Real and the Camino de Cruces

The first was the Camino Real, an overland route that linked Panama City with Nombre de Dios (and with Portobelo, when Nombre de Dios was abandoned in 1597). Its name, which translates to "royal road," was rather regal for what was essentially a mule trail, only part of which was paved. It was brutal and muddy, and where it crossed over the foothills it grew so steep that travelers had to climb through the muck on their hands and knees.

The second was the Camino de Cruces, known in English as the Las Cruces Trail. This was an overland route from Panama City to Venta de Cruces, a village on the Río Chagres about a third of the way across the isthmus. The trail was wider than a man is tall during the Spanish Colonial era, and it was paved with flat stones. From Venta de Cruces, it became a water route, with cargo moved by boat or barge up and down the Chagres, which flows into the Caribbean. Fuerte San Lorenzo was built at the mouth of the Chagres to defend it. Because this route was considerably farther west than the Camino Real, goods had to be transported by sea between the mouth of the Chagres and Nombre de Dios or Portobelo to the east. The whole trip took one to two weeks each way.

Though an easier and cheaper route, especially for shipping heavy loads, the Camino de Cruces was more vulnerable to pirate attack than the Camino Real, which had the natural protection of the jungle for much of its length.

The Spanish established the Camino de Cruces in 1527 and it was still being used up until the mid-19th century. The 49ers used it in their own hunt for treasure, as they rushed to the gold fields of California. It was finally abandoned with the building of the Panama Railroad in the 1850s. The village of Venta de Cruces is now at the bottom of the Panama Canal, but part of the Camino de Cruces is still intact and can be walked. The Camino Real was abandoned in 1826.

Gold gets all the attention in romantic tales of Caribbean pirates and Spanish galleons, but silver made up the bulk of the riches Spain looted from South America, mostly from the mines of Peru. By the end of the 17th century, Spain had tripled the amount of silver in circulation throughout the world. An estimated 60 percent of it came through Portobelo alone.

Trade Fairs

This silver, and other treasures from the New World, were traded at massive fairs held at Nombre de Dios and Portobelo. Spanish merchants from Europe and South America converged at the fairs for several weeks each year, more or less, during which they exchanged treasure for European finished goods, which included everything from nails to fine cloth. Merchant ships heading across the Atlantic to and from Spain were escorted by the Spanish navy.

The first organized fair was held in 1537. At their peak, the fairs surpassed those held anywhere else in the world. Bars of silver were stacked high in the streets, but the presence of the heavily armed Spanish fleet kept pirates away.

Not so between fairs. Despite its great importance to the Spanish Empire, the isthmus was neglected and never adequately defended against pirates. Panama was always treated as a notch below, say, Peru, a wealthy and powerful viceroyalty. Panama had the lower administrative rank of *audencia* and was governed by a president.

The trade fairs and treasure shipments marked the first time Panama became a crucial link in world commerce, a role it has continued to play over the years—as a route for the 49ers, as the site of the Panama Canal, and as an international banking capital. One can even see the Colón Free Zone, along the coast where the ruins of the Spanish fortifications still stand, as a kind of descendent of the Spanish trade fairs.

After 1628, these fairs diminished in importance along with the declining fortunes of the Spanish Empire. They were finally abandoned in 1739.

Elizabethan Pirates and Privateers

Lack of funds, poor planning, and procrastination have been blamed for the fact that Panama was constantly sacked and looted throughout the Spanish era.

Nombre de Dios was always a bad choice for a port—the harbor was shallow and exposed, and it would have been hard to defend even if it had had better fortifications. Sir Francis Drake attacked it in 1572, and would likely have sacked it then if he had not been wounded during the conflict. Still, he and his men went on to ambush a mule train on the Camino Real loaded down with so many tons of silver they couldn't carry it away. They buried it instead and made off with some gold. The Spanish dug up the silver before Drake could return for it.

Drake's many exploits on the isthmus as a young adventurer during this period read like something straight out of "Treasure Island." As historians have pointed out, one gets a sense he had an enormously good time tweaking the Spanish. He had help in his adventures from *cimarrones,* escaped African slaves who lived in hidden towns in the jungle and also delighted in harrying their former Spanish masters.

Drake returned to the isthmus years later for more adventures, but he fell sick and died on Jan. 28, 1596, and was buried at sea in a lead-lined coffin near Portobelo. Expeditions have searched for that coffin, but it has never been found.

The Spanish abandoned Nombre de Dios and moved west to Portobelo in 1597, before the fortifications were even completed. Portobelo was a far better location for an important port town. The harbor was long and narrow, surrounded by hills. The Spanish fortified it heavily, but the design was poor from the beginning and constant redesigns over the years didn't seem to help matters much.

Portobelo was barely completed by the time the English pirate William Parker attacked and looted it in 1601. It was sacked and rebuilt several times over the next two hundred years.

Morgan and the Sacking of Panama City

The Welsh buccaneer Henry Morgan took Portobelo and held it for ransom in 1668. He did so by landing his troops at night some distance from Portobelo and attacking the fortifications by land. The defenders' cannons, pointing out to sea, were useless. Still, it was a vicious battle. At one point, Morgan's men used Spanish priests and nuns as human shields, forcing them to erect scaling ladders against the fort walls. The Spanish governor ordered the poor hostages shot down. When Morgan captured the city, he tortured its inhabitants if they refused to reveal where they had hidden their goods. The Spanish finally paid him a ransom of 100,000 pieces of eight to get him to leave.

As this tale suggests, the buccaneers of the 17th century earned a reputation as a far crueler, bloodier, and less dashing lot than the Elizabethan privateers of the previous century.

Morgan was determined to sack and loot Panama City, and he knew where to start his raid. There was another Caribbean fort, Castillo de San Lorenzo el Real, better known today as Fuerte San Lorenzo. It was built near the mouth of the Río Chagres. An imposing cliff there overlooks the river mouth and the sea, the perfect place for a fortress. Oddly, however, the fort was made of wood and its buildings had thatched roofs. As bizarre as it sounds, even the fort's gunpowder was stored in a thatched hut. When Morgan invaded the isthmus, he was able to sack and destroy San Lorenzo, even though the Spanish knew he was coming, by shooting flaming arrows over the walls. He then proceeded up the Chagres by canoe and sacked Panama City. The city was burned to the ground—whether by Morgan or the Spanish is still a matter of debate—and later rebuilt at it a more defensible location eight kilometers farther west. This second Panama City still stands, as an historical

part of modern-day Panama City known as Casco Viejo or Casco Antiguo.

The Scottish Colony

One of the stranger and more tragic episodes during this period was the doomed Scottish colony of New Edinburgh. It was the dream of an entrepreneur named William Paterson, who convinced the Company of Scotland, an overseas trading company created by the Scottish parliament, to invest hundreds of thousands of pounds in his scheme to establish a colony on the Caribbean coast of the Darién. He argued the colony would be ideally situated to become a trading center between Europe and Asia and would help transform Scotland's struggling economy. In July of 1698, Paterson and 1,200 colonists set sail for the Darién. Those who survived the crossing arrived in the Darién on November 2nd. They built a fort, Fort Saint Andrew, on a long, narrow bay they named Calidonia, a name it retains to this day. The colonists were completely unprepared for life in the tropical rainforest, and the colony was a debacle. The first attempt at settlement was abandoned in less than a year, and only a third of the colonists made it back to Scotland. Attempts were made to reestablish the colony, but incompetence, in-fighting, battles with the Spanish, opposition from the English, shipwrecks, and disease brought an end to New Edinburgh by 1700. Scotland, deeply in debt, was forced in 1707 to give up dreams of independence and empire, and joined England to form Great Britain.

THE TUMULTUOUS 19TH CENTURY

With the decline of the Spanish Empire and the drying up of the treasures of the Inca Empire, Panama became a colonial backwater. When independence movements swept through Latin America, Panama eventually got caught up in the tide.

Independence from Spain

On November 10, 1821, residents of the little town of La Villa de Los Santos on the Azuero

Peninsula wrote a letter to Simón Bolívar complaining of mistreatment by the Spanish governor and asking for his help. This *primer grito de la independencia* (first cry for independence) is commemorated as a national holiday in Panama.

This was followed 18 days later by a meeting in Panama City in which Panama broke away from Spain and joined Colombia in an uneasy union that for a while included Venezuela and Ecuador. November 28 is celebrated in Panama today as the first of several steps toward independence.

In 1826, Bolívar called a congress, held in what is now the Casco Viejo section of Panama City, in an attempt to create a union of Latin American republics. The Congress of Panama took place from June 22 to July 15. Though Bolívar himself did not attend and the talks ended in failure, the attempt is still considered an important moment in Latin American history.

The isthmus of Panama was in turmoil through much of the 19th century. It attempted three times between 1831 and 1841 to break away from Colombia, but each time it failed.

The Prestán Uprising

One of the bloodiest incidents of the 19th century in Panama was the so-called Prestán Uprising of 1885. Depending on whom one chooses to believe, Pedro Prestán was either a revolutionary martyred in the cause of freedom or a rabble-rousing mulatto with an irrational hatred of foreigners, especially white ones. When a former president of the department of Panama, Rafael Aizpuru, tried to seize power in Panama City, Colombian troops were dispatched to the city from the Caribbean side of the isthmus, leaving the city of Colón largely undefended. Prestán took advantage of this, reportedly leading a band of machete-wielding men in a looting spree along Front Street. He then took hostages, whom he threatened to kill if the United States warship *Galena*, at port in Colón, landed troops. He also demanded he be given a shipment of arms that had been smuggled by ship and were waiting for him in the harbor.

The commander of the *Galena* had been ordered not to interfere in Panama's domestic affairs unless the Panama Railroad was threatened, which so far it hadn't. The American consul, one of Prestán's hostages, promised to turn over the weapons. Prestán released the hostages, but the *Galena* towed the steamer with the cargo of guns away from shore before Prestán could get access to them.

On March 31, Colombian troops returned from Panama City and battled Prestán's men at Monkey Hill, just outside the city. Routed, Prestán allegedly set fire to Colón as his men retreated. The city, which was built almost entirely of wood, burned to the ground, leaving at least 18 dead and thousands homeless. The Colombian troops rounded up dozens of Prestán's men and executed them. Prestán himself was tried and hanged in Colón, above the railroad tracks. Aizpuru, whose own failed rebellion in Panama City left dozens dead, was sentenced to 10 years in exile.

The War of a Thousand Days

The isthmus was also the scene of major battles in the War of a Thousand Days (1899-1902), a Colombian civil war fought between the Liberal and Conservative parties.

One of the most important of these was the battle of La Vieja Negra, fought outside the city of David in western Panama on March 31, 1900. Liberals who had taken refuge in Nicaragua from the ruling Conservative party invaded Panama from the west, captured David, and defeated better- trained and -equipped Conservative forces at La Vieja Negra, after which they marched on Panama City and were defeated. A peace treaty was signed on July 26, 1900, but was quickly broken. Bloody battles continued to flare up around the isthmus. Colombia called on the United States to intervene, and the war finally came to an end with the signing of a peace treaty aboard the warship *U.S.S. Wisconsin* on November 19, 1902.

Though the Liberals lost the war, Panama considers the leaders of the Liberal forces to be heroes and founding fathers of the country. These include Belisario Porras, the civilian head of the isthmian forces, and Victoriano Lorenzo, who commanded an army of his fellow *cholos* (people of Indian descent but Latino culture) that played a key role in many of the battles. Porras would later serve as president three times when Panama finally became an independent country. Although the peace treaty was supposed to grant the combatants amnesty, Lorenzo was executed by firing squad on May 15, 1903, which Panama remembers as one of the darker days in its history.

GOLD RUSH DAYS

The California gold rush brought Panama back onto the world stage in another quest for treasure. The fastest way to get to the gold fields was to cross at Panama, but it was hardly the easiest. Thousands made their way by foot or mule across the 50 miles of the isthmus by way of the muddy, brutal Camino de Cruces, the same trail used by the Spanish during their own bout of gold fever. Untold others died attempting it, of cholera, dysentery, yellow fever, malaria, and the other dangers that made the Panama route notorious.

If a railway could be built across the isthmus, it would make the crossing faster and far safer for the 49ers who, not incidentally, would be willing to pay a small fortune for the privilege. A forward-thinking U.S. merchant named William Henry Aspinwall negotiated a treaty with Nueva Granada to build just such a railway shortly before the California gold rush began.

Though only 47.5 miles long, the railroad was an incredibly costly undertaking, both in dollars and lives. It was said that every railroad tie represented one worker dead from disease. That's a wild exaggeration, but thousands did die building the little railroad through the jungle. In 1852, a cholera epidemic struck so quickly that workers died on the tracks, to be eaten by ants and land crabs. So many died that the Panama Railroad company started a lucrative side business shipping cadavers preserved in barrels to medical schools and hospitals around the world. Engineers had to contend with the powerful Río Chagres, which could rise 40 feet overnight, and with obstacles such as the seemingly bottomless Black Swamp.

When the railroad was completed in 1855, it included 304 bridges and culverts. The company was able to charge $25 in gold for a one-way trip, a huge sum for the day.

The massive influx of foreigners on the isthmus, some of them rather rough characters, caused some conflicts. The worst incident occurred in April of 1856, when an allegedly drunk train passenger who had just arrived in Panama City grabbed a slice of watermelon from a black vendor and refused to pay for it. This sparked the so-called Watermelon War, a day of rioting that had racial, anti-American, and class overtones. It left at least 16 dead, almost all North Americans, and caused extensive damage to railroad property.

THE PANAMA CANAL AND INDEPENDENCE FROM COLOMBIA

For hundreds of years, visionaries had dreamed of building a canal across the isthmus. Even the early Spanish colonists toyed with the idea until King Philip II allegedly declared that if God had wanted a canal joining the oceans, he would have put one there Himself.

The French Canal

The French were the first to undertake the challenge, in 1882. The moving force behind the effort was Ferdinand de Lesseps, a charismatic diplomat with no engineering background who was basking in the glory of leading the successful effort to build the Suez Canal. He insisted that building a sea-level canal at Panama would be far easier. After all, Suez was twice as long.

But this was Panama, and a sea-level canal here meant digging through mountains, not sand, and contending with its tropical diseases, fierce heat, torrential rains, and forbidding terrain.

The French failed disastrously. It has been estimated that 20,000 workers died, mostly of disease, during the seven-year French effort. The French canal company ran out of money in 1889, and the ensuing financial crisis nearly bankrupted France.

The U.S. Canal

The United States had long toyed with building its own canal. It bought out the French concession, but clashed with the government of Nueva Granada (i.e., Colombia) over payments and the granting of rights over the proposed waterway. When negotiations stalled, the United States, under President Theodore Roosevelt, decided to support a small independence movement in Panama spearheaded by a few prominent Panamanians and Panama Railroad officials. In a display of literal "gunboat diplomacy," America sent a warship to Panama to intimidate the Colombian forces on the isthmus. On November 3, 1903, Panama declared its independence from Nueva Granada.

It was a remarkably peaceful civil war. Bloodshed was likely averted by a fast-thinking Panama Railroad official. He convinced a Colombian general who had just landed with his troops in Colón that it was only fitting that he and his officers should ride in a special train car ahead of his men, who were left stranded in Colón. When the officers arrived in Panama City, Panama-based Colombian soldiers who had been bought off by the revolutionaries took them prisoner. The only casualty during the whole conflict was a Chinese shopkeeper, asleep in his bed, who was killed by an errant shell from a Colombian gunboat. A second shell killed a donkey in a slaughterhouse. By November 6, the revolution was over.

The United States immediately signed the controversial Hay–Bunau-Varilla Treaty with the new Panamanian government, which gave America the right to build a canal in Panama. It would become a source of contention for decades to come that no Panamanian signed the treaty. The official signatory for Panama was a Frenchman, Philippe Bunau-Varilla, the former director of and major shareholder in the French canal effort. The revolutionaries had reluctantly agreed to let him negotiate with Washington on their behalf as an "envoy extraordinary." He signed the treaty in New York before the Panamanian delegation even arrived.

The treaty granted the United States control "in perpetuity" over the canal and a 50-by-10-mile strip of land surrounding it. The United

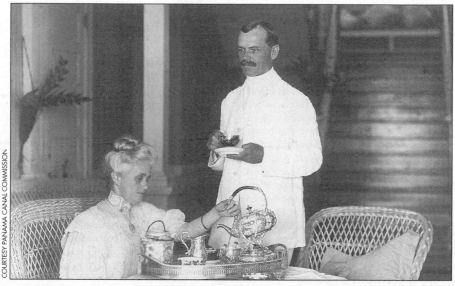

Colonel and Mrs. David D. Gaillard having tea at their home on the banks of Culebra Cut

COURTESY PANAMA CANAL COMMISSION

On May 20, 1913, two steam shovels met at the bottom of the Culebra Cut, now known as the Gaillard Cut.

States paid the new country of Panama $10 million, plus an annual payment of $250,000. The French canal company received $40 million for all the equipment, infrastructure, and excavation it left behind, much of which proved useful to the Americans.

The American effort was quite different from the French one. Instead of a sea-level ditch, the U.S. plan called for a lock canal that would lift ships over the isthmian land mass. The plan was designed by John Stevens, a brilliant railway engineer, and seen to completion by his successor as chief engineer, George W. Goethals. All work on the canal had to be halted, however, until disease could be controlled. Under the leadership of a forward-looking sanitary officer named Dr. William Gorgas, the Americans eliminated yellow fever from Panama, brought malaria and other deadly diseases under control, and introduced clean water and modern sanitation to the isthmus.

The canal was a colossal task. It required an excavation three times as massive as that at Suez. And among other challenges, the builders had to cut right through nine miles of mountains at the continental divide, a job overseen by David Gaillard, for whom the resulting Gaillard Cut is named. The lock chambers were among the largest structures ever made by man. The mighty Río Chagres was contained by the largest earthen dam in history, forming the largest manmade lake in the world. The canal is still considered one of the most extraordinary engineering feats of all time.

The U.S. canal effort cost $352 million and took 5,600 lives, most of them West Indians who made up the bulk of the labor force. But the canal opened for business on August 15, 1914, under budget and ahead of schedule.

THE NEW NATION

The first president of the new Republic of Panama was Dr. Manuel Amador Guerrero, an elderly, well-respected medical doctor from a prominent Panamanian family and the leader of the little band of revolutionaries. Panama was a kind of democracy, but leaders inevitably came from the wealthiest, whitest families.

One of the biggest challenges to the new republic was an independence movement among the Kunas of the San Blas Islands. The Kuna declared their independence from Panama in February of 1925 and announced the creation of their own country, the Republic of Tule. A brief war ensued that left about two dozen dead. The United States intervened and presided over a peace treaty between Panama and the Kunas that gave the latter the semiautonomous status they retain to this day. The other indigenous peoples of Panama have slowly gained similar control over their ancestral lands over the years through the establishment of *comarcas* (reservations). Some are still fighting for *comarca* status.

Arnulfo Arias

A figure who loomed large in Panamanian politics through much of the 20th century was Arnulfo Arias Madrid, a Harvard Medical School graduate from a family of provincial farmers. Along with his brother, Harmodio Arias Madrid, he was a leading figure in a group called Acción Comunal that overthrew the president, Florencio Harmodio Arosemena, in a bloody assault on the presidential palace in 1931. (Note: many of the major figures in Panamanian politics have similar names, including many who are not remotely related.) Arosemena was replaced by Ricardo J. Alfaro, a choice acceptable to Acción Comunal. The following year, Arnulfo's brother was elected president. The United States decided not to intervene in any of this. It was the country's first successful coup.

But it was hardly the last. Arnulfo Arias himself, ironically enough, endured them incessantly. He was elected president of Panama at least four times (voter fraud makes the official outcome in two elections hard to confirm) between 1940 and 1984. Each time he was either deposed or forbidden to take office by the *Policía Nacional* (National Police) or its successor, the *Guardia Nacional* (National Guard).

Arnulfo, as he is known in Panama, was a charismatic populist who espoused a vehement brand of nationalism known as *Panameñismo*. He was also a fascist sympathizer during World War II who was determined not only to rid the isthmus of North Americans but also of fellow citizens he deemed undesirables. Nevertheless, he was beloved by many of Panama's poor and disenfranchised, who saw him as a counterweight to the power of the oligarchy.

In 1941, at the beginning of his first aborted administration, he introduced a new constitution that replaced the one instituted in 1904. Among other things, it increased the presidential term of office to six years. But it's most notorious for blatantly racist provisions that forbade the immigration of blacks from non-Spanish-speaking countries, as well as Chinese, Indians, and Arabs. It also stripped those already in the country of their citizenship. It was replaced with yet another constitution five years later, after he was overthrown the first time. But Arias is also credited with establishing many of Panama's most important institutions, such as the social security system, and expanding the rights of some of its citizens.

The Rise of the National Guard

The commander of the National Police, José Antonio Remón Cantera, militarized and increased the power of the force and served as kingmaker (and breaker) for several Panamanian presidents before running for president himself. In a strange series of events, he first opposed and then installed Arnulfo Arias as president in 1949, declaring, without presenting evidence, that the election of the year before should have found Arias the victor. Arias' second attempt at wielding power deteriorated rapidly, and demonstrations against him turned so violent he was forced to hole up in the presidential palace with his most loyal supporters. Two officers of the National Police were shot dead on the steps of the palace under mysterious circumstances. The murders were to prove emblematic of the enmity that would exist for the rest of the century between the *arnulfistas* and the National Police, later the National Guard. Arias was removed from power a second time.

Remón decided it was time to become president himself. He was elected in 1952 and began a campaign of social and economic reforms that was cut short in 1955 when he was machine-gunned to death at a horse-racing track on the outskirts of Panama City. All kinds of conspiracy theories have been put forth about who was behind the assassination. One even points the finger at the American mobster "Lucky" Luciano. Panama City's racetrack was renamed in Remón's honor.

EMERGING NATIONALISM

Tensions between Panama and the United States flared up repeatedly through much of the 20th century. Again and again, especially in the early days of the republic, the U.S. intervened in the domestic affairs of the country. Because of the strategic and economic importance of first the Panama Railroad and then the Panama Canal, the United States has insisted on reserving the right to play a hand in the destiny of the isthmus in treaty after treaty.

Tensions occasionally erupted in violence. When the Panamanian national legislature met in 1947 to consider a treaty that would allow the United States to continue to use military bases outside the Canal Zone, 10,000 protestors took to the streets and clashed with Panama's National Police, with deaths on both sides. The legislature rejected the treaty unanimously. Violent anti-U.S. demonstrations flared up again in 1958 and 1959.

The Flag Riots

The most infamous incident, though, were the so-called Flag Riots of 1964. The United States had agreed to fly the Panamanian flag alongside the U.S. one in a few places in the Canal Zone, even though some feared (and others hoped) this would throw U.S. sovereignty over the Zone into doubt. In an attempt to avoid controversy, the governor of the Canal Zone decided to take down some flagpoles in the Zone altogether. One of these spots was Balboa High School. A group of high school students objected to this, and before the pole could be removed they raised a U.S. flag themselves. When a group of Panamanian college students heard of this, they organized a march to the high school and attempted to lower

the U.S. and raise the Panamanian one. A scuffle broke out, during which the Panamanian students claimed their flag had been torn.

What happened after that will probably forever be a source of passionate debate, depending on one's sympathies and prejudices. What everyone can agree on is that rioting, looting, and destruction followed, mostly along Fourth of July Avenue, which separated Panama City from the Canal Zone. In the end, two dozen people were killed and millions of dollars of property destroyed. The Panamanians who died are officially considered martyrs in Panama, and January 9th is still a national day of mourning in their honor. Fourth of July Avenue was renamed Avenida de los Mártires.

In the wake of this terrible clash, President Lyndon B. Johnson announced that the United States would undertake negotiations with Panama on an entirely new canal treaty.

A NEW TREATY

In 1968 Arnulfo Arias was again elected president. He took office on October 1 and immediately called for the turnover of the canal to Panama and attempted to take control of the National Guard. The second move was a mistake. A military junta deposed him on Oct. 11 and, ironically enough, he fled to the Canal Zone for protection. He had served 11 days in office, his shortest term yet.

Omar Torrijos

After a period of chaos and demonstrations, a National Guard colonel named Omar Torrijos Herrera assumed power. He was himself the subject of an attempted coup by three rival colonels when he took a trip to Mexico early in his rule. When he learned of this, he returned to Panama, rallied supporters in the western city of David, and marched on the capital. He regained power and sent the colonels into exile.

Torrijos had himself promoted to general and became a remarkably popular figure. Though a military dictator, he was also a populist who flirted with socialist ideas—he had a friendly re-

COURTESY PANAMA CANAL COMMISSION

President Jimmy Carter and General Omar Torrijos signing the 1977 Panama Canal Treaties

lationship with Fidel Castro—and instituted sweeping social reforms. Though he installed a figurehead president, Demétrios Lakas, everyone knew who was really in charge. In 1972 he introduced yet another new constitution that confirmed him as head of a powerful central government and curtailed civil rights. He ordered the redistribution of land to the *campesinos,* greatly expanded public health programs, reformed the school system, built roads and bridges in rural areas, and laid the groundwork for Panama's emergence as an international banking center. Some of these changes came at the expense of the oligarchy.

For all these accomplishments, however, corruption and nepotism blossomed under Torrijos, and the bodies of his political enemies are still being dug up around the country.

One of the things that helped ensure Torrijos' popularity was his focus on a new treaty that would turn control of the canal over to Panama. Negotiations began with the Nixon and Ford administrations, but progress was slow until Jimmy Carter took office in 1977. On September 7 of that year, Torrijos met Carter in Washington,

D.C., to sign two new Panama Canal treaties. The first called for a gradual turnover of the canal to Panamanian control, to allow the small country time to absorb the massive undertaking. Panama gained complete jurisdiction over the canal and former Canal Zone at noon on December 31, 1999. The second one, the Neutrality Treaty, bound the United States and Panama to guarantee the canal's neutrality in peace or war and allow unimpeded transit of the ships of all nations. The United States reserved the right to act against any perceived threat to the canal but not otherwise intervene in the domestic affairs of Panama. This second treaty was open-ended and is still in effect, and it continues to be a source of discontent in Panama from time to time. Two-thirds of the Panamanian people voted in favor of the new treaties, a weaker show of support than expected.

To gain support in Washington for the treaties, Torrijos had agreed to begin a process of democratization. He stepped down as the official head of government but retained ultimate authority by retaining his position as head of the National Guard. He allowed Arnulfo Arias to return to Panama and start rebuilding his political support.

The constitution was amended in October 1978 to weaken the power of the executive branch somewhat and increase that of the Asamblea Legislativa, the national legislature. The legislature voted in Aristides Royo, a candidate backed by Torrijos, as president.

The first political party granted official recognition was the Partido Revolucionario Democrático (democratic revolutionary party) or PRD, which was controlled by Torrijos and his supporters and would come to be known as the National Guard's party. National elections were held in 1980. Opposition parties gained some representation in the national legislature, but Torrijos ensured that most seats were reserved for the PRD.

Noriega Takes Power

On July 31, 1981, Torrijos died in a small plane that crashed in the mountains above El Copé in central Panama. The area has since been turned into a national park named in his honor. Rumors that the crash was arranged by one of his political rivals circulated immediately. A period of turmoil followed, with a parade of military figures succeeding each other in power.

By 1983, General Manuel Antonio Noriega had firm control of the National Guard, which he soon renamed the *Fuerzas de Defensa de Panamá* (Panama Defense Forces), and the country as a whole. Torrijos had spotted Noriega's potential early in his own military career, and when he became dictator he had put Noriega in charge of military intelligence. Despite this long association, some speculated that Noriega was behind the death of Torrijos. The contrast between the two dictators could not have been more stark. Torrijos was a handsome, charismatic man who had inspired loyalty among his supporters and enacted many popular programs. Noriega's pockmarked face earned him the nickname *cara de piña* (pineapple face), and he ruled through fear.

In the 1984 elections, the Noriega-controlled PRD nominated Nicolás Ardito Barletta Vallarino, a former World Bank vice president with a degree in economics from the University of Chicago. Opposing him was the indefatigable Arnulfo Arias. Barletta was elected president in

what was widely agreed to be a fraudulent vote count. The United States decided to recognize him anyway.

But in September 1985 a horrific event occurred that began Noriega's spectacular fall from power. Dr. Hugo Spadafora, a colorful and charismatic Noriega opponent who had been a guerrilla fighter in Africa and a protégé of Torrijos, decided to return to Panama by bus to challenge Noriega's hold on power. He claimed to have information on Noriega's illegal dealings throughout Latin America that would force him from power. He took a bus from the Costa Rican border towards Panama City on September 13, but he was stopped near the town of Concepción and forced off the bus. He was subsequently tortured and beheaded, his decapitated body later found in a river across the border in Costa Rica. Suspicion immediately fell on Noriega.

The following year, the Pulitzer-Prize-winning investigative reporter Seymour Hersh began breaking stories in the New York Times that detailed a laundry list of shady dealings by Noriega: that he had long been a CIA asset, that he was deeply involved in drug dealing and money laundering, that he'd rigged the 1984 election, that he did intelligence work for Cuba, that he was implicated in the murder of Spadafora. When the Iran-Contra scandal broke, Noriega emerged as a vital player who was said to have a cozy relationship with Oliver North, CIA director William Casey, and other Iran-Contra figures. He was accused of helping the Contras with everything from shipping arms to planning sabotage operations in Nicaragua. Noriega was proving an increasing embarrassment, first to President Ronald Reagan and then President George H.W. Bush, whom Noriega had known since Bush's days as CIA director in the 1970s.

Operation Just Cause

A new election was held on May 7, 1989, with a Noriega-backed candidate named Carlos Duque running against Guillermo Endara, a lawyer and protégé of Arnulfo Arias, whose long political career had finally ended the year before, when he died at age 86. Panama always elects two vice-presidents, and Endara's running mates were Guillermo "Billy" Ford and Ricardo Arias Calderón.

The election was a sham. Votes were bought, eligible voters were turned away from the polls, ballots were destroyed. Jimmy Carter, who had flown to Panama as an election observer, held a press conference at a Panama City hotel and declared that "The government is taking the election by fraud." He said the opposition had won by a margin of three to one.

Endara and his two running mates led a protest march three days later that was attacked by Panama Defense Forces troops and Noriega goons. Demonstrators were blasted with buckshot and teargas. Endara was knocked unconscious by an attacker wielding a steel pipe, and Arias Calderón and Ford were beaten and shot at. Images of the bloodied candidates were beamed around the world.

By now, some officers of the Panama Defense Forces were becoming nervous at what seemed to be Noriega's increasingly erratic behavior. Major Moises Giroldi decided to mount a coup, with tentative support from a suspicious Washington. On October 3, 1989, Giroldi and his supporters took Noriega hostage at his headquarters, the Comandancia, but hesitation and confusion allowed Noriega time to phone his most loyal troops, who surrounded the Comandancia and engaged in a firefight with the rebels. Noriega prevailed and the coup plotters were tortured and executed. The Bush administration denied having any involvement with the coup attempt, despite considerable evidence it had encouraged the coup, then declined to give it support at the vital moment.

Periodic violent clashes between the Panama Defense Forces and U.S. military personnel traveling outside the Canal Zone reached a low point when a U.S. Marine Corps lieutenant, Robert Paz, was shot dead in Panama City on December 17. Three days later, on December 20, 1989, President Bush ordered an invasion of Panama, dubbed Operation Just Cause. It left somewhere between 200 and 4,000 civilian dead. The true number may never be known, as it was in the in-terest of the United States and the subsequent Panamanian government to downplay the number, and of those with other political agendas to inflate it. The hardest-hit area was El Chorrillo, an impoverished neighborhood of wooden tenements and anti-Noriega sentiment that lay right next to the Comandancia. It was swept by a fire that left an untold number dead and thousands homeless.

Noriega escaped and sought asylum at the residence of the papal nuncio, the representative of the Vatican in Panama, on Christmas Eve. U.S. troops surrounded the house and "psychological operations" personnel blasted loud rock music to keep him from getting any rest. He surrendered on January 3, 1990, and was flown to Florida. On July 2, 1992, he was sentenced to 40 years in a Miami prison on drug and racketeering charges. The sentence was later reduced to 30 years. In 2004, a federal judge recommended the former dictator's release because of his "advancing age"—he was then 70—but the request was turned down. As this book went to press, he was expected to be released in 2007. If so, he faces jail time in Panama, which has called for his extradition and where in 1995 he was convicted in absentia of murdering the leaders of the 1989 coup attempt.

A NEW DEMOCRACY

Guillermo Endara, who had been robbed by Noriega of the presidency in 1989 and brutally beaten along with his vice-presidential candidates in the protests that followed, was finally sworn in as president during the invasion. His term was a period of instability, as Panama worked to recover from the devastation of the invasion, and the U.S. economic sanctions that preceded it. A final military coup was attempted and failed. The Panama Defense Forces were disbanded, and today Panama no longer has a military. But crime increased in Panama while order was restored and a new civilian police force organized.

Endara—a figure of some fun in Panama because of his obesity, lack of political experience, and infatuation with his young, attractive wife—managed to serve out his term and democracy took hold in Panama.

Endara was succeeded in 1994 by Ernesto Pérez Balladares, a member of the PRD, the party of Noriega and Torrijos. He won with 33 percent of the vote in an election that also featured Mireya Moscoso, the widow of Arnulfo Arias, and Rubén Blades, the famous salsa singer and actor. The election was considered fair.

The PRD attempted to distance itself from the Noriega years, but during the Balladares administration it continued to face accusations of drug trafficking, money laundering, and corruption. Balladares, popularly known as *El Toro* (the bull), enacted free-market reforms that sparked protest in Panama and caused his popularity to suffer. He attempted to change the constitution to allow him to run for a second term, but Panamanian voters defeated the proposal by a two-to-one margin.

In 1999, Moscoso ran again for the presidency on the ticket of the Partido Arnulfista (PA) or Arnulfista Party. This time her main opponent was Martín Torrijos, the young son of the late dictator, who represented the PRD. Moscoso won and became Panama's first female president. A peaceful democracy proved to be well established as full control of the Panama Canal was turned over to Panama at noon on December 31, 1999.

The new millennium began with things looking pretty bright for Panama. The Panama Canal was in the middle of a billion-dollar expansion and was increasingly being run as a business, its raised tolls making a major contribution to the economy. New construction was transforming the Panama City skyline and, thanks to Balladares, the road system throughout the country had been greatly improved.

But the downturn in the world economy hit Panama's services sector hard. Moscoso also generated a great deal of animosity, and not just from her PRD rivals. Her administration, like the one before it, was plagued by accusations of corruption. Environmentalists complained her policies were wreaking immeasurable damage for short-term gain. She did little to endear herself to the poor people among her supporters when, early in her administration, she presented each of the 72 members of the national legislature with a Cartier watch as a "Christmas present."

But in 2001 the Moscoso administration established a *Comisión de la Verdad* (truth commission) to investigate the disappearance of 110 people under the Torrijos and Noriega dictatorships. Forensic anthropologists dug up human remains all over the country, and in its final report the commission concluded that 70 of the cases it investigated were murders and the other 40 were still missing.

Moscoso's term ended in 2004. Martín Torrijos ran a second time for the presidency and this time was elected. He took office on September 1, 2004. The new century of Panamanian political life was beginning to look quite familiar: an ongoing power struggle between the Arnulfistas and the PRD.

Government and Economy

Panama is a constitutional democracy. The chief executive is the president, assisted by two vice presidents, all of whom are elected to a single five-year term. The *Asamblea Legislativa* (legislative assembly) is the national legislature, currently consisting of 71 members in a unicameral (one house) body. Legislators serve five-year terms that run concurrently with the presidential term. There is also a supreme court consisting of nine justices who serve 10-year terms, as well as several superior courts and courts of appeal.

For much of Panama's history, however, the government was essentially controlled by the oligarchy, the military, or both. Especially during the military dictatorship that lasted from the 1968 coup to the 1989 U.S. invasion that removed Noriega from power, the president was often a figurehead, and neither the legislature nor the courts held much independent power.

Every election from 1994 on has been widely considered free and fair, with less controversy surrounding them than, for instance, recent U.S.

COURTESY PANAMA CANAL COMMISSION

The administration building in Balboa Heights is the headquarters of the Panama Canal Authority.

elections. Though corruption and influence peddling are still acknowledged to be problems, Panama's democracy appears healthier and more firmly entrenched than ever before. Suffrage is "universal and compulsory"—that is, everyone 18 years and older is required to vote in all national elections.

Panama either adopted a new constitution or amended an existing one several times during its first 100 years, usually motivated by expanding or contracting the government's power and citizens' rights or realigning its relationship with the United States, particularly concerning U.S. intervention in Panama's affairs and its rights in the Canal Zone. New changes to the constitution were working their way through the national legislature as this book went to press.

The central government has also loosened its control over large sections of the country through the creation of *comarcas*, or semiautonomous reservations for the country's indigenous peoples.

Panama's gross domestic product in 2003 was $12.88 billion. Unlike its Central American neighbors, Panama's economy depends mainly on an extensive services sector, not agriculture. About three-quarters of its GDP comes from the Colón Free Zone, international banking, the Panama Canal, ports, ship registry, tourism, and related services. Agriculture comprises just 8 percent of GDP. The main agricultural exports are bananas, rice, coffee, sugarcane, and shrimp. Panama's largest trading partner, by far, is the United States.

Panama has always been a "dollarized" economy, meaning its currency is tied to the U.S. dollar. In fact, Panama's paper currency, officially known as the balboa, *is* the dollar.

The economy took a major hit towards the end of the 1990s with the departure of U.S. military personnel and their dependents (and dollars), but Panama Canal revenues have helped soften the blow in the last few years. The canal took in a record $257.9 million in 2003, thanks mainly to an increase in tolls. Many in Panama hope tourist dollars will eventually more than make up for the loss; major tourist developments are transforming the former Canal Zone and other parts of Panama.

The Free Zone and the banking sector have also experienced a slump in recent years, driven in part by a downturn in the world economy and increased competition abroad, though the slide appears to be slowing and the Panamanian economy as a whole recovering. GDP grew a reported 4.1 percent in 2003, led by a boom in construction.

Panama generally has low inflation (1.4 percent in 2003). But its unemployment rate has been high in recent years. In 2003 the official unemployment rate for workers 15 and older was 13.4 percent, a small improvement over the year before. Public sector debt hovers around $8.9 billion, or two-thirds of GDP. More worrisome still is the poverty rate.

Though one of the region's most affluent countries, Panama has one of the most unequal distributions of wealth in the world. An estimated 1.2 million Panamanians, about 40 percent of the population, live in poverty. Half of these people live in extreme poverty, trying to get by on less than $1 a day. At the other extreme, a widely quoted study claimed in 2004 that just 80 people accounted for half of Panama's total GDP.

People

Panama's 1911 census, the country's first, estimated its population at just 336,742. By the 2000 census, it had grown to 2,839,177.

Despite high unemployment and a downturn in the economy in recent years, Panamanians remain prosperous by Latin American standards. A primary-school education is compulsory, and nearly 93 percent of the population aged 15 and older can read and write. Average life expectancy at birth is 72 years, about the same as Hungary. Women outlive men by nearly five years. However, there is a wide gap between the comparatively few rich and large number of poor people.

Panamanians often identify themselves by their family's province of origin, each of which has regional stereotypes associated with it. There are nine provinces: Bocas del Toro, Chiriquí, Veraguas, Herrera, Los Santos, Coclé, Panamá, Colón, and Darién. There are also a number of indigenous reservations or *comarcas,* and in recent years the national legislature has been adding more by carving territory in existing provinces.

The most densely inhabited part of the country borders the Panama Canal, an area that encompasses Panama City and Colón and the most developed parts of the provinces (Panamá and Colón) that contain them. More than one-third of Panama's population lives in the greater metropolitan area of Panama City alone, if one includes the sprawling barrio of San Miguelito.

Most of the rest of Panama's population is concentrated on the Pacific hills and lowlands of the isthmus, particularly in the so-called central provinces of Coclé, Herrera, Los Santos, and Veraguas. This area, particularly the Azuero Peninsula, is considered by many Panamanians to be their heartland because of its preservation of traditional folklore and crafts, the Spanish colonial architecture that can still be found in its provincial cities and towns, and its long agricultural history. It occupies in the Panamanian imagination a place somewhere between that occupied by the Old West and the Great Plains in the gringo one. Not surprisingly, given its early settlement, it's also the most severely deforested part of Panama.

The province of Chiriquí contains the fertile mountains of western Panama and the country's second largest city, David (pop. 77,734 in the central city, 124,280 in the entire district), in its humid lowlands. *Chiricanos* have a strong regional identity and are proud of their beautiful homeland. It's sometimes said that they consider themselves *Chiricanos* first and Panamanians second. Stickers depicting the provincial flag adorn the windows of many homes and the bumpers of many cars, and fake Chiriquí "passports" are sometimes sold as novelties in stores. The area around Volcán Barú, Panama's highest mountain, has been experiencing a tourist boom in recent years, particularly the cozy town of Boquete.

Bocas del Toro also feels somehow separate

from the rest of Panama, but here it takes the form of neglect. Bocatoreños often complain of being treated as a backwater province. It is one of the few places in Panama that still cannot rely on a steady supply of clean water, which is one of the grievances that spark occasional demonstrations. Paradoxically, the islands of Bocas del Toro are developing rapidly thanks to a tourism explosion greater than any part of the country outside Panama City.

The Darién (which traditionally includes both Darién province and the eastern side of Panama province) to the east and the Caribbean slope to the north are still mostly forested and lightly populated, though that's changing rapidly.

As the soil of the central provinces has been depleted and cattle ranchers have taken over, slash-and-burn farmers in the central provinces have been forced since about the 1950s to push farther east and north to find new farmland, often following the building of new roads. These *colonos,* as the internal migrants are known, soon exhaust the new land as well, which is again taken over by cattle ranchers. Loggers also follow the roads, accelerating the deforestation. All this has sometimes resulted in clashes with indigenous peoples, who not surprisingly consider this an invasion of their land and the destruction of their way of life.

Panama is a young country: nearly one-third of the population is 14 years or younger, and just 6 percent are older than 64.

INDIGENOUS PEOPLES

While pockets of the indigenous peoples of the isthmus can be found all over the country, either clinging to vestiges of their way of life or assimilating fully into the Panamanian mainstream, most still live on their ancestral lands. *Comarcas* (semiautonomous reservations) are still being established.

Most Kuna (pop. 62,000) live in one of three *comarcas.* The largest of these is Kuna Yala, or the San Blas Archipelago, which includes a strip of mainland and a string of nearly 400 coral islands that extends down the eastern Caribbean coast

from Colón province to the Colombian border. The other two Kuna *comarcas,* Madungandí and Wargandí, are on the Caribbean slope of the Darién rainforest. The Kunas refer to themselves as Tule, though they recognize the name Kuna as well. The name is sometimes spelled "Cuna," but that's now considered anachronistic.

The Emberá (pop. 22,000) and Wounaan (pop. 7,000) live in *comarcas* on both the Caribbean and Pacific slopes of the Darién. They are culturally similar but speak different languages. In the past they have been known collectively as the Chocos, but the name is seldom used today. Emberá-Wounaan is preferred when speaking of them as a group.

The Ngöbe (pop. 170,000) and Buglé (pop. 18,000) have traditionally been known as the Guaymi, but the name is increasingly falling out of favor. Ngöbe-Buglé is preferred when speaking of them collectively. Like the Emberá and Wounaan, they are culturally similar but speak different languages. They are by far the largest indigenous group in Panama. Most live in the mountains of western Panama. In 1997, they gained their own, enormous *comarca,* carved out of the provinces of Chiriquí, Bocas del Toro, and Veraguas.

The remaining recognized indigenous people are the Naso, also known as the Teribe (pop. 3,800), who live along the rivers on the mainland of Bocas del Toro and are trying to gain *comarca* status; the Bri Bri (pop. 2,500) who also live in Bocas del Toro; and the Bokota (pop. 993), whose few surviving members live in eastern Bocas del Toro and northwest Veraguas.

Most indigenous people make a living through subsistence farming, fishing, and hunting. The Kuna and Emberá-Wounaan are also able to bring in some cash through the sale of their handicrafts, which are prized by collectors around the world. Many Ngöbe-Buglé work on coffee plantations in the Chiriquí highlands. Indigenous peoples are increasingly experimenting with tourism, especially ecotourism, to improve their economic conditions. By far the most experienced at this are the Kuna, who have allowed foreign tourists on their islands for decades.

Unemployment, poverty, illiteracy, and poor health are consistently highest among the indigenous people. An estimated 95 percent live in poverty, most in extreme poverty, defined as trying to get by on less than $1 a day. Poorest of all are the Ngöbe-Buglé.

ETHNIC MAKEUP

Panama is a remarkably diverse country by Central American standards, thanks to its surviving indigenous peoples and its status as an important transit point for international commerce for more than 500 years. While most of the arrivals during that time came from Spain and sub-Saharan Africa, Panama also has a substantial population of immigrants from around the world, especially China, India, the Middle East, Central Europe, and North America.

Of these, the longest-established group is the Chinese, who first came over to build the Panama Railroad in the 19th century. Many stayed to open shops and restaurants, and today they are in all walks of life. The traditional community is cohesive enough in Panama City to support three newspapers, three temples, a small Chinatown, a cultural center, and a radio station. People of Chinese descent also can be found throughout the country. Some estimates put their number at high as 150,000, or 5 percent of the total population.

People of African origin have lived on the isthmus since the 16th century. In Panama, a distinction is made between *Afro-Colonials,* the descendents of Spanish slaves, and *Afro-Antillanos,* who came later from the Caribbean islands. The latter are generally referred to as West Indians by English-speakers on the isthmus.

Afro-Colonials who escaped from their Spanish masters were known as *cimarrones,* and they built secluded villages, or *palenques,* along the eastern Caribbean coast and the Darién jungle. Some of these still exist today.

The *Afro-Antillanos* include Jamaicans brought over to dig the French Canal, banana-plantation workers from Jamaica and the Colombian islands of San Andrés and Providencia who settled in Bocas del Toro, and workers from around the West Indies who supplied most of the labor for the Panama Canal. Most of this last group, which numbrd 20,000 in all, came from Barbados.

Race and Class

The ethnic breakdown of Panama is generally thought of as being about 65–70 percent *mestizo* (mixed Amerindian and Caucasian) and 8–10 percent Amerindian, with the bulk of the remaining population consisting of those of African and/or European descent. These estimates are quite rough and have recently been called into question, with one local DNA study concluding that 75 percent of Panama's "common gene pool" are of African and Amerindian origin and just 25 percent from Europe. Estimates of the number of smaller minorities, such as those of Chinese, Indian, and Middle Eastern ancestry, are even more unreliable.

Race relations on the isthmus are complex. Most Panamanians, whether officially *mestizo* or not, are the product of a mixture of different ethnicities, and the country is increasingly proud of being a *crisol de razas* (racial melting pot). Some of the country's legendary national heroes are of African and Amerindian descent.

But a racial pecking order lingers in Panama, tied closely to socioeconomic class. The country has traditionally been ruled by an oligarchy drawn from the elite families, many of whom have light skin and European features and can trace their ancestry back to Spain. They still wield a great deal of power in Panama and tend to marry within other elite families. They are known disparagingly by other Panamanians as *rabiblancos* (white tails).

The indigenous peoples and those of African descent are among the nation's poorest, and they still find it difficult to move up in society. As late as 2002, Panama found it necessary to pass a law forbidding discrimination against minorities in commercial establishments, sparked by repeated incidents of blacks being turned away at the door of bars, discos, and restaurants.

In 1941 the national legislature passed a new constitution that stripped English-speaking blacks (meaning the *Afro-Antillanos* or West Indians) and other non-Latino minorities of their Panamanian citizenship. It also outlawed the immigration of new arrivals from the English-speaking West Indies, as well as China, India, and the Middle East. The constitution was overturned in 1946.

Afro-Antillanos in particular had an uneasy existence on the isthmus during much of the 20th century. They faced discrimination both in the Canal Zone and Panama but had largely lost their ties to the Caribbean islands from which they came. As the years have gone by, most have adopted Spanish as their first language and assimilated more fully into mainstream Panamanian society. The process has sped up with the decline and disappearance of the U.S. Canal Zone, where many families had lived and worked since canal construction days.

The military dictatorship that took power in 1968 was the most serious challenge to the rule of the oligarchy, opening up opportunities for those of different ethnicities and lower socioeconomic classes to rise to positions of power. A relatively large middle class began to emerge. In modern times especially, academic achievement, professional success, and other new sources of societal clout can sometimes overcome the traditional obstacles of race and family connections.

CULTURE

In part because of the long U.S. presence in Panama and in part because of its even longer role in world commerce, Panama has been quicker to "internationalize" than many of its Latin American neighbors. Siestas, for instance, are not really a part of daily life, and in many ways Panama City today has more in common with Miami than it does with, say, Madrid.

But for all Panama's diversity, the country's dominant culture does derive directly from Spain. The extended family is by far the most important social unit. Taking care of one's family comes first, and family-oriented occasions such as baptisms, Mother's Day, and birthdays are treated as important celebrations. Most hotels, especially outside Panama City, are still oriented to accommodate fairly large Panamanian families that share the same room for a weekend or holiday retreat rather than foreign couples or singles exploring the country. Panama is also a quite child-friendly country, all the more so since such a high percentage of the population is younger than 14.

There is a strong feeling of national pride in Panama. Panamanians often express a sense that their country is somehow different from others in the region, in part because of Panama's unique geographical position and unusually rich history for such a small place. That sense may be best summed up in the popular phrase that is in essence Panama's national motto: *puente del mundo, corazón del universo* (bridge of the world, heart of the universe).

Family and Society

Home is sacrosanct, and it's quite possible to be friends with someone for years without setting foot in his or her home. Dining with the middle- and upper-classes of Panama City usually means meeting at a restaurant. To be invited to someone's house or weekend country home is generally something special and can mean you're considered family. Outside Panama City, especially among the *campesinos* (country people, farmers), entertaining at home is more typical.

Whom one is related to is still extremely important in determining status in Panamanian society. Panama is a small enough country that the names of the prominent families are widely known. Even in nonelite circles, the family names of one's father and mother can help one get ahead or hold one back.

This, of course, has its downsides. In recent years, there has been increasing concern in Panama that putting the interests of family and self first can hurt the society as a whole. Nepotism, corruption, *amiguismo* (cronyism), and conflicts of interest have been serious problems in Panama throughout its history.

In 2002, Panama's then-president, Mireya Moscoso, repeatedly and publicly defended nepotism as a long-established tradition in Panama. Transparency International found in 2003 that

Panama ranked squarely in the middle on its Corruption Perceptions Index of 133 countries, based on surveys of academics, business people, and risk analysts. Panama's level of corruption was deemed about the same as that of China, Sri Lanka, and Syria.

There have been attempts in recent years to address these problems through new anti-corruption commissions, press exposés, and transparency laws designed to stop illegal deals, subject once-secret government and business negotiations to public scrutiny, and remove from the public payroll so-called *botellas* (literally, "bottles"—well-connected appointees without the skill or inclination to do their assigned jobs).

Many of these efforts have been dismissed as cynical or halfhearted, though some have produced results. But reformers in Panama maintain that an attitude of *juega vivo* (roughly, "live game" or "the game of life") is still firmly rooted in daily life. *Juega vivo* refers to a belief that one should grab any opportunity life presents, even if ethically or legally shaky.

Men and Women

Machismo is a fact of life in Panama. But it's not as pronounced as in some other Latin American countries, and stereotypical sex roles have begun to break down in modern times. Women are now in more positions of power outside the home; in 1999, Panama even elected its first female president (albeit one best known for being the widow of a popular male politician). Still, boys tend to be given more freedom during their upbringing, men work in the fields and women in the home in rural areas, and the tradition of married men having a mistress and even an entirely separate family has not died out; women are still expected to dress and act in "feminine" ways, and men on the street think nothing of openly ogling any attractive woman who passes by.

Manners and Mores

Foreigners often comment on how laid-back and peaceful Panamanians are—except behind the wheel. One word any visitor is likely to hear often is *tranquilo* (calm, peaceful, easy-going), used both as an injunction (as in, "take it easy") and as expression of praise (as in, "what a peaceful place"). It says a lot about what's valued in Panama.

But boisterous celebrations are also extremely popular. Panamanians take time off seriously, and the calendar is filled with national holidays, religious observances, and other excuses to party. The entire country comes to a halt for big celebrations, such as Carnaval. Parties often last all night and feature music played at ear-shattering volumes. Those who can afford it have cottages at the beach or in the mountains, or *fincas* (literally farms, but often just a country home on a sizable piece of land) that they use for weekend getaways or extended holidays.

Another important word to know is *dignidad* (dignity). Treating others with politeness and respect is extremely important in Panama, and slights are taken seriously.

On the other hand, Panama is also quite a tolerant place, and a laissez faire attitude prevails. While, just as in any other country, there is racism and discrimination, people of different nationalities, religions, and lifestyles have generally been left in peace. Open homosexuality is still a ways in the future, but gays have begun to assert their rights, and gay bars and clubs aren't subject to raids and official harassment. While abortion is officially illegal in this Catholic country (punishable by up to three years in jail for the woman and up to six years for the practitioner), it's surreptitiously available at some clinics. Birth control is practiced by a majority of the sexually active. Prostitution is legal and regulated by the government.

Perceptions of Time

Among the hardest things for visitors to adjust to, especially those from North America and northern Europe, are local attitudes toward time. As in many other Latin American countries, showing up later than an agreed-upon time is normal, even expected. It's not unusual for guests at a sit-down dinner party to show up an hour or two after the appointed hour.

There's also ample opportunity for culture clashes concerning appointments. As in other

Latin American countries, foreigners trying to do business in Panama often complain of the *mañana* syndrome: putting off for a vague future time what would seem possible to do right now. Miscommunications are common. What a visitor may interpret as a commitment to call or show up somewhere without fail may actually have been intended only as a polite expression of intent to help out if nothing more urgent comes up.

Panama and the United States

Not surprisingly, the United States generates a range of feelings in Panama. The United States has intervened in the affairs of the isthmus constantly since its own early days as a republic. The United States has repeatedly used the isthmus to further its own strategic and commercial interests, and for most of the 20th century had military bases and a largely foreign community planted in a 500-square-mile zone that bisected the country and over which Panama had little control.

Students, politicians, activists, and nationalistic citizens regularly denounced the U.S. presence on the isthmus as imperialistic and paternalistic, quite often with good cause, though sometimes Panama's leaders used the U.S. presence as a bogeyman to deflect attention from domestic problems.

Some in Panama had largely positive feelings about the U.S. presence. Others were indifferent. Still others were ambivalent, seeing the United States as instrumental in helping Panama gain independence but selfishly robbing it of true self-determination, of spurring great improvements in health and welfare on the isthmus but keeping most of the spoils for itself, of propping up but then removing the military dictatorships that ruled the country for decades.

What most can now agree on is that the end of the Canal Zone and the closing of the U.S. military bases have made possible a healthier and more equal relationship between the two nations. There's a widespread sentiment in Panama that the country did not gain full sovereignty until December 31, 1999, when it gained full control of the Panama Canal. *Soberania* (sovereignty) is still a word one hears

often in Panama, and its importance to many is undeniable. When the Panamanian government created a new national park through a swath of the Panama Canal's watershed, it named it Parque Nacional Soberania. There is even a beer called Soberana (sovereign) that appeared during the negotiations over the new Panama Canal treaty and which is still consumed today. Evidence of the U.S. presence in the former Canal Zone has been steadily eroded, with streets renamed and English-language signs removed.

American pop culture took hold long ago, apparent in everything from the Hollywood movies playing at the multiplexes, to the popularity of American fast-food franchises, to the clothing and music tastes of young people. Baseball, basketball, and, to a more limited extent, American football have long been popular in Panama. European football (soccer) has only come into its own in recent years. For wealthier Panamanians, Florida is a popular shopping destination, and U.S.-style malls have sprouted up in and around the major cities in the last few years. Middle- and upper-class students often go to the United States for college and graduate school.

SPORTS

Panama has produced a considerable number of outstanding world athletes and a few bona fide legends. Many of them have come from the ranks of Panama's poorest families.

Panama is known for producing great boxers, the best known of whom is Roberto Durán. Nicknamed *Manos de Piedra* (hands of stone), he held world titles in four weight categories: lightweight, welterweight, junior middleweight, and middleweight. He earned the welterweight title in a famous match against Sugar "Ray" Leonard in June 1980. But his career took a sharp downward turn during a rematch with Leonard in November of that same year. Durán, after being taunted repeatedly by a fast-moving Leonard, told the referee during the eighth round that he wanted to stop the fight. The two words he spoke to end the match, *No más* (no more), would haunt the rest of his career and cause an uproar back home. The words are better remembered today than the fact Durán went on to win two more world titles. His best days behind him, a car accident finally forced him to retire in 2002 at the age of 51. He is considered one of the best boxers in history, with 104 wins in 120 fights, 69 of them knockouts.

Panama has also produced champion horse-racing jockeys, by far the most famous of whom is Laffit Pincay Jr. In 1999 Pincay broke Willie Shoemaker's record for career wins. He rode until April 2003, when a fall during a race left him with a broken neck and forced him to retire at the age of 56. By then, he had racked up an astonishing 9,530 victories.

But in sheer volume of great athletes, Panama's biggest contribution to world sports has been the disproportionate number of major-league baseball players. These include Hall-of-Fame first baseman Rod Carew, who retired in 1986 with 3,053 career hits. He was born on a train going from Colón to Panama City and was named Rodney after the doctor who delivered him. The current stars (at the time of writing) include New York Yankees pitcher Mariano Rivera, Boston Red Sox pitcher Ramiro Mendoza, Montreal Expos catcher Einar Díaz, and Chicago White Sox left fielder Carlos Lee. Other current major leaguers include José Macías, Olmedo Sáenz, and Bruce Chen.

Panama's greatest international football (soccer) star to date is forward Julio César Dely Valdés, who earned the nickname "Panagol" for his striking prowess while playing for Nacional de Montevideo in Uruguay. He spent much of his career playing in Spain and Uruguay before retiring in 2004 at the age of 37. He's considered one of the best football players to come out of Central America.

At the 2004 Olympics in Athens, the Panamanian runner Bayano Kamani came in fifth place in the 400-meter hurdles. That was an impressive achievement for a small country not known for its runners, and Kamani was hailed as a national hero.

ARTS AND CRAFTS

Panama takes great pains to preserve its traditional music forms, dances, costumes, crafts, and customs. It also has a vibrant contemporary arts and entertainment scene with roots in its unique history.

While music and dance are extremely popular, one often hears complaints in Panama that the fine arts and literature play far too small a role in daily life.

A number of painters have received at least some international recognition, though Panama's most widely known artistic creations are the work of anonymous indigenous artists, especially the Kuna with their *molas* and the Emberá-Wounaan with their tagua and cocobolo carvings and woven baskets.

Music and Dance

Given its geographical location, it's not surprising that a wide variety of music is popular in Panama. Dance clubs may spin a salsa, cumbia, merengue, or reggae number, then follow it up with a Latin pop music hit, a bit of electronic dance music, or a rock song in English or Spanish. What may be more surprising is how strong a hold Panamanian folkloric music still has on the country, both in purist and modernized forms.

Important instruments in folkloric music include the accordion, *los tambores* (wooden drums with the top covered by cowhide), *la caja* (a small wooden drum with both sides covered with hide), la *mejoranera* (a small, five-stringed guitar), *la bocona* or *socabón* (a four-stringed guitar), *la guáchara* or *churuca* (a gourd-shaped instrument played by scraping an implement across notches carved into it), maracas, and violins. Folkloric music can be instrumental or feature singing, the most distinctive element of which is the *saloma*, a Panamanian form of yodeling. The music is an acquired taste for those who didn't grow up listening to it.

Folkloric music is often accompanied by traditional dances, the most famous of which is the drum-based *el tamborito*. This is Panama's national dance, with many regional variations, and

COURTESY PANAMA CANAL COMMISSION

The *pollera* is Panama's beautiful embroidered national dress. Each one takes six months or more to make.

is usually what is performed for visitors or on other special occasions when there is a folkloric dance performance. Women dress in beautiful hand-embroidered *polleras* and the men in either long-sleeved white *camisillas* and black pants or a colorful embroidered shirt and pants cut off below the knees. In either case, the man wears some variety of traditional Panama hat, often the *sombrero pintao*. All of these hats are quite different from the so-called Panama hats that are made in Ecuador.

Other important dance-music forms include the *mejorana*, a type of song accompanied by the *mejoranera*, and the festive dance music performed by *murgas* (strolling bands of musicians) during Carnaval.

All these folkloric traditions come from Panama's central provinces, particularly the Azuero Peninsula. Other traditional dance forms include the *congos*, derived from Africa and still performed occasionally by descendents of African slaves, and the *balsería*, which is really something between a festival and an extreme sport performed by the indigenous Ngöbe-Buglé peoples;

it involves throwing balsa poles at the legs of participants, often with painful results.

Music rooted in Panama's folkloric traditions has changed with the times and evolved into what is known as *música típica* or simply *típico*, a dance-music form that features traditional elements such as accordion and yodeling but has a livelier beat, modern lyrics, and an almost pop sensibility. It's enormously popular in Panama. Its biggest stars include the accordionists Osvaldo Ayala and Ulpiano Vergara and the brother-sister duo Samy and Sandra Sandoval.

Panama's most famous musician outside its own borders is the salsa star, actor, and politician Rubén Blades. He first gained fame for his work with salsa legend Willie Colón before launching a solo career notable for both his politically conscious lyrics and musical innovation. He ran an unsuccessful campaign for the presidency of Panama in 1994.

Another international music star is Danilo Pérez, an innovative jazz pianist noted for blending Latin, African, and other influences with established jazz forms. Both he and Blades spend a great deal of their performance time abroad, and concerts in Panama are special events.

El General (born Edgardo A. Franco) had some reggae-influenced, Spanish-language dance hits in parts of the United States and Latin America in the early 1990s.

Danceable blends of rap, reggae, rock, dancehall, and calypso have become hugely popular in the last few years, with a Spanish-language rap-reggae style that features driving beats and often sexually suggestive lyrics predominating. One of its biggest stars is El Rookie, who has enough street cred to make a video that featured rival street gangs.

Panama has a sizable rock scene, with a number of bands of varying skill performing original songs and covers in Spanish and English. Los Rabanes have met with the greatest success outside of Panama, with tours in Latin America and the United States. Other popular bands include Son Miserables, Os' Almirantes, the long-established Los 33, newcomers Señor Loop, and Big Fat Hen.

Jazz and classical music draw urban sophisticates to occasional performances at concert halls and restaurants in Panama City. Panama has also been trying to establish regular music festivals, including an annual Panama Jazz Festival, held in Panama City during the dry season.

One of the most popular local jazz performers is the singer Barbara Wilson. High-toned cultural events—such as performances by the 60-person national symphony orchestra, the national ballet, and visiting arts groups—are generally held in the Teatro Nacional or Teatro Balboa. Smaller groups sometimes perform in the intimate Teatro Anita Villalaz. These kinds of performances are rare outside of Panama City.

Fine Arts

Panama has a number of notable artists. An important early figure is the painter and sculptor Roberto Lewis (1874-1949), known for his paintings of Isla Taboga and his sweeping murals, which depict romantic scenes drawn from history and mythology. The latter still adorn the Teatro Nacional, the presidential palace, and the Es-

cuela Normal Juan Demóstenes Arosemena in the provincial city of Santiago.

Alfredo Sinclair (b. 1915) and Guillermo Trujillo (b. 1927) are widely considered two of Panama's great master painters. Their work has been displayed around the world. Other major figures include Manuel Chong Neto (born 1927), whose paintings often features fleshy women with birds, and Juan Manuel Cedeño (1914-1997), a disciple of Lewis. Important younger artists include Isabel de Obaldía (b. 1957), noted for her paintings as well as her glass art, and Brooke Alfaro (b. 1949), whose subjects include the marginalized of Panamanian society and who now works mainly in video.

Making generalizations about any diverse group of artists is difficult, but it's striking how many of Panama's best-known painters make use of warm, vivid colors and dreamlike or primitive elements in their work.

Other popular and widely collected artists include Sheila Lichacz, whose main subjects are the *tinajas* (clay pots) that date from pre-Colombian days and are folkloric icons throughout Panama. She is relatively well-known outside of Panama, but some art aficionados in her home country were surprised in 2003 when her work was exhibited at the Smithsonian in Washington, D.C. Al Sprague (b. 1938), a Panama-born American who was an art teacher at Balboa High School in the former Canal Zone, is popular locally and among former Zone residents for his paintings, drawings, and prints of the Panama Canal, the Canal Zone, and daily life in Panama.

Some of Panama's finest art is made by its indigenous people, though these works are usually made anonymously and sold as souvenirs. The carved tagua nuts, cocobolo statues, and woven baskets of the Emberá-Wounaan have begun to receive the international fame long accorded the *molas* of the Kuna people. A few Emberá, Wounaan, and Kuna artists now sign their work.

Literature

Panamanian literature has made a relatively small splash beyond the country's borders, perhaps in part because traditionally much of it has been inward-looking, drawing inspiration from distinctly Panamanian themes of national identity and history, the country's natural beauty, and daily life on the isthmus. Even in Panama it can be hard to find books by Panamanian authors, whose works are often printed cheaply in modest, limited editions. Panama's literary output leans heavily towards poetry and short stories, followed by novels and essays and, to a far lesser extent, plays. Nearly all of it is in Spanish.

Ricardo Miró (1883-1940) is the country's most revered poet, often referred to as "El Poeta de Panamá" and for whom the country's most prestigious literary awards are named. His most famous poem is "Patria," an ode to his beloved country. He also produced short stories and novels. Other notable early poets include María Olimpia de Obaldía (1891-1985), whose main theme was family life, and Amelia Denis de Icaza (1836-1911), most famous for her patriotic "Al Cerro Ancón."

One of the country's most important literary figures in the 20th century was Rogelio Sinán (1902-1994), the penname of Bernardo Domínguez Alba. Sinán is remembered for the breadth and quality of his work, which included short stories (particularly "A la Orilla de Las Estatuas Maduras"), novels (most notably "Penilunio"), poetry, and even a children's play, "La Cucarachita Mandinga." Other major figures of the period included the poets Ricardo J. Bemúdez (1914-2000), Demetrio Korsí (1899-1957), Demetrio Herrera Sevillano (1902-1950) and Stella Sierra (1917-1997).

Novelists and short-story writers have come to the forefront in the modern era. Prominent current authors include Ernesto Endara (b. 1932), known especially for his short stories and plays; Rosa María Britton (b. 1936), a physician whose novels include "El Señor de las Lluvias y el Viento" (1984) and "Todas Íbamos a Ser Reinas" (1997); and the prolific Enrique Jaramillo Levi (b. 1944), whose works include the short-story collection "Duplicaciones" (1990) and many other short stories, poems, and essays. He is also a scholar and cultural promoter who has probably done more than any other living person to bring attention to Panamanian literature. He is the editor of "Maga," a Panamanian literary review.

The historical novels of Jorge Thomas, the penname of the lawyer Juan David Morgan (b. 1942), are relatively easy to find in Panama, especially "Con Ardientes Fulgores de Gloria" (1999).

Panama City has an active theater scene, and works by Panamanian and foreign playwrights are staged frequently. Plays range from hoary classics to experimental pieces. One playhouse, the aging Teatro Guild de Ancón in the former Canal Zone, still offers plays in English.

RELIGION

An estimated 85 percent of Panamanian are Roman Catholic. Various sects of Protestantism have made inroads over the years, accounting for most of Panama's other followers of organized religion.

Catholicism is taught in public schools unless parents request that their children be exempted. Catholic holidays, festivals, and rites are widely observed. However, many Panamanian Catholics take a "cafeteria" approach to church doctrine. Birth control, for instance, is widely available and practiced throughout the country. And Panama has a long history of religious freedom and tolerance.

Judaism and Islam have significant minority followings and a long history in Panama, particularly in the cities. Islam is believed to have first came to the isthmus with African slaves in the 16th century. The first Jewish congregation in Panama, Kol Shearith, celebrated its 125th anniversary in 2001. Panama City has one of the world's seven Baha'i Houses of Worship, as well as a prominent Hindu temple. The Greek Orthodox Metropolitanate of Central America is based in Panama. Many of Panama's indigenous peoples still practice their traditional religions to some degree.

LANGUAGE

The official language of Panama is Spanish. English is the major second language, but it's not as widely spoken as one might think given the long United States presence in the country and Panama's role in world commerce and finance. In fact, even in Panama City it seems harder to find someone fluent in English than it was 25 years ago.

A nationalistic emphasis on Spanish, combined with the exodus of U.S. civilians and military personnel when the Canal Zone disappeared, has led to a steady erosion in English on the isthmus. Even the large English-speaking West Indian immigrant populations, which learned Spanish as a second language when they came to the isthmus, are gradually losing their English skills as they become fully assimilated into the Panamanian mainstream.

The role of English in Panamanian life is still a touchy subject. A major controversy erupted in 2002 when a proposal to make English an official second language of business was floated in the national legislature, with many denouncing it as unconstitutional and impractical.

But the greatly diminished U.S. presence on the isthmus has helped make English less of a political hot potato. There's a growing belief in Panama that English skills are crucial to the survival of its services-oriented economy. The point was driven home in 2002 when the HSBC Bank tried to open a 600-person call center in Panama. Of the 1,600 applicants, only 41 were fully bilingual in English and Spanish. The bank set up the call center in Malaysia instead. That same year, a Panamanian official estimated that only about 2 percent of government employees speak English well.

In 2003 the Panamanian government passed a law requiring the teaching of English in all primary and secondary schools. This immediately raised concerns about finding enough qualified teachers to meet the demand. How well this new effort will fare remains to be seen.

All that said, English-speaking visitors usually have little trouble getting around even if they don't speak Spanish. It's not hard to find someone who speaks at least some English, especially in the fancier hotels and restaurants.

Outside of Panama City, English is mostly widely spoken along the Caribbean coast, particularly in Bocas del Toro. There are few English speakers in the rural areas and *comarcas*. In some of the *comarcas*, even Spanish is not universally spoken.

Panama's indigenous people still speak their traditional languages to varying degrees. Ngöbere (spoken by the Ngöbe) and Kuna (spoken by the Kuna) are probably the least endangered, mostly because of the sheer number of speakers.

Those who speak neither Spanish nor English will have a harder time getting around, as no other European languages are widely spoken on the isthmus, let alone languages from other parts of the world. Panama City, Bocas town on Bocas del Toro, and, to a lesser extent, Boquete have the greatest mix of international residents and visitors.

Some descendents of Chinese immigrants in Panama City and larger towns in the interior still speak their ancestral languages, especially Hakka and Yue (Cantonese). Arabic and Hebrew are among the other languages with a foothold in cosmopolitan Panama City.

So-called Panamanian Creole English (PCE) is still spoken among the descendents of immigrants from Jamaica, Barbados, San Andrés, Providencia, and other West Indian islands. Most speakers live in Colón, the former canal area, Panama City, and Bocas del Toro, whose distinctive regional variation of PCE is called Guari-Guari. It's almost impossible for uninitiated speakers of standard English to understand PCE.

Getting There and Away

Most visitors come to Panama by air, and it's usually no bargain. Except for occasional promotions, such as an airline inaugurating a new route, it's rare to see fares dip much below standard rates.

The cheapest way to get to Panama from North and Central America is by bus, so long as one has lots of time and doesn't mind a bit of adventure and discomfort. It's also possible to drive from North America all the way to the Darién Gap, a popular adventure for intrepid road warriors that can require considerable planning and resourcefulness. There are no roads between Colombia and Panama, and no ferry service. The only safe way to travel between Panama and South America is by air. There is no international rail service to any country.

Reservations should be made far in advance for travel around holidays and festivals, particularly Christmas and Carnaval. Planes and buses are generally more crowded during the dry season, which is high season for both in-country and foreign tourists and summer vacation for Panamanian students. November is filled with national holidays, which can make travel logistics trickier.

Remember that visitors to Panama must be able to show proof of a return or onward ticket. In practice this is rarely enforced, especially with neatly dressed travelers, but visitors can be turned away at the border without it.

The departure tax to leave the country is $20. For those flying out of the country, it is now generally included in the price of the air ticket.

CHARTER FLIGHTS AND PACKAGE DEALS

All-inclusive packages that include charter flights are proving increasingly popular, especially with Canadians and Europeans, and can be a good deal for families and couples who don't mind traveling with the herd and having accommodations, meals, and activities all concentrated at one place.

The all-inclusive resorts generally offer tours of the surrounding attractions for an extra fee, but visitors should expect to spend most of their time at or near the hotel. At the time of writing, the best of these were the Royal Decameron Beach Resort and Casino and the Gamboa Rainforest Resort, which offer both package deals and "a la carte" stays. The Barceló Playa Blanca, close to the Decameron, is another good possibility.

BY AIR

Panama has good air connections with destinations throughout the Americas and parts of the Caribbean and Western Europe.

Travel to and from anywhere farther east, including Australia and Asia, is more complicated and will probably require at least one change of plane and/or airline. At the time of writing, few European and no Asian, African, Middle Eastern, or Australian airlines were offering passenger service to Panama.

Note: the information in this section is particularly subject to change. Carriers add and drop service to Panama frequently. However, routes dropped by one airline are generally picked up by another.

In mid-2004, Panama regained it "Category 1" International Civil Aviation Organization (ICAO) rating following an inspection by the U.S. Federal Aviation Administration. This means Panama's civil aviation authority again meets all international safety standards (its ratings slipped in 2001), paving the way for new flights to the United States.

Carriers serving Panama with nonstop or connecting flights include:

U.S. airlines: American, Continental, and Delta.

European airlines: Iberia and Air Madrid.

Central American and Caribbean airlines: Copa, TACA, LACSA, and Cubana.

South American airlines: Avianca, Lloyd Aero Boliviano, and West Caribbean Airways.

Know Panama

TRAVEL TIP: TO SAVE MONEY, BE FLEXIBLE

Avoid peak times

Fares go up and flights get more crowded around major holidays, especially Christmas and Carnaval, and in the dry season, which lasts from December to April. Book well in advance to get seats and decent fares. Fall and spring are good times to hunt for discounted tickets, since these are low seasons both in Panama and many countries that fly there. Unfortunately, these months also bring a lot of rain to Panama.

Midweek travel can mean lower prices, as can meeting minimum and maximum stay requirements. Such restrictions have traditionally made less difference for travel to Latin America than other destinations, but this seems to be changing. Sometimes the only way to discover deals is to plug in different dates and see what fares pop up.

Break it down

Experiment with creative routings. For instance, flights to San José, Costa Rica, are more frequent and can be half as expensive as those to Panama, which is just a quick flight or cheap bus trip away.

Try pricing domestic and international segments separately, especially during promotions. Determine cities offering nonstop flights to Panama, then calculate different fare possibilities from your location. For instance, total travel time from San Francisco to Panama is about the same through any U.S. gateway, so one might as well see which route is cheapest. Multiple stops can also mean lower prices. But allow enough time to make connecting flights. This is especially important on the return trip; those flying back to the United States, for example, must clear customs and immigration at the first port of entry, which can take an hour or more.

Consider an Air Pass

Air passes are an often-overlooked option. These are sold only through travel agencies or participating airlines and are not available to everybody. For instance, the All America Airpass offers discounted airfare on flights throughout Latin America, but only those who live outside the Americas are eligible. Typically, one must buy air passes in conjunction with an international ticket to and from the coverage area.

Two air passes of possible interest are Grupo TACA's Latin AirFlex Program (sometimes called the TACA Airpass) and Copa's Hop Over Fares (or the Copa Airpass).

TACA's pass is sold only in Europe, Asia, Australia, and Israel. It carves the Americas into a series of "zones" based roughly on the distance between two points. Prices are based on zones and the number of "coupons" (flight segments) you buy. For instance, for the 2004-2005 pass, a coupon for a flight between Panama City and Mexico City cost $125 in economy class, not including taxes and surcharges. There are restrictions, such as a minimum and maximum number of coupons (3-16 at the time of writing) and a $75 surcharge if you arrive in Central America on a non-TACA flight.

Copa Airline's Hop Over Fares are similar, but with steeper prices and a smaller network of destinations. It's valid for flights throughout Central America, South America, and the Caribbean, but the only U.S. destination is Miami. There is a minimum and maximum number of coupons (2-9 at the time of writing), but no penalty for arriving in Central America on a non-Copa flight.

Passes come and go yearly, and rules and participating airlines are in constant flux. Getting current information about them can feel like a hunt for the Holy Grail. Travel agents or even airline reservation agents may not know about the program, or mistakenly think it has been terminated. Places to start searching include www.allairpass.com and www.airtimetable.com. Copa and TACA have offices around the world; see their websites for a list.

Figure out a rough itinerary before buying any air pass to make sure it really is a good deal and offers the routings you want.

© WILLIAM FRIAR

Passengers arrive in Puerto Piñas. Small planes are sometimes the only practical way to get around.

Most of the airlines listed above have so-called "codeshare" agreements with other carriers, meaning flights booked on one airline may actually be operated by a partner airline that's supposed to meet similar standards of quality and safety. For instance, Copa, Panama's national airline, has a well-established codeshare alliance with Continental Airlines, as well as a more recent agreement with Mexicana. Copa's own fleet, fairly large by Latin American standards, flies to 30 destinations in 20 countries. It's a growing airline that's getting increasingly positive reviews.

Grupo TACA, a consortium of major Central American airlines that includes El Salvador's TACA and Costa Rica's LACSA, has codeshare agreements with a number of carriers, including American Airlines, Air France, Iberia, and Copa. Grupo TACA also has an alliance with Panama's largest domestic airline, Aeroperlas.

International Airport

Panama's only international airport is Aeropuerto Internacional de Tocumen (tel. 238-2700 switchboard, 238-2736 flight information, 238-2782 general information). Its airport code is PTY. Commonly referred to simply as Tocumen (toe-KOO-men), it's about 25 kilometers east of downtown Panama City.

Travelers leaving the country must pay a $20 per person departure tax at the airport. It's now usually included in the price of the ticket. There's no tax for children ages 2 and younger.

Tocumen doesn't give visitors the best first impression of Panama City. It's dreary and a bit worn, though a multimillion-dollar expansion and modernization program may eventually make the place less of an embarrassment to a country that likes to think of itself as "the bridge of the world, heart of the universe."

The airport has a branch of the Banco Nacional de Panamá (tel. 238-4161 or 238-4178, 7 A.M. to 11 P.M. daily). It's one of only two places in the Panama City area that exchange a wide variety of currencies, so those who need to change foreign currency into U.S. dollars (Panama's currency) should do it here. Among the many currencies the bank is not equipped to exchange are

Know Panama

THE WORLD HAS TWO PANAMA CITIES

When booking a flight, make sure it's for Panama City in the Republic of Panama, and not Panama City, Florida. I've heard more than one tale of visitors from the United States and United Kingdom ending up in that Florida beach town. They were—briefly—pleasantly surprised at how short the flight from Miami was, though they wondered why the plane was so small. When making a reservation, be sure to verify the correct destination. And when the ticket or e-ticket arrives, double-check that it has the airport code for Tocumen International in Panama City, Republic of Panama: PTY.

Those who use the Internet to search for flights should also note that pull-down menus on airline websites, especially those in Spanish, sometimes list Panama under "Ciudad de Panamá," "Tocumen," "Aeropuerto Omar Torrijos Herrera" (the international airport's erstwhile name), and so on.

---

those of Australia, Holland, Italy, Belgium, Ecuador, Nicaragua, and El Salvador. The commission charged varies by currency.

There's an IPAT information booth between the *migración* (immigration) desks and the *aduana* (customs) area that may or may not be staffed. It carries a few hotel fliers but little else.

There's a Cable and Wireless office (7 A.M.–7 P.M. daily) near the ticket counters upstairs that sells phone cards and has fax, Internet, and long-distance calling services. There's an ATM nearby, next to the escalators.

An airport information booth, the Centro de Información y Servicios, is near the Copa wing of the airport. Those who made purchases at the Colón Free Zone can pick them up at the *Equipaje Acompañado* office, which is downstairs and to the right of the main terminal as one faces the main terminal, next to the police office.

A number of duty-free and other shops are in the departure lounge. They carry a variety of electronics, liquor, clothing, some souvenirs, and so on. The only dining options are a couple of greasy-spoon cafeterias, in the departure lounge and upstairs from the check-in counters in the terminal.

For those with time to kill, the hardworking kids at the shoeshine stand offer an excellent, thorough shine for $1.50.

David's Aeropuerto Enrique Malek, in western Panama, once offered international service by small, short-haul planes to and from Central American destinations, but this service has been suspended. The future of old U.S. military airfields was still in limbo as this book went to press.

Airport Transportation

Though Panama City is just a 25-kilometer drive from Tocumen, there's no satisfactory public transportation to and from it.

Taxis are available on the ground floor of the terminal, beyond customs, immigration, and baggage claim. To be sure of getting a licensed driver, look for the booth with the "IPAT, Servicios de Transportes Taxi" sign near the exit. The fare to Panama City is $25 for one or two persons. There's an extra charge of $2.40 to pay for the toll road, but it's well worth the savings in time. Most destinations in the former Canal Zone—including Amador, Albrook, Corozal, Clayton, and Pedro Miguel—run $28-35 for one or two people. Other fares available at the booth for one or two persons include Gamboa ($45), Colón ($65), and the Riande Aeropuerto Hotel and Resort ($5), which is two kilometers away and a good option for those who just want a place to rest during a quick layover. Those passing through Panama who have a long layover can get a tour of the Panama Canal for $60. More ambitious tours are also offered. Add $10 to all these fares for a third person. Pay at the booth and take the receipt. Your driver will be pointed out to you, most likely a neatly dressed man with a clean, late-model car. It's not customary to tip taxi drivers in Panama. Panama City taxis should charge about $20-25 for the trip back to the airport, but settle on the price before getting in the cab.

It may be possible to get better rates from other characters hanging around the terminal, especially when split with fellow travelers, but there's a chance of ending up with an unscrupulous driver and getting ripped off or worse.

A few hotels in Panama City offer airport pickup and drop-off for less than the cost of a taxi; ask when you make room reservations.

It's possible to take a bus into the city, but it's a hassle and should only be attempted by those on a tight budget. Buses do not stop at the terminal. To catch one requires hauling your luggage outside the grounds of the airport. There's a bus shelter on the roundabout a hot and humid half-kilometer away on the main road. The fare is $.25 for a more-frequent non-air-conditioned bus, but it's well worth coughing up extra change for an air-conditioned bus if one passes by. The final stop is at Plaza Cinco de Mayo in downtown Panama City, a trip that can take an hour and a half in traffic. Buses that travel along the Corredor Sur are far quicker; look for a sign that says *corredor* painted on the bus. Buses run frequently but erratically. There is no luggage storage compartment; you'll have to squeeze on with all your gear. I don't recommend attempting all this at night, which is quite likely when your plane will arrive.

On the return trip, Tocumen-bound buses can be caught in front of the artisans' stands on Plaza Cinco de Mayo. Air-conditioned buses pass in front of the nearby Caja de Seguro Social, the hulking government building to the east, between Calle 23 and Calle 24 on Avenida Justo Arosemena. Note: The area around this building is not safe at night, and travelers should be alert even in the daytime. The building of new highway ramps and the creation of new bus routes may change the bus stops. Plaza Cinco de Mayo is the best bet for finding a bus around this area. Buses to and from Tocumen also stop at the Gran Terminal de Autobuses in Albrook, which is a safer option for those arriving or leaving at night. Be sure the bus stops near the airport (none go into it). Passengers are dropped off with their luggage at the same roundabout outside the airport.

Rental cars are available at the airport. All the major companies have offices here, including Hertz, Avis, Thrifty, Dollar, Alamo, National, and Budget. Only those planning road trips outside Panama City should fool with them, though, because driving and parking in the city is a hassle.

The quickest route between Tocumen and Panama City is by way of the Corredor Sur, a toll highway to the airport that starts on the eastern outskirts of the city, than on the congested surface streets. The toll is $2.40 to the end of the line. The Corredor Sur section of the drive takes only a few minutes, but heavy traffic in Panama City can slow getting to or from the highway. Allow at least an hour to drive between Tocumen and most parts of the city, more during the height of morning and evening rush hours.

From the United States and Canada

Panama's gateway cities in the United States are Atlanta, Houston, Los Angeles, Miami, Newark, New York City (JFK), and Orlando. There were nonstop flights between all of them and Panama City at the time of writing. Those coming from other U.S. cities will have to make one stop en route, and in some cases more.

The busiest route is Miami-Panama City, with several daily nonstop flights each way. The flight takes a little less than three hours. Copa is the only airline that flies nonstop to Orlando, with four weekly flights.

The major carriers offering nonstop service from U.S. gateway cities are American (from Miami), Continental (Los Angeles, Houston, Newark), Copa (Miami, New York City, Los Angeles, and Orlando), and Delta (Atlanta).

Many visitors from the West Coast of the United States are surprised to discover they have to fly not just south but considerably east to get to Panama. (Look at a world map: Notice that Panama City is actually slightly east of Miami.) Those traveling from the San Francisco Bay Area, for instance, most often take connecting flights through Houston, Atlanta, or Miami.

Note: At the time of writing, Continental was

booking connections through Houston that were virtually impossible to make. Try to allow at least two hours to connect through any U.S. airport.

Air fares between the United States and Panama fluctuate, though bargain fares and packages are not as easy to come by as they are in, for instance, tourist-saturated parts of the Caribbean. Expect to pay around $400 to $700 round-trip from most U.S. cities. Flights out of Miami and Houston tend to be on the cheaper end of the scale. The least expensive West Coast flights usually originate in Los Angeles, though the difference is generally not great enough to make it worthwhile for those outside of Southern California to route their trip through LAX.

Except for charters, there are no direct flights from Canada to Panama. Those flying to or from Canada will most likely have a stop in the United States or Mexico. Advance-purchase fares hover around C$1,000. Flights out of Toronto are generally cheaper than from other cities. Canadians are a major market for package deals that often include charter airfare. These can be very good value for those who like all-inclusive resorts. Check with a travel agent or contact any resort hotel listed in this book for current offers.

From Mexico

All the U.S. carriers that fly into Panama City also fly into Mexico City, but that doesn't mean they fly *between* Panama City and Mexico City. At least, not directly: American's Mexico-Panama flights require a circuitous stop in Miami, for instance. It makes more sense to fly with the Latin American carriers. Expect to pay between around $400 and $600 round-trip; nonstops are more expensive.

Copa, which has a codeshare agreement with Mexicana, offers two daily nonstops between Panama City and Mexico City, as well as four weekly nonstops to and from Cancun. The airlines of Grupo TACA also fly out of Mexico City: TACA itself offers connecting service through El Salvador, and LACSA has flights that connect through Costa Rica. Lloyd Aero Boliviano flies five times a week between Panama City and Mexico City and twice weekly between Panama City and Cancun.

From Central America and the Caribbean

Getting to Panama by air from most Central American capitals generally means taking the "milk run" down the Central American isthmus; expect to make at least one stop en route, possibly more. The exceptions are Costa Rica and El Salvador, both of which have regular nonstop flights to and from Panama City.

The major carriers for flights within Central America are Grupo TACA and Copa. Both airlines fly between most Central American capitals and Panama City. Only TACA offers regular service between Belize and Panama, with a stop in El Salvador. Advance-purchase round-trip fares to and from most places are around $300-$400, though prices vary quite a bit and deals are often available through the airlines' websites.

From Costa Rica: There are plenty of flights between Panama City and San José, Costa Rica, all of which are nonstop. Advance-purchase fares are about $200-300 round-trip, with the cheaper fares available through website deals and other promotions. The flight takes about an hour, or closer to two on a small plane. Note that Costa Rican time is always an hour behind Panama time.

Grupo TACA has two daily flights, Copa has three, and little West Caribbean Airways has one. West Caribbean's fleet consists of two jets and several turboprop planes, but their fares are competitive with the larger carriers. Also, one-way tickets on West Caribbean are actually cheaper than round-trips, which is often not the case.

From the Caribbean: Copa flies between Panama City and Cuba, Jamaica, Puerto Rico, and Haiti. TACA flies to Cuba. Cubana, Cuba's national airline, flies between Panama City and Havana on Monday, Wednesday, and Friday. West Caribbean Airways flies between the Colombian island of San Andrés on Mondays and Fridays. (A number of Panamanians, particularly in Bocas del Toro, have roots in San Andrés.) Travel to and from other parts of the Caribbean generally requires flying

AMERICANS IN CUBA

I t's against U.S. law for U.S. citizens to engage in "any transaction related to travel to, from, and within Cuba" except in certain narrowly defined situations, and usually only with a license issued by the Treasury Department.

U.S. citizens can get into trouble if they visit Cuba as tourists. In the past, travelers have gotten around this requirement by visiting as "journalists" or "researchers" or by flying through third countries—such as Canada, Mexico, and, yes, Panama—and asking Cuban authorities, delighted to have gringo tourists, to stamp their tourist cards instead of passports. But George W. Bush's administration has tightened the rules. An April 22, 2004, State Department warning had an ominous tone:

"Transactions related to tourist travel are not licensable. This restriction includes tourist travel to Cuba from or through a third country such as Mexico or Canada. U.S. law enforcement authorities have increased enforcement of these regulations at U.S. airports and pre-clearance facilities in third countries. Travelers who fail to comply with De-

partment of Treasury regulations will face civil penalties and criminal prosecution upon return to the United States."

Violators are subject to a $65,000 fine and possible jail time, though the main targets usually have been corporations and tour operators; traditionally only a few individuals were penalized each month, with far smaller fines. But the Bush administration has cracked down on violators. New restrictions were added in July 2004 that include a greater focus on individual travelers, sparking controversy even among some anti-Castro Cuban expatriates (they can now visit family members in Cuba just once every three years, for instance). Rules will probably continue to shift, especially during U.S. election seasons. Would-be visitors should research regulations carefully. Start with the latest State Department advisories, available at www.state.gov, and guidelines on so-called "licensed travel" compiled by the Treasury Department's Office of Foreign Assets Control, available at www.treas.gov.

through Miami or doing some island-hopping by small plane after arriving at one of the gateway islands.

A visit to Cuba is a popular add-on for travelers to Panama. Standard round-trip air fare from Panama starts at around $400, but package deals that include airfare, three nights' accommodation, some meals, airport transfers, and tours can be had starting at less than $600. European and Canadian visitors sometimes route their trips to Panama to include a visit to Cuba on the way over or back. There are severe restrictions on visits to Cuba by U.S. citizens. (See the "Americans in Cuba" sidebar.)

It's also possible to fly to Aruba or Curacao on Avianca, but this requires going through the airline's hub in Bogotá, Colombia.

From South America

Panama has good connections with much of South America, particularly Colombia. Flights will most likely be on a Central American or

South American airline; few other carriers fly directly between South America and Panama. Continental, for instance, operates only one nonstop between Panama City and South America, to Guayaquil, Ecuador. But tickets can still be booked through an airline's codeshare partners. American Airlines has an especially extensive network of South American flights operated either by itself or its partners.

Copa flies between Panama City and Colombia (Bogotá, Barranquilla, Cali, and Cartagena), Argentina, Venezuela, Peru, Chile, Brazil, and Ecuador (Quito and Guayaquil). Other airlines that fly between Panama and South America include Avianca, Grupo TACA, Lloyd Aero Boliviano, Aires, and West Caribbean Airways.

Colombia and Ecuador are less than two hours from Panama City, and standard round-trip, advance-purchase fares can generally be had for about $250 to Colombia and $350 for Ecuador. Promotional deals can cut fares considerably, especially for popular routes. Even nonstop flights to or from the most distant locations, such as Argentina and Brazil, take at least seven hours and can cost anywhere from $600-$900 for advance-purchase fares.

From Europe and the United Kingdom

The only European airlines offering direct service to Panama are the Spanish carriers Iberia and the new, discount Air Madrid. (Spain accounts for the largest share of European visitors to Panama.) They fly to Panama only from their hubs in Madrid, but Iberia has good connections with other parts of Europe and beyond.

The best deals are sometimes available through carriers that don't fly directly between Europe and Central America. Often this requires no more than one stop. U.S. carriers that fly to both Europe and Panama offer connecting flights through their East Coast hubs in the United States, namely Continental (Newark), American (Miami), and Delta (Atlanta). British Airways and Air France also offer flights in conjunction with codeshare partners. Both Air France and Lufthansa were said to be considering service to Panama, so there may be more options by the time you read this.

Expect to pay around 700–800 euros for round-trip tickets between most European countries and Panama. Lower fares may start to appear if Panama becomes a hot tourist destination, as many are gambling it will. Consider buying an air pass if you plan to travel elsewhere in the Americas (see the sidebar "Travel Tip: To Save Money, Be Flexible").

A good way to compare all current routings and fares is through a Web travel search service such as www.expedia.co.uk. Those in the United Kingdom should also check out Journey Latin America (tel. 44 (0) 20 8747 3108, flights@journeylatinamerica.co.uk, www.journeylatinamerica.co.uk), a knowledgeable, London-based tour operator and travel agency that books flights to Panama, sells several kinds of air passes, and offers a few adventure-oriented Panama tours. Its website has lots of current information.

From Elsewhere in the World

There is currently no direct service between Panama and Asia, Australia, Africa, and the Pacific. However, Asian carriers attempt Panama routes from time to time, so this may well have changed by the time you're ready to travel. Getting to Panama from points east of Europe generally means flying to San Francisco, Los Angeles, or Mexico City and connecting there with Panama-bound flights. It's usually a quite expensive proposition. Try to find a good travel agent or be prepared to do a fair amount of independent research to find reasonable fares. Round-the-world tickets or travel using an air pass may prove to be the most economical way to go. (See the sidebar "Travel Tip: To Save Money, Be Flexible.")

BY LAND

There are three border crossings between Panama and Costa Rica: at Paso Canoas on the Pacific side of the isthmus, at Río Sereno in the highlands, and at Guabito-Sixaola on the Caribbean coast. Paso Canoas, which is on the Interamerican Highway, is by far the most traveled. The Guabito-Sixaola crossing is used mainly by those traveling to and from Bocas del Toro. The Río Sereno crossing is rarely used and is not always open to foreign visitors.

The Interamerican Highway comes to an end at the town of Yaviza in eastern Panama, where the famous Darién Gap begins. There are no roads linking Panama with Colombia and the rest of South America, and no car-ferry services. Travelers generally must fly from Panama to Colombia and continue their journey from there.

By Private Vehicle

It's possible to drive the entire length of the Interamerican Highway (often referred to as the Pan-American Highway outside of Central America) from North America to Panama, but this is a long, serious trek and there's always some risk of encountering bandits, brutal roads, and dyspeptic border guards. The only book I know of on the subject is "Driving the Pan-American

Highway to Mexico and Central America," by Raymond and Audrey Pritchard (Costa Rica Books, 1997), and it's quite out of date. Making the trip requires serious planning and a well-equipped vehicle. Allow about three weeks from the Mexican border to Panama at a reasonable pace. Bear in mind that North American auto insurance policies don't apply south of the border.

Cars rented in Costa Rica cannot be driven in Panama, and vice versa. Even trying to drive cars registered in one of the countries across the border into the other is a nuisance and a source of continuing squabbles. It's not worth the hassle for a short trip; take the bus instead.

R.V. convoys occasionally make pilgrimages down the Interamerican Highway. The only true R.V. park in Panama is XS Memories (tel. 993-3096, fax 993-3069, xsmemories@hotmail.com, www.xsmemories.com) in Santa Clara, about a two-hour drive west of Panama City. It has 12 hookups for campers and mobile homes and can provide current information for those interested in shipping vehicles to South America.

By Bus

Inexpensive, relatively comfortable buses make daily trips from southern Mexico, Guatemala, Honduras, El Salvador, Nicaragua, and Costa Rica to Panama. This is, obviously, quite a long haul—nearly four solid days from the Mexico-Guatemala border, including two overnight stays in El Salvador and Nicaragua. Few take buses the whole way. Buses between San José, Costa Rica, and Panama City are popular, however.

Know Panama

CENTRAL AMERICA BY TORTOISE

A unique way to travel the Interamerican Highway is by **Green Tortoise** (U.S. tel. 415/956-7500, tel. 800/867-8647 in the United States outside San Francisco Bay Area, tortoise@greentortoise.com, www.greentortoise.com). These trips cram 30 or more adventurous people onto a bus that serves as vehicle, dorm, and rec room for days or weeks. Camping outdoors is possible on some nights.

Most trips are in the United States, but several Central American adventures are offered every year through a Green Tortoise affiliate. The Central America Trek runs once a year between Cancun and Costa Rica, usually around February or March. It runs in a different direction each year. The trip lasts 21-day and costs about $1,100. That's a lot, but the price includes lodging (on the bus and camping) and most meals (which passengers help prepare). There are also trips within Costa Rica and between Costa Rica and Nicaragua.

Those who end up in Costa Rica at the right time should consider the Carnaval Trip, an 11-day jaunt from San José to Panama for the Carnaval celebration. This is an ideal way to celebrate Carnaval because there are no worries about hotel availability, and the group can look out for one another if someone gets too *borracho*. The itinerary varies, but it should include a stop in Las Tablas, the biggest party spot, and may include visits to Bocas del Toro, Panama City, El Valle, etc. Unfortunately, the trip was "on hiatus" in 2005 but with enough interest it may be back in 2006.

I've ridden with the Green Tortoise several times (though never to Panama), and it's made for some of the most memorable adventures I've had in all my travels. For those with the right attitude, it can be a blast. But there's little privacy, lots of close contact, and itineraries can change overnight. This is not a normal bus trip. Think of it as a backpacking trek on wheels. Even for those who don't mind occasional discomfort and marginal hygiene, the difference between a great trip and a very long one depends on one's compatibility with the drivers and other passengers. Go with the flow or don't go at all.

Contact Green Tortoise through the listings above or write for a brochure: Green Tortoise Adventure Travel, 494 Broadway, San Francisco, CA 94133, USA.

The website for Tica Bus (www.ticabus) has thorough information in English and Spanish about the routes, which may be useful even for those who choose not to travel with them.

Two bus companies, Tica Bus and Panaline, make one daily trip between Panama City and San José, Costa Rica. Both leave from the Gran Terminal de Transportes, Panama City's main bus terminal in Albrook. Try to make reservations at least three weeks ahead of time during the dry season and on holidays. At other times, booking about four days ahead of time should be fine. Tickets must be bought and reservations made in person at one of the company's offices or reservation agencies; bring passports. Travelers can check two pieces of luggage and take one carry-on at no extra charge.

Transport is by large, long-haul air-conditioned buses with toilets and reclining seats. The trip costs $25/$50 one-way/round-trip on either line and takes about 16 hours, which usually includes a lengthy stop at the Paso Canoas border crossing to go through immigration and customs, as well as a half-hour or so break at the Hotel Pyramidal complex in Santiago, about halfway across Panama. There's a cafeteria, restaurant, pharmacy, ATM, and other services at the complex.

Note: Costa Rica time is always one hour behind Panama time. Times listed below are all local. Tica Bus veterans should also note that the bus no longer picks up or drops off passengers at the Hotel Ideal in Panama City. Panaline now arrives at the Hotel Caribe in Panama City, not the Gran Hotel Soloy.

Tica Bus (tel. 314-6385 in Panama City, San José tel. 506/22-8954, ticabus@ticabus.com, www.ticabus.com) leaves from the Albrook bus terminal at 11 A.M. daily, arriving in San José around 3 A.M. the next day. The San José bus stop is at the north corner of Iglesia La Soledad, on Avenida 4 between Calle 9 and Calle 11.

The bus from San José to Panama City leaves from the same corner at 10 P.M. daily, arriving at Panama City's Gran Terminal de Transportes at 4 P.M. the next day.

The Tica Bus booth is in the Gran Terminal de Transportes (the Hotel Ideal office is closed). It's open 8:30 A.M.–6 P.M. Monday–Friday, 8:30 A.M.–4 P.M. Saturday, and 9 A.M.–2 P.M. Sunday.

Panaline (tel. 314-6382 at the Gran Terminal de Transportes and tel./fax 227-8648 at the Hotel Caribe in Panama City, San José tel. 506/256-8721) leaves from the Albrook bus terminal at noon daily. The bus stops at the Paso Canoas border crossing around 8 P.M. and arrives in San José around 4-5 A.M. the next day. The bus drops off passengers in San José 200 meters north of Hospital San Juan de Dios, near Terminal Coca Cola. Note that this is a rough part of San José, so be alert upon your arrival at such an early hour.

Buses from San José leave from the same spot at 1 P.M. daily and arrive around 5-6 A.M. the next morning at the Hotel Caribe in the Calidonia neighborhood of Panama City, not the Albrook bus terminal. Tickets can be bought either at the bus terminal or the Hotel Caribe. Both offices are open 8 A.M.–5 P.M. daily. The Hotel Caribe is at Avenida Perú and Calle 29 Este. It's a worn place and not good value for the money; better budget hotels are nearby. There's an Internet café and international call center on the premises.

A third bus company, **Agencia Tracopa** (tel. 775-7269 or 775-0585 David, tel. 727-6581 Paso Canoa, San Jose tel. 506/222-2666) has one bus departure from David to San José daily, at 8:30 A.M. The trip takes about eight hours and costs $12.50. The bus lets passengers off at the sketchy Coca-Cola bus terminal in San José. Tracopa's office at the David bus terminal is open 7:30 A.M.–noon and 1 P.M.–4 P.M. Monday–Friday, 7:30 A.M.–2 P.M. Saturday, and 7:30 A.M.–noon Sunday.

Tica Bus also links Panama with Nicaragua ($36 one-way), Honduras ($56-64), Guatemala ($69), and Tapachula, Mexico ($84), which is near the Guatemalan border. Connections are pretty good between Panama and Nicaragua.

Theoretically, one could make the trip to or from Managua in a brutal 30 hours or so either way, including a layover of just an hour or two in San José if timed right. Trips to or from El Salvador, however, require an overnight stay in Nicaragua, and trips starting or ending anyplace farther north require overnight stays in both Nicaragua and El Salvador. Passengers are free to break their travel anywhere and catch a bus on another day, but they must book reservations ahead of time for the onward journey.

Panaline's service to Nicaragua was suspended at the time of writing; it was only making the trip between Costa Rica and Panama.

BY SEA

Cruise Ships

The Panama Canal is one of the top cruising destinations in the world, though "destination" is not really the right word. More than 150,000 people transit the canal each year, but most never set foot in Panama itself. Panama has been trying to change that in recent years. It now has two cruise-ship ports on the Caribbean side of the isthmus near Colón, and an entire cruise-ship complex under construction at the Amador Causeway on the Pacific side near Panama City. A cruise-ship terminal and other facilities have been completed at Amador, though ships must still bring passengers ashore by tender boats.

The main Panama Canal cruise season begins in October, when ships end their Alaska cruises. They head down south and transit the canal to position themselves for their Caribbean and Panama Canal cruises. The main season lasts until the end of the dry season, around mid-April. A canal transit takes 8-10 hours. Ships sometimes visit Panama's islands, especially those of Kuna Yala.

By Yacht and Cargo Boat

Panama has long been a haven for yachties, who come to transit the canal and explore the islands and beaches. It may come as a surprise, then, that facilities for yachts are still quite limited. Slips are scarce and haul-out facilities can be quite crude. Marinas near the canal include the Panama Canal Yacht Club, at Cristóbal near the Caribbean entrance to the canal, and the Balboa Yacht Club and Flamenco Yacht Club, at Amador near the Pacific entrance to the canal. The famous and funky

wooden clubhouse at the Balboa Yacht Club, alas, burned down a few years back. Today it consists of little more than moorings, a dock, and a burger stand. The new Isla Flamenco Yacht Club has the most extensive and modern facilities, but they're expensive.

Other long-established ports and anchorages include Pedregal, Boca Brava, Puerto Mutis, and Isla Taboga on the Pacific side of the isthmus and Bocas del Toro, Portobelo, Isla Linton, and José del Mar (a.k.a. José Pobre) on the Caribbean side. Yachts also frequent the Islas Perlas and several islands in the Golfo de Chiriquí, but with the exception of Contadora and a few other islands, most of these spots are uninhabited and lack even rudimentary marinas.

Facilities vary dramatically outside the canal area. The two new marinas in Bocas del Toro, Bocas Yacht Club and Marina Carenero, can accommodate large yachts and perform limited maintenance work, and both are right in the middle of all the Bocas action. José del Mar and Boca Brava, on the other hand, are remote though lovely spots offering little more than a place to anchor and get a bite and a beer.

The San Blas Islands (Kuna Yala) are a popular yachting destination, but yachties should be prepared to pay a small fee when anchoring off islands in the archipelago. The waters out there can be treacherous; this is a place for skilled, experienced sailors. Transiting the canal by yacht is a complex and time-consuming process. An increase in tolls has made transiting a quite expensive proposition. The minimum cost is $600, for yachts up to 50 feet. Many yachts need to take on additional crew at the canal (see below) to help handle lines.

An indispensable guide for yacht owners is "A Captain's Guide to Transiting the Panama Canal in a Small Vessel," by David Wilson. Wilson is an experienced sailor who lives in Panama and has transited the canal dozens of times. The booklet is a nuts-and-bolts guide to putting a yacht through the canal without damaging it—a very real hazard—as well as navigating the canal's considerable bureaucracy. The book is available through Blue

EXPEDITION AND ADVENTURE CRUISES

For those who can afford it, a trip on a small, adventure-type cruise ship can be a terrific way to explore Panama, particularly its more inaccessible parts. These ships are quite different from mammoth "Love Boat"-style cruise ships. For one thing, they're small, usually less than 200 feet long with accommodations for 100 passengers or fewer. They're really more like mega-yachts than ships.

Because of this they can give visitors a much more intimate and eco-friendly experience of the natural surroundings than larger ships can. They can visit places the bigger ships can't, and many use Zodiacs and other small watercraft to get to even more remote spots. They also tend to be more oriented towards adventure travel and the natural and human history of the places they visit. Some offer scuba-diving, snorkeling, sea kayaking, waterskiing, and other active sports. Cruises generally run only in the dry season.

These cruises also tend to cater to those interested in learning about the human and natural history of the destinations in some depth. Trips typically include lectures by historians and naturalists who travel with the passengers, as well as local naturalist guides at the ports of call. On some cruises, interested passengers are given a suggested reading list ahead of time.

Cruises are offered both by small-ship lines and by travel operators that charter vessels for their expeditions. Ships and itineraries vary widely. Some are quite high-end, with luxuries and rates comparable to the fanciest of the conventional lines. Travel Dynamics, for instance, offers long expedition cruises that send passengers out on Zodiacs and kayaks on

some days but always brings them back to a sleek ship with staterooms and suites featuring marble bathrooms and the like. The more humble vessels of American Caribbean Canadian Line (ACCL), on the other hand, are comfortable but offer food, accommodations, and amenities that are deliberately kept simple. Rates on these lines can be a small fraction of that offered by the high-end cruises. Those prone to sea sickness should note that one tends to feel the sea far more on any of these small vessels than on the massive cruise ships.

Destinations in Panama can include places that are hard to get to by any other means, such as Isla Coiba and the more remote and pristine parts of Kuna Yala (the San Blas Islands). Those eager to explore a place like the Darién, however, should note that even these expedition ships tend to include only a visit to the rather touristy Emberá "village" of La Chunga. It's a colorful place and the river trip to it is beautiful and adventurous enough for most people. But truly experiencing the Darién usually means a multi-day, somewhat rugged trek most cruises can't accommodate. Be sure to get details from the tour operator before choosing a cruise.

The more prominent operations are listed below. Itineraries and the vessels used change frequently, so contact the operators or a travel agent for current offerings.

American Canadian Caribbean Line offers an 11-night cruise aboard the 100-passenger *Grande Caribe* that explores both sides of the isthmus. The ship has a bow ramp that allows landings directly on small islands. The itinerary includes the Isla Perlas, Kuna Yala, coastal Darién, Portobelo, Isla

Water Books and Charts in Ft. Lauderdale, Fla. (www.bluewaterweb.com), Islamorada Internacional (a nautical charts and equipment store in Balboa; see the Panama City chapter), or by mail from Panama. Contact information: tantoes@pobox.com. Mailing address: Tantoes, S.A., PMB PTY 2611, P.O. Box 025207, Miami, FL 33102-5207. Full disclosure: Wilson is a family friend, but he really does know his stuff.

Joining a Crew

Landlubbers looking for a free canal transit can sometimes join a yacht as a line handler. This is not a pleasure cruise, however. Don't consider this unless you're fairly strong, respond quickly to orders, and are prepared to get a little training. Yachties sometimes pay for the service, but not if there are enough volunteers around. Yachts are sometimes required to stop in the middle of the canal, sometimes for the night, so be prepared for

Taboga, and a Panama Canal transit. Rates start at $2,800 per person, plus port charges of $250. The line also offers cruises between Belize and Panama that do not transit the canal, starting at $1,400 per person. Tel. 800/556-7450 or 401/247-0955, info@accl-smallships.com, www.accl-smalships.com. Mailing address: ACCL, P.O. Box 368, Warren, RI 02885.

Clipper Cruise Line has 9-day cruises that focus on Costa Rica but include a canal transit and a stop along the Pacific coast of the Darién. Clipper has been guaranteeing a daylight transit of the canal by treating it as an included shore excursion, using a local vessel for the transit and returning passengers to its own ship (most likely the 140-passenger *Yorktown Clipper*) at the end of the day. Rates start at about $2,800 per person. Itineraries that don't include a canal transit are also available. Tel. 800/325-0010 or 314/655-6700, clipper@clippercruise.com, www.clippercruise.com. Mailing address: Clipper Cruise Line, 11969 Westline Industrial Drive, St. Louis, MO 63146-3220, USA.

Cruise West offers cruises that last a week to 10 days and generally combine visits to both Panama and Costa Rica. Panama destinations can include a canal transit, Kuna Yala, the Pacific coast of the Darién, Portobelo, and Coiba. Rates start at about $3,400 per person for a cruise that includes a canal transit. Shorter, less expensive Costa Rican cruises can include a visit to Coiba. Cruises are aboard the 100-passenger *Pacific Explorer*. Tel. 888/851-8133 or 206/441-8687, Info@cruisewest.com, www.cruisewest.com. Mailing address: Cruise West, 2301 Fifth Ave., Seattle, CA 98121-1856, USA.

Linblad Expeditions generally combines its Panama itineraries, aboard the 60-passenger *Sea Voyager*, with visits to Costa Rica. The Panama portion can include a canal transit and visits to Lago Gatún, the Islas Perlas, Coiba, and the Pacific coast of the Darién. Rates start at around $3,700 for itineraries that include a transit. Tel. 800/397-3348 or 212/765-7740, explore@expeditions.com, www.expeditions.com. Mailing address: Linblad Expeditions, 720 Fifth Ave., New York, NY 10019, USA.

Tauck World Discovery offers 11-day tours that include six nights aboard the 90-passenger *Le Levant*. Panama destinations include Kuna Yala, a canal transit, the Pacific coast of the Darién, and Coiba. Rates start at $4,200, including the land portion of the tour. Tel. 800/788-7885 or 203/899-6500, info@tauck.com, www.tauck.com. Mailing address: Tauck World Discovery, 10 Norden Place, Norwalk, CT 06855, USA.

Travel Dynamics International offers itineraries that include a month-long cruise aboard the 106-passenger *Orion* down the Pacific coast of South America and around Cape Horn to the Falklands. The Panama portion includes a canal transit and visits to Isla Barro Colorado in Lago Gatún and Isla San José in the Perlas archipelago. Rates start at $13,000 per person, including airfare. Shorter cruises are also available. Past itineraries have also included more extensive exploration of Panama. Tel. 800/257-5767 or 212/517-7555, www.traveldynamicsinternational.com. Mailing address: Travel Dynamics International, 132 East 70th St., New York, NY 10021, USA.

the possibility of sleeping onboard. The transit is a one-way trip, so if you need to get back, figure out ahead of time how you're going to do it. The yacht owner sometimes coughs up the bus ($2) or cab fare (about $40).

The best places to look for needy yachts are the Balboa Yacht Club or the Flamenco Yacht Club, on the Pacific side of the isthmus, and the Panama Canal Yacht Club, on the Caribbean side. Ask around. Note: The Panama Canal Yacht

club is right next to Colón. It's dangerous to wander anywhere outside the grounds of the club.

It may also be possible to sign on as a crew member on a yacht for a longer trip, but this is not common, especially for those who aren't experienced sailors. Ask around at any of the yacht clubs. The dock master will likely know who's going where and/or is in need of new crew members. It's also sometimes possible to pay for passage. Local authorities are keeping a wary eye on this practice, however, out of concern people are slipping illegally in and out of the country. Travelers with recreational drugs—which they should definitely not have in Panama anyway, as it can land them in jails for years—should get rid of them before boarding a boat. If the yacht is stopped and any drugs are found aboard, both the traveler and the yacht owner are going to be in big trouble. It's foolish, and grossly unfair to the owner.

The truly adventurous sometimes strike a deal for passage on a cargo boat, such as the Colombian trading vessels that ply the waters of Kuna Yala or the Kuna-owned boats that travel the same route. WARNING: I strongly advise against this. For one thing, some of these boats are barely seaworthy rust buckets, and the gentle waters one encounters near shore can turn remarkably rough very quickly. The seas around Kuna Yala are particularly dangerous given the number of shallow reefs lurking like depth charges throughout the archipelago, not to mention the powerful winds that blow through at times. There are lots of shipwrecks there to prove it, and at least two

lives have been lost from yachts out there in the last few years. Second, Panama is a popular transshipment point for drugs coming up from South America. If you're unlucky enough to be aboard a vessel intercepted with a few tons of cocaine in the hold, you'll have some tricky explaining to do. Boats are also sometimes caught with less-sinister but no-less-illegal contraband.

Those still interested are best off asking at the Voyager Youth Hostel in Panama City, which has up-to-date information on the ins and outs of cheap travel to South America, including by cargo boat. Be sure to check out their notice board. At the very least, don't board any boat that doesn't have life jackets, well-equipped lifeboats, and a captain who inspires confidence. All of this goes for yachts as well.

Those who insist on hitching a ride should know it's tough to join a boat in Kuna Yala. Many a tourist ends up stranded in El Porvenir because they've heard that's the place to hop on a boat. It's much easier to arrange from Colón or Isla Grande.

Getting Around

It's easy to get almost anywhere in Panama by bus or small plane. Commercial boat service, ironically for a country that owes so much to its waterways, is harder to come by.

The main roads in Panama are generally in good shape, and they've been much improved in recent years. The nation's major artery is the Interamerican Highway, or Interamericana, which in Panama stretches from the Costa Rican border along the Pacific slope of the isthmus all the way to the town of Yaviza in the Darién, where all roads stop.

The Interamericana is a divided highway from close to Panama City to Aguadulce. From there to the city of David there are poorly maintained sections with monster potholes, detours, and washouts. However, work is proceeding on extending the divided highway all the way to David. The easternmost section of the highway to the Darién is not paved all the way. At the time of

writing it was still only drivable all the way to Yaviza in the dry season, and then only with great effort and a good four-wheel drive or bus. At other times it's almost impossible to get much beyond Metetí.

Buses offer the cheapest way to explore most parts of Panama and are the best option for many travelers. Rental cars are a viable option for those who can afford it, are in a hurry, plan to travel extensively beyond the cities, and are up for the many hazards of driving in Panama. Panama's domestic airlines offer the fastest way to get from point A to point B in many parts of Panama, and for some of Panama's most remote places they're the only reasonable option.

BY AIR

Panama is dotted with airstrips served by a network of small commercial prop planes and jets.

© BONNIE KAY SPINDLER

"airport" in Kuna Yala

The longest flights take about an hour (not including interim stops) and cost no more than $120. There are several flights a day along some popular routes.

Note that the planes are essentially air taxis that often make several stops, and not always in the order you expect. Flights to Bocas del Toro province, for instance, always stop at both Changuinola and Bocas del Toro town, though which comes first varies. Planes to Kuna Yala sometimes go island-hopping down the archipelago, landing at several airstrips. Make sure to get off in the right place.

Panama City has the country's main domestic airport, Aeropuerto Marcos A. Gelabert, in the Albrook neighborhood a short drive from downtown. Most taxi drivers won't know it by name: ask to go to the *aeropuerto en Albrook*. Be sure to stress Albrook, or you may be taken to Tocumen International Airport. (Note: Some old maps still show the domestic airport in Punta Paitilla, but the airport was moved to its current location in 1999.)

The majority of flights originate from and end at this airport. Those who want to fly between other parts of Panama will most likely need to change planes in Albrook. There are, for instance, no direct flights between Bocas del Toro to Kuna Yala (the San Blas Islands). Panama's domestic carriers are not really set up for complicated itineraries, and flights don't sync up well. It's usually best to think of Panama City as your base and plan side trips that begin and end there.

There are three regular domestic carriers: Aeroperlas (and its subsidiaries, Aero Taxi and Ansa), Turismo Aéreo, and Mapiex Aero (a.k.a. Aero).

Mapiex Aero and Aéreo Turismo had formed a "strategic alliance" as this book went to press, and it's possible they may have merged by the time you visit. Aeroperlas's two subsidiaries, Aero Taxi and ANSA, fly to Kuna Yala, but they've steadily been losing their separate identities—all flights on them can be booked through Aeroperlas.

Aeroperlas (tel. 315-7500, fax 315-7580, info@aeroperlas.com, www.aeroperlas.com) is the oldest and largest of the airlines, with the most routes and passengers.

Turismo Aéreo (tel. 315-0279 or 315-0300, fax 315-0300) flies only to Contadora, Isla San José, the Darien and Kuna Yala (the San Blas Islands).

Mapiex Aero (tel./fax 315-0888, reservaciones@aero.com.pa, www.aero.com.pa) flies only to David and to Bocas del Toro province (Bocas del Toro town on Isla Colón and Changuinola). The airline is sometimes known simply as Aero.

Note: As this book went to press, the U.S. State Department was still issuing a travel warning that "called into serious question the safety standards of small air carriers flying domestic routes" in Panama. It recommended that travelers consider other means of domestic transportation, but that's not always possible.

I've had some white-knuckle flights, and friends have had even more exciting rides. Crashes do occur, including fatal ones. On the other hand, the views are spectacular. And given the road, sea, and other possible hazards to get to some remote destinations—including Kuna Yala, the Darién, and even Bocas del Toro—it may very well be the safest way to go.

Weight Limits

The baggage weight limit on domestic flights is 25 pounds (11.25 kilograms). Note that this is total weight, including both checked luggage and carry-ons. Do not try to slip by with more; planes are sometimes dangerously overloaded. Passengers are sometimes also asked to report their own body weight. If anything, err on the side of inflating your weight just to be safe.

Fares

Domestic airlines that fly the same route match each others' fares, which don't fluctuate from day to day and go up slowly from year to year. The round-trip fare is always double the one-way fare. Children between ages 2 and 5 generally pay half fare; infants usually fly free. Try to make reservations at least several days in advance, and reconfirm the reservation 72 hours before the flight. Be at the airport at least an hour before the scheduled departure time.

BY BUS

Panama's buses are the backbone of its transportation system. Except for the relatively few

Panama's buses are roving works of art.

© BONNIE KAY SPINDLER

able to afford cars, Panamanians rely on buses to get just about everywhere. They're cheap, run frequently, and are generally fast—sometimes too fast. The only ones not worth fooling with, except for those on a starvation budget, are buses within Panama City. They crawl across the city's congested streets, and anybody who can afford it takes the inexpensive taxis instead.

Many buses, especially in rural areas, run from dawn to dusk. There are few night buses except in the cities and a few major long-distance routes. There are also few expresses. Generally one can take any bus that goes at least as far as one's destination. For instance, to get from Panama City to Penonomé one can take a bus with a final destination of, say, Aguadulce or Santiago, both of which pass by Penonomé.

Panama's biggest bus terminal, not surprisingly, is in Panama City: the Gran Terminal de Transportes, in the Albrook neighborhood not far from downtown. It's possible to get a bus there to the most remote parts of the republic, often without any changes.

The other major hubs are Santiago and David. The hubs on the Azuero Peninsula are in Chitré and Las Tablas.

Reservations are seldom necessary (and not always possible) except to be sure of getting on a particular bus leaving at a certain time.

BY BOAT

Organized ferry and water-taxi service is available between Panama City and Isla Taboga and sometimes Contadora, and between the mainland and Isla Colón in Bocas del Toro province. Other than these services, boat transportation for travelers is generally more casual and arranged on an ad hoc basis.

Boats are the main means of regional transportation within the archipelagos of Bocas del Toro and Kuna Yala (the San Blas Islands). They are also the main way to get around the densely forested parts of the Darién and mainland Bocas close to rivers, especially in the rainy season when the rivers are more easily navigable.

The Bocas archipelago is the only place with anything resembling scheduled, cheap, commercial boat transportation among the islands. Boat transportation everyplace else is usually a matter of tracking down a fisherman or enterprising local boat owner and negotiating a price for a tour or extended trip. This can get expensive quickly. Tours are generally charged by the hour per group; the price for longer trips is based on distance, with gasoline the biggest expense. The price always includes the boat, a captain (and crew, if needed), and fuel. As always, agree on a price ahead of time.

Transportation is generally in exceptionally long wooden dugouts called *piraguas,* though fiberglass boats (*botes*) are also used in some places. Both come equipped with outboard motors. For long trips especially, check the horsepower of the motor, and ask if there's a backup motor and life jackets (*salvavidas*). *Piraguas* are actually the preferred form of transportation on the river. Long dugouts

A REAL LIFESAVER

If you know ahead of time you'll be making any trips on open ocean or even fast-flowing rivers, bring a life jacket with you to be on the safe side. Few boats are equipped with them, and even the larger ferry services don't always have enough for all passengers. These are light and easy to carry in your luggage, and during safe stretches of water they make a convenient cushion over the hard wooden planks that serve as seats. At the end of the trip, donate the jacket to the boatman; hopefully someone else will use it to make their own trip safer. This leaves extra room in your luggage for souvenirs on the way back home. Those who forget to bring one down to Panama should be able to find them in a sporting goods, home-supply, or department store in the larger cities. Try Novey or a Do It Center in Panama City.

used on the ocean are similar, but they have higher sides and an angled prow to break the waves. Short dugouts called *cayucos* are powered by a single wooden paddle and are all too easy for inexperienced paddlers to flip; it's unlikely you'll find yourself in one except for a very short trip.

Chartered sailboats, fishing or diving trips, and other outdoor activities on more substantial boats are easy to come by, but they tend to be quite expensive.

It's possible to take a partial or complete transit of the Panama Canal every Saturday via small vessel. See the Panama Canal chapter for information.

BY RAIL

The only passenger rail service in the country is on the recently rebuilt Panama Canal Railway, which runs between Corozal, a few minutes' drive north of downtown Panama City, and Colón. Some Panamanian businesspeople use it as a commuter service, but for most travelers it's a day excursion, and getting there is all the fun. See the Panama Canal chapter for information.

Know Panama

A slow, rickety banana train runs the 21 kilometers between Changuinola and Almirante. Plantation workers are its only regular passengers, but travelers who time it right should be able to get a ride for $1. See the Bocas del Toro chapter.

BY TAXI

Taxis are everywhere in Panama, especially Panama City. They're clearly marked and are nearly always small, brightly painted Japanese cars. Fares are based either on a series of zones established by law or on long-established prices for particular routes. There are no metered taxis in Panama.

Taxis are also cheap, and drivers do not expect a tip. It's rare to pay more than $2 or $3 even for long rides in Panama City. Fares in other cities generally top out at $.50 or $1. Rides outside the cities are more negotiable and more expensive, though it's rare to pay more than $20 even for a long trip on bad roads. Most shouldn't cost more than $5-$10.

In rural areas, the taxis are sometimes pickup trucks, occasionally converted into a kind of homemade minibus. These are especially useful for travel on dirt or badly maintained roads.

Fares are nearly always per ride, not per person, though occasionally taxis running specific routes, especially the converted pickups, operate more like buses than taxis and do charge by the head. Always agree on a price ahead of time, and clarify that it's a total price, not a per-person price.

Taxis can be hired by the hour for tours, though few taxi drivers speak much English. This can be a good option for those who want to cover a lot of ground in a short amount of time and would like the driver to wait between stops. Again, agree on a price ahead of time and don't pay until the end of the tour.

Taxi drivers throughout the country are usually honest, decent, hardworking folks. However, the chance of encountering an unscrupulous character goes up somewhat in the more touristy parts of town and around the posher hotels. I try to walk away from these areas before hailing a taxi.

In Panama City, so-called "tourist taxis" (they have "SET" license plates) hover around the more expensive hotels. These are larger, air-conditioned cars that are authorized to charge several times the going rate. It's a pricey way to go, but may be of interest to those who want a more comfortable ride and the security of a lot more metal around them on the capital's chaotic streets. Those who want the cheaper ride can just walk down to a main street and hail a cab.

Taxi drivers tend to drive fast and aggressively, and their cars have the dents to prove it. Buckle in and hope for the best. If a driver is making you uncomfortable, a firm but polite *Despacio, por favor* ("slow, please") should help a bit. If it doesn't, demand to be let out and get another taxi.

It's usually easy to find a cab night or day, and the international hailing sign of the raised arm works just fine. There are so many taxis eager for business that they often tap their horn at pedestrians to get their attention. This can get to be a little annoying if you're just out for a walk, but it's just an advertisement for business, not harassment.

At night, it can be worth calling for a radio taxi rather than waiting on the street. Many hotels, restaurants, and bars will be happy to call one for you.

RENTAL CARS AND DRIVING LAWS

Do not bother with rental cars for travel within Panama City or any other urban area. It's far easier, cheaper, and more convenient to take taxis. But renting a car is a reasonable option for longer trips.

Visitors can drive in Panama for 90 days with a driver's license from their home country; there's no need to get an international or Panamanian driver's license or permit. Be prepared to present both your driver's license and passport if stopped by the transit police for any reason.

Two kinds of insurance are obligatory when driving a rental car in Panama. Different rental companies call them by different names, but they're essentially collision and robbery insurance (called something like *renuncia a daños o*

IF THE CHICKEN CROSSES THE ROAD

Among the many road obstacles intrepid drivers are likely to encounter on the back roads of Panama are suicidal chickens. Chickens are definitely free range in the countryside, and they have a way of blundering out into the road with no notice. If you hit one, you are expected to find the owner and pay him or her for the pummeled poultry. Seriously. Make the effort to do the right thing, since for many people chickens are an important means of subsistence. The going rate is $5 per befouled fowl. You are, of course, then welcome to take the roadkill with you, if you have a means of preparing it. More likely you'll turn the deceased over to the grieving farmer. Also be on the lookout for dogs—an alarming number of them only have three legs due to tangles with traffic.

perdida or *cobertura de colisión y robo* and comparable to collision damage waiver—CDW—in the United States) and insurance against liability for harm to third parties (called something like *cobertura de daños a terceros o responsabilidad civil* or *suplemento de seguro de responsabilidad contra terceros*). Other kinds of insurance are optional. Your credit card, home auto insurance, or travelers' insurance may include some car-rental protection, but be sure to check ahead of time that it covers driving in Panama. When I have to rent a vehicle in Panama, I err on the side of too much rather than too little insurance.

Drivers and passengers are required by law to wear seatbelts. Cars are not yet required to have airbags, so ask if your car has them.

It's against the law to drive while talking on a cell phone. If you need to make a call, pull over. It's also illegal to drive without a shirt—seriously, you'll get ticketed for this.

Rental car agencies in Panama do not allow customers to take cars out of the country. Visitors are allowed to drive foreign-registered vehicles within Panama for up to 90 days.

Panama's streets are increasingly choked with enormous SUVs, so consider that when contemplating renting a subcompact car. For some more remote, rugged areas, a four-wheel-drive vehicle with high clearance is a must to navigate rough, rocky dirt roads and small streams. In the rainy reason, some roads will be impassable no matter what you're driving. Four-wheel-drives tend to be popular, so be sure to make a reservation for these well ahead of time. If you're unused to driving these vehicles, bear in mind many have a high center of gravity and it's disturbingly easy to flip them over on sharp turns or when dodging road obstacles, both of which pop up often on Panama's roads. Four-wheel drives are known in Panama as *cuatro por cuartos* (four by fours), *vehículos con doble traccion* (vehicle with double traction), or simply *dobles*.

Rental cars are most widely available in Panama City, but they can also be found in David and a few other places. In Panama City, the highest concentration of offices is in the Vía España area, though there are branches dotted around the city and at the international airport. Rates are about the same and sometimes cheaper than they are in the United States, and promotions are often available, including packages that combine a car rental with domestic flights and/or hotel stays. These can be great deals.

The major companies are Hertz, Avis, Thrifty, Dollar, Alamo, National, and Budget. Which one is best changes so rapidly, depending on current local management, it's impossible to recommend one over another. Vehicles rented in Panama City should be reasonably well-maintained. Outside the capital things are dicier. I once rented a car in David from a major U.S. agency and was presented with a muddy old clunker.

BY BICYCLE

Panama is not a bicycle-friendly country. There are no bike lanes, few places to rent bikes, and only a handful of areas it's even marginally safe to venture out on a bike. A trailblazing friend is determined to build a bike trail through Parque

Natural Metropolitano in Panama City, and it may actually exist by the time you visit.

If not, the best bet for a reasonably safe workout are the hilly loop roads above Boquete, though even here it's important to keep a sharp eye out for speeding trucks and cars. The Calzada de Amador is a good place for a flat, leisurely ride with great views. Isla Colón in Bocas del Toro is pretty much the only place that lends itself to biking as a sightseeing activity.

There are few bike shops and rental places in the country. The main place in Panama City to rent bikes at the time of writing was Alquiler de Bicicletas Moses on the Calzada de Amador, which not coincidentally is pretty much the only place in Panama City it's safe to ride them. Bikes can also be rented in Gamboa, Santa Clara, Farallón, El Valle, Boquete, and Bambito. Do not expect high-quality bicycles at any of these locations. Rentals tend to be basic mountain bikes or clunky old road bikes. Bike rentals are usually around $2-$5 an hour.

Some true adventurers (masochists?) have biked all the way from North America to the Darién Gap.

HIKING

Panama is a great place for hikes, both casual day trips and major back-country treks. There are very few developed campsites in the country, however, and few rangers to help out stranded hikers. Trails are often rugged and rudimentary.

Never, ever hike in the forest alone. Go with a qualified naturalist guide. It's surprisingly easy to get lost, and in some parts of Panama—such as the Darién—getting lost can be fatal. Also, rainforest trails can be very slippery, and you don't want to be stuck alone in the forest with even a twisted ankle. I'm embarrassed to admit how many times I've wiped out on what looked like an easy trail or gentle stream crossing.

Appropriate gear is key to a safe, enjoyable hike in the tropics. Always camp in a tent, even on the beach, to prevent insect and possible vampire-bat bites. Treat even small scratches with antibiotics; wounds quickly become infected in the tropics.

HITCHHIKING

Hitchhiking is not common in most parts of Panama, and it's just as dangerous here as it is in your own country.

ORGANIZED TOURS

There are many tour operators and guides in Panama, of wildly different quality. Companies appear and disappear constantly, and I've encountered many a "guide" who hasn't a clue what he or she is talking about. Even the more established companies can be hit or miss.

The ones listed below are among the most prominent and well-established, and I have indicated the ones I recommend highly. In addition to arranging tours, many operators can also make hotel and travel arrangements. Those especially interested in nature travel should be sure to sign up with a group that uses qualified naturalist guides; ask about credentials. See specific destination chapters for more possibilities.

Ancon Expeditions

Ancon Expeditions (P.O. Box 0832-1509 WTC Panama City, Republic of Panama, tel. 269-9414 or 269-9415, fax 264-3713, info@anconexpeditions.com, www.anconexpeditions.com) is Panama's top nature-tour company. It's known for employing some of Panama's best naturalist guides, particularly in the Darién. These include Hernan Araúz, Rich Cahill, Iván Hoyos, and Rick Morales, all of whom I've traveled with and can recommend. They're also all fluent in both English and Spanish. Hernan (one of Panama's top birding guides and Darién experts) and Rich are particularly experienced, with multiple trans-Darién treks and many shorter adventures to their credit. They're a blast to travel with, filled with a sense of fun and adventure but always responsible and safety-conscious. I've learned a lot from both. Ancon Expeditions also runs some unique ecolodges, including ones in Cana, Punta Patiño, and Bocas del Toro. Tours range from easy day trips to ambitious, multi-day treks through the forest. The company occasionally organizes ocean-to-ocean adventures through the heart of the Darién. Recently added is a week-long trip that includes a multi-day hike along what remains of the historic Camino Real, which once stretched from Panamá La Vieja across the isthmus to Portobelo.

Chiriquí River Rafting

Chiriquí River Rafting (Entrega General, Boquete, Chiriquí, Panama, tel. 720-1505, cell 618-0846, fax 720-1506, rafting@panama-rafting.com or panamarivers@cwpanama.net, www.panama-rafting.com) is a safety-conscious, highly professional operation. I've had great experiences with them. They primarily run white-water rivers in the western highlands, but they also offer tamer river trips.

Ecocircuitos

This company (tel./fax 314-1586, cell 617-6566, fax 708/810-9350 in the U.S., Annie@ecocircuitos.com, www.ecocircuitos.com), based at the Country Inn and Suites in Amador, offers a wide range of short and multi-day tours around the country. It hires friendly and accommodating guides who speak English and Spanish.

Exotics Adventures

This group (tel. 223-9283, cell 673-5381, info@panamaexoticsadventures.com, www.panamaexoticsadventures.com) is led by a Frenchman named Michel Peuch. I have not yet traveled with him, but he comes highly recommended by people whose opinion I trust and respect. Unusual offerings include a fast and arduous ocean-to-ocean Darién trek and a kayak trip in Bocas del Toro. He offers a range of other tours, including some that are far less strenuous.

Gold Coast Expeditions

This operation (tel. 441-4339, cell 635-2292, gold-coast@cwpanama.net, http://goldcoastpanama.homestead.com) is run by Skipper and Jill Berger, longtime residents of the Caribbean side of the former Canal Zone. They offer a variety of snorkeling/diving, sailing, and sightseeing trips around Panama, with the Caribbean side of the canal area a specialty. Popular trips include kayaking excursions around Portobelo and the lower Río Chagres.

Iguana Tours

Iguana Tours (P.O. Box 6655,, Panama 5, Republic of Panama, tel. 226-8738, 226-1667, or 226-4516, fax 226-4736, iguana@sinfo.net, www.nvmundo.com/iguanatours) specializes in trips to Isla Iguana off the Azuero Peninsula, but it offers a range of tours all over the country.

José Saenz

José (based in Panama City, Republic of Panama, cell 614-7811 tel. 263-7604, Bocasfrog@yahoo.com) is a taxi driver, but if you spend any amount of time in Panama you'll realize he's an important part of the tourist infrastructure. I highly recommend him, as do many others. He's punctual, responsible, polite, dependable—and a safe driver. These are qualities to prize among Panama taxi drivers. He'll pick you up or drop you off at Tocumen International Airport for $20, and if you give him enough notice he'll even make hotel reservations for you. He charges $8 an hour for Panama City tours. He also does tours all over Panama, including Chiriquí, the Azuero Peninsula (his specialty; that's where he's from), and Bocas del Toro. Rates for this vary. Besides his air-conditioned cab, he has access to a 14-passenger minibus and a pickup truck with a double cabin for surfboards and such. He speaks pretty good English.

Nattur Panama

This group (Apartado 5068, Balboa-Ancon, Republic of Panama, tel. 442-1340, fax 442-8485, panabird@cwpanama.net, www.natturpanama.com) is headed by Willie Martinez, who is recognized as one of the very best birding guides in Panama. The company offers a range of nature tours throughout the country. Its unique offerings include stays at Martinez's own ecological retreat, Willie Mazu, in the species-rich Fortuna area. The group is working on setting up a similar retreat near Colón. It also offers a popular boat tour on the Río Chagres near the Caribbean entrance to the Panama Canal.

Know Panama

Panama Travel Experts
Many of this group's (tel. 265-5323, fax 265-5324, 877/836-5300 or 707/226-2640 in the U.S., reservations@panamatravelexperts.com, www.panamatravelexperts.com) offerings are higher-end multi-day packages that include stays at luxury hotels, but it also offers less expensive day tours.

Pesantez Tours
Pesantez (P.O. Box 55-0716, Paitilla, Republic of Panama, tel. 263-8771, 223-5374, or 263-7577, fax 263-7860, pesantez@sinfo.net, www.pesantez-tours.com) is a long-established company that enjoys a solid reputation. It specializes in tours of Panama City and cultural tours rather than nature trips.

San Blas Sailing
This outfit (P.O. box 89-9838, Panama City, Republic of Panama, tel. 232-7598, cell 674-8860, info@sanblassailing.com, www.sanblassailing.com) arranges memorable multi-day yacht tours of Kuna Yala (the San Blas Islands). Though not cheap, these trips are not as expensive as one might expect and offer good value. For those who don't have yachts of their own, it's the best way to explore and enjoy the islands.

Scubapanama
Scubapanama (tel. 261-3841 or 261-4064, info@scubapanama.com, www.scubapanama.com) is Panama's biggest dive operator. Common offerings include diving around Portobelo, a dive in both oceans in a single day, and diving in the Panama Canal.

Twin Oceans Dive Center
This is a newer dive operation (tel. 448-2067, info@twinoceans.com, www.twinoceans.com) that's impressed me with its professionalism. It's based in Portobelo but sometimes offers dive tours to Coiba and other locations.

TOLL ROADS
Panama has three toll highways: the Corredor Norte, the Corredor Sur, and the Autopista Arraiján-La Chorrera. The Corredor Sur links Tocumen International Airport and central Panama City. The Corredor Norte extends north from Panama City about a third of the way across the isthmus toward Colón. Both of these latter highways were begun in the 1990s and are still works in progress to some degree. Supposedly the Corredor Norte will one day be extended all the way across the isthmus, creating another overland link between the two oceans, but wrangling between the Panamanian government and the Mexican contractor behind the project has stalled the expansion for years now.

Tolls on the corredors are based on distance driven, the amount collected in increments at toll plazas along the way. Payments are made in cash or through an electronic debit system that only regular commuters bother with. Most tolls are around $1 or less.

The Autopista Arraiján-La Chorrera, completed in 1981, is Panama's oldest toll road. It's on the Interamerican Highway west of Panama City. The toll plaza is about 30 kilometers west of the Puente de Las Americas (Bridge of the Americas), and the toll for a passenger car is $.50.

Tolls on all three highways are collected in either direction. Take the receipt the attendant hands you and hold onto it until you exit the highway. Tolls are higher for larger vehicles.

Visas and Officialdom

Entry requirements for tourists to Panama are a muddle. Rules are in flux, and government officials often seem the last people one can count on for accurate information. It's possible to call a half-dozen consulates and get a half-dozen contradictory answers to basic questions.

That said, getting into and out of Panama is generally not a problem, particularly for those who fly. U.S. citizens in particular can visit the country with remarkably little hassle: all they need is a passport and a $5 tourist card bought at the airport on the way in.

Things are trickier for citizens of some other countries, or for those interested in more than just playing tourist for a few weeks. Below are official requirements for most travelers at the time of writing. Check with the nearest Panamanian consulate in your own country for current rules (or at least what they think are the current rules). Good luck.

VISAS AND TOURIST CARDS

Entry requirements for foreign tourists depend on the nationality of the visitor. Some foreign nationals need only present a passport that is valid for at least six months after the date of entry. Others must also have either a visa or tourist card. Warning: Requirements for particular nations change constantly. In recent years Panama has tinkered with its general entry and exit requirements, adding to the confusion. Check with the nearest Panamanian consulate or embassy for current requirements. Double warning: some of these officials are themselves confused about the requirements. If you don't get a satisfactory answer, try again later and pray for a more savvy official.

Theoretically, U.S. visitors can visit Panama with proof of citizenship other than a passport, such as a birth certificate. In practice, though, having a passport will make dealing with officials much easier. It also may be difficult to return to the United States without one.

Tourists must also be able to show proof of having at least $500 (a credit card or travelers checks should do it) and a return or onward travel ticket out of Panama. In practice, this rule will probably not be enforced, especially for clean, neatly dressed North Americans and Western Europeans. Bedraggled backpackers may get more attention. Bus passengers arriving at Paso Canoa without proof of onward travel are sometimes required to buy a bus ticket back to Costa Rica, whether they intend to use it or not.

Those traveling on a tourist card are allowed to stay in Panama for 90 days, extendable for another 90 days. There are different limits for other kinds of visas. Extending a stay requires getting something called a *prórroga de turista* (tourist extension), and it's a bureaucratic nuisance. See below.

Note: In 2004, Panamanian immigration officials announced their intention to reduce tourist stays to 30 days, extendable for another 60 days, to stem the flow of foreigners on tourist visas who were working illegally in the country. There was considerable confusion about this new rule even before the government changed hands in late 2004. By spring 2005, it appeared the new administration was going to revoke the new rule and allow tourists to stay 90 days without a *prórroga*. In any case, most tourists can probably count on being able to stay 30 days without hassle or additional paperwork.

Countries whose citizens need neither a visa nor a tourist card to enter Panama include: Argentina, Austria, Belgium, Chile, Costa Rica, Denmark, Finland, France, Germany, Great Britain, Hungary, Israel, Italy, Luxembourg, Poland, Portugal, Spain, Switzerland, and Singapore. Warning: This list is especially subject to change; check with the consulate or embassy in your country for current requirements.

Tourist Card

The tourist card is a simple document that can be bought at the port-of-entry airport (from the airline) during check-in or at the border upon arrival into Panama. It costs $5. It's better

Know Panama

to buy it ahead of time to avoid possible border hassles, such as local officials running out of them. Airlines that fly to Panama from U.S. ports of entry know the drill well and should have ample stocks of the cards. Those flying to Panama from another country may want to check with the airline—preferably the ticketing desk at the port-of-entry airport, which is most likely to know what you're talking about—to make sure they have them. Those traveling by bus should ask about it when making a reservation. If they don't have the cards, though, it shouldn't be a problem to buy one on arrival in Panama. However, anyone eligible for a tourist card is also eligible for a stamped visa, which may be the best option for those traveling to Panama by land, sea, or an unusual air routing. See below.

At the border crossings with Costa Rica, tourist-card-eligible travelers who arrive without one are sometimes required to buy a $10 *timbre* (stamp) in lieu of it. See the border-crossing entry for details.

Those with tourist cards need to keep it with their passport during their stay in Panama and should be prepared to present both to the police or other officials at any time.

Countries whose citizens can travel to Panama on a tourist card include: Australia, Canada, Colombia, Japan, Mexico, Norway, New Zealand, South Korea, Sweden, Taiwan, and the United States.

Authorized Visa

Citizens of some countries need a so-called *visa autorizada* (authorized visa). It is only available through a Panamanian consulate or embassy, which decides whether to approve the visa application. Most countries on this list are in Africa, the Middle East, Eastern Europe, and Asia.

Confusingly, stated requirements can vary by consulate, so double-check with the nearest one before beginning the process to make sure to have all the required documents in order. But even the loosest interpretation of the rules makes applying a lengthy hassle, and they sure aren't designed to make the applicant feel welcomed

with open arms. Begin the process at least 30 days before the start of travel.

Applicants will probably need to present:
1. A completed one-page application form.
2. A valid passport.
3. A current bank/financial statement.
4. A letter from a local "sponsor" in Panama. (It may be worth arranging at least one tour with a Panamanian guide company or tour operator and have them supply this letter for you—again, start this process well in advance, as getting this letter may be a nuisance. Don't pay for the tour until the letter's supplied.)
5. A copy of the proposed itinerary. (Some consulates warn travelers not to buy a travel ticket until the visa is authorized, in case it isn't, but others require proof of a round-trip ticket. In that case, make sure the ticket's refundable.)
6. Two passport-size photographs.
7. A photocopy of the "identification card" from your home country (include both a photocopy of your passport's information pages and any national ID card to be on the safe side).
8. A money order for $115 made out to "Consulate General of Panama."
9. Proof of employment in the home country.

Countries whose citizens can only travel to Panama with an authorized visa include: Bangladesh, Cuba, Haiti, Hong Kong, India, Pakistan, the People's Republic of China, Russia, and South Africa.

Stamped Visa

Panama also issues a so-called "stamped visa" that lets travelers enter the country multiple times over the course of a year. These are only available through a Panamanian consulate or embassy, and as the name implies it consists of a stamp placed in the traveler's passport. Travelers must present the passport and a money order for $60 made out to "Consulate General of Panama."

Citizens of some countries are required to get a stamped visa. Those who are eligible to travel to Panama on a tourist card can also opt to get the visa instead if they want. This is a good option for those planning to travel to Panama by land or through an unusual air routing. Tourist cards may be hard to come by ahead of time in these cases, so a stamped visa in the passport can avoid possible hassles at the border.

Countries whose citizens must have a stamped visa to travel to Panama include: Cyprus, the Czech Republic, the Dominican Republic, Egypt, Peru, and the Philippines.

Extended Stays

Tourists who want to extend their stay beyond that authorized by their original tourist card or visa must apply for a *prórroga de turista* (tourist extension) at an immigration office, and in recent years that's become a serious nuisance. Gather all the materials needed and start the application process about four working days before the visa or tourist card expires. Wear your nicest clothes and be unfailingly polite.

The main office in Panama City is the Ministerio de Gobierno y Justicia, Dirección de Migración y Naturalización (Avenida Cuba and Calle 29 Este, tel. 207-1806, 8 A.M.–1 P.M. Mon.–Fri. for tourist services). Try to come first thing in the morning, as getting the process started can take a couple of hours. There's an information booth near the front entrance. There's also a small *relaciónes públicas* (public relations) office on the right just before the stairs down to the main hall where the lost and confused, at least those who speak Spanish and are excessively polite, may get some help.

A nearby Internet café (@rquinet, Calle 29 Este between Avenida Cuba and Avenida Perú, next to Hotel Benidorm) can make photocopies. The massive El Machetazo store a block up (Avenida Perú between Calle 28 Este and Calle 29 Este) has a photo booth in the cosmetics section, one floor up towards the back of the store, where one can have four passport-sized photos made for $2.10.

Applicants must submit:

1. Their passport and tourist card or visa.
2. A photocopy of the passport pages that show the applicant's photo, personal details, and latest entry stamp for Panama.
3. A photocopy of the tourist card or visa.
4. A sponsorship letter from a Panamanian or foreign resident, along with a photocopy of the sponsor's *cédula* (national identity card) and a photocopy of his or her latest telephone or utilities bill.
5. A photocopy of a return or onward-travel ticket that's valid for a year.
6. Proof of one's own financial solvency (e.g., travelers checks or credit cards) or that of one's sponsor (e.g., proof of employment or social security payments)
7. Two passport-size photos.
8. A payment of $1 to open a file and $15 to make the *carnet de prórroga* (ID card).

Applicants need to fill out a simple Spanish form (those who don't speak Spanish may want to bring a phrasebook). The whole procedure generally takes four working days, and applicants may be required to leave their passport (be sure to make an extra photocopy or two for yourself).

There are other immigration offices around the country, including one in David, one in Chitré, and two in Bocas del Toro, but the main Panama office is best equipped to deal with foreign tourists.

Tourists can get up to 90 more days in Panama through this process. Note that getting the full extension is not guaranteed. The number of days granted is at the discretion of immigration authorities.

After the extension expires, tourists have a two-day grace period to leave the country. The penalty for staying beyond that, interestingly, is apparently not that bad. Tourists whose stay has expired are required to pay a *multa* (fine) before leaving the country. The fine is $25 for overstaying a month, $30 for two months, $40 for three months, and so on, up to $300 for overstaying by a year.

Violators pay the *multa* at the immigration office, are given a receipt to show upon leaving the country, and have an eight-day grace period to finally clear out. Do not try to leave the country without this receipt, as you may get stopped at the border. Straightforward as this all sounds, it's still not a good idea to get enmeshed in the cogs of the Panamanian bureaucracy by overstaying your official welcome. Rules change, and border officials and police officers may not take kindly to a tourist who's been hanging around their country illegally. Those who just can't get enough of Panama should either leave the country and come back on a fresh tourist card or visa, or else go through the considerable bureaucracy of having their visitor status changed while in-country.

Tourists who extend their stay, by the way, no longer have to go through the additional hassle of getting a *paz y salvo* (a document that certifies one doesn't owe Panama taxes) and *permiso de salida* (exit permit). These are now only required for some locals and resident expatriates.

LIVING AND WORKING IN PANAMA

It's tough to get a permit to work in Panama. The country has high unemployment and the government wants jobs to go to Panamanians, not foreigners. However, foreign investors and retirees are welcome to make their home in Panama if they meet certain conditions.

Coming to Panama as anything other than a tourist requires considerable paperwork, the services of a Panamanian lawyer, and certification by a Panamanian consulate. The process is time-consuming. Allow several months for the paperwork to make its way through the system, and try to get a lawyer who specializes in immigration law.

The biggest and most established law firms include: Morgan and Morgan; Galindo, Arias, and López; Arias, Fábrega, and Fábrega (ARIFA), and Icaza, González-Ruiz, y Alemán (IGRA). One place to start a hunt for a Panamanian lawyer is the visitor-information website www.panamainfo.com. Some of the more prominent firms are listed there. The website www.legalinfo-panama.com has detailed legal tips, articles, books for sale, and lists of Panamanian attorneys. It's mostly written in Spanish (Spanish-speakers can search *trámites* for all kinds of entry requirements), but some of it is in English as well. Note that the site is very attorney-oriented, so it recommends just about every move one takes in Panama be done with a lawyer's help.

A useful book for those planning a move to Panama is "Living in Panama," by Sandra Snyder. It covers the daily realities of life in Panama, particularly Panama City, and includes tips on everything from registering a car to choosing a school to how to pay the phone bill. Those in the United States can buy it by mail ($19.95). It's also available in some local stores in Panama ($16.95). Contact information: tel. 264-0567, whosnew@wnpan.org, tantoes@pobox.com, or sts panama@pobox.com, www.wnpan.org. Mailing address: Tantoes, S.A., PMB PTY 2611, P.O. Box 025207, Miami, FL 33102-5207. (Full disclosure: Sandra is a family friend, but her knowledge of the subject is solid. She has lived in Panama for years and is so plugged into the local scene some Panamanians turn to her for tips.)

Residency for Foreign Retirees

Foreign retirees who want to make their home in Panama must get a *visa de turista pensionado* (pensioned tourist visa). Retirees are required to hire a lawyer to handle the process. Fortunately, Panama wants relatively affluent retirees so the requirements are not nearly as onerous as in some other countries. These include a recent medical evaluation certifying the applicant is in good health, an HIV test, proof of retiree status, and a monthly pension of at least $500, plus $100 for each dependent the retiree wants to bring along. The dependents also need a clean bill of health. Sometimes proof of not having a police record in the home country is also required. The lawyer will explain the kind of documentation needed, as well as the photos, passport photocopies, and other bureaucratic fodder that must be supplied.

After the applications are submitted, retirees should be given a provisional I.D. good for three months. If the application is approved, they will be given a permanent I.D. card. This must be renewed after one year of residency.

Benefits of *turista pensionado* status, besides the right to live in Panama, include the right to import up to $10,000 worth of possessions for personal use duty-free, as well as the duty-free import of a vehicle every two years. A huge plus for retirees, both foreign and domestic, are discounts at restaurants and hotels, for transportation and many medical services, and for some financial dealings. These can range from 10 percent to 50 percent.

Another visa for retirees is the *visa de rentista retirado* (retired financier visa), intended for those who don't have a pension per se but have an independent income coming in. Applicants must show a monthly income of $750, and the process of certifying that is somewhat more complicated.

Retirees are allowed to invest in Panama but are not allowed to work except under certain special circumstances.

Work Permits, Temporary Visitor Visas, and Immigrant Visas

Work permits are generally only granted if a Panamanian company has offered the applicant a job, and even then only if it can be proved no Panamanian could do that job. The permits are issued by Panama's labor ministry, el Ministerio de Trabajo y Desarrollo Laboral, and getting one requires a good Panamanian attorney. The applicant must then apply for a temporary visitor visa, again with legal help. Executives who want to work in the Zona Libre de Colón, technical and scientific experts, and qualified candidates interested in working at one of the Ciudad del Saber (City of Knowledge) projects have the best chance of being approved.

Investors who want to live and do business in Panama must meet several other conditions, not the least of which is proof of having at least $100,000 in capital, and the hiring of at least three Panamanian employees.

Anyone with assets of at least $100,000 can apply for an immigrant visa, even without job prospects.

EMBASSIES AND CONSULATES

Panama City is home to the embassies and consulates of quite a number of countries. But some major nations are missing: Australia, for instance, advises its citizens to contact the Australian embassy in Mexico if they need help. A few countries with embassies or consulates in Panama City include:

- **Canada:** World Trade Center, Calle 53 Este in Marbella, tel. 264-9731, fax 263-8083, www.dfait-maeci.gc.ca/panama/menu-en.asp
- **Colombia:** World Trade Center, Calle 53 Este in Marbella, tel. 264-9266 (embassy), tel. 223-3535 (consul general), fax 223-1134, www.embajadadecolombia.org.pa/
- **Costa Rica:** Avenida 2 Sur/Samuel Lewis, tel. 264-2980, 264-2937 (consulate), fax 264-6348 (Costa Rica also has a consulate in David: Calle C Sur and Avenida 2 Este Avenida, tel. 774-1923)
- **Cuba:** Calle 33 and Avenida Cuba, tel. 227-5277 or 227-0359, fax 225-6681
- **El Salvador:** Avenida Manuel Espinosa, tel. 223-3020
- **France:** Plaza de Francia in Casco Viejo, tel. 211-6200, fax 211-6235
- **Germany:** World Trade Center, Calle 53 Este in Marbella, tel. 263-7733, fax 223-6664
- **Great Britain:** Swiss Tower, Calle 53 Este in Marbella, tel. 269-0866, fax 223-0730
- **Guatemala:** Vía Argentina, tel. 269-3406, fax 223-1922
- **Mexico:** Calle 58 and Avenida Samuel Lewis, tel. 263-4900 or 263-2159
- **Nicaragua:** Avenida Manuel E. Batista, tel. 269-6721 or 223-0981
- **Spain:** Calle 33 and Avenida Perú, tel. 227-5122, fax 227-6284
- **United States:** Avenida Balboa between Calle 37 and Calle 38, tel. 207-7000, fax 227-1964, http://usembassy.state.gov/panama; visas to U.S.: Torre Miramar, Avenida Balboa and Calle 39, tel. 207-7000 or 207-7030

BORDER CROSSINGS

There are three border crossings between Panama and Costa Rica: at Paso Canoa on the Pacific side of the isthmus, at Río Sereno in the highlands, and at Guabito-Sixaola on the Caribbean coast. Paso Canoa, which is on the Interamerican Highway, is by far the most traveled. The Guabito-Sixaola crossing is used mainly by those traveling to and from Bocas del Toro. The Río Sereno crossing is rarely used, and foreign travelers are not always allowed across.

The Interamerican Highway comes to an end at the town of Yaviza in eastern Panama, where the famous Darién Gap begins. There are no roads linking Panama with Colombia and the rest of South America. At the time this was written, the civil war in Colombia had made the one Panamanian border crossing with Colombia, at Puerto Obaldía at the very eastern tip of the Caribbean coast, too dangerous to attempt even when it's actually open. Those who want to go to Colombia from Panama should fly.

General Considerations

On arrival at any border crossing, be prepared to present immigration officials with an onward ticket out of Panama and evidence of having $500. These aren't often asked for, but officials have the right to refuse entry to anyone without them. Arriving at the border looking clean, neatly dressed in long pants and good shoes (e.g., no sneakers, flip-flops, sandals, etc.), and generally solvent and respectable increases one's chances of being waved through without incident. A credit card should be sufficient to prove the money requirement. Those without an onward or return ticket can generally buy a one-way bus ticket back to Costa Rica at the border for about $10 and then just toss it out later if not needed, but if no international-bus driver is around travelers may be stuck. Better to buy some kind of ticket ahead of time.

Paso Canoa tends to be the strictest border crossing, and when a bus arrives the whole immigration and customs process can be a drawn-out nuisance. Sixaola-Guabito is generally friendlier and far more casual. There's a good chance you'll be waved in with a smile and just a cursory glance at belongings and passport. Río Sereno is also casual, but it's rarely used by foreigners and is the least equipped to handle them.

Try to arrive at the border during regular business hours to avoid a lengthy wait at the border for immigrations and customs officials to show up. Borders are open every day.

Tourist Cards vs. Timbres

Those who need a visa to enter Panama must get one ahead of time; they'll be turned back at the border otherwise. Those who only need a tourist card should try to get one before visiting Panama, but if that's not possible the cards are generally available at the border for $5.

If border officials run out of them, which sometimes happens, the recourse is to buy a stamp (*timbre*) for $10 at the government-run Banco Nacional de Panamá (BNP). Note: This option is only available for those eligible to enter Panama on a tourist card. The visitor must then return to an immigration office and have an official stick the *timbre* into the passport and give it the seal of approval. This is easy to do at Paso Canoa and Río Sereno (at least when the banks are open), but it's more of a nuisance at Guabito-Sixaola. There are no banks nearby, so visitors must get one at the BNP in Changuinola or Isla Colón and then stop by the immigration office in either town to have it validated. It's best to do this as soon as possible, though there are immigration offices in David and Panama City if for some reason it's not possible to get this taken care of in Bocas. Some visitors just stick the *timbre* in their passport without bothering with the immigration office and have been able to travel around and leave the country without incident. But it's best to go through the whole process and let the officials assure you everything's in order. Those who try to leave the country without proper documentation are subject to fines and real bureaucratic hassles.

Paso Canoa

The border crossing at the decaying town of Paso Canoa is on the Interamerican Highway and is the route taken by the great majority of visitors coming from or going to Costa Rica by land. It's about an hour by bus or car west of David, the provincial capital of Chiriquí Province.

Going through formalities on both sides can be surprisingly quick or painfully slow. Count on an hour or two for the whole process and hope for the best.

Those arriving by bus tend to encounter the most inconvenience. Passengers are generally expected to hand-carry their luggage across the border for inspection on either side. Also, processing a busload of visitors takes time, especially if the bus arrives early in the morning.

It's impossible to get lost crossing over, but the offices aren't well marked. Small boys may offer to help navigate for a small tip. This may be worthwhile if the procedures are baffling or if you just want to stop the other kids from bugging you. About $.25 should make your assistant happy.

Those exiting Costa Rica need to buy a little stamp for the equivalent of about $.70 from an office on the Costa Rican side. The official should take either colones or dollars. Panamanian officials have apparently decided this is a nifty idea and now charge $1 on their side of the border.

Immigration, customs, an IPAT government tourism office, a post office, and a branch of Banco Nacional de Panamá are all next to each other at the border. The immigration and customs "offices" consist of ticket-booth-style windows in the wall of the building. At the time of writing there were plans for a fancy new customs/immigration complex, but it was unclear when this would actually be built.

Tourist-card-eligible visitors who arrive without one should go to immigration before buying the card. After the officials check the passport, go to the IPAT office (tel. 727-6524, 6 A.M.–11 P.M. daily) around the corner to buy the card for $5. Be sure to have small bills—they can't make change for anything bigger than a $20. After buying the card, return to immigration and customs to complete the process. If they are out of cards (which really shouldn't happen), go to the Banco Nacional de Panamá (8 A.M.–3 P.M. weekdays, 9 A.M.–noon Sat.) to buy a *timbre* for $10. It has an ATM, but they don't change Costa Rican colones. Those who need to should look for a man wandering around carrying a money pouch. If changing money on the streets of a grungy border town doesn't sound like a smart thing to do—and it probably shouldn't—change colones into dollars before entering Panama.

There are plenty of buses and taxis about 50 meters past immigration/customs. For more information see the Golfo de Chiriquí chapter.

Sixaola-Guabito

This border crossing is used primarily by those traveling between Costa Rica and Bocas del Toro. Sixaola is the border town on the Costa Rican side; Guabito is on the Panamanian side. The border itself runs down the middle of the Río Sixaola. Travelers must cross over a short, rickety railroad bridge, either by foot or in a vehicle. Pedestrians should look out for traffic, missing handrails, and gaps in the planking.

The Panamanian border post is on an elevated railway trestle on the edge of the Río Sixaola. The immigration office (tel. 759-7019, 8 A.M.–noon and 12:30 P.M. to 6 P.M. daily) is right on the train tracks next to the bridge that crosses the river. Travelers can only enter and leave Panama when the office is open. Note that Panama time is always one hour ahead of Costa Rican time.

For those who can enter Panama on a tourist card, there's a representative of IPAT, Panama's tourism bureaucracy, in the immigration office who sells them ($5), but it's best to get one in Costa Rica ahead of time if at all possible. If they're out of tourist cards, eligible travelers can instead buy a *timbre* (stamp) for $10 at the Banco Nacional de Panamá in Changuinola or in Bocas town and then get it validated at the immigration office in either town. Those who need a visa to enter Panama will be turned away at the border if they don't have one.

The IPAT representative has nothing else to offer except a friendly smile, if you're lucky. The customs office is right next to the immigration office. Travelers usually find border formalities here quick and laid-back.

There are no hotels, no appealing places to eat, and almost no services in Guabito. The nearest place with significant services is Changuinola, about a 20-minute drive away.

Those entering Panama without onward transportation should walk down from the railroad tracks to get a bus or taxi after clearing customs and immigration. Taxi drivers and unofficial "tour guides" sometimes try to over-charge new arrivals or take them to hotels that pay them a commission, so be cautious. See the Bocas del Toro chapter for transportation information and tips on logistics.

Río Sereno

This little-used border crossing is a possible alternative to Paso Canoa for those coming from or going to the western highlands of Panama. However, it's rarely used and it not always open to foreigners. There's nothing much of interest for tourists there, and you're likely to be the only foreigner in town. It's a far prettier spot than Paso Canoa, but it's not really set up to deal well with foreign visitors, it's out of the way for any destination but the area around Volcán, and the road leading east into Panama is quite dangerous. It's a better idea all around to cross over at Paso Canoa.

Those crossing over to Panama need to first buy an exit stamp for about $.70 at the store the Costa Rican immigration officer will point out. They take colones or dollars.

The Panamanian immigration/customs office (tel. 722-8054, 7 A.M.–7 P.M. daily) in Río Sereno is on a hill above the town plaza. It's near the radio tower and shares a building with the police station. Tourist-card-eligible visitors who arrive without one will probably need to buy a $10 *timbre* at the Banco Nacional de Panamá branch on the town plaza, then walk back up the hill to immigration.

The nearest major junction for onward travel in Panama is at Volcán, 42 kilometers east of the border. The drive, on a beautiful but dangerous road, takes nearly two hours. The pickup-taxi ride costs about $20, and you'll be sharing the ride. Buses from Río Sereno run from 5 A.M. to 5 P.M. every 45 minutes to Volcán (around $3) and David (around $4).

There is one basic but okay place to stay for those unlucky enough to get stranded at the border. See the Río Sereno entry in the Western Highlands chapter for more information.

BRIBES AND SCAMS

Panama has a history of corruption in the public sphere that in recent years it has acknowledged and taken steps to address. The problem isn't going to disappear in the foreseeable future, however. Still, it's unlikely most tourists will find themselves in a situation where a bribe is expected.

The possible exception is being stopped by a police officer, usually for a traffic violation, and being encouraged to pay the "fine" on the spot instead of going to the trouble of paying it at the courthouse. How to handle this is a judgement call. Some adamantly refuse to pay a bribe out of principle. Sometimes the officer will lose interest and let the violator go; other times this leads to a time-wasting visit to the local courthouse. Paying or offering a bribe is illegal, and theoretically it can get a visitor in far more serious trouble. Others find paying a few dollars the easiest way to deal with the nuisance.

In recent years, there have been reports of travelers being stopped by police repeatedly while driving in western Panama. This occurs between Divisa and David on the Interamerican Highway. They are accused, rightly or not, of speeding or not staying within the lane and then told to pay a "fine" of $20. Some have refused to pay and are let go; others pay, only to be stopped again farther down the road. The police reportedly spot likely-looking tourists as they drive by and radio ahead to their confederates to stop them. Those driving in western Panama should obey the speed limit and all other traffic rules and try as much as possible not to look too touristy.

Those interested in buying real estate in Panama should proceed carefully. Land scams have been a problem in recent years, especially with the tourist and retiree boom in Bocas del Toro and Boquete. Be especially cautious of timber schemes and other get-rich-quick scenarios. If it looks too good to be true, it's probably a scam. A great deal of land in Panama is untitled, which makes buying it tricky and in some cases legally precarious—don't "buy" a piece of land from someone who doesn't actually own it. The craziest thing of all is people buying into Panama sight unseen. Besides the danger of getting ripped off, Panama is not a place everyone would want to live or invest in. To avoid disappointment, get to know the country first.

Scams against regular tourists are still not much of a problem. Most visitors are more likely to be ripped off by a fellow foreigner than by a Panamanian. But stay alert and be cautious with overly friendly strangers.

POLICE

Panama's police force is a lot less intimidating now than in the days of the military dictatorship. Law-abiding visitors are unlikely to have any bad dealings with the police. In fact, Panama is so eager to protect tourists and give them a positive impression of the country there's a whole detachment of 200 police offers, known as the Policía de Turismo (tourist police), dedicated to watching out for them in Panama City. They're generally bicycle cops, easy to spot in their khaki uniforms with short pants. They're most visible in the Casco Viejo section of the city, where the force is headquartered.

Transit police sometimes crack down on certain offenses on busy stretches of road. They're usually on the lookout for speeders, those making illegal turns, drivers talking on cell phones, etc. Drivers signal that the transit police are staking out an area by flashing headlights at each other. I sometimes flash lights to slow down reckless drivers even when no cops are around.

The police also sometimes set up roadblocks to check drivers' licenses and registrations. This is normal and no cause for alarm. If a police officer stops you, be unfailingly polite and friendly. Be prepared to hand over your passport and driver's license. Police officers rarely speak English, which some resident expatriates and visitors use to their advantage when stopped for a traffic violation, feigning an inability to speak Spanish in the hopes the officer will lose patience and just wave the driver on instead of handing out a ticket.

Know Panama

Conduct and Customs

Despite Panama's undeserved reputation, among those who've never been there, as a dangerous country, you'll likely find it a remarkably mellow and low-key place to travel. It's extremely rare to encounter hostility or belligerence. Courtesy is considered quite important, however. Panamanians may take offense if they feel they're not being treated with proper dignity and respect.

Foreigners sometimes complain that the Panamanians they encounter in stores and offices seem unfriendly or sullen. This complaint is most often made about Panama City; in the countryside, visitors are frequently overwhelmed by the warmth and friendliness they encounter. If you feel you're being treated rudely, do not raise your voice or snap at the offending party—this will get you absolutely nowhere. Be patient and polite, and take your business elsewhere next time. Similarly, the less you expect punctuality and speediness the happier you will be.

As in other Latin American countries, machismo is a fact of life in Panama. Women may find they have to deal with unwanted male attention. See the "Women Traveling Alone" section for details.

DRESS AND APPEARANCE

Panama is in some ways a rather formal and conservative country. Neat dress, good grooming, and cleanliness are expected. It's against the law to drive or walk down a city street without a shirt; violators are subject to fines. What constitutes a "city" street is broadly defined: Shirtless travelers have been ticketed for walking down the main street in Bocas town, a place that hardly qualifies as an urban setting in most people's minds. Sneakers are not considered acceptable footwear in most restaurants, bars, and nightclubs. Wearing shorts can get one kicked out of a government office or church. Dress is more relaxed at the beaches of the interior, where shorts and casual clothes are the norm.

Suits have largely replaced guayabera shirts as business and semiformal wear for middle- and upper-class Panamanian men, made practical by the widespread use of air-conditioning in the cities. Women tend to dress as elegantly as their budget will allow, and two-piece suits or conservative dresses are the norm for professional women. Less-affluent city dwellers and *campesinos* take pains to dress as neatly as they can.

Children wear uniforms to school, and, though spiky modern hairstyles and casual clothes have made some inroads in recent years, it's rare to see even teenagers take their fashion sense too far. Though long-haired kids are no longer hauled off by the police for a haircut, as they were during the military dictatorship of the 1970s, people are still judged by their appearance to a great extent. Expensive or at least dressy clothes, a neat hairstyle, and accessories make a stronger impression here than in more casual countries such as the United States.

Mochileros (backpackers) sometimes get a bad rap in Panama as an unkempt and disreputable lot that travel so cheaply they add little to the economy. There's little animosity, but one occasionally senses a mild distrust. To this day, most tourism efforts are pitched at the affluent, and some shudder at the thought of Panama being overrun with foreign backpackers, as they believe Costa Rica has been. This attitude seems to be softening somewhat as more real backpackers arrive and they're not as scary as feared, more efforts are being made to accommodate them. Still, those traveling on a frugal budget will likely feel more welcome if they do their best to look especially neat and respectable, and stash the backpack in a safe place when possible. It's tempting to wear skimpy, sloppy clothes in the Panamanian heat. Resist the temptation.

ETIQUETTE

Formality extends to etiquette as well. Titles are taken seriously (such as *Doctor* or *Doctora* for a

physician, *Licienciado* for an attorney or even someone who holds a bachelor's degree, *Profesor* or *Maestro* for a teacher, *Ingeniero* for an engineer, etc.). If known, they should be used in introductions or correspondence. Courtesies in writing and speech tend to be more elaborate in Panama than in English-speaking countries. Some allowances will be made for foreigners, but try to make up for any gaps in eloquence with cordial body language.

Women often greet each other and men with air kisses. Unlike some other Latin American countries, men rarely greet each other with an *abrazo* (hug) unless they are on quite friendly terms. Handshakes are the norm, but these tend to be far lighter (some say limper) than in other countries. A crushing handshake is considered aggressive.

It's not typical in Panama to greet someone with an *hola* (hello). This is considered quite casual and, especially if the person is unknown to you, not very polite. The main greetings are *buenos días* (good morning), *buenas tardes* (good afternoon), and *buenas noches* (good evening). In casual situations this is often shortened to a simple *buenas*, which conveys a tone somewhere between "hey" and "howdy." It's become fashionable in recent years, for some reason, to say "ciao" when parting.

Courtesy may be less elaborate among the poor working classes of the city and the country, but being polite is just as important. Even more so, in some ways. It's considered extremely insulting to address someone of perceived lesser status as though they're inferior. Use formal terms of address (e.g., *usted* vs. *tú*) with all strangers at first, but be especially sensitive about not lapsing into casual forms with someone who's performing a service for you.

Many Panamanians are proud of their country and do not take kindly to criticism of Panama and things Panamanian. Complaints they may make to each are one thing, complaints from a foreigner are quite another. This is especially true when it comes from U.S. citizens, not surprising given the long and complicated relationship between the two countries.

Tips for Travelers

OPPORTUNITIES FOR STUDY

The easiest way to study in Panama is through an exchange program with the student's home university. But there are several other options as well.

With the possible exception of casual, short-term programs, visiting students must travel with a special visa. Student visas are a kind of temporary visitor visa, with many of the same requirements as other visas (HIV test, criminal record report, medical certificate of good health, letter of sponsorship, etc.). Applicants must also show proof of acceptance into the academic program and evidence of "economic solvency." The process generally requires a lawyer, but presumably the academic institution will help with the process.

Florida State University has had a satellite program in Panama for decades that draws students from Latin America, the United States, and Canada. Instruction is in English. Students can enroll in bachelor's and associate's degree programs in environmental studies, international affairs, Latin American and Caribbean studies, and the social sciences, offered in collaboration with the **Ciudad del Saber** (City of Knowledge) at Clayton. The university is also experimenting with a variety of environmental sciences and archaeological projects at the Linton Island Research Station, near Isla Grande on the Caribbean side of the isthmus. FSU-Panama now occupies what was once the campus of Canal Zone College, a community college at the foot of the Bridge of the Americas near the Pacific entrance to the Panama Canal. Note: Don't confuse this program with the FSU campus in Panama City, Florida. For information, write Florida State University - Panama, P.O. Box 6-4794 El Dorado, Panama 6A, Republic of Panama, or contact the university at tel. 507/314-0367, admissions_fsupanama@fsu.edu, http://international.fsu.edu/.

The **Smithsonian Tropical Research Institute** (STRI) coordinates a variety of short-term and long-term fellowships for undergraduate, graduate, and postdoctoral students that are offered by the Smithsonian Institution and STRI itself. For information on STRI fellowships, write the Smithsonian Tropical Research Institute, Office of Education, Apartado 2072, Balboa, Panama or contact tel. 212-8031, fellows@tivoli.si.edu, www.stri.org. For information on Smithsonian Institution fellowships in Panama, contact Smithsonian Institution, Office of Fellowships, P.O. Box 37012 Victor Bldg. 9300, MRC 902, Washington, DC 20013-7012, tel. 202/275-0655, siofg@ofg.si.edu, www.si.edu.

The **Ciudad del Saber** (City of Knowledge) in Clayton hosts a variety of academic programs in a number of disciplines. For information, write Ciudad del Saber, Apartado Postal 83-0645, Zona 3, Panama City, Republic of Panama or contact 317-0111, iperurena@cdspanama.org or cgvergara@cdspanama.org, www.ciudaddelsaber.org.pa.

Panama has several universities, the most prominent of which is the **Universidad de Panamá**, opened in 1935, which offers a wide array of degree programs. Through its main campus in Panama City and extension programs around the country, it has about 74,000 students. Instruction is in Spanish. Foreigners interested in attending must apply through the university's Secretario General. For requirements and application details, write Universidad de Panamá, Ciudad Universitaria, Dr. Octavio Méndez Pereira, El Cangrejo, Republic of Panama or contact up@up.ac.pa, www.up.ac.pa.

A Florida-based non-profit called the **Institute for Tropical Ecology and Conservation (ITEC)** has a biological field station in Bocas del Toro. See the Bocas del Toro chapter for information.

VOLUNTEER OPPORTUNITIES

Those interested in doing volunteer work in Panama will most likely have to come up with a scheme of their own. Few formal volunteer programs exist as of yet. The best way to start is to find a place or a cause one is interested in and

Know Panama

TIPS FOR RESPONSIBLE TRAVEL

An overseas trip is supposed to be fun, not an exercise in political consciousness. But visitors will get more out of Panama, and help keep it an enjoyable destination for others, if they make at least some effort to get to know the place and how their actions may affect it.

Start by reading up on the fascinating history of Panama, which for hundreds of years has earned its reputation as the "crossroads of the world," and by learning a bit about its flora and fauna.

It would be nice to think it goes without saying that buying souvenirs made from the body parts of endangered animals—jaguar teeth, tortoiseshell jewelry—is a big no-no. If not, remember that possessing these products is a serious crime in Panama, punishable by fines and jail time. Trafficking in *vida silvestre* (wildlife) is punishable by 6 months to two years in jail. Note this includes *all* animals found in the wild, not just endangered species. The same thing goes for possession of pre-Columbian pottery and other historic artifacts. Collecting these is known as *huaqueria* (roughly, "grave robbing") and is illegal. Obviously, it's also illegal to eat endangered animals; do not partake of tortoise eggs or the like. Do not buy jewelry made from coral, which is being severely damaged in Panama. Leave intact shells on the beach; they're potential homes for a variety of sea creatures.

Think about what you eat in Panama. Lobster, for instance, has been terribly over-harvested in the San Blas Islands (Kuna Yala). You'll be tempted to try one on the islands, but bear in mind that what was once a subsistence food for the Kuna is now in danger of extinction, which would have serious consequences for the Kuna and their environment. And it's not just in the San Blas you should consider this: Poor lobster divers sell their catch to fancy restaurants in Panama City. If nothing else, avoid lobster during the mating season, which runs from March to July. Consider that a female lobster carries thousands of eggs, but divers scoop up the expectant moms right along with the other lobsters. It'd be a shame if your dinner meant the end of a whole generation of baby lobsters.

Among the many other reasons not to eat beef is the fact that cattle ranching is not at all sustainable in Panama. It has led to massive deforestation and the destruction of entire habitats. Carnivores should cut down in Panama.

Personal recreational watercraft (Jet Skis and the like) panic marine life, shatter the tranquillity of other beachgoers, and pollute the environment. Resist the temptation to go for a spin.

Be skeptical of tour operators and hotels that advertise themselves as eco-conscious. Ask them exactly what they mean by that, and what kind of environmentally conscious services they offer.

Because hotels and tour operators know that "eco" can spell money for them, they have an incentive to exaggerate just how ecologically con-

---

then pitch a volunteer plan to the director, highlighting your skills. Many will be happy for the free labor.

The **Canopy Tower** (see the Panama Canal chapter) accepts volunteers willing to work at the tower in exchange for room, board, and a stipend of about $400 a month. Volunteers are expected to take on a full range of responsibilities at the tower. Management prefers volunteers willing to stay at least three months. Those interested should send an email to the tower's owner, Raúl Arias de Para, at birding@canopytower.com. He speaks fluent English.

Hotel y Cabañas Los Quetzales (see the West-

ern Highlands chapter) sometimes uses volunteers to help run the hotel. **Voyager International Youth Hostel** in Panama City and the **Purple House Hostel** in David are other possibilities. Those interested can also try one of the universities or research institutes (see "Opportunities for Study").

The environmental non-profit **ANCON** sometimes takes volunteers as well. The best approach is to send ANCON a letter or email detailing skills and saying when you'd like to come down and how long you'd like to stay. Try to be as specific as possible about how you think you can help. Write ANCON, Apartado 1387, Panamá 1, República de Panamá, or email scious their operations are. This is not yet a big problem in Panama, but it's easy to see how it could become one if nature tourism really takes off in the country. To help readers make informed decisions about who to go with, this book attempts to highlight the features of a place or an operation likely to appeal to a low-impact tourist (e.g., small-scale, locally owned hotels that tread lightly on their surroundings) as well as those features that may be off-putting (e.g., a private zoo on the property).

Environmentally sensitive tourism is so new to Panama it's hard for tourists to be entirely pure about where they stay and how they travel. Even Panama's finest ecotourist lodges have their shortcomings. One place I visited in the highlands seemed great; it even composted and recycled its waste, which is all but unheard of in Panama. As I was leaving, though, a friend pointed out the necklace worn by the son of the Ngöbe-Buglé caretaker: It appeared to be made of jaguar teeth.

Because there's no way to know for sure how old those teeth were or where they came from, and it would be unfair in any case to blame the owners of the lodge for the traditional ways of its caretaker, I still recommend this place. More disturbing was a hike I took with a native guide who worked for another lodge. He was a terrific guide, a gentle soul who loved the beauty that surrounded him and was eager to share his knowledge. One morning, though, we came across what we thought might be a rare owl. Hoping to give my companions and me a look at the owl in flight, he threw a stick at it.

It's tricky to know how to handle something like this. If we had told the owner of the lodge about this incident, there was a very real possibility the guide, a poor man with a wife and several small children, would have been fired on the spot. We chose to ask him politely not to throw sticks at animals in the future.

The answer is almost definitely not to boycott those places and tour outfits that don't fit all our criteria for a low-impact, environmentally aware operation. Probably the most useful thing to do is to seek out those that are on the right track, and through our own actions encourage those qualities we like and discourage those we don't. Most of the best operations are owned and run by intelligent businesspeople who take great pride in what they're trying to accomplish. Don't be afraid to give them feedback, including criticisms. They're all still trying to figure out just what it is low-impact tourists want, and they'll likely be eager to hear your comments.

Nature tourists to Panama in the next few years may well play a critical role in shaping the future of Panamanian tourism. If entrepreneurs see a demand for responsible, low-impact nature travel, and they are shown that it can pay, in a few years there may be more simple eco-lodges and fewer sprawling five-star resorts.

ancon@ancon.org. More information is available from the ANCON website: www.ancon.org or by calling tel. 314-0062.

The **Spanish by the Sea** program in Bocas del Toro (tel. 757-9518, info@spanishbythesea.com, www.spanishbythesea.com) can sometimes organize volunteer work. Possibilities include a sea-turtle conservation project. See the Bocas del Toro chapter for more information.

WOMEN TRAVELING ALONE

This is a tough one. Women who travel alone in Panama are likely to be safer than in many other countries, but it's still not the safest way to go. On the one hand, it's unusual for any traveler to face serious harassment in Panama. It's an easygoing, live-and-let-live kind of place. On the other hand, it is a macho country, and women are subject to lots of cat-calling, honking horns, smooching noises, and other obnoxious behavior from dudes on the street. Generally, that's as aggressive at it gets, but it can certainly make women who travel alone feel unsafe, sometimes with good reason.

Women are most likely to encounter this nonsense in Panama City. Some women have also reported unwanted attention in Bocas del Toro and Boquete, where a sudden influx of foreign tourists has collided with provincial attitudes, and to some extent in David. A woman friend was practically stalked in Bocas by a few eager guys a couple years back, so much so she cut her visit short. Women who travel alone should be especially alert in Bocas and Panama City. The Calidonia and Casco Viejo neighborhoods of Panama City are not the best places for women traveling on their own.

Panamanian women who get bothered on the street tend to ignore the culprits completely. That's probably the best tack to try at first. Try not to lose your cool. Knowing at least some Spanish and appearing confident and at home can also help diffuse unpleasant encounters. Befriend fellow visitors and travel in groups if possible. Cabs are probably safer than walking at night, but avoid taking them alone. Women who go to bars and discos alone are often assumed to be looking for sex, and there will be no shortage of guys eager to help out.

GAY AND LESBIAN TRAVELERS

Panama is a quite tolerant and open-minded place for a predominantly Roman Catholic Latin American country. I've yet to hear a story, for instance, about a police raid on a gay club. However, gays and lesbians are still for the most part closeted. Same-sex affection on the streets would cause a sensation at best, an ugly encounter at worst. Homosexuality is not illegal in Panama, but neither is it legally protected.

Foreigner status (and, by implication, access to relative wealth and power) will also help protect gay and lesbian travelers from harassment. Gay and lesbian acquaintances in Panama say they've never felt threatened, but it's hard to know how much of this is just the natural immunity that comes from having power in a society that's sharply divided between the haves and have-nots. Poorer gays do sometimes get beaten and harassed, and they have little protection or legal recourse.

The visibility of gays and lesbians has increased in recent years. Local soap operas, enormously popular in Panama, have introduced gay characters who are portrayed in a positive light, and one of the hosts of a popular TV chat program, "La Cocoa," is an openly gay man who goes simply by Harold and has become something of a household name. Gays have also been allowed to enter floats in Panama's Carnaval celebration in recent years, complete with a Carnaval queen in drag.

In 2001, after a three-year battle, Panama gained legal recognition for its first gay and lesbian organization, La Asociación de Hombres y Mujeres Nuevos de Panamá ("the association of new men and women of Panama"). AHMNP advocates the rights of "sexual minorities," including gays, lesbians, bisexuals, and transgendered people. It also aims to provide education about preventing sexually transmitted diseases and support for those infected with HIV.

The organization is still finding its legs and doesn't even have an office yet. For more information, contact Ricardo Beteta (AHMNP), Apartado Postal 87-0002, Zona 7, Panama, Republic of Panama, tel. 633-8890, amigoglbt@hotmail.com, www.farraurbana.com (look for the AHMNP tab). There are also AHMNP chapters in Colón, Santiago, and Chiriquí province.

Information on parties, clubs, and events aimed at the GLBT crowd is available at www.farraurbana.com and www.chemibel.com.

For more information on international gay rights issues, check out the International Gay and Lesbian Human Rights Commission (www.iglhrc.org) and the International Lesbian and Gay Association (www.ilga.org). Neither group has much information specifically on Panama, however.

ACCESSIBILITY FOR DISABLED TRAVELERS

Disabled travelers will not find Panama an easy country to maneuver around. Accessibility and the rights of the disabled are new concepts in Panama.

In 1999, Panama passed Ley 42, which guarantees equal opportunity for and makes it illegal to discriminate against disabled people in employment, education, services, transportation, health services, and so on. That same year,

Panama signed the Organization of American States' Inter-American Convention on the Elimination of all Forms of Discrimination Against Persons with Disabilities.

However, according to an international disabled-rights group, the Center for International Rehabilitation (www.cirnetwork.org), Panama so far has done little to enforce compliance with either agreement, or other disability-rights laws that are on the books.

Even in the fanciest hotels and restaurants it's unusual to encounter ramps, handrails, and other accommodations for people with disabilities. Ley 42 requires making both public and private buildings accessible, but advocacy groups estimate that to date only about 5 percent of public buildings meet the requirements. I know of only one hotel in the entire country, Los Capitanes in El Valle, that consciously designed some rooms to be accessible.

The modern infrastructure of Panama City makes it perhaps the easiest place for those with disabilities to get around. The abundance of elevators and taxis help, though almost all taxis are rather cramped and there are no taxi services geared towards those with wheelchairs. Conditions quickly become difficult in the countryside, particularly in the Darién or any of the island groups, where paved roads disappear, transportation is often by small boat, and it can be somewhat challenging for just about anyone to get around.

Some information on accessible travel worldwide is available at www.access-able.com, though at the time of writing they did not have Panama-specific tips.

SENIORS

Seniors are treated with deference and respect in Panama, where the old-fashioned honorifics *don* and *doña* are sometimes still used for venerable older people. Panamanian seniors and foreign residents are entitled to discounts as high as 50 percent on a whole range of services, but unfortunately these are not available to visitors. It never hurts to ask for a *descuento* (discount), but

those who do will usually be asked to show a Panamanian identification card.

TRAVELING WITH CHILDREN

Panama is a child-friendly country. There are many young families in the country, so lodgings often include little playgrounds, child-oriented activities, guest rooms with multiple beds, etc.

Vaccination recommendations and other preventative-care measures are often different for small children than for adults. Visit the U.S. Centers for Disease Control's website at www.cdc.gov or ask your doctor for information.

Panama's warm weather and abundance of outdoor-recreation possibilities makes the country a great place for kids. But parents need to be especially alert when traveling around Panama given the comparatively fewer safeguards for children than in more developed countries (missing handrails, sudden drop-offs, chaotic traffic, etc).

Kids are welcome just about everywhere, but a few hotels and other establishments do not allow or at least discourage bringing children. These are usually ecolodges that don't want the wildlife disturbed or are concerned about children falling off boardwalks into the water. I do not recommend taking small children to most parts of the Darién or to Kuna Yala (the San Blas Islands) because of the rugged conditions and possible dangers from wildlife. Rats, for instance, are a fact of life in the San Blas Islands, and while the risk of a bite is small, rustling in the rafters has been known to shatter more than one worried parent's rest.

Since 1995 Panama City has had a nighttime curfew for those under age 18. Unattended minors are supposed to be off the streets 8 P.M.–6 A.M. Sunday–Thursday and 11 P.M.–6 A.M. Friday–Saturday. Exceptions are made for students and young workers, but only with proper documentation. The curfew is aimed at residents, but theoretically foreign minors could be stopped by the police if unaccompanied by a parent or legal guardian. Violators are taken to a police station until picked up by their parents, who are subject to a fine.

TRAVELING WITH PETS

Bringing a pet to Panama is a bad idea unless one is planning a lengthy or permanent stay. Dogs and cats must be quarantined for 40 days, though a recent law allows for home quarantine in lieu of a stay in a kennel. Travelers on the road will obviously not be able to provide a home in which to quarantine the pets, so kenneling at the quarantine office may be the only option. There is also considerable paperwork involved that may require the help of a lawyer

or at least a relocation-service agent. (José Saenz, one of the guides listed under Organized Tours, provices this service.) The process can't be started any sooner than 10 days before the pets are shipped, because all documents must be as up-to-date as possible. Requirements include a certificate of good health and a payment of $130. Leaving the country with a pet requires a whole other round of permissions. Requirements are more stringent for birds and other animals. Contact a Panamanian consulate for current requirements.

Health and Safety

It's extremely unlikely you'll contract a serious disease in Panama. Health conditions are generally good, especially for a developing nation. For instance, the country has not had a single report of polio since 1972, yellow fever since 1974, diphtheria since 1981, or cholera since 1993. Panama City and the former Canal Zone are particularly safe.

However, those planning to spend a considerable amount of time in rural areas, especially if camping, can do several things to stay healthy.

The most important of these is to avoid insect bites as much as possible. Always use insect repellent in the countryside, particularly in the evenings and early mornings. Sleep in screened-in rooms or use mosquito netting. Wearing long-sleeved shirts and long pants will also reduce insect bites. See below for other tips. If you're only planning to spend a few days in these areas and know you'll be sleeping under mosquito nets or in screened-in rooms, you may not want to fool with malaria prophylaxis.

For current information on health conditions in Panama, contact the Centers for Disease Control in Atlanta, Georgia, at 877/FYI-TRIP or www.cdc.gov.

BEFORE YOU GO

Make preparations for any needed vaccinations or anti-malaria medication as far ahead of time as

possible. Some vaccinations can't be administered at the same time, and some anti-malaria meds need to be started a week or two before traveling.

The information that follows is meant to give travelers general guidelines on staying healthy in Panama. It's drawn from a number of public-health sources, but it's not intended as medical advice and is certainly no substitute for profession medical care in case of emergency. Do not attempt to diagnose or treat yourself for any illness.

Vaccinations and Other Prophylaxis

Note that many physicians unfamiliar with Panama except for a vague and dated notion the place is synonymous with "tropical disease" go overboard in prescribing all kinds of unneeded preventative measures. Many a visitor who plans only to visit Panama City and the Panama Canal area comes loaded with expensive anti-malaria medications that serve little purpose other than to amuse their fellow travelers and hosts.

What kind of precautions to take depends largely on where travelers plan to go and what they plan to do. Those who will spend most of their time in Panama City and the Panama Canal area probably do not need more than minimal protection. Those planning a trek across the Darién may want every defense against disease they can find.

Health conditions and vaccination recommendations can change quickly, so check current requirements and advisories through the CDC (www.cdc.org) or your doctor.

All visitors should make sure their routine immunizations are up to date, especially against measles-mumps-rubella and tetanus-diphtheria. The incidence of these diseases in Panama is low to nonexistent, but the CDC recommends everyone be current on their immunizations against them, including non-travelers.

The CDC also recommends that travelers to Central America be vaccinated against Hepatitis A and, in some cases, Hepatitis B. A rabies vaccination is recommended for those who expect to come in contact with animals, wild or domestic. The CDC suggests typhoid fever vaccinations for those traveling in Central America, though the chance of contracting it in Panama seems remote.

Those planning to travel to rural parts of Panama, especially near the Costa Rican or Colombian border, should probably be vaccinated against yellow fever and may want to consider anti-malaria medication.

Panama recommends but still does not require that most visitors be vaccinated against yellow fever. There is a far greater risk of someone bringing yellow fever to Panama than of catching it there (the last known case in Panama was in 1974). But travelers, especially those planning to travel to or from South America or other regions known to have the disease, should strongly consider getting vaccinated, for their own protection and that of others as well as to avoid border hassles.

Warning: Despite the lack of a clear policy requiring yellow-fever vaccinations, Panamanian authorities have been known to vaccinate those arriving from infected countries at the airport if the traveler cannot present a yellow-fever certificate, at a cost of $10. Better to take care of this before leaving home. Be sure to bring a properly stamped and signed international yellow-fever certificate, which the person administering the vaccine should give you. Panamanian health officials also urge vaccinations for those planning to travel in Kuna Yala (the San Blas Islands) and the Darién, especially anywhere near the Colombian border (travelers shouldn't go that far into the Darién in any case).

There is no vaccine for malaria, but there are several kinds of anti-malaria drugs meant to be taken daily or weekly before, during, and after travel to an endemic area.

Visitors to most parts of Panama should not need to take them. However, outside of Panama City and the area around the former Canal Zone there is a slight risk of contracting malaria. The risk is greatest in the Darién and the Comarca de Kuna Yala (San Blas Islands and mainland). The highest-risk areas west of the Panama Canal are the rural parts of Bocas del Toro and Veraguas provinces.

Many travelers even to these areas don't take anti-malaria medication unless they plan to spend a fair amount of time in remote villages or sleep somewhere that doesn't have screened-in rooms. The true risk is almost impossible to measure, so think about the kind of traveling you want to do and discuss options with your physician.

There is a chloroquine-resistant strain of malaria in the Darién and Kuna Yala. Mefloquine, doxycycline, or atovaquone/proguanil is recommended for those planning to spend a significant amount of time in these regions. Chloroquine is considered effective against any strains found west of the Panama Canal.

These medications go by an assortment of brand names, which can cause confusion. Some anti-malaria medications have serious side effects and are not recommended for everyone (e.g., pregnant or breast-feeding women). They can also make one more susceptible to sunburn. Some of the contraindications are unusual—mefloquine, for instance, is not recommended for those with a history of depression—so do some research and quiz your doctor carefully. To be effective, travelers must continue to take the medications anywhere from a week to a month after returning home.

INSECTS AND ARACHNIDS

Insects generally come second (after snakes) in the list of creatures tropical neophytes worry about. But most parts of Panama are not nearly as buggy as one might think, and certainly can't compare to, say, the mosquito swarms of Alaska in the summer.

Mosquito populations are kept down around populated areas because of the potential risk of mosquito-borne diseases. Still, mosquitoes can be a nuisance in certain places, especially in the rainy season. Dusk and dawn tend to be active times. Insect repellent and long-sleeved shirts and pants are effective at keeping mosquitoes at bay. Sleep in tents or screened-in rooms to avoid bites at night.

Sand flies (a.k.a. sand fleas, no-see-ums) are locally known as *chitras* and can be a real irritation. They love to bite feet and ankles and can cause itching for hours. To avoid infection, try not to scratch. Mosquito repellent sometimes seems ineffective against the annoying little buggers. They tend to like beach spots without breezes, especially near mangroves, and dine in force in the early evenings. The Caribbean side of the isthmus seems particularly susceptible to them, especially parts of Bocas del Toro (there's actually a Sand Fly Bay off Isla Colón). Some claim *chitras* like pale skin, so start working on a leg tan as soon as possible. Keeping feet covered with shoes and socks provides some protection. Anti-inflammatory and itch-relieving creams, such as hydrocortisone, can help with the irritation after bites. Eurax is locally popular for the itching, as is coconut oil. *Chitras* can spread leishmaniasis (see entry), so it's a good idea to minimize exposure as much as possible.

Chiggers are a type of parasitic mite that hikers can pick up wandering through a field or grassy area. They often climb up the hikers' legs and like to burrow into the skin around the elastic bands of underwear or pants. Once they latch on, they stay attached for days and cause their hosts to itch like crazy. Insect repellent on the clothes, especially around the legs and feet, can offer some protection. Experienced hikers often tuck their pants into their boots and seal them off with masking tape to keep the things out. Some also sprinkle powdered sulfur into their boots to ward them off.

In general, be careful where you put your hands and feet when hiking. Many plants have sharp spines and the like and may harbor aggressive ants, poisonous caterpillars, and other nasties.

There's a reasonable chance of coming across a scorpion, especially in rural and semi-rural areas. Usually the sting isn't dangerous, but it's quite painful. Ditto for some spider bites. To be on the safe side, shake out your shoes and clothes before putting them on. When I'm traveling in the countryside, I stuff my socks into my shoes before going to bed at night and shake them out in the morning. In the canal construction days, workers slept with their boots under their pillows. Tarantulas and other large spiders sometimes make an appearance, which is more startling than dangerous; if you leave them alone, they'll do likewise.

Panama has Africanized bees—the so-called "killer bees"—which can be aggressive and dangerous. Keep well away from any bees you come across. If you disturb them and they start chasing you, try to run through dense brush. They will have a hard time following. Do not jump into a body of water to escape them; they will wait for you to surface. (I know someone who died precisely this way in Panama—when he came up for air, the bees got down his throat.)

Stay out of the way of ants. Some, such as the bullet ant, have ferocious stings, and less-nasty ones can still swarm over an unsuspecting hiker remarkably quickly.

INSECT-BORNE DISEASES
Dengue Fever
Dengue fever is a viral infection that gets little press but is becoming an increasingly serious public health threat around the world, including the Americas. It's spread through a bite from infected mosquitoes, and so far the only way to prevent it is to keep mosquito populations down and avoid mosquito bites as much as possible. There is no vaccine against the disease and no specific medications to treat it, but anyone who suspects an infection should get medical attention immediately. It's a serious illness, and in some cases can be fatal if untreated.

Both dengue fever and DHF are caused by four distinct but closely related viruses.

The main carrier is the *Aedes aegypti,* the same mosquito responsible for yellow fever, but it is also carried by the *Aedes albopictus,* a resilient, adaptable mosquito colloquially known as the Asian tiger mosquito because of its coloration: black with white stripes.

Aedes aegypti is endemic to Panama, but *Aedes albopictus* originated in Asia and has only recently spread to other parts of the world, including the United States. It was not discovered in Panama until 2002.

The disease comes in two forms. Classic dengue fever is characterized by high fever, nausea, vomiting, headache, and pain in the back, joints, and eyes. Pain can be intense, which is how the disease earned the ominous nickname "breakbone fever." Symptoms are often milder for younger children. Recommended treatment includes pain medications, rest, and drinking lots of fluids under a doctor's care while the virus runs its course.

Dengue hemorrhagic fever (DHF) is a far more serious form of the disease. It can be fatal if not properly recognized and treated. With good medical care, however, the mortality rate is generally less than 1 percent. Symptoms include a fever that lasts 2 to 7 days, accompanied by symptoms that are easily confused with those of other illnesses, such as nausea, vomiting, headache, and stomach pain. This stage is followed by signs of hemorrhage, including a tendency to bruise easily, bleeding nose or gums, and sometimes internal bleeding. Without treatment, this stage can be followed by circulatory failure, shock, and death.

Both dengue fever and DHF are caused by four distinct but closely related viruses. All four now exist in Panama. Infection by one type provides no immunity against later infection by another type.

Dengue epidemics are becoming increasingly common in the Americas. In 1993 Panama had its first reported case of dengue in nearly 50 years. An aggressive public-health response has so far prevented a major outbreak, but in recent years the country has averaged several hundred annual cases of classic dengue and a handful of DHF cases. Cases of classic dengue have dropped off sharply since 2002.

Dengue thrives in poorer urban areas, and many reported cases in Panama since 1993 have occurred in the sprawling San Miguelito district on the outskirts of Panama City. Two people died of DHF within a month of each other in mid-2004, both in Colón province.

Yellow Fever

Yellow fever was the most dreaded disease in Panama until a massive sanitation and public health program eliminated it from the isthmus in 1906. While it has never had a serious resurgence in Panama (the most recent known case was in 1974), the country has to be constantly on guard against the possibility. Panama provides a perfect home for the disease and its local vector, the *Aedes aegypti* mosquito. Relaxed sanitation standards helped the mosquito reestablish itself on the isthmus in 1985, which sparked a new public-health push to control it. So far, the mosquito has brought with it dengue fever but not yellow fever.

The biggest concern is that the disease will be brought to the country by foreign visitors from a neighboring country that still has the disease, such as Colombia, which experienced a yellow-fever outbreak in 2004 that killed several people.

Yellow fever symptoms typically come in two phases. The first is characterized by fever, intense muscle pain, nausea, headache, chills, and vomiting. For about 15 percent of sufferers, there is a drop-off in symptoms that is followed in a few days by a return of the fever, and sometimes jaundice (hence the name "yellow fever"), stomach cramps, vomiting, and hemorrhaging. About half of these latter patients die within 10-14 days after the onset of the first symptoms. There is no cure, but most people do survive a yellow-fever attack. Those who do are immune to the disease thereafter, which is a mild consolation. Seek medical help immediately at the first sign of symptoms.

Malaria

Malaria is a tenacious disease that has not been entirely eradicated either in Panama or most of the rest of the world where it's endemic. But it was drastically reduced during Panama Canal construction days as a result of the same sanitation program that eradicated yellow fever. It's been kept at bay ever since.

Chloroquine-resistant strains of the disease exist in eastern Panama, but any strain found west of the Panama Canal is not believed to have acquired immunity to this medication.

Symptoms of malaria usually do not appear until at least a week after infection from the bite of an *Anopheles* mosquito. Flu-like symptoms such as fever, chills, headache, muscle pain, and fatigue are common. Malaria can also cause anemia and jaundice. Symptoms can be intense or quite mild. Those infected may not realize it for some time, which is dangerous. Malaria is a serious disease and potentially fatal if not treated quickly. The U.S. Centers for Disease Control urge any traveler to an endemic area to get medical care immediately at the first sign of fever or flu-like symptoms for a full year after returning home. Be sure to tell the doctor where you've been.

Leishmaniasis

Leishmaniasis is a parasitic disease spread by bites from infected sand flies. The type most commonly found in Latin America is known as cutaneous leishmaniasis, which is characterized by skin sores and is far less serious than visceral leishmaniasis, which attacks the internal organs but is found primarily in Brazil, Africa, and southern Asia.

There is no vaccine for leishmaniasis; the best way to avoid the small chance of contracting it in Panama is to reduce contact with sand flies as much as possible. The only travelers likely to be at risk in Panama are adventurous types who travel far off the beaten track.

Sores develop weeks or even months after the victim is bitten by an infected sand fly. The sores may be painless, and they may or may not scab over. Untreated sores can last from weeks to years and develop into prominent craters on the skin. Anyone who suspects an infection should see a tropical-medicine specialist for diagnosis and treatment.

American Trypanosomiasis (Chagas' Disease)

Chagas' disease is a parasitic infection carried by triatomine bugs (blood-sucking insects sometimes known as the assassin, cone nose, or kissing bug). The parasite, *Trypanosoma cruzi*, often produces a small sore at the point where it enters the body. If this happens around the eye, the eyelid may become swollen. Other symptoms can include a fever and swollen lymph nodes, but infection can be asymptomatic. There is no vaccine against the disease. Those who suspect they might be infected should see a tropical-medicine specialist for diagnosis and treatment. Chronic infections can cause damage to the heart and intestines and even death.

It's rare for travelers to contract Chagas' disease, in Panama or anywhere else. The bugs tend to infest ramshackle buildings made of palm thatch, mud, or adobe, especially those with lots of nooks and crannies in the walls and roof. The disease can also be spread through transfusions of blood that has not been screened for the parasite.

Panama has found about 500 cases of Chagas' disease in the entire country in the last 25 years, and the Pan American Health Organization has noted a marked decline in the presence of the disease since 1993. Central Panama seems more vulnerable to the disease than other parts of the country.

RABIES

The chance of catching rabies is remote, but the consequences of doing so are extreme. There is no cure for rabies, and it's fatal. Only one person in history has ever recovered from a full-blown case of rabies: a girl who was bitten by a bat in the rural United States in late 2004 and treated with a bold experimental technique that could easily have killed her.

Rabies is almost always transmitted by an animal bite. Any mammal can be a carrier, but in Central America one should be particularly wary of vampire bats, feral or aggressive dogs and cats, and monkeys.

In Panama, most cases of rabies in humans are

caused by bat bites. In 2002, a 69-year-old woman and her daughter, residents of the community of San Juan Demóstenes Arosemena in Colón province, died from rabies after being bitten by a vampire bat. The last confirmed rabies cases before that occurred in 1995, again from bat bites.

The CDC recommends rabies vaccines for travelers to Latin America who expect to spend considerable time outdoors in rural areas at night or in the evening, even if the trip is brief. This is especially true for those who like to explore caves.

Anyone bitten or scratched by an animal should immediately wash the wound with plenty of soap and water and iodine, if available. Don't panic: most suspect mammals, even violent ones, do *not* have rabies. The animal should be captured—if possible to do so without risking further attacks—and taken to a medical center for testing. Those potentially exposed to rabies need a series of shots, usually given over the course of a month. This is true even if the victim has had a pre-exposure rabies vaccine. The recommended series of injections these days are no more painful than flu shots. Prompt treatment after exposure can nearly always prevent rabies infection.

Most people bitten by vampire bats do not realize it at the time. The bat usually approaches its victims at night, while they're sleeping (yes, just like in all those B-movies). It lands next to the victim and waddles over to a vulnerable spot. The bat drools onto the site before biting it. The saliva contains an anesthetic and an anticoagulant that lets the bat bite its victim without waking it and lap up the blood that trickles steadily out. Human victims generally don't discover they've been bitten until the next morning, when they find a clump of dried blood near the wound site.

Disgusting? You bet. That's why I recommend travelers sleep only in a tent or screened-in room in rural areas, including beaches and forests. This is especially true around cattle, a favorite blood supply for vampire bats.

An experienced naturalist guide I know was bitten by a vampire bat during a Darién trek a few years ago. It was a hot night, and he left a small opening in his tent. That was all the bat needed. My friend got his round of shots and spent an unpleasant month waiting to see if he'd die. Luckily, he didn't.

"Endemic zones" for rabies in Panama include Chilibre, eastern Panama province, La Chorrera, the Darién, the district of David in western Panama, and various spots along the Interamerican Highway.

Symptoms of rabies include paralysis, spasms of the swallowing muscles in the presence of water (hydrophobia), delirium, and convulsions, followed by coma and death.

STOMACH AILMENTS

Gastrointestinal complaints such as dysentery, giardia, E. coli infections, and even so-called "traveler's diarrhea" are far less common among travelers to Panama than in most parts of Latin America.

It's safe to drink water out of the tap almost everywhere in the country. The destination chapters alert you to the few places where that still wasn't a good idea at the time of writing, such as some parts of the Darién and Bocas del Toro. Never drink untreated water from a stream or lake, no matter how pristine it looks.

Hygiene standards in restaurants tend to be fairly high, particularly in Panama City. You're unlikely to get so much as a stomachache. But if a place looks dirty or unpopular, you're probably better off going elsewhere. Street-vendor fare is somewhat riskier. Make sure whatever you munch has just been fried at high temperature. It's not a good idea to eat ice cream and other milk- or water-based sweets sold by street vendors.

The CDC warns that certain fish and shellfish served in tropical countries can contain biotoxins even when well cooked. Barracuda has the highest level of these toxins and should always be avoided. Other possibilities include red snapper and sea bass. I've never heard of anyone in Panama being poisoned by these delicious fish, but if you experience stomach distress accompanied by a sudden change of temperature, weakness, or other unusual symptoms after eating fish, get medical help.

Mild traveler's diarrhea doesn't usually need to be treated with anything more than fluids, rest, and a modest diet of bland foods. Anything more serious, such as bacterial or amoebic dysentery, needs to be treated with drugs and requires a visit to the doctor.

HANTAVIRUS

There was an outbreak of hantavirus pulmonary syndrome in Las Tablas and Guararé in Los Santos province in late 1999 and early 2000 that infected a dozen people and left 3 dead. It forced the cancellation of the Carnaval celebration in Las Tablas that year. Panama's biggest Carnaval is held in Las Tablas, and the cancellation was a major blow to the local economy.

Hantavirus is an infectious disease most often spread through the inhalation of particles from the feces, urine, or saliva of infected rodents. However, person-to-person infection is also possible. The disease is characterized by fever, headache, and muscle pain followed by hypotension, shock, difficulty breathing, and pulmonary edema (fluid in the lungs). It's a serious disease and the fatality rate can be above 50 percent. There is no treatment, cure, or vaccine. However, getting health care immediately, especially oxygen therapy, greatly increases one's chance of recovery. Anyone who has been around rodents and experiences shortness of breath and fever should tell a doctor immediately.

Hantavirus was first discovered in the Four Corners region of the western United States in 1993, and before the Las Tablas outbreak it had not been diagnosed in Central America. A major public-health push, in coordination with the U.S. Centers for Disease Control, appears to have largely contained the disease so far, though officials remain vigilant about the possibility of a major flare-up, especially around Carnaval time. In 2003, there were five more cases, in Los Santos and Veraguas provinces. Two were fatal. Three more cases appeared in Los Santos in 2004 near Carnaval time, but the celebration was not canceled that year.

The chance of contracting hantavirus are exceedingly low, especially for those who avoid contact with rodents. Mice and rats infest some lodgings in the Panamanian countryside, especially the cheaper places. It's probably worth splurging for better digs in Los Santos province, since that's where the disease erupted in Panama. Rats are a fact of life in Kuna Yala, unfortunately, and it's not unusual to hear them rustling in the rafters of tourist huts or running along the beach at night. Clean up messes and keep all food packed away at night.

SEXUALLY TRANSMITTED DISEASES

Panama has an estimated 30,000 people living with HIV, which, given the country's small population, gives it the third-highest rate in Central America. HIV in Panama is more often transmitted through heterosexual than homosexual sex. According to a United Nations agency in Panama, HIV rates have skyrocketed 500 percent in the last decade. At the current rate of increase, HIV is expected to infect 2 percent of the population by 2010.

The sexually adventurous should also remember that other STDs are serious and not necessarily easily treatable. An antibiotic-resistant strain of gonorrhea, for instance, is on the rise around the world.

Those who want to experiment should at lest be sure to get a hepatitis B vaccination and always use condoms and other safer-sex methods.

OTHER DISEASES

Panama has seen flare-ups of viral meningitis, pertussis (whooping cough), and tuberculosis in recent years, but travelers are at little risk of contracting them.

SUN

Remember that Panama is just eight degrees north of the equator, and it's easy to get sunburned amazingly fast. Pale northerners have been known to get a nasty sunburn after just a half hour out in the noonday sun. Try to stay in the shade between noon and about 3 P.M. Don't be fooled by mild or cloudy days. Even if you don't feel hot, ultraviolet rays are frying you. Always wear sunscreen. Be especially careful when out on the water, which reflects sunrays like a mirror. (Ever had a chin burn?) Sunglasses and a hat are also a good idea. Drink lots of waters to avoid dehydration even when it feels humid.

OCEAN DANGERS

A rip current, sometimes erroneously referred to as an "undertow," is created when surf gets trapped on its way back out to sea, often by a sandbar. Pressure builds up until a concentrated stream of water rips a hole in the sandbar and water surges back out in a narrow channel, sometimes at impressive speed. It's similar in effect to pulling the plug on a bathroom drain.

Be on the lookout for patches of muddy, dark, or disturbed water, which can indicate a rip. If you feel yourself being pulled out to sea, don't panic and don't try to fight against the current—it's stronger than you are. Instead, swim with the current but try to veer off at a 45-degree angle to it. Contrary to popular belief, rip currents don't drag swimmers under or sweep them out to sea. They are typically short and narrow and swimmers should be able to swim out of the channel fairly quickly. Tired or poor swimmers should just float with the current until it weakens, then swim parallel to shore to escape it. Stay calm and conserve your strength. Once you escape the rip current, swim back to shore.

Panamanians often prefer to bathe along stretches of beach with muddy sand and little surf, knowing from experience how powerful those majestic, rolling waves on the picture postcard beaches can be. Waves can get enormous on some of Panama's beaches and give swimmers a real pounding. Use common sense and don't wade in past your shins when the surf is high, and look out for hidden rocks and reefs.

Shark attacks are highly unlikely, particularly in the Caribbean. The Pacific sea snake is one of the most toxic creatures in the world, but the chances of coming across one are slim—I've only ever seen one in all my years of swimming in

Panama, and it was dead, washed up on the shore. Barracudas may be scary-looking, but they're not generally aggressive toward humans. However, do not wear shiny jewelry while swimming or diving. The flash of the sun off jewelry looks to a barracuda like the scales of a fish, and they may dart in the direction of it.

Look out for sea urchins and fire coral, and never touch any other kind of coral; it'll scrape you up and cause serious damage to the coral. Shuffle your feet on entering or exiting the water to avoid stepping on a hidden ray.

HYPOTHERMIA

The chance of contracting hypothermia in a tropical country such as Panama may seem slim, but it can get quite chilly in the highlands, even in the Darién, something not all travelers are prepared for. Do not go hiking in the highlands, particularly around Volcán Barú, in just shorts and a T-shirt. It can get down to freezing at the top of Barú even when it's sweltering hot far down the volcano. Bring warm, waterproof clothing to change into if it gets wet and chilly, which it often does.

Hypothermia is caused by a drop in the body's core temperature, so it's possibly to become hypothermic even in milder conditions. To avoid hypothermia, stay dry, dress warmly, avoid alcohol and rapid changes of temperature, and drink lots of water.

Early warning signs of hypothermia include loss of coordination, inability to concentrate, and involuntary shivering. If the afflicted person continues to shiver even when bundled up, the hypothermia is more serious.

WILD ANIMALS

Almost every hiker new to the tropics worries about snakes. As has been mentioned several times throughout the book, it's rare to come across a snake while hiking and extremely rare to be bothered by one. The chances of coming across one near any population center are even smaller, partly because Panamanians are aggressive about exterminating snakes in their midst. However, be cautious around leaf and trash piles even in the cities, just in case.

There are several things hikers can do to make it even less likely they'll be bothered by a slithering critter.

First, be careful stepping over tree falls, which attract snakes (not to mention stinging insects). Also be careful around piles of dried leaves. Before gathering any to start a fire, shuffle boot-clad feet through them.

This should go without saying, but don't play with snakes in the tropics. Some people seem irresistibly drawn to disturbing the creatures, which usually just want to be left alone. A European tourist I was hiking with in the Darién once tried to use his walking stick to prod a baby fer-de-lance we came across. The fer-de-lance is a deadly pit viper, and even the babies can be lethal. They can also be extremely aggressive and quick when disturbed. The guide and I managed to save the guy from his foolish, possibly suicidal, curiosity.

In the extremely unlikely event of being bitten, try not to panic. All that accomplishes is to increase one's heart rate and pump any injected venom faster through one's system. Poisonous snakes don't always inject venom when they strike. Obviously, get to the nearest hospital as soon as possible. If possible without risking further bites, kill the snake and take it with you to be identified. Do not try slashing at the wound and sucking out the poison, as usually this is ineffective and can actually make things worse. Keep the site of the wound below the heart and head if possible.

Do not feed, tease, or get too close to monkeys. Some can be aggressive if they feel threatened and fling feces, bite, or otherwise attack. If bitten by a monkey, get medical help immediately. They can carry rabies and other nasty diseases.

Peccaries, a kind of wild pig, are a concern in the more remote forests, particularly in the Darién. Because their natural predator, the jaguar, has been hunted to near extinction, peccary populations have exploded in some areas. They sometimes descend on a spot by the hundreds and tear everything up. They can run surprisingly fast and have fearsomely sharp teeth. Those un-

lucky enough to get in the path of a herd should climb the nearest tall tree and stay there until they move on.

TRAFFIC ACCIDENTS

Traffic accidents pose by far the greatest hazard for visitors to Panama. Traffic in Panama tends to be chaotic, road conditions poor, and enforcement of driving laws lax. About one person a day is killed on the roads, which is a lot for a country of less than 3 million people, many of whom don't have cars. Be alert at all times on the road, and if you're a passenger don't be shy about asking a speeding driver to slow down.

If you're involved in an accident, do not move the cars—it's against the law. Stay on the scene until the *tránsito* (transit police) arrive. If someone is injured or it's otherwise an emergency, call the police emergency number (104) or the fire department (103). Once the *tránsito* arrive they'll fill out a report that will include your description of the accident. Be fully cooperative and polite. Contact your insurance company or the car-rental agency as soon as possible.

Panamanian attitudes toward safety in general tend to be far more relaxed than those in, say, Northern Europe and North America. Accidents, including traffic accidents, are the second leading cause of death in Panama, after cancer.

LOCAL DOCTORS, CLINICS, AND HOSPITALS

Panama has world-class medical facilities and doctors, many of whom were trained in the United States and speak English. Even those without medical insurance can receive good care for far less than it would cost them in the United States. It's possible to get a checkup from, say, a specialist trained at Johns Hopkins for about $35.

The best medical facilities are in Panama City. See that chapter for more information. The hospitals in David are also reputed to be good, though I have no personal experience with them. See the Golfo de Chiriquí chapter for information.

Note: U.S. Medicare does not cover medical care outside the United States.

Condoms and other non-prescription means of birth control are available at pharmacies. To avoid a visit to a local doctor, those taking birth-control pills should being a sufficient supply to last while visiting Panama.

Centros de Salud (health centers) and small rural hospitals are scattered throughout the country, though they can be poorly staffed and equipped. Serious medical problems should be treated in Panama City if at all possible. Those planning adventurous travel in remote spots may want to consider buying travel insurance that includes emergency evacuation provisions. I strongly advise all travelers to buy at least basic travel insurance.

ILLEGAL DRUGS

Panama is famous for its marijuana (e.g., the "Panama Red" of hippie anthems) and notorious as a transshipment point for cocaine. Don't let that fool you into thinking the consumption of illegal drugs is treated casually in Panama. If you're caught you could very well find yourself spending years in a squalid, overcrowded prison.

Simple possession of even a small amount of marijuana or any other drug is punishable by a minimum of one year in prison. Those caught with more than a tiny bit of a drug are assumed to be trafficking in it, and punishment is correspondingly harsh. Anyone caught buying or selling drugs is looking at 5 to 10 years behind bars.

Dealers have been known to set up gullible tourists for a bust, sometimes in the hope of sharing a bribe with a corrupt cop. Resist all temptations to sample the local products. It's an extremely foolish risk to take.

CRIME

Panama is by and large a peaceful, mellow place despite its undeserved reputation as some sort of danger zone. You'll likely be safer in Panama City than you would in any city of comparable size back home. Violent crime against tourists and affluent Panamanians is still so unusual that when it does happen it's huge news and causes lots of local hand-wringing about the decline of Panamanian society.

Property theft and other kinds of non-violent crime are the main concern for the haves, and even this is mainly a problem for those who live in the cities, not travelers.

However, extreme unemployment and poverty make Colón, historically Panama's second most important city, unsafe for any outsider. There's an excellent chance of getting mugged if you wander around here. Avoid that city altogether for the foreseeable future.

Even in Panama City, avoid the poorest neighborhoods, such as El Chorrillo and Curundu, and be alert in transitional ones, such as the historic Casco Viejo area.

Because of reports of robberies at the secluded Madden Dam (on Lago Alajuela), I do not recommend that travelers visit it even in groups. I have also heard the occasional unconfirmed report of robberies in the national parks around Panama City, but this does not yet appear to be a major problem. Just do not hike alone, which is never a good idea anyway.

Rural areas are generally quite safe, but do not leave valuables even in a locked car when going for a hike in remote spots.

As tourism increases, it's probably inevitable that scams and crimes against tourists will increase as well. I've been hearing more reports lately of thefts from beaches while tourists are out swimming or surfing. These generally occur at the more popular surfing spots, such as the north side of Bastimentos in Boca del Toro. Again, this is not a major problem, at least not yet, and even the "scams" usually amount to being overcharged for a taxi ride or taken to a hotel one is not interested in. Be alert and use common sense when traveling in the relatively more touristed parts of Panama.

Information and Services

MONEY

Panama's currency is the balboa. The balboa's rate of exchange has always been tied to the dollar, with one dollar equal to one balboa. In fact, Panama does not print paper money, so the U.S. dollar is legal tender in Panama. Panamanian coins (one-, five-, 10-, 25-, and 50-cent pieces) are the same size, weight, and color as the U.S. ones and are used interchangeably with them. The only difference is what is printed on the faces; except for the one-centavo coin and special-edition coins, heads is always a portrait of Balboa and tails is always the shield of Panama. The one-centavo coin has Urracá, a fierce indigenous chief who won many battles against the conquistadors. You may see prices quoted with either a "B/" or "$" before them. Both mean the same thing.

Despite Panama's status as a world banking capital, it's tough to exchange foreign currencies almost everywhere in Panama. Try to bring only dollars to Panama.

Changing Money

Those who can't avoid changing money in Panama have only a few options. One is the branch of Banco Nacional de Panamá in Tocumen International Airport (6 A.M. to 1 P.M. daily). Another is Pancambios (Vía España, tel. 223-1800, 8 A.M.–5 P.M. Mon.–Fri.), a small office in central Panama City tucked at the back of the Plaza Regency next to Plaza Concordia. It exchanges Costa Rican colones, euros, British pounds, and Canadian dollars for U.S. dollars. Panama City's main Western Union office is down the street from Pancambios in the Plaza Concordia shopping complex (Vía España, tel. 800-2224, 8 A.M.–8 P.M. Mon.–Sat., 10 A.M.– 5 P.M. Sun.). It exchanges Latin American currencies only.

There's a roaming money changer on the streets of the Panama/Costa Rican border crossing at Paso Canoa who exchanges dollars and colones.

Banks

Banks are generally open from 8 A.M. to 2 or 3 P.M. weekdays, 9 A.M. to noon on Saturdays. ATMs are located throughout Panama and are by far the easiest way to access cash; look for red signs that read *Sistema Clave*. Some find service at the state-run Banco Nacional de Panamá (BNP) to be slower and more bureaucratic than at private banks, but BNP is sometimes the only option in more remote areas.

Financial Services

Panama's extensive financial services sector is focused on offshore banking, not serving short-term visitors. Try not to get involved with bank transfers and such during your stay, as it'll most likely be an expensive exercise in bureaucratic frustration. For those who must wire money to or from Panama, the best option is to use Western Union or Moneygram, which have many outlets throughout the country.

Travelers Checks

Travelers checks are difficult to cash in Panama. Merchants are reluctant to accept them since banks, unconscionably, treat them as foreign checks and put a 45-day hold on them before the merchants' accounts get credited. Meanwhile, since of course travelers checks are essentially cash, the banks rake in interest on the "float." Banking reforms may have changed this unfair practice by the time you visit, but travelers checks are generally more nuisance than they are worth. The Banco Nacional de Panamá is often the only place one can cash them. Trying to cash anything other than American Express checks is even more difficult. Given the ubiquity of ATMs, it's better to rely on cash cards than travelers checks in Panama. It's still a good idea, however, to bring some travelers checks as a backup, or as way to prove economic solvency when crossing borders.

Credit Cards

Credit cards are widely accepted in the cities, especially in the more upscale hotels and restaurants and most stores of any size. Visa and Mastercard are the most widely accepted. Other cards can generally only be used in the most cosmopolitan establishments, such as five-star hotels. Simpler hotels and restaurants are often cash only, as are most personal services (taxis, tour guides, small outfitters, etc). The farther away one gets from an urban center, the less likely it is credit cards will be accepted. Bring lots of small bills to more remote parts of Panama, such as the Comarca de Kuna Yala (San Blas Islands), where credit cards are not accepted and larger denominations are hard to break. Casinos can be a good place to break larger bills. Some businesses in Bocas del Toro still impose a surcharge on credit-card purchases; ask ahead of time.

Taxes and Tipping

A 10-percent tourism tax is added to hotel room bills. Room prices quoted in this book include the tax unless specified. Panama sales tax is 5 percent. The departure tax for those leaving the country is $20. For those flying out of the country, it is now generally included in the price of the air ticket.

It's customary to tip 10 percent in restaurants. Bellhops, porters, and others who perform special services should be tipped. How much to tip depends on the service and the discretion of the tipper. Anywhere from $.25 to $1 should do it for minor services. Porters at the international airport expect a buck a bag. Taxi drivers do not expect a tip.

In rural areas, park rangers and other workers sometimes provide guide services, cook food, tote luggage, etc., for campers and hikers. It's good karma to tip at least $5 a day for these services on top of the camping or transportation fees.

Bargaining and Discounts

Haggling is not the norm in Panama. It's sometimes possible to get a slight break on major purchases, such as expensive electronics, or on handicrafts, such as *molas,* but don't expect much. Crafts sellers will sometimes start out with an inflated price but they quickly come down to a firm offer and are unlikely to budge. It's always worth seeing if there's some kind of *descuento* (discount), though. There may be a price break

for buying more than one item; those willing to buy two or more *molas,* for instance, can sometimes get a break.

Senior and student discounts are generally only available to Panamanians and resident expatriates, not visitors. In fact, in some places, such as the national parks, there is a two-tier system of fees, with foreigners expected to pay more than residents. It may be possible to get a student or senior discount at museums and the like, though the entrance fee is usually so small to begin with it's probably not worth bothering with.

MAPS

Good tourist maps of Panama and Panama City are hard to come by. Every issue of the freebie tourist magazine "Focus Panama" contains foldout maps of the country, Panama City, Colón, and David. The city maps aren't terribly detailed, but they can be useful. The magazine is widely distributed to hotels, restaurants, and shops frequented by tourists.

The best country map of Panama is a 1:800,000-scale one published by **International Travel Maps and Books** (ITMB), in Vancouver, Canada. It also contains insert maps of the Panama Canal area and central Panama City. The city map is not very detailed, and anyone planning to explore the city in depth will find it of limited use. The entire map is also getting out of date and does contain some errors, particularly in the Darién.

Those planning to drive around the country will find the map indispensable, however. Make sure to get the most recent, fourth edition, published in 2001. The map can be ordered through the company directly if you can't find one at your local travel bookstore or map shop. In Panama it is available in stores frequented by tourists, including some Panama City bookstores. ITMB is working on a new 1:500,000-scale map of the country that may be finished by the time you're ready to travel. Contact ITMB at 530 W. Broadway, Vancouver, Canada V5Z 1E9, tel. 604/879-3621, itmb@itmb.com, www.itmb.com.

Other maps of various quality are available in Panama, especially Panama City. Best bets in

Panama City include Exedra Books, Libreria Argosy, and El Hombre de la Mancha bookstores, Farmacia Arrocha drugstores, or Gran Morrison department-store outlets.

The **Instituto Geográfico Nacional Tommy Guardia** (Vía Simon Bolívar/Transístmica, tel. 236-2444 or 236-1844, fax 235-1841, www.mop.gob.pa, 8 A.M.–3:30 P.M. Mon.–Fri.) in Panama City sells a wide variety of physical, political, and topographical maps of the country, including a nine-sheet 1:12,500 scale map just of Panama City. The prices are low, but most of its maps are too large and detailed to be of use to most visitors. Many of the more popular maps, including ones of central Panama City, are frequently unavailable. It doesn't sell tourist maps. The place is affectionately known as "Tommy Guardia" and most taxi drivers should know it. It's on the north side of the Transístmica directly across the street from the Universidad de Panamá. The **Islamorada Internacional** store in Balboa is an excellent resource for those who need nautical charts. See the Panama City chapter for details.

TOURIST INFORMATION

Large-scale tourism is still a new concept for Panama, and getting good, accurate, and current tourist information in the country is not always easy. Take everything you read and hear with a grain of salt, as much of the material out there is more interested in promoting tourism and selling real estate than giving balanced information.

The best way to get current information on Panama before a trip is through the Internet. A good place to start is www.panamainfo.com, an enthusiastically pro-Panama-tourism site that consistently has the most up-to-date information of any of the overview sites. It's written in both English and Spanish. Panama's government tourism sites are www.visitpanama.com and www.ipat.gob.pa. They contain some useful information, such as an updated schedule of festivals and holidays. For other websites, including umbrella sites for particular regions, see Resources.

The Panamanian newspaper with the best and most extensive coverage of tourist destinations

and promotional deals is La Prensa, a daily widely available throughout the country. It has a good website that gives free access to most of its content, including its archives: www.prensa.com.

Panama's government tourism agency, the Instituto Panameño de Turismo (Panamanian Tourism Institute), widely known as IPAT (EE-pot), has long had a reputation for providing little actual information to tourists. Each change of government brings new optimism that IPAT will be galvanized into action, usually with mixed results at best. What will happen under the new Torrijos regime will probably take a couple of years to figure out, but one of its first acts when it took power was the rather bold move to appoint the internationally famous salsa star and actor Rubén Blades to head the institute (Torrijos and Blades are chums).

IPAT has both small information booths and massive tourist-information complexes known as CEFATIs (*Centro de Facilidades Turisticas e Interpretación*, which roughly translates to tourist and interpretative centers) dotted around the country. These sometimes have minimally informative printed information, but the attendants often know surprisingly little about the area's attractions and rarely speak anything other than Spanish. CEFATIs are sometimes worth a visit for their displays on the history and culture of the given area.

IPAT's administrative headquarters is in the Atlapa Convention Center next to the Hotel Caesar Park off Vía Israel, but they're not really set up to deal with actual visitors. Their contact information is: Instituto Panameño de Turismo, Centro de Convenciones Atlapa, Vía Israel, San Francisco, Apdo. 4421, Zona 5, Panama, Republic of Panama, tel. 800/231-0568 or 866/9-PANAMA (in the United States or Canada), tel. 800-IPAT (in Panama), infotur@ns.ipat.gob.pa.

Film and Photography

Good quality cameras are widely available around Panama, particularly Panama City. Don't expect great deals, though—the equipment is probably at least as expensive as it is back home. Good places to shop for photo equipment in Panama City are the walking section of Avenida Central, along Vía España, and at the huge Panafoto store on

Calle 50. The latter is also a good bet for photo processing. It's not worth shopping for photo equipment in the Colón Free Zone unless you're in the market for a dozen cameras or so. Film is easy to come by; try any of the pharmacy chains, such as the omnipresent Farmacia Arrocha.

Bring a couple of large, sturdy plastic bags to wrap the camera in to protect it from Panama's sudden torrential downpours and sloshing from boat trips, as well as sand and salt near the ocean. The country's heat and humidity are hard on cameras and film; try to keep them in as cool a place as possible. Also, allow time for the camera to adjust from the air-conditioned indoors to the steamy outdoors.

Disposable cameras are widely available, waterproof disposable cameras less so. Bring a disposable underwater camera or a waterproof case from home if you expect to spend much time snorkeling or diving; the photo possibilities can be spectacular.

Always ask permission before taking someone's picture. Snapping away at a "colorful local" is a good way to offend someone's dignity. Do not take photos of police or sensitive government installations. See the Kuna Yala chapter for information on taking photos of Kunas.

The light is usually best in the early morning and late afternoon, but the sun rises and sets fast near the equator so work quickly. The scenery can get washed out by the sun around midday.

COMMUNICATIONS AND MEDIA

Panama has a relatively free and aggressive press, certainly in comparison with the days of the military dictatorship, which controlled and censored the press either directly or through intimidation and violence. But Panama continues to be widely criticized for restrictive and antiquated laws that, for instance, make it a criminal offense for a journalist to "insult" public officials, even if the criticism is factually accurate. Newspaper reporters, TV journalists, and editorial cartoonists continue to be arrested and fined for these and other "offenses." While jour-

nalists are usually released quickly, international press-freedom organizations have denounced the laws and worry about the chilling effect it has on the media. Physical attacks, threats, and harassment of journalists sometimes occur as well. Despite new transparency laws, it remains difficult for journalists to get access to many government documents and records that are publicly available in other countries.

As in the United States and elsewhere, there is also concern about concentration of media ownership in the hands of a powerful few, including those with their own political agendas.

Newspapers

Panama has an abundance of Spanish-language daily newspapers, all headquartered in Panama City but most of which are widely available throughout the country. Panama's various news outlets tend to have allegiances to parties, political stances, and families, which can color what they cover and how they cover it.

The best of the bunch is La Prensa, which is comparable to a major U.S. daily. It has a bewildering array of weekly supplements, on everything from fashion to health, and does the best job of any paper in covering tourism and other topics likely to be of interest to visitors. El Panamá América or La Estrella de Panamá are fallbacks if La Prensa is sold out. Panama also has popular tabloids, notably La Crítica and El Siglo, which specialize in gory, sensationalist crime stories and inflammatory political topics.

Sadly, Panama's one remaining English-language newspaper, the muckraking Panama News, is no longer available on the newsstands except for occasional special editions. But it survives on the Internet as a labor of love by its gadfly editor, Eric Jackson (www.thepanamanews.com). A newer English-language news site is the Isthmian (www.isthmian.net), edited by Okke Ornstein, a Dutch expatriate who, like Jackson, delights in taking on controversial topics and butchering sacred cows. He really lets loose in his rather profane online newsletter, Noriegaville (www.ornstein.org).

There are also three well-established Chinese-language newspapers that cater to those in the large Chinese immigrant population who haven't lost their ancestral tongue.

Television and Radio

For years Panama had just two television stations: RPC (channel 4) and TVN (channel 2), as well as the U.S. armed forces station (SCN, channel 8 on the Pacific side of the isthmus, and channel 11 on the Caribbean side). The armed forces stations disappeared with the closing of the American bases, but several other networks, including Telemetro (channel 13, which is owned by the company that owns RPC) have popped up in recent years. The entire country is increasingly plugging into "cable" television—actually satellite TV—through DirecTV and the plethora of Spanish- and English-language stations it offers.

The country's airwaves are crammed with the sounds of radio stations, most offering típico, Latin pop, and mainstream American rock. There's not a single one I can recommend these days.

Telephone Services

The country code for Panama is 507. Do not dial 507 when making calls within the country. Cellular phone numbers generally begin with the number "6." These can be more expensive to call, but they're often the best way to contact someone.

The emergency number for the police (*policía nacional*) is 104. The emergency number for the fire department (*bomberos*) is 103. In smaller communities, these numbers don't always work; you have to dial a local number instead. Ask a resident or call directory assistance for help. Directory assistance (*asistencia al directorio*) is 102. The national operator can be reached at 101. To reach the international operator, dial 106.

There is no true "911"-type emergency response for medical emergencies. There are private-ambulance services, however. The two major ones in Panama City are SEMM (tel. 264-4122 for emergencies) and Alerta (tel. 269-9778 or 800-0911 for emergencies).

Pay phones pop up in the most unlikely places, including dirt-poor villages and islands in the middle of nowhere. Long-distance calls within the country generally cost no more than 15 cents

per minute. Instructions on using modern pay phones are in English and several other languages, but finding one that actually works can sometimes be a problem. Also, many of these phones accept only prepaid calling cards.

Panama's main telephone service provider, Cable and Wireless (C&W), sells two different kinds of "Telechip" prepaid phone cards. One is a stored-value card that contains a computer chip and only works with specially designed public telephones that have a slot to receive the cards. The cards come in denominations of $3, $5, $10, and $20. The "Telechip Total" card instead uses a coded number and can be used in any phone, making it far more flexible. It's especially useful in remote parts of Panama, where coin-operated pay phones are rarely emptied and can become choked with coins, making them impossible to call out on except with a phone card. The Telechip Total card comes in the same denominations as the regular Telechip cards, except for an additional $1 card. Both kinds of cards are sold in C&W offices around the country, as well as in vending machines outside many of the offices, and in some stores (look for signs or stickers on storefronts). A recently introduced "Telechip Internacional" is the same as the Telechip Total card, but it has better rates for international calls. It comes in denominations of $5, $10, and $20. Note that both the Telechip Total and Telechip Internacional expire within 15-60 days. Higher denominations generally last longer, but the international card has a lower overall lifespan.

Some Internet cafés offer international calling and fax services. Calls can be quite reasonable (e.g., $.15 per minute to the United States) but check carefully before sending or receiving a fax. International fax service isn't that common at most of these places, and the charges can be steep, especially to send. It's not unusual to be charged $1 a page to receive and up to $5 a page to send, plus international dialing charges. The high-end hotels tend to have business centers with computer and phone services.

The international access code for placing direct calls from Panama is "00" followed by the country code. The country code for the continental United

States or Canada is 1, the United Kingdom is 44, Spain is 34, Germany is 49, France is 33, Australia is 61, Costa Rica is 506, Nicaragua is 505, Colombia is 57, and Mexico is 52. Check a local phone book or call the international operator (106) for other access codes and for help making a call.

Mail Service

Mail between Panama and other countries is not too speedy. A postcard sent from Panama takes at least five to 10 days to reach the United States, longer to more distant destinations. Postcards to the United States cost $.25. Airmail letters weighing up to 20 grams (0.7 ounces) cost $.35. Add $.05 to the above for Canada addresses, $.10 for European ones, and $.15 for addresses in Asia, Africa, and Oceania. Some of the more expensive hotels sell stamps. Note that bulky packages sent to or from Panama sometimes get "lost" in the mail.

Do not put cellophane (Scotch) tape on envelopes; the post office may refuse to accept it, or return international mail that has tape on it. One explanation I've heard for this strange rule is that it discourages thieves from opening mail and then resealing the envelope to hide the crime.

Post office hours are generally 7 A.M. to 6 P.M. weekdays, 7 A.M. to 5 P.M. Saturday. Post offices are closed on Sunday.

Another oddity about mail in Panama is there is no home delivery; even in modern Panama City, everyone must have mail sent to an *apartado postal* (post-office box). Frustrations with slow and sometimes unreliable postal service has driven many who can afford it to subscribe to private mail and courier services, some of which are only slightly more satisfying.

There are a number of international mailing and shipping stores in Panama City. Mail Boxes Etc. has outlets around the city, including one at Vía España and Calle 61 and one in the Albrook Mall next to the Gran Terminal de Transportes. They also have fax services.

Internet Access

Internet cafés are increasingly common in Panama. You will have little trouble finding one in the cities, and they're beginning to pop up in

fairly remote areas as well. Charges are rarely more than a dollar or two an hour, often less. Most of these cafés use Windows-based machines. Macintoshes are sometimes available as well.

WEIGHTS AND MEASURES

Panama uses the metric system, though auto fuel is sold by the gallon, and pounds, inches, and feet are still sometimes used interchangeably with their metric equivalents.

Electricity

Panama's voltage is almost universally the same as it is in the United States: 110 volts. Sockets are two-pronged, and U.S. appliances don't need an adapter. There are still a few remote places that use 220 volts, however, so if there's any doubt, ask before plugging in. Note that short blackouts and power surges are common in Panama. Those traveling with sensitive equipment, such as a laptop computer, may want to bring a surge suppresser.

Time Zone

Panama is on Eastern Standard Time. (There is no daylight savings time in Panama, so the time difference with U.S. destinations changes by an hour during daylight savings time in the United States.) Put another way, Panama time is five hours behind Greenwich mean time. Panama is always one hour ahead of Costa Rica, something to remember when crossing the border.

HOLIDAYS

If you are in Panama around Christmas, New Year's, Carnaval, Semana Santa (the week leading up to Easter), or the November independence holidays, be prepared for celebrations and business closures even on days that are not officially listed as holidays. Also note that when holidays fall on a weekday they are often celebrated on a Monday to create a long weekend. From October through November every city, town, and tiny village has a drum corps and marching band that practices incessantly. Some will find the incessant drumming colorful. Others will find it maddening.

Check with IPAT (see Tourist Information) for exact dates of holidays that change yearly, and for a current list of the many other festivals, fairs, religious observances, and regional celebrations that take place somewhere in the country just about every week. The major national holidays are:

• January 1st: *Año Nuevo* (New Year's Day)
• January 9th: *Día de los Mártires* (Martyr's Day)
• The four days leading up to Ash Wednesday: *Carnavales* (Carnival)
• Friday before Easter Sunday: *Viernes Santo* (Good Friday)
• May 1st: *Día del Trabajo* (Worker's Day)
• November 3rd: *Separación de Panamá de Colombia* (Independence from Colombia)
• November 4th: *Día Nacional de la Bandera* (Flag Day)
• November 10th: *Primer Grito de Independencia de España* (First Call for Independence from Spain)
• November 28th: *Independencia de Panamá de España* (Independence from Spain)
• December 8th: *Día de Las Madres* (Mothers' Day)
• December 25th: *Navidad* (Christmas)

WHAT TO BRING

See the *Discover Panama* chapter for general tips on appropriate clothing for Panama. A good pair of binoculars adds a lot to any nature trip, especially for those with the slightest interest in spotting birds. They should be fairly powerful and have a wide aperture—binoculars with a narrow aperture make spotting creatures far too difficult. The minimum usually recommended by naturalist guides is 7x32, with "7" being the power and "32" the aperture.

If you forget something, it's easy to find just about anything vital in Panama, especially Panama City. The kiosks around the Terraplén in Casco Viejo are a good bet for army-surplus boots and other rugged gear.

Suggested General Gear List

1. Raingear. A lightweight poncho is good for hiking and boat trips, especially if it rains. Bring a small, collapsible umbrella for the cities.
2. A hat, preferably with a wide brim to cover the neck and a some means of keeping it from blowing off in a boat or high wind, such as a cord with a clamp.
3. Warm-weather clothes should be loose, thin cotton or moisture-wicking, quick-drying artificial fabric. Jeans are popular in Panama, but many visitors will find them hot, and they're slow to dry if they get wet.
4. For forest hikes, bring at least one set of khaki, green, or gray clothing. White and bright colors scare off wildlife.
5. Bring at least one long-sleeved shirt to ward off mosquitoes and sun. Bring long pants for the same reason, and to look respectable in populated areas away from the beach.
6. A warm, semi-dressy jacket, sweater, or shawl can be useful in city restaurants and shops, where air-conditioning is often set at Arctic temperatures.
7. Shorts should be at least medium-length.
8. Bathing suit. Women should bring a thigh-length bikini wrap of some kind to cover up upon leaving the beach.
9. Cargo pants, especially ones with legs that zip off to convert to shorts, are useful, especially for hikers.
10. Be prepared for wet, chilly weather in the highlands. Bring layers of warm, waterproof synthetics.
11. One or two dressy outfits for going out in the cities. For women, this can be a black cocktail dress, with some kind of wrap to keep from freezing. For men, a button-down shirt and nice slacks is usually good enough. Go easy on the jewelry. It can be risky to wear in some parts of the cities and a nuisance to deal with in the countryside.
12. Those planning to snorkel or scuba-dive should consider an underwater disposable camera or underwater camera case.
13. Lots of film or memory sticks.
14. Flip-flops.
15. Reef sandals/Tevas for boat trips
16. A couple of Nalgene-type water bottles.

17. Flashlight and/or head lamp with extra batteries and bulb.
18. Lots of plastic ziplock bags to protect sensitive gear from sudden downpours, or splash during boat trips. Be sure to double-bag cameras and passports.
19. Money belt/pouch for travel in the sketchier urban areas.
20. Two photocopies of passport information, photo, and entry-stamp pages, kept separately from the passport.
21. Daypack.
22. A small backpack with internal frame is best for travel on domestic flights, buses, and boats.
23. Spare pair of glasses and/or glasses prescription.
24. Sunglasses.
25. Sunscreen.
26. Insect repellent. It can be surprisingly hard to find strong repellent in Panama. Be sure to bring some. The best stuff, arguably, contains a high concentration of DEET and is easy to find at camping or Army surplus stores. (Note: DEET is not safe for small children.)

Trekking Gear

Those planning treks or long hikes should bring sturdy hiking boots. U.S. Army-surplus boots are the footwear of choice for Darién treks. The U.S. military experimented with jungle survival and warfare techniques over many years in Panama, so there are actually Army boots with "Panama treads" that feature quick-mud-release soles. They can be hard to find these days, but they're worth searching for. They take a while to break in. The treads of other boots can get clogged with sticky mud instantly, giving them the traction and usefulness of roller skates in the jungle. A popular alternative, widely used by those who live in the forest, are Wellington boots. These are especially useful in the rainy season.

Adventure-travel companies generally bring most bulky gear that clients need, including tents. They'll usually take care of providing clean water, too, but it can be a good idea to bring along water-purification tablets or a high-quality water purifier just in case.

The list of additional gear below is for those expecting hardcore, multi-day treks and includes some items that may not be obvious but can come in surprisingly handy. It was compiled with the help of Hernan Araúz, a highly experienced Darién guide. Warning: This gear list is not meant to suggest the inexperienced can go for a jungle trek without an experienced, professional guide. That is an extremely dangerous thing to do. Much of the gear listed below, such as machetes and first-aid kit, will likely be the responsibility of the guide.

1. Lighter.
2. Sewing kit.
3. Spare boot laces.
4. Extra batteries for all electronic gear.
5. Swiss Army knife or similar.
6. Small machete.
7. Tent or tarp.
8. Spoon.
9. Prescribed medication (always keep these on your person).
10. Hand disinfectant. It's important to wash hands before eating in the Darién and other remote spots.
11. A first-aid kit that contains: anti-diarrhea medications (such as Imodium or Lomatil), Pepto-Bismol or similar, a supply of oral-rehydration solution packages, skin creams such as Neosporin or Triderm, hydrogen peroxide, antihistamines, pain medications such as ibuprofen or aspirin, snake antivenin, Ace bandages, antibiotics, burn cream, condoms, eardrops, eyedrops, gauze, and medical tape.
12. MREs (Meals, Ready to Eat) in case you get stranded.
13. Small, lightweight hammock.
14. Belt.
15. Pillow or inflatable cushion for riding in *piraguas*.
16. A small shortwave radio, book, and/or CD player can stave off boredom at night, which comes early in the forest, since there's little else to do.
17. Earplugs.
18. biodegradable soap/shampoo.
19. An extra pair of prescription eyeglasses.

Spanish Phrasebook

Your Panamanian adventure will be more fun if you use a little Spanish. Panamanian folks, although they may smile at your funny accent, will appreciate your halting efforts to break the ice and transform yourself from a foreigner to a potential friend.

Spanish commonly uses 30 letters—the familiar English 26, plus four straightforward additions: ch, ll, ñ, and rr, which are explained in "Consonants," below.

PRONUNCIATION

Once you learn them, Spanish pronunciation rules—in contrast to English—don't change. Spanish vowels generally sound softer than in English. (Note: The capitalized syllables below receive stronger accents.)

Vowels

a — like ah, as in "hah": *agua* AH-gooah (water), *pan* PAHN (bread), and *casa* CAH-sah (house)

e — like ay, as in "may:" *mesa* MAY-sah (table), *tela* TAY-lah (cloth), and *de* DAY (of, from)

i — like ee, as in "need": *diez* dee-AYZ (ten), *comida* ko-MEE-dah (meal), and *fin* FEEN (end)

o — like oh, as in "go": *peso* PAY-soh (weight), *ocho* OH-choh (eight), and *poco* POH-koh (a bit)

u — like oo, as in "cool": *uno* OO-noh (one), *cuarto* KOOAHR-toh (room), and *usted* oos-TAYD (you); when it follows a "q" the **u** is silent; when it follows an "h" or has an umlaut, it's pronounced like "w"

Consonants

b, d, f, k, l, m, n, p, q, s, t, v, w, x, y, z, and **ch** — pronounced almost as in English; **h** occurs, but is silent—not pronounced at all.

c — like k as in "keep": *cuarto* KOOAR-toh (room), Tepic tay-PEEK (capital of Nayarit state); when it precedes "e" or "i," pronounce **c** like s, as in "sit": *cerveza* sayr-VAY-sah (beer), *encima* ayn-SEE-mah (atop).

g — like g as in "gift" when it precedes "a," "o," "u," or a consonant: *gato* GAH-toh (cat), *hago* AH-goh (I do, make); otherwise, pronounce **g** like h as in "hat": *giro* HEE-roh (money order), *gente* HAYN-tay (people)

j — like h, as in "has": *Jueves* HOOAY-vays (Thursday), *mejor* may-HOR (better)

ll — like y, as in "yes": *toalla* toh-AH-yah (towel), *ellos* AY-yohs (they, them)

ñ — like ny, as in "canyon": *año* AH-nyo (year), *señor* SAY-nyor (Mr., sir)

r — is lightly trilled, with tongue at the roof of your mouth like a very light English d, as in "ready": *pero* PAY-doh (but), *tres* TDAYS (three), *cuatro* KOOAH-tdoh (four).

rr — like a Spanish r, but with much more emphasis and trill. Let your tongue flap. Practice with *burro* (donkey), *carretera* (highway), and Carrillo (proper name), then really let go with *ferrocarril* (railroad).

Note: The single small but common exception to all of the above is the pronunciation of Spanish **y** when it's being used as the Spanish word for "and," as in "Ron y Kathy." In such case, pronounce it like the English ee, as in "keep": Ron "ee" Kathy (Ron and Kathy).

Accent

The rule for accent, the relative stress given to syllables within a given word, is straightforward. If a word ends in a vowel, an n, or an s, accent the next-to-last syllable; if not, accent the last syllable.

Pronounce *gracias* GRAH-seeahs (thank you), *orden* OHR-dayn (order), and *carretera* kah-ray-TAY-rah (highway) with stress on the next-to-last syllable.

Otherwise, accent the last syllable: *venir* vay-NEER (to come), *ferrocarril* fay-roh-cah-REEL (railroad), and *edad* ay-DAHD (age).

Exceptions to the accent rule are always marked with an accent sign: (á, é, í, ó, or ú), such as *teléfono* tay-LAY-foh-noh (telephone), *jabón* hah-BON (soap), and *rápido* RAH-pee-doh (rapid).

BASIC AND COURTEOUS EXPRESSIONS

Most Spanish-speaking people consider formalities important. Whenever approaching anyone for information or some other reason, do not forget the appropriate salutation—good morning, good evening, etc. Standing alone, the greeting *hola* (hello) can sound brusque.

Hello. — *Hola.*
Good morning. — *Buenos días.*
Good afternoon. — *Buenas tardes.*
Good evening. — *Buenas noches.*
How are you? — *¿Cómo está usted?*
Very well, thank you. — *Muy bien, gracias.*
Okay; good. — *Bien.*
Not okay; bad. — *Mal* or *feo.*
So-so. — *Más o menos.*
And you? — *¿Y usted?*
Thank you. — *Gracias.*
Thank you very much. — *Muchas gracias.*
You're very kind. — *Muy amable.*
You're welcome. — *De nada.*
Goodbye. — *Adios.*
See you later. — *Hasta luego.*
please — *por favor*
yes — *sí*
no — *no*
I don't know. — *No sé.*
Just a moment, please. — *Momentito, por favor.*
Excuse me, please (when you're trying to get attention). — *Disculpe* or *Con permiso.*
Excuse me (when you've made a boo-boo). — *Lo siento.*
Pleased to meet you. — *Mucho gusto.*
How do you say . . . in Spanish? — *¿Cómo se dice . . . en español?*
What is your name? — *¿Cómo se llama usted?*
Do you speak English? — *¿Habla usted inglés?*
Is English spoken here? (Does anyone here speak English?) — *¿Se habla inglés?*
I don't speak Spanish well. — *No hablo bien el español.*
I don't understand. — *No entiendo.*
How do you say . . . in Spanish? — *¿Cómo se dice . . . en español?*

My name is . . . — *Me llamo . . .*
Would you like . . . — *¿Quisiera usted . . .*
Let's go to . . . — *Vamos a . . .*

TERMS OF ADDRESS

When in doubt, use the formal *usted* (you) as a form of address.

I — *yo*
you (formal) — *usted*
you (familiar) — *tu*
he/him — *él*
she/her — *ella*
we/us — *nosotros*
you (plural) — *ustedes*
they/them — *ellos* (all males or mixed gender); *ellas* (all females)
Mr., sir — *señor*
Mrs., madam — *señora*
miss, young lady — *señorita*
wife — *esposa*
husband — *esposo*
friend — *amigo* (male); *amiga* (female)
sweetheart — *novio* (male); *novia* (female)
son; daughter — *hijo; hija*
brother; sister — *hermano; hermana*
father; mother — *padre; madre*
grandfather; grandmother — *abuelo; abuela*

TRANSPORTATION

Where is . . . ? — *¿Dónde está . . . ?*
How far is it to . . . ? — *¿A cuánto está . . . ?*
from . . . to . . . — *de . . . a . . .*
How many blocks? — *¿Cuántas cuadras?*
Where (Which) is the way to . . . ? — *¿Dónde está el camino a . . . ?*
the bus station — *la terminal de autobuses*
the bus stop — *la parada de autobuses*
Where is this bus going? — *¿Adónde va este autobús?*
the taxi stand — *la parada de taxis*
the train station — *la estación de ferrocarril*
the boat — *el barco*
the airport — *el aeropuerto*
I'd like a ticket to . . . — *Quisiera un boleto a . . .*

first (second) class — *primera (segunda) clase*
roundtrip — *ida y vuelta*
reservation — *reservación*
baggage — *equipaje*
Stop here, please. — *Pare aquí, por favor.*
the entrance — *la entrada*
the exit — *la salida*
the ticket office — *la oficina de boletos*
(very) near; far — *(muy) cerca; lejos*
to; toward — *a*
by; through — *por*
from — *de*
the right — *la derecha*
the left — *la izquierda*
straight ahead — *derecho; directo*
in front — *en frente*
beside — *al lado*
behind — *atrás*
the corner — *la esquina*
the stoplight — *la semáforo*
a turn — *una vuelta*
right here — *aquí*
somewhere around here — *por acá*
right there — *allí*
somewhere around there — *por allá*
street — *calle*
highway — *carretera*
bridge; toll — *puente; cuota*
address — *dirección*
north; south — *norte; sur*
east; west — *este; oeste*

ACCOMMODATIONS

hotel — *hotel*
Is there a room? — *¿Hay cuarto?*
May I (may we) see it? — *¿Puedo (podemos) verlo?*
What is the rate? — *¿Cuál es el precio?*
Is that your best rate? — *¿Es su mejor precio?*
Is there something cheaper? — *¿Hay algo más económico?*
a single room — *un cuarto sencillo*
a double room — *un cuarto doble*
double bed — *cama matrimonial*
twin beds — *camas gemelas*
with private bath — *con baño*

hot water — *agua caliente*
shower — *ducha*
towels — *toallas*
soap — *jabón*
toilet paper — *papel higiénico*
blanket — *frazada; manta*
sheets — *sábanas*
air-conditioned — *aire acondicionado*
fan — *abanico*
key — *llave*
manager — *gerente*

FOOD

I'm hungry — *Tengo hambre.*
I'm thirsty. — *Tengo sed.*
menu — *lista; menú*
order — *orden*
glass — *vaso*
fork — *tenedor*
knife — *cuchillo*
spoon — *cuchara*
napkin — *servilleta*
soft drink — *refresco*
coffee — *café*
tea — *té*
drinking water — *agua pura; agua potable*
bottled carbonated water — *agua mineral*
bottled uncarbonated water — *agua sin gas*
beer — *cerveza*
wine — *vino*
milk — *leche*
juice — *jugo*
cream — *crema*
sugar — *azúcar*
cheese — *queso*
breakfast — *desayuno*
lunch — *almuerzo*
dinner — *cena*
the check — *la cuenta*
eggs — *huevos*
bread — *pan*
salad — *ensalada*
fruit — *fruta*
mango — *mango*
watermelon — *sandía*

papaya — *papaya*
banana — *plátano; banana*
apple — *manzana*
orange — *naranja*
lime — *limón*
fish — *pescado*
shellfish — *mariscos*
shrimp — *camarones*
meat (without) — *(sin) carne*
chicken — *pollo*
pork — *puerco*
beef; steak — *res; bistec*
bacon; ham — *tocino; jamón*
fried — *frito*
roasted — *asada*
barbecue; barbecued — *barbacoa; al carbón*

SHOPPING

money — *dinero*
money-exchange bureau — *casa de cambio*
I would like to exchange traveler's checks. —
    Quisiera cambiar cheques de viajero.
What is the exchange rate? — *¿Cuál es el tipo de*
    cambio?
How much is the commission? — *¿Cuánto cuesta*
    la comisión?
Do you accept credit cards? — *¿Aceptan tarjetas de*
    crédito?
money order — *giro*
How much does it cost? — *¿Cuánto cuesta?*
What is your final price? — *¿Cuál es su último precio?*
expensive —*caro*
cheap — *barato; económico*
more — *más*
less — *menos*
a little — *un poco*
too much — *demasiado*

HEALTH

Help me please. — *Ayúdeme por favor.*
I am ill. — *Estoy enfermo.*
Call a doctor. — *Llame un doctor.*
Take me to . . . — *Lléveme a . . .*
hospital — *hospital*

drugstore — *farmacia*
pain — *dolor*
fever — *fiebre*
headache — *dolor de cabeza*
stomach ache — *dolor de estómago*
burn — *quemadura*
cramp — *calambre*
nausea — *náusea*
vomiting — *vomitar*
medicine — *medicina*
antibiotic — *antibiótico*
pill; tablet — *pastilla*
aspirin — *aspirina*
ointment; cream — *pomada; crema*
bandage — *venda*
cotton — *algodón*
sanitary napkins — use brand name, e.g., Kotex
birth control pills — *pastillas anticonceptivas*
contraceptive foam — *espuma anticonceptiva*
condoms — *preservativos; condones*
toothbrush — *cepilla dental*
dental floss — *hilo dental*
toothpaste — *crema dental*
dentist — *dentista*
toothache — *dolor de muelas*

POST OFFICE AND COMMUNICATIONS

long-distance telephone — *teléfono larga distancia*
I would like to call . . . — *Quisiera llamar a . . .*
collect — *por cobrar*
station to station — *a quien contesta*
person to person — *persona a persona*
credit card — *tarjeta de crédito*
post office — *correo*
general delivery — *entrega general*
letter — *carta*
stamp — *estampilla, timbre*
postcard — *tarjeta*
aerogram — *aerograma*
air mail — *correo aereo*
registered — *registrado*
money order — *giro*
package; box — *paquete; caja*
string; tape — *cuerda; cinta*

AT THE BORDER

border — *frontera*
customs — *aduana*
immigration — *migración*
tourist card — *tarjeta de turista*
inspection — *inspección; revisión*
passport — *pasaporte*
profession — *profesión*
marital status — *estado civil*
single — *soltero*
married; divorced — *casado; divorciado*
widowed — *viudado*
insurance — *seguros*
title — *título*
driver's license — *licencia de manejar*

AT THE GAS STATION

gas station — *gasolinera*
gasoline — *gasolina*
unleaded — *sin plomo*
full, please — *lleno, por favor*
tire — *llanta*
tire repair — *reparación de llantas*
air — *aire*
water — *agua*
oil (change) — *aceite (cambio)*
grease — *grasa*
My . . . doesn't work. — *Mi . . . no sirve.*
battery — *batería*
radiator — *radiador*
alternator — *alternador*
generator — *generador*
repair shop — *taller mecánico*

VERBS

Verbs are the key to getting along in Spanish. They employ mostly predictable forms and come in three classes, which end in *ar, er,* and *ir,* respectively:

to buy — *comprar*
I buy, you (he, she, it) buys — *compro, compra*
we buy, you (they) buy — *compramos, compran*
to eat — *comer*
I eat, you (he, she, it) eats — *como, come*

we eat, you (they) eat — *comemos, comen*

to climb — *subir*
I climb, you (he, she, it) climbs — *subo, sube*
we climb, you (they) climb — *subimos, suben*

Got the idea? Here are more (with irregularities marked in **bold**).

to do or make — *hacer*
I do or make, you (he she, it) does or makes — **hago,** *hace*
we do or make, you (they) do or make — *hacemos, hacen*

to go — *ir*
I go, you (he, she, it) goes — **voy, va**
we go, you (they) go — **vamos, van**

to go (walk) — *andar*
to love — *amar*
to work — *trabajar*
to want — *desear, querer*
to need — *necesitar*
to read — *leer*
to write — *escribir*
to repair — *reparar*
to stop — *parar*
to get off (the bus) — *bajar*
to arrive — *llegar*
to stay (remain) — *quedar*
to stay (lodge) — *hospedar*
to leave — *salir* (regular except for **salgo,** I leave)
to look at — *mirar*
to look for — *buscar*
to give — *dar* (regular except for **doy,** I give)
to carry — *llevar*
to have — *tener* (irregular but important: **tengo, tiene,** *tenemos,* **tienen**)
to come — *venir* (similarly irregular: **vengo, viene,** *venimos,* **vienen**)

Spanish has two forms of "to be." Use *estar* when speaking of location or a temporary state of being: "I am at home." "***Estoy en casa.*** " "I'm sick." "***Estoy enfermo.*** " Use *ser* for a permanent state of being: "I am a doctor." "***Soy doctora.*** "

Estar is regular except for ***estoy,*** I am. *Ser* is very irregular:

to be — *ser*
I am, you (he, she, it) is — ***soy, es***
we are, you (they) are — ***somos, son***

NUMBERS

zero — *cero*
one — *uno*
two — *dos*
three — *tres*
four — *cuatro*
five — *cinco*
six — *seis*
seven — *siete*
eight — *ocho*
nine — *nueve*
10 — *diez*
11 — *once*
12 — *doce*
13 — *trece*
14 — *catorce*
15 — *quince*
16 — *dieciseis*
17 — *diecisiete*
18 — *dieciocho*
19 — *diecinueve*
20 — *veinte*
21 — *veinte y uno* or *veintiuno*
30 — *treinta*
40 — *cuarenta*
50 — *cincuenta*
60 — *sesenta*
70 — *setenta*
80 — *ochenta*
90 — *noventa*
100 — *ciento*
101 — *ciento y uno* or *cientiuno*
200 — *doscientos*
500 — *quinientos*
1,000 — *mil*
10,000 — *diez mil*
100,000 — *cien mil*
1,000,000 — *millón*
one half — *medio*

one third — *un tercio*
one fourth — *un cuarto*

TIME

What time is it? — *¿Qué hora es?*
It's one o'clock. — *Es la una.*
It's three in the afternoon. — *Son las tres de la tarde.*
It's 4 A.M. — *Son las cuatro de la mañana.*
six-thirty — *seis y media*
a quarter till eleven — *un cuarto para las once*
a quarter past five — *las cinco y cuarto*
an hour — *una hora*

DAYS AND MONTHS

Monday — *lunes*
Tuesday — *martes*
Wednesday — *miércoles*
Thursday — *jueves*
Friday — *viernes*
Saturday — *sábado*
Sunday — *domingo*
today — *hoy*
tomorrow — *mañana*
yesterday — *ayer*
January — *enero*
February — *febrero*
March — *marzo*
April — *abril*
May — *mayo*
June — *junio*
July — *julio*
August — *agosto*
September — *septiembre*
October — *octubre*
November — *noviembre*
December — *diciembre*
a week — *una semana*
a month — *un mes*
after — *después*
before — *antes*

—Courtesy of Bruce Whipperman, author of *Moon Handbooks Pacific Mexico.*

Suggested Reading

Some of the books listed below are out of print or most readily available in Panama, but even these can generally be special-ordered through bookstores or the Internet.

General Information

De La Espriella, Ricardo III. *Panamá: Resumen Histórico Ilustrado del Istmo, 1501–1994,* Colombia: Antigua Films, 1994. A slender coffee-table book with historic photos and brief summaries of major events in Panama's history. In Spanish.

Friar, William. *Portrait of the Panama Canal: From Construction to the Twenty-First Century.* Portland: Graphic Arts Center Publishing, 2003. A photo-essay book by the author of this travel guide.

Navarro Q., Juan Carlos. *Panama National Parks.* Panama: Ediciones Balboa. A beautiful coffee-table book depicting Panama's national parks. In English and Spanish.

Salvador, Mari Lyn (ed.). *The Art of Being Kuna: Layers of Meaning Among the Kuna of Panama.* A hefty coffee-table book with fascinating photos and scholarly essays on Kuna life, culture, art, beliefs, and history. The best introduction to the Kunas and *molas.*

History, Politics, and Current Events

Anderson, Dr. C. L. G. *Old Panama and Castilla del Oro.* New York: North River Press, 1911. A fascinating, in-depth account of the Spanish conquest and pirate history of Panama, written by a medical doctor who worked for the Panama Canal during its construction.

Buckley, Kevin. *Panama: The Whole Story.* New York: Simon and Schuster, 1991. Solidly reported and well written, this is the most reliable account of the U.S. invasion that removed Noriega from power in 1989.

Díaz Espino, Ovidio. *How Wall Street Created a Nation: J.P. Morgan, Teddy Roosevelt, and the Panama Canal.* New York: Four Walls Eight Windows, 2001. An impassioned polemic about behind-the-scenes dealings leading to Panama's separation from Colombia and the 1903 Panama Canal treaties.

Dyke, Tom Hart and Winder, Paul. *The Cloud Garden: A True Story of Adventure, Survival, and Extreme Horticulture.* Guilford, Connecticut: Lyons Press, 2004. An alternately funny and horrifying account of two backpackers kidnapped by guerrillas in the Darien jungle in 2000.

Howarth, David. *The Golden Isthmus.* London: Collins, 1966. Also published as *Panama: Four Hundred Years of Dreams and Cruelty.* Contains fascinating tidbits on the exploits of Spanish conquistadors, Elizabethan adventurers, and bloody buccaneers. Becomes unreliable as it enters the modern era.

Howe, James. *A People Who Would Not Kneel: Panama, the United States, and the San Blas Kuna.* Washington: Smithsonian, 19998. Gives interesting insights into the history and culture of the Kuna.

Lindsay-Poland, John. *Emperors in the Jungle: The Hidden History of the U.S. in Panama.* Durham, North Carolina: Duke University Press, 2003. Investigative journalism examining the history of U.S. military involvement in Panama.

McCullough, David. *The Path Between the Seas: The Creation of the Panama Canal, 1870-1914.* New York: Simon and Schuster, 1977. The definitive history of the Panama Canal. An astonishing book that reads like a thriller.

Prebble, John. *The Darien Disaster: A Scots Colony in the New World, 1698-1700.* New York:

Holt, Rinehart, and Winston, 1968. A readable account of the doomed Scottish attempt to establish a colony in the Darien jungle.

Nature and Wildlife

Forsyth, Adrian and Miyata, Ken. *Tropical Nature: Life and Death in the Rain Forests of Central and South America.* New York: Simon and Schuster, 1995. An introduction to tropical ecology.

Kircher, John. *A Neotropical Companion: An Introduction to the Animals, Plants, & Ecosystems of the New World Tropics.* Princeton: Princeton University Press, 1999. A detailed explanation of just about anything you'd like to know about the New World tropics. Reading it will deepen hikers' experience of the forest.

Ventocilla, Jorge; Herrera, Heraclio; and Nunez, Valerio translated by King, Elisabeth. *Plants & Animals in the Life of the Kuna.* Austin: University of Texas, 1995. This book is notable for describing flora and fauna, forest life, and environmental destruction in Kuna Yala from the point of view of the Kuna themselves, often in their own words.

Wong, Marina and Ventocilla, Jorge. *A Day on Barro Colorado Island.* Panama: Smithsonian, 1995. A slim volume that contains an overview of the flora and fauna of the island and a detailed trail map.

Field Guides

Reid, Fiona A. *A Field Guide to the Mammals of Central America and Southeast Mexico.* New York: Oxford University Press, 1998.

Ridgely, Robert S. and Gwynne, John A. Jr. *A Guide to the Birds of Panama.* Princeton: Princeton University Press, 1989. Though overdue for an update, this is still the Bible of Panama bird-watching. Also contains information on birds found in Costa Rica, Nicaragua, and Honduras.

Travel Guides

Pritchard, Raymond and Audrey. *Driving the Pan-American Highway to Mexico and Central America.* Costa Rica: Costa Rica Books, 1997. Quite out of date, but at the time of writing the only guidebook on driving to Panama from North America.

Wilson, David. *A Captain's Guide to Transiting the Panama Canal in a Small Vessel.* Panama: Tantoes, 2002. A technical guide for yachties. Available through www.bluewaterweb.com.

Zydler, Nancy Schwalbe and Tom. *The Panama Guide: A Cruising Guide to the Isthmus of Panama.* Port Washington, Wisconsin: Seaworthy Publications, 2001. A guide to yachting destinations along both sides of the isthmus, with detailed tips and 187 charts.

Life in Panama

Henderson, Malcolm. *Don't Kill the Cow too Quick: An Englishman's Adventures Homesteading in Panama.* Lincoln, Nebraska: iUniverse, 2004. Homespun account of an expatriate couple's adventures building their retirement dream in Bocas del Toro.

Knapp, Herbert and Mary. *Red, White, and Blue Paradise: The American Canal Zone in Panama.* New York: Harcourt Brace Jovanovich, 1984. An account of life in the old Canal Zone from a couple who lived it.

Snyder, Sandra. *Living in Panama.* Panama: Panama Relocation Services/PanAmCham, 2002. A thorough guide for expatriates moving to Panama, covering everything from dinnerparty etiquette to registering cars. Available through www.wnpan.org.

Internet Resources

Travel

www.bocas.com

This visitor-information site for Bocas del Toro contains listings for many hotels, restaurants, and services as well as some background information on Bocas.

www.bocasmarinetours.com

Bocas Marine and Tours is a Bocas del Toro water-taxi service, but its site also contains useful, frequently updated maps of the Bocas archipelago and mainland, transportation schedules, and facts about Bocas. The Bocas town map is printer friendly.

www.boomersabroad.com/panama.html

This is an overview site for those interested in retiring or investing in Panama. It takes a more measured approach than similar sites, which can be aggressive about hyping Panama.

www.legalinfo-panama.com

This site contains detailed legal information for those interested in moving to or doing business in Panama, as well as listings of lawyers and law firms. It's in Spanish with some English content.

www.panamainfo.com

Panamainfo is a frequently updated visitor-information site that accentuates the positive. It's most useful for those traveling on a moderate and above budget but also contains general information for destinations around Panama.

http://travel.state.gov

The web site of the U.S. State Department contains general entry requirements and travel warnings for U.S. citizens traveling abroad, listed by country.

www.visitpanama.com

The official site of Panama's government tourism institute, IPAT. It's in English and Spanish. IPAT also has another, Spanish-only website: www.ipat.gob.pa.

www.journeylatinamerica.co.uk

Journey Latin America is a London-based tour operator and travel agency that's a good place to start for those going to Panama from Europe and points east.

Ecotourism

www.ancon.org

ANCON is Panama's largest environmental organization. The site contains some information on the country's national parks and a list of endangered species. In Spanish only.

www.panamaaudubon.org

The Panama Audubon Society organizes frequent bird-watching trips that are open to foreign visitors and listed on its site, which is in Spanish and English.

www.stri.org

The web site of the Smithsonian Tropical Research Institute contains information on its projects and installations, including Barro Colorado Island. It also shows live video from user-controllable web cams set up on Barro Colorado and Parque Natural Metropolitano.

News Sites

www.theboquetetimes.com

The Boquete Times is a fledging operation run by gringo expatriates. It covers the town of Boquete and surrounding areas.

www.isthmian.net

The Isthmian is a muckraking web-only newspaper. At the time of writing it had suspended operation due to legal challenges in Panama, but it may resume publication.

www.noriegaville.com
A collection of news and hard-hitting opinion by Okke Ornstein, the Dutch journalist behind the Isthmian. His critical view of life in Panama is a stark contrast to the rah-rah sites.

www.thepanamanews.com
The original muckraking English-language newspaper in Panama, the Panama News is now online only.

www.prensa.com
Panama's best Spanish-language newspaper. Free registration allows access to its extensive archives.

Government
www.conpahouston.com
The FAQ section of the website for the Panamanian consulate in Houston contains more reliable information on requirements for visiting and moving to Panama than other foreign ministry sites.

www.pa
General Panamanian government site with telephone listings and links to government ministries and organizations, including the tourism and culture institutes. In Spanish.

www.pancanal.com
The website for the Panama Canal Authority contains news and history about the Panama Canal, and tide tables for Balboa and Cristóbal. But its coolest features are the live video feeds from the web cams set up at Miraflores Locks, Gatun Locks, and the Centennial Bridge over Gaillard Cut.

Miscellaneous Information
www.canal1.net
Lists tide tables (click on "Tabla de Mareas"), not to mention lottery results. In Spanish.

www.cdc.gov/travel/
The U.S. Centers for Disease Control list comprehensive immunization information and health advisories for destinations around the world.

www.cia.gov/cia/publications/factbook/ geos/pm.html
The U.S. Central Intelligence Agency lists detailed statistics and background information on Panama here.

www.czbrats.com and http://lostparadise.com
Nostalgia sites for Zonians, containing photos, stories, and memorabilia from the former Canal Zone.

www.paginasamarillas.com
Online telephone book for Panama and other Latin American countries.

Index

Acknowledgments

for my mother

Finishing this book ended up being a longer, bumpier, and more painful road than any I've driven in Panama, and that's saying something.

Many people helped smooth the way and gave me guidance when I got lost, more than I can mention here. Many others were nameless friendly strangers I met along the way who answered boneheaded questions, pointed the way, or lent a hand when I needed one. Though their names do not appear below, I thank them all.

Most of all I need to thank my family, whose unwavering support and encouragement have gotten me through some tough slogs. Then there are the folks who have become like family — especially Mary Coffey, Sandra Snyder, and David Wilson — except that family members would never put up so cheerfully with such incessant demands.

As always, special thanks and *abrazos* go to Egbert N. ("Beets") Grazette and Clotilde O. de Guerra, who remind me about the important things in life, and who make that life so much more pleasant when I'm in Panama.

Karen Said was a crucial support to me at the end of this project. I can't thank her enough for her wisdom, kindness, and generosity of spirit.

Among the countless hard-working folks in Panama who were unbelievably generous with their time and support, I can't forget to mention Jane Walker, Barry Robbins, Rich Cahill, Hernan Araúz, Marco Gandasegui, Schoschana Crouwel, Jon Hanna, and Andrea Aster. Bonnie Spindler was a great traveling companion and photographer. I was buoyed through the bulk of my research and writing by the patience and unselfish assistance of Candice McFarland back in the States.

This book grew out of an earlier work, and the help I was given then helped make this one possible. Among those I remain grateful to are Leslie Zellers, Scott Doggett, Teresa Tulipano, and Roberto Roy.

I also am grateful to everyone at Avalon Travel Publishing for their patience and professionalism, most especially Kay Elliott, my long-suffering editor, and Marisa Solís, her even-longer-suffering predecessor.

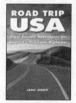